THE BLUE GUIDES

BLUE GUIDE

FRANCE

IAN ROBERTSON

With 60 Town Plans

Ernest Benn Limited
London

W. W. Norton & Company Inc.
New York

First Edition 1984

Published by Ernest Benn Limited
Sovereign Way, Tonbridge, Kent TN9 1RW

© Ernest Benn Limited 1984

Printed in Great Britain

Published in the United States of America by
W. W. Norton & Company Inc.
500 Fifth Avenue, New York, N.Y. 10110

ISBN *Cased* 0 510-00144-0   0 393-01662-5 (U.S.A.)
ISBN *Paper* 0 510-00143-2   0 393-30069-2 (U.S.A.)

'I have not onely seene severall Countries, beheld the
nature of their climes, the Chorography of their Provinces,
Topography of their Cities, but understood their severall
Lawes, Customes and Policies; yet cannot all this perswade
the dulnesse of my spirit unto such an opinion of my self, as
I behold in nimbler & conceited heads, that never looked a
degree beyond their nests'.—*Sir Thomas Browne.*

PREFACE

This Blue Guide to France breaks new ground for the series, although the country has been covered previously, in five separate volumes which, with the exception of the Editor's radically revised version of that dealing with the N.W. of France, have been unavailable for decades. The capital and the Île de France are already described in detail in *Blue Guide Paris and Environs* (5th edition; 1983), which will continue to be published as an individual volume. This area is here given a *very condensed* description, which is intended for travellers whose object is not Paris for herself but Paris as a brief stage in the exploration of the rest of France. Corsica, a visit to which is usually considered a separate excursion, is not included, although it is administratively part of France.

To compose a single-volume guide to so large a country has posed several problems, perhaps not all of them satisfactorily resolved. The Editor has concentrated, in addition to its topography in general, on the cultural background—its art, and architecture, and history: the lack of certain minutiae (previously included in some regional guides) will, it is hoped, not be regretted, such as the temperatures and medicinal qualities of spa waters; the generating capacities of hydro-electric stations; and the positions of refuge-huts among Alpine or Pyrenean peaks, for example. It retains the form which over the years has been found the most satisfactory way of describing a country, by following a series of routes and sub-routes, since it is on these that the traffic of history has travelled and on which most places of old foundation stand. They are still likely to be the most interesting, although not necessarily the fastest or most beautiful course. When a motorway exists near one of these it is mentioned at the start of the route concerned.

For the sake of convenience the volume has been arranged in 13 sections, with occasional overlappings. It need hardly be emphasised—especially in the case of the longer routes—that it is virtually impossible to visit all the monuments described and hope to cover the route in the same day, but they will suggest a general direction which it may be convenient to follow.

Hotel and restaurants are to be found throughout most of France, although there are areas where they are thinner on the ground. As several reliable publications issued annually concentrate on these it has been considered superfluous to list any in this guide; but see p 57. Towns are described for sightseeing on foot, almost always the most convenient and enjoyable way of getting about, more so since so many pedestrian precincts have been formed in recent years, and a complement of 60 schematic town plans has been drawn, which should give the visitor a good idea of their general layout. **Doug London** has been entrusted with the cartography, while *John Flower* has drawn the plan of Paris.

The numerous town plans in the *red* Michelin Guide—a useful companion to the present volume—will give more detailed indications of the points of entry or exit, of one-way streets, car-parks, garages, the situation of Tourist Offices (S.I.) and Post Offices (P.T.T.), and a selection of hotels and restaurants, etc. It is essential that the traveller has a general map of France, and more detailed motoring maps of the areas through which he intends to tour or explore in depth, and advice on these is given on p 50.

While the Editor has travelled extensively throughout France on several occasions in recent decades, and again during the last 2-3 years in the service of this guide, not every road has been followed, nor every locality visited, but a substantial proportion of the descriptions have been revised in the light of personal observation on the spot and familiarity with actual conditions. However, he knows from experience that sudden and unexpected changes can occur immediately he has turned his back. Although endeavouring to keep abreast of all the most recent changes and re-arrangements of museums, etc., inevitably the latest facts are not always forthcoming, and getting advance information accurate enough to print is virtually impossible. Times of admission to monuments and museums are not included: to do so would inevitably misinform the traveller in a high proportion of cases, but to avoid disappointment he should make advance enquiry at any S.I.

The practice of 'starring' the highlights has been continued, for although it is subjective and inconsistent, such asterisks do help the hurried traveller to pick out those things which the general consensus of opinion (modified by the Editor's personal prejudices, admittedly) considers he should not miss. In certain cases a museum has been starred rather than individual objects among those described, when the standard of its contents is remarkably high; likewise, a particularly attractive village or view has been so marked. It has been suggested that he might also include 'daggers' to indicate what would be better avoided, for even when discounting chauvinism and provincial pride, not all French geese are swans. Not infrequently, in spite of illusion-dispelling experience, the Editor has been disappointed by expecting too much of some 'local lion', and would rather save others the wasted journey by assuring them that it is not worth the time or trouble. Indeed, he would as much welcome a recommendation from a reader to delete a church or château—for example—which in his view does not merit inclusion, as having an omission pointed out to him. Well can he sympathise with Aldous Huxley, who when writing of uncritical guides remarked: 'For every traveller who has any taste of his own, the only useful guide-book will be the one he himself has written. All others are an exasperation—they make him travel long miles to see a mound of rubbish; they go into ecstasies over mere antiquity', etc.

Selection indeed remains the touchstone by which guide-books are judged, and it is hoped that this new volume, in spite of certain inevitable inadequacies, will lead the traveller to whatever is most worth seeing in the way of landscape, art and architecture, etc., at the same time providing sufficient historical and cultural context.

Certain townscapes have changed radically during recent years; too many have had 'the treatment', being surrounded by unsightly blocks of apartments which have succeeded in destroying the entire equilibrium of the place; and yet—'plus ça change et plus c'est la même chose'—very often the Editor's own adverse reaction to a place merely confirms the view of earlier critical travellers—whether it be Smollett, Arthur Young, Murray, or Augustus Hare—and certain 'asides' have been slipped in, when trenchantly underlining such views.

The laying of an *autoroute* has in certain cases enabled an area to regain its former calm and provinciality; the same highway may have brought a once sequestered district near—sometimes far too near—the beaten track. Once 'tourist blight' has attacked a place, and the profit motive is the principal consideration, then the traveller in search of France's great cultural heritage and 'qualité de la vie' will hurry on elsewhere (unless there is some exceptional treasure which cannot be overlooked); but occasionally the balance is precarious, although there is now more awareness of the dangers of over-exploitation of obvious attractions. More emphasis is given to conservation and restoration, and providing discreet amenities; more encouragement to the exploration of the country's lesser known sites and monuments: indeed it is only by very deliberately breaking away from the paths pursued by the majority and turning onto uncluttered byways that one can get a deeper feeling for and understanding of France.

This is not intended to be a guide to the sophisticated delights of casinos, crowded beaches and yacht plaisances; nor does it attempt to provide information with regard to pot-holing, underwater-fishing, hang-gliding, bird-watching, naturist reserves, camping-sites, winter-sports facilities, or the pleasant occupation of canal-cruising: the Government Tourist Offices, and local S.Is (see p 53) are far better equipped to give up-to-date advice on all such subjects. Likewise, the descriptions of high mountain regions are limited to pointing out the main summits, for the serious climber will have his more specialised sources of information.

Like others in the Blue Guide series, it sets out to provide the discriminating traveller with a balanced account of certain characteristics of a country which will make his visit to it that much more rewarding, without omitting (except perhaps deliberately) anything that will be conspicuous by its absence which might appeal to the intelligent visitor, and without being so exhaustive as to leave him with no opportunity of discovering many additional pleasures for himself. He will frequently find that there is almost always more to a place than the description specifies.

Apart from being a distillation of the present Editor's Blue Guide to *Paris and Environs*, and including a further revision of *Loire Valley, Normandy, Brittany* (4th ed.; 1978), this guide is largely based on Findlay Muirhead's *North-Eastern France* (2nd ed.; 1930), L. Russell Muirhead's *Southern France* (2nd ed.; 1954), and Stuart Rossiter's *The South of France* (1st ed.; 1966; a revision of the E. half of the former work and the relevant part of the pre-war *French Alps*).

Its preparation has depended almost entirely on the Editor alone (in spite of occasional kind and encouraging French enquiries after the *équipe*), and certain unintentional omissions are unavoidable, since France offers an 'embarras de richesse' that can never be encompassed in a single tome, and he alone is responsible for all inexactitudes, shortcoming, inconsistencies, and solecisms.

Acknowledgement must be made however to several functionaries of the Ministère de la Jeunesse, des Sports et des Loisirs (on which the Direction du Tourisme depends), who have eased his path, among them *Philippe Doyon* in Paris, *René Bardy*, in London, and *Henri Gassan* in Madrid; and, likewise of the Ministère de la Culture et de la Communication (Direction du Patrimoine), in particular *Hubert Landais*, *Chantal Meslin-Perrier*, and *Geneviève Ravaux* (Direction des Musées de France); *Claude Soalhat* (Directeur de Service Commercial de la Réunion des Musées Nationaux); *Jean Fosséyeux* (Caisse Nationale des Monuments Historiques et des Sites); also to the Cultural Counsellors at the French Embassy, London; *Beatrice Massenet* (La Demeure Historique), and *Yolande de Lacretelle* (Vieilles Maisons Françaises).

Material assistance has been gratefully received from *J. Henderson McCartney* (McCarta, London), and *Jacques Monteil* and *Dominique*

Wintrebert (IGN; Paris); from *F. G. Whiston* (Michelin, London); *John Healey* (British Rail, Paris); and the Directors of the Institute Nationale de la Statistiques et des Études Économiques, Paris.

Almost all conservateurs of museums, when available, have been helpful, and while it may be invidious to particularise, I must mention *Matthieu Pinette* (Autun), *Dominique Serena* (Arles), *Danièle Giraudy* (Antibes), *Philippe Comte* (Pau), *Jean Favière* (Strasbourg) and *Christine Debrie* (St-Quentin). *Roseline Bacou* (Cabinet de Dessins, Musée du Louvre), and *Fabienne de Sèze* (Musée des Arts Décoratifs, Paris), have encouraged and advised on numerous occasions.

Thanks must be extended to the following individuals who have provided the Editor with information, assistance, or hospitality: *M. Blanchard* at Martel; *Robert Fuster*, at Dijon; *Jacqueline Bret*, and *Jacques de Place*, Lyon; *Louise Danvers*, at Épernay; and *Bertrand de Saulieu*.

Julian Brind has contributed the introduction to the Wines and Spirits of France.

In acknowledging the advice and assistance extended to the Editor in his search for the several illustrations which are a feature of this and other newly edited Blue Guides, the following must be thanked both for their patience and for providing prints: The French Government Tourist Office in London; Mrs Hill and the staff of the Conway Library, Courtauld Institute of Art (whose fine photographic library is invaluable), and John Sunderland at the Witt Library; William Joll, Thos. Agnew & Sons, Ltd; Adam Hogg, Christie, Manson & Woods Ltd; Messrs Richard Green; Max Rutherston, Sotheby & Co.; the directors of The Parker Gallery; and Kenneth F. Banner.

Paco and Olga Mayans, Alain and Françoise Bertrand, and Arthur and Marion Boyars have continued to provide welcome refuges to the Editor on his travels, while Francis Chapelet, and Tony and Clair Forster have also kindly offered hospitality and advice. Marie-Thérèse, my wife, has philosophically undertaken the arduous task of driving many thousands of kilometres throughout France, sharing both the vexations and pleasures of intensive travel and the many secluded months of the guide's gestation, during which time I have received every support and encouragement from Timothy Benn, John Beer, Paul Langridge, and Tom Neville, who have patiently guided me, and throughout have given all practical assistance, while Giles Johnson has also helped considerably with the proof-reading, bringing several errors and discrepancies to my notice.

Blue Guides: their History

Although over half a century has now elapsed since there was any direct collaboration, there are many who assume that there is still a close connection between the English **Blue Guides**, published by **Ernest Benn Ltd**, and the French **Guides Bleus**, published by *Librairie Hachette*, and it may be convenient therefore to include here an explanatory note. Further confusion has been caused by the translation into English of some of Hachette's editions under the title *World Guides*, apart from others under the title 'Les Guides Bleus'.

Prior to the outbreak of the First World War, the English editors of the German *Baedeker Guides*, marketed from 1908 by T. Fisher Unwin, were *Findlay* and *James Muirhead*. During 1915, with influential backing, the editors acquired the copyright of the majority (with one exception—'India') of the famous 'Red' *Hand-Books* published by *John Murray*, the standby of English travellers to the Continent and elsewhere for the previous three-quarters of a century; they also bought the copyright of a series published by *Macmillan*, who were to market the new series, the first of which was announced for publication by *Muirhead Guide-Books Limited* by early 1916. In the following year an agreement for mutual co-operation with *Hachette et Cie* of Paris was entered into: the French house, who had previously published the blue cloth bound *Guides-Joanne*—named after their first editor *Adolphe Joanne* (1813–81) who was succeeded by his son Paul (d. 1922)—were to handle a translation of a guide to 'London', which was in fact the first 'Guide Bleu'; this, and other volumes originating with Muirhead, were entitled *The Blue Guides* (further distinguishing them from *red* Baedekers and Murrays). In 1921 an adaptation—not a direct translation—of Hachette's Guide Bleu to 'Paris et ses Environs' (edited by Marcel Monmarché) was published in London, another example of the collaboration between the two firms, who made a new agreement in 1927, which lasted for six years, when it lapsed. *Litellus R. Muirhead* acted as assistant editor at this period. Meanwhile, in 1931, editorial control of the Blue Guides was transferred from Macmillan to *Benn Brothers*, who in 1926 had bought T. Fisher Unwin (who were again handling Baedekers after the war, but Baedekers then transferred to Allen and Unwin).

In 1934 *L. Russell Muirhead* (1896–1976), Findlay Muirhead's son, became Benn's Blue Guide editor, and from 1954 he was assisted by *Stuart Rossiter*, who succeeded him as editor of the series in 1963, under whom the present editor undertook the revision of his first Blue Guide—to Spain—in 1971. For 28 years, until shortly before his death in December 1982, Rossiter had been intimately associated with the editing of the Blue Guides, taking personal responsibility for the revision and compilation of several volumes, among them *London*, *England*, and, in particular, *Greece*, for which he was perhaps best known, which, continuing the tradition, combined scholarship with utility. He brought a high quality of writing and critical editing to the series, his criteria and standards being those which other editors have sought to emulate, and for which the discriminating readers of Blue Guides likewise will be indebted.

In 1975 *Paul Langridge* assumed the general editorship, since when the series has grown spectacularly with the publication of entirely new guides to *Moscow and Leningrad*, *New York*, *Egypt*, *Istanbul*, *Portugal*, *Cyprus*, and *Florence*, among others.

CONTENTS

ROUTE MAPS 72-77

TOWN PLANS

EXPLANATIONS

Type. The main routes are described in large type. Smaller type is used for most sub-routes, excursions, or deviations, for historical and preliminary paragraphs, and (generally speaking) for descriptions of greater detail or less importance.

Asterisks indicate points of special interest or excellence; two stars are used sparingly.

Distances, total and intermediate, are measured in kilometres, and total route distances are also given in miles. Road distances along the routes themselves record the distances between the towns and villages, etc., described, but with the re-alignment of roads, one-way systems, and by-passes, it is almost certain that these will vary from those measured by motorists on their milometers, and are at best approximate. **Altitudes,** and the measurement of buildings, and archaeological sites, etc., are expressed in metres. While most of the recent changes in road numbers have been incorporated, some may still be in the process of alteration.

The **Population** figures given (in round figures) are based on the census of 1982, but it should be noted that in the case of some larger cities this may not include the entire conurbation or 'agglomération' of which it may be the centre. Figures are not given for places with fewer than 5000 inhabitants.

Anglicisation. Place-names and the names of kings, etc. retain their French spelling—*Lyon*, rather than Lyons; *Marseille*, rather than Marseilles—but although it may be inconsistent, certain regions—*Brittany*, rather than Bretagne; *Burgundy*, rather than Bourgogne—remain anglicised.

Abbreviations. In addition to the generally accepted and self-explanatory forms, the following occur in this guide:

Av. = Avenue	R = Room
C = Century	r. = right
Blvd = Boulevard	Rte = Route
IGN = Institut Géographique National map number	St, Ste, SS = Saint or saints
l. = left	S.I. = *Syndicat d'Initiative* or Tourist Office (in spite
M = Michelin map number	of the fancy titles
m = metres	some have chosen to
N.-D. = Notre-Dame, Our Lady	give themselves).
Pl. = Place or Plan	

The sign ◊ immediately after certain monuments and buildings indicates that the *Caisse Nationale des Monuments Historiques et des Sites* is responsible for them; see p 69.

HISTORICAL INTRODUCTION

The foundations of modern France may be said to date from the passage of the Alps by the Romans in 121 B.C., and the establishment of the province (Latin *provincia*; modern *Provence*) of *Gallia Narbonensis*. Important remains such as the Pont du Gard, and the splendid theatres and amphitheatres at Nîmes, Arles, and Orange, are still extant. But the whole of France as we now know it did not become subject to Rome until after *Julius Caesar's* decisive defeat of *Vercingetorix* at *Alésia* in 52 B.C. *Lutetia*—the capital of the *Parisii*, an insignificant Gallic tribe—was nominated by Caesar as the rendezvous for deputies from conquered *Gaul*. In spite of occasional local revolts, Rome gradually imposed her government, roads, speech, and culture on Gaul. By c. A.D. 250 the country had become partially Christianised, but within a few years began the first of a series of Barbarian invasions, among them the *Visigoths*, and *Burgundians*. The invaders gradually became assimilated and were later employed in defending the frontiers of the declining Empire. But they wearied of their alliance with the degenerate Gallo-Romans, and after the repulse of *Attila* and his Huns at the *Catalaunian Fields* (near Chalons, in 451), became virtually masters of the land, the most powerful tribe being the *Salian* FRANKS under their leader *Merovius*.

Merovius's grandson, *Clovis I* (481 – 511), defeated both *Syagrius*, the Roman governor of Soissons, in 486, and a decade later the *Alemanni* at *Tolbiac*. He then adopted the Christian religion, being baptised at *Reims*, and in 508 made *Paris* his official capital. According to Frankish custom, the kingdom was divided on his death between his three sons into *Austrasia* (between the Meuse and the Rhine), *Neustria* (the territory to the N.W., from the Meuse to the Loire), and *Burgundy* (to the S.), and although the Merovingians remained in control, the dynasty was weakened by internicine warfare during the next two centuries. Eminent among the Merovingians were *Chilperic I* (king of Neustria from 561 – 84), and *Dagobert* (king of Austrasia from 622, and of all France from 628 until his death in 638). *Charles Martel* (714 – 41; an Austrasian) defeated at Poitiers in 732 the invading Moors or Saracens, who had overrun Spain during the previous two decades, but despite their reversal, the Moors continued to plague Provence among other southern territories.

Carolingians

Pepin (le Bref; 751 – 68)
Charlemagne (768 – 814)
Louis (le Débonnaire; 814 – 40)
Charles (le Chauve; 840 – 77)
Louis II (le Bègue; 877 – 79)
Louis III, and Carloman (879 – 82)
Carloman (882 – 84)

Charles (le Gros; 884 – 87)
Count Eudes (887 – 98)
Charles (le Simple; 898 – 922)
Louis IV (d'Outremer; 936 – 54)
Lothaire (954 – 86)
Louis V (le Fainéant; 986 – 87)

In 751 *Pepin*, Martel's son, deposed *Childeric III*, the last Merovingian, and founded a new dynasty, the Carolingians. He was succeeded by *Charlemagne*, who, in alliance with the Pope, extended his dominion over Germany and Italy, and was crowned 'Emperor of the West' or 'Holy Roman Emperor'. Charlemagne moved his seat of government to *Aix-la-Chapelle*. Not only a great ruler, he also presided over a remarkable revival of learning and education. However, the system of dividing territories on the death of kings was to cause the eventual disintegration of the empire, and in 843, by the *Treaty of Verdun*, those areas which were to form modern France were transferred to his grandson *Charles le Chauve*. Further division ensued, and France became little more than a collection of independent feudal states, controlled by dukes and counts. The situation was further aggravated by the invasions of Scandinavian or Norse pirates; by 912 the VIKINGS had settled in *Rouen* and had carved out the duchy of *Normandy* for themselves, having meanwhile besieged Paris (885). In 888 *Eudes*, duke of France and count of Paris, deposed *Charles le Gros*, but the Carolingian dynasty continued to stagger on for another hundred years. It was to be a century of disunity for France, distinguished politically by the growth of Norman power, and religiously by the foundation in 910 of a Benedictine abbey at *Cluny*, later to gain fame and influence.

Capetians

Huges Capet (987– 96)

Robert (le Pieux; 996– 1031)

Henri I (1031– 60)

Philippe I (1060– 1108)

Louis VI (le Gros; 1108– 37)

Louis VII (le Jeune; 1137– 80)

Philippe Auguste (1180– 1223)

Louis VIII (le Lion; 1223– 26)

Louis IX (St Louis; 1226– 70)

Philippe III (le Hardi; 1270– 85)

Philippe IV (le Bel; 1285– 1314)

Louis X (le Hutin; 1314– 16)

Jean I (1316; died 4 days old)

Philippe V (le Long; 1316– 22)

Charles IV (le Bel; 1322– 28)

Hugues Capet was elected by the nobles at *Senlis* in preference to any more incapable Carolingians, and he and his successors proceeded to make Paris the base of a centralising policy by which they might control the disunited country. This policy frequently brought them into conflict with independent spirits, one of whom, *William, Duke of Normandy*, in 1066 invaded and conquered England. The marriage in 1152 of the future *Henry II* of England to *Eleanor of Aquitaine* (the divorced wife of Louis VII), whose dowry brought Henry about one-third of France, was to cause a power struggle between the two countries which lasted three centuries.

Meanwhile, in 1095 *Urban II* preached the *First Crusade* at Clermont; in 1098 the abbey of *Cîteaux* was founded; in 1115 *Clairvaux* was founded by *St Bernard*, who in 1146 was to preach the *Second Crusade* at *Vézelay*. This religious enthusiasm was in part the reason for the Jews in France being expelled by *Philippe Auguste* in 1182, while in 1209 commenced the sanguinary *Albigensian Crusade* against the *Cathars* of Languedoc, which convulsed the southern half of the country. *Simon de Montfort*, with *Dominic Guzman* (later canonised), one of the leaders of the crusade, although victorious at the battle of Muret (1213), was killed before Toulouse five years later. A university was established here in 1229, partly as a bulwark of orthodoxy to counteract the possible recrudescence of heresy; others had been founded at Orléans and Montpellier, previously the home of an influential school of medicine, while that at Paris, at which Abelard had taught, was granted its first statutes by *Innocent III* in 1208.

In 1214 Philippe Auguste inflicted a heavy defeat on the allies of *John* of England at *Bouvines*, thus winning back a large part of the lost provinces (Normandy and Anjou), although the former was not formally surrendered until 1259, by *Henry III*, after his defeat by

Louis IX at *Saintes*. Louis, canonised in 1297, was a great crusader, and eventually lost his life at Tunis. The period between 1150 and 1300 was one of great expansion and building, and most of the major cathedrals of France were being erected or reconstructed, apart from numerous other churches. The second half of the 13C saw the establishment of a large number of *bastides* or new towns in the S.W. of the country by both English and French magnates, many of which are still recognisable by their grid pattern of streets. The same period likewise experienced the considerable growth of many of the older cities apart from Paris, among them those of Rouen and Montpellier, each containing as many as 40,000 inhabitants by the beginning of the 14C. It has been estimated that prior to the ravages of the *Black Death* in 1348, the population of Toulouse was 35,000, and of Tours, 30,000. Orléans, Strasbourg, and Narbonne had about 25,000 each, and Amiens, Bordeaux, Lille, and Metz, approximately 20,000 each, while Beauvais, Bourges, Dijon, Douai, Lyon, Marseille, Reims, and Avignon had between 10,000 and 20,000 each.

In 1309 *Clement V*, expelled from Rome, established himself at *Avignon*, where the popes remained until 1377, their place being taken by two anti-popes, not driven out until 1403.

House of Valois

Philippe VI (1328–50)	Louis XII (le Père du Peuple;
Jean II (le Bon; 1350–64)	1498–1515)
Charles V (le Sage; 1364–80)	François I (1515–47)
Charles VI (le Bien-Aimé;	Henri II (1547–59)
1380–1422)	François II (1559–60)
Charles VII (le Victorieux;	Charles IX (1560–74)
1422–61)	Henri III (1574–89)
Louis XI (1461–83)	
Charles VIII (l'Affable;	
1483–98)	

With the death in 1328 of *Charles IV*, the direct branch of the Capetian dynasty became extinct.

The claim of *Philippe de Valois*, cousin of Charles IV, to the throne was disputed by *Edward III* of England, who invaded France, thus precipitating the 'Hundred Years' War (1337–1453). He routed the French at *Crécy* (1346); at *Poitiers* (1356) he inflicted a further defeat on them, and captured *Jean II*. By the *Treaty of Brétigny* (1360) France surrendered *Aquitaine*, while Edward renounced all claim to the French crown; but before long desultory warfare between the two countries broke out again, and continued until the French had won back a large part of their lost territory, largely due to the tactics of *Du Guesclin*. Charles V was able to bring back some sort of order to his kingdom, but his weak-minded son became the pawn of rival regents, and for the next 40 years France suffered from dissentions between the aristocratic party, the *Armagnacs*, and the Burgundians, the popular party. Jean II had made his fourth son—*Jean sans Peur*—Duke of Burgundy.

In 1415 *Henry V* of England invaded France, and, supported by the Burgundians, defeated the French at *Agincourt*. By the *Treaty of Troyes* (1420) he received the hand of *Catherine*, Charles VI's daughter, together with the right of succession to the throne. Indeed, from 1420, when Henry entered Paris, until 1436, the English controlled the city, although Henry himself died at Vincennes in 1422, only seven weeks before the death of *Charles VI*. *Charles VII*, by himself no match for the English and Burgundians, found a champion in *Jeanne d'Arc* (Joan of Arc; 1412–31), who, after a brilliant campaign, defeated the English at *Orléans* in 1429. In the following year she was captured by the Burgundians at *Compiègne*, handed over to the English, and, condemned as a heretic by a court of French ecclesiastics, was burned at the stake at *Rouen*. Nevertheless, the successful revolt she had inspired continued; Paris was retaken in 1436, and in 1453, with the defeat and death of 'Old John Talbot', the *Earl of Shrewsbury*, at *Castillon*, E. of Bordeaux, little remained of the once extensive English possessions in France except Calais.

With the reign of *Louis XI*, the change from the medieval social system to the modern state was accelerated. Provincial 'Parlements', in addition to those already established at Toulouse and Grenoble, were set up at Bordeaux and Dijon, a policy later extended to Rouen, Aix-en-Provence, and (in 1554) Rennes. A brilliant and unscrupulous politician—and relieved of the menace of England, then occupied with the domestic 'Wars of the Roses'—Louis proceeded to crush the great feudal lordships which encroached on his territory, the most threatening being that of *Charles the Bold* of Burgundy ('le Téméraire; 1433–77). The *Peace of Péronne* (1468) gave the Burgundians a momentary advantage, but in 1475 Louis managed to alienate Charles' English allies by the *Treaty of Picquigny*. After Charles' death before the walls of *Nancy*, Louis soon overwhelmed his lesser adversaries, bringing *Arras*, the *Franche-Comté*, *Anjou*, and *Maine* into direct allegiance to the crown. In 1481, after the death of *Count René*, Duc d'Anjou, *Provence* also became part of France. In 1484 the first meeting of the *Estates-General* was convened at *Tours*, near which, in the Loire valley, several châteaux were being rebuilt as royal residences.

The following half century was principally occupied by indecisive campaigns in Italy, the only tangible result of which—particularly during the reign of *François I*—was the establishment in France of the cultural concepts of the Italian Renaissance. Among the more important literary figures of the period were *Marot*, *Rabelais*, *Du Bellay*, and *Ronsard*.

Charles VIII and *Louis XII* were successive husbands of *Anne de Bretagne*, whose dowry, the important duchy of *Brittany*, was united to France in 1532 on the death of her daughter, who had been married to François I. The reign of *Henri II* saw the acquisition of the *Three Bishoprics* (Metz, Toul, and Verdun), while *Calais* fell to the *Duc de Guise* in 1558. In the last year of his reign Henri concluded the *Treaty of Cateau-Cambrésis* with Philip II of Spain, thus ending the Italian wars.

The short reign of *François II*, who when still dauphin (aged 10) had married *Mary Stuart*, Queen of Scots, was followed by that of his brother *Charles IX*. At the instigation of *Catherine de Médicis*, his bigoted and domineering mother, Charles signed the order for the massacre of protestant Huguenots on the *Eve of St Bartholomew* (23 Aug. 1572). Catherine was mother also of *Henri III*, and of *Marguerite de Valois*, the first wife of *Henri of Navarre*. From 1560 until the promulgation of the *Edict of Nantes* in 1598, the country was ravaged sporadically by the Religious Wars of the *League* (La Ligue). In 1589 the ultra-Catholic *Henri, Duc de Guise* was murdered at *Blois* by Henri III, against whom he had been an overt rebel. The king himself was assassinated at *St-Cloud* the following year.

House of Bourbon

Henri IV (le Grand; 1589–1610)	Louis XV (le Bien-Aimé; 1715–74)
Louis XIII (le Juste; 1610–43)	Louis XVI (1774–92)
Louis XIV ('le Roi Soleil'; 1643–1715)	Louis XVII (never reigned)

The parents of *Henri IV* (of Navarre) were *Jeanne d'Albret* (daughter of *Marguerite of Navarre*) and *Antoine de Bourbon*, of the Bourbon branch of the Capetian dynasty, descending from *Robert of Clermont*, sixth son of Louis IX. A Protestant, Henri eventually defeated the Catholics at *Ivry* (1590), but was unable to enter the besieged capital until 1594, after he had ostensibly abjured his faith with (it is said) the cynical remark that 'Paris vaut bien une messe'. Nevertheless, despite his conversion, he granted Protestants freedom of worship by the *Edict of Nantes*. Among the many who joined in the general recognition of Henri as the legitimate heir to the throne was *Montaigne*, whose 'Essays' were published in part in 1580. However, with Henri's assassination by *Ravaillac* in 1610, religious restlessness returned, and the admirable reforms and economies instituted by *Sully*, his able minister, were brought to nothing by the extravagant favourites of young *Louis XIII* (whose mother, *Marie de Médicis*, Henri had married in 1600 after his divorce from Marguerite de Valois).

On Henri's death, Marie became Regent, but in 1624 *Card. Richelieu* (1585–1642) took over the reins of government. His main aim was the establishment of absolute royal power in France, and also of French supremacy in Europe. A great bigot, he suppressed all Protestant influence in politics, capturing their stronghold, *La Rochelle*, in 1628. Anyone defying Richelieu suffered severe penalties, and numerous fortresses throughout the country were dismantled in the process of repression. The cardinal then turned his attention to the House of Habsburg, which under the *Emperor Charles V* had been encroaching on the frontiers of France, and, in alliance with *Gustavus Adolphus* of Sweden, Richelieu involved France in the *Thirty Years' War*. The campaigns of the *Grand Condé* (1621–86; a member of a collateral branch of the Bourbons) resulted in the temporary acquisition of *Picardy*, *Alsace*, and *Roussillon*. *Anne of Austria*, consort of the king since 1614, gave birth to the future Louis XIV in 1638.

Richelieu had been succeeded meanwhile by *Card. Mazarin* (1602–61), who carried on his predecessor's policies. Although France was assured of the possession of Alsace and the Three Bishoprics by the *Treaty of Westphalia* in 1648, the expenses of campaigning were crippling. Civil war broke out, known as the *Fronde*, from which no one—the insurgents, Mazarin, Condé, or Marshal Turenne (1611–75)—emerged with much credit. During the Fronde, Condé (who had defeated the Spanish at *Rocroi* in 1643), allied himself with Spain, who had not subscribed to the Treaty of Westphalia, but Turenne's victory at the *Battle of the Dunes* forced Spain to accept the *Treaty of the Pyrenees* (1659), formally ceding Artois and Roussillon.

On Mazarin's death in 1661, *Louis XIV*, who had succeeded as a minor in 1643, decided to govern alone, duped by the conviction that 'L'État c'est moi'. The nobility were reduced to ineffectual courtiers, and the king selected his ministers from the *Haute bourgeoisie*, some, such as *Colbert* (1619–83), being very able. He then launched a series of costly wars of self-aggrandisement, which although they eventually increased the territory of France—its frontiers fortified by *Vauban* (1633–1707)—were to bring his long reign to a disastrous close. At the same time his indulgence in such extravagant projects as the building of a palace fit for the 'Roi Soleil' at *Versailles*, where Louis had chosen to transfer his court in 1672, further beggared the country. Here were gathered most of the great artists of this and succeeding epochs, while among composers *Lully* (from 1652 until his death in 1687), *Couperin*, and (in the following reign) *Rameau*, provided music to entertain the court. Paris, which had by now grown to a metropolis containing some 500,000 inhabitants, had become one of the cultural centres of Europe. *Corneille, Racine, Molière, La Fontaine, Boileau*, and *Pascal* (the latter associated with the activities of the reforming *Jansenists*) made their home there, while the salons of *Mme de Rambouillet* and *Mme de Sablé* had become the influential intellectual rendezvous of such figures as *La Rochfoucauld*, the *Scudérys*, and *Bossuet*. Meanwhile, in 1685, Louis had revoked the Edict of Nantes, an opprobrious act which again imposed Catholicism on the country.

The king's preoccupation with 'La Gloire' involved him first in the rapid campaign of 1667–68, which secured the possession of several towns in *Flanders*; while the *Dutch War* of 1672–78 ended in the *Peace of Nijmegen* and the absorption of the *Franche-Comté*. Less successful were the campaigns against the *League of Augsburg* (or the *Grand Alliance*; 1686–97), and the *War of the Spanish Succession* (1701–13), in which French forces suffered repeatedly at the hands of *Marlborough* and *Prince Eugène* (at *Blenheim* in 1704; *Ramillies* in 1706; *Oudenard* in 1708; and *Malplaquet* in 1709), although *Villars* won a victory at *Denain* (1712) after the withdrawal of the English from the war. 'If greatness of soul consists in a love of pageantry, an ostentation of fastidious pomp, a prodigality of expence, an affectation of munificence, an insolence of ambition, and a haughty reserve of deportment; Lewis certainly deserved the appellation of Great. Qualities which are really heroic, we shall not find in the composition of his character'. Such was Smollett's condemnation, for one. Life at court during the latter part of the reign and subsequent regency (under *Philippe, duc d'Orléans*; 1715–23) is brilliantly recorded in the 'Memoires' of the *Duc de Saint-Simon*. Several bad harvests decimated the peasantry—who formed four-fifths of the population of 20,000,000 in 1700—but colonial trade improved, and merchants thrived in such provincial centres as Bordeaux, Nantes, and Marseille.

The marriage in 1725 of *Louis XV* to *Maria*, daughter of *Stanislas Leczinski* (the deposed king of Poland), drew France into the *War of the Polish Succession* (1733), and further ruinous wars followed, including that of the *Austrian Succession* (in which Louis was allied with *Frederick the Great of Prussia* in opposition to England and Holland, who supported the cause of *Maria Theresia*, Empress of Austria). In spite of *Saxe's* brilliant victory at *Fontenay* (1745) the French gained little, while the English improved their position as a maritime power, and Prussia likewise gained in strength. The *Seven Years' War* (1756–63), in which France was allied to Austria, was a military disaster for France, and saw the loss of her flourishing colonies in India, North America, and the West Indies. By 1788 the cost of these wars had created a situation whereby three-quarters of the State expenditure was being spent on reducing the national debt and on defence! A customs-barrier raised round Paris, at the instigation of powerful and rapacious farmers-general of taxes, only fostered further discontent in the capital.

But in spite of the general degradation of his court, and the corruption and negligence rife among his administrators, the reign of Louis XV was made illustrious by some of the greatest names in French literature—*Voltaire, Rousseau, Montesquieu, Marivaux*, the *Encyclopédistes* (*Diderot*, and *d'Alembert*, etc.)—who frequented the fashionable salons of the *Marquise de Lambert, Mme de Tencin, Mme du Deffand, Mme Geoffrin*, et al. But many of the philosophers vehemently attacked both the establishment and the clergy, and their ideas undoubtedly helped to sow the seeds of revolution. At the same time, the expulsion of the Jesuits in 1764, after years of struggle with the Jansenists, removed one of the pillars of the *Ancien régime*.

On his accession, *Louis XVI* found the populace critical of his predecessor's extravagance and lack of military success, but was too weak to cope with the interminable financial crises (in spite of the reforms initiated by *Turgot* from 1774, and *Necker* from 1777). Economic problems were precipitated by bad harvests, particularly in 1787–88, when there were grain riots in many French towns, including Paris and Grenoble. These crises inspired reforms which, if accepted, would adversely affect the privileged estates ('les Privilégiés'): the upper ranks of the clergy (the First Estate), and the majority of the nobility (the Second Estate) therefore rejected them. Meanwhile, Louis' foreign policy, if it could be called such, which supported the American colonies in their struggle for independence from England, was not only financially disastrous, but indirectly did much to disseminate democratic ideals.

In an attempt to reform methods of taxation—for les Privilégiés held innumerable hereditary rights by which they avoided paying taxes, yet levied them to their own advantage—the king convoked an assembly of the *États généraux* or States General. The 1165 deputies elected met at *Versailles* on 5 May 1789, for the first time since 1614. The first political act of the Third Estate, the Non-privilégiés (which numbered almost 600) was the creation of a *National Assembly* (17 June), which, meeting separately in the Salle de Jeu de Paume on the 20th, swore not to disband until a constitution had been given to the country which would limit royal autocracy, and guarantee liberty, equality, and fraternity. Three days later *Mirabeau* defied the king: 'Nous sommes ici par la volonté du peuple et . . . on ne nous arrachera que par la force des baïonnettes'; and on 9 July, reinforced by many of the clergy and a minority of the nobility, the renamed *Assemblée constituante* set to work to frame such a constitution. But two days later Necker, who had promised further financial reforms, was dismissed by the king, and it was feared that this gratuitous act would be followed by the dissolution of the Assembly.

The Revolution. The citizens of Paris—and also in the provinces (at Dijon, Rennes, Lyon, Nantes, and Le Havre)—were provoked into more open rebellion, culminating in the storming of the Bastille on 14 July, but while the next few months saw numerous reforms, there was little political or economic stability, and tensions heightened. In an attempt to avoid bankruptcy, Church lands were nationalised. Many of the nobility sought asylum abroad while the going was good. The king and his unpopular consort, *Marie-Antoinette*, were virtually prisoners in the Tuileries; they attempted to flee the country, but were arrested (at *Varennes* in June 1791) and brought back ignominiously to Paris. On 1 Oct. 1791 a new Legislative Assembly was formed, which in the following April declared war on Austria to forestall foreign intervention. The Assembly was at first swayed by the moderate *Girondins*, but the following year the extreme *Jacobins* under *Danton, Robespierre*, and *Marat*, siezed power, and, as the *National Assembly* (meeting on 20 Sept., the day on which the victory of *Valmy* turned the tide of war in France's favour), established the *Republic*.

On 21 Jan. 1793 Louis XVI was executed in the Place de la Révolution, an act soon followed by the setting-up in March of the dictatorial *Committee of Public Safety*, which, suspicious of the moderate party, ruthlessly suppressed all suspected of royalist sympathies. The guillotine was in constant action. In July Marat was assassinated, and even the Dantonists found themselves to be a moderating force, opposed to the even more sanguinary *Hébertists*. But Robespierre, chief architect of the *Reign of Terror*, brooked no rivals, and early in 1794 both *Hébert* and Danton were guillotined. However, after further weeks of ferocious intimidation, the reaction came, and on 27 July Robespierre's own head fell.

By the following year the Girondins were again in control, although the Royalists continued to make determined efforts to change the course of events, particularly in the *Vendée*, where they were eventually suppressed by *Hoche*. On 28 Oct. 1795 a *Directory* of five assumed power. One of the five was *Barras*, to whom the young Corsican general, *Napoleon Bonaparte* (1769–1821), owed his promotion as general of the Interior. During the next four years French republican armies under Bonaparte won notable successes abroad, especially in campaigns in Italy against the Austrians (whom he was to crush at *Marengo* on 14 June, 1800). Returning to Paris after his failure to destroy the British fleet at the *Battle of the Nile*, Bonaparte found the tyrannical Directory generally detested, and with the help of the army and of *Siéyès*, established the *Consulate* by a *Coup d'état* on 9-10 Nov. 1799. Bonaparte became First Consul, assisted by Siéyès and *Roger Ducos*. A new constitution awarded him the consulate for life, but such was his personal ambition that he caused himself to be declared 'Emperor of the French', and was crowned Napoleon I in Notre-Dame by Pope Pius VII (18 May, 1804). A *Civil Code*, largely retaining the liberal laws of the Revolution, was laid down.

First Empire. Faced by a new coalition of England, Austria, and Russia, Napoleon shattered the last two at *Austerlitz* in 1805, and imposed on them the humiliating *Peace of Pressburg*, but his fleet had been virtually destroyed at *Trafalgar* only six weeks earlier. In the following year Prussian armies were cowed at *Jena* and *Auerstadt*, and a further campaign against Russia was ended by the *Treaty of Tilsit*, which brought temporary peace to the Czar. Austria attempted to renew the struggle, but suffered disastrous defeats at *Essling* and *Wagram*. The subsequent *Peace of Vienna* (1809) marked perhaps the apogee of the emperor's power.

Meanwhile, his brother *Joseph* had been imposed on the Spaniards, whose guerrilla methods of carrying on the war in the Peninsula were to cause a continual drain on Napoleon's reserves of power. England sent two expeditionary forces to assist the Spaniards, and under *Wellington* they inflicted a series of defeats on the French, culminating in the battles of *Vitoria* (1813), and—on French territory itself—*Toulouse*. Napoleon himself had just returned from the suicidal invasion of Russia, where the 'Grande Armée', although successful at *Borodino*, was virtually annihilated at the crossing of the Beresina by 'Generals January and February'. The Prussians, having recovered from their previous defeats, were able to retaliate at *Leipzig* (Oct. 1813), and entered France. Paris itself surrendered to the Allies (31 March, 1814); the emperor abdicated at Fontainebleau, and retired to the island of Elba.

The Bourbons were restored, but the *Treaty of Paris* (30 May, 1814) cut the empire down to size. During 'the Hundred Days' (26 March-24 June, 1815), Napoleon made a desperate attempt to regain absolute power, having claimed at Grenoble (en route to Paris from Elba) that he had come to deliver France from 'the insolence of the nobility, the pretentions of the priests, and the yoke of foreign powers'. His defeat at *Waterloo* (18 June), and subsequent banishment to St Helena, where he died in 1821, enabled the king—*Louis XVIII* (1814–24)—to resume his precarious throne, which he was only able to retain by repressive measures: the University of Paris, for example, was supervised by the clergy! The reign of his successor, *Charles X*, whose reactionary *Ordinances of St-Cloud* suppressed the liberty of the press and reduced the electorate to the landed classes, only proved that the bigoted Bourbons could 'learn nothing and forget nothing'. The '*July Revolution*' of 1830 lost him his throne.

House of Orléans. *Louis-Philippe* (1830–48; son of '*Philippe-Égalité' d'Orléans* of the Revolution) was chosen as head of the 'July Monarchy', and the upper middle class, who had striven for power since 1789, now achieved it. Most of the urban populace, however, still lived in pestilential conditions: some 19,000 Parisians of a total of about 900,000 died in an outbreak of cholera in 1832. The total population of France was then about 32,500,000. The only other towns of any size were Lyon and Marseille, with about 115,000 each, and Bordeaux and Rouen with about 90,000 each. France was still essentially a country dominated by agriculture and by a rural population. The 'citizen-king' surrounded Paris with a ring of fortifications in 1841–45, but these could not defend him against the mass of his people. Socialist ideas were spreading, but the conservative policy of *Guizot* opposed any reforms, and in the '*February Revolution*' of 1848 Louis-Philippe was overthrown. In the elections that followed, which introduced universal male suffrage, the electorate leapt from 250,000 to 9,000,000. Among famous literary figures during the first half of the century were *Balzac, Chateaubriand, Hugo, George Sand, Stendhal, Flaubert, Gautier,* and *Sainte-Beuve*.

A *Second Republic* was set up by the provisional government, and *Louis Napoleon* (Bonaparte's undistinguished and indolent, but shrewd and cynical nephew, who as pretender had already made two abortive attempts to regain the throne) was elected Prince-President by almost 75 per cent of those who voted; but such was the sentimental prevalence of the idea of empire, that in Dec. 1851 a *coup d'état* (involving the temporary imprisonment of some 30,000 in opposition) led to his election as the *Emperor Napoleon III* some months later, thus inaugurating the *Second Empire*. Having adopted the clever but misleading motto of 'L'Empire c'est la paix', he proceded to embroil the country in a succession of wars, first in the *Crimea* (1854–56), and then in Italy, which he undertook to deliver from

Austrian oppression, afterwards unchivalrously demanding *Savoy* and *Nice* in recompense. In 1870 Napoleon III declared war on Prussia, the inglorious campaign virtually ending with the capitulation of *Sedan*, where the king himself was taken prisoner and deposed. He died in exile at Chislehurst (England) in 1873.

Third Republic

Presidents in office:

1871–73 Adolphe Thiers	1906–13 Armand Fallières
1873–79 Maréchal MacMahon	1913–20 Raymond Poincaré
1879–87 Jules Grévy	1920 Paul Deschanel
1887–94 Sadi Carnot	1920–24 Alexandre Millerand
1894–95 Jean Casimir-Périer	1924–31 Gaston Doumergue
1895–99 Félix Faure	1931–32 Paul Doumer
1899–1906 Émile Loubet	1932–40 Albert Lebrun

Gambetta and *Thiers* were largely instrumental in forming the *Third Republic*, which had been proclaimed (4 Sept. 1870) while German troops were advancing on Paris. After a four-month siege and much suffering and famine, Paris capitulated on 28 Jan. 1871. Order was not re-established until the *Communard Insurrection* (18 March-29 May) had been crushed at the cost of pitched battles in the streets, in which 3-4000 Communards were killed and several public buildings destroyed. Retaliatory measures included the summary execution of 20-25,000 Parisians, mostly of the working classes; and in addition some 4-5000 were deported. Thiers, who was ultimately responsible for these mass killings, was then declared President. An amnesty bill, introduced by Gambetta, was—expediently—not adopted until 1880.

By Sept. 1873 the occupying troops had gone, but France was left to pay a heavy war indemnity, and lost the provinces of *Alsace* and *Lorraine*. Various political crises, embittered by the reprehensible *'Dreyfus affair'* (1894–1906), coloured much of the period up to the outbreak of the *First World War*, differing facets of which were well described by *Zola*, and later by *Proust*. An 'Entente Cordiale' between Britain and France was established in 1904, putting an end to colonial rivalry, and paving the way for future cooperation. In 1903 the 'Loi sur les Associations' was passed, and in 1905 the Church was separated from the State, both essential measures to counteract the pernicious influence the ecclesiastics and religious orders still had on education.

War with Germany broke out on 3 Aug. 1914. French troops were dramatically reinforced at the *Marne* by some 11,000 men rushed to the front in Parisian taxis, but although the capital was saved from another occupation, ten departments were overrun, and the attrition of three long years of trench warfare followed. In 1916, with the *Battle of the Somme* and the French stand at *Verdun*, the tide began to turn against Germany, but at an appalling cost (on both sides) in men's lives. On 11 Nov. 1918 an armistice was signed. The provinces lost by France through the *Treaty of Versailles* in 1871 were restored, although *Clemenceau*, the 'Tiger', France's Prime Minister, wanted more. Nothing, however, could compensate for the staggering loss of manpower during the war years. For every ten Frenchmen between 20 and 45, two had been killed—a total of 1,300,000. Slowly the country recruited her strength, even if, politically, she showed little initiative. Her defence was concentrated on the construction of a costly and supposedly impregnable barrier along the German frontier—the *Maginot Line* (named after a minister of war)—which was immediately side-stepped by invading armoured divisions at the outbreak of the *Second World War* (Sept. 1939), thus underlining the sagacity of the French high command.

Demoralised French forces, in no state to resist, and not capable of mounting a successful counter-attack, capitulated to the triumphant Reich, while a high proportion of the British expeditionary force managed to re-cross the channel from *Dunkerque* (27 Mar.-4 June, 1940) in a fleet of open boats sent to its rescue. The Germans proceeded to occupy the northern half of the country and the Atlantic coast, overrunning the rest of France after 11 Nov. 1942. For the remainder of the war, the underground *Resistance Movement* bravely did what it could to thwart the collaborating policies of the 'Vichy Government', presided over by the octogenarian *Marshal Pétain*, hero of Verdun, and *Pierre Laval*, among others.

Meanwhile a provisional government had been set up in London by *Gén. Charles de Gaulle* (1890–1970), and Free French forces co-operated in the liberation of France. Allied troops disembarking in Normandy and in the South of France (on 6 June and 15 Aug. 1944, respectively) converged on Paris, which was freed by late August. But an armistice with Germany was not signed until 8 Mar. 1945. The occupying troops were after a fierce campaign driven from French soil, and France was able to participate in the victory celebrations.

In Oct. 1946 the *Fourth Republic* was proclaimed, of which *Vincent Auriol* (1947–54), and *René Coty* (1954–58) were presidents. Women now had the vote, and proportional representation was adopted. Slowly, despite many changes in government, and despite defeat in Indo-China and Revolt in Algeria, the country was restored to economic prosperity after the physical and moral devastation of war. In 1957 a *Common Market* (EEC) was established, in which France, West Germany, Italy, and the Benelux countries were founder members.

Fifth Republic

1958–69 Charles de Gaulle	1974–81 Valéry Giscard d'Estaing
1969–74 Georges Pompidou	1981– François Mitterand

In 1958 de Gaulle prepared a new constitution, which was approved by a referendum, and the general was elected the first president of the new republic by universal direct suffrage, for a period of seven years. The powers of the head of state were considerably—some would say inordinately—increased: he nominates the prime minister, who in turn recommends the members of the government; he can make laws and refer decisions of major importance to popular vote by referendum; in extreme cases he has the power to dismiss the National Assembly.

In 1962 Algerian independence was proclaimed, since when a remarkable number of Algerians can be seen in the industrial towns of France. In 1965 de Gaulle was returned to power with enthusiasm, but with a reduced majority. In May 1968 a serious 'Student Revolution' took place in Paris, which precipitated overdue educational reforms. The following year de Gaulle was succeeded by *Pompidou*, who died in office in 1974. His successor was *Giscard d'Estaing*, whose somewhat cavalier attitude to the mass of his countrymen produced a reaction, and a swing to the Left, with *Mitterand* moving into the Élysée. But, like the Bourbons, the Socialist regime appears also to have 'learnt nothing and forgot nothing'. Mitterand immediately alienated many of his supporters by the inclusion of Communist ministers in the government, a devious manoeuvre which in turn will no doubt provoke reaction.

Administration

France is now divided in 96 *Départements* (including Corsica; 20 A/B), and each has its number, the majority of these being formed arbitrarily, for administrative purposes, in 1790, out of the old provinces or military governments, and with certain exceptions are named after some natural feature, often a river.

At the beginning of the 17C there were twelve *Grands gouvernements*, or provinces, namely: *Auvergne, Bourgogne, Bretagne, Champagne, Dauphiné, Guyenne* (which had since 1052 included the duchy of Gascogne), *Île de France, Languedoc, Lyonnais, Normandie, Picardie,* and *Provence.* Prior to 1789 the new provinces of *Alsace, Artois, Franche-Comté, French Flanders, Lorraine,* and *Corsica,* were ceded or annexed to the *Domaine royale.* Many of the older gouvernements had by then split up, and in 1789 there were over thirty areas known as *intendances,* often still termed provinces, the function of *gouverneurs* after 1636 being largely superceded by the king's provincial inspectors of justice, police, and finance, and known as *intendants.*

Each department is administered by a *préfet,* appointed by the President, and assisted by a *conseil général,* and its main town is the seat of the *préfecture.* Départements are sub-divided into *arrondissements,* each with it *sous-préfet* and its sous-préfecture. The team *préfet* has recently been changed under the Socialist regime to the dour title of *Commissaire de la Republique.* The *canton,* a sub-division of the arrondissement, is the judicial unit, under a *juge de paix.* The canton included a number of *communes* or parishes, each presided over by a *maire,* and the commune—of which there are some 36,400—is the administrative unit of local government.

In 1972, in an attempt to break the administrative stranglehold of Paris, the départments were grouped into 22 *Régions* (including one for Corsica), which, although they may assist the bureaucratic machine, are confusing to most people, as their boundaries cut across areas once reasonably well understood. For example, the region denominated *Pays de la Loire* comprises départments 44 (Loire-Atlantique), previously part of Brittany; 53 (Mayenne), and 72 (Sarthe), originally forming Maine; 49 (Maine-et-Loire), previously Anjou; and 85 (Vendée), previously part of Poitou. As far as this guide is concerned, although tabulated below, these administrative regions are ignored.

Population. The total population of mainland France (not including Corsica), according to the census of 1982, was in round figures, 54,000,000. The population of Corsica was 230,000. See also note on p 19.

The **Departments** of mainland France are listed below, together with the *Préfecture,* and in brackets, the administrative *Région.* This is followed by the name of the former Province, in those cases where it differs from the modern region.

01	Ain: *Bourg-en-Bresse* (Rhône-Alpes)—Bourgogne
02	Aisne: *Laon* (Picardie)—Île-de-France
03	Allier: *Moulins* (Auvergne)—Bourbonnais
04	Alpes-de-Haute Provence: *Digne* (Provence-Alpes-Côte-d'Azur)—Provence
05	Hautes Alpes: *Gap* (Provence-Alpes-Côte d'Azur)—Dauphiné
06	Alpes-Maritimes: *Nice* (Provence-Alpes-Côte d'Azur)—Comté de Nice
07	Ardèches: *Privas* (Rhône-Alpes)—Languedoc

08	Ardennes: *Charleville-Mézières* (Champagne-Ardenne)—Champagne
09	Ariège: *Foix* (Midi-Pyrénées)—Comté de Foix
10	Aube: *Troyes* (Champagne-Ardenne)—Champagne
11	Aude: *Carcassonne* (Languedoc-Roussillon)—Languedoc
12	Aveyron: *Rodez* (Midi-Pyrénées)—Guyenne et Gascogne
13	Bouches-du-Rhône: *Marseille* (Provence-Alpes-Côte d'Azur)—Provence
14	Calvados: *Caen* (Basse-Normandie)—Normandie
15	Cantal: *Aurillac* (Auvergne)
16	Charente: *Angoulême* (Poitou-Charentes)—Angoumois
17	Charente-Maritime: *La Rochelle* (Poitou-Charentes)—Aunis et Saintonge
18	Cher: *Bourges* (Centre)—Berri
19	Corrèze: *Tulle* (Limousin)
21	Côte d'Or: *Dijon* (Bourgogne)
22	Côtes-du-Nord: *St-Brieuc* (Bretagne)
23	Creuse: *Guéret* (Limousin)—Marche
24	Dordogne: *Périgueux* (Aquitaine)—Guyenne et Gascogne
25	Doubs: *Besançon* (Franche-Comté)
26	Drôme: *Valence* (Rhône-Alpes)—Dauphiné
27	Eure: *Évreux* (Haute-Normandie)—Normandie
28	Eure-et-Loir: *Chartres* (Centre)—Orléanais
29	Finistère: *Quimper* (Bretagne)
30	Gard: *Nîmes* (Languedoc-Roussillon)—Languedoc
31	Haute-Garonne: *Toulouse* (Midi-Pyrénées)—Languedoc
32	Gers: *Auch* (Midi-Pyrénées)—Guyenne et Gascogne
33	Gironde: *Bordeaux* (Aquitaine)—Guyenne et Gascogne
34	Hérault: *Montpellier* (Languedoc-Roussillon)—Languedoc
35	Ille-et-Vilaine: *Rennes* (Bretagne)
36	Indre: *Châteauroux* (Centre)—Berri
37	Indre-et-Loire: *Tours* (Centre)—Touraine
38	Isère: *Grenoble* (Rhône-Alpes)—Dauphiné
39	Jura: *Lons-le-Saunier* (Franche-Comté)
40	Landes: *Mont-de-Marsan* (Aquitaine)—Guyenne et Gascogne
41	Loir-et-Cher: *Blois* (Centre)—Orléanais
42	Loire: *St-Étienne* (Rhône-Alpes)—Lyonnais
43	Haute-Loire: *Le Puy* (Auvergne)—Languedoc
44	Loire-Atlantique: *Nantes* (Pays de la Loire)—Bretagne
45	Loiret: *Orléans* (Centre)—Orléanais
46	Lot: *Cahors* (Midi-Pyrénées)—Guyenne et Gascogne
47	Lot-et-Garonne: *Agen* (Aquitaine)—Guyenne et Gascogne
48	Lozère: *Mende* (Languedoc-Roussillon)—Languedoc
49	Maine-et-Loire: *Angers* (Pays de la Loire)—Anjou
50	Manche: *St-Lô* (Basse-Normandie)—Normandie
51	Marne: *Châlons-sur-Marne* (Champagne-Ardenne)—Champagne
52	Haute-Marne: *Chaumont* (Champagne-Ardenne)—Champagne
53	Mayenne: *Laval* (Pays de la Loire)—Maine
54	Meurthe-et-Moselle: *Nancy* (Lorraine)
55	Meuse: *Bar-le-Duc* (Lorraine)
56	Morbihan: *Vannes* (Bretagne)
57	Moselle: *Metz* (Lorraine)
58	Nièvre: *Nevers* (Bourgogne)—Nivernais
59	Nord: *Lille* (Nord—Pas-de-Calais)—Frandre
60	Oise: *Beauvais* (Picardie)—Île-de-France
61	Orne: *Alençon* (Basse-Normandie)—Normandie
62	Pas-de-Calais: *Arras* (Nord-Pas-de-Calais)—Artois
63	Puy-de-Dôme: *Clermont-Ferrand* (Auvergne)
64	Pyrénées-Atlantiques: *Pau* (Aquitaine)—Béarn
65	Hautes-Pyrénées: *Tarbes* (Midi-Pyrénées)—Guyenne et Gascogne
66	Pyrénées-Orientales: *Perpignan* (Languedoc-Roussillon)—Roussillon
67	Bas-Rhin: *Strasbourg* (Alsace)
68	Haut-Rhin: *Colmar* (Alsace)
69	Rhône: *Lyon* (Rhône-Alpes)—Lyonnais
70	Haute-Saône: *Vesoul* (Franche-Comté)
71	Saône-et-Loire: *Mâcon* (Bourgogne)

72	Sarthe: *Le Mans* (Pays de la Loire)—Maine
73	Savoie: *Chambéry* (Rhône-Alpes)—Savoie
74	Haute-Savoie: *Annecy* (Rhône-Alpes)—Savoie
75	Ville de Paris: *Paris* (Île-de-France)
76	Seine-Maritime: *Rouen* (Haute-Normandie)—Normandie
77	Seine-et-Marne: *Melun* (Île-de-France)
78	Yvelines: *Versailles* (Île-de-France)
79	Deux-Sèvres: *Niort* (Poitou-Charentes)—Poitou
80	Somme: *Amiens* (Picardie)
81	Tarn: *Albi* (Midi-Pyrénées)—Languedoc
82	Tarn-et-Garonne: *Montauban* (Midi-Pyrénées)—Guyenne et Gascogne
83	Var: *Toulon* (Provence-Alpes-Côte-d'Azur)—Provence
84	Vaucluse: *Avignon* (Provence-Alpes-Côte-d'Azur)—Comtat Venaissin
85	Vendée: *La Roche-sur-Yon* (Pays de la Loire)—Poitou
86	Vienne: *Poitiers* (Poitou-Charentes)—Poitou
87	Haute-Vienne: *Limoges* (Limousin)
88	Vosges: *Épinal* (Lorraine)
89	Yonne: *Auxerre* (Bourgogne)
90	Territoire-de-Belfort: *Belfort* (Franche-Comté)—Alsace
91	Essonne: *Évry* (Île-de-France)
92	Hauts-de-Seine: *Nanterre* (Île-de-France)
93	Seine-Saint-Denis: *Bobigny* (Île-de-France)
94	Val-de-Marne: *Créteil* (Île-de-France)
95	Val-d'Oise: *Pontoise* (Île-de-France)

The 21 mainland **Régions**—the department of which they are comprised being shown in brackets—are as follows, together with their administrative capitals.

Alsace (67; 68); Strasbourg
Aquitaine (24; 33; 40; 47; 64); Bordeaux
Auvergne (10; 15; 43; 63); Clermont-Ferrand
Basse-Normandie (14; 50; 61); Caen
Bourgogne (21; 58; 71; 89); Dijon
Bretagne (22; 29; 35; 56); Rennes
Centre (18; 28; 36; 37; 41; 45); Orléans
Champagne-Ardennes (08; 10; 51; 52); Châlons-sur-Marne
Franche-Comté (25; 39; 70; 90); Besançon
Île-de-France (75; 77; 78; 91; 92; 93; 94; 95) Paris
Haute-Normandie (27; 76); Rouen
Languedoc-Roussillon (11; 30; 34; 48; 66); Montpellier
Limousin (19; 23; 87); Limoges
Lorraine (54; 55; 57; 88); Metz
Midi-Pyrénées (09; 12; 31; 32; 46; 65; 81; 82); Toulouse
Nord-Pas-de-Calais (59; 62); Lille
Pays de la Loire (44; 49; 53; 72; 85); Nantes
Picardie (02; 60; 80); Amiens
Poitou-Charentes (16; 17; 79; 86); Poitiers
Provence-Alpes-Côte d'Azur (04; 05; 06; 13; 83; 84); Marseille
Rhône-Alpes (01; 07; 26; 38; 42; 69; 73; 74); Lyon

Regions

THE WINES OF FRANCE

by *Julian Brind*

France produces a high proportion of the world's finest wines. So wide a field cannot possibly be covered in a few pages, and the reader requiring detailed studies is referred to the selective list of books on French Wines on p. 50. For Map of the main wine-producing areas see p 37.

History. The *Vitis Vinifera* via appears to have been known in Persia, and later in Egypt (c. 5000 B.C.). By c. 600 B.C. vines were being planted in Provence by Greek settlers, although the Romans were to a larger extent responsible for the expansion of the vineyards, particularly in what is now known as Languedoc and Roussillon, with Narbonne an important base for the manufacture of storage recepticals. Vienne, in the Rhône valley, was another thriving centre for the wine trade. With the growth of the Empire more vineyards were laid out, particularly along river valleys, whose banks were cleared to provide easier communication between the main centres, and later planted by the local inhabitants. Many of these were Gallo-Roman farmers—often also pressed into service as legioneers—who pursued this occupation when not engaged in the domination of native tribes. The Rhône valley was thus developed during the 1C A.D., while in the following century areas near present-day Bordeaux, and in Burgundy and the Saône valley, were planted. By the 4C the valleys of the Rhine and Mosel were under cultivation, and vineyards were laid out on the banks of the Seine and Loire. Wine was preserved from turning into acetic acid by the admixture of honey and herbs (the incidental origin of *Vermouth*), for although recepticals were sealed, the use of corks was not general until c. 1750.

After the demise of the Empire, the Church controlled the production of wine, partly for the pleasure of drinking and also to provide wine for celebrating mass. The Benedictines in particular extended the areas under cultivation, notably at the monastic centre of Cluny in Burgundy. Later, Crusaders returned from the Middle East with Pinot and Gamay vines, which now produce the fine wines of Champagne, Burgundy and Beaujolais, and also the Muscat variety, which was developed in Roussillon, near Frontignan, and Rivasaltes.

With the marriage of Henry II to Eleanor of Aquitaine in 1152, England become more involved in the import of wines from France. The vineyards of the Loire as well as those of Bordeaux came under English control, while the vineyards in England went into a decline. Bordeaux wine, often a light red in colour, and known as clairette, was anglicized as *Claret*. By 1453 the English crown had lost virtually all her French possessions, and her traders were at a disadvantage; indeed, Scottish importers found favour, and some of the best claret cellars could be found in Scotland: it was then that the English started importing Rhine wines, and later, wines from Portugal.

Meanwhile, although the import of wines from France was sporadically prohibited due to hostilities, or restricted by high duties, the quality of French wines continued to improve. By the 18C the use of cork stoppers enabled wines to be matured slowly in bottles rather than in vats or casks, and in 1781 vintage wine was first bottled and laid down by *Château Lafite*. In 1786 Pitt's commercial treaty with France facilitated once more the importation of her wines, although during the period of the Revolution and subsequent Napoleonic Wars French wines were rarely shipped across the Channel. However, in 1860 Gladstone lowered the duty on French wines, and imports rose again. Clarets were by now often sophisticated by the addition of stronger wines from Cahors, or Hermitage, and even by brandy, while the better Bordeaux wines began from 1855 to be listed in order of quality, a classification which still holds good. (The only change was in 1973, when Mouton Rothschild joined the highest class of Châteaux-Lafite, Latour, Margaux, and Haut Brion.) The sweet white Sauternes were likewise classified, but those of the rest of the Gironde area were only classified in 1955. The hierarchy of growths (*crus classés*) can be confusing, each area varying in its terminology.

Meanwhile, in the 1870s, European vineyards were attacked by two devastating enemies—the first a mildew known as *Oidium Tuckeri*; then the *Phylloxera* aphid, imported unsuspectingly by keen viticuluralists on cuttings from America (where it is indigenous), a microscopic louse which, living on the sap, bleeds the plant to death. The biologists of the Botanical Gardens at Kew were the first to analyse and resolve the problem, and the European vineyards were saved from extinction by the resourceful grafting of European shoots onto vines of American stock, which were found to be resistant to the disease, having thicker and tougher bark. The mildew was counteracted by the development of sprays. At the same time, Louis Pasteur's experiments with the alcoholic fermentation of wine emphasized the importance of clean and controlled fermentations by the correct yeast, thus enabling better wines to be produced.

Jealous of their reputation as producers of quality wines, several vineyard owners would bottle their wines on the premises to prevent the fraudulent abuse of appellations, for in the late 19C and early 20C numerous blended wines were being sold under prestigious names. In 1936 the Institut National des Appellations d'Origine, in conjunction with the French government, passed the first 'Appellation Contrôlée' laws, specifying—for example—the geographical titles, grape types, pruning methods, alcoholic content, and production per hectare, etc. of the various varieties. Since then, legislation has been extended to qualify various levels of quality which may be attained. The lowest level is the *Vin de Consumation Courante* (VCC), or 'vin ordinaire'; then the recently introduced *Vin de Pays*; next the *Vin Delimité de Qualité Superiéur* (VDQS); and finally those with an *Appellation Contrôlée* (AC).

With the independence of Algeria in 1966, several French wines became noticeably lighter, particularly in the Midi, where poor wines, low in alcoholic content, had previously been bolstered by the addition of heavy and stronger Algerian reds. Since then, helped by government subsidies, producers in the Midi, among others, have been making tolerable wines in their own right, some of them much improved in quality, a tendency extending throughout the main wine-producing areas.

The most northerly vineyards are those of **Champagne**, known for fine sparkling white (or rosé) wines produced on the rolling predominantly chalk hills around Reims and Épernay. Originally still wines, the 'sparkle' was supposedly introduced by Dom Perignon, a Benedictine monk from Hautvilliers, during the years 1668–1715, although 'Blanquette de Limoux' (S. of Carcassonne, in the Aude) also lays claim to introducing the method. The 'Méthode Champenoise' is that which induces a second fermentation in the bottle, a complex process which the interested traveller will find described in detail in Patrick Forbes' study of Champagne; and a visit

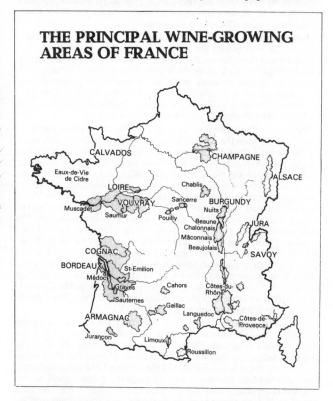

THE PRINCIPAL WINE-GROWING AREAS OF FRANCE

to one of the houses of the better known manufacturers is advised. *Vintage Champagne* is a wine produced from one year, although a blend from different villages in the region area; non-vintage Champagnes are a blend of wines from different years. The grapes used are normally a combination of the red *Pinot Noir* and the white *Chardonnay* variety, the latter being used on its own to manufacture the *Blanc de Blancs Champagne*.

Alsace. This area, parallel to the W. bank of the Rhine, is protected by the Vosges mountains, the lower E. slopes of which, being comparatively dry and warm, produce some excellent white wines named after the grape variety rather than a place name. During the German occupation of Alsace after 1870, the Alsatians were obliged to produce in bulk for blending with the wines of the lower Rhine and Moselle, and it was only in 1945 that AC was instituted. Alsatian wines are generally dry, and the grape varieties are divided into 'noble' grapes and the more ordinary. The cheaper wines are known as

'*Zwicker*', a blend of both types, the more expensive being '*Edelzwicker*', from noble grapes only. Among the finest are the *Riesling* grape wines, while the *Gewürztraminer* produces a wine with an individual spicy flavour as its name suggests. Other noble grapes are the *Pinot Gris* (also known as *Tokay d'Alsace*, for it is believed to have been imported from Hungary), *Muscat d'Alsace*, and *Sylvaner*. Among the more ordinary grapes are *Pinot Blanc*, *Chasselas*, *Müller-Thurgau*, and *Knipperle*.

Jura. This wine-producing area is centred on Arbois and Château Chalon. Its *Vins jaunes* are matured in wood for at least six years under a yeast film lying on its surface, the same 'flor' that lies on that of a Fino sherry. Its *Vins de Paille* are so-called from the process of drying the grapes on straw mats, and are likewise powerful, rich, long-lived wines. A variety of other wines—red, white, and rosé—of individual flavour are also found, but the volume produced is small and they are therefore comparatively highly priced.

Burgundy. There are four main areas. The finest wines (reds and whites) come from the *Côte d'Or* (between Dijon and Chagny, to the S.), divided into the *Côte de Nuits* and *Côte de Beaune*. The former includes the vineyards of *Gevrey-Chambertin*, *Chambolle-Musigny*, *Vosne-Romanée* and *Nuits St-Georges*; the latter includes the villages of *Pommard* and *Volnay*, and the white wine-producing villages of *Meursault*, *Puligny-Montrachet*, and *Chassagne-Montrachet*. These double-barrelled names have come about by linking the original village name to that of its most famous adjacent vineyard. The Burgundians have recently extended their vineyards towards the summit of this range of hills, and have been granted the Appellation *Hautes Côtes de Nuits* and *Hautes Côtes de Beaune*, but although good wines, they are lesser than those of the traditional areas. Some 20km E. of Auxerre is the town of *Chablis*, the centre of another small district producing white Burgundy. Here the noble *Chardonnay* grape produces a delicate wine lighter than those of the Côte de Beaune, but it does not age so well.

Most of the famous vineyards of Burgundy are split up into small holdings, some growers having rows only of vines in several of the better-known vineyards. This is a form of insurance, because the region is subject to devastating hail storms, which when they strike can destroy the crop in a localized area, although the hazard is partly counteracted by resorting to hail guns, spraying hail clouds, or netting the vineyards, which is also a protection against birds. The main cause of this fragmentation of property was the division of ecclesiastical estates among peasant proprietors after the Revolution, and Burgundy, with Cluny as a centre, was particularly affected in this respect. This makes the shipping houses (Latour; Bouchard, et al.) influential and important, for they buy in quantity from the small growers with differing wines, which are then blended to produce a 'house style', each different from his competitors, so it is incumbent on the consumer to select the 'house style' he prefers.

To the S. of the Côte d'Or are the gentler slopes of the *Côte Chalonnais*, taking their name from Chalon-sur-Saône. The soil is rich and therefore less suitable for producing fine wines, and although made from the same grapes, these wines rarely have the same quality as other Burgundies, nor do they age so well. Only wines from the communes of *Givry*, *Mercurey*, *Montagny*, and *Rully* are allowed the Appellation Chalonnais rather than merely Bourgogne. Rully is a centre for the production of sparkling white wines, and Montagny produces white Burgundies exclusively. The other villages concentrate on red wines.

The **Mâconnais**, further S., is best known for the white wine appellations of *Pouilly-Fuissé, Pouilly-Loche,* and *Pouilly Vinzelles,* particularly the first, but in a good year any of them make a delicious white Burgundy that in quality can approach those from further N. The southerly commune of *La Chapelle-de-Guinchay* has the privilege of calling its wines either *Mâcon* or *Beaujolais,* although the vintner will usually list the white as Mâcon and the red as Beaujolais. A small amount of Beaujolais Blanc is produced in this northernmost district of Beaujolais. The Mâcon red or what can be a Mâcon Supérieur (if the natural degree of alcohol is high) may add the commune name, as with *Mâcon-Lugny,* while the appellation *'Bourgogne Passe-Tout-Grains'* allows a blend of *Pinot Noir* and *Gamay* grapes, producing wines light in body, but which do not age well.

There was a saying that 'three rivers flow into Lyon: the Rhône, the Saône, and the Beaujolais', for great quantities of each year's wine were consumed in that city before the fashion spread to Paris. Beaujolais is a wine to be drunk young and fresh, with perhaps the exception of those from *Morgan* and *Moulin-a-Vent,* which can take some ageing. They would be allowed the appellation Bourgogne Rouge if the grape used was the Pinot, and are still considered Burgundies, but these are very different, for here the *Gamay* grape is grown, and on a granite soil. The Beaujolais region is on a latitude where a marked change in climate, and in the way the vines are pruned, becomes noticeable. Although wires are still seen, the traditional 'lower Gobelet' pruning is prevalent. The wines are classified into four main groups: those of ordinary *Beaujolais,* with less than 10% alcohol; *Beaujolais Superieur,* with more than 10%; *Beaujolais Villages,* from a blend of wines from c. 30 communes; and the top nine distinctive Beaujolais *crus,* from *Brouilly, Côte-de-Brouilly, Morgon, Chiroubles, Fleurie, Moulin-a-Vent, Chenas, Julienas,* and *St-Amour.*

Savoy. To the W. of Annecy and N. of Annemasse respectively are the small appellation areas of *Seyssel* and *Crépy.* Seyssel is either a dry or sparkling white wine mainly from the *Chasselas* vine, but also from the *Roussette.* Crépy wines are normally from the Chasselas grape and produce dry and naturally pétillant white wines.

Côtes-du-Rhône. Between Lyon and Avignon, where the sun-baked valley broadens, the vineyards of the Côtes-du-Rhône precariously hug the cliffs on either side of the river, with an occasional break where the site or soil is unsuitable. The dominant element of the soil is granite, which in conjunction with the heat of the summer sun produces strong wines. Most of the finer are made from one grape, or sometimes a blend of two or three grapes, the principal variety being the *Syrah* (perhaps originating in Persia), which gives firm robust wines that are inclined to be hard, and occasionally a small proportion of white *Viognier, Marsanne,* or *Roussanne* is blended to soften them. Among other red grape varieties permitted are *Grenache, Carignan,* and *Mourvèdre.* From N. to S., those wines of note are as follows: *Côte-Rotie,* robust reds which age well, and *Condrieu* and *Château-Grillet,* which are similar in that they are vigorous dry whites with a yellow hue. The former is best drunk young, and may be had in a semi-sweet style. Château-Grillet is a very small appellation and rarely seen; it is always dry and has more finesse than Condrieu. After a break in the wine-growing area, one approaches the town of Tain-l'Hermitage. *Crozes-Hermitage* is a fine full red which ages quite well but is a lesser wine than its near neighbour, *Hermitage* itself, the greatest wine of this group, full and powerful, which ages beautifully. A good strong white is also produced, which will last up to 15 years. Slightly further S., near Valence, lie *Cornas* and *St-Péray*, the former producing wines similar to Hermitage, but not so perfumed and elegant; they tend to be hard, and so age well. St-Péray produces white spirited wines with body, but they do not age so well. Some vineyards in the area make dry or semi-sweet sparkling wines. Some 15km further S., off the main road, lies *St-Joseph*, producing delicate red wines but with less body than Hermitage, while its whites are likewise lighter. Some 50km E. of St-Joseph lies *Die*, where a little-known semi-sparkling white is made from the *Clairette* and *Muscat* grapes, called *Clairette-de-Die*.

Further down the Rhône valley, where it broadens out, the wines of *Châteauneuf-du-Pape* and *Tavel* dominate the appellations. Châteauneuf-du-Pape is made from a blend of up to 13 varieties of grape and has a full rich complex character as might be expected, but it does not age so well as Hermitage. Tavel produces one of the best rosés of France, made mainly from the *Grenache* grape, and a dry wine preferably drunk chilled. Among other noteworthy rosés are those of *Lirac* and *Chasclun*, while *Gigondas*, *Cairanne*, and *Vacqueyras* also produce good rosés, reds, and whites. *Beaumes-de-Venise* and *Rasteau* produce sweet fortified dessert wines.

The vineyards of the **Côtes de Provence**, recently granted AC status, produce unexceptional wines with a high alcoholic content, but which are perfectly enjoyable, mostly rosés and reds. Certain small areas in the region are recognized for more notable wines, among them those of *Palette*, near Aix-en-Provence, while *Cassis*—on the coast—produces a good rosé, as does *Bandol* which also produces a good red. *Bellet*, above Nice, produces notable whites, rosés, and reds.

The **Midi**, including the plain of Languedoc and part of Roussillon, and covering the departments of Gard, Hérault and Aude, contains extensive wine-growing areas, the quality of which has been improving during recent decades. Some districts such as the *Côtes-de-Roussillon* and *St-Chinian* have been granted AC, as has the *Clairette-de-Bellegard*, a small light yellow wine made from the *Clairette* vine. The best red wines in the Gard are from the *Costières-de-Gard*, which has VDQS status. In the Hérault the vineyards in the neighbourhood of Montpellier and Beziers produce vast quantities of ordinary reds, apart from the superior dry white *Clairette-du-Languedoc* (AC), and a wine known as '*Rancio*', an acquired taste. Other wines from the area are the sweet fortified *Muscat-de-Lunel* and *de-Frontignan*.

The Aude contains the AC wines of Côtes-de-Roussillon and the VDQS wines of *Corbières* and *Minervois*, partly in the Hérault. They are mostly rough reds made from the *Grenache* grape. *Banyuls*, near the Spanish border, produces a sweet natural wine which becomes Rancio when aged; it is also known for a sweet fortified muscat wine, as is nearby *Rivesaltes*. To the N.W., still within the Aude, is the *Blanquette-de-Limoux*, a wine made from the *Mauzac* and *Clairette* grapes and made sparkling by the 'Methode Champenoise'; the still variety, also AC, is sold as *Limoux Nature*.

Gaillac, on the Tarn to the W. of Albi, is another wine-producing centre with still or sparkling whites of no great distinction although awarded AC. They were once appreciated by Plantagenet kings. Another historically popular wine is that of *Cahors*, on the Lot, further N.W., once a hard and very dark tannic wine, since softened and lightened. Cahors is also the name given to the grape of the area, which is also grown in small quantities near Bordeaux, and known as *Malbec* or *Cot*.

There are some notable wines in the Lot-et-Garonne, covering the area between Gaillac and Bordeaux, among them reds, and some whites, produced from the classic Bordeaux vines on the *Côtes-de-Duras*, while similar wines come from the *Côtes-de-Buzet* and *du-Marmandais*. S.W. of the Garonne lie the vineyards of **Armagnac**, where the *La Folle Blanche* and *St-Emilion* grapes produce an individual brandy which the Gascons claim to be superior to Cognac, although the same grapes are used. The Armagnac still is continuous, but the spirit is rectified at a much lower degree than in the pot still of Cognac, and is also matured in Armagnac oak. The Region was marked out in 1909, being largely in the department of Gers; its main centres are Condom, Auch and Eauze, the last, in Bas Armagnac, producing the best wines on a mainly sandy soil. Other subdivisions are *Tenareze*, and *Haut-Armagnac*. As in Cognac, the various types are sold as '3 Star', VSOP, Extra Veille, etc., apart from the occasional Vintage Armagnac.

To the S.W., near Pau, are the vineyards of *Jurançon*, the whites of which are of considerable individuality, the produce of the *Manseng*, *Petit Manseng* and *Courbu* vines. The grapes are collected very late, after they have been attacked by the *Pourriture Noble* (noble rot; cf. Sauternes and Barsac), so that the grape sugar is concentrated. The sweeter wines are left up to four years in wooden casks, and are of more interest than the dry wines from the area.

Bordeaux. The vineyards of Bordeaux are the most extensive fine wine-producing areas of France, and unlike those of Burgundy (which produces much less wine), they are large properties whose wines are usually sold under the name of the château—among them those of *Lafite*, *Latour*, *Margaux*, *Haut-Brion*, *Mouton-Rothschild*, etc., which are world renowned. One reason for the difference in their size was that the estates had been long established by powerful landowners including a number of English, Scots and Irish descent (such as *Château Talbot*, *Smith-Haut-Lafite* and *Haut-Brion*, the last said to be derived from O'Brien); several English firms are still engaged in the Bordeaux trade.

Between the rivers Garonne and Dordogne, which converge N. of Bordeaux to form the broad estuary of the Gironde, lies an area known as **Entre-Deux-Mers**, better known in England for its dry white wines, although in fact more red than white is produced, but neither are exceptional. The greatest concentration of great red wines is to be found on the W. bank of the Gironde in the low undulating district known as the **Medoc**, where the communes of *St-Estephe*, *Pauillac*, *St-Julien* and *Margaux*, among others, are dotted with châteaux whose names are famous for their vineyards. Around the city of Bordeaux itself lies the area known as **Graves**, its gravelly soil producing great wines such as those of *Château Haut-Brion* among others only a little less prestigious. Graves also produces reasonable dry and medium whites. Another important area lies around *St-Emilion*, to the E., producing such great wines as *Château Cheval-Blanc* and *Château Ausone*. From contiguous *Pomerol* are those of *Château Petrus*, while those of nearby *Fronsac* are similar in style to St-Emilion if not so refined. On the E. bank of the Gironde lie the vineyards of *Blaye* and *Bourg*, offering a variety of good value wines compared to the better known and more expensive appellations mentioned.

S. of Bordeaux, on the S. bank of the Garonne, are the vineyards producing the sweet wines of **Sauternes**, most famous of which is that of *Château Yquem*, and *Barsac*. Adjacent to Barsac are the wines of *Cérons*, with those of *Loupiac* and *St-Croix-du-Mont* on the opposite bank. The grapes are attacked by the *pourriture noble* or—to be biologically correct—the micro-organism known as *Botrytis cinerea*, which punctures its skin; this then shrivels, and the sugar content concentrates, to produce an exceptional naturally sweet wine.

Among the 'noble' grapes of the Bordeaux region are the red *Cabernet—Sauvignon*; the *Merlot*, producing less tannin; and the lesser used *Cabernet Franc*, *Malbec* and *Petit-Verdot*. For white wines, the *Sémillon, Sauvignon, Muscadelle* and *Merlot Blanc* are grown, the Sémillon being that used for the Sauternes, etc.

Some distance to the E. of Bordeaux are the wines of *Bergerac*, few of which are of great distinction, although the sweet *Monbazillac* is notable; other appellations are *Haut-Montravel, Côtes de Montravel* and *Rosette* (semi-sweet wines), and the red *Pécharmant*.

The region producing **Cognac** is extensive, centred on the town of Cognac, although the headquarters of some houses are at nearby Jarnac. Prior to 1600, the wines of the Charente were thin and acidic, and it is said that the best Cognac comes from the worst wine. This is distilled in the original and picturesque copper 'swan's neck' stills seen sitting on brick furnaces. The vapours condense to produce a '*brouillis*' of about 25% alcohol, which is redistilled; the result, known as the '*bonne chauffé*' (75% alcohol), is later aged in Limousin oak casks, where much of it evaporates. The remainder is eventually blended with other Cognacs to achieve the desired style, for the differing areas around Cognac—depending on the proportion of chalk in the soil—produce differing qualities. The six *crus* established in 1909 are *Grande Champagne* (from a delimited district S.E. of the town), *Petite Champagne, Borderies* (to the N.W.), *Fins Bois* (N.E.), *Bons Bois, Bois Ordinaires* (towards the coast). The *St-Emilion* grape is the commonest used, although *La Folle Blanche* and *Colombard* are also allowed. The various styles are '3 Star', aged 3 years or more; VSOP (Very Special Old Pale), at least 4 years old, but usually aged between 7-12 years; and older blended Cognacs called Reserve, XO, Cordon Bleu, Napoleon, etc.

Both *Vins-de-Pays-Charentais* and the sweet *Pineau-des-Charentes*, fortified with brandy to a strength of 16.5-22% alcohol, are also promoted, the latter being either white or rosé, depending on the grapes used.

The wines of the middle and lower **Loire** valley vary considerably in style and character, and while lighter than those of Bordeaux or Burgundy, they can be very refreshing; few, apart from sweet *Vouvrays*, age well. The **Muscadets**, subdivided into the AC areas of *Muscadet de Sèvre-et-Maine, Muscadet Côteaux-de-la-Loire* and *Muscadet* (in descending order of quality) are found near Nantes, where they make a delightful accompaniment to fish and shell-fish dishes, and should be drunk when young and fresh. The *Muscadet-sur-Lie* is sometimes seen, an unfiltered wine with an unusual bitter but refreshing taste.

Anjou is best known for its rosés, made from the *Groslot* vine, or from the better *Cabernet-Sauvignon* and *Cabernet-Franc*, in which case the bottles are labelled Anjou Rosé-de-Cabernet. Red and white wines are also produced; the sweeter whites are preferable to the dry, the richest among them being from the *Côteaux-du-Layon*. Among other AC areas are *Anjou*, *Côteaux-de-la-Loire*, *Savennières*, *Bonnezeaux*, *Côteaux-de-l'Aubance*, *Quarts-de-Chaume*, *Côteaux-de-Saumur* and *Saumur*. Saumur itself recently became an important centre for the production of mainly dry sparkling wines, although there is also a sparkling wine with the more general appellation of Anjou.

To the N. of Angers is the AC *Côteaux-du-Loir* (a tributary of the Loire), where rosés and whites which are sometimes pétillant are produced, both being excellent; the reds are poor in quality. Further up the Loir are the white wines of *Jasnières*, slightly sweet, and rich and velvety in texture.

Touraine. The AC include *Bourgueil* and *St-Nicholas-de-Bourgueil* (restricted to reds from the *Cabernet Franc* grape, and rosés); *Touraine-Azay-le-Rideau* (restricted to white); and *Chinon*, of which the reds are best; *Touraine-Amboise*, *Touraine-Mesland*, *Montlouis* and *Vouvray*, the last two being similar, although Vouvray produces perhaps the finest wines of the region. They will vary from year to year, but have more depth and richness than the other whites, and may be dry or sweet, still, semi-sparkling or sparkling, the last being produced by the Methode-Champenoise. The main grapes grown are the *Cabernet Franc* and *Cabernet Sauvignon*, although Gamay is also used for the reds, and *Chenin Blanc* for the whites.

Near the Loire are the small appellation areas of *Quincy* and *Reuilly*, which have the same style as the Pouilly-Blanc-Fumé and Sancerre appellations further up the river; both produce dry white wines from the *Sauvignon* grape, even if of no great distinction. The *Pouilly-Fumé*, from Pouilly-sur-Loire, is a dry white made from the Sauvignon grape, and with a slightly smoky character (whence its name), which should not be confused with the *Pouilly-Fuissé*, a white Burgundy made from the *Chardonnay* (see p. 38). A lesser but pleasant white wine made from the *Chasselas* grape is also produced in the area. On the opposite bank of the Loire lies *Sancerre*, known for its crisp white from the *Sauvignon* grape, similar in style to the Pouilly-Blanc-Fumé but also occasionally producing rosés and reds from the *Pinot Noir*.

Calvados, an eau-de-vie distilled from apples, will be found in Normandy, where the Cider is also ubiquitous, while the many other fruit-based alcohols in France include *Kirsch*, from cherries; *Mirabelle*, from plums; and *Poire William*, from pears.

The sign *'Dégustation'* is an invitation to taste wine. Sometimes a modest charge is made, but there is no obligation to buy. Travellers wishing to bring wine back to England should first check with the regulations as to how much they are allowed duty free, and the duty and VAT chargeable on additional quantities, which must be declared on passing Customs. Tourist Offices in wine-growing areas can advise travellers where one can buy wine and which châteaux may be visited without appointment, but it should be noted that few *vignerons* will have much time to attend to the casual visitor during the *vendage*, the Autumn wine harvest.

FRENCH ARCHITECTURE

Among the more important archaeological sites in France are *St-Blaise* (near Martigues), *Entremont* (near Aix-en-Provence), *Ensérune* (near Béziers), the alignments at *Carnac* in Brittany, and the recently excavated sites at *Marseille*; not to mention *Lascaux* in the Dordogne, where a replica of its famous cave-paintings was opened in 1983 adjacent to the original cave, closed to the public on account of the risk of further deterioration.

Perhaps the earliest extant remains of architectural significance in what is now France are the ROMAN theatres, amphitheatres, and other monuments in Provence and the Rhône valley, notable among which are those at *Fréjus, Arles, Nîmes* (together with the neighbouring *Pont du Gard*), *Glanum* (near St-Rémy), *Orange, Vaison-la-Romain, Vienne* and its transpontine suburb of *St-Romain-du-Gal*, and *Lyon*. Other relics of consequence may be found as far afield as *Autun, Besançon, Bavay* (near Valenciennes), *Narbonne, Cimiez* and *La Turbie* (above Nice), *Dax, Die, Limoges, Paris, Périgueux, Reims*, and *Saintes*.

By the 4C A.D. the Gallo-Romans were building basilicas, that at *St-Bertrand-de-Comminges*, on the N. slope of the Pyrenees, being the earliest, and several baptisteries, such as those at *Poitiers, Fréjus, Vénasque, Riez*, and *Le Puy*. During the Merovingian and Carolingian periods several towns grew in importance, both as centres of religious life, and later as commercial entrepots, among them *Clermont* (where a cathedral existed from c. 450), and *Tours* (where St-Martin dated from c. 472). Others were *Chalon-sur-Saône, Metz, Troyes, Langres, Beauvais, St-Omer, Arras, Le Mans, Angers, Toulouse*, and *Auxerre*. The 10C frescoes in the crypt of *St-Germain* at Auxerre are perhaps the earliest extant examples of French medieval painting; the original church on this site did not survive the Scandinavian invasions. That of *Germigny-des-Prés* (near St-Benoit-sur-Loire), with its Byzantine-type mosaic, and *St-Philibert-de-Grandlieu* (S.W. of Nantes) are among the few churches remaining from this early period.

The 11C onwards was a great era of building of churches in the **Romanesque** style, usually barrel-vaulted in stone, and there are several regional variations, such as those of Poitou, Provence, Normandy, and Burgundy. In Aquitaine large domes were constructed, as with the cathedrals at *Cahors, Périgueux, Angoulême, Poitiers* (St-Hilaire), and *Souillac*, although also seen at *Fontevraud, Le Puy*, and elsewhere. Other individual styles are those of Auvergne (with their geometrical incrustations), Alsace, and Roussillon.

Among the more architecturally interesting examples of surviving churches of this epoch in Normandy are the two abbeys at *Caen*; those at *Fécamp, Mont-St-Michel*, and *Rouen* (St-Ouen); and the cathedrals of *Bayeux, Évreux*, and *Coutances*. There are of course several notable ruins extant, such as those of *Jumièges*.

In Burgundy, the churches of *St-Philibert* at *Tournus*, and those at *Paray-le-Monial* (contemporary with *Cluny*, of which little remains), *Saulieu, Beaune*, and *Vézelay*, and the cathedrals of *Langres*, and *Autun* (whose sculptor, *Gislebertus*, is one of the few whose name is known) are all remarkable, and most of them contain a wealth of carving, as do several smaller churches.

In Poitou and Saintonge there are several outstanding buildings, among them *St-Savin-sur-Gartempe, Fontgombault,* and *Aulnay;* while to the S.E. of Bordeaux is the notable ruin of *Sauve-Majeure.* Further E., in the Auvergne, the churches at *Conques, St-Nectaire, Issoire, Orcival,* and *Clermont-Ferrand* (N.-D.-du-Port), are among the more remarkable. In Languedoc there is the great brick-built pilgrimage church of *St-Sernin* at *Toulouse,* with its radiating chapels and octagonal bell-tower, the prototype of many in the area.

In Provence the usually smaller churches of this period are notable for their exterior decoration, often using Classical motives, such as that of *St-Trophime* at *Arles,* or at *St-Gilles,* among several others. Among cloisters, those at *Elne* (S. of Perpignan), and at *Moissac* (N. of Toulouse) are but two of the more interesting, both remarkable for their sculptural details.

The **Gothic** style, concentrating on verticality, and solving the considerable constructional problems thus created, evolved during the 12C, and continued to do so until it merged with the architectural innovations of the Renaissance in the 16C. Rib-vaulting, a characteristic of the style, was first applied to a building as a whole by Anglo-Norman architects (as at Durham), while one of the first Norman churches to be entirely covered in this way was that *Lessay* in the Cotentin peninsula. During the first half of the 12C several churches in Paris and the Île-de-France were similarly vaulted—often only partially so—such as *St-Martin-des-Champs* in the capital, and at *Morienval,* shortly followed by the cathedral at *Sens* and the church at *St-Germer-de-Fly,* and the influential rebuilding of *St-Denis* (commenced 1137); and during the next 45 years at *Noyons, Senlis, Laon, Soissons,* and *Paris* (Notre-Dame), the last serving as the prototype for the cathedrals at *Bourges* and *Le Mans,* while that of Laon influenced the building of *St-Rémi* at *Reims,* and *Notre-Dame* at *Châlons-sur-Marne.*

In the Plantagenet domain to the W., the rib-vaulting took on a different and more domical form known as the ANGEVIN, as in the cathedrals of *Angers* itself, and *Poitiers.* A third and more austere type of Gothic was produced by the Cistercian reform, carried out at *Cîteaux* itself (since destroyed), and at *Pontigny, Noirlac,* and *Fontenay,* etc. Other Cistercian monasteries which may be visited are those at *Fontfroide* (near Narbonne), and in Provence, the 'three sisters' of *Le Thoronet, Sénanque,* and *Silvacane;* while of the chartreuses of the Carthusians, that at *Villeneuve-lès-Avignon* (still the object of restoration) is notable. (The more famous *Grande-Chartreuse*—N.W. of Grenoble—dates almost entirely from the 17C.)

The 13C saw the construction of some of the greatest examples of Gothic architecture, among them the magnificent cathedrals of *Chartres, Reims,* and *Amiens* (all begun between 1194–1220), followed at *Beauvais* (unfinished) by a development known as the 'rayonnant' style, seen likewise at the *Ste-Chapelle* in Paris. A feature of these churches was the increased amount of space devoted to stained-glass; this provided very explicit representations of Old and New Testament scenes, etc., which might impress the largely illiterate congregation.

In the southern provinces of France, recently ravaged by the destructive Albigensian crusade, the rib-vault was not in general use (although tried out in the porch at *Moissac* in 1130–40, and in the nave of the cathedral at *Toulouse* in c. 1211) until the last decade of the 13C, at *Bayonne, Clermont-Ferrand, Limoges, Rodez, Car-*

cassonne (St-Nazaire), and *Narbonne* (unfinished). The wide span of the vault at *Toulouse* was partly imitated at *St-Bertrand-de-Comminges*, *Perpignan*, and *Albi* (beung 1282). The facade and nave of the cathedral of *Strasbourg* were reconstructed in the mid 13C, but the tower was not completed until the 15C.

From the 11C the feudal barons of France had been defending their lands by the erection or reconstruction of substantial fortresses, improved by the innovations of returning Crusaders, and numerous towns had likewise provided themselves with defensive walls. Among the more remarkable of the latter extant—although often rebuilt and restored—are those at *Provins*, and *Carcassonne* (13C), *Aigues-Mortes* (late 13C), *Angoulême*, *Avignon* (14C), and *Langres*, apart from several smaller sites in Brittany, such as *St-Malo*, *Guérande*, *Dinan*, *Vannes*, *Vitré*, *Concarneau*, and *Fougères*. Many other towns retain their fortifications in part, or at least their gates, and sometimes—as at *Cahors*, or *Orthez*—their fortified bridges. Unfortunately many of the finer medieval castles or *châteaux* were dismantled in consequence of Richelieu's orders during the third decade of the 17C, although several remarkable examples may still be seen, often spectacularly sited, such as *Château Gaillard*, *Loches*, *Chinon*, *Angers*, and *Saumur*; while others—as at *Pierrefonds*—suffered from the over-enthusiastic attentions of *Viollet-le-Duc* in the mid 19C.

In the S.W. of France many 'new towns' or *bastides* were planted during the later period of the English occupation (late 13C), often laid out on a grid pattern and walled. Some were also established by the French. Among many fine examples are *Monpazier*, *Monflanquin*, *Domme*, *Villefranche-de-Rouergue*, *Villeneuve-sur-Lot*, *Grenade-sur-Garonne*, *Cologne-de-Gers*, and *Fourcés*.

Among other notable extant examples of domestic architecture of this period are the *House of Jacques Coeur* at *Bourges*, the *Palace of the Popes* at *Avignon* (both mid 14C), the *Hospital* at *Tonnerre* (late 13C), and the *Hôtel-Dieu* at *Beaune* (mid 15C).

The 15C and even part of the 16C is the era of FLAMBOYANT GOTHIC, recognised by an elaboration of vaulting techniques, the absence of capitals, and prolific decoration for its own sake: the cathedrals of *Tours*, and *Moulins*, *St-Maclou* at *Rouen*, the church at *Brou* (Bourg-en-Bresse), *Notre-Dame* at *Caudebec*, *N.-D.-de-l'Épine* (E. of Châlon-sur-Marne), and the early 16C cathedral at *Auch* being notable examples. The choir of the latter also contains some of the more remarkable wood-carvings in France, although the stalls at *La Chaise-Dieu*, *Albi*, *Amiens*, *Brou*, *Montbenoît*, *Rodez*, *Metz*, *Thann*, and *St-Bertrand-de-Comminges* also come to mind. The cathedrals of *Treguier*, *Quimper*, and *St-Pol-de-Leon* in Brittany, although dating from this period, are still 'Rayonnant' in style, the Flamboyant appearing only in the 16C.

The **Renaissance**. In 1527 François I, on returning from captivity in Madrid, set about rebuilding and decorating his hunting-lodge at *Fontainebleau* in the Italian taste which had so much impressed him during his earlier visits to the courts of Italy. To this end he commissioned Italian artists, among them *Rosso* and *Primaticcio*, who were to prove influential on French art in general.

Among the prominent architects of this fruitful period—one in which residential rather than defensive châteaux were being built—were *Pierre Chambiges*, *Philibert de l'Orme* (a friend of Rabelais), *Jean Bullant*, *Pierre Lescot* (who rebuilt the Cour Carrée of the Louvre), *Nicolas Bachelier*, and several members of the *Du Cerceau* family. Among the more striking examples of such châteaux are *Chambord* (commenced 1519, and another favourite of François I's), *Azay-le-Rideau*, and *Chenonceau*, all near the Loire valley, while *Ancy-le-Franc*, in Burgundy, is the only surviving building in France erected by *Serlio*. Numerous other châteaux were also being 'modernised' if not rebuilt.

The next generation of architects included *Étienne Martellange* (who had a great influence on the 'Jesuit style'), *Salomon de Brosse*, *Jacques Le Mercier* (who enjoyed the patronage of Richelieu), *Louis Le Vau* (responsible for Fouquet's château of *Vaux-le-Vicomte*, and in part for the drastic changes at Versailles), *François Blondel*, *Libéral Bruant* (designer of Les Invalides, and the church of *St-Louis* in the Hôspital de la Salpêtrière, Paris), *Pierre Bullet*, and notably *François Mansart*, whose grand-nephew *Jules Hardouin-Mansart* was the favourite architect of Louis XIV, for whom he created the final version of the *Palace* at *Versailles*. To *André Le Nôtre* are attributed the design of the gardens of Versailles, and of numerous other parks and gardens throughout the country. The military engineer *Sébastien de Vauban* was at the same time transforming the defences of France by re-designing its frontier fortresses. Among the more redoubtable, the ground-plans of which are still very obvious, are the forts or bastions of *Lille*, *Le Quesnoy*, *Toul*, *Neuf-Brisach*, *Besançon*, *Mont-Dauphin*, *Perpignan* (and neighbouring *Salses*, originally laid out in 1497), *Villefranche-de-Conflent*, and *Bayonne*.

The 17th and 18Cs were also great centuries of town-planning, and among the several imposing squares and promenades laid out in the provinces which are still extant are those at *Aix-en-Provence*, *Bordeaux*, *Dijon*, *Montpellier*, *Nancy*, *Nantes* and *Rennes*.

Among the more individual architects of the 18C were *Pierre Lassurance*, *Germain Boffrand*, *Jacques Gabriel* and his son *Ange-Jacques*, *Emmanuel Héré* (largely working at Nancy and Lunéville), *Richard Mique*, and *Jacques-Germain Soufflot* (architect of the *Panthéon* at Paris), who with *A.-T. Brogniart* lead a movement back to Classicism. Others included *Victor Louis*, *Claude-Nicolas Ledoux* (responsible for the design of the salt-works at *Arc-en-Senans*, among several other remarkable buildings), and *Jean-François Chalgrin*, who designed the *Arc de Triomphe* in Paris (begun 1806).

In general the architects of the 19C were less distinguished, although there were some exceptions, among them *Fontaine*, often working in collaboration with *Percier*, *Louis Visconti*, *Henri Labrouste*, *Lassus*, *Viollet-le-Duc* (responsible for much restoration and rebuilding of medieval remains), *Charles Garnier* (architect of the *Opéra* in Paris), and the engineer *Gustave Eiffel*, designer of numerous bridges apart from the tower which bears his name.

While the functional concrete structures of *Auguste Perret*, 'Le Corbusier', et al, may have their admirers, most 20C French buildings—in Paris, at least—reflect forms of engineering rather than of architecture, and although a few retain their individuality, such as the *Palais de Chaillot* (1937), too many recent erections impress merely by their height (such as the *Tour Montparnasse*) or as curious examples of 'pop' architecture, such as the *Centre Beaubourg*, with its 'ossature métallique', a design chosen from some 680 projects, which reflects either a sad lack of architects of any quality, or of aesthetic judgement among selection boards.

Glossary of Architectural and Allied Terms

Acajou, mahogany

Androyne, passage between houses in bastides

Arc-boutant, flying buttress

Archivolt, series of mouldings forming the ensemble of an arch

Ardoises, slates

Autel, altar

Bastide, a settlement established, by both the French and English, in the S.W. of the country during the 13-14Cs, usually on a rectangular grid plan round a central arcaded square, and usually fortified; in Provence the term applies to a countryhouse

Boiseries, decorative woodwork

Carrefour, crossroads

Carrelages, floor tiles

Caissons, en, coffered

Chemin de ronde, battlement walk

Chevet, exterior of an apse; also *Abside*

Colombages, à, half-timbered

Colombier, devecote

Colonnette, little column for a vaulting shaft

Communs, outbuildings

Contreforts, buttresses

Corbels, wooden or stone projections supporting a beam or parapet, and often elaborately carved

Cornières, The arcades of the 'place' in bastides

Corps de logis, main residential part of a château

Dessus de porte, a painting above a door

Donjon, keep

Dosserets, pillars subsidiary to the pilaster of a compound pier

Douves, moat; wet or dry

Ébéniste, cabinet-maker

Échauguette, fortified corner turret, or bartizan turret

Émail, enamel

Escalier, staircase; *a vis*, spiral

Flèche, spire

Grenier, granary, or attic

Hôtel, mansion; *Hôtel de Ville*, town hall, *Hôtel-Dieu*, the principal hospital in many towns

Hourds, wooden sentry walks

Jeu de paume, a real tennis-court

Jubé, rood-screen

Lambris, wainscoting

Lucarnes, dormer windows

Mairie, town hall or municipal building; also *Hôtel de Ville*

Mandorla, pointed oval-shaped frame used as an aureole in medieval sculpture and painting; also a *Vesica*

Mansard roof, roof of which each face has two slopes, the lower steeper than the upper, named after the architect François Mansart (1598– 1666)

Narthex, an ante-nave, porch or vestibule to a church or basilica

Nacre, mother of pearl

Nef, nave

Oeil-de-boeuf, circular, sometimes oval, window (bull's eye)

Oppidum, Gallo-Roman settlement, usually on a fortified ridge or plateau

Pièce d'eau, an expanse of water, usually ornamental

Poivrettes, pepper-pot turrets

Pont-levis, drawbridge

Porte-cochère, carriage gateway

Poutres, beams or joists

Rez de chaussée, ground floor

Tierceron, curved rib in Gothic vault springing from the same point as the intersecting diagonal rib, and rising to the end of the ridge-rib

Tympanum, space, often decorated, between door lintel and arch

Vermeil, silver-gilt

Vitrail, stained-glass window

Voussoires, wedge-shaped stones used in constructing arches or vaults

Note. The following emblems may be seen blazoning the walls, etc., of châteaux, particularly in the Loire valley, associated as follows:

A field of ermine 'tails' (often combined with Franciscan cords) = Anne of Brittany

An ermine *passant* = Anne of Brittany or Claude of France

A swan pierced by an arrow = Claude of France

A porcupine *statant*, crowned = Louis XII

A salamander *passant*, crowned = François I

BIBLIOGRAPHY

The number of books in English on French topography, history, and culture is extensive, and the very brief list appended (containing also one or two titles in French) does not pretend to be more than a compilation of works which may be found useful for reference or in providing general background. Unfortunately a general bibliography entitled 'How to Find Out About France: a Guide to Sources of Information', by *J. Pemberton* (1966) is in several respects out of date. There are of course numerous lacunae, and this list reflects the compiler's personal interests and tastes, although not every title has been read by him. Most of the volumes have been published within recent decades, or if not, the date of their first edition is given in brackets, and most of them contain comprehensive bibliographies for further reading. Certain titles are also mentioned in passing in the text.

The French reader's attention is drawn to two notable series: the *Histoires des villes de France*, published by *Privat* of Toulouse; and the reprints of regional histories published by *Editions Jeanne Lafitte* of Marseille. *Guénégaud*, in Paris, is one of several publishers of topography.

History and General: *D. G. Charlton* (ed.), *France, a Companion to French Studies (2nd ed.,); *O. Brogan*, Roman Gaul; *J. Drinkwater*, Roman Gaul; *John Le Patourel*, The Norman Empire; *P. S. Lewis*, Later Medieval France; *J. Huizinger*, The Waning of the Middle Ages (1924); *Alain Decaux* and *André Castelot*, *Dictionnaire d'Histoire de France PERRIN*; *R. Briggs*, Early Modern France, 1560–1715; *Henry Adams*, Mont Saint-Michel and Chartres (1911); *E. C. Lodge*, Gascony under English Rule (1926); *Joan Evans*, Life in Medieval France; *J. Calmette*, The Golden Age of Burgundy; *Richard Vaughan*, Philip the Bold, John the Fearless, Charles the Bold; *J. Shirley* (trans. and ed.), A Parisian Journal, 1405–1449; *E. Leroy Ladurie*, Montaillou; *Jonathan Sumption*, The Albigensian Crusade; *A. R. Lewis*, The Development of southern French and Catalan Society, 718–1050; *Amy Kelly*, Eleanor of Aquitaine and the Four Kings; *Aldous Huxley*, The Devils of Loudun; *Georges Duby* (ed.), Histoire de la France Urbaine, (and with *A. Wallon*), Histoire de la France Rurale; *F. L. Carsten* (ed.), The Ascendency of France, 1648–1688 (New Cambridge Modern History, Vol. V); *W. C. Scoville*, The Persecution of the Huguenots and French Economic Development; *Saint-Simon*, Historical Memoirs (trans. and ed. by Lucy Norton); *Alfred Cobban*, A History of Modern France (1715–1962); *O. Hufton*, Bayeux in the Late 18C; *J. McMasters*, French Ecclesiastical Society under the Ancien Régime: a Study of Angers in the 18C; *Norman Hampson*, A Social History of the French Revolution; *Corelli Barnett*, Bonaparte; *J. M. Thompson*, The French Revolution; *Rodney Gallop*, A Book of the Basques; *Joseph Duloum*, Les Anglais dans les Pyrénées (1739–1896); *D. W. Brogan*, *The Development of Modern France (1870–1939); *Theodore Zeldin*, *France, 1848–1945, The French; *J. Ardagh*, The New France; *Gordon Wright*, France in Modern Times, 1760 to the Present; *Michael Howard*, *The Franco-Prussian War.

Topography: *Bryan Morgan*, Fastness of France (Massif Central); *Freda White*, Three Rivers of France, Ways of Aquitaine, West of the Rhône; *Philip Oyler*, The Generous Earth (although describing a fast receding way of life); *Hilaire Belloc*, The Pyrenees (1909); *James Pope-Hennessy*, Aspects of Provence; *Douglas Goldring*, The South of France; *Augustus Hare*, N.E. France, N.W. France, S.E. France, S.W. France (1890–95); *Maurice Beresford*, New Towns of the Middle Ages; *P. Howarth*, When the Riviera was Ours.

Art and Architecture: *Anthony Blunt*, Art and Architecture in France, 1500–1700; *W. von Kalnein* and *M. Levey*, Art and Architecture of the 18C in France; *Ian Dunlop*, The Cathedral's Crusade; *Allan Bramham*, The Architecture of the French Enlightenment; *Pierre Lavedan*, French Architecture; *Otto von Simson*, The Gothic Cathedral; *Joan Evans*, Monastic Architecture in

France (1500–1700), Romanesque Architecture of the Order of Cluny, Art in Medieval France; *V. R. Markham*, Romanesque France (1929); *Ed. Zodiaque*, Glossaire de termes techniques; *Hubert Fenwick*, The Châteaux of France; *G. Ring*, A Century of French Painting, 1400–1500; *Basil Taylor*, French Painting; *P. H. Michel*, Romanesque Wall-painting in France; *Alan Borg*, Architectural Sculpture in Romanesque Provence; *K. J. Conant*, Carolingian and Romanesque Architecture, 800–1200; *R. Branner*, Burgundian Gothic Architecture; *R. H. Wilenski*, French Painting.

Literary: *Paul Harvey* and *J. E. Heseltine*, *The Oxford Companion to French Literature; *J. M. H. Reid*, The Concise Dictionary of French Literature; *L. Cazamian*, A History of French Literature; *P. E. Charvet* (ed.), A History of French Literature (6 volumes); *John Lough*, Writer and Public in France, from the Middle Ages to the Present Day; *Enid Starkie*, Gautier to Eliot: the Influence of France on English Literature, 1851–1939.

Miscellaneous: *P. Morton Shand*, A Book of French Wines; *Alexis Lichine*, Guide to the Wines and Vineyards of France; *E. Penning-Rowsell*, The Wines of Bordeaux; *J. Livingstone-Learmonth* and *M. C. H. Master*, Wines of the Rhône; *Patrick Forbes*, Champagne; *Cyril Ray*, Cognac; *Elizabeth David*, French Provincial Cooking; *E. E. Benest*, Inland Waterways of France; *I. Cazeaux*, French Music in the 15C; *J. R. Anthony*, French Baroque Music; *Martin Cooper*, French Music from the Death of Berlioz to the Death of Fauré; *L. Wylie*, Village in the Vaucluse; *J. L. Reed*, The Forests of France.

Maps

The traveller is advised to obtain at least one of the following three maps for general planning: the *Michelin* Map 989 or the *Institute Géographique National* (IGN) Map 901, both at 1:1,000,000, the latter being usefully supplemented by the 'cultural' Map 902 (principales richesses historiques et artistique). It is essential to acquire the latest editions of all maps, which will incorporate the most recent changes.

For travellers wishing to explore specific areas in some detail, the IGN *Série verte* is excellent, covering the whole of mainland France in 72 sheets at 1:100,000 (or 1cm for 1km), each map covering an area approx 90 by 100km. Alternatively, their *Série rouge*, which pinpoints the position of numerous churches, châteaux, scenic roads, and viewpoints, etc., may be found preferable, supplementing Map 902 listed above. These cover the country in 15 sheets at 1:250,000.

These maps, and the Michelin series nos 230–45 (see below) are referred to by number at the start of each route in this Guide.

IGN also publish several other series of maps concentrating on *Forest areas, National* and *Regional nature reserves and parks, Mountain regions,* and *Islands.* The walker may find IGN 903 (Sentiers de Grande Randonnée) helpful. IGN also publish a topographical series at 1:50,000, and a new *Série bleue* at 1:25,000, which should be completed by 1986. All these, and numerous more specialist maps including relief maps, and maps of mountain regions published in conjunction with *Editions Didier-Richard*, may be seen and bought from their saleroom at 107 Rue la Boétie, 75008 Paris (*Métro* Franklin D. Roosevelt), or McCarta Ltd, 122 King's Cross Road, London WC1 X9DS, should they not be readily available from good bookshops.

Travellers concentrating on **Paris**, or making excursions thence, will find the environs covered by IGN 90 (1; 100,000); their 'Région d'Île de France: patrimoine artistique', at 1:150,000; the Série rouge 103, or nos 8, 9, 20, and 21 of the Série verte, of considerable assistance; likewise Michelin maps nos 101 (outskirts of paris, at 1:50,000) 196 (Environs of Paris, at 1:100,000); or 237 (the Paris region) at 1:200,000. For central Paris, one cannot do better than acquire Michelin 12, Plan de Paris (1: 10,000), also available in a convenient Atlas form (11), together with a street index, etc., which will supplement the maps in *Blue Guide Paris and Environs*.

Michelin likewise cover mainland France in a new series of 16 sheets, mostly rectangular in form, and at 1:200,000 (1cm for 2km), numbered 230–45. They cover a larger area, and are in many ways more convenient than the regular series of 39 sheets (nos 51-87; 91-2), most of which open horizontally, and may be supplemented by nos 93 and 195.

These are published by Pneu Michelin, 46 Av. de Breteuil, 75341 Paris, and are available in the U.K. from the Michelin Tyre Co. Ltd, 81 Fulham Road, London SW3, or through any good bookshop.

These, and other general maps of France, together with other specialist maps, *should* be stocked by, or may be ordered through, Stanfords, 12-14 Long Acre, London WC2; the AA, Fanum House, Leicester Square, London WC1, etc.

PRACTICAL INFORMATION

Formalities and Currency

Passports are necessary for all British and American travellers entering France. British passports, valid for ten years, are issued at the Passport Office, Clive House, Petty France, London SW1, and from certain provincial offices, or may be obtained for an additional fee through any tourist agency. *British Visitors' Passports* (valid one year), available from Post Offices in the UK, are also accepted. No visa is required for British or American visitors, but should any foreigner intend to remain in France for more than three months, he should apply in advance to the nearest French Consulate, or if already in France, to the Préfecture de Police in the department in which he is residing, or to the Préfecture de Police (Service des Étrangers) in Paris (7 Blvd due Palais, 4e). Procedures are at present in the process of revision.

Custom House. Except for travellers by air, who have to pass customs at the airport of arrival, or those travelling on international expresses, where their luggage is examined in the train, luggage is still liable to be scrutinized at the frontier, or ports of departure and disembarkation. Provided that dutiable articles are declared, bona-fide travellers will find the French customs authorities (*douaniers*) courteous and reasonable.

It is as well to check in advance with French Consulates or Tourist Offices before starting out as to the latest regulations with regard to the importation of firearms, whether sporting or otherwise.

Embassies and Consulates, etc. *British Embassy*, 35 Rue du Faubourg St-Honoré, 8e, Paris; the *Consulate* is at 105–109, some 5 minutes' walk to the W. There are consulates at Le Havre, Bordeaux, Lille, Lyon, and Marseille; *British Chamber of Commerce*, 6 Rue Halévy, 9e; at the same address is the *British Colony Committee for Paris and District*, who produce a 'Digest of British and Franco-British Clubs, Societies, and Institutions in France'; *British Council*, 9 Rue de Constantine, 7e.

American Embassy, 2 Av. Gabriel, 8e (just N. of the Pl. de la Concorde) with consulates at Lyon, Marseille, Bordeaux, Strasbourg, and Nice; *Canadian Embassy*, 35 Av. Montaigne, 8e, with consulates at Bordeaux, Marseille, and Strasbourg; *South African Embassy*, 59 Quai d'Orsay, 7e; *Australian Embassy*, 4 Rue Jean Rey, 15e; *New Zealand Embassy*, 7ter Rue Léonard-de-Vinci, 16e; *Irish Embassy*, 4 Rue Rude, 16e.

Security. No objects of any value should be left visible in the interiors of cars parked in underground car-parks, or overnight near hotels, for example, which is merely tempting providence. Women should beware of bag-snatchers. In general, it is advisable to deposit any valuables with the manager of one's hotel, against receipt. Normally, however, with a reasonable amount of circumspection the tourist will find his property respected. The police should be applied to in case of any trouble.

Currency Regulations. In Oct. 1979 the British Government announced the suspension of exchange controls. There is now no restriction on the amount of sterling the traveller may take *out* of Great Britain, but it is advisable to enquire in advance at one's bank as to the latest regulations with regard to the export or re-export of money from France, for proof in the form of a 'declaration of entry' may be required if the sum involved is in excess of 5000 francs, particularly since restrictive ordinances have been applied by the Socialist regime.

Money. The monetary unit is the *franc*, subdivided into 100 *centimes*. Bank notes of 10, 20, 50, 100, 200 and 500 francs are in circulation, and there are also coins of 5, 10, 20, and 50 centimes, 1 franc, 2 francs, 5 francs, and 10 francs.

Branches of most French banks are open from 9.00 to 16.30 from Mon. to Fri.; most branches close on Sat. morning, but some central branches of the principal banks may have a 'bureau de change' open from 9.00 to 12.00. At some main-line stations, the 'bureaux de change' are open daily from 6.30 or 7.30 to 22.00 or 23.00. Those at the international airports operate a daily service from 6.00 to 23.00.

Larger hotels will also accept travellers' cheques, but they will give a lower rate of exchange. It is advisable to obtain a sufficient supply of French change for incidental expenses before leaving home, particularly if arriving in France during a week-end. It is also often worth while to 'shop around', for different banks give different rates of exchange.

Approaches to France; transport and motoring in France

France may be reached directly from Great Britain by a variety of ways, although a car taken across the Channel will render the tourist independent of other forms of transport in France. There are several rapid rail and ferry services from London to the Channel ports, and onwards to the larger centres, where there are usually car-hire facilities. The quickest but least interesting means of transit is by air: see below.

Travel Agents. General information may be obtained gratis from the *French Government Tourist Office*, 178 Piccadilly, London W1.

They have offices in the United States at 610 Fifth Av., New York, with branches at 645 N. Michigan Av. Chicago; 9401 Wilshire Blvd, Beverly Hills; 360 Post Street, San Francisco, 2050 Stemmons Freeway, Dallas: their Canadian office is at 1840 Ouest, Rue Sherbrooke, Montreal, with a branch at 372 Bay Street, Toronto.

Any accredited member of the *Association of British Travel Agents* will sell tickets and book accommodation. As some once-reliable firms appear to concentrate on 'groups' rather on the individual private traveller, the latter is advised to contact one of the many good but smaller organisations offering a personal service. They are warned that some agents have chosen to impose an additional charge when booking open-dated return air tickets not originally issued by themselves, and it is preferable to visit the individual airline's offices in such cases.

Rail and Ferry Services. Numerous and frequent Passenger and Car Ferry services are operated by British and French Railways, Town-send Thoresen, Southern Ferries, Normandy Ferries, etc. from

British to Northern French ports. For the latest information about services available, inquiries should be made to the *Sealink Car Ferry Centre*, 53 Grosvenor Gardens, London SW1. Those wishing to make use of the various **Hovercraft** services should be warned that the quality of service may be erratic in adverse weather conditions.

The *British Railway Travel Centre*, Rex House, Lower Regent Street, London SW1, provides travel tickets, sleeping-berth tickets, seat reservations, etc. on Continental as well as British Transport services. The offices of *French Railways*, (SNCF, or Société des Chemins de Fer Française) adjacent to the French Tourist Office in Piccadilly, are equally helpful, but do not actually sell tickets. Both can provide the prospective traveller with full details of the variety of services available, together with their cost, including **Motorail** (car-carrier) expresses, mostly with sleeping-cars, etc.

To avoid considerable inconvenience and irritation on train journeys, travellers are advised to check their tickets closely at the point of issue, particularly as to their validity (including the return trip), and should make sure that the '*Global*' charge has been made, including all possible supplements, etc.

Service *on board* some passenger **Ferries** has deteriorated, more attention being given to the selling of 'bingo' tickets than to the comfort of passengers, who are frequently treated like cattle. Often required to queue during the crossing for 'Passport control' (a procedure which could be simplified with ease if some administrator gave it his attention), travellers are then left to disembark with their luggage without the least form of organisation or even an attempt to control their movement to the gangways. Those finding conditions unacceptable should complain without compunction to the purser while on board, and on their return by writing to higher authorities (such as the European Rail Traffic Manager, Eversholt House, London NW1): otherwise no improvement can be expected.

The Paris office of *British Railways* is at 12 Blvd de la Madeleine, 9e.

Motorists driving in France will save much trouble by joining the *Automobile Association* (Fanum House, Basingstoke, Hants RG21 2EA) the *Royal Automobile Club* (83 Pall Mall, London SW1), the *Royal Scottish Automobile Club* (17 Rutland Sq., Edinburgh), or the *American Automobile Association* (8111 Gatehouse Road, Falls Church, Virginia 22042). These organisations will provide any necessary documents, as well as information about rules of the road abroad, restrictions regarding caravans and trailers, advice on routes, and arrangements regarding delivery of spare parts, insurance, etc. Motorists who are not the owners of their vehicle should possess the owner's permit for its use abroad. The use of safety-belts is now compulsory in France. Children under ten may not travel in the front seat (unless the car has no back seat). Both the A.A. and R.A.C. have offices in Paris, the former c/o the *Touring Club de France*, 6-8 Rue Firmin Gillot, 15e; the latter at 8 Pl. Vendôme. The insurance facilities offered by *Europ Assistance* should be taken advantage of. It is advisable to buy maps in advance of the tour.

A variety of approaches from the Channel ports to Paris are described in Section I of this Guide. Drivers should have a good idea of exactly where in Paris they are making for, and it is as well to familiarise oneself in advance as to which exit (*sortie*) to aim for prior to entering the 'Ceinture' or Blvd Périphérique (and likewise with the by-passes of other cities). These are usually well indicated some distance in advance, but care must be taken to be in position to make one's exit well before bearing off the motorway.

Those wishing to avoid Paris altogether will find Rtes 28A and 103A, for example, useful, although there are of course several alternatives—from Beauvais to Évreux or Dreux, or Beauvais to Senlis, Meaux, and Provins, for example.

Parking is restricted in most large towns, and many are now provided with underground car-parks (but see Security, p 52). A certain amount of circumspection is necessary, for the police, if feeling officious, may either fine one or have the car towed away; ill-parked foreign cars are removed as ruthlessly as native ones, and may take hours to recover from the '*fourrière*' or pound, and at a considerable charge; there will be a heavy fine to pay in addition.

The sign '*Seulement Riverains*', indicating that the road is private, should be respected.

Motorways in France are mostly toll roads (*autoroutes à péage*), unlike those in the U.K., and can on occasion provide a useful and rapid alternative to what may be congested main roads, and those in operation are listed at the start of routes near which they run. Some *bridges* (such as that at Tancarville) also charge a toll. Most service areas are well managed, and the distances between petrol-stations are usually indicated.

Many towns, large and small, are now provided with by-passes or ring-roads, and travellers wishing to visit the place in question must keep a sharp look-out for the turning marked 'Centre Ville'.

In winter certain routes described in this Guide will be impracticable, although most of the main roads will be kept clear of snow, and it is advisable to make enquiry beforehand if intending to drive in mountainous districts, including the Massif Central.

There are several regular **Bus** or **Coach services** from the U.K. to various destinations in France, notably the service provided by *Euroways*, and details may be obtained from the Victoria Coach Station, London SW1, British Rail Travel Centres, or the French Government Tourist Office, etc.

Regular **Air Services** between England and France are maintained by *Air France* working in conjunction with *British Airways*. Full information regarding flights from London and other cities in the U.K. may be obtained from British Airways, Dorland House, Lower Regent Street, London SW1, and from Air France, 158 New Bond Street, W1. *British Caledonian* (215 Piccadilly, W1, and 29A Royal Exchange, Threadneedle Street EC3) provides a service to Paris, while several charter companies are also in operation. Tourist offices can likewise inform one of the regular international flights from European cities to those in France, and of direct services from New York, and Montreal, etc., to France. Internal or domestic services are maintained by *Air Inter*, 232 Rue de Rivoli, Paris 1er, and branches. Most airports have car-hire facilities, and taxi services.

British Airways have Paris offices at 91 Av. des Champs Elysées and 34 Av. de l'Opéra; *Air France* offices are at 119 Av. des Champs-Elysées; *British Caledonian* at 5 Rue de la Paix, 2e.

The main airports in France served by Air Inter, and others, are (apart from Paris): Lille, Metz, Strasbourg, Mulhouse, Brest, Quimper, Lorient, Rennes, Nantes, Limoges, Clermont-Ferrand, St-Étienne, Lyon, Grenoble, Bordeaux, Biarritz, Pau, Tarbes, Toulouse, Perpignan, Montpellier, Nîmes, Marseille, Toulon-Hyeres, Frejus-St-Raphael, and Nice.

The *British Rail Travel Centre*, or *French Railways* (see above) can advise on the variety of services available on French Railways (SNCF). There are several lines from the Channel direct ports to other towns than Paris, including overnight trains from Calais to the Côte d'Azur. The main railway termini in Paris, all on *Métro* lines, have most of the facilities required by the traveller, including left-luggage offices (*consigne*) or lockers, and information bureaux. The SNCF provide an unusually efficient service. They also can advise on train or coach tours, self-drive car hire, and bicycle hire, etc. There are also the new high-speed TGV trains (*Train à Grande Vitesse*) from Paris to Lyon and Avignon, and to Dijon, Besançon, etc., and these lines are rapidly extending.

Gare d'Austerlitz, serving the Région Sud-Ouest (Tours, Bordeaux, Toulouse, Bayonne, the Pyrenees, etc.).

Gare de l'Est for the Région Est (Reims, Metz, Strasbourg, etc.).

Gare de Lyon for the Région Sud-Est (Lyon, Dijon, Provence, Côte d'Azur, etc.), including the new *Trains à Grande Vitesse* or TGV.

Gare Montparnasse, terminus for the Région Ouest (Brittany, La Rochelle, etc.).

Gare du Nord for the Région Nord (Lille, etc.), and also for boat-trains to Boulogne, Calais, and Dunkerque).

Gare St-Lazare, another terminus of the Région Ouest (Normandy lines, Rouen, and boat-trains to Dieppe, Le Havre, Cherbourg, etc.).

Note. French Railways have abolished ticket control at platform barriers. Passengers purchasing a ticket *in France* must themselves punch-and-date-stamp (or '*composter*') their ticket in an orange red-coloured machine at the platform entrance *before* boarding the train. Those inadvertently failing to do so are liable to pay a supplementary fee/fine to the inspector. This procedure does not apply to tickets purchased outside France.

For public transport within Paris, including the fast exterior lines of the RER (*Réseau Express Regional*), see *Blue Guide Paris and Environs*. Here the buses (*autobus*) and the underground railway (*Métro*) are controlled by the RATP (*Régie Autonome des Transports Parisien*), with offices at 53bis Quai des Grands-Augustins (just S. of the Pont Neuf), and a branch in the Pl. de la Madeleine (on the E. side of the church), which can give details of coach tours to sites in the environs, while Tourist Offices can provide information of coach tours into the provinces.

Postal and Other Services

Most **Post Offices**, indicated by the sign **P.T.T.**, are open from 8.00 to 19.00 on weekdays, and until 12.00 on Sat. Correspondence marked 'poste restante' may be addressed to any post office (preferably the *Bureau de Poste* of the town in question), giving the départment number before the name of the town, and is handed to the addressee on proof of identity (passport preferable). Letters may be sent registered ('recommandé') for a small fee, and are likewise not delivered without proof of identity. The whereabouts of post offices are shown on the town-plans of the *red* Michelin guide, although the actual addresses are not given. However, by enquiring for the P.T.T. (pronounced P as in pet, and the two Ts as tay tay), one will be given directions, usually towards the town centre.

Letter-boxes are painted yellow. Postage stamps (*timbres*) are sold at all post offices and most tobacconists.

Telephones. The telephone service in France has been much improved. Public call-boxes may be found at most post offices, métro stations, cafés, restaurants, and at some bus stops (taxiphones). With patience and sufficient small change one should have little difficulty in making the right connection. France is in S.T.D. communication with the British Isles, and most of Europe, etc. Reversed-charge calls ('P.V.C.') are accepted. Some call-box instruments are constructed to take 'jetons' only, which have to be bought at the counter near which the telephone is installed. Note that the charge for calls made from hotels is frequently higher than those made from public telephone boxes. When calling abroad, one must wait after dialling the prefix 19 (international) for a change in the dialling tone before continuing.

If telephoning the U.K. from France, dial 44 after the tone change, and then the area code (but omit the zero) and number required. A list of essential telephone numbers (bank, insurance company, family, etc.) including area codes should be carried abroad with one as a precautionary measure. When calling the provinces from Paris, or from one department to another, the prefix 16 is first dialled, followed, after a change of tone, by a 2-figure department code, and then the 6-figure number. The latter only is required when dialling within the same department. For directory enquiries, dial 12; for operator, 13; telegrams, 14; police, 17; and fire, 18.

Information Bureaux. Most towns have a local *Syndicat d'Initiative* (indicated in this Guide by the initials S.I.). They often provide useful information with regard to accommodation (without actually recommending specific hotels), local events, sporting facilities, times of admission to museums, and châteaux, etc. Many of the major towns have an *'Accueil de France'* tourist office, with their head office at 127 Av. des Champs-Élysées, Paris (and subsidiary branches at some main line railway stations), who can also make hotel bookings throughout the country.

Hotels and Restaurants: Food and Wine

The availability of accommodation is *not* indicated in this Guide. All forms and categories of accommodation can be found throughout France, and as there are several annual publications which concentrate on hotels and restaurants, etc., travellers are advised to acquire the latest edition of one or two such volumes. Among the more reliable are the *'red guide'* published by *Michelin, Kléber, Gault-Millau*, the *Logis de France* (available gratis from the French Government Tourist Office), and the *Guide des Relais Routiers* (with a London office at 354 Fulham Road, SW10), the latter being unpretentious but usually providing a comfortable bed, and good value for money.

Other publications, including one produced by Michelin, cater for the requirements of campers and caravanners. Bed-and-breakfast accommodation, and camping sites on working farms, etc. will be found listed in a handbook entitled 'Gîtes de France', available from the French Government Tourist Office; while a 'French Farm and Village Holiday Guide', produced in collaboration with the Fédération Nationale des Gîtes Ruraux de France', is published by Duo Publishing Ltd, 1 Hermes Street, London N1, who also produce 'The Young Traveller's Guide to France', the acquisition of which is recommended to students in general.

Branches of the Office de Tourisme de Paris (see p 57) will endeavour to make on-the-spot bookings *in Paris*, although it is prudent to book in advance either directly or through a travel agency, for hotels are often full during the tourist season, particularly at Easter and during the course of exhibitions, trade fairs, etc. They can also make hotel bookings throughout the country, and local S.Is can also provide brochures listing accommodation in their areas. It is wise during certain seasons to book in advance of weekends, and it should be noted, when touring, that many hotels fill up comparatively early in the evening, as in most cases travellers will be settling in prior to the evening meal; obviously this does not apply to the same extent with those hotels without restaurants.

All **Hotels** are officially classified by the *Direction de Tourisme*, and their grading is shown by stars, depending on their amenities and the type of hotel, from 4-stars 'L' (luxury) to 1-star (plain but comfortable). Hot and cold running water will be found in all bedrooms, but only a proportion of hotels in the 1-, 2-, and even 3-star categories have rooms with a private bath and W.C. en suite, although many more will provide a shower and bidet. Similarly, many hotels have no restaurant, although almost all will provide a continental breakfast: but see below.

Charges vary, of course, according to the grade of hotel and the time of year, being at their highest from mid-June to mid-Sept. In most hotels (especially when quoting 'en pension' terms) 15 per cent is now added to the bill for 'service'—whether provided or not—and certainly when the bill is marked 'service et taxes compris' (s.t.c.) no additional gratuity is expected.

It should be noted that a number of large establishments have been built at some considerable distance from the centre of the larger towns and cities (which may be all very well for groups and those attending trade fairs, etc., but inconvenient for the tourist), and it is advisable to make certain in advance as to the exact situation of the hotel in question before booking; and likewise, in his own interest, the traveller should have a very precise understanding as to the charge before taking possession of his room, particularly in view of the fact that too many—in the larger towns—appear to be geared to the 'expense-account' visitor. Valuables should be deposited with the management in exchange for a receipt. See also *Security*; p 52.

'I wonder not at the *French*, for their dishes of frogges, snailes, and toadstools . . .', wrote Sir Thomas Browne in 'Religio Medici', while a century later Joseph Baretti, an intimate of Dr Johnson's circle, when travelling on the Continent, remarked 'Let it be dinner-time, and I care not a fig for the difference between macaroni and roast-beef, herring and frogs, the olla and the sourcrout; a very cosmopolite in the article of filling one's belly', and the present-day tourist in France cannot do better than follow such sound advice, savouring the palatable regional dishes in preference to the routine 'International' menu, and preferably in establishments patronised by the locals. **Restaurants** of every kind and category are to be found without much difficulty throughout the country, and they have been officially graded to indicate that they adhere to certain criteria. Although the prices tend to be comparatively high, very often (but no means always) one will obtain better value for money than in some other countries who do not take the ritual and etiquette of eating so seriously, and who are prepared to accept lower standards.

At most restaurants the day's set menu, 'à prix fixe', is available, with a certain choice of dishes, and at a much lower price than 'à la carte', even if somewhat unimaginative in the more modest establishments; and this is displayed, with prices, at the entrance, and should be perused in advance. Frequently there is more than one selected menu to choose from, apart from the recommended 'plat du jour', even if the cheapest is so uninspired that the client is thus obliged to take one at a higher price.

The **wine**, either *rouge*, *blanc*, or *rosé*, in bottles or carafes, is usually very fair at most restaurants, while many can provide a liberal choice of superior wines at relatively high prices. When dining *à la carte*, the traveller should not allow the suggestions of the waiter, however plausible, to add more dishes to the menu than he really wants; the slightest additions (for vegetables, for example) can easily swell the bill by a disproportionate amount. The bill (*l'addition*), which should be carefully scrutinised, should be in writing; the normal 15 per cent gratuity is now usually included in the price of a set menu; this is not so if one has chosen à la carte, but any misunderstanding can be avoided by asking 'Le service est-il compris?'. If no gratuity has been included, the waiter may be rewarded with some 10-12 per cent of the bill, according to the quality of service: less where a considerable proportion of the total is for a single bottle; but see also *Tipping*, p 71.

There are, of course, a number of French gastronomic guides (see above) listing a great range of eating-places throughout France, among them the better-known 'rosetted' and 'de luxe' restaurants where French cookery *should* reach its perfection—at a price which few can afford—but it must be admitted that the traveller without inside knowledge will often have better value for his money at the less pretentious establishments.

Unfortunately there is a tendency, particularly in areas frequented by tourists rather than by a regular clientele, to serve stereotyped meals of a mediocre quality for the prices charged. Some restaurants, which can easily be avoided, also assume that piped music is conducive to a better appetite. It will be noticed that many restaurants are closed on Sundays, and (in Paris) during August. It is advisable to book a table in advance at the better-known or more fashionable restaurants.

Among numerous restaurants near main roads, notable are the characteristic '*Courte-Paille*' restaurants, concentrating entirely on grills, the situation of which is shown on a map in the *Guide des Relais-Routiers*.

Cafés are usually found in the main streets or in or near the main 'Place' of towns, and in the season tables and chairs may be set out on the adjacent pavement (known as the 'terrasse')—or behind a glazed conservatory/observatory. The *café* or *café crème* is usually very good, but tea-making is still a perfunctory performance. A 'Continental breakfast' or *'petit déjeuner'* may be obtained in the mornings at many cafés, with fresh rolls, *croissants*, or *brioches*, and butter, with coffee or—less frequently—chocolate.

The usual order for a small beer is a *demi*; draught beer is *à la pression*. It is cheaper to stand at the bar; prices are automatically raised if one subsequently takes a seat. The waiter should not be paid after each drink, but just prior to the time one wishes to leave. Travellers are warned that the prices charged at some pretentious cafés or patisseries for a mere coffee, beer, *vin ordinaire*, or other beverage, are quite exorbitant, and it is always as well to check before order-ing, to avoid an unpleasant shock.

The standard of toilet facilities in restaurants, brasseries, bistros, bars and cafés, is improving; they are not all the Stygian bogs they once were, but towels (paper or otherwise) are often hard to come by. However, when there is reason for complaint—likewise in hotels— travellers should not hesitate to do so, both to the proprietor and the next S.I. they pass.

One of the great pleasures of wandering through any provincial town in France is to see the range and quality of the provisions displayed in its shops and stalls, both tempting the eye and stimulating the palate, and a promise of a good meal to which one may look forward to without apprehension.

When touring, much time and money may be saved by having pic-nics en route, buying bread (*pain*; *pain de seigle*, rye bread; *pain complet*, wholemeal) at the *boulangerie*; *tranches* (slices) of the local patés, which each have their particular characteristics, at the *char-cuterie*, together with slices of their hams, *galantines*, *saucissons*, or a carton of *rillettes*. A range of fresh cheeses (*fromages*), many locally produced, may be seen at the *crémerie*, while few will be able to resist entering the *patisserie*. A *traiteur* is a shop producing a variety of prepared dishes. Fresh fruit in all its variety may be selected from a *primeur* or *marchand de legume*, or from the market stalls, a visit to which is both an education and a reassuring experience, while a bot-tle or two of wine from the *marchand de vins* will not be overlooked. Beware of carrying *terrines* for any distance on a hot day, for the jel-ly will melt; and likewise bottles of cider, the contents of which may well spurt out on opening . . . Bottles of water, etc. may be found in most *supermarchés*, *épiceries* (grocers) and elsewhere.

It would be foolish to even attempt to describe in a few pages the gastronomy of France, or even a resumé of the 'Nouvelle Cuisine'. Its many regions have their individual ways of preparing their specialities, and within recent decades—particularly since the publication of Elizabeth David's cookery books, which have been the stand by of all who love French food—there has been a growing knowledge and appreciation of its qualities. When referring specifically to the cuisine of Normandy, she remarked that the traveller unacquainted with it might get the impression that perhaps the inhabitants of that rich region lived on nothing else but duck paté and Tripes *à la mode de Caen*. . . while the great slabs of butter from Isigny or Gournay, and the bowls of thick cream in the crémeries, and such a variety of cheeses on display, would make one wonder how the Normands could resist the excess of cholesterol; but perhaps the ubiquitous Calvados eau-de-vie assists more than somewhat in its digestion!

A few warning words may not come amiss: it should be remembered that in the provincial towns of France the main meal of the day is at noon, and that any specialities which may have been available at midday are unlikely to be on the evening menu; nor are these specialities cooked every day, or prepared at a moment's notice. The *bouillabaisse* of Provence, the *cassoulet* of Languedoc, the *brochet au beurre blanc* of the Loire, or the *coq au vin* of Bur-gundy about which one may have read, are usually only produced on special occasions, feast days, and holidays, and the tourist may well be disappointed by what may be passed off as a regional delicacy produced perfunctorily merely to attract gullible customers. It should also be appreciated that several specialities are very seasonal, depending on the availability of essential ingredients; nor is it sensible to request a Provençal *chou farci*, a *cassoulet toulousain*, or a *gratin dauphinois* on a hot August day. High summer is not the best moment for freshly made pork products and patés, and few of the great French cheeses will then be found in their prime condition. It should also be noted that fresh spring vegetables—although seen in profusion when driving through parts of Brittany, for example—are not always as much in evidence on menus as they should be, a sad situation caused perhaps not so much by the time taken and the cost involved in their preparation, but by the fact that a high proportion of the production is already committed to the canning industry. Indeed, as Elizabeth David sagely remarked: 'A flourishing tradition of local cookery implies also genuine local products; the cooks and the housewives must be backed up by the dairy farmers, the pig breeders and the pork butchers, the market gardeners and the fruit growers, otherwise regional cookery simply retreats into the realms of folk-lore'.

Travellers have every right to expect a variety of fish and shell-fish on the Atlantic and Mediterranean coasts, and they will rarely be disappointed, whether it be tunny or the *chipirones* of the Basque country, the latter being little squids cooked in their own ink; the lamprey of Bordeaux; the pickled herrings of Boulonge; the mackerel of Dieppe; or the *palourdes gratinées* or *farcies* of Brittany, likewise the home of the *cotriade* or fish stew, other varieties of which are the *chaudrée* of La Rochelle, the *pochouse* of Burgundy, and the *bourride* of Provence, where a *brandade de morue*, creamed salt cod with olive oil and garlic, may also be relished.

Inland one will find the Pyrenean trout, among others in mountainous areas, such as the *omble-chevalier* in the Alps, while *quenelles de brochet*, a pike dumpling, may be sampled in the Jura. In the Loire valley, carp, pike, or shad, among other river fish, may be served *au beurre blanc* or with a sorrel souce, *à l'oseille*, which can be delicious; in Alsace the river fish may be served with a white wine sauce, *au riesling*.

From the salt marches of the Médoc or Cotentin peninsulas comes succulent *pré-salé* lamb; the hams of Bayonne, the Morvan, and the Massif central, are notable; while in the Dordogne are found *maigret de canard* (a fillet of duck), apart from *confits*—potted and preserved duck or goose— together with *foie gras*, the latter also a speciality of Alsace. Further S.W. is the home of the *dinde aux marrons* (turkey stuffed with whole chestnuts), while the corn-fed chickens of Bresse, and the wild-fowl of the Sologne, and elsewhere, are all remarkable. Nor is there any lack of venison and wild boar in the Ardennes, among other sequestered areas.

Different regions will have their individual ways of preparation, whether it be the *poule au pot à la crème Normande* (poached in a butter and cream sauce), or *farci en daube à la Berrichone*. At Tours one will be offered *noisettes du porc aux pruneaux*; in Normandy, *côtes de porc Vallée d'Auge* (grilled, with cider sauce); in Burgundy, and not only there, one might prefer *boeuf bourguignonne*, Charolais beef stewed in red Burgundy.

Soups and vegetable dishes are also found in variety of forms, from the *garbure* of the W. Pyrenees, a thick soup of cabbage, pimento, potatoes, and haricot beans, to the *potage Lorraine*, of potatoes and leeks. From the Basque country too comes the *piperade*, made with tomatoes, onions, and pimentos, and served with eggs fried in olive oil; in Provence its place is taken by the *ratatouille*. In the Dordogne one will come across *pommes sarladaises*, potatoes cooked with goose fat and truffles; in Alsace there is the *tarte aux vigneronnes*, a potato pie, not forgetting the *zewelwaï* or onion tart—nor *choucroute* or sauerkraut; in Picardy the *flamiche* or leek tart is found; in Provence the *pissaladière*, an anchovy tart.

One should allow one's curiosity to get the better of caution, and whenever available, select a dish that is both regional and seasonal. If in doubt, do not be shy of asking advice. Mistakes will, of course, be made, or a dish will be served which is not at all what one might have been expecting or to one's taste; but without taking an occasional 'risk', the traveller will pass through a country, the gastronomic pretensions of which are undeniable, losing marvellous opportunities of indulging oneself in the one of the more gratifying pleasures of life.

Many French culinary terms and processes are universally known, but to assist those not so well acquainted with some of the more common foods, etc., a representative list is appended with their English equivalents

Les Potages, Soups

Bouillon, broth
Consommé, clear soup
Crème, thick soup
Aigo boulido, a provençal soup, the main ingredients of which are garlic, herbs, and yolk of eggs
Garbure, thick cabbage or vegetable soup from S.W. France
Soupe au pistou, a vegetable soup of garlic, basil, and herbs, eaten in the Nice region
Cotriade, a Breton fish soup, a variation of which is the *Chaudrée* of La Rochelle

Hors-d'Œuvre and Salads

Crudités, raw vegetables, usually sliced, chopped, or grated
Tapénade, a purée of black olives, capers, anchovies, tunny-fish, etc., from the provençal *tapéno*, for capers
Salade Niçoise, with tomato, anchovy, onions, and olives
Salade Cauchoise, of potatoes, celery, and ham
Salade panachée, mixed salad
Salade verte, green salad; also *Salade simple*, or *de saison*
Salade de riz aux tomates, rice and tomato salad
A *Salade Lyonnaise* in fact consists of a variety of meats, seasoned and with an oil, vinegar, shallot, and parsley dressing, and served on separate dishes.

Les Oeufs, Eggs (including some hot hors d'œuvre)

à la coque, soft-boiled; *mollets*, medium-boiled; *durs*, hard-boiled; *sur le plat*, or *au plat*, fried; *pochés*, poached; *en cocotte*, baked in a remekin; *brouillés*, scrambled
Omelette aux fines herbes, savoury omelette; *au jambon*, ham omelette, etc., and an infinite variety of others
oeufs durs soubise, hard-boiled eggs with an onion and cream sauce
piperade, a concoction of eggs and green peppers, tomatoes and onion, from the Basque country and Béarn
Quiche Lorraine, cream and bacon tart
Tarte à l'Oignon, or *Zewelwaï*, onion and cream tart, from Alsace
Pissaladière, provençal onion and anchovy pie
Gratin Dauphinois, sliced potatoes cooked in cream
Gratin savoyard, similar, but with the addition of eggs and cheese

Le Poisson, les Coquillages et Crustacés
(or **Fruits de Mer**), etc., Fish and Shellfish

not forgetting such delicacies as *Cuisses de grenouilles*, frogs' legs; and
Escargots, snails
Alose, shad
Anchois, anchovies
Anguille, eel
Bar, bass
Barbou, brill
Baudroi, angler fish
Bellon, a type of oyster
Blanchaille, whitebait, a dish of which is *friture*, deep fried
Brochet, pike, often the base of *quenelles*
Calmars, inkfish
Carpe, carp
Chipirones, squid
Colin, hake
Coquilles St-Jacques, scallops
Crevettes, prawns or shrimps
Daurade, sea bream
Ecrevisse, fresh-water crayfish
Encornet, squid
Éperlans, smelts
Espadon, swordfish
Harengs, herrings
Homard, lobster
Huîtres, oysters
Lamproie, lamprey
Langouste, crawfish or lobster; *langoustine*, Dublin Bay prawn
Lotte, burbot (a kind of eel)
Loup, a kind of sea bass
Maquereau, mackerel
Merlan, whiting
Mérou, brill
Morue, salt cod (see *brandade*, below); fresh cod is *Cabillaud*
Moules, mussels
Mulet, grey mullet
Omble-Chevalier, char
Palourdes, clams; also *Praires*
Poulpe, octopus
Raie, skate (often served 'au beurre noir', with black butter)
Rouget, red mullet
St-Pierre, John Dory
Saumon, salmon; *fumé*, smoked
Thon, tunnyfish or tuna
Truite, trout

Bouillabaisse, said to be at its best at Marseille, for in the gulf are caught the
racasse, *roucau*, and *St-Pierre*, the three fish essential to its success, with the
addition of unions, oil, garlic, and saffron, etc.
Brandade, a cream of pounded salt cod, from Nîmes
Aïoli, a mayonnaise of vinegar, oil, and pluverised garlic, often eaten with fish
Bourride, a Provençal fish stew, to which *aïoli* is added
Quenelles, fish (often pike) or meat dumpling roll, served in a souce
Tain, a dish of vegetables, eggs, and fish, flavoured with cheese and garlic,
from Carpentras
Pochouse seurroise, a Burgundian fish stew

Les Viandes, Meat

Agneau, lamb; *gigot*, leg of lamb; *carré d'agneau*, cutlets
Boeuf, beef; *queue de boeuf*, ox-tail; *Rosbif*, roast beef; (*Bifteck* is a *franglais*
word which has been in use since 1786)

Cochon de lait, sucking-pig
Mouton, mutton
Porc, pork; see below
Veau, veal; *ris de veau*, sweetbreads
Viandes froides, cold meats

Meat may be ordered *bleu*, very rare; *saignant*, underdone; *à point*, medium; or *bien cuit*, well done
daube, a stew; other forms are *pot-au-feu*, and *marmite*
Cassoulet, a stew of mutton, pickled pork, sausages, and possibly goose, and haricot beans, originating in Castelnaudary
Beckenoff, a port and mutton pie from Alsace, baked with potatoes
Among general terms are:
Basquaise, with tomato and pimento
Bercy, with wine and shallots
Bourguignonne, cooked in red wine, with bacon, mushrooms, and small onions
Cauchoise, with cream, calvados, and apples
Chasseur or *forestière*, with mushrooms
Lyonnaise, with onions
à la meunière, cooked slowly in butter
à la nivernaise, with a glazed carrot and onion garnish
Normande, with a cream sauce
Parmentier, with potatoes
Périgourdine, with truffles and/or *foie gras*
Provençale, with oil, tomatoes, and garlic

La Charcuterie, Pork products and cooked meats, etc.

Andouille, smoked chitterling sausage; and *ouillettes*, a smaller version
Boudin, black pudding (or white if pork-based); *boudin blanc*, chicken mousse
Cervelles, brains
Foie, liver
Jambon, ham; *jambon cuit*, York Ham; *fumé* or *cru*, smoked; *de Bayonne*, salt-cured
Pieds de porc, pigs' trotters
Rillettes, potted shredded pork; in *Rillons* the pieces of port are larger
Rognons, kidneys
Saucisses, sausages; *saucisson*, salami sausage
Terrines, potted meants

Les Volailles et le Gibier, Poultry and Game

Alouettes, larks
Bécasse, woodcock
Caille, quail
Canard, duck; *canard sauvage*, wild duck; *caneton*, duckling (those of Duclair and Nantes are reputed)
Cerf or *Chevreuil*, venison
Dinde or *dindon*, female and male turkey
Faisan, pheasant
Grives, thrushes
Lapin, rabbit
Lièvre, hare
Oie, goose; *paté de foie gras* is made from goose liver; a *confit d'oie* is a conserve of goose preserved in its own fat: both reputed in Alsace and Aquitaine
Palombes, wood-pigeons
Perdreau or *perdrix*, partridge
Pintade, guinea-fowl
Pluviers, plovers
Poulet, chicken; *poularde*, capon (those of Bresse being reputed)
Sanglier, wild boar; *marcassin*, a young wild boar
Sarcelle, teal

Les Légumes et Aromates, Vegetables and Herbs

Ail, garlic; *aioli*, a mayonnaise of pulverised garlic, vinegar, oil, etc.
Artichauts, globe or leaf artichokes; *fonds*, hearts; *Topinambours*, Jerusalem artichokes
Asperges, asparagus
Aubergine, egg plant
Betterave, beetroot
Blettes, chard
Céleris, celery
Carottes, carrots
Céleri-rave, celeric; *céleri-rave rémoulade*, in mustard sauce
Cerfeuil, chervil
Champignons, cultivated mushrooms. Other common edible fungi are *Cèpes* (boletus edulis), *Chantarelles* or *Girolles*, and *Morilles*
Chicorée, Belgian endive (or witloof); *chicorée frisée* or *scarole*, curly chicory
Chou, cabbage; *chou rouge*, red cabbage; *choux de Bruxelles*, Brussels sprouts
Choucroute, sauerkraut (at its best in Alsace)
Choufleur, cauliflower
Ciboulettes, chives
Concombre, cucumber
Cornichon, gherkin
Courge, marrow; *Courgettes*, baby marrows
Cresson, watercress
Échalotes, shallots
Endives Belges; see above
Épinards, spinach
Estragon, tarragon
Fenouil, fennel
Fèves, broad beans
Genièvre, baies de, juniper berries
Haricots blancs, white haricot beans; *haricots verts*, French beans; *Flageolets*, green beans
Huile d'Olive, olive oil; *huile de noix*, walnut oil
Laitue, lettuce; *salade*, green salad
Lentilles, lentils
Mâche, lamb's-lettuce or corn-salad
Navets, turnips
Oignons, onions
Oseille, sorrel
Persil, parsley
Petits pois, green peas
Pissenlits, dandelions
Poireaux, leeks
Pois chiches, chick peas
Poivre, pepper
Poivrons, sweet peppers (pimentos)
Pommes de terre, potatoes
Raifort, horseradish
Riz, rice
Romarin, rosemary
Truffes, truffles

Ratatouille, a Provençal mixture of aubergines, tomatoes, onions, and peppers, stewed in oil, and served hot or cold

Les Fromages, Cheeses

There are numerous regional varieties, and the initials c, e, and g indicate whether they are produced from cow (*vache*), ewe (*brebis*), or goat-milk (*chèvre*). Only some of the more usual types are listed.
Normandy: *Bondon, Camembert, Livarot, Pont-l'Évêque, Boursin* (all c)
N. France, and Île-de-France: *Mimolette, St-Paulin, Brie, Coulommiers* (all c)
Brittany: *Port-du-Salut* (c)
Touraine, and Poitou: *St-Paulin* (c), *Chabichou*, and *Ste-Maure* (both g)

Berry, and Burgundy: *Valençay* (g), *St-Florentin*, and *Epoisse* (both c)
The Pyrenean region produces several, mostly cow, but also ewe-cheeses
The Causses, to the N.E., produce the renowned *Roquefort* (e), and *Pelardon des Cévennes* (g)
The Auvergne is noted for the *Bleu-d'Auvergne*, *Cantal*, *St-Nectaire*, and *Fourme-d'Ambert* (all c)
In Alsace and Lorraine are the *Carré-de-l'Est*, *Munster*, and *Rocollet* (all c)
The Franche-Comté produces the *Comté*, and further S., the *Bleu-de-Bresse* (both c)
Savoy is noted for *Beaufort*, *Emmental*, *Reblochon*, and *Tomme* (all c); in the Lyonnais and Dauphiny, the *Rigotte-de-Condrieu* (c), the *Picodon*, and *St-Marcellin* (both g) are reputed; and in Provence, the *Banon* (g)

There are of course any variety of cream cheeses, such as the *Petit-Suisse*, and numerous processed forms, some encrusted with grape-pips, or walnuts, or dusted with pepper, etc. It is worth while savouring, at least, the local productions.

The *Fondue Savoyarde* consists of melted cheese (often the *Vacherin*), wine, and kirsch, kept at a sizzling temperature, into which cubes of bread are dipped.

Note that cheese is always eaten *before* the dessert in France.

Les Desserts, Dessert (and also fruit and nuts, etc.)

Abricots, apricots
Ananas, pineapples
Bananes, bananas
Cannelle, cinnamon
Cassis, black current
Cerises, cherries
Citron, lemon
Coings, quinces
Figues, figs
Fraises, strawberries; *fraises des bois*, wild strawberries
Framboises, raspberries
Fruits confits, crystallised fruit; *fruits en compote*, stewed
Groseilles, red or white currants; *Groseilles à Maquereau*, gooseberries
Marrons, chestnuts; *marrons glacés*, candied chestnuts
Mendiant, a plate of mixed almonds, raisins, etc.
Miel, honey
Mûres, mulberries; *mûres de ronce*, blackberries
Myrtilles, bilberries
Noisettes, hazel-nuts
Noix, walnuts
Pamplemousse, grapefruit
Pêches, peaches
Poires, pears
Pommes, apples
Pruneaux, prunes (those of Agen being reputed); *pruneaux fourrés*, stuffed with almond paste (from Tours)
Prunes, plumes; *Mirabelles*, small yellow plumes; *Reine-claudes*, greengages
Raisins, grapes; *raisin sec*, raisin
Sucre, sugar
Crème brulée, caramel rice; *crémets*, a confection of thick cream and egg yolks
Flan, cream caramel
Glaces, ice-creams
Pâte d'amande, almond paste or marzipan; *pâte des prunes*, plum paste; *pâte de coings*, quince paste, etc.
Soufflés hardly require introduction

In Auvergne one will find the *milliard*, a kind of batter pudding containing black cherries; further W., in the Limousin, one may enjoy *clafoutis*, a backed custard filled with black cherries

Patisseries et Confiseries, Pastries, Cakes, and Confectionery

Berlingots, pyramid-shaped sweets
Confiture, jam; *confiture d'orange*, marmalade
Crêpes dentelles, pancakes. Crêperies have proliferated in several regions of France, and offer an interesting and succulent variety of fillings in their pancakes
Croissant, a crescent-shaped rich bread roll
Dragées, sugared almonds
en brioche, baked in dough
en croute, baked in a pastry case
Galettes, a biscuit; in Brittany a type of pancake
Gâteaux, cakes, *gâteaux secs*, biscuits; also *Gâteau Breton*, *Gâteau Basque*, etc.
Gaufres, waffles
Macarons, almost paste macaroons
Nougatines, caramelised ground almonds
Pain d'Épices, spiced honey-cake or gingerbread
Petits fours, fancy biscuits

Pain, bread, is usually bought at *Boulangeries*; there are numerous forms and varieties, the most common perhaps being the *baguette*, a long roll of medium thickness, also thinner, known as a *ficelle*; the *épi* is of more irregular shape; there is also the larger *pain campagne*, etc.

Monuments and Museums:
Churches and Châteaux

Much has been done in recent years to modernise and reform the provincial museums of France, in which many masterpieces have long lain secluded, and several others are undergoing overdue reorganisation—the Musée Granet at Aix, the Musée Calvet at Avignon, the Musées du Château des Rohan at Strasbourg and the museums of Bordeaux come to mind. It would be invidious to mention certain others where such reformation is still an aspiration. Some fine new buildings have also been constructed—such as that at Caen, the Musée de la Civilisation Gallo-Romaine at Lyon, or the extension to the Musée Dobrée at Nantes, while some remarkable transformations have taken place at Metz, Besançon, the Musée Bonnat at Bayonne, and the Musée des Augustins, Toulouse, for example. Several museums of great importance have been installed in buildings notable in themselves—such as the Musée du Petit Palais, Avignon, or the Maison de l'Outil, at Troyes.

In the 'Répertoire des musées et collections publiques de France', published in 1982 by the Éditions de la Réunion des musées nationaux, Paris, some 1350 museums (including several châteaux, and cathedral treasuries, and a large number of very slight interest) are listed, and although the Editor has visited in person a high proportion of the more important collections in the service of this Guide, it is quite possible that he may have overlooked a smaller museum of quality, or not given sufficient notice of others, while some important work may not be listed, because under restoration or on exhibition elsewhere. There are a many important collections which deserve visiting, notable among which are the museums of Colmar (d'Unterlinden), Dijon (Beaux-Arts), Lille (Beaux-Arts), Montpellier (Fabre, and Atger) and Rouen (Beaux-Arts); also of interest are those at Agen, Annecy, Arles, Auch, Autun, Castres, Chalon-sur-Saône, Épinal, Grenoble, Nancy (Historique Lorrain), Pau, and St-Tropez (l'Annonciade). Of more specialised interest are those of Angers (Château d'Angers; tapisseries); Adrien-Dubouché, at Limoges (ceramics); Tissues, and Arts Décoratifs, and de l'Imprimerie, Lyon; de l'Empéri, Salon (military); Tautavel (N.W. of Perpignan; prehistory); the Naval Museum at Toulon, or de l'Impression sur Étoffes, Mulhouse (printing on fabrics). Others concentrate on specific artists, such as Albi (Toulouse-Lautrec), Antibes (Picasso), Montauban (Ingres), Nice (Matisse), St-Quentin (Delatour), Honfleur (Boudin), or Valence (Hubert Robert). Every year new collections are being inaugurated, such as the Musée d'Art Moderne, at Troyes.

As a general rule, the NATIONAL MUSEUMS are *closed on Tuesdays*, but there is no general rule with regard to others, and the traveller should make enquiries at any S.I. concerning times of admission. Many museums will be closed between 12.00 – 14.00. It may be remarked that visitors coming from countries where they are used to entering musuems free of charge may sometimes baulk at paying the fee imposed. In fact, in many cases, the charge is in no way disproportionate to the size and quality of the collections to be seen, an increasing number of which are being reformed and displayed with imagination and taste. Unfortunately this is not always so, and the same charge can apply to museums and monuments whose conservateurs appear to remain unconcerned as to whether they are giving value for money, and who are insensitive to the comparative excellence of other collections.

It may also be mentioned that although considerable work seems to have gone into the preparation and production of lavishly illustrated catalogues, selling at high prices, of *temporary* exhibitions, few of the important museums—perhaps because so many of them are undergoing drastic change—publish good general catalogues or inventories of their *permanent* collections of use to the discriminating visitor, for whom the few 'Publications scientifiques' available are both too detailed and highly priced, and who find the slighter booklets too superficial, a situation which it is hoped will be improved before too long. Indeed, there are signs of this, with the publication by the *Editions de la Réunion des musées nationaux* of several general catalogues of collections. A list of catalogues printed by this organisation is available from any bookstall of the national museums.

Many, but by no means all, churches and cathedrals are freely open all day, or at least until dusk, but the depredations of vandals and pilferers have precipitated the closure of others, although usually there is some indication as to the whereabouts of the local guardian. Some will be closed between 12.00 and 14.00. Crypts, choirs, towers, treasuries, etc. in some churches may be viewed between specific hours only, or on specific days, but *if* the sacristan can be found, he may be persuaded to allow entry at other times. A fee for entry is still considered a perquisite of the local guardian of some village churches, particularly if it contains murals, or some other object of special interest, which might be an excuse to extort francs from the interested visitor, but this is by no means always so.

It will be noticed that the altars of many churches have been moved from their traditional place to a more central position nearer the crossing—in accordance with recent liturgical reform—but only a proportion have taken the opportunity of ridding themselves of the tasteless clutter of 19C or more modern decoration, Stations of the Cross, insipid statues, and other furniture, which so often detract from the aesthetic appeal of the building in question. At the same time it is encouraging to find so much work being carried out in the way of tasteful and restrained restoration of a large number of the smaller churches of France, apart from the more obvious cathedrals, and a special note of admiration should be recorded and every encouragment given to those entrusted with the work of preservation.

Regrettably the same cannot be said so frequently with regard to many of the famous châteaux, although there are of course impressive exceptions, and the discriminating visitor may occasionally be disenchanted, indeed disappointed, on approaching for the first time a building seen previously in photographs. While, in extenuation, it is appreciated that the amount of restoration which it is possible to undertake is largely dictated by economic considerations, it is unfortunate that in some cases, in spite of the fee for entry charged, one is given the strong impression that little interest is taken in the upkeep of the building or in making it more inviting. The temptation is great to embark on a general condemnation of the present stultifying situation with regard to 'conducted tours'. It must be observed, however, that while it is appreciated that the effective supervision of and communication with groups, large or small, presents problems of organisation, the intelligent foreign visitor will frequently find it an imposition to be herded round a château. An additional frustration is the amount of time wasted in waiting for a group to accumulate, and often the guides are both verbose and uninformative. If the building concerned were provided with informed guards rather than guides (which can always be provided by the local S.I. or the proprietor for those who prefer their presence), and the exhibits properly labelled, far more visitors would feel inclined to continue their tour of châteaux after their first few illusion-dispelling experiences.

The châteaux industry is no longer a cottage industry, and the tourist intending to visit more than a few is recommended to obtain in advance the brochures provided by *La Demeure Historique*, 55 Quai de la Tournelle, 75005 Paris, or *Vieilles Maisons Françaises*, 93 Rue de l'Université, 75007 Paris, which will give details of times and days of admission, etc. Likewise the *Caisse Nationale des Monuments Historiques*, Hôtel de Sully, 62 Rue St-Antoine, 75003 Paris, may be applied to, who also publish a number of informative guides, including the recently published 'Ouvert au Public', and organise lecture tours, etc., among other bodies. But usually a local S.I. or tourist office will be able to provide sufficient information to enable one to plan one's visits, particularly in the Loire valley, for which a brochure in English is available listing the fees charged or otherwise and details of 'spectacles de son et lumière', and other such 'manifestations', together with information with regard to coach-tours from Paris to a number of representative châteaux.

Most châteaux will be closed one day a week, but, depending on the mood of the owner (if in residence) or of the guardian (if the building is vacant, some of whom will expect a 'pourboire'), the seriously interested visitor may gain admittance. The privacy of the owners of châteaux should also be respected, and in certain cases, when this has been abused, a notice to the effect that the guardian will not even answer the bell, may be affixed to the gate (as at *Josselin*). Sometimes they will be guarded by a Cerberus-like individual—as at Fontenay—whose obtuseness (at least when approached by the Editor) is to be experienced to be believed.

A torch, and a pair of binoculars, will be found useful equipment when exploring the recesses of churches and cathedrals, and perusing the details of capitals and stained-glass windows, etc.

General Information

Sports. General information about a variety of sporting events or facilities in France may be obtained from Government Tourist Offices, or from the Direction de la Jeunesse et des Sports, 17 Blvd Morland, 75004 Paris. They can also advise on the capacities of the French sporting federations to assist the visitor, who is recommended to apply well in advance to the offices of his *own* home club or sporting organisation (whether it be hunting, shooting, or fishing; golf or tennis; sailing or underwater swimming, mountaineering or winter-sporting; motor-racing, or bicycling; polo, or hang-gliding; canoing, riding, or hiking, which may be his interest): they may well be able to give more practical information.

French Government Tourist Offices can provide information with regard to **Canal-cruising** (Tourisme fluvial), and details as to when canals may be closed for cleaning, etc. (*chomages*). Various maps, etc. are available from Editions Maritimes et d'Outre-Mer, 17 Rue Jacob, 75006 Paris; Editions du Plaisancier, B.P. 27, 69641 Caluire Cedex; and from the IGN.

Beaches. To protect the holiday-maker against the unpleasant if not dangerous after-effects of pollution on some French beaches, the local health and environment authorities are now—in the face of opposition from commercial interests—attempting to give them temporary gradings based on their daily monitoring. Where the bacterial level of the sea-water is high enough to be a serious health hazard, the beach in question should be marked by the display of a *purple flag*.

Medical advice. Travellers are advised to check with British Social Security authorities with regard to health cover under form E111. Medical advice, and first aid, are available from pharmacies, recognisable by their *green* cross.

Details of **Military Cemeteries**, usually well indicated by *green* signposts, a constant remainder in Normandy and northern France of those who died there during the First and Second World Wars, may be obtained from the Commonwealth War Graves Commission, 2 Marlow Road, Maidenhead, Berks SL6 7DX; Tel.: (0628) 34221. This organisation can also provide an overprinted Michelin Map, sheet 51, on which are shown the position of all *First* World War cemeteries and memorials in the area, apart from other material of interest. The American Battle Monuments Commission address is 68 Rue 19 Janvier, 92380 Garches, France; and the Canadian Veteran Affairs Bureau, Wellington Street, Ottawa. A guide to those of the 1914–18 War is provided in 'Before Endeavours Fade', by R.E.B. Coombs.

Music Festivals. The main annual music festivals in provincial France take place in Aix-en-Provence, Besançon, Bordeaux, Caen, Lyon, Metz, Nice, Orange, Prades, Avignon, Strasbourg, Vaison-la-Romaine, St-Donat, Saintes, and Tours. Travellers wishing to plan a tour to take in such a festival should make enquiries well in advance from National Tourist offices, who can advise on the booking of seats, and also accommodation, which should also be booked as early as possible.

Right of Way. Travellers may be surprised that Republican Frenchmen apparently appear so preoccupied with the defence of their privacy and property, in contrast to some other countries where he is not so constrained. Among the variety of signs displayed at the entrance of domaines, etc., in an attempt to intimidate undesirable trespassers, the most frequently seen are: *Defense d'entrer*; *Passage interdit*; *Propriete privé*; *Interdit au public*; *Maison peagée*; *Chasse gardée*; *Chien mechant*, etc. Although without legal implication, such injunctions should nevertheless be respected.

Working Hours, etc. It will be found that in France work starts earlier than in the U.K., and generally meals are also begun at an earlier hour. Although there is a movement towards the 'English' week-end, some food shops in the larger towns are open on Sunday mornings, and remain open later on weekday evenings; but they are likely to be shut on Mondays.

Public Holidays. Jan. 1 (*Jour de l'An*; gifts—*étrennes*—exchanged); Easter Monday; Whit Monday (*Pentecôte*); Ascension Day; 1 May (with Lily of the Valley sold in the streets); 8 May (commemorating the end of the war in Europe); 14 July (Fête Nationale); 15 Aug. (*Assomption*); 1 Nov. (*Toussaint*; All Saints' Day); 11 Nov. (Armistice Day); and 25 Dec. (*Noël*; Christmas). Banks are likely to shut at noon on days preceding public holidays.

If any of these falls on a Sunday, the following day is taken as a holiday; if falling on a Tuesday or Friday, the intervening Monday or Saturday is also taken, making a 'long weekend' or *pont* (bridge).

Metric System. The decimal system of weights, measures, and coins, was legalized in France in 1801, and became obligatory in 1840. The *mètre* is the unit of length, the *gramme* of weight, the *are* of land-measurement, and the *litre* of capacity. Greek prefixes (*déca-*, *hecto-*, *kilo-*, *myria-*) are used with these names to express multiples; Latin prefixes (*déci-*, *centi-*, *milli-*) to express fractions: kilomètre = 1000 mètres; millimètres = 1000th part of a mètre.

For approximate calculations the mètre may be taken as 39 inches; the litre as 0.22 gallons or 1¾ pints; the hectare as 2½ acres; 150 grammes as 5 oz.; and 5 kilomètres as 3 miles (or 8km as 5 miles).

Tipping. However anachronistic may be this stultifying system of rewarding waiters, taxi-drivers, cloakroom attendants, et al., who now invariably expect more than they merit for the quality of service often grudgingly given, it still persists. However, many restaurants and hotels have replaced it by adding 10-15 per cent (no less) to the bill, leaving little room for discussion, even when the 'service' has been indifferent or merely perfunctory.

Any series irregularity should be reported, without compunction, to Tourist Offices, or to the director of the local S.I.

Guernsey

Jersey

Ushant

Roscoff
St-Pol-de-Léon
Tréguier
Paimpol
Lannion
43 B
Le Folgoët
42
42
42
St.-Malo
Morlaix
Guingamp
Dinard
3
Brest
43 A
41
Brieuc
42
Dinan
Huelgoat
Carhaix-Plouguer
Lamballe
41
Crozon
Rostrenen
Pleyben
44
Loudéac
Locronan
44
Quimper
Pontivy
45
46 A
Josselin
40
Concarneau
Ploërmel
Quimperlé
Pont-l'Abbé
46 B
Hennebont
Rochefort-en-Terre
Lorient
46 A
Vannes
40
Auray
la Roche-Bernard
47
Carnac
46 A
Quiberon
46 B
Belle Ile
la Baule
St-Nazaire

Ile de Noirmoutier

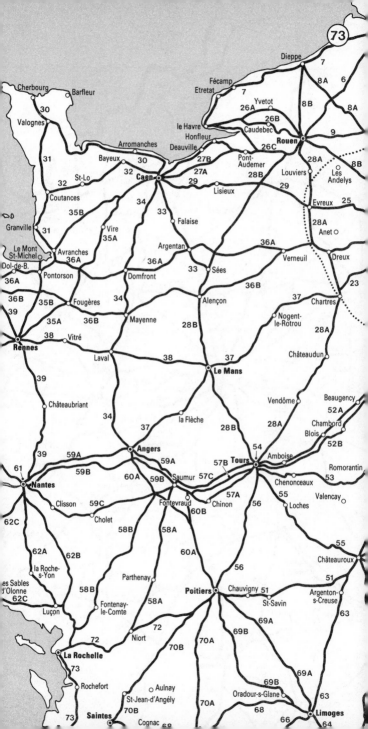

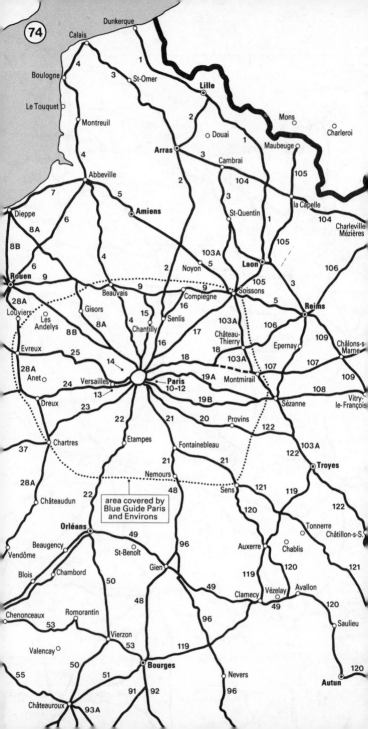

I THE CHANNEL PORTS TO PARIS: FLANDERS; ARTOIS; PICARDY

Like Chaucer's young squire, at 'some tyme in chivalrye, in Flaundres, in Artoys, and in Picardie', Englishmen throughout the centuries have been only too familiar with the North of France, an area admittedly more of interest for its historical associations than its landscapes, although several towns—such as Arras, Douai, or St-Omer—are characteristic. Crécy was fought in *Picardy* (Fr. Picardie); Agincourt in *Artois*, corresponding roughly to the present department of Pas-de-Calais, and deriving its name from the Atrebates, whose capital was Arras. Its countship reverted to the French crown in 1659. Many of its towns were close to the British front in 1914, a remarkable feature of which—Vimy Ridge—deserves a visit, as were those in French *Flanders* (Fr. Flandres), abutting it to the N. (see also Section IX), extending along the Franco-Belgium frontier from the coast at Dunkerque to the Ardennes, and including the industrial areas centred on Lille and Valenciennes. The ancient countship, which included Belgium and Dutch Flanders, was united to Burgundy in 1385, and passed under Austrian and Spanish domination, until France finally secured her share in 1713 after the long resistance of Villars to Marlborough on 'La Bassée Lines'. Much of the area was devastated during the First World War, and most of the military cemeteries in the British sector may be seen here; see p 70. The department of the Somme partially represents Picardy; lower Picardy, which included Beauvaisis, Soissonais, and Laonnais, was later considered part of the *Île de France*; see Section II.

1 Dunkerque to Reims via Lille, Le Quesnoy, and Laon

265km (164 miles). D 916. 9km Bergues—18km *Cassel*—8km. Hazebrouck lies 6km S.—D933. 13km *Bailleul*—12km *Armentières*—16km **Lille**—C27 and N49. 46km **Valenciennes**—N934. 18km *Le Quesnoy*—23km *Chapeau-Rouge* crossroad—D946. 18km *Guise*. 9km D967. 29km **Laon**—N44. 46km **Reims**.

Maps: IGN 2, 4, 9, or 101. M 236.

Motorway. The A25 to Lille may be entered just S. of Dunkerque. It can be conveniently joined 15km S.E. of Cassel, to avoid possible congestion in industrial areas N.W. of Lille.

DUNKERQUE (anglicised as *Dunkirk*; 73,600 Dunkerquois), busy terminus of cross-Channel ferries, the northernmost town of France, and its third port, is famous as the base from which the British Expeditionary Force was evacuated in May-June 1940.

Dunkerque, the 'church of the dunes' (Duine-kerke), traditionally founded in the 7C by St Eloi or Eligius, assumed its present Flemish name in the 9C. Here, in the 13-16Cs, the Counts of Flanders were often gratuitously attacked by the French kings; more celebrated sieges were those of the 17C, when the place was captured in turn by Condé (1646), aided by Van Tromp and the Dutch fleet; by the Spaniards (1653); and by Turenne (1658) after the Battle of the Dunes. It was then ceded to Cromwell in return for the services of the Ironsides to the victors; but two years after his restoration Charles II—already financially embarrassed—sold it to Louis XIV. The corsairs of Dunkerque, led by Jean Bart (1651–1702), a native, and the Chevalier de Forbin (1656–1733), played their part in later wars, and in punishment for their depredations the harbour works were twice dismantled under treaties imposed by England. It resisted a siege by the Duke of York in 1793–94.

An advance base of the Dover Patrol in the First World War, it was repeatedly shelled and bombed. In late May 1940 it was encircled by the Germans, but in spite of continuous strafing, by 4 June between 340,000 and 366,000 men, British and French, were embarked on fleets of ships of all sizes—perhaps as many as 765 altogether—shuttling across the Channel from the beaches just E. of the port, left littered with abandoned material. It again suffered severely when a pocket of German resistance during the period Sept. 1944 to 9 May, 1945, since when it has revived and flourished, with the construction of new port installations, extensive docks, etc.

Just N. of the rebuilt central *Pl. Jean-Bart*, embellished by a statue by David d'Angers, stands *St-Eloi* (16C; but much restored), in which Bart was buried. Opposite rises the *Belfry* (c. 1440; 58m high), also restored. Further N. is the *Hôtel de Ville* (with a *War Museum*), beyond which is the octagonal *Tour de Leughenaer*, a relic of the port's 14C defences.—To the E., in the *Pl. du Gén. de Gaulle*, is the *Museum*, housing several paintings of the Dutch and Flemish Schools; a panel of Delft tiles depicting the bombardment of the town in 1695; and numerous ship models, etc.

For the road W. to *Gravelines* and (43km) *Calais*, see Rte 3.—The Belgian frontier lies 14km E.—For *Veurne*, 7km beyond, see *Blue Guide Belgium*.

We follow the D916 S. over the flat *Watteringues*, drained by canals and dikes, to (9km) **Bergues**, a small partly-walled frontier fortress of character, frequently besieged, but which resisted an English attack in 1793. Its rebuilt *Belfry* replaces its 16C predecessor destroyed in 1944. Also rebuilt are the *Hôtel de Ville* (in the 17C taste), and brick-built *St Martin* (16C); the adjacent *Museum*, in a building of 1630, contains some paintings of quality. To the E. of the town centre stand two towers of the 11C abbey of *St-Winoc*.

11km to the E. lies *Hondschoote*, a frontier village of Flemish type, with a Renaissance *Hôtel de Ville* and an early 17C brick church, with a belfry of 1513.—From *Oost-Cappel*, 6km S., one may cross the frontier to *Poperinge*, 12.5km S.E.; *Ieper* **(Ypres)** lies 12km further E.: see *Blue Guide Belgium*.

The D916 crosses the A25 motorway S. of Bergues, beyond which the r.-hand fork leads 28km S.W. to *St-Omer*; see Rte 3.—Bearing l. we approach (7km) *Wormhout*, 2.5km W. of which, at *Esquelbecq*, characteristically Flemish, is a moated *Castle* of 1610, and a 16C church.

8km **Cassel**, perched on a solitary hill 175m above the plain, retains a restored *Grand' Place* of some interest, with the *Hôtel de la Noble Cour* (16-17C) containing a small museum, and the *Hôtel Lenglé de Schoebeque* (1634). *Notre-Dame* dates from 1298. The terrace of the former castle provides an extensive view, one which in Thicknesse's time would take 'the pen of a poet like Virgil to describe, or a Gainsborough to delineate'. An 18C windmill is preserved.

The Roman station of *Castellum Menapiorum* remained a fortress during the medieval period. Three battles were fought beneath its walls: in 1071, between rival counts of Flanders; in 1328, when Philippe de Valois defeated the Flemish and seized the place; and in 1677, when the success of the Duc d'Orléans over William of Orange largely decided the Peace of Nijmegen the following year. Here the Duke of York marched his 10,000 men up the hill only to march them down again, during the Flanders campaign of 1793–94. Cassel was the H.Q. of Gén. Foch in 1914–15, and of Gen. Plumer (2nd British Army) in 1916–18. Fighting here in May 1940 delayed the German advance on Dunkerque.

Descending from Cassel, we drive S.E., at 8km leaving *Hazebrouck* 6km to the S.

This market town of 20,500 Hazebroukois, a familiar centre of communications during the 1914–18 War, has a Classical *Hôtel de Ville*; a small *Museum* in an Augustinian convent (1518–1616); and *St-Eloi*, which lost its openwork spire in 1940.—The road continues S. through the *Forêt de Nieppe*, which covered the town against the German advance of April 1918, to (12km) *St-Venant*, just W. of the Lys battlefield; see below. *Lillers* lies 9km S.W.; *Bethune* 14km S.E.; see Rte 3.

After 9km the D933 crosses the motorway, with a view N. of the *Mont des Cats* (158m; crowned by a Trappist monastery rebuilt after 1918), to enter (4km) *Bailleul* (13,400 Bailleulois), a lace-making town of ancient origin, with a neo-Flemish *Hôtel de Ville*, its belfry on a 12C base, and a small *Museum* with a good ceramic collection.

We now cross an area over which the *Battle of the Lys* was fought (9-15 April, 1918) to (12km) **Armentières**, an industrial town of 26,000 inhab., which for 3½ years lay only 3km behind the British trenches, and was virtually destroyed during the battle, in which some 30-40,000 gas shells were fired into it.

8 German divisions advanced just S. of the town against two British separated by one Portuguese division. Armentières was surrounded, and Hazebrouck and Béthune threatened, but the enemy were eventually compelled to withdraw some four months' later, although the town was not liberated, by Plumer's 2nd Army, until 2 Oct.

Its *Grand' Place*, once known as 'Eleven o'clock Square', for the clock of the Hôtel de Ville had stopped at this hour during an early bombardment, is embellished by a belfry, etc.

5.5km N. lies *Ploegsteert* ('Plug Street'), with its wood, for which see *Blue Guide Belgium.*

On quitting Armentières, the road crosses the lines of the former British and German trenches to traverse *Lomme* and the outer suburbs of (16km) **Lille**; see Rte 2.

The recommended way out of Lille is the A1 motorway, off which, at 5km, we bear l., and after a further 2km veer r. onto the C27.—The A27 continues due E. to (20km) **Tournai**; see *Blue Guide Belgium.*

The road shortly pass near (l.) the village of *Bouvines*, famous as the site of Philippe Auguste's decisive victory of 27 July 1214 over the German Emperor Otto IV and his English allies.—Adjacent lies *Cysoing*, with the vaulted foundations of a castle of the Merovingian kings.

17km *Orchies* (l.), once fortified, has a rebuilt Renaissance belfry.—10 km W., at *Mons-en-Pévèle*, the Flemings were defeated by Philippe IV in 1304.—18km S.W. lies **Douai**; see Rte 3.

The road turns E. to skirt (r.) the *Forêt de Marchiennes*, after 6km passing the restored 15C castle of *Leloire*.

3km. The l.-hand fork leads 6km to the spa of **St-Amand-les-Eaux** (16,400 Amandinois), on the Scarpe, noted for its faience. In the *Grand' Place* are relics of its once famous Benedictine abbey founded in 647, in which Hucbald (840-930), the musical theorist, studied. The 82m-high Baroque tower dates from 1626–40. The *Échevinage*, in the Flemish Renaissance style, contains a room decorated with paintings by Louis Watteau. Doric *St-Martin* dates from 1787. The main road may be regained 4km S.

The *Forêt de Raismes* is traversed. It covered the British left at Mons in Aug. 1914, and was among the final obstacles overcome in the Allied advance four years later.

18km. **VALENCIENNES** (40,900 Valenciennois), an important industrial town on the Escaut, and a market for sugar-beet, has little to interest the traveller except the museum.

Named after one of the three Roman emperors called Valentinian, it was in the 15C the capital of a principality later absorbed into the county of Hainault. It was several times taken and retaken in 16-17C wars, finally surrendering to Louis XIV in 1677. In 1793 it made a heroic resistance under Gén. Ferrand to the Anglo-Austrian army, but was abandoned during the retreat from Mons in 1914, and became the H.Q. of the German lines of communication until recaptured by the Canadians on 1 Nov. 1918. Considerable damage was done to its industrial installations during the war, and it again suffered severely in 1940 and 1944.

Valenciennes was the birthplace of Baldwin IX, count of Flanders and Emperor of Constantinople (1171–1206); Henry VII of Germany; Jean Froissart (c. 1337–c. 1410), the chronicler; the composer Claude Lejeune (1528–1600); the artists Antoine Watteau (1684–1721), J.-B. Pater (1695–1736), and Henri Harpignies (1819–1916); and J.-B. Carpeaux (1827–75), the sculptor.

In the town centre stands the rebuilt *Hôtel de Ville*, preserving a facade in the Flemish Renaissance style (1867), to the W. of which is rebuilt *St-Géry* (partly 13C); adjacent is the *Library*, containing several incunables and MSS of interest.

To the E. is the **Musée**, overlooking the Blvd Watteau.

Some rooms are closed; and some labelling requires revision, but the following paintings are notable: *Jan Mandyn*, Temptation of St Anthony; *Reymerswael*, The tax-collector; attrib. *F. Bunel*, Procession of the League; *anon. Dutch* Male portrait (1611), and Female portrait; *Van Dyck*, St Matthew, and St Paul; *Rubens*, Elias and an angel, and Deposition, etc.; *De Crayer*, several paintings; *Frans II Pourbus*, Marie de Medicis; *Abraham Jansens*, Crucifixion; *D. Vinckeboons*, Diana and Acteon; *P. Snayers*, Attack of brigands, etc.; *anon. Dutch* Shipwright and family; *Jérôme Jansens*, Scène galante; *Jan Brueghel*, Landscape; several *Flemish* Still-lifes, and Flower-paintings; *School of Van de Meulen*, Siege of Valenciennes; *Carreño*, Charles II of Spain; *Pourbus*, Elisabeth of France; *C.J. Crec*, Carnival Scene; *Watteau*, Scène galante, Portrait of Pater; *Pater*, Marguerite Pater, and Scène galante; *De Troy*, Jean de Julienne; *Louis Watteau*, Morning, Midday, Afternoon, and Evening, and Country scenes; representative works by *Hubert Robert, J.-B. Mallet, Pissarro, Harpignies, Lepine, Corot, Boudin*, et al. *Carpeaux*, numerous busts, including those of Gounod, Princess Matilde, Prince Imperial, etc.

To the S., facing the Blvd Carpeaux, and flanked by the Parc de la Rhonelle, is the 13-15C *Tour de la Dodenne*.

Condé-sur-l'Escaut, 13km N., giving its name to the Condé branch of the Bourbons, preserves a castle of 1411 and 17C ramparts. It was the birthplace of the composer Josquin des Prez (c. 1450–1521). Between here and Belgian frontier, 5km beyond, is the 18C *Château de l'Ermitage*, built by the Duc du Croy.

At *Famars*, 5km due S. of Valenciennes, are the curious remains of a Roman fortress (*Fanum Martis*), flanked by round towers.

The N30 leads N.E. from Valenciennes to meet the frontier at 12km, 21km beyond which lies *Mons*; see *Blue Guide Belgium*.

Driving S.E., we reach a road junction at 11km, and bear r. for (7km) *Le Quesnoy*; see below.

The l.-hand fork leads 12km E. to **Bavay**, its *Hôtel de Ville* of 1784 surmounted by a 16C belfry, of interest for its Roman remains. Roman *Bagacum*, capital of the Nervii and second only to Reims among the towns of N. Gaul, stands at the intersection of several Roman roads. It was totally destroyed in the 5C, but on its site rose another fortress, often besieged during the Flemish wars until 1654, when it was dismantled by Turenne. It was Sir John French's advanced H.Q. during the opening stages of the battle of Mons.

Since 1942 an area immediately W. of the town has been excavated, revealing a cryptoporticus and forum, etc.; adjacent is a *Museum* displaying the artefacts found on the site.—*Pont-sur-Sambre*, 9km S.E., is the supposed place of Julius Caesar's victory over the Nervii in 57 B.C.; while 5.5km N.E. of Bavay lies the battlefield of *Malplaquet*, where on 11 Sept. 1709 Marlborough and Prince Eugène defeated Marshal Villars.—For *Mauberge*, 14km due E.; see Rte 105.

Le Quesnoy (5400 Quercitains), ancient *Quercetum*, a characteristic brick-built fortress attractively sited among trees and adjacent to a small lake, has sustained several sieges, notably by the Austrians in 1793, the penultimate of which was in Nov. 1918, when its German garrison surrendered to the New Zealanders, who scaled its walls with ladders in medieval fashion. It held out again the Germans from 17-24 May, 1940.—2km E. stands the 13C castle of *Potelle*.

We drive S. to (16km) *Landrecies*, skirting (l.) the extensive *Forêt de Mormal*, which divided into two columns the British army retreating from Mons on 25 Aug. 1914: the 1st Corps retiring to the E., and the 2nd to the W., while the German vanguard executed a forced march through its glades to deliver a surprise attack at Landrecies. This village was the birthplace of Joseph Dupleix (1697–1763), who established French power in India.

At 7km the N43 (see Rte 104) is reached at the Chapeau-Rouge crossroads, and shortly after, the Sambre à l'Oise Canal is twice crossed before entering (18km) **Guise** (pron. Gu-ise; 6300 Guisards), an ancient town and cradle of a ducal family, and birthplace of Camille Desmoulins (1760–94). An engineering factory was established here in 1846 by J.-B.-A. Godin on the 'familistère' lines advocated by Fourier, run by a communistic colony of c. 40 families. Here on 30 Aug. 1914 Von Bülow's advance was checked by Gén. Lanrezac; it was damaged in fighting in Oct. 1918. The huge 16C brick *Fortress* encloses remains of an 11C castle.

The road continues S. across sugar-beet fields through (24km) *Crécy-sur-Serre*, later passing near (r.) the ruins of a 14-16C castle at *Aulnois-sous-Laon* as (14km) **Laon** itself is approached, the upper town on its commanding ridge; see Rte 105. For the road S.E. hence to (46km) **Reims**, see Rte 3.

2 Lille to Senlis, for Paris

A. Lille

LILLE (174,000 Lillois; 54,800 in 1801; 75,800 in 1851), ancient capital of French Flanders, and préfecture of the Nord, is the centre of one of the most flourishing commercial and industrial conurbations in France, but comparatively few relics of its past remain to interest the traveller; nevertheless, its museum contains a quantity of canvasses, some of which are of quality.

After a stormy period common to Flemish frontier towns, it began to prosper in the 15C under the dukes of Burgundy, even if racked by Spanish occupation in the 16th and early 17C. It was recaptured in 1667 and promptly re-fortified by Vauban. In 1708 it was starved into submission by Marlborough, in a siege which Sterne's Uncle Toby and Corporal Trim followed in the 'Gazette' and on the bowling green, and in which Col Henry Esmond distinguished himself. Here,

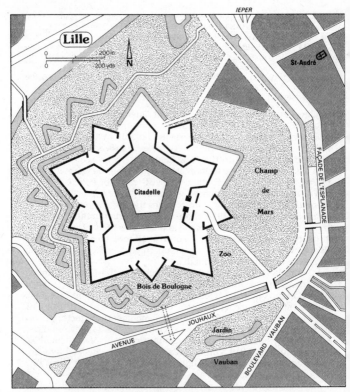

later in the century, Thicknesse was grossly overcharged for his horses' fodder, but notwithstanding 'the many mortifications they met with', remained in the town—'by many called Little Paris'—for a week. In 1792 it withstood a siege and ten days' bombardment by the Austrians. The Paris-Lille railway was inaugurated in 1846.

During the Franco-Prussian War it became the centre of an 'entrenched camp' defended by eleven forts, but after 1880 these defences fell into disuse and were finally condemned in 1911. Lille capitulated to the Germans on 12 Oct. 1914, and was not liberated until 18 Oct. 1918, when it was outflanked by the capture of Menin and Douai. The deportation of 25,000 of its citizens in April-May, 1916, was the culminating point of the tyranny under which Lille lived during *this* occupation, while in that latter month a munitions depot in the S.E. rampart exploded, killing 200 and destroying whole streets. Not being shelled by the Allies, it became a favourite resort of German officers on leave—'heroes of the Lille front'—for whom a variety of entertainment was organised, the newly completed theatre being converted into an opera-house for the more refined. It suffered considerably from bombing during the years 1940–44.

Here were born J. B. Monnoyer (1634–99), the flower-painter; C. J. Panckoucke (1736–98), creator of the 'Moniteur universel' (1792), and initiator of the 'Encyclopédie méthodique'; Gén. Faidherbe (1818–97), whose attempted resistance to the Prussians was crushed at St-Quentin; the composer Édouard Lalo (1823–92); Carolus-Duran (1837–1917), the artist; and Gén. Charles de Gaulle (1890–1970).

The centre of Lille is traversed from N.W. to S.E. by the wide Blvd de la Liberté, at a central point in which is the *Pl. de la République*,

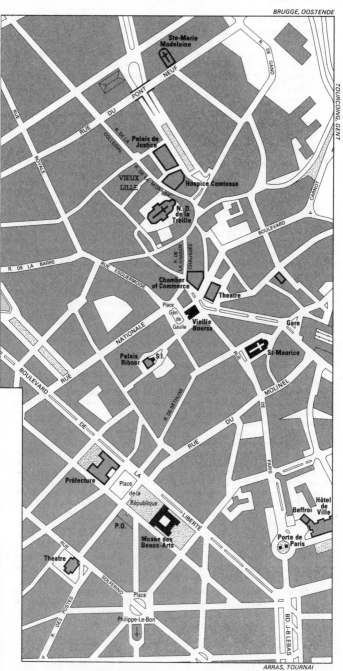

flanked by the pompous *Préfecture* (1869), and opposite, the **Palais des Beaux-Arts** (1892), a mausoleum of a building containing several departments: Numismatics; *Ceramics; Archaeology (notable in which is the Censer of Lille, of c. 1120, and a series of enamels); a notable collection of Drawings, the majority left to the town by its native artist J.-B. Wicar (1762–1834); and an extensive collection of general Antiquities, medieval sculptures, altarpieces, woodcarvings, and works of art of the Flemish Renaissance.

Remarkable among the Paintings (many of them donated by Antoine Brasseur—1819–86—born in Lille) are: *Dirk Bouts*, Paradise, and Hell; *Wallerant Vaillant*, Male, and Female portraits, and of a Young artist; *anon. 16C Flemish*, The Baptist preaching; attrib. *Pourbus*, Male portrait; *J. Bellegambe*, The Mystic Bath; *School of Dirk Jacobsz*, Male, and female portraits; *anon.* Virgin and Child and two angel musicians; *Roelant Savery*, Flower-piece; *Jordaens*, Temptation of the Magdalen; *Rubens*, Martyrdom of St Catherine, Deposition, and Ecstasy of the Magdalen; *Van Dyck*, Marie de Medicis, and Crucifixion; *Jan Siberecht*, two Pastoral scenes; *Snyders*, Bitch and puppies; *D. Teniers*, Temptation of St Anthony, and Gypsies; *Frans Franken*, Cavalry scene; *Momper*, View of the Alps; *Seghers*, St Jerome; *Paul Bril*, Shipwreck of Jonas; *Van der Meer*, Return from the chase; *W. de Geest*, J.-M. de Nassau; attrib. *J. Van Loo*, Triumph of Silenus; attrib. *J.G. Cuyp*, Family portrait; *Nicolas Maes*, Young woman; *Pieter Codde*, Conversation piece; *Jan van Goyen*, Skating scene; attrib. *Dirk Hals*, Trictrac party; *J. van Ceulen*, Portrait; *School of Jan Massys*, Tarquin and Lucrecia; *Amberger*, Charles V; *anon. 17C Dutch*, Young girl reading by candlelight; *Salomon Koninck*, Male portrait; *Ruysdael*, Cornfield; *Pieter de Hooch*, Young woman and servant; *Bosch*, Concert in the egg; *J.A. Rootius*, Female portrait; *B. van der Helst*, Male, and Female portraits; *Jan Steen*, Village scene; *R. Brakenburgh*, Scène galante; *Dirck Barendsz*, Female portrait; *Bart. di Giovanni*, Virgin and Child; *Barthel Bruyn, the Elder*, Male portrait; *Barthel Bruyn, the Younger*, Male, and Female portraits; *School of Cranach*, Derision of Christ; *Nicolas Neufchatel*, Johann Neudorfer and his son; *School of Patinir*, The Flight into Egypt; *after Roger van der Weyden*, Philippe le Bon; *anon. mid 16C Dutch*, Portrait of Johanna van Crudingen; *Pieter Codde*, Melancholy, and The theologian; *Van Honthorst*, Female portrait; *Lawrence*, Gen. Sir John Cuppage; attrib. *Miereveldt*, Female portrait; *A. Palamedes*, Dutch family portrait; *Jan Fyt*, Jesus at the house of Martha and Mary; *J.C. Verspronck*, Young man; *Corneille de Vos*, Male portrait; *Emmanuel de Witte*, Interior of the New Church at Delft; *J. Vernet*, Marine view; *Ph. de Champaigne*, Nativity; a curious *anon. mid 17C* Last Supper; *Georges de la Tour*, Mme Pelerin; *Watteau*, Fête au Colisée, View of Lille, Fiddler, and Street vendor; *E. Liénard*, Female portrait; *Wilkie*, The Earl of Kellie; *David*, Belisarius; *Boilly*, The triumph of Marat, and Portraits of Houdon, Robespierre, etc., and of Isabey's studio; *Delacroix*, Medea; *Courbet*, Afternoon at Ornans; *Fantin-Latour*, Self-portrait; *Monticelli*, two Scenes; *Carolus Duran*, Woman in black, and M. Tempelaere; *Henner*, Dead Christ; *Renoir*, The road from Versailles to Louveciennes; *Goya*, The letter, and The old woman; *El Greco*, St Francis, and The Mount of Olives; *Tintoretto*, A senator; attrib. *L. Costa*, Young girl; *Ribera*, St Jerome; and characteristic works by *Guardi, Canaletto, Géricault, Corot, Sisley, Boudin, Monet, Lepine, Lebourg, Guillaumin, Jongkind, Vuillard*, et al, and *Buffet*, two Nudes.

The transverse boulevard leads S.E. to approach the *Pl. Volant*, embellished by the *Porte de Paris*, an arch erected in 1682 to commemorate Louis XIV's capture of Lille. It is dominated by the 106m-high tower of the *Hôtel de Ville* of 1933.

From the N.E. side of the Pl. de la République we may follow the pedestrian Rue de Béthune, continued by the Rue du Sec-Arembault, to reach **St-Maurice**, one of the few old buildings in Lille (14-15C; remodelled in 1872), with a spacious five-aisled interior.

The Rue de Paris leads N.W. to the *Pl. du Théâtre*, flanked (r.) by the *Théâtre* of 1914, and the *Palais de la Bourse*, with its tower (both by L. Cordonnier); opposite the former is the rear facade of the **Ancienne Bourse**, a late but good example of the Flemish Renaissance (1652; by Julien Destré), richly decorated, but spoiled by the row of shops abutting it, and with a mutilated arcaded courtyard.

Continuing N. past the new Bourse, we may follow the Rue de la Grande Chaussée (in which are some of the more sophisticated shops), continued by the Rue des Chats-Bossus, to the triangular *Pl. du Lion d'Or*, with several old houses in the vicinity.

From its N.W. corner leads the picturesque Rue de la Monnaie. To the l. is the 17C *Hôtel de la Monnaie*; to the r. the 17C **Hospice Comtesse**, founded in 1236 by Jeanne de Flandres, and recently restored. It contains a late 15C *Salle des Malades*, and a *Museum* of local history and decorative art.

A lane beside the Hospice leads to the *Palais de Justice* (1969), some distance N. of which, in the Rue du Pont-Neuf, is the domed church of *La Madeleine* (1675–1715).

A passage opposite the Hospice leads to *N.-D. de la Treille*, commenced in 1854; never completed, and better if demolished.

Returning towards the old Bourse, we may veer r. along the Rue de la Bourse to enter the *Grand' Place* (or Pl. du Gén. de Gaulle), the main centre of animation, retaining on its S. side the *Grand' Garde* of 1717, with its elaborate facade.

From its N.W. corner leads the Rue Esquermoise, continued by the old Rue Royale, to the W. of which stands *St-Catherine* (1538), containing a Martyrdom of that saint, by Rubens.

From the S.W. corner of this square the *Pl. Rihour* is shortly entered, where the old **Palais de Rihour**, the 15C residence of Jean le Bon, with its Gothic chapel, stair-turret, and guardroom, now houses the S.I.—A short distance to the W. is *St-Étienne*, built for the Jesuits in 1696, whence the Blvd de la République is regained.

At the N.W. end of this thoroughfare is the *Citadel*, surrounded by gardens, a pentagonal fortress by Vauban, still in part preserving its 17C aspect. The interior may be seen from the inner gate, on applying to the guard.

The district between Lille and the Belgian frontier is largely occupied by the contiguous industrial complex of **Roubaix** (101,900 Roubaisiens), which imperceptibly merges with **Tourcoing** (97,100 Tourquennois). The latter has a small *Museum*, and was the birthplace of the composer Albert Roussel (1869–1937). Both can be by-passed by following the A1 motorway N., entered just S.E. of Lille.—*Comines*, on the border N.W. of Tourcoing, was the birthplace of the historian Philippe de Comines (c. 1445–1511).

For **Courtrai**, 15km N.E. of Tourcoing, and *Menen* (*Menin*), just N. of the frontier, see *Blue Guide Belgium*.

B.   Lille to Senlis

182km (113 miles). A1 motorway for 37km, then N50 for 13km to **Arras**—N17. 22km *Bapaume*—20km *Péronne*—30km *Roye*—60km **Senlis**.

Maps: IGN 2, 4, 9, or 101. M 236, 237.

Motorway. The A1 leads directly from Lille to Paris, beyond Arras providing easy access to Amiens, Compiègne, and Senlis.

Travellers wishing to visit *Vimy Ridge* en route should bear r. off the motorway either after 21km, or 27km, to *Lens* (see Rte 3), there turning S. onto the N17 for **Arras**, from which one diverges r. to ascend the ridge to the S.W.: see p 97.

LILLE TO BÉTHUNE AND ST-POL-SUR-TERNOISE (64km). The A25 motorway leads W., off which we shortly turn onto the N41 to (22km) *La Bassée*, situated at the head of the canal from Aire, first cut in the 13C. It was seized by the Germans in Oct. 1914, and remained for almost four years one of the strongest points in their front, held by Prince Rupprecht of Bavaria. Through La Bassée ran the trenches of Villars in 1708–11, which proved impregnable by frontal assault, and led to stalemate between the French army and that of Marlborough, who was advancing from the conquest of Flanders.—7km N. lies *Neuve-Chapelle*, captured in the battle of 10-12 March 1915, when the British front was carried forward at a cost of 13,500 casualties. Monuments in the area also commemorate Indian and Portuguese losses.—The road running S. of La Bassée traverses the battlefield of Loos: see p 95.—13km. *Béthune* (see Rte 3), beyond which the N41 bears S.W. through the mining town of *Bruay* to (12km) *Divion*, 7km S.E. of which is the picturesque moated **Château d'Olhain* (15-16C).—Crossing the ancient Chaussée Brunehaut, after 13km, the D916 from Lillers is met 4km prior to entering *St-Pol*, for which see Rte 3.

We follow the A1 S., at 8km passing (l.) the airport.

4km. *Seclin*, 2km W., has a large restored church with a pre-Romanesque crypt, while to the S. of the town is its 17C *Hospital*, with a 15C chapel of its predecessor.

9km. *Lens* (see Rte 3) lies 13km S.W.

8km. **Douai** (see Rte 3) lies 9km S.E.

10km. The motorway continues S., off which we bear r. to (13km) **Arras**; see Rte 3.

The N25 leads S.W. from Arras to (35km) *Doullens*; see Rte 3.

The N17 leads S. from Arras to (15.5km) *Ervillers*, beyond which we traverse a region fought over in March 1918, when the 3rd Army front was penetrated at several points by German masses, while *Bullecourt*, some 10km N.E., beyond the motorway, was the centre of a bitter struggle in May 1917, when the Australians there seized part of the *Hindenburg Line*.

6.5km. **Bapaume**, once fortified, has been rebuilt since virtually levelled during the First World War.

It was abandoned by the Germans in March 1917, but recaptured by them a year later, and finally regained by New Zealanders in the **'Second' Battle of Bapaume** (21 Aug.– 1 Sept. 1918), in which the 3rd and 4th British Armies drove 35 German divisions across the Somme battlefield, capturing 34,000 prisoners. Here in 1180 Isabelle de Hainaut and Philippe Auguste were married.

BAPAUME TO AMIENS (47km). The D929 drives S.W., after 6km reaching the battle area of 1916, with the *Butte de Warlencourt* prominent to the l., a tumulus which held up the advance on Bapaume in Nov. that year. *Flers*, some 4km to the S.E., was captured in the first attack with tanks (15 Sept. 1916). —6km. *Pozières*, in the military cemetery of which is a memorial to some 14,700 missing, lies on a ridge taken by the Australians in July 1916.—5km N.W., beyond *Thiepval*, is a memorial to another 73,300 missing.—2km N. lies *Beaumont-Hamel*, adjacent to which is a Memorial Park. The village was taken in the **Battle of the Ancre** (13-15 Nov. 1916).—The church at *Mailly-Maillet*, 4km W., has a notable portal.—Continuing S.W. from Pozières we cross *La Boisselle*, near which a huge mine crater has been preserved, the explosion of which signalled the start of the battle of the Somme; see below.

7km. **Albert** (11,500 inhab.), entirely rebuilt since 1918, was known as *Ancre* prior to 1619, when Charles d'Albert, Duc de Luynes, to whom it had been presented by Louis XIII, graced it with his name. Unfortunately, the ugly late 19C church has been reconstructed exactly as it was, together with the gilt image which surmounted it. In the Autumn of 1914 the Germans established themselves in strong positions on chalk ridges just E. of the town, but it was not until 1 July, after a bombardment of hitherto unequalled intensity, that the British 4th Army began operations known as the **Battle of the Somme**. The French gained ground on both banks of the meandering river some 10km S., but the assault on *Gommecourt* (c. 16km N.) was unsuccessful. The 5th Army then entered the battle, and by the 26th *Combles* (17.5km E., adjacent to the present motorway) was in Allied hands, and the French were at the gates of *Péronne*. The advance was continued some 9km N. of Albert on 13-15 Nov. (Battle of the Ancre), in which a further 7000 prisoners were taken, making a total of 38,000 men and 125 guns captured since 1 July. The German retired behind the powerful *Hindenburg Line*, until, in March 1918, their great offensive pushed the British back, Albert falling into their hands on the 27th. By 4 April the enemy claimed the capture of 90,000 prisoners and 1300 guns. But their massed attacks on the slopes W. of Albert were defeated, and the ruined town was recaptured on 22 Aug. after the *Battle of Amiens.*—Beyond Albert, the straight switchback road traverses (14.5km) *Pont-Noyelles*, site of an indecisive battle in 1870, to enter (12.5km) **Amiens**; see Rte 5.

Quitting Bapaume, the N17 passes below the A1, and A2, and traversing (11km) *Rancourt*, scene of desperate fighting in 1916, and passing (l.) *Mont St-Quentin*, a formidable position changing hands three times in 1917 – 18, enters (9km) **Péronne** (9900 Péronnais), situated at the confluence of the Cologne and the Somme. The 13C *Château* is partly surrounded by 16-17C additions; the rebuilt Mairie houses the *Musée Danicourt*, with interesting collections of ancient coins and jewellery.

Petrona or *Petronia* originated in an abbey founded by or for Scottish monks, its first abbot being St Fursy (d. 650; cf. Lagny). In the 9C the Counts of Vermandois made it their capital, and built a keep in which Charles le Simple was twice imprisoned and died of starvation in 929. Charles le Téméraire of Burgundy occupied the town in 1465, and there imposed on Louis XI the humiliating Treaty of Péronne (1468), as graphically described in 'Quentin Durward'. It was besieged by the Duc de Nassau in 1536, when it was successfully defended, the local heroine, Catherine de Poix, slaying a Spaniard with her own hand, and—in the words of Scott—'preserved the proud name of Péronne la Pucelle, until the Duke of Wellington, a great destroyer of that sort of reputation, took the place in his memorable advance upon Paris in 1815'. It surrendered to the Prussians on 9 Jan. 1870 after 12 days' bombardment. It was fought over in 1917 – 18 and largely destroyed, and was also damaged in the Second World War.

The D944 leads 10km S.E. to meet the N29 18km W. of *St-Quentin*; see Rte 3 and p 100.

PERONNE TO COMPIEGNE VIA HAM AND NOYON (67km). An alternative road to the N17 is the D937, which traverses a plateau E. of the Somme, where although comparatively little fighting took place, the villages were ruthlessly mined in the German retreat of March 1917. At 7km we cross the N29 and pass through (3.5km) *Athies*, its church preserving a good 13C portal. It was the site of a Merovingian palace.—12.5km **Ham** (6400 Hamois), on the canalised Somme, is an ancient but rebuilt town with a 15C *Castle*, ruined by the Germans in 1917, in which several state prisoners were mewed up, the most famous of whom was Louis Napoleon (later Napoleon III), who escaped hence disguised as a workman in 1846, after six years' confinement. *Notre-Dame* dates from the 12-13C. Ham was the birthplace of Gén. Foy (1775 – 1825).

The D932 leads S. via (10km) *Guiscard*, with relics of an 18C château, to (10km) **Noyon**; see Rte 5.—The N32 leads S.W. through what was once a devastated area of the French battlefield, where in 1918 the rupture of the Allied centre was repeatedly attempted, to (10km) *Ribecourt*, and 14km beyond, *Compiègne.*—A pleasanter road (D165) turns l. in the S.W. suburb of Noyon to traverse the *Forêt d'Ourscamp*. The first r.-hand fork leads to the former *Abbaye d'Ourscamp*, founded in 1129 on the site of a 7C monastery; it preserves a ruined 12C church, a 13C infirmary, and several 18C buildings.—Regaining the D165 we continue through the *Forêt de Laigue* to *Choisy-au-Bac*, 3km N. of which is the late 15C château of *Le Plessis-Brion*, and shortly enter **Compiègne**, for which see *Blue Guide Paris and Environs*, or Rte 16.—**Senlis** lies 32km S.W.

The N17 continues S. from Péronne, crossing the Somme, and after 7km, the N29, at rebuilt *Villers-Carbonnel*. At 11km *Nesle* lies 7km S.E., the *Nigella* of Dagobert (7C), and of importance during the medieval period; its 12C abbey church has been rebuilt in a Romanesque style.

11km. *Roye* (6700 inhab.), ancient *Rhodium*, on the Avre, has a late-Gothic church battered almost beyond recognition during the First World War, when scarcely a building survived.

The N17 crosses the A1 to reach a road junction at 4km. The r.-hand fork (D930) leads 14km to *Montdidier*; see Rte 5.—We fork l. past (2.5km) *Tilloloy*, with a restored 17C château and Renaissance church.

15km. The D935 forks S.E. across the A1 to (16.5km) **Compiègne**; see *Blue Guide Paris and Environs*, or Rte 16.—To the E., the valley of the Matz was the scene of critical fighting in March and June 1918, prior to the Allied offensive.

12km. *Estrées-St-Denis*, domain of Gabrielle d'Estrées, mistress of Henri IV.

At 3.5km we cross the N31 (see Rte 9), and 11km beyond reach *Pont-Ste-Maxence*, for which, and **Senlis**, 12km beyond, see *Blue Guide Paris and Environs*, or Rte 16.

3 Calais to Reims via St-Omer, Arras, and St-Quentin

279km (173 miles). N43. 40km **St-Omer**—43km *Béthune*—D937. 30km **Arras**—D939. 36km *Cambrai*—N44. 39km **St-Quentin**—46km **Laon**—45km **Reims.**

Maps: IGN 1, 2, 4, 9, or 101. M 236, 237.

Motorway. The A26 has been completed from a point W. of St-Omer to its junction with the A1 E. of Arras; it will be extended towards Calais, and to St-Quentin, and eventually to Reims itself.

CALAIS (76,900 Calaisiens), the nearest French town to England, and busy terminus of cross-channel ferries, is divided into maritime *Calais-Nord*, lying between the harbour (to the E.) and the *Citadel* (to the W.), and the more extensive suburb of *St-Pierre* (or *Calais-Sud*), long devoted to the mechanical production of tulles and lace, although its manufactures have been diversified.

It emerges into History in the 12C, playing a prominent part in the early struggles between England and France. After an obstinate defence, it was taken by Edward III in 1347, and remained in English hands until 1558, when its garrison was expelled by the Duc de Guise at the head of 30,000 troops, a humiliation which caused Mary Tudor to say that the name 'Calais' would be found graven on her heart at her death; and the story is told of the six burghers, headed by Eustache de St-Pierre, who—as shown in Rodin's sculptured group—wearing halters about their necks, offered themselves to Edward III as a ransom to save the port from destruction, which (together with their lives) was spared due to the intercession of Queen Philippa. Mary Stuart, the young widow of François II, sailed hence for Scotland in 1561; and here Louis XVIII landed in 1814 to assume the French crown. A number of weavers from the rival lace-making town of Nottingham settled in Calais at various times.

The famous *Hôtel Dessein* (which stood near the Hôtel de Ville), where the opening scene of Sterne's 'Sentimental Journey' is set, was in its time 'very elegant' and 'not inferior to any tavern in England', according to Philip Thicknesse (even if, as he found out later, the drains from the military hospital ran beneath it, which were both dangerous and offensive), and with its 130 beds and half that number of servants, made a great impression on all English travellers on first landing in 'La Belle France'. A theatre and shops were attached, and M. Dessein profited greatly, in addition, both as banker and in hiring post-chaises to his clients.

But, as with most frontier towns, Calais has had its critics. John Murray, in his 'Hand-Book for France' (1843: a direct predecessor of this Guide), had remarked that an English traveller of the time of James I described it as 'a beggarly, extorting town: monstrous dear and sluttish'; and, Murray added, 'this description holds good down to the present time'. It was one in which few, unless they were obliged to, would spend much time.

It was an important British base during the First World War, and in consequence suffered from bombing raids in 1917–18. The old town was razed during the Second World War, but has since been re-built. The once widely-read novelist Pigault-Lebrun (1753–1835), and the essayist Paul Léautaud (1872–1956) were born here; while Nelson's Lady Hamilton died in poverty in 1815 at No. 27 Rue Française, and was buried in the public cemetery.

The *Avant-Port*, with the *Gare Maritime*, lies immediately N. of the town, while further E. is the hovercraft terminus (*Gare Aéroglisseur*). Opposite the former is the fishermens' quarter of *Le Courgain*, partially rebuilt in the old style, to the W. of which is *Fort Risban*, beyond which is the extensive beach.

To the S. is the central *Pl. d'Armes*, retaining the heavily-buttressed *Tour du Guet*, a watch-tower built by Philippe de Boulogne in 1224, restored in 1806, and used as a lighthouse until 1848. ''Tis monstrous high', wrote Sterne, 'and catches the eye so continually, you cannot avoid taking notice of it, if you would'.

Hence the Rue Royale leads S. past (l.) the Parc Richelieu, with a *Museum* and picture-gallery (including water-colours by Bonington, and examples of the Dutch and Flemish Schools), and an important collection of lace. Brick-built *Notre-Dame* (14-15C; restored) to the N.E., shows strong Tudor influence.

Continuing S. over the *Pont George-V*, with a view to the W. of the *Citadel* (1560), we pass (r.) the *Gare Centrale*. Beyond (l.), opposite the Parc St-Pierre, stands Rodin's **Monument to the Burghers of Calais* (1895; see above), behind which rises the ponderous mass of the *Hôtel de Ville* (1910–23), a tasteless brick edifice in a Flemish Renaissance style, with an equally barbarous belfry.

Threading our way down the congested Blvd Jacquard, named after Joseph Jacquard (1752–1834; cf. Lyon), the inventor of the power-loom, we reach a road-junction, at which the N1 leads r. to **Boulogne**; see Rte 4.

We turn l. and shortly fork r. onto the N43.

CALAIS TO DUNKERQUE (43km). The N1 leads E. between sand-dunes and flat inland meadows intersected by canals, or '*watergands*', to cross the canalised Aa at (22km) **Gravelines** (11,600 inhab.). This ancient fortress, which preserves its 16–17C ramparts, and a late 16C church, was the scene of the battle in which Count Egmont defeated the French under Marshal de Thermes in 1558, while on 29 July 1588 the Spanish Armada was dispersed off Gravelines by the English fleet, after being driven out of Calais roads by fire-ships. A nuclear power-station and extensive port installations are under construction between this point and *Dunkerque*, on the W. outskirts of which one may turn r. to gain the A25 motorway; see Rte 1.

The N43 crosses an uninteresting level tract as far as (14km) *Le Pont-d'Ardres*, with a bridge of 1754 over two canals.

5km. *Ardres*, an ancient town with a lake, lime-trees, a picturesque triangular Place, and 14C church, was occupied by François I during the conference known as 'The Field of the Cloth of Gold' (or Camp du Drap d'Or), held at *Balinghem*, 3km W., in 1520.—*Guînes*, 6km further W., in English hands from 1352 to 1558, was the residence of Henry VIII during these meetings.

At *Licques*, 10km S.W., are ruins of a Premonstratensian abbey.

Continuing S.E. from Ardres, we shortly meet an entrance to the A26 motorway, and after 10km pass (l.) the imposing church-tower of *Bayenghem-lès-Eperlecques*.

13km. **ST-OMER** (15,500 Audomarois), a quiet town on the Aa, described rather unkindly in the 1840s as 'a very dull place', in fact retains several objects of interest, although its ramparts have virtually disappeared. An elaborate system of waterways flanks its N.E. side.

St-Omer is named after a 7C bishop of Thérouanne, founder of the abbey of St-Bertin. Hereward the Wake met his wife Torfrida here. Suger (1081–1151), abbot of St-Denis, was a native of the town, which underwent many sieges (including two by the English, in 1337 and 1339) before being annexed to France in 1677. Invested by Marlborough and Prince Eugène in 1711, it was saved by Jacqueline Robins, the local heroine, who brought in a boatload of arms and provisions at the risk of her life. St-Omer was the British G.H.Q. from 12 Oct. 1914 to 31 March 1916. Sir John French, and later Sir Douglas Haig, lived at No. 37 Rue St-Bertin, and Lord Roberts died (14 Nov. 1914) at No. 50 Rue Carnot. From 1917, when it became the British Royal Flying Corps H.Q., it suffered heavily from both bombing and shell-fire; it was likewise damaged by bombing during the period 1939–45.
It was the birthplace of Jean Titelouze (1563–1633), the organist and composer; and Alphonse de Neuville (1836–85), a war-artist during the Franco-Prussian campaigns.

N.E. of the central *Pl. Foch*, with the *Hôtel de Ville* of 1840, stands *St-Sépulchre* (14-15C), with a beautiful stone spire. Off the S.W. corner of the square is the *Musée Henri-Dupuis*, with a good ornithological collection; to the W. the Blvd Vauban overlooks the umbrageous *Public Gardens*, in which are remains of 17C ramparts, while a few steps S. brings one to the W. entrance of ***Notre-Dame** (13-15C), perhaps the most interesting church in Artois, and a cathedral between 1559 and 1801. The tower and S. portal, with its 15C statue of the Virgin and sculptured Last Judgement, are the main features of the exterior.

The well-glazed and spacious interior, with two Flamboyant rose-windows in the transepts, contains numerous ex-votos, and 15-16C tombs, among them, in the S. aisle, that of Eustache de Croy (d. 1538) by Jacques Dubroeucq. Some original paving is preserved here; also a 13C group of Christ, the Virgin, and St John. Off the S. transept are the tomb of St Erkembode (d. 742), and a clock dated 1558, while in the N. aisle is the 13C cenotaph of St. Omer. Both transepts and the well-panelled *Choir* have galleries of slender grey marble columns. Four sections from a Flemish altar-piece are exhibited in the N. ambulatory. Many of the chapels retain their Renaissance grilles, while the *Organ-case* is profusely carved. The *Treasury* is in the S.E. tower.

N. of the apse is the former *Bishop's Palace*, now Law Courts.

No. 14 Rue Carnot, leading N.E. from the adjacent *Pl. Victor-Hugo*, is the *Hôtel Sandelin*, an attractive building of 1766, housing the **Museum**.

Notable are an *anon.* Crucifixion of c. 1480; *School of Gerard David,* Holy Family; *Momper,* Alpine landscape, and other Flemish landscapes; *Jan Steen,* Joker;
Terboch, Male, and Female portraits; *Thomas de Keyser,* Elisabeth Van der Aa,
and Hendrick Kerburg; *Eliasz Dickenoy,* Old woman; and two paintings by *L.-L.*
Boilly.
    Other rooms contain medieval sculpture, some painted; furniture; alabasters;
10-11C ivories; an enamelled and gilt bronze pedestal for a cross (c. 1185);
faience from St-Omer and St-Amand, and an important collection of Delft ware.
Other sections are devoted to a curious collection of clay pipes; arms; and local
archaeology.

Turning S.E. from the Pl. Victor-Hugo, we pass (r.) the Jesuit *Chapel*
of the Lycée (1639), and the *Library* (its entrance in the parallel Rue
Gambetta), containing valuable early MSS and some 200 incunables.
To the l. in the Rue St-Bertin stands *St-Denis,* rebuilt 1714, with a 15C
choir and 13C tower. Almost opposite are the buildings of the
Hôpital Militaire (1726).

Formerly a school for the Roman Catholic youth of Great Britain, it was founded
by the Jesuits in 1592, and removed successively to Bruges (1762), Liège (1773),
and finally (in 1794) to Stonyhurst in Lancashire. Titus Oates, John Carroll (first
R.C. bishop in the United States), and Daniel O'Connell, were among its pupils.

At the far end of the street stand the ruins of the abbey-church of *St-*
Bertin, largely destroyed since 1830 'by the municipal administration, under pretence of giving employment to workmen' (according
to Augustus Hare); the lower half of a 15C tower, and a few arches of
the nave, subsist. Childéric III, last of the Merovingians, died in the
abbey in 755.

To the N.E., beyond the station and suburbs of *Haut-Pont* and *Lyzel,* lie the
'*watergangs*', a labyrinthine system of canals among the marshes constructed by
the earlier amphibious Flemish-speaking inhabitants; the land thus reclaimed
('*lègres*') is devoted to market-gardening.—At *Clairmarais,* 4.5km N.E., are the
remains of a Cistercian abbey where Becket took refuge in 1165 after his quarrel with Henry II.
    Some 6km S.W. of St-Omer, off the N42, is the modern Benedictine abbey of *St-*
Paul-de-Wisques, retaining a 15C tower, and 18C buildings.—Further S. stood a
V1 missile base, in 1944.

ST-OMER TO ABBEVILLE (85km). The D928 leads S.W., after 5km passing near
Esquerdes (3km W.) with a church of interest, partly 12C.—5km. *Bientques,* 7km
S.E. of which, on the ancient highway, known as the 'Chaussée Brunehaut', lies
the village of *Thérouanne,* once an episcopal town of importance, Gallic *Taruen-*
na, razed by Charles V in 1553.—At *Enguinegatte,* 4km further S., in an
endeavour to raise the siege of Thérouanne, the French were routed by Henry
VIII and Maximilian at the *Second Battle of the Spurs* (1513), in which the
chevalier Bayard, when captured, was set free without ransom by the
English.—Continuing S.W. from Bientques, at 8km we pass (r.) *Merck-St-Liévin,*
and after a further 4km, *Fauquembergues,* both with churches of some
interest.—14km. *Ruisseauville,* 2km S. of which lies *Azincourt,* where on St
Crispin's Day (25 Oct.) 1415, Henry V won the momentous but sanguinary victory better known as **Agincourt,** over the French. The Constable d'Albret fell into a snare by drawing up his army in a narrow plain between two woods, where it
was ambushed and taken in flank by the English archers, and their crowded
ranks were broken or put to flight after a struggle of only three hours' duration.
The French are said to have left 10,000 slain on the field, while among the
prisoners was the poet Charles d'Orléans.—*Tramecourt,* just to the E., retains an
ancient brick and stone château, while *Ambricourt,* further E., was the scene of
Georges Bernados's novel 'The Diary of a Country Parson', whose author
(1888–1948) spent much of his youth at *Fressin,* some 9km to the W., with a
Flamboyant church.—The D928 shortly descends through woods into the valley
of the Canches at (14km) **Hesdin,** founded by Charles V in 1554 after the

destruction of its predecessor the previous year, the remains of which lie some 5km to the S.E. The *Hôtel de Ville* dates from 1629, and its hall-church from 1563–85. The Abbé Prévost (1697–1763), author of 'Manon Lescaut', was born here, and was educated by the Jesuits.—Some of the illustrious victims of Agincourt are buried in the 13-16C abbey-church of *Auchy-lès-Hesdin*, 5km N.E.—At 17km the r.-hand turning leads 5km to **Crécy**; see Rte 4.—2km. The brick and stone château of *Brailly-Cornehotte* (1775) lies 2km r.—2.5km. **St-Riquier**, 9.5km S., is noted for its fine Gothic *Church (mainly 16C, after a fire in 1487), lavishly adorned with sculptures, and a treasury of interest. The abbey was founded c. 645 and endowed by Dagobert and Hugues Capet, and rebuilt in the 16-18C. Richelieu was once abbot. The town suffered several sieges, in that of 1536 it was defended by a regiment of women under the local heroine Becquétoille.—14km (9km S.W. of St-Riquier) brings us to **Abbeville**; see Rte 4.

Continuing S.E. from St-Omer, the N43 traverses (4km) *Arques*, whence the N42 leads 18km due E. to *Hazebrouck*; see Rte 1. On the adjacent *Canal de Neuffossé* is the *Ascenseur de Fontinettes*, a remarkable hydraulic lift (1888), which until 1967 performed the work of five locks.—At *Blendecques*, 3km S. of Arques, are ruins of an abbey founded in 1186 and rebuilt in the 18C.

14km. **Aire** (10,000 Airois), a drab town on the Lys, was an ancient fortress. It retains the charming *Hôtel du Baillage* (c. 1600), and a *Hôtel de Ville* of 1724, while *St-Pierre*, rebuilt in the 16C and restored since 1944, with an imposing tower, shows three different stages of Gothic architecture.

At *Isbergues*, 4.5km S.E., the 15C church is reputed to be the burial-place of St Gisela, a sister of Charlemagne.—The 12C church of *Guarbecque*, 4.5km beyond, has a remarkable belfry.

12km. **Lillers** (9500 Lillérois), on the western fringe of an extensive mining and industrial zone—one will observe the slag-heaps—was much damaged by bombardment in 1918. Here, in the 12C, the first *Artesian well* (so-called after the province of Artois) is said to have been sunk, and may still be seen in the courtyard of the old Dominican monastery. The 12C church of *St-Omer* has suffered from restoration in the past, and has again been restored. The 12C 'Christ du Saint-Sang' is normally behind the altar.

At *Ham-en-Artois*, 3.5km N.W., is the ancient abbey of *St-Sauveur*.

LILLERS TO AMIENS (83km). The D916 turns S. across the motorway, and after 7km of jolting pavé road crosses the ancient 'Chaussée Brunehaut' and reverts to a smoother surface beyond *Cauchy-à-la-Tour* (l.), birthplace of Marshal Pétain (1856–1951), whose heroism at Verdun was tarnished by his craven surrender to Hitler in 1940.—4km. *Pernes*, where in 1793 the insurrection known as the 'Petite Vendée' broke out, to be bloodily suppressed by Joseph Lebon.—3km. *Bours* (l.) has ruins of a 16C château.—10km. **St-Pol-sur-Ternoise** (6300 Saint-Polais), an old market-town with a chequered history, developed in importance during the First World War as a railway junction, and jointly with Calais, was the final home (in 1920–21) of the shrunken G.H.Q. of British troops in France and Flanders. It was briefly occupied by the Germans in 1914, and was later shelled at long range.—10km. *Nuncq*, 3km W. of which is the brick and stone château of *Flers* (1780).—3km. *Frévent*, on the Canche, has a 16C church, while 1km S.E. stands the château of *Cerquamps* (c. 1740) adjacent to the site of a Cistercian monastery founded in 1137, but demolished at the Revolution.—13km S.W. lies *Auxi-le-Château*, with a ruined 12C castle and an interesting Flamboyant church.—8.5km. *Lucheux*, 6km E., has a church of c. 1130, a picturesque belfry, and a ruined 12-17C castle.—6.5km **Doullens** (7900 Doullennais), much damaged in the Second World War, lies at the confluence of the Authie and the Grouches. In the new *Hôtel de Ville* took place the conference of March 1918 at which the Allies decided to confide the supreme command on the Western Front to Mar-

shal Foch. The former *Town Hall*, with a graceful belfry, dates from the 15-17C;
of *St-Pierre* (13-15C), only an arcaded nave remains. Local antiquities and paintings may be seen in the *Musée Lombart*, housed in an old convent.—Climbing
S., the 16-17C *Citadel* is passed.—14km. *Naours*, 3km W., is known for its extensive range of caves or '*muches*', used by refugees in former wars. Some 2km of
underground streets, three chapels, stables, and storerooms, etc. have been excavated, some dating to perhaps the 9C.—After 5km, just beyond *Villers-Bocage*,
with a 16C Entombment in its church, we may briefly diverge past the château
of *Bertangles* (1747) before descending into the valley of the Somme at **Amiens**,
near (r.) what remains of its *Citadel* (1598). Bearing l., and shortly passing (r.) the
University buildings on the site of the old Hôtel-Dieu, and (l.) the ancient church
of *St-Leu*, the town centre is approached, dominated by its cathedral; see Rte 5.

Continuing E. from Lillers, after 13km **Béthune** (26,100 inhab.) is
entered, an industrial town in a swampy district at the junction of the
Lawe with the Bassée Canal, formerly the seat of a lordship of Artois,
and a fortress. It was the birthplace of the trouvère Conon (Quesnes)
de Béthune (d. 1224). The town, which remained in British hands
from Oct. 1914 until the Armistice, was much damaged in April
1918. A restored 14C *Belfry* dominates its central *Grand' Place*, N. of
which is the rebuilt mid 16C church of *St-Vaast*.

BÉTHUNE TO DOUAI AND VALENCIENNES (80km). The N43
leads E.—After 3km the N41 forks l. to (10km) *La Bassée* (see Rte 2),
at 4km traversing *Cambrin*, from which 'Harley Street' ran N. to
Givenchy on its slight ridge, a key position and pivot of the British
retreat of April 1918; *Festubert*, further N., was fought over in Dec.
1914, and again in May 1915.

The N43 bears S.E., passing (r.) *Labourse*, with a church dating
from the 9C, to enter the Lens coalfield, at 11km skirting (l.) *Loos-en-
Gohelle*, which gave its name to the **Battle of Loos**, lasting from 25
Sept. to 13 Oct. 1915, in which the 1st and 4th British Corps took
part, gaining some ground, taking 3000 prisoners and 26 guns, but
losing three divisional commanders, while at 'Dud Corner' cemetery
the *Loos Memorial* commemorates some 20,700 'missing'.

4km. **Lens** (pron. Lons; 38,300 Lensois), which may be by-passed to
the N., since 1850 a coal-mining town of no attraction, surrounded
by shale-heaps and brick-built miners' dwellings known as 'cités' or
'corons'. In 1648 Condé defeated the Spaniards beneath its walls, but
it has only belonged to France since 1659. It was captured by the
Germans in Oct. 1914, and remained in their hands for four years,
during which time mining continued on both sides until devastation
and systematic flooding by the enemy made it impossible. It was
damaged by bombing in 1944.—The N17 leads S. to (7km) **Arras**, see
below, providing an approach to *Vimy Ridge*, commanding it to the
W.

Turning due E. on the motorway, an industrial belt is avoided,
before bearing S.E. to (23km) **DOUAI** (44,500 Douaisiens), on the
canalised Scarpe, an important industrial town of historic interest,
retaining a number of old houses, although severely damaged in
both world wars.

Roman *Duacum*, a place of note under the earliest Counts of Flanders, was in
1479 fruitlessly besieged by Louis XI after the death of Charles le Téméraire. In
1710 it surrendered to Marlborough after a resistance of 52 days, only to be
retaken by Villars in 1712, and restored to France by the Treaty of Utrecht. It
was a hotbed of English Roman Catholicism during the reigns of Elisabeth I and
James I, a college being founded by Card. Allen in 1568 for the training of
'seminary priests', many of whom returned to England by stealth and paid the

penalty with their lives. The R.C. English translation of the Old Testament, first published here in 1610 (together with the New Testament, published in Reims in 1582) is known as the 'Douay Bible'. Its university, founded by Philip II in 1562 during the Spanish occupation, its faculties transferred to Lille in 1887, has been re-established. Its ramparts were demolished in 1891. The town remained in German occupation during most of the First World War, until their evacuation in the face of the British advance, when several quarters were mined and numerous houses set alight. It was the birthplace of the artists Jean Bellegambe (1470–1534), and Edmond Cross (1856–1916); probably of Jean de Boulogne (Giovanni da Bologna; 1524–1608), the sculptor; and the poetess Marceline Desbordes-Valmore (1786–1859).

The town centre is somewhat cramped, and—if approaching from the W.—it is advisable to follow the Rue de la République, circling to the N.E. The Rue des Chartreux leads r. off this, in which stand the 16-18C buildings of the former *Chartreuse* and the *Hôtel d'Abancourt-Montmorency* (1559–1608), once used as barracks, but now attractively accommodating the *****Museum**, which can no longer be condemned—as it was by Augustus Hare—as containing 'an unusual amount of rubbish, in gaudy frames, crowded together'.

Among more notable works are an *anon*. 15C Florentine 'Cour d'Amour'; *J. Mandyn*, Trial of Job; *Coxie*, Christ carrying the cross; *Carracci*, Flagellation; *Brueghel*, Village brawl; *J. Massys*, Tobias; *Teniers the elder*, Scene of sorcery; portraits by *Van Dyck* and *P. Moreelse*; *A. Govaerts*, Holy Family; *T. Verhaecht*, Mountain landscape; *Ruisdael*, Forest scene; *A. Cuyp*, Young child; and works by *Veronese*, *Jan van Scorel*, *C. Engelbrechtsz*, and *Bellegambe*. Also, portraits by *Nattier*, including that of the Marquise de Dreux-Brézé, and *Heinsius*; *Vivien*, pastel Portrait of Bacqueville de la Potherie; *Delacroix*, Bellinger; *David*, Mme Tallien; *Cross*, Portrait of his wife; and characteristic works by *Corot, Jongkind, Sisley, Pissarro*, and *Lebourg*. The Plan of Douai in 1769, and a series of Alabasters will also be noticed.

At No. 53 Rue St-Albin, adjacent, are collections of natural history and archaeology.—Hence we may work our way S. past *St-Jacques* (1706), once the church of English Benedictines. The street opposite leads across the Scarpe to the *Palais de Justice*, with a facade of 1789, and containing the former chamber of the Parlement of Flanders (1709–13), beyond which rises domed *St-Pierre*, with an organ-loft of 1760, and massive tower (1512–1686). Turning S. along the Rue de Bellegambe the *Hôtel de Ville* is reached, partly 15C, partly from 1860, divided by a typical five-storeyed Flemish *Belfry* (1380–1410), 54m high.

To the S.E. is the rebuilt *Pl. d'Armes* (in which No. 70, the *Maison du Dauphin*, of 1754, houses the S.I.), and beyond, near the *Porte de Valenciennes* (1453 and 17C) stands restored *Notre-Dame* (13-15C).

Turning W. from the Hôtel de Ville, and forking l., the Scarpe is re-crossed to the *Pl. St-Amé*, S.W. of which, at No. 35 bis Rue d'Arras, is the *Library*, containing over 300 incunables, and important MSS, including a Biblia Pauperum, a Book of Hours of Sir Thomas More (with an autograph dedication to Bp John Fisher), Roger Bacon's 'Opus Tertium', etc.—Further S.E. stands the 14C *Porte d'Arras*; to the N.W. the Rue d'Esquerchin leads back to the Rue de la République.

Flines-lez-Râches, 11.5km N.E., site of a Cistercian abbey founded in 1231, preserves its church (13C, with a 12C tower), and remains of fortifications.

The N43 leads S.E., traversing a district flooded by the Germans on their final retreat in Sept.-Oct. 1918, to (26km) **Cambrai**; see Rte 104.

We now follow the N45 to (12km) *Auberchicourt*, and fork r. for (9km) *Bouchain*, on the Scheldt, which underwent a celebrated siege in 1676, when the entry of Duc Philippe d'Orléans was followed by the arrival of the Prince of Orange with a relieving force. The massive *Tour d'Ostrevent* is a relic of the former castle.—By turning l. onto the N30, and by-passing (l.) at 7km industrial *Denain* (21,900 Denaisiens), on the l. bank of the Scheldt, famous for the victory of Villars over Prince Eugène in 1712, after 10km **Valenciennes** (see Rte 1) is entered.

From Béthune, we follow the D937 S. below the motorway and through (6km) *Noeux-les-Mines*, a mining town lying close behind the front during 1914–18, its shale-heaps providing 'observation posts' of trench warfare.—12km. *Souchez*, to the E. of which rises the 'pimple' at the N. extremity of *Vimy Ridge* (see below), and to the N.W., the spur of *N.-D. de Lorette*, with its cemetery and monument, a height won by the French in May 1915. Below, to the S., is the remains of a church of 1524 at *Ablains-St-Nazaire*.

At 3.5km we may turn l. to adjacent *Neuville-St-Vaast*, 3km N.E. of which, beyond the motorway, lies **Vimy Ridge* (now wooded), which resisted a French attack in the summer of 1915, but which, after a long bombardment, was taken by assault by the Canadian Corps commanded by Gen. Byng on 9-10 April, 1917. It is now dominated by the twin pylons of the *Canadian Memorial* (1936), on *Côte 145*, commanding an interesting panorama. 60,000 Canadians of the 425,000 who took part in the First World War, died in the battle, 11,000 of whom have no known graves.

An area of trenches and tunnels has been preserved close by, with somewhat artificial-looking 'concrete' sandbags and duckboards, but giving an impressive idea of what conditions must have been like at that time, and also the proximity of the confronting lines. The whole area is tastefully conserved, and sheep graze over the hummocky battlefield, pocked by shell-holes, but it is wise to keep to the well-defined paths, which are clearly indicated, for unexploded shells and grenades may still be in evidence.

Regaining the main road, we turn l., with a view (r.) of *Mont-St-Eloi*, on which stand the ruined 17C towers of an Augustinian abbey founded in the 7C. In the intermediate valley lay a Royal Flying Corps landing-field.

We shortly fork l. to enter (8.5km) *Arras*, first crossing the river Scarpe, and following an avenue, to the r. of which lies the Grand Place.

ARRAS (45,400 Arrageois), préfecture of the *Pas-de-Calais*, a flourishing town largely rebuilt since being shattered by four years of close-range bombardment during the First World War, and by bombing in the Second, preserves two squares of great character, apart from other objects of interest.

Roman *Nemetacum* was the capital of the Atrebates, from whom, like the province of Artois, it derives its name. Its bishopric was founded by St Vaast (Vedast) in the 6C. Peace was signed here in 1414 between the Armagnacs and Burgundians prior to the battle of Agincourt; a second treaty (1435) detached the latters from their English alliance; and a third (1482) established a new N. frontier of France. After a century and a half of Spanish and Austrian domination—from the accession of Maxmilian I in 1493—Arras was captured by the French in 1640; and in 1654, under Turenne, it successfully resisted a Spanish army commanded by Condé. It was noted from an early period for its cloth and its now extinct manufacture of tapestry hangings ('*arras*'), which thrived in the 16C.

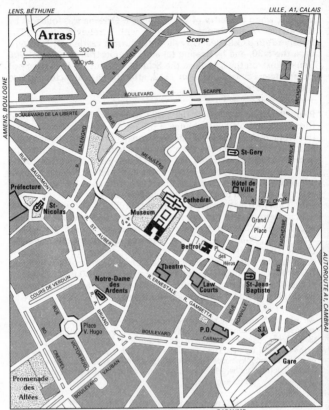

It was briefly in German hands (15-30 Sept. 1914), and then formed a salient in the front line, being included in the British sector in 1916. The first great aerial battle took place just to the S.E. on 10 Nov. 1916, when 70 planes were engaged, six of the enemy (out of 40) being brought down. The **Battle of Arras**, of which the seizure of Vimy Ridge was an important part, opened on 9 April 1917, in which some 13,000 prisoners and 200 guns were captured in the first stage of the advance E., and compelled a German retreat S. of Lens, but the hostile armies became locked in bloody and indecisive fighting astride the Scarpe after the 23rd. The Arras front was violently attacked on 28 March 1918 by three German divisions, which failed to break through the Allied defences; while on 26 Aug. commenced an Allied movement E. along the Cambrai road, which by 2 Sept. had overwhelmed the *Wotan Line*, causing a precipitate German retreat, in which they lost 16,000 prisoners and 220 guns. A rearguard action was fought here by the British in 1940 during the retreat to Dunkerque.

Arras was the birthplace of Jean Bodel (fl. early 13C), the writer, and of the trouvères Gautier d'Arras (12C), and Adam de la Halle (c. 1235– c. 87); Maximilien de Robespierre (1758– 94); Joseph Lebon (1765– 94), who, once a local curé, introduced the 'Terror' into the town; and F.-E. Vidocq (1775– 1857), who later in a venal life set up a Criminal Investigation Department for the French police, confirming the wisdom of 'setting a thief to catch a thief'. Arras is reputed for its *andœuillettes*.

The ***Grand' Place** is once again the pride of Arras, its entire rebuilding and restoration having recently been completed: approx.

one-third had been destroyed. It is surrounded by 155 picturesque brick and stone Flemish houses in the late 17C taste, varying in size and design, but uniform in style, with arcaded and gabled roofs. Beneath the square are some of the largest '*boves*' or cellars of Arras, which once offered its civilians some security from bombardment: those at No. 8 may be visited. Others may be seen in the Rue Pasteur, further S.

From its S.W. corner we reach the very similar **Petit Place** or *Pl. des Héros*, likewise reconstructed, flanked by the *Hôtel de Ville*, rebuilt in the original early 16C style, with a Gothic facade and graceful 75m high belfry (the former dated from 1443 – 1554).

Near its S.E. corner is rebuilt *St-Jean Baptiste* (1565 – 84), in 1793 the Temple of Reason, and seat of Lebon's revolutionary tribunal.—A short distance S.W. of the Hôtel de Ville is the *Palais de Justice* (1724), from which one may approach, via the Rue Paul-Doumer, the buildings of the *Abbaye de St-Vaast* (1754), a frequent residence of the notorious Card. Édouard de Rohan, in the S. wing of which is the **Museum** (with pictures 'more than usually bad', in Augustus Hare's opinion, and many will agree).

These include several huge canvases by *Ph. de Champaigne, Jouvenet, Restout*, et al; *Jean Bellegambe*, Adoration, and Christ and the executioners; *G. Baglioni*, Apollo and the Muses, part of a series painted in 1620; *Charles Desavary*, View of the Grand' Place in 1878; *J.-B. Isabey*, Portrait of Charlotte de Robespierre; *Paul Bril*, The hunt; *Corot*, Cottages near Arras; and works by *Constant Dutilleux* (1807 – 65). Among the more curious objects in the extensive collection are the original metal Lion from the summit of the belfry (1554); a maquette of Arras (1716); a 12C mosaic tombstone; the macabre tomb of Guille Lefrançois (1446); and an early 14C Funerary mask of a young woman. The ceramic collection is notable.

Abutting the N. end of the abbey buildings is the restored *Cathedral*, a somewhat frigid Classical edifice of 1755 – 1833, by Contant d'Ivry, remarkable only for its size, and succeeding the older abbey church.

S.W. of the Rue Paul-Doumer is the *Théâtre* (1785), adjacent to the main transverse street, which leads N.W. towards the *Préfecture* in the former *Bishop's Palace* (1780), near which is restored *St-Nicolas* (1846), occupying the site of the original cathedral, demolished at the Revolution.

From the latter we may return S. to visit the regularly planned *Basse-Ville*, with a pyramid of 1779 in its octagonal *Pl. Victor-Hugo*, from which an avenue leads S.W. past the Promenade des Allées to the huge *Citadel*, erected by Vauban in 1674. To the N. is the British military cemetery and *Arras Memorial* to 35,900 missing; and near by, the *Mur des Fusillés*, a memorial to 200 Frenchmen shot here during 1941 – 44.

For the road S. towards *Peronne* and *Paris*, see Rte 2.

The N39 leads E.S.E., a straight road of Roman origin, shortly passing (r.) *Observation Ridge*, and (l.) *The Harp* and *Telegraph Hill*, from which the *Hindenburg Line* swung S. and then S.E., and crosses an area fiercely contested in April-May 1917, and in March-August 1918. *Mouchy-le-Preux*, to the l. of the road just beyond (7km) the A1 motorway, provided the Germans with a commanding view of the Allied lines.

18km. We cross the *Canal du Nord* at *Marquion*, scene of a Canadian victory in Sept. 1918, and then the A26 and A2 motorways before entering (11km) **Cambrai**; see Rte 104.

The N44 leads S., passing just E. of an area of heavy fighting in the region of the *Hindenburg Line* (known to the Germans as the '*Siegfried Line*'), a powerful system of field-works constructed in 1916–17, which extended from near Arras towards the Chemin-des-Dames, S. of Laon. It was breached on a wide front during the **First Battle of Cambrai** (20 Nov. 1917) some 10km S.W. of Cambrai, but Ludendorff's counter-attack on the 30th pushed back the British towards *Gouzeaucourt*, 6.5km S.W. of the road junction 11km S. of Cambrai, where we fork S.E. for *St-Quentin*; see below.

In the following March this sector resisted a German offensive, and the same area was fought over again during the **Second Battle of Cambrai** (27 Sept.-5 Oct. 1918), when the Hindenburg Line was again breached—between Cambrai and St-Quentin—the 1st and 3rd Armies taking 36,000 prisoners and 380 guns.

At (7.5km) *Masnières* a successor of the canal bridge is crossed, the collapse of which under the weight of a British tank fatally delayed the advance of 20 Nov. 1917, and a long hill is ascended before forking l. at 3.5km to re-cross the *Scheldt Canal.*—2km N.E., on the far bank, lie the gutted ruins of the Cistercian abbey of *Vaucelles.*

The road now crosses what was another sector of the *Hindenburg Line*, after 13km passing (r.) a monument. Some 1200 Americans were cut off here on 29 Sept. 1918 after breaking through the enemy front at adjacent *Bony.*—3.5km *Bellicourt*, near which is the S. entrance of the *Bellicourt Tunnel*, a canal tunnel pierced in 1810, which was connected by shafts with the Hindenburg Line further W., forming one of its strongest points.—After 2.5km we pass (r.) the *Riqueval Bridge*, which survived the fighting here, and (1.5km) *Bellenglise* (r.), where on 29 Sept. 1918 the British crossed the canal.

9.5km **ST-QUENTIN** (65,100 St-Quentinois), an animated industrial town on the r. bank of the Somme, severely damaged in the 1914-18 war, preserves an interesting church and museum.

Roman *Augusta Veromanduorum* derives its name from the Christian missionary Caius Quintinus, beheaded here in 287, whose tomb later attracted pilgrims. Its capture on St. Lawrence's Day (10 Aug.) 1557 was the success which Philip II of Spain commemorated by building the Escorial. Three years later St-Quentin formed part of the dowry of Mary, Queen of Scots. It resisted the Prussian attack of 8 Oct. 1870, but Gén. Faidherbe's army was defeated by Goeben on the 19 Jan. 1871. It remained behind the German front from late Aug. 1914 until 1 Oct. 1918, when entered by Gén. Debeney's forces. On 21 March 1918 some 64 German divisions attacked the British front in overwhelming force (at least two to one), and breaking through W. and S.W. of the town, claimed some 45,000 prisoners in this **Second Battle of the Somme** (or of **St-Quentin**); it was not again approached by the Allies until the following Sept., being outflanked by the British thrust at Bellenglise (see above).

It was the birthplace of Loyset Compère (c. 1450–1518), the composer, while his colleague Jean Mouton (c. 1475–1522) died here; better known natives were Maurice-Quentin Delatour (1704–88), the pastellist; Babeuf (1760–97), the socialist leader in the Revolution; and Antoine-Nicolas de Condorcet (1743–94), the mathematician and philosopher, in fact born at *Ribemont*, 14km S.E.

The central *Place* is flanked by the restored *Hôtel de Ville*, with a Flamboyant facade of 1509, 18C tower, and carillon.

A short distance S.E. is an important *Entomological Museum*, containing a collection of 600,000 butterflies, etc.; to the N.E. stands the spacious 13-15C collegial church of *St-Quentin*, one of the finest Gothic buildings in N. France, tastefully restored. The nave, with its maze (1495) is flanked by aisles which are prolonged as far as the apse; traces of murals may be observed in the 2nd N. chapel; the *Organ-loft* dates from 1690–1703.

Both the Petit Transept and Grand Transept have rose-windows, the latter retaining a quantity of 16C glass on its N. side, more of which is in the clerestory, while that in some of the radiating apse-chapels dates from the 13C. A Tree of Jesse, a sculpted Deposition, and a well-carved Knight and his wife will be noted. St Quentin is said to be buried in the 11C crypt beneath the choir.

A few minutes' walk N.W. along the Rue Raspail brings one to the **Musée Antoine-Lécuyer** (at No. 28 in the street of that name), containing a remarkable *Collection of no less than 87 pastels by *Maurice-Quentin Delatour* (sometimes printed de La Tour) among other 18C French paintings, and more recent work, etc.

Among the portraits by *Delatour* are those of Jean d'Alembert; Marc-René Argenson; Camargo, the dancer; Crébillon *père*; Charles Pinot Duclos; Mme Favart; Mlle Marie Fel; Marie-Josèphe de Saxe; Charles Parrocel, the artist; the Marquise de Pompadour; Jean Restout, the artist; Jean-Jacques Rousseau; the Maréchal de Saxe; and a Self-portrait. Also a portrait of Delatour by *Perronneau*, and a bust of the artist by *Lemoyne*.

For the road hence to *Soissons* and *Troyes*, see Rte 103A.

The N44 leads S., at 21km forking l. to by-pass *La Fère*, an ancient fortress at the confluence of the Serre and Oise, with a small museum of Dutch and Flemish art. The road traverses the N.E. part of the *Forêt de St-Gobain*, in which (r.) are the remarkable late 14C buildings of the priory of *Le Tortoire*, to pass (l.) *Crépy* (where a treaty was signed in 1544 between François I and Charles V), just N.W. of which, on the N. slope of the *Mont de Joie*, was the site of the three 'Big Bertha' gun emplacements, which in 1918 fired upon Paris at a range of 132km (82 miles). At least one was silenced by French artillery.

We approach **Laon** (see Rte 105), preferably entered by bearing r. 4km prior to reaching its ridge, and turning l. through *Semilly*.

From just E. of Laon the road bear S.E. to (17km) *Corbeny*, 4km S.W. of which lies *Craonne*, site of Napoleon's victory over Blücher on 6-7 March, 1814, and virtually destroyed during the First World War.—At 9km we cross the Aisne at *Berry-au-Bac*, overlooked by *Côte 108*, and continue S.E. past (r.) *Cormicy*, once a fortress with ramparts, and skirting (r.) the *Massif de St-Thierry* and village of *St-Thierry*, with a restored porch of a 12C church, and 18C château.—18km. **Reims**; see Rte 106.

4 Calais to Paris via Boulogne, Abbeville, and Beauvais

278km (173 miles). N1. 34km **Boulogne**—38km *Montreuil*—44km **Abbeville**—42km *Poix*—44km **Beauvais**—76km **Paris**.

Maps: IGN 1, 3, 8, or 101, 103. M 236, 237

For **Calais**, see Rte 3.

The longer alternative coastal route (42km) may be followed by taking the D940 immediately W. of Calais, skirting the shore, shortly after passing a monument to Louis Blériot's first cross-Channel flight in 1909. (In the *Bois de Fiennes*, 13km due S. of Calais, an obelisk marks the spot where the balloonists J.P. Blanchard and Dr J. Jeffries descended in 1785, after crossing the Channel.)—9.5km. *Sangatte*, near which the S. end of the proposed Channel Tunnel may one day emerge.—4km. *Cap Blanc-Nez* (134m high), with an obelisk commemorating the Dover Patrol of the First World War, offers extensive views. To the S.W., beyond the resort of (7km) *Wissant*, stands the lower *Cap Gris-Nez*, the nearest point to England (29.5km N.W.), whose cliffs may be discerned with ease in clear weather. There are numerous relics of German block-houses and gun emplacements in the area.—11km. *Ambleteuse*, with a 17C fort, from which on 5 Jan. 1698 James II disembarked on his flight from England. The resort of *Wimereux*, with the ruined *Fort de Croy* (1803) is traversed prior to entering **Boulogne**; see below.

On quitting Calais, the N1 traverses open downland to the S.W. to (21km) *Marquise*, with a 12-16C church and extensive marble quarries.—8km. *Wimille*, where in the cemetery of the 12-13C church are buried Pilâtre de Rozier and M. Romain, whose 'Montgolfier' balloon took fire and fell here during another attempt to cross the Channel in 1785 (see above).—We shortly pass (r.) the marble *Colonne de la Grande-Armée* ◇ (1841; 53m), surmounted by a statue of Napoleon, a grandiose monument to the projected invasion of England, restored since damaged in 1944, beyond which the 'Haute Ville' of Boulogne is approached; see below.

BOULOGNE (or *Boulogne-sur-Mer*, to give it its correct title; 48,300 Boulonnais), an important fishing-port—mainly herrings—is also a busy terminus of cross-Channel ferries, being a main transit port for cars to and from England, the *Gare Maritime* and *Hover-port* lying to the W. of the estuary.

Roman *Gesoriacum* derives its name from *Bononia*, which was perhaps the Roman citadel. Hence in 43 A.D. the Romans crossed the Channel to commence their conquest of England. It was the capital of a line of counts until acquired by the astute Louis XI in 1478, who piously placed it under the suzerainty of the Virgin. It was nevertheless captured by Henry VIII in 1544, but sold back to France six years later. From 1801 the 'Camp de Boulogne' was the centre of Napoleon's preparations for the invasion of England, and the floating dock behind the Gare Maritime was originally excavated to hold the growing flotilla of flat-bottomed boats collected for this purpose, but the project was partially neutralised by the Battle of Trafalgar (21 Oct. 1805).

Later in the 18C century Boulogne became the resort of English duellists and a refuge of French debtors, and had a considerable English colony—as many as 5000 at one time—among them Col Newcome, who in his fallen fortunes, occupied quarters 'in a quiet grass-grown old street in the Old Town'. In June 1763 Smollett's books were seized here by the customs and sent to Amiens to be examined: 'a species of oppression which one would not expect to meet in France, which piques itself on its politeness and hospitality'. The poets Charles Churchill (1731–64) and Thomas Campbell (1777–1844) died here, the former on a visit to the exiled John Wilkes. Le Sage (1668–1747), author of 'Gil Blas', died at No. 3 Rue du Château, while Gen. San Martin, the 'liberator' of Argentina, also died at Boulogne, in 1850. Philip Thicknesse (1719–92), Louisa Stuart Costello (1799–1870), and Richard Martin (1754–1834), known as 'Humanity Martin', and founder of the RSPCA in 1824, are among those buried here.

The first troops of Sir John French's army disembarked here on 14 Aug. 1914, and although temporarily evacuated during the retreat from Mons, it was the main channel for drafts of British troops and reinforcements throughout the war. It was heavily bombed during 1917–18, and suffered likewise in the Second World War, when 85 per cent of the town was damaged.

Among natives were Godefroy de Bouillon (d. c. 1100) and his brother Baldwin (d. 1118), kings of Jerusalem; Frédéric Sauvage (1786–1857), who applied the principle of the screw to steamers; Charles-Augustin Sainte-Beuve (1804–69), the critic; and the two actors Coquelin. 'Jenny' Dacquin (1811–95; the 'Inconnue'), daughter of a local notary, corresponded regularly with

Mérimée from 1831–70. Manet painted there on several occasions during the 1860s.

On the E. bank of the Liane lies the *Basse-Ville*, with most of the hotels and shops, from which the Quai Gambetta leads N. past four blocks of buildings ranged in echelon to the Plage, above which stands the ruined *Tour d'Ordre*, for which a Roman origin is claimed, and relics of a brick fort built by the English in 1545.

From the *Pont de l'Entente-Cordiale*, the Rue de la Lampe and Grande Rue ascend past (r.) *St-Nicolas* (13-18C), and the *Museum*, its main collection being that of Greek pottery, which it is proposed will be moved to the Château. The **Haute Ville*, about 420m by 320m, is enclosed by *Ramparts*, still practically perfect, built in 1231 on Gallo-Roman foundations by Count Philippe Hurepel, reinforced in the 16-17C, and surrounded by gardens.

It was here, wrote Smollett in his usual splenetic vein, that the 'noblesse' lived, who starved in dark holes in order to have the wherewithal 'to purchase fine clothes and appear dressed once a day in the church, or on the ramparts. . . stimulated by the vanity of being seen'. Here also was a convent where English girls were sent for their education.

Entering by the *Porte des Dunes*, the *Pal. de Justice* (1852) is passed to approach the *Pl. Godefroy-de-Bouillon*, where streets from the four town gates converge, with the *Hôtel de Ville* (1754 and 1894), its belfry on a 13C base; to the S. is the 18C *Hôtel Desandrouins*.—A short distance N.E. stands the massively-domed and ill-proportioned basilica of *Notre-Dame*, erected in 1827-66 on the site of the 13-15C cathedral destroyed at the Revolution, the re-vamped Romanesque crypt of which may be visited. An object of veneration in the former church—until 1793, when it was burnt—was a wooden statue of the Virgin which miraculously entered the port in the 7C in a boat without a crew! Passing through the adjacent *Porte de Calais*, and turning r., we have a view of the exterior of the *Château*, in which Louis Napoleon was confined for several days after his attempted insurrection against Louis-Philippe in 1840.

The N42 leads 14km E. past (l.) *Le Wast*, with a Romanesque church, and 4km beyond, the huge 18C *Château de Colembert*.—From *La Chapelle*, 7km along this road, a pleasant detour may be made by diverging r. through the *Forêt de Boulogne* (see IGN 417) to *Crémarest*, there turning S. through *Questrecques* to regain the N1 at *Samer*; see below.

From the Haute Ville, the main road descends steeply to (5km) *Pont-de-Briques*, where the restored 18C château was an occasional residence of Napoleon in 1803-5.

PONT-DE-BRIQUES TO ABBEVILLE VIA ÉTAPLES (81km, without detours). After 5km a road leads W. off the D940 to *Hardelot-Plage*, with a sandy beach backed by high pine-clad dunes, and ruins of a castle probably built by Philippe Hurepel in 1231. The main road continues S., skirting the dunes and (r.) a War Cemetery (11,300 British graves) prior to entering (16.5km) **Étaples** (11,300 inhab.), on the estuary of the Canche, and probably the site of the important Gallo-Roman port of *Quentovic*. Until 1914 an ancient but sleepy fishing-village visited by artists for the sake of its picturesque harbour, early in the war it became an important British base and departure point for reinforcements, and the site of several base-hospitals. It was the birthplace of the humanist Jacques Lefèvre d'Étaples (1450– 1537).—**Montreuil** (see below) lies 13km further up the valley.

An airport on the far bank of the river serves the fashionable resort of **Le Touquet** (5400 inhab., rising to over 30,000 in summer) further W., encircled by thick pine-woods, above which two lighthouses are conspicuous, while among the trees (planted in 1855) are numerous bungalows and villas on the outskirts of the regularly built town, bounded by a promenade skirting the beach. It has most of the concomitant attractions of an expensive resort, including a golf-course, polo-ground, yacht basin, 'Centre Sportif', heated pools, etc.

The D940 continues past (13km) *Berck* and *Berck-Plage*, a watering-place notable for its hospitals and sanatoria devoted to diseases of the bones, beyond which the road bears S.E. and again S. to (19km) *Rue*, with a richly decorated Flamboyant *Chapelle du St-Esprit* (15-16C), part of a Gothic church demolished in 1826.

Hence one may regain the main route some 5km S.E., or continue S. to (8km) *Le Crotoy*, a small port on a promontory overlooking the Somme estuary. Joan of Arc was imprisoned by the English in its former castle, while Jules Verne lived from 1865–70 at No. 9 in the street which bears his name. The sandy expanse at the river mouth, although treacherous, is noted for its wildfowl.—*St-Valéry*, retaining fragments of its gates and ramparts, lies to the S., where in 1066 William the Conqueror, having set out from *Dives*, was forced to wait on his first attempt to gain the English coast, finally sailing hence on 27 Sept. of that year.—From Le Crotoy the road turns S.E., skirting the marshes, to by-pass (7km) *Noyelles-sur-Mer*, just E. of which a cemetery where are gathered 870 Chinese members of the British forces who died in an epidemic in 1918; note the pagoda. The Somme, to the S., here canalized, was crossed at the former ford of *Blanquetaque* (Blanche-tache) by Edward III's army prior to the battle of Crécy, which took place some 17km N.E.—13km. **Abbeville**; see below.

From Pont-de-Brique, the N1 bears S.E. past (10km) **Samer**, known for its strawberries, with a cobbled triangular *Place* containing several 18C houses, and a 15C church.—2km to the N.E. lies *Wierre-au-Bois*, where Sainte-Beuve spent much of his youth, and where his parents are buried.—Turning S. we approach (23km) *Montreuil*, with a good view of its brick ramparts as we descend into the valley of the Canche.

Montreuil, situated on the N. slope of a plateau overlooking the river, derives its name from a small monastery founded in the 7C by St Saulve, Bp of Amiens. The town once stood nearer the sea, as its earlier name, Montreuil-sur-Mer emphasised, and was later a staging post on the road from Calais to Paris, as described in Sterne's 'Sentimental Journey'. In 'Tristram Shandy' Sterne suggested that the handsomest thing about the place was the inn-keeper's daughter!

The former abbey-church of *St-Saulve*, with an admirably sculptured porch, possesses a well-vaulted nave of the 12-13th and 16Cs, sustained by octagonal columns with interesting capitals. To the N. is the *Hôtel-Dieu* (restored 1860), which since its foundation in 1200 has been managed by Augustinian nuns; its Flamboyant *Chapel* retains Renaissance panelling. The *Ramparts*, converted into a tree-lined promenade, afford extensive views. At their N.W. extremity is the *Citadel*, rebuilt in the 17C around the ruins of a 13C Castle. From March 1916 to April 1919 the British G.H.Q. enjoyed what has been styled a 'remote centrality' at Montreuil, the commander-in-chief occupying the *Château de Beaurepaire*, c. 5km S.E.

On the N. bank of the Canche, at *Neuville*, is a Carthusian monastery reconstructed in 1872, while at *Montcavrel*, 6km N.E., is a naveless Flamboyant church of interest.

The N39 leads S.E. along the l. bank of the river to (24km) *Hesdin* (see Rte 3), off which at (5km) *Brimeux*, the D129 leads 9.5km N.E. to *Humbert*, where the church contains oak statues of angels (13C); while at *Beaurainville*, 5km beyond Brimeux, stands a ruined *Tower* in which Harold of England, after being wrecked on the coast in 1064, was imprisoned by Guy of Ponthieu, until released on the intercession of William the Conqueror.

The N1 leads S. to (13km) *Nampont,* there crossing the marshes of
the Authie, where a moated 15-16C château, may be seen among the
trees. Here occurred the episode of the dead ass in Sterne's 'Sentimental Journey'.

NAMPONT TO ABBEVILLE VIA CRÉCY (c. 40km). While a slightly shorter
detour may be made by driving direct to Crécy on the D27, it is recommended
that one follows the minor D192 along the S. bank of the Authie past (6km) the
*Abbeye de Valloires, founded in the 12C but largely rebuilt in 1756 following a
series of fires. It is now a remand home, but may be visited; the church contains
baroque decoration by Pfaffenhoffen, and two 13C tombs.—We traverse the
village of *Argoules,* and continue along the valley to (9km) *Dompierre,* with a
14C church; to the N. lie the ruins of the 12C abbey of *Donmartin.*—Turning S.
through *Wadicourt,* the base of the so-called *'Moulin Édouard III'* is passed (l.),
whence the English king watched the progress of the **Battle of Crécy** (named
after the village of *Crécy-en-Ponthieu* immediately to the S.W.), where on 26
Aug. 1346 Edward III, with 20,000 men, defeated the French army of Philippe VI,
three times as numerous, for undisciplined and badly led, their repeated attacks
withered before the ravaging fire of the English archers. Edward the Black
Prince won his spurs in the contest, but the story that he adopted the 'Prince of
Wales's feathers' and the motto 'ich dien' from the badge of the blind King John
of Bohemia, who fell in the mêlée, is without historical foundation. According to
Southey, who visited the site in 1838, 'all English who travelled in this part of the
country made a point of going to Cressy'.—The road continues S.W. through the
Forêt de Crécy, intersected by numerous glades, before rejoining the N1 some
7km N. of *Abbeville.*

9km. *Rue,* see above, lies 5km W., beyond the *Château d'Arry*
(c. 1760).

The N1 skirts the W. limits of the *Forêt de Crécy,* and after 21km
enters the brick-built suburbs of *Abbeville.*

Those wishing to drive direct to *Amiens,* by-passing Abbeville, may fork l. onto
the D32 at *Nouvion* (13km before Abbeville) for (16km) *St-Riquier* (see Rte 3) to
meet the N1 at *Ailly-le-Haut-Clocher;* see Rte 5.

ABBEVILLE (26,000 Abbevillois), an historic town now largely
devoted to the manufacture of textiles, lies mainly on the r. bank of
the Somme. Its old centre, 'disagreeably built. . . with a greater air of
antiquity than I remember to have seen', which in Young's view
would have 'long ago been demolished' if in England, was in fact
practically destroyed by German bombs in 1940, and although
restored, is of slight interest.

Originally an abbey farm (*Abbatis Villa*), fortified by the 10C, it was the site of a
treaty in 1259, whereby Henry III ceded Normandy to France. As the ancient
capital of Ponthieu, it passed into English hands at the marriage of Eleanor of
Castile to Edward I in 1272, and remained so until 1477, apart from a brief inter-
val under the dukes of Burgundy. In 1527 François I and Card. Wolsey here signed an offensive and defensive agreement against the Emperor Charles V. During
the greater part of the First World War Abbeville was the H.Q. of the British
lines of communication, and suffered from air raids in 1918.

Philippe Hecquet (1661–1737), who served as Le Sage's model for 'Doctor
Sangrado' in 'Gil Blas', was a native of Abbeville, while the archaeologist Jacques Boucher de Perthes (1788–1868) long resided here. It was also the home of
numerous distinguished engravers, among them Claude Mellan (1598–1688),
François de Poilly (1623–93), Jean Daullé (1703–63), Jacques Aliamet
(1726–88), Jacques Beauvarlet (1732–97), Jean-Charles Le Vasseur
(1734–1816), François Dequevauviller (1745–1807), and Émile Rousseau
(1831–74). Both Bonington (in 1823) and Ruskin painted at Abbeville.

Just W. of the central *Pl. de l'Hôtel-de-Ville* stands restored **St-
Vulfran,** a late-Gothic buiding commenced in 1488, interrupted in

1539, and left unfinished, the central portal of the Flamboyant N. front of which contains a lion rampart with the royal arms, symbolizing the union of England and France by the marriage in this church of Mary Tudor and Louis XII (1514; who died three months later). The doors are carved in the Renaissance style. The first statue on the l. of the r.-hand portal is a good figure of Charity. The twin towers, with the watch-turrets, and the slightly leaning *Tour St-Firmin*, flanking the N.E. transept, are notable.

N. of the Place is the *Musée Boucher-de-Perthes* (Rue du Beffroi), with portraits by Largillière, et al. and some 3000 engravings (see above), apart from archaeological and natural history sections of interest.—Further N.E. is *St-Sépulchre* (15C), containing an impressive Entombment, while to the S.E. is *St-Gilles* (1485; restored), beyond which, on leaving the town, we pass (l.) the brick and stone *Château de Bagatelle* (18C), preserving good *boiseries*.

For roads hence to **Amiens**, **Rouen**, and **Le Havre**, see Rtes 5, 6, and 7, respectively.

On quitting Abbeville, the D901 traverses (9km) *Pont-Rémy*, with a 15C château remodelled in 1837 in the 'Troubador' style, before climbing the S. slope of the Somme Valley, passing (r.) the *Oppidum des Catélis*. The village of *Bailleul*, 4km S.W., was the original home of the Bailliol family, which gave two kings to Scotland, and its name to an Oxford college.

10km. *Airaines*, a village ravaged in 1940, preserves two churches of interest (12-15C) and the ruins of two castles, in the vicinity of which are remains of Roman entrenchments.—At 4km we pass (r.) the château of *Tailly* (early 18C), which was owned by Marshal Leclerc de Hautecloque (1902–47).—18km. *Poix-de-Picardie*, an ancient village with a 16C hill-top church, 2km S.W. of which, at *Blangy-sous-Poix*, is a 12C church with an octagonal belfry.

25km. *Marseille-en-Beauvaisis*.

Some 11km S.W. stands the attractive hill-top village of * **Gerberoy**, which deserves the detour. Repopulated by an artistic colony headed by Henri le Sidaner (1862–1939), it was once an important fortress on the frontier of the Duchy of Normandy and the kingdom of France, and here in 1079 William the Conqueror was wounded in a skirmish with his son Robert. It was the birthplace of the composer Eustache du Caurroy (1549–1609). The former collegiate church contains good stalls and statues.

Hence one may return 2km to follow the D133 S.E. to (21km) *Beauvais*, which is 19km from Marseille on the D901.

For *Beauvais*, and the road hence to **Paris**, see—in detail, but in the reverse direction—*Blue Guide Paris and Environs*. The main points of interest are given below. For the road from Rouen to *Soissons* via Beauvais, see Rte 9.

BEAUVAIS (54,100 inhab.), préfecture of the *Oise*, has been largely rebuilt since indiscriminate incendiary bombing by the Germans in 1940. Its centre is dominated by the * **Cathedral of St-Pierre**, which, had it been completed, would have been the largest Gothic church in the world; its choir and transepts, forming one of the most ambitious masterpieces of medieval architecture, were in construction between 1227 and 1578. Notable are the facades of the transepts, and the lofty *Choir*, containing good 16C glass, while 13C glass can be seen in some ambulatory chapels.—Adjacent is the *Galerie Nationale de la Tapisserie*, ◊ devoted to a display of *Beauvais tapestry* (made

on a horizontal or 'low' warp, unlike *Gobelins*, which is made on a
vertical or 'high' warp and is woven from the reverse side).—To the
W. is the *Museum*, containing a good collection of Gothic sculpture,
etc.—A few minutes' walk to the S. brings one to ***St-Étienne***
(12-16C), with a W. tower of 1598. The contrast between the
Romanesque nave and late Gothic choir is striking, while a rose-
window representing the Wheel of Fortune, and a Tree of Jesus window, are both remarkable.

Driving S.E. on the N1, after 4km we pass (r.) the 13-16C church of
Allonne, and after 28km fork r. to cross (6km) the Oise 3km N.E. of
L'Isle-Adam. The road skirts the *Forêt de L'Isle-Adam*. At 15km
Écouen lies 4km to the S.E. (see Rte 15), while some 4km W. after
5km lies hill-top *Montmorency*, with its associations with Rousseau.

The road traverses several *banlieus* or suburbs after c. 6km veering E. of **St-Denis** (see Rte 14) to meet the A1 motorway, which we
follow to (4km) the *Porte de la Chapelle* and the Blvd Périphérique
6km due N. of *Notre-Dame*. See Rtes 10-12, or *Blue Guide Paris and
Environs*.

5   Abbeville to Amiens and Reims

203km (126 miles). N1. 47km **Amiens**—D934. 43km *Roye*—20km
Noyon—14km. *Blérancourt*—D6. 23km **Soissons**—N31. 56km **Reims**.

Maps: IGN 3, 4, 9, or 101. M 236, 237.

For **Abbeville**, see Rte 4.

An alternative to the N1 is the D218, turning l. off the D901 11km S.E. of Abbeville through *Liercourt*, with a Flamboyant church, and following the S. bank
of the Somme.—6.5m. At *Long*, on the far bank, beyond numerous ponds covering the valley floor, is a Louis-XV château.—9km. *Hangest*, with a 12-16C church
containing furniture from the partially restored *Abbaye du Gard* (founded
1137), is shortly passed (l.) prior to traversing (7.5km) *Picquigny*, situated below
the ruins of its castle. Here, in 1475, a peace was signed between Edward IV
and Louis XI, the mistrustful monarchs (according to Comines) exchanging hand-
clasps through a palisade erected on the bridge.—13km. *Amiens*; see below.

The N1 traverses (12.5km) *Ailly-le-Haut-Clocher*, with a largely 13C
church, and (9.5km) *Flixecourt*, 5km beyond which it bears l. past the
prehistoric site of *Belloy-sur-Somme*, and later (r.) the ancient *Camp
de Tirancourt*, known as 'Caesar's Camp', to reach the centre of
Amiens after 20km.

AMIENS (136,400 Amiénois; 52,100 in 1851; 90,800 in 1901),
préfecture of the *Somme*, is a busy industrial and textile centre on
the S. bank of the canalised Somme. Much of the old brick-built
town, replete with its historical associations, and encircled on three
sides by boulevards marking the site of earlier ramparts, was
destroyed during 1940–44.

Ancient *Samarobriva*, chief town of the *Ambiani*, a Belgic tribe converted by St
Firmin the Martyr in the 4C, later became the capital of Picardy, its government
being shared by its counts and bishops. From 1435–77 it belonged to the Duke
of Burgundy, and later fell into Spanish hands, but was twice recaptured by
Henri IV (in 1594 and 1597), who on the latter occasion was assisted by 4000
English troops under Sir Arthur Savage. The 'Mise of Amiens' was a decision
given in 1264 by Louis IX as arbiter in a dispute between Henry III and his
English barons headed by De Montfort, which failed to bring peace. Edward III
did homage here for Guyenne in 1329, and in 1550 a peace treaty was signed

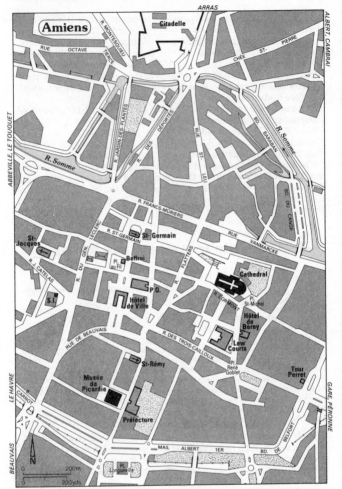

here between Edward VI and Henri II. A more famous treaty concluded in 1802
between France and Britain, Spain, and Holland, marked a brief pause in the
Napoleonic Wars. Its population was then 40,300.

It was entered by the Germans (under Manteuffel) in 1870; they again occupied the city for twelve days in 1914, until driven back to a line some 30km E.,
where the front was stabilised. It was then a vital link in allied communications,
which made it the target for a sudden thrust by the Germans converging from St-
Quentin and Cambrai in March 1918, which was only halted at *Villers-
Bretonneux*, 16km E.; see pp 100 and 111. Civilians were evacuated, and Amiens
was subjected to a destructive artillery bombardment. Some 400 of these guns
and 13,000 prisoners were taken when the town was disengaged by the counter-
attack of 2-10 August.

Among natives were Peter the Hermit (d. 1115); Vincent Voiture
(1598–1648), a habitué of the Hôtel de Rambouillet; the polymath Du Cange
(1610–88); the poet and dramatist J.-B.-L. Gresset (1709–77); Pierre Choderlos
de Laclos (1741–1803), author of 'Les Liaisons dangereuses' (1782); J.-B. de

Lamarck (1744–1829), the naturalist; J.-B.-J. Delambre (1749–1815), the astronomer; Édouard Branlay (1844–1940), the physicist; the sculptor Nicolas Blasset (1600–59); and the cabinet-maker Charles Cressent (1685–1768). Jules Verne (1828–1905) spent most of his life in Amiens, where he died.

Specialities are its 'pâtés de canard', 'macarons', and 'sucre d'orge'.

What remains of the old town is dominated by the *Cathedral of Notre-Dame, which exhibits, earlier than any other building in N. France, the tendency towards the Flamboyant.

The present church, the largest in France *in area*, erected on the site of a Romanesque cathedral destroyed by fire in 1218, and was begun two years later for Bp Evrard De Fouilloy by Robert de Luzarches, and the nave and W. front were completed before 1238. Thomas and Regnault de Cormont continued the work at intervals during the 13C. The chapels of the nave date from 1292–1376; the upper parts of the towers and the W. front from the 15C; and the spire (112m high) from 1529. The whole was 'restored' in the 1850s under the supervision of Viollet-le-Duc. Protected by sandbags during the First World War, the exterior carvings escaped serious damage, although the edifice was struck by nine shells.

Exterior. The *W. Facade, with its deeply recessed portals, presents an imposing array of sculpture, and—despite its grimy condition—deserves close inspection (cf. Ruskin's 'Bible of Amiens'). It is flanked by two towers, unequal in height, dating respectively from c. 1366 (S.; 62m) and (N.; 67m) from the early 15C. Above the gallery over the portals are statues representing the Kings of Judah, and then a rose-window, the delicate tracery of which, like the upper part of the facade, dates from the 14-15C. The central portal contains on its central pier a 13C statue of Christ, while in the pediment is a relief of the Last Judgement; the 150 statues in the vaulting represent the celestial hierarchy; a figure of St Michael surmounts the gable. The Virgin trampling a monster appears in the r.-hand porch; the pediment depicts her Entombment and Assumption. The *Porche de St Firmin*, dedicated to that martyr, who is represented on the central pier with a figure of Idolatry beneath his feet, has a pediment depicting the discovery and translation of his relics.

S. Facade. The colossal statue of St Christopher will be noted, while between the windows of the 14C chapels are two rows of statues; more—somewhat stereotyped — statues embellish the N. Facade, while the *Lady Chapel*, in the centre of the seven radiating chapels of the apse, is decorated with ugly 19C seated statues.

Interior. Its simplicity is enhanced by its great height (42m) in proportion to its width, its dimensions being 143m long and 65m wide across the transepts. The arches between its 126 pillars rise to almost half the total height, above which a richly foliated string-course runs round the entire church below the triforium, above which again is a clerestory of unusual height. The rose-windows, with their elaborate tracery, offer a rich display of glass, but only a proportion of it dates from the 15-16Cs.

Nave. The oak organ-loft (1422) was unfortunately redecorated in 1836; the organ itself dates from 1425. In the 3rd bay are two remarkable tombs with bronze effigies, of Bp Evrard de Fouilly (1222; r.) and Bp Geoffroi d'Eu (1236). The 18C pulpit is by Dupuis of Amiens, also responsible—together with Blasset, and others—for the statues and decoration of the aisle chapels. At the W. end of the S. aisle is a monument to Antoine Niquet (d. 1652).

The *Transepts* have groined vaulting of c. 1270, the earliest in France, and good rose windows. In the S. Transept are marble reliefs illustrating the Life of the Virgin, above which are four depicting the Life of St James the Great in elaborate early 16C frames.—In the N. transept, opposite the 12C font, is a relic said to be the head of the Baptist, brought from Constantinople in 1206 and enshrined in a repellent 19C reliquary.

The *Choir*, on a higher level, with 18C wrought-iron railings, contains 110*Stalls, carved in 1508–19 under the direction of Ernoul Boulin, Alexandre Huet, and Antoine Avernier, present 3650 figures in 400 scenes from the Old Testament, the Life of the Virgin, trades and crafts, etc.

The *Ambulatory*. The choir-screen (1489–1530) is richly decorated with arcading and restored stone reliefs, painted and gilt, depicting (S. side) the legends of St Firmin and St Saulve, and N., the history of the Baptist. Opposite the Lady Chapel is a monument to Canon Lucas, founder of the orphanage of Les Enfants Bleus, with an 'enfant pleureur', one of Blasset's better works (1628).

The *Pl. Notre-Dame* provides a view N. over the narrow streets of the quarter of St.-Leu, divided by canals and streams entering the Somme, while further E. are the low-lying *Hortillonnages*, a curious area of market-gardens and orchards irrigated by a network of canals, much of it only accessible by boat.

From the cathedral apse one may follow the Rue Victor-Hugo to No. 34 (l.), the *Hôtel des Berny* or *des Trésoriers de France* (1634), with a small regional museum; opposite is the *Pal. de Justice* (1874), on the site of the abbey of St-Martin-aux-Jumeaux, which itself replaced a chapel said to mark the spot where St Martin divided his cloak with a beggar.—To the W. beyond gardens, stands the 15C brick and stone *Logis du Roi*, and the *Maison du Sagittaire*, the Renaissance facade of which has been re-erected here.—A passage leads S. to the Rue des Trois-Cailloux, a main thoroughfare, with the facade only remaining of the *Théâtre* (1780).

To the E. is the railway station, with the adjacent *Tour Perret*, an ugly 26-storey concrete construction by Auguste Perret (1874–1954; cf. Le Havre).

Turning W. on reaching the Rue des Trois-Cailloux, we shortly reach the central *Pl. Gambetta*, from which the Rue de la République leads S. past (r.) *St-Rémi* (containing sculpture by Blasset), behind which are relics of the cloister of the Convent of the Cordeliers, to reach the **Musée de Picardie**, installed in a pompous pillared edifice of 1869.

The Ground Floor is devoted to archaeological collections, including a square 12C font; a miscellaneous range of medieval sculpture and furniture, among them some good alabaster figures, and the tomb-statue of Robert de Bouberch (15C).—The staircase, decorated the canvases by *Puvis de Chavannes*, ascends to a series of rooms housing the extensive art collections, remarkable among which are examples of the work of the *Amiens School* (c. 1525), including a jousting scene and the Balance of Justice.

These were formerly in the possession of the Confrérie du Puy Notre-Dame, an ancient society which enlisted the aid of literature and painting in the glorification of the Virgin, and which, from 1452 until the 17C, was presented by the Maitre of the Confrérie with a painting representing the theme of the verse or 'palinod' propounded by him for that year. The majority of examples in this curious collection, which hung in the cathedral, were destroyed by the canons; their frames should be noted.

Among later works are Seascapes by *Van Goyen*; *Frans Pourbus the younger*, The Five Senses; *Salvator Rosa* (?), Landscape; *anon. Flemish* Deposition (late 15C); *Aart de Gelder*, Esther's Repast; *Frans Hals*, Pasteur Langelins; *El Greco*, Male portrait (with an unusually fat face); *Maurice Quentin Delatour*, pastel Self-Portrait; *Chardin*, four Still-lifes; Landscapes with ruins by *Panini*, and *Hubert Robert*; also Pierrots by the latter; *Longhi*, Venetian senator; representative works by *Guardi*, and *G.-B. Tiepolo*. A room is devoted to nine Hunting scenes, similarly framed, by *Boucher, Parrocel, Van Loo, Lancret, De Troy*, and *Pater*, which were originally painted for the Gal. des Petits Appartements du Roi at Versailles. Among 19C works are *Isabey*, Mont St-Michel; *Jongkind*, View of Harfleur; a Portrait by *Winterhalter*; and Revolutionary scene, by *Delacroix*.

Opposite the museum stands the *Préfecture*, in the buildings of the *Intendance* (1761); while adjacent is the *Library*, containing c. 1200 MSS of the 9-16Cs, and 300 incunables.

Just W. of the Pl. Gambetta is the *Hôtel de Ville* (1600; with a facade of 1760), altered in the 19C, in which the Treaty of Amiens was signed in 1802. Behind it (l.) is the 15C *Bailliage*, with dormer windows and Renaissance details; and further N., the 14C *Beffroi*, a square tower with a round upper storey added in 1746. Beyond stands *St-Germain*, an elegant 15C building, restored.

From the *Pl. Léon-Gontier*, to the W. of the Hôtel de Ville, the Rue Jean-Catelas leads some distance N.W. towards the Blvd Faidherbe and the *Promenade de la Hôtoire*, a public park with a lake and zoo.

For roads from Amiens to *Neufchâtel-en-Bray*, for **Rouen**; see Rte 8A.

AMIENS TO BEAUVAIS (60km). The N1 leads S. to (32km) *Breteuil*, with remains of an abbey retaining its 12-13C church. The Gallic capital of *Bratuspantium*, mentioned by Caesar, may have been sited a short distance to the S., near *Vendeuil-Caply.*—At *Folleville*, 9km N.E., is a ruined 15C château and a church containing the splendid **Tomb* of Raoul de Lannoy (d. 1513) and his wife, by Antonio della Porte and Pace Gaggini.—The D916 leads S.E. to (33km) *Clermont* (see Rte 15, and *Blue Guide Paris and Environs*), and **Senlis**, 26km beyond; see also Rte 16.—The N1 continues S.W. from Breteuil to (21.5km) *Guignecourt* (r.), with an 11-16C church, and **Beauvais**, 6.5km beyond; see Rte 4, and *Blue Guide Paris and Environs.*—Beauvais may also be approached from Amiens by the D210, which at 19km passes 2.5km E. of *Conty*, with an interesting 15-16C Flamboyant church, with good sculpture in the interior, some by François Cressent, father of the great cabinet-maker.

AMIENS TO COMPIÈGNE (71km). The D935 forks r. off the N29 some 6km S.E. of Amiens, following the valley of the Avre past (r. at 3km) *Boves*, with a ruined 12C castle, to (27km) **Montdidier** (6300 Montdidériens), said to derive its name from the Lombard king Didier, imprisoned here in 775 by Charlemagne. Ravaged during the battles of 1918, when its two interesting old churches were almost entirely destroyed, it was the birthplace of Antoine-Augustin Parmentier (1737 – 1813), who introduced the potato into France.—*Cantigny*, 6km W., was recaptured by American forces on 28 May, 1918, their first intervention on the active front; while *Méry-la Bataille*, c. 14km S.E., was the scene of Mangin's defensive victory in that June.—At *Maignelay-Montigny*, 14km S.W. of Montdidier, is a fine Gothic church with bold and original vaulting, finished in 1516 by the elder Vast, an architect of Beauvais cathedral.—The churches of **St-Martin-aux-Bois* (13C), and *Ravenel*, with a Renaissance tower, c. 5km S.E., and S.W. respectively of Maignelay, are also of interest.—The D935 continues S.E. from Montdidier to meet the N17 (see Rte 2) at (16km) *Cuvilly*, where we turn r., and after 2.5km fork l.—Shortly crossing the A1 motorway, **Compiègne** is entered after 16.5km; see Rte 16, and *Blue Guide Paris and Environs*.

AMIENS TO ST-QUENTIN (74km) The N29 leads S.E., after 6km bearing l. to (11km) *Villers-Bretonneux*, where a French defeat in Nov. 1870 enabled the Prussians to enter Amiens. On 23 April 1918 it was attacked by four German divisions and 15 tanks; the British front was broken, and the town briefly seized, but in the tank battle which ensued the German tanks were driven back, and the place was recovered, thwarting the attempted advance on Amiens. On 8 Aug. 1918 Gen. Rawlinson's 4th Army, including the Canadian, Australian, and 3rd Corps, supported by cavalry, low-flying aircraft, and some 400 tanks, in conjunction with the French 1st Army on the r., overran the plateau E. of the town, in the first day capturing over 13,000 prisoners and 400 guns. This **Battle of Amiens** convinced Ludendorff that victory was impossible, and on the 14 Aug. he advised his government to seek for peace. The *Australian National War Memorial* lies to the r. of the road leading N. to (4.5km) **Corbie** at the confluence of the Ancre with the Somme, here flowing through a marshy valley. Both *St-Pierre* (1502 – 1740), and *St-Étienne* (11-13C) are relics of an influential Benedictine abbey founded in 657. *N.-D. de l'Assomption* (15-16C) in *Le Neuville*, on the r. bank of the Ancre, preserves a remarkable sculptured portal, the tympanum of which depicts the Entry into Jerusalem.—At 23km we cross the A1 motorway, and 4km beyond, a turning to *Péronne*, 7km N.E.; see Rte 2.—19km. *Vermand*, on a spur overlooking the Omignon, is believed to have been the capital of the Veromandui, and possessed an abbey founded c. 1100, between which and (11km) **St-Quentin** (see Rte 3) the now obliterated *Hindenburg Line* is crossed.

From Amiens the D934 leads due S.E. to meet the A1 motorway after 40km, and traverses *Roye* (see Rte 2) 2km beyond.

20km. **NOYON** (14,200 Noyonnais), an historic cathedral town, was severely damaged in both World Wars, but its beautiful Transitional cathedral has been well restored and deserves inspection.

Ancient *Noviomagus* was the seat of the bishops of the Vermandois, and among its early bishops were St Médard (531) and St Eloi (640–59). Chilperic was buried here in 721, and Charlemagne was here crowned king of Neustria (768), while Hughes Capet was elected king of the Franks here in 987. The Germans entered Noyon on 1 Sept. 1914, and until 1917 it remained the nearest occupied town to Paris, 100km S.W., Clemenceau reminded his countrymen in a much-quoted phrase that 'Messieurs les Allemands sont encore à Noyon'. The bombardments it suffered in March 1917 and Aug. 1918 laid it in ruins. Violent fighting took place in its streets in June 1940, and prior to its liberation by American troops on 1 Sept. 1944, it was again bombarded. It was the birthplace of Jean Calvin (1509–64), and the sculptor Jacques Sarrazin (1592–1660).

The **Cathedral of Notre-Dame*, the fifth church on this site, was commenced c. 1150, and virtually completed by 1220, although lateral chapels were later added, one of which contains good carved panelling, and another, fine vaulting. The narthex contains a porch mutilated in 1793. The transepts end in absides. The high altar, with its gilt cherubs, is by Godot (1757). A number of dependencies are preserved, including one arm of the cloister, and the *Chapter Library*.

In a square to the S.W. is a reconstructed house on the site of Calvin's birthplace, with a small museum devoted to the reformer; to the S.E. is the rebuilt *Hôtel de Ville* of 1485–1523.

Hence we continue to follow the D934 S.E. through (9.5km) *Cuts*, birthplace of the humanist Pierre Ramus (1515–72), to (4.5km) **Blérancourt**, where two pavilions survive of a *Château* built by Louis XIII by Salomon de Brosse, which since 1929 has housed a *Museum of Franco-American Co-operation*, based on the collections of Miss Anne Morgan.

BLÉRANCOURT TO LAON VIA COUCY-LE-CHÂTEAU (c. 45km). This attractive alternative route follows the D934 E. to (15km) **Coucy-le-Château**, best approached from the S. after circling beneath its ramparts. The ridge-top village was named after its famous 13C **Castle* ◊ bought c. 1400 by Louis d'Orléans, dismantled by Mazarin in 1652, and wantonly blown up by the Germans in 1918. Its chief feature was a huge cylindrical *Keep*, 65m high and some 31m in diameter.—*Folembray*, 3km N.W., gave its name to a treaty between Henri IV and the Duc de Mayenne, which in 1596 put an end to the Catholic League.—**Soissons** lies 17km due S.—From the village of Coucy we continue E., traversing a high-lying plateau covered by the *Forêt de St-Gobain*, one of the principal defensive bastions of the German front, not abandoned until Oct. 1918.—A l.-hand fork leads to (11km) *St-Gobain* itself, celebrated for its royal mirror factory established in 1685/92 at the instance of Colbert.—By forking r. off this road after 5km, one may turn r. at crossroads 3km beyond, and descend to view at 2km the imposing 18C buildings of the former abbey of *Prémontré*, the mother house of the Premonstratensian order, founded in 1120, now accommodating a psychiatric establishment.—Returning to the crossroads and turning r., in 4km we reach the D7, and turn r., after 2km passing near (l.) the ruins of the 11C abbey of *St-Nicolas-aux-Bois*. The D7 continues E. to meet at 11.5km the N44 just W. of **Laon**, where we turn r. and then l. through *Semilly* to reach the upper town; see Rte 105; *Reims* lies c. 47km S.E., see Rte 3.

From Blérancourt we turn S.E. onto the D6 for (23km) **Soissons**; see Rte 17 or *Blue Guide Paris and Environs*.

From Soissons the N31 is followed to the E., above the bank of the

Map p 74 BATTLE OF THE BRESLE **113**

sluggish river Aisne before bearing r. up the Vesle valley, where the
Americans saw action in July-Sept. 1918, to (18km) *Braine.*

During the **Battle of the Aisne** (13-14 Sept. 1914) the British front extended
28km to the E., from the outskirts of Soissons to *Bourg-et-Comin*, 12.5 km N.E. of
Braine, but the planned advance was checked on the S. slopes of the ridge N. of
the river, along which runs the *Chemin des Dames*; see Rte 105. Haig's 1st Corps,
on the r., distinguished itself in the fighting, but an attempt to carry the German
positions by assault on the 18 Sept. was abandoned, and early in Oct. the British,
relieved by French reserves, proceeded to the Flanders front.

Braine preserves the much damaged and restored abbey-church of
St-Yved, built for the Premonstratensians in 1180–1216, and
modelled on the cathedral of Laon.—2km. S. are the ruins of the 13C
Château de la Folie.

8km. *Bazoches* (r.) with relics of a 13-16C castle, and *Fismes*, 4km
beyond, are traversed. The latter, of Roman origin, has a largely
reconstructed 12C church, seriously damaged both in 1914 and
1940.—27km. **Reims**; Rte 106.

6   Abbeville to Rouen

99 km (61 miles). N28. 25km *Blangy*—29km. *Neufchâtel-en-Bray*
—45km **Rouen**.

Maps: IGN 3, 7 or 8, or 101, 103. M 236, 237 or 231.

Quitting **Abbeville** (see Rte 4), after 10km the road by-passes (l.)
Huppy, with a 16C church and 17C château, in which Col Charles de
Gaulle established his provisional H.Q. on 29 May 1940, being pro-
moted général three days later.

4km. *St-Maxent*, with an ancient *Mill*, restored, is traversed, 6km
beyond which a l.-hand turning leads 3km to *Rambures*, with an imposing brick-built castle (15C).—The main road shortly descends
steeply into the valley of the Bresle at (2.5km) *Blangy-sur-Bresle*,
rebuilt since its destruction in 1940.

Aumale, see Rte 8A, lies 23km S.E., reached by ascending either
bank of the charming valley of the Bresle.

BLANGY TO EU (20km). We may descend the valley on either side of the Bresle,
which here forms the border between Picardy and Normandy.—*Gamaches*, 8km
N.W. on the r. bank, has an interesting 12-15C church, beyond which are slight
remains of the abbey of *Lieu-Dieu*, founded by the Cistercians in the 12C. 12km.
Eu, see Rte 7.

The **Battle of the Bresle**. This river line was, in accordance with Gén.
Weygand's orders, to be held at all costs, and the British 51st and the French 31st
Divisions remained here from 6-9 June 1940, but by the 9th the Germans had
reached the Seine at Rouen, and retreat to the S. was cut off. By the
10th—withdrawal across the Seine having been sanctioned too late—two
brigades were sent to Le Havre to embark for England, the main force retreating
W. to hold the line of the Arques and the Béthune flowing towards Dieppe. But
meanwhile the Germans had reached the coast near Veulettes, leaving little
alternative but to withdraw to the area round St-Valéry-en-Caux and Veules.
Many village cemeteries between the Bresle and the coast contain little groups
of graves of those who fell in the retreat.

From Blangy, the N28 continues S.W., traversing part of the *Haute
Forêt d'Eu*, after 26km descending to (3km) *Neufchâtel-en-Bray*, a
small agricultural town noted for its cheese ('bondon'), and named
from a former castle built in 1106 by Henry I. In 1940 the Germans

destroyed much of the town, including the former Benedictine abbey buildings. *Notre-Dame* (12-16C; restored), with a large unfinished tower, contains an Entombment of 1491.—5.5km N.W. stands the imposing Renaissance château of *Mesnières-en-Bray*.

Continuing S.W., after 9km we bear l. away from the extensive *Forêt d'Eawy*, and in 32km reach the N.E. suburbs of Rouen, there commencing the descent into the Seine valley, following the Rue Louis-Ricard past *St-Ouen* to reach (4km) the quays.

ROUEN (105,100 Rouennais; already 100,300 in 1851), the ancient capital of the duchy of Normandy, and the préfecture of the department of *Seine-Maritime*, lies mainly on the N. bank of the river, partly encircled by hills, while suburbs fan out on the opposite bank. In spite of appalling damage caused in the Second World War, it is one of the most interesting of French cities, even if young Ruskin's estimation of it as being '*the* place of North Europe as Venice is of the South' is an exaggeration. Only a few decades earlier Young had condemned it as a 'great ugly, stinking, close, and ill-built town which is full of nothing but dirt and industry'. Its churches and museums, its few quaint streets and old houses, some hundreds of which have been the object of tasteful restoration, add to its present interest and charm, while it is also noted for its duck paté and sugar candy made with apples.

Roman *Rotomagus* was the capital of the Celtic Veliocassi; its first bishop was St Mellon (c. 260), a Welshman. Sacked in 841 by Scandinavian pirates under Ogier the Dane, it became in 912 the capital of the duchy of Normandy, established by Rollo, an ancestor of William the Conqueror, the latter dying here in 1087. In 1189 and 1199 respectively Richard I and his brother John were crowned dukes of Normandy in the cathedral. John, the last duke (who had his nephew Prince Arthur murdered in the castle here), was expelled by Philippe Auguste, who entered the town unopposed. Captured by Henry V in 1419 after a long siege, it remained in English possession until 1449, during which period Joan of Arc was condemned as a heretic by a court of French ecclesiastics and burnt at the stake (1431), Bp Cauchon, her accuser and judge, and Richard, Earl of Warwick, president of the court which tried her (and later Lieutenant-Governor of Normandy), died here in 1442 and 1439 respectively. In the Religious wars of the 16C the town was ravaged in turn by Huguenots and Catholics. Charles II stayed here on his journey from Fécamp to Paris. Southey, who visited it in 1838, complained of its unsavoury alleys, where 'all variety of unclean smells are blended', even if 'The Cathedral and the other Churches which rival it in beauty... [were] magnificent objects'. Its population in 1831 was 88,000.

It was occupied by the Germans for almost eight months in 1870–71. In Aug. 1914 part of the British Expeditionary Force disembarked at Rouen, a staging camp for reinforcements landing at Le Havre or ascending the river by steamer; it was also the site of several base hospitals. In June 1940 the Germans bombed and set fire to the old town between the cathedral and the river, while in 1944 Allied air attacks continued the destruction. It was liberated on 29 Aug. 1944.

Pierre Corneille (1606–84) and his brother Thomas (1625–1709) were born here; likewise the botanist Guy de la Brosse (d. 1641); Robert de la Salle (1643–87), explorer of the Mississippi; J.-F. Blondel (1705–74), the architect; the artists Jean Jouvenet (1647–1717), Jean Restout (1692–1768); and Théodore Géricault (1791–1824); Fontenelle (1657–1757), the centenarian savant; the composer François Adrien Boïeldieu (1775–1834); the hispanist and connoisseur Jean Charles Davillier (1823–83); and Gustave Flaubert (1821–80). Edward Hyde, Lord Clarendon (1609–74) completed his 'True History' and died in exile in Rouen, while the Belgian poet Émile Verhaeren (1855–1916) was killed in a railway accident at the station. Simone de Beauvoir taught philosophy at the Lycée Jeanne d'Arc in 1933–37.

A convenient spot from which to visit the major monuments is the central *Pl. de la Cathédrale*, on the W. side of which is the *Bureau des*

Finances (1509; by Roulland le Roux), now accommodating the S.I. To the N. is a modern conference-hall.

The ****Cathedral** (Notre-Dame), one of the most beautiful churches in France, dates almost entirely from the rebuilding started in 1201, and illustrates the phases of Gothic architecture from that date to 1514, when the elaborate **W. Front* was completed.

The building has been admirably restored after extensive war damage by a team of some hundred craftsmen working under the supervision of Albert Chauvel, architect of the Monuments Historiques.

The central doorway, with a Tree of Jesse and several decapitated statues, was built by Roulland le Roux in 1514, and is flanked by the 12C *Porte St-Jean* and *Port St-Étienne*, with decoration of 1370–1421 by Jean Périer and Jean de Bayeux. These, with the 12C *Tour St-Romain* (81m) on the l., are the sole relics above ground of the Romanesque cathedral, burnt in 1200; the upper part of the tower, added by Guillaume Pontis in 1477, was partially burnt in 1944. The Flamboyant *Tour de Buerre* (76m; carillon), also by Pontis (1485–1507), was paid for by selling indulgences to eat butter in Lent. The original wooden *Spire* surmounting Roulland's central lantern (c. 1524–23) was replaced in 1544 by Robert Becquet's; this was destroyed by lightning in 1822, after which the present cast-iron structure was erected.

The **Portal des Libraires* (c. 1275–1300; by Jean Davy) on the N., is so-called from the booksellers' stalls which once crowded its forecourt; the *Portal de la Calende*, on the S., is likewise rich in sculptured detail. The bays and chapels of the S. aisle and the 14C *Porte des Maçons* were practically destroyed in 1944.

The *Interior*, 135m long including the Lady Chapel, is 28m high. The *Nave* (1201–20; by Jean d'Andely), well proportioned and uniform in style, has 20 clustered columns surmounted by pointed arches, while above the triforium is a balustraded gallery. The rose-window of the W. front contains 16C glass. The central lantern-tower (51m) combines elegance of design with boldness of execution. The stained-glass in both aisles range in date from the 13th-16C, the earliest being in the N. aisle. Note also the curious range of upper colonettes in the aisles.

In the N. transept, with a charming Renaissance staircase, the destroyed rose-window has been faithfully reconstructed. The *Chapel of St-Romanus*, in the S. transept, contains glass of 1521 illustrating the story of that saint, while the adjoining *Chapel of Jeanne d'Arc* contains her statue by Saupique.

The *Choir*, with its plain round pillars, was, with the transepts, erected c. 1220–30. Its surviving **Stalls*, carved by Philippe Viart in 1457–69, have been restored. The lower windows contain early 13C glass of the Chartres School; in the upper windows is 15C glass brought here from destroyed *St-Vincent*. The high altar is embellished by gilt angels by Caffieri from the same church.

Behind the altar steps descend to the *Crypt* of the 11C cathedral (completed in 1062). It included part of an ambulatory and an E. apsidal chapel (where a leaden casket contains the heart of Charles V). The crypt was discovered as a result of the bombing, and refutes the widely-held theory that 11C Norman churches were built without ambulatories. Adjoining is a slightly later square crypt beneath the present sanctuary.

In the *Ambulatory* (S. side) are the effigies of Duc Rollo (d. 932) and Richard I (Coeur-de-Lion; d. 1199), whose hearts are interred below. The S.E. *Chapel of St-Barthélemy* has a 15C stone screen and wrought-iron door. On the N. side are effigies of Richard's elder brother Henry (d. 1183), and William Longsword (d. 943). All these effigies are 13C, except that of Rollo, which is a copy of the original (fragments preserved in the Treasury), too badly damaged in 1944 to be restored. On the raised floor of the choir, near Henry's tomb, a plain slab marks the grave of John, Duke of Bedford (1389–1435), regent of France. In the wall opposite is the Romanesque tomb of Abp Hugh, abbot of Reading (d. 1164).

The *Lady Chapel*, enlarged in 1302–20, preserves its original 14C glass, and 15C windows from St-Vincent. Here is the Renaissance **Tomb of the two Cardinals Amboise*, designed by Roulland le Roux, but with numerous statues by other hands; also the tomb of Louis de Brézé (d. 1531), husband of Diane de Poitiers, with the kneeling figure of his widow. Adjoining is the restored late-Gothic tomb of Pierre de Brézé (d. 1465).

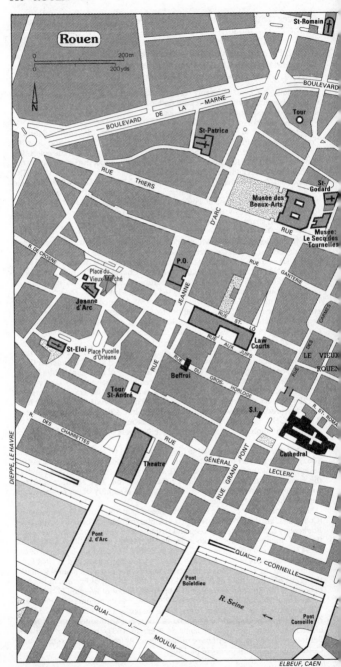

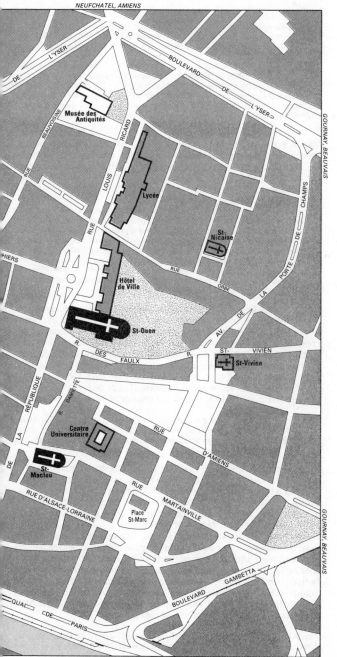

The Rue de Change skirts the S. facade of the cathedral, passing the entrance to the 15-18C *Archbishop's Palace*. Adm. may be requested to visit the Gothic rooms on the ground floor, including the vaulted Kitchens, and Great Hall, with good ironwork, and containing paintings of Rouen, Le Havre, Dieppe, and Gaillon, by Hubert Robert.

A lane opposite leads down to the Renaissance *Monument de St-Romain* (1542), where the *'fierte'* or reliquary of that saint was yearly raised for the worship of the crowd by a condemned prisoner released on the recommendation of the cathedral chapter, a custom discontinued in 1790. Adjacent are part of the 17C walls of the old *Halles*. Of the buildings once flanking the quays, the *Porte Guillaume-Lion* (1749) alone survives, and may be seen a short distance further E.

The picturesque Rue St-Romain, skirting the N. side of the cathedral, retains several ancient houses, including the restored *'Vieille Maison'* of 1466. An inscription (r.) recalls that this wall was part of the chapel in which Joan of Arc was sentenced and in which her innocence was proclaimed 25 years too late.

The narrow streets of this quarter contain a large number of quaint half-timbered houses of great age, the beams and gables of many protected by tiles, and admirable work continues with their careful preservation and restoration, which makes the centre of Rouen—like Troyes or Dijon—still one of the most attractive and interesting of French cities to wander through, either by day or night, in spite of the ravages it has sustained. In 1525 an ordinance was promulgated forbidding the erection of buildings with storeys overhanging the streets, already narrow and dark enough, and as a general rule those thus built were erected prior to that date.

Crossing the Rue de la République, we see ahead the Flamboyant Gothic W. front of *St-Maclou* (1437–1521), designed by Pierre Robin, with a remarkable bow-shaped facade of five pinnacled arches. The spire was added in 1868, replacing the earlier one destroyed in 1794. The richly decorated doorways, and delicately carved doors (cleaner on the interior), are noteworthy; also the Renaissance stained-glass and organ-loft (by Jean Goujon; 1521) with its openwork stone spiral staircase (1512). Severe damage was done to the E. end and S. side of the church in 1944.

To the N.E. of its apse is the entrance to the *Cloister* or *Aître St-Maclou* (1526–33), with wooden galleries decorated with sculptured friezes of skulls, etc., surrounding a quadrangle which was used as a plague cemetery as lately as 1780.

From the W. front of St-Maclou, with its restored neighbouring houses, the narrow Rue Damiette leads N., in which, in No. 30, the *Hôtel d'Aligre* or *de Senneville* (17C) lived Lord Clarendon; see above. The timber-framed *Hôtel d'Etancourt*, its courtyard crossed by a street, with facades embellished by seven statues, is passed (l.) before reaching the S. facade of St-Ouen.

St-Ouen, although more uniform in style and fractionally larger than the cathedral, is a dull building in comparison, however perfect may be its architectural proportions and elaborately buttressed its soaring fabric. Its choir was begun in 1318, and the nave dates mainly from the 15C, above the crossing of which rises the central tower (82m), with an octagonal lantern. Two towers flank the W. front, an uninspired restoration of 1851. On the S. is the 14C *Portail des Marmousets*, named after its grotesque carvings.

The *Interior* (137m long, and 33m high) is singularly devoid of decoration, and there is an almost total absence of horizontal lines, and the E. windows, arranged in tiers, add to the impression of loftiness created by the arcades of the nave, although the vertical lines of the piers are broken by statue-niches. The choir, with stalls of 1615, is enclosed by good 18C railings; and there survives some 14C *Stained-glass* in the choir and ambulatory, which also contains (in the 2nd N. chapel) the tomb of Alexandre of Berneval (d. 1440), architect of the church. Some 15-16C glass embellishes the nave clerestory, and transepts, but only a proportion of the 80 windows have been replaced. The organ is reputed for its tone.

A short distance to the E. stands *St-Vivien* (15C), with a stumpy stone steeple, while of *St-Niçaise*, N. of the latter, only a 16C choir with some glass of the same period, remains.

On the N. side of St-Ouen, facing the otherwise unimpressive *Pl. du Gén.-de-Gaulle*, is the *Hôtel de Ville*, in restored 18C buildings of the abbey. A passage between it and the church leads to gardens affording a good general view of St-Ouen, while abutting its N. transept is a survival of an earlier Romanesque church.

The Rue Louis-Ricard climbs N. from the Place, passing (r.) the *Chapel* (1614–56) of the *Lycée*, once a Jesuit college, which numbered amongst its pupils Pierre and Thomas Corneille, La Salle, Bernadin de St-Pierre, Flaubert, Corot, Delacroix, Maupassant, and André Maurois.

Beyond, to the l., is the **Musée des Antiquitiés**, occupying the buildings of a 17C convent and its cloisters (apart from a modern extension). In addition to the collection of carved beams, pilasters, etc. rescued from destroyed buildings, are examples of 12-13C Limoges enamel reliquaries; 13-15C ivories, among them a charming Virgin; a series of Nottingham alabasters; medieval chests and furniture; and a large Roman mosaic pavement from Lillebonne.—A *Natural History* collection is housed adjacent.

From the Pl. du Gén. de Gaulle the Rue Thiers leads W. to the *Musée des Beaux-Arts (r.) facing the umbrageous *Sq. Verdrel*, containing one of the better provincial collections.

RR1-6 *Gerard David*, Virgin and Saints; *Perugino*, Adoration of the Magi, Baptism, and Resurrection (part of the predella of the altarpiece from San Pietro at Perugia); *anon.* 15C *Spanish* Flagellation; *Guercino*, Visitation; *Marten de Vos*, Story of Rebecca (on six panels), also David and Abigail; *Luca Giordano*, The Good Samaritan; *Caravaggio*, Flagellation; *School of Ribera*, St Zachary; *Velázquez*, Man with a globe; two paintings of St Sebastian nursed by Irene, by *Georges de la Tour* and *Nicolas Regnier* respectively.

RR7-11 are devoted to the Dutch and Flemish Schools, remarkable among which are an *anon.* 17C Portrait of an old lady; *Nicolas Neufchâtel*, Male portrait; *T. de Keyser*, The music lesson; *Gerard Ter Borch*, The tap-room; *Jan Steen*, Wafer-seller; a series of still-lifes and flower-paintings; Landscapes, including one by *Paul Bril*; Views of Rouen by *Van Ruysdael*, and *Jan van Goyen*, and another dated between 1592 and 1619 by an *anon. Flemish* artist; and a Naval combat by *Wilhem van de Velde*.

RR12-18 *Clouet*, Bath of Diana; *Poussin* the Storm; *Vivien*, Pastel portrait of Samuel Bernard; *Fragonard*, Les Lavandières; and examples of the art of *Hubert Robert*; also *George Morland*, Horse and cart in a landscape; *A. Ch. G. Lemonnier* (1743–1824), The first soirée chez Mme Geoffrin (1755); *J.P. Houel*, (1735–1813), Cave serving as a warehouse at Dieppedalle.

RR19-23 19C French School, including works by *Boilly*, among them a Portrait of Boïeldieu; *Louis David*, Portraits of Songeolier, and of A young boy; *Ingres*, La belle Zélie (mouth smudged); *Vigée-Lebrun*, Mme Grassini as Zaire; *Géricault*, Portrait of Delacroix, and other works; *Paul Huet*, View of Rouen; *Corot*, Landscapes; *Sickert*, The music-hall. Adjacent is a room containing Sketches by *Delacroix*, and in another his sensational painting of Trajan the Lawgiver.

RR24-28 Impressionists, including works by *Monet* and *Boudin*; *Renoir*, Woman with a looking-glass; *Caillebotte*, At the café; *Lépine*, Paris suburb under snow; *Sisley*, two Views of the Seine, The church at Moret, Marly under snow, and Floods; Landscapes by *Albert Lebourg* (1849–1928, at Rouen); an early *Dufy* of The beach at Ste-Adresse.—**R29** five works by *Dufy*, and Portrait of J.E. Blanche by *J.-L. Forain*.—Canvases by *Puvis de Chavannes* adorn the staircase.

In a room to the l. on the FIRST FLOOR are a series of *Portraits* of his contemporaries by *J.E. Blanche* (1861–1942), among them those of Bergson, Claudel, Cocteau, Drieu la Rochelle, Gide, Giraudoux, Max Jacob, Maeterlinck, Mauriac, Maurois, Paul Morand, Montherlant, the Comtesse de Noailles, Radiguet, 'Les Six', Stravinsky, and Valéry.—Adjacent is a large room containing examples of French religious art of the 17C, including canvases by *Jouvenet*; and an Adoration, and Deposition, by *Laurent de la Hyre*.

RR30-33 contain *Rouen faience* (1550–1800) a remarkable collection acquired by the town in 1864.

In the S. Wing a series of rooms contains collections of silver, jewellery, watches, fans, and nécessaires; Oriental jades, Japanese ivories, bronzes, lacquer, cloisonné, and pewter, etc. In other sections are prints by *Debucourt* and others, and pastels by *Hubert Robert* and *Fragonard*. Among the sculptures are busts by *Pajou, Lemoyne, Houdon* (Diderot in 1771), and *Caffieri* (terracotta model for a bust of Pierre Corneille).

In the former church of *St-Laurent* (1444–1554), immediately behind the Museum, is installed the ***Musée Le Secq des Tournelles**, a remarkable collection of *Ironwork*, attractively displayed (press button to see objects on moving belts), including two iron chairs (1595) from Guernica (Vizcaya), and a stair-rail from the château de Bellevue (Meudon).

Among smaller objects are shop-signs; locks and keys; boxes and safes; door-furniture, and grilles; knives, scissors, and razors; lecterns; domestic and kitchen implements; scales, measures, compasses; and irons; tools; stays; jewellery, buckles, and combs; seals and key-rings; smoking accessories; plaques, etc. Some stained-glass (15-16C) from destroyed St-Vincent, with designs by Jean and Engrand Leprince (c. 1525) is also here.

Immediately to the N. is *St-Godard*, beyond which, in the Rue Beffroy, is the restored 17C *Hôtel Caillot de Coquereaumont*.—A short distance N.W. stands the *Tour Jeanne-d'Arc*, relic of the castle built by Philippe Auguste, where the 'Maid' appeared before her 'judges', while the site of the tower in which she was imprisoned is marked by a tablet in the Rue Jeanne d'Arc, further W., in the courtyard of which are its foundations. This thoroughfare leads N. to the art-nouveau *Railway Station*, just E. of which is *St-Romain* (1676–1730).

Just N.W. of the Sq. Verdrel stands *St-Patrice*, with some good 16C glass.

The Rue Jeanne d'Arc leads downhill past (r.) the Rue des Bons-Enfants, preserving some old houses (Fontenelle was born at No. 100 in 1657). To the l. is the 19C facade of the *Law Courts*, behind which, in the Rue dux Juifs, extends the famous **Palais de Justice**, an impressive specimen of late-Gothic architecture, which although largely rebuilt or restored, still shows signs of its mutilation in 1944, when the central part of the building was left a mere shell behind its Flamboyant **Facade*, and the Salle des Séances, built in 1508 for the Parlement of Rouen by Roulland le Roux and Roger Ango, was destroyed. The Salle des Pas Perdus (1499) was likewise destroyed, but not—such is Fate—the r. wing, built in 1842–52.

The parallel street to the S.—much restored and part of it a pedestrian precinct—derives its name from the **Grosse Horloge*, a striking group of buildings including a Renaissance *Gatehouse* (1527) spanning the street, with an elaborate clock-face (with a single hand), a tall belfry of 1389, and a little 17C corner pavilion with a fountain of 1732. The belfry, which preserves the mechanism of the clock,

A lithograph of the Rue de la Grosse Horloge, by Thomas Shotter Boys

may be ascended for the view. Immediately to the E., on the corner of the Rue Thouret, is the old *Town Hall* of 1607.

To the W., across the Rue Jeanne d'Arc, is the site of the *Pl. du Vieux-Marché*, surrounded by restaurants. This whole area has been drastically reconstructed, with a neo-medieval market-hall, a 15C facade from the Abbaye de St-Armand (on the W. side), relics from St-Vincent, etc., and a chapel marks the site of the pyre where on 30 May 1432 Joan was burnt.

The Rue de Crosne leads W. from the Place to the 18C *Hôtel-Dieu*, some few minutes' walk away, where Flaubert's father was a surgeon. The building in which the author was born has been converted into a *Museum* devoted to him, also containing a section on the History of Medicine; cf. *Croisset*.

19C *St-Gervais*, to the N. of the Hôtel-Dieu, covers a Carolingian crypt, in which St Mellon was buried c. 311, and in the priory which stood here William the Conqueror died in 1087 from the injuries received at Mantes in falling off his horse.

Some distance to the W. of St-Gervais, on the *Mont-aux-Malades*, is a 12C church founded by Henry II and dedicated to St Thomas of Canterbury, near which is Romanesque *St-Jacques* (restored).

At No. 4 Rue de la Pie, S.W. of the Pl. du Vieux-Marché, is the birthplace of Pierre Corneille and his brother Thomas, now the *Musée Cornélien*.

Just beyond the S.E. corner of the Place, in the *Pl. de la Pucelle*, is the *Hôtel de Bourgtheroulde* (pron. Bou-troude), a mansion of 1537 now occupied by a bank. The facade of the inner court is decorated with reliefs, some worn, of 'triumphs' and scenes from the Field of the Cloth of Gold (cf. Rte 3).—Adjacent stands the derelict protestant church of *St-Eloi* (16C).

S.E. of this Place is the restored *Tour St-André* (1542), facing the Rue Jeanne d'Arc.

Turning r. here, we shortly reach the quays, passing (l.) the modern *Théâtre*.—Opposite, the *Pont Jeanne-d'Arc* spans the Seine to the industrial and residential suburb of *St-Sever*, with its high-rise blocks of flats. To the W. is the new *Pont Guillaume-le-Conquérant*; to the E., the *Pont Boïeldieu*, and beyond, the *Pont Corneille*, joining the *Île Lacroix* to both banks. Between the two are the buildings of the *Centre Administratif* (1966), with the clean lines of its 79m tower dominating the area.

It was on the quays here that young Marc Isambard Brunel first saw, to his wonder and delight, the component parts of a huge steam-engine, just landed from England, which caused him to say to himself, so reported John Murray: 'When I am a man, I will repair to a country where such machinery is made'.

Some distance S.W., in the suburb of *Le Petit-Quevilly*, is the *Chapel of St-Julien* (c. 1183; restored), originally attached to a leper-hospital founded by Henry II, and exhibiting a characteristically English wall-arcade and remarkable 12-13C ceiling-paintings.

In the suburb of *Le-Petit-Couronne*, to the W. of the main road (N138), some 8km S. of central Rouen, at No. 60 in the street named after him, is the half-timbered *Manoir de Pierre Corneille* (of 1544), the rural retreat of the dramatist from 1639 until his death, containing a few personal relics. At the door is the stone he used to mount his horse, but the thatched bakery is a reconstruction.—Continuing S., we pass oil-refineries and traverse *Le-Grand-Couronne* to reach *Moulineaux*, with a 13C church containing a carved 15-16C *Rood-screen*, and good 13C glass above its altar.

For roads from Rouen to *Dieppe* and *Paris*, see Rte 8; to *Le Havre*, Rte 26; to **Caen**; Rte 27; to **Tours** via *Le Mans*, Rte 28; and for *Beauvais* and *Soissons*, Rte 9.

7 Abbeville to Dieppe and Le Havre

175km (108½ miles). D925. 32km *Eu*—33km **Dieppe**—32km *St-Valéry-en-Caux*—32km **Fécamp**—17km D940. *Étretat*—28km **Le Havre**.

Maps: IGN 3, 7, or 102. M 236, 231.

The D925 drives S.W. from **Abbeville** (see Rte 4), shortly traversing the plateau of Vimeu, an ancient 'Pays' dotted with châteaux, windmills, and orchards.—At 8.5km *Moyenneville*, with a church of interest, lies 4km S.E.

23.5km **Eu** (8700 inhab.), where in 1053 William of Normandy and Matilda were married; and the birthplace of the sculptors François and Michel Anguier (1604–69, and 1612–86, respectively). Its predecessor, Gallo-Roman *Augusta*, under excavation, lies to the E.

of the town. The central *Pl. Carnot* is flanked by *St-Laurent*, originally built in 1186 – 1230 and dedicated to St Laurence O'Toole (d. at Eu
in 1180), Abp of Dublin. It has no towers, but is otherwise a
characteristic Norman church of its period, while the exterior of the
choir is a rich example of the Flamboyant style.

The *Choir*, enclosed by a stone balustrade of 1540 – 80, contains four bronze
urns (on marble columns), two bearing the arms of the Orléans, the others those
of the Prince de Dombes and of Catherine of Cleves, wife of Henri, Duc de Guise
(see below). Above the high altar is the shrine of St Laurence, whose restored effigy lies in the 12C crypt with members of the house of Artois (13-15C). The
Lady Chapel contains a Virgin attrib. to François Anguier; an ambulatory chapel
contains a 15C sculptured Entombment.
    To the W. stands the *Château* (incorporating the *Hôtel de Ville*), which is en-
tirely modern except for the r. wing, begun in 1578 by the Duc de Guise and continued after 1661 by Mlle de Montpensier. Largely destroyed in 1795, the
edifice, a favourite residence of Louis-Philippe, was repaired in 1821. He twice
received Queen Victoria here, in 1843 and 1845, the earlier date being the first
occasion since 1520 on which an English sovereign had visited a French 'cousin'.
In 1902 the château, apart from the r. wing and chapel, was destroyed by fire. Its
park was laid out by Le Nôtre.
    To the S. of the Pl. Carnot is the restored *Chapel* (1642) of the *Collège*, built in
1582 by Catherine of Cleves, and formerly owned by the Jesuits, in which are
the cenotaphs of Catherine (d. 1633) and her husband, Henri of Guise,
assassinated at Blois in 1588.

    4km to the N.W. lies **Le Tréport** (6600 inhab.) a small port of little natural at-
traction, but long popular as being the nearest bathing resort of Paris, whose
populace would flock there in their thousands. During the occupation of
1940 – 44 the Germans built extensive fortification here and did considerable
damage. Cliff-top *St-Jacques* is a much restored Flamboyant building (16C) with a
19C porch sheltering a Renaissance portal; the elaborately vaulted interior has
pendant bosses. Behind it are remains of an abbey of 1036 dedicated St-Michel,
like the more famous island abbey at the opposite extremity of Normandy.

9.5km. *Criel-sur-Mer*, 6.5km S.E. of which is the interesting 12-16C
church of *St-Martin-le-Gaillard*.—Beyond Creil the road traverses a
dull plateau to (10km) *St-Martin-en-Campagne*.

Hence a minor road bears r. to skirt the coast via *Berneval-sur-Mer*, destroyed in
1944, and the site of a Canadian landing in 1942, where their commandos were
decimated; a more successful assault was made at adjacent *Belleville*.—The
resort of *Puys*, further W., was made fashionable by the younger Dumas, whose
father died here in 1870. Lord Salisbury spent his summers here from 1870 – 95.
Nearby is the *Camp de Cesar*, or *Cité de Limes*, inhabited until the Middle Ages.

12km. Dieppe; see Rte 8.

DIEPPE TO VEULES-LES-ROSES VIA THE COAST (26km). More attractive than
the inland road, the D75 ascends the plateau behind the castle at Dieppe, and
traverses (4.5km) *Pourville*, where another Canadian landing in 1942 effected a
complete surprise, and they were able to reach the crossroads at *Le Petit-
Appeville*, 2km up the valley of the Scie. Here begins the *Aqueduc de Toustain*, a
dry subterranean canal dug in 1558 to lead its waters to the town and castle of
Dieppe.—The road turns inland, after 3km passing (l.) the *Manoir d'Ango*, built
by Jehan Ango in 1530 – 45, with a curious dovecot.—The 13-16C church of the
adjoining village of *Varengeville* contains 16-17C tombs; in the cemetery are
buried the composer Albert Roussel (1869 – 1937) and Georges Braque
(1882 – 1963), the latter a frequent visitor, who designed some stained-glass windows here.
    A lane leads N. to *Vastérival*, overlooking the shore. Both here and further W.
at *Ste-Marguerite*, troops under Col Lovat raided the coast with complete success
on 19 Aug. 1942, climbing inland along narrow gullies worn by streams cutting
through the chalk cliffs, and killing or capturing the crew of a German battery.
The rebuilt *Phare d'Ailly*, on a promontory between the two villages, replaced

an 18C lighthouse destroyed in 1944, except for its tower. *Ste-Marguerite* has a Romanesque church preserving a 12C apse with interlaced arches, rare in Normandy, and an altar of c. 1144.—A long descent leads to the mouth of the Saâne, and *Quiberville-Plage*, with an exceptionally untidy sand and pebble beach.—Beyond the villages of *St-Aubin* and *Sotteville-sur-Mer* (with cliff views) lies *Veules-les-Roses*, with extensive watercress beds. 16C *St-Martin* has a 13C tower; the sacristy is surmounted by a curious stone chimney in the shape of a double cross, and the nave roof (1609) is also of unusual design. A 16C cross adjoins the ruins of *St-Nicolas*. Over 3000 Allied troops were evacuated here in June 1940; cf. *Battle of the Bresle*, Rte 6.

The D925 climbs S.W. from Dieppe onto the chalky wind-blown plateau known as the *Pays de Caux* or *'Plateau cauchois'*, which occupies the triangle between Dieppe, Le Havre, and Rouen. It is intersected by steep dry valleys, with bold white cliffs facing the Channel (some with relics of German fortifications), and is dotted with numerous small and ancient villages—with names frequently ending in -ville—most of them with churches of interest, and many with 16C churchyard crosses. Also typical are the half-timbered farms, usually surrounded by wooded embankments containing some acres of orchard, a pond, and various out-buildings, and often entered by a 'monumental' gateway.

17km. *Bourg-Dun* has a *Church retaining its fine 13C tower, a Romanesque N. aisle and transept, an early Gothic nave, a Flamboyant S. transept, and a Renaissance font-cover.—*Lunerary*, 4km S., was a cradle of Protestantism, whence many pamphlets sent by Calvin from Geneva were distributed.—7km. *Veules-les-Roses* (see above), to the S. of which, at *Blosseville*, the 16C church has contemporary glass and a 12C tower.—Further S., at *Silleron*, is an attractive 16C manor.

8km. **St-Valery-en-Caux**, a small fishing-port, preserves a house of 1540 opposite the W. end of the bridge. During the retreat of 1940, when much of the town was destroyed, although c. 1300 men had previously been evacuated by sea, over 800 of the 51st Div. and the 2nd French Cavalry Div. were trapped on the beach and were compelled to surrender.—6km W., to *Conteville*, where Napoleon once planned to establish a naval base, a nuclear power-station is under construction.

The main road turns inland to (12km) **Cany-Barville**, amid beech-woods, with an 18C *Market-hall* and *Mairie*, and a *Church* rebuilt in the 16C, with a 13C tower.

Beyond the church of *Barville* (2km S.), prettily placed on an island in the Durdent, is seen the imposing château of *Cany* (1640, with later flanking pavilions). To the S.E. of the latter lies *Grainville-la-Teinturière*, birthplace of Jean de Béthencourt (d. 1425), who established the first European settlement in the Canaries, some 5km beyond which, at *Auffay*, is a charming château of c. 1450.

From Cany-Barville, the road leads due W., at 8km passing 4km N. of the abbey of *Valmont*, with the ruined late-Gothic transepts and 16C choir of its church, while the Renaissance *Lady Chapel* of c. 1525 contains 16C glass, a stone group attrib. to Germain Pilon, and tombs of the Estoutevilles. On the S. bank of the Valmont stands the castle of that family (15-16C), preserving a Norman keep.

12km. **Fécamp** (21,700 Fécampois), confined, like Dover, in a narrow valley between chalk cliffs, is a busy port whose fleet engages in cod-fishery. It contains several canning factories, and is famous for its Benedictine abbey and distillery.

Its legendary foundation is placed in the 1C A.D., when a hollowed trunk of a fig-tree landed here, transporting a leaden box containing drops of the Holy Blood, a miracle which soon attracted a stream of pilgrims. It was the site of a Gallo-Roman oppidum; and here St Waninge founded a monastery c. 633, later destroyed by Norman pirates, and replaced by a Benedictine abbey in the 10C. The port suffered in competition with Le Havre after the 16C. Charles II landed here in Nov. 1651, having embarked at Shoreham after his flight from Worcester. During the Second World War it was damaged by the Germans. Maupassant (1850–93) was born at No. 82 in the quay named after him, although immediately taken to the château of Miromesnil (near Dieppe), where his birth was registered. He often returned to Fécamp, which served as the background to a number of his works.

From the central *Pl. Thiers*, flanked by *St-Étienne* (1500, with a facade and tower of 1887), the Rue J.-Huet leads to the abbey-church of ***La Trinité**, a fine example of early Gothic, but with its interior defaced with whitewash—a fact commented on by Augustus Hare in 1895—and its glass unrepaired.

Dating mainly from 1175-1225, it replaced an earlier church almost entirely destroyed by fire in 1168. The restored S. porch is late 13C. The crossing is surmounted by a square lantern tower (early 13C); the 18C facade is undeniably incongruous. The *Lady Chapel*, by Jacques le Roux of Rouen, was added after 1489, while the energetic Abbot Bohier was responsible for commissioning the Renaissance embellishments from Giralamo Viscardo and other Genoese artists.

Steps descend into the *Interior* (126m long; 22m high). The triforium is pierced with quatrefoils, while sculptures between the 8th and 9th bay of the dignified nave indicate the position of a 15C rood-screen, figures from which flank a painted stone Renaissance group of the Death of the Virgin (c. 1495) in the S. transept. A slab in the Baptistry covers the lead coffins of Richard I, Duke of Normandy (946–96; born at Fécamp) and his son Richard II (d. 1026), two benefactors of the abbey, who in 1162 were reburied here in the presence of Henry II.

The *Choir*, recalling the Abbaye aux Hommes at Caen, retains a high altar of 1751, with a Renaissance altar in white marble (1507) by Viscardo behind it, both beneath a 18C gilt canopy. The ambulatory chapels are remarkable for their Renaissance stone *Screens (best on the S.), and abbots' tombs (11-14C), notably that of Guillaume de Ros (d. 1107). Note the elaborate clock of 1667 in the N. transept. A damaged tabernacle (1505; by Viscardo) behind the high altar is reputed to contain the precious blood; see above.

Abutting the N. side of the church, part of the 18C monastic buildings houses the *Hôtel de Ville*. Just to the N. the Rue de l'Inondation (sic) leads shortly to the *Fontaine du Précieux-Sang*, which wells forth in the courtyard of No. 12 Rue de l'Aumone.

The Rue Alexandre-Legros leads W. from La Trinité, in which No. 21 is the *Municipal Museum*, containing models of fishing-boats, and local bygones. Further W. is the entrance to the *Benedictine Distillery* (r.), occupying extensive mock-antique buildings, parts of which may be visited. In the 16C the liqueur was made by the monks as a cordial for the sick: its modern manufacture is an interesting and more sophisticated process. A *Museum* exhibits some 14-16C ivories, Nottingham alabasters, 16C polychromed statues, a collection of locks, and remnants of the rood-screen from the abbey.

FÉCAMP TO TANCARVILLE VIA BOLBEC (40km). Although the D925 to (13km) *Goderville* is the direct road, the D73 (from the W. front of La Trinité) is preferable, in that it leads directly to the **Château of Bailleul*, c. 12km S.E., a fine Renaissance building containing paintings attrib. to Memling, Rembrandt, Hobbema, and Frans Hals.—*Goderville* lies 6km S.W., whence we follow the D910 S.E. past a manor of the Henri-II period near *Beuzeville-la-Grenier*, one of several interesting old mansions in the district.—12km. *Bolbec*; see Rte 26A.—*Lillebonne* (see Rte 26B) lies 10km S.E., and *Tancarville* (see Rte 26C) 15km S.

From Fécamp, the D940 leads S.W., off which a sinuous minor road hugs the coast through *Yport*, often described by Maupassant, to (17km) **Étretat**, a small flint-built resort attractively sited on a cliff-encircled bay. Eugène Isabey painted there; Alphonse Karr sang its praises; and Offenbach erected the 'Villa d'Orphée' with the profits of 'Orpheus in the Underworld', and partly composed his 'Tales of Hoffmann' here in 1879.

On entering the town we pass (l.) *Notre-Dame*, with a 12C door-way with carved capitals, spoilt by a tympanum added in 1866. The dark 12C nave, with cylindrical columns and round arches with geometrical mouldings, gives way to the 13C crossing and choir; the lantern tower is of the same date.

The reconstructed *Market-hall* is passed before reaching the sea-front, damaged during the German occupation, relics of whose defensive fortifications are still in evidence. The pebbly beach is flanked by two towering masses of white *Cliffs*, each pierced by a natural arch; that to the N.E. known as the *Porte d'Amont*; that to the S.W., the *Porte d'Aval*.

The rocks and caves at the cliff base may be approached by steep descending paths, or along the beach at low tide. The Falaise d'Amont is surmounted by a rebuilt chapel and a monument and museum dedicated to Nungesser and Coli, who were lost in their attempt to fly the Atlantic from E. to W. in 1927.

In the opposite direction (beyond oyster-beds hollowed out of the rock in 1777 for Marie-Antoinette) is the *Manneporte*, another rock arch accessible at low tide from the bay called the *Petit-Port*, beyond the Falaise d'Aval. A cliff path continues past the *Pointe de la Courtine* to the *Cap d'Antifer*, a bold promontory 110m high, with a lighthouse.

Near *Criquetot-l'Esneval*, 8.5km S.E. of Étretat, the farm of *Alezonde* is said to have belonged to Sir John Fastolf, regent of Normandy in 1423; while André Gide (1869–1951) is buried—and was apparently married, in 1895—at *Cuver-ville*, 3km N. of the latter.

From Étretat the D940 drives S.

At 4km a lane turns r. to *Bruneval*, where a breakwater protects an oil-tanker terminal under construction. In a daring night raid here (27 Feb. 1942) British paratroops destroyed a German radar station and captured vital equipment, in which they suffered only slight casualties, and were taken off by waiting naval craft.

The main road continues S.W. to enter *Ste-Adresse*, a W. suburb of **Le Havre** after 24km; see Rte 26A.—Le Havre can be avoided by turn-ing l. off the D940 9km S. of Étretat for (5km) *St-Martin-de-Bec*, with a 16C lakeside château, to meet 5km beyond, the D925, where one turns r. for (2.5km) **Montivilliers**, an industrial town formerly famous for its cloth. It retains a Romanesque *Church* (relic of an ab-bey founded in the 7C) with a 16C N. aisle and choir vault; also a fine W. tower and two W. porches, one Romanesque, surmounted by a 'geometrical' Gothic window; the other is Flamboyant. The contrast between the two periods of architecture in the nave, with its pulpit of 1671, is curious. At the W. end of the N. aisle is a large oriel; in the choir are eleven 15C Nottingham alabasters. The crypt (according to Augustus Hare) contains the skeletons of 130 nuns!

6.5km due S. lies **Harfleur**, at the mouth of the Lézarde, now little more than an industrial suburb of Le Havre.

Throughout the Middle Ages it was one of the chief ports of France, and here Henry V landed before Agincourt (1415), but in 1435 the English were driven out by Jean de Grouchy, lord of Montérolier and 104 peasants. In 1485 Henry of

Richmond embarked here for Milford Haven. The silting up of the mouth of the Seine, and the competition of Le Havre, reduced its importance, but since the construction of the Canal de Tancarville, and the establishment of an arsenal, rolling-mills, and oil refineries to the S.E., it again materially flourishes.

Late 15C *St-Martin* has a conspicuous stone **Spire* (83m high) and elaborate N. porch; the W. door dates from 1635. Some ancient tombs, pendant bosses, and a Renaissance organ-loft may be seen in the interior. Adjacent is the château (1653), now the *Hôtel de Ville*.

For **Le Havre**, and the road E. to *Tancarville*, see Rte 26.

8 Dieppe to Paris

A. Via Gournay-en-Bray and Gisors

173km (107½ miles). D915. 36km *Les Hayons*—18km. *Forges-les-Eaux*—20km *Gournay-en-Bray*—25km **Gisors**—36km **Pontoise**—N14. 38km **Paris**.

Maps: IGN 3, 8, or 103. M 231, 237.

DIEPPE (36,400 Dieppois), a busy cross-Channel terminus, with a deep and commodious harbour containing several inner basins, and a seaside resort, lies at the mouth of the Arques between two ranges of chalk cliffs. Its fishing-fleet is of considerable importance.

It probably originated in the Gaulish and Roman settlement of the *Cité de Limes*, to the N.E. In the 10C it was colonised by Norse adventurers, to whom it owes its name (in allusion to the *depth* of its harbour). The earliest castle here was erected by Henry II. Like St-Malo, it was long the lair of privateers, whose exploits included the pillaging of Southampton (1338), a blockade of Lisbon (1530), and voyages of discovery as far afield as Iceland and the Gold Coast; and many Dieppois were among the first settlers in Canada. Under François I (who visited the castle in 1535) the port became the most flourishing in France, with 60,000 inhabitants, and the local manufacture of carved ivory from imported tusks dates from this period. John Knox took refuge here in 1553, and may have written here (if not at Geneva) his 'blast' against the 'monstrous Regiment of Women' (1557).

Its large Protestant population suffered by the Revocation of the Edict of Nantes (1685), while in the previous year the town was ruthlessly bombarded by an English fleet returning from an unsuccessful attack on Brest, and it was later largely rebuilt. Voltaire disembarked here on his return from exile in England in 1729. The first cross-Channel ferry service from Dieppe plied to Brighthelmston in 1790. It became a fashionable resort c. 1820, when visited by the Duchesse de Berry, and was painted by Bonington, Cotman, and Turner.

In 1939–40 it was the medical base for the B.E.F., and on 19 Aug. 1942 was the target of a raid by approx. 6000 Allied troops, mostly Canadians. Although landings were made here and on neighbouring beaches (from Berneval to St-Marguerite), at the cost of heavy casualties it was found that the German defences were well-nigh impenetrable.

Among Dieppois are Jehan Ango (1480–1551), privateer and merchant prince; Jean Cousin, one of the claimants to the discovery of Brazil (1488); and Abraham Duquesne (1610–88), the Calvinist admiral who vanquished De Ruyter off Sicily. Sickert made Dieppe his headquarters in 1899–1905, living at *Neuville*, on the outskirts (and after 1911 moving to *Envermu*, 15km due E.), and the artistic colony here was frequented by Camille Pissarro, J.-E. Blanche, and Ludovic Halévy.

From the N.E. corner of the central *Parc Jehan Ango*, laid out on the site of an earlier basin, with the new *Hôtel de Ville* (and S.I.), the Quai

Duquesne leads to the *Gare Maritime* and landing-stage for the cross-Channel ferries. Further N. is the long Blvd de Verdun, beyond which, on the far side of gardens, is the parallel Blvd Foch, skirting the beach.—To the W. is the *Porte du Port d'Ouest*, a restored relic of the old town walls, passing through which we reach *St-Rémy* (1522–1640), recently restored, with immense round piers in its choir showing strong Renaissance influence in their capitals. The 18C organ is noteworthy.

Immediately to the S. is the Grande-Rue, partially a pedestrian precinct, off which rises **St-Jacques** (13-16C), exhibiting in the transeptal facades the purest Norman-Gothic style.

The W. end was heavily restored in the 19C, but the mutilated W. portal dates from the early 14C. Two curious gargoyles decorate the N. angle of the facade. To the S. is a square 15C tower; the rest of the building is hidden behind flying buttresses. At the W. end of the S. aisle is an admirable stone screen (1612), and a modern copy of the Entombment in the church at Eu. There is some delicate tracery in the choir, while in the ambulatory is a worn Renaissance frieze depicting the adventures of Dieppois merchants (over the entrance to the sacristy; N. side); in a chapel of the S. side is Jehan Ango's tomb.

Just beyond the W. end of the Grande-Rue, the Rue de Chastes, continued by a flight of steps, ascends N. to the **Castle**, dominating this end of the town, and offering extensive views. It may also be approached by a road further W. It dates from the 15C, but has been considerably restored, again after damage caused by the Germans prior to their retreat in 1944. The cylindrical keep, originally isolated, was erected in the 14C. The castle now houses a **Museum**, on the Ground Floor of which is a collection of ship models and marine views.

FIRST FLOOR. Paintings by *Eugène Isabey, Pissarro, Sickert,* and *J.-E. Blanche; Asselineau,* View of Dieppe c. 1880; *anon.* View of the Rue St-Rémy c. 1830; *Ruysdael,* Landscape; and works by *Boudin* and *Dufy.* Other rooms contain furniture, including a finely-carved oak bed; collections of pre-Colombian pottery, and **Carved ivories*; and the first piano (a Pleyel) of Saint-Saëns (1835–1921) among other souvenirs of the composer, whose father was a local farmer. By the exit is the *Donation Georges Braque*, with a number of works by the artist (1882–1963; cf. Varengeville).

DIEPPE TO AMIENS (107km). The D1 leads S.E. from the E. side of the harbour to (6.5km) *Martin-Église*, with a 12-13C church, and shortly beyond passes an obelisk commemorating the battle of 21 Sept. 1589, in which Henri IV decisively defeated the Leaguers under the Duc de Mayenne.—We follow the Béthune valley to (24.5km) *Mesnières-en-Bray* and (5km) *Neufchâtel-en-Bray;* see Rte 6. Hence the D135 continues S.E. via (41km) *Gerberoy,* to **Beauvais,** 21km beyond; see Rte 4.—*Forges-les-Eaux* (see below) lies 17km S.E. of Neufchâtel.—We climb uphill to the E. shortly forking r. onto the N29 for (26km) **Aumale,** on the Bresle, which suffered severely in 1940. The restored *Church* (1508–1610) shows some Renaissance features, the main portal being ascribed to Jean Goujon, above which rises a square tower with a staircase turret and a balustrade with statues of the Apostles. The vaulting in the apse, with pendants ending in statues of saints, is noteworthy. The *Hôtel de Ville* dates from the 15th and 17Cs. Henri IV, defeated here by the Spaniards in 1592, escaped wounded from the battlefield.—17km. *Poix-de-Picardie* (see Rte 4), beyond which the road veers N.E. towards (28km) **Amiens;** see Rte 5.

A recommended alternative to the main road, which may be joined 15km S.E. of Dieppe, is the D154, which after 6km traverses **Arques-la-Bataille,** famous for its battle and its ruined **Castle*, founded in the 11C by an uncle of William the Conqueror, and completely rebuilt in its present form by Henry I in 1123.

The English were finally expelled in 1449, and although François I visited the castle, it fell into disuse after the 17C, and was used as a quarry until purchased by the State in 1868, which saved it from further depredations, although it was damaged in 1944. Southey thought it 'altogether the finest ruin of its kind' he ever saw. The W. end, with the present entrance, was strengthened in the 16C by enormous double towers; at the E. end is the 12C keep, with 14C additions to guard the entrance bridge. It is still an attractive ruin, surrounded as it is by a deep moat although situated on a hill, and a footpath on the narrow exterior rampart affords a good view.

The large *Church* (1515– 1633), is, in spite of its date, a graceful example of Late Gothic, and contains a fine rood-loft and choir-screen of 1540 and a Renaissance timber roof with carved pendants. The choir preserves some 16C glass.

Continuing up the valley of the Varenne, at 9km we meet the D915 and turn l., skirting the extensive *Forêt d'Eawy.*—After 15km the road passes near the villages of *Fresles* and *Bully* (to the N.E. and E. respectively), both with churches containing notable 14-15C statues.—7km. *Les Hayons*, on the N28, which is crossed; c. 12km beyond, a l.-hand turning leads to the ruined abbey of *Beaubec*, founded in 1127, and restored in 1450 after a fire in 1383, and sheltered by the *Bois de l'Épinay*.

6km. **Forges-les-Eaux**, an old chalybeate spa visited by sufferers from anaemia, etc., has three principal springs, named La Royale, La Reinette, and La Cardinale, commemorating the visit in 1632 of Louis XIII and Anne of Austria, accompanied by Richelieu, in search of a cure for the queen's apparent sterility; six years passed, however, before the desired prince (Louis XIV) was born!

12.5km. 4km W. stands the château of *Brémontier-Merval* (1620– 30), N. of its church, containing sculpture from the vanished abbey of Bellozanne.

7.5km. **Gournay-en-Bray** (6500 inhab.), a market town on the Epte, is a centre for the manufacture of cream cheese known as 'petite suisses'. It was much damaged in 1940, but *St-Hildevert* preserves its Romanesque nave and Gothic choir (c. 1200), both with remarkable capitals, and a notable Renaissance organ-loft.—*Gerberoy* (see Rte 4) lies only 11.5km N.E.; and the N31 leads 30km E. via *St-Germer-de-Fly* to **Beauvais**; see Rte 9.

Continuing due S. from Gournay, the valley of the Epte is followed to (25km) *Gisors*, at 17km traversing *Sérifontaine*, its 12-16C church containing a well-carved 16C retable, and 4km beyond, *Eragny-sur-Epte*, which gave its name to the Eragny Press (London, 1894– 1914); Lucien Pissarro and his father lived at adjacent *Bazincourt* from 1884. For *Gisors*, and the road hence to **Paris**, see—in detail, but in the reverse direction—*Blue Guide Paris and Environs*. The main points of interest are given below.

GISORS (8900 inhab.), the former capital of the *Vexin Normand*, a territory long contested by the English and French, preserves the remarkable 13-16C church of ***St-Gervais-St-Protais**, to the N. of which are the extensive ruins of its ***Castle**, dominating the town, commenced in 1097 by William Rufus. Its keep rises from a mound in the centre of the enceinte, surrounded by 12 towers overlooking the double fosse, while the cylindrical *Tour du Prisonnier* is 29m high.

Hence the D915 leads S. It may be regained after making a brief DETOUR to the E. via *Trie-Château*, where in 1767 Rousseau, when guest of the Prince of Conti, finished writing his 'Confessions'. The road continues through *Chaumont-en-Vexin*, to the S.E., with a fine Renaissance tower to its Gothic church.

The D915 continues S.E., traversing (18km from Gisors) *Chars*, *Marines*, and *Cormeilles-en-Vexin*, each with churches of interest, before entering (18km) **Pontoise**, now part of the larger conurbation of *Cergy-Pontoise*. Pontoise was the ancient capital of the Vexin Français, but the older town now contains little of moment other than the church of *St-Maclou*, with a 12C choir and transepts, and nave and facade of the 15-16C, containing features of interest.—Relics of the 13C abbey of *Maubuisson* lie to the E., on the far bank of the Oise.

Hence we follow the N14 S.E. towards Paris, or join the A15 motorway; alternatively one may turn S. to cross the Seine at *Conflans-Ste-Honorine*, and after traversing the *Forêt de St-Germain*, enter **Paris** from the W. via *St-Germain-en-Laye*; see *Blue Guide Paris and Environs*, or Rte 14.

B. Via Rouen and the N14

190km (118 miles). N27. 61km **Rouen**—N14. 32km *Écouis*. **Les Andelys** lies 8km S.—32km *Magny-en-Vexin*—27km **Pontoise** —38km **Paris**.

Maps: IGN 3, 8, or 103. M 231, 237.

For **Dieppe**, see Rte 8A. Following the Av. Gambetta due S., the road bears r. after 3km, and after another 3km passes (r.) *Offranville*, where the artist J.-E. Blanche (1861-1942) died on his estate; the church dates from 1517.

To the l. is the 17C *Château de Miromesnil*, once the property of Louis XVI's minister of that name, and later of Guy de Maupassant's father, passed before climbing onto the *Plateau de Caux*.—16km. *Auffay*, with an interesting 12th to 17C church, lies 5km S.E.

7km. *Tôtes*, where the *Hôtel du Cygne* sheltered Maupassant when writing 'Boule-de-suif', and Flaubert in search of local colour for 'Madame Bovary'.

St-Victor-l'Abbaye, 6km E., retains the 13C chapter-house of a Benedictine foundation of 1051, and a 13C statue of William the Conqueror on the apse of its church.

9km. *Clères* lies 5.5km E., with a 15-16C château, and a collection of vintage cars.

4km. The old road descends a wooded valley to enter the industrial N. suburbs of Rouen, but it is advisable to bear S.W. to join the A15, descending directly to the river-bank and quays of **Rouen**; see Rte 6.

For the road leading along the Seine valley to Paris, and the autoroute, see Rte 8C.

The N14 drives S.E., soon climbing above the Seine, with retrospective views, and at 11km traverses *Boos* (pron. Bô), with remains of a nunnery and 16C *Dovecot.—13km. *Fleury-sur-Andelle*.

An attractive DETOUR may be made hence by turning S.W. down the valley past *Radepont*, with the ruins of a medieval castle captured from King John by Philippe Auguste in 1203, and not far beyond, the ruins of the Cistercian nunnery of *Fontaine-Guérard*, founded by Robert, Earl of Leicester, in 1198.—*Pont-St-Pierre*, further down the valley, has a château of c. 1500, and a 13C church containing 16-17C woodwork. The *Côte des Deux-Amants* (view) overlooks the Seine to the S.W., here controlled by the Amfreville lock.—Following the N.

bank of the river *Les Andelys* is approached (see below) from which the N14 may be regained 13km further E.

8km. *Écouis*, where the conspicuous *Church*, with its twin towers, founded c. 1310 by Enguerrand de Marigny, contains some remarkable 14C wood and stone sculptures, notably a St Veronica; Renaissance choir-stalls with 14C seats; a 15C Ecce Homo; a Burgundian Annunciation; and a portrait effigy of Abp Jean de Marigny (d. 1351).

Les Andelys lies 8km S., approaching which, near the hamlet of *Noyers*, are remains of a *Roman Theatre*, which measured 120m in diameter, etc. The twin towns of **Les Andelys** (8200 Andelysians), together with the rest of the route to Paris, are described in detail in *Blue Guide Paris and Environs*. Its most interesting building is *Notre-Dame*, 13C, with later additions. It contains 16C glass and an Entombment, a carved Renaissance organ, and several paintings by *Quentin Varin*, the first master of Nicolas Poussin (1594–1665), born in the neighbouring hamlet of *Villers-sur-Andelys*.

Hence a road climbs steeply to the impressive ruins of *Château-Gaillard, built by Richard I in 1196. The main road may be regained 13km to the E., by the D125 12km S.E. of Écouis.—*Hacqueville*, 4km N. of this junction, was the birthplace of Marc Isambard Brunel (1769–1849), the engineer.

3km. *Les Thilliers-en-Vexin*, 15km N.E. of which lies **Gisors**; see Rte 8A.—We traverse (7km) *St-Clair-sur-Epte*, where a treaty in 912 between Rollo and Charles le Simple established the river as a boundary of the Duchy of Normandy, and 7km beyond, by-pass (l.) *Magny-en-Vexin*, in which 16C *St-Martin* contains several monuments of note.

Hence the road continues S.E. passing at (8km) *Guiry-en-Vexin* (r.) a 17C château attrib. to *François Mansart*; and (6km) *Vigny* (r.) with a Renaissance château with pepper-pot towers, built by Card. Georges d'Amboise.—After 3km we reach a junction 10km prior to **Pontoise** (see Rte 8A), where, by turning 14km S.W., the A13 motorway may be joined (see Rte 8C), providing a convenient approach to central **Paris**.

C. Rouen to Paris via the N15 or A13

135km. (84 miles). N15. 18km *Pont-de-l'Arche*—24km *Gaillon*—14km *Vernon*—24km **Mantes**—55km **Paris**.

Maps: IGN 3, 8, or 103. M 231, 237.

The A13 motorway offers a more rapid route, and can be used in conjunction with the N15, particularly after Mantes, and may be joined c. 10km S.W. of *Rouen*; see Rte 6. It shortly crosses a loop of the Seine and traverses, among others, the *Forêt de Louviers*, before striking S.E. to Mantes, later swinging S. towards Versailles, to enter Paris at the Porte d'Auteil.

We follow the N15 along the N. bank of the Seine, at 10.5km turning l. to cross one of its numerous serpentine loops, and then the river at (7.5km) **Pont-de-l'Arche**, which owes it name to a bridge constructed by Charles le Chauve in the 9C to approach his palace; the bridge was last rebuilt in 1954. There are scanty remains of ramparts, and some half-timbered houses, while *St-Vigor* (1500–85) preserves good

contemporary glass, and choir stalls from *Bonport*, a ruined abbey
2km W., founded by Richard I in 1190 (in fulfilment of a vow made
while swimming the Seine with his horse, so it is said).

The road traverses the *Forêt de Bord*, and passes between **Louviers**
(4.5km S.; see Rte 28A) and (l.) the new town of *Le Vaudreuil*, briefly
running parallel to the motorway before veering away to (24km)
Gaillon which, and the road beyond, is described in detail in *Blue
Guide Paris and Environs*, but in the reverse direction, and partly in
Rte 25.

The N15 approaches and skirts the Seine to (14km) **Vernon**
(23,500 inhab.), an old town much damaged in 1940, and where the
Allies threw bridges across the river in Aug. 1944. It nevertheless
preserves several half-timbered houses, while 14-15C *Notre-Dame*,
with an elaborate W. front, contains several features of
interest.—**Giverny**, long the home of Claude Monet, with its charming *Gardens* and lily-ponds, lies some 4km S.E. on the far bank of
the Seine.—10km further E. is *La Roche-Guyon*, with the château of
the La Rochefoucauld family, where the author of the 'Maximes'
(1665) wrote a large part of his work.

Continuing to skirt the l. bank of the river, and crossing the *Corniche de Rolleboise*, we pass (14km) *Rosny*, and (6km) **Mantes**, for
which see Rte 25, and for the continuation of the N13 to **Paris**.—The
A13 motorway may be joined just S. of the town.

9 Rouen to Beauvais, Compiègne, and Soissons, for Reims

175km (108 miles). N31. 50km *Gournay-en-Bray*—30km **Beauvais**
—26km *Clermont*—31km **Compiègne**—38km **Soissons**.

Maps: IGN 8, 9, or 103. M 237.

For **Rouen**, see Rte 6. Climbing E. from Rouen through the industrial
suburb of *Darnétal*, after 16km we pass (r.) the moated *Château de
Martainville* ◇ (c. 1485), with a folk museum and large dovecot, 6km
beyond which is *Vascoeuil*, attractively sited in the Andell valley,
with the restored brick château '*de la Forestière*', a residence of the
historian Michelet.

Ry, 3km N.W., with a carved wooden Renaissance church-porch,
was the 'Yonville-l'Abbaye' of 'Madame Bovary'.— Some 5.5km
beyond, the Flamboyant *Church* at *Blainville*, founded 1489, contains carved stalls and 15C statues.

From Vascoeuil a DETOUR may be made by bearing S.E. through the *Forêt de
Lyons* to (11km) **Lyons-la-Forêt**, delightfully situated among beech woods, and
the birthplace of both Enguerrand de Marigny (1260–1315) and Isaac de
Benserade (1613–91), the laureate of the 'Précieuses'; the latter's home being
near the *Market-house*. Henry I died here in 1135. The *Church*, with a late-14C
alabaster Pietà and other sculpture, dates mainly from 1479.—Some 5km S. lie
the ruins of the Cistercian abbey-church of *Mortemer* (cons. 1209).—At *Le Tron-
quay*, 3km N. of Lyons, was born the engineer Nicolas Brémontier (1738–1809),
who was responsible for the reafforestation of the Landes, S. of
Bordeaux.—Hence we regain the N31 at *La Feuillie* (11km E. of Vascoeuil), with
a 13C church.

17km. *Gournay-en-Bray*; see Rte 8. Hence we bear S.E., after 6km
passing (2km r.) **St-Germer-de-Fly**, a village preserving the somewhat

Map 74   CLAIRIÈRE DE L'ARMISTICE **133**

shabby remains of an ancient abbey, the *Church* of which was begun shortly before 1150, and strikingly illustrates the transition from Romanesque to Gothic. From behind the choir a passage leads to the *Sainte-Chapelle* of 1259–66, an imitation, on a reduced scale, of that at Paris.

24km. **Beauvais**; see *Blue Guide Paris and Environs*, or Rte 4.

We continue E., after 5.5km bearing l., later traversing the *Forêt de Hez-Froidment* (see IGN 407), passing (r.) the 13-16C church of *Agnetz* just prior to entering (20km) *Clermont*; see *Blue Guide Paris and Environs*, or Rte 15.

After 16km the N17 is crossed, and then the A1, to enter (15km) **Compiègne**; see *Blue Guide Paris and Environs*, or Rte 16.

The N31 leads E. through the *Forêt de Compiègne* (see IGN 403), after 6km reaching the 'Clairière de l'Armistice', with a railway-coach, identical to that of Marshal Foch, later destroyed by the Germans. In the original coach German plenipotentiaries, who had presented themselves previously at Rethondes, signed the Armistice of 11 Nov. 1918. Hitler forced the French to sign an armistice in the same carriage in June 1940.

The road follows the S. bank of the Aisne, passing near several 12-13C churches, to approach (32km) **Soissons**; see *Blue Guide Paris and Environs*, or Rte 17. For the road hence to **Reims**, 56km E.; see Rte 5.

II   PARIS AND THE ÎLE DE FRANCE

10   Paris

A. General

The 16 routes in this section contain far more condensed descriptions than elsewhere in the Guide, as the area is described in detail in *Blue Guide Paris and Environs* (last edition, 1983), compiled by the Editor of this Guide, to which readers are referred. The following outline routes will, it is hoped, provide sufficient information for those travellers whose visit to Paris is merely a brief stage in the more thorough exploration of France as a whole.

Paris, the capital of France, lies on both banks of the *Seine*, near the centre of the so-called Paris Basin. Its height above sea-level varies from 25 to 130m, and its distance from the sea is 150km (or over 320km by the windings of the river). The Seine, the third in length of the four great rivers of France, enters the capital some 500km from its source, and describes a curved course through the city, at the same time forming two islands, the *Île St-Louis* and the larger *Île de la Cité*. Much of the attraction of Paris stems from the way the river, with its numerous bridges, has been used to unite rather than divide the northern or Right Bank (*Rive Droite*) and the southern or Left Bank (*Rive Gauche*); indeed, the two are much more nearly of equal importance than the N. and S. banks of the Thames. Unlike London, Paris was always (until c. 1919) bounded by a definite line of ramparts, which although they have been demolished and their sites built upon, served to contain its population, denser than in any other European city and enclosed an area of 7800 hectares. The line of the 19C defensive walls can be imagined by following the exterior Blvd Périphérique.

The total municipal population of *Paris*, according to the census of 1982 was—in round figures—2,170,000 a notable proportion of which was made up of foreigners, many from the poorer nations of Europe, but also including large numbers of Algerians, Tunisians, Moroccans, and others from Black Africa, as confirmed by recent demographic surveys. Those interested in such figures are advised to contact that useful and helpful organisation, the *Institut National de la Statistique et des Études Économiques* (INSEE), its head offices at 18 Blvd Adolphe Pinard, 14e, and with its centre for the Île-de-France in Tour Gamma A, 195 Rue de Bercy, Paris 12e (easily approached from the level of the Gare de Lyon).

With the growth of Paris, the old department of the Seine was by a decree which took effect in 1968, subdivided into four departments: *Ville-de-Paris*; *Hauts-de-Seine* (préfecture *Nanterre*); *Seine-St-Denis* (préfecture *Bobigny*); and *Val-de-Marne* (préfecture *Créteil*). The old department of *Seine-et-Oise* was similarly divided into three: *Val-d'Oise* (préfecture *Cergy-Pontoise*); *Yvelines* (préfecture *Versailles*); and *Essonne* (préfecture *Évry*). At the same time the department of *Seine-et-Marne* (préfecture *Melun*) was incorporated to make up what is now known as *La Région d'Île-de-France*.

The topography of Paris can perhaps be best understood by taking the **Pl. de la Concorde** as a focal point, although historically the *Pl. du Parvis-Notre-Dame* (from which kilometric distances are measured) might be more appropriate. Hence (and elsewhere) we can appreciate the artistic town-planning of the past, which deliberately allowed vistas from one bank of the river to extend to the far bank in further impressive perspectives. Indeed it is these great perspectives that are particularly memorable about Paris, but visitors are warned that because of the sheer scale of many of its monuments, and the extensive sweep of many such vistas, it is only too easy to underestimate distances, and one should not attempt too much sightseeing in a day.

Turning to the N.W., we can see the *Arc de Triomphe* at the far end of the *Champs-Élysées*; in the opposite direction, the immense bulk of the *Louvre* beyond the gardens of the *Tuileries*. This is flanked to the N. by the *Rue de Rivoli*, which with its continuation, the *Rue St-Antoine*, leads to the *Pl. de la Bastille*. It is perhaps this diagonal axis, more than the river, which cuts Paris into two almost equal parts.

Central Paris contains twenty municipal districts, or *Arrondissements*, each with its Maire and Mairie, or town hall, which are important administrative and topographical entities, their names and numbers conveying far more than that of a municipal borough or mere postal district in London.

A few only of the more important and interesting buildings and museums in *central* Paris, which should not be missed on a brief visit, are described in Rtes 10B-12. For a more detailed description the reader is referred to *Blue Guide Paris and Environs*, in which such obtrusive monuments as the Eiffel Tower, Tour Montparnasse, the Opéra, Arc de Triomphe, and Sacre-Coeur, are covered, together with several museums of interest not only to the specialist, such as the Cabinet des Médailles et des Antiques of the Bibliothèque Nationale, the Musée Jacquemart-André, Musée Nissim de Camondo, Musée National des Arts et Traditions Populaires (at the N. end of the Bois de Boulogne), Musée de la Marine (in the Palais de Chaillot), and the oriental collections of the Musée Guimet and Musée Cernuschi. Several new museums, such as that devoted to Picasso in the restored Hôtel Salé, and the Science Museum at La Villette, will be detailed in forthcoming editions of this companion volume, which likewise describes a number of churches of architectural interest, among them Val-de-Grâce, St-Louis (part of the Hôpital de la Salpetrière), St-Sulpice, and St-Gervais-St-Protais; also the Château de Vincennes, with its imposing keep, in which died Henry V of England, among the *embarras de richesse* that Paris itself has to offer.

B. Île de la Cité

MÉTROS: *Pont-Neuf; Châtelet; St-Michel; Cité.*

The *Île de la Cité*, the earliest inhabited part of the capital, and long the royal, legal, and ecclesiastical centre, lies in the Seine like a ship, the 'Pointe' as its prow, and *Notre-Dame* as its poop, moored to either bank by numerous bridges, the *Pont-Neuf*, the oldest (1607), crossing the W. extremity of the island, embellished with a statue of Henri IV.

To the E. of this is the *Pl. Dauphine*, beyond which, on the N. bank, is the entrance to the much-restored ***Conciergerie,**◊ one of the world's famous prisons, occupying part of the lower floor of the Palais de Justice, and originally the residence of the 'Concierge', chief executive of the Parlement, and its historical associations are numerous.

From the *Salle des Gardes*, a handsome vaulted room dating from the 14C, a spiral staircase in the r.-hand corner was climbed by Marie-Antoinette and some 2275 other prisoners on the way from their cells to the Tribunal. The four-aisled Gothic *Salle des Gens-d'Armes* was the original 'Salle des Pas-Perdus', said to be so-called because the victims of the Revolution walked through it to the Cour du Mai and execution. Near its far end an open spiral stair leads to the *Cuisines de St-Louis* (14C), also vaulted, with four huge fireplaces. One is also shown the *Galerie des Prisonniers*, the windows of which look out onto the *Cour des Femmes*, where the female prisoners took exercise, and the scene of the massacres of Sept. 1792; also the original door (but in a different position) of Marie-Antoinette's cell, where the queen remained from 2 Aug. to 16 Oct. 1793. Adjacent is that of Robespierre. Several souvenirs may be seen in the *Chapel*—with a gallery for prisoners—including a blade of the guillotine.

The Blvd du Palais, to the E., is flanked by the **Palais de Justice**, incorporating the hall of the medieval palace in which in 1431 the coronation banquet of Henry VI of England was celebrated, and among other rooms the *Chambre Dorée*, perhaps originally the bedroom of Louis IX, and later used by the Parlement, in contempt of which Louis XIV here coined the epigram 'L'État, c'est moi'. The Revolutionary Tribunal, with Fouquier-Tinville as public prosecutor, sat here in 1793.

A vaulted gateway leads from the *Cour du Mai* to approach the *Sainte Chapelle*, ◇ built in 1243–48 by Louis IX as a shrine for miscellaneous relics, and ascribed to *Pierre de Montreuil*, but overrestored in the mid 19C. It was often the scene of royal marriages, and Richard II of England was here betrothed in 1396 to Isabelle of France.

The building, remarkable for the impression of lightness it conveys, consists in fact of two superimposed chapels, the lofty and luminous stained-glass windows of the upper being particularly noteworthy. The 86 panels from the Apocalypse in the large rose were a gift of Charles VIII, while other windows represent scenes from the Old and New Testaments, the Legend of the Cross, etc.

Turning E. from the Cour du Mai, and turning r., we approach the W. Front of *Notre-Dame*, and the entrance (r.) to the *Crypte Archéologique*, ◇ uncovered during excavations since 1965, and one of the more interesting relics of old Paris extant. The site is exceptionally well displayed, with sections illuminated by press-button lighting, and with explanatory notes printed both in French and English. One may see the foundations of the late 3C *Gallo-Roman rampart*, and further E., of the 6C Merovingian cathedral of St-Étienne (founded by Childebert), together with those of several other medieval buildings, and relics of hypocausts, etc.

The foundation-stone of *Notre-Dame* was laid in 1163, and the building, replacing an earlier church on this site, was virtually completed during the 13C. Its inception was due to Maurice de Sully, Bp of Paris (d. 1196), and it replaced the cathedral of St-Étienne (see above).

Here in 1430, at the age of ten, Henry VI of England was crowned king of France; and here were celebrated the marriages of François II to Mary Stuart (1558), Henry of Navarre to Marguerite de Valois (1572), Charles I of England (by proxy) to Henrietta Maria (1625); Napoleon I and Joséphine were crowned here in 1804, and Napoleon III and Eugénie de Montijo were married here in 1853. The reigns of Louis XIV and Louis XV brought deplorable alterations, while further destruction was caused during the Revolution, and it was not until 1845 that a thorough 'restoration' was begun by Lassus and Viollet-le-Duc.

Key to map on following pages

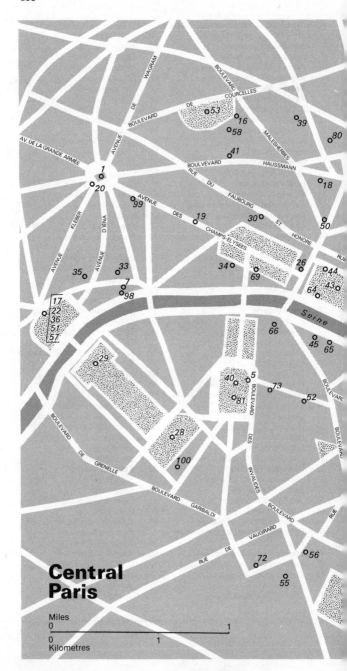

Central Paris

Miles
0 _____ 1
0 _____
Kilometres 1

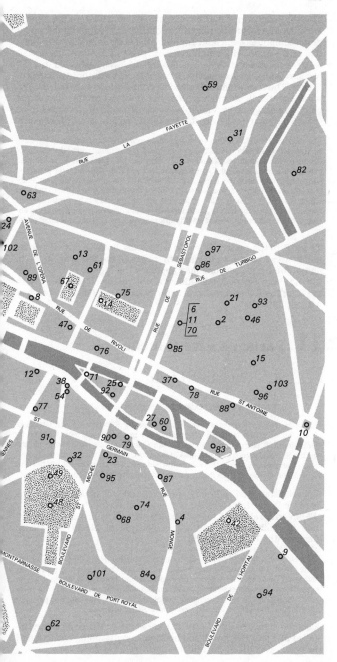

The W. Front forms one harmonious whole, although the central *Porte du Jugement* was ruined by Soufflot in 1771. Only the upper tier of sculptures is ancient. To the l. is the *Porte de la Vierge*; to the r. that of *Ste-Anne*, with sculptures mostly late 12C. Above the portals is the reconstructed *Gallery of the Tree of Jesse*, destroyed in 1793 because the Parisians assumed the sculptures to be those of kings of France. The rose-window, flanked by double-windows within arches, is surmounted by an open arcade. The *Towers*, with their grotesque gargoyles designed by Viollet-le-Duc, were originally intended to be crowned by spires; also notable are the flying buttresses of the *Apse*.

The *interior* (130m long, 48m wide, and 35m high) consists of a nave of ten bays of great purity of design, flanked by double aisles continued round the choir. Of the three *Rose-windows*, retaining their original 13C glass, the N. is the best preserved and finest. The *Choir* was modified in 1708–25, and later attracted Viollet-le-Duc's restoring hand, but 78 of the Stalls remain. Geoffrey Plantagenet, son of Henry II, was buried in front of the high altar in 1186, to the S. of which is a statue of Louis XIII, by *Coustou*; that of Louis XIV is by *Coysevox*. On the S. side of the *Ambulatory*, containing the tombs of several prelates, is the entrance to the *Treasury*, a somewhat indifferent collection of ecclesiastical plate, etc.

To the E. of the cathedral lies the *Île St-Louis*. Both islands are convenient bases from which to visit either bank of the Seine. From the E. end of the Île St-Louis one may approach the *Marais* with ease; see Rte 12. From Notre-Dame either the *Quartier Latin* (see Rte 11), to the S., or the *Centre Beauborg*, to the N. (see Rte 12) may be reached without difficulty.

11 Paris: La Rive Gauche

A. Quartier Latin

MÉTROS: *St-Michel; Odéon; Maubert-Mutualité.*

The Latin Quarter derives its name, conferred by Rabelais, on the language spoken by its earlier students: the argot of the present day is more difficult to comprehend. It occupies the site of Roman *Lutetia*, and its main thoroughfare was the Rue St-Jacques (the Roman *Via Superior*), until the Blvd St-Germain was driven transversely across the area in the mid 19C. The busy Blvd St-Michel (the *Via Inferior*) divides it from its W. extension, covered in Rte 11B.

A short distance S.E. of the *Pl. St-Michel*, and S.W. of the *Pl. du Parvis de Notre-Dame*, from which it is approached via the *Petit-Pont*, stands ***St-Séverin**, rebuilt in the 13-16C on the site of an oratory of the time of Childebert I, and where Foulque of Neuilly-sur-Marne preached the Fourth Crusade.

The main W. portal (early 13C), was brought piecemeal from a destroyed church in the Cité in 1837; its upper storeys date from the 15C; the tower, also 13C, was completed in 1487. The interior impresses by the breadth of its double ambulatory, while the most striking details are the ribs of the vaulting and the choir triforium, which approach English Perpendicular in style. The apse was partially classicised in the 17C at the expense of Mlle de Montpensier.

A short distance to the S. is the entrance to the ***Musée de Cluny**, installed in a late 15C hôtel, and housing an outstanding collection of the arts and crafts of the Middle Ages.

In 1515 it became the residence of Mary Tudor (1496–1533), daughter of Henry VII and later widow of Louis XII, when she was known as 'La Reine Blanche' from the white mourning worn by her as queen-dowager. James V of Scotland was lodged here before his wedding with Madeleine, daughter of François I, in 1537.

The inventory of the museum now approaches 23,000 items, only a proportion of which are on display. Notable is its collection of *Tapestries*, among them the famous series of 'millefleurs' known as 'La Dame á la Licorne (or Unicorn), probably woven in the southern Netherlands for Jean Le Viste just prior to 1500. At the far end of the ground floor are steps descending to the *Frigidarium* of the Gallo-Roman baths, still preserving its vault, unique in France, and probably dating from c. 217. The *Chapel*, vaulted from a central pillar, is likewise remarkable.

From opposite the entrance, one may continue S. along the ascending Rue de la Sorbonne, passing (l.) *Ste-Ursule de la Sorbonne*, rebuilt at the expense of Card. Richelieu (d. 1642), and containing his dramatic tomb, designed by *Le Brun*, and sculptured by *Girardon* (1694).

On reaching the Rue Soufflot, to the W. rises the grandiose bulk of the **Panthéon**, ◊ situated on the highest point of the Left Bank. Designed by *Soufflot*, it was completed in 1789, and shortly after it was decreed that it should be a burial-place of distinguished citizens.

Externally imposing, it is built in the shape of a Greek Cross, 100m long, 82m wide, and 83m high to the top of its majestic dome. The pediment above the portico is the masterpiece of *David d'Angers*, representing France between Liberty and History. The interior, coldly Baroque, of slight interest, contains monuments to Diderot and the Encyclopaedists, and Rousseau, among others; and the crypt preserves the remains of Rousseau, Voltaire, Victor Hugo, Zola, Braille, Bougainville, et al.

Immediately to the N.E. stands ***St-Étienne-du-Mont** (1492–1586, with a later portal); the picturesque porch on its N. side dates from 1632. The interior retains its beautiful fretted *Rood-screen* of 1535, and late 16C glass. The graves of Pascal and Racine are by the entrance of the Lady Chapel, while the artist Le Sueur is likewise buried here. The *Windows* of 1609 in the adjacent Charnier are notable, mostly designed by *Léonard Gautier*, one of which depicts the Mystic Wine-press.

B. St-Germain-des-Prés

MÉTROS: *St-Michel; Odéon; Mabillon; St-Germain-des-Prés.*

From the Pl. Edmond-Rostand, at the W. end of the Rue Soufflot (see above), one may bear N.W., skirting the *Jardin du Luxembourg*, to reach the ***Palais du Luxembourg**, with its heavily rusticated masonry, built by *Salomon de Brosse* for Marie de Médicis in 1615–27, and enlarged in the 19C before housing the French Senate. The *Cabinet Doré* is its most interesting room, but the series of paintings devoted to the Life of Marie de Médicis, by Rubens, which once hung in the palace, are now in the Louvre.

From its N. entrance, one may descend the wide Rue de l'Odéon, bordered by 18C houses, to reach the Blvd St-Germain. A short distance to the W. rises ***St-Germain-des-Prés**, retaining considerable remains of Romanesque work, but much mutilated over the centuries and only recently restored. It is all that remains of a

Benedictine abbey founded in 558 by Childebert I, who is buried there.

The W. porch dates from 1607, put preserves the jambs of a 12C door and a battered lintel depicting the Last Supper. The interior is architecturally interesting for the combination of the Romanesque style with the first attempts at the Gothic style in the choir. It contains the tombstones of Descartes (d. 1650), removed from Ste-Geneviève in 1819, and that of Nicolas Boileau (d. 1711), removed from the Sainte Chapelle.

From just N.E. of the building, one may traverse the picturesque *Pl. de Furstemberg*, and continue N. along the Rue de Seine to approach the **Institut de France**, surmounted by its gilded dome, designed by *Le Vau* and erected in 1662–74 as a college, in accordance with Card. Mazarin's will. It is now the home of the Académie Française, founded by Richelieu in 1635, and houses the *Bibliothèque Mazarine*.

The adjacent *quais* provide extensive views across towards the *Palais du Louvre* (see Rte 12), which may be approached by the *Pont du Carrousel*, to the W.

C.   The Fauborg St-Germain

MÉTROS: *Chambre des Députés; Solferino; Invalides; Varenne.*

By continuing W. along the S. bank of the Seine from the *Pont du Carrousel* (spanning the river from the *Palais du Louvre*), one passes, beyond the *Pont Royal*, the **Musée d'Orsay**, or *du XIXᵉ* (Dix-neuvième) *Siècle*, in the process of installation in the gutted *Gare d'Orsay* (1900), an all-too-solid structure, which will contain a variety of French 19C paintings and sculptures at present distributed among several museums.

With the *Jardin des Tuileries* on the far bank, we may continue W. past (r.) the *Palais de la Lègion d'Honneur* (1786) and the *Palais-Bourbon* (1722; but since radically changed), accommodating the Assemblée Nationale, equivalent to the British House of Commons. Hence the *Pont de la Concorde* leads N. to the *Pl. de la Concorde*; see Rte 12.

We reach, a short distance further W., the *Esplanade des Invalides*, at the S. end of which is the majestic ***Hôtel des Invalides**, founded in 1671 as a home for disabled soldiers, and which at one time housed 4000 pensioners. It was erected to the designs of *Libéral Bruant*, and was continued by *J. Hardouin-Mansart*. The dormer windows of the dignified facade, over 200m long, take the form of trophies, each different, while the equestrian bas-relief of Louis XIV above the central door is by *Pierre Cartellier*. Opposite the entrance to the Cour d'Honneur is the simple but imposing *Church of St-Louis*, beyond which is the ***Dome des Invalides** (1675–1796), below which lies the *Tomb of Napoleon* (1769–1821), designed by *Visconti*, in which the Emperor was placed in 1861, forty years after his death at St Helena, although his remains were brought to the Invalides in 1840. In surrounding chapels lie the tombs of Joseph Bonaparte, Vauban, Foch, Lyautey, La Tour d'Auvergne, and Turenne.

The extensive buildings also house the ***Musée de l'Armée**, one of outstanding collections of military souvenirs and of arms and armour of its kind; the subsidiary *Musée des Plans-Reliefs*, in its attics, should not be overlooked.

Immediately to the E., with its entrance in the Rue de Varenne, is the *Hôtel Biron* (1730; by *Aubert* and *Gabriel*), a fine example of the type of mansion erected in the Faubourg St-Germain—extending E.—during the 18C, many of them now converted to house embassies or government offices. It now contains an impressive collection of the sculpture of Auguste Rodin (1840–1917).

12 Paris: La Rive Droit

A. Pl. de la Concorde to the Pl. du Louvre

MÉTROS: *Concorde; Tuileries; Palais-Royal; Louvre.*

Occupying a central position on the Seine midway between the *Étoile* and the Île de la Cité, is the impressive **Pl. de la Concorde**, in the centre of which rises the *Obelisk of Luxor*, presented by Mohammed Ali to Louis-Philippe in 1831, and originating at Thebes in Upper Egypt (13C B.C.). The site was occupied by a guillotine during the Revolution, which claimed the life of some 1119 victims, including Charlotte Corday, Marie-Antoinette, Philippe-Égalité, Mme Roland, Hébert, Danton, Mme Élisabeth, Robespierre, and Louis XVI (21 Jan. 1793). Unfortunately it is often congested by swirling traffic, and one can no longer, as Arthur Young did when visiting the square in 1787, feel clean 'and breath freely'.

To the S. is the facade of the *Palais-Bourbon* (see above); to the N., between two handsome mansions designed by *Gabriel* in 1763–72, at the end of the Rue Royale, stands the church usually known as the **Madeleine** (1806–42) with a majestic Corinthian colonnade, but with an interior of slight interest. Towards the W. extends the long Av. des Champs-Élysées, at first flanked by gardens, and ascending gently towards the huge *Arc de Triomphe*. In the opposite direction extends the *Jardin des Tuileries*, adorned with a wealth of statues, in the N.W. corner of which is the *Jeu de Paume* (previously displaying a collection of Impressionists, now in the *Musée du XIXe Siècle*; see Rte 11C); to the S.W. is the *Orangerie*.

The *Palais du Louvre* may be approached hence through the gardens, or via the arcaded Rue du Rivoli, skirting its N. side, and passing near the impressive **Pl. Vendôme** (approached by the Rue de Castiglione), its uniform mansions designed by Hardouin-Mansart, in the centre of which rises the *Vendôme Column* (1810; in the style of Trajan's Column in Rome).

The Rue de Rivoli reaches the N.W. wing of the Palais du Louvre at the Pl. des Pyramides, just N. of which stands **St-Roch** (1653–1735), in which Corneille, Diderot, Le Nôtre, Mme Geoffrin, and Cherubini are buried. This mid 19C wing now houses the ***Musée des Arts Décoratifs**, an outstanding collection of decorative and ornamental art too often overlooked by visitors.

Between this wing and the long S. wing overlooking the Seine lies the *Jardin du Carrousel*, and the small *Arc du Triomphe du Carrousel*, built in 1806 to commemorate Napoleonic victories. Hence we obtain a good general view of the ***Palais du Louvre**, one of the world's most magnificent palaces, originating as a fortress in the 12C, and which later became a royal residence. It was largely rebuilt by François I, and then extended. Louis XIV, preoccupied with Versailles, lost interest in the building, and it was not until 1754 that Louis XV commissioned *Gabriel* to renovate and restore the edifice. Its W. wing was demolished in 1871 after being fired by the Communards. It has contained a museum since 1793.

The main entrance is in the Pav. Denon, on the N. side of the S. wing. The older palace comprises the buildings around the courtyard further E., much of it rebuilt by *Le Vau* after 1660, while its exterior E. facade was the work of *Claude Perrault* (1670).—Facing it is the church of *St-Germain-l'Auxerrois* (13-16C).

The ****Musée du Louvre**, in the process of drastic reorganisation, will eventually extend into part of the N. wing, recently vacated by the Min. des Finance. Its extensive and unsurpassed collections are devoted to Paintings (and Drawings); Greek and Roman antiquities; Egyptian Antiquities; Oriental (or rather middle-eastern) antiquities; Objets d'Art (including furniture), and Sculpture. The building and its contents are described in detail in the *Blue Guide to Paris and Environs*.

While it is invidious to mention individual masterpieces in the collections, for so many are outstanding, and some—such as *da Vinci's* Monna Lisa or the *anon.* Venus 'de Milo'—too often the target of milling crowds, notable among the PAINTINGS, in which the French School naturally predominates, are several canvases by the following: Poussin, Claude Lorrain, Georges de la Tour, Louis le Nain, Chardin, Watteau, Boucher, Greuze, David, Gros, Ingres, Géricault, and Delacroix, all of whom are well represented. Among foreign schools, it is rich in examples of the work of Rembrandt, Memling, Van Dyck, and Rubens; Zurbaran, Ribera, and Murillo; Botticelli, Mantegna, Perugino, Veronese, Titian, Raphael, and Guardi; Cranach the Elder, and Holbein the Younger, et al.

The GREEK AND ROMAN (and ETRUSCAN) collection contains numerous important sculptures, sections of friezes, mosaics, monumental vases, bronzes, jewellery, arms, and utensils, etc., and extensive collections of Antique pottery from the 10C to 4C B.C., figurines, and glassware, etc.

The department of EGYPTOLOGY preserves several outstanding sculptures (such as the so-called 'Scribe accroupi'), funeral steles, effigies, statuettes, and several rooms devoted to smaller objects such as Ushbati figures, mirrors, scarabs, votive offerings, jewellery, and pottery, etc., together with a section of Coptic antiquities.

Notable among the 'ORIENTAL' Antiquities are the *Codex of Hammurabi* (c. 1800 B.C.) and the *Moabite Stone* (842 B.C.), together with Sumarian and other Babylonian antiquities, including reliefs from the palace of Darius; also Phoenician and Assyrian antiquities, etc.

OBJETS D'ART. Several rooms are devoted to Medieval and Renaissance Goldsmiths' work, ivories, enamels, bronzes, medals, and ceramics, etc.; tapestries, and furniture (mostly 18C; by Boulle, Cressent, Oeben, Cramer, Riesener, and the Jacob family); also collections of watches and clocks, snuffboxes, silverware, jewellery, Sèvres porcelain, etc.

SCULPTURE. Partly of the 'Gothic' period, together with examples of the German and Italian Schools (among the latter being works by Donatello, and Michelangelo). Among French sculptors are representative works by Germain Pilon, Goujon, Coysevox, Pigalle, Caffieri, Houdon, Pradier, Rude, Barye, et al.

B. From the Pl. du Palais Royal to the Pl. des Vosges

MÉTROS: *Palais Royal; Louvre; Halles; Rambuteau; Châtelet; Hôtel de Ville; St-Paul.*

Immediately N. of the Pl. du Palais Royal stands the **Palais-Royal**, originally the 'Palais Cardinal', having been built by J. Lemercier for Richelieu in 1634–39, who bequeathed it to Louis XIII. It passed through the hands of several architects during succeeding centuries, but its arcades and gardens provide a delightful backwater. During the Revolutionary period they were the scene of unbridled licence and revelry.

From the Pl. du Louvre, immediately E. of the Palais du Louvre, the Rue de Louvre leads N. past (r.) the *Bourse du Commerce*, a circular mid 18C building abutted by a column, a relic of a residence built for Catherine de Médicis in 1572.—Further N.E. stands ***St-Eustache** (1532–1637), and partly rebuilt in the 18C. Its interior is a striking example of classical forms with a Gothic plan, and it contains a remarkable organ. Both Colbert and Rameau were buried here.

To the S. of the church, until its recent demolition, stood *Les Halles*, the main market of Paris, succeeded by a characterless pedestrian precinct and commercial premises still under construction. By continuing E. across the Blvd de Sébastapol, we reach an unattractive but much promoted scaffolding-like glazed structure known variously as the **Centre Beauborg** or *Centre Pompidou*, apart from other less complimentary names. It contains, nevertheless, an important **Collection of Modern Art* on its 3rd and 4th levels.

Hence, from its N.E. corner, the Rue Rambuteau, continued by the Rue des Francs Bourgeois, lead E. past the *Hôtel de Soubise* (1.; 1712), accommodating the *Archives Nationales*, and one of the many fine mansions in the area known as the **Marais**, long the most fashionable residential quarter of Paris until the creation of the Faubourg St-Germain in the early 18C.—A short distance further E. is the ***Musée Carnavalet**, with important collections illustrating the history of Paris, while the building (1544; later altered by *Mansart*) was once the residence of Mme de Sévigné.—Not far beyond lies the attractive ***Pl. de Vosges**, a spacious quadrangle surrounded by 39 houses of red brick with stone facings built on a uniform plan over arcades in the first decade of the 17C.

It occupies the site of a residence of the Duke of Bedford after the death of Henry V, and in 1559 it was the scene of the fatal tournament in which Henri II was accidentally killed by Montgomery, and in consequence abandoned by his widow, Catherine de Médicis.

13 Paris to Versailles

ROAD. The fastest approach is the A13 motorway, off which turn l. at the first exit after traversing the St-Cloud tunnel.

RAIL. A convenient approach is the new RER line running along the S. bank of the Seine, where the train may be boarded at, for example, *St-Michel, Gare d'Orsay, Invalides, Champ-Mars*, or *Javel*, etc., a branch of which has its terminus at *Versailles-Rive Gauche*, the station nearest the palace.

BUS 171 from the *Pont des Sèvres*, served by MÉTRO.

An alternative road is that following the N. bank of the Seine to the Pont de Sèvres, there crossing the river and taking the N10 to (9km) Versailles. Immediately to the N. at *Sèvres* is the most famous *Porcelain Factory*, moved here from Vincennes at the instance of Mme de Pompadour. Here is a sale-room and *Musée Céramique* (also displaying other than Sèvres ware); the workshops may also be visited.—Slightly further on is the *Parc of St-Cloud*, ◊ the royal château of which was burned down in 1870.

Note that the *Palace* of Versailles is closed on Mondays, although the gardens are open every day until dusk. The town of **Versailles** (95,200 inhab.; 25,000 in 1801; 55,000 in 1901), the préfecture of *Yvelines*, with its imposing avenues converging on the palace, which overshadows it in interest, still seeks to retain its royal cachet.

It emerged from obscurity when Louis XIII built a hunting-lodge here, enlarged c. 1630. In 1661 Louis XIV conceived the idea of erecting a trophy of self-glorification in the form of a vast palace, the cost of which impoverished France: *tant pis*. Le Vau restored and embellished the original building, while Le Brun superintended its interior decoration, and after 1676 Jules Hardouin-Mansart remodelled the whole, which was extended by two huge wings, producing an immense facade with a total length of 580m. Meanwhile Le Nôtre laid out the Gardens, in which the Grand Trianon was commenced in 1687, and the Petit Trianon completed some 80 years later. The seat of government had been transferred to Versailles in 1682.

Here in 1783 the independence of the United States was formally recognised by England, France, and Spain. Here in June 1789 the States-General constituted themselves into the National Assembly; on 6 Oct. the Paris mob marched on the palace, massacred the bodyguard, and carried the royal family to the Tuileries. It was re-occupied in 1814 but later fell into some disrepair, being used as a hospital by the invading armies during the Franco-Prussian War. On 25 Feb. the Third Republic was proclaimed here; here on 28 June 1919 the Peace Treaty with Germany was signed. It was the Allied G.H.Q. for some months after Sept. 1944.

Among buildings of interest in Versailles itself are (to the N.E. of the palace) *Notre-Dame* (1684), and just beyond, the *Musée Lambinet*, containing sculptures by Houdon, a native of the town, and other works. Immediately to the S. of the palace is the *Grand-Commun*, built to house a swarm of minor officials; while off the Av. de Sceaux is the *Jeu de Paume*, where deputies of the Third Estate adjourned in 1789, swearing not to separate until they had given France a proper constitution.—Slightly further S. is the somewhat frigid *Cathedral of St-Louis* (1754).—Opposite the main front of the palace are the *Grandes* and *Petites-Écuries*, the royal stables, once accommodating 2000 carriages and 2500 horses, later barracks, and in the process of being converted to other uses.

The ***PALACE OF VERSAILLES** is open every day from 9.45-17.00 except Mondays, but only the State Apartments can be traversed without restriction; most of the other suites of rooms may only be visited in guided groups (some with an English-speaking guide), and one should enquire at the entrance vestibule for details: normally there is little delay in waiting for a group to collect. It is as well to check in advance on times of admission to the Trianons. Some tourists attempt what is virtually impossible in endeavouring to visit the entire palace, the gardens, and the Trianons in the same day.

The main entrance is to the r. of the *Cour Royale*, but it is worth walking over first to the *Cour de Marbre* at its far end, which courtyard was the nucleus of the palace before its later transformations.

Adjacent to the vestibule is the **Chapel**, with its colonnade of Corinthian columns, completed by Robert de Cotte in 1710; beyond are the *Salles du XVIIᵉ Siècle*, containing an impressive collection of portraits, views of Versailles and other palaces by P.-D. and J.-B. Martin, and of sieges by Van der Meulen, etc. At the far end of this N. wing is the restored **Opéra** (1753-70; by Gabriel). Ascending to the FIRST FLOOR, we return S., continuing through a series of galleries, and with a striking view of the chapel from an upper vestibule, to enter the *Salon d'Hercule*, where Swiss Guards used to be posted to prevent the intrusion into the *State Apartments* of 'those freshly marked by smallpox, the shabbily dressed, petitioners, begging friars, and dogs'. The following six rooms retain most of their original decoration, executed under the supervision of Le Brun, the *Salon de Mars* containing Gobelin tapestries designed by him illustrating the Life of Louis XIV. The *Salon de la Guerre* is next entered, serving as an antechamber to the magnificent **Galerie des Glaces**, 73m long and lighted by seventeen windows, facing which are as many mirrors.

To the r. are the *Cabinet de Conseil* (transformed in 1755), and the *King's Bedchamber* (in which Louis XIV died), overlooking the Cour de Marbre. Here took place the ceremonial 'lever' and 'coucher' of the king, who used to lunch daily at a little table placed by the middle window. It was from the balcony here that Louis XVI and Marie-Antoinette showed themselves to the mob on 6 Oct. 1789. Adjacent is the *Oeil-de-Boeuf*, so-called after its windows, where courtiers assembled to await admission to the king.

Off the Cabinet de Conseil is a suite of private apartments constructed after 1738 to provide Louis XV with a retreat from the tedious etiquette of his court, for (to quote Richard Ford, when describing the royal palace at Madrid) 'nothing is more tiresome than a palace, a house of velvet, tapestry, gold and bore. . . '. The *Queen's Bedchamber* (in which both Marie-Thérèse and Marie Leczinska died—in 1683 and 1768 respectively—and where took place many confinements of the queens of France), is adjacent to the *Salon de la Paix*. Overlooking the interior courtyard are the cramped private apartments of Marie-Antoinette. To the E. is the *Salle des Gardes de la Reine*, where the revolutionaries burst in to apprehend the royal couple, having ascended the adjoining *Escalier de Marbre*.

From the loggia across the landing one may visit the *Apartments of Mme de Maintenon*, in which a collection of 16C portraits by Corneille de Lyon and artists of the School of Clouet are displayed.—On the floor above are the *Attiques de Chimay* and *du Midi*, in which are installed outstanding collections of historical paintings illustrating the early Napoleonic period, and should not be overlooked: they included numerous fine paintings by Bacler d'Albe, Lejeune, Lefèvre, Bagetti, Gérard, David, Taunay, et al among other portraitists and war-artists of the era.—Also on these upper floors are the diminutive suites in which Mme du Barry, and Mme de Pompadour were installed.

On the first floor of the *S. Wing*, mutilated by Louis-Philippe, is the *Galerie des Batailles* formed by demolishing most of the rooms previously there, and now displaying a sad collection of huge canvases representing French military achievements, perhaps the best of which is Delacroix's 'The Battle of Taillebourg': Thackeray considered them among 'the worst pictures that eye ever looked on'. The galleries on the floor below are likewise of slight interest, although they contain certain works by H. and C. Vernet, and Gros.

On descending the Escalier de Marbre, one may visit the *Salles de XVIIIᵉ Siècle*, overlooking the gardens, the apartments of the dauphin and dauphine, and other members of the royal family. They have been repeatedly altered, and now preserve a number of portraits by Nattier and Vigée-Lebrun, among others. One room is devoted to 'American Independence', with portraits of Washington (after C.W. Peale) and of famous Americans, painted by G.P.A. Healy.

The **Gardens of Versailles* are entered by a passage-way just W. of the main entrance. Laid out originally by Le Nôtre in 1661 – 68, they are essentially formal, with geometrically planned vistas, tree-lined walks, terraces, parterres, lakes and ponds, and embellished with fountains and statuary of infinite variety. The planting of trees was later considerably extended, so that what we now see are basically the gardens of Louis XV and Louis XVI.

To the S., beyond the *Parterres du Midi*, steps descend to the *Orangery*; to the W. beyond the *Parterres d'Eau*, are the *Marches de Latone*, providing vistas of both the palace and gardens, whence the *Tapis Vert* leads to the *Bassin d'Apollon*, in the centre of which is the impressive group of Apollo's Chariot, by Tuby. Further W. is the *Grand Canal*, scene of Louis XIV's boating parties, the transverse arm of which extends N. towards the Grand Trianon. To the N. of the palace the *Allée d'Eau* leads to the *Bassin de Neptune* (1740).

The most direct approach to the Trianons for the pedestrian to follow leads from the Bassin de Neptune via the Av. de Trianon, approx. 20 minutes' brisk walk. The **Grand Trianon** is a miniature palace on one floor, built for Louis XIV in 1687 as a retreat from the formality of court life. It was redecorated by Napoleon, who frequently stayed there after his marriage with Marie-Louise, and much of the Empire furniture he installed still remains. It was the object of extensive renovation in the 1960s.

We pass to the E. the *Musée des Voitures* before reaching the recently restored **Petit Trianon**, built by Gabriel (1751 – 68) as a country seat for Louis XV and Mme de Pompadour, who did not survive its completion, and it was then occupied by Mme du Barry. It was a favourite residence of Marie-Antoinette and was subsequently occupied by Pauline Borghese. Here, so Thicknesse was told, the king 'had a little garden... where he picks his own salad, makes his own soup, and enjoys the conversation of a few select friends, without the plague, impertinence, and above all, the parade that generally attends royalty.' Here also is a *Theatre*, and octagonal *Belvedere*, among other pavilions; while a few minutes' walk to the N.E. brings one to the *Hameau*, a sort of theatrical village built to gratify Marie-Antoinette's taste for 'nature' as popularised by Rousseau, although apart from churning butter, the queen left the work of the farm to real, not royal, peasants.

14 St-Denis; Malmaison; St-Germain-en-Laye

St-Denis is conveniently approached by MÉTRO to the *St-Denis-Basilique* terminus. This N. suburb of Paris (91,300 inhab.) has few attractions, but the contents of the **ABBEY OF ST-DENIS**, ◇ a short walk from the métro, are of historical interest.

It was founded c. 475, and rebuilt by Dagobert. A more substantial mid 8C church was replaced by another built by Suger, of which the W. porch, one tower, and the apse (c. 1144) survive; most of the rest of the edifice dates from 1231 – 81. With the exception of Philippe I, Louis XI, Louis-Philippe, and Charles X, all the French kings since Hughes Capet are buried here, and in 1422 the body of Henry V lay in state here on its way from Vincennes to Westminster Abbey, with which St-Denis may be compared as a royal mausoleum. At the Revolution many of the tombs were rifled, and later was drastically restored, and the fabric of the building somewhat disfigured.

Among the more important tombs which may be seen on what is a too rapid conducted tour are those of François I and Claude de France (S. transept); Henri II and Catherine de Médicis (N. transept); and Louis XII and Anne of Brittany (N. aisle). The Crypt was constructed round the original Carolingian 'martyrium', the site of the grave of St Denis and his companions, and preserves the sarcophagi of Louis XVI and Marie-Antoinette, among other later royalty; the ossuary on the N. side contains royal bones thrown into a pit in 1793.

To the S. are restored monastic buildings (18C), beyond which is the *Musée d'Art et d'Histoire*, preserving the reconstituted *Pharmacy* of the Hôtel-Dieu; the Study of the poet Paul Éluard (1895–1952), born in St-Denis; a collection of drawings, many by Daumier, and rooms devoted to the Paris Commune (1870–71), etc.
For the road hence to *Écouen* and *Chantilly*, see Rte 15.

Malmaison, to the W. of central Paris, is approached by road (N13) from the *Pont de Neuilly*, or by 158A bus from *La Défense* (on the RER from Auber or Étoile), to within a few minutes' of the château.
The *CHÂTEAU OF MALMAISON*, built in 1622, and enlarged in 1800, was the home of Josephine Bonaparte from 1798, and here she retired after her divorce in 1809, and died five years later.

It passed through various hands until sold to the philanthropist Daniel Osiris in 1896, who refurnished it and bequeathed the mansion to the State as a Napoleonic museum, to which further acquisitions have since been added. It now approximates its original appearance, and, preserving numerous souvenirs of the Empress and Napoleon, it is certainly one of the more interesting collections to be seen in the vicinity of the capital.

Among notable objects are books from the Emperor's personal library, re-assembled since dispersed; the 'Table d'Austerlitz'; the camp-bed on which Napoleon died, in a room hung with the brocade which covered his catafalque, etc. Other rooms preserve souvenirs of Queen Hortense (mother of Napoleon III) and Eugène de Beauharnais, Josephine's children by her first marriage.

The *Coach-house* shelters Napoleon's '*dormeuse*' used at Waterloo; the adjacent pavilion contains collections of caricatures, medallions, and snuffboxes, etc. propagating the Napoleonic legend.

A few minutes' walk to the N.E. is the **Musée du Château de Bois-Préau**, an annexe to the main collection, containing many more objects of interest, including several portraits by Gérard, and Marchand's sketch of the dead emperor, and other mementoes of the Napoleonic dynasty.

The tomb of Joséphine lies in the church of *Rueil*, nearby; that of Hortense in a chapel opposite.

St-Germain-en-Laye, further W., is rapidly approached from central Paris by the RER, the station of which is close to the château; alternatively by the N13, or N190 from the *Pont de Neuilly*.
St-Germain-en-Laye (40,800 inhab.), birthplace of Claude Debussy (1862–1918), grew up round the strategically sited castle, which commands this reach of the Seine to the W. of Paris.

The 12C fortress was entirely rebuilt in the mid 16C, except for the keep and chapel, and here Louis XIV was born (1638) and his father died five years later. It was the residence of the widowed Henrietta Maria of England, and after 1688 of the court in exile of James II (who compared the extensive view from the Terrace to that from Richmond), who died here in 1701. His tomb, containing only his heart, lies in the church opposite the castle.

The château houses the important **Musée des Antiquités Nationales*, with a series of rooms devoted to prehistoric collections, and others on the first floor concentrating on Roman and Merovingian Gaul.

To the N. extends the *Forêt de St-Germain.*—Some 5km further N. lies **Maisons-Laffitte**, with its well-furnished *Château*, ◊ by François Mansart, completed in 1651.—At *Chambourcy*, 4km W. of St-Germain, known for its white cheese, are the tombs of the Chevalier d'Orsay and the Countess of Blessington.

Some 4km S. stood the royal château of *Marly*, built by Jules Hardouin-Mansart for Louis XIV as an occasional retreat while Versailles was 'aired'. It was destroyed at the Revolution, but vestiges of the park remain. The famous hydraulic 'Machine de Marly', constructed to raise water from the Seine to carry it by aqueduct to Versailles, was dismantled in 1967.

For roads from St-Germain to *Évreux*, and *Gisors* and *Rouen*, see Rtes 25, and 8 respectively, the latter in reverse.

15 Paris to Clermont via Écouen and Chantilly

64km (40 miles). N16. 20km—**Écouen**—21km **Chantilly**—23km *Clermont*. Chantilly may also be approached by the N17 and D924A; see Rte 16.

Maps: IGN 9, or 103. M 196 or 237.

From the *Porte de la Chapelle*, the N16 drives N. and circles round (l.) **St-Denis** (see Rte 14) to reach **Écouen**, overlooked by the magnificent Renaissance ***CHÂTEAU D'ÉCOUEN**, restored to house the ***Musée National de la Renaissance**.

It was commenced c. 1535 for the Constable Anne de Montmorency, and among artists employed there were Jean Goujon and Jean Bullant. To the l. of the central courtyard is the *Chapel*, from which a series of rooms on the ground floor is traversed, several of them with remarkable chimney-pieces in the style of the School of Fontainebleau. Notable are the collections of carved wood plaques and panels; pear-wood statuettes; bronze figurines; metalwork, arms and armour, cutlery, and door-furniture; mathematical instruments, and watches; and sculptures.—The First Floor continues the display of furniture, enamel plaques, tile pavements, majolicas, etc., two notable series of tapestries, among them the Labours of Hercules, and the story of David and Bathsheba (Brussels; 16C). Other sections will be opened progressively.

At 10km a l.-hand fork leads through *Luzarches*, with a mid 16C church of interest, preserving parts of its 12C predecessor.—*Chantilly* is 10km N.

A DETOUR may be made to **Royaumont**, 6.5km N.W., with the considerable remains of a great Cistercian abbey, founded in 1228, in the dismantled church of which Louis IX was married in 1234; the beautiful **Refectory*, its vaulting sus-

tained by five monolithic columns, contains the tomb of Henri of Lorraine, by
Coysevox.—*Chantilly* lies 8.5km N.E.

Chantilly (10,200 inhab.), the 'Newmarket' of France, where race-
meetings have been held since 1836, is likewise famous for its
château, approached via the Rue du Connétable, passing (r.) *Notre-
Dame* (1692) and the ***Grande-Écuries** (1740), with room for 240
mounts.

The ***Château de Chantilly** consists of two connected buildings
standing by a carp-stocked lake, and contains the ***MUSÉE CONDÉ**,
one of the most interesting collections within easy reach of Paris,
especially rich in French paintings and illuminations of the 15-16Cs.

It came into the possession of the Montmorency family in 1484 and passed to the
Grand Condé (1621– 86) in 1632. The *Petit Château* was erected c. 1560 for the
Constable Anne de Montmorency, probably by Jean Bullant. The *Grand
Château* was reconstructed by Mansart on the site of an earlier mansion (in
which Molière's 'Les Précieuse ridicules' was first performed in 1659), but
destroyed at the Revolution. It was entirely rebuilt by the Duc d'Aumale
(1822– 97), who bequeathed the domain and his art collection to the Institute de
France.

The *Galerie des Cerfs* is first traversed, hung with 17C Gobelins
tapestries of hunting scenes, and then the *Galerie de Peintures*, with
portraits of Mazarin and Richelieu by *Philippe de Champaigne*, and
of Colbert by *Nanteuil*, to reach the *Rotunda*, with a mosaic from
Herculaneum, and paintings by *Clouet*, *del Sarto*, *A. Carracci*, and
Piero de Cosimo.—Hence we turn into the *Galerie de Logis*, with a
magnificent collection of French portrait drawings, many by *Corneille de Lyon*. From the *Rotonde de la Minerve* we return along an
exterior gallery, with a series of rooms displaying Greek and Roman
antiquities, and an interesting series of paintings to reach the *Salle
Caroline*, containing works by *Greuze*, *Watteau*, and *Nattier*,
amongst others, while in the adjoining room are more paintings,
largely of the *Schools of Clouet* and *Corneille de Lyon*.

Re-crossing the Galerie de Peintures, the *Galerie de Psyche* is
entered, with 42 sepia *Stained-glass windows representing the
Loves of Cupid and Psyche, probably designed in 1541 by Michiel
Coxie for Écouen. On the walls are other portrait drawings, ascribed
to *Clouet* or *Jean Perréal*. The adjacent *Santuario* contains Raphael's
'Madonna of the House of Orléans', and The three Graces, and
reproductions of 40 miniatures from the *Book of Hours of Étienne
Chevalier* (ascribed to *Jean Fouquet*, and executed in 1453– 60).
Beyond is the *Cabinet des Gemmes*.

The *Tribune* is then traversed, decorated with views of country
seats of the Duc d'Aumale (including Twickenham), and a variety of
good paintings, even if some of them are of doubtful attribution, to
regain the Galerie des Cerfs.

The richly decorated and furnished apartments of the *Petit
Château* are then visited, among them the *Salon des Singes*, with
chinoiserie wall-panels by Christophe Huet. The long *Galerie des Actions* is devoted to scenes of battles fought by the Grand Condé (including Rocroi, Nördlingen, and Lens), painted by *Sauveur Lecomte*
in 1686– 96, together with portraits and busts.

Retracing our steps, the *Cabinet des Livres* or *Library* is next
entered, preserving numerous remarkable bindings, and reproductions of the magnificently illuminated **Très Riches Heures du Duc de
Berri*, executed c. 1415 by *Pol de Limborg* and his brothers. The

delicate originals (together with those of the above-mentioned Étienne Chevalier miniatures), although preserved here, are understandably no longer on general view.

On reaching the principal staircase, we turn r. along the *Galerie de la Chapelle*, with drawings by *Dürer*, *Domenichino*, *Piombo*, and *Raphael*, to enter the *Chapel*, many times rebuilt, in which is the mausoleum of Henri II de Condé (d. 1662), with mid 16C *boiseries* and stained-glass brought from Écouen, together with an altar by Jean Bullant and Jean Goujon.

The *Park* was largely laid out for the Grand Condé by Le Nôtre, and is embellished by several buildings, including the *Maison de Sylvie* to the S.E. (the name being given by Théophile de Vau to Marie Félice Orsini, Duchesse de Montmorency, who hid the poet here when he was condemned to death in 1623 for his licentious verses). It was rebuilt in 1684, and was later the scene of a romantic affair between Mlle de Clermont and M. de Melún, who was killed in 'a hunting accident'. To the N. is a *'Hameau'* (1776), and to the W., near the stables, the *Jeu de Paume* of 1757, containing carriages, etc.

The *Forêt de Chantilly*, of 2100 hectares, extending to the S. and S.E., is intersected by numerous roads or sandy tracks (in the interest of the training-stables), the latter being closed to cars.

10km to the E. lies **Senlis**; see Rte 16; 5.5km to the N.W. is the notable 12C *Church of St-Leu-d'Esserent.

The N16 leads N. from Chantilly past the industral town of (8km) **Creil** (36,100 inhab.) and *Nogent-sur-Oise*, on the far bank of the river, also by-passed.—At 9km the road passes 2km W. of *Liancourt*. It was a Duc de Liancourt who made the celebrated retort when Louis XVI remarked (on the evening of 14 July 1789), on hearing of the disturbance in Paris, 'Mais c'est une révolte': 'Non, Sire, c'est une révolution!'.

At 7km **Clermont** (8700 inhab.) is reached, on a hillside above the Brèche, on the summit of which are the ruins of its *Castle*, twice captured by the English, in 1359 and 1434, which was the birthplace of Charles IV, le Bel, in 1294.

For the road on to *Breteuil* and **Amiens**, see Rte 5, in reverse.

16 Paris to Senlis and Compiègne

75km (46 miles). N17 to (44km) **Senlis**—D932A. 31km **Compiègne**.

Maps: IGN 9, or 103. M 196 or 237.

The A1 motorway also provides a rapid approach to Senlis.

Leaving Paris by the *Porte de la Villette* the N17 at 16km passes (l.) the old airport of *Le Bourget*, where the *Musée de l'Air*, with a notable collection of 140 aircraft, largely from 1919, but including earlier flying machines, has been installed.—A short distance beyond, the modern airport of *Charles de Gaulle* is passed to the r.

At 18.5km the D924A forks l. for (9.5km) **Chantilly**; see Rte 15.

Traversing part of the *Forêt de Chantilly*, at 9.5km we enter **SENLIS** (15,300 inhab.), which retains several attractive old alleys within the Gallo-Roman ramparts of the Silvanectes, and a cathedral of interest.

Probably built on the site of *Ratomagnus*, Senlis was a royal residence from the time of Clovis to Henri IV. Hughes Capet was elected 'Duc des Francs' here in

987; in 1358 it was the scene of a massacre of nobles by the Jacquerie. It was briefly in German hands in Sept. 1914, who set fire to some streets and plundered the town, which was also damaged in 1940.

A stretch of its medieval ramparts survives to the S.E., while in the town centre is the *Hôtel de Ville*, rebuilt in 1495, from which the Rue du Châtel leads into the Gallo-Roman enceinte, of which 16 towers remain, although many are hidden by abutting houses. It approaches the *Hôtel des Trois-Pots*, first mentioned in 1292, but with a 16C facade, the entrance to the ruined castle, the *Priory of St-Maurice* (14C), a *Hunting Museum*, and the cathedral.

The *Cathedral* was built in 1155–84 (almost coeval with St-Denis and Nôtre-Dame, Paris), its S. tower surmounted by a 13C spire. The central door of the W. facade is embellished with statues and reliefs. The transepts were rebuilt in the mid 16C after a fire, and display Renaissance tendencies; the five E. chapels and the side portals date from the same period.

The interior preserves a beautiful triforium gallery, and a splendid 16C vault in the E. chapel of the S. transept. The late 14C *Chapter-house*, with a remarkable central pillar, and the octagonal *Sacristy*, a relic of the original church, are both notable.

To the E. is the former *Bishop's Palace*, behind which is the former church of *St-Pierre* (now a market) with a Flamboyant facade of 1516, one tower with a dome of Renaissance date, and the other partly Romanesque, with a spire of 1432.

To the W. of the town are the relics of a *Gallo-Roman amphitheatre*; 2.5km S.E. are the picturesque ruins of the *Abbaye de la Victoire*, founded by Philippe Auguste to commemorate the Battle of Bouvines (1214), and rebuilt in the 15-16C.

The N17 continues N. through the *Forêt d'Halette* to (12km) *Pont-Ste-Maxence*, taking its name from a bridge over the Oise built here by Perronet in 1785 and rebuilt since its destruction in 1940. The *Abbaye de Moncel*, E. of the town, partly 14C, is almost entirely preserved, with the exception of its church.—For the road beyond, see Rte 2, in reverse.

The D932A leads N.E., at 11.5km passing 2km N.W. of **Raray**, with a 17C château preserving a remarkably decorated *Courtyard*, which served as the location for Cocteau's film 'La Belle et le Bête.—5.5km. *Verberie*, an ancient town once residence of Merovingian and Carolingian kings, is traversed, some 10km to the E. of which, at *Champlieu*, ◊ are several Gallo-Roman remains.

Skirting the W. side of the *Forêt de Compiègne*, at 14km **COMPIÈGNE** (43,300 inhab.) is entered, the *Compendium* of Latin chronicles, so called from its position on the 'short cut' between Beauvais and Soissons (see Rte 9), and later a country seat of the Frankish kings.

Joan of Arc, leading a sortie in 1430, was captured here by the Burgundians, who sold her to the English. It was briefly occupied by the Germans in Sept. 1914, and bombarded by them in June 1918, while in June 1940 a large section of the town was destroyed by German bombs.

The **Palace**, extensive in area, designed by Gabriel under Louis XV, is an example of French neo-classical decadence. It originated in a hunting-lodge, and became a favourite royal residence: here Marie-Antoinette was received by Louis XVI in 1770, and Marie-Louis by

Napoleon I in 1809, who restored the place. Here, during the frequent visits of Napoleon III, the fatuities of court junketings reached their zenith.

The interior, through which groups are escorted, contains several handsomely decorated apartments, many of them retaining the Empire furniture installed here by Napoleon I. The *Galerie de Bal*, resplendent in its ugliness, and the series of rooms designated the *Musée du Second Empire* are also included in the tour. A collection of veteran cars and other early vehicles may be seen in the adjoining *Musée National de la Voiture et du Tourisme*.

In the town stands the Flamboyant *Hôtel de Ville* (1509), which R.L. Stevenson condemned as 'a monument to Gothic insecurity', containing an extensive collection of tin soldiers and several dioramas of battles.—To the W. is the *Musée Vivenal*, with an important collection of Greek vases, apart from Mennecy and Chantilly porcelain, 12-13C ivories, and items of local interest.

For the road N.E. to (24km) *Noyon*, and beyond, see Rte 2, and for **Noyon** itself, Rte 5.—For the *'Clairière de l'Armistice'*, 6km E., see the last section of Rte 9.

12.5km S.E., on the far side of the forest, is the huge and commanding bulk of the **Château de Pierrefonds**, ◇ (1407), long considered one of the outstanding examples of medieval military architecture, but a critical reaction to Viollet-le-Duc's criteria of restoration (after 1857) has since taken effect. The powerfully constructed fortress is nevertheless impressive, and may be visited.—For *Morienval*, 8.5km S.W., and *Crépy-en-Valois*, see Rte 17; likewise *Villers-Cotterêts*, 16km S.E.

17 Paris to Soissons

104km (64 miles). A1 for 14km from the *Porte de la Chapelle*, there bearing r. to join the N2—20km *Dammartin-en-Goële*—39km *Villers-Cotterêts*—25km **Soissons**.

Maps: IGN 9, or 103. M 196 or 237.

The N2 bears N.E. not far S. of the *Charles de Gaulle airport*, to approach hill-top *Dammartin-en-Goële* (l.).

A DETOUR may be made hence to **Ermenonville**, 9km N., famous for its association with Jean-Jacques Rousseau (1712–78), who died in a pavilion (no longer existing) of the 18C château of the Marquis de Girardin, and was buried on the *Île des Peupliers*, near the S. end of the lake in the adjacent park. The sandy soil of the area has earned it the soubriquet 'Désert'.—Some 2.5km further N. lies *Chaalis*, with the remains of a Cistercian abbey founded in 1136, visited by Tasso in 1570. The main building now contains a somewhat miscellaneous collection of antiquities, etc., and several paintings of doubtful attribution.—The main road may be regained at *Nanteuil*, 10km E. of Ermenonville.

14km (from Dammartin) *Nanteuil-le-Hardouin*.

Hence another DETOUR may be made to **Crépy-en-Valois**, 12km N.E. on the D136, the capital of *Valois*, an appanage of the royal family, preserving part of its medieval fortifications. It suffered severely in the Hundred Years' War, and was sacked by the English in 1431. The imposingly timbered *Grande Salle* of the old castle now contains an *Archery Museum*.—9km N., on the D335, lies **Morienval**, its *Church, with three Romanesque towers, preserving early 12C Gothic vaulting.—*Pierrefonds* (see Rte 16) is 8.5km further N.E.—The main road may be regained by turning E. up the valley just S. of Morienval via the restored 13-14C château of *Vez*, and the imposing ruins of the 12C abbey of *Lieu-Restauré*, in which a Flamboyant Rose-window survives.

25km (from Nanteuil), to the S. of its by-pass, lies **Villers-Cotterêts**, almost surrounded by the extensive *Forêt de Retz*.

In June 1918 it saw the opening action of Gén. Mangin's offensive, in which 20,000 German prisoners and 400 guns were captured. It was the birthplace of Alexandre Dumas (père; 1802– 70), who is buried here, and a small museum is devoted to the family. Parts of its *Château* (1522– 45), built by Philibert Delorme and Jacques and Guillaume Le Breton for François I (to replace a castle burnt down by the English in 1429), may be visited.

At *La Ferte-Milon*, 9km S., with the impressive ruins of its castle, was born Jean Racine (1639– 99).

Continuing N.E., the N2 is shortly regained.—At 7km the imposing ruins of the Cistercian abbey of *Longpont* lie 4km to the r.

18km. **SOISSONS** (32,200 inhab.), although one of the oldest towns in France, contains comparatively few relics of its past importance.

It is believed to have been the *Noviodunum* of Caesar, and was later the second capital of *Gallia Belgica*. Clovis defeated its Roman governor in 486, and in 511 it became the capital of the kingdom of *Neustria*. Pepin le Bref was proclaimed king here in 752; Charles le Simple was defeated outside its walls in 923; and in 948 it was captured by Hugues le Grand. It was frequently besieged during the Hundred Years' War. It suffered severely in bombardments in 1870 and after the final retirement of the occupying Germans in Aug. 1918, whose gunners revenged themselves on its smoking ruins, when only 500 of its former 15,000 inhabitants remained.

Its two most important monuments surviving are the *Facade of the former abbey of **St-Jean-des-Vignes**, founded in 1076 and dismantled in 1804. Its imposing but dissimilar towers, completed in 1506, dominate the remaining dependencies, including a 13C cloister and 14C refectory.

Further N. is the **Cathedral**, considerably restored when not rebuilt, dating largely from the 12-13C, with a 14C tower. The *Choir*, completed in 1212, and the transepts, escaped serious injury in 1918. The *S. transept* (1177), is the oldest and most beautiful part of the building, with an apsidal ending and, above its graceful arcades, two triforium galleries beneath a loftily placed clerestory.

N. of the main square are remains of the former abbey of *St-Lèger*, housing the provincial museum.—The 9C *Crypt of St-Médard*, to the E., on the far bank of the Aisne, contains the tombs of Clotaire (c. 561) and Sigebert (d. 575), son and grandson respectively, of Clovis.

For roads from Soissons to *Noyon* and *Amiens*, and to *Compiègne* and *Beauvais*, see Rtes 5, and 9, respectively, in reverse. For *Reims*, likewise, see the latter part of Rte 5. For the road from *St-Quentin* to *Troyes* via Soissons, see Rte 103A, and from Soissons to **Laon**, 35km N.E., Rte 105.

18 Paris to Meaux and Château-Thierry

91km (56 miles). N3. 45km **Meaux**—20km. *La Ferté-sous-Jouarre*
—26km **Château-Thierry**.

Maps: IGN 9, or 103. M 196 or 237.

Meaux may also be approached rapidly by bearing N. off the A4
motorway, which continues N.E., with an exit just N. of *Château-
Thierry*, to *Reims*: see also Rte 19.

MEAUX (45,900 Meldois), the main attraction of which is the old
quarter near the cathedral, was originally a stronghold of the Meldi,
a Gallic tribe, commanding an abrupt bend of the Marne. It was later
the capital of the *Haute-Brie*. It is reputed for its cheese, and mustard,
although the latter is now manufactured at Lagny; see Rte 19. Some
9000 peasants were massacred here during the revolt of the Jacquerie in 1358. It was twice besieged by the English in the 15C. The
reactionary preacher Jacques-Bénigne Bossuet (1627–1704) was
bishop here from 1681.
   The *Cathedral is a beautiful but weather-worn 12-16C building,
with a Flamboyant W. front and slated stump of a tower. The 13C N.
portal has bas-reliefs representing the Life of St Stephen. The interior
is elegant and airy, in spite of the short nave. Bousset is buried in the
Choir, although his *Monument* is in the N. nave aisle.
   To the N. is the *Bishop's Palace* (15-17C), with a 12C chapel, now
housing a *Museum*. In the garden is a pavilion known as the 'Cabinet
de Bossuet', where he composed many of his sermons and polemical
works.—To the E. is the *Old Chapter-house* (restored), dating from
the 13C, with a picturesque covered exterior staircase (15C woodwork). The episcopal gardens are flanked by a section of the *Town
Wall*, incorporating Roman work.
   Continuing E. from Meaux, at 8km we pass 2km N. of the ruins of
the château of *Montceaux* (1560), built by Philibert Delorme for
Catherine de Medicis, and altered by Henri IV for Gabrielle
d'Estrées; it was dismantled in 1798.—Passing beneath the motorway, at 12km *La Ferté-sous-Jouarre* is entered, 3km S. of which, at
Jouarre, are the important remains of the Merovingian *Crypt (634)
of its once-famous Benedictine abbey, of which a 13C tower survives. It contains porphyry and jasper columns, surmounted by
white marble capitals, and the notable sarcophagi of sundry saints
(one hypothetically an Irish princess); the decoration of the walls,
etc. is also remarkable. For adm. enquire at the abbey, 9 Rue Montmorin.

The D407, continued by the D933, leads 33km E. from La Ferté to *Montmirail*, a
small town which was the birthplace of Paul de Gondi, Card. de Retz (1614–79),
preseving a mid 16C château. It was the scene, on 11 Feb. 1814, of Napoleon's
victory over the combined forces of Russian and Prussia.—For the road hence to
Sézanne and **Troyes**, see Rte 103A; for that continuing E. to **Châlons-sur-Marne**,
see Rte 107.

The N3 turns N.E. from La Ferté to **Château-Thierry**, also approached by the longer but more attractive riverside route. Sheltering
below its castle-crowned hill, guarding a crossing of the Marne, the
old town of 14,900 Castelthéodoriciens, was the birthplace of the
fabulist Jean de la Fontaine (1621–95).

Said to be named after a fortress built here for Thierry IV (d. 737), a Frankish king, it was later held by the counts of Champagne. It was captured by the English in 1421, by the Emperor Charles V in 1544, and by the Leaguers in 1591, and pillaged in 1652 during the War of the Fronde. It was bombarded in 1814, and was the scene of bitter fighting in June – July 1918; it also suffered during 1940.

It preserves a 16C belfry, two medieval gateways, and several old houses, while to the W. of the central Place stands *St-Crépin* (15-16C), with a heavy square tower.

22km N.E., via the D967, is *Fère-en-Tardenois*, the British G.H.Q. during the **First Battle of the Aisne** (Sept. – Oct. 1914), and the scene of fierce fighting in May – Aug. 1918. It retains a robustly pillared *Market-hall* of 1552, and a 15-16C church.—3km. N.E. lie the ruins of the 13C castle of *Fère*, approached by a Renaissance galleried viaduct of five arches, 20m high, built by Jean Bullant.—3km E. is a large U.S. military cemetery.—Paul Claudel (1868 – 1955) was born at neighbouring *Villeneuve-sur-Fère*, to the S.E.

For roads from Château-Thierry to **Épernay**, and **Reims**, see Rte 106.

19 Paris to Sézanne

A.   Via Champs and Coulommiers

111km (69 miles). N34. 21.5km **Champs**—39.5km *Coulommiers* —50km *Sézanne*.

Maps: IGN 21, 22, or 103. M 196 or 237.

The A4 motorway, driving E. from the *Porte de Bercy* towards Reims, now facilitates the exit from Paris in this direction, providing an exit for *Champs*, off which we later turn onto the N43.

From the *Porte de Vincennes*, after passing (r.) the *Château de Vincennes* (see Rte 10A), the N.E. corner of the Bois is crossed before reaching the suburb of *Nogent-sur-Marne*, where a surviving market pavilion from the former Paris Halles (1856; by Victor Baltard) has been re-erected on an esplanade overlooking the river, and converted into a theatre and exhibition hall. Watteau died at Nogent in 1721, while Louis Daguerre (1787 – 1851), who gave his name to the daguerreotype, died at *Bry-sur-Marne*, further E.

The *Château de Champs, ◇ built in 1707 by J.-B. Bullet, was the residence of the Princesse de Conti (daughter of Louis XIV and Louise de la Vallière), and in 1757 of Mme de Pompadour. The *Gardens* were laid out by Claude Desgots, a nephew of Le Nôtre. Its furniture and furnishing, and the several good paintings it contains, make it one of the more rewarding châteaux to visit in the immediate environs of Paris. Notable are the Salon Chinois and Blue Boudoir, decorated by Christophe Huet.

The road continues through (8km) **Lagny** (18,300 inhab), ancient *Latiniacum*, in which *St-Pierre* (or *N.-D. des Ardents*), the choir of an unfinished abbey-church of the 13-14C, is of interest.—We pass S. of *Coupvray*, birthplace of Louis Braille (1809 – 52), and shortly veer S.E.; the **Battle of the Ourcq** (Sept. 1914) took place to the N. and E.

Coulommiers (12,300 Columériens), the ancient *Columbariae*, a busy market town, and the birthplace of the artist Jean de Boulogne (1591 – 1634), retains two pavilions of 1631 (by François Mansart) of the château built by De Brosse for the Duchesse de Longueville, described in Mme de la Fayette's 'La Princesse de Clèves', and demolished in 1737; to the N.E. of the town are several dependencies of a Commandery of the Templars, now part of a Hospital farm.

The N34 ascends the plateau and continues due E. to (14.5km) _La Ferté-Gaucher_, also approached by the more picturesque D66 following the river valley.—At 18km we meet the N4, and shortly after pass (l.) the 16-17C château of _Esternay_.—The road skirts (r.) the _Forêt de la Traconne_, and after 14km enters **Sézanne**, lying amidst vineyards, its 15-16C church retaining a Renaissance S. portal and upper windows, and a good stone reredos. Its andouillettes are reputed.

For the road hence to **Troyes**, see Rte 103A; for that to _Vitry-le-François, Bar-le-Duc_, and **Nancy**, see Rte 108.

B.   Via Rozay-en-Brie

This faster but duller road (N4) drives E. from the _Porte de Picpus_, passing near several châteaux of comparatively slight interest, at 51km by-passing (r.) _Rozay-en-Brie_, an attractive village with traces of fortifications, and a 13C church restored in the 16C, with a 12C belfry.—2km S. is the château of _La Grange-Bléneau_ (16-17C), which belonged to Lafayette from 1799 until his death in 1834, and retains his library; he received Pitt here in 1802.

At 10km further E. the D231 forks r. for **Provins**, 21km S.E.; see Rte 20.—Continuing E., at 12.5km _Beton-Bazoches_ is traversed, with a 12C church, 21km beyond which we meet the N34 14km W. of _Sézanne_; see above.

20 Paris to Provins

84km (52 miles). N19. 29.5km _Brie-Comte-Robert_—34km _Nagis_—20.5km **Provins**.

Maps: IGN 21, or 103. M 196, or 237.

Driving S.E. from the _Porte Picpus_, and traversing _Créteil_, préfecture of _Val-de-Marne_, at 21.5km we pass (l.) the château of *Gros-Bois, built by the Duc d'Angoulême at the beginning of the 17C and sumptuously furnished during the First Empire by Marshal Berthier.

8km. _Brie-Comte-Robert_, a small town founded in the 10C, lies on the rich _Plateau de la Brie_, famous for its cheese, and preserves the ruins of its castle, and remains of an old _Hospital_ (1207), while St-Étienne (13C, later altered) contains features of interest.

25km. After passing the petrol refineries of _Grand-Puits_, _Nangis_ is traversed, 4.5km beyond which, 1km S. of the road, is the remarkable *Church_ of **Rampillon**, with its sculptured portal and tower attributed to the Templars.—Of equal importance is that at *St-Loup-de-Naud, 4km S.E. at 11.5km, partly 11C, with a well-preserved sculptured portal of the 12C.

4.5km. **PROVINS** (12,700 Provinois), one of the most attractive towns within easy reach of Paris, once the capital of the _Brie_, with an important fair.

It was ruined by a plague in 1373, by the English wars, and the Wars of Religion. Among its natives were the trouvères Guyot de Provins (12C) and Thibaut IV, Comte de Champagne (1201–53). Its crimson roses were introduced into the coat-of-arms of Edmund of Lancaster (1245–96), when he married the widow of Henri le Gros, Comte de Champagne.

The upper town is still partially surrounded by well-preserved **Ramparts**, well-seen approaching from Paris, and it is recommended to fork l. to enter the old town by the *Porte de Jouy*, first passing the *Porte St-Jean* and the so-called 'Brèche des Anglais', through which the English forced their way in 1432. A short distance from the central *Pl. du Châtel* is the **Grange-aux-Dîmes**, a 13C tithe-barn of two vaulted storeys, now containing a lapidary collection. To the S.E. rises the curiously constructed **Tour de Cèsar*, a massive early 12C keep on a motte surrounded by a rampart added by the English during their occupation.

Further downhill stands **St-Quiriace*, begun in 1160, with an unfinished nave and early 12C choir, and 13C triforium. The cupola of 1665 over the crossing replaces a belfry destroyed by fire. (St Quiriace was a converted Jew, of which there were once many in Provins, who assisted the Empress Helena in her search for the True Cross.)

An *Archaeological Museum* has been installed in a Romanesque house in the Rue du Palais, to the N.—The upper town commands a good view of the **Hôpital Général**, on the far side of the valley, built on the site of a monastery of the Cordeliers, of which a 14-15C *Cloister* and *Chapter-house* survive, while the heart of Thibaut V is preserved in the wooden barrel-vaulted *Chapel*.

The Rue St-Thibaut, in which are several ancient houses, descends into the lower town. To the N. of the *Pl. du Gén-Leclerc* stands *Ste-Croix*, with a 13C nave and aisles, and 16C choir; further E. is *St-Ayoul* (11-16C), with a 12C portal, and woodcarvings by P. Blasset (1612–63), who is buried here. N. of the latter is the *Tour N.-D. du Val* (1544), surviving from an earlier cloistered church.

For the road from Provins to **Troyes**, see Rte 122.

18km S.W., on the road to *Montereau-Faut-Yonne*, at *Donnemarie*, are remains of ancient fortifications, and a 12-13C **Church* and two galleries of a 16C cloister; and 3km beyond, to the S., the ruins of the Cistercian abbey of *Preuilly*, founded in 1118 by Stephen Harding, Abbot of Citeaux (a native of Sherborne, in Dorset).

21   Paris to Fontainebleau, for Sens or Nemours

117km (72 miles). N6. 46km *Melun*. **Vaux-le-Vicomte** lies 6km N.E.—N6. 18km **Fontainebleau**—10km *Moret-sur-Loing*—8km *Montereau-faut-Yonne* lies 4km N.E.—35km **Sens**.
   The N7 leads S. from Fontainebleau to (15km) *Nemours*.

Maps: IGN 21, or 103. M 196 or 237.

The A6 motorway provides a rapid route to a point 16.5km N.W. of Fontainebleau, later passing within 2km of Nemours. This alternative route bears S.E. not far S. of Paris to bypass (l.) *Orly Airport*, and some 37km beyond, the N37 forks l. to (16.5km) *Fontainebleau*.—A r.-hand turning just after leaving the motorway, leads S.W. past (5.5km) the château of *Courances*, to *Milly-la-Forêt*, with an 11-12C church, a ruined 12C castle, and *Market-hall* of 1479; also a 12C

Chapel restored and decorated by Jean Cocteau (1889–1963), who died here.—To the S. of this approach road to Fontainebleau lie the imposing château of *Fleury-en-Bière*, and the village of **Barbizon**, now the sophisticated resort of artists emulating the School of painters who made it their headquarters in the 19C, among them Millet, Théodore Rousseau, Corot, Diaz, and Daubigny. The first two were buried at *Chailly-en-Bière*, just N. of the main road, where Bazille, Monet, Renoir, Sisley, and Seurat also painted.—For **Fontainebleau**; see below.

The N6 traverses the *Forêt de Sénart* prior to reaching (46km) **Melun** (36,200 Melunias), préfecture of *Seine-et-Marne*, and of Gallo-Roman foundation (*Melodunum*). It was the birthplace of the humanist Jacques Amyot (1513–93). The oldest part of the town lies on an island in the Seine, connected to either bank by bridges rebuilt since blown up during the heavy fighting here in 1944, when 15-16C *St-Aspais*, on the N. bank, was also damaged. *Notre-Dame*, on the island, founded in 1031, was much altered in the 15C.

6km N.E., off the D215 stands the château of ***Vaux-le-Vicomte**, built by Le Vau for Nicolas Fouquet (1615–80), Louis XIV's superintendant of finance. Molière's 'Les Fâcheaux' was performed on the occasion of the extravagant fête given here on 17 Aug. 1661 in honour of the young king, which also precipitated Fouquet's downfall. The sumptuously furnished rooms, including the impressive domed *Grand Salon*, contain several portraits of interest. The formal *Gardens* were one of Le Nôtre's first commissions.—3km further E. is the ruined 12-14C castle of *Blandy*.

A direct road (N105) leads S.E. from Melun to (30km) *Montereau-faut-Yonne*; see below.

The N6 leads due S. from Melun through part of the *Forêt de Fontainebleau* to (18km) **FONTAINEBLEAU** (18,800 Bellifontains), taking its name from *Fons Blandi* or *Fontaine de Bland*, and one of the pleasantest resorts in the neighbourhood of Paris, although one may quote Arthur Young, who visited the place in Sept. 1787, who remarked that the landlord of the inn there 'thinks that royal palaces should not be seen for nothing; he made me pay 10 livres for a dinner which would have cost me not more than half the money at the Star and Garter at Richmond'.

It is mentioned as a royal hunting-seat as early as 1137, and was later fortified. Thomas Becket, then in exile, consecrated the chapel of St-Saturnin in 1169. Although Philippe IV was born and died here, it was later deserted for the Loire. It owes its present form to François I, who assembled a group of Italian artists (among them Serlio, Rosso, Primaticcio, Vignola, and Nicolo dell'Abate) to rebuild and decorate the palace, which continued during the reign of Henri IV, whose son Louis XIII was born here. Christina of Sweden retired here in 1657; here Louis XIV signed the Revocation of the Edict of Nantes (1685); and it was visited by Peter the Great in 1717 during the minority of Louis XV. The palace was restored by Napoleon, who confined Pope Pius VII here. Napoleon abdicated here in 6 April 1814, only to return here (20 March 1815) via Grenoble from Elba to review his guard before leading them to the Tuileries. Louis-Philippe likewise restored it, in his usual questionable taste. From 1941 it was the H.Q. of Von Brauchitsch, until liberated by Patton in Aug. 1944, after which it became the H.Q. of the Allied powers in Europe for some years.

The Rue Royale (in which No. 15 contains a small military museum) and the Blvd Magenta converge on the *Pl. du Gén. de Gaulle*, facing the W. front of the palace, in which the doorway of the *Hôtel du Card. de Ferrare* is an authentic work by Serlio.

The exterior of the ***PALACE DE FONTAINEBLEAU**, composed of many distinct buildings erected over the years, is plain compared with its richly decorated interior. The main entrance is approached via the *Cour des Adieux* (after Napoleon's farewell to the Old Guard on 20 April 1814), also known as that 'du Cheval Blanche', from the cast of a Roman equestrian statue which once stood by the horseshoe-shaped staircase by Jean du Cerceau (1634), ascending to the FIRST FLOOR. The interior is visited in groups.

To the l. of the *Vestibule* is the *Chapelle de la Sainte-Trinité*, built by Philibert Delorme, in which Louis XV and Marie Leczinska were married in 1725.—To the r. are the *Apartments of the Queens-Mother*, occupied by Catherine de Médicis, Anne of Austria, and Marie-Thérèse (and later by Pius VII), among which the main bedroom; the *Galerie des Fastes*, with its carved foliage; and the *Galerie des Assiettes*, decorated with Sèvres plates, are notable.

Opposite the entrance is the 64m-long *Galerie François-Ier*, of 1528–44, one of the few rooms extant of that period. Beyond, we traverse (r.) the *Salle des Gardes* and *Escalier du Roi* (by Gabriel; 1749), the upper part once the bedroom of the Duchess d'Étampes, to reach the splendid *Salle de Bal*, by Philibert Delorme, in which the interlaced monograms and emblems of Henri II and Diane de Poitiers are ubiquitous. The mythological paintings were designed by Primaticcio and executed by dell'Abate (1552).

Returning to the Salle de Gardes, first traversing the *Salon de St-Louis*, in the original castle keep, a series of *Royal Apartments* on the N. side of the *Cour Ovale* are visited, among the more interesting of which is the *Salon Louis XIII*, with paintings by Ambroise Dubois, and facing N., the *Appartements de la Reine* (or de Marie-Antoinette, whose chose the decorations), built between 1545 and 1565. Notable are the *Queen's Bedroom* and the *Salle du Trône* (previously the king's bedroom), with a ceiling of the time of Louis XIII and a copy of Philippe de Champaigne's portrait of that king.

The imposing *Salle du Conseil*, decorated by Boucher and C. van Loo, among others, with a bay added in 1773, is traversed before entering the *Apartments of Napoleon I*, abutting the *Galerie François-Ier*, partly furnished in Empire style, and containing several Napoleonic relics.—On the floor below are the *Petits Appartements de Napoleon et de Joséphine*, preserving their Louis-XV and Louis-XVI decoration, and more Empire furniture and Napoleonic souvenirs.

Admission to other parts of the palace is normally only granted on specific request to the conservateur.

The *Jardin de Diane* may be visited from the N.E. corner of the entrance courtyard, while to the S.E. of the main block of buildings extends the *Parterre*, and further W., the *Jardin Anglais*, laid out for Napoleon. Thomas Coryate, passing through Fontainebleau in 1605, was amazed to see ostriches running wild somewhere in these gardens! Beyond the parterre is the Park, with a canal dug for Henri II.

Some distance to the E. beyond the walls, lies the suburb of **Avon**, with a 13-16C church in which are the tombs of Monaldeschi (Christina of Sweden's favourite, whose assassination she had ordered), Ambroise Dubois, the artist, and the naturalist Daubentin; while in the cemetery lies Katherine Mansfield (1888–1923), who died near here while under the malign influence of Gurdjieff.—At *Valvins* (1.5km N.E. of the railway-station), lived Mallarmé (1842–98), from 1884 until his death. He is buried in its cemetery.

The ***Forest of Fontainebleau**, surrounding the town, approx. 17,000 hectares in extent, although traversed by a number of good roads, is best explored on foot. Its thick glades and picturesque wildernesses of rock interspersed by sandy clearings, make it a pleasant place for excursions; two of the more attractive sites are the *Gorges de Franchard*, and *d'Apremont*, some 4km W. and N.W. respectively of the *Carrefour de la Libération*.

For the road S. to *Nemours*, see below.

The N16 leads E. from the *Carrefour de l'Obélisque* (S.E. of the palace), from which at 6.5km the l.-hand fork traverses **Moret-sur-Loing**, retaining two 14C gates among other relics of its fortifications, while in the castle-keep of 1128 Fouquet was imprisoned for some months in 1664. *Notre-Dame* has a good 15C portal, and contains some remarkable wood-carvings. Sisley (1840 – 99) spent the last four years of his life at No. 9 Rue du Château; Pissarro painted here in 1901 – 2.

At 6km beyond Moret, **Montereau-Faut-Yonne** (19,500 inhab.) is by-passed, where Jean sans Peur, Duke of Burgundy, was in 1419 assassinated by partisans of the Dauphin, afterwards Charles VII. A statue of Napoleon, between the restored 18C bridges, commemorates his defeat of the Germans here in Feb. 1814.

The road follows the valley of the Yonne, at 24km passing a l.-hand turning for the Renaissance château of *Fleurigny* (c. 1526), 13km E.—11km **SENS** (pron. Sánss; 27,500 Senonais), which was described by Thicknesse as 'a large ragged ancient city, but adorned with a most noble cathedral well worthy of the notice of strangers'.

It was the chief town of the Senones, a powerful Gallic tribe, which was evangelised in the 3C, and became the seat of a widely-spread archbishopric to which even Paris was suffragan until 1627. The council at which St Bernard secured the condemnation of the doctrines of Abélard, met here in 1140; in 1234 Louis IX was married to Margaret of Provence in the cathedral. Du Perron (1556 – 1618), the religious controversialist, was Abp of Sens. During the Wars of Religion, its citizens were enthusiastic supporters of the League. Becket spent part of his exile (from 1166) here; the architect William of Sens was born here, as was the poet Rutebeuf (d. 1285). Marivaux lived some years in the town, as did Mallarmé in 1857 – 60.

The old town is surrounded by a pleasant oval of wide tree-lined boulevards, some parts of which are flanked by medieval *Walls*, of which an isolated tower and postern of 1260 survive.

In the centre rises the ***Cathedral of St-Étienne**, begun c. 1130, and after 13-14C alterations, completed in 1520. Several of its features were reproduced at Canterbury by William of Sens, to whom the rebuilding of the E. end of the English cathedral was entrusted in 1175.

The W. front was ruthlessly mutilated in 1793, only the figure of St Stephen on the main pillar of the central portal escaped, being protected from the general destruction by the words 'La Loi' engraved on the book in his hand.

The **Stained-glass* throughout is good. In a chapel to the l. of the choir is the *Tomb of Dauphin Louis* (1729 – 65), father of Louis XVI, by G. Coustou; also notable are the reliefs from the destroyed tomb of Card. Duprat, archbishop of Sens in 1525 – 35, and the kneeling statues of two other archbishops (1636). The *Treasury* contains the vestments and mitre of Becket.

Immediately to the S. is the *Palais Synodal* ◊ (13C), restored in 1860 by Viollet-le-Duc; further E., beyond a vaulted passage with a Renaissance doorway, is the mid 16C *Archbishop's Palace.*—Several old houses survive in the Rue de la République, and Rue Jean-Cousin (named after the 16C artist, born at *Soucy*, 6km N.E.).

The N60 leads 65km E. to **Troyes**; see Rte 122.
For roads to **Auxerre**, *Vézelay*, *Avallon*, and *Autun*, see Rte 120; for **Dijon**, via *Tonnerre* and *Montbard*, see Rte 121.

The N7 leads due S. through the forest from Fontainebleau, at 8km bypassing (l.) *Grez-sur-Loing*, its 12–16C church containing Romanesque capitals. Louise de Savoie (1476–1531), mother of François I, died in its castle, now ruined. R.L. Stevenson moored his canoe here after his 'Inland Voyage' (1876), and Frederick Delius (1862–1934) lived here from 1897 until his death.

7km. **Nemours** (11,700 inhab.), ancient Nemoracum, once the capital of the *Gatinais*, was fortified at an early date, and between 1420 and 1437 was in English hands. Eleuthère-Irénée, one of the family of Du Pont of Nemours, founded in the State of Delaware a factory which formed the basis of the chemical 'empire' which bears his name.

The fortified *Château* (15C; parts dating from the 12C), defending the river crossing, has been restored to house a local *museum*; another *Museum* devoted to the prehistory of the Île de France, has been recently inaugurated further E. The *Grand Pont* commands a view of the apse of 16C *St-Jean Baptiste*, with a fan-vaulted nave and pendant bosses. There are several quaint old houses in the vicinity.

NEMOURS TO SENS (46km). The D225 leads E. below the motorway, at 16km reaching crossroads, 2km N. of which is the fortified church of *Lorrez-le-Bocage-Préaux*; 5km S. lies **Égreville**, with a 13-15C *Church* and 15C *Market-hall*. The Duchesse d'Étampes—Anne de Pisseleu—mistress of François I, lived in the 16C château, where Jules Massenet (1842–1912) passed his last years; he is buried in the cemetery.—8km. *Chéroy*, with a medieval tithe-barn, 6km N.E. of which is the 16C château of *Vallery*, where the great Condé was brought up; the fine tomb of his father, Henri II de Condé, is in the church which he founded.—22km. **Sens**.

For roads from Nemours to **Bourges**, and to **Nevers** and **Moulins**, see Rtes 48, and 96, respectively.

22   Paris to Orléans

116km (72 miles). N20. 10km **Sceaux**—40km **Étampes**—68km **Orléans**.

Maps: IGN 20, or 103. M 196, or 237.

The A10 motorway provides a rapid route, which may be joined S. of Sceaux. later veering S.W. Sceaux may also be approached by the RER from Paris, stopping at *Sceaux* or *Bourg-la-Reine*.

The N20 drives S. from the *Port d'Orléans*.

The **Château de Sceaux** ◊ is a 19C building replacing the sumptuous 17C residence which was in the first half of the 18C the scene of the literary and artistic court of the ambitious Duchesse du Maine (1676–1753). Here Voltaire wrote three of his tragedies, and works by Racine, Molière, and Lully were performed in the adjacent *Orangerie*, built by J. Hardouin-Mansart (1684; restored). The château houses the ***Musée de l'Île de France**, containing a wealth of material illustrating the history and topography of the region, depicting the appearance of, and life in, the environs of the capital in past centuries.—The extensive *Park* was laid out by Le Nôtre, to the N.W. of which, in the old churchyard, are buried the fabulist Florian (1755–94), and Pierre and Marie Curie (1859–1906 and 1867–1934 respectively), the discoverers of radium.

13.5km. *Longpont-sur-Orge*, 2km l., has a *Church of interest, begun c. 1060, its W. front with a 13C portal surmounted by a 15C rose-window, while the nave, remodelled in the 12C, has fine Romanesque arches and foliate capitals, and a blind triforium.

Montlhéry is shortly passed, dominated by its cylindrical *Keep* (13-15C), ◊ a relic of a famous fortress dating from 991, and 4km beyond, *Arpajon* (l.) is by-passed.

Dourdan, 20km S.W., Gallo-Roman *Dordincum*, has a royal *Castle*, rebuilt by Philippe Auguste in 1220; in its predecessor was born Hugues Capet (c. 941).

8km. *St-Sulpice-de-Favières*, 2.5km r., has an elegant *Church of 1260–1320, with an exceptionally fine tower and choir.—The N20 climbs the once notorious hill known as the 'Côte de Torfou', and approaches (11km) **ÉTAMPES**, an ancient town of 19,500 inhab., called *Stampae* in the 6C, strung out along the Orléans road, and dominated by a huge 12C *Keep*, where Philippe Auguste confined his queen, Ingeborg of Denmark (c. 1176–1236), for 12 years (1201–13). Geoffroy St-Hilaire (1772–1844), the naturalist, was born here.

In the town centre is *St-Basile* (15-16C), retaining an elaborate Romanesque W. door and 12C tower. The Rue de la République leads S.E. to *N.-D. du Fort*, with a tall 12C steeple, and preserving much 11C work in its nave. *St-Martin*, at the S.W. extremity of the town, has a beautiful apse, and a dangerously leaning 12-13C tower displaying Renaissance decoration.

10km E. lies *Farcheville*, with a château and well-preserved fortifications of 1291.

An alternative road to Orléans is the D921 to (32km) **Pithiviers**, a rather dull old town, with a municipal *Museum*, and *Transport museum*, 6km E. of which is a ruined castle of c. 1236 of some interest at *Yèvre-le-Châtel*.—The D152 bears S.W., later traversing the *Forêt d'Orléans*, to (42km) **Orléans**.

The N20 continues S.W. from Étampes across the monotonous but fertile Beauce plateau, at 32km by-passing *Toury*. A monument here commemorates Blériot's first monoplane flight (on 31 Oct. 1908) to *Artenay*, some 13km S., 20km. beyond which we enter **Orléans**; see Rte 50.

At *Le Puiset*, 6km W. of Toury, is a beautiful 12C church, and ruins of a castle which defied Philippe I but was destroyed by Louis VI. Most famous of its robber-barons was Hugh de Puiset (d. 1195), nephew of King Stephen, and Bp of Durham.

23 Paris to Chartres

103km (64 miles). N306. 40km *St-Rémy-lès-Chevreuse*—21km *Rambouillet*—D906. 23km *Maintenon*—19km **Chartres**.

Maps: IGN 20, or 103. M 196, or 237.

The A11 motorway bearing S.W. off the A10 provides a rapid direct route from Paris, while the N10 leading S.W. from Paris via *Versailles* and *Rambouillet*, is likewise fast, as is the N118, circling S. from near the *Bois de Boulogne* to join the A10 motorway, but although the places they pass near are detailed in *Blue Guide Paris and Environs*, few are of great moment. The route described below, although slower, is of more interest.

The N306 leads S.W. from the *Porte de Châtillon*, eventually descending into the *Vallée de Chevreuse* and reaching *St-Rèmy-lès-Chevreuse*.

A DETOUR may be made hence to **Port-Royal-des-Champs**, 6km N.W., where stood the celebrated abbey, founded in 1204, which played an important part in the religious history of France, being the headquarters of the Jansenists. Racine spent the years 1655–58 here. In 1709, the Machiavellian Jesuits obtained a Papal bull authorizing the demolition of the abbey and the dispersal of its inmates, mostly elderly nuns, who were given a quarter of an hour to pack and leave. The *Musée National des Granges de Port-Royal*, devoted to the history of Jansenism, may be visited.

The village of *Chevreuse* is shortly traversed, dominated by the imposing ruins of the *Château de la Madeleine*, once the home of the intriguing Marie de Rohan, Duchesse de Chevreuse (1600–79), an enemy of Richelieu.

4km W. lies the splendid château of *Dampierre*, rebuilt for the Duc de Luynes by Jules Hardouin-Mansart in 1683, with a park laid out by Le Nôtre.

At 7km S.W. of Chevreuse we pass some 3km E. of the ruins of the Cistercian abbey of *Les Vaux-de-Cernay*, founded in 1118, of interest, but adm. is rarely granted.—**11.5km Rambouillet** (22,500 inhab.), where since 1897 the *Château* ◇ has been the official country residence of the Président of the Republic. Only one tower of the original 14C castle survives. François I died here in 1547; here Charles X signed his abdication in 1830. Louis XVI was a frequent visitor, but Marie-Antoinette found it unbearably dull. To amuse her the *Laiterie de la Reine* was built.—To the S.E. and N.W. extends the *Forêt de Rambouillet* (some 13,100 hectares), perhaps better explored from *Montfort-l'Amaury*, 19km N.; see Rte 24.

We now follow the D906 through (14km) *Épernon*, with a 13C vaulted cellar and large late Gothic church, 9km beyond which is *Maintenon*. The *Château* was given by Louis XIV in 1674 to Françoise d'Aubigné (1635–1719), later Marquise de Maintenon, who in 1683 became his second wife. Restored since damaged in 1940, it preserves a 13C keep and two 14C towers, but is mainly a 16C building.—Bearing S.W., the road shortly passes the ruins of an aqueduct designed to bring water from the Eure to Versailles, a project never completed.

19km **Chartres**; see *Blue Guide Paris and Environs*, or Rte 28A.

24 Paris to Dreux

84km (52 miles). N12. 46km **Montfort-l'Amaury** lies 2km S.—17km *Houdan*—21km **Dreux**.

Maps: IGN 20, or 103. M 196, or 237.

The A12 and N10 converge a short distance S.W. of Versailles, where we diverge onto the N12.—2km N.E. of this intersection stood the military academy of *St-Cyr*, founded by Napoleon in 1808 but destroyed in 1944.

5km. *Pontchartrain*, with a château built by François Mansart, 7km beyond which the crossroad 2km N. of **Montfort-l'Amaury** is reached. This small town was the seat of the counts of Montfort, notable among whom were Simon IV (d. 1218), the ruthless leader of the

Albigensian Crusade, and Simon V (1208–65), Earl of Leicester, and is now a fashionable week-end retreat. *St-Pierre* contains remarkable 16C glass and elaborate roof-bosses, while a short distance N.W. is the *Old Cemetery*, preserving a 15C gateway and three 16-17C galleries. The Rue St-Laurent leads uphill to the *Porte Bardouel*, the most conspicuous section of the town walls, overlooked by the ruins of the *Castle* (10th and 15C). The nearby *Villa de Belvédère* was the home of Maurice Ravel (1875–1937) from 1921, and contains a small museum devoted to the composer.

At *Les Mesnuls*, 4km S.E., is a château built in 1530 and altered by Marshal Villars.

17km. Houdan, preserving a 12C keep of a castle of the Montforts, several old houses, and a handsome 15-16C church with an impressive apse.

Hence a DETOUR may be made to **Anet**, 16km N.W., famous for its **Château*, built by Henri II for Diane de Poitiers in 1555. Philibert Delorme was the architect, and its decoration was entrusted to Jean Goujon, Germain Pilon, and Benvenuto Cellini. It later passed to the Duchesse du Maine, but the greater part was demolished in 1808–11. The entrance gate, in the form of a triumphal arch, is adorned with a copy of Cellini's Nymph of Fontainebleau and a clock surmounted by a sculptured stag-hunt. The W. wing, and chapel also survive; the latter, on the plan of a Greek cross, contains reliefs by Goujon. Diane's tomb was rifled in 1795, but her body was rescued and buried outside the E. end of the parish church.—*Ivry-la-Bataille*, on the N. bank of the Eure, owes it name to the decisive victory gained by Henri IV over the Duc de Mayenne's forces in 1590, during the Wars of the League.

DREUX (33,800 Drouais), lies 22km W. of Houdan, and 19km S.W. of Anet, the latter road traversing the *Forêt de Dreux*.

The capital of the Gallic tribe of the Durocasses, it was in the Middle Ages the headquarters of a powerful line of counts, and although the county passed to Charles V in 1378, it was not formally united to the French crown until 1556. Henry V occupied the town in 1421. The 'Journée de Dreux', in 1562, was one of the most sanguinary battles of the Religious wars, in which Montmorency and Guise defeated the Huguenots under Louis de Condé. Its fortifications were dismantled by Henri IV in 1593, after a stubborn siege, and the place later passed by marriage to the Orléans branch of the Bourbons. Several members of the Métezeau family of architects were born here, as were Antoine Godeau (1605–72), the poet Jean Rotrou (1609–50), and the composer and chess-player Danican Philidor (1726–95).

On the N. side of the central Place stands *St-Pierre* (13-17C), largely the work of the Métezeau family, preserving a fine but mutilated W. doorway of 1524 flanked by two 16C towers, one unfinished, while the interior contains several features of interest.—On the W. side of the square is the sturdy Renaissance ***Beffroi** (1537), facing the Grande Rue. At the far end of this street rises a hill surmounted by the Orléans mausoleum, or *Chapelle Royale St-Louis* (1816), enlarged and completed by Louis-Philippe (1773–1850), in his usual decadent taste, who is also buried there, his remains and those of his wife being transferred here in 1876 from Weybridge, their home in exile in England. It contains a number of ostentatious tombs of members of that 'illustrious' family, and funerary sculptures by Chapu, Pradier, Walhain, and Princess Marie d'Orléans (d. 1839).

For the road from Évreux to *Chartres* via Dreux, see Rte 28A; for roads from Dreux to *Argenton*, and *Alençon*, see Rtes 36A and B.

25 Paris to Évreux

96km (59 miles). A13 to (56km) **Mantes**—15km N13—25km **Évreux**.
Those taking in *St-Germain* en route (see Rte 14), may join the
motorway 8.5km N.W.

Maps: IGN 8, 103. M 196, or 237.

At 44km we bear r. off the motorway to (2km) **MANTES** (43,600 inhab.), an industrial town hardly deserving its soubriquet 'la Jolie'.

It was burned in 1087 by William the Conqueror, whose horse is said to have
trodden on a cinder, causing the fall from which the corpulent king died at
Rouen. Philippe Auguste died here in 1223. It was again sacked, by Edward III, in
1346, and finally passed to France in 1440. Gabrielle d'Estrées was frequently
visited here by Henri IV.

*Notre-Dame** (12-13C) resembles its namesake in Paris in style. Its
rose-window, and the gable over the S. doorway will be noted; the
upper gallery and part of the N. tower are mid 19C additions, while
the 14C *Chapelle de Navarre*, vaulted from a central pier, is
remarkable.
    To the E., opposite the remains of an ancient bridge, survives the
14C *Porte aux Prêtres*; while to the W. the *Tour St-Maclou* is a relic of
an earlier church.—The composer Ernest Chausson (1855–99) was
killed in a bicycle accident near his villa at *Limay*, on the far bank.

About 1.5km N.W. is the interesting church of *Gassicourt* (restored), with a late
12C nave and 13C choir and transepts.
    For the road hence to **Rouen**, see Rte 8C, in reverse.

Hence one may either regain the motorway, bearing off it after
15km, or follow the N13, after 6km traversing **Rosny-sur-Seine**, birthplace of Henri IV's minister Maximilien de Béthune, Duc de Sully
(1560–1641), to whose château here the king retired after the battle
of Ivry; additions were made by the Duchesse de Berry, a later
owner, in 1818–26.—The road climbs the *Corniche de Rolleboise*
before descending through *Bommières-sur-Seine*, to bear W. away
from the river, at 22km passing (r.) *Pacy-sur-Eure*, with a 12C church.

The D386 leads N.W. hence along the charming Eure valley through *Cocherel*,
scene of Du Guesclin's victory over English and Navarrese troops in 1364, to
(16km) *La Croix-St-Leufroy*, where a moated castle of 1620 is the abbot's lodge of
a former abbey. For **Louviers**, 10km beyond, see Rte 28A.

18km. **ÉVREUX** (48,700 Ebroïciens), préfecture of the *Eure*, stands
on three branches of the Iton, and preserves a cathedral of interest,
and is noted for its rillettes, quenelles, poultry, and cider.

Gallo-Roman *Mediolanum* probably occupied a plateau site some 5km S.E., but a
town, with its theatre, existed on the present site in the time of Augustus. A
bishopric was founded by St Taurinus in the 4C, and walls were built a century
later. It was burned by Henry I, who received the bishop's permission to do so on
condition that he rebuilt the cathedral. Prince John of England treacherously
massacred its principal citizens in 1193, and in 1365 it was again burned. In 1427
Charles VII bestowed the countship on Sir Charles Stuart of Darnley, sieur
d'Aubigny, commander of his Scottish bodyguard. It experienced another
devastating fire in June 1940, on being indiscriminately bombed by the Germans.

The ***Cathedral**, many times ruined, rebuilt, and restored since the 12C, presents a curious but interesting assembly of successive phases of architecture. The main (Renaissance) facade, with its rose-window, dates from 1591; the N. facade is Flamboyant; the spire of the central tower, of 1467, was destroyed in 1940.

The Romanesque nave arcades date from the rebuilding of Henry I, the upper part being reconstructed after a fire in 1194; the E. chapel is noticeably more sumptuous. The aisles were added in the 14C, some chapels preserving 13C glass, but most of the window tracery dates from the 15-16Cs. The 15C glass in the *Lady Chapel*, together with other glass in the ambulatory (with its Renaissance screen), and the 14C *Choir-stalls*, are likewise notable. The transepts contain open triforiums with Flamboyant arches, and 16C rose-windows; the restored Gothic cloister is entered from the S. transept.

To the S. is the former *Bishop's Palace* (from 1481), now housing the *Museum*, with Gallo-Roman antiquities, Rouen faience, Limoges enamels, English alabasters, and a portrait of Angélique Arnauld by Philippe de Champaigne, and more modern paintings.

The old town *Moat* and *Ramparts* may be skirted by a walk leading N. to the Flamboyant *Tour de l'Horloge*.

The Rue de Verdun leads W. from the cathedral, reaching (r.), soon after meeting the Rue Josephine, the church of the vanished abbey (founded in 1026) of **Ste-Taurine**; the W. front is mid 18C, but the general effect is that of a 14C building. Note the 16C glass in the fine 14C choir, just to the N. of which is preserved the **Shrine of St-Taurinus* (13C).

For the road hence to **Caen**, see Rte 29; for that from Rouen to *Chartres* via *Évreux* and *Dreux*, Rte 28A.

III NORMANDY; MAINE

The ancient duchy of **Normandy** (Fr. Normandie) owes its name to its occupation in the first half of the 10C by the Norsemen (Normands), although the names of its pre-Roman tribes survive in corrupted form in those of several towns and districts, among them the Caletes (Caux), the Veliocasses (Vexin), the Eburovices (Évreux), the Bajocasses (Bayeux), Lexovii (Lisieux), and the Abrincatui (Avranches). The Norse conquest was of more consequence than the previous incursions of Scandinavian pirates, which had begun c. 820 with sporadic pillaging raids, and by the Treaty of St-Clair-sur-Epte (911) Rollo (Rolf, or Rou in French), the Viking chief of these settlers, secured a concession to the region he had overrun, and embracing Christianity, made Rouen his capital. He was succeeded by William 'Longsword' (931–42). This political bridgehead established, further hordes of Vikings (and Danes from Ireland and England) poured in, sometimes actually invited, as in 1013, when Olaf the Norwegian and Lacman the Swede were called in by Duc Richard III to assist him against the odious Odo of Chartres. In 1014 Olaf was baptised at Rouen prior to returning home to carry the new faith to his fellow-countrymen. Integration continued, and the French language was adopted, although certain place-names have obvious Norse roots.

In 1066 Duc William (1035–87) set out to conquer England, landing at Pevensey in Sussex, and defeating Harold, as graphically depicted in the Bayeux Tapestry. The Norman-French feudal system, with its strong centralised monarchy, was introduced there, and likewise the French language and the Norman type of Romanesque architecture, and the Anglo-Norman state rapidly evolved, resulting in the fact that 'it was no longer the duke of the Normans who reigned in England, but the King of the English who reigned in Normandy'. A considerable Anglo-Norman literature came into being; Robert Wace, a clerk of Caen, for one, composing the 'Brut d'Angleterre', a history of the kings of England (c. 1155), and the 'Roman de Rou', another chronicle of the dukes of Normandy (1160); Breton legends were introduced into Normandy; the story of Tristan and Isolde was chanted before the dukes at Fécamp. Less than a century later, Normandy had become the heart of a great Angevin dominion that stretched from the North Sea to the Gulf of Gascony, and from the Scottish border to the Pyrenees. Norman adventurers had also settled in S. Italy, where they established the Kingdom of the Two Sicilies. In 1204, after a long struggle, the mainland of Normandy was itself reconquered by the Kings of France, the duchy accepting the rule of the Capets; Henry III formally surrendered the Norman title in 1259. The region was re-occupied by the English, and intermittently ravaged by both factions during the Hundred Years War (1346–1450). Its administrative unity was not finally ended until the Revolution. The coast N. of Caen was the scene of the Allied invasion of France in June 1944, and it was here that most of the serious fighting of the liberating campaign took place.

Western Normandy was abutted to the S. by **Maine** (now the departments of *Sarthe* and the non-Breton part of *Mayenne*). Its hereditary countship, created by Hugues Capet in the 10C as a buttress against Norman incursions, retained its independence, although at the time acknowledging the suzerainty of William the Conqueror. It was united to adjacent *Anjou* (see Section V) by the marriage of its heiress with Fulk (or Foulques) of Anjou, father of Geoffrey Plantagenet, and passed with the other possessions of John to Philippe Auguste. It was the scene of frequent battles during the Hundred Years War, the English only being finally expelled from Le Mans in 1447, and the province was united to the royal domain in 1481. It was invaded by troops from La Vendée in 1793, and resistance to the Revolution was maintained there for seven years by the Chouans. One of the last battles of the Franco-Prussian War took place near Le Mans (Jan. 1871).

26 Le Havre to Rouen

A. Via Yvetot

86km (53 miles). N15. 30km *Bolbec*—21km *Yvetot*—35km **Rouen**.

Maps: IGN 7, or 102. M 231.

Although not the most attractive route, it is faster than Rte 26B; but those wishing to drive rapidly from Le Havre to Rouen are advised to follow Rte 26C.

LE HAVRE (200,500 inhab.; 16,000 in 1801; 130,200 in 1901), although the second port of France (after Marseille), and well-placed at the mouth of the Seine, is of little attraction to the visitor without commercial or maritime interests. Few would have agreed with its chauvinistic native Casimir Delavigne, who declared that 'after Constantinople, there was nowhere so beautiful'. Of the older town, which Murray described as having 'no fine buildings, nor historical monuments', little remained after the ravages of the Second World War, during which some 5000 civilians were killed, and since then it has been virtually rebuilt in an impersonal lack-lustre style under the supervision of Auguste Perret (1874–1954). The docks—covering an immense area S. of the town—have been given a new lease of life, and with their modern equipment, are indeed imposing, while the harbour is still the terminus of transatlantic traffic and some cross-Channel ferries. Guided tours of the docks may be arranged by the S.I.

Founded by François I in 1516 as *Havre-de-Grâce*, it was handed over by the Huguenots to Elizabeth I in 1562, but was recaptured in the following year from the Earl of Warwick by Charles IX. In 1694 it was bombarded and besieged by the English and Dutch fleets. It was long an important emporium for imported cotton and coffee. Sir Sidney Smith was captured here in 1796 when attempting to cut out a French warship lying under its defensive batteries. Under Napoleon it was raised to the rank of a first-class naval harbour. The Havre Athletic Club of the English residents introduced Rugby football into France in 1872.

In the First World War part of the British Expeditionary Force landed here in Aug. 1914, and the seat of the Belgian Government after the fall of Antwerp and Ostend was at adjoining *Ste-Adresse*. During the Second World War it was the target of countless attacks which destroyed most of the centre and the dock installations, the latter being finally blown up by the Germans before their surrender on 13 Sept. 1944, after a siege of several days.

Le Havre was the birthplace of Madeleine de Scudéry (1607–1701), author of 'Le Grand Cyrus'; Bernadin de St-Pierre (1737–1814), author of 'Paul et Virginie'; the poet Casimir Delavigne (1793–1843); Frédérick Lemaître (1800–76), the actor; René Coty (1882–1962); the Swiss composer Arthur Honegger (1892–1955); and among painters, Raoul Dufy (1877–1953), Othon Friesz (1879–1949), and Jean Dubuffet (1901–). Boudin worked here in his youth in a picture-framer's shop, and was given drawing lessons by Millet. In 1858 he himself adopted Monet (then living in Ste-Adresse) as his pupil.

Slightly to the W. of the *Gare Maritime*, and overlooking the *Arrière Port*, stands the **Musée des Beaux-Arts**, an uninspiring building (1958) in which the contents are neither well-framed nor well-lit.

In addition to a number of works of no great merit, it contains 296 paintings by *Eugène Boudin* (1824–98), among them his 'Pardon of St Anne la Palud', of 1852 (cf. p 281). Other canvases include: *Terbruggen*, Vocation of St Matthew; *De Keyser*, Seated man, and Seated woman; *Van de Velde*, Ship weighing anchor; *Greuze*, 'L'accordée du village'; *Jean de Boulogne*, Denial of St Peter; *anon.* (after

1697) Farewell of the Italian Comedians after their suppression; *G.-A. Decamps*, Masons; Landscapes by *Georges Michel*; *Harpignies*, Banks of the Loire; *Constable* (?), Landscape; *Charles L'Huther* (1895–98; the master of Dufy), three Portraits; Townscapes by *Pissarro* (Views of Le Havre, Honfleur, and Southampton, etc.), *Jongkind*, and *Monet* (Westminster Abbey). In a lower gallery are numerous examples of the work of *Dufy*, including a Portrait of his brother (1902).

The Rue de Paris leads N. from the Quai de Southampton to the central *Pl. du Hôtel de Ville*, passing (r.) *Notre-Dame* (1574–1638), showing an incongruous mixture of late-Gothic and Renaissance, with a late-Renaissance main portal and a charming earlier N. portal.—A few minutes' walk N.E., crossing a bridge onto the former Île St-François, brings us to the church of that name, dating from 1542, with later additions; and, in the adjoining street, the *Musée de l'Ancien Havre* (with local historical collections) occupying a late 17C house.

The *Hôtel de Ville* was completed in 1957. Hence the busy Blvd de Strasbourg leads E. to the *Railway Station*, with its prominent tower (cf. Amiens), passing (l.) the *Sous-Préfecture* and *Pal. de Justice* (1880).—The wider, garden-lined Av. Foch leads W. to the Blvd Albert-Ier, skirting the beach and passing near the all-too-conspicuous octagonal concrete tower of *St-Joseph* (1957), by *Perret.*—To the N.E. stands the *Fort de Tourneville*; to the N.W., the *Fort de Ste-Adresse*, dominating this residential suburb, while overlooking the cliffs is the lighthouse of *La Hève*. The airport is further N.

For the road to *Étretat*, *Fécamp*, and *Dieppe*, see Rte 7, in reverse.

The N15 drives E. shortly passing near (l.) the church of *St-Honorine* in the suburb of *Graville*, a relic of a fortified abbey, its 13C chapterhouse containing a collection of sculpture and archaeology. In addition to the 12C central tower, a ruined N.W. tower survived the damage of 1944, and is contemporary with the nave (11-12C), with crudely carved cushion capitals. The 13C choir has been over-restored.

The road veers N. of the *Harfleur* (see Rte 7), at 14km passing 3km S. of the 16C-18C château of *Filières*, with its beech-avenue, to (10km) **Bolbec** (12,600 inhab.), also by-passed, with a church of 1773 by *Patte*, several 18C houses in the Rue de la République, and, behind the Hôtel de Ville, two sculptures originally at Marly.—*Lillebonne* (see Rte 26B) lies 10km S.E.

At 16km we traverse *Valliquerville*, with a fine 16C church tower, 2km S. of which, beside the church of *Allouville*, is an oak-tree, said to be 1000 years old, containing two superimposed chapels.

5km. **Yvetot** (10,900 inhab.), also by-passed, a textile town largely destroyed by fire in the 18C, and with its centre rebuilt since further ravages in 1940–44, including a round church (*St-Pierre*; 1956), with stained-glass by Max Ingrand. It is in the centre of the Caux region (see p 124), portrayed with 'romantic realism' by Flaubert, but the curious title of 'Roi d'Yvetot'—'Se levant tard, se couchant tôt, dormant fort, bien sans gloire'—has never been satisfactorily explained, although the seigneurs of Yvetot have been invested with that rank since the 15C at least.

The new *Pont de Brotonne*, 12km S., and just E. of *Caudebec* (see Rte 26B), will improve communications between Dieppe and Normandy S. of the Seine.

3.5km after leaving Yvetot the N15 bears r., shortly passing within 3km of *Motteville* (l.), with a 12-17C church, and château of the time of Henri IV; Mme de Motteville (1621–89), a friend of Henrietta-Maria of England, left interesting Memoires.

14.5km *Barentin* is an industrial town in the valley of Ste-Austreberthe, here crossed by a railway viaduct (1846) by Joseph Locke (1805–60), constructor of the Paris-Rouen-Le Havre railway line.—The adjoining town of *Pavilly*, to the N., has a 13C church and 11C chapel, relics of a nunnery founded in the 7C, whose first abbess was St Austreberthe.

There is a 13-17C château at *Limésy*, 5.5km further N.

We join the A15 motorway S.E. of Barentin, by-passing *Maromme*, birthplace of Marshal Pélissier (1794–1864; C.-in-C. at the siege of Sebastopol), and *Déville*, where in 1731 Voltaire wrote his tragedy 'La Mort de César', and shortly enter (16km) **Rouen**; see Rte 6.

B.   Via Lillebonne and Caudebec

89km (55 miles). N182. 27km *Tancarville*—D982. 10km **Lillebonne**—16km *Caudebec*—at 10km *Jumièges* lies 3.5km S.—4km *Duclair*—20km **Rouen**.

Maps: IGN 7, or 102. M 231.

The N182 and the parallel road to the S. (which traverses port installations, petrol refineries, and factories constructed on the reclaimed flats between the Canal de Tancarville and the Seine estuary) converge 20km E. of Le Havre, to skirt steep cliffs, surmounted by the striking little church of *St-Jean-d'Abbetot* (11C), with wall-paintings both in its choir (13th and 16C) and crypt.—Passing beneath the Tancarville suspension bridge (see Rte 26C) the road bears N.E. below the village of *Tancarville* and its *Castle* (before 1103; but the existing ruins date mostly from the 13C, with 15C additions), and adjoining *Château-Neuf* (1710–17), once occupied by Marshal Suchet.

10km. **Lillebonne** (9700 inhab.), the ancient capital of the Gaulish Caletes, from whom the *Pays de Caux* takes its name, occupies the site of the Roman station of *Juliobona*. The *Roman Theatre*, 110m in diameter, probably dates from the time of Hadrian (c. A.D.120), but little masonry remains except the walls use for supporting tiers of seats.—The ruined *Castle*, founded by William the Conqueror, preserves a fine cylindrical keep and other towers, with part of the enceinte, all dating from the 12-13C reconstruction. A feature of the plan is the walls across the moat connecting the main enclosure with one of the towers, repeated at Flint, in Wales.—The 16C *Church*, with a tall spire, has a 19C choir containing 17C stalls from the Cistercian abbey of *Valasse*, c. 2.5km N.W., founded in 1177, retaining some 17-18C dependencies and its original chapter-house.

The road climbs E. onto a plateau above the Seine, dropping down at 16km to *Caudebec*; see below.

The D428, turning S., follows the old N. bank of the Seine, passing the oil-refineries of *Port-Jérôme*, to (17km) *Norville*, with an over-restored15C château and 15-16C church with a tall steeple.—5.5km. *Villequier*, sheltered by wooded hills, was the scene in 1843 of the boating accident in which Victor Hugo's eldest daughter Léopoldine and her husband were drowned by the tidal bore or 'mascaret', which is now a rare occurrence, although the river is particularly treacherous at this point. The house in which Hugo lived, now a museum, stands on the quay, and several tombs of the family lie in the cemetery of the 16C church, preserving glass of 1521–1611 and its original font.—4.5km. *Caudebec.*

Caudebec-en-Caux, in a delightful setting, has been entirely rebuilt since 1940, when the Germans set fire to the place, virtually destroying the picturesque timber-built town which had once been the capital of the Pays de Caux, although a few old houses survive in the Grande Rue; the restored *Maison des Templiers* (in the Rue de la Boucherie, E. of the church) is a good example of 13C secular architecture. *Notre-Dame is an attractive Flamboyant-Gothic church of 1426–1515, built on the plans of Guillame Letellier.

Its square tower is crowned by a rebuilt octagonal spire, which rises in three stages like a papal crown. The triple porch, recalling that of St-Maclou at Rouen, is a work of great delicacy, and shows some Renaissance features. The openwork balustrade surrounding the building is carved in the form of letters 1m high which spell out part of the 'Magnificat' and 'Salve Regina'. Among the fine 15-16C glass, the window over the N. doorway contains English glass representing the Virgin with SS. George, Catherine, and Michael, and with the arms of Fulke Eyton, the donor, captain here in 1435–47. Also notable are an organ-loft of 1559, a 16C font, and a lectern of 1656. The choir-stalls and the Louis-XIII woodwork at the entrance of the 1st S. apse-chapel are from St-Wandrille (see below), while adjacent is an early 17C Entombment below a carved canopy; the *Lady Chapel* preserves elaborate pendant keystones.

A short distance downstream stands the pilgrimage-chapel of *N.-D. de Barival*, rebuilt in the late 17C, while 2.5km to the N.W. is 16C *Ste-Gertrude*.

Immediately E. of Caudebec the Seine is spanned by the new *Pont de Brotonne* (toll), the only one between Tancarville and Rouen, which will ease communications between the Channel ports and Normandy S. of the Seine, which here makes a wide loop to the N., in which lies the extensive *Forêt de Brotonne*, part of a nature reserve, traversed by several minor roads and sheltering a number of village churches of varying interest.

Just E. of the bridge, a l.-hand turning leads shortly to the village of **St-Wandrille**, with a 11-13C church, and its ruined Benedictine *Abbey*, named after a muscular 7C saint called Wandregesilus, a disciple of St. Columbanus. Its medieval prosperity waned in the 16C, and in 1631 the central tower collapsed. After a restoration by the reformed Benedictines of St-Maur, the abbey was suppressed at the Revolution, and its buildings used as a spinning-mill. In 1863 it was puchased and further mutilated by the Duke of Stacpoole. Reoccupied by misogynist monks from 1894 to 1901, when they were again expelled, it became the residence from 1905–14 of Maurice Maeterlinck. The Benedictines returned in 1931. The name Fontenelle, inscribed over the entrance, was the original name of the place.

Visitors are conducted round the 'ruins', but the Cloisters may only be entered by males; even they are excluded from the 12C Refectory, with its blind arcading and 16C wooden roof. One is condescendingly allowed to hear the Gregorian chant in the *Church*, a 15C tithe barn transported piecemeal from La Neuville-du-Bosc in the Eure in 1969 and re-erected beyond the site of the original *Abbey Church* (1248–1342), little of which remains except part of the N. transept—and it is somewhat disappointing, even as a ruin, when compared with *Jumièges* (see below)—nevertheless, it is possible to trace its plan: a nave of seven bays and a choir of great length, with 15 ambulatory chapels. Excavations have revealed the foundations of a Romanesque crypt of 1108–31, and ambulatory. A Romanesque doorway leads to the 14-15C cloisters, on the N. side of which, near an elaborately carved 16C Lavatory, is the closed door of the same period, which leads to the Refectory. The remaining buildings are mostly

17C.—Some minutes' walk away, reached by turning down the valley, and then skirting the abbey wall, is the chapel of *St-Saturnin* (c. 1050), with herring-bone masonry.

Regaining the main road, the unprepossessing ship-building yards of *Le Trait* are passed, also with a 16C church and ruined 12C castle, before reaching (c. 11.5km from Caudebec), the r.-hand turning for Jumièges at *Yainville*, with a fine wooden roof to its Romanesque church.

At 3km the parish church of *St-Valentin* is first passed, consisting of a 12C aisled nave connected in a makeshift fashion with an unfinished choir of 1539. Near by is the restored 17C *Château*, once the Abbot's Lodging.

The romantically sited ruins of the great Benedictine ***Abbey of Jumièges**, ◊ resembling Fountains Abbey in its dignified seclusion, are indeed imposing.

The abbey was founded in 654 by St Philibert, and soon after, the Duke of Bavaria and his son, captured by Charlemagne, were sent here, where they were buried. The fate of these prince-monks is the probable origin of the legend that the 'Énervés de Jumièges', two sons of Clovis II, hamstrung in punishment for revolting against their mother Bathilde, who were received into the abbey.

The building of the present church, begun by Abbot Thierry c. 1020 (after the refoundation by William Longsword), was continued by Abbot Robert II, who became archbishop of Canterbury in 1051. The consecration of Abbot Robert III in 1067 took place in the presence of the Conqueror. Sacked during the Religious Wars, the abbey was dismantled at the Revolution and used as a quarry. The heart of Agnes Sorel, mistress of Charles VII, is buried in the N. transept; see below, and also *Loches*.

Of the *Church* (c. 1020–67) there survives the W. porch; two W. towers, now spireless, but still 51m high, square in their lower storeys and octagonal above; and the roofless nave and aisles. The great semicircular arch which supported the W. wall of the central tower is also still standing, but of the choir, rebuilt in the 13C, there only remain two apsidal chapels and fragmentary walls. A 14C vaulted passage connects it to the adjoining church of *St-Pierre*, rebuilt in 1330 but preserving the W. end and the two N. bays of the Carolingian church. Other remains include the 12C *Chapter-house*, and a dank vaulted undercroft.

Regaining the main road, and bearing N.E., we pass (l.) the Renaissance *Château de Taillis* before entering (4km) *Duclair*, a small river-port, famous for its ducks.

Duclair may also be approached by following the riverside road beyond Jumièges, which shortly turns N. through *Le Mesnil-sous-Jumièges*, with remains of a manor (incorporated into a farm) where Agnès Sorel died in 1450. The road then skirts the wooded r. bank of this wide lobe of the meandering Seine.

The *Church* of Duclair, with its Romanesque tower and 16C slated spire, although restored in 1860, preserves a Romanesque nave of which four columns are of Gallo-Roman marble. The choir is 14C, but the aisles are a 16C addition. It contains four 14C statues from Jumièges, and later statuettes.

Beyond Duclair, the road again circles to the S. before entering (9km) *St-Martin-de-Boscherville*, where the **Abbey Church of St-Georges*, founded by Raoul de Tancarville (tutor and chamberlain to William the Conqueror), is a fine example of early 12C Romanesque.

The low central tower (restored) is surmounted by a slated spire; the two elegant W. turrets are among later additions (c. 1300). The aisles and choir are covered by a groined vault; the apse vault shows a few primitive ribs. The capitals are worthy of note, particularly a curious unfinished centaur, and two jousting knights (in the S. transept). One may also visit the early-Gothic *Chapter-house* (1157–1211), entered by a triple Romanesque archway with historiated capitals.

The direct approach hence to Rouen is made by ascending due E. through the *Forêt de Roumare* to the high-lying dormitory suburb of *Canteleu*, whence a panoramic view of **Rouen** is obtained on the descent to its W. outskirts; see Rte 6.

A pleasant DETOUR—at least in its first half—may be made from St-Martin by following the r. bank of the Seine on one of its many coils along the valley, skirting the umbrageous promontory immediately W. of Rouen. At the château of *La Rivière-Bourdet* (1668) at *Quevillon*, 4km S., Voltaire wrote part of the 'Henriade' (1723–25).—The road circle through (7km) *Sahurs*, with the *Chapelle de Marbeuf* of 1525, and a delightfully sited Romanesque church; on the far bank, above *Moulineaux*, rises the ruined *Castle* of Robert le Diable; see Rte 26C.—Hence we bear N.E. through (5.5km) *Val-de-la-Haye*, where in 1840 Napoleon's remains, returned from St Helena, were trans-shipped to a boat which conveyed them to Paris.—Continuing N. parallel to the industrial S.W. suburbs on the far bank, *Dieppedalle* is traversed, with caves in the chalk cliffs which once served as depots for 'gabelle' salt, before reaching *Croisset*. Here, adjacent to a paper-mill, is the riverside *Pavillon Flaubert*, where the novelist wrote many of his works, and died in 1880. The interior, with personal mementoes, may be visited; his library is preserved in the *Hôtel de Ville*.—The W. suburbs of **Rouen** are shortly entered; see Rte 6.

C.   Via the Pont de Tancarville and the A13

The first 27km of this route duplicates Rte 26B. We then ascend the high N. bank of the Seine before crossing to its lower S. bank by the impressive *Pont de Tancarville (toll), completed in 1959, and the first to span the river W. of Rouen, communication between the two banks previously relying entirely on a series of ferries. Its length is over 1500m, with a central span of 600m.

To the S. of this suspension bridge is the low-lying *Marais Vernier*, a tract of alluvial land reclaimed from the Seine in 1607 by Henri IV's Dutch workmen, who had constructed the Digue des Hollandais.

The r.-hand turning at the S. bank leads 9km to *Foulbec*, whence one may turn r. for (16km) *Honfleur* (see Rte 27B), or continue ahead to (23km) *Pont-l'Évêque*; see Rte 27A. *Caen* lies 44km further W.

At the far end of the bridge we bear l., after 4km passing (l.) **Quillebeuf**, a decaying fishing-port and the old capital of the *Roumois*, which was the first town to greet Henri IV as king of France, when for a time it assumed the name of Henricarville. Here in 1607 landed the Irish earls Tyrone and Tyrconnell, exiled from their estates. *Notre-Dame* has a sturdy central tower and good doorway; the choir is a 16C addition to the 12C nave. The half-timbered *Maison Henri-IV* (16C), with its courtyard, may be seen in the Grande Rue.—S. of the town, the N182 forks r. for (14.5km) *Pont-Audemer*; see Rte 27A.

Forking l., in 10km we meet the A13 motorway and bear E., skirting (l.) the nature reserve centred on the *Forêt de Brotonne*.—After 23km the ancient river-port of *La Bouille*, with a restored 15-16C church containing some contemporary glass, is passed to the l.—At *Yville-sur-Seine*, 7km N.W., is an 18C château once belonging to the financier John Law.

Continuing E., the road shortly passes (l.) the ruins of the *Castle* of Robert, Duke of Normandy (d. 1035), known as 'le Diable', and father of William the Conqueror, beyond which we turn off the motorway onto the N138 to approach **Rouen**; see Rte 6.—For the road hence to **Paris**, see Rte 8B.

27 Rouen to Caen

A. Via Pont-Audemer and Pont-l'Évêque

123km (76 miles). N138. After 14km the A13 motorway is briefly followed before turning off onto the N175.—36km **Pont-Audemer**—9km *St-Maclou*—19km *Pont-l'Évêque*—45km **Caen**.

The excursion to *Honfleur*, adding 13km to this itinerary, may be made with ease from St-Maclou, and the road may be regained at Pont-l'Évêque, a worth-while detour for those whom the sophisticated pleasures of the 'Côte Fleurie' (described in Rte 27B) may hold little attraction.

The A13 motorway may be followed all the way to Caen by those in a hurry.

Maps: IGN 7, or 102. M 231.

The N138 passes close to (r.) *Le Petit-Quevilly* and *Le Petit-Couronne* (see p 122) on quitting Rouen, before traversing the *Forêt de la Londe*. After reaching the motorway, the ruined *Castle* of Robert le Diable is passed (r.) prior to turning off and traversing *La Bouille* (see Rte 26C), beyond which we pass beneath the motorway to (13km) *Bourg-Achard*.

13km. *Appeville-Annebault*, 5.5km S., has a church of 1518, and the ruined *Château* of 1522–46 constructed by Adm. d'Annebault, the defender of Turin against the Emperor Charles V.—2.5km beyond is the hillside village of *Montfort-sur-Risle*, with a church and ruined castle, both 11C.—For *Le Bec-Hellouin*, 10km further S., see Rte 28B.

4km. *Corneville-sur-Risle*, often called Corneville-'les-Cloches' after Planquette's operetta, has a church with a restored Romanesque facade.

6km. **Pont-Audemer** (10,200 inhab.), a charmingly situated and attractive old river-port on the Risle, although damaged in 1940–44, preserves a number of half-timbered houses in the alleys on either side of its main street, many of them built over a network of little tributaries of the river, where stood its tanneries. It was the birthplace of the composer Guillaume Costeley (c. 1531–1606). James II spent the night here in 1690 en route for Paris after his defeat at the Boyne. The 11C Castle, overlooking the town to the N., was razed by Du Guesclin after a siege in the early 14C, in which cannon were used for the first time in France.

In the broad Rue de la République stands ***St-Ouen**, which although unfinished, is a monument to the bold ambition of its 15C builders. The unbalanced W. front has two incomplete towers, on the smaller of which is a beautiful two-light window with a balustrade and pre-Renaissance ornaments. The lofty and richly decorated nave has a fine triforium, above which is an apology for a clerestory. The 6th N. chapel retains glass of 1556, but much of the rest suffered in a fire in 1913. The font is noteworthy, while the low 11C choir preserves some Romanesque capitals, and others altered at the Renaissance.

Some distance S., beyond the railway, is *St-Germain* (11-12C), altered in the 13th and 15Cs, and mutilated in the 19C.

9km. *St-Maclou*, with a Romanesque belfry, where the D180 leads N.E. to *Honfleur*; see Rte 27B.

12km. *St-André-d'Hébertot*, where the chemist L. N. Vauquelin (1763–1828/9) was born and buried; the *Château*, with a tower of 1612, has an 18C facade.

7km. **Pont-l'Évêque**, seriously damaged in 1944, takes its name from a bridge over the Touques built by a bishop of Lizieux, and still preserves several old houses in the Grande Rue and the Rue Vaucelles, its continuation, where No. 68 is a 16C posting-inn retaining its courtyard. The town is famous for its cheese, which is mentioned as early as 1230 in Guillaume de Lorris's 'Roman de la Rose'. Flamboyant *St-Étienne* has lost its old glass. Further S. is the *Hôtel de Ville* in the 18C *Hôtel Brilly*, near which are the 15C buildings of the former *Convent des Dames Dominicaines de l'Île*.

The D579 leads 17km S. up the valley of the Touques to *Lisieux* (see Rte 29, at 11km passing near *Norolles*, with a 16C château and 17C manor, and 2km beyond, the restored 10C church of *Ouilly-le-Vicomte* (l.).

The N177 leads 11km N.W. down the valley to *Deauville* and *Trouville* (see Rte 27B), passing at (5km) *Canapville* a 15C manor, and later (r.) the ruins of a castle once the residence of William the Conqueror at *Bonneville-sur-Touques*.—At adjacent *Touques*, once of importance, William Rufus embarked on his way to assume the English crown. The foundation stone of *St-Thomas* was laid by Becket; disused *St-Pierre* has a 12C lantern tower.—The 16C *Manoir de Méautry*, to the S. of the village, shelters the Rothschild stud.—At *St-Arnault*, on the far bank, is an ancient priory and 11-15C chapel.

4km S. of Pont-l'Évêque, beyond the motorway, is the cheese-making village of *Pierrefitte-en-Auge*, with a painted ceiling of 1645 in its church, whence one may regain the main road by turning W. through *St-Hymer*, with a 12-14C church and priory, later a hot-bed of Jansenism in Normandy.

Continuing W. on the N175, at 8km *Beaumont-en-Auge*, with a former priory church, birthplace of the Marquis de Laplace (1749–1827), the astronomer, lies 2km N.—Some 4km beyond is the manor of *Glatigny*, partly of 1338.

8km. *Dozulé*, a village conserving several houses of chequered brick, beyond which, to the N. of the motorway, is the château of *Criqueville* (1584).—At 10km we cross the Dives and traverse *Troan*, with remains of a Benedictine abbey founded in the 11C by Roger de Montgomery, and enter an area fought over in 1944, after 8km passing (r.) *Démouville*, where the artist Rex Whistler (born 1905) was killed when serving with the Guards armoured division, to approach the W. outskirts of **Caen**; see Rte 29.

B. Via Honfleur and Trouville-Deauville

125km (77 miles). N138 and N175 to (53km) *St-Maclou*—D180.
15km **Honfleur**—N513. 15km **Trouville-Deauville**—17km *Dives-sur-Mer*—1km *Cabourg*—24km **Caen**.

Maps: IGN 7, or 102. M 231.

For the road to *St-Maclou*, see Rte 27A.

Hence the D180 leads N.W. to (9.5km) *Fiquefleur*, 3km to the N.E. of which lie the ruins of the *Abbaye de Grestain*, the traditional burial-place of Arlette, mother of William the Conqueror (cf. Falaise).

5.5km **HONFLEUR** (8500 inhab.), an old fishing-port, has been spared the worst of modern disfigurement by the absence of a bathing-beach. It retains a number of attractive streets with tall timber and slated houses, which have long made it the delight of artists in search of the picturesque, lacking in most other resorts on this coast. Unfortunately, it tends to become crowded with trippers.

Mentioned as being walled in the 13C, Honfleur fell to Edward III in 1346, who used it as a port of embarkation after the treaty of Brétigny (1360). The French regained the town in 1387, but from 1418–49 it was again in English hands. Hence Paulmier de Gonneville set sail to explore the South Seas in 1503–05, and Samuel de Champlain on his voyages to Canada (1603–07). The *Vieux Bassin* was begun in 1668 by Duquesne, and later extended; in the 1830s it exported some 7000 dozen eggs weekly to England, besides butter and fruit.

Among Honfleurais are Pierre Berthelot (1600–38), the navigator; Frédéric Le Play (1806–82), the educationalist; Eugène Boudin (1824–98), whose father was a fisherman, and who acted as a cabin-boy at the age of ten on river-trips to Rouen (cf. Le Havre); the humorist Alphonse Allais (1855–1905); Henri de Régnier (1864–1936); and Eric Satie (1866–1925). Mme d'Aulnoy (1651–1705) was probably born at *Barneville-la-Bertrand*, some 5km S.W.

The *Vieux Bassin* is flanked by quaint, irregularly built 16-17C houses, some having been reconstructed near the *Musée du Vieux-Honfleur*, installed in the former church of *St-Étienne*, and adjoining the old prison. In the parallel Rue de la Ville, to the E., is the old *Grenier à Sel*, where salt was stored when the '*gabelle*', its tax, introduced by Colbert, was in force. Overlooking the N. entrance of the basin is the *Lieutenance*, a block of 16C buildings with tiled roofs and corner turrets, incorporating the *Porte de Caen*, a relic of the town's fortifications, beyond which is the *Avant-Port*, the anchorage of the fishing-fleet.

Immediately to the W. is the unique timber-built *Church of Ste-Catherine*, a 15C shipwright's masterpiece, consisting of two unequal naves, with a lean-to aisle on either side. The Renaissance panels of the organ-loft, the 15C lectern, and some 17C wooden statues are worth inspection, even if its banners are a distraction. A detached belfry is supported by wooden stays.

To the N. the Rue Haute and parallel Rue de l'Homme-de-Bois preserve half-timbered houses, while to the l. of the latter is the *Musée Eugène Boudin*, with a representative collection of his paintings together with works by *Courbet, Huet, Isabey, Jongkind, Monet, Dufy*, et al.

A short distance E. of the Vieux Bassin stands *St-Léonard*, with a fine 16C portal; the rest of the church was rebuilt after a disastrous fire in the 17C.

Honfleur is dominated by the wooded slopes of the *Côte de Grâce*, approached via the Rue des Capucins, leading N.W. from the W. front of Ste-Catherine, and affords splendid views. The chapel of *N.-D. de Grâce*, although offending all canons of the taste of the time (1600–15), charms by its rustic originality.

The D579 leads S.W. from the Vieux Port to regain the N175 for Caen at (16km) *Pont-l'Évêque*, passing at 2.5km roads (r.) to *Barneville*, with a Romanesque church, and l. to *Gonneville-sur-Honfleur*, with a 13C church.

Following the coast road (D513), we shortly pass *Vasouy*, its church with a 12C nave and 16C doorway, and the 16C *Manoir de Conti*; the church at (5.5km) *Pennedepie*, built by the Templars, contains 14C statues and 16C English alabasters.

2.5km. *Cricqueboeuf*, with an ivy-covered church, lies N. of the *Forêt de St-Gatien*; at low tide a mussel-bound reef known as the *Banc du Ratier* is uncovered.—2km *Villerville*, a small resort with a beach of sand, shingle, and rock. The shore stretching from here to Cabourg is known as the 'Côte Fleurie'; the 120m cliff to the W. is one of the highest on the Calvados coast.

5.5km. **Trouville-sur-Mer**, and contiguous **Deauville**, on the opposite bank of the Touques, which is all that physically divides them, have a combined population (out of season) of c. 12,000 inhab.; during the 'Season' they attract a 'mondain' and cosmopolitan crowd, perhaps less smart at Trouville than its once aristocratic neighbour, but both have still great pretensions to sophistication.

Trouville became fashionable as a watering-place in the mid 19C. It was visited by Dumas père in 1831, and frequently by Flaubert. Isabey was one of the first to paint there; in 1865 Whistler stayed there with Courbet; in 1870 Monet with Boudin, the latter dying at his villa in Deauville in 1898. In 1848 Louis-Philippe lay hidden for 30 hours in the house of Victor Barbey before his departure from Honfleur for England; in 1870 the Empress Eugénie sought safety in flight by embarking on Sir John Burgoyne's yacht.—*Deauville* owes its origin more to the toils of fashion set by the speculating Duc de Morny during the Second Empire.

They both sport Casinos—that at *Trouville* also housing a local museum—'piscines', hydropathic or 'thalassothérapie' establishments, and what not, but share the railway station, airport (some 7.5km to the E.), racecourses, etc. Both have splendid sands flanked by 'Promenades des Planches', or plank-walks, although *Deauville* displays broad gardens between its serried ranks of hotels and the sea. There are numerous tennis courts, night-clubs, and other attractions where one may whittle away the time; a yacht basin communicates with the river, on the l. bank of which a complex of apartments have been built over the water, with adjacent moorings protected by moles, a prestigious development known as *Port-Deauville*. Yet, with all its cachet, out of season its chessboard pattern of streets and vacant lawns capture a feeling of desolation not equally shared with *Trouville*, which enjoys a much longer period of animation.

The church of *St-Laurent* in *Vieux-Deauville*, inland, preserves a Romanesque apse.

Hence a series of minor resorts are traversed, after (8km) *Villers-sur-Mer* turning inland behind the *Vaches-Noires*, a line of dark clay and marl cliffs rich in fossils, which continues as far as Houlgate.—The church at *St-Pierre Azif*, 6km S.E. of Villers, is of some interest, while in the churchyards of *St-Vaast-en-Auge* and *Brucourt* (4km S. of Villers, and 4km S. of Dives, respectively) are buried some of the British airborne troops who were the spearhead of the 1944 landings.

7km. *Houlgate*, another small resort, lies between the *Butte de Houlgate* (122m; to the E.), and the *Butte de Caumont* (130m), the latter dominating the adjacent industrial town of **Dives-sur-Mer** (5700 inhab.), once, until its river silted up, an important port, from which

William the Conqueror (with—so it was claimed even allowing for medieval exaggeration—50,000 men-at-arms and 200,000 other ranks; but probably c. 7000 altogether) originally set sail on his conquest of England (cf. St-Valéry). A list (inscribed in 1862) of the names of the principal officers on this expedition may be seen at the Flamboyant *Church* (14-15C), with its sculptured porch and 11C crossing, a relic of an earlier building. Dives also preserves a 15-16C *Market-hall*, the 17C *Manoir de Bois-Hibou*, and a 16C house now the *Hostellerie Guillaume-le-Conquérant*.

On the W. bank of the Dives, lies **Cabourg**, which was condemned by Augustus Hare as 'a most dreary bathing-place', but which, nevertheless, had sufficiently gay attraction to be visited frequently by Marcel Proust between 1907–14, who partially used it as a model for 'Balbec' in 'A l'ombre des jeunes filles en fleurs', a fact avidly seized on by its exploiters: indeed, the *Grand Hôtel* has recently been refurbished in an attempt to recreate a suitably elegant *fin-de-siècle* atmosphere. Although a D-Day objective of the Allies in 1944, it was not taken until mid-August. The most obvious feature of Cabourg is its plan of nine avenues—later subdivided—radiating fan-wise from the hub of the *Jardins du Casino* and adjoining Grand Hôtel, N. of which the Blvd des Anglais skirts the fine sandy beach, along which Proust and his grandmother battled against the wind, when not 'Swanning' around.

Both roads from Cabourg to Caen traverse one of the bloodiest battlefields in the campaign following the Invasion of France in June 1944, in which *Ranville*, immediately S.E. of the *Pegasus Bridge* (so-named in honour of the 6th Airborne Div.), was the first to be liberated from the Germans. 2566 graves lie in the British military cemetery.

The **Battle of the Lower Orne**; see also Rte 30. In the very early hours of 6 June 1944, units of the British Airborne Div. landed in three sectors on the E. side of the Orne, near *Ranville*, *Varaville*, and *Touffréville*. To the first force was assigned the task of capturing intact the double bridge over the Caen Canal and the river Ranville and *Bénouville*, while the others were to destroy the bridges across the Dives and its tributaries from Troarn to Varaville, and an impenetrable enemy strong-point at *Merville* on the coast.

These objectives were all achieved on D-Day, and after two days' desperate fighting a semicircular bridge-head covering Ranville, *Le Mariquet*, and *Hérouville* was established. The Germans counter-attacked in and near *Bréville* on the 10th in an attempt to drive a wedge between the E. and W. parties of this Division, and only after further ruthless fighting was Bréville captured on the 11th. The position was consolidated, but the Division suffered heavy casualties holding the line before the general order to advance E. towards Le Havre was given on 17 August.

The main road drives S.W., at 5.5km skirting *Varaville*, the scene of a disastrous defeat of Louis d'Outremer by the Normans in 945, with a feudal motte and a church with a 13C choir.

7.5km. *Ranville* lies 2.5km to the r.—After 4km we pass the steel-works of *Colombelles* before entering the E. suburbs of **Caen**; see Rte 29.

The alternative D514 drives due W. from Cabourg past *Merville-Franceville*, a small resort amid dunes, before bearing S.W. through an area noted for its wildfowl at the mouth of the Orne, where extensive sand flats are uncovered at low tide, to reach, after 13.5km, the E. end of the *Pegasus Bridge* just N. of *Ranville* (see above). Crossing the Orne and the Canal de Caen, we turn l. past the *Château de Bénouville*, by Ledoux, the chapel and gardens of which may be visited.—**Caen** lies 10km beyond; see Rte 29.

28 Rouen to Tours

A. Via Chartres

268km (166 miles). N15. 25km—N154. 4km **Louviers**—22km
Évreux—29km *Nonancourt*—N12. 14km **Dreux**—N154.35km
Chartres—N10. 44km **Châteaudun**—40km **Vendôme**—55km
Tours.
Maps: IGN 8, 19, 26, or 102. M 237, 238.

This route is one convenient approach to the Loire Valley from the
Channel ports and Rouen, taking in the cathedral towns of Évreux
and Chartres. It should be noted however that the towns of *Chartres*,
Évreux, and *Dreux* themselves are described in detail in *Blue Guide
Paris and Environs*, their main monuments only being listed below,
and in Rtes 25 and 24 respectively.

For the first 25km of this road, see Rte 8C.

4km. **Louviers** (19,400 Lovériens), a cloth-manufacturing town,
preserves a church of interest, but most of its old houses were burnt
down in June 1940. The centrally placed *Hôtel de Ville* contains
various local collections, including Rouen porcelain.

Nôtre-Dame, a short distance to the S., with an unfinished N. tower
begun in 1411, was altered and enlarged in the 15-16C. In contrast to
its plain W. front, with a 14C portal, and the square E. end (early
13C), the **C. Front* and porch, with its Renaissance doors (1528) are
an elaborate masterpiece of Flamboyant Gothic, with a profusion of
niches, crockets, pinnacles, and gargoyles.

Within, the nave and aisles are 13C, with 15C outer aisles, and contain 15-16C
glass; the design of the triforium and clerestory is unusual, while the earlier
choir was strengthened c. 1500 to support the central tower. Among works of
art two English alabaster panels for which enquire, two paintings of 1645 by
Jean Nicole, a local artist, and an Esternat tomb (after 1465), are notable.

Continuing S. we shortly pass *Pinterville*, with an 18C château, once
the residence of Bernadin de St-Pierre (1737–1814), author of 'Paul
et Virginie'; there is another attractive late 16C château at (5km) *Ac-
quiny*, where the church, adjoined by a curious oratory, contains
good 18C *boiseries*; the cemetery chapel preserves late 15C glass in
the English style.

17km. **Évreux**; see Rte 25.—*Conches-en-Ouche* lies 18km S.W.; see
Rte 28B.

Hence we drive due S. on the somewhat monotonous N154 for
18km before turning l. to by-pass *Nonacourt*, 1km S., which grew up
round a castle built in 1113 by Henry I, where in 1189 Philippe
Auguste and Richard I signed a treaty determining their share in the
Third Crusade. Henri IV slept here the night before the battle of Ivry
(1590). Here, in Nov. 1715, the local post-mistress saved the life of
James Francis Edward, the 'Old Pretender', who otherwise would
have been assassinated by hirelings of the Earl of Mar, as described
by Saint-Simon (whose home at *La Ferté-Vidame* lies 31km S.W.; cf.).
The church (1511) contains some good glass and an organ-loft, both
16C.

13km S.E. lies **Dreux**; see Rte 24.

DREUX TO NOGENT-LE-ROTROU (65km). The D928 leads S.W. through (21km)
Châteauneuf-en-Thymerais, the old capital of the *Thimerais.*—7km. *Senonches*,

with a 15th and 17C château preserving its 12C keep, lies 10km W. among its
woods, whence the road may be regained to the S.—14km. *La Loupe*, a small
market town, with part of a castle built under Henri IV, is traversed, before we
meet the N23 and enter (22km) *Nogent-le-Rotrou*; see Rte 37.

From Dreux the road continue S. to (35km) **CHARTRES** (39,200
Chartrains), prèfecture of *Eure-et-Loire*, famous for its magnificent
**Cathedral, largely 13C, with a crypt surviving from its
predecessors. Among its more striking features are the two towers,
the Romanesque steeple to the S., and the crocketed N. spire, or
'Clocher Neuf' of 1507–13; the rich lateral portals; the wealth of its
brilliant stained glass; and its three rose-windows. The style
throughout the nave and choir is the most vigorous early Gothic,
and the grandeur of proportion is enhanced by an extreme sobriety
of sculpture, although the choir itself is enclosed by an elaborate
sculptured stone screen, begun in 1514.

To the N., in the former *Bishop's Palace*, is the *Museum*, containing several paintings of quality and a series of enamels by Léonard
Limousin.—To the S. is an attractive quarter of ancient houses, many
restored; and further S.E. stands *St-Pierre*, with a massive 12C tower
and apse, 13C nave, and 14C choir, and notable for its flying buttresses and stained-glass.

For roads hence to **Orléans**, and **Le Mans**, see Rtes 49 and 37 respectively.

CHARTRES TO CHÂTEAU-RENAULT VIA MONDOUBLEAU (124km). The
D921 leads S.W. to (25km) *Illiers* (recently renamed **Illiers-Combray**), a little
town on the Loir, which here divides the Beauce from the Perche-Gouët, with a
14C church. It is the 'Combray' of Proust's 'À la recherche du temps perdu',
where the author spent childhood holidays with his uncle and aunt, M. et Mme
Amiot ('tante Léonie'), whose house, No. 4 Rue du Docteur-Proust, is preserved
as a literary shrine (and 'centre de documentation proustienne'); for details, refer
to George Painter's 'Marcel Proust; a Biography', vol. 1 (1959).—The main road
may be regained at *Châteaudun*, 29km S., via *Dangeau*, with a good 11-12C
church.

Crossing the A11 motorway, we enter (13km) *Brou*, with some ancient houses
and a partly 12C church.—At *Frazé*, 8km N.W., is an attractive late 15C
château.—24km. *Arville*, with a 12C church, preserves some of its medieval
walls, and (3.5km) *St-Argil* has a 15-16C château, 2km beyond which (r.) is a fortified manor of similar date.—5.5km. *Mondoubleau*, with considerable remains
of its castle, notably a ruined 12C keep, and also the 16C *Porte Vendôme*.—At
adjacent *Cormenon*, with a 16C church preserving a fine E. window, and several
old houses, died Piganiol de la Force (1669–1753), author of 'description historique et géographique de la France' (1715), and 'Description de la Ville de Paris et
de ses environs' (1742), precursors of more modern guides. *Vendôme* lies 28km
S.E. of Mondoubleau, via *Le Temple*, with its 12C Templar church, with 16C additions.

9km. *Mon Plaisir*, on the direct road between Le Mans and Vendôme.—**St-
Calais** lies 9km W., an ancient town, overlooked by relics of its 11C castle and
motte. *Notre-Dame*, with a Renaissance W. front (1549) and three W. bays of the
nave in the same style; the E. parts date from 1425, while the S. tower, with a fine
steeple, was erected in 1622. On the r. bank of the Anille is the *Hôtel de Ville*,
with a gabled facade and a belfry. From the Benedictine monastery here came
Bp William de St-Carilef (d. 1096), the builder of Durham cathedral.

From Mon Plaisir we descend the Braye valley to the S.W. through (4.5km)
Savigny-sur-Braye, and bear l. for (15.5km) *Montoire-sur-le-Loir*.—A minor road
continues S.W. from Savigny, after 7km passing 3km S.E. of the imposing
château of *Courtanvaux* (1467–98), by Jacques de Berziau, enlarged in the early 16C, and restored in 1815.—*Pont-de-Braye* (see p 185) lies 8km further S.E.

Montoire, with a ruined castle, has a *Hôtel de Ville* and other buildings of
Renaissance date, while the *Chap. St-Gilles* (11C) contains murals of c. 1300. 15C
St-Oustrille is disused. At the railway station here Hitler met Pétain and Laval in

Oct. 1940 ('l'entrevue de Montoire').—At **Lavardin**, 2.5km S.E., the 12C church contains *Wall-paintings* of the 12th and 14Cs; the ruined *Castle* preserves its 14C donjon, surrounded by three lines of ramparts, while the residential portion includes the remains of a grand staircase (15C). For a description of the Loir valley from Vendôme to La Chartre, see p 185.—The D9 continues S., at 12km passing (r.) the 18C *Château du Fresne*, to approach (8km) *Château-Renault*; see below.

The N10 leads S. from Chartres to by-pass (3km r. at 25km) *Alluyes*, with a remarkable medieval castle, and (5km) *Bonneval*, an ancient town still preserving relics of its ramparts. *Notre-Dame* is a good example of 13C Gothic, while the ruined 12C church and abbot's lodge (1490) of the Benedictine *Abbey*, founded in 857, lie to the S. (adm. on application).

After 6.5km we pass (l.) the *Château des Coudreaux*, which in 1570 belonged to Renée de France, patroness of Clément Marot, and later to Marshal Ney. Shortly beyond, *Marboué*, with an elaborate 15C steeple, is traversed.

7.5km. **CHÂTEAUDUN** (16,100 Dunois), the older part of which, Gallo-Roman *Castrodunum*, was built on a spur between the Loir and a tributary valley, has earned its device 'Extincta revivisco' from the number of disastrous fires it has survived, the most recent of which were those of 1870, when it was pillaged by the Prussians after a stubborn resistance, and in 1940, when German incendiaries rained down on the Madeleine and sub-préfecture. Jean, Comte de Dunois (1403–68), the 'Bâtard d'Orléans', took his title from the district of which Châteaudun was the chief town.

The *Castle*, ◊ acquired by the State from the Duc de Luynes in 1939, stands at the point of the promontory. It probably dates from the 12C, even if the inscription over the door of the imposing cylindrical keep (45m high) assigns it to Thibaut le Tricheur (966–78), Count of Blois. Adjoining the keep is the late-Gothic *Sainte-Chapelle*, built by Dunois after 1451, containing 15 contemporary *Statues*, most of them lifelike figures of female saints (among them Mary of Egypt), remarkable for their expressiveness; a smaller figure in armour is said to be Dunois himself. In the S. side-chapel is a 15C wall-painting of the Last Judgment.

The main body of the castle comprises two wings: the Gothic W. wing (from 1460), and the N. wing of 1510–18, begun by François d'Orléans-Longueville (d. 1513); their two staircases afford a comparison of contrasting styles.
   Within, the sparsely furnished rooms are interesting for their architectural detail: the elaborate ceiling of the upper chapel; the chimney-pieces of the *Salles des Gardes* (Longueville wing); and the delicately sculptured vaulting-pier of the Renaissance staircase. One is conducted round the covered sentry-walk encircling the top-most storey of the fortress, which provides plunging views. Its precipitous walls, broken by string-courses, are well seen from the Fauborg St-Jean, to the N.W.

Several old houses survive in the streets leading S. to *La Madeleine*, a large irregular 12C building with a curious Romanesque portal in the N. wall, and an apse of 1529.—S.E. of the central square is *St-Valérien* (12-13C), with a 15C spire, beyond which is the charming early-Renaissance entrance to the cemetery.

The D955 leads S.E. to (48km) *Orléans*, traversing the fertile but uninteresting Beauce plateau, passing (l.) at 6.5km a Romanesque church of interest at *Lutz-en-Dunois*.

12km. *Cloyes-sur-le-Loir*, its church with a good 15C belfry, was, with Châteaudun, visited by Zola in search for background to 'La Terre' (1877).

Montigny-le-Gannelon, 2km N., an ancient village with the ruined 12C *Porte Roland* remaining in its walls, suggests some connection with Ganelon, who betrayed Roland at Roncevaux. The château was rebuilt under Louis XII and enlarged in the 19C.

A pleasant DETOUR along the E. bank of the winding Loir leads S. to (15km) *Morée*, with old houses, including a 15C tithe barn, bearing S.W. from which the main road is regained beyond *Fréteval*, where in 1194 Richard I won a battle against Philippe Auguste, with an 11C keep and 12C church.

4km S. of Cloyes we pass (l.) the 16C *Château de Rougemont*, and skirt the *Forêt de Fréteval*. The neighbouring *Tour de Grisset* is probably Gallo-Roman in origin.

14km. VENDÔME (18,200 Vendômois), an interesting old town, once famous for its tanneries, is built on the branching Loir at the foot of a steep castle-crowned hill.

By the 10C it was an independent countship strong enough to send an expedition to help with rebuilding of Oporto (in Portugal) after its destruction by the Moors. The aggressive Count of Anjou, Geoffroi Martel, temporarily acquired the Vendômois, but in the Hundred Years War it remained a frontier province between the French and English spheres of influence. By 1375 it had become a fief of the Bourbon family, but by 1586 Henri IV had to capture it by main force from the Leaguers, and in revenge hanged the governor and slighted the castle. He then granted the town to César de Vendôme (1594–1665), his son by Gabrielle d'Estrées, whose line was extinguished in 1712. It was the birthplace of Marshal de Rochambeau (1725–1807), who assisted Washington in the capture of Yorktown.

The central *Pl. St-Martin* is overlooked by the Renaissance *Tour St-Martin, relic of a church which collapsed in 1850 (now containing the S.I.); No. 24 is a 15C house.

The Rue de l'Abbaye cuts through the former abbey guest-house and leads to *La Trinité, originally the church of an abbey founded by Geoffroi Martel. In front of the admirable facade, a masterpiece of the early 16C by Jean de Beauce, stands the detached *Belfry, over 79m high, with a stone spire (mid 12C), often regard as the model for the 'Clocher Vieux' at Chartres.

Within, the nave increases in age from W. to E., with four bays of the late 15C, two of c. 1450, and two of c. 1350. The unusually lofty triforium is remarkable. The transepts retain their 11C walling, and four capitals of the same date survive at the crossing; but the vaults and windows are none of them older than the 13C. The ritual choir has late 15C stalls with *Misericords, and is surrounded by an early Renaissance screen.

The stained-glass of the clerestory is 14C, and in the 2nd S. chapel of the ambulatory is a 12C *Window of the Virgin; below is a Renaissance figure of St Bienheuré, who is said to have evangelised Vendôme in the 6C. The inscription and the tears carved on the lower N. side of the choir-screen refer to a vanished relic brought back from Jerusalem by Martel. Opposite, in the N. transept, is some 16C glass.

To the S. are the 14C sacristy, part of a wing of the 14-15C cloister, and some 18C buildings (but including the 14C chapter-house) occupied by the local *Musée*. Behind the apse is the *Abbot's Lodging* (15-16C), and behind that again are some sections of the town wall.—From a lane leading N. through gardens not far beyond the apse, a picturesque view of the *Porte d'Eau* is obtained.

Regaining the main street, one may turn l. to the *Pl. du Château*, whence steps ascend to the ruined *Porte de Beauce* and the castle;

this may also be reached by car by a lane leading l. off the Blois road (D957). The **Castle**, a stronghold of the Counts of Vendôme, dates from the 11C, although altered in the 14th and 17Cs.

It occupies a rectangular enclosure on a plateau which falls abruptly away to the river on the N.; to the W. it is protected by the St-Lubin ravine, and on the E. by a deep ditch. The S. side is strengthened by three semicircular bastions, and on the E. is the *Tour de Poitiers*, a large semicircular tower regarded as the keep, with 16C dungeons. The enceinte also contains the foundations of the 11C collegiate church of St-Georges, destroyed during the Revolution: excavations have discovered the tombs of Antoine de Bourbon (d. 1562) and Jeanne d'Albret (d. 1572), parents of Henri IV.

Turning W. from the Pl. du Château along the Rue Ferme, we reach (r.) the *Pont St-Georges* and the late 14C ***Porte St-Georges**, a picturesque gateway flanked by two heavy round towers and fortified with machicolations and battlements ornamented by medallions, etc. of the 16C.—Hence the Rue de la Poterie leads past (r.) the *Hôtel de Ville* to cross an arm of the Loir at the 16C *Hôtel du Saillant*; near by is the *Hôtel de Gennes* (1575).

Further N. is *La Madeleine* (1474), with a crocketed stone spire, and good glass of 1529. Hence the Rue St-Jacques leads E. past the *Lycée Ronsard*, built in 1639 by Duc César as a college of Oratorians on the site of the hospital of St-Jacques, whose Flamboyant ***Chapel** is still extant. A monument within encloses the duke's heart, and his portrait (attrib. to Van Dyck) is in the parlour. Balzac was a pupil here c. 1810, and describes his schooldays in 'Louis Lambert'; the site of Ronsard's residence in the Rue St-Jacques is indicted by a bust of the poet.

A village with the significant name of *Areines*, 3km E., marks the site of the Gallo-Roman settlement of *Vindocinum*; its little Romanesque church is decorated with 12C wall-paintings.

VENDÔME TO BLOIS (32km). The D957 runs due S.E. across the monotonous plateau here called the 'Queue de la Beauce' via (15km) *Le Breuil*, to the E. of which at the château of *Frechines*, Lavoisier had his laboratories.—At 5.5km we pass (r.) a dolmen, and later traverse *Fossé*, where the château was once the home of Mme de Staël.—*Blois* lies 7km beyond, on the far side of the A10 motorway; see Rte 52A.

VENDÔME TO LA CHARTRE-SUR-LE-LOIR (c. 47km). An interesting excursion may be made by following the N. bank of the Loir to (9km) *Le Gué-du-Loir*, where the old manor of *La Bonaventure* has long been fabled to be one the country houses frequented by Antoine de Bourbon, Ronsard, and their circle.—On the S. bank of a loop of the river here is the *Château de Rochambeau*, the marshal's ancestral home; he is buried in the cemetery of the adjacent village of *Thoré.*—Near (7.5km) *Les Roches-l'Évêque* are a number of troglodyte dwellings, 4km beyond which we reach *Montoire*; see p 182.—Hence we continue along the N. bank of the river to (6.5km) *Trôo*, with remains of ramparts and a 12C *Church with historiated capitals and 15C *boiseries*. There is a huge tumulus close by.—The 10-12C church at *St-Jacques-des-Guérets*, on the S. bank, contains remarkable 13-15C frescoes.—Continuing W. from Trôo, we traverse (6.5km) *Le Pont-de-Braye*, and 2km beyond turn l. for (2km) *Couture*, just S. of which is the *Manoir de la Possonnière*, a richly decorated Renaissance mansion adjacent to the site of one in which Pierre de Ronsard (1524– 85) was born.—The l.-hand turning 2km N. of Couture shortly leads past the château of *Poncé*, half burnt down during the Revolution, but preserving its magnificent staircase of 1542; the 12C village church contains contemporary murals.—9km. *La Chartre-sur-le-Loir*; see p 189.

From Vendôme the N10 climbs onto the 'Queue de la Beauce', and heads S.W., at 11km passing (r.) the Louis-XIII château of *Le Plessis-St-Armand*, and 15km beyond, *Château-Renault*, a small leather-working town, preserving a 12C keep.

20km. To the l. is the huge chestnut-roofed *Tithe Barn* (c. 1220) at *Meslay*, once the property of the abbey of Marmoutier, and recently the site of music festivals.—The church of *Parçay-Meslay*, on the far side of the A10 motorway, has 12C wall-paintings.—Skirting (l.) the airport, the road shortly commences the descent into the Loire Valley and (9km) **Tours**; see Rte 54.

B.   Via Alençon and Le Mans

274km—(170 miles). N138. 58km **Bernay**—54km *Nonant-le-Pin*—12km **Sées**—21km **Alençon**—49km **Le Mans**—80km **Tours**.

Maps: IGN 7, 18, 19, 25, 26, or 102, 106. M 231, 232.

We follow the N138 S., and the A13 motorway briefly, at 19km turning S.W. through the *Forêt de la Londe* to (7km) *Bourgtheroulde* (pron. Bou-troude), with a 15C church tower, and relics of its château, destroyed in 1794.—3km S. is the 17C château of *La Mésangère*, once belonging to the daughter of Mme de la Sablière.

5km. The early 16C *Château de Tilly*, by Claude Le Roux, with ruins of a 12C castle adjacent, lies 3km W. at *Boissey-le-Châtel*.

8.5km. A r.-hand turning leads in 2.5km to **Le Bec-Hellouin**, ◇ with the *Remains* of what was once a powerful abbey, moved to this site in 1040, having been founded in 1034 by Herluin or Hellouin at Bonneville-Aptot, 5km to the N.E. Bec reached the height of its fame in the late 11C under Lanfranc of Pavia and Anselm of Aosta, both of whom became archbishops of Canterbury. Its decline was hastened by the Hundred Years War, after which the rich abbacy passed into the hands of influential families. It revived for a time with the reformation of St Maur (1626), and became a centre of Jansenism, numbering among its inmates the Abbé Prévost (1697–1763), author of 'Manon Lescaut'. In 1792 the monks were dispersed, and the buildings used as a cavalry depot. They again briefly accommodated British troops in 1944, and since 1948 have been inhabited by Benedictines, who have converted the vaulted refectory into a church, in which lies the 11C tomb of its founder.

The bell-tower (1475) and a few 13C arches are the sole relics of the immense church, demolished in 1809–17 for its stone, and only the 17-18C buildings remain. The 14-16C parish church contains some good sculpture.

Some 11km W. stands the attractive 18C *Château de Launay*.

3.5km. *Brionne*, overlooked to the E. by a ruined feudal keep, lies in the valley of the Risle. Its 14-15C church contains sculpture from Bec, and a font of 900 A.D.; disused *St-Denis* retains a 12C tower.

Climbing out of the valley, at 6km we cross the N13 (see Rte 29), and 9km beyond, enter **Bernay**, a thriving town of 11,000 inhab. at the confluence of the Cosnier and Charentonne, once noted for its horse fairs and cattle breeding, and preserving several 16C houses. Alexandre de Bernay, the 12C trouvère, was the first to use (in his 17,952-line epic of 'Alexander the Great') the 12-syllable verse since known as 'Alexandrine'.

Ste-Croix, destroyed in 1357 (by Carlos II of Navarre), was rebuilt in 1374, and enlarged in 1497, when the tower was added. The choir has double aisles, and contains more statues from Bec, the provenance likewise of some 15C tombstones, among them that of Guillaume d'Auvillars, near the sacristy. Note also the Renaissance and 17C woodwork of the organ and pulpit.

The *Hôtel de Ville* occupies the 17C buildings of an abbey founded in 1031 by Judith of Britanny, grandmother of William the Conqueror. In front is a statue commemorating Jacques Daviel (1693– 1762; born at *La Barre-en-Ouche*, 18km S.), discoverer of the operation for cataract. The *Abbot's Lodge*, of chequered brick and stone, houses the *Musée*, with collections of Rouen ware, Norman furniture, and Gallo-Roman silver, etc. the secularised *Abbey Church* (much mutilated and under restoration) was built c. 1015– 40, but its vaults are 17C.—*N.-D. de la Couture* (14-15C), some distance S. of the railway station, preserves an elaborate wooden roof of English type, and black and white chequered walls.

13km S.E. is the imposing brick and stone château of *Beaumesnil* (1633– 40).

We continue S.W. above the Charentonne valley, after 11km entering *Broglie*, originally Chambrais, which owes its name (pron. Broï, but locally Brog-lee) to a Piedmontese family to whom it was given in 1716. The W. front, choir, and parts of the nave of *St-Martin* are Romanesque, but the rest dates from the 15-16C. A bronze bust to the N. commemorates Augustin Fresnel (1788– 1827), the physicist and optical inventor. The 17C *Château*, abutted by remains of a medieval castle, houses the laboratory of the brothers Maurice and Louis-Victor de Broglie, the titled physicists. (The death of the late Prince de Broglie is still an unresolved mystery.)

Orbec, 11km W., preserves a number of old houses, a 15C *Hospice-chapel*, and a church of the same date containing restored 16C glass.

8km. *Montreuil-l'Argillé*, 3km S.E., has an 11-12C church, and 16C baillaige.—23km. *St-Evroult-de-Montfort*. The church preserves a Romanesque lead **Font* (c. 1180), one of four in France, with reliefs of the Labours of the Months and Signs of the Zodiac.

13km to the E. lies *St-Evroult-N.-D.-du-Bois*. Odericus Vitalis (1075– 1142), the chronicler, was a monk at the abbey here, of which some arches of its 13C church, the entrance-porch, and the abbot's lodging, remain (under restoration).

2km. *Gacé*, with a 16C château formerly owned by the Marshal de Matignon (1647– 1739), is traversed, and 12km beyond, *Nonant-le-Pin*, with a 17C church, and the birthplace of the courtesan Alphonsine Plessis (1824– 47), better known as Marie Duplessis, prototype of Marguerite Gautier in 'La Dame aux Camélias' of Dumas *fils*.—*St-Germain-de-Clairefeuille*, 1.5km N.E., has an interesting 14-15C church containing a 16C choir-screen painted in the Flemish style.

For the cross-road (N26) see Rte 36A.

12km. **Sées** (pron. Sé), also by-passed, is an ancient but declining episcopal town, retaining several 17-18C mansions, and known for its little ***Cathedral**, replacing a church burnt by Henry II in 1174. The nave is early 13C; the choir dates from the time of Bp Jean de Bernières (1278– 94), and has affinities with the English Perpendicular style. The W. front, clumsily buttressed in the 16C, and a good deal mutilated in 1793, has 14C doors. Its spires have been the object of recent restoration.

The proportions of the interior are remarkably good, and the lofty cylindrical columns of the nave are impressive, with a curious triplet design in the triforium. The square-framed rose-windows in the transepts are notable for their tracery, and some 13C glass remains in the *Chap. of St-Latuin*, in the N. transept, and also in the clerestory of the choir. In the S. aisle is a reconstructed 13C well-head. The graceful *Choir* contains stalls and altar of 1785.

A statue opposite the W. front commemorates Nicolas Conté (1756–1805), a native of *St-Cénery* (5km S.E.), the inventor of 'lead' pencils.—Behind the cathedral is the former *Bishop's Palace* (by Joseph Brousseau; 1778).—Some distance down the main street are the reconstructed Gothic ruins of *St-Pierre*; its tower remains intact. To the E:, the 18C buildings of the former *Abbey de St-Martin*, have a relief of the saint above the doorway; adjacent is the apparently derelict church of *N.-D.-de-la-Place*, which contained 16C reliefs in gilt and coloured stone.

Sections of the road beyond Sées have been improved, as the great *Forêt d'Écouves* is skirted (r.), and an extensive area designated a Nature Reserve is traversed.

21km. **ALENÇON** (32,500 Alençonnais), préfecture of the *Orne* (although situated on the Sarthe), and on the confines of Normandy and Maine, has long been famous for its manufacture of tulle and lace ('point d'Alençon'). The quarter near the station suffered from bombardment before the town was liberated in Aug. 1944. Strenuous efforts have been made to restore the few remaining old houses which deserve such attention.

A very ancient town on an important crossing of trade routes, it became the seat of a countship, and later of a duchy held by the Valois family. Having fallen into the hands of the Count of Anjou in 1040, it was besieged in 1048 by William 'the Bastard' (later 'the Conqueror'), who, enraged by the ribald jeers of its defenders in allusion to his origin, caused the hands and feet of thirty prisoners to be hacked off and flung into the castle as an earnest of the fate that awaited all who continued to resist, and the garrison forthwith surrendered.

Its lace industry was fostered by Colbert, who introduced it from Venice. Among its natives were Catherine des Jardins, Mme de Villedieu (1640–83), whose novels once had a vogue; Jacques-René Hébert (1757–94), the revolutionary editor of the violently anticlerical 'Le Père Duchesne'; and Thérèse Martin (1873–97; cf. Lisieux).

From the *Pl. Gén.-de-Gaulle* (the main road junction to the N.E., near the station), the Rue St-Blaise passes (r.) the *Préfecture*, in a building of 1630–77, known as the *Hôtel de Guise* during the residence of Elisabeth d'Orléans, Duchesse de Guise in 1676–96.

Hence the Grande Rue continues S., passing (l.) the *Maison d'Ozé*, a fine old mansion dating back to 1450, built by Jean du Mesnil, a defender of the town against the English; Henri IV stayed here in 1576.

Adjacent rises **Notre-Dame**, the facade of which is remarkable for its richly decorated *Porch* (1506–13) by Jean Lemoyne. The Flamboyant buttresses will be noted. The nave and aisles were begun in 1475, but the choir and transepts were rebuilt in 1745–62 by Perronet after a fire, and the blend of styles is unfortunate. Above the triforium are admirable stained-glass windows of 1511–45.

The Grande Rue continues past (l.) the Rue du Pont-Neuf, at No.13 in which is a lacemaking school and saleroom, to Flamboyant *St-Léonard* (1489–1505).—Hence the Rue Porte-de-la-Barre, with a charming 15C house (r.) leads past the park, whence we turn r. to the enlarged *Pl. Foch*, where the *Palais de Justice* occupies the remains of the castle, consisting of the *Tour du Chevalier* (late 14C) and a huge 15C gateway with imposing battlements. Its W. side is flanked by the *Hôtel de Ville* of 1783.

To the N., in the restored buildings of a former Jesuit college, the

Musée des Beaux-Arts et de la Dentelle has been housed since 1981; adjacent is its chapel.

On the GROUND FLOOR are several large canvases by *Philippe de Champaigne*, *Jouvenet*, and *Simon Vouet*, and a room devoted to temporary exhibitions.

A more general collection of French 16-19C paintings may be seen on the floor above, together with characteristic works of the Dutch and Flemish schools, etc. Among individual works may be listed: *Ribera*, Christ carrying the cross; *Aved*, Portrait of Néel de Christot, Bp of Sées; *Vigée-Lebrun*, Mme de Polignac; and *Géricault*, Shipwreck. The SECOND FLOOR is devoted to *Lace*. Other sections are in the course of installation.

Just E. of the Place is the circular glass-domed *Corn-Market*, beyond which we may follow the pedestrian Rue aux Sieurs to regain the Grand Rue near *Notre-Dame*.

At *Lonrai*, 5km. N.W., is a 16C château, the birthplace of Jacques, Comte de Matignon (1525–97) and of Marshal Charles de Matignon (1647–1739).

For the road from Alençon W. to *Mayenne* (N12), see Rte 36B.

An attractive DETOUR may be made into the so-called *Alpes Mancelles* to the S.W. through *St-Céneri-le-Gérei*, its Romanesque church containing 13C frescoes, to (20km) *St-Léonard-des-Bois*, delightfully situated village, there turning S.E. through (12km) *Fresnay-sur-Sarthe*, picturesquely sited on a rocky height above the river. Its ruined castle walls enclose gardens, and the Romanesque and Gothic church has carved oak doors in its 16C portal.—There are churches of interest at *St-Christophe-du-Jambet*, 6km. S., and at *Ségrie*, 4km beyond, whence one may regain the N138 9km to the E.

At 11km S. of Alençon, *Bourg-le-Roi* lies 4km E., with ruins of a castle built by William Rufus, and 6km beyond this turning we pass (l.) *St-Germain-sur-Sarthe*, with an 11C church and round tower, before reaching (7km) *Beaumont-sur-Sarthe*, an old fortified town guarding the river crossing, retaining its castle keep.—At *Vivoin*, 2km E., is a handsome 13C church and ruins of a Benedictine priory, partly restored.—*Ballon*, 9km further S.E., preserves a conspicuous 15C keep.

At 5.5km *St-Marceau* is traversed, where the chapel of *St-Julien* has six 16C stained-glass windows, to approach, some 20km S., the N. suburbs of *Le Mans*, where we get a good view of the old fortified enceinte dominating the river on descending to the Sarthe.—For **Le Mans**, see Rte 37.

For roads hence to *Laval*, and **Angers** or *Saumur*, see Rtes 38, and 37 respectively.

LE MANS TO TOURS VIA LA CHARTRE-SUR-LE-LOIR (86km). The D304 leads S.E. through (15.5km) *Parigné-l'Évêque* to *Le Grand-Lucé*, 11.5km beyond, with a handsome château of 1760. The road skirts (r.) the oak *Forêt de Bercé*, and at (8.5km) *St-Pierre-du-Lorouër* descends into the valley of the Loir, with a view (r.) of the *Château de Bénéhart*, a medieval stronghold altered in the 16C.—8.5km. *Le Chartre*; see p 185 for the road E. hence to *Vendôme*.

Hence the road continues S.E. through (10km) *Chemillé-sur-Dême*, with a 11-15C church, and *Beaumont-la-Ronce*, 10km beyond, its château, of various dates, preserving a 12C keep.—After 17km we join the N10 3km prior to reaching the Loire at **Tours**, see Rte 54.

The N138 drives S. from Le Mans, passing the motor-racing circuit, to be avoided during the season, and beyond (21km) *Écommoy* traverses the hilly *Forêt de Bercé*, with some magnificent glades of oaks, which may be entered by turning l. at (9km) the Carrefour de St-Hubert.

11km. *Château-du-Loir*, where *St-Guingalois* (i.e. Winwaloe), with a 13-14C E. end, has an over-restored Romanesque crypt.—We shortly cross the Loir to (5km.) *Dissay-sous-Courcillon*, birthplace of Philippe Dangeau (1638–1720), whose 'Mémoires' throw light on the court of Louis XIV.

At *Bueil-en-Touraine*, 5.5km S.E., the collegiate church of 1470 contains tombs of the Bueil family, among whom was the poet Honorat de Beuil, Seigneur de Racan (1589–1670), one of the original members of the Académie Française, who rebuilt the imposing *Château de la Roche-Racan*, to the r. of the road 9.5km S. of Dissay. He was born at *Aubigné-Racan*, 13.5km W. of Château-du-Loir, beyond *Vaas*, ancient *Vedacium*, with the 12-15C church of a Premonstratensian abbey.

La Roche-Racan may also be approached by a pleasant by-road leading directly S. from Dissay through *St-Christophe-sur-le-Nais*, with a good 14-16C church, and (8.5km) *St-Paterne-Racan*, where the church contains a notable 16C Adoration from the ruined Cistercian abbey of *La Clarté-Dieu*, 2km W., founded in 1240 by a bequest of Peter des Roches (d. 1238), Bp of Winchester.

11km. *Semblançay* (2km r.) preserves the ruins of the 12-13C castle of Jacques de Semblançay, treasurer of François I, who in 1527 was unjustly hanged for peculation.

7.5km. Not far N. of *Mettray*, 1.5km E., is the remarkable dolmen known as the *Grotte aux Fées*.

We shortly join the D959 and 4km beyond, the N10, and descend to the Loire at (7km) **Tours**; see Rte 54.

C. From Rouen to Le Mans via Verneuil and Mortagne-au-Perche

195km (121 miles). N138 for 13km, then fork l. onto the D238 for (7km) *Elbeuf*—D840. 18km *Le Neubourg*—22km *Conches-en-Ouche*—14km *Bréteuil*—11km **Verneuil-sur-Avre**—N12. 36km, there forking S. to (3km) *Mortagne-au-Perche*—D938. 17km *Bellême*—54km **Le Mans**.

Maps: IGN 7, 18, 19, or 102. M 55, 60.

After traversing the S. suburbs of Rouen and the *Forêt de Rouvray*, at 13km fork l. over the A13 motorway to regain the Seine at *Orival*, with a partly subterranean church.

7km. **Elbeuf** (17,400 Elbeuviens), is an old clothworking town now devoted to general industry, which, although it suffered bombardment in 1940, was comparatively unharmed. André Maurois (the pseudonym of Émile Herzog; 1885–1967), was born and lived thirty years here.

On entering the town we pass (r.) *St-Étienne*, rebuilt after 1517, with a 17C facade, containing remarkable early 16C *Glass*; good 17-18C woodwork; and a font made from marble brought from Herculaneum by the Duc d'Elbeuf (1750).—A short distance beyond, the Rue Guynemer (l.), with an old house at No. 64, leads to *St-Jean*, rebuilt in the 17C, with a graceful tower and Baroque facade of 1708, and preserving some 16C glass from its predecessor.—The *Hôtel de Ville*, on the quay, contains an ornithological collection.

Traversing woods on climbing S.W. onto a plateau, we enter *Le Neubourg*, 23km beyond, a small market town which in 1160 was the scene of the marriage of Henry, son of Henry II, to Louis VII's daughter, Marguerite. King John burnt the place down in 1198.

4km N.E. stands the magnificent château of *Champs-de-Bataille* (1686–1701), perhaps named after a skirmish between local gentry in which the Comte de Créqui defeated his brother-in-law, and containing a collection of furniture and works of art, and paintings by Mignard, Van Loo, Drouais, and Fragonard, in its well-panelled rooms.

4km. To the l. stands the 18C *Château d'Omonville*, retaining its original interior decoration, 1km beyond which we cross the N13; see Rte 29.

17km. **Conches-en-Ouche**, formerly Douville, is an attractive village above a loop of the Rouloir. The 'shell-shaped' hill on which it stands may have suggested its name, but a more probably derivation is from Conques in Languedoc, whence the relics of St Foy are said to have been brought c. 1035.

From the N. we ascend the main street, passing (l.) the *Hospital*, in which are incorporated Romanesque arches and part of the church of a former Benedictine abbey. *Ste-Foy* (15-16C), with a Flamboyant choir, and a spire added in 1851, is noteworthy for its 16C *Stained-glass*, that in the apse being ascribed to Romain Buron, an artist of the Beauvais school, apparently working from German models. It also contains 15C English alabasters, and good carved doorways.—There are some old timbered houses opposite the church, while a terrace behind it provides a good view of the ruined keep and remaining defences of the 12C castle.

14km to the W. lies *La Ferrière-sur-Risle*, with a 14C *Market-hall*; and 4km beyond stands the keep of *Thevray* (1489), one of the last to be built.—The imposing château of *Beaumesnil* (1640), with Baroque decoration, is 4km N. of the latter.
The D830 leads S.W. from Conches to (37km) *L'Aigle* (see Rte 36A), first traversing the *Forêt de Conches* and the valley of the Risle to (28km) *Rugles*, the centre of the pin industry of France, its 15-16C church with a splendid Flamboyant tower.—That at *St-Sulpice-sur-Risle*, 6km beyond, contains 14C glass, and 16C furniture.

The D840 leads S. from Conches, skirting its forest (r.) to (14km) *Breteuil*, with a small lake, and a partly Romanesque church containing a 16C organ-loft.—The imposing *Château de Chambray* (c. 1580), in its park, is some 8km due E.

11km. **Verneuil-sur-Avre** (6900 inhab.), is a curious old town fortified by Henry I c. 1120, under whose walls was fought a bloody two-day battle in 1424 ending in the victory of the Duke of Bedford over Charles VII assisted by a Scottish force, which briefly confirmed the English supremacy N. of the Loire. Both Archibald, 4th Earl of Douglas, and John, Earl of Buchan, were killed.

To the N. of the town centre is disused *St-Jean*, with a well-timbered roof, to the S.E. of which is *La Madeleine*, a 12C foundation with a Flamboyant *Tower* (c. 1470–1525) surmounted by an octagonal lantern, and nearly 60m high, dwarfing the rest of the building. This is entered through a Renaissance porch, and contains some 15-16C sculpture and glass.

To the S., the Rue de la Madeleine preserves several old houses, including one of the 15C on the corner of the Rue du Canon, leading to the cylindrical *Tour Grise*, a short distance to the W. of which is seen the slender spire of *Notre-Dame* (12C, with 15C and later additions), containing an impressive collection of 16C sculpture and a grotes-

quely carved stoup. More old houses survive in the lanes to the N.,
while to the S.W. stands the convent of *St-Nicolas*.

4.5km. S.E. lies *Reuil-le-Gadelière*, where Maurice Vlaminck (1876– 1958) lived
from 1925 and died, and is buried in the village cemetery.
  For the road from Verneuil to *Argentan*, see Rte 36A.

VERNEUIL TO NOGENT-LE-ROTROU (59km). The D941 leads due S. to (14km)
La Ferté-Vidame, with the ruins of a château belonging to the family of the Duc
de Saint-Simon (1675– 1755), where he retired in 1723 to write most of his
'Mémoires'; Louis-Philippe constructed a tasteless château near by in
1845.—15km S.W. is *Longny-au-Perche*, long famous for its horse-fairs, with a
fine late Gothic church, remains of a 17C château, and an interesting
Renaissance cemetery chapel.—Hence the D11 at 12km passes W. of the 17C
Château de Vore, where Helvetius lived, to (2km) *Rémalard*, with an 11-15C
church.—We turn l. 10km beyond for *Nogent*; see Rte 37.

For the road from Verneuil to (36km) the turning 3km N. of
Mortagne-au-Perche, see Rte 36B.

39km. **Mortagne-au-Perche**, an old town once known as
Mauritania, in a district famous for its breed of powerful draught
horses ('*percherons*'), was the birthplace of E. A. Chartier
(1868– 1951), the writer and philosopher, better known under his
pseudonym of 'Alain'. Some 150 percheron families emigrated to
Canada in 1627 under the auspices of Richelieu, to assist in the
establishment of the Compagnie de la Nouvelle France. Augustus
Hare condemned the place as 'utterly uninteresting'.

A small regional *Museum* is housed in the *Porte-St-Denis*, a relic of
a fort of 1411, adjacent to which is *Notre-Dame* (1494– 1536;
restored), with pendant keystones in its nave, and 18C *boiseries* from
the Chartreuse de Valdieu. To the S. is an arcaded *Market-hall*; to the
E. a *Hospital* occupies the Franciscan convent founded by Comtesse
Marguerite de Lorraine (d. 1521).—The church at *Loisé*, 1km E., contains 16C glass and more woodwork from Valdieu.

We drive due S., after 12km traversing the *Forêt de Bellême*, in
which a Roman fountain discovered in 1607 is passed, to enter (5km)
Bellême, the ancient fortress of a line of ruthless counts, who in 1082
assumed the title of Comtes d'Alençon. It preserves a gateway of its
15C castle; two towers are reconstructions; others have been built
round. The *Hôtel de Ville* occupies the 17C *Bailliage*. *St-Sauveur* was
rebuilt between 1675– 1710. Also of interest are the 11C chapel of
St-Santin, and late-Gothic *St-Martin*, in a suburb to the N.W.

Roger Martin du Gard (1881– 1958) lived for many years at the *Château du Tertre*, 1km N.E., where he died.—5km S. is the moated *Château des Feugerets* (16C).
  For the road from Nogent-le-Rotrou to *Alençon* via *Bellême*; see Rte 37.

Hence we bear S.W. to (26km) *Bonnétable*, with a handsome moated
castle of 1478 (restored in 1888).—The château of *St-Aignan* lies
c. 8km N.W.

28 km. **Le Mans**; see Rte 37. For the roads hence to **Tours**, see Rte
28B.

29 Évreux to Caen

121km (75 miles). N13. 72km **Lisieux**—49km. **Caen**.

The A13 motorway from Paris, which may be joined 25km N. of
Évreux, provides a rapid alternative for those wishing to drive direct
to Caen.

Maps: IGN 8, 18, or 102. M 231.

From **Évreux** (see Rte 25 or 28A) we drive N.W., at 20km crossing
the D840 (see Rte 28C), and 4km beyond, the D133.

8km S.W. lies *Beaumont-le-Roger*, a charmingly situated village on the Risle
damaged by bombing in 1940–44 (owing to its proximity to a German airfield),
in which the nave of *St-Nicolas* was partly destroyed. The 14-16C church has a
square tower on which a wooden soldier called 'Regulus' strikes the hours.
Nearer the station is the former church of *Notre-Dame* (16C); while to the N.W.
is the priory of *La Trinité*, with enormous buttresses, founded in 1080 by Roger
de Vieilles, who gave the place his surname. A passage, formerly vaulted,
ascends to a terrace and the scanty ruins of the 13C priory church; that at
Beaumontel, 1km beyond, has a 15C stone spire.—The main route may be
regained to the N.W. via (7km) *Serquiny*, whence a road leads W. up the valley
to *Bernay* (see Rte 18B) passing near *Fontaine-l'Abbé*, with a Louis-XIII
château.—2km N. of Serquiny, where the church has a Romanesque doorway
and some 16C glass, the Romanesque chapel of *St-Éloi* adjoins a 16C house at
which Mme Récamier and Chateaubriand frequently stayed.

4km. *Harcourt*, 3.5km N., is the cradle of the family of that name,
where their *Château*, largely rebuilt in the 17C but flanked by 14C
towers, stands in a park of coniferous trees.

At 6.5km the Risle is crossed, and 4.5km beyond, the N138 (see
Rte 28B). The next r.-hand turning leads 3km to *Berthouville*, near
which, in 1830, was found the silver hoard of Mercurius Canetonen-
sis now in the Cabinet des Médailles of the Bibliothèque
Nationale.—To the l. of the N13 is the Romanesque church of
Boisney, altered in the 16C.

19km. *L'Hotellerie*, from which a by-road leads N.W. to approach
the 16-17C châteaux of *Fumichon*, and *Ouilly-du-Houley*.

14km. **LISIEUX** (25,800 Lexoviens), until the Second World War a
most interesting old Norman town, with its cathedral and quaint
timbered houses, is now less so. Much was destroyed in essential
Allied air attacks (particularly that of 6-7 June 1944, and in the con-
sequent fire), and the once picturesque quarters have since been
almost entirely rebuilt.

Gallo-Roman *Noviomagus*, capital of the Lexovii, became the seat of a bishop in
the 6C (suppressed in 1802). It was starved into submission to Geoffrey Plantagenet in 1141, after a long siege, and in 1152 was the scene of the momentous
marriage of Henry II and Eleanor of Aquitaine, but by 1203 it was again in
French hands. Pierre Cauchon, the accuser and judge of Joan of Arc, was bishop
here from 1432–42. It was the home from 1877 of Thérèse Martin (1873–97),
born at Alençon, who suffered from hallucinations, and died of tuberculosis, and
in 1925 was canonised as Ste-Thérèse de l'Enfant-Jésus.

To the N.E. of the central *Pl. Thiers* stands the former cathedral of
*St-Pierre, which escape the bombing. Begun c. 1170 by Bp Arnoul,
it is the oldest Gothic church in Normandy, contemporary with that
at Sens and the choir of Canterbury. The fabric was practically completed by the end of the 12C, although the ambulatory dates from
c. 1225, and the N. and S. aisle-chapels were added in the 14th and

15Cs respectively. The impressive Lady Chapel is also of the latter date.

The W. Front, with a mutilated central doorway, above which is an ornate window, and two fine side doorways, is flanked by dissimilar towers. The unfinished N. tower is 13C; the S. tower, notwithstanding its Romanesque appearance, dates from the 16C, and has a spire of 1579. The S. transept is entered by the 12C *Portail du Paradis*, between two heavily pinnacled buttresses. The crown of the central lantern tower dates from 1452.

The *Nave*, almost 20m high, and making with the choir a total length of 109m, is a dull but dignified Gothic hall in the purest 12C style. The large cylindrical piers have foliated capitals, while against the exterior walls of the later aisles are clustered pillars. The N. transept contains some mutilated tomb-statues (12-13C) and glass of the 12C (E. side), 13th, and 16Cs. The Choir has 16C stalls. The *Lady Chapel*, built by Cauchon, who was buried here, although his mutilated effigy now lies in the S. transept, contains eight 15C reliefs (restored), probably from the rood-screen destroyed in 1682.

Adjoining the cathedral is the former *Bishop's Palace*, its facade overlooking the Place being a brick and stone construction of the Louis-XIII period. On the r. are the *Law Courts*, with a classical portico, containing the 17C *Chambre Dorée*, with a painted ceiling of 1643. Steps mount to *Public Gardens*.

In the Rue Henri-Chéron, S. of St-Pierre, are a few old houses and the 18C *Hôtel de Ville*, to the S. of which is *St-Jacques* (1496– 1501), restored since gutted in 1944.

A short distance further S. is the *Carmelite Convent* in which Thérèse Martin passed the last eight years of her life, whose relics attract pilgrims, especially Bretons.

On a hill S.E. of the town centre, approached by the Av. Ste-Thérèse, stands the monstrous domed *Basilique Ste-Thérèse*, an ostentatious stone pile built in a neo-Byzantine-Romanesque style by Cordonnier in 1929– 54, with a more recent detached belfry. The interior, consisting of a wide nave and transepts decorated in a manner in striking contrast to the simplicity prescribed by its dedicatee, is garishly glazed; the huge *Crypt* has mosaic-work in less strident colours. It is usually crowded on 15 Aug. and 30 Sept., when it is as well to avoid the town altogether.

7km S.E. is the 16C château of *Le-Mesnil-Guillaume*, and 2km beyond, the ruined château of *Mailloc* (burnt out in 1925), with four corner towers.

There are several attractive *manoirs* or '*gentilhommières*' in the vicinity of Lisieux, among the most picturesque being that of **St-Germain-de-Livet* (15-16C), 7km S., to the l. of the D579 (see below), and that at *Fervaques* (15-17C), 7km beyond, on the Touques.

LISIEUX TO GACÉ (45km). The D579 leads S. to (18km) *Livarot*, in the lush valley of the Vie, known for its butter and cheese, to the N.W. of which is *St-Michel-de-Livet*, commanding wide views.—At *Bellou*, 7km E., is a picturesque 16C manor, and another at *Chiffretot*, 3km beyond.—6km. *Ste-Foy-de-Montgommery* has given its name to an illustrious Norman and English family, not all unassuming; a grass-grown motte marks the site of their castle.—*Lisores*, 2km E., has a museum devoted to Fernand Léger (cf. Argentan) in the family farm.—3km. *Vimoutier*, practically destroyed in the fighting of August 1944, is a small market town dealing in fruit, butter, and the cheese named after *Camembert*, a village 5km S.W., where a statue commemorates Marie Harel, who in the latter half of the 18C discovered the famous recipe.—Further W., on the Argentan road, near *Champeaux*, stands the old farm of *Le Ronceray*, birthplace of Charlotte Corday (1768– 93).—Crossing into and ascending the valley of the Touques, at 18km (from Vimoutier) we enter *Gacé*, on the N138; see Rte 28B.

LISIEUX TO FALAISE (45km). The D511 forks l. just W. of the town to (14km) *St-*

Julien-le-Faucon, 2km N.W. of which is the moated manor of *Grandchamp;* another beyond (r.) an attractive farm, lies at *Coupesarte,* 2km S.E.—*Mesnil-Mauger,* 5km beyond the former, standing at the confluence of the Viette and Vie, has a 12C church with a 15C lead font, and a 15-16C moated farm.—Romanesque *Ste-Marie-aux-Anglais* (2km S.) preserves 13C wall-paintings.—At 4.5km from St-Julien we get a panoramic view over the Dives valley to the W.—1km S.E., at *Vieux-Pont,* is an 11C church partly rebuilt in '*petit appareil*' of the period, with a noteworthy 16C group of the Trinity.

6.5km **St-Pierre-sur-Dives,** a small market town, possesses a *Church* formerly attached to a Benedictine abbey founded in 1046. The original edifice, destroyed by Henry I in 1107, was rebuilt after 1145, of which the S.W. tower is a survival; the remainder was again rebuilt both in the 13-14Cs and in 1501–38, and contains carved 16C stalls. The 13C *Chapter-house* (apply Mairie) preserves the contemporary tiled floor from the choir. The adjoining abbey buildings (17C) are now dwellings. The medieval *Market-hall* has been restored.—On leaving the town the 18C château of *Carel* is passed (r.), the road continuing S.W., after 6km turning away from *Courcy* (4km E.), with the ruins of a 12C castle, and a 12C choir to its church.—4km. To the r. are the remains of the priory of *Perrières,* with a restored late 12C barn.—At 8.5km we meet the N158, and turn l. for (1.5km) **Falaise;** see Rte 33.

Quitting Lisieux, the road climbs out of the valley of the Touques, at 5.5km passing (r.) a British military cemetery, and (2km) *La Boissière.* To the N.E. is *Pré-d'Auge,* an important ceramic and tile-making centre in the 16-17Cs.

3.5km N.W. is the former 17C abbey of *Val-Richer,* later converted into a residence by François Guizot (1787–1874), buried at near-by *St-Ouen-le-Pin.*—André Gide was mayor of the neighbouring village of *La Roque-Baignard* in 1896–99, and lived in the château there.

We bear S.W. through (2km) *La Houblonnière,* with a 15-16C fortified château, to (7.5km) *Crèvecoeur-en-Auge,* with a 16C manor; to the W. is the *Manoir de-la-Planche,* with another just S. of it.

At *Cambremer,* 5km N.E., with a 16C manor, the church has a massive Romanesque tower.

The N13 circles to the N.W.—3km. Carrefour St-Jean, 3km N. of which is the charming *Manoir de Victot-Pontfol,* with a stud of racehorses founded in the 18C.—The valley of the Auge is crossed, deservedly reputed for its cider and cattle, and at 8km the road passes 5km N. of the Italianate *Château de Canon* (1764), where the geologist Elie de Beaumont (1798–1874) was born and died.

Beyond (4.5km) *Moult* we enter the zone of battle round Caen, which left many villages in the area sadly battered: *Airan,* for example, just to the S., preserves little more than the Romanesque W. portal of its church.—At *Vimont,* 2.5km W. of Moult, a column commemorates the victory won by William the Conqueror over the rebel barons of his duchy at *Val-ès-Dunes* (1047).—3.5km *Frénouville,* near which an extensive Gallo-Roman and Merovingian necropolis has been discovered, is traversed, to approach the S.E. suburbs of (10.5km) *Caen.*

CAEN (117,100 inhab.; 44,800 in 1901), originally *Cadomus,* from the Celtic *Catumagus* (battlefield), and préfecture of the *Calvados,* stands on the Orne some 15km from the sea, and has not been unattractively rebuilt in a 'traditional' style (in Caen stone) since the destruction of the greater part of the town in the summer of 1944; see Rte 30, and p 180. It nevertheless preserves one of the finest Romanesque churches in France, and its numerous monuments and important university once earned it the title of the 'Norman Athens', while Mme de Sévigné described it as 'la source de tous nos plus beaux esprits'.

Its local building stone was long exported to England, while discoveries of iron ore in the neighbourhood before the First World War led to its industrial development and added to the importance of its harbour; both blast furnaces and port installations have been almost entirely rebuilt during recent decades.

It was of minor importance until William of Normandy and his wife Matilda settled their residence there and founded their respective abbeys, and William's body was brought to Caen from Rouen at his death. It prospered in the 13C, an attraction to the invading army of Edward III in 1346, when the uncooperative burghers were systematically pillaged, and Edward's ships returned home from Ouistreham laden with loot. Caen was again captured, by Henry V, in 1417, and remained in English hands until the disaster of Formigny in 1450, when Dunois compelled the Duke of Somerset and his garrison of 4000 to surrender the castle. After surviving the usual depredations of the Religious Wars, Caen became at the Revolution a stronghold of the Girondins, and it was in the Paris diligence that Charlotte Corday set out hence to assassinate Marat. In 1801 its population was 30,900.

Following the landings on the Normandy coast on 6 June 1944, it was subject to continuous bombardment until liberated: the left bank of the Orne on 9 July; the right, ten days later.

Among famous Caennais are François de Malherbe (1555–1628), and the poet Regnault de Segrais (1625–1701); Bp Huet of Avranches (1630–1721), the original editor of the Delphin Classics; Jean Restout le Vieux (1663–1702), and Robert Tournières (1668–1752), artists; Daniel François Auber (1782–1871), the composer; and the mariner Jean Vauquelin (1726–63).

Wace, the 12C author of the 'Roman de Brut' and 'Roman de Rou', probably taught at Caen; Christopher Plantin, apprenticed printer at Caen, left here for Antwerp in 1549; St Jean Eudes (1601–80), founder of the Eudistes, died here, as did 'Beau' Brummell (1778–1840), appointed Consul in 1830 (when the town had an English colony of a thousand or so); deprived of his post as a measure of economy in 1832, he went bankrupt, and although friends secured his release from prison, George Bryan Brummell later fell ill and died in the local asylum. Arcisse de Caumont (see Bayeux) lived here from 1841 to 1873.

The hub of Caen is still the extensive remains of its enormous **Castle**, started by William the Conqueror, covering an area of high ground dominating the N. of the town. It is still practically surrounded by its massive 12C walls, attractively framed by wide green swards, but little remains of the huge deeply moated keep, to the N. of the enceinte. From its S. entrance one may ascend the ramparts for the view, with, prominent to the E., the disused church of *St-Sépulchre* (18C; with a Romanesque doorway), where, during the occupation, the town's archives were housed.

Beyond the entrance is the *Chapel* (12th and 15C; its W. end restored), and adjacent a memorial cross dated 1066–1966! Further on is the *Échiquier* (c. 1100; restored), one of the earliest secular buildings in Normandy surviving. To the N.E. is the 14C *Porte des Champs*.

Some distance N. of the ramparts are seen the clean lines of the new *University* buildings, commenced in 1954.

The University, founded in 1532 for Henry VI by the Duke of Bedford, preserves the Déesse Mère, a Gallo-Roman statue unearthed at St-Aubin-sur-Mer by the Germans, and the Thorigny marble, a red marble pedestal found at Vieux, which originally bore a statue (erected in 238 A.D.) of Titus Semnius Solemnis, a native of Vieux, once president of the Assembly of the three Gauls, then held annually at Lyon.

On the S.W. side of the enceinte is housed the *Musée de Normandie* (1960), with various sections devoted to the arts and crafts of the region from the Gallo-Roman period to present; mostly they relate to pottery, costumes and coifs, weaving and lace, popular art, metalwork, and the production of butter and cheese.

To the E. is the unobtrusive **Musée des Beaux-Arts*, installed in a well-designed edifice built round a courtyard (1971).

RR1-5 *Perugino*, Marriage of the Virgin, and St Jerome in the desert; *Cosimo Tura*, St James; *Van der Weyden*, Virgin and Child; *Cima da Conegliano*, Virgin and Child between St George and St James; *Barnato de Modena*, Calvary; *Antwerp Mannerist* (1505–15), Virgin and Child with St Catherine; *Veronese*, Judith and Holophernes; *Cornelius van Haarlem*, Venus and Adonis; *School of Martin van Cleeve*, Flemish fair; *Pourbus I*, Last Supper (sepia); *Frans Floris*, Female portrait; *Poussin*, Death of Adonis; *Sebastien Bourdon*, Gypsy encampment; *anon. Flemish* Portrait of James I of England; *Daniel Seghers*, Virgin and Child surrounded by a garland of flowers; *Gérard de Lairesse*, a baroque Conversation of St Augustin.

RR6-8 are devoted to the Collection of Pierre-Bernard Mancel (1798–1872), born in Caen, who also acquired a number of other masterpieces displayed in the museum. These include *Cornelius van Ceulen*, Female portrait, among others; Landscapes by *Ruysdael*, *Van Goyen*, and *Jan Asselyn*; *Van Ostade*, Interior of an inn; *Jacob Duck*, Family concert; *Adrien Brouwer*, Topers; *Van Dyck*, Male

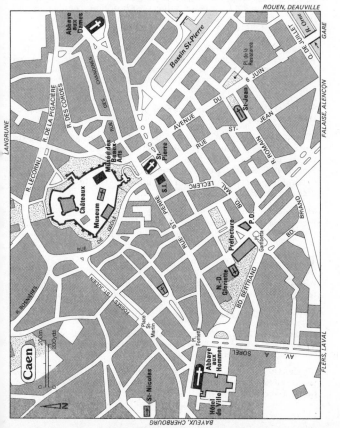

portrait (1630); *Rubens*, St Sebastian and St Maurice (small sketch); *Lancret*, Family in park; *Luis Paret y Alcázar*, View of Fuenterrabia.

R9 *J.-B. Martin* ('des batailles'), Siege of Besançon; *Van der Meulen*, two paintings of the Passage of the Rhine; *Philippe de Champaigne*, Vow of Louis XIII, and Annunciation; *Rigaud*, Portraits of Marie Cadenne, and the Comte de Gacé.—**RR10-11** are devoted to miniatures, porcelain, and furniture.—**RR12-15** *Robert Tournières*, Portraits of Grodon, the sculptor, and Audran, the engraver, a Magistrate, and of Two Epicures; *Oudry*, Wild boar defending young; *anon.* French 18C Still life (of salsify and a leg of lamb); *Robert Lefèvre*, Self-portrait, and others including those of Grétry, and of Mme Récamier; *Martin Drolling*, Visiting the poor; *Géricault*, Three jockeys; *Louis Lottier* (1815–82), Church of St-Pierre, Caen; Landscapes by *Corot*, *Boudin*, and *Lépine*; Views of ports, by *Bonnard*, and *Vuillard*; *Courbet*, Woman with jewels.

In basement rooms are relegated a collection of modern works, including some by *Luis Fieto*, and a number by *Dufy*. A specially designed *Cabinet des Estampes* containing an extensive collection of prints, among them numerous examples of the art of *Callot*, may also be visited.—The *Ceramic Collection* is largely devoted to the manufactures of Delft, Rouen, Moustiers, and Strasbourg.

Immediately below the castle stands **St-Pierre**. Its spire of 1317 and the roof of the nave were both destroyed in 1944, the former by a naval shell, and have been rebuilt. The 13C tower, a model of lightness, was able to withstand bombardment in 1563. The Flamboyant W. porch is surmounted by a good rose-window; while the *Apse (1518–45; by Hector Sohier), with ornate 'candelabra' pinnacles, is one of the most remarkable examples of Renaissance work in Normandy.

There is a striking contrast in styles between the plain Gothic nave (14C), without transepts, and the richly ornamented E. end of the 16C choir. The nave vault changes after the first five bays to the Flamboyant, with pendant bosses, as in the choir. A balustrade runs the whole length of the church, altering in pattern after the fifth bay. The capital of the 3rd N. column in the nave is embellished with subjects from chivalric romance. The Renaissance apse provides almost a surfeit of elaborate roof-bosses and other decoration; the niches in the apsidal chapels are noteworthy.

Immediately to the W. (adjacent to the S.I.) is the gateway to the restored *Hôtel d'Escoville* (1540). From this point one may see, looking S.E. along the Rue St-Jean, the W. tower, with a noticeable tilt, of Flamboyant *St-Jean*. Restored after grave damage in 1944, it has a decorated gallery surrounding the interior. The tower above the crossing remained unfinished.

This whole S. quarter of the town, which until early 18C was still an island, has been almost entirely rebuilt.—Further S. is the river Orne, on the far bank of which is *St-Michel-de-Vaucelles*, with a 12C tower; the facade and pulpit date from 1780.

To the E. of St-Pierre, beyond the *Tour Guillaume-le-Roy*, a relic of the town wall, is the N. end of the *Bassin St-Pierre*, connected both with the Orne and the *Canal Maritime* (1857; enlarged 1920), running parallel to the l. bank of the Orne to *Ouistreham*; see Rte 30.

From this point one may follow the Rue Basse to the E.

This eventually leads (c. 10 minutes) to the so-called *Manoir de Nollent* (or *des Gens d'Armes*), with a crenallated wall of c. 1540, adorned with medallions, and two battlemented towers with statues.

By shortly turning l. off this street, and climbing uphill, we soon reach the *Pl. Reine-Matilde*, dominated by *La Trinité*, better known as the **Abbaye aux Dames**.

Founded in 1062 by Matilda, wife of the Conqueror, as a nunnery for noble ladies, the concrete result of a vow to perform some great work on behalf of the Church. The vow was imposed by the Pope on the intercession of Lanfranc in order that the excommunication laid on the pair for having married without papal dispensation (as cousins, being within the prohibited degrees), might be lifted. Their daughter became its second abbess.

The main entrance is flanked by two square towers once crowned with spires; the central tower bears a small belfry. Unfortunately this W. front was subjected to a too-rigorous restoration in 1851–61, and retains little of its original masonry, and the result detracts from the quality of the building as a whole.

The Interior is nevertheless typical of the best 11C Norman work, with its great semicircular arches, grotesque capitals, and blind triforium, although the nave vault is late 12C. In the S. transept is a charming 13C Gothic chapel with delicate ribs and columns resting on original Norman work. The Romanesque *Crypt* is a forest of columns with sculptured capitals; the *Choir* is entirely Romanesque, and its quadripartite groined vaulting (1110), like that of the aisles, ranks among the earliest in Normandy. In the centre of the choir is the *Tomb of Matilda* (d. 1083), violated in 1562 and again in 1793, and only the black marble slab is original. Almost overcome by the new altar is the tombstone of Anne of Mont-morency (d. 1388).—The adjacent *Hôtel-Dieu* occupies the former abbey buildings (18C).

Returning W. along the Rue des Chanoines, the scant remains of 12C *St-Gilles* are passed (r.), the rest of which was destroyed in 1944, to regain the Castle.

Skirting the castle gardens by following the Rue de Geôle N.W., we see (l.) the *Maison de Quatrans*, a half-timbered house dating from 1380, altered in the 16C, and recently when restored.—Turning l. down the Rue des Croisiers, then r., and l. again, we pass at No. 6 in the Rue des Cordeliers, the *Hôtel de Colomby* (17C), before reaching disused *Vieux-St-Sauveur*, preserving its 12C tower.

Just beyond is the charming *Pl. St-Sauveur* (once the Pl. du Pilori), with a statue of Louis XIV by Petitot, and flanked by several 18C houses, notably No. 20. At the far end stands the *Palais de Justice* (1784–87), its facade cleaned, facing the *Pl. Fontette*.

A recommended route to follow is to turn uphill to the r. immediately after entering the Pl. St-Sauveur, to the *Pl. St-Martin*, at the S.W. end of the tree-lined *Fosse St-Julien*, for the view hence of the towers of the *Abbaye aux Hommes*; see below.—The Rue St-Martin leads down to the *Pl. de l'Ancienne Boucherie*.

The Rue St-Nicolas branches r. off this street through a district retaining some pleasant 18-19C houses to **St-Nicolas**, built in 1083. The three-arched Romanes-que porch is unusual; the apse and apsidal chapels of the transept retain their original conical stone roofs; the tower was added in the 15C.

The ****Abbaye aux Hommes**, more correctly the church of St-Étienne, destined by William the Conqueror as his resting-place, was virtually finished and dedicated by him a decade before his death in 1087, and Abp Lanfranc was its first abbot. It is a Romanesque edifice of the first rank, notwithstanding the Gothic additions that were made in the early 13C, and its restoration in the 17C. It is again undergoing a thorough and more scholarly restoration.

The severe W. *Front* (c. 1096) is pierced by three Romanesque portals and ten round-arched windows, entirely without ornamentation. The two imposing *Towers are Romanesque work as far as the base of their spires, which with their surrounding bell-turrets belong to the 13C. The low central tower has a modern conical steeple. The *Apse* makes a striking effect with its radiating chapels, flying buttresses, and four turrets, best seen from the Pl. Louis-Guillouard, to the S.E.

Interior. The proportions of the *Nave* exhibit the austerity and grandeur of the Norman Romanesque style, while the *Choir* is an early example of Norman Gothic, slightly later than Fécamp and Liseux. The deep *Chapelle Hallebout*, in the N. aisle, was added in the 14C; the large clock in the N. transept dates from 1743. A tablet in the N. ambulatory commemorates the shelter given by the church to some thousands of Caennais during the battle of 1944. On the S. side another commemorates the ninth century of the birth of the Conqueror, his grave marked by a plain marble slab in the pavement near the altar. This was violated by the Huguenots in 1562, and again in 1793, and has long been empty. The 18C angels on the high altar are attrib. to *Coysevox*; the choir stalls are of 1622. The sacristy occupies an elegant 13C chapel in the S. transept.

Some restored 13C buildings are seen to the S.W. of the entrance.

Adjoining St-Étienne are former abbey buildings of 1704–24, with spacious cloisters, now occupied by the *Hôtel de Ville*. It contains good *boiseries*, an imposing staircase, and several paintings (by Restout, Lépicié, and others).

From the *Pl. Fontette*, to the E. of the church, one may regain the centre by following the Rue Ecuyère, retaining several old houses, among them No. 9 (Renaissance), and Nos 42 and 44 (15-18Cs), which, beyond the *Pl. Malherbe*, is continued by the Rue St-Pierre; see below.

From the *Pl. Louis-Guillouard*, S. of the Pl. Fontette, the Blvd Bertrand leads S.E. past (l.) the severely damaged church of *Vieux-St-Étienne* (13-16C), with a charming octagonal tower of the 15C; beyond is the 'Roman Renaissance' church of *N.-D.-de-la-Gloriette* (1684–87). Further along the street, to the l., are several administrative buildings, including the unobtrusive new *Préfecture*.

The Rue Arcisse-de-Caumont leads E. from *Vieux-St-Étienne* to the Pl. Malherbe. Malherbe was born at No. 126 Rue St-Pierre, in which Nos 52 and 54 are half-timbered 16C houses.—To the l. is *N.-D.-de-la-Rue-Froide* (also known, incorrectly, as *St-Sauveur*), with a double nave (14-15C) and two apses, one 15C, the other a remarkable work of 1546, probably by Hector Sohier. The Gothic tower is surmounted by a stone spire influenced by that of St-Pierre. The main portal has 15C doors.

The Rue Froid, flanking its W. side, contains several attractive old houses, many in the course of restoration.—We may turn r. further along the Rue St-Pierre to reach the Blvd du Gén.-Leclerc, a centre of animation, opposite which stands the Renaissance *Hôtel de Than* (1520; restored) not far N.E. of which is the apse of *St-Pierre*.

Several routes diverge from Caen, among them that along the Western Calvados Coast (including the Normandy Beaches), and to *Cherbourg* (Rte 30); to *Bayeux*, *St-Lo*, and **Coutances** (31); to *Alençon*, for **Le Mans** (33); to **Angers** (34); and to **Rennes** (35).

30 Caen to Cherbourg via the Western Calvados Coast

150km (93 miles). D514. 13km *Ouistreham*—17.5km *Courseulles-sur-Mer*—14km **Arromanches**—10.5km *Port-en-Bessin*—34km *Isigny-sur-Mer*—N13. 11km **Carentan**—13km *Ste-Mère-Église*—17km **Valognes**—20km **Cherbourg**.

The recommended detour from Valognes to *Barfleur* will add 32km to the distance, while those driving direct from Caen to Courseulles or Arromanches will likewise reduce the distance. Arromanches may be visited with ease from Bayeux (see Rte 32, and also for the road hence to Isigny).

Maps: IGN 6, or 102. M 231. Foldex also publish a map of the Normandy battlefields.

The department of *Calvados*, the coast of which in fact extends from Honfleur (to the E.) to Isigny, is named after a vessel of the Spanish Armada, the 'Calvados' (or 'Salvador'?), said to have been wrecked on the long reef off Asnelles in 1588; just W. of Arromanches, this is known as the *Fosse d'Espagne*. The beaches are mainly sandy, or with patches of rock and seaweed, and its little resorts, of slight interest in themselves (many were severely damaged after D-Day), are less pretentious than those further E.; indeed, it was only after June 1944 that this coast—between Riva-Bella and 'Omaha Beach'—became overnight the focus of world attention, and still retain many relics of that historic invasion.

The beaches here, from E. to W., are now known as 'Sword' (from Riva-Bella to St-Aubin); 'Juno' (from St-Aubin to Asnelles); and 'Gold' (from Asnelles to Port-en-Bessins), all of which were in the British sector. Further W. extended those of 'Omaha' (from Port-en-Bessins to Isigny); and 'Utah' (N.W. from Isigny to Quineville), which formed the American sector.

The **Battle of Normandy**. On 6 June 1944, after many months of intensive preparation for operation 'Overlord', Allied forces landed on the coast of Normandy. The 21st Army Group, commanded by Gen. *Bernard Montgomery* (1887–1976), consisted of the U.S. 1st Army (*Lt-Gen. Omar Bradley*) and the British 2nd Army (*Lt-Gen. Dempsey*), including airborne troops, and Canadian and Allied contingents.

The 6th Airborne Div., including glider-borne troops, were dropped some hours before dawn in the area E. of the Orne, and captured intact the bridges over the Orne and the canal at *Bénouville* (the 'Pegasus Bridge'; see the latter part of Rte 27B), silenced a coastal battery at *Merville* near the river mouth, and destroyed three bridges over the Dives. The U.S. 82nd Airborne Div. had meanwhile entered *Ste-Mère-Église*, on the Cherbourg road. The low-lying land adjacent to the rivers Merderet and Douve had been flooded by the Germans. The 101st U.S. Airborne Div. were scattered over a wider area than planned, but, although thereby losing considerable equipment, they pushed S. towards *Carentan*, a point of convergence for the two American groups.

The 50th Div. of XXX Corps, the 8th Armoured Brigade, and No. 47 Royal Marine Commando landed on 'Gold' Beach between the strongholds of *Le Hamel* (Asnelles) and *La Rivière*, and by the evening the bridgehead of the 10th Div. was approx. 10km by 10, and they were in command of *Arromanches*, where the 'Mulberry' prefabricated harbour was to be established. From 'Juno' Beach, at the mouth of the Seulles, the 3rd Canadian Div., together with the 2nd Armoured Div., took *Bernières* and *Courseulles* after sharp fighting, and reached *Bretteville-l'Orgueilleuse* on the Caen-Bayeux road, only to withdrawn to the main divisional line about 8 to 10km inland.

On 'Sword' Beach, within range of German guns at Le Havre, the 3rd British Div. of I Corps, the 27th Armoured Brigade, and British and French Commandos, landed at *Lion-sur-Mer* and *Colleville-Plage*, and entered *Biéville*, within 6.5km of Caen, but were forced to withdraw through lack of support. The landings at the most easterly point were slowed up by small-arms fire from *Riva-Bella* until this was silenced by No. 4 Commando.

Commandos of the 1st Special Service Brigade, traversing the inland village of *Colleville*, contacted the airborne troops at Bénouville by 13.30 on D-Day, but infantry reinforcements did not get through for another eight hours. From a German strongpoint near *Douvres* (where their radar station held out until 17 June), a small force was able to slip through to *Luc-sur-Mer*, between the Canadians and the 3rd British Div., but before reinforcements could reach them, an immense British glider-force arrived (at about 21.00) to relieve the paratroops and confuse the enemy.

The No. 47 Commando, after a march of 20km through enemy territory, captured *Port-en-Bessin* before dawn on 8 June, and the British 7th Armoured Div. entered *Tilly-sur-Seulles*, S.E. of Bayeux, the same day, but lack of infantry support compelled them to withdraw. The Canadians reached *Authie*, 5.5km N.W. of Caen, on 7 June, but were driven back, and did not enter the village again until 8 July, for the German 7th Army has sent their strongest reinforcements towards this area near the Orne. On 9 June the British linked up with U.S. troops at 'Omaha' Beach.

Little resistance was met by the Americans on 'Utah' Beach, and by nightfall all the enemy had been accounted for, and contact had been made with the 101st Airborne Div. The disembarkation on 'Omaha' Beach had been an arduous affair, and their infantry here, with no armour in support, encountered the full impact of a German division ready for action.

Bad weather following the initial landings enforced some days' delay in further offensive movements on the part of the Allies, and the gales of 19-21 June caused extensive damage to the 'Mulberry Harbour'. The Germans were able, meanwhile, to bring up reinforcements in the Caen area to support the four Panzer divisions between Caen and the Bocage. The British thrust S. through difficult country to recapture Tilly-sur-Seulles on the 18 June, while further British and Canadian forces were also doggedly gaining ground towards Caen itself, most of which was in their hands by 9 July, although the Germans clung to the suburbs on the r. bank of the Orne until the 19th.

It was at this point that Montgomery ordered the VIII British Corps (whose landing had been much hampered by stormy weather) to swing forward between Tilly and Caen towards the Caen-Falaise road, 'to pull the enemy on to the 2nd Army so as to make it easier for 1st Army to expand and extend', and a bridgehead was established across the Orne on 28 June.

By the end of June there were eight Panzer divisions in Normandy, seven and a half of which were engaged with the British 2nd Army.

On 18 June the Americans had reached *Barneville*, on the W. coast of the Cotentin, thereby cutting off the enemy in the N. of the peninsula; they then advanced N. through *Montebourg* and *Valognes* to the outer defences of *Cherbourg* (21 June).

The month of July was occupied principally in small advances against stubborn resistance, especially in the Bocage. On 18-20 July the I British Corps, then E. of Caen, pushed as far S. as *Bourguébus*. Meanwhile, the Americans had slowly advanced towards *Granville* and *Avranches*; but on 6 Aug. the Germans made a violent counter-attack westwards from their front between *Vire* and *Mortain* in an attempt to cut off the Americans around Avranches; to neutralise which, Montgomery order the Canadian 1st Army (*Lt-Gen. Crerar*) to capture *Falaise* and threaten the German rear. After bitter fighting this objective was gained on 17 Aug. The Germans withdrew in the face of this flank attack, allowing the Americans under *Gen. Patton* to thrust S.W. through *Mayenne*. German divisions were annihilated or captured piecemeal, and on 19 Aug. the Americans and the Canadians joined forces near *Chambois* (12km N.E. of Argentan): the Battle of Normandy was virtually over.

The cost had been high. It has been calculated that the Allied ground forces had approx. 210,000 casualties, which included some 37,000 killed; total German losses must have been 400,000 men, half of which were prisoners, plus 20,000 vehicles, 1500 field-guns, and 1300 tanks.

For the inland road from Caen to *Arromanches*; see below.

The D514 drives N.E. from Caen (see Rte 29) parallel to the Canal de Caen and the Orne, at 9km passing (r.) the 18C *Château de Bénouville* (by *Ledoux*) and the 'Pegasus Bridge', captured intact on the first day of the Normandy Landings.—4km. *Ouistreham*, the ancient port of Caen, and time-honoured landing-place of English expeditions against the city, and where Royal Naval 'frogmen' swam in to clear the canal of obstacles in 1944, retains a Gothic church with a good W. facade.—Contiguous *Riva-Bella*, a villa-resort flanked by fine sands from which the tide recedes some 2km, preserves a massive German blockhouse and other relics of the Occupation and Invasion.

Immediately to the W. is the *Colleville-Montgomery Plage*, an important beach on D-Day, perpetuating the name of the C-in-C of the 21st Army Group, while a short distance beyond (l.), near the village church of *Hermanville-sur-Mer*, with a Romanesque nave and Gothic choir, is a British military cemetery.

6km. *Lion-sur-Mer*, with a party 12-13C church and 16C château, is another family resort, off which extensive reefs are uncovered at low tide, beyond which we pass *Luc-sur-Mer* and *Langrune-sur-Mer*, 3km inland from which, at *Douvres*, is a Romanesque church tower surmounted by a 13C Gothic spire. The 13C church of Langrune has a fine tower likewise. Another may be seen beyond *St-Aubin-sur-Mer* at *Bernières-sur-Mer*, 4km W., with a partly 12-13C church.—2.5km. *Courseulles-sur-Mer*, off which a dozen ships were deliberately sunk on D-Day to form a temporary harbour until the 'Mulberry' was ready; a blockhouse is preserved here. On the W. bank of the Seulles, at *Graye*, King George VI, accompanied by Winston Churchill, landed for some hours on 16 June.—6km. *Ver-sur-Mer*, with a sand and pebble beach, was virtually destroyed in 1944; remains of the 'Atlantic Wall' thrown up by the Germans, may still be discerned. The older inland village has a Romanesque church tower of four storeys, with blind arcades.

8km. **Arromanches**, with a good sandy beach and cliffs to the E. and W., was the site of the famous prefabricated '*Mulberry*' *Harbour*, which, towed piecemeal from England in the form of 146 caissons (over half a million tonnes of concrete), was to form, with its pierheads and jetties, the means of reinforcements on a colossal scale—some 2,500,000 men, 500,000 vehicles, and 4,000,000 tonnes of material in the following three months. Numerous traces of the harbour, locally known as '*Port Winston*', are still visible, while models in the *Musée du Débarquement* here graphically display and explain its importance in June 1944 and subsequent weeks. A film, with English commentary, may be seen.—*Ryes*, 4.5km S., has a 12-13C church.—**Bayeux** (see Rte 31) lies only 10km S.W. of Arromanches.

CAEN TO ARROMANCHES, VIA CREULLY (29km). The D22 leads N.W. past (5km) *St-Contest*, where Gen. Rommel briefly had his H.Q., and where the Romanesque church survived the fighting, to (4.5km) *Cairon*, just S. of which, at *Lasson*, is a Renaissance château, and a church with an imitation Romanesque tower of the 18C; that at adjacent *Rosel* is 12-15C.

Just beyond Cairon, the D170 turns r. for *Courseulles*, providing an approach via *Thaon* to *Fontaine-Henry*. By turning r. and then l. on leaving *Thaon*, one may follow a lane to the disused 12C *Church* (not to be confused with the other church further W.), until lately a barn, but preserving noteworthy decoration.—Returning to the village, and turning l., we shortly enter *Fontaine-*

Henry; the Renaissance château, with its high, steeply-pitched roof and elaborate decoration, is certainly picturesque from the gates, but its interior hardly deserves attention, having been mutilated in the 19C. Hence our road may be regained further W. at _Pierrepoint_, just S.W. of which is the attractive 17C château of _Manneville_, beyond _Lantheuil_.

From Cairon, the D22 continues N.W. via (9km) _Pierrepont_ (see above) to (3km) _Creully_, with a 12C church, and an adjacent 12-16C château (now the Mairie) with a slender staircase tower and ruined enceinte; it once belonged to Robert of Kent, natural son of Henri I, and later to Colbert.—At _St-Gabriel_, 2km S.W., is a ruined priory with a 12C gateway, 15C refectory, and 12C choir to its church. There is an attractive 17C manor at _Brécy_, just S. of St-Gabriel.—On the far bank of the Seulles at Creully we pass (l.) the château of _Creullet_, in the gardens of which Montgomery briefly parked his caravan, and on the 12 June 1944 conferred with Churchill.—The road now bears N. through _Crépon_, and _Meuvaines_, both with Romanesque churches, the latter containing 15C statues, to approach **Arromanches**; see above.

From Arromanches, the coast road traverses _Manvieux_, with an old church, to (6km) _Longues-sur-Mer_, preserving considerable remains of the 13-16C Benedictine abbey of _Ste-Marie_, founded in 1168. A lane to the r. approaches the cliff-edge, providing extensive views, and with remains of German bunkers and batteries, etc.—5km. _Port-en-Bessin_, a small fishing-port at the mouth of the Dromme, protected by granite moles, is situated in a hollow beneath high cliffs. The damaged _Tour Vauban_ is a relic of a project to fortify the harbour in the 17C and later. The port was used as a petrol depot in the early days of the Landings.—_Huppain_, just to the W., has a Romanesque church; immediately S. of which, at _Villiers-sur-Port_, are the ruins of a 12-16C priory.

7km. _Colleville-sur-Mer_, with a practically rebuilt Romanesque church with a good tower, is slightly inland from the E. end of 'Omaha' Beach, where American forces landed on 6 June 1944. The 'Mulberry Harbour' here was rendered virtually useless after a storm of unprecedented violence which started on the 19th. Some of the fiercest fighting occured between here and (6km) _Vierville-sur-Mer_, another little resort largely destroyed at the time, inland from which is the _Château de Vaumicel_, a Renaissance manor now a farm.

The coast road hence via _Grandcamp-Maisy_, with a small harbour and dismantled fort, to (21km) _Isigny_ is of slight interest.

Isigny-sur-Mer, severely damaged before its capture by the Americans on 9 June 1944, a small port on the Aure close to its junction with the estuary on the Vire, gives its name to the butter produced in this part of Normandy. The church preserves a 13C tower and choir, while the _Hôtel de Ville_ occupies an 18C château.

On crossing the Vire, the N13 enters the _Cotentin_, and (11km) **Carentan** (6900 inhab.), the Gallo-Roman _Crociantonum_, derived from the Celtic _Carentomagus_. The medieval town was burnt in 1346 by Edward III, and again, accidentally, in 1679. It is now an important market for dairy produce and cattle, but would be of slight interest was it not for Flamboyant _Notre-Dame_, the 14C *Tower of which is crowned by a graceful 15C spire; the W. door dates from the 12C.

The interior is less uniform in style. The low nave (14-15C), with foliated capitals, is separated from the lofty 15-16C choir (with its cumbersome 18C reredos) by a late Romanesque crossing. The Renaissance choir screen and stalls are noteworthy, also the quaint paintings on wood in the two N. choir chapels, and a niche in the N. transept. In the nave are two small Flamboyant doorways, and—in the N. aisle—a 16C doorway embellished with skulls.

CARENTAN TO LA HAYE-DU-PUITS (24km). The D903 leads due W., passing at 11.5km near (r.) *Coigny*, connected by a long avenue with the 18C *Château de Franquetot*, a residence of the dukes of Coigny.—To the S. extend the *Marais de Gorges*, flooded by the Germans in 1944.—8.5km. To the l. rises *Mont Castre*, with remains of a Gallo-Roman camp, and 4km beyond we reach *La Haye-du-Puits*, 8km N. of *Lessay*; see Rte 31.

CARENTAN TO COUTANCES (33km). The D971 leads S.W. to *Périers*, severely damaged in 1944, but preserving its 13C church tower.—Early 14C murals have been uncovered in the church at *Marchésieux*, 10km due E.; for *Lessay*, 10km N.W., see Rte 31. **Coutances** lies 15km S. of Périers; see Rte 32.

CARENTAN TO QUETTEHOU VIA 'UTAH' BEACH (38km). We turn r. off the N13 3.5km N.W of Carentan to (6.5km) *Ste-Marie-du-Mont*, its Romanesque church with 14C additions, 1km beyond which the main road turns N.W. parallel to the coast, which may be skirted by continuing ahead to *La Madeleine*, with a monument on a blockhouse to the 1st Engineer Special Brigade. Between this point and the *Dunes de Varreville*, 4km N.W., is the stretch known as *'Utah' Beach*, where mass landings took place on D-Day; see above. The American troops were able to reach *Barneville*, on the W. coast of the Cotenton peninsula by the 18 June, before swinging S. to *St-Lô* and *A vranches*. We pass several relics of the 'Atlantic Wall' before turning inland at (21km) *Quinéville*.

Off the coast here took place the sea **Battle of La Hougue** (or La Hogue; 19-23 May 1692), between the French under Tourville, and the English and Dutch under Edward Russell (later the Earl of Orford), the first encounter occurring off Barfleur, after which part of the French fleet escaped to St-Malo. Of the remainder, some were burnt in the Cherbourg roads, but the majority were destroyed by Sir George Rooke off the anchorage of La Hougue, an action fought under the eyes of the exiled James II, who here saw vanish his last hope of regaining the throne.

At the N. end of the bay lie *Quettehou*, with a 13C church, and *St-Vaast*, a little fishing-port, with oyster-beds, facing the *Île de Tatihou* (accessible at low tide); both the island and the promontory of La Hougue retain fortifications constructed on the plans of Vauban after the battle.—To the E. of Quinéville is the offshore *Îles St-Marcouf*, where a British naval post in 1793 paralysed sea communications between Cherbourg and Le Havre.—*Montebourg* (see below) lies 7km inland.

The N13 drives N.W. from Carentan through (4km) *St-Côme-du-Mont*, its 11C Romanesque church with a fine apse and archaic capitals; note the door-lintel on the exterior of the S. transept illustrating the fable of the fox and the crane. The 14C tower and vaulting have been rebuilt since 1944. Several churches in the area have Romanesque details.

9km. **Ste-Mère-Église** was the focal point of the landings of the U.S. 82nd and 101st Airborne Divisions on the night of 5-6 June 1944. An *Airborne Museum* may be visited, while the largely 13C church contains a memorial window.—10km. *Montebourg*, practically rebuilt since 1944, has a restored 14C church with a fine spire.

7km. **Valognes** (7000 inhab.) was a town of some importance in the 17-18Cs, and although much damaged in 1944, still preserves several elegant grey stone mansions of the genteel provincial aristocracy satirised in Le Sage's 'Turcaret' (1709).—Near the S.E. entrance of the town, the Rue des Capucines leads E. to the suburb of *Alleaume*, with a little 14C church with a Romanesque arcade and bas-relief incorporated in its S. wall. Some minutes' walk beyond, to the S.E., is the ruin known as the *Vieux-Château*, in fact a relic of the Gallo-Roman town of *Alauna* (also reached from the main road via the Rue du Vieux-Château), but its theatre is no more.

Little remains of the centrally situated church of *St-Malo*, to which a modern nave has been added. Hence the Rue des Religieuses leads S.E., passing the *Hôtel de Grandval*, where Barbey d'Aurevilly often resided, towards the 17C dependencies of a former Benedictine abbey, now a *Hospital*.—A lane leading S. from the apse of the church shortly meets the ironically named Rue Petit-Versailles, on the r. of which is a small 15C manor; to the l., facing the Rue Barbey d'Aurevilly, is the splendid facade of the **Hôtel de Beaumont* (c. 1750).

The main road continues N.W. to (20km) **Cherbourg** (see Rte 31). passing (at 9km) near *Brix* (l.), said to be the ancestral home of the Bruce family, whose descendants became kings of Scotland.

The more interesting, and recommended, DETOUR is that from Valognes to Cherbourg via Barfleur, approached by driving N.E. on the D902 through (3km) *Tamerville*, the Romanesque church of which has an octagonal tower, to (12.5km) *Quettehou;* see above.—At *La Vast*, 6km N.W., the 15C church has contemporary glass, while that at *Réville*, 3km to the r. of the main road, is also of interest, beyond which several characteristic Norman manor-farms are passed.

9.5km **Barfleur**, an attractive fishing-port and small sailing resort on a rocky inlet, was until the end of the 12C one of the most frequented ports of communication between Normandy and England, and it was here, in 1120, that the 'White Ship' (on which were William, only son of Henry I, and over 100 young nobles) struck a rock not far from the shore, the butcher Bérold being the only survivor from the wreck. At the harbour entrance stands a 17C church with a massive tower, while the town itself preserves a number of pleasant old houses.

From *Gatteville*, 2km N.W., with a 12C church rebuilt in the 17C, one may visit the lighthouse on the *Pointe de Barfleur*, the N.E. extremity of the Cotentin, from the summit of which the lights of the *Isle of Wight*, c. 112km distant, are occasionally visible.

Driving W. from Barfleur, we pass (5km) *Tocqueville*, its château a residence of Alexis de Tocqueville (1805 – 59), author of 'Democracy in America' and other historical works.—From (5km) *St-Pierre-Église*, with an 18C château, and 17C church incorporating parts of its 12C predecessor, one may skirt the coast or continue W. on the main road, passing (r.) the airport of *Maupertus*, and descend past *Tourlaville*, with a 14C church and Renaissance château, 5km before entering **Cherbourg;** see Rte 31.

31   Cherbourg to Avranches via Coutances

130km (81 miles). N13. 20km **Valognes**—D2. 15km *St-Sauveur-le-Vicomte*—D900. 11km *La Haye-du-Puits*—8km **Lessay**—D2. 21km **Coutances**—D971. 29km **Granville**—D973. 26km **Avranches.**

Maps: IGN 6, 16, or 102. M 231.

CHERBOURG (30,100 inhab.), the terminus of the Southampton ferry, and an important naval base and commercial port, lies below a range of hills, the nearest of which, the *Montagne du Roule* (112m) overlooks the inner basin. Its harbour, unlike the natural roadstead at Brest, has been formed by the construction of a series of breakwaters some 3km from the shore, between the *Île Pelée* and the *Pointe de Querqueville* to the W. These, with the completion of a dredged channel in 1933, permitted Atlantic liners to berth alongside the Gare Maritime.

Little is known about the port prior to the 10C, but it grew in importance under Philippe Auguste, and was several times attacked by the English, being occupied by them from 1418–50. Although fortified by Vauban in 1686, it was again raided by an English fleet in 1758, when its arsenal was destroyed and its ships burnt. Nathaniel Wraxall, who landed here in 1775, condemned it as 'a wretched collection of houses crowded together in a sandy valley...', while thirteen years later Young complained that he was there 'fleeced more infamously than at any other town in France'. Construction of the *Digue*, begun by Louis XVI, was not completed until 1853, and its defences not until 1858. In the previous year Queen Victoria was received here by Napoleon III on the occasion of the opening of the railway from Caen.

The British 52nd Div. was evacuated from Cherbourg on 15-16 June 1940, and the Germans entered the town two days later. In June 1944 the Germans, isolated here by the Americans (see Rte 30), carried on their work of demolition while putting up a stout defence, the harbour forts only capitulating on 29 June. Cleared of contact mines, the port was soon in use as a vital supply base, and was the terminus of a petrol pipe rapidly laid across the Channel from the Isle of Wight known as 'PLUTO' (Pipe Line Under The Ocean).

Jean Hamon (1618–87), the Jansenist doctor and preceptor of Racine, was born here, as was Georges Sorel (1847–1922), the exponent of revolutionary syndicalism.

To the N.W. of the *Avant-Port* stands La Trinité (1423–1504), a restored Flamboyant church disfigured by the addition (in 1825) of a heavy square tower. The S. porch retains some delicate tracery. Painted reliefs decorate the balustrade below the clerestory, and 15C niches adorn the four piers of the crossing, two of which bear fragments of a 14C English alabaster altarpiece.

On the W. side of the undistinguished *Pl. de la République* is the **Musée Thomas Henry**, where, until suitable premises are constructed, a small collection of paintings are displayed.

These include: *Van de Meulen*, Skirmishing; *Jan Massys*, Tipplers; *Adrien van de Kabel*, two Landscapes; *A. Hanneman*, Female portrait; *Frans II Franken*, Christ and the woman taken in adultery; *Master of the Legend of St Ursula*, Virgin enthroned; *Paul Bril*, Landscape; *Jan van Kessel*, miniature Still-lifes; *H.C. Vliet*, Interior of the Old Temple, Delft; *Teniers*, Monkeys at an inn; *Jordaens*, Adoration of the Magi (two versions); *Chardin*, Still-lifes; *anon.* Flemish triptych of the Deposition; *J.-F. Millet* (born at Gruchy, 15km N.W.; see below), Self-portrait, and other Portraits.

A short distance to the W. is the *Parc Emmanuel-Lias*, with hot-houses and a collection of exotic trees and shrubs, whence the Rue de l'Abbaye leads to the entrance of the *Arsenal* (closed to prying foreigners). The few 12-13C remains of the *Abbey de Voeu*, founded by the mother of Henry II, were destroyed in 1944.

The *Fort du Roule* (1854), surmounting the Montagne du Roule, strengthened during the Occupation, contains a *Museum* devoted to the Liberation of Cherbourg and the Cotentin.

There are several routes S. from Cherbourg, converging on *La Haye-du-Puits*, and the *Excursion to the Cap de la Hague*, with its impressive coastal scenery (described below) may be combined with that via *Carteret*, adding approx. 40km to the journey.

CHERBOURG TO THE CAP DE LA HAGUE. We turn off the D901 5km W. of Cherbourg onto the D45, traversing *Querqueville*, with a 10-11C chapel beside its church, to pass (l.) a 16C château at _Nacqueville_.—10.5km. _Gréville-Hague_, with a 12C Transitional church, lies just S. of the hamlet of _Gruchy_, birthplace of Jean-François Millet (1814–75); the neighbouring cliffs are curiously broken up by steep watercourses.—Some 4km beyond Gréville we cross _Mont Pali_ (109m) before following the road round the N. side of the _Cap de la Hague_, the N.W. extremity of the Cotentin peninsula, separated from _Alderney_ (in French known as _Aurigny_) by the dangerous strait of the _Raz Blanchard_, 16km wide: see _Blue Guide The Channel Islands_.—At _Auderville_ we turn S.E. to (5km) Jobourg, 2km to the W. of which is the precipitous cliff of the _Nez de Jobourg_ (128m high). The road skirts an _nuclear power-station_, the building of which has caused considerable opposition in the area, and the ancient line of fortifications known as the _Hague-Dicke_, which once walled off the promontory, before entering (5km) _Beaumont_, where the 15C church has a round tower.—Hence one may turn S.W. through _Vauville_, with its high dunes, and _Biville_, providing a good view of the _Channel Islands_, to regain the main road leading S. 3km E. of _Beaumont_. Hence the D904 may be joined 11km S. near _Benoîtville_; see below.

CHERBOURG TO LA HAYE-DU-PUITS VIA CARTERET (58km). The D900 is followed for 6km, before forking l. onto the D904 to traverse _Virandeville_, with a feudal tower, and (l.) the restored 16 _Château de Sotteville_ to reach (12km) _Benoîtville_, and, 3km beyond, the viewpoint of _Les Pieux_.—There is a small harbour at _Diélette_, 6km N.W., S. of which is _Flamanville_, with a château of 1660, in the grounds of which stands a pavilion erected as a retreat by the Marquis de Flamanville for Jean-Jacques Rousseau, who preferred the less inaccessible hermitage at Ermenonville (less than 50km N.E. of Paris).

From Les Pieux, the main road continues S., at 16km reaching the junction for _Carteret_, 1.5km W., on its rocky headland, with extensive dunes to the N. It is the nearest harbour to _Jersey_ (some 22km S.W.; launches to _Gorey_ in summer), and was liberated on 18 June 1944 by the Americans driving W. from 'Utah' Beach, cutting off the Germans further N. in the Cotentin.—Regaining the main road, _Barneville-Carteret_ is traversed, with a Romanesque church containing remarkable capitals, and (20km) _La Haye-du-Puits_.—At 6km a road leads r. to **Portbail**, a small harbour at the mouth of the Ollonde, where 11C _Notre-Dame_ has a 15C battlemented tower; the remains of a 3-4C _Baptistry_, and _St-Martin_, with a 12C doorway, are of interest. Cpt. C. Lindbergh landed on the S. side of the estuary after his first solo transatlantic flight in 1927.—A road is under construction from Portbail to _Lessay_ (see below), skirting the neighbouring beaches.

CHERBOURG TO ST-SAUVEUR-LE-VICOMTE VIA BRICQUEBEC (38km). The D900 climbs S. and then S.W. before forking r. past (7km) _Martinvast_, with a 12C church and a château rebuilt in the 19C. Attractive undulating country is traversed in (17km) **Bricquebec**, an ancient town retaining its 14C _Castle_ with a well-preserved ten-sided keep, and a fortified and turreted enceinte. It was taken from the Estouteville family after Agincourt and given to William de la Pole, Earl of Suffolk, who parted with it to ransom himself from the French in 1429. The 11C doorway of the old church survives.—2km N. is the Trappist monastery of _N.-D. de Grâce_ (1824.)—14km _St-Sauveur_; see below.

The N13 ascends S.E. to (20km) **Valognes**; see the latter part of Rte 30.—Here we turn S. through (6km) _Colomby_, with a curious rectangular church (early 13C) with a octagonal spire, to (9km) _St-Sauveur-le-Vicomte_, severely battered when the Americans crossed the Douvre here on 16 June 1944. Its damaged castle, with a 13C keep, was given by Edward III to Sir John Chandos, who built one of its gateways. The restored church, rebuilt in the 15-16C, contains a stone Ecce Homo (16C). Jules-Amédée Barbey d'Aurevilly (1808–89), the flamboyant reactionary novelist and critic, was born here.

The road shortly crosses the _Marais de la Sangsurière_, after 8km passing 1.5km W. of the Premonstratensian abbey of _Blanchelande_, founded in 1155, its extensive property still partially surrounded by walls.

3km. _La Haye-du-Puits_, much of it rebuilt since 1944, retains slight relics of its 11C castle keep, with 16C additions, progressively demolished in the 1820s and '30s to provide road-building material.

8km. **Lessay** lies on the edge of 'landes' or heaths, long the scene of an annual horse-fair. The *Church* is an admirable specimen of Romanesque architecture (11-12C, with later vaulting), well restored after war damage, in which its central tower was destroyed. Note the superimposed galleries surrounding the interior. The buildings of the former abbey are 18C.—The church at *St-Germain-sur-A*y, on the estuary 6km N.W., preserves a Romanesque font and capitals.

21km. **Coutances**; see Rte 32; also approached by a coast road.

Although the D7 leads S. across country to (47km) *Avranches*, our route follows the D971 S.W., at 4km passing (r.) *Orval*, where the church has a Romanesque church and crypt.

3km. *Montmartin-sur-Mer* lies 4.5km W., 3.5km N.W. of which, at *Regnéville*, is a ruined tower of a 13C castle, while 2km S.W. lies *Hauteville-sur-Mer*. Among the sons of Tancred, Lord of Hauteville, were Robert Guiscard (1015–85), conqueror of Southern Italy and Sicily, whose brothers Guillaume 'Bras-de-Fer' and Roger helped to establish Norman domination in Apulia and Sicily respectively.

9km. *Bréhal*, just E. of which is the Renaissance château of *Chanteloup*, attrib. to Hector Sohier.

10km. **GRANVILLE** (15,000 Granvillais), a small fishing-port overlooked by the Haute Ville on its rugged headland, and with a newer Basse Ville sprawling inland, has been somewhat misleadingly styled 'the Monaco of the North'!: Young considered it 'a close, nasty, ugly, ill-built hole'. The tide rises and falls here as much as 14m at some seasons.

The English fortified the promontory in 1439, but were driven out three years later, and its ramparts were dismantled in 1689 only to be rebuilt in 1715–50. The natural harbour was improved in the 16C, whence its privateers regularly harassed English shipping, and in 1695 an English fleet retaliated by bombarding the place. In 1793 Granville's resistance to the Vendean army, 20,000 strong, was such that La Rochejaquelein was obliged to raise the siege. The English again bombarded the town in 1803.

Heinrich Heine spent four successive summers here in the 1830s, but Murray found its attractions few, remarking that 'the stranger desirous to rescue himself from *ennui* must repair to the noble Pier, begun in 1828'. It was liberated on 30 July 1944, and in the Sept. Gen. Eisenhower briefly had his H.Q. here. The artist Maurice Denis (1870–1943) was born at Granville.

Motor-boats ply to the offshore *Îles Chausey* in summer, and to *Jersey*; for details enquire at the S.I.

To approach the *Haute Ville* from the central *Cours Jonville*, follow the Rue Paul-Poirier to the *Pl. Foch* (with the casino), to the N.E. of which is the beach. One may ascend steps behind the casino, or preferably follow the Rue des Juifs to the *Grande Porte* (17C, but altered), containing a small *Museum* of local antiquities and bygones.

The Haute Ville, preserving some 18C houses in its narrow streets, is entirely surrounded by ramparts. At its W. end is the granite church of *Notre-Dame* (15-17C). Passing out through the Grande-Porte and turning r., one may either walk down to the *Avant-Port* (and thence back to the Cours Jonville), or by keeping to the r., visit the *Lighthouse* at the *Pointe du Roc*, commanding a splendid view of the *Îles Chausey* (16km distant), *Cancale* on the Brittany coast, and the *Pointe de Champeaux*, which masks *Mont St-Michel*. Relics of German pill-boxes and gun-emplacements are still evident.

GRANVILLE TO AVRANCHES VIA THE COAST (33km). This slightly longer alternative to the main road skirts the rocky coast, traversing several small resorts, among them (3.5km) *St-Pair-sur-Mer*, with a fine sandy beach. The church, founded in 540 by St Padarn (Paternus) on the site of the tomb of St Gaud of Évreux, preserves a Romanesque bay beneath the tower, and has a 14C spire and choir.—The D911 continues through (8km) *Carolles*, with the 12C church-tower of the old village inland, and shortly provides a good distant view of *Mont St-Michel* (see Rte 36A) before descending to (4.5km) *St-Jean-le-Thomas*, a quaint hamlet where the sea retires for over 2km at low tide.—6.5km. *Genêts*, with a 12-14C church, overlooks an expanse of sand extending across the bay to *Mont St-Michel*. While these *may* be crossed on foot, a guide is essential, as there are dangerous areas of quicksand.—The road bears E., and N. of *St-Léonard*, with relics of a former priory, to (10.5km) **Avranches**; see below.

The D973 drives due S.E. from Granville, at 10km passing (3.5km E.) the Premonstratensian abbey of *La Lucerne*, preserving the ruins of its plain church (1164–1220; partly rebuilt), with a 14C square tower, and in the rebuilt cloister, a late 12C lavatory.

16km. We get a good view of its remaining ramparts on the N. side of **AVRANCHES** on approaching the town (10,400 inhab.), well sited on the slopes and summit of a hill (104m).

It was formerly the capital of the Gaulish *Abrincatui*, or *Abrincates*. Here in July 1639 broke out the ferocious revolt of the 'Nu-Pieds', peasants who in opposition to the '*gabelle*' or salt-tax, had armed themselves and established a camp beneath its walls, while their mysterious leader, Jean Nu-Pieds, proclaimed in every parish that the monopolists should be punished by death. The movement spread far and wide—as far as Caen and Rouen—but Marshal Gassion was despatched against them, and after a desperate resistance the Nu-Pieds were crushed. There was an English colony here for some decades from 1830, of which a neglected cemetery is a relic.

The VIII American Corps entered Avranches on 30 July 1944, and here Gen. Patton briefly set up his H.Q. before leading the 3rd American Army in an offensive sweep S. of the Mortain pocket; see p 222. Gén. Valhubert (1764–1805), who fell at Austerlitz, was born here.

The focal point of the town is the *Pl. Littré*, named in honour of the lexographer Émile Littré (1801–81), whose family were natives. To the N.E. of the *Hôtel de Ville* is the *Musée*, containing several MSS, incunables, and binding of interest, many of them from Mont St-Michel.—Further W. is the *Palais de Justice*, the former bishop's palace, rebuilt since a fire in 1899, but retaining its 14-15C chapel and part of its 12C walls.

Beyond is the so-called *Plate-forme*, the site of the cathedral, which was demolished and its stone sold in 1836, with the exception of a 15C column, after its partial collapse in 1796. A slab, surrounded by a chain, indicates the spot where in 1172 Henry II knelt before the papel legates to make atonement for precipitating the murder of Becket. The view hence is good but inferior to that commanded by the Jardin des Plantes; see below.

To the N.E. remains of the *Castle*, including the crenellated keep, while to the E. of the Place is *St-Gervais-St-Protais* (18C), preserving 12-13C reliquaries.

A few minutes' walk S. of the Place via the Rue du Docteur-Gilbert, passing rebuilt *St-Saturnin* (with a 15C bas-relief in the N. transept) and granite *N.-D. des-Champs* (19C), leads to the *Jardin des Plantes*. Its terrace (where an 11C portal is preserved) overlooking the estuary of the Sée, commands a superb *View over the bay of Mont St-Michel, with the abbey outlined on the horizon.

The *Pl. Patton*, to the S.E., is the site of that paranoic general's H.Q., with trees and earth imported from the U.S. surrounding a monument with a sententious inscription.

For the road S. from the important junction of (7km) *Pontaubault*, see Rte 35B, and for **Mont St-Michel**, Rte 36A.

32 Caen to Coutances, via Bayeux and St-Lô

90km (56 miles). N13. 28km **Bayeux**—D572. 32km **St-Lô**—D972. 27km **Coutances**.

Maps: IGN 6, or 102. M 231.

On the N.W outskirts of **Caen** (Rte 29) we pass (r.) the ruins of the *Abbaye d'Ardenne*, including the church with a 13C nave in pure Norman-Gothic style, and fragments of conventual buildings incorporated into farms.

9km. To the N. lies *Rots*, with an interesting but damaged Romanesque church; for *Rosel* (1.5km beyond), see Rte 30.

2.5km. *Norrey-en-Bessin*, 1.5km S., has a 13C church, restored since 1944, with a remarkable choir. The building, which closely resembles the Early English style, has a pentagonal apse, with a carved frieze above its blind arcade, flanked by two semicircular chapels with tall conical stone roofs, a curious design not uncommon in the district.

The next r.-hand turning off the N13 leads in 3km to *Secqueville*, its Romanesque church with an elegant 13C spire, which was a refuge of Robert FitzHamon, a partisan of Henry I, when pursued by Robert of Normandy.—For other churches and châteaux further to the N.W., see Rte 30.

5.5km. A short DETOUR may be made via *Audrieu*, 3.5km S., with a good 12C church, 4.5km beyond which is *Tilly-sur-Seulles*, with an 11C church, which survived the sanguinary battle in the vicinity in 1944; the adjacent British military cemetery is one of several in the area.—The detour may be slightly extended by driving N.W. on the D6, and shortly forking l. to take in the *Abbaye de Mondaye*, with a church of 1720 incorporating classical decoration by Eustache Restout, including a terracotta group of the Assumption; it also serves as a memorial chapel to British dead in the Battle of Normandy; see Rte 30. Hence the D6 may be regained, where we turn l. for Bayeux, (10km beyond the turning for Audrieu).

BAYEUX (15,200 inhab.), the former capital of the *Bessin*, standing on the river Aure some 10km from the coast, is a peaceful old episcopal town preserving a beautiful cathedral, but whose name is more often associated with the 'Bayeux Tapestry''.

Roman *Augustodorum* became the headquarters of the Gallic *Baiocasses*, where a bishopric was founded c. 360 by St Exuperantius (Exupère or Exupery). It was occupied by the Normans in the 10C, and Odo, half-brother of the Conqueror, later became its bishop, since when its history has been comparatively uneventful, although Henry I burnt the place in 1105, and it was ravaged by Huguenots in 1562. It was the first French town to be liberated in 1944, on the 7 June, by the 50th (Northumbrian) Division.

Among Bayeusains—*not* béotiens—are Alain Chartier (1385–1433), the poet; Jean de Brébeuf (1592–1649), missionary to the Hurons; Marguerite Weimer (1787–1867), better known as Mlle George, the actress; the antiquary Arcisse de Caumont (1802–73); and the artists Robert Lefèvre (1756–1830), and P.-F.

Delaunay (1759–89). Nicolas de Clèmanges, archdeacon of Bayeux c. 1420, was one of the first of the earliest French advocates of the Reformation.

The centrally sited **Cathedral** is perhaps the most perfect example of Norman Gothic existing. It is an imposing and somewhat austere edifice, an impression heightened by the sombre grey of the local stone used in its construction. The W. towers, piers and arches of the nave, and crypt, date from c. 1077, but the bulk of the building is 13C, with later additions.

The two Romanesque *Towers* at the W. end are surmounted by 13C spires. The central doorway, altered c. 1760, is flanked by two side portals. each with a tympanum, the sculptures in which are unfortunately much worn. The S. side of the nave (13C) has flying buttresses, pinnacles, balustrade, and chapels of the 14C; the tympanum of the S. transeptal porch (mid 13C) depicts the story of Becket, and the small two-arched portal (early 13C) has a 14C door. The *Apse* is notable for its beautiful blind arcading and the deep-set chapel windows.

The *Central Tower* was added in the 15C, but a neo-classical cupola of 1714 endangered its foundations. Southey, who visited the cathedral in 1838, had noted that 'workmen were going on with their repairs during the service and officiating priests taking snuff with the most complete unconcern'. Then, c. 1850 a proposal was mooted to pull down the whole tower and most of the transepts, but the under-pinning of the tower-piers, attempted at the protest of the locals, was successfully accomplished in 1857, after which the present upper storey, inadequate although safe, was added.

The interior is 102m long and 22m high. Steps descend from a side door at the W. end of the *Nave*, impressive with its irregularly spaced Romanesque piers, its diaper work above the sculptured spandrels, its elaborate arch-mouldings, and its delicate 13C trefoiled arcade surmounted by a clerestory of narrow lofty windows. The W. window, with 15C glass presented by the Guild of Cooks, is concealed by the organ, below which are seen carved and gilded 18C W. doors. Above the 5th arch on the N. side is a finely carved stone balcony. The pulpit (1787) is a striking example of the taste of the time.

The *S. transept* is decorated with 15C murals (with the exception of 19C daubs of the murder of Becket). The piers at the crossing are 13C. The raised *Choir*, of the same period, has clustered pillars and an elegant triforium. On the vaults are painted medallions of early bishops; the stalls (1588) and the bishop's throne of 1682, are noteworthy. The columns behind the Louis-XVI altar were fluted in the 18C. Between the choir and ambulatory is a wrought-iron grille of 1682 and 1772. Some of the choir chapels contain 15-16C paintings, and are connected by a gallery at window-level.

The *Crypt*, entered from the N. ambulatory, with squat pillars, curious capitals, and traces of 15C wall-paintings, is a survival of the 11C building.—The 13C *Chapter-house*, at the N.W. of the church, retains a few 13C frescoes and floortiles arranged as a maze; the *Treasury* is normally closed.

Opposite the S. door of the cathedral is the entrance to the 18C *Ancien Évêché*, the bishop's palace from 1802–1906. The *Ancien Seminaire* of 1693 in the Rue de Nesmond, a short distance to the E., has since 1983 housed, in specially constructed airtight showcases, the **Bayeux Tapestry**, depicting the Norman Conquest of England from the Norman point of view.

Also known as the 'Tapisserie de la Reine Mathilde', this strip of woollen embroidery on coarse linen is neither tapestry nor the work of Matilda, but more likely an Anglo-Saxon origin, and presented by the queen to Bp Odo c. 1080 if not commissioned by that bellicose prelate himself. This great historical 'document'—50cm wide and 68.5m long—was first recorded in an inventory of cathedral property in 1476, and used to be unwound by the yard, as from a haberdasher's roller, and subjected to the fingers as well as the eyes of the curious. In 1792 it was saved from being used as a waggon-cover by an observant officer, and Napoleon caused it to be exhibited in the main towns of France to drum up support for his projected invasion of England. During the Second World

A section of the 'Bayeux Tapestry'

War it was stored in the Château du Sourches, N.W. of Le Mans.

Earphones may be hired for those who require a blow by blow account, although each of its 58 scenes is captioned in dog-Latin. The events so dramatically portrayed range from the promise of Edward the Confessor to leave the throne to William, to the death of Harold of Hastings, but the embroidery is also of considerable value in its naive delineation of arms, costumes, ships, and fortifications of the period; the subsidiary marginal scenes also deserve attention.

The *Chapel* (c. 1250) has close affinities to the Early-English style.

Off the Rue des Chanoines, to the N.W., affording a good view of the cathedral towers, the Rue Bourbesneur leads to the umbrageous *Pl. Gén.-de-Gaulle*, passing (No. 10; l.) the late Gothic and Renaissance *Maison du Gouverneur*, in need of restoration.

To the N.E. of the cathedral is the attractive *Cour des Tribunaux*, with a huge plane tree planted in 1797, and flanked by 13-16C buildings of an earlier *Bishop's Palace*, now law courts, the chapel of which, of 1516, has a Renaissance painted ceiling.

On the N. side is the *Musée de Peinture*, a miscellaneous collection, among which is a curious painting by *Pourbus the Elder* of a Fancy-dress ball at the court of Charles IX, with named portraits of the artist, the king, Henri de Guise, Catherine de Medicis, etc. Other sections contain lace and porcelain.

From just E. of the cathedral, the Rue Larcher leads past the 18C *Hôtel de Ville* to the Rue St-Martin, the main thoroughfare, in which survive several old houses in various stages of decrepitude (see No. 60), including the half-timbered 15C building housing the S.I.; also Nos 5, 6, 13, 18, 39-41. Others may be seen in the Rue Franche and Rue Gén.-de-Dais (No. 41), both leading off the Rue St-Martin, while further N. off this street are the buildings of a former *Ursuline convent* (17-18C) and the *Manoir de la Caillerie* (1647).

The D516 leads N.E. to (10km) **Arromanches** (see Rte 30) passing—on the outskirts of Bayeux—near *St-Vigor-le-Grand*, with a 13C gateway and chapel of a priory founded by Odo; the church preserves an 11C marble bench upon which it was customary for bishops-elect of Bayeux to take their seat.

The narrow D104 leads N. to (7km) *Longues-sur-Mer* (see Rte 30), off which, after 3km, at the attractive hamlet of *Vaux-sur-Aure*, a lane leads N.W. to the fortified *Manoir d'Argouges*, 3km to the W. of which (beyond the direct road from Bayeux to Port-en-Bessin), at *Maisons*, is a 15-17C château.

BAYEUX TO ISIGNY (31km), for the Cotentin peninsula; see Rte 30. This continuation of the direct road from Caen to Cherbourg (N13) leads W. to (6km) **Tour-en-Bessin**, with a *Church preserving a splendid Romanesque W. door and nave, 13C steeple, and a three-apsed choir (14C) with stone sedilia of the English type, rare in France, while on the S. side of the chancel are 12C *Carvings* depicting the Labours of the Months.—9.5km. *Formigny*, with a Romanesque and 13C church, was the scene of the decisive French victory of 1450 (commemorated by a chapel of 1486), by which the English were driven out of Normandy, and practically ended the Hundred Years War. Sir Thomas Kyriel, the English commander, a veteran of Agincourt, took little account of the superior numbers of the French, and while engaged in attacking the army of the Comte de Clermont, was assaulted from the rear by the Constable de Richemont, with disastrous consequences.—'*Omaha*' *Beach* (see Rte 30) lies 4km N.—5km. *Longueville*, just N. of which is the former abbey-church of *Deux-Jumeaux*, with an 11C choir and tower, and later dependencies.—11.5km. *Isigny-sur-Mer*, for which, and the road beyond, see Rte 30.

From Bayeux the D572 is followed to the S.W., past (r.) a British military cemetery, and through *St-Loup-Hors*, its 12-14C church with a Romanesque tower, passing shortly beyond, to the l., *Guéron*, with a Romanesque church and 16C château and manor.

At 9km we by-pass (l.) *Noron-la-Poterie*, with manufactures of the traditional Norman salt-glazed earthenware.—The next r.-hand turning, at (1.5km) *La Tuilerie*, leads to (4km) *Campigny*, with a Renaissance château, now a farm, and a church containing 14-16C monuments.—*Castillon*, 2km S. at this turning, occupies a once-fortified site, 4km to the S.W. of which lies **Balleroy**, with a moated *Château* of 1626–36 built by Mansart, with ceilings by Mignard, in its attractive park.—One may regain the main road at *L'Embranchment*, the junction of seven roads on the edge of the *Forêt de Cérisy*, in which Gen. Montgomery briefly had his H.Q.

Another brief DETOUR may be made through the woods to (6km due W.) **Cérisy-la-Forêt**, famous for its abbey founded in 1030 by Robert I. The *Church*, N.E. of the village, is 11C with 13-15C alterations. The emplacement of the pillars of the original nave can be seen. It retains a good apse and choir, and 15C stalls, and is adjoined by some 13-15C monastic buildings.—Regaining the D572 5km S., we turn r. for St-Lô, passing to the r. on entry, the *Haras* or National Stud.

ST-LÔ (24,800 inhab.), préfecture of the *Manche*, is named after St Lô or Laudus, a 6C bishop of Coutances. It was the birthplace of Urbain Le Verrier (1881–77), the astronomer, and the novelist Octave Feuillet (1812–90).

The old town was situated on a fortified promontory overlooking the Vire, and its restored walls are best seen from the N., but this naturally strong position made it the target of incessant bombardment in early July 1944, which wrought havoc with the town, the ruins of which were entered by U.S. forces on 18 July.

Unfortunately, apart from the imposing *Ramparts*, which can now be viewed to advantage, the place retains little of interest except for heavily restored **Notre-Dame** (14-16C), with its blind arcading. The S.W. doorway, the grotesque carvings on the choir, and an exterior pulpit on the N. side, are noteworthy, while in the spacious interior the 16C choir retains some stained-glass presented to the town by Louis XI in reward for beating off an incursion of Bretons in 1467.

A short distance E., in the *Pl. de Hôtel-de-Ville*, the doorway of the prison is preserved as a memorial to members of the Resistance, who, incarcerated by the Germans, were left to their fate during the battle. The adjacent *Museum* accommodates works by *Corot* and *Boudin*, et al, and eight 16C tapestries of 'Les Amours de Gombaut et de Macé'.—Further E. is *Ste-Croix*, rebuilt in a Romanesque style in 1860, incorporating one original Romanesque doorway.—A Franco-

American *Memorial Hospital*, embellished with a mosaic by Fernand
Léger, stands to the S.W. of the town. Samuel Beckett acted as a
storekeeper and interpreter at the Irish Red Cross Hospital at St-Lô in
1946.

ST-LÔ TO (34km) VILLEDIEU-LES-POÊLES, FOR AVRANCHES. The D999 leads
S.W., after 22km skirting the W. slope of *Mt Robin* (276m) before reaching
(2.5km) *Percy*, a village which was the cradle of the earls and dukes of Northumberland.—6km to the E. lie the interesting ruins of the Benedictine abbey of
Hambye (founded c. 1145), including the church *Choir in the earliest Norman
Gothic style, with an ambulatory of c. 1400, and 13C chapter-house. Louis
d'Estouteville, the defender of Mont St-Michel, is buried here, with his wife
Jeanne Paynel or Paganel, whose arms appear on the entrance-porch.—Hence
one may turn S. to *Villedieu-les-Poêles*, 9.5km S.W. of Percy; see Rte 35B.

Continuing W. from St-Lô, on the D972, at 6.5km we pass 3.5km N.
of *Canisy*, with a château built by François Gabriel.—10.5km.
Savigny, 3.5km S.W., has 14C frescoes in its church.

10km. **COUTANCES** (13,400 inhab.), an ancient hill-top town, the
three towers of its fine cathedral conspicuous from afar, was bombed
in 1944 (when the cathedral miraculously escaped serious damage),
and the centre has been largely rebuilt.

Under the name *Constantia*, Gaulish *Cosedia* was fortified in 296 by Constantius
Chlorus, and became the centre of a diocese which included all the *Constantinus
Pagus*, later known as the *Cotentin*. This region was the cradle of numerous
Anglo-Norman families, among them the Beaumonts, Grevilles, Carterets,
Bruces, Nevilles, Bohuns, Percys, and Pierponts. Coutances itself has a long
history of sieges, and in 1639 was a centre of the 'Nu-Pieds' (cf. Avranches). The
trouvère André de Coutances was a native, and Saint-Évremond (1613–1703)
was born in the neighbourhood.

The Gothic **Cathedral** occupies the site of a church consecrated
c. 1056 by Bp Geoffroy de Montbray, and most of the present structure dates from the early 13C, except for the Lady Chapel and S.
nave chapels, which were added about a century later. Free from
over-exuberant ornament, it is remarkable for the elegance of its
proportions.

The W. facade is flanked by two *Towers rebuilt in the 13C, and crowned by
magnificent spires encircled by slender pinnacled spirelets. The huge central
Lantern-tower above the crossing is also seen to great advantage from the interior. Above the middle portal is a large Gothic window surmounted by a richly
decorated gallery. The tracery of the W. window and the elaborate S. doorway
(at the base of the S.W. tower) were damaged in 1944.—A good view of the apse
may be obtained from the gardens behind the cathedral.
    Interior. The church is 94m long and 23m high. The nave and choir are
separated from the aisles by clustered pillars, the vaulting shafts being carried
down to the base of the piers. The blind triforium is of original design. The
chapels in the aisles, all of which deserve examination, are remarkable for the
open screens of mullioned tracery that connect them. In the *Chapel of St Francis*
(last in the S. aisle) is a wooden carving of the Betrayal, and canopied screenwork
with mutilated figures (14C). The monumental organ-case, with caryatids, dates
from the 17C. There is (restored) 13-16C glass in the transepts, some of it in the
oldest style of black on a grey ground.
    The shafts and arcading in the choir aisles and the groining of the chapels
deserve perusal, for there is no church in France where this important detail in
Gothic work is more ingeniously treated.—In the apse are six coupled cylindrical
pillars placed with great art to support stilted arches; and in the westernmost ambulatory chapel is a 14C frescoe (restored). The *Lady Chapel* contains a 14C
Virgin, from *St-Nicolas*.

In front of the cathedral is the *Pl. du Parvis*, a few steps W. of which

The Lantern-tower of the cathedral at Coutances, from the crossing

are the *Gardens* of the *Hôtel Morinière*, charmingly laid out in the 17C taste. Within the gateway is a small *Musée* containing an antique bronze of the emperor Hadrian, etc.—Below the gardens, in the Faubourg des Pilliers, to the N.W., are remains of an *Aqueduct*, consisting of five Gothic arches (1322; rebuilt 1595).

From the Pl. du Parvis the Rue Tancrède leads N. to *St-Nicolas* (restored since 1944), mostly 16-17C, with an 18C lantern, and the plain Gothic tower of its predecessor.

The Rue Geoffroy de Montbray leads S. from the cathedral to *St-Pierre*, rebuilt c. 1500, with an early Renaissance central tower and octagonal late Gothic W. tower with a Renaissance lantern; the interior is notable for the balustrade that takes place of a triforium, and for the graceful and ornate Corinthian central lantern.—Some distance further S., in the valley of the Guerney, stands the *Hôtel-Dieu*, founded in 1209, preserving the elegant 15C steeple of the Augustinian church.

The D44 leads W. to (8km) *Tourville*, birthplace of Adm. de Tourville (1642–1701), passing at 2.5km *Gratot* (r.) with a 15-16C château and church. *Blainville-sur-Mer*, to the N.W., was the birthplace of Marcel Duchamp (1887–1968), a leader of the Dada movement.—*Coutainville*, a small resort amid dunes, to the W. of Tourville, provides a distant view of both the Îles Chausey and *Jersey*.

For the road S. from Coutances to *Granville*; see Rte 31.

33 Caen to Alençon, for Le Mans

101km (62 miles). N154. 34km **Falaise**—23km **Argentan**—23km **Sées**—21km **Alençon**.

Maps: IGN 18, or 102. M 231.

At first the road from **Caen** (Rte 29) traverses dull country, at 5km passing (r.) *Ifs*, whose church, with a stone pulpit of 1685, lost its 13C spire in 1944; one of several churches in the area which suffered damage at the time, among them that at *Cintheaux*, 10km beyond, which was desecrated by S.S. troops prior to their departure. Near by is a Canadian military cemetery; and 3km further S., a Polish cemetery.—Some 5km E., on the road to *St-Pierre-sur-Dives*, is a monument to the British Columbia Regiment, which, suffering high casualties, held 'Côte 140' on 10 Aug. 1944.—3.5km W. of the main road is the *Château d'Outrelaise* (c. 1600).

7km. *Potigny*, with a late 12C church, 1.5km to the E. of which is the *Brèche au Diable*, where the Laizon penetrates a wooded ravine, above which is the sententious monument of the Comédie Française actress Marie Jolie (d. 1798).

Beyond Potigny we pass *Soulangy*, and *Aubigny*, both with churches of interest, the latter containing kneeling statues of six 16-18C nobles, adjacent to which is a 17C château.

The road descends into the valley of the Ante, dominated to the S. by (9km) **FALAISE** (8800 Falaisiens), famous for its castle defending a rocky spur with precipitous cliffs (*falaises*); to the W. rises Mt *Myrrha*. Much of the town has been rebuilt since 1944. It had already suffered from bombardment that June, and was further damaged before its liberation by the Canadians on 17 August, the turning-point of the fighting in Normandy (see Rte 30), while the Germans made a final retaliatory air attack after their evacuation of the district.

The castle was a favourite residence of the first dukes of Normandy, who built it. Robert 'le Diable', stimulated by the sight of Arlette, the tanner's daughter, washing linen at a fountain below, took seignorial advantage. The resultant bastard was in his later years known as William 'the Conqueror' (1027–87) and it was from Falaise that he organised his expedition to England. By the Treaty of Falaise (1174) William the Lion acknowledged the suzerainty of the English crown over Scotland, a claim abandoned by Richard I in 1189 on being paid off. Henry V took Falaise in 1417, but the French recaptured it in 1450. In 1590 Henri IV gained it after a desperate defence by the Ligueurs. One of the severest battles of the Normandy campaign of 1944 was fought here in the area known as the Falaise 'Gap' or 'Pocket'.

It was the birthplace of the poet Vauquelin de la Fresnaye (1536–1606/8), and the dramatist Antoine de Montchrétien (c. 1575–1621).

Before entering, a pleasant walk (or drive) may be taken by following a lane to the W. below the *Town Walls* (restored) past the 13C *Porte des Cordeliers*, and an attractive manor, ascending by the '*Fontaine d'Arlette'* below the castle, and skirting its S. wall to reach the *Pl. Guillaume-le-Conquérant*. The costume of the statue of William (by Rochet; 1851) was copied from the Bayeux Tapestry.

This *Place* may also be conveniently approached by turning r. off the main road along the Rue St-Gervais, passing (r.) a lane leading to the *Porte Philippe Jean* (1740). *St-Gervais*, consecrated in 1123, with a 12C tower, was largely rebuilt in a florid Gothic style, with flying buttresses on the N. side and round the apse. The S. side of the nave is Romanesque; the N., 13C. The 16C choir, with a strong inclination to the r., was damaged in 1944.

The ungainly church of **La Trinité**, in the main square, preserves 13C transepts, but was rebuilt after the siege of 1417, and not finished until 1540. It has a remarkable Renaissance porch, while a triangular baptistry (originally a porch) projects from the W. end. The nave has a balustraded gallery and some interesting capitals on the S. side. The apse (damaged), with its Renaissance flying buttresses, is carried over the street.

Near its E. end is the former *Hôtel-Dieu* (c. 1200; rebuilt 1764), one restored wing of which is occupied by the *Tribunal*; the other, a ruined Gothic hall which served as the hospital chapel, was probably the *Salle des Malades*, a rare medieval relic.—The *Hôtel de Ville* of 1785 preserves six late Bronze Age helmets found in 1832 on the *Monts d'Eraines*, some 7km N.E.

Adjacent is the entrance to the *Castle, a magnificent ruin, preserving its 13C enceinte and main gateway flanked by towers. Although a shell penetrated the 4m-thick walls of the *Tour de Talbot* (when it was being used as an observation post by the Germans), little of the massive structure was destroyed in 1944. In the 12C Norman *Keep* (restored 1869), rising abruptly from the cliff edge, the cell is shown in which William 'the Bastard' was born, according to tradition. The walls are impressively solid, and the few Romanesque windows remaining retain their interesting capitals. It is surpassed in elevation by the *Tour de Talbot* (35m), dating from the reign of Philippe Auguste but at one time supposed to have been erected by 'Valiant Talbot' when Lord Warden of the Norman Marches (1427–50).

Some vestiges of fortifications may be seen to the N.E. of the town, including the fragmentary *Port Maudit*, and beyond St-Gervais, the ruins of *Porte St-Laurent*.

In the suburb of *Guibray*, to the E., preserving some old houses, an annual horse-fair had taken place for c. 900 years until abandoned in the 1920s; *Notre-Dame* has a Romanesque apse and W. door (restored).

5km to the W. lies *Noron-l'Abbaye*, where the 13C church retains its Romanesque belfry; while *Bazoches-au-Houlme*, 10km S. of Falaise, was the birthplace of Rémy de Gourmont (1858–1915), in the *Château de la Motte*.

The N158 continues S.E., traversing the *Bois de St André*, secreting the ruins of an old abbey, to (15km) *Brévaux*, just W. of which is the manor of *Commeaux* (c. 1520).—2km. *Occagnes*, preserving a good 12C church tower.

6km. **ARGENTAN** (18,000 inhab.), on the river Orne, has been virtually rebuilt since its destruction during the summer of 1944: it was at *Chambois*, only 12km N.E., that the 'pincers' of the Allied armies met on 19 August (see Rte 30).

It was at Argentan that Henry II rashly remarked that he would be well rid of that 'turbulent priest', which sent four officious knights to assassinate Becket at Canterbury (1170). Argentan long manufactured lace in friendly rivalry with Alençon—in particular the famous 'point d'Argentan'—the production of which revived after 18C pattern instructions were discovered in 1874. It was the birthplace of the artist Fernand Léger (1881–1955); see *Lisores*.

Forking half-l. on entering the town from the N., we pass (r.) *St-Martin* (1480–1550), with an octagonal tower, contemporary glass, and a notable triforium in the choir.—The adjacent *Hôtel de Raveton* was briefly occupied by Charles X on his way to exile in England, while James II took temporary refuge at No. 17 in the nearby Rue Pierre-Ozanne after witnessing the defeat of the French fleet at La Hogue in 1692; se Rte 30.

The 15C *Tour Marguerite*, a relic of ramparts, stands on the S. side of the Rue de la République. Further S.E. are the Rue des Vieilles-Halles and parallel Rue St-Germain, in which some old houses survive, including the 18C *Maison Dieu*.

*St-Germain, in the process of restoration, was begun in 1410 in the Flamboyant style (nave), but the apse, with its curious flying buttresses, was only completed in 1606 by Jacques Gabriel, and the N. tower (by Guillaume Grété and Thomas Oliver), with its cupola, not until 1641. The Renaissance lantern surmounting the central Gothic tower was shot away in 1944. The 15C porch contains 16C statues.

The light interior has good triforium balustrades, and the elaborate choir vault, the ironwork screen (1742), and the 17C stalls, are noteworthy, but the ugly modern altar and organ detract from the general effect. Note the donkey carved on a pier of the crossing. The Renaissance apse chapels have depressed arches and clumsy vaults. Of the paintings and sculptures that decorated the church, a 15-16C stone Pietà survives.

To the S. is the *Pl. du Marché*, with the 14C *Chapelle St-Nicolas* and contemporary turreted *Château*, both restored, and remains of the 12C keep.

For the cross road hither from Dreux, and hence to *Dinan*, see Rte 36A.

The N158 bears S.E., at 15.5km passing just S. of the picturesque *Château d'O*, with an E. wing of brick and stone, Gothic in form but Renaissance in detail, of c. 1500, a 16C S. wing, and W. wing of 1770.

Médavy, 4km N., has an 18C château with two cylindrical gate towers; *Almenêches*, 3km beyond, formerly possessed a Benedictine abbey founded in the 7C, and retains the handsome Renaissance *Abbey Church*, with bas-reliefs of 1679.
  To the S. of the main road, a lane leads to the late 16C *Manoir de Clérai*, moated and turreted.

7.5km. **Sées**; see Rte 28B, and likewise for the road S. to (21km) **Alençon**.—**Le Mans** lies 49km further S.

34   Caen to Angers

211km (131 miles). D562. 57km **Flers**—21km *Domfront*—35km **Mayenne**—N162. 25km **Laval**—30km *Château-Gontier*—43km **Angers**.

Maps: IGN 18, 17, 25, or 102, 106. M 231, 232.

The road from **Caen** (Rte 29) follows the winding valley of the Orne to (8.5km) *St-André-sur-Orne* (r.), 4.5km W. of which lies *Vieux*, the ancient capital of the Viducasses, where Gallo-Roman remains have been discovered, including the Thorigny marbles, now at the University of Caen.

17.5km. *Thury-Harcourt*, rebuilt since 1944, was once the seat of a Norman barony, raised to a duchy by Louis XIV. The 17C château, together with its archives belonging to the Duc d'Harcourt, was deliberately burnt by the Germans on their retreat. The church preserves an imposing 13C facade.—Some 12km W. rises *Mont Pinçon* (365m), the capture of which by the 43rd Division on 6 Aug. 1944 was one of the decisive actions in the break-out from Normandy; on its S. slope is the former priory of *Le Plessis-Grimoult*, with an early Gothic W. tower.

We now enter an attractive craggy and wooded district somewhat fancifully called the 'Norman Switzerland', in which (10km) *Clécy* is a good centre for excursions, just N.E. of which is the 16C *Manoir de Placy*, while some 7km to the E. is the *Château de la Pommeraye.*—Further to the S.E. are the *Gorges de St-Aubert*, traversed by the upper Orne.

9km. *Condé-sur-Noireau*, a small textile town rebuilt in a traditional style since its virtual destruction in 1944, with restored *St-Martin*, preserving its 12th and 15C choir. It was the birthplace of the Antarctic navigator Dumont-d'Urville (1790–1842).—Some 7.5km N.W. is the lakeside *Château de Pontécoulant* (16-18C).

12km. **Flers** (19,400 inhab.), is another flourishing textile town, likewise much rebuilt, its main attraction being the moated *Château* (16-17C), with two corner towers, and its park and lake. It was a Royalist headquarters during the Chouan rebellion, and now contains a small museum.

7km to the N.E. rises isolated *Mt Cerisi* (264m), with ruins of a castle; further S. in the valley are relics of the abbey of *Belle-Étoile*, founded in 1215.—15km due W. of Flers, beyond *Mt Crépin* (305m), lies *Tinchebray*, a small town which was the birthplace of that pioneer of Surrealism, André Breton (1896–1967). Here, in 1106, Robert of Normandy, son of the Conqueror, was defeated by his younger brother, Henry I, passing the rest of his life (d. 1134) in custody in England. The chapel of *St-Rémy* has a 12C choir, fortified transepts, and Romanesque tower.

21km. **Domfront**, situated on a height above the Varenne, was once one of the strongest fortresses in Normandy.

In 1574 the Comte de Matignon took it from the Protestants, and their leader, Gabriel, Comte de Montgomery (1530–74) was sent to the scaffold at Paris. It was he, formerly a captain of the Scottish guard, who had mortally wounded Henri II in a tournament in 1559. The older town, still with its ancient ramparts, was comparatively undamaged in 1944, and retains some pleasant lanes.

The ruined *Castle*, on the edge of a 60m-high precipice, was built c. 1011 by Guillaume de Bellesme, and was taken by William the Conqueror. Here Henry II received the papal nuncios sent to reconcile him with Becket. The 13C casements are shown on request, and the gardens command a good view. To the N.W. is restored *N.-D. sur l'Eau*, a Romanesque edifice of c. 1100, with a good tower and apse, containing numerous tombs.

There are several 14-18C manor-houses in the neighbourhood, while at *Lonlay-l'Abbaye*, 9km N.W., the restored 13-14C church of a Benedictine abbey founded c. 1020, retains transepts of c. 1100, a 15C porch, and 16C stalls and sculptures; the nave was never built.

For *Bagnoles-de-l'Orne*, 22km E., and *Mortain*, 25km W., see Rte 36A.

We continue S., at 23km traversing *Ambrières*, and 12km beyond, enter **Mayenne** (14,300 inhab.), a quiet little textile town straddling the steep banks of a river of the same name. To the N. of the central bridge is *Notre-Dame*, founded in 1100, but badly damaged in 1944, with its choir rebuilt in a Gothic style in the 19C; there is a crypt beneath the apse. The adjoining main street leads uphill to the *Hôtel de Ville* of 1660.—To the S. of the church is the much rebuilt *Castle*, retaining some towers and a 13C chapel. It was captured by William the Conqueror in 1068, and in 1425 endured a three months siege by the English under the Earl of Salisbury. On the l. bank of the river is Romanesque *St-Martin*, with an over-restored interior.

Of interest in the vicinity are the remains of the Cistercian abbey of *Fontaine-Daniel* (founded 1204), some 6km S.W.
    For the cross-road from Alençon to *Fougères*, see Rte 36B.

We follow the N162 S., at 13.5km passing some 4km N.E. of *Châlons-du-Maine*, birthplace of Jules Renard (1864–1909), author of 'Poil de Carotte'.

After 11km we cross the motorway and 5.5km beyond, enter **Laval**; see Rte 38.

LAVAL TO CHÂTEAUBRIANT (67km). The N171 drives S.W. to (30km) *Craon*, with a large *Château* (1774–77; by Pommeyrol).—9.5km to the S.E. is the partly ruined *Château de Mortiercrolle*, built by Pierre de Rohan before 1500, a moated quadrilateral with a fine gatehouse.—Continuing S.W. from Craon, we traverse *Renazé*, with slate quarries, to reach (21km) *Pouancé*, pleasantly sited on a lake formed by the Verzée, with ruins of a 13-15C castle, and a 15C gateway.—5km S. in the woods are relics of the 13C priory of *Primaudière*.—**Châteaubriant** lies 16km W, of Pouancé; see Rte 39.

The N162 drives S., skirting the E. bank of the Mayenne, at 9km passing just E. of the Trappist abbey of *Port-du-Salut*, where the strong 'Port-Salut' cheese is manufactured, after 20km entering **Château-Gontier** (8400 Castrogontériens), a town founded in 1007 by Fulk Nerra.

In the more modern quarters on the E. bank of the river is *La Trinité* (17C), by Pierre Corbineau. The chapel of the Collège, *N.-D. du-Genneteil*, opposite, is a restored Romanesque church. The large *Hôtel-Dieu St-Julien*, by the bridge, founded in 1206, was rebuilt in 1879.

On the r. bank, the Grande Rue, with several old houses, ascends past (l.) the local *Musée*, and (r.) near *St-Jean*, an early 11C building restored since damaged by enemy action in 1940, with heavy square piers and a crypt of three naves. Some late 11C frescoes have been uncovered.—The adjoining gardens and riverside quays are notable for their splendid trees.

7km S.W., at *Chemazé*, is the *Château de St-Ouen*, built for Guy Le Clerc, confessor of Anne of Brittany, in 1505–15; the imposing square tower is ascended by a lavishly ornamented spiral staircase, and many rooms retain magnificent chimney-pieces.

Several châteaux are passed by the main road, mostly to the E., near the Mayenne river, among them, at 8km, *de Magnannes* (late 17C), and 5km beyond, *du Percher*.—3km. The *Château du Bois-Maubourcher*, with its lake, lies to the l., 6km beyond which we reach *Le Lion-d'Angers*, with the 18C *Château de l'Isle-Braint*, and a church with a Romanesque tower.

8km. The restored 15C **Château of Le Plessis-Macé**, with 11C

walls, and moat, and with a 16C chapel added by the Du Bellay family, is 1.5km to the S.W.

The main road veers S.E., and 14km beyond this turning, after
crossing the A11 motorway, enters **Angers**; see Rte 59A.

35   Caen to Rennes

A.   Via Vire and Fougères

174km (108 miles). N175. 25km *Villers-Bocage*—5km, where we
follow the D577 to 29km **Vire**—25km **Mortain**—D977. 14km *St-
Hilaire-du-Harcouët*—28km (partly on the D177) **Fougères**—N12.
48km **Rennes**.

Maps: IGN 6, 16, 17, or 102. M 231, 230.

Immediately beyond the S.W. suburbs of **Caen** (Rte 29) *Bretteville-
sur-Odon* is traversed, near which are the quarries of Caen stone.
The area to the S. of the main road was the scene of savage fighting
in June-July 1944, culminating in the recapture of 'Côte 112' by the
43rd (Wessex) Div., with a monument; see p 202.

25km. *Villers-Bocage*, entirely rebuilt, shortly beyond which we
veer S. through broken country, skirting *Mont Bremoy* (r.; 361m), into the valley of the Souleuvre, and after 34km enter the dairying and
textile centre of **Vire** (14,500 Virois). This old capital of the *Bocage*,
situated on a hill, to the S.W. of which the river Vire sweeps beneath
wooded cliffs, was devastated by Allied bombing in 1944, but the
15C *Tour de l'Horloge* survived, supported by a 13C Gothic gateway
with two flanking towers, once the main entrance to the old centre.
It is well-known for its andouillettes and pastry. The *Tour St-Sauveur*,
relic of another gate, is preserved in the Rue Chausée, together with
another old tower to the S. *Notre-Dame*, at the W. end of the street, is
an undistinguished 13-16C building, which was severely damaged.
There is a good view of *Vaux-de-Vire* from the neighbouring terrace,
while at the end of the spur to the S., inaccessible on three sides, and
originally separated from the town by a deep ditch, stands the ruined
Castle, built by Henry I, and dismantled by Richelieu. Another view-
point is the *Rocher des Rames*, to the W., approached by the Rue des
Cordeliers, N.W. of the church.

The valley of the Vire, now somewhat industrialised, is known as 'Les Vaux de
Vire', which gave its name to the lively songs (mainly in praise of cider, and of
his native province) of Olivier Basselin, who had a fulling-mill here in the 15C.
These songs, edited and added to by Jean Le Houx in the late 16C, eventually
gave rise to the term 'vaudeville'.

At *St-Sever-Calvados*, 13.5km W. on the road to Villedieu-les-Poêles (see Rte
35B) is the interesting abbey *Church* (13-14C), with a detached 17C tower, of a
monastery founded in the mid 6C. To the S. extends the *Forêt de St-Sever*.

Beyond Vire, the road undulates over the hills to (13km) *Sourdeval*, a
village burnt by the Germans, to the W. of which the valley of the
Sée offers some attractive scenery, to (12km) **Mortain**, likewise
severely damaged during the German attack of 6 August 1944; see
p 230. Sited on a hill above the gorge of the Cance, with views of
wooded crags across the valley, Mortain was once the seat of a
powerful feudal family descended from Robert de Couteville, half-

brother of the Conqueror. The Abbé Breuil (1877–1961), the archaeologist, was born here.

To the N. of the town, to the E. of the road from Vire, is the former *Abbaye Blanche*, founded in 1115 for Benedictine nuns, but a Cistercian house since 1147. Most of the buildings date from the 19C, but the 13C chapter-house, the late 12C chapel, and part of the Romanesque cloisters may be visited.—Near by is the *Grande Cascade*, an unusually large waterfall for Normandy; while an attractive walk may be taken via the little Romanesque church of *Le Neufbourg* and the *Petite-Cascade* on the Cançon, just before this tributary stream joins the Cance.

The granite church of *St-Evroult* (13C), betraying a Breton influence in its severity, survived unscathed. A doorway on its S. side, with sawtooth moulding, appears to date from a previous building (1082); a 14C tower, pierced by lancets, stands at the S.E. corner. The symmetrical arcading of the nave is continued in the choir, in which are stalls with 15C misericords.

A good view may be had from a rocky height (314m) some distance S.E. of St-Evroult, on which stands the *Chapelle St-Michel*.
For the road hence to (25km) *Domfront*, see Rte 36A.

We turn S.W. into the Sélune valley to (14km) *St-Hilaire-du-Harcouët*, rebuilt since 1944. For the road hence to *Pontaubault*, 20km W., see Rte 36A.

The D977 leads due S., at 6km passing 3km W. of the ruined abbey of *Savigny-le-Vieux*, in its sequestered site, where the monastic order of Savigny, merged with the Cistercians in 1147, was founded by Vitalis de Savigny in 1114. Furness Abbey was their principal house in England.

6km. *Louvigné-du-Désert*, 1.5km S.W. of which, in the chapel of the early 17C château of *Monthorin*, are the tombs of Raoul II de Fougères (d. 1194), Françoise de Foix (cf. Châteaubriant) and the hearts of Gén. de Lariboisière (d. 1812) and his son.—6km S.E., at *Mausson*, is an interesting castle, modernised in the 16C.

8km S. of Louvigné we enter the *Forêt de Fougères*, containing several megalithic monuments, and once populated by *sabotiers* living in curious little huts, where they carved the beech-woods into sabots.

8km. **FOUGÈRES** (25,100 Fougerais), an ancient town on the borders of Brittany, largely engaged in the manufacture of shoes, preserves its older town on an escarpment overlooking the Nançon, below which (unusually) stands its imposing feudal castle; parts of the walls joining the two still exist.

The frontier fortress was one of the nine great Breton baronies. Henry II razed the castle in 1166, and the town fell to the English on several other occasions, notably in 1449, when they were commanded by the Spanish adventurer Surienne. In 1428 the barony was purchased by Jean V, Duke of Brittany, and it remained incorporated in the duchy until the marriage of Claude de France with François I.
Mercoeur occupied the town for the League in 1589–98. Most of its timber houses were destroyed by fires in the 18C. In 1792 the anti-Revolutionary conspiracy of La Rouërie ended with the execution of 13 citizens, although in the following year the army of the Vendée temporarily captured the place. Damage was caused to the modern town in two air attacks in June 1944.
Juliette Drouet (1806–83) was born here and often visited by Victor Hugo; Chateaubriand and De Musset were also frequent visitors, and Balzac describes the town in 'Les Chouans'.

An interesting approach to the castle is that descending from the old town, more specifically from the umbrageous *Pl. aux Arbres* adjacent to late Gothic *St-Léonard* (15-16C), with a modern facade flanked by a tower completed in 1637; the baptistry is 12C.—A 14-15C *Belfry* stands some distance to the N., beyond which is the *Tribunal* (1741); parts of the *Hôtel de Ville*, to the S., date from the 14-16C.

From the Pl. aux Arbres, with its extensive *Views*, the *Escalier de la Duchesse-Anne* descends steeply to the Nançon and the lower town, in which several 16C houses survive, particularly in the *Pl. du Marchix* and Rue de Lusignan. The latter leads to **St-Sulpice**, begun 1410, although the nave was not completed until the 16C, and the choir dates from 1734 – 63. The interior, with two 15C altarpieces sculptured in the granite walls, preserves the 11C(?) statue of N.-D.-des-Marais, retrieved from the marshes in the 14C. Among the grotesque carvings on the exterior of the S. doorway, note that of the fairy Melusine, emblem of the Lusignan family, and its mythical foundress.

To the N. it is dominated by the massive curtain wall of the *Castle, surmounted by a rampart walk; the whole has been freely restored. To the N.E. is the 14-15C *Porte Notre-Dame*, flanked by two machicolated towers, and forming the most important relic of the town walls, to the W. of which is a rampart pierced by a water-gate through which the Nançon rushes, forming a moat on the S. side of the castle only, although a loop of its former course once entirely surrounded the fortifications.

Making the circuit of the exterior in a clockwise direction, we pass in succession the square 13C *Tour du Cadran*; the semicircular *Tours Raoul* and *Surienne* (both late 15C); the four-storeyed **Tour Melusine**, built by Hugues de Lusignan in 1242; the *Tour Gobelin* (12-14C), outside which is the disused postern-gate; and the small *Tour Guibé* (late 13C), joined by a rampart to the strong *Tour de Coigny*.—The interior may be visited (guided), passing first through the *Tour de la Haye-St-Hilaire*, which like the *Tours de Guémadeuc* (r.) and *du Hallay*, date from the 12C. The ruined archway gives access to the great court, now tree-shaded.

Hence one may ascend the Rue de la Pinterie, largely rebuilt since 1944, which climbs parallel to the old ramparts, of which the 15C *Tour Nichot* survives.

For the road hence to *Dol-de-Bretagne*, see Rte 36B; for *Vitré*, 29km S., Rte 38.

Continuing S.W., the N12 leads past (20km) *St-Aubin-du-Cormier*, where in 1488 François II, the last duke of Brittany, was defeated by La Trémoïlle in a battle which dealt with the death-blow to Breton independence. The 13C castle was immediately dismantled by Charles VIII, who married the duke's daughter, Anne.

The road shortly traverses the *Forêt de Rennes*, at 27km entering the Breton capital itself, for which see Rte 39.

B. Via Avranches and Mont St-Michel

190km (118 miles). N175. 79km *Villedieu-les-Poêles*—22km **Avranches**—7km *Pontaubault*, just beyond which one turns r. to (15km) **Le Mont St-Michel**—D976. 9km *Pontorson* (itself 15km S.W. of Pontaubault)—N175km. 58km **Rennes**.

Maps: IGN 6, 16, or 102. M 231, 230.

For the first 30km, see Rte 35A.

18km beyond this junction, where we fork r., a r.-hand turning leads 8km N.W. to *Torigni-sur-Vire*, with the shell of a château built in the 16C by the Maréchal de Matignon and held until the Revolution by his family, who became princes of Monaco.

11km. The main road now by-passes *Pont-Farcy*, crosses the Vire and, climbing out of the valley, 19km beyond enters **Villedieu-les-Poêles** in the valley of the Sienne, owing its surname to the manufacture of hammered copper utensils—'*dinanderie et quincailleries*'—which has been its main occupation for several centuries. It retains numerous old houses and courtyards, while a bellfoundry may be visited in the Rue du Pont-Chignon.

An attractive winding road (D999) leads S.E. hence to (35km) *St-Hilaire-du-Harcouët*, and beyond to *Fougères*; see Rte 35A.

The N175 continues S.W. to (22km) **Avranches** (see Rte 31), and 7km beyond, *Pontaubault* on the river Sélune, which Southey considered was not a place 'where any who had ever passed through it would halt by choice'.

The D998 leads hence to (33km) Fougères via (12km) *St-James*, on a spur above the Beuvron, once commanded by a castle erected by William the Conqueror, where the 15C church incorporates a doorway from its Romanesque predecessor, while the 13C entrance to the cemetery is from a demolished church. An American military cemetery lies 1.5km E.
  A direct road (D140) leads S. from Pontaubault to regain the N175 after 22km, 1km S. of *Antrain*; *Pontorson* is 15km S.W.: for both, see below. A new road is under construction, which will by-pass Pontorson and Dol, to cross the Rance estuary N. of Dinan.

We shortly turn r. onto the D43 to skirt the estuary of the Sélune, with a view towards *Mont St-Michel*, to approach which one turns r. after 13km to follow the long causeway, built in 1879, joining the mount to the mainland, at the far end of which are obligatory car-parks (fee).

**LE MONT ST-MICHEL is one of the great natural curiosities in France, and as such, is rarely free from swarms of trippers, particularly in summer. Once resigned to this phenomenon, most visitors will find the imposing site and the exploration of the great Abbey itself merits the detour.

The isolated granite cone, almost 80m high, rises abruptly from the sands, against the base of which are plastered the village houses, above which a series of immense buttresses flank the ancient abbey perched on the summit. Its historical associations are hardly inferior in interest to its physical appearance, by day or night, particularly at high tide when the moonlight is reflected in the surrounding waves. Unfortunately its insularity is constantly threatened by the retirement of the sea from the bay, and the encroachment of the '*herbu*'.

The *Bay of Mont St-Michel* measures some 21km in width between Cancale in Brittany and Granville in Normandy, and consists of a vast sandy tract ('La Grève'), which the rising tide covers with great rapidity. **N.B.** Although *long excursions* may be made over the sands at low tide, it is *essential* to go accompanied by a guide, not only because of such tidal dangers, but also on account of the not infrequent areas of quicksand. One of the scenes in the 'Bayeux Tapestry' depicts Harold rescuing some Norman soldiers from such quicksands at the mouth of the Couësnon when on their march against Duc Conan of Brittany. A tour *round the base of the Mont* by the sands can be made on foot at low tide in approx. 30 minutes, but some wading through shallows may be necessary. At

Mont-St-Michel, by David Roberts

high tide one may make the more attractive circuit by water. For further information with regard to guides, and for the hire of boats, apply at the S.I. near the entrance to the Mont.

On its W. flank one will pass the *Tour Gabriel* (1534); on the N.W., the *Chapelle St-Aubert* (13-14C); and on the N. side is the *Fontaine St-Aubert*, said to have been discovered in the 8C and used for the water supply of the monastery during the following seven centuries.

To the N. of the Mont is the quaintly shaped islet of *Tombelaine*, where a chapel and cell of the abbey were established in 1137. The English several times seized this vantage point, but were finally expelled in 1450 by the Constable de Richemont. In the 17C Fouquet acquired the islet and converted the priory into a château, but after his disgrace in 1666 it was demolished, and only ruins remain.

Mont St-Michel was originally called 'Mont-Tombe', and like Tombelaine (see above) was doubtless one of the sea-tombs whither, according to Celtic mythology, the souls of the dead were ferried in an invisible barque. In 708 an apparition of St Michael the archangel to St Aubert, Bp of Avranches, command-ed the building of an oratory on the summit of this rock, which gave place to a Carolingian church in the 10C, and a Romanesque basilica in the 11-12Cs. In 966 Richard I of Normandy installed Benedictines here, who provided several vessels for the Conqueror's fleet a century later. In 1047 a chapel on St Michael's Mount in Cornwall was placed under their control by Edward the Confessor. By the 12C, under its abbot Robert de Torigni, it became a celebrated seat of monkish learning. In 1166 Henry II held court here and received the homage of the turbulent Bretons he had subdued. In 1203 the French king sent an expedi-tion against the Mont, when some of its dependencies were burnt, for which depredation Philippe Auguste later compensated the monks royally, and with the proceeds the 'Merveille' was built; while Louis IX, who visited the abbey in 1254, contributed to the cost of its defensive works; indeed it increasingly took on the character of an ecclesiastical fortress, with a garrison maintained at the joint charge of both king and abbot. It was the only stronghold which held out when the rest of Normandy was overrun by Henry V's armies, and withstood two sieges under Louis d'Estouteville (in 1417 and 1423), and a third English assault was beaten off in 1434. In 1469 Louis XI added to the prosperity of the monastery by instituting the royal order of St Michel. Noël Beda, head of the Collège de Montaigu in Paris from 1499, was banished here by François I for his officiousness, where he died in 1536. In 1591 it successfully resisted Mont-gomery and his Calvinist troops.

In 1622 the vitiated confraternity were replaced by the reformed (but Philistine) congregation of St Maur, who divided the refectory into two storeys of dormitory cells. From 1790 to 1863 it was a State prison, and only after 1874, when it passed into the hands of the Commission des Monuments Historiques, did its restoration commence.

'Mont-Saint-Michel and Chartres', by Henry Adams, is still of interest.

At the far end of the causeway a wooden footbridge leads to the *Porte de l'Avancée*, the only opening in the ramparts, within which (l.) is the *Corps de Garde* (1531), housing the S.I. A second gatehouse is flanked by two bombards abandoned by the English in 1434, while an inner gate, the picturesque *Porte du Roi* (15C) is surmounted by a house used as the Mairie, and preserves its portcullis, battlements, and carvings of shells and salmon that figure respectively as abbey and town emblems.

The Grande Rue, the only street, is overhung by gabled houses almost entirely occupied by souvenir shops and/or restaurants, among which the *Mère Poulard* had a time-honoured reputation for its omelettes and pré-salé mutton. Some distance uphill (l.) is the *Parish Church*, founded in the 11C, just beyond which is a restored house said to have been built by Du Guesclin in 1366 for his wife Tiphane Raguenol. A Romanesque portal in a garden wall, further on, is a relic of the earliest fortress.

The street now becomes stepped on approaching the **Abbey*, ◇ with its enceinte of crenellated walls, the steep final flight of which is known as the *Grand-Degré*, which ascends to the only entrance, a fortified gateway beneath the late 14C *Châtelet*.

Any attempt by the guide to hurry one through the abbey should be resisted, and it should be noted that the itinerary described below is not necessarily followed in that order, nor are all parts of the building shown to visitors, such as the 11C Dormitory, the 11-12C Promenoir des Moines, and the oubliettes.

The *Escalier du Gouffre* ascends to the *Salle des Gardes*, with the ticket kiosk, beyond which is the *Aumônerie* (where, if not in the Salle des Gardes, visitors await the next conducted tour, which set off every 15 minutes in the season), a Gothic vaulted hall with a cen-tral row of pillars, which served as a victualling hall as well as almonry, and contains the lower opening of a shaft by which provisions were hauled up to the refectory.

The tour is commenced by climbing the 90 steps of the *Grand-Degré Intérieur* to the terrace of the church, skirting (r.) the exterior of the Choir, and l., the restored *Abbot's Lodge*, connected by bridges. Further on (r.) is the rebuilt *Cistern*, and at the top of the steps the terrace known as the 'Saut-Gautier', after an unfortunate prisoner who went mad and leapt from it! Passing a 13C side portal of the church, the main *Terrace* is reached, on the wind-blown side of the destroyed bays of the nave. The *Views *away* from the facade, added after 1780, are superb, and the river Couësnon is seen far below meandering through the sands and 'herbu'.

The *Church consists of two parts: the Norman Romanesque nave and transepts in the massive style of 1020–1135 (restored since it was divided horizontally by floors like the refectory), in which the r.-hand aisle retains its Romanesque barrel-vaulting; the l.-hand aisle its ogival vaulting; and the Flamboyant *Choir*, replacing its Romanesque predecessor, which had collapsed in 1421. The latter dates from 1456–1521, and is surrounded by an ambulatory and radiating chapels containing 16C sculptures, and is supported by enormous flying buttresses adorned by a profusion of pinnacles. The mouldings of the arches are carried down the piers, uninterrupted by capitals. The lofty clerestory is pierced by large windows, and the triforium is glazed.

From the second chapel to the r. a stair ascends to an outer platform, from which the remarkable *Escalier de Dentelle* leads to an upper balustrade, but this is not normally shown. The church is surmounted by a spire of 1895, rising 152m above sea level, topped by a gilded St Michael and the Dragon, by Frémiet.

The *Cloister is next entered, forming the W. half of the upper storey of the 'Merveille', as the monastery proper is frequently called, its immense three-storeyed N. facade dating from 1203–28.

The cloisters are supported by a double row of pointed arches resting on slender granite pillars, leaving a narrow groined vault between the rows, the pillars of the outer arches placed opposite the point of the inner. Their capitals are of a plain bell form with a circular abacus, common in English work, but rare in France, and the spandrels are filled with a variety of carved foliage and flowers. On the S. side is the *Lavatory*, while the large arches to the W. were to have been the entrance to a chapter-house, which was never built.

To the E. is the *Refectory (1225), a large hall lighted by tall narrow windows, and with a restored wooden roof; the floor awaits restoration. On the wall to the r. is the stone Lector's Seat. Dishes were raised from the kitchens through a circular aperture.

Returning through the cloister, we descend through a series of passages to the *Chapelle de St-Étienne* (12C, with 13C vaulting), off which a huge wooden wheel used for hoisting victuals is shown. Another corridor leads to the *Crypte des Gros-Piliers* (15C), suitably named after its massive cylindrical columns, which support the choir; in its corner are the capacious cisterns. Other 11-12C crypts preserve parts of the 10C Carolingian church.

The *Salle des Chevaliers* (below the cloister), an imposing hall of four finely vaulted aisles of 1215–20, was originally the scriptorium, but after 1469 used for the early chapters of the Order of St. Michael.

Beneath the refectory is the *Salle des Hôtes* (1213), the main guest-chamber, with two huge fire-places, and a central row of columns. On a lower level is the *Cellier* (below the Salle des Chevaliers), and beneath the Salle des Hôtes, the *Aumônerie*, whence the Salles des Gardes is regained.

To the r. of the exit, a lane passes a small *Museum*, and the arcaded *Maison de la Truie qui File*, to regain the Grande Rue; alternatively one may descend directly to the causeway by a flight of steps; or continue W., climbing down to the *Terrasse de la Gire*.

A third descent may be made from the Grand-Degré, passing (l.) the entrance to the abbey gardens (fee), before turning l. and down to the 14C *Tour du Nord*, thence passing in turn the *Tour Boucle* (mid 15C), *Tour Cholet*, *Tour Basse*, *Tour de la Liberté*, and *Tour de l'Arcade*.

Driving S. from Mont St-Michel, at 9km *Pontorson*, an important road junction, is traversed, whose late 12C church contains a Renaissance stone reredos with mutilated sculptures of the Passion.—For the road W., see Rte 36A.

12km. *Antrain*, with a 12th and 16C church, and a 17C tower, 1km S. of which is the handsome 16C *Château de Bonne-Fontaine.*—4km. *Tremblay*, with an 11-12C church, and a turreted house of 1578, beyond which the N175 continue S. up the valley of the Couësnon, later entering that of the Rance as it approaches (41km) **Rennes**; see Rte 39.

36   Dreux to Dinan

A.   Via Argentan, Domfront, and Dol-de-Bretagne

286km (177 miles). N12. 35km *Verneuil*—N26. 23km **L'Aigle**—32km *Nonant-le-Pin*—22km **Argentan**—D924, D916. and D908. 55km *Domfront*—D907. 25km *Mortain*—D977. 14km *St-Hilaire-du-Harcouët* —20km *Pontaubault*. **Mont St-Michel** lies 15km to the W.—N175. 15km *Pontorson*—N176. 19km **Dol-de-Bretagne**—26km **Dinan**.

Maps: IGN 8, 18, 16, 17, or 102. M 231, 230.

For **Dreux**, see *Blue Guide Paris and Environs*, or Rte 24. Hence the N12 leads W., by-passing (14km) *Nonancourt* (see Rte 28A), 8km N.W. of which is the 16-18C *Château de Hellenvilliers.*—At 11km (l.) *Tillières-sur-Avre*, the oldest of the Norman dukes' frontier strongholds facing France, having been founded by Duc Richard II early in the 11C, and strengthened by Henry I. Nothing remains of the castle except the terraced site and a round tower adjoining the town gate. The restored 16C church has a choir-vault decorated in a pagan Renaissance style (1546).

Continuing W., we shortly pass N. of *Montigny*, its church containing a memorial to F.-X. de Montmorency-Laval (1623–1708), first bishop of Canada, prior to reaching (10km) *Verneuil sur-Avre*; see Rte 28C.

The N26 drives due W. hence to (23km) **L'Aigle** (10,200 inhab.), said to be named after an eagle's nest found on the site of its former castle, and largely engaged in the manufacture of pins and needles (*aiguilles*), a busy little town on the Risle. A shower of meteorites fell here in 1803, which was one of the first authenticated by scientists.

St-Martin has a richly sculptured square W. tower (16C), while on the S. is a lower *Tour de l'Horloge* (12C), the same date as the exterior of the apse. The mid 16C vaulting of the S. aisle is notable.—Less interesting is 15C *St-Jean-Baptiste*, its tower decorated with statues, and containing a 17C reredos. The *Mairie* is housed in the château of 1690, where models of the Battle of Normandy are displayed; see Rte 30.

31km. *Nonant-le-Pin*; see Rte 28B.

7km. *Le Pin-au-Haras*, with a finely situated château of 1728 by J. Hardouin-Mansart, well-known for its stud, 1km to the W. of which, at *Le Vieux Pin*, is a charming Louis-XIII priest's house.—*Exmes* (Roman *Oximum*), a decayed local capital, its church with a 12C choir, lies 3.5km N.E.

5km. *Le Bourg-St-Léonard* has an imposing château of a c. 1763, 5km N. of which, at *Chambois*, with a 12C church and magnificent keep built by Guillaume de Mandeville before 1189, took place the historic meeting of the N. and S.W. pincers of the Allied armies on 19 Aug. 1944, which virtually marked the end of the Normandy campaign; see Rtes 30, and 33, the latter likewise for **Argentan**, which is entered 10km W., beyond the *Forêt de Gouffern*.

The D916 bears S.W. through (9km) *Écouché*, its church with a beautiful choir and transepts, begun in 1529 to rival St-Germain at Argentan, but left unfinished; adjoining are remains of a 13C nave.—We fork l. for (11km) *Rânes*, with an early 16C tower to its château.—For *Carrouges*, 11km S.E., see Rte 36B.

13km. *La Ferté-Macé*, a small industrial town, the sacristy of its 19C church occupying the 12C tower of its predecessor. Here, in 1917 e.e. Cummings was imprisoned, as described in 'The Enormous Room'.

Hence a brief DETOUR may be made to the small spa of **Bagnoles-de-l'Orne**, picturesquely sited in the thickly wooded valley of the Vée only 6km S.W. It was earlier named Bagnoles-les-Eaux, and the mineral baths of *Balneum* were probably known to the Romans.—2km S. is the charming 16-18C *Château de Couterne* or *du Fay*.—The main road may be regained by driving N.W. through the *Forêt des Andaines*.

20km. *Domfront*; see Rte 34.—4km after leaving Domfront, we pass 1.5km N. of the *Manoir de la Saucerie*, with a splendid 14C gatehouse.—The next r.-hand turning leads 4km N. to *Lonlay-l'Abbaye*; see p 220.—11km. *Barenton*, a hilltop village, to the N.E. of which, in the adjacent *Forêt de Lande-Pourrie*, German tanks were massed before their offensive of 6 Aug. 1944; see Rte 30.—Skirting the contiguous *Forêt de Mortain*, we reach *Mortain* itself after 9km, and bear S.W. thence to *St-Hilaire-du-Harcouët*; for both see Rte 35A.

The N176 continues W. via (16km) *Ducey*, with an old bridge on the Sélune and a château built in 1624 for Gabriel de Montgomery the younger, to *Pontaubault*, 4km beyond (see Rte 35B); or, alternatively, one may make a slight detour to the S. along the river valley here damned by the *Barrage de Vézins*.

15km. *Pontorson*, 9km S. of *Mont St-Michel*; see Rte 35B. A new road is under construction, which will by-pass Pontorson, Dol, and cross the Rance estuary N. of Dinan.

19km. **DOL-DE-BRETAGNE** a characteristic old town on the borders of Brittany; no longer merely 'a long street. . .without a glass window', which gave such 'a horrid appearance' when Arthur Young traversed it in 1788.

St Samson, abbot of Caldey (according to legend), fleeing from the Saxon invaders of his own country, founded the monastery of Dol before 557. Nominoë, who was crowned king of the Bretons here in 848, created the archbishopric, independent of Rome, whose see was suppressed in 1790. An important frontier fortress, it successfully resisted William the Conqueror in 1075, but Henry II took it in 1164, and in 1203 John burnt down the old cathedral. In the 16C it sided with the Leaguers, and with the Royalists at the Revolution, when the Vendeans gained one of their last victories here in 1793.

The Grande-Rue-des-Stuarts intersects the place, retaining several old arcaded and gabled houses, among them the *Maison de Palets (perhaps as early as the 11C), a rare example of domestic Norman Romanesque, with its original round-arched windows; the 15C Maison de la Guillotière (restored to house a small collection of wooden statues of Breton saints, etc.); and the Maison de Trois Bécasses, with elaborate dormers and a curious device of gloves and birds, is also of interest.

To the N.W. stands the *Cathedral, remarkable for the English character of its Norman Gothic style, occupying the site of the Romanesque church destroyed by John.

It dates principally from the early 13C (nave) and the late 13th-14C (choir). The severe W. front, much restored and hardly worthy of the building, is flanked by two towers, of which that on the N. (Vieille Tour; rebuilt 1520), although unfinished, is notable for the beauty of its graduated buttresses. The S. tower, of various periods, has a low 17C corner-turret and lantern. The squat central tower above the crossing dates from the 14C. Little remains of the W. portal except for four slender columns and a worn architrave with foliage patterns. On the S. facade is the projecting Grande-Porche, the date of which is indicated by the keystone bearing the arms of Bp Coeuret (1405–29), while the charming Petit-Porche shows the bishop's canting arms—a heart—on the central column.

The Nave is remarkable for the disposition of its pillars and their shafts, attached on the E. and W., and detached on the N. and S. A triforium passage encircles the whole, with a rather less simple design in the choir than in the nave. The clerestory, plain in the nave, has plate-tracery in the choir. In the N. transept is the *Tomb of Bp Thomas James (1482–1504), a Renaissance work executed for a nephew of the bishop by the Florentine brothers Antoine and Jean Juste, who afterwards founded a celebrated school in Tours. It has been mutilated, but preserves some beautiful friezes, including fantastic animals.

Off the S. aisle is a charming little 13C chapel with quaint corbels. In the S. transept is a curiously carved stoup. The Choir, with clustered columns, has 14C stalls and a 16C bishop's throne. The great E. window contains late 13C glass. The rectangular ambulatory has one apsidal chapel.

A good general view of the building may be obtained from the gardens to the N.E., on the site of the former ramparts (Les Douves), also commanding a good view towards Mont Dol, 3km N., a bold granite rock (64m) overlooking the surrounding 'marais'.

A number of prehistoric remains have been found in the vicinity of this height, once a pagan sanctuary, later affording a refuge to several apostles of Brittany. It also figures in the Bayeux Tapestry. On its S. slope is a 12-15C church, from which a track ascends to the summit.

The Bay of Mont St-Michel lies only 8km N., whence a road follows the shore to the W. of the Cancale; see Rte 39, likewise for St-Malo, 24km N.W. of Dol.

2km. S. of Dol, to the E. of the D795, rises the Pierre du Champ-Dolent, an imposing menhir fabled to mark the site of a legendary battle ended by the falling of the stone from Heaven.

The N176 continues S.W. from Dol to (26km) **Dinan**; see Rte 41.

B. Via Alençon, Mayenne, and Fougères

292km (181 miles). N12. 35km *Verneuil*—36km *Mortagne-au-Perche* lies 3km S.—39km **Alençon**—61km **Mayenne**—44km **Fougères**— D155. 51km **Dol-de Bretagne**—N176. 26km **Dinan**.

Maps: IGN 8, 18, 17, 16, or 102. M 231, 232, 230.

For the road from Dreux to *Verneuil*, see Rte 36A. Hence our route bears to the S.W. through a wooded countryside, after 20km traversing the *Forêt du Perche*.

5km. *Tourouvre*, 2km r., was one of the principal villages in this area to send emigrants to Canada during the reign of Louis XIV, and in 1891 was visited by Honoré Mercier, a Canadian Prime Minister, as commemorated in a window in St-Gilles; another depicts Julien Mercier and 80 families setting out for the colony in 1650.

A cross-road 5km further W. leads 4km N. to the once-famous monastery of **La Grande-Trappe**, beautifully situated in the forest, among oak glades and lakes. It was founded c. 1140 by Rotrou III, count of Perche, who had previously erected an oratory on the spot in memory of his wife and brother-in-law, lost in the wreck of the 'White Ship' (cf. Barfleur). The house was affiliated to the Cistercians in 1147, but owes its celebrity to the severe rule enforced by the Abbé de Rancé, who reformed the order drastically in 1662, enjoining perpetual silence (except in prayer), total abstinence from flesh, fish, and wine, and laborious manual occupations, which is still enforced. Their ascetic and taciturn character did not save them from expulsion in 1792, but a number of monks returned in 1815 and rebuilt the monastery, the parent house, which was again reconstructed in 1884–92. The Trappists, being a non-proselytising order, survived the 'Loi des Congrégations' of 1901, which did much to sweep clean the Augean stables of monasticism.—The *Church*, in a 13C Gothic style, the elaborately decorated reliquary chapel, chapter-house, and refectory, etc. may be visited by male guests only.

The D930 leads S. from this cross-road to regain the N12 3km N. of *Mortagne*.

At 15km S.W. of the turning for Tourouvre, we leave *Mortagne-sur-Perche* (see Rte 28C) to our l., and continue to (38km) **Alençon**; see Rte 28B.

10km beyond Alençon the *Butte Chaumont* (378m), rising to the N., commands a wide view, while to the S.W. the *Forêt de Multonne* covers *Mont Souprat* (385m).

At 8km **Carrouges**, a hilltop village known for its *Château*, ◇ lies 11km to the N. Owned by the Le Veneur family from 1450 until 1936, this huge moated quadrilateral is mainly 15th and 17C, with a tall-roofed 16C gatehouse. It contains a charming oratory and decorations by Maurice Gabriel (c. 1650). The 15C Collégiale is now a barn.

The main road skirts the N. flank of the *Mont des Avaloirs* (417m), the highest point in N.W. France.

From (6km) *Pré-en-Pail* the D176 forks r. to (18km) *Couterne*, 5km S. of *Bagnoles-de-l'Orne* (see Rte 36A), and *Domfront*, 19km beyond.

12km. *Javron-les-Chapelles*, with a 13C church.

Lassay, 13km W., has a splendid feudal *Castle*, rebuilt in its present form by Jean de Vendôme in 1458, with a later barbican. The living quarters in the two N. towers were altered in the 17C, and the bridge of 1749 replaced a drawbridge. The whole was restored in the 19C.—The picturesque ruin of the *Château de Bois-Thibault* (mid 15C) lies 1km N.W.; those of the *Château du Bois-Froult*, to the W.—One may regain the main road 15km S.W., just after passing (l.) the 14-16C *Château du Fresne*.

25km. **Mayenne**; see Rte 34.

Hence the N12, after 7km, skirts the N. side of the *Forêt de Mayenne*, extending to the S.W., and 17km beyond traverses *Ernée*, picturesquely situated on the river of the same name, which grew up round a castle, its site now occupied by a church of 1697.—*Vitré* (see Rte 38) lies 19km S.W.

After 8.5km *La Pellerine* (r.) is by-passed, where the Vendean leader Lescure died in 1793, and just beyond we enter Brittany, descending the Couësnon valley to (15.5km) **Fougères**; see Rte 35A, and below.—**Rennes** lies 48km S.W.

The D155 traverses the small 'pays' of Coglès to (26km) *Antrain* (see Rte 35B), beyond which traversing the *Forêt de Ville-Cartier*, and at 16km passing 3km N. of the 15C castle of *Landal*, with a restored keep.—9km. **Dol-de Bretagne**, for which and the road beyond see Rte 36A.

FOUGÈRES TO DINAN VIA COMBOURG (71km). After 21.5km we turn l. off the D155 through (2km) *Tremblay* (see Rte 35B), and follow the D796 W. to (23.5km) **Combourg**, a grey old town retaining some 16C houses and the 14-15C *Castle* where Chateaubriand passed his boyhood, as described in his 'Mémoires d'Outre-Tombe', and now containing a small museum of relics. In 1788, the year the 20-year-old Chateaubriand went to Paris, Arthur Young passed through Combourg, the country round which had for him 'a savage aspect' and the people 'almost as wild as their country'. Combourg itself he censured as being 'one of the most brutal filthy places that can be seen; mud houses, no windows, and a pavement so broken as to impede all passengers, but ease none—yet here is a chateau, and inhabited; who is this Monsieur de Chateaubriant, the owner, that has nerves strung for a residence amidst such filth and poverty? Below this hideous heap of wretchedness is a fine lake, surrounded by well wooded enclosures'. It has seen improvements since, and the castle is seen at its romantic best from the far side of its lake.—Hence one continues W., after 13km crossing the N137 (see Rte 39), and 11km beyond, enter **Dinan**; see Rte 41.

37 Chartres to Le Mans and Angers

208km (129 miles). N23. 54km **Nogent-le-Rotrou**—21km *La Ferté-Bernard*—44km **Le Mans**—42km **La Flèche. Saumur** lies 51km S. on the D938.—47km **Angers**.

Maps: IGN 19, 25, or 102, 106. M 237, 232.

The A11 motorway, entered S. of Chartres, now provides a rapid route to Le Mans, and is being extended S.W. thence to Angers, which will then connect with the already completed stretch between Angers and Nantes.

For **Chartres**, see *Blue Guide Paris and Environs*, or Rtes 23 and 28A.

The N23 drives due W. across the monotonous Beauce plateau to by-pass (19km) *Courville-sur-Eure*, birthplace of the prolific songwriter C.F. Panard (1674–1765), 7km N.W. of which, at *Pontgouin*, is a 13C church and relics of a former castle of the bishops of Chartres; Sully died at the 15-17C château of *Villebon*, 7km S.; see below.

We now enter the *Perche-Gouët*, a pleasanter countryside of copses, orchards, and old houses, skirting (r.) the *Forêt de Champrond*, before reaching (17km) *Montlandon*, with its ruined feudal tower.

The church at *Frétigny*, 6km S.W., contains 12–13C murals, 7km S. of which, at lakeside *Thiron*, another retains a good early Gothic nave.

The road descends into the valley of the Huisne at (18km) **Nogent-le-Rotrou** (13,200 Nogentais), an interesting old market town, the birthplace of the poet Rémi Belleau (1528–77). The Duc de Sully (1560–1641), Henri IV's minister, who had acquired the overlordship of Nogent in 1624, was first buried here (cf. Sully-sur-Loire), and his *Tomb*, by Boudin, may be seen in the *Hôtel-Dieu* in the Rue de Sully. Adjacent is *Notre-Dame* (13-14C), with an earlier portal; to the W. is riverside *St-Hilaire* with a tower of 1560, and a notable 13C choir. The S. end of the main street is commanded by the *Castle* of the counts of Perche, with a gateway of 1492 and massive early 11C keep, now housing the local *Museum*. Below it, to the W., stands *St-Laurent* (15-16C), containing a 16C Entombment, the ruins of the priory of *St-Denis*, and the *Tribunal*, in a 16C mansion, one of several old houses in the area.

NOGENT-LE-ROTROU TO ALENÇON (62km). The D955 leads W. to (22km) *Bellême* (see Rte 28C), passing several attractive manors both N. and S. of the road, among them those of *Lormarin*, and *Courboyer*, approached by turning r. 11km from Nogent; by turning l. 2.5km beyond one may visit (4km S.) the considerable remains of the priory of *Ste-Gauburge*, with its 13-16C church, and the picturesque fortified manor of *L'Angenardière* (15C). The main road may be regained via *St-Cyr-la-Rosière*, its church containing a 17C terracotta Entombment.
15km. **Mamers** (6700 Mamertins), a small market-town which fell to the English in 1359, and 1417, while its walls were razed by Salisbury in 1428. Its churches have been much rebuilt—10km. *Neufchâtel-en-Saosnois*, 2km N. of which lie the picturesquely sited ruins of the abbey of *Perseigne*, founded 1145, beyond which we climb through the *Forêt de Perseigne* to reach (15km) **Alençon**; see Rte 28B.

Continuing S.W. from Nogent, we pass (r.) at 9km the ruins of the 11C abbey of *N.-D.-des-Clairets*, to reach (12km) **La Ferté-Bernard** (10,100 inhab.), birthplace of the 15C architect Jean Texier, and Robert Garnier (1534–90), the poet. In the central Place stands 15-16C *N.-D. des-Marais*, of which the elaborate exterior of the choir is effective; its glass; the vaulting of the apsidal chapels, containing bas-reliefs; and the organ-loft (all of c. 1535), are notable.

The *Halles* (1536); 15C *Porte St-Julien*, W. of the church; and the *Tour des Moulins* in the upper town, a survival of its fortifications, are of interest.

15km S.E., beyond the motorway, is the walled hilltop village of *Montmirail*, with a *Castle*, altered in the 15th and 18Cs, which was the residence of the lords of the Bas-Perche, the first of whom, Guillaume Gouët, gave his name to the district, the *Perche-Gouët*. It was the scene of a meeting in 1168 between Henry II and Becket, whom Louis VII tried in vain to reconcile. To the l., 7km beyond, is the 15-16C château of *Glatigny*, birthplace of Card. Jean du Bellay (1492–1560), the friend of Rabelais.

We shortly cross the A11 motorway, at (19km) *Connerré* passing 2km W. of a large passage-grave, the *Pierre-Couverte*, not far N. of which is the *Pierre-Fiche*, a pierced menhir.—After 10km the *Camp d'Auvours*, lies to the N., where in 1908 trial flights were made by Wilbur Wright (1867–1912).—A road junction is reached at 5km, the l.-hand fork by-passing Le Mans to join the N23 further S.W.

The r.-hand fork, after 7km leads past (l.) a turning for the *Abbaye de l'Épau*, c. 3km from the centre of Le Mans.

The original abbey, founded in 1230 by Berengeria of Navarre, the widow of Richard I (whom she married at Limassol, in Cyprus), was burnt down in 1365 by the Manceaux to prevent the English from fortifying it, and the present buildings (restored) date largely from the late 14C, consisting of the *Church* (to which the tomb of the foundress has been returned from the cathedral), with its great transepts and E. rose-window; a vaulted sacristy, and cellar; the chapter-house, and remains of the cloister, with the lavatory, dormitory, etc.

LE MANS (150,300 Manceaux; 27,100 in 1851; 100,500 in 1946), former capital of *Maine*, and now the Préfecture of the *Sarthe*, is a flourishing market town, and industrial centre. The older fortified nucleus, with the cathedral, overlooking the river Sarthe, is in the process of restoration; the modern centre has been much rebuilt.

The probable capital of the Gallic Cenomanni was in Roman occupation by the 3C, and was soon after evangelised by St Julian. Seized by William the Conqueror, it was an important centre of the Norman and Angevin dominions and a favourite city of Henry II. It was besieged five times during the Hundred Years' War, finally falling to the French in 1481. In 1562 it was devastated by the Huguenots, and by the Vendeans under La Rochejaquelein in 1793, who made their last stand here, being driven out after a bloody battle in its streets with the Republican troops of Marceau and Westermann. During the Franco-Prussian War, the disastrous defeat of Chanzy's 2nd Army of the Loire to the S. and E. of the town (11 Jan. 1871) rendered hopeless all further attempt to relieve Paris. It was bombed on several occasions during the Second World War.

Le Mans was the birthplace of Henry II (1133–89), the first Plantagenet king of England; Jean le Bon (1319–64), king of France; the painter Marc Duval (c. 1530); Jacques Peletier (1517–82), humanist and initiator of the 'Pléiade'; Dom Guéranger (1806–75), founder of the abbey of Solesmes; Léon Bollée (1870–1913), famous in the early history of the motor-car and aeroplane; Arnold Dolmetsch (1858–1940), the exponent of, and reviver of interest in, medieval music; and the composer Jean Francaix (1912–). Antoine de Saint-Exupéry was a pupil at the Jesuit Collège de Sainte-Croix in 1909–14.

Sports cars converge on the Circuit du Mans (S. of the town) in late June and Sept., when the area is best avoided by non enthusiasts. It also contains a *Museum of veteran cars.*

A number of roads meet at the *Pl. des Jacobins*, just S. of the cathedral apse, to the E. of which is the Promenade des Jacobins (parking), flanked to the N. by the *Jardin de Tessé*. The former bishop's palace here houses the **Musée de Tessé**, a rather miscellaneous collection, but containing several works of interest.

Notable is the **Portrait of Geoffrey Plantagenet*, Count of Anjou and Maine, and father of Henry II, a fine work in champlevé enamel (12C) from his tomb in the cathedral, with one of the earliest known representations of armorial bearings. Among other exhibits are: *Philippe de Champaigne*, Vanity (a still life), and Adoration, and Dream of Elijah (previously in the N.-D.-de-la-Couture; see below); *Jean de Boulogne*, St John; *Georges de la Tour*, Ecstacy of St Francis; attrib. *Ferdinand Bol*, Male portrait; attrib. *David*, Portrait of the Revolutionary Michel Gérard and his family.

The Pl. des Jacobins provides a striking view of the elaborate apse of the cathedral, with its paired buttresses set at an narrow angle, which are unique in Gothic architecture, rising above the fortified enceinte.

The ***Cathedral** (dedicated to St Julian) is approached hence by a flight of steps on the site of a Roman wall.

Three distinct parts will be discerned; the Romanesque nave (11-12C); the choir (completed 1254), one of the boldest conceptions of the 13C; and the transepts, rebuilt together with the insignificant tower in the 14C (S.) and 15C (N.). The somewhat clumsy S. porch covers a portal flanked by 12C statues resembling those in the Portail Royal at Chartres. Adjacent is a little Romanesque doorway, while at the S.W. corner stands a menhir of red sandstone. The W. front, with

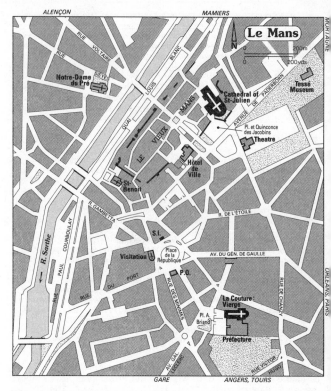

two small side portals and a large central doorway, has preserved its Romanesque aspect.

Interior. The *Nave* and aisles, with their particoloured stonework (whitewashed over in 1767 by the 'improving' Bp Luis-André de Grimaldi), are essentially Romanesque, although the main arcade has pointed Transitional arches (12C), above which, however, the original 11C round arches may still be traced. The carved capitals are purely Romanesque; so are the triforium and clerestory, but the vault is a late 12C addition. Most of the stained-glass in the great W. window, and in some of the aisle windows, is among the oldest in France (before 1150), but in 1562 some 57 windows in the apsidal chapels were broken, among others, during the general destruction and mutilation of the church by the Huguenots, and it is extraordinary that these others survived.

The *S. transept* has an open triforium and three fine windows, and contains a 16C organ-case. The glass in the rose-window of the N. transept, also with a good triforium, dates from 1430. In the baptistry, with its curious vault, are the tombs of Charles d'Anjou, Count of Maine (d. 1472), by Francesco Laurana, and of Guillaume du Bellay (d. 1543), viceroy of Piedmont under François I, an elegant work by an Italian sculptor.

The **Choir*, with a double ambulatory of unequal height (as at Bourges and Coutances), is in the purest Gothic style. The little blind arcades round the base of the piers are an uncommon feature. The stalls are restored but still interesting work of 1575. The glass in the upper windows dates from the 13-14C. In the first S. chapel is a 17C Entombment; and in the *Sacristy*, a handsome Gothic room vaulted from a central pier, are panels from the choir. Colourful tapestries hang above the choir and stalls and on adjacent pillars at the crossing.

Immediately N. of the cathedral is the *Pl. du Card. Grente* or *du Château*, named after William the Conqueror's keep, of which nothing remains, although parts of two 14C gate-towers survive in the Rue du Château. Opposite the menhir stands the *Hôtel du Grabatoire* (1528–42), formerly the canons' infirmary, and now the *Bishop's Palace*; No.3, with scallop shells, is the 16C *Maison du Pèlerin*; and No.5, the *Tour du Cavalier* (14C). Paul Scarron (1610–60), the husband of Mme de Maintenon, and honorary canon of the cathedral, is supposed to have occupied No.1 in the adjacent *Pl. St-Michel*, opposite the S. transept.

Hence one may follow the Rue Bérengère into the picturesque but ramshackle old town; No.11, known as the *Maison de la Reine Bérengère*, but in fact dating from 1495, houses a small museum with a good collection of faience, including local Ligron and Malicorne ware; No.20, opposite, is called the house of the 'Deux Amis' after its quaint pillar.

We cross the small square bridging the cutting pierced in 1857 through the hill to link the Pl. du Jacobins with the bank of the Sarthe, and named the Rue Wilbur-Wright, whose statue, by Landowski, stands at its S. end (cf. p 234). Beyond is the *Maison du Pilier Rouge* (No.45 Grande Rue), and further on (No.69), the *Maison d'Adam et Eve*, built in 1525.

There are other interesting 16C houses in the Rue de l'Écrevisse (*Hôtel de Vignobles*) and Rue St-Honoré (*Hôtel Perot*), leading l. to the *Pl. St-Pierre*, and the 18C *Hôtel de Ville*, with a charming garden, and remains of a 14C tower. The adjacent school covers the 13C crypt of the collegiate church of *St-Pierre-la-Court*.

On the N. side of the Grande Rue, the Rue St-Pavin or du Bouquet, with their tumbledown houses, lead down to the Rue de Vaux.—To the l., the *Escalier de la Grande-Poterne* climbs down to the river, providing a good view of the 4C *Gallo-Roman Walls*. Fragments of 14C walls are seen in the riverside gardens.

On the far bank of the Sarthe, approached by the rebuilt *Pont Yssoir*, is *N.-D. du-Pré*, a restored Romanesque building (with a 19C tower), interesting for its 12C capitals, both of the main columns and of the particoloured blind arcading along the walls. On the S. side is a curious 16C relief depicting the translation of the relics of St Scolastica hence to *St-Benoît* (due S. on the other bank), a church entirely rebuilt in 1905. Its 11C crypt contains the tomb of St Julian, whose cell exists in the corner of the *Pl. de l'Éperon*, N.E. of the Pl. de la République.

The *Pl. de la République* may be reached directly by flights of steps descending from the S. end of the Grande Rue. This main square (with the S.I. on its N. side) is surrounded by a somewhat heterogeneous collection of buildings, among them the *Church of the Visitation* (1737), with a balustrade in the interior designed by Anne-Victoire Pillon, a Visitandine sister.

From its S. side the Blvd René-Levasseur leads shortly to the *Pl. Aristide-Briand*, with the *Préfecture* of 1770 on the site of abbey buildings, and occupying the cloister of adjoining **N.-D.-de-la-Couture** (or '*de Cultura Dei*'). It dates mainly from the 12th and 14Cs, although the earliest parts are 10C. Two unfinished towers flank the late 13C *Porch*, decorated with statues of six apostles, with numerous statuettes in the archivolt; the Last Judgment appears below the tympanum; the doors are 15C.

The aisleless *Nave* (the first bay of which is disfigured by 19C decoration), dating from the latter half of the 12C, has groined vaulting slightly domed in the Angevin manner, and Romanesque windows. Opposite the pulpit is a Virgin attrib. to Germain Pilon, and 16-18C tapestries are exhibited on the walls. The *Choir* itself is imposing; the ambulatory and one of the apse chapels are early Romanesque, with good capitals on the S. side. The upper parts are of the 12C, and the other chapels are later. The six 12C *Statues* serving as supports for the apse vault are probably unique in France. The *Crypt* under the choir is 10C, with eight re-used columns (one with an inverted capital as a base). Beneath the altar is the tomb of St Bertrand (d. 616), founder of the church.

From behind the building, one may follow the Rue Bertholet to the Rue du Chanzy.—By turning l. here, the Pl. des Jacobins may be regained without crossing the concrete jungle of the new city centre.

At the S. end of the Rue Chanzy is the church of *Ste-Jeanne-D'Arc*, which is in fact part of the great hall of the *Hospital of Coëffort*, a foundation of Henry II (1180), and resembling the Hôtel-Dieu at Angers. It served for years (until 1951) as a barrack-store.

For the road W. from Le Mans to **Rennes**, and *Mayenne*, see Rte 38; for **Tours**, see Rte 28B.

LE MANS TO ANGERS VIA SOLESMES (108km). The most interesting route is that which forks l. off the N157 23km W. of Le Mans (shortly after crossing the motorway) to follow the D21 to (12.5km) *Brûlon*, birthplace of Claude Chappe (1763–1805), the physicist who invented the French aerial telegraph.—After 6.5km we turn l., passing the *Château de Verdelles* (1490), to (5km) *Asnières-sur-Vègre*, its church containing remarkable 13C murals.—Here we turn l. again through *Juigné-sur-Sarthe*, preserving old houses, to (7km) **Solesmes**, the abbey buildings of which are better seen from across the river as we approach than at close quarters, for although they were conceived in the style of the mid 12C (at least in the view of their architect), they were erected only in 1880–98.

Founded in 1010 as a priory, the Benedictine community was re-established here in 1830 by Dom Guéranger, under whom it became the headquarters of the Order in France. It was abandoned after the decree of 1901, but re-occupied in 1922. It is famous for its Gregorian chant, which may be heard in the church daily. The *Church* was almost entirely rebuilt in the 15-16C, and in 1865 was provided with a large choir in the 15C style, with 16C stalls. Of interest, but rather cramped together, are the series of sculptures which may be seen in the transepts: the *Entombment* (1596), a composition of eight figures attrib. to Michel Colombe, to the S.; and to the l., on the altar, beneath a Renaissance colonnade, a 16C relief of the Massacre of the Innocents, and of the Flight into Egypt. The N. transept contains an *Entombment of the Virgin* (16C), above which is another group representing the Assumption; also Jesus in the Temple. An English alabaster has been incorporated in the altar. On the r. of the chapel is the Dormition of the Virgin, with her Coronation above.

We continue S.W., at 3km traversing *Sablé* (12,700 inhab.), with a château, rebuilt in 1715, approached by a fortified 14C gatehouse, following the D309 to (10.5km) *St-Denis-d'Anjou*, with a *Halles* of 1509, a church preserving 16C wall-paintings and stalls, and a *Mairie* in a 15C mansion.—5.5km. *Miré*, whose church has a painted vault (15C). At 7km the D768 passes 5km W. of *Châteauneuf-sur-Sarthe*, its church with characteristic 13C vaulting, 4km N.E. of which, at *Brissarthe*, Robert le Fort, count of Anjou, was slain in battle against the Normans in 866.—Continuing S., we pass (l., after 6.5km) the *Château de la Hamonière* (15C and c. 1575).—4.5km beyond, a l.-hand turning, after 4km, approaches the *Château du Plessis-Bourré*, a wide-moated quadrilateral with corner towers, built in 1473 for Jean Bourré, treasurer to Louis XI.—Regaining the main road we shortly reach *Feneu*, there forking l. for (17.5km) **Angers**; alternatively we may make our way S. along lanes in the Sarthe valley.

An alternative to the main road FROM LE MANS TO LA FLÈCHE (see below) is the D23, running approx. parallel to and W. of the N23, passing at (5km) *Allonnes*, on the S.W. outskirts of Le Mans, the site of a Gallo-Roman villa.—13km. *La Suze-sur-Sarthe*, where the river is crossed by a nine-arched bridge built under Henri IV; its church occupies the chapel of the ruined 15C château.—13km. *Malicorne*, preserving some old turreted houses, a 12C church, and a château

visited by Mme de Sévigné; its pottery is of some local importance. Bearing S.E.,
we reach *La Flèche* after 16km.

LE MANS TO SAUMUR VIA LE LUDE (91km). At *Arnage*, 8km S., we fork l. onto
the D307, traversing woods to (21km) *Pontvallain*, where Du Guesclin defeated
the mutinous army of Sir Robert Knolles in 1370.—14km. **Le Lude**, famous for its
***Château**, a quadrilateral with a huge machicolated tower at each corner. The
N. wing (late 15C) has a Gothic facade and an equestrian statue of Jean de
Daillon (d. 1480), its founder; the remarkable Renaissance S. wing overlooks the
park; the E. facade dates from the time of Louis XVI. It contains a collection of
furniture, family portraits, and costumes, a charming oratory, and a series of
frescoes of Italian workmanship. The park skirts the Loir for almost 2km, and is
the scene of 'Son et Lumière' spectacles in the summer.—For the road hence to
Tours, see below.
    At 10km S. are (l.) the ruins of the 12C Cistercian abbey of *La Boissière*, and
12.5km beyond, the road passes 5.5km E. of *Mouliherne*, with a remarkable
12-13C church.—7.5km. *Vernantes*, where the mairie occupies a former church,
still retaining its 12-15C steeple and a singular monument of the 17C châtelains
of *Jalesne*, a mansion W. of the village.—After 10km, on emerging from
pinewoods, we get a good view of the Loire valley ahead before meeting the
N147 5km N.E. of **Saumur**, with its castle dominating the far side of the river; see
Rte 58.

LE LUDE TO TOURS (50km). The D306, continued by the D959 leads S.E. to
(17km) *Château-la-Vallière*, which provided the title of Duchesse de la Vallière
(in 1667) for Louise de la Baume Le Blanc, mistress of Louis XIV. The lake to the
S. is known as the *Lac de Valjoyeux*, S.E. of which is the ruined castle of *Vau-
jours*.—At 12km we pass (l.) the 13-16C moated *Château de la Motte-Sonzay*, and
continue S.E. over the thinly peopled wooded plateau of the *Gâtine Tourangelle*
to (21km) **Tours**; see Rte 54.

The N23 drives S.W. from Le Mans, shortly entering a well-wooded
district, and traverses several small villages, at 30.5km passing (r.)
Ligron, known for its pottery.

6km. The D13 leads l. to (4km) the charming late 15C *Château du Gallerande*,
and 4km beyond, *Luché-Pringé*, its church preserving a fine 13C choir.

5.5km **La Flèche** (16,400 Flèchois), an old town on the r. bank of the
Loir, became a fief of the Bourbons in 1536, and owes much of its
prosperity to Henri IV, who founded the *Prytanée Militaire* in 1604.

This college, in a street N. of and parallel to the Grande Rue, was managed by
the Jesuits until 1762, when it was transformed into a preparatory school for the
École Militaire in Paris, and it is still a school for the sons of men in the services
being 'educated' for a military career. Amongst its pupils have been Descartes,
La Tour d'Auvergne, and Galliéni.

The restored *Chapel* (1622) contains an elaborate but unattractive
high altar by P. Corbineau (1663), with an Annunciation by Restout.
In a niche above the gallery in the N. transept are the intermingled
ashes of the hearts of Henri IV and Marie de Médicis, which were
burnt by the Republicans in 1793.
    To the S. in the central square, is *St-Thomas*, with a 12C crossing
and 15C choir; and further S., by the bridge, the *Hôtel de Ville* occupies the old *Château des Carmes*, practically rebuilt after a fire in
1919.

To the E. of the Prytanée is the *Hospital*, preserving a 17C cloister, 1km N. of
which, in the village of *St-Germain-du-Val*, was born the composer Léo Delibes
(1836–91), while the neighbouring *Château d'Yvandeau* was the residence of
David Hume in 1735.—In the W. suburbs, behind the cemetery, the *Chapelle de
N.-D.-des-Vertus*, with a Romanesque portal, contains some charming
Renaissance woodwork.—3km. N.W., at *Vernon*, is the *Cours des Pins*, a 15-16C

manor, the birthplace of Lazare de Baïf (d. 1547), patron of the Pléiade, and father of one of its members.

Le Lude (see above) lies 20km E. on the D306.

LA FLÈCHE TO SAUMUR (51km). The D308, continued by the D938, leads due S. through woods to (18km) **Baugé**, an ancient town on the Couasnon, with a fine *Castle*, rebuilt in 1430, with a beautiful turret staircase. To the N.E., the *Hospice St-Joseph* preserves its 17-18C *Pharmacy*; the *Chapelle des Incurables*, in the Rue de la Girouardière, contains a remarkable double-armed Cross brought from Constantinople to the abbey of La Boissière in the 13C as a piece of the True Cross. It is the heraldic emblem of the House of Anjou, later adopted by the House of Lorraine, and better known as the Cross of Lorraine.—*Le Vieil-Baugé*, 2km S.W., with an 11C church, was the scene of a battle in 1421, when Thomas, Duke of Clarence was defeated and killed fighting against Charles VII aided by the Scots under John Stewart, Earl of Buchan.

Continuing S. we pass (r.) the Renaissance *Château de Landifer*, and at 6km, *Cuon*, with a curious 12C church-tower and the *Château de la Grafinière*.—12km. *Longué-Jumelles*, 10km beyond which we fork r. for (5km) **Saumur**; see Rte 58.

From La Flèche, the N23 bears W. through (7.5km) *Bazouges-sur-le-Loir*, with a *Château* built by Baudoin de Champagne, chamberlain to Louis XII, and a church with a painted 15C ceiling.—5.5km. *Durtal*, with a late 16C *Château* retaining two towers of its feudal predecessor, beyond which we veer S.W., skirting the *Forêt de Chambiers* and after 12km pass (r.) the ruined late 15C *Château de Verger*.—22km. **Angers**; see Rte 59A.

38   Le Mans to Rennes

144km (89 miles). N157. 75km **Laval**—After 20km fork r. onto the D857 for (15km) **Vitré**, regaining the N157 17km beyond, and 17km prior to **Rennes**.

Maps: IGN 19, 17, 16, or 106. M 232.

A branch of the A11 motorway bears W. a short distance N.W. of Le Mans to by-pass Laval, later veering S. of Vitré.

For **Le Mans**, see Rte 37.

LE MANS TO MAYENNE (74km). The D304 leads N.W. to (33km) *Sillé-le-Guillaume*, with a massive 15C Castle on the site of an earlier one taken by William the Conqueror and later besieged by the earls of Richmond, and Arundel. The church has a good 13C portal and crypt. To the N. is the *Forêt de Sillé*, on the slopes of the granite chain of the *Coëvrons*, the highest point of which is the *Gros-Richard* (357m), S. of the main road 18km beyond. Just W. of *Bais*, 3km beyond, is the 14-16C *Château de Montesson*.—7km. At *Jublains*, 5km S.W., are remains of a Roman Camp or fort, and thermae, whence one may regain the main road just E. of **Mayenne**; see Rte 34.

On crossing the Sarthe by the *Pont Yssoir* (with retrospective views of the old fortified town overlooking the river), we bear away from Le Mans across the fertile *Champagne Mancelle*, succeeded beyond the Vègre by the heaths of the *Charnie*, similar to those of Brittany. Many of the village churches have early Gothic details and contain terracotta statuary.

At 21km a r.-hand turning leads c. 7.5km to the huge *Château de Sources* (1761–80).—We shortly skirt the S. border of the *Forêt de la Grande Charnie*.

22km. A short DETOUR may be made hence to the hilltop village of *Ste-Suzanne*, 8km N., with square bastioned walls, and the 11C keep of its castle, which withstood a siege by William the Conqueror, but which was dismantled by the Earl of Salisbury in 1425; the 'new' castle dates from the 17C; View.—**Évron**, 7km N.W., has a remarkable Romanesque and Gothic *Church, founded in 648. The tower and most of the nave is 12C; two bays, the transepts, and the choir with its ambulatory chapels, are admirable Gothic work of the 13-14Cs. One chapel preserves 12-13C frescoes.—Against its W. end is a massive abbey building of 1726; the arches of the market support the Mairie.—5km to the N.W., and S.E., respectively, are the *Châteaux du Rocher* (14-15C), and *de Montecler* (1585– 1610), while c. 1km W. is that of *La Roche-Pichemer* (15-16C).—S. of the latter lies *Montsûrs*, birthplace of André de Laval (1410– 65), a companion of Joan of Arc, with the slight remains of its castle, burnt by the English in 1430.—The N157 may be regained 11km S. via *La Chapelle-Rainsouin*, containing good 15-16C sculpture in its church.

3km W. of the turning for Ste-Suzanne, *St-Jean-sur-Erve* is by-passed.

The *Grottes de Saulges*, stalactite caves inhabited in palaeolithic times, may be visited in the valley to the S., the most interesting of which are the Grottes de Rochefort and à Margot, from which the main road may be regained at *Vaiges*, 7km W. of St-Jean.

The N157 continues W., at 17km passing (r.) the quaint village of *Bonchamp-lès-Laval*.

5km. **LAVAL** (53,800 Lavallois), préfecture of the *Mayenne*, and formerly a textile centre, is now devoted to general industry. The older town is attractively situated on the r. bank of the Mayenne, here 73m wide, its castle dominating the *Pont Vieux*.

The Castle, founded c. 1020 by a seigneur named Guy II—whose descendants retained the countship until the Revolution—was captured by the English under Talbot in 1428, but was retaken the following year. After the usual vicissitudes of the Religious Wars, it submitted to Henri IV in 1594. Henri de Rochejaquelein's Vendean army (which had seized the place at bayonet-point) gained a brilliant victory over the Republican army at *La Croix-Bataille*, just S. of the town, but was obliged to retreat the following Dec. after the disaster at Le Mans. It was in this neighbourhood that the first bands of 'Chouans' (see p 242) were organised. Among natives were Ambrose Paré (1517– 90), the surgeon; Henri Rousseau, 'Le Douanier' (1844– 1910); and Alfred Jarry (1873– 1907), author of 'Ubu Roi', etc.

The main thoroughfare crosses the rebuilt *Pont-Neuf;* on the W. bank is the spacious *Pl. du 11-Novembre*, from the S. side of which the Rue des Déportés leads to the *Pl. de la Trémoïlle*, flanked by the *Palais de Justice*, a freely remodelled Renaissance structure of 1508– 42. To the S. is the **Vieux-Château**, occupied by the *Musée*. Used as a prison from 1792– 1909, it preserves little of its original 11-12C work except the crypt and *keep; the façade overlooking the Mayenne is 13C, but the whole bears evidence of repeated alteration. The interior façade has Renaissance windows. A statue commemorates Béatrice de Gavre, who married Guy IX in 1289. She brought with her the Flemish weavers who established the textile industry.

The timber-vaulted *Grande Salle* contains tombs of the lords of Laval, brought from the abbey of Clermont, among them those of Countess Béatrix, daughter of Arthur II of Brittany and Yolande de Dreux, the widow of Alexander III of Scotland. Other rooms display collections of ironwork and ceramics, etc., and views of Laval by J.-B. Messager (1814– 85); on the Ground Floor is a collection of Naive Art, misleadingly named *Musée Henri-Rousseau*, for it contains only one of his canvases.

A few paces W. is the inelegant **Cathedral**. Its nave and crossing date from 1070–1160; the N. transept and N. side of the choir from the 16C, and the rest mainly 19C. Notable are the tomb of Bp Ouvrin of Dol (d. 1357), a triptych attrib. to Pieter Aertsen, and several Aubusson tapestries.

Near its S.E. corner is Rue de la Trinité, with the 16C *Maison de Clermont*, with six wooden figures on its façade; to the S.W. rise the two towers of the *Porte Beucheresse* (14-15C), from which the narrow Rue des Serruriers leads E. to approach a section of town walls, S.E. of which is the *Jardin de la Perrine*, sloping down to the river, where a willow weeps over the *Tomb of Henri Rousseau*.

The Rue Renaise leads N.W. from the cathedral through further relics of walls, to approach *N.-D.-des-Cordeliers* (from 1387), and *St-Martin*, largely Romanesque, but both are of slight interest.

The Grande Rue (with the Renaissance *Maison du Grand-Veneur*) descends towards the 13C *Vieux-Pont*, with its Gothic arches, from a point not far E. of the cathedral. On the E. bank here is *St-Vénérand* (1485–1500), with a heavy classical pediment; on its pulpit is a view of the town in relief. To the N. of the church, the *Préfecture* occupies the 18C buildings of the Jacobin convent.—1km S. of the Vieux-Pont, on the W. bank, rises the graceful spire of 1534 of *N.-D. d'Avénières* (1140–70).

At *Pritz* (pron. Priss), 2km N. of Laval, is a restored Romanesque church containing 13C frescoes, etc.

Just past *St-Ouën-des-Toits* (13km N.W., on the D30, for *Fougères*, 35km beyond), to the r. of the road, lies the *Closerie des Poiriers*, a farm once occupied by the brothers Cottereau, nicknamed 'Chouan' because they imitated the cry of an owl ('chat-huant') as a signal on their smuggling expeditions. Jean Chouan is said by some to have organised a band of peasants to resist the Republican authorities after 1792, whence the term 'Chouan' came to mean the insurgents in general, later extended to include all intransigent supporters of the dwindling royalist cause in western France.

The N157 leads W. from Laval, at 12.5km passing a road (r.) leading 4km to the partially restored *Abbey of Clermont*, founded c. 1150, with a large Cistercian church and other dependencies.

At 7.5km we bear r. for (15km) *Vitré*, here crossing from Maine into the old *Duchy of Brittany*.

A pleasant DETOUR may be made by turning l. after 4km onto the D110 to visit the **Château des Rochers**, restored in the 17th and 18Cs. It was a favourite residence of the Mme de Sévigné (1626–96), who visited it nine times between 1654 and 1690, and dated 267 of her letters from it or Vitré. One may visit the octagonal Chapel, constructed in 1671 by her uncle the Abbé de Coulange, the 'Cabinet Vert', with her portrait by Mignard and other souvenirs, and the garden, laid out by Le Nôtre, with a sundial and a semicircular wall returning a double echo ('un petit rediseur de mots jusque dans l'Oreille'). The large park, with its fancifully named avenues, is not enclosed.—Mlle du Plessis, one of her bêtes noires, lived at *Argentré-du-Plessis*, 3.5km S., now on the far side of the motorway.—Hence we follow the D88 N.W. to Vitré.

VITRÉ (13,500 Vitréens), an ancient and picturesque old town above the Vilaine, preserves several 15-16C houses, parts of its ramparts, and an imposing castle, which dominates the sharp W. angle of its walls.

In the 13C part of the countship of Laval, it was subsequently held by the Montfort, Rieux, Coligny, and La Tremoïlle families. The Colignys turned it into a Huguenot stronghold, and in 1589 it resisted a five months' siege by the Duc de Mercoeur, chief of the Leaguers in Brittany. The States of Brittany assembled here several times in 1655–1706, and piquant details of such meetings are given in a letter of Mme de Sévigné (see above).

The best views of the town and its defences are obtained from the Fougères road, entering Vitré from the N., from the *Tertres Noirs*, a wooded knoll just to the N.W., and from the direction of Rennes.

The *Castle, erected at the end of the 11C, was rebuilt in the 14-15Cs, the best period of Breton military architecture, but has since been 'restored'; the interior may be visited; see below. The old town is best approached by the Rue Beaudrairie (climbing N. from the *Pl. de la Liberté*, near the railway station), containing a number of half-timbered houses with gables and carvings, off which (l.) is the Rue d'Embas, with the curious *Hôtel du Bol d'Or*. The next turning leads to the *Pl. du Château*, and the castle entrance.

Beyond the drawbridge we pass under the gate-tower to enter the triangular ward; to the r. is the Romanesque doorway of the original chapel, and the *Hôtel de Ville* (1913), flanked externally by three towers. The turreted *Tour St-Laurent*, or keep, contains a collection of local antiquities, and an elaborate chimneypiece of 1538. The *Tours de l'Argenterie* and *de la Chapelle* (with a Renaissance oriel), both on the S.W., house collections of furniture and farming implements, etc.

Beyond, the N.E. corner of the Place, is *Notre-Dame, a Flamboyant Gothic building (15-16C) noteworthy for an exuberance of pinnacles, gables, grotesque carvings, its tall spire (a later addition), and exterior pulpit. It preserves some Renaissance glass, and a triptych of 1544 with 52 Limoges enamels.

Steps descend from the N.W. corner of the square to the *Poterne St-Pierre* and exterior *Promenade du Val*, skirting the **Town Walls**, following which one may re-enter the town at the *Pl. de la République*, with an old tower.—The Rue de Paris, with several attractive old houses, leads E. to the cemetery, in which stands the belfry of the former church of St-Martin.

From just W. of the latter Place we may bear l. along the Rue Poterie, flanked by slate-covered and timber houses, often with projecting upper storeys supported on wooden pillars, to reach the Rue Garangeot, there turning downhill to regain the Pl. de la Liberté.

Continuing W., at 7.5km the road passes 4km S. of *Champeaux*, where the plain Gothic church contains Renaissance glass, curiously carved stalls of 1530, and a handsome tomb embellished with the naked statues of Guy d'Épinay and his wife (c. 1553; 1567); in the adjoining chapel is the tomb of their daughter Claude (d. 1554).

At 9.5km we regain the N157.

Châteaugiron, with a number of old houses, and the imposing ruins of its castle, where in 1472 a treaty of alliance was signed between François II of Brittany and Edward IV, lies 9km S.W.

16km. **Rennes** (see Rte 39), on the approach to which (r.) the new University buildings are passed.

IV Brittany

Brittany (Fr. *Bretagne*), the ancient duchy consisting of the granitic W. peninsula of France, whose name is still generally used to designate the region, comprises *Haute Bretagne*, and the sea-girt Celtic fastness of *Basse Bretagne*, with its striking coastal scenery, where the Breton tongue still partially persists. The interior, with its undulating gorse-covered heaths, retains a few scattered remnants of the primeval Armorican forest, inextricably pervaded by the legends of Merlin and King Arthur. To the S.W., near Carnac, are grouped the more important rude stone monuments for which Brittany is famous. Here, in the far W., may be seen survivals of Breton costume and coifs, relics of its superstition and piety, and its characteristic ossuaries and calvaries; see below.

Little is known of the race, perhaps of Ligurian stock, responsible for the erection of the megaliths, but more light is thrown on the peninsula with the coming of the Celts (c. 6C B.C.), and it became known as *Armorica* (armor, near the sea). It was inhabited by various tribes, among them the Namneti (around the mouth of the Loire), the Redones (in the Vilaine Valley), the Curiosoliti (near the valley of the Rance), the Osismi (on the Atlantic coast), and the Veneti (on the gulf of Morbihan); the latter were virtually exterminated by Julius Caesar, who considered them serious rivals to Roman trade with Britain and the Mediterranean. Although it prospered under the Romans, Armorica was eventually ruined by the demands of Imperial taxation, and on their withdrawal it was left to the mercy of raiding pirates. The first British settlers, fugitives from the Picts and Scots, landed on the Breton coast c. 460, and later emigrants, including bands fleeing from the Saxons and Angles, continued to arrive during the following two centuries, and Bretagne, as it became known, with its half-Christianised groups of colonies with their British princes, institutions, and speech, became a rallying-ground of Celtic sentiment only yielding grudging allegiance to the Frankish kings.

Their first successful revolt, against Charles le Chauve, took place in 843 under Nominoë, who was crowned king of the Bretons at Dol. But, largely due to the Norman invasions, this kingdom broke up on the death of his nephew Salomon (d. 874), although later united by Count Alain of Vannes and his godson Alain Barbe-Torte ('Wrybeard'), who expelled the Normans in 938. Few other rulers of the region emerge from the swirling mists of Breton legend, who contented themselves with the titles of dukes of Brittany and a nominal sway over the feudal countships of Léon, Cornouaille, Penthièvre, Rennes, etc., from which in their turn the baronies of Fougères, Vitré, and the eastern frontier held their fiefs.

After the accession of William the Conqueror as king of England, Brittany was forced gradually into the position of a subordinate state between France and England, bargaining with each in turn, only to be used as a battleground for both. Duc Conan III was defeated by his rebellious nobles in 1148, while Conon IV (le Petit) sought the aid of Henry II, in whose favour he abdicated in 1166. Arthur of Brittany, who was probably murdered by John at Rouen in 1203, was the son of Constance (Conan's daughter) and Geoffrey VI Plantagenet, Henry's third son. His half-sister was married to Pierre de Dreux, who became the first of a new line of dukes under French protection.

The death of Duc Jean III in 1341 precipitated a fierce War of the Succession, in which Jean de Montfort (d. 1345) and his wife Jeanne of Flanders ('Jeanne la Flamme') claimed for fief of Brittany against Jeanne, wife of Charles de Blois and Duc Jean III's official heir. The struggle developed into a trial of strength between Edward III (who took the part of de Montfort) and Philippe VI (of France; uncle of Charles), and most of the towns in the region were sacked. Among those who served in the ranks of Charles was the redoubtable Bertrand de Guesclin (c. 1320–80), who was taken prisoner at the decisive Battle of Auray (1364), when his master fell.

The younger Jean de Montfort now became Duc Jean IV, but his claim was opposed by Olivier de Clisson (1336–1407), who had at first served the English, but who went over to Charles V in 1370. Feuding continued sporadically, and the Constable de Richemont (1393–1458) later became Arthur III of Brittany, while Duc François I (1442–51) is remembered for having handed over his brother Gilles de Bretagne—on a charge of favouring the English—to a mortal enemy, who obligingly starved him to death in 1450.

During the reign of Duc François II (d. 1488), young Henry Richmond (later Henry VII of England) and his uncle Jasper Tudor, Earl of Pembroke, sought refuge in Brittany after the Battle of Tewkesbury (1474), and were there detained as prisoners for fourteen years. The heiress of François II was Anne of Brittany (1477–1514), 'la petite Brette', who was married to two French kings in succession—Charles VIII and Louis XII—becoming queen of France, but also remaining duchess of Brittany. Her eldest daughter, Claude, was invested with the duchy, and brought it in dowry to her husband, afterwards François I of France. The province was united to France in the person of their son, Henri II, in 1547, although the formal union had taken place in 1532, on the death of Claude. The Breton people retained their own 'parlement' until the Revolution, at all times jealously claiming the fulfilment of the marriage contract by which Louis XII pledged himself and his heirs to respect 'the liberties, franchises, usages, and customs' of the duchy, and the risings against infringements were numerous; the nobles, under Mercoeur, even calling in the Spaniards to aid them during the wars of the Ligue, while the imposition of the 'gabelle' or salt tax under Louis XIV incited the insurrection of the 'Bonnets Rouges', the cruel suppression of which brought some comments of ironical pity for the 'poor Bretons' from Mme de Sévigné.

During the Revolutionary period, the grandsons of the same priest-ridden peasantry lay ambushed behind their oaktrees in defence of their faith, thus prolonging until the early days of the Consulate the wars of the Vendée and the 'Chouannerie'. It was on the Breton coast at Quiberon that the ill-conceived counter-revolutionary expedition of 1795 was landed under the protection of a British fleet. The political fusion of Brittany with France was only completed in the 19C, but the province still remains a stronghold of parochialism and catholic fervour with which Ireland, with its kindred climate and racial origins, offers perhaps the closest parallel, remaining inflexible in its opposition to the secularising tendencies of the State; in recent years there has been a quaint revival of 'regionalism', and even bids for 'independence' by the more stiff-necked.

During the Second World War guerrilla bands harrassed the occupying German garrisons, whose naval bases at Brest, Lorient, and St-Nazaire were strongly fortified and provided with vast concrete submarine-shelters, which made them the essential target of heavy Allied air attacks, in which they suffered severely. On 1 Aug. 1944 Gen. Patton's 3rd U.S. Army, breaking through the German line at Avranches, had within a fortnight liberated almost the whole peninsula, much of it by then under the virtual control of the 'Forces Française de l'Intérieur'. Brest itself was not taken until 18 Sept., and the garrisons in the 'pockets' of Lorient, Quiberon, and St-Nazaire did not surrender until the following May.

The Breton dialects, all founded upon the Celtic, are many, and have inspired a rich popular literature. Many place-names resemble those in Wales or Cornwall; among the more common prefixes are *Lann* or *Lan* (llan), 'church-place', confirming the grant of land to a church-builder; *Plou* or *Ple*, 'the parish', indicating the settlement of an immigrant clan; and *Tre*, 'the homestead', about which a hamlet grew; while *Loc* is an abbreviation of 'locus penitentiae', a hermitage; and *Pen*, as in Welsh, signifies 'a head'. The uniformity of civilisation has caused the once colourful costume to be only displayed on occasional festivals, buttressed by the cult of 'folklore', although the provincial coifs of the women, with their curious local differences in design, are more frequently seen, particularly on Sundays. No longer are the peasants dressed in reversed goatskins, which once gave them such a savage appearance, and reminded earlier travellers of Robinson Crusoe. Most of the better examples of the 'lits-clos', or closed bedsteads, have found their way from farmhouses to museums or private collections, and the ancient 'biniou' or bagpipe, with its melancholy drone—often depicted in stained-glass windows or woodcarvings—is less frequently heard than of yore, although it has its champions.

Much credulity and superstitution remains, especially in relation to the megalithic monuments, of which Brittany possesses the greatest wealth in Europe, particularly in the form of a single upright stone or 'menhir', of which there are some thousands extant, some rudely carved, and some with the addition of Christian symbols. They are occasionally seen in a row or in parallel alignments, as at Carnac. The 'cromlech' are menhirs arranged in the form of a circle, sometimes found at the end of an alignment. The 'dolmen' is formed by one or more flat stones laid horizontally on the tops of upright stones, the whole composing a roughly roofed (and wholly or partly enclosed) chamber, usually sepulchral, and it is likely that dolmens as we see them represent chambered tumuli stripped of their earthen covering by erosion. The *'allée couverte'*, or covered way, is a variant of the dolmen or an approach to it. The *'tumulus'*, or barrow, was used for burial long after the period when the menhirs were set up. The *'lech'*, often seen in Breton churchyards, is merely a small menhir regularly cut. The stone is sometimes of portable dimensions, and inscriptions are frequent, while a variety of 'rocking-stones' and 'ringing-stones', some of them artificially placed, also exist. Other relics of the imperfect assimilation of pagan superstition with Christian rites are the ubiquitous ossuaries and calvaries, characteristic of Breton churchyards.

The *Ossuaries* or *'reliquaires'* are bone or charnel-houses intended for the preservation of those exhumed from cemeteries to make way for later arrivals, and may be seen attached to the church or in the form of a detached building in the adjacent cemetery, and extant examples date from the late 15C to 1773. Mostly dating from the 16th and 17Cs are the equally ubiquitous stone *Calvaries*, to be seen not only in cemeteries and near churches, but at numerous crossroads, etc. Many are merely single crosses, but may include subsidiary statuettes; others are more elaborate groups on elevated platforms. Among the more remarkable are those at Plougastel-Daoulas, Guimiliau, Pleyben, Plougonven, and St-Thégonnec. Analogous are the *'Pardons'*, annually celebrated at numerous churches, chapels, and shrines, particularly in the department of Finistère, which are purported to be religious ceremonies or processions, but they have been much corrupted and commercialised, even if they continue to attract flocks of pious pilgrims eager to pay their devotions and present their offerings to the saint in question, of which there are legion (even if not recognised by Rome). The 'Seven Saints of Brittany' are Malo, Samson, Briocus, Tugdual, Paul Aurelian, Corentin, and Paternus (Padarn), representing the dioceses of St-Malo, Dol, St-Brieuc, Tréguier, St-Pol-de-Léon, Quimper, and Vannes, respectively. But as almost every British or Irish immigrant who founded a church was locally canonised, the list of Breton saints is as endless as their legends are ingenuous.

39 St-Malo to Rennes and Nantes

191km (118 miles). N137. 69km **Rennes**—D163. 55km **Châteaubriant**—D178. 67km **Nantes**.

Maps: IGN 16, 24, or 105. M 230.

ST-MALO (47,300 Malouïns; also the French equivalent for Falkland-islanders, this figure also including the contiguous resorts of *Paramé* and *St-Servan*), a Channel-port and holiday resort occupying a granite promontory at the mouth of the Rance opposite Dinard, is still an important base for the Atlantic cod-fishery. The old walled town, once a strong fortress on this rock-bound coast, has since 1944 been largely rebuilt in an innocuous style approximating to the original, for it was three parts destroyed.

In the 6C the islet was a retreat of Abbot Aaron, who gave refuge here to St Maclou or Malo, a Welshman, one of the earliest bishops of Aleth (now St-Servan). It was long a bone of contention between the kings of France, the dukes of Brittany, and the English, and the later depredations of its privateers provoked reprisals from the latter in 1693, 1695, and 1758.

In 1944 the area was fortified by the occupying Germans, who were cut off there by the American advance into Brittany, and refused to surrender when surrounded. The ensuing bombardment, which began on 6 Aug., was followed by uncontrollable fires, and it was reduced to ruins. After a week the civilians were evacuated, and the garrison gave in the following day, although some continued to hold out until 2 Sept. Here, in May 1951 Guy Burgess and Donald Maclean landed on the Continent en route to Moscow.

Among its natives were Jacques Cartier (1491–1557), explorer of the coast of Canada; Porcon de la Barbinais (1636–65), the 'French Regulus', who returned to die at Algiers, whence he had been liberated on parole; Duguay-Trouin (1673–1736), the mariner; Robert Surcouf (1773–1827), the privateer; Mahé de la Bourdonnais (1699–1755), governor of the French East Indies, who captured Madras in 1746; Moreau de Maupertuis (1698–1759), the geometer and philosopher, whose quarrel with Voltaire is celebrated; François-René de Chateaubriand (1768–1848); and Félicité-Robert de Lamennais (1782–1854; 'Monsieur Féli' to his friends), the controversial religious writer.

Launches run regularly to Dinard and Dinan, and many excursions are available during the summer.

Roads converge on the *Esplanade St-Vincent* (with the S.I.), at the W. end of the *Sillon*, a narrow isthmus joining the walled enceinte to the mainland, skirted to the N. by a broad sandy beach. To the N. of the Esplanade rises the **Castle**, a quadrilateral with a triangular annexe called 'La Galère' pointed towards the E.

The *Great Keep*, overlooking the sea and forming part of the earliest town wall, was breached in 1378 by the Duke of Lancaster; the *Little Keep* dates from the 15C. To the W. is a high curtain wall and gate-tower, with its watch-turrets, flanked by the massive *Tour Générale* and *Tour Quiquengrogne*, built by Anne of Brittany, beyond which the *Porte St-Thomas* leads to the Grande Plage. It now houses a *Museum* of local history.

The town is entered through the twin gateways of the *Porte St-Vincent*, one a modern reproduction of the early 18C original; over the l. gate are the arms of St-Malo; over the r., the ermine of Brittany. The adjacent *Pl. Chateaubriand* is the main focus of animation.—Hence the Rue St-Vincent leads into the centre of the enclosed town, passing the former cathedral of **St-Vincent**, the S. transept of which was damaged beyond repair in 1944. It has a Renaissance W. front, with 18C additions, and a 15C central tower.

The massive pillars of the 12C nave support early Gothic vaulting; the graceful square ended choir of c. 1310 is surmounted by a beautiful triforium with trefoiled arches and flanked by chapels. The aisles, also with their chapels, were rebuilt in the 16C; the stoup has grotesque figures in relief.

To the N.W. is the *Hôtel de Ville* (1953); to the N., the *Chapelle St-Aaron* (1621), said to be on the site of the original anchorite's cell.—Beyond the former are steps ascending to the ramparts and the *Tour Bidouane*: on this side the walls date mainly from the 15-16C.

To the N.E., on its rocky isle, is the *Fort National* (by Vauban; 1689), accessible at low tide, as is the **Île du Grand-Bé**, to the N.W., approached by a causeway leading from the *Porte des Champs-Vauverts*, to the S. On the N. side of the island is the plain granite *Tomb of Chateaubriand*—'solitary in death, as he affected to be in life'; you are warned not to loiter here if the tide is coming in.—Some 3.5km out to sea is the larger *Île de Cézembre*, said to have been a refuge of St Brendan of Ireland between 520–30.

Regaining the ramparts, wind permitting, one may make a *Tour of the Walls; in an anti-clockwise direction, a good view of Dinard on the far side of the estuary is obtained from the projecting *Bastion de Hollande*, while in the distance to the W. is *Cap Fréhel*. Although of medieval foundation, the ramparts were substantially rebuilt in the 17C and later, the restored S. Wall, beyond the *Môle des Noires*, dating from 1708–34. To the S. the harbour mouth is defended by *Fort St-Servan*. At the S.E. corner is a group of 17-18C houses of the 'armateurs' which escaped destruction in 1944; while S. of the *Gare*

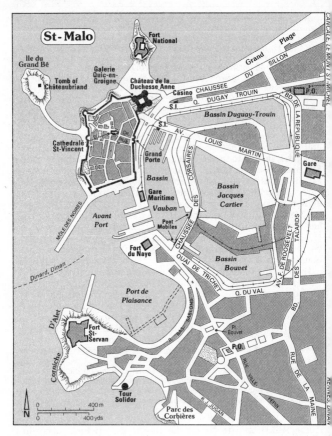

Maritime is the large *Écluse du Naye*, a regulating lock which makes the inner harbour independent of the tide, which here rises to 13-15m above low-water mark, owing to the influx of the ocean tide added to that of the Channel. Turning N. we pass the *Grande-Porte*, facing E., with its castellated Gothic towers, to regain the Porte St-Vincent.

For *St-Servan*, see below. For the coast road from St-Malo to **Morlaix**, see Rte 42.

ST-MALO TO CANCALE AND LE MONT ST-MICHEL (60km). Traversing *Paramé*, which, apart from its sandy beach, is of no interest, one can either take the direct road to (14km) **Cancale**, a pleasantly situated fishing-port, noted for its oysters, or via the coast road, which bears l. past sandy bays and jagged promontories to the *Pointe du Grouin*, with its lighthouse, the W. extremity of the bay of Mont St-Michel.—Hence we skirt the bay, after (10km) *Le Vivier-sur-Mer* (8km N.

of *Dol*; see Rte 36A), crossing the flat *Marais de Dol*, which with its lines of wind-swept osiers, lies well below high-water level. It was probably submerged in the 9C, and reclaimed from the sea in the 12C, although its protective embankments were not completed until the 18C. Its 'pré-salé' lamb is reputed.—22km. *Pontor-son*, 9km S. of *Mont St-Michel*; see Rte 35B.

The road from St-Malo to Rennes first traverses **St-Servan**, on the S. side of the port, the promontory of which was the site of the Gallo-Roman town of *Aleth*, to the S. of which is the triangular *Tour Solidor*, ◊ built by Jean IV of Brittany in 1382, the restored interior housing a *Musée de Cap-Horniers*, or windjammers.

To the r. at 5km is a turning for the **Usine maré-motrice de la Rance* (1966), a hydro-electric station and dam harnessing the strong tidal flow of the estuary, and providing a road-bridge across the Rance.—**Dinard** (see Rte 42) lies 3.5km N. on the far bank.

At 10km the direct road to **Dinan** (see Rte 41), 17km S.W., forks r., beyond which the approach-road to a new bridge over the estuary is crossed and later, the N176, to enter woods, where to the l. beyond *Tressé* is a remarkable 'allée couverte'; to the r. at (4km) *St-Pierre-de-Plesguen* is a château once occupied by Lamennais and his disciples.—5km. The *Château de la Bourbansais* (1583; with later in-terior decoration) is passed (l.) as we approach (15km) *Hedé*, a hilltop village with a ruined castle and over-restored church—At *Les Iffs*, 6km W., the Flamboyant church preserves good 16C glass; at the castle of *Montmuran*, razed by Henry II in 1168, and later rebuilt, Du Guesclin was knighted (1354), and married his first wife, Jeanne de Laval.

22km. **RENNES** (200,400 Rennais; 39,500 in 1851; 98,500 in 1936), the sedate old capital of Brittany, and préfecture of the *Ille-et-Vilaine*, stands at the juncture of the canalised Ille and the Vilaine, the latter dividing the town into two approx. equal halves. Few medieval buildings survived the great fire of 1720, after which the place was rebuilt in reddish granite on a more formal plan designed by Robelin. Still the administrative capital of Brittany, and an impor-tant market for agricultural and dairy produce, its commercial ac-tivities and industrial installations have expanded in recent years. The Faculté des Lettres of its University is preoccupied with Breton culture and the study of Celtic languages. Augustus Hare somewhat unfairly castigated it as 'being the dullest, as it is almost the ugliest, town in France'.

The capital of the *Redones* became the focus of Roman roads, but did not emerge as the capital of Brittany until the late 10C; it was in dispute between Jean de Montfort and Charles de Blois, and in 1356 its siege by Henry of Lancaster was raised by Du Guesclin, who supported Charles. In the earlier cathedral Henry of Richmond swore to marry Elizabeth of York (1483) when he obtained the English crown. Rennes has always been jealous of the privileges of Brittany; and here the revolt of the 'Bonnets Rouge' broke out in 1675 in protest against taxes not authorised by the Breton Parlement, which was transferred to Vannes for 15 years; in 1762 the distinguished lawyer Caradeuc de la Chalotais (1701–85; who was born here) was imprisoned for supporting the Parlement's action in dissolving the Jesuit order in Brittany against the will of Louis XV.

At first hostile to the Revolution, it later became a base for Republican opera-tions against the army of the Vendée, but its mayor, Jean Leperdit, saved it from the excesses of the Terror. In 1846 its population was 39,200. In 1899 Capt. Alfred Dreyfus's sentence of deportation was here commuted to ten years' im-prisonment. In 1940 and again in 1943–44 it was heavily bombed, with con-siderable loss of life. It was liberated by American troops on 4 Aug. 1944. Some Bretons have clamoured for more regional independence during recent decades, but this remains a typically Celtic idealistic aspiration. Few of its natives have risen to great fame: among them were La Motte-Picquet (1720–91), the mariner; and the reactionary Gén. Boulanger (1837–91). Marbode, the Latin poet, was bishop of Rennes (d. 1123).

A short distance E. of the central *Pl. de la République*, bridging the Vilaine (with the S.I.), facing the Quai Émile-Zola, in the former university buildings, are the museums. The important ***Musée de Bretagne** (l. of entrance) comprises an attractively designed series of interlinked rooms, where one may trace the history of the Breton people from the earliest times, the items being well-displayed and described.

Sections are devoted to the Gallo-Roman and medieval periods; ceramics; historiated capitals; etc. Note the tomb-statue of J. Guibe (early 16C), and a granite Virgin and Child from Lesneven. Further rooms display a range of Breton furniture, and prints of the area; the *Galerie 1789–1914* contains Breton costumes, agricultural implements and domestic utensils, and sections on fishing, crafts, and musical instruments; and lastly, Contemporary Brittany, with maps and plans of the region showing its industrial expansion, etc.

Stairs ascend to the ***Musée des Beaux-Arts**.

R1 *Mariotto di Nardò*, Martyrdom of SS Laurence and Blaise; *Leonardo da Vinci*, Two drawings of drapery; *School of Fontainebleau*, A Woman between Youth and Old Age; *Van Heemskerk*, St Luke painting the Virgin; *Pauwels Franken*, Venetian fête; *Louis de Caulery*, Dance at the court of Henri IV; *anon. French*, Dance at the Valois court (c. 1580); *Veronese*, Perseus delivering Andromeda; and *Flemish* portraits.

R2 *Jordaens*, Crucifixion; *Cornelis Gysbrecht*, Still Life; *Van Kessel*, Entry into the Ark; *Lod. Carraci*, Martyrdom of St Peter; *Honthorst*, St Peter's denial; *Georges de la Tour*, *Nativity; *Loubin Baugin*, Plums; *Laurent de la Hyre*, Old Testament scenes; *Frans II Franken*, Meal at the house of Simon; *Philippe de Champaigne*, Penitent Magdalen; *J.-B. Monnoyer*, Flower paintings; *Jan Mijtens*, Marriage of the Elector of Brandenbourg with Louise-Henriette de Nassau, 1646; *Théobald Michau*, Landscapes; *Van Ostade*, Farm scene; *Salomon Konik*, Alchemist cutting his nails; *Frans I van Mieris*, Double portrait; *Wouverman*, Horse-fair; *Lely*, Mlle de la Vallière, with angelic children.

R3 *Chardin*, Still Lifes; three of 18C French trompe-l'oeils; *Robert Tournières*, Louis-Henri de Bourbon; *J.-F. Colson*, Portraits of the Comte, Comtesse, and Marquise de Pire; *Desportes*, Wolfhunt; *Greuze*, Head of a young girl.—**RR4-5** contain 19-20C works, including landscapes by *Boudin*, and *Sisley*; *Gauguin*, Still Life with oranges; *Picasso*, Woman's head (1924). Other rooms are devoted to Breton artists, among which two views of Rennes by *Édouard de Gernon* (1811–78) are noteworthy.

In the gallery surrounding the courtyard is a selection of faience from Rouen, Quimper, La Rochelle, Le Croisic, Nevers, and Strasbourg, etc. A small collection of Greek, Egyptian, Coptic, and Etruscan antiquities is also shown. Note two bronze plaques from an equestrian statue of Louis XIV by *Coysevox*, demolished at the Revolution.

Behind the Musées is *Toussaints*, formerly a Jesuit chapel (1624–57), and the *Lycée* in which the Dreyfus appeal was heard. The caricature original of Alfred Jarry's 'Ubu' was a master here, where Jarry was a pupil.

Regaining the Pl. de la République, one may cross to the *Pl. de la Mairie*, on the E. side of which is the convex facade of the **Théâtre** (1856), complementing the horseshoe-fronted **Hôtel de Ville** (1734–43; by Jacques Gabriel), opposite. The central niche originally held a statue of Louis XV, and later a group symbolising the union of Brittany with France, blown up by 'separatists' in 1932.

A short distance from S.E. is *St-Germain*, Gothic and Renaissance, containing the tomb of the Breton historian Bertrand d'Argentré (d. 1590).

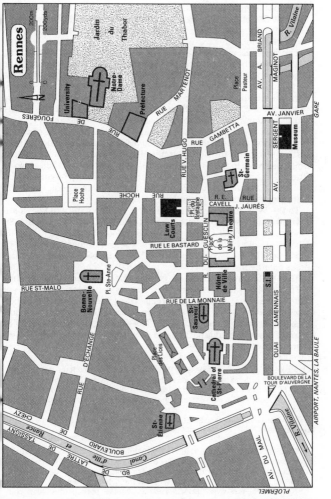

From the N.E. corner of the Place we approach the 18C *Pl. du Palais*, overlooked to the N. by the ***Palais de Justice**, formerly the Parlement-house, begun in 1619 from the designs of Salomon de Brosse, and completed by Cormeau c. 1654.

The corner pavilion are surmounted by leaden allegorical figures (copies of the originals), and its entrance is flanked by statues of worthy members of the local bar. The stair (1726; by Gabriel) ascends to the *Salle des Pas-Perdus*, with a carved and gilt wooden ceiling; the *Grande Chambre du Parlement*, with a ceiling by Pierre Dionis painted by N. Coypel, has painted and gilded boiseries by Pierre Maillé. Intervening chambers also contain woodwork of 1669, paintings by Jouvenet, and decorations by Ferdinand (1709).

Hence the Rue Victor-Hugo runs E. to the Rue Gambetta, where, overlooking gardens, are the arcaded buildings of the former *Abbaye de St-Georges*, founded in 1018 and rebuilt in 1670 by the abbess, Madeleine de la Fayette (whose name appears in iron lettering on the facade).

The street ascends to the *Sq. de la Motte* and the *Préfecture* (1715), beyond which is the former abbey church of *Notre-Dame* or *St-Melaine*, founded in the 11C but poorly rebuilt in the 14C; the base of the tower is Romanesque although masked by a 17C facade. Formerly the bishop's palace, the adjacent buildings are occupied by the *Académie*, behind which are 17C cloisters. To the E. extend the attractive *Jardins du Thabor*, likewise a legacy of the abbey.

The Rue St-Melaine leads W. to the *Pl. Hoche*, to the N. of which the *Library* (preserving illuminated MSS of interest) occupies a former seminary; further W. is unfinished *St-Aubin*. Several ancient houses survive in the adjacent square, including one of 1586 at No. 7 Rue St-Michel, which leads hence to the *Pl. St-Michel*, beyond which is Doric *St-Sauveur* (17-18C), containing an organ-loft from St-Georges; Fauré was organist here in 1866–70.

To the W. is the apse of the cathedral, in the vicinity of which are several characteristic houses, among them Nos 3 and 8 in the Rue St-Guillaume (N.), and further S., the 18C *Hôtel de Blossac* (6 Rue de Chapitre), and *Hôtel de Talhouët* (19 Rue des Dames; birthplace of Adm. de la Motte-Picquet), near which is disused *St-Yves*, which served as a cathedral in 1754–92.

The **Cathedral** itself is a commonplace pseudo-Ionic edifice (1787–1844), which Southey considered ruder than any he had yet seen in France, Dol excepted. It replaced a former church which collapsed, preserving two towers begun in 1541 like the two side portals, but not completed until 1703. The uninviting interior is only of interest for a *Reredos (last chapel of S. aisle), a masterpiece of German 15C woodcarving.

Opposite its W. front is the derelict *Porte Mordelaise*, by which the dukes of Brittany and the bishops of Rennes made their state entry into the town; to the N.W. is the *Pl. des Lices*, in which the *Hôtel du Molan* (No. 34) dates from 1689; further W. is *St-Étienne* (17C), with a tiled dome, once the chapel of an Augustinian convent.

For roads from Rennes to **Brest** via *Pleyben*, and to **Vannes**, see Rtes 44 and 40 respectively.

RENNES TO NANTES VIA THE N137 (107km). Of slight interest, this direct road leads due S. through (32km) *Bain-de-Bretagne*, 14km beyond which we pass (r.) *Le Grande-Fougeray*, with the ruined keep of its 13C castle.

Langon, approached via *Port-du-Roche*, on the Vilaine 9.5km due W., with a 12-15C church, preserves the *Chapelle Ste-Agathe, perhaps the oldest complete building in Brittany (key at the mairie). Of Gallo-Roman origin, it appears to have been a sanctuary of Venus Genitrix prior to its conversion to Christian use, but its dedication to St Agatha (who miraculously recovered after having her breasts cut off) dates only from c. 1700; legend claims that the marsh to the E. engulfed an ancient city.

Continuing S. from Le Grande-Fougeray, at 7km we traverse *Derval*, 2.5km N.E. of which is the ruined keep of *St-Clair* which in the 14C belonged to Sir Robert Knolles.—At 14km *Blain* (see Rte 46) lies 13km S.W.—The N137 continues S. to (40km) **Nantes**; see Rte 59A.

The D163 drives S.E. from Rennes to (55km) **Châteaubriant** (14,400 Castelbriantais), an old town in the valley of the Chère, passing to the r. on approaching from this direction, *St-Jean-de-Bère* (11C), with features of interest.

Châteaubriant takes its name from a stronghold founded in the 11C by Brient, count of Penthièvre, a successor of whom married Jeanne de Beaufort, and from this Châteaubriant-Beaufort family the author Chateaubriand claimed descent. In 1488 La Tremoïlle burnt the town and shattered the castle.

It was replaced by another built by Count Jean de Montgomery-Laval, which was the scene of the alleged murder of Françoise de Foix (1495–1537), his wife and the former mistress of François I. In 1852 the Duc d'Aumale, who inherited the castle in 1830, presented it to the department. The Germans shot 27 political detainees here in Oct. 1941 in reprisal for the death of their commander at Nantes.

The *Castle consists of two parts, the Renaissance *Château-Neuf* (with the *Palais de Justice* and a small *Museum*), and remains of the old, remodelled in the 11-15C, preserving its huge keep approached by a gateway with drum towers. In the inner court are the 12-13C chapel and the *Grand-Logis*, rebuilt (after 1488) and restored since damaged in 1944.

A DETOUR may be made to the E. of Châteaubriand to *Pouancé*, a once-walled town by its lake, with a ruined 13-15C castle, 5.5km S. of which are the relics of the priory of *La Primaudière*, founded in 1207; 10km further S. is the *Château de la Motte-Glain*, built for Pierre de Rohan in 1496–1513, whence one may regain the main route some 18km S.W.

19km. *La Meilleraye* (3km S.E.) preserves the nave of its church, part of a Cistercian monastery founded in 1145, now Trappist, with 18C buildings. The road beyond follows the valley of the Erdre, partly occupied by a series of navigable lakes to approach (37km) **Nantes**; see Rte 61.

40 Rennes to Vannes

106km (66 miles). N24. 60km **Ploërmel**—N166. 46km **Vannes**.

Maps: IGN 16, 15, or 105; also 501, for the Morbihan. M 230.

For **Rennes**, see Rte 39.

At 33.5km *Plélan-le-Grand*, on the S. verge of the *Forêt de Paimpont* (6500 hectares), is crossed.

This, the last relic of the primeval forest of Armorica, is celebrated under the name of *Brocéliande* in chivalric romances, both Welsh and Breton. Hither it was that Merlin withdrew from the court of King Arthur, to be spellbound by the fairy Vivien, 'the lady of the lake', by whom, according to one legend, he was made to vanish into a thornbush. Merlin's Spring (or *Fontaine de Barenton*) lies near its N.W. border.

6km to the N.W. is the village of *Paimpont*, with the church and 17C dependencies of a monastery founded in the 7C, overlooking its lake.—3.5km. *Les Forges de Paimpont*, also with its lake, is by-passed prior to traversing the *Camp de Coëtquidan*, the 'combined training' centre of the French military forces established here after the Second World War, after their buildings at *St-Cyr* had been destroyed. 13km. *Campénéac*, 3km N.E. of which is the moated 15C castle of *Trecesson*, while 6km N. is the romantic *Val-sans-Retour* on the S.W. edge of the forest.

9km. **PLOËRMEL** (7300 Ploërmelais), a town of fallen fortunes, retains several picturesque old houses.

It derives its name from St Armel or Armagillus (died c. 562), a Welsh or Cornish hermit who evangelised the district. The decree of 1240 banishing the Jews from Brittany was published here. Edward III captured the place in 1346 and left as governor Richard Bembro (or Bamburgh), who was killed in the Battle of the Thirty (see below). The French burnt it in 1487, except for the Carmelite monastery outside its walls. Calvinism later gained a footing here, and an attack by the Leaguers was defeated in 1594. It was damaged by bombing in 1944, when the old market-hall was destroyed.—One of Meyerbeer's light operas was named the 'Pardon de Ploërmel' (1869).

The central *Place* is named after the abbé Jean-Marie de Lamennais (a brother of the more controversial figure), who in 1824 founded here the Institut des Frères de l'Instruction Chrétienne, the buildings of which preserve the old steeple of the Ursuline chapel.

To the E. is late Gothic *St-Armel (1511–1602), with a massive square tower, the upper part dating from 1733–41.

On the S. side are gabled chapels with mullioned windows. The N. front has a rich Renaissance doorway with depressed arches, the buttress on the r. being carved with grotesque bas-reliefs, while the gable above is surmounted by a line of chimeras, and the crosses of Christ and the two thieves. To the l., on the re-entrant of the choir and the N. transept, is a gargoyle of a naked female mounted on a dog.

The *interior* is remarkable for its remaining stained glass, including a superb Tree of Jesse in the S. aisle. In the S. transept is the granite tomb of Duc Philippe de Montauban (d. 1415) and his wife, and a marble effigy, perhaps of Jeanne, Viscountess of Léon (died c. 1330), from the Couvent des Carmes, provenance likewise of those of dukes Jean II (d. 1305), and Jean III (d. 1341) on the N. side of the choir.

The apse overlooks the *Pl. d'Armes*, in which stands a statue of Dr Guérin (1816–95), a pioneer of surgical dressing.

Among old houses are the *Maison Bigarré* in the Rue des Francs-Bourgeois (N. of the church), where James II is traditionally said to have spent Christmas in 1690; and in the neighbouring Rue Beaumanoir, facing each other, the Renaissance *Maison des Marmousets*, and the medieval *Hôtel des Ducs de Bretagne.*—In the Rue du Val, leading N. from the Pl. Lamennais, the Gendamerie occupies the *Couvent des Carmes*, founded 1273; adm. on application.

PLOËRMEL TO HENNEBONT (75km). The N24 leads W., at 9km passing the *Pyramide de Mi-Voie*, a granite obelisk (1823) commemorating the 'Battle of the Thirty', in which in 1351 Jean de Beaumanoir, captain of the castle of Josselin, with thirty Breton noblemen, defeated a like number of English, Flemish, and Breton knights commanded by Richard Bembro; the names of the victors are inscribed, but that of Beaumanoir is given as Robert by an error borrowed from Froissart, who omitted to mention the combat at all in his earlier editions.—3km. **Josselin**, an attractive old village overlooking the Oust, spanned by a bridge which commands a good view of the castle rising from the rock. It was the seat of the countship of Porhoët, which in the 13C was held by the Lusignan family until purchased by Olivier de Clisson (1336–1407) in 1370, whose *Tomb*, with that of his wife, Marguerite de Rohan, is in *N.-D. du Roncier*. The *Castle*, one of the finest structures of its kind in Brittany, preserves only four round towers and the curtain wall (on older foundations) dating from Clisson's reconstruction; the keep and remaining towers were dismantled in 1629 by Richelieu's order when occupied by Henri de Rohan, a Huguenot. The inner facade is a masterpiece of Flamboyant sculpture in the obdurate granite, with its gargoyles and rows of dormer windows linked by a delicate parapet in the tracery of which the Rohan motto is reiterated. Dating from c. 1510, it replaced the quarters demolished by Duc François in 1488 as a punishment for Jean de Rohan's adherence to the cause of France. The interior contains a few good family portraits and other pictures, and a sumptuous 16C chimneypiece, and may be visited when adm. is permitted: see p 69.—*Pontivy*, see Rte 44, lies 34km N.W.

6.5km. **Guéhenno**, 5km S., has a *Calvary* of 1550 with a particularly good

The inner facade of the château of Josselin

series of sculptures depicting the Passion, including two soldiers who appear to be guarding the adjoining ossuary.—*St-Jean-Brévelay*, 8.5km beyond, is named after St John of Beverley (Abp of York; d. 721), whose relics were brought here by Saxon refugees.—The village of *Colpo* (8km further S.W., on the direct road from Locminé to Vannes) was built by Princess Elisa Bacciochi (d. 1869), who was exiled to her château there by her cousin Napoleon III.

17.5km. **Locminé**, which owes its name (Locmenec'h, 'the cell of the monks') to a monastery founded in the 7C by St Columbanus, invoked on behalf of imbeciles and madmen, who in hope of a cure used to be chained up in the crypts of the 16C *Chapel* dedicated to him; the parish church is of the same date; a house in the adjacent square preserves ancient effigies.

16km. *Baud.*—1km beyond, to the l. of the road, is the so-called *Vénus de Quinipily*, a semi-naked statue over 2m high, resembling a figure of Isis, standing on a pedestal above a granite trough. The original idol, known as 'Groac'h er Couard' (the witch of La Couarde), was dug up on the Montagne de Castennec (see below), where St Gildas may have buried it as being a heathen image. During the Middle Ages it was worshipped with more or less pagan rites by peasant women wanting an easy childbirth and by girls seeking husbands, etc., and was several times overthrown and finally destroyed by the ecclesiastical authorities as detracting from the devotion of their own images. The present figure, a somewhat modified version, was rudely sculpted for Pierre de Lannion, lord of the manor, and set up here in the 18C.

11km N. of Baud, a turning l. off the Pontivy road leads shortly to the Flamboyant chapel of *St-Nicodème*, 2km W. of which is the chapel of *St-Nicolas-des-Eaux* (1524), on the Blavet; 2km beyond which is the *Grotto of St-Gildas*, at the foot of the *Montagne de Castennec*, occupied as an oratory by that saint and St Bieuzy (Budoc), who summoned the faithful by means of a ringing-stone now in the church of *Bieuzy*, 2km further W.—3km beyond, at *Melrand*, is a striking *Calvary*.

Hennebont (see Rte 46) lies 23km S.W. of Baud.

Turning S.W. from Ploërmel, we pass (r.) at 7km the *Château de Crévy*, its enceinte partly 13C, overlooking the Oust and just beyond, a road leading 16km S.E. to *Malestroit*, an ancient fortress preserving several Gothic and Renaissance houses, and a double-naved 12-15C church. The road soon traverses the desolate *Landes de Lanvaux*, over which are scattered fallen menhirs, among other megalithic monuments, after 12km passing (r.) the ruins of the château of *Rohéan*, and then that of *Brignac*, with a 15C tower, to enter (10km) *Elven*.

The manor of *Kerlo*, 3km W., was the property of the family of Descartes, who once resided there.—Continuing S.W. we pass (r.) the ruins of the château of *Largoët*, called *Les Tours d'Elven*, with a 15C round tower and 14C keep 40m high, where in 1474–76 Henry of Richmond (later Henry VII) and his uncle the Earl of Pembroke were confined by the Marshal des Rieux (cf. *Suscinio*).

16.5km **VANNES** (45,400 Vannetais), *Gwened* in Breton, préfec-ture of the *Morbihan*, preserves a number of attractive houses in the old quarter near the cathedral, and is a good centre for excursions in the area; see below.

Vannes was originally the capital of the *Veneti*, a maritime tribe that headed the Armorican league against Caesar, which was compelled to surrender after the naval victory in 56 B.C. of Decius Brutus (later Caesar's assassin). St Paternus was its first bishop (446). Canao, one of the counts of British origin who ruled here, gave asylum to Cramme, the fugitive son of Lothair I, but was defeated and killed by the Frankish king in 559, and Cramme and his family were captured and burned (at Le Guildo; see Rte 42). In the 9C it was the capital of the short-lived kingdom of Brittany.

In 1342 it was four times besieged. Duc Jean IV (de Montfort) built the castle of L'Hermine and made it his habitual residence, where he held to ransom his enemy Olivier de Clisson. Jean V invited the fanatic Spanish Dominican St Vicente Ferrer to Vannes, who died here in 1419. In the years 1487–91 it changed hands several times, in the struggle to retain independence, but in 1532 the union of Brittany with France was proclaimed here before the States assembled in the presence of François I.

Mme de Sévigné stayed in the bishop's palace (since demolished) in 1689. In 1759, during the Seven Years' War, a force was concentrated here for a pro-jected descent on England, neutralised by Hawke's naval victory off Quiberon. The neighbouring parishes took the Royalist part during the Revolution, and it was partially as an example that the principal prisoners taken at Quiberon were executed at Vannes in July 1795 by Parisian volunteers, after local regiments had refused to carry out the sentence.

Aramis, in Dumas *père's* 'Le Vicomte de Bragelonne', was Bp of Vannes, but few of her more historical natives have been notable.

From the *Pl. Maurice-Marchais*, to the N.W. of the walled centre, with the 19C *Hôtel de Ville* and a 17C chapel, the Rue Émile-Burgault leads E. to the quaint *Pl. Henri-IV*, enclosed by old gabled houses. Here rises the 13C **Cathedral**, rebuilt on the site of a church burnt by the Normans; it was later remodelled in the Flamboyant style, notably the N. portal, and drastically 'restored' in the 18C. The W. front dates from 1873, and is of little merit.

The nave has lost much of its character, but retains a good 17C organ-case. Among tombs in the aisle-chapels are those of Bp de Bertin (d. 1774), by Fossati, and in the 2nd chapel in the N. aisle lie the bones of the émigrés shot in 1795; the N. transept contains the tomb of Vicente Ferrer (1347–1419; canonised 1455). The *Choir* preserves a high altar and two statues of apostles by Fossati, and a 17C lectern; the Lady Chapel (1546) the tombs of Bps de Rosmadec (d. 1646), and d'Argouges (d. 1716), a friend of Mme de Sévigné.

The Rue des Chanoines, with the archdeaconry (No. 24), occupied by Queen Henrietta Maria in 1644, leads past the N. facade (with re-

mains of a Renaissance cloister, and a circular chapel of 1537); the
parallel Rue St-Guenhaël descends past the S. front, and they converge before reaching the early 15C *Porte-Prison*, a fragment of the
old fortifications, flanked by machicolated towers.—Further N.E. is
St-Patern, rebuilt 1727–1825, with a striking pulpit.

Passing through the gate one may turn r. to get a view of the remaining 14-17C **Walls**, well-preserved, and making a delightful picture when seen from the umbrageous *Promenade de la Garenne*, S. of
the gardens of the *Préfecture*. It was on this promenade that 22 of the
prominent émigrés captured at Quiberon, including Sombreuil and
Bp Hercé of Dol, were shot.

Opposite the far end of this esplanade is the *Porte-Poterne* (1680),
adjacent to a quaint timbered wash-house, beyond which is the *Pl.
Gambetta* and the shallow tidal harbour, where the Morbihan launches start (for details of excursions, enquire here or at the S.I., 29 Rue
Thiers).

The W. quay is formed by the *Promenade de la Rabine*, opposite
which is the former bishop's palace (from 1629). There is a
Renaissance house at 2 Rue du Port, leading N.W. hence to the Rue
Thiers, which skirts the W. side of the old town.—Passing through

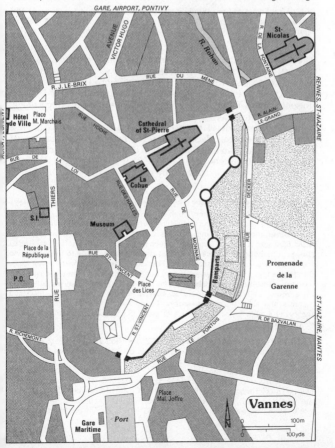

the *Porte-St-Vincent*, a classical gateway of 1704, the Rue St-Vincent, in which Hoche had his headquarters in 1795, ascends past the triangular *Pl. des Lices*, with a market and a turreted 17C house. At its apex (l.) opposite some modern buildings, is an overhanging house with two grotesque figures known as 'Vannes and his wife'. In the adjacent Rue de Noé is the *Château Gaillard*, where the Parlement of Rennes met from 1456 to 1532, now occupied by the ***Musée Archéologique**.

The Salle des Etats contains prehistoric weapons and utensils from Carnac and Locmariaquer, and a remarkable collection of ornaments in turquoise-matrix; here also is a fine Aubusson tapestry of 1671. An adjoining room displays English alabaster reliefs (15C), a 14C (?) ivory goblet, and 16C embroidered dalmatics, etc.; the Cabinet des Pères du Désert, on the floor above, has painted panelling of c. 1640.

Turning r. at the end of this lane the *Pl. de la République* is reached, while in the Rue Thiers, to the l. on ascending, is the *Hotel de Limur (from which the *Musée*—with paintings by Delacroix, Vigée-Lebrun, and Van Loo—is in the process of moving), beyond which is the Pl. Maurice-Marchais is regained.

In *N.-D. du Loc* at *St-Avé*, 4km N.E., with an old Calvary, are a group of 15C English alabasters, and a Crucifixion of 1550 with carved and painted figures.—The D199 leads 5km S. to *Séné*, home of the amphibious 'Sinagots', the boatmen of the gulf.

The **Gulf of Morbihan** ('the little sea' in Breton) is a broad expanse of tidal water with deep tributary creeks and numerous shoals and islets opening onto the Atlantic by a strait no more than 1.5km wide. Strong currents impede the passage of sailing-craft, and at low tide noisome mudbanks are exposed; but at high water the effects of colour and light are impressive.

The Morbihan is of relatively recent formation, for encroachments of the sea have taken place within recorded history and submerged megaliths have been found in addition to the numerous monuments remaining on the islets.

The following two excursions by road cover the areas of most interest.

VANNES TO LARMOR-BADEN (15km). The D101 leads S.W., continued by the D316 direct to (14.5km) *Larmor-Baden*, off which several minor roads lead to the shore, at the *Pointe d'Arradon* (views); to *Port-Blanc*, the nearest point to the **Ile aux Moines**, the largest island, at the S. end of which is an irregular stone circular, 85m across, and the largest cromlech in France; to the E. is the *Île d'Arz*, its church containing four fantastic Romanesque capitals, while to the S. are two menhirs and a ruined passage grave. **Larmor-Baden** itself, with oyster-beds, stands on a promontory between the gulf and the Rivière d'Auray opposite *Locmariaquer* (see Rte 47). Offshore is the islet of *Gavr'Inis* (goat island), with a remarkable late-Neolithic *Tumulus, approached by a gallery with inscribed menhirs and slabs (torch necessary). To the W. is the *Île Longue*, with a somewhat similar barrow; while on *Er Lanic* (S.) is a double cromlech, partly submerged.

VANNES TO PORT-NAVALO, VIA SARZEAU (34km one way). Fork r. 6km E. of Vannes onto the D780, which skirts the E. bank of the gulf past (14km) the 18C *Château de Kerlévenan* to *Sarzeau*, 3km beyond, with a conspicuous church-tower of 1626 and several 17-18C houses, in one of which, on the Suscinio road, was born Alain-René Le Sage (1668–1747), author of 'Gil Blas'.—The picturesque ruins of the 13-14C ***Castle of Suscinio**, 3.5km S.E., was the birthplace of the Constable de Richemont (Arthur III of Brittany; 1393–1458); between the years 1471–83 it was the intermittent enforced

residence of Henry of Richmond (cf. *Elven*). There remain the inner walls flanked by five machicolated drum towers and a square tower on the side nearest the
sea.—**St-Gildas-de-Rhuys**, 6.5km S.W. of Sarzeau, gives its name to the peninsula
or 'Presqu' Île', which separates the gulf of Morbihan from the open sea. Here
stood the Benedictine abbey founded by Gildas (the earliest if not the most accurate of British historians), who came here, probably from Glastonbury, and
died in 570. St Felix rebuilt the abbey after its devastation by Normans, and one
of its later abbots was Abélard, against whose strict rule the disorderly monks
rebelled in 1138. The church, the nave and tower of which were rebuilt in the
17C, preserves its Romanesque choir and transepts, with 11th and 12C apsidal
chapels bearing curious external reliefs. Within, the capitals (including several
now used as stoups) are remarkable. In the N. transept are the tombs of sundry
saints, including that of Gildas, behind the altar.

Some 10km to the N.W., beyond the *Butte de Tumiac* (with a partially restored
late-Neolithic tumulus), from the summit of which Caesar is supposed to have
watched the defeat of the Veneti (cf. Vannes), and which certainly commands a
wide view, lies the harbour of *Port-Navalo*. On the opposite side of the strait is
Locmariaquer; see Rte 47.

Those not returning to Vannes may fork l. just beyond *Kerlévenan* to reach
the N165 19km E.; see Rte 46.

41 Dinan to Morlaix via St-Brieuc and Guingamp

140km (87 miles). N176. 37km **Lamballe**—N12. 19km **St-Brieuc**
—32km **Guingamp**—52km **Morlaix**.

Maps: IGN 16, 14, or 105. M 230.

DINAN (14,200 Dinannais), the old town of which retains an almost
entire circuit of walls, lies above the head of the Rance estuary in attractive hilly country, and preserves a number of picturesque old
houses and streets, making it a favourite centre for excursions into
surrounding areas of Brittany; indeed Southey 'had seen no town
more beautifully situated'.

Fortified by the dukes of Brittany, it was attacked by the English in 1344 and
1364, on the first occasion being burnt, on the second its fate was determined by
the result of a duel between two champions, in which Du Guesclin vanquished
Sir Thomas of Cantorbéry, and the English army withdrew. In 1598 it was occupied by Henri IV; and between 1643 and 1717 the States of Brittany met eight
times at Dinan. During the War of American Independence an Irish regiment in
the French service was quartered there, while Baedeker remarked at the turn of
this century that it had a large English colony (of about 350). Among its natives
were the diarist Charles Pinot Duclos (1704–72); Auguste Pavie (1847–1925),
the explorer of Indo-China; and the Breton bard Théodore Botrel (1868–1925).

Launches ply from the Vieux-Pont (below the viaduct) to St-Malo in summer:
for details apply to the S.I., 6 Rue de l'Horloge.

The focus of traffic is the *Pl. Duclos*, near the N.W. corner of the enceinte, flanked by the *Hôtel de Ville*, S. of which the Promenade des
Petits-Fossés skirts the W. side of the *TownWalls (13C and later), retaining 15 of their towers and gates, the circuit of which is recommended.—From the Place the Grande Rue passes (l.) *St-Malo*, with a
choir and transepts of 1490, a Renaissance S. portal and a mid 19C
nave, to reach the *Pl. des Cordeliers*, in which are several old houses.
To the l. is the 15C gateway to the former *Couvent des Cordeliers*,
preserving its cloisters. Hence the Rue de la Lainerie is continued by
the largely 16C *Rue du Jerzual*, which descends steeply to the 14C
Porte du Jerzual.

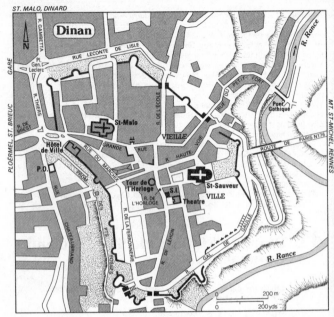

The energetic should climb down the quaint Rue du Petit-Fort to the *Pont-Vieux* (only one arch of which is old) to the quay below the granite *Viaduct de Lanvallay* spanning the Rance. From its foot the town may be regained by flights of steps and a winding path ascending to the *Jardin Anglais*, a terrace on the E. side of the ramparts offering plunging views.

A short distance down the Rue du Jerzual, a r.-hand turning leads to **St-Sauveur**, a Romanesque and Gothic edifice with a mutilated 12C W. portal surmounted by a 15C gable pierced by a Flamboyant window. The tower of 1557 has a wood and slate belfry added in 1779. The 12C capitals and the arcading of the S. wall are notable, as is the 15C window in the N. aisle. A 12C stoup supported by four headless figures contains a carved fish; the heart of Du Guesclin (d. 1380) is preserved in the N. transept. Note the keystones in the E. chapel, and the piscinas in the ambulatory chapels.

To the N.W. is the *Pl. de l'Apport*, preserving characteristic old houses, whence one may follow a street S. past the 15C *Tour de l'Horloge* (with the S.I. opposite) to approach the *Porte St-Louis* (1620), W. of which is the **Castle* (1382–87), comprising the huge oval keep and massive round *Tour de Coëtquen*; it now contains local historical collections.

Hence the Rue du Château leads N. to the *Pl. du Guesclin*, beyond which is the *Champs-Clos*, to regain, via the wide Rue du Marchix, the Pl. Duclos.

A recommended EXCURSION (by foot or car) is that to the charmingly situated village of **Lebon**, in the valley of the Rance c. 2km S. of the Porte St-Louis. It preserves an old bridge, a ruined 13C castle, and ruins of a priory, the restored church of which contains 15C stalls with painted panels, curious stoups, and Beaumanoir tombs; the 14C refectory and 17C cloisters may be visited also.

Rennes (see Rte 39) lies 52km S.E. of Dinan, approached by the D2 and D27, via (21km) the high-lying village of *Bécherel*, W. of which is the 17C *Château de Caradeuc* with its park, once owned by La Chalotais, 5km beyond which (l.) lies *Les Iffs*; see also Rte 39.

The D766 leads due N. to (18km) *Dinard* (see Rte 42) passing (l.) shortly after quitting Dinan the 15C *Château de la Coninnais*, with a feudal keep, and the pic-turesque ruins of the *Château de la Garaye* (16C).

DINAN TO PLOËRMEL (68km). The D766 leads S.W. to (21.5km) *Caulnes*, just W. of the *Château of Couëlan* (1672; enlarged 1777), 2.5km beyond which we cross the N12, and 10km further S., *St Méen*; see Rte 44.—14km. *Mauron*, the scene of a battle in 1352 won by the Bretons and English followers of the Countess de Montfort over the French allies of Charles de Blois, beyond which the road skirts the W. edge of the *Forêt de Paimpont* (see Rte 40) to (20km) *Ploërmel*.

DINAN TO LAMBALLE VIA PLANCOËT (43km). Just W. of Dinan the D794 forks r., at 8km passing (l.) an octagonal tower, perhaps the most notable Roman ruin in Brittany, which may represent the 'Fanum Martis' of the Theodosian Table. Vestiges found near *Corseul*, 2.5km beyond, suggest that it occupies the site of the capital of the Curiosolites, an Armorican tribe. To the r. of the church choir is immured a Roman cippus dedicated to Silicia by her son Januarius, whom she (emulating Monica, the mother of St Augustine) had followed from Egypt.—To the W. are the ruins of the 12C *Château de Montafilan*.—6.5km. *Plancoët*, picturesquely sited on the tidal Aguenon, where in a house on the r. bank Chateaubriand used to spend holidays with his grandmother. While the main road continues hence to (26km) *Lamballe*, a more interesting alternative is the D28, leading S.W. through the *Forêt de la Hunaudaye*, beyond (8.5km) *Pléven* passing (l.) the massive ruins of the pentagonal moated *Castle of La Hunaudaye* (1378, with Renaissance additions).

The N176 drives W. across the *Landes de Plélan* to cross the lake of the Aguenon at 22km, beyond which we bear N.W. to (15km) **Lam-balle** (10,100 Lamballais), an old town sited on a hillside above the r. bank of the Gouëssan.

It was the capital of the counts of Penthièvre from 1134 to 1420; here in 1591 the Calvinist leader François de la Nouë was mortally wounded. Marie Antoinette's friend, Louise de Savoie, executed in Paris during the September massacres of 1792, was the wife of the Prince de Lamballe, only son of the Duc de Bourbon-Penthièvre. Young passed that way in 1788 and remarked that 'above fifty families of noblesse' lived there in winter, and that there was 'probably as much foppery and nonsense in their circles, and for what I know as much happiness, as in those of Paris. Both would be better employed in cultivating their lands and rendering the poor industrious'.

W. of the central *Pl. du Martrai* is Flamboyant *St-Jean*, with a recess-ed W. portal with unusual capitals and an attractive octagonal tower added in the 17C.—The Rue Notre-Dame ascends steeply N.E. past the *Maison du Sénéchal de Penthièvre* to ***Notre-Dame**, restored in the mid 19C, with a rectangular choir rebuilt in 1371 by Charles de Blois, and aisles added in the 15C. The square central tower dates from 1595.

The W. portal, with grotesque capitals, and the double N. portal, beneath a deep-ly recessed round arch, date from the late 12C, while the impressive nave with its massive pillars with foliated capitals, and wooden roof, is 13C. The double triforium on the N. side of the choir and the balustrading on both sides will be noted, and likewise the carved and painted **Screen* from a 16C rood-loft, and the organ-loft above.

A promenade to the N. occupies the site of the castle, dismantled by Richelieu in 1624.—The Rue du Dr Calmette leads N. from the main square, continued by the Rue St-Martin past a stud-farm to the much-restored church of *St-Martin*, with a dark nave of 1084, belfry of 1555, and a grotesquely-carved cross-beam in its 16C S. porch.

LAMBALLE TO ROSTRENEN (72km). At 12.5km W. the D10 bears l. off the old road, after 6km passing (l.) the elliptical *Camp de Péran*, a good example of a vitrified fort of the Early Iron Age.—6km. The D790 forks r. to (8km) *Quintin*, standing on a hill above an expansion of the Gouët, preserving several old granite houses in its main Place, and the 15C *Porte Neuve*, the most conspicuous relic of its ramparts; the *Castle* was rebuilt in 1662 and 1775.

Continuing S.W., the road shortly passes the 18C *Château de Robien* to traverse (16km) *Corlay*, its castle dismantled in 1598, known for its 'double bidets' or large cob horses, said to descend from Arab steeds brought back by Crusaders crossed with English stallions.—8.5km. *St-Nicolas-du-Pélem*, 6km N.W. of which, at *Lanrivain*, is a *Calvary* of 1548, and further N., in 17C *N.-D.-de-Guiaudet*, a curious recumbent Virgin.—One may regain the main road by turning S. near the rocky gorge of *Toul-Goulic*, in which the Blavet descends in rapids and for a time disappears.—15.5km. *Rostrenen*; see Rte 44.

18km. ST-BRIEUC (51,400 Briochins), préfecture of the *Côtes-du-Nord*, was described by Augustus Hare as a 'clean but exceedingly dull town', and in the latter respect it has little changed. It stands on a plateau some 4km from the estuary of the Gouët and the small tidal port of *Le Légué*, damaged in 1944. It was famous for its markets, and in recent years factories and refrigeration depots have been built in the area to handle the early vegetables of the Léon district and elsewhere in Brittany, to the extent that it is now difficult to get served with fresh spring vegetables.

St Briocus, a Welsh missionary to Armorica, settled here in the 6-7C, and the cathedral is built on the site of his tomb. Olivier de Clisson entered the town in 1375, and from the cathedral held its citizens at bay; in 1394 the Briochins in turn took the building, holding out against his besieging troops for 15 days. The States of Brittany met here for the last time in 1768. During the Terror, both Chouans and 'les bleus' (the Republicans) contested bitterly for the place, and in 1799 the Vendeans achieved a coup of liberating a band of condemned Royalists from the prison. Auguste Villiers de l'Isle-Adam (1840–89) was born here.

To the N.E. of the central *Pl. du Guesclin* are the gardens of the *Grandes Promenades* and the *Palace de Justice*, overlooking the ravine of the Gouëdic, while a few minutes' walk to the N.W. through the old town brings one to the **Cathedral**, facing the *Pl. Gén. de Gaulle*.

It was begun in the 13C, but its two sieges necessitated extensive repairs, and in the 18C it was partially rebuilt, and later completely restored. The W. front, relieved by a Flamboyant rose-window, is flanked by two austere fortified towers. The 13C porch is a restoration, as is the contemporary *Porche du Martray* on the N. side. Note the humpbacked figure with sealed lips at the N.W. angle of the N. transept.

The massive 13C pillars at the W. end of the nave give place to slender 15C columns further E. The organ-case dates from 1540. In the S. aisle, beyond the granite tomb of Bp Le Porc de la Porte (d. 1620), is a florid Gothic chapel containing the *Tomb of St-Guillaume*, with a good 15C statue, and a carved wooden altarpiece by Corlay. Several 15-16C tomb-niches will be noticed. The pillars at the entrance to the choir display four Romanesque capitals from an earlier church; the elegant triforium dates from the 15C.

To the W. is the modern *Préfecture*, enclosing in its l.-hand courtyard the former canonry of *Maison du St-Esprit*, with a late Gothic turret; to the l. is the 16-18C *Hôtel de Maillé*.

To the S.E. of the cathedral is the 18C pavilion of the *Hôtel de Bellecize*, the former bishop's palace.—To the N. of the Place, in the

neighbourhood of the *Pl. du Martray*, are several irregular old lanes:
noteworthy are the corner house (10 Rue Fardel), and No. 15, the so-
called *Hôtel des Ducs-de-Bretagne*, a restored Renaissance house of
1572. Nos 32 and 34 in this street, 9 Rue Quinquains, and 9 Rue St-
Pierre, are other characteristic examples of 16-17C Breton domestic
architecture.

Some 3..5km N.E., beyond *Cesson*, is a *Tower* erected by Jean IV of Brittany in
1395, blown up in 1598, and ringed by a double line of moats cut in the rock.
   For the coast road hence to *Paimpol* and *Treguier*, see Rte 42.

Continuing W., at 18km the N12 by-passes (r.) **Châtelaudren**, a
cider-making town on the Leff, where 14C *N.-D.-du-Tertre* contains
15C paintings on wood (unfortunately indistinct), and *St-Magloire*
preserves some old glass and an altarpiece carved by the prolific
Breton wood-carver Yves Corlay, who died here in 1776.

   14km. **GUINGAMP** (9500 Guingampais), also by-passed, is an important road junction on the river Trieux, and was once the capital of
the duchy of Penthièvre. The Gorsedd of the Breton Bards was
founded here in 1909 on the initiative of Charles Le Goffic and
Anatole Le Braz (1859–1926; born at Fuault, c. 30km S.W.). Little is
now seen of the 'gateways, towers, and battlements, apparently of
the oldest military architecture; every part denoting antiquity and in
the best preservation', which Arthur Young remarked on in 1788,
although some turrets of the 15C *Castle* survive to the W. of the *Pl.
du Verdun*, to the N. of which is the old *Hôtel-Dieu*, founded by
Charles de Blois and rebuilt in 1699 in the Breton Renaissance style
(restored); its chapel has a facade of 1695–1709. Next to a turreted
Renaissance house stands **N.-D.-de-Bon-Secours**, a striking Gothic
and Renaissance edifice, its W. front flanked by a 14C *Tour de
l'Horloge* and 16C *Tour Plate*. The spire of the central tower (14C)
was damaged by shell-fire in 1944. Its 16C W. portal is decorated by
statues of the Apostles; on the N. and S. facades are Gothic portals; to
the N. is the **Grande Porche* (14C; restored 1854), now forming a
chapel.

The gloomy interior is of interest for its blend of styles due to the 16C rebuilding
of the S. aisle by Jean Le Moal after the collapse of the S. tower. The bays and
triforium on the N. of the nave are Gothic; those on the S., Renaissance. The flying buttresses are carried boldly into the interior of the aisles and choir, while a
narrow crossing beneath the belfry separates the nave abruptly from the choir.
The four massive piers here, the oldest part of the church, are embellished with
the heads of beasts and grotesques. In the S. transept is the tomb of Pierre Morel,
Bp of Treguier in 1385. The choir, noteworthy for its graceful columns, contains
the tomb of Roland Phélippes (14C), seneschal of Charles de Blois, with his effigy
in armour. The ambulatory, of unusual plan, was added in 1462–84.

Beyond the *Pl. du Centre* are several Gothic houses, and the
Renaissance *Fontaine de la Pompe*, restored in 1743. Fragments of
town walls are visible a short distance to the W. of the adjacent Rue
des Carmelites.

The suburban village of *Ste-Croix*, on the S. bank of the Trieux, grew up round an
Augustinian abbey founded c. 1135, the ruins of which are now occupied by a
farm, above the entry of which is inscribed a 'lettre de sauve-garde' received
from Louis XV in 1736 (not 1636 as the inscription states!); at the far end of the
courtyard is the former abbot's lodging (1530); on the r. the ruined church.

GUINGAMP TO CARHAIX-PLOUGUER (48km). The D787 leads S.W., at
10.5km passing 4km E. of *Gurunhuel*, with a *Calvary*; at *Bourbriac*, 6.5km E., the
church preserves the granite sarcophagus of St Briac.—7.5km *Bulat-Pestivien*,

4km l., with a Renaissance chapel, its sculptured porch and carvings of skeletons engaged in everyday occupations (on the sacristy wall) being remarkable, whence one may regain the main road 5km W.

10km. *Callac*, once noted for its quarterly horse-fairs, 10km W. of which, in remote *Plourac'h*, is a fine village church, with an elaborately decorated 16C porch.—The road now descends the valley of the Hyères to (20km) **Carhaix-Plouguer**; see Rte 44.

The main road leads due W. from Guingamp, passing at 2.5km N. of *Grâces* (beyond the by-pass), with a handsome chapel of 1512 containing beautifully carved beams depicting a variety of amusing subjects. A reliquary preserves the remains of Charles de Blois (1319–64), brought here in 1605.

The D767 shortly forks r. for (10km) *Bégard*, which grew round a Cistercian abbey of 1130, of which slight ruins remain; there are several tall menhirs in the neighbourhood. *Lannion* lies 18km further N.W.; see Rte 42.

The N12 passes at 9km the isolated hill of *Menez-Bré* (302m), crowned by a chapel, and 7.5km beyond, by-passes *Belle-Isle-en-Terre* (its inn described by Young as 'a villainous hole'), just N. of which, at *Locmaria*, is a good 16C rood-loft; there is another example at *Loc-Envel*, 3.5km S.

7.5km. *Keramanac'h*, an ancient commandery of the Knights Hospitallers.

6km N. is *Plouaret*, with a large square; adjacent to the 16C church is a curious antique sculpture (possibly Roman) of a horseman trampling a female dragon.—Some 6km N.E. of Plouaret is the *Chapelle des Sept-Saints*, rebuilt in 1714 on a dolmen forming a crypt, where images of the Seven Sleepers of Ephesus are said to have appeared miraculously.

5km. *The Étang du Moulin Neuf* is skirted, beyond which the N12 enters the department of *Finistère*.—7km S. lies the old village of *Guerlesquin*.—A winding descent followed by a steep climb, to be avoided by a new road under construction, brings one to (11km) *Plouigneau*, 6km S. of which, at **Plougonven**, is a remarkable *Calvary of 1555, one of the finest in Brittany, with vividly sculptured groups, whence one may drive 11.5km N.W. to **Morlaix**, 10km due W. of Plouigneau. *Morlaix* is also by-passed by a road circling to the N. across its estuary; see Rte 43A.

42   St-Malo to Morlaix via the Coast

200km (124 miles), approx.; the distance will be considerably more if every detour and indentation of the rocky coast are followed. The main route traverses (12.5km) **Dinard**—D786—20km *Le Guildo* —4km *St-Cast* lies 4km r.—9.5km *St-Aide*—40km **St-Brieuc**— 28.5km *Plouha*—17km **Paimpol**—15km **Treguier**—18km **Lannion**. *Perros-Guirec* lies 12km N.—38km **Morlaix**.

Maps: IGN 61, 14, or 105. M 230.

On crossing the Rance estuary just S. of *St-Servan* (see Rte 39), fork r. for **DINARD** (10,000 inhab., out of season), long a favourite summer resort, with a mild climate, in the vicinity of which are several attractive rocky bays. It was frequented in particular by English tourists at the turn of the century (Gerald Brenan spent three school holidays there), when there was even a resident British consul, and it still re-

tains a somewhat faded *fin-de-siècle* air, even if it has all the usual installations and distractions expected of such places.

For details of excursions, by launch or coach, enquire at the S.I., opposite the
casinos. The airport of *Pleurtuit* is some 6km S.

The centre of 'high life' is the *Plage d'Écluse*, N. of the casinos, a sandy beach and promenade lying between the *Pointe du Moulinet* (E.;
Views), and the *Pointes de la Malouine* and *du Grouin* (with cliff
walks) to the W. On the far side of the former is the *Porte
d'Émeraude*, from which the long Promenade du Clair de Lune skirts
the Anse de Dinard, the larger bay; the Av. George-V runs parallel to
and W. of this esplanade, at the N. end of which is the *Aquarium* and
Musée Marine, containing souvenirs of Dr Charcot (1867–1936)
and the voyage of the 'Pourquoi Pas'; at its S. end is the Plage du
Prieuré, named after a priory founded in 1324 by Olivier and Geoffroy de Montfort, of which a ruined chapel remains.

   Now contiguous with Dinard is *St-Énogat*, named after an early
bishop of Aleth (cf. St-Malo); to the W. of its crescent bay a path leads
to the *Grotte de la Goule-aux-Fées*, accessible at low tide.—Immediately to the W. is **St-Lunaire**, situated at the foot of the *Pointe du
Décollé*, separating two sandy beaches, beyond which a headland
commands views of the reef-strewn bay. The older town, inland,
preserves a restored 11-16C church of some interest.

   The road traverses several small resorts, skirting the *Baie de Lan-
cieux*, and the neck of another promontory ending in a jagged reef,
on which is *St-Jacut-de-la-Mer*, to *St-Guildo*, with its 'ringing-stones',
and picturesque ruined castle on the traditional site of the place
where Prince Cramme and his family were burnt in 559 (cf. Vannes).

A by-road shortly bears r. through *Pen-Guen* to (4km) **St-Cast**, with its sandy
beach, between which and the inland village a column near the 'Cimetières des
Anglais' commemorates the skirmish of 1758, when a landing party from an
English fleet was decimated by the Duc d'Aiguillon's troops. Extensive sea views
may be enjoyed from the headlands at either end of the main plage.

4.5km. **Matignon**, which preserves the motte of the original castle of
a family providing France with two marshals.—There is a 13C octagonal tower at *Montbran*, 6km W.
   The road descends by the head of the *Baie de la Frênaye*, and
climbs to (6.5km) *St-Aide*.

6.5km N.E. is the *Fort de la Latte*, the medieval stronghold of the Counts de
Matignon, 'modernised' in the 17C, N.W. of which are the red granite cliffs and
rock-stacks of *Cape Fréhel*, whence one may regain the main road by following
the corniche S.W. via *Sables-d'Or-les-Pins*.

The D786 bears S.W. beyond St-Aide, off which several roads lead
down to minor resorts, such as the little port at *Erquy* (r. at 8km), and
5km beyond we pass (l.) the 17C *Château de Bienassis*, with its double moat.

To the W. lies *Pléneuf*, where the poet and dramatist Jean Richepin (1849–1926)
is buried, and the resort of *Le Val-André*, with a fishing-harbour of *Dahouët* adjacent.

5.5km. To the l. is the 15C chapel of *St-Jacques*, with interesting exterior sculpture—2.5km. **Lamballe** (see Rte 41) lies 11km S.E.
   7km *Les Ponts-Neufs*, a hamlet on the Gouessant, with an embankment of Roman origin, is traversed 4km prior to meeting the N12,

which skirts the head of the *Anse d'Yffiniac*, where the sea recedes 6.5km at low tide, on the sands of which, in 937 took place a decisive battle in which Alain Barbe-Torte (Wrybeard), the Breton leader, crushed the Northmen.

St-Brieuc (see Rte 41) is by-passed on a viaduct spanning the Gouët, off which the N786 forks r. to *Binic*, a small resort with a tidal harbour, 13.5km N.W. of St-Brieuc.

6.5km W. is *N.-D. de-la-Cour*, with the recumbent effigy in armour of Guillaume de Rosmadec (d. 1640) and remarkable windows depicting scenes from the life of the Virgin, in 15C costume.

7km. *St-Quay-Portrieux*, combining a fishing-port with a family resort, is named after St Kea, a 6C Welsh missionary, 8km beyond which, at *Plouha*, many adherents of Charles I took refuge after the battle of Naseby.—The 13C chapel of *Kermaria-an-Isquit*, 4km W., with a 14C porch supported by apostles, contains 15C English alabasters, a mural of the Dance of Death, and quaint statuettes.—Some 6km further W. beyond the D6, is *Lanleff*, with a ruined late 11C baptistry.

The road traverses (5km) *Lanloup*, with a picturesque 16C church, and, 10km beyond, the ruins of the Premonstratensian abbey of *Beauport*, founded in 1202, the refectory dating from the 13C, and other dependencies from the Renaissance, while the main facade of the church is Early English in character.

2km. **Paimpol** (8400 inhab.), a typical Breton longshore fishing-port, whose Atlantic cod-fisheries have been largely superseded by oyster cultivation and the production of early vegetables, but whose traditions are preserved in Pierre Loti's 'Pêcheur d'Islande' (1886), and in the songs of Théodore Botrel (1868–1925). Henry of Richmond embarked here in 1483 on his abortive descent on England. A national Merchant Marine School was established here in 1963. Just W. of the harbour is the *Pl. du Martray*, with a 15C turreted house, and further W., the belfry of 1768 of a former church.

A good view of the town may be obtained from the *Tour de Kerroc'h*, on the N. side of the inlet, near *Ploubazlanec*, with a curious ossuary in its churchyard and the *Mur des Disparus en Mer*, inscribed with the names of those drowned.—Further N.E. is the *Pointe de l'Arcouest*, beyond which is an archipelago of rose-granite rocks and the larger *Île de Bréhat* (launches from Paimpol or from the Pointe), on the N. extremity of which is a rebuilt lighthouse. Its community is scattered amongst a labyrinth of drystone walls (as in the Aran Islands, off the Irish coast), among whom may be descendants of the English who several times occupied the place in the 15-16Cs.

From Paimpol the D786 drives due W. to cross the Trieux at (5km) *Lézardrieux*, 8km S. of which is the late 15C château of *La Roche-Jagu* overlooking the estuary; 8km N. is *Pleubian*, its church with an exterior pulpit (16C), beyond which extends the 3km.-long shingle causeway of the *Sillon de Talbert*.

10km **TRÉGUIER**, a picturesque cathedral town, stands above the confluence of the Guindy and Jaudy.

Said to be founded in the 6C by St Tugdual or Tudwal, son of a Welsh prince, it was the seat of a bishopric created by king Nominoë in 855, which existed until the Revolution, a canon of which was the Abbé Siéyès (1748–1836), author of several forceful essays in 1788–9, including 'Qu'est-ce-que le Tiers État?'. Ernest Renan (1823–92), author of a rational 'Vie de Jésus', whose 'Souvenirs d'Enfance et de Jeunesse' contains interesting descriptions of the place, was born here, but the erection of his statue in the cathedral square offended devouter citizens, who set up a Calvary as a counter-measure.

The former **Cathedral was begun c. 1300 but only finished in the 15C, and preserves two fragments of an earlier edifice, the 13C W. Porch, and the Romanesque *Tour d'Hastings*, above the N. transept. The S. transeptal tower has an 18C openwork spire 63m high; and a third tower surmounts the crossing. Both the S. porches are of interest; that of the nave has elaborate tabernacle-work within.

Interior. Each pair of piers in the nave is of a different design, and the varied patterns of the triforium and clerestory, throughout the church, are most attractive. The modern glass is not so appealing. Richly decorated chapels flank the aisles, in which are 15C tombs; two knights on the S. side, a cleric on the N. The *Chapelle au Duc*, in the N. aisle, contains that of Jean V of Brittany (d. 1442). The Christ to the r. of the entrance is similar to that at St-Pol de-Léon.

The N. transept contains Romanesque arches and capitals; in the S. transept are a 14C stoup, 17C panel of St John the Evangelist, and a naive carved group of St Yves between the Rich Man and the Poor. Of the carved oak choir-stalls (1648), the first two depict St Tudwal and St Yves. The high altar, which was a notable work of 15C woodcarving, has been stolen recently. The rose-windows of the ambulatory chapels are remarkable. A doorway leads from the N. transept to the elegantly arcaded **Cloisters* (1461–79), providing a good view of the Tour d'Hastings.

Adjacent to the W. portal is the former *Bishop's Palace*, in the gardens behind which is the tomb of Anatole Le Braz (1859–1926), the Breton author.

The *Pl. du Martray* and the old Rue Ernest-Renan, which descends from behind the cathedral to the quay, offer good examples of 17C Breton domestic architecture.

Beyond the S. suburbs is *Minihy-Tréguier*, to approach which we pass the 15C *Tour St-Michel*, the steeple of a destroyed church. In the graveyard of Minihy's largely 15C church is the Gothic Table-tomb of St Yves (Yves Hélory de Kermartin, 1253–1303; patron of reactionary lawyers), beneath which credulous Bretons used to crawl on their knees at the Pardon des Pauvres.

7km N. is the 15-16C *Chapelle St-Gonéry*, with a 9C tower, containing the tomb of Bp Guillaume de Halgouët (d. 1602); while beyond adjacent *Plougrescant* are reef-fringed headlands.

At (5.5km) *Pont-Losquet*, S.W. of Tréguier, the tiny fishing harbour of *Port-Blanc* lies 8.5km N.W., the occasional residence of Le Braz, Botrel, and Ambroise Thomas.—3.5km S. of this junction is *La Roche-Derrien*, at the head of the Jaudy estuary, where took place a battle in 1347 in which Charles de Blois was taken prisoner by followers of Jeanne de Montfort and the English; slight remains subsist of an 11C castle; the 13-14C church contains a Renaissance altarpiece.—There is a late 15C church of interest at *Runan*, 8km S.E.

For the DETOUR to the '*Côte de Granite Rose*', one may follow the D6 directly W. from Pont-Losquet to (16km) **Perros-Guirec** (7500 inhab.), an old-fashioned resort built on a headland, the church of the old village preserving a 12C nave with interesting capitals.—The coast road shortly passes *La Clarté*, with a 15C chapel, before reaching *Ploumanac'h*, on the E. side of a jagged land-locked bay of chaotic heaps of rose-red granite rocks. To the N. are the *Pointe de Squéouel*, and the offshore *Sept-Îles* (both with lighthouses), the latter now a sea-bird sanctuary.—It was off the coast here that the oil-tanker 'Torrey Canyon' ran aground in March 1967, causing the widespread pollution given the name 'marée noire'; cf. Portsall, and Ushant.

Continuing W. we traverse *Tourony*, where on the island *Château de Costaërès*, Sienkiewicz wrote part of 'Quo Vadis', and **Tregastel Plage**, a small resort enjoying one of the more attractive sites on the Breton coast. The inland

village has a 12-13C church and 17C ossuary, and preserves the tomb of Le Goffic (cf. Lannion) with a relief by Bourdelle.—The corniche road veers S.W., passing (l.) the megalithic monuments of *Kerguntuil* before reaching *Penvern*, inland
from which is a Telecommunication Research Station.—The offshore *Île-Grande*,
also with dolmens, is now joined to the mainland by a bridge.—The road shortly
traverses the resort of *Trébeurden*, with its granite rocks and islands, commanding a view over the *Baie de Lannion. Lannion* itself lies 9.5km S.E.

At 12.5km (from Pont-Losquet) we enter **Lannion** (17,200 Lan-
nionais), a characteristic Breton town astride the Léguer, built up in
recent years, which was the birthplace of Charles Le Goffic
(1863– 1932), the poet and novelist.

The Rue des Augustins ascends from the widened bridge to the *Pl.
Gén. Leclerc*, with the *Hôtel de Ville*, where the *Maison du Chapelier*,
with curious projecting turrets, is the best of a group of slate-faced
15-16C houses; some others are in lanes to the N.E., while the 17C
facade of the chapel of a former Ursuline convent may be seen in the
Rue Jean-Savidan, leading S.E. *St-Jean-du-Bally* (16-17C, with an unfinished tower of 1519) stands just N.W. of the central Place.

Overlooking the town to the N. is the 12-16C church of *Brélevenez*, approached
by a long flight of steps off the Rue de la Trinité, containing a 14C group of the
Virgin and six saints, granite font, and a restored 11C crypt with an 18C Entombment.

On the l. bank of the river stands the picturesque *Hospice*, occupying a former
convent. A riverside road leads hence to *Loguivy* (2.5km N.W.), where the
Gothic church contains a carved wooden relief of the Nativity, with bagpipe-
players in Breton costume. In the cemetery is a curious Renaissance fountain,
and outside it is a statue of the founder, St Yvi.

S.E. of Lannion, approached by lanes leading l. off the D11, are the overgrown
ruins of the 14C castle of *Coatfrec*, 2.5km E. of *Ploubezre*, from which the
Chapelle de Kerfons (1559, with a Renaissance rood-loft), and the ruined castle of
Tonquédec (14-16C), an irregular polygon flanked by round towers, in the valley
further E., may be visited. The manor of *Kergrist*, further S., to the l. of the D11, is
notable.

The D786 leads S.W. from Lannion to (11km) *St-Michel-en-Grève*,
beyond which its sandy bay is skirted to (5km) *St-Efflam*, named after
a 6C British or Irish hermit whose 16C tomb lies in the church of
Plestin-les-Grèves, 2km beyond, a rectangular building of 1575, with
cross-vaulted aisles.—To the N. is *Locquirec*, with a small harbour, a
picturesque 17C church, and several sandy beaches.

7km. *Lanmeur* (r.) has a modern church built over the crypt (?8C)
of the church of *Kerfeunteun*, an ancient town on this site destroyed
by Norman pirates. The cemetery chapel of *Kernitron* here has a
Romanesque portal, 13C nave and transepts, and a 16C choir.

Prior to entering *Morlaix*, 13km S.W., a DETOUR may be made to **St-Jean-du-
Doigt**, 7.5km N.W., its churchyard containing a chapel of 1575 and Renaissance
fountain. The church itself dates from 1440– 1513, a handsome Flamboyant
building with a lavishly decorated interior, its treasury containing a reliquary
said to enclose a finger of the Baptist, after which the village is named.

2km N.W. is *Plougasnou*, its 16C church with a remarkable porch, beyond
which is *Primel-Trégastel*, near its high red granite headland, with a harbour and
relics of German fortifications.—Hence one may follow by-roads to the W. to
Plouézoc'h (also reached directly from Plougasnou), in the neighbourhood of
which is the recently excavated megalithic site of *Bonnenez*.—The D76 leads
9km hence along the estuary to *Morlaix*, passing near *Ploujean*, but the former
estate of Marshal Foch has been largely superseded by an airport.

For **Morlaix**, see below.

43 Morlaix to Brest

A. Via Landerneau

65km (40 miles). N12. 13km *St-Thégonnec*—4km *Guimiliau* lies 4km
S.—4km *Lampaul-Guimiliau*—4km *Landivisiau*—D712. 16km
Landerneau—20km **Brest**.

This route takes in some of the more remarkable *Calvaries* between
Morlaix and Landivisiau. Others are described, to visit which will
add slightly to the total distance.

A faster motorway (N12) drives direct between the two towns,
c. 60km apart.

Maps: IGN 13, or 105. M 230.

MORLAIX (19,500 Morlaisiens), is attractively sited in a deep valley
spanned to the N. by a monumental two-storeyed railway viaduct
(and further N., a road bridge), and although some distance from the
open sea, has a small tidal harbour. The town centre retains a few old
slate-faced houses, but most of the 'crazy, but picturesque constructions' here were demolished in the early 19C.

Known to the Romans as *Mons Relaxus*, Morlaix later belonged to the counts of
Léon, whose kingdom (according to Breton legend) was the Lyonesse of the Arthurian romances. It was besieged and captured in 1187 by Henry II for his ward
Arthur of Brittany. During the Hundred Years' War it frequently changed hands,
and was pillaged by the Earl of Surrey's raiding force in 1522. Mary, Queen of
Scots, after landing at Roscoff (see Rte 43B), made a solemn entry here in 1548. It
later took the part of the Leaguers, and the castle was stormed for Henri IV in
1594. It was slightly damaged by bombing in 1943 in an attempt to destroy the
viaduct.
    Among its natives were Gén. Moreau (1763–1813), the victor of
Hohenlinden; and the poet Tristan Corbière (1845-75). Gén. Dupleix, the adversary of Clive in India, spent his childhood in the old manor of *Pennanru*, just N.
of the town, where his father was director of the tobacco factory. Gén. Weygand
(1867–1965) was buried here.
    Occasionally the local women wear a 'lobster-tail' head-dress with the hair
plaited at the nape. The arms of Morlaix bear the punning motto 'S'ils te mor-
dent. mord-les' ('a bite for a bite').

Roads converge on the long tree-planted *Pl. des Otages*, flanked to
the S. by the *Hôtel de Ville* (1838), and dominated by the *Viaduct* of
1864 (285m long and 58m high). To the E. is *St-Melaine*, founded in
1150 and rebuilt in 1489; the tower and belfry were completed in
1574. Its wooden ceiling will be noted, with carvings depicting the
vices of monks; likewise the organ-loft, and font cover.
    Beyond the viaduct is the *Pl. Cornic*, named after Charles Cornic-
Duchêne (1731–1809), a local privateer, continued by the new *Pl.
Charles de Gaulle*, built over the river, on the E. side of which is an
imposing 17C mansion. The harbour is flanked by quays, that to the
E. leading shortly to the *Fontaine des Anglais*, said to mark the spot
where some 600 of Surrey's followers, loaded with booty, were ambushed. Opposite is the *Tobacco Factory*.
    From the *Pl. Souvestre*, S. of the Hôtel de Ville, one may follow the
pedestrian **Grande Rue*, a quaint and characteristic street preserving some 16C shopfronts: note also the grotesque statues of a
bagpipe-player and a man in his shirt. It ends at the *Pl. des Halles*,
recently cleared, overlooked to the W. by the Rue du Mur (named

from the old town wall, W. of which is the *site* of the castle). Here is the much-restored *Maison de la Duchesse-Anne* (No.30; 16C). The interior has a curious lantern-roofed courtyard in which a spiral stair-case ascends round a carved newel.

Hence the Rue Basse climbs to *St-Mathieu*, rebuilt in 1824, but re-taining a Renaissance tower of 1548 with charming decorations (E. side). A door in the S. aisle opens onto a small esplanade with a *Calvary*, and the chapel of *N.-D. du Mur*. Near by is the *Pl. des Jacobins*, with the former Dominican or *Jacobin Convent* founded in 1237, remodelled in the 15C, used as lodging for Mary Stuart, and as a Jacobin club during the Revolution. In the 13C church, preserving a rose-window, is installed the *Musée*, a somewhat miscellaneous collection of paintings, sculpture, and architectural fragments.

The Rue au Fils leads hence to meet the Rue Ange de Guernisac, in which No.13, and 2 Venelle au Son, opposite, are of interest, to regain the Pl. des Otages.

On a height to the W., near the railway station, stands *St-Martin-des-Champs*, founded 1128 but rebuilt in the Doric style on the eve of the Revolution.

MORLAIX TO QUIMPER (81km). The D785 turns S. c. 5km S.W. of Morlaix through (5.5km) *Pleyber-Christ*, with a many-gabled church with a portal of 1666, and 4km beyond, near the 12C Cistercian abbey church of *Le Relecq* (4km S.E.) with an incongruous facade of 1785.—7km. The Huelgoat-Landerneau crossroads: see Rte 44. To the r. rises the *Roc'h Trévezel* (365m) on the main ridge of the *Monts d'Arrée*. To the l. on the descent is the *Reservoir de St-Michel* filling the once marshy basin of Botmeur, with a 'Centrale Nucléaire' on its bank—in the centre of the Parc Régional d'Armorique! The road climbs again past the *Signal de Toussaines* (384m; the highest point in Brittany), and round the *Montagne St-Michel* (380m), providing extensive views in clear weather.—16km. *Brasparts*, with a fine spire and church porch, and a *Calvary* depicting St Michael and the Dragon (all 16C).—11km **Pleyben** (see Rte 44). Hence one may follow the old road S. to (33km.) **Quimper**, also approached by the N165, joined 6km to the W.; see Rte 45.

The N12 climbs S.W. to (12km) **St-Thégonnec**, where a monastery was founded by St Tigernach (d. c. 550), Bp of Clogher and Clones (in Ireland). The churchyard contains a remarkable *Ossuary* of 1675 with a crypt containing an Entombment of carved and painted wood (c. 1700), a *Calvary* of 1610, where among numerous statuettes is one of Tigernach with his cart drawn by the wolf who ate the saint's ass, which he then tamed and harnessed. The church, with a steeple of 1563 and Renaissance tower, preserve exuberantly carved woodwork.

We turn l. 4km W. for **Guimiliau**, named after king Miliau of Cornouaille, murdered by his brother c. 531, and later canonised. Here is another striking *Calvary* (1581), with a carved frieze and plinth crowded with figures in 16C costume, some depicting scenes from the life of Christ. The *Ossuary* dates from 1648; the 17C *Church* has a remarkable *S. Porch* (1617) sculptured in black Kersanton granite; note the Creation; likewise the carved beams, font-canopy, and W. gallery.

Lampaul-Guimiliau (4km W.). The late-Gothic church has a good porch-tower of 1573 and well-carved S. porch: it would seem that many local villages attempted to outshine their neighbours in the quality of carving in churchyards and porches. Within are six 17C wooden *Altarpieces*, an Entombment of 1676, font-cover of 1651, etc. The naive carving on the rood-beam, choir-rail, and stalls are worthy of examination; note also the banner-cupboards.

The Calvary at St-Thégonnec (1610)

Landivisiau (4km N.W.; 8100 inhab.), the rebuilt church of which retains its sculptured **Porch* of 1554. The adjacent 15C *Fontaine de St-Thivisau* is embellished with statues taken at the Revolution from the tombs of the lords of Coatmeur.—The churches of *Lambader* (8km N.) and *Bodilis* (5km N.W.) have features of interest.

The D172 leads W. past the picturesque *Moulin de Brézal* to (11.5km) *La Roche-Maurice*, below its ruined château. The E. window (1529) of its Gothic and Renaissance **Church* is a remarkable composition depicting a variety of personages in contemporary costume and armour; the Rohan lozenges are prominent. Also notable are the sculptured frieze in the nave and aisles, and rood-loft. Death aims his arrow at a line of figures on the Ossuary of 1640.

The church porches at *La Martyre* (5km S.E.; named after the king-martyr St Salomon), and at *Ploudiry*, adjacent, are notable; likewise the church at *Pencran*, S. of *Landerneau*.

4.5km. **Landerneau** (15,500 Landernéens), pleasantly sited at the head of the estuary of the Elorn, was the feudal capital of the *Pays de Léon*; and its provincial pretensions have made it a butt: the expression 'il y aura du bruit dans Landerneau' being sarcastically used to characterise news of trivial importance, while proverbial reference is made to the 'lune de Landerneau' since a Breton gentleman in the time of Louis XIV (adverting to a weather-vane in his native town) stoutly maintained that the moon at Landerneau was bigger than that at Versailles!

The river is spanned by the picturesque *Vieux Pont* (1510), and is partly bordered by old houses, notably the Rohans' mansion; others may be seen in the Quai de Léon, Rue du Commerce, and Pl. du Marché. On the S. bank stands *St-Thomas-de-Cantorbéry*, with a tower of 1607, and Renaissance *Ossuary* (1635).—*St-Houarneau*, preserving its sculptured porch of c. 1600, was moved to its present site on the N. bank in 1860.

The church at *Trémaouézan* (8km N.; beyond the N12) has features of interest.

7km S., to the W. of the D770 to *Daoulas* (see Rte 44) at *Dirinon*, is a chapel of 1577, containing the tomb of St Nonna (6C), daughter of king Brecan of Wales, whose abduction by the Welsh prince Kérétic led, according to the Breton legend, to her flight into Armorica and the subsequent birth of St David of Wales. The adjoining church has a spire of 1593. Murals depicting the history of St David (in the costume of 1676) may be seen in the church of *St-Divy*, N. of the D712, some 6km W. of Landerneau.

20km. **BREST** (160,400 Brestois; 27,000 in 1801; 84,300 in 1901), on the N. shore of an almost land-locked roadstead forming one of the finest natural harbours of Europe, with an important fortified naval port and dockyards, is of little interest to the ordinary traveller. It suffered heavily from air attacks in 1940–44, and has been largely rebuilt. It has also the reputation of being the rainiest of French towns.

Mentioned in the 9C as a '*bourgade*' of the counts of Léon, it grew in importance, Duc Jean IV observing that 'he is not duke of Brittany who is not lord of Brest'. In 1342 Edward III seized the place on behalf of Jean de Montfort, and it remained in English hands, resisting sieges by Du Guesclin and De Clisson, until Richard II sold the castle in 1396. It passed to France at the marriage of Anne of Brittany to Charles VIII in 1491.

The dockyard was founded by Richelieu in 1631, further implemented by Colbert (who replaced the wooden wharves by masonry), Duquesne, and De Seuil, and an Anglo-Dutch attack under Adm. Berkeley (1694) failed in the face of Vauban's defences. James II sailed hence in March 1689 with a French force to invade Ireland, and returned here after his defeat at the Boyne in July the following year. 26 Girondin deputies for Finistère were executed here during the Terror. Its convict hulks were long notorious, but the establishment was transferred to Cayenne in 1860.

In 1940 Brest served as an evacuation port until the entry of the Germans on 19 June, and for the next four years (particularly while the battle-cruisers 'Scharnhorst' and 'Gneisenau' sheltered there) it suffered incessant bombing. Almost half the town was destroyed, including the old centre, and over 1000 civilians were killed, 400 of them by a mysterious explosion in a huge shelter only days before the American entry on 18 Sept. 1944, after a five week siege.

Louis-Nicolas van Blarenberghe (1716–94), the military and marine painter, was born here; Charles Louis du Couëdic (1740–80), a naval hero, was buried in the church of St-Louis (destroyed by the Germans).—In the ruined *Château de Kérouaille* (5km N.W.) was born Louise-Renée de Penancoët de Kérouaille (1649–1734), who came to England as a maid 'of honour' and became the mistress of Charles II, by whom she was created Duchess of Portsmouth.

For motor-launch excursions, etc., enquire at the S.I., Pl. de la Liberté.

Most roads entering Brest converge on the *Pl. de Strasbourg*, in its N.E. suburbs, from which the congested Rue Jean-Jaurès leads downhill to the central *Pl. de la Liberté*, where a boulevard occupies the site of Vauban's ramparts. By turning S. here we reach the tree-planted Cours D'Ajot (1769) offering views over the harbour, the breakwaters, and the *Brest Roads*, which communicate with the open sea by the strait or *Goulet de Brest*, scarcely 2km wide.

To the W. stands the 13C **Castle** with several 15-16C towers, replacing a Roman fort, fragments of which are incorporated into the bases of towers and lower courses of ramparts on the town side. Restored, it accommodates the *Préfecture Maritime* and a *Naval Museum*. The Girondin deputies were confined in the machicolated towers flanking the gateway; and in the dungeons beneath, English prisoners, during the War of the Austrian Succession (1740–48).

To the N.W. is the *Pont Mobile de Recouvrance* (1954), replacing a swing bridge of 1861 across the Penfield estuary, to the N. of which is the *Arsenal Maritime* (foreigners not admitted), rebuilt since its virtual destruction during the war. Adjacent to the W. end of the bridge is the *Tour Tanguy*, with a museum of local history; further W. stood the German submarine shelters.

The Rue de Siam (so named in 1686 in honour of the Siamese embassy sent to Louis XIV) leads N.E., the busiest thoroughfare of the rebuilt 'old' town, to regain the Pl. de la Liberté, passing (r.) in the Rue Traverse, the *Musée Municipal*, containing marine views, Breton scenes, and works of the Pont-Aven school, etc.

For the road hence to *Le Conquet*, 24km W., see p 276, in reverse.

B. Via St-Pol-de-Léon and Le Folgoët

79km (49 miles). D173. 21.5km **St-Pol-de-Léon**. **Roscoff** lies 5km N.—D10 and D125. 31.5km *Lesneven*—D788. 2km **Le Folgoët**—4km **Brest**.

The several detours described will add to the total distance.

Maps: IGN 13, or 105. M 230.

The less interesting D769 bears l. 4.5km N.W. of Morlaix, later veering N. near (l.) the ruined castle of *Penhoat* to skirt the W. bank of the Penzé estuary to *St-Pol*.

The D173 continues to follow the W. bank of the Morlaix estuary, turning W. 2.5km S. of *Carantec*, on its promontory.

To the E. is the island fort of *Le Taureau*, built in 1542 to defend the roadstead, and strengthened by Vauban; it was also used as a state prison, in which Le Chalotais (1765) and Auguste Blanqui (1871) were confined.—To the N. is the *Île Callot*, with a rebuilt chapel founded in the 6C to commemorate the repulse of Norman pirates.

9.5km. **ST-POL-DE-LÉON** (8000 Saint-Politains), a quiet old market town preserving a number of stone mansions, and the former seat of the barony of *Léon*, is named after St Paul Aurelian, a Welsh monk, who founded a monastery on the Île de Batz (see below) in 530, and became bishop of Léon. It grew into a religious centre, whose riches naturally attracted a descent of Norman pirates in 875. It was attacked by the English in 1375, who burnt the Kreisker. Michel Colombe, the sculptor (1431–1512), was a native of the see of St-Pol.

Passing (r.) the *Cemetery* (with its chapel and rows of 16C ossuary niches), we reach the town centre, dominated by the splendid open-work *Spire* (77m high) of the Gothic *Chapelle du Kreisker*, dating mainly from the late 14th-15C, and which later served as a chapel for the *Collège de Léon* (1787), opposite.

The square central tower surmounted by the spire (which recalls that of St-Pierre at Caen) has served as a model for many Breton churches. The W. facade has three large windows; below the six windows of the S. facade is a shallow porch decorated with foliage; the N.W. porch is embellished with foliage and statues. The irregularity of the ground plan and the inclination of the main axis to the r. will be noticed. The roofs are of wood except at the crossing, where four massive piers support the tower. The cross-vaulted aisles, of unusual width, are flanked by tomb-niches.

The Rue Gén.-Leclerc, in which are several old granite houses, leads to the *Pl. Budès de Guébriant* and the former *Cathedral*, one of the outstanding churches of Brittany.

The nave and aisles date from the 13–early 14C; the choir and transepts were remodelled in the mid 15C; the ambulatory was doubled and the radiating chapels were added in the course of the 16C. The W. facade, with two towers crowned by spires of unequal height, has a portal surrounded by a platform, and at the base of the S. tower is a portal known as the 'lepers' door'. The S. porch contains a double doorway of the 15C; the S. transept an admirable 14C rose-window, above which is a balcony and a kind of exterior pulpit.

Interior. The stone *Nave* contrasts with the later granite choir. The Renaissance organ-case, a 12C sarcophagus (serving as a stoup) passes for the tomb of Conan Mériadic (d. 421), the earliest Breton king, and tempera paintings of angels on the vault of the crossing, will be noticed; noteworthy in the *Choir* are the ogee arches of its triforium, the stalls of 1512, and a curious little piscina, while above the latter is a 17C carved palm-trunk; a black marble slab in front is said to mark the tomb of St Paul Aurelian.

The *Ambulatory* contains several bishops' tombs, mostly 17C, among which is that of Fr Visdelou (d. 1671; chaplain to Anne of Austria), with a characteristic statue; an 18C painting of the Virgin interceding for St-Pol, with a view of the town; and the tomb of a certain Amice Picard (1599–1652), who is said to have subsisted for the last 18 years of her life on nothing but eucharistic wafers! Note also the ossuaries to the l. of the choir.

To the N. is the former Bishop's Palace, now the *Hôtel de Ville*, while behind the church is the early 16C *Maison Prébendale*, displaying the pet dragon of St Paul Aurelian.

ST-POL TO ROSCOFF (5km N.). Passing the '*allée couverte*' of *Keravel*, we enter **Roscoff**, a small port where Mary, Queen of Scots (when a child of five years, eight months) landed in 1548 on her way to be affianced to the Dauphin. On 10 Oct. 1746 the Young Pretender, fleeing after Culloden, also disembarked here, after two pursuing ships were beaten off by a privateer from St-Malo. It was a smugglers' lair during and after the Napoleonic wars, and is now the terminus of a ferry from Plymouth.

On the r. of the main street is the *Hospital* of 1573, near which in the 'Enclos des Capucins' grows a celebrated *Fig-tree*, planted c. 1620. Beyond is Flamboyant Gothic *N.-D.-de-Kroaz-Baz*, with a Renaissance tower of 1550. The ships and cannon carved on the exterior emphasis the town's maritime importance. Adjacent are two 17C ossuaries, and the tomb of Dorothy Silburne (d. 1820), a friend to the French émigré clergy. The 16C organ-case and pulpit, and the 15C English alabasters in the N. aisle, are notable.

There are several 17C houses close by and in the Rue Amiral-Réveillère, leading to the tidal harbour, in which No.25, with its courtyard, is known as that 'of Mary Stuart'. The neighbouring *Marine Biological Station* and aquarium are of interest, while the *Pointe de Bloscon* provides a fine view of adjacent reefs and the offshore *Île de Batz*, with its lighthouse.

ST-POL TO LESNEVEN VIA THE D788 (31km). The road drives S.W. to (14.5km) *Berven*, with a simple 'triumphal arch' leading to the church, with a Renaissance tower of 1576 and grotesque gargoyles (E. end), and carving on its aisle beams.—1.5km. *Mengluez*, 2km N. of which is the ruined *Château de Kergonadeac'h* (1605).—3km S. stands the ***Château de Kerjean**, ◇ enclosed by rectangular ramparts 6m thick, flanked by a deep moat. Largely of 1553–1618, it was partly destroyed by fire in 1710. A Renaissance portal with fluted columns admits to the charming inner court, with three wings and a portico, noteworthy also for its well; the interior contains a *Breton Museum*.—The main road hence may be regained at *Lanhouarneau*, with an ossuary adorned by an Ionic colonnade, and a Renaissance church porch in which are figures of the Apostles, while within is seen blind St Hervé (d. 575), led by his wolf.—For *Leneven*, 9km W., see below.

The coast road leads due W., after 5km passing (r.) several manors, and the 15C *Château de Kerouzéré*.—10km. *Plouescat*, with a 16C market-hall, beyond which we skirt the sandy *Grève de Goulven* to reach **Goulven**, its 15-16C church with a good steeple of local type.—*Brignogan*, 6km N.E., is a small resort, with an 8m high menhir and lighthouse.—The D10 leads 16km W. to *Plouguerneau*, see below.

From Goulven the D175 turns inland to (7km) *Lesneven*, 2km beyond which is the imposing church of ***Le Folgoët** (dated 1422, according to an inscription).

It was erected on the site of a hovel of a local idiot named Salaün or Solomon, but more usually known as the Folgoët, who lived here beside a spring, (which now rises below the altar), and for forty years in the mid 14C begged his bread in the district with the invocation 'Ave Maria'. From his tomb a white lily miraculously appeared, its golden stamens forming the same words!

The N. tower is a fine example of Breton Gothic. The double S. portal is richly ornamented. On the S. side of the choir projects a chapel remarkable for its *Porch*, with delicately carved figures of the Apostles in Kersanton granite, and a statue of Duc Jean V, who raised the church to collegial rank. The rather heavy interior contains a magnificent Flamboyant *Rood-loft* between the nave and the choir, supported by flying buttresses; the E. rose-window is notable, and also a charming statue of St Margaret.

Brest, see Rte 43A, lies 26km S.W.

LE FOLGOËT TO LE CONQUET VIA THE COAST. This circular route takes in most of the villages on this N.W. promontory of France, many of which may also be reached direct from Brest. The coast of Léon, which fringes this bare and rather featureless plateau, is itself low and rocky, with innumerable small sandy beaches and offshore reefs and islets, marked at night by the intermittent flashes of lighthouses. The harvesting and burning of seaweed (for fertilisers and alginates) is still a local industry, and the resultant smoke may hang like a pall over the landscape on occasions. Menhirs, dolmens, and other megalithic monuments abound, but are not always easy to locate. Among characteristic local dishes are 'cotriade' (fish soup) and 'caillebottes', resembling Cornish cream.

Plouguerneau lies 14.5km N.W. of Le Folgoët. It was here that Jean de Montfort embarked in 1345 to seek English aid against Charles de Blois. The beam from the 75m high lighthouse on the *Île de la Vierge*, to the N.W., can be seen over 40km away.—Hence we turn S.W. across the *Aber-Wrac'h* estuary past (l.) the 17C *Château de Kerouartz*, to *Lannilis*, beyond which the parallel estuary of *Aber-Benoît* is skirted to reach *Ploudalmézeau*, with its 18C steeple; the porchtower of c. 1620 at adjacent *Lampaul-Ploudalmézeau* is notable.

Portsall, 3km N.W. of the former village, and a small fishing-harbour and resort, was the scene of disaster in March 1978, when the Liberian-registered but American-owned tanker, the 'Amoco Cádiz', went aground, its steering disabled, causing some 230,000 tonnes of crude oil to be washed ashore on the coast here, causing immense ecological damage, and precipitating the more rigorous control of shipping off this dangerous cape.

Continuing S.W., the coast road passes the ruins of the 13C castle of *Trémazan*, with its four-storeyed keep, via *Argenton* to (8km) *Porspoder*, where St Budoc landed, having sailed from Ireland on a 'floating stone'. Legend relates that this 6C saint was a son of the beautiful Azénor, daughter of a count of Léon, who was imprisoned in the castle of Brest in consequence of her stepmother's calumnies, and then thrown into the sea in a barrel. After being nourished for five months by her guardian angel, she gave birth to St Budoc, and they were both cast up safe and sound on the Irish shore.

From Argenton the D68 leads S.E. towards *Brest*, at 8km passing the well-restored Breton Renaissance Château of *Kerouézel.—Lanrivoaré*, just beyond, named after an early missionary to Armorica, has within its cemetery a curious walled and paved enclosure in which, according to legend, an entire tribe was buried after being massacred by heathen neighbours. No one has been buried there since. A cross here, with the Virgin below it, has in front eight round stones, said to be loaves thus transformed by St Hervé (cf. Lanhouarneau), nephew of St Rivoaré, to punish a baker who refused to give him alms.—The main coastal road circles the muddy estuary of *Aber-Ildut* before turning S., at *Plouarzel* passing a turning for the *Pointe de Corsen*, the W. extremity of the French mainland.—4km E. is the *Menhir de Kerloas, the tallest in Finistère (almost 13m), until comparatively recently resorted to as a cure for sterility.—10.5km S. of Plouarzel lies **Le Conquet**, finely situated on one of the W. extremities of Brittany, with a small fishing-port, where in 1404 and again in 1513 English squadrons were beaten off, but in 1558 they successfully burnt the town, except for eight houses (which still exist) belonging to English subjects. It is a port of call for vessels from Brest to the *Île d'Ouessant* (anglicised as *Ushant*), which lies some 19km N.W. On the intermediate island of *Molène* are interred victims of the wreck of the 'Drummond Castle', which in 1896 struck the nearby *Pierres Vertes* and sank with the loss of 400 lives. A more recent wreck was that of the 272,000 tonne oil-tanker 'Olympic Bravery', which ran aground off Ushant in Jan. 1976 (cf. Portsall, above). Some 30,000 ships of varying tonnage round the archipelago every year.

Rock-bound **Ushant** (7km by 4km), known to the Bretons as *Enez-Heussa* ('Isle of Terror'), is now denominated part of the Parc Régional d'Armorique, and has an ornithological station. It is said to have been occupied by druidesses before the arrival of St Paul Aurelian. The customs and costumes of its somewhat inter-bred population are curious. The women, wearing loose hair and short skirts, were the only tillers of the soil, and for centuries chose their partners in marriage. Fishermen lost at sea were given a ceremonial funeral, their empty graves being marked with a cross. The lighthouse or *Phare de Créc'h*, on its rugged N.W. side, has a beam visible for c. 50km.

Adm. Keppel fought an indecisive naval action off Ushant against the Comte d'Orvilliers in 1778, while on 'the Glorious First of June' of 1794 Adm. Howe sank ten and captured seven of Villaret de Joyeuse's fleet in the same area.

4km S. of Le Conquet is the *Pointe de St-Mathieu, where the head of that saint is said to have been brought from Ethiopia and landed by Breton sailors. On the rocky promontory are the ruins of a large church (1157–1208), the successor of a monastery founded in the 6C by St Tanguy, which later became a Benedictine abbey. The Pointe was a favourite landing-place on the sea-route between England and its provinces in Aquitaine.—The coast road leads E. hence through *Le Trez Hir*, with views S.E. towards Camaret on the Crozon peninsula (see Rte 45), later passing N. of the *Pointe du Petit Minou*, and *Ste-Anne-du-Portzic*, the popular plage of the Brestois. Passing the rebuilt Naval College and crossing the Penfeld estuary, we reach the Castle of **Brest**; see Rte 43A.

44   Rennes to Brest via Rostrenen

239km (148 miles). N12 for 32km, then N164. 10km *St-Méen*—43km *Loudéac*—47.5km **Rostrenen**—20.5km **Carhaix-Plouguer**—36km **Pleyben**—6km N165. 14km *Le Faou*—10.5km *Daoulas*—20km *Brest*.

Maps: IGN 16, 14, 13, or 105. M 230.

This road is the main E.–W. artery of central Brittany, off which several subsidiary roads lead N.W. and S.W. towards the respective coasts of the Breton peninsula. For the road from Rennes to *Vannes*, see Rte 40; for Rennes to *St-Malo*, Rte 39 in reverse.

The direct road from Rennes to *Dinan*, 52km N.W., forks l. off the N137 11km from Rennes for (20km) *Bécherel*, to the W. of which is the 17C *Château de Caradeuc*, with its park, once owned by La Chalotais.—**Dinan** lies 21km N.W.; see Rte 41.

The N21 drives N.W., at 30km by-passing *Montauban*, and (r.) its château, with two 15C towers, and 2km beyond forks onto the N164 for *St-Méen*, 10km S.W.—The N12 continues N.W. to (45km) **Lamballe**; see Rte 41.

St-Méen-le-Grand retains interesting remains of an abbey founded by St Maine (Mewen or Mevennus; d. c. 617), a Welsh companion of St Samson of Dol. The square tower dates from the late 12C; the nave was built c. 1300, and the choir and transepts are early Gothic. The 13C tomb of the founder, and that of Abbot Coetlogon (15C), are notable features.

After 10km the road skirts the *Forêt de la Hardouinais* (r.), where in 1450 Gilles de Bretagne was murdered, and after 7km traverses *Merdrignac*.

MERDRIGNAC TO ST-BRIEUC (54km). The D6 leads N.W. to (17km) *Collinée*, c. 9km N.E. of which, on the N. edge of its forest, is the Cistercian abbey of *Boquen*, founded in 1137, and restored by Trappists in 1937, where the corpse of Gilles de Bretagne was buried.—The road continues N.W. from Collinée, at 5km passing (l.) the hilltop 19C chapel of *N.-D.-de-Bel-Air*, on the highest point of the *Landes du Mené*, and 5km beyond, Gothic *N.-D.-du-Haut*, containing statues of six 'healing saints': Mamert (healing colic), Lubin (rheumatism), Houarniaule (fear), Méen (madness), Hubert (dog-bite), and Yvertin (headache).—8km. **Moncoutour**, once an important Breton stronghold, where the Chouan leader Boishardy held out for two years against Republican forces. 16C *St-Mathurin* has a good Renaissance tower and glass of 1538. The 18C *Château des Granges* has replaced the feudal castle; 5km E. is the restored *Château de la Touche-Trébry* (16C); 6km N.W., the *Château du Colombier*.—The N12 may be gained 15km N., between *Lamballe* and *St-Brieuc*.

The N164 leads W., later skirting the *Forêt de Loudéac* (2450 hectares), sheltering wild boar and deer, to traverse (27km) *Loudéac* itself.

LOUDÉAC TO GOURIN VIA PONTIVY AND LE FAOUËT (87km). The N168 leads S.W. to (22km) **Pontivy** (14,200 Pontiviens), an ancient town on the Blavet, its picturesque lanes contrasting with the regularity of the quarters to the S., laid out after 1806 and known as 'Napoléonville' until 1871, for this staunchly Republican town was chosen by Napoleon as the military headquarters of Brittany. Gén. de Lourmel (1811–54), who fell at Inkerman, was a native. At its N. end is the *Castle*, built by Jean de Rohan in 1485, the enceinte now surrounded by a grassy moat. Pontivy became the capital of the Duchy of Rohan, created in 1603, and the Rohan mascles are displayed on the columns of the doorway of Flamboyant *N.-D.-de-la-Joie*, further S. Between the castle and church is the quaint *Pl. du Martray*, in which, and in adjacent streets, several characteristic

15-16C houses, and 17-18C mansions, are preserved. The Rue du Pont descends past the *Hospital* (partly 16-17C) incorporating one of the town's gateways.—Hence we turn W. through *Stival*, with the 16C chapel of *St-Mériadec* to (21km) *Guéméné-sur-Scorff*, and follow the D782 to (12.5km) **Kernascléden**, with a Flamboyant Breton *Chapel* of 1420– 64, with sculptured porches, handsome rose-windows, and 15C murals.—Passing near the 16th and 18C *Château de Pontcallec*, we bear W. to (14.5km) **Le Faouët**, a small town in one of the wildest regions of Brittany, with a late 16C timber and slate *Halles*, and 13C ossuary adjoining 1ts 16C church. There are several chapels in the vicinity, the more interesting being those of *St-Barbe* (1489; 2km N.E.), and *St-Fiacre* (2.5km S.), the latter with a remarkable carved and painted rood-loft of 1480.—17km N.W. is *Gourin*, a market and quarrying town on the S. slopes of the main ridge of the *Montagnes Noires*, whence one may regain the N164 13km N.W. via the D301, passing near the chapel of *N.-D. du Crann* (1532) possessing good mid 16C glass.

Driving W. from Loudéac (to be by-passed), at 19km the N164 leaves *Mur-de-Bretagne* to the S. and skirts the *Lac de Guerlédan*, with the *Forêt de Quénécan* extending beyond.—12.5km. To the l. lie the ruins of the abbey of *Bon-Repos*, founded 1172, and 6km S. those of the *Château de Salles*, overlooking its lake: to the N. are the *Gorges du Daoulas*.—16.5km. **Rostrenen**, a small hilltop town, with a market-square bordered by 16-18C houses. *N.-D.-du-Roncier*, with a tower of 1677, preserves an earlier porch containing wooden statues of the Apostles.—5.5km S.W. is the *Château de Coat-Couraval*.

10.5km. **Carhaix-Plouguer** (9100 Carhaisiens), an important road junction, market town, and dairying centre.

Gallo-Roman *Vorgium* was of consequence under the kings of Cornouaille, but the derivation of its name from Ker-Ahès (the house of Ahès, daughter of King Gradlon) is fanciful. Conomor or Comorre, a savage 6C chieftain, here decapitated his wife Tréphime and his son Trémeur, and as the victims were traditionally believed to walk around with their heads under their arms, they acquired a local reputation as saints.

La Tour d'Auvergne (Théophile-Malo Corret; 1743– 1800), 'first grenadier of France', was a native, descended from an illegitimate branch of the family whose name he was allowed to assume in 1771.

Several old houses may be seen in the vicinity of the *Pl. de la Mairie*, just S. of the town centre, to the N. of which is 16C *St-Trémeur*, while further W. is the more interesting church of *Plouguer*, partly Romanesque, with a tower of 1546.

CARHAIX-PLOUGUER TO LANDERNEAU (FOR BREST) VIA HUELGOAT (66km). The D764 winds N.W. for 17km, where we fork l. for (3.5km) **Huelgoat**, an attractively sited lake-side village somewhat spoilt by exploitation, surrounded by wooded hills and ravines, with an argentiferous lead mine worked from the 15C until 1914. The Iron Age 'Camp d'Artus', and several caves, a loganstone, the menhir of *Kerampeulven*, and other natural curiosities are visited by pedestrians. In the central Place is a 16C church containing a naive group of St Yves between the Poor man and the Rich.

The road hence to *Pleyben* (D14) leads S.W. through (7km) **St-Herbot**, its *Chapel* a fine example of 15-16C Breton architecture, preserving features of interest, but deserving restoration; adjacent is a *Calvary* of 1571. The choir contains the tomb and effigy of St Herbot, the patron of cattle, and on the day of his Pardon peasants presented the idol with tufts of hair from their beasts' tails to secure protection for their herds.—The road goes on via *Loqueffret* and *Lannédern*, both with typical Breton churchyard monuments.

From Huelgoat the D764 traverses the Parc Régional to (13.5km) cross the Morlaix-Pleyben road (see p 270) near *Roc'h Trévezel* before descending past (5km) *Commana*, its church with a good porch of 1650; to the S. of the road is the *Allée couverte' of *Mougau*.—10km. *Sizun*, with a cemetery entered through a 'Triumphal Arch' of c. 1588; its contemporary *Ossuary* is in the form of a chapel;

the church contains woodwork of interest.—At 9km we pass near *La Martyre* (see Rte 43A) prior to reaching **Landerneau**, 8km beyond.

Bearing S.W., the N164 passes (10km) *Cléden-Poher*, with a 16C *Calvary* and ossuary, and church with features of interest.—The church and *Calvary* at *St-Hernin*, 5km S.E., is noteworthy.—12km. *Châteauneuf-du-Faou*, with its church dedicated to St Teilo (c. 550; Bp of Llandaff), lies 2km S., beyond which rises the long chain of the *Montagnes Noires*.

14km. **Pleyben**, a small town with a remarkable *Calvary*, commenced c. 1550, its numerous figures in contemporary costume. The church, with wood-carvings of interest, has a Renaissance porch-tower of 1591 and a curious sacristy of 1779; the cemetery is entered through a 'Triumphal Arch' of 1725; its *Ossuary* is late Gothic, with elegant paired arches surmounted by ogees.

We meet the new Brest–Quimper road (N165) 6km W., much improving communications in the area; *Châteaulin* lies 4km beyond, for which, and the *Crozon peninsula* further W., see Rte 45.

14km. **Le Faou** (pron. 'Fou'), its main street lined with old slate-faced houses, and with a 16C church, is by-passed to the l.; to the r. is *Rumengol*, with a church of 1536 dedicated to *N.-D.-de-Tout-Remède* ('cure-all', in Breton 'Reme-holl', a pun on Rumengol), its interior profusely decorated.

10.5km. **Daoulas** preserves relics of a 12C abbey, including *Cloisters* (occupied by Franciscan nuns), one of the most interesting Romanesque survivals in Finistére. The church, with an ossuary and 16C porch, has been restored; the chapel of *St-Anne*, beyond the cemetery, is noteworthy.—Travellers *from* Brest will turn through Daoulas to visit the *Crozon peninsula*; see Rte 45.

8.5km. **Plougastel-Daoulas** (l.), a town of little attraction, having suffered severely in 1944, preserves adjacent to its rebuilt church a famous *Calvary* (1604; restored), which rivals that at Guimiliau.

In front is an altar with statues of saints; the encircling frieze of naive but spirited sculpture presents bas-reliefs of the life of Christ, while on the platform the drama of the Passion is depicted by over 150 figures.

Some names on adjacent tombstones confirm the settlement here of Spanish followers of the Duc de Mercoeur after the wars of the League, and until comparatively recently the inhabitants of this neighbourhood were inclined to more colourful costumes than elsewhere in Brittany, but the old superposed waistcoats and skirts are no longer worn.

Several 15C chapels, among them those of SS Adrien, Guénolé, and Christine, lie 4.5km S.W., containing quaint statues.

We shortly cross the Elorn estuary by the two-storeyed *Pont-Albert-Louppe* (1930; 900m long), one arch restored after its destruction by the Germans.—For **Brest**; see Rte 43A.

45 Quimper and the neighbouring Coast

Without suggesting that Quimper itself is necessarily a good base from which to visit the S. part of the Breton peninsula, it is convenient to describe this area in three short excursions commencing from Quimper. A number of the places described can of course be approached direct from Quimper, or vice versa.

Maps: IGN 13, or 105. M 230.

QUIMPER (pron. Kam-pair; 60,200 Quimpérois), an ancient cathedral town and riverport at the confluence or meeting ('Kemper') of the Steir and the Odet, was once the capital of *Cornouaille*, and is now préfecture of *Finistère*.

Traces of a Roman settlement have been found at Locmaria and elsewhere, but Quimper is said to have been founded in the 5C by king Gradlon, who brought the name Cornouaille (Cornwall) from Britain, and made St Corentin the first bishop of the see. The countship was united to the duchy of Brittany in 1066. The town, walled since the 13C, suffered in the wars of succession, being sacked in 1344 by Charles de Blois, and besieged by Jean de Montfort (1345). Its faience, manufactured in Locmaria, was originally imitated from Rouen ware.

Quimper was the birthplace of Voltaire's antagonist Elie Fréron (1718–76); René Laënnec (1781–1826), inventor of the stethoscope; probably of Yves de Kerguëlen (1734–97), navigator of the South Seas; and of the poet and painter Max Jacob (1876–1944).

For details of motor-launch excursions, enquire at the S.I., near the cathedral.

The **Cathedral* is the most complete Gothic cathedral in Brittany, despite 19C 'restoration' and additions.

The work of almost three centuries (1239–1515) it exhibits Breton characteristics in all its phases. Between the two towers, their spires erected by local subscription in the mid 1850s, is an equestrian statue of king Gradlon; the Flamboyant W. portal of 1425 is embellished with 19C sculptures. The heraldic devices of the lion of the De Montfort family holding aloft the arms of Brittany, will be noticed.—The S. portal, likewise Flamboyant, and the N. front, retain features of interest.

On entering from the W. the pronounced inclination of the choir to the l. is evident. The *Nave* has a trefoil-headed triforium, surmounted by a clerestory with Flamboyant windows containing restored 15C glass. The *Pulpit* (1676) depicts the life of St Corentin; here and elsewhere the patron is shown carrying the miraculous fish which supplied his daily meal and daily reappeared in the pool near his cell. The aisles contain the tombs of sundry bishops; those in the ambulatory chapels are of more interest. The choir, with a vault of 1410, contains some early 15C glass beside garish modern windows.

The **Musée Breton*, installed in the former *Bishop's Palace*, to the S., contains in its courtyard the reconstructed 13-15C cloisters; the gardens, with relics of ramparts, command a good view of the cathedral. The museum contains an extensive collection of tombs, among them that of Troilus de Mondragon (16C) and sculptures, both in wood and stone, the remarkable *Menhir of Kervadel*, and several Gallo-Roman antiquities. A staircase of 1530 ascends to upper floors displaying collections of Breton furniture, including '*lits clos*', coifs and costumes, and local faience, etc.

On the N. side of the *Pl. St-Corentin* is the **Musée des Beaux-Arts**, recently reorganised, with a few good paintings (apart from the usual martyrdoms and allegories), mostly French and Flemish, among them portraits by *Drolling*, *Vigée-Lebrun*, and *Chassériau* (of Mlle Cabarrus), and characteristic works by *Oudry*, *Corot*, *Boudin*, et al, and with a small section devoted to *Max Jacob*.

The Rue Kéréon, in which several old houses are preserved, leads W. to a bridge over the Ateir, close to which (l.) is a section of the fortified enceinte, with a corbelled turret. Beyond is *St-Mathieu*, with a good 16C E. window, and other old mansions in the adjacent *Pl. Terre-au-Duc*.—On the S. bank of the Odet rises thickly wooded *Mont Fruqy*; to the E. of the *Préfecture* here is a 15C wooden house (in the Rue Ste-Catherine). A few minutes' walk W. alongside the riverside *Allées de Locmaria* brings one to the faience factory, with a small

Museum; beyond is an 11-15C church and the 17C buildings of the former priory.

QUIMPER AND THE CROZON PENINSULA VIA LE FAOU. The N165 will provide a rapid drive N. to (41km) *Le Faou*; see Rte 44.

The old D720 to *Châteaulin* passes en route a 15C chapel and striking mid 16C *Calvary* at *Quilinene*, some 11.5km N. of Quimper, and that of *St-Vennec*, 5km beyond, also with a *Calvary*, preserving a curious naive statue of St Gwen, miraculously endowed with three breasts with which to suckle her saintly triplets, Guénolé, Jacut, and Vennec.—At (12km) *Châteaulin*, 15-16C *Notre-Dame*, on its hillock, contains several naive statues.—16km. *Le Faou*.

The D791 leads W. from Le Faou, climbing above the estuary of the Aulne, with views of the headland of *Landévennec*, approached by turning r. beyond (11km) the *Pont de Térénez*.

The village of **Landévennec** preserved the ruins of the **Abbey* founded by St Winwaloe (or Guénolé) in which King Gradlon is said to have been buried in the 6C. It was dismantled at the Revolution, but Benedictines have recently undertaken the erection of a new abbey adjacent. Of the old church there remains the Romanesque portal, bases of walls and piers, a curious Romanesque tomb, and the apse with three chapels, the effigy of the last resident abbot (d. 1522), and a 16C statue of the founder.—One may regain the main road just N. of *Argol*, with a typical church and enclosure.

The **Crozon Peninsula** (or *Presqu'île*), separating the *Rade de Brest* from the *Baie de Douarnenez*, with its spectacular coastal views, is an interesting corner of Brittany, but bathers are warned of its treacherous currents, and tourists should heed the military notices.—16km. *Crozon* itself, birthplace of the actor Louis Jouvet (1887–1951), is of slight interest.—3km S. lies the small fishing-port of *Morgat*, visited for its fine beach, caves, and cliff scenery, 7.5km beyond which are the cliffs of *Pointe de la Chèvre*, and 5km W., *Pointe Dinan*.—From Crozon we continue 15km W. to **Pointe de Pen-hir*, with impressive sea views, prolonged by a series of isolated granite masses known as the *Tas-de-Pois*.—Turning N. from the headland, the road skirts (l.) the *Alignment of Lagatjar* (143 menhirs), long ago overturned by an earthquake, and set up again in 1928.

Camaret-sur-Mer, à small fishing port and resort, is protected by a long natural breakwater, on which stands a Flamboyant chapel and the *Château Vauban* (1689), which played its part in the naval battles of 1694, when an Anglo-Dutch fleet was repulsed with heavy loss (cf. Brest). Off the roadstead here Robert Fulton conducted his earliest, but unsuccessful, experiments in submarine warfare (1801).

Hence a pleasant DETOUR may be made along the peninsula of *Roscanvel* to the *Pointe des Espagnols* (12km N.), which owes its name to a Spanish force which entrenched itself here in 1593 until expelled by Marshal d'Aumont, assisted by some 1800 English troops sent by Queen Elizabeth; Adm. Frobisher was fatally wounded in the assault. The views N.E. towards Brest, and of the ships anchored in the roads, are impressive. Driving S. along the E. side of the promontory, we pass the offshore islands of *Trébéron* and *des Morts*. Further E. is the little port of *Le Fret*, whence Jeanne de Navarre, regent of Brittany, set sail in 1402 to marry Henry IV. In the vicinity are nuclear-submarine and fleet air arm bases.

Regaining Crozon, we drive E., after 5.5km forking r. towards the isolated hill of *Menez Hom*, to the summit of which a road ascends (330m; view), on the S. slope of which is a chapel noted for its interior woodwork and statues. Here we turn S. to (9.5km) *Plonévez-Porzay*.

To the W., near its wide beach, the 19C chapel of **Ste-Anne-la-Palud** contains a

16C statue of St Anne, who, according to legend, was born in Cornouaille of royal lineage, but fled to the Holy Land to escape from a brutal husband. Its Pardon, in which pilgrims camped out on the adjacent sands, was the subject of a painting by Boudin (of 1852) in the museum at Le Havre.

4km S. is ***Locronan**, an ancient and well-preserved village named after St Ronan, a 5C Irish missionary. It has a late 15C *Church* with a massive tower, containing a number of 16-17C wooden figures, a good 15C E. window, and a pulpit of 1707 painted with scenes from the life of St Ronan; his tomb, and an Entombment (both 16C) are in the *Chapelle du Pénity*.

Plogonnec, with a Renaissance church tower, lies 3.5km S.E.; and **Quimper** is 13.5km beyond.—*Douarnenez*, see below, is 10km W. of Locronan.

QUIMPER TO THE POINTE DU RAZ. The D765 leads N.W. to (22km) **Douarnenez** (17,800 Douarnenistes), a thriving fishing-port and canning-centre, which although well-sited on a wide bay at the mouth of the Port-Rhu estuary, is not an attractive town, and its narrow streets are flanked by mean little houses.

It owes its name to the priory of St Tutuarn, founded on the offshore island of *Tutuarn-Enez*, now called *Île Tristan* (no adm.), which almost closes the mouth of the estuary. The connection of the islet with the lover of Isolde (or Iseult) is legendary, although some remains near *Plomarc'h*, just E. of Douarnenez, are described as those of the palace of king Mark. In the wars of the League, Fontenelle (d. 1602), a freebooter who had captured the town, held out on the island, which he had fortified, for three years (1595–98).

The 15C *Belfry* in the S. suburb of the *Ploaré* is notable.

From the central *Pl. Gabriel-Péri*, the Rue Anatole-France descends to the r. past the 16C *Chapelle St-Hélène* to the enlarged harbour, which although malodorous at low tide, is a hive of activity when the fishing fleet comes in. Hence a boulevard circles the promontory 'en corniche' before turning S., where crossing the estuary, we traverse *Tréboul*, with its smaller harbour and the beach of *Sables-Blancs*.

A minor road leads W. to approach the *Pointe du Raz* via the bird sanctuary of *Cap Sizun* and *Cléden-Cap Sizun*, with a good 16C steeple.

The main road (D765) turns W. just S. of Douarnenez, after 9km passing (r.) the 13C chapel of *N.-D. de Kérinec*, with a *Calvary* incorporating an open-air pulpit, beyond which *Confort*, with a handsome 16C Gothic church, is traversed.

7.5km. **Pont-Croix**, a village of white-washed granite houses at the head of the Goyen estuary, has an imposing 15C church, **N.-D. de Roscadon*, with a well-carved S. porch, and a belfry-tower crowned by a 65m-high spire. It retains the nave, with unusually slender columns, and a double N. aisle of the choir of its Romanesque predecessor. Its 15C baptistry contains 18C figures; a chapel N. of the apse a 17C Last Supper with carved reliefs in Roman dress.

5.5km. **Audierne**, with a hill-top church (16-17C), is an ancient port with a quaint old harbour at the mouth of its estuary, largely occupied by lobster-boats.—Hence we continue W. past (4.5km) *St-Tugen* (l.), with a chapel dedicated to St Eugène or Eoghan (d. 618), Bp of Derry, regarded as a protector against mad dogs, with his statue among other naive sculptures.—6.5km. *Plogoff* has a church dedicated to St Kea or Collédoc, a Welsh missionary bishop, said to have been the spiritual advisor to Queen Guinevere.

5km beyond is storm-beaten ***Pointe du Raz**, an 80m-high

headland identified with Ptolemy's *'Gobaeum Promontorium'*.

Below its W. extremity is a chasm known as the *Enfer de Plogoff*, against which high seas thunder; to the N. is the *Baie des Trépassés* (of the departed), named after the druids' custom of sending their dead hence for burial on the offshore *Île de Sein* (see below), or alternatively from the number of victims of shipwreck cast ashore. At the head of the bay is a marshy lagoon supposed to be the site of the maritime city of Ys, traditionally submerged in the 5C as a divine punishment for the debauchery of Ahès, daughter of king Gradlon, but some Gallo-Roman remains near the neighbouring hamlet of *Troguer* are the only evidence for the story.

Some 8km due W. is the small reef-bound **Île de Sein**, flat and treeless, with two lighthouses and a population of a few hundred fishermen and their wives. Until converted from the practice by the Jesuits in the 17C, they flourished on the trade of 'wrecking', and were known as 'sea-devils'; they have since shown their bravery in rescuing shipwrecked mariners (notably the crew of the British naval brig 'Bellissima' in 1835), while in 1940 the entire active male population took to their boats and joined Free French forces in England, aiding the escape of some 3000 sailors and soldiers in the process. Six years later Gén. de Gaulle in person presented the Cross of Liberation to the islanders.

In the 'bourg' near the harbour the 'streets' are only 1m wide, as much for economy of space as for protection against the wind. Adjacent to the modern church are two menhirs, relics of the druidic burial-place of *'Enez Sizun'* or 'Isle of the Seven (Sleepers)' of Breton legend.—Enquire at *Audierne* for the times of ferries thence.

From Audierne we follow the D784 S.E. through *Plouhinec*, with a 14C belfry, to (10km) *Plozévet*, the church with Romanesque nave-arcades and a 16C choir, and thence to **Quimper**, 25km due E.—*Pont-l'Abbé* is 22km S.E.; see below.

QUIMPER TO PONT-L'ABBÉ AND THE POINTE DE PENMARC'H.

The D785 leads 19km S.W. parallel to the more interesting D20 skirting the Odet estuary, to **Pont-l'Abbé** (7700 inhab.), the attractively sited 'capital' of the *Bigouden*, an ancient Breton tribe once inhabiting this S.W. corner of the peninsula.

Strictly speaking, the word 'Bigouden' is the name for the bizarre headdress of the women, which consists of a high cylindrical lace coif, underneath which the hair was held up tight by a small bonnet. Their black bodices and the black waistcoats of the men are embroidered with arabesque patterns in yellow and orange, elaborate costumes which may occasionally be seen at Sunday mass, market days, and Pardons.

It preserves a 13C round tower of the *Castle* of the Barons du Pont, commanding the bridge originally built by the abbots of Loctudy, and some 17C buildings housing the *Hôtel de Ville*. The tower contains the *Musée Bigouden*, illustrating local regional life, and coifs. The Gothic *Church*, with an unusual belfry of wood and slate (17C), further E., preserves notable E. and W. windows, altar-tombs of local seigneurs, and a sculpted Annunciation. Some old houses flank the shady *Pl. Gambetta*, S. of the central *Pl. de la République*. On the opposite bank of the estuary are the ruins of the church of *Lambour*, with a good portal and 13C capitals.—2.5km S.W. is the restored 16C castle of *Kernu*.

Hence one may drive W. 8km to the lonely chapel of *N.-D.-de-Tronoën* (14C), with a weatherworn 15C *Calvary*, the prototype of many in Brittany.—5km S. lies **Penmarch**, now a small village, which four centuries ago rivalled Nantes as a seaport, but declined with the failure of the off-shore fishery, its main source of wealth. Its curious 16C church of *St-Nonna* (after the Irish missionary St Ninidh) was built by local privateers—note the maritime motifs in the sculptures—and has an unfinished W. tower in addition to the characteristic gable-belfry.—*Kérity*, a small fishing-port 2km S.W., has a restored church which belonged to the Knights of St John, beyond which, on the *Pointe de Penmarch*, stands the granite *Phare d'Eckmühl* (1897), 60m high, with a visibility of 56km.—2km N. is **St-Guénolé**, with its harbour, and *Musée Préhistorique*, adjacent to various megalithic monuments, and containing a representative collection of Bronze Age weapons and ornaments, etc. found in Finistère.

Returning to Penmarch, one may drive E. past the fishing villages of *Guilvinec* and *Lesconil*, to (14km) **Loctudy**, a small resort. Its church has a Romanesque edifice with curious capitals, but masked by an unattractive 18C facade.—We pass the 16C Château of *Kérazan* (housing a school of textile crafts, etc.) to regain *Pont-l'Abbé*, 6km N.W.

Hence the excursion may be extended by turning E. onto the D44, crossing the wooded estuary of the Odet by a toll-bridge (1972) to (11km) *Bénodet*, a well-sited and popular resort with a yachting harbour and sandy beach.—**Quimper** lies 15km N.

The *Odet Estuary* may also be explored by boat. Launches run regularly from Quimper to Bénodet, and irregularly to Loctudy, and also to the *Îles de Glénan*, a sea-girt reef of nine islets, with an old tower, marine laboratory, lighthouse, sailing school, bird sanctuary, etc.

BÉNODET TO CONCARNEAU (21km). The D44 leads E. to (8km) *Fouesnant*, noted for its cider, its coifs, and *Church*, largely 12C.—*Beg-Meil*, 5.5km S.E., a resort of scattered villas among trees, with a sandy beach and rocky coves, was visited by Proust and Reynaldo Hahn in 1896.—*Concarneau* (see Rte 46) lies across the bay, approached from *Fouesnant* via *La Forêt-Fouesnant*, with an old manor, 16C church and *Calvary*.

46 Quimper to Nantes

A. Via Quimperlé, Auray, Vannes, and La Roche-Bernard

227km (141 miles). D765. 22km *Rosporden*—26km **Quimperlé**—D62. 23km **Hennebont**—N265. 28km **Auray**—N165. 18km **Vannes**—40km **La Roche-Bernard**—70km **Nantes**.

Auray, *Carnac*, and *Quiberon* are described in Rte 47; *Vannes* and the *Morbihan* in Rte 40; and the coastal road between *Concarneau* and *Lorient*, and the *Brière* (with *La Baule* and *St-Nazaire*) in Rte 46B.

The N165 provides a rapid route from Quimper to *Auray*, but bypasses most places of interest, although *Quimperlé* and *Hennebont* themselves can be approached from it with ease.

Maps: IGN 13, 15, 24, or 105. M 230.

For **Quimper**, see Rte 45. 22km. **Rosporden**, a market town on the Aven, known for its curious local coifs, with a particularly fine 14C church spire, and (11km) *Bannalec*, are traversed, beyond which we pass S. of the old castle of *Quimerch*, encircled by double moats.

13km. **QUIMPERLÉ** (11,700 Quimperlois), the old town of which stood on an island at the confluence of two streams (meeting—'kemper', as at *Quimper*). Here stood an abbey, the 18C cloisters of which are partly occupied by municipal offices. Théodore Hersant de la Villamarque (1815–95), the Breton scholar, was born here; while *Arzano* (9.5km N.E.) was the scene of 'Marie', the chief work of the pastoral poet Auguste Brizeux (cf. Lorient).

Immediately N. of the *Pl. Nationale* is ***Ste-Croix**, one of the most curious edifices in Brittany.

An almost exact reconstruction of the Romanesque building (1029–83) founded by Alain, count of Cornouaille, it was partly destroyed in 1862 by the subsidence of the belfry tower. The plan of the rotunda, with its three apsidal projections forming a cross, emulates that of the Holy Sepulchre at Jerusalem. The facade is 18C, and the detached tower has been rebuilt.

The *Ambulatory*, with two small apses, forms a ring round three parts of the central rotunda, off which opens the larger E. apse. The W. doorway is framed in a delicately carved but mutilated Renaissance *Rood-screen* (1541). Beneath the choir is an 11C *Crypt*, with Romanesque capitals showing Byzantine influence. Here are the 15C tombs of Abbot Lespervez, and St Gurloes (d. 1057), the first abbot, who is invoked against gout!

The Rue Brémond-d'Ars leads N., with (r.) the 15C doorway of ruined *St-Colomban* and some old timbered houses and dilapidated 17-18C mansions; the double staircase (l.) is a relic of the Court of the King's Lieutenant.—Opposite St-Colomban a lane flanked by some grotesquely quaint hovels leads to the *Pont Salé*, beyond which in the upper town, buttressed by houses, is *St-Michel* (14-15C), with a Flamboyant N. porch.

S. of the town is the former Dominican *Abbaye Blanche*, founded in 1255 by Blanche de Champagne, consort of Duc Jean I, rebuilt in the 17C, in which the elder Jean de Montfort (d. 1345), ancestor of the later dukes of Brittany, is buried.

Le Faouët, see Rte 44, lies 21km N. on the D790.

12km. *Pont-Scorff*, the *Mairie* of which is in a handsome Renaissance mansion, is traversed, and 11km beyond, **Hennebont** (13,100 inhab.), an ancient fortress and decayed river-port on the Blavet, which suffered considerably in 1944–45 when it was occupied by the Americans during the siege of the Lorient 'pocket'.

In 1342 Jeanne de Montfort, 'la Flamme', was besieged here by Charles de Blois, and saved by the timely arrival of an English fleet under Sir Walter de Manny sent to her aid by Edward III. The English garrison was put to the sword by Du Guesclin in 1372.

Conspicuous in the central square is the tower of Gothic *N.-D. du Paradis* (1513–30), with a graceful W. portal. The 13-15C *Porte du Broc-Erec'h*, the gateway to the *Ville-Clos*, was gutted in 1944, and the destructive fire revealed a stretch of 15C *Town Wall* descending towards the river.

The Cistercian *Abbaye de la Joie*, 1km N., founded in 1279, with slight remains, is now a stud-farm.—For *Baud*, 23km N.E., see Rte 40; for *Carnac*, 30km S.E., see Rtes 46B, and 47.

28km. **Auray**, for which, and its surroundings, see Rte 47.

18km. **Vannes**; see the latter part of Rte 40.

VANNES TO NANTES VIA REDON AND BLAIN (124km). The N166 leads N.E., shortly bearing r. onto the D775, at 25km passing 3km N. of *Questembert*, preserving several old houses and a covered *Market* of 1675. A monument commemorates a battle here in 888, in which Alain le Grand defeated 15,000 Normans (?Northmen, or Viking pirates), only 400 of whom escaped to their ships!—At 2km the l.-hand fork leads 7.5km to *Rochefort-en-Terre, a singularly attractive and characteristic Breton village overlooking the Arz, with a long street of 17C granite houses and an old *Market-hall*. The *Castle* was twice destroyed, by the Leaguers in 1594 and the Chouans in 1793, but a 13C gateway survives, and the 17C buildings have been restored. *N.-D.-de-la-Tronchaye* has an interesting N. front with large Gothic windows (1553); the interior, of four aisles, contains stalls of 1590, parts of a rood-screen, painted statues, and a 17C stone altarpiece.—There are several megalithic monument near the *Bois de Brambien*, towards *St-Gravé*, 6km N.E.

Hence we continue E., having regained the D775, to (29km) **Redon** (10,300 Redonnais), at the crossing of the Vilaine and the Nantes-Brest canal. The Grande Rue has several quaint old houses, while *St-Sauveur* belonged to a Benedictine abbey founded early enough to be destroyed by the Northmen in 869. Since a fire in 1782 the Gothic S.W. tower has remained isolated from the rest of the building. The rounded angles of the low central 12C *Tower* are unique in Brittany (and probably in France). The design of the triforium is notable, while the nave has been restored in a plain Romanesque style. Adjacent are 17C abbey buildings, with a cloister. Chestnuts, for 'marron glacés' are exported hence in some quantity.

The D164 leads S.E. along the flank of the Isaac valley, at 24km skirting the beautiful *Forêt du Gâvre* (4500 hectares), to enter (9km) **Blain** (7400 inhab.), with a well-preserved *Castle* said to have been founded in 1104, but the oldest part is the huge *Tour du Connétable*, built by Olivier de Clisson in 1380. The cylindrical *Tour du Pont-Levis* was later added, and a residential wing after 1551. The Protestant leader Henri, first Duc de Rohan (1579–1638), son-in-law of Sully, was born here. Hence one may follow the D42 S.E. for (35km) **Nantes**.

The N165 continues S.E. from Vannes, at 23km by-passing *Muzillac*, 2.5km S. of which is the *Abbaye de Prières*, with a restored tower; a chapel contains the effigies of the founder (in 1250), Duc Jean I, and Isabel of Castile (d. 1328), wife of Jean III.

At 15km the road passes S. of *Marzan*, with a quaint *Market-house*, and crosses the tidal Vilaine (view) on a bridge rebuilt since 1944 (the successor to a suspension bridge under construction when Southey passed that way in 1838, destroyed in 1912), to **La Roche-Bernard**, an old town preserving several ancient mansions, and once famous for shipbuilding. In 1795–80 it was known as 'La Roche-Sauveur', in memory of Joseph Sauveur, the district president, murdered by a royalist mob. James II, en route to Brest in 1689, was entertained here by the Duc de Chaulnes, lieutenant-governor of Brittany.—For the area S. of the road, and the *Grande-Brière*, see Rte 46B.

At 10km we pass (l.) the 15C *Château de la Bretesche*, rebuilt after being burnt during the Revolution.—By-passing (9km) *Pontchâteau*, the road runs parallel to a long range of low hills known as the *Sillon de Bretagne*, to approach **Nantes**, 50km S.E.; see Rte 59A.

B. Via the Coast: Concarneau, Lorient, La Baule, and St-Nazaire

270km (168 miles). D783. 23km **Concarneau**—14km Pont- Aven—17km **Quimperlé**—D265. 20km **Lorient**—D165. 36km Auray—18km **Vannes**—40km **La Roche-Bernard**—D774. 17km Guérande. La Croisic lies 11km S.W.—D92. 6km **La Baule**—17km St- Nazaire—N171. 28km N165. 34km **Nantes**.

Several detours are also described, which will add to the distance.

Quimperlé is described in Rte 46A; *Auray, Carnac,* and *Quiberon*, in Rte 47; and *Vannes* and the *Morbihan* in Rte 40.

Maps: IGN 13, 15, 24, or 105, also 501 for the Morbihan, and 308 for the Brière. M 230.

For **Quimper**, see Rte 45.

23km. **Concarneau** (18,200 Concarnois), a thriving fishing-port, with large canning factories for both tunny and sardines, and vegetables, is attractively sited on the E. shore of the bay of *La Forêt*, with small but frequented beaches, and preserves its imposingly fortified *Ville Close* on an island site between the *Avant* and *Arrière Ports*, reached by a bridge from the central *Pl. Jean-Jaurès*, with the S.I. It was visited twice by Flaubert, in 1847 and 1875.

Its earliest ramparts date from the 14C, when the English were besieged here by De Guesclin, and were later reconstructed by Vauban. We pass through two gateways, separated by a kind of barbican, to reach the Rue Vauban (spoilt by over-exploitation by the souvenir industry), which traverses the length of the island, off which lead lanes. Here a fee is charged to ascend the rampart walk, although other sections of the massive granite walls further E. may be reached without any such imposition. A *Fishing Museum* may be visited.

Out to sea lie the *Îles de Glénan* (see p 284); for excursions, enquire at the S.I.

Pont-Aven, a picturesque village, lies in a rocky valley at the head of its estuary, above which are water-mills, the romantic *Bois d'Amour*, and the rustic chapel of *Trémalo*. It was here in 1888 that Paul Gauguin informally established the so-called 'School of Pont-Aven', although he migrated to *Le Pouldu* the following year; see below. In fact several French and English artists had preceded him, including Berthe Morisot in 1866, while in 1896 it was visited by Ernest Dowson, the poet. Théodore Botrel (1868–1925) is buried here.—3km S., on the W. bank, is the 15-16C *Château de Henan*, with a tall hexagonal keep.

Quimperlé, see Rte 46A, lies 17km E.; and *Lorient* is 20km further S.E.

PONT-AVEN TO LORIENT VIA THE COAST (50km). At (4.5km) *Riec-sur-Belon*, near the head of its estuary, famous for its oysters, we turn r. through (11.5km) *Clohars-Carnoët*, S.E. of which is *Le Pouldu*, where in 1889 Gauguin, disgusted with the influx of visitors to Pont-Aven, stayed for a franc a day at the auberge of 'Marie Poupée'.—The main road passes (l.), prior to crossing the Laïta estuary, the ruins of the abbey of *St-Maurice*, founded in 1170, to the N. of which is the *Forêt de Carnoët*, in which are the relics of a castle said to have been built by the ferocious Conomor (cf. Carhaix-Plouguer).—8.5km. *Guidel*, which is close to the direct road to *Lorient*.

Turning r., we follow the coast road via *Fort-Bloques*, with a view of the offshore *Île de Groix*, 8km S., cliff-bound and treeless, known to the Bretons as Enez-Groac'h (Witch's Island), which may be visited by launch from Lorient.—At *Larmor-Plage*, at the mouth of the Lorient estuary, we turn N., with a view (r.) of three colossal and virtually indestructible *German Submarine Shelters* (1941–43), built of reinforced concrete and hardly damaged by bombardment.

They are now named after Gén. Stosskopf, an engineer officer, who ostensibly collaborating, communicated information about the movements of U-boats to the Allies until eventually betrayed and shot. Adjacent are the new commercial and fishing harbours.

LORIENT (64,700 Lorientais), one of the main French naval bases, largely rebuilt since the last war, stands on both banks of the Scorff at its confluence with the Blavet, which form its estuary. It was never of great interest to the ordinary traveller: Young found it 'so full of fools, gaping to see a man-of-war launched' that he could get no bed for himself nor stable for his horse, while Murray remarked in 1843 on the 'monotonous dullness of its dirty streets, whose meagre houses look as though they were built merely to be knocked down'—which they were, exactly a century later! Its *Naval Dockyards* and *Arsenal* are not accessible to foreigners.

About 1628, merchants trading with India from the old port of Blavet (Port-Louis) built a few warehouses here, but the settlement did not receive its name (L'Orient) until 1664, when letters patent were granted by Louis XIV to the French East India Company (Compagnie des Indes) for the establishment of shipbuilding-yards. The Company became a potent maritime power, and reached the height of its prosperity towards the middle of the 18C, when it owned 35 ships of the largest class. An English attempt against Lorient under Adm. Lestock and Gen. Sinclair miscarried in Oct. 1746, although 7000 troops were landed; but the French loss of Bengal (1753) and internal mismanagement led to the failure of the Company, and the port passed to the Crown, to be re-fortified under Napoleon, by which time the warehouses 'of several stories and all vaulted in stone, in a splendid style and of vast extent', were virtually empty.

Lorient was four-fifths destroyed in the Second World War, as the submarine base established here by the Germans attracted the heaviest air attacks, notably in Jan.-Feb. 1943 (see above). During the American relief of Brittany (Aug. 1944) the garrison entrenched itself here in a 'pocket' and what was left of the town and its surroundings was further devastated in an artillery duel which lasted until the German surrender on 8 May 1945.—The Breton poet Auguste Brizeux (1803–58), of Irish extraction, was born here.

For **Hennebont**, 9km N.E., see Rte 46A.

LORIENT TO AURAY VIA PORT-LOUIS (47km). On crossing the Blavet, turn r. to **Port-Louis**, so-named by Richelieu to flatter his sovereign. It had been in Spanish hands from 1590 until ransomed by France at the Treaty of Vervins (1598), who built the *Citadel*, extended in 1616–36. Here were confined Louis Napoleon in 1836, several Communards in 1871–72, and members of the Resistance in 1941–44. The *Town Walls* of c. 1650 rise picturesquely from the beach; to the S.E., the long sandy shore is a gunnery-range.—This is skirted to the E., passing 5km S. of *Merlevenez*, with a well-restored Romanesque church, to cross the *Rivière d'Etel*, an estuary here forming a curious inland sea.

To the N. on the far bank is a little island on which is the Romanesque chapel of *St-Cado*, named after a prince of Glamorgan who settled here in the 5-6C; the causeway by which it is approached is said to have been built by the Devil in a single night, in response to an offer by St Cadoc who promised to yield to him the soul of the first to cross it. At daybreak the casuistical Welshman let his cat out onto the causeway, which the Devil in his fury attempted to destroy; the saint, in preventing him, slipped on a slimy rock, and left what is now pointed out by the pious as the 'Glissade de St-Cado'.—**Auray**, see Rte 47, lies 14km due E.

Travellers preferring to continue S.E. to *Carnac* or *Quiberon* will fork r. onto the D781 to (10.5km) *Plouharnel*, past the small fishing port of *Etel*, with several megalithic monuments in its vicinity, and after *Erdeven* pass (l.) the **Alignment of Kerzerho*, with over 1000 stones standing, and a short distance beyond, *Crucuno* (l.) with two dolmens, one of them the largest in the Morbihan. For *Plouharnel*, and the area in general, see Rte 47.

From Lorient, the N165 by-passes *Hennebont* (see Rte 46A), and circles S.E. to approach **Auray** (see Rte 47), there turning due E. to (18km) **Vannes** (see Rte 40), beyond which we follow the road to (40km) *La Roche-Bernard*; for the direct road hence to **Nantes**, see Rte 46A.

Turning S. onto the D774, we enter the *Parc Naturel de Brière*, a curious peaty plain, 7000 hectares in extent, once a lagoon, and now intersected by dikes and flooded in winter. Here and there rise islets with their thatched cottages, whose inhabitants still subsist largely on fishing and fowling, for their monopoly of peat-cutting is restricted to a short summer season.

From (8km) *Herbignac*, the market for the N. part of the Brière, a
road running E. and S.E. to *Montoir* serves several of these amphibious villages, typical of which is *Île de Fédrun*.

17km. **Guérande** (9500 inhab.), an interesting old town preserving
almost intact its circuits of *Walls, 15C on earlier foundations, retaining six towers and four gateways; that of *St-Michel*, facing E.,
houses the *Mairie* and a collection of local costumes. In the centre is
St-Aubin, outwardly much-restored, with a 15C exterior pulpit. The
nave, mainly 12C, has historiated capitals; the transepts and choir
are 15-16C. A treaty signed on the altar in 1365 acknowledged Jean
de Montfort as Duc Jean IV of Brittany, who in 1384 built the chapel
of *N.-D. la-Blanche* in the *Pl. du Pilori*.

Piriac, on a promontory 12km N.W., was described by Zola as 'un
trou perdu, au bout du monde'.

A new road now connects Guérande with the N171 N. of St-
Nazaire, at its junction with the approach to the Loire
bridge.—Another road leads directly to *La Baule*, 6km S.

GUÉRANDE TO LA BAULE VIA LE CROISIC. This detour takes one through the
old village of *Saillé*, on the edge of extensive salt-marshes, lying several metres
below high water level, where sea-water is let in to evaporate, when it is heaped
up by the '*paludiers*'. Circling to the S. we traverse *Batz-sur-Mer*, its church
tower of 1677 dominating the area, to enter the old fishing-port of **Le Croisic**,
near the end of its peninsula, its harbour facing the inland gulf and protected by
the artificial promontory of *Penbron* opposite. After the French naval defeat off
Quiberon in 1759 it was bombarded for three days by English ships. It retains
several 17-18C houses, and its *Mairie* occupies the late 16C *Hôtel d'Aiguillon*,
with a small naval museum. Flamboyant *N.-D. de Pitié*, with a 17C lantern, and
graceful N. porch, and the picturesque *Poissonnerie*, are other buildings of
note.—Some good cliff scenery is commanded by a road circling the *Pointe de
Croisic* and skirting the S. side of the peninsula to the yachting centre of *Le
Pouliguen*, on the W. side of the canal which alone divides it from *La Baule*.

La Baule (14,700 inhab.), the largest and most fashionable resort on
the so-called 'Côte d'Amour', was founded c. 1906 among pine trees
originally planted to moor the shifting dunes: in fact it partly occupies the site of the old village of *Escoublac*, whose inhabitants had
been diven inland by the encroaching sands. The extensive beach is
bordered by a wide promenade, the W. end of which is reserved for
pedestrians. Like most summer resorts, it has its casino, tennis
courts, golf-courses, and other distractions. The painter Édouard
Vuillard (1868– 1940) died here.

To the E. is the contiguous resort of *Pornichet*, whence one may
drive direct to *St-Nazaire*, or follow the slightly longer but more attractive road skirting the *Pointe de Chémoulin*.

ST-NAZAIRE (68,900 Nazairiens), practically destroyed in the Second World War, is of little interest to the ordinary traveller,
although as a port and shipbuilding centre it has made a remarkable
recovery.

Work on the harbour has revealed the probable location of *Corbilo*, the pre-
Roman port of the Veneti (not at *Couëron*, as was long assumed). In the Middle
Ages a castle defended the ducal harbour here—there had been a port at the
Loire mouth for centuries—but it was not until the mid 19C, when the increasing
size of vessels made access to Nantes less convenient, that St-Nazaire was
developed: the population rose from 3000 to 40,000 between 1850 and 1940.
The great dock or *Bassin de Penhoët* was opened in 1881. It was a temporary
base of the British Expeditionary Force in 1914, and part of the American contingent disembarked here in 1917.
On 17 June 1940, during the evacuation of France, the 'Lancastria', with 6000

British troops on board, was sunk off St-Nazaire by German planes, with the loss of 3000 lives. Five days later the Germans occupied the place, which became one of their main U-boat bases. On 27/28 March 1942 a British commando raid took the enemy completely by surprise. The old destroyer 'Campbeltown', filled with high explosive timed to detonate some hours later, was forced into the dock entrance, and duly blew up. Landing-parties fought a fierce 48-hour battle in the streets. Further destructive explosions led to savage reprisals on the civilian population. The Germans then fortified the area, but for the next two years the port was regularly attacked from the air; and as the 'St-Nazaire pocket' it held out against the Americans from Aug. 1944 until the garrison finally surrendered on 12 May 1945. The Harbour works were found to be mined, but they failed to explode.

The sole relic of the past is the so-called *Dolmen* (actually a trilithon) in the Rue du Dolmen, leading N.E. from the *Pl. Marceau*. To the E. of this square may be seen the huge *Submarine Shelter* erected by the German 'Todt Organisation', which resisted all air attacks. Visitors are not permitted to enter the dockyard or harbour, but a good idea of their extent may be obtained by driving N. from the shelters to regain the main road to Nantes to the N.E., beyond the entrance to the ***Pont de St-Nazaire** (1975; 3356m. in length; toll), which provides an alternative route to Nantes S. of the Loire; see below.

The fast but uninteresting N171 passes N. of *Donges*, an ancient riverside port once the capital of the Brière, now surrounded by petrol refineries, to join the N165 for Nantes (34km S.E.) just beyond (25km) *Savenay*, where in Dec. 1893 the last remnants of the royalist army of the Vendée was defeated by Kléber.

Alternatively, one may follow the old road (D17), which runs along the crest of the *Sillon de Bretagne*, the long range of low hills running S.E. towards **Nantes**; see Rte 61.

NANTES MAY ALSO BE APPROACHED VIA PORNIC (68km) by crossing the new bridge to *Mindin*, where Charles Edward Stuart embarked on 'La Doutelle', which carried him to Scotland in 1745.

Hence a minor road follows the S. bank of the Loire to (57km) Nantes via (11km) *Paimboeuf*, a decayed seaport, and 25km beyond, S. of the riverside hamlet of *La Martinière*, birthplace of Napoleon's police chief Joseph Fouché (1759–1820), before meeting the D751; see below.

The road from Mindin passes several minor resorts backed by pinewoods, later leaving the rocky *Pointe de St-Gildas* to the W. as it approaches (21km) **Pornic** (8700 Pornicais), on a creek providing a natural harbour (ferries to the *Île de Noirmoutier;* see Rte 62B). Its 13-14C *Castle* was forfeited by Gilles de Rais and devastated during the Breton wars of succession; Browning's 'Gold Hair' is a 'story of Pornic'.—The coast road continues to *Bourgneuf-en-Retz* (13km S.W.; see Rte 62B).—Turning E., at 12.5km we pass S. of the ruined castle of *Princé*, another haunt of Gilles de Rais, and 20km beyond pass (r.) the N. edge of the *Lac de Grand-Lieu*, a reedy expanse of 7000 hectares noted for its fish and water-fowl. Skirting the airport of *Château-Bougon*, and by-passing *Rézé*, site of a Gallo-Roman oppidum on the hill to the r., we cross the Loire to **Nantes**; see Rte 61.

47 Auray, Carnac, and Quiberon; Belle-Ile

Plenty of time should be allowed for the exploration of the numerous megalithic monuments to be seen in the area, the more important of which are described. Not every dolmen, etc. is detailed, but most of them are well signposted.

Maps: IGN 15, or preferably 501. M 230.

Auray (10,200 Alréens), on the *Rivière d'Auray*, the estuary of the Loc, noted for its oysters, is an old-fashioned town, which, like *Vannes* (18km E.; see Rte 40), is a convenient base from which to explore this fascinating part of Brittany.

A decisive battle here in 1364 secured the dukedom of Brittany for young Jean de Montfort, later the son-in-law of Edward III. Du Guesclin was taken prisoner by Sir John Chandos, and Charles de Blois was killed.—At *Kerléano*, on the S.W. outskirts, was born and buried (at least his remains, after his skeleton had been mounted on wire by Larrey) the 'last of the Chouans', Georges Cadoudal (1771–1803). Benjamin Franklin landed on the quay at Auray in 1776.

From the central *Pl. de la République*, with the 18C *Hôtel de Ville*, the Rue du Lait leads to *St-Gildas* (1624; with contemporary altar-pieces); the Rue du Père-Éternel leads S. to the *Promenade du Loc*, where a belvedere occupies the site of a castle demolished in 1558. In the transpontine suburb are several sombre overhanging 15-17C houses, and *St-Goustan*, largely rebuilt but retaining a Gothic porch.

Some 2km N., to the W. of the D768, is the 18C *Chartreuse*, rebuilt on the site of a monastery erected to commemorate the battle of 1364, but ravaged by fire in 1968, when occupied by a home for female deaf mutes, when the *Funerary Chapel* (1823; abutting the Hospital chapel of 1720) was badly damaged. It contains the tomb of 952 royalists who were made prisoner after the disastrous Quiberon landing (see below) and afterwards shot (Aug. 1795) by Hoche's Republican troops on the so-called Champs des Martyrs to the N.E., with its expiatory chapel of 1829; cf. Vannes.

The excursion may be extended by turning N.E. to (4km) **Ste-Anne-d'Auray**, which since 1623 has been the resort of Breton pilgrims, a peasant named Yves Nicolazic having been instructed by the mother of the Virgin to erect a chapel on the site where she stated one had stood some 924 years earlier. Two years later a statue (probably a Celtic or Gallo-Roman image) was discovered there, and the Carmelites were soon promoting the cult. The 17C dependencies are more attractive than the ostentatious basilica of 1865–78 (which contains some 15C English alabaster panels).

The D28 leads 8km S. to a road junction.

The l.-hand fork leads to (5km) *Locmariaquer*, on the outskirts of which a path leads r. to the passage-grave of *Mané-Lud*, with inscribed supports. Nearer the village is the *'allée couverte'* and dolmen of *Mané-Rutual*, enclosed by a wall. On the r. at the entrance to the village a path approaches the granite **Men-er-Groac'h*, which was the largest menhir existing (20m) until struck by lightning in the 18C; it now lies prostrate, and its four fractured pieces, one of which is 13m long, are estimated to weigh 345 tonnes. Beside it is the **Dol-ar-Marc'ha-dourien* or 'Table des Marchands', a dolmen approached by a passage and supported at one end by a conical inscribed menhir.

Locmariaquer ('the place of the Virgin Mary') is an attractive little port near the mouth of the Rivière d'Auray, its church containing good 12C capitals.—1km S. is the **Tumulus de Mané-er-Groc'h*, a barrow hollowed out in the shape of a funnel, with an entrance at its base. At the extremity of the peninsula is the '_allée couverte_' of the _Pierres-Plates_, with more inscribed stones, and a good view across the mouth of the _Golfe du Morbihan_; see Rte 40.

Returning to the road junction, we turn l. to cross the mouth of the Rivière de Crach and traverse the little harbour of _La Trinité-sur-Mer_, with oyster beds.

8km. CARNAC, a village world-famous for its ancient stone monuments—the 'giant stones of Carnac... bearded with lichen, scarr'd and grey' of Matthew Arnold. The resort of _Carnac-Plage_, planted with pines, and with a sandy beach on 'the sickle sweep of Quiberon Bay' is almost contiguous to the S.—In the centre of the old village is 17C _St-Cornély_ (Cornelius, the patron of horned cattles in S. Brittany; cf. _St-Herbot_), with a good spire and interior features of interest. Cattle are drawn up for presentation before the church prior to being driven through the streets in procession at its Sept. fair and Pardon.

Adjacent is the *_Musée Miln-Le Rouzic_, with an unrivalled collection of artifacts, largely from excavations in the locality.

It was founded by James Miln (1819–81), a Scotsman whose interest was aroused by the stone monuments in the area, and who commenced digging in 1874. His finds were classified and greatly increased in the pre-historic field by Zacharie Le Rouzic (1864–1939), who, starting as Miln's assistant, became a distinguished archaeologist. His detailed description of the megalithic monuments in the neighbourhood may be obtained at the museum, now controlled by the University of Rennes.

A short distance N.E. stands the *_Tumulus de St-Michel_, a barrow 120m long, 65m broad, and 12m high, built of uncemented stone blocks, and surmounted by a rebuilt chapel providing a view of the alignments to the N. The earliest excavations, in 1862, led to the discovery of a subterranean dolmen, with calcined bones, jewels, and other remains, but since then the interior galleries have been 'reconstituted'. Mounds to the E. mark the site of a Gallo-Roman villa first unearthed by Miln.

The megalithic monuments here are the most extensive of their kind, among which the ****Alignment of Carnac** comprises no less than 2730 standing and fallen menhirs to the N. and N.E. of the village and among neighbouring hamlets.

Many theories have been advanced concerning their origin, once naively assumed to be the burial-ground of some great forgotten battle, and in the 18C they were seriously explained as marking the site of a Roman encampment, the stones being set up to protect their tents from the wind! A local tradition suggests that they were the serried ranks of warriors miraculously turned to stone in the act of pursuing St Cornelius to the shore. Le Rouzic, while recognising their funerary character, believed that they were astronomically arranged to indicate the direction of sunrise at the solstices and the equinox, and thus to fix the periods for ceremonies of an ancient cult of solar worship.

The erection of menhirs commenced in the middle-Neolithic period (before 2000 B.C.), while the first dolmens date from the late-Neolithic era (2000–1200); the last megaliths may perhaps be assigned to the latest Bronze Age (c. 750 B.C.). In recent centuries, especially in the early 19C, much damage was done by seekers after gold ornaments, and many menhirs were thrown down and dolmens unroofed. With the creation of the Historic Monuments Commission in 1879, restoration was put in hand, but unfortunately the work was often carried out in an amateur fashion, and several menhirs were re-erected upside down.

Immediately N. of the village, beyond the D196, is the **Alignment of**

Part of the alignment of Le Ménec

Le Ménec, its W. end a hemicycle of 70 mehirs partly embedded among the houses and gardens of the hamlet of that name, while 11 rows extend to the N.E. roughly parallel to the road towards the cross-road (D119).—Hence a circuit of 8km passes a series of other monuments. Continuing E. along the D196 we pass (l.) the **Alignment of Kermario** of 10 rows, in which likewise the largest stones are at the W. end.—Shortly a lane to the r. leads to the château of *Kercado*, in the park of which is a fine chambered tumulus.—Beyond a farm on the l. begins the *Alignment of Kerlescant*, 13 rows preceded by an irregular ring of menhirs, and ends near *Kerlescant*, beyond which we turn l. onto the D186, although the alignment is continued as far as some rows of smaller stones known as *Le Petit-Ménec.*—On turning l. 2km N., beyond *Le Moustoir* we pass (r.) an excavated barrow surmounted by a menhir, and continuing S.W., one may return to *Carnac*.

3km N.W. of Carnac lies *Plouharnel*, an old village with a 16C chapel containing an alabaster Tree of Jesse, to the N.E. of which are the dolmens of *Kergavat*, and those of *Rondossec*, *Vieux-Moulin*, and *Kerbérenne*, with menhirs.—At the village of *St-Barbe*, 2km N.W., Gén. Hoche established his camp among the dunes to meet the landing at Quiberon; see below.

For the area between Plouharnel and *Etel*, to the N.W., see p 288.—The return journey to Auray may be made by the D768, leading N.E. past the dolmens of (l.) *Runesto* and *Mané-Kerioned*, and (r.) *Keriavel*, and (4km) *Crucuny*, with an excavated barrow surmounted by a menhir, before skirting the head of the Crach estuary.—9km. **Auray**.

PLOUHARNEL TO QUIBERON (15km). Skirting the sandy bay of Plouharnel, where the sea recedes some 4km at low tide, the road veers S. along a narrow isthmus of dunes and salt-marshes, to traverse (6km) *Penthièvre*, with an 18C fort guarding the narrowest part of the 'Presqu'ile', only 275m wide, where a monument commemorates 50 Frenchmen shot here in July 1944 by the Germans, who held out in the peninsula for 11 months in 1944–45, destroying the pinewoods previously planted to moor the dunes.

The *Bay of Quiberon*, to the E., was the scene of a decisive battle between Caesar's triremes and the leather-sailed fleet of the Veneti in 56 B.C.; and in Nov. 1759 of the daring action in which Hawke destroyed the French fleet under Conflans, shattering any plans for an invasion of England.

The isthmus widens just before *St-Pierre-Quiberon*, where there is an alignment of 21 menhirs and a stone circle.—5.5km beyond, somewhat exposed at the S. extremity of the peninsula, lies **Quiberon** itself, a fishing-port and small resort, with some impressive coastal scenery to the W. along the 'Côte Sauvage'; while to the E., on the far side of the sheltering *Pointe du Conguel*, is *Port-Haliguen*, where steamers for *Belle-Île* berth in stormy weather. A statue of Gén. Hoche (1768–97) in the town centre of Quiberon recalls the ill-judged expedition of June-July 1795 which he was sent to quell, the Convention having received prior warning of such a descent.

Some 10,000 French 'émigrés', some of them *ci-devant* noblemen and ostensibly converted Republican prisoners-of-war, were disembarked at the base of the peninsula under the protection of Commodore Warren's squadron. They were joined by bands of Chouans (see p 242), but some of the rank and file mutinied, and in spite of the brave resistance of a force under Sombreuil, the royalists were either driven ignominiously into the sea or obliged to lay down their arms, for owing to rough weather the English ships could not approach the shore, and under 2000 reached the safety of their decks.

The *Îles de Houat* and *de Hoëdic*, two peaks of a submarine granite ridge connecting Quiberon to Le Croisic, lie 15km and 22km S.E., respectively, and may be visited by vedette (enquire at the S.I. in the Pl. Hoche). The former is fertile and flowery, and was the first refuge of St Gildas, who returned to die there in 570; the latter is flat and barren. There are dolmens and menhirs on both.

14km to the S.W. of Quiberon lies *Belle-Île**, the largest of the Breton islands, some 18km from N.W. to S.E., and 10km wide, consisting largely of a bare and exposed slaty plateau intersected by valleys in which subtropical plants flourish.

It belonged to the counts of Cornouaille, one of whom presented it to the abbey of Ste-Croix, Quimperlé, in the 9C. In 1548 an English fleet of 36 sail was driven off, but in 1573, after the monks had sold the island to the de Retz family, a raid was successful. Several further attacks were made, notably by Adm. Tromp (1673), who was obliged to re-embark the men he had landed, and by Adm. Keppel and Gen. Hodgson, who captured the island in 1761. This English occupation lasted two years, after which it was restored to France by the same treaty which gave Nova Scotia to England. A number of Nova Scotian families then migrated to Belle-Île, where they introduced the potato some years before Parmentier had popularised its cultivation in France.

Nicolas Fouquet was the owner of the island prior to his arrest in 1661; it was later rented for a time by the French East India Company (cf. Lorient). Adm. Willaumez (1763–1845) and Gén. Trochu (1815–96) were born on Belle-Île. Here Dumas *père* laid several scenes of his 'Vicomte de Bragelonne' as well as the tragic death of Porthos (in the caves of Locmaria).

Steamers from Quiberon or Lorient enter the picturesque harbour of *Le Palais*, on the N.E. coast, the principal town, the ramparts and *Citadel* of which, built in 1572 by Marshal de Retz, and strengthened by Fouquet and Vauban, give it an imposing aspect. The founder of the church of *St-Géran* has been identified by Baring-Gould with the Geraint of Arthurian legend.

1km N.W. is the massive *Château Fouquet*, in which Fouquet never stayed, but in which Barbès and Blanqui were imprisoned in 1848.—Some 7km beyond is the little fishing-port of *Sauzon*, and near the *Pointe des Poulains*, a dismantled fort long occupied as a summer residence by Sarah Bernhardt.—2.5km W. of

Sauzon is the *Grotte de l'Apothicairerie, one of the natural curiosities of Brittany, named for the regularity with which cormorants' nests are ranged on its ledges.—Turning S.E., two menhirs are passed to approach the central crossroads of the island, near its airstrip.—To the S.W. is the high-lying *Grand-Phare* (1826; view), below which is the fiord-like *Port de Goulphar.*—At the E. end of Belle-Île is *Locmaria*, with the *Pointe de Kerdonis* to the N.E., whence one may regain Le Palais by skirting the *Plage des Grands Sables*, the scene of Tromp's landing.

V   THE LOIRE VALLEY: ORLÉANAIS; TOURAINE; POITOU; VENDÉE

The *Loire* (not to be confused with the *Loir*, its northern tributary), in its lower reaches traversing several historic provinces and rich and fertile regions, is inferior in beauty to the Seine, although near its banks are found several of the more imposing châteaux of France, or at least, the more promoted. Swollen in winter and spring, and subject to devastating floods (its right bank requiring a protective dyke or *levée* between Blois and Angers), and even changes of bed, in summer it shrinks to a placid stream flowing lazily through unsightly sand banks, making navigation difficult at all seasons, and often impossible.

The **Orléanais** includes, to the N., the *Beauce*, 'the granary of France', and to the S., the barren *Sologne*, rich in game. Its adhesion to the Armagnac cause invited its invasion by the Burgundians and English, the subsequent siege of Orléans being raised by Joan of Arc in 1429. The province was united to the French crown in 1495. The first Duc d'Orléans, a son of Philippe I of Valois, died without issue; Louis, brother of Charles VI, founded a second ducal line, and his son Charles d'Orléans, the poet (1394– 1465; who had been taken prisoner at Agincourt and remained 25 years in captivity in England), was father of Louis XII. The third creation began and ended with Gaston (1608– 60), brother of Louis XIII. Louis-Philippe, who ascended a precarious throne in 1830, and his father Philippe Égalité (1747– 93; the fifth duke of an undistinguished line), traced their descent from Philippe (d. 1701; brother of Louis XIV, whose son was the Regent (d. 1723) described in Saint-Simon's 'Memoirs'.

Touraine, now the department of *Indre-et-Loire*, takes its name from the Gallic tribe of the Turones. It has been styled 'the garden of France' from the fertility of its valleys, especially along the left bank of the Loire, by which it is intersected. No longer can one write, as did Wraxall two centuries ago when admiring the countryside here, that although there was 'much magnificence' there was 'still much distress. One princely chateau surrounded by a thousand wretched hamlets: the most studied and enervate luxury among the higher orders of society, contrasted with beggary and nakedness among the people'. Although annexed to the royal domain by Philippe Auguste in 1203, it was not definitively united to the crown until 1584, under Henri III. It was a favourite residence of the Valois and Bourbons until the time of Louis XIV, who preferred the sands and morasses of Versailles to such sites as Blois, Amboise, Chenonceau, Chambord, or Loches, while further W. stand Azay-le-Rideau, Chinon, and Fontevraud (where lie Henry II, Eleanor of Aquitaine, and Richard I, 'Coeur-de-Lion'). Its associations with French history are endless.

Anjou, to the W. (almost entirely represented by *Maine-et-Loire*), with its capital at Angers, owes its historical importance to the fortunes of its 9-11C counts, Fulk the Red, Fulk the Good, and Fulk Nerra (the Black), among others. Count Geoffrey V Plantagenet married Matilda of England in 1125, and when his son Henry II ascended the throne in 1154 the provinces of Anjou, Maine, and Normandy passed to England. They were forfeited only fifty years later, in 1204, by John. In 1290 the counts of Valois assumed the title of dukes of Anjou and Maine, and in 1328 were united with the crown under Philippe VI. Charles of Anjou, a brother of Louis IX, established an Angevin dynasty on the throne of Naples in 1266, which lasted until the expulsion in 1442 of King René, who was also Duc d'Anjou, and the father of Margaret, wife of Henry VI of England.

S. of the Loire lies **Poitou**, named from the Gallic Pictones or Pictavi (corresponding to the departments of *Vienne*, *Deux-Sèvres*, and *Vendée*), a battleground for contending tribes. Alaric II, king of the Arian Visigoths, was defeated and slain near Poitiers in 507 by Clovis the Frank. More famous was the battle of Poitiers of 732, when Charles Martel decisively repulsed the Moorish invasion from Spain. Poitou was later included in the duchy of **Aquitaine**, which Eleanor brought, as part of her dowry, to Henry II after her divorce from Louis VII. Although it was recovered by Philippe Auguste, it was briefly regained by the English at the Treaty of Brétigny after the Black Prince's victory at Poitiers in 1356. In 1369 it was recaptured by Du Guesclin, eventually becoming an appanage of the dauphin, who was proclaimed Charles VII at Poitiers in 1423.

In the following century Protestantism made numerous converts in Poitou, and the province was profoundly disturbed in the ensuing Religious Wars, some measure of tranquility returning with the Edict of toleration signed at Nantes by Henri IV in 1958. The district of **La Vendée** (or Bas-Poitou), on the Atlantic coast, was notorious during the Revolutionary wars for its stubborn adhesion to the monarchy and for the obstinate guerrilla warfare waged against Republican forces until its 'pacification' by Hoche.

48 Nemours to Bourges

148km (92 miles). N7. 33km **Montargis**—N7 and D940. 39km **Glen**—30km *Aubigny*—46km **Bourges**.

Maps: IGN 21, 27, or 108; also 415. M 237, 238.

For **Nemours**, see Rte 21.

An alternative road to *Montargis* is the D40, following the W. bank of the Loing to (15km) **Château-Landon**, on a bluff over the Fusain valley, and the birthplace of ancestors of the Plantagenets. *Notre-Dame* (11-14C), with a 13C tower, is notable, and the view from the terrace adjoining the main square of the ancient fortifications, and the ruined Romanesque tower of *St-Tugal*, is impressive. At the E. end of the village are the ruins of the abbey of *St-Séverin*, founded by Childebert in 545.—Hence one may join the N7 9km S.E.—The next l.-hand turning leads shortly to *Ferrières*, with an 11-15C abbey church, remarkable for a rotunda formed of eight columns at the crossing, and for its 16C glass.—*Montargis* is 12km S. of this turning; see below. For other monuments of minor interest in the area, see *Blue Guide Paris and Environs*.

NEMOURS TO CHÂTEAUNEUF-SUR-LOIRE (62km). The D403 leads S.W. through the *Gatinais*, a region famous for its honey, at 14km passing 7km E. of *Puiseaux*, and (l.) *Arville*, with churches of interest, to (9km) *Beaumont-en-Gatinais*, with a late 16C *Market-house*, and remains of its castle.—The church of *Boësse*, 3km N.W., is notable.—The road bears S. to (17km) **Bellegarde**, passing some distance E. of *Beaune-la-Rolande* and *Boiscommun*, both with notable churches.—Bellegarde (called Soisy-aux-Loges until its elevation to a duchy in 1646) preserves the massive 14C keep of its castle, together with several pavilions erected c. 1717 by the Duc d'Antin, son of Mme de Montespan, one of which is the mairie. The *Church*, with a Romanesque facade, contains good paintings and *boiseries*.—*Lorris*, 14km S.E., birthplace of Guillaume de Lorris (d. c. 1235), author of the first part of the 'Roman de la Rose' (cf. *Meung*), has a 12-13C church containing 15C choir-stalls and a Renaissance organ-loft, and a 16C *Hôtel de Ville*.—The N60 leads S.W. from Bellegarde through the *Forêt d'Orléans* to (23km) *Châteauneuf-sur-Loire*; see Rte 49.

An exit from the A6 (driving S.E. towards Auxerre) and the N7 converge 18km N. of Montargis, skirting its forest before entering the town.

Montargis (17,600 Montargois), an industrial town at the confluence of several streams and canals, was the medieval capital of the *Gatinais*. It was the birthplace of Mme Guyon (1648–1717), the Quietist; and the artist Anne-Louis Girodet-Trioson (1767–1824); the younger Mirabeau (1749–91) was born in the neighbouring *Château de Bignon*.

Little remains of the 11-15C *Castle*, for centuries used as a royal nursery; the church of *La Madeleine* has a nave of 1160, 15-16C chapels, and a 16C choir completed by Jacques Androuet du Cerceau for Renée de France, daughter of Louis XII. The *Hôtel de Ville* contains a small *Museum*, while in the adjacent gardens is a bronze statue of the legendary 'Dog of Montargis', which identified

his master's murderer in the ranks of Charles VIII's army as it marched through the town, and afterwards slew him in judicial combat.

16.5km. The ruins of the Gallo-Roman *Amphitheatre of Chenevière*
lie just N. of *Montbouy*, 7km E.; see Rte 96.

8km. The N7 bears l.; see Rte 96.—The N940 forks r. for (13.5km)
Gien (16,800 inhab.), once a quaint old town on the Loire, here crossed by a 16C bridge, but much damaged in 1940–44, and partly
rebuilt in the traditional style. Its *Castle*, approached by stepped
alleys, rebuilt in 1494 by Anne de Beaujeau, is of patterned red and
black brick within stone frames. It sheltered Anne of Austria, young
Louis XIV, and Mazarin during the Fronde (1652), and now contains
a *Hunting Museum*, including paintings by Desportes. The 15C
clock-tower of a former church is adjacent. Gien is noted for its
faience factory (1820; W. of the town) and its leather fair, said to date
from 581.

For the riverside road skirting the Loire, see Rte 49.—20km.
Argent-sur-Sauldre, with a turreted castle and 15C church with a
graceful spire, lies on the E. verge of the *Sologne*, with its woods and
meres, 8km S.E. of which is the 15C castle of *Blancafort*.—8km.
Aubigny-sur-Nère, preserving some 15-16C houses—note the
reticulated tiling—and a 12-14C *Church* containing good 15C glass
and 16C choir-stalls. The 15-16C *Château*, a residence of the
Duchess of Portsmouth after 1673 (cf. Brest), is occupied by the
Mairie.

9km S.E., on the edge of the *Forêt d'Ivoy*, is the *Château de la Verrerie*, begun
c. 1430 by John Stuart, a scion of the Scottish royal house, the lordship of
Aubigny having been presented by Charles VII to his father, Sir John Stewart of
Darnley (d. 1429) in return for services at the battle of Baugé (1421). It was completed by Robert Stuart, Maréchal d'Aubigny, in 1525.

14km. *La Chapelle-d'Angillon*, birthplace of Henri Alain-Fournier
(1886–1914), author of 'Le Grande Meaulnes', retains the handsome
Château de Béthune, with an 11C keep repaired by Sully.

5km S.E. is *Ivoy-le-Pré*, birthplace of the chemist Nicolas Leblanc
(1742–1806).—*Henrichemont*, 6km beyond, was built on a regular plan by Sully
in 1608, and named after Henri IV.

12km. 5km S.E. is the *Château of Menetou-Salon*.

20km. **BOURGES** (79,400 Berruyers), once the capital of *Berry* and
now préfecture of the *Cher*, the old centre of which rises on a hill
above the sluggish Yèvre, dominated by its imposing cathedral,
preserves a number of medieval houses, while industry expands on
its outskirts.

Roman *Avaricum* derives its name from the Gallis *Bituriges* who flourished here.
It was from c. 250 governed by its archbishops, passing later to a line of counts
and viscounts from whom Philippe I purchased it in 1101. No subsequent royal
dukes of Berry left a male heir, so a ducal line was never established. The most
distinguished was Jean (1340–1416), son of Jean le Bon, and the 'Maecenas of
the House of Valois'. His patronage of artists was continued by Jacques Coeur
(1400–56), the financier and merchant. It was the capital of the dominions of
Charles VII, then at their lowest ebb, and both he and Louis XI often made it
their residence, the latter being known to the English as 'the King of Bourges'.
The university founded in 1463 became a centre of legal learning under Alciati
of Milan and Cujas of Toulouse, and in 1531 numbered Calvin among its pupils.

Jacques Coeur was born here, and died on the island of Chios. Other natives
were Louis XI (1423–83); Louis Bourdaloue (1632–1704), the preacher; and the
artist Berthe Morisot (1841–95). Don Carlos, the Spanish pretender and

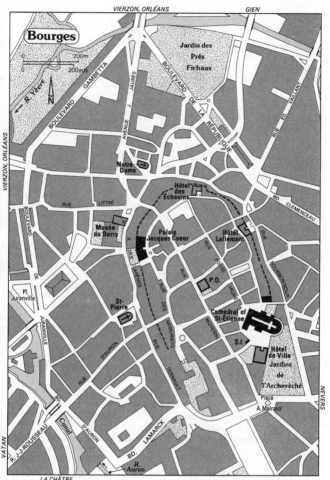

younger brother of Fernando VII (cf. Valençay) was held here under surveillance after the First Carlist War.

Roads from the N.E. converge on the *Pl. St-Bonnet*, with a 16 church. From the *Pl. Gordaine*, with its quaint gabled houses, just to the S., the Rue Bourbonnoux ascends towards the cathedral, passing (r.) the *Hôtel Lallemant* (late 15C), with additions in the Renaissance taste, and preserving several interesting features, a vaulted kitchen, and richly ornamented oratory, etc.

The **Cathedral**, St-Étienne, one of the most remarkable of Gothic buildings, was designed in 1172 and evidently modelled on that of N.-D.-de-Paris, but the experience of 29 years led to the introduction by its unknown architect of certain improvements; the triforium was reduced in importance, additional height being given to the inner aisles. No transepts were constructed, although a false transept was added in the 14C, and removed by Viollet-le-Duc. Work began c. 1192 and it was consecrated in 1224.

The *W. Front*, 55m wide, is pierced by five *Portals, and has two unequal towers: the *Tour de Beurre* (N.; 65m high) dates from 1508–40, its predecessor having collapsed in 1506; the *Tour Sourde* (58m high) dates from the 14C but was never completed; adjacent is a buttress tower formerly used as a chapter prison. Chapels were later added between a number of buttresses.

The tympanum of the late 13C central portal is adorned with a *Last Judgment in high relief, with (r.) the Damned being hurled by demons into the Devil's gaping maw, and the Blessed being led to the Gates of Paradise by St Peter. The two portals on the r. depict the histories of St Stephen, and St Ursinus (its first bishop), where a few beheaded figures survive; those to the l. were rebuilt c. 1515. Above is a window added in 1370, by Guy de Dammartin, illustrated in a miniature included in the 'Trés Riches Heures du Duc de Berry'.

The side doorways, although preceded by porches contemporary with the rest of the building, are survivals of a previous cathedral; that on the N. is sculptured with scenes from the life of the Virgin; that on the S. is more elaborately decorated than any other part of the edifice. The doors themselves are 15C.

The *Interior* (110m long; 40m wide; and 40m high) is lighted by 141 windows, containing superb *Stained-glass dating from the early 12C (from the earlier church) to 1619. The rose in the W. window was glazed in 1392; the lower panels c. 1450. The organ at the W. end dates from 1667. The glass in the lst and 4th chapels on the r. is by Jean Lécuyer (1520; 1532); that in the 3rd comes from the Sainte Chapelle of Duc Jean, demolished in the mid 18C. The *Choir Chapels* and the windows between them contain magnificently glowing glass of 1215–20, by two *Maîtres Verriers*, while on either side of the E. chapel are kneeling statues of Duc Jean and Jeanne de Boulogne, his second wife, previously in the Sainte Chapelle. Three statues from the mausoleum of the Laubespine family, by Philippe de Buyster (17C) kneel in a chapel off the N. aisle; and beyond the adjacent chapel is the door to the *Sacristy* constructed at the expense of Jacques Coeur by his son Abp Jean Coeur; the arms of the family appear in the tympanum. The kneeling statue of Marshal de Montigny, by Michel Bourdin (1633), and a window of 1619, are in the 1st chapel on the N. aisle.

The *Crypt* ◊ contains the tomb-statue of Duc Jean (by Jean de Cambrai), and an Entombment of c. 1520. A stair at the N.E. corner leads to a vaulted passage, a survival of the mid 9C church.

Immediately to the S. is the *Hôtel de Ville* (1681; by Jean Bullet), once the archbishop's palace; the garden front dates from 1871; the gardens themselves, designed by Le Nôtre, command a fine view of the cathedral apse, where the small chapels with 'extinguisher' roofs are a curious feature; the parapet and upper pinnacles are 19C additions.—To the W. is the *Cité-Administrative* and late 18C *Préfecture*. A Romanesque doorway at No. 28 Av. H.-Ducrot is the only relic of the collegiate church of *St-Ursin*.

Just N. of the cathedral is the *Grange aux Dimes*, a restored 13C tithe barn, passing which one may descend the narrow Rue Molière to follow the Rue Branly, circling to the W., in which is the *Hôtel des Échevins*, preserving a late 15C stair-turret; while the adjacent *Lycée Alain-Fournier* occupies the site of the Collège Royale de Ste-Marie, founded 1500 and rebuilt by Martellange in 1620–40.

A short distance beyond is the *Palais de Jacques-Coeur**, one of the more remarkable examples of mid 15C domestic buildings extant, but over-restored in 1928–38 in an attempt to right mutilations during its use as the Palais de Justice between 1820 and 1923.

The entrance front is pierced by a gateway with a postern beside it; the knocker is a replica of the original. Above is a canopied niche which formerly held an equestrian statue of Charles VII, flanked by dummy windows from which sculptured half-figures, probably of Jacques Coeur and his wife, look out. The mullions of a higher window form the outline of two hearts and a fleur-de-lys.

*One of the two sculptured half-figures on the entrance front
of the Palais de Jacques-Coeur*

The portal is embellished with hearts and scallop-shells, emblems of the builder
and his device 'A vaillans coeurs riens impossible'. Two of the three richly
decorated stair-turrets facing the arcaded central courtyard display motives of
the proprietor's commercial interests; those on the tympanum of that to the r. indicate its use as the kitchen entrance.

Visitors are conducted through the kitchens (where an ingenious water-
heating system is pointed out), and dining-hall, with its minstrels' gallery. Stairs
ascend to the little-restored *Salle du Trésor*, with a complicated lock on its iron
door and delicately carved scenes from the romance of Tristan and Isolde on one
console of its vaulted roof. The *Chambre de l'Argentier* preserves some 17C wall-
painting and a sculptured angel above its damaged chimneypiece; the *Great Hall*
contains a reconstruction of the tomb of Duc Jean, smashed in 1793, together

with some of the original weepers from its pedestal (by Étienne Bobillot and Paul Mosselman). The *Chambre des Galées* is named after the relief of a fully-rigged galley above its door. The galleries surrounding the chapel have restored chimneypieces and ceilings vaulted like an inverted ship's hull; the Chapel ceiling preserves its original paintings.

Steps to the S. descend to the *Pl. Berry*, from which one may see the Gallo-Roman walls forming the foundation to the severe W. front of the palace.—To the S. is 12C *St-Pierre-le-Guillard*, re-vaulted in the 15C, and containing the grave of Cujas.—The *Hôtel Cujas* (1515), the former residence of the jurisconsult, is N. of the Pl. Berry, beyond the *Palais de Justice* (previously the Grand Séminaire), and now houses the **Musée de Berry**.

The depressed entrance archway retains its delicately sculptured frieze; on the r. outside is a medieval money-changer's booth. Among the sculpture is a Crucifixion from the cathedral rood-screen, demolished by the Philistine chapter in the 18C; other collections are devoted to prehistoric and Gallo Roman antiquities, including a 7C sarcophagus. The *First Floor* displays ceramic collections, including rustic ware from La Borne, in the Berry, and paintings by the local artist Jean Boucher (1568–1633), etc.

Beyond the *Pl. Planchat* the Rue Gambon leads W., in which stand the richly decorated *Maison de la Reine Blanche* (16C; No. 19) and the *Hôtel-Dieu* (No. 32), with its Renaissance doorway.—To the N.E. of the Place is *Notre-Dame*, with a square tower and S. porch altered in 1640 when its Ionic attic was added. In the neighbouring Rue Pellevoysin, and the Rue Mirabeau (leading E. to regain the Pl. St-Bonnet) are several characteristic old houses.

For roads from Bourges to *Châteauroux* and **Poitiers**, to **Brive**, and **Clermont-Ferrand** via *Montluçon*, see Rtes 51, 91, and 92 respectively; for roads hence to *Tours*, and to *Auxerre* via *La Charité* and *Clamecy*, see Rtes 53, and 119, in reverse.

49   Chartres to Avallon via Orléans, Gien, and Clamecy

259km (161 miles). N154. 52km *Artenay*—N20. 21km **Orléans**—N60. 25km *Châteauneuf-sur-Loire*, for **St-Benoît** and 18km *Sully*—D951. 23km **Gien**—D592. 10km *Briare*—N7. 17km—D957. 16km *St-Armand-en-Puisaye*—39km **Clamecy**—D951. 23km **Vézelay**—15km. **Avallon**.

Maps: IGN 20, 27, 28, or 103, 108; also 306, and 409, 411. M 237, 238, 243.

For **Chartres**, see *Blue Guide Paris and Environs*, or Rte 28A.

Driving S.E., soon after passing the A11 motorway we pass 2.5km S. of **Brétigny**, where in 1360 the treaty was signed whereby Jean le Bon, paying a ransom of 3 million crowns to regain his liberty lost at the Battle of Poitiers, surrendered the whole of S.E. France to Edward III, who in return, renounced all claims to the French crown.

37km. *Allaines-Mervilliers*, 2km S. of which a disused church preserves a remarkable 12C sculptured tympanum said to represent St-Fiacre refusing the Scottish crown.

After 8km the road crosses the A10, and 6km beyond by-passes *Artenay*, with a prominent domed steeple.—*Loigny-la-Bataille*, some

8km. W. of the motorway, was the site of a battle during the Franco-Prussian War (Dec. 1870); while *Patay* (15km S.W. of Artenay) was the scene of Joan of Arc's victory over the English in 1429, in which John Talbot, Earl of Shrewsbury, was taken prisoner.

20km. **Orléans**; see Rte 50.

The N60 skirts the N. bank of the Loire, traversing (10km) *Chécy*, where Joan of Arc crossed the river in 1429 prior to making the assault on Orléans. She defeated the English a few weeks later at *Jargeau*, on the far bank 8km E., where the church has an early Romanesque nave and 16C choir with contemporary stalls.

7km. *Châteauneuf-sur-Loire*, a pleasant riverside town preserving a park and parts of a château rebuilt by the statesman Phélypeaux de la Vrillière (d. 1681), whose magnificent Italian tomb may be seen in the church, although both tomb and church, containing a good organ, were damaged in 1940. A small *Museum* devoted to fishing and navigation on the Loire may be visited.

We fork r. immediately to the E. for (4.5km) **Germigny-des-Prés**, a village famous for its *Church*, built in 806 as an oratory by Theodulphus, Bp of Orléans. Originally on the plan of a Greek cross, with four apses, it was provided with a nave in the 15C, and was too drastically restored in the 1860s. The magnificent *Mosaic* in the semi-dome of the E. apse, discovered by chance in 1841, is believed to be a 5C work transported from Ravenna; fortunately preserved almost intact, it represents the Ark of the Covenant supported by cherubim. It also contains a free-standing 7C piscina, 11C font, and 15C Pietà; its glass has been replaced by alabaster.

5km. **St-Benoît-sur-Loire**, a decayed town, once with a community of 15,000, is famous for its Benedictine abbey founded in the 7C under the name of *Fleury*.

It was re-named after the exploit of the abbot Mummolus and the monk Aigulf, who in 655 (after the spoliation of Monte Cassino by the Lombards in 589) brought hence the body of St Benedict. It became a centre of learning from the time of Charlemagne, its monks gaining a reputation for their skill as illuminators; its most famous pupil was Gerbert (Pope Sylvester II; 935–1003).

The existing church was dedicated by Innocent II in 1131. Its decay dates from 1486, when a succession of titular abbots began to exhaust its resources, one of whom, the Protestant Odet de Châtillon (elder brother of Coligny), openly pillaged the treasury; the sack of the abbey by Condé's troops in 1562 was a blow from which it never recovered, although in 1627 Richelieu introduced there the reformed Benedictine order of St. Maur. The monastic buildings were destroyed in 1792, with the exception of the church. Restoration was put in hand in 1836 and has continued intermittently. The poet Max Jacob (1876–1944) lived here for twenty years prior to his deportation and death in the German internment camp at Drancy. A new Benedictine abbey has flourished here since 1959.

The ****Church**, one of the most remarkable Romanesque edifices in France, was begun before 1079, and completed in 1218; the central tower is a late 19C reconstruction. It is 95m long, and the double transeptal plan is unusual at so early a date.

Preceding the facade is an aisled *Narthex of three bays (late 11C), with groined vaulting and huge piers with vigorous capitals, supporting a vaulted chamber which was deprived of its upper storey and spire by François I in 1527 as a punishment for the opposition of the monks to the appointment of Chancellor Duprat as titular abbot. The lintel of the N. doorway depicts the transportation of St Benedict's remains from Monte Cassino.

The aisles were vaulted in 1160, but the groined vaulting of the nave was not completed until 1218. The ritual choir contains stalls of 1513 with grotesquely carved canopies; the Italian mosaic pavement was presented by Duprat in conciliation, and the remodelled tomb is that of Philippe I (d. 1108), with a recumbent figure on a slab supported by lions. The *Capitals* in the raised apse are noteworthy.

Sully-sur-Loire (5800 inhab.), 8.5km S.E., lies on the far bank of the river spanned by a bridge replacing one twice blown up in June 1940, when the town was savagely bombed while refugees were streaming S., and in June 1944 by Allied aircraft attacking the retreating Germans.

It was raised to the rank of duchy when Maximilien de Béthune, Baron de Rosny, Henri IV's minister, bought the lordship in 1606 from the La Trémoïlle family (Georges de La Trémoïlle had been the favourite of Charles VII). Here Sully wrote his memoirs, and his descendants, enriched by his economies, held court. Voltaire, exiled from Paris, stayed in the castle in 1716 and 1719. It was the birthplace of Maurice de Sully, (d. 1196), later Bp of Paris, and responsible for the rebuilding of Notre-Dame.

The moated *Château*, restored since 1940, a four-squared stronghold with corner turrets, dates from the mid 14C. The E. wing, with a separate moat, includes the *Petit-Château*, rebuilt by Sully, and a modern edifice replacing a pavilion burnt down in 1918. The magnificent chestnut roof of 1363 will be noted.

The D948 drives due S. via (15km) *Cerdon*, with a 13C church, to (11km) *Argent-sur-Sauldre*, on the D940 to **Bourges**; see Rte 48.

We follow the D951 S.E., passing, on the far bank, a nuclear power-station, to recross the Loire at (23km) **Gien**; see Rte 48.
The road skirts the r. bank to traverse (8km) *Briare*, from which a canal, 58km long, was constructed in 1604–42, linking the Loire with the Seine, in 1890 being connected with the Canal latéral à la Loire by an aqueduct over the river.—We meet the N7 2km beyond the town, and after 15km turn l. at *Neuvy-sur-Loire*, onto minor roads.
16km. *St-Amand-en-Puisaye*, with a brick and stone Renaissance château.—Some 10km N.E. are the moated château of *Ratilly*, and a large Flamboyant church at adjacent *Treigny*.—The main road (D957) continues S.E. through *Entrains-sur-Nohain*, Roman *Interamnes*, with a 13-16C church where several Gallo-Roman antiquities have been found, and traverses undulating wooded country to (39km) **Clamecy**; see Rte 119.
Here we cross the Yonne and follow the D951 E., climbing away from the valley and through the hills and woods to approach (23km) **Vézelay**, and **Avallon**, 15km beyond; for both see Rte 120.

50 Orléans to Châteauroux

137km (85 miles). N20.—79km **Vierzon**. **Bourges** lies 33km S.E.—58km. **Châteauroux**.

Maps: IGN 26, 35, or 106. M 238.

A motorway (A71) is under construction, bearing off the A10 just W. of Orléans, and running parallel to the N20, which will veer S.E. to Bourges just prior to Vierzon.

ORLÉANS (105,600 Orléanais; 47,440 in 1851), préfecture of the *Loiret*, and situated on the r. bank of the Loire at the most northerly point of its course, has long thrived as an important centre of communication between the Loire and Paris. The older town, surrounded on three sides by boulevards laid out on the site of former walls, is of interest for is historical associations, of which few tangible memorials remain, even fewer since the bombing of 1940; in the 18C it was 'one of the largest and pleasantest cities in France', according to Nugent, while Southey, who visited it in 1838 on his tour of N.W. France, remarked that it disappointed him more than any other place in the course of his journey.

Probably the Gallic *Genabum* taken by Julius Caesar in 52 B.C., it appears in the 3C as a flourishing town under the name of *Aurelianis*. In 451 its citizens, headed by St Aignan, the bishop, maintained a successful defence against Attila, but in 498 it fell to Clovis, who there held the first council assembled in France. In 613 it was united with Neustria.

In 1344 it was the capital of a duchy given as appanage to a younger son of Philippe I, and on several occasions it has been conferred on cadet branches of the royal family; see p 296.

The heroine of Orléans is Joan of Arc (Jeanne d'Arc; 'La Pucelle; 1412–31; cf. *Domrémy*), who entered the city in the teeth of the occupying English army on 29 April 1429, and raised the siege within eight days, a feat which materially influences the outcome of the war.

During the Religious wars, Condé made it the Prostestant headquarters, and it was during the fruitless siege of 1563 that François, 2nd Duc de Guise was assassinated by Poltrot de Méré. In 1594 it was in the hands of the Leaguers, and fell to Henri IV only after he had come in person to direct operations. During the Revolution Orléans was abandoned to the excesses of Collot-d'Herbois and Barrère. In 1870–71 it was occupied for 3½ months by the Prussians. The old centre was bombed by the Italians in 1940; and in 1944 the quarter near the station was severely damaged in Allied air attacks.

Among its natives were Robert the Pius (996–1031); Étienne Dolet (1509–46); Baptiste Du Cerceau (c. 1545–90) the architect; Michel Corneille the Elder (1601–64), the artist; and Charles Péguy (1873–1914), the poet and essayist. Another local 'pucelle' was Thérèse Levasseur (b. 1721), long the mistress of J.-J. Rousseau; while in 1791 it was visited by Wordsworth, who there left Antoinette Wallon with a natural daughter. Proust did his military service here in 1889–90.

The hub of the old town is the *Pl. du Martroi*, in the centre of which is an equestrian *Statue of Joan of Arc*, by Foyatier (1855), restored in 1950 by citizens of New Orleans. To the S. are two classical pavilions, one of which (1759) contains the archives of the duchy; the other (1865) houses the Chamber of Commerce.—To the E., at 11 Rue Ste-Anne (leading N.) is the '*Maison des Oves*', perhaps by Du Cerceau, with its courtyard.

Continuing E. along the Rue d'Escures, preserving some 17C mansions, we pass (r.) the brick-built Flamboyant church of *St-Pierre-du-Martroi* (1501–90), and the gardens behind the Hôtel de Ville, with the 15C doorway of the *Chapelle St-Jacques*, brought here from the Quartier des Halles.

The **Hôtel de Ville** occupies the mid 16C *Hôtel Groslot*, decorated with caryatids in the style of Jean Goujon beneath its balconies; François II died here on 5 Dec. 1569.

In the Rue de la Bretonnerie, leading N.W., is the early 16C *Hôtel de la Vieille-Intendance*, and *Palais de Justice* of 1824.

The **Cathedral of Ste-Croix**, to the S.E., is a curious example of the persistence of the Gothic tradition. After the destruction by fire of its Romanesque predecessor, a new church was begun before 1287, but the Calvinists of Théodore de Bèze toppled its central tower by

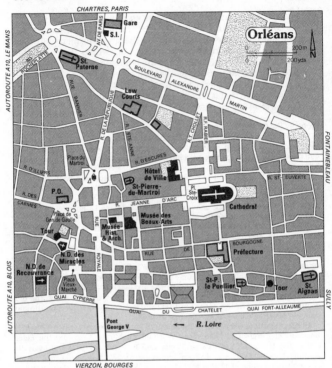

undermining the piers of the crossing, and set the ruins alight; and it was a condition of his absolution by the Pope that Henri IV, ostensibly converted from Protestantism, commenced its reconstruction.

Of this medieval edifice, only the apse chapels and two 16C bays in the middle of the nave remain, although the foundations of three previous buildings (8-12C) may be seen in the crypt. The choir was begun by Henri IV, and the transeptal facades were completed in 1679 by Pierre Martellange, and display the 'Roi Soleil' in their rose-windows. The W. front, with its two 'wedding-cake' towers, was begun by Trouard in 1767 and continued after 1787 by A. Paris, and is embellished with sculptures by Houdon and Pajou, among others. Work on the nave and aisles continued until 1829, while as an afterthought, the central spire was added by Boeswillwald in 1858.

In the interior, the choir-stalls of 1706, designed by Hardouin-Mansart and Gabriel, and executed by Jules Degoullons, are notable, but little else; it also contains the grave of Sir William Douglas, killed fighting the English at Verneuil in 1424.

Relics of the 'Old Cemetery', with three walks of a 16C cloister, survive to the N.—Further E. is a *Lycée* built over the 10-11C crypt of *St-Avit*; and (r.) the former *Bishop's Palace*, with vestiges of Gallo-Roman walls in its garden.—Some distance further E. stands *St-Euverte*, with an ungraceful 16-17C tower, 15C nave, and earlier choir.

From the S. side of the cathedral the Rue Pothier leads to the *Préfecture*, passing (l.) the *Salle des Thèses* (1450), a rare survival of French medieval academic building (adm. on application to the Préfecture).

A lane to the E. of the Préfecture leads shortly to *St-Pierre-le-Puellier*, partly 11-12C, to the E. of which is the *Tour Blanche*, sole relic of the medieval fortifications; and beyond is *St-Aignan*, mutilated in 1565, but with impressive flying buttresses, and a crypt of 1029 of some interest.

The pedestrian Rue de Bourgogne leads W. from the Préfecture past the *Maison Hector de Saucerre* (1544; restored) to the Rue Louis-Roguet in which (turning r.) the **Musée des Beaux-Arts** occupies the *Hôtel des Créneaux*, its courtyard flanked by a *Belfry* of 1448.

Remarkable among the collections are: *F. Bol*, Male portrait; *Francisque Millet*, Mercury and Argus; *J.E. Hensius*, M. et Mme de la Rivière; an *anon*. 15C Adoration; *School of Clouet*, the Duc d'Orléans as a child; *Matteo di Giovanni*, Virgin and Child; *Jouvenet*, Mlle de Scudéry; *Jean Valade*, pastel Portraits; *C.-A. Coypel*, Self-portrait; *Perronneau*, Hubert Drouais, and other portraits; and portraits by *Nattier*; Philippe de France (*anon*. 17C); *Claude Deruet*, The Four Elements; *Lubin Baugin*, St Gregory; *Philippe de Champaigne*, St Charles Borromeo; *Le Nain*, Bacchus and Ariadne; *Claude Lefebvre*, Le Nôtre; *Pierre Patel*, Landscapes; *Van Loo*, Louis XV, and Philippe d'Orléans; *J.-B. Santerre*, Le Jardinière; *Martin Drolling*, Self-portrait, and of his Wife; *Robert Lefèvre*, Portrait of Guérin; *Girodet-Trioson*, Female portrait; *David*, The governess; characteristic works by *Boucher, Lancret*, and *Fragonard*; *Gauguin*, Landscape (1873), and a still-life entitled 'Fête Gloanec' (1888).—In basement rooms are: *Isaac van Ostade*, Traveller attacked; attrib. *Velasquez*, St Thomas; *Roelant Savery*, Noah's Ark; *Jacob Grimer*, Eremetical scenes; *A. Roslin*, Portrait of Daubenton; *Van Valkenborgh*, Fête in a park; *Momper*, Snow scene. A room is devoted to *Max Jacob* (cf. *St-Benoît*). Among sculptures are *Houdon*, Bust of La Fontaine; *Germain Pilon*, Bust of Bp Morvilliers; and a 15C Virgin and Child. The collection of prints and drawings is extensive.

In the parallel Rue Ste-Catherine is the *Hôtel Cabu* (1530), gutted in 1940, restored to house the *Historical and Archaeological Museum*, containing what was saved from the disaster, including Gallo-Roman *Bronzes* from the Treasure of Neuvy-en-Sullias; medieval wooden figures; and a collection of Orléans ware.

There are several ancient houses in the area between this point and the river, including the 16C *Maison de la Coquille* in the Rue du Pierre-Percée.

The Rue Royale, designed by Jean Hupeau and built in 1754–70, and reconstructed since 1940, leads S. from the Pl. du Martroi to the *Pont George V* (1761; by Robert Soyer).—By following the quay to the r., and turning r. along the Rue de la Recouvrance, we pass *Notre-Dame* (1519) and the *Hôtel Toutin* (1540; with a colonnaded courtyard), N.E. of which are the remains of *St-Paul*, with a detached belfry of 1629 which survived the holocaust of 1940. The facades of several other old houses may be seen in the Rue du Tambour, leading off the *Pl. du Gén. de Gaulle*, further N., in which stands the so-called *Maison Jeanne d'Arc*, where Joan is said to have lodged briefly in 1429.

For roads to *Gien*, and along the N. and S. banks of the Loire to *Tours*, see Rtes 49, and 52A and B, respectively.

The N20 leads S., shortly crossing the Loiret at *Olivet*, probably a resurgence of an underground branch of the Loire, but apparently with its source in the park of the *Château de la Source*, to the E., rebuilt in 1632, where in 1720 Bolingbroke retired after his negotiations with the Old Pretender. Here he received Voltaire and heard him read his 'Henriade'; here also, in 1815, Marshal Davout signed the warrant for the dispersal of the survivors of the army of Waterloo. Adjacent are the new University buildings and the new town of *La Source*.

We now enter the **Sologne**, formerly a marshy plain, but although preserving numerous meres, providing scope for both the wildfowler and conservationists, it is largely drained and wooded, but is sparsely populated. Several churches have wooden porches characteristics of this melancholy and isolated district.

21km. *La Ferté-St-Aubin*, with a 12th and 16C church, and château rebuilt in 1635–50 to the designs of Fr. Mansart, with additions by Marshal Lowendal (1700–55), a later owner.—The D922 leads directly hence to (45km) *Romorantin* via (34km) *Millançay*, with remains of a Roman camp.

15km. *Lamotte-Beuvron*, long a rendezvous of 'chasseurs', has a château converted by Napoleon III into a penal farm-colony.—20km. *Salbris*, 8.5km S.W. of which is the château of *La Ferté-Imbault* (16-17C; restored).

The D944 leads directly S.E. to (50km) *Bourges*, at (14km) *Nançay* passing S. of a radio-astronomy station.

23km. **Vierzon** (34,900 Vierzonnais), by-passed to the W., an important but uninteresting town on the Cher, with manufacturers of agricultural and industrial machinery, glass, and porcelain, etc. It was the birthplace of the inflamatory socialist writer Félix Pyat (1810–89). The town preserves a few 16C houses, a 15C gate, and a church of the 12th and 15Cs.

For the road hence to **Bourges**, 33km S.E., see Rte 53.

VIERZON TO LE CHÂTRE (79km). The D918 leads due S., in the S. suburbs passing 7km W. of *Brinay*, its church choir decorated with 12-13C murals.—11.5km. *Lury-sur-Arnon*, with a 12C keep and fortified gateway.—6.5km. *Reuilly*, noted for its white wines, its church preserving a crypt said to be Merovingian, and with a Renaissance mansion, beyond which (l.) is the *Château de la Ferté-Reuilly*, an imposing composition by Mansart (1659).—16km. **Issoudun**; see Rte 51.—The roads ascends the Théols valley to (14km) *Meunet-Planches*, on either side of which are visible traces of the Roman road from *Argentomagnus* (Argenton-sur-Creuse) to *Avaricum* (Bourges), here known as the 'Levée de César'.—At 3km we pass, 3km S.E., *Bommiers*, its 12C church containing 16C stalls, and the adjacent ruins of the castle of *Bourg-le Château*.—At 21km we meet the D943 between Vic and Nohant, 7km N. of **Le Châtre**; see Rte 91.

The N20 bears S.W. through (10km) *Massay*, with a striking abbey church, partly 12C.—6.5km. The quaint village of *Graçay*, 6.5km W., has several dolmens in its vicinity.—10.5km. *Vatan*, with a 19C church preserving relics of its predecessor, and a *Vintage Car museum*, is traversed, beyond which the road strikes across country to (30km) **Châteauroux**; see Rte 51.

51 Bourges to Châteauroux and Poitiers

187km (116 miles). N151. 38km **Issoudun**—29km **Châteauroux**—60km *Le Blanc*—18km **St-Savin**—19km **Chauvigny**—23km **Poitiers**.

Maps: IGN 35, 34, or 106. M 238, 232.

Driving S.W. from **Bourges** (Rte 48) parallel to a Roman road to the N., at 15km we traverse *St-Florent-sur-Cher*, a small iron-working town with a restored 15-16C château and remains of a Roman bridge, to (11km) *Chârost*, with a Romanesque church known as the 'Église Rouge' from the ironstone with which it is built. The 16C château was the residence of Armand de Béthune (1738–1800), the liberal Duc de Chârost, who abolished all seigniorial rights prior to the Revolution.

12km. **Issoudon** (15,200 Issoldunois), noted for its leather manufacturers and red and rosé wines, was the Gallo-Roman *Exoldunum*, and in the 12C a fortress disputed by Philippe Auguste and Richard I. The revocation of the Edict of Nantes (1685) expelled its once numerous Protestant population (contemptuously nicknamed '*parpaillauds*') and ruined its prosperity. The name of the central *Pl. du 10-Juin* (or du Marché) recalls the date of the destructive bombing in 1940.

The 12th and 16C *Porte du Beffroi* on its W. side separate it from the *Pl. Voltaire*; beyond, to the l. is the *Hôtel de Ville* (1731), behind which are some vestiges of the medieval ramparts and the cylindrical keep or * *Tour Blanche* (1202) of the castle, with an imposing vaulted hall. On the other side of the main square is 15C *St-Cyr*, with a fine 16C window, to the S.E. of which the Rue Basse leads to the *Hospice St-Roch*, in the chapel of which are two * *Trees of Jesse* in relief (15C); it now houses a municipal *Museum* and an old *Pharmacy*, etc.

For the road hence to *Le Châtre*, see Rte 50.

The N151 continues S.W., at 20km passing some 5km N. of *Diors*, where the remains of a 13C château, with a 15C tower, contain a *Museum* devoted to the Franco-Prussian and two World Wars.

8km. **CHÂTEAUROUX** (54,000 Castelroussins), the busy industrial préfecture of the *Indre*, with manufacturers of textiles, tobacco, and machinery, is not particularly inviting, and has been provided with a by-pass; nevertheless it contains a few monuments of interest.

It owes its name to a castle erected by Raoul le Large, lord of Déols, in the 10C. As part of Eleanor of Aquitaine's dowry, it became a fief of the English crown, but eventually passed to the Condé family (1612), and here the widow of the Grand Condé, disgracefully treated by her husband and son, died in 1694. It was presented by Louis XV, with the title of duchess, to the youngest of the three de Mailly sisters. Gén. Bertrand (1773–1844), Napoleon's aide and biographer, was born here; Jean Giraudoux (1882–1944) was partly educated here (1893–1900).

A short distance N. of the central *Pl. Gambetta* is the *Musée Bertrand*, installed in a mansion of 1767 in which the general died, with Napoleonic souvenirs and other collections of local interest. Opposite stands *St-Martial* (13th and 15C; restored), with a Renaissance belfry. To the N.E. in the *Pl. St-Hélène* is the former *Église des Cordeliers* (13C), with a wooden vaulted roof.

The Rue du Marché leads S.W. from the museum towards the *Hôtel de Ville* (1821), which contains in its library the oldest extant MS. of the 'Chanson de Roland'.—Further W. (beyond *Notre-Dame*, built in 1882 by André Dauvergne, architect also of *St-André*, 1876, S.E. of the Pl. Gambetta, an edifice in the '13C style', with two spires), is the **Château Raoul**, now part of the *Préfecture*, a picturesque 15C building; to the E. is the *Porte St-Martin*, the main gateway to the castle.

Of interest also is the suburb of **Déols** (once the capital of Berry), approached by the Av. de Paris, leading N. from the centre. To the r., on the far bank of the Indre, are the remains of the famous Cluniac abbey-church, consecrated in 1106 and sacked by the Huguenots in 1569, of which a magnificent Romanesque * *Tower*, 54m high, with a conical stone spire, survives; and at its base, some beautiful 12C arcading. The 15C *Porte de l'Horloge* was part of its old ramparts.—*St-Étienne*, with a 12C nave, 15C aisles, and an incomplete 16C tower, contains an image which has been the object of pilgrimage since 1187. The Gallo-Roman *Crypt* preserves the tomb of St Ludre, a marble sarcophagus of the 3C, and that of his father Leocade, the senator and founder of Déols.

For the road from Châteauroux to **Limoges**, see Rte 63; for that to *Loches* a..id **Tours**, see Rte 55 in reverse; and to **Clermont-Ferrand** via *Guéret* and *Aubusson*, Rte 93.

The D943 leads 36km S.E. to *La Châtre*, ascending the Indre valley, here known as the 'Vallée Noire' via (14km) *Ardentes*, Roman *Alerea*, with a 12C church, and 16km beyond, *Nohant*; see Rte 91.

The N20 drives S.W., traversing the W. edge of the *Forêt de Châteauroux* to (15km) *Lothiers*, where the N151 forks r.—For *Argenton*, 15km beyond, see Rte 63.—At 15km we reach the Creuse at *St-Gaultier*, with a 12C church, and skirt its N. bank to (14.5km) *Ciron*, with a 12C 'lanterne des morts', opposite which rise the towers of the 14C castle of *Romefort*. There are several megalithic monuments in the *Brenne*, a marshy area to the N., described on p 333.

14km. **Le Blanc**, ancient *Oblincum*, is a pleasant old market-town astride the Creuse, in the upper part of which are a modernised castle and 17C *St-Étienne*; in the lower town is *St-Génitour*, with a Romanesque tower and square-ended choir, 13C nave, and 15C aisles.

8km N.W., approached by the D950 following the r. bank of the river, is **Font-gombault**, an attractive village with an important *Abbey*, founded in 1091. Occupied originally by Benedictines, and in 1849–1903 by Trappists, it has reverted to the former order. The ruined nave of the Romanesque *Church* (1091–1141) was completely and tastefully rebuilt during the Trappist occupation. The three archways in the W. front, with rich sculptures, are notable, but more so the apsidal *Choir*, with its beautiful triforium, curving ranges of columns, and five subsidiary chapels. The monastic dependencies include a chapter-house, cloister, refectory, etc., all of the 15C.—For *Angles-sur-l'Anglin*, some 9km N.W., see Rte 56.

9km. *Ingrandes*, where we cross the Anglin, has ruins of a castle.

The D50 lead N.W. hence up the valley to (15.5km) *Angles* via (2km) *Plain-courault*, with a 15C manor and *Chapel* of 1291 decorated with quaint murals, and *Mérigny*, on the opposite bank, beyond which is the rebuilt château of *Rochbellusson*, and further on, dominating a picturesque reach of the stream, the *Château de Puygirault*.
Some 11km S. of Ingrandes is the village of **Villesalem**, with a remarkable mid 12C Romanesque *Church*, recently well restored, once a priory of the order of Fontvraud, and worth the detour.

9km. **St-Savin**, on the Gartempe, one bridge over which is 13C, is famous for its abbey, founded in 811 by Charlemagne over the tomb of the hermit St Savinus. Its murals were first brought to general notice by Mérimée in his 'Notes d'un voyage dans l'ouest de la France' (1836), written when he was Inspector General of Historical Monuments.

The *Abbey Church* (c. 1080), with a handsome tower and crocketed spire (94m; 14-15C) and a lower central tower, is decorated in the porch, nave, and apse with life-size *Mural Paintings* (11th and 13C) depicting the stories of Genesis and Exodus, the triumph of the Virgin, and (in the porch) the Last Judgement, with Passion scenes in the chamber above. The 13C paintings in the crypt relate to the legend of St Savinus and St Cyprian. The floor of the church is below the level of the entrance, and the W. end seems to have been separated from the rest to form a narthex. The columns were unfortunately coloured to simulate marble in the 19C. Parts of the abbey buildings date from 1640; the 15C abbot's lodge (restored) is now private property.

The D11 leads 18km S. to *Montmorillon* (see Rte 69A) via *Antigny* and *Jouhet*, both villages with churches of interest.

18km. **Chauvigny** (6700 inhab.), picturesquely sited on the E. bank of the Vienne, was a strong fortress in medieval times, and still possesses the ruins of five *Castles*, built on the same plan, a square flanked by turrets. At the S. point of the spur above the town is the massive *Château Baronnial* (12th and late 14C), a seat of the bishops of Poitiers, who were lords of Chauvigny; then come the *Châteaux d'Harcourt* (13-15C), *de Montléon* (12th and 15C), *de Gouzon* (partly 11C), and the *Tour de Flins*.—Also in the upper town is *St-Pierre* (12C; restored), with an early 13C tower, and richly decorated both without and within, its grotesque *Capitals* being remarkable.—Romanesque *St-Martial*, further N., is now a barn.

In the lower town, the tri-apsidal Romanesque church of *Notre-Dame* (also restored) contains good capitals, and a late 15C wall-painting of the Bearing of the Cross, with attendants popes and saints.

About 1.5km S. is *St-Pierre-les-Églises*, preserving 13C paintings, beyond which in the rocky *Vallée des Goths*, is the curious *Grotte de Gioux*.—For *Civaux*, 13.5km beyond, see Rte 69A.

Some 13km N.E. is the remote ruined abbey of *N.-D.-de-l'Étoile*, founded in 1124; for the D749 N.W. to *Châtellerault*, see p 335.

Continuing W., at 6km we pass (r.) *Jardres*, with a 14C steeple, and 4km beyond traverse *St-Julien-l'Ars*, with a restored castle.—4km N. is the *Château de Bois-Doussé*, with Renaissance details. After another 8km the new University buildings of Poitiers are passed (l.) prior to descending through the Fauburg de Pont-Neuf to the river Clan. For **Poitiers**, see Rte 56.

52 Orléans to Tours

A. North of the Loire, via Blois

115km (71 miles). N152. 18km *Meung-sur-Loire*—7km **Beaugency** —32km **Blois**—34km **Amboise**—24km **Tours**.

The route is followed by the A10 motorway running parallel some 3km to the N. between Orléans and Blois, and then some 10km apart, providing rapid approaches to Blois, Amboise, and Tours.

Maps: IGN 26, or 107. M 238.

Although the route described below follows the N. bank of the Loire, this can be combined with ease with that running parallel to the S. bank (see Rte 52B), for the river is crossed at a number of points. A good compromise is to follow the N. bank to *Beaugency*, there crossing to take in *Chambord*, and re-crossing to visit

Blois, before returning to the S. bank to *Beauregard* (and *Cheverny*), *Chaumont*, *Amboise*, and *Chenonceau*.

Note. With such an 'embarras de richesses' many travellers are in a quandary as to which châteaux of the number open to the public they should visit in the time at their disposal, and a few words of advice are given on p 67-9 of this Guide. It is almost impossible to give any overall indication of which may or may not be open, depending on the season, but as a very general rule, the better known châteaux of the Loire Valley are *open every day* throughout the year, although some will close on a *Tuesday* or another day each week, except during the summer. It is *strongly recommended* that the traveller planning to visit them—including those described in Rte 57, and elsewhere in the region—should first acquire from any of the larger S.Is in the area (or when in London or Paris) a copy of the latest brochure detailing times of admission, and entitled 'Val de Loire'. An English language version is also produced.

Driving S.W. from **Orléans** (Rte 50), we traverse (5km) *La Chapelle-St-Mesmin*, with a Merovingian crypt, and (7.5km) *St-Ay*, well-known for its wine, to reach *Meung-sur-Loire*, with the 13C church of an abbey founded in the 6C, the 11C tower and a curious fortified edifice adjoining it being relics of its predecessor. The former castle of the bishops of Orléans retains some 13C towers, while the *Porte d'Amont* is a survival of its 14C ramparts. François Villon was incarcerated in the episcopal prison here in 1461. It was the birthplace of Jean de Meung (c. 1260–1305), author of the second part of the 'Roman de la Rose' (cf. Lorris).

6km. **BEAUGENCY** (7300 inhab.), in spite of modern suburbs, a charming old riverside town, once walled, and long disputed between French and English. It was the Council of Beaugency (1152) which annulled the marriage of Louis VII and Eleanor of Aquitaine, that enabled her to marry Henry II, thus adding her extensive possessions to his dominions in France.

Turn l. a short distance beyond the remains of ramparts (r.) near the E. entrance to the town. Passing beneath the 13C *Tour de l'Horloge* we reach (r.) the charming *Hôtel de Ville (c. 1525). Turning l. at the end of the Rue du Change, and then r., we pass the *Château* (see below) before reaching the *Bridge*, a long irregular structure of 26 arches of varying date, restored since war damage, which commands a good view of the town. On the quay is the *Tour du Diable*, and 18C dependencies of an abbey founded in 580 and burnt by the Huguenots in 1567.

Ascending a lane S. of this tower, we reach its church, *Notre-Dame*, largely Romanesque, with a sham vault provided some 100 years after the fire; it was here that the Councils of Beaugency assembled.—To the W. is the *Tour de César*, the keep, once connected to the residential wing of the *Castle* (14-15C), now housing a small *Museum* of regional exhibits.

A few paces S.W. on the far side of an attractive square is the heavily buttressed *Tour St-Firmin* (1530), the tower of a church destroyed at the Revolution.—A lane to the l. leads to the *Porte Tavers* (12C) and the Promenade of the Petit-Mail.—To the r. the Rue de la Sirène leads to the *Maison des Templiers*, a good example of Romanesque domestic building, whilee to the W. is the *Pl. du Martroi* (beyond which is disused *St-Étienne*; 11C); the Rue Nationale is regained a short distance N.

7km. *Avaray*, with a moated castle which belonged to the Montgomery family before 1581, but entirely built after 1736 except for its 13C corner towers. The view across the Loire is disfigured by a *Centrale Nucléaire*.—6km. *Mer*, its church with a Flamboyant tower.

At **Talcy**, 9km N.W., is the *Château ◊ built c. 1520 by Bernardo Salviati, cousin of Catherine de Médicis (a frequent visitor), and father of Ronsard's 'Cassandra'. It preserves a 12C keep, and contains good furniture; note also the old winepress and a huge dovecot.

5km. *Suèvres*. The 12C nave of *St-Christophe* was added to an older aisle (?7C), with a herring-bone brickwork facade; 10-16C *St-Lubin* was built on the foundations of a Roman temple.—6km. *Menars*, with an 18C *Château* completed by Soufflot for Mme de Pompadour.

BLOIS (49,400 Blésois), préfecture of the *Loir-et-Cher*, lies largely on the N. bank of the Loire, its historic castle commanding the narrow streets and quaint houses of the lower town, some of it seriously damaged in 1940, particularly in the vicinity of the bridge.

In feudal times it was the seat of a line of counts, including Thibault I, Le Tricheur ('the trickster'; d. 978), who erected the earliest keep, and Stephen, William the Conqueror's grandson, who became king of England (1135–54). In 1397 it passed to the house of Orléans, and to the crown in 1498, when Louis XII, born in the château, succeeded to the throne. Charles d'Orléans held court here in 1440–65. Blois was a favourite residence of both Louis XII (whose widow, Anne of Brittany, died here in 1514) and François I. Henri III summoned the States General to Blois in 1576 and again in 1588, when their antagonistic attitude revealed a danger which he attempted to avert by assassinating the Duc de Guise and his brother the Cardinal. Catherine de Médicis, the king's mother and counsellor, died in the château a few days later. Marie de Medicis was imprisoned at Blois for two years (1617–19) by her son, Louis XIII, whose brother Gaston d'Orléans (d. 1660) attempted to set up a rival court here, but with indifferent success. In 1699 Addison visited Blois in order to learn French.

Among natives were Peter of Blois (d. 1200), the chronicler; the physicist Denis Papin (1647–1710); and the historian Augustin Thierry (1795–1856).

Most roads converge on the circular *Pl. Victor-Hugo*, which commands a good view of the François-I wing of the château (see below), by which it is overlooked. To the N. is *St-Vincent-de-Paul*, a former Jesuit church (1626–71) containing monuments erected in 1677 to Mlle de Montpensier and her father, Gaston d'Orléans. To the W. is the Renaissance *Pavillion d'Anne de Bretagne* (housing the S.I.), with the timbered *Orangerie* adjoining, which formerly stood in the castle gardens. Further W. is the *Tour de Guise*, a relic of medieval ramparts.

From the S. side of the Place one ascends to the *Pl. du Château*, once a fortified forecourt to the **Château**, an irregular quadrilateral enclosing a spacious courtyard.

It consists of four distinct parts: facing the Place is the *Louis-XII Wing*, in the late Gothic style, with a brick facade of 1503, flanked to the r. by the rebuilt gable of the *Salle d'États* (13C). It is embellished with curiously sculptured corbels and dormer windows, and the main entrance is surmounted by a Flamboyant niche containing a (mid 19C) statue of Louis XII, whose emblem, the crowned porcupine, is here obsessively repeated as an ornament.

Wraxall, writing after his visit in 1775, remarked that the castle was 'tending to decay...', and it is still hard to overlook the general state of dilapidation which the building exhibits; as yet little appears to have been done to clear the shabby interior of its disastrous mid 19C decoration (although a thorough restoration was no doubt then very necessary, for, after decades of neglect, it had been used as barracks from 1788 to 1841). Arthur Young, who passed that way in 1787, observed that the 'murders or political executions perpetrated in this castle... were inflicted on and by men that command neither our love nor our veneration. The character of the period, and of the men that figured in it, were alike disgusting. Bigotry and ambition, equally dark, insidious, and bloody, allow no feelings of regret. The parties could hardly be better employed than in cutting each others' throats'.

Visitors are taken round in groups, a time-consuming and not always very rewarding procedure. Having acquired a ticket, one awaits a guide in the central courtyard.

To the l., a _Musée d'Art Religieux_ has been installed, with a collection of paintings and sculpture above, notable among which are a Portrait of Marguerite de Bourbon, by _Corneille de Lyon_; _Nicolas Mignard_, Louis XIV aged eight; _Pierre Mignard_, Mme de Montespan and the Duc de Maine; _Lemoyne_, terracotta Busts of the architect Gendrier, and of Charpentier, the sculptor.

Beyond is the _Galerie de Charles d'Orléans_, and the _Chapelle de St-Calais_ (c. 1480), three bays of which were demolished by Charles d'Orléans. The adjoining terrace provides a wide view (with the château of _Beauregard_ in the distance). To the r. is the massive _Tour de Foix_, a relic of the earlier fortress, and traditionally regarded as the astrological observatory of Catherine de Médicis.

To the S.W. is the _Gaston d'Orléans Wing_, designed by Mansart (1635), but left unfinished at the accession of Louis XIV. Its dignified Classical style contrasts with its ornate Renaissance neighbour, which it awkwardly abuts, part of which was destroyed in its construction. The remarkable _Staircase_ is crowned by an elaborate elliptical cupola by Mansart. This wing was not touched after 1841, when the rest of the castle was 'restored'.

To the N. is the *_François-I Wing_ (1515–24), possibly built under the direction of Domenico da Cortona. The exterior facade is a masterpiece of its period, with its finely proportioned double loggias in the Italian manner, surmounted by a gallery close under the roof, while its uniformity is broken by a row of gargoyles above and in the smaller projections below. The pavilion in the Classical style is the termination of the Gaston d'Orléans wing; the adjacent _Tour des Oubliettes_, although outwardly transformed in the 16C, belongs to the original fortress. The inner facade is encrusted with Renaissance ornamentation (everywhere displaying the ubiquitous salamander emblem of François I), from which projects the octagonal openwork stair-turret, likewise lavishly decorated, the work of Jacques Sourdeau and his son.

Groups are conducted up this spiral to the FIRST FLOOR (and locked in!). Here are the apartments once occupied by Catherine de Médicis, including her bedroom (in which she died on 5 Jan. 1589), oratory, and study (its panelling concealing secret hiding-places); Marie de Médicis is said to have escaped from the castle in 1619 through a window in this study. An exterior gallery gives access to the _Tour des Oubliettes_, with a cell at the door of which the Card. du Guise was murdered. In the centre of the floor is a well 9m deep. Before ascending to the second floor one is shown the _Salle des États_, a spacious Gothic hall 30m long, 22m broad, and 18m high, divided by 13C arcades.

The _Apartments of Henri III_ are reached by a staircase in the thickness of the 13C wall or by the _Escalier des Quarante-Cinq_, named from the 45 'gentlemen-in-waiting' who were accomplice to the premeditated murder of the Duc de Guise (surnamed 'le Balafré' from the scar on his face) and his brother (23-24 Dec. 1588). The _Salle des Conseil_ has two over-restored fireplaces, at one of which Guise was warming himself when summoned to the degenerate king's presence and his own assassination.

Steps descend from the E. end of the Place du Château to the _Pl. Louis-XII_, whence the narrow Rue St-Lubin leads W. past 15-16C houses to approach _St-Nicolas_ (1138–1210). Its crossing is vaulted by an unusual ribbed dome, and crowned with a lantern; the capitals and corbels deserve notice, as does the altar-piece of c. 1460 depicting scenes from the life of St Mary of Egypt.

Between the church and the river a _Hospital_ occupies 18C abbey buildings.—To the N.E. is the _Pont Gabriel_ (rebuilt 1717–24), decorated with the so-called _Pyramide_, sculptured by Nicolas Cousteau.

From the semicircular Place at the N. end of the bridge-head, one may turn r. off the Rue Denis-Papin (which with its extension, the Rue Porte-Côté—which leads back to the Pl. Victor-Hugo—is the busiest street in the town) to the Rue Fontaine-des-Élus, in which the *Hôtel de Jassaud* (No. 5) is one of the more interesting houses in this 'Vieux Quartier'. To the N. in the Rue du Puits-Châtel, are the *Hôtel Sardini* (No. 7), and No. 5, dating from the time of Louis XII.

Parallel to the N., the Rue des Papegaults (No. 10 in which is the *Hôtel Belot*) ascends to the **Cathedral of St-Louis**. Largely rebuilt in 1678 in a kind of Flamboyant Gothic, it preserves its N.W. tower on a 12C base (with an interesting inscription), Renaissance upper storeys and a W. doorway, also of Renaissance date.

Murray suggested that it was 'not worth entering', but those who do so will find in the S. aisle some marble bas-reliefs, one a fragment of the tomb of the mother of Stanislas Leczinski (d. 1727); two others, by Louis Larembert (1660) are from the other tombs. Below is a 10C crypt. Behind the cathedral is the former Bishop's Palace (18C) occupied by the *Hôtel de Ville*.

From the cathedral one may return to the Pl. Victor-Hugo either by descending the narrow Rue Pierre-de-Bois, with 15C houses, one bridging the street, to the Rue des Juifs, also with characteristic houses, bringing us to the junction of the Rue Denis-Papin and the Rue Porte-Côté (from which a monumental stair ascends); or, alternatively, by following the Rue du Palais W. to the statue of Denis Papin (for whom the French claim the discovery of steam power) at the head of the steps. Hence, skirting gardens, the Rue St-Honoré continues W. past the *Hôtel d'Alluye, a Renaissance building due to Robertet, finance minister under François I, with a double gallery in its courtyard, and in the restored interior, a magnificent chimney-piece. At the end of this lane, the Rue Porte Chartraine descends to the Rue Porte-Côté.—Further to the W. is the *Hôtel de Guise*, 8 Rue Chemonton.

The N152 continues S.W., skirting the river, to (16km) *Escures*, where one may cross the Loire to *Chaumont* (see Rte 52B), the château of which is seen high above the far bank.—The church of *Mesland*, 7km N.W., contains 16C sculpture in the style of Michel Colombe, and retains a remarkable portal of c. 1120.—More sculpture of the same style is seen at *Limeray*, 1.5km to the r. as we approach (18km) the transpontine suburb of **Amboise**, on the far bank; see Rte 52B.

2km. *Négron*, with a restored 13C barn, and *Mairie* occupying a partly 12C building, is traversed, 9km beyond which we pass S. of *Venou-sur-Brenne*, with a good 12C church enlarged in the 16C.—4km. *Vouvray*, famous for its white wines, the cellars of which may be visited.—4km. *Rochecorbon* (r.), dominated by a remarkable 14C tower known as the *Lanterne de Rochecorbon*. A *Museum* contains exhibits illustrating the wine trade, and 17-19C furniture.

2km further W., just short of the motorway, are the slight remains of the abbey of **Marmoutier**, founded by St Martin of Tours, and once one of the most influential in France, its site now occupied by a convent.

Almost all the buildings were demolished in 1818 except for the 13C *Portail de la Crosse*, and the turreted boundary-wall. Visitors may view (entry in the Rue St-Martin) the 12C *Tour des Cloches*; the *Chapel of the Seven Sleepers*, a cruciform excavation, in which St Gatien celebrated his first mass, containing the tombs of the seven disciples of St Martin, who all died on the same day (as he had foretold); the *Cell of St-Léobard*; and the *Repos de St-Martin*, a primitive 'dug-out' chapel favoured by that saint.

The suburb of *Ste-Radegonde* has a part-Romanesque church; that of *St-Georges* dates from the 11C.—We may cross the Loire slightly further W. to enter Tours near its cathedral, or alternatively traverse the N. suburb of *St-Symphorien*, with a church preserving a 12C crossing and choir, to approach **Tours** by the *Pont Wilson*; see Rte 54.

B. South of the Loire, via Chambord, Cheverny, Chaumont, and Amboise

130km (81 miles). D951. 15km *Cléry*—24km. Turn l. onto the D112 for (6.5km) **Chambord**, 18km S. of which, via *Bracieux*, lies **Cheverny**.—D765. 7.5km N.W. **Beauregard**—D77. 7.5km *Les Montils*—D7 and D751. 9.5km **Chaumont**—18km **Amboise** (14.5km S.E. of which is **Chenonceau**)—24km **Tours**.

Maps: IGN 26, or 107. M 238.

The preliminary paragraphs of Rte 52A also apply to this route.

The road leads S.W. to **Cléry**, of slight interest apart from the somewhat dilapidated basilica of *Notre-Dame*, a Flamboyant edifice rebuilt by Louis XI in fulfilment of a vow made at the siege of Dieppe; of its predecessor, destroyed by the English in 1428, a low tower on the N. side survives.

The *Tomb of Louis XI* (1423–83), on the N. side of the last bay of the nave, is so sited that the kneeling statue faces N.-D. de Cléry (by Michel Bourdin; 1622), replacing the original image destroyed by the Huguenots in 1563; the rest of the monument, which disappeared at the Revolution, is a late 19C reconstruction. In the vault below is the sarcophagus the king had made during his lifetime, which still contains his remains and those of his wife Charlotte of Savoy.

In an adjacent vault is the tomb of Tanneguy du Chastel, who died in saving Louis' life at the siege of Bouchain (1477); on the opposite side of the nave a tombstone covers the heart of Charles VIII. A 15C chapel contains the tomb of Dunois (d. 1468), the companion of Joan of Arc.

7km. *Lailly-en-Val*, where died the philosopher Condillac (1715–80); **Beaugency** lies 5km W.; see Rte 52A.—At 10km we pass close to a *Centrale Nucléaire*, and not far beyond turn off for Chambord.

The ****Château de Chambord**, ◊ a grandiose product of the Renaissance, stands on the banks of the Cosson in a park of 54km² of forest tract, encircled by a wall nearly 35km round. Its imposing appearance, the great staircase, and extraordinary roof, where one walks as among streets, are its main points of interest.

The rebuilding of the château, originally merely a hunting-lodge of the counts of Blois, was begun for François I c. 1519, and 1800 workmen are said to have been employed upon it for 15 years. Jean Le Breton and Pierre Nepveu (surnamed Trinqueau) were assisted by Jacques and Denis Sourdeau, and Domenico Boccadoro. François I had a predilection for the place, and spent most of his later years here. Later kings made various alterations and additions—Stanislas Leczinski of Poland, who occupied it during the years 1725–33, filled up the moats;

A late 17C view of the château of Chambord

while the Marshal de Saxe, to whom it was given in 1748, certainly did not improve it.

In 1792 the London Society of Friends made a proposal to establish a school there, but later Napoleon gave it to Marshal Berthier, from whose widow it was bought in 1821 and offered to the infant Duc de Bordeaux (1820–83), who later assumed the title of Comte de Chambord. On his death it was bequeathed to the princes of Bourbon-Parma, but as Elie de Bourbon was an officer in the Austrian army the estate was sequestered in 1914, and in 1932 was purchased by the State.

The château consists of an outer quadrangle with massive cylindrical towers at its four corners, on the N.W. side of which rises an imposing square donjon, with similar but taller towers, and crowned with a fantastic profusion of dormers, chimneys (decorated by diamonds of slate to simulate marble), lanterns, and pinnacles, surmounted by a lantern over 30m high. This central block is divided into three perfectly proportioned storeys by plainly moulded string-courses. The *Porte Royale* in the low S.E. wing admits to the *Cour d'Honneur*.

Interior. Outstanding is the *Great Staircase, remarkable for the unique arrangement of its two spiral stairways, which start at different elevations, wind around the same central shaft and never meet, a conceit some have attributed to Leonardo da Vinci. It is situated in the centre of the inner courtyard of the donjon, at the intersection of the four main *Salles des Gardes*, which are arranged in the form of a Greek cross, and whose vaulted ceilings are decorated throughout with the salamander and initials of François I. It ascends to the spacious *Terraces* (views) at the foot of the lantern (a replica of the original, taken down at the turn of the century), whose elegant arched buttresses support a belvedere and campanile crowned by a huge fleur-de-lys. Two smaller spiral staircases ascend near each end of this wing at the corners of the *Cour d'Honneur*.

Parts of the building are under restoration; others await their turn. The rooms are sparsely furnished except for the *Chapel*, hung with tapestries, the *Appartements de Louis XIV*, arranged and furnished under the Restoration, with souvenirs of the Comte de Chambord, tapestries, and portraits (some of them contemporary copies) by *Largillière, Rigaud, Mignard, Clouet*, etc.; and the

Cabinet de Travail.—On the FIRST FLOOR is a room containing an enormous
stove of Dresden ware (contributed by de Saxe), and the hall in which took place
the first performance of Molière's 'Monsieur de Pourceaugnac' and 'Le
Bourgeois Gentilhomme' (in 1669 and 1670 respectively). A suite of rooms here
has been recently decorated, and among works of art displayed are a painting of
Louis XIV at Chambord (a copy of Van de Meulen's original in the Grand
Trianon), and a number of interesting old plans of the château.

A *Hunting Museum* (an extension of that in the *Hôtel de Guénégaud* in Paris)
has been installed on the SECOND FLOOR, including a series of engravings by
Jan van der Straet (Stradanus; 1536–1605). In a hall on the Ground Floor are
kept the state-carriages hopefully intended by the Comte de Chambord for his
entry into Paris as king in 1873. In an adjoining room hangs a set of six
*Tapestries, the 'Histoire des chasses du Roi François', after Laurent Guyot
(Paris; late 16C).—The enormous stables have accommodation for 1200 mounts.

The route is continued by driving S. through the park (which in Arthur Young's view was admirably suited for growing turnips, rather
than preserved for sporting nobles), and the adjacent *Forêt de
Boulogne*, to (8km) *Bracieux*, with its old market-hall. Hence the
D102 turns W. past the *Château de Villesavin*, on the far bank of the
Beuvron, built in 1537 by Jean Le Breton, with a chapel containing
16C frescoes, and a 16C dovecot, to (9.5km) *Cour-Cheverny*.

The *Château de Cheverny*, built in 1634, is a well-furnished
residence standing in a large park, and heralding, in its general plan,
the Louis-XIV style. Near the entrance an outbuilding houses a small
Hunting Museum; adjoining are the kennels and parts of an early
16C manor-house. The baying hounds now accompany the pink-
coated huntsmen who (for a fee) will blow their horns to amuse
coachloads of tourists, a vulgar expedient with which few expect to
be greeted.

The *Dining Room* contains a series of curious paintings by Jean Mosnier, a
native of Blois, from the history of Don Quixote (1638); the *Grand Salon*, its furniture upholstered with Aubusson tapestry, and the *Petit Salon*, with Flemish
tapestries after Teniers, have 17C decorations.—A sculptured stone staircase
ascends to the *Appartement du Roi*, where the *Salle des Gardes* with an imposing
chimney-piece, contains Gobelins tapestry representing the Rape of Helen; in
the *King's Bedchamber* are more paintings by Mosnier (Perseus and Andromeda,
and Theagenes and Chariclea), and an early 17C tapestry illustrating the
Odyssey.

4km N.W., a turning l. off the D956 leads to the *Château de
Beauregard* (1545–53), built for Jean du Thier, a minister of Henri II
and friend of Ronsard, and enlarged in 1631–38.

Of particular interest is a *Gallery containing 363 historical portraits, many unique, (and including one of Rabelais), painted by Jean Mosnier for Paul Ardier,
quartermaster-general, and mounted here between 1617 and 1638. Notice also
the Delft tiles depicting an army on the march. Some good 17C furniture is
displayed in an adjacent room, together with a 16C Brussels tapestry of the wedding of Henri IV. Adjoining is the oak-panelled *Cabinet des Grelots*, with three
hawk's bells (the device of Du Thier) on the ceiling, a motive used throughout its
decoration. The S. front is adorned with terracotta medallions.

From adjacent *Cellettes* the D77 leads S.W. via *Les Montils*, preserving a 12C gateway and keep built by Thibault le Grand, to
Chaumont-sur-Loire.

An alternative route from Cheverny is the D52, leading S.W. to (11.5km)
Fougères-sur-Bièvre, where the *Château*, ◇ founded in the 11C, was rebuilt
from 1470 onwards, uninfluenced by the Renaissance; its chimneypieces and
wooden ceilings are remarkable.—*Les Montils*, see above, lies 7km N.W.

The *Château de Chaumont, ◇ sited on a cliff above the Loire, is approached from the village entrance by an ascent—some 10 minutes' walk—through the park. It is a good example of a Gothic structure to which Renaissance details have been applied. A drawbridge gives access to a courtyard surrounded by three unequal wings: the fourth, overlooking the river, was demolished in 1739, an expedient followed at Saumur. Note Louis XII's porcupine on the r.; the interlaced 'Cs' of Charles and Catherine d'Amboise, the cardinal's hat of Georges d'Amboise, and the 'Ds' of Diane de Poitiers, are also conspicuous.

Founded in the 10C by Count Odo I of Blois, it was entirely rebuilt after 1466 by Pierre d'Amboise and his sons Charles I (d. 1481) and Charles II (d. 1511), who added the S. and E. wings. After 1560 Catherine de Médicis lived here for a few years, before forcing Diane de Poitiers to accept Chaumont in unfair exchange for Chenonceau. The estate later passed through the hands of Jacques Le Ray, who here established a terracotta factory under the direction of J.-B. Nini (1717–80), an Italian artist, whose portrait medallions are highly-considered likenesses. Le Ray's son gave sanctuary here in 1810 to Mme de Staël during her persecution by Napoleon. About 1833 its 'restoration' was undertaken by the Comte d'Aramon, who collected most of the furniture now displayed. The Princess de Broglie, the last private owner, sold the château to the State in 1938.

From the waiting-room, groups traverse rooms which still await the removal of their depressing 19C decoration, preserving historical relics, etc. More interesting are those on the FIRST FLOOR, reached by a spiral stair, and containing 15-16C paintings and decoration. Notable is the Salle des Fêtes, with a *Floor of Sicilian majolica tiles depicting hunting scenes. Among exhibits here are a set of tapestries representing the sun and planets; bronze andirons attrib. to Cellini; a fine chimneypiece retaining its original polychrome; and a copy of a painting of Catherine de Médicis when young. A balcony leading off her bedroom overlooks the Chapel, where some *15C murals may be seen near the altar.—Behind the château are the *Stables, with saddlery and harnesses displayed, and the riding-school, in which Nini set up his kiln in 1772, and where four years later Benjamin Franklin sat for his portrait in clay.

The N751 continues downstream to (18km) **AMBOISE** (11,400 inhab.), an old town, the 4C *Ambatia*, lying on the S. bank of the Loire, spanned here by a bridge crossing the Île St-Jean, with a disused 12C chapel. On the quay are the Hôtel de Ville (1505), containing a local Museum; St-Florentin (1484), with a Renaissance belfry; and a Fountain (1968) designed by Max Ernst. To the S. of the adjacent Pl. Gén. Leclerc is the 14-15C Tour de l'Horloge, whence some minutes along the pedestrian Rue Nationale will bring one to St-Denis (12-16C), containing historiated capitals, a 16C Entombment, and a recumbant figure called 'La Femme Noyée' in the style of Primaticcio. There is a Postal Museum in the Rue Joyeuse, leading S. from this street.

The Beaubruns, a family devoted to portrait-painting in the 16–17Cs, lived at Amboise.

The town is dominated by the *Château, perched on the corner of a rocky plateau, its terrace supported by thick walls flanked by two formidable bastions, each of which contains a vaulted spiral incline which may be ascended by carriage. The present buildings are only a fragment of the extensive fortress which stood here in the 15C.

A castle existed in 496, when Clovis and Alaric II had a reconciliatory interview on the Île St-Jean. Under Charles VII (1434) it became a royal residence, and Charles d'Orléans died here in 1465. Charles VIII (1470–98, who was born here and died here), was responsible for a complete reconstruction, commenced in 1492, and carried on by François I, who in 1539 here entertained the Emperor Charles V. In 1560 the Huguenots, led by La Renaudie and inspired by Condé, made a determined attempt to seize François II, held here by the Guises, and the failure of the conspiracy, known as the 'Conjuration d'Amboise', precipitated the most horrible carnage. Amboise ceased to be a royal residence. It was later used as a State prison, and fell into the hands of Roger Ducos, Napoleon's colleague in the Consulate, who demolished the S. and W. wings (apart from the chapel) and the castle-church of St-Florentin. It later became the property of the Orléans family, and since 1950, when the Law of Exile was repealed, a residence of the Comte de Paris.

A sloping covered passage ascends from the town to the terrace, on the edge of which is the Gothic *Chapelle St-Hubert, finished in 1493 and restored since 1940, when it was slightly damaged, its spire suitably decorated with antlers. On the lintel is a delicately carved Vision of St Hubert and the legends of St Christopher and St Anthony, perhaps by Corneille de Nesve. Under the pavement of the N. transept are the supposed remains (transferred from St-Florentin; see above) of Leonardo da Vinci (1452–1519), who had been invited to Amboise by François I.

The *Logis du Roi* has a handsome exterior facade profusely adorned with dormers and pinnacles. From the *Salle des Gardes*, an open gallery communicates with the *Tour des Chevaliers* (or *des Minims*), with a vaulted spiral *Ramp which ascends from the Loire to the roof (view; including one of the *Balcon des Conjurés*, with ironwork from which some hundreds of La Renaudie's followers were hung. Hence one descend to the imposing *Salle d'États*, sustained by four pillars carved alternately with fleurs-de-lys and Anne of Brittany's ermines; note also their capitals, and the chimney-piece. The smaller *François-I Wing* has a suite of rooms containing good furniture (some 15C) and Aubusson tapestries, etc. On the FIRST FLOOR are rooms decorated in the Louis-Philippe taste, with 19C portraits of members of the Orléans family, five of them by Winterhalter.

The *Tour Hurtault*, across the gardens, also has a spiral ramp. A bust of da Vinci marks the site of the castle-church, to the N. of which is a doorway with the porcupine emblem of Louis XII, on the lintel of which Charles VIII is supposed to have hit his head, the resulting concussion causing his death.

The Rue Victor-Hugo leads E. to the 15C manor of **Le Clos-Lucé**, where Leonardo spent the last four years of his life. It now contains some 40 remarkable *Models, constructed by IBM from his sketches of inventions, which are of historical and technical interest.—The *Château Gaillard*, beyond, belonged to Charles de Guise, Card. of Lorraine (1525–74).

AMBOISE TO CHENONCEAUX (15km). The D81 leads directly S.E., but the more interesting D31 drives due S., at 2.5km passing (r.) the *Pagode de Chanteloup*, built in 1775–78 by Le Camus for the Duc de Choiseul in emulation rather than imitation of Chamber's pagoda at Kew, and restored in 1916. The château of Chateloup, built by Robert de Cotte and later used as a sugar-beet refinery by Chaptal, the chemist, was demolished in 1823.—Traversing the *Forêt d'Amboise*, the road descends to (6km) *La Croix-en-Touraine*, 6km. E. of which is the village of *Chenonceaux* (retaining its ultimate x), with the **Château de Chenonceau** partly spanning the Cher, for which see Rte 53.—**Loches** (see Rte 55), lies 27km S. of La Croix, via (9km) *Sublaines*, near which are mounds called the *Danges*, said to have been raised by Clovis and Alaric II to mark the boundary between their respective dominions (cf. Amboise), later travelling traversing the *Forêt de Loches* and descending into the Indre valley.

The D751 leads W. from Amboise to (13km) *Montlouis*, noted for its white wines (as is *Vouvray*, on the far bank; see Rte 52A).—11km. **Tours**; see Rte 54.

53 Tours to Bourges via Chenonceaux and Romorantin-Lanthenay

126km (78 miles). N76. 28km *Bléré*, 3km beyond which cross the Cher to *Civray*, and turn r. for (3.5km) **Chenonceaux**—9.5km *Montrichard*—17km *St-Aignan* (on the S. bank)—14km *Selles-sur-Cher*—8.5km D724. 9.5km **Romorantine-Lanthenay**—D922. 8km *Villefranche-sur-Cher*—N76. 8.5km *Mennetou-sur-Cher*—16.5km **Vierzon**—16km *Mehun-sur-Yèvre*—17km **Bourges**.

Maps: IGN 26, 27, or 106. M 238.

On crossing the Cher immediately S. of **Tours** (see Rte 54) we turn l. through *St-Avertin*, ancient *Ventiacum*, and called Vençay until the 16C, the 11C church of which has a choir added in the late 15C by a Scotsman, John de Coningham, who built the neighbouring *Château de Cangé*. St-Avertin was the birthplace of Christopher Plantin, the printer (1514–89).

4km. *Larçay*, preserving remains of a Gallo-Roman castellum, 2km beyond which is *Véretz*, with a monument to the pamphleteer Paul-Louis Courier (1772–1825), who upheld the rights of the peasants against the petty oppression of the church and officialdom, but who was murdered by a farm-labourer he had dismissed near his country house in the adjacent *Forêt de Larçay*.

On the far bank of the Cher is the rebuilt *Château de la Bourdaisière*, the probable birthplace of Gabrielle d'Estrées (1573–99), whose mother was of the family of Babou de la Bourdaisiére, a powerful clan in 16C Touraine.

4km. 3km S. is the priory of *St-Jean-du-Grais*, of which survive a Romanesque tower, 15C refectory, and a remarkable Gothic chapter-house with a dorter above.

The N76 passes several minor châteaux before entering (12km) *Bléré*, with its 12th and 15C church surmounted by a stone spire, and Renaissance *Hôtel du Gouverneur*, 3km beyond which we cross the river to *Civray* and *Chenonceaux*.

The ****Château de Chenonceau** (without the final x) is famous for both for its architecture and for its unique and romantic position across the umbrageous Cher.

Thomas Bohier, deputy treasurer-general for Normandy, having in 1513 purchased an old manor and mill on the N. bank of the river, refaced the principal tower, and then demolished the rest, before building a new residence on the foundations of the mill (from 1515). He died in 1523 before its completion, having carved among its decoration the prophetic motto 'S'il vient à point, me souviendra'. His wife Catherine Briçonnet continued the work, but in 1535 their son was obliged to surrender the domain to the crown in payment of his father's debts.

Henri II gave the château to Diane de Poitiers in 1547, who commissioned Philibert Delorme to construct the bridge across the Cher. At the king's death (1559) Catherine de Médicis forced Diane to exchange it for Chaumont, and under her instructions the somewhat uninspired upper storeys were added in 1580 to Delorme's bridge; her other alterations were removed during 19C restorations. It was her favourite residence, and here she fêted her son François II and Mary, Queen of Scots, his child bride. At her death (1589) Catherine bequeathed it to Louise de Vaudémont, Henri III's widow, who died here in 1601.

Between 1601 and 1730, when it became the property of the Farmer-General Dupin, the fabric was allowed to fall into disrepair, but its new owner revived its splendour and threw open its doors to the distinguished 'salon' of Mme Dupin,

The château of Chenonceau in 1843, by Justin Duvrié (detail)

which included Montesquieu, Buffon, Bolingbroke, Voltaire, Mme de Boufflers, Mme de Tencin, and Mme du Deffand; Rousseau lived here in 1747 as tutor to the son of the house. It escaped the ravages of the Revolution, owing to the respect which the aged Mme Dupin (d. 1797) commanded. Since 1913 it has been the property of the Menier family, chocolate manufacturers, who have kept the place in tasteful order.

An avenue of plane trees leads up to the forecourt, to the r. of which are the extensive stables of Catherine de Médicis, known as the *Bâtiments des Dômes*. On the r. beyond a drawbridge, stands the 15C *Tour des Marques*, as refaced by Bohier. A second bridge crosses to the main building, a square pavilion flanked by corbelled towers and richly ornamented in the early Renaissance taste. The sober classical gallery which springs from the S. facade is built above the five-arched bridge across the Cher, and was intended to have been terminated on the far bank by another pavilion, but the work was cut short by the death of Catherine.

On each floor four large rooms open from the vestibule. On the GROUND FLOOR a handsome door on the l. leads to the old *Salle des Gardes*, which has a ceiling of painted rafters showing the device of Catherine de Médicis, and Flemish tapestries representing the Rape of Helen, etc. A carved door communicates with the *Chapel*, where an English inscription is said to date from the days of Mary Stuart. The *Chambre de Diane de Poitiers* contains 15C Flemish tapestries and a chimneypiece ascribed to Jean Goujon. Next to it is the *Cabinet Vert*, adjoining a small *Library* (view) with a fine coffered ceiling. Hence one may visit the *Long Gallery*, 60m in length, with a series of bow windows overlooking the river; the ceiling preserves a section with curious funerary decoration from the chamber of Louise de Vaudémont.—Steps descend to kitchens in the basement.

The *Chambre de François-I*, on the r. of the vestibule, contains Louis-XIII furniture, a case with autographs of 'Dianne de Poytié' and Gabrielle d'Estrées, a portrait of Diane by *Primaticcio*, and the Three Graces (in fact the Mlles de Nesles) by *Van Loo*.—Adjoining is the *Grand Salon*, with a portrait of Mme Dupin by *Nattier*, the Infant Jesus with St John, by *Rubens*, and a portrait of Samuel Bernard, by *Mignard*; Aubusson tapestry covers the chairs.

An Italianate staircase ascends to a series of restored rooms on the FIRST FLOOR. The upper floor of the *Long Gallery* is embellished with 17C Audenarde tapestries.—On the N. bank of the Cher are the well-kept gardens, 'á la française'.

The riverside road leads E. through *Chissay-en-Touraine*, with an imposing Renaissance château, to **Montrichard** (pron. Mon-trichard), overlooked by remains of the *Castle, of which the keep was built by Fulk Nerra and reconstructed in the 12C, and with outer ramparts dating from the 13th to 15Cs. Below is the 15-16C *Hospice*, behind which is a tower of the old town wall.

In the W. suburb of **Nanteuil** is an interesting *Church with 12C transepts and a triple Romanesque apse, a 13C nave, a two-storeyed Lady Chapel, and two richly decorated 15C doorways. The corbels supporting the nave-vault are carved to represent the heads of kings and bishops. In and near the main street are several old wooden-beamed houses, while in *Ste-Croix*, with a good 12C doorway, was celebrated the ill-starred marriage of Louis XII and Jeanne de France (1476).

5.5km S., off the D764, is the ruined abbey of *Aiguevive*, its church in a fair state of preservation, with an exquisitely sculptured 12C W. doorway. The great window above dates from c. 1400, and the rest of the fabric, including the central tower, is late 12C.—6km further S.W. is the 15C château of *Montpoupon*, altered in the 18C.

7.5km N.E. lies *Pontlevoy*, site of a Benedictine college founded in 1034 and refounded by Richelieu, partly burnt by the Germans in 1940; of the abbey buildings, mainly 18C, with part of a 17C cloister, and 15C chapel, etc., several features of interest survive.

7km. The *Château du Gué-Péan*, 3.5km N.E. preserves four 14-15C towers and two Renaissance pavilions, well furnished, with a chimneypiece by Germain Pilon, and several paintings and autographs of interest.—3km. *Thézée*, on approaching which we pass relics of a large Gallo-Roman structure.

7km. **St-Aignan**, in the S. bank of the Cher, preserves several 15-16C houses in the vicinity of its 12C *Church, with a tower over its crossing, and containing remarkable capitals. There are contemporary murals in the 15C Lady Chapel, and earlier examples in the crypt.—A long flight of steps ascends to the *Château* of the Beauvillier family, with ruins of an older castle adjoining.

Regaining the N. bank, we continue E. to (14km) **Selles-sur-Cher**, an old town preserving a number of ancient houses, and a 12-14C *Church* with long Romanesque transepts with apsidal chapels, two of which are decorated on the exterior with a frieze depicting the story of St Eusice. In the riverside park are two *Castles, a 12-13C fortress and a Renaissance château (built for Philippe de Béthune, younger brother of Sully), the pavilions of which, connected by a gallery, contain good furniture and decoration.

14.5km. S. lies **Valençay**, with its sumptuous Renaissance *Château, begun in 1540 for Jacques d'Estampes and completed in the 17C. In 1805 it was acquired by Talleyrand, who died here in 1838. From 1080–14 it was occupied by Fernando VII of Spain during his captivity in France. It consists of an elegant and lofty pavilion with corner turrets, and two lower wings each terminating in a cylindrical tower surmounted by a lanterned dome; from the larger of which, the *Veille Tour*, a later wing runs back, ending at the *Tour Neuve*. A vaulted passage through the central pavilion gives access to the arcaded *Cour d'Honneur*. Some souvenirs of Talleyrand, of slight interest, and the bedroom of Fernando, may be seen.—Steps descend to the (private) *Jardin de la Duchesse* and the extensive park, which includes part of the *Forêt de Gâtine*; the public gardens are remarkably unkempt.—The main route may be regained via *Chabris*, 13km N.E., its church incorporating ancient, perhaps Carolingian, sculptures in its N. transept.

From Selles, one follows the valley of the Sauldre N.E., at 8.5km bearing l. from the N76, which continues E. to (8.5km) *Villefranche-sur-Cher*; see below.—9.5km. **Romorantin-Lanthenay** (18,200 inhab.), an ancient cloth-working town (Rivus Morantini), preserving several characteristic old houses. On the island site stands *St-Étienne*, mainly 13C, with a 12C central tower, and 15C aisles. The bridge to the N. commands a view of the remains of the 15C *Castle*, in which François II signed the edict to prevent the establishment of the Inquisition in France. On the N. bank are the Renaissance *Hôtel de Rère* and *Hôtel St-Pol* (c. 1500), and two 16C timber-framed houses. To the E. is the *Hôtel de Ville*, containing the *Musée de la Sologne* (cf. p 307-8).

9km W. is *Lassay-sur-Croisne*, with a good 15-16C church, and the neighbouring moated *Château du Moulin* (1480– 1502), built by Jacques de Persigny for Philippe du Moulin, Charles VIII's captain at the battle of Fornovo (1495).—The early Renaissance château of *Trécy* is 5km E. of Romorantin.

The N76 is regained 8km S. at *Villefranche-sur-Cher*, its 12C church preserving good capitals.—8.5km. *Mennetou-sur-Cher*, a curious old town with steep winding streets and old houses, still partly encircled by 13C ramparts with gateways and towers. The church has an interesting 13C choir with Angevin vaults.—The 12-13C church at *St-Loup*, 2.5km W. on the far bank, contains murals.

Traversing (16.5km) **Vierzon**, (see Rte 50), we continue E. to (16km) **Mehun-sur-Yèvre** (7200 inhab.), ancient *Magdunum*, with the ruins of a castle rebuilt by Jean, Duc de Berry before 1390 (in whose 'Tres Riches Heures' it is illustrated), and bequeathed by him to Charles VII, who was crowned here in 1422 and died here in 1461. He was visited by Joan of Arc in 1429 and 1430, who is said to have lodged in what is now the *Hôtel Charles VII*; the *Tour Charles-VII* (behind the 11-12C church, with a restored 15C chapel) is a relic of the fortress; the *Porte de l'Horloge*, flanked by towers, is a survival of the 14C ramparts.

17km. **Bourges**; see Rte 48.

54 Tours

TOURS (136,500 Tourangeaux; 33,500 in 1851; 80,000 in 1946), the ancient capital of *Touraine* and the préfecture of the *Indre-et-Loire*, was situated on a narrow tongue of land between the Loire and Cher, but within recent decades its growth has been such that its suburbs have spread along the N. and S. banks respectively of both rivers. It is a lively place, famed for the purity of its French, the quality of its food, and the mildness of its climate, and for those who prefer a city to a small town or village as a base for the exploration of the châteaux of the Loire, it is a pleasant and convenient centre.

The Loire contributes less to the attraction of the town than might be expected, for in summer a great part of its channel is left high and dry. From the rebuilt *Pont Wilson* (replacing the *Pont de Pierre* of 1777), which partially collapsed in 1978, the Rue Nationale, leading S., divides the Cathedral quarter to the E., the original site of Tours, from the contiguous town of Châteauneuf, restored since the Second World War, and now the most picturesque part of the old centre. Modern factories on the outskirts are portents of a prosperous material future.

Gallic *Altionos*, on the N. bank of the Loire, was moved to the opposite bank and renamed *Caesarodunum* by the Romans. Its present name first appears in the form *Urbs Turonum* in the 4C, by which time Christianity had been introduced by St Gatien or Gratian, and spread by its third bishop, St Martin. It was taken by the Visigoths in 473 and recaptured by Clovis in 507. To the W. of its walls arose the independent borough of *Châteauneuf*, formerly called *Martinopolis*, being the site of that saint's tomb and basilica, which, twice pillaged by the Normans, was not protected by ramparts until 906, and only incorporated with Tours in 1354.

The first French chronicler, Gregory of Tours (d. 594), and Charlemagne's preceptor Alcuin (d. 804) made the town a centre of learning in the early Middle Ages. In the 11C it was seized by Fulk Nerra, and through his descendant Henry II Touraine became a fief of the English crown until 1242, when it was made over to the French. *Plessis-lès-Tours* was a favourite residence of Louis XI. The area became an important centre of silk production, but its prosperity was ruined by the Religious Wars, being repeatedly devastated, and it only flourished again after Henri IV came to the throne (1589). It had previously been bestowed as an appanage on Mary Stuart and her short-lived husband, François II.

The Livres Tournoises, a currency in general circulation in France for some centuries until the Revolution, ceased being minted here only in 1772. In 1870 the National Defence Government sat here for three months, after which the place was bombarded by the Germans and later occupied by them. In 1917–18 it was the chief supply base for the American army. It was seriously damaged in June 1940, and bombed on numerous occasions during the next four years, while its bridges were destroyed by the Germans in retreat.

It was the birthplace of Bérenger (998–1088), the heresiarch; Marshal Boucicault (1366–1421), taken prisoner at Agincourt; the artists Jean Fouquet (c. 1415–81), Jean Bourdichon (1457–c. 1521), and François Clouet (1510–72), and the engraver Abraham Bosse (1602–76); René Rapin (1621–87), the poet and historian; Louise, Duchesse de la Vallière (1644–1710), mistress of Louis XIV; the poet Philippe Néricault-Destouches (1680–1754); Honoré de Balzac (1799–1850); Georges Courteline (1858–1929), the satirist; and the sculptor François Sicard (1862–1934). Michel Colombe, the sculptor, died here in 1512, and Giov. Fr. Rustici, the Florentine artist, in 1554; while Anatole France died at his villa in the N.W. suburb of St-Cyr in 1924.

The S.I., at the Pl. du Mar.-Leclerc, by the railway station, can give full information on times of adm. to châteaux in the area, etc. (see p 000, and preliminary paragraphs of Rte 52A).

The hub of the town is the *Pl. Jean-Jaurès*, at the intersection of the Rue Nationale, continued S. by the Rue de Grammont, and the Blvds Béranger (W.) and Huerteloup (E.), the latter laid out on the site of earlier ramparts. At its N.E. corner is the *Hôtel de Ville* (1905), with its campanile and allegorical statuary, behind which is its modern extension; to the N.W., the classical *Palais de Justice* of 1845, and adjacent, the *Post Office*. The Rue Nationale itself, laid out on a uniform design in 1786, has been largely rebuilt after its devastation in 1940, in which Balzac's birthplace (No. 39) was destroyed.

The Rue de la Préfecture leads r. off this to the *Préfecture*, which occupies the buildings of a former Visitandine convent, with its 18C gates, passing which we reach the small *Pl. François-Sicard*, on the E. side of which is the old *Archbishop's Palace* (17-18C), with parts of an earlier structure built on to the Gallo-Roman town wall. The material for the portal, with its Doric columns, belonged to a 17C triumphal arch. It now accommodates the **Musée des Beaux-Arts**. The garden, with a magnificent cedar of Lebanon near the entrance, is open all day. The extensive collections, dispersed throughout a series of 35 rooms on three floors, many of them also displaying furniture and decorations, some from Chanteloup (see p 320), contains comparatively few works of great merit, but among the more notable are the following:

GROUND FLOOR: attrib. to *Niccolo di Tommaso*, Martyrdom of St Agatha;

anon. Head of a monk (previously attrib. to Fouquet); *Quentin Metsys*, Virgin and Child; *anon. English* Portrait of William Cecil, Lord Burghley; two Nottingham alabasters; *Mantegna*, *Resurrection, and *Jesus in the Garden, two paintings which made up with the 'Christ between two thieves' (in the Louvre) the predella of the altarpiece at San Zeno in Verona (1460); *Moroni*, Male portrait; also a collection of Greek ceramics.

FIRST FLOOR: a series of engravings by *Abraham Bosse*; note the fine 17C chimney-piece with carytids (R7); R9, the *Salle des États*, was the meeting-place of the States General on three occasions in the 15-16Cs; *Rembrandt*, The flight into Egypt (1627); *Tocqué*, Portrait of the Duc de Richelieu; *Largillière*, two Self-portraits; representative works by *Lancret*; *Boucher*, Silvia fleeing from the wolf; *Perroneau*, Self-portrait; *Antoine Vestier*, Portrait of a veteran; *L.-M. van Loo*, Portrait of Mlle Sallé; *J.-P. Houel*, Views of the Loire; and among the sculpture, a bust of J.-F. de Vallières by *Lemoyne*.

SECOND FLOOR; *C.-A. Demachy* (1723–1807), and *Antoine Rougeot* (1740–97), Views of Tours; Portraits by *Alexandre Roslin*; *Louis Boulanger*, Portrait of Balzac in his dressing-gown; and among sculptures, *Bourdelle*, Bust of Anatole France.

Immediately N. of the museum stands the **Cathedral**, of comparatively modest dimensions (96m long and 29m high), the construction of which lasted from 1220 to 1547. The choir is 13C, and the transepts c. 1400. The nave, narrower than the choir, was begun in the early 14C.

The *W. Front, commenced 1426, with its three Flamboyant portals and great central window, is flanked by two slightly dissimilar towers crowned by Renaissance cupolas. All the statues except a few high up on the towers were destroyed at the Revolution, and the building only just survived total demolition. A number of replicas were inserted in their place in 1850.

The *Interior* contains some magnificent *Stained-glass*, particularly in the choir and N. transept. In the first choir-chapel on the r. is the *Tomb of the two infant sons of Charles VIII and Anne of Brittany, a Renaissance work of 1506 previously in St-Martin. The Royal Staircase, supported by a curious skeleton vault, is in the N. tower.

Adjacent is the *Cloître de la Psallette*, ◊ preserving three walks, containing ecclesiastical antiquities and 13-14C murals.

In the *Pl. Grégoire-de-Tours*, behind the cathedral, is the 12C gable of the old archbishop's chapel, with a 16C open-air pulpit. Adjoining is a 16C house showing the arms of the Chapter. The whole quarter is interesting, and remains of the *Gallo-Roman Wall* (4C) may be seen at No. 11 Rue Blanqui, or (on application) at 4 Rue des Ursulins.

The Rue Lavoisier leads from the cathedral to the bank of the Loire, passing (r.) the *Tour de Guise* (12th and 15C), all that remains of Henry II's castle, taking its name from the son of 'Le Balafre', who was imprisoned here after his father's assassination at Blois.—The Rue Colbert leads W., on the r. of which, in the Rue des Jacobins is their ruined church of 1260; in the parallel *Pl. Foire-le-Roi* are several old houses, including (No. 8) the *Hôtel Babou de la Bourdaisière*, the mansion of Philibert Babou (d. 1529), finance minister to François I and Henri II.

At the junction of the Rue Colbert with the Rue Nationale, a quarter devastated in 1940, is *St Julien*, the church of an abbey founded in the 5C, but dating from 1255–59 with the exception of the W. towers and parts of the N. transepts, which are Romanesque, and two 16C E. chapels. A century and a half ago it was temporarily used as a coach-house for diligences.—On its N. side is a 12C *Chapter-house*, where the Parlement de Paris met in 1589. The vault is supported by four central columns, and above is the 16C dorter. Here is installed the interesting *Musée du Compagnonnage*

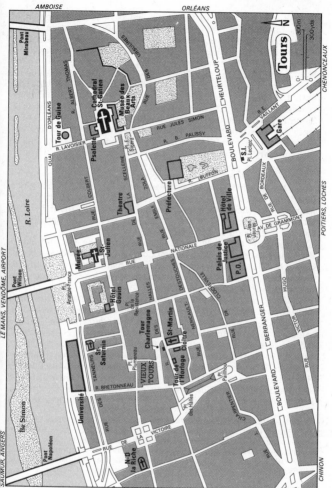

(Journeymen artisans; cf. *Troyes*), while on the opposite side of the
cloister garth (with its 16C press) a *Wine Museum* has been set up in
the vaulted *Cellarium* (12C).

To the S. of the Rue Colbert, in the Rue Jules-Favre, are two surviving facades of interest: the Renaissance *Hôtel de Baume de
Semblançay*, and early 18C *Palais du Commerce*.

On the W. side of the Rue Nationale, the Rue du Commerce
traverses an area largely rebuilt, in which survives (r.) the early-
Renaissance facade of the *Hôtel Gouin* (1440), now housing the re-
formed *Musée Archéologique*, with interesting collections of the
Gallo-Roman and medieval period, including on the first floor,
Rousseau's experimental laboratory from Chenonceau, etc.—Fur-

ther W., in the centre of the oldest and most picturesque part of
Tours, tastefully restored since 1940, is the ***Pl. Plumereau**, retaining several 15C houses. The whole districct deserves exploitation,
either by day or night, when its medieval impact is stronger. Immediately to the N., an ancient cemetery has been excavated. To the
N.E. of the Place, the Rue Paul-Louis-Courier leads off the Rue du
Commerce, in which Nos 10 (**Hôtel Binet*) and 17 (*Hôtel Juste*) are
both 15C: No. 15 (**Hôtel Robin-Quantin*), with two late 16C courtyards, leads through to the parallel Rue Littré, in which (r.) stands *St-
Saturnin* (1473) and the *Pl. des Carmes*. Between this point and the
river are the modern buildings of the University's *Faculté des
Lettres.*—An alley leads N.E. to the ***Rue Briçonnet**, with the *Hôtel de
Pierre du Puy* (No. 16; late 15C), and Nos 29 and 31 (late 13C) of interest.

We shortly regain the Pl. Plumereau, from the S.W. corner of
which the Rue du Grand-Marché leads to the Rue Bretonneau, with a
late 15C court at No. 22, extended to the S. by the *Pl. du Grand-
Marché*, with the **Fontaine de Beaune* (1511), attrib. to Michel Colombe.—Some distance to the W. is *N.-D.-La-Riche*, originally 'La
Pauvre', with good 15-16C glass.

To the S.W. of the Pl. du Grand-Marché is the Rue des Trois-
Escritoires, where No. 7, the *Hôtel Cottereau*, has a 16C courtyard.
Hence the Rue de Châteauneuf (also reached directly from the Pl.
Plumereau) leads E.; No. 11 is the mansion of Jean Briçonnet, the
first mayor of Tours (1462).

On the N. side of the neighbouring *Pl. de Chateauneuf* is the *Hôtel
de la Croix-Blanche* (14-15C) incorporating the former church of *St-
Denis* (15C). To the S. rises the so-called *Tour Charlemagne* (12-14C;
somewhat over-restored), which in fact buttressed the N. transept of
the old *Basilica of St-Martin*; the *Tour de l'Horloge* (or du Trésor;
11-13C)—a short distance S.W., on the S. side of the Rue des Halles—
being the S. tower of its W. front. Between the two runs the Rue des
Halles, following almost exactly the axis of the nave. One walk of the
Renaissance cloister (1508–19) now incorporated in the *Couvent de
Petit-St-Martin*, may also be seen (apply at No. 3 Rue Descartes).

These fragments are all that remain of the magnificent church erected in 1175
(the third on this site) over the tomb of St Martin, and destroyed in 1802. The
crypt containing the tomb, rediscovered during excavation in 1860, beneath
which are two ancient chapels, lies below the choir of the present *Basilica*
(1887–1924), built in a repellant and ill-conceived 'early-Christian' style by
Laloux, a local architecture, with monolithic nave columns of Vosges granite.

Turning E. down the Rue des Halles one may regain the Rue Nationale at its central point.

Environs

Among places of interest in the intermediate neighbourhood are the château of
Le Plessis-lès-Tours, best approached via the Rue d'Entraigues, leading W. just S.
of the Pl. Jean-Jaurés to the *Jardin Botanique*, and its prolongation, which also
passes (r.) *La Rabaterie*, a 15C house described as that of Olivier Le Daim, both
barber and minister of Louis XI.

The *Château*, originally a mansion of the Maillé family of Luynes, preserves a
brick and stone wing apparently rebuilt by Louis XI after 1463, whose daughter
Jeanne de France was born here in 1464. In 1589 Henri III and the future Henri
IV had a momentous interview at Le Plessis which united Royalists and
Reformers against the League and the Guise faction. After serving as a farm-

house and latterly as a serological institute, it has been restored as a *Museum of the Touraine Silk industry*. The chimneypiece in the *Salle des États* and the panelled room in which Louis XI is believed to have died in 1483, are of interest.

To the S., beyond the railway and nearer the Cher, are slight remains of a *Convent of Minimes*, the oldest in France, founded in 1482 by Francesco da Paola, who has been summoned here by Louis to console his dying hours. His services were retained by Charles VIII and Louis XII, and he died in the convent in 1508, being canonised in 1519.

By following the road N. alongside the railway embankment for 1.5km, one reaches the ruins of the *Prieuré de St-Cosmé* (approached directly from Tours by the quays on the S. bank of the Loire; 3km), founded in the 11C. It preserves part of its church, the 12C refectory with its lector's pulpit, and other dependencies restored after war damage. Ronsard was prior here from 1565 and died here in 1585. His tomb was rediscovered in 1933, and a simple slab marks his reinterment in the choir. A small museum may be visited.

For roads from Tours to **Bourges**, and to **Châteauroux**, see Rtes 53, and 55; to **Poitiers**, and to **Saumur**, Rtes 56, and 57; and to *Orléans*, and *Chartres* or *Le Mans*, Rtes 52, and 28, in reverse.

55 Tours to Châteauroux via Loches

111km (69 miles). N143. 41km **Loches**—22km *Châtillon-sur-Indre*—48km. **Châteauroux**.

Maps: IGN 26, 34, or 106. M 238.

6km S. of **Tours** (Rte 54), the N143 turns S.E. across the A10 to traverse the *Forêt de Larçay* on its chalk plateau before descending to (14.5km) *Cormery*, a substantial village on the Indre, which grew up round a Benedictine abbey founded in the 8C, of which part of the Romanesque *Tour St-Paul* and one 15C chapel survives of the church, also part of the 14-15C cloister, the 14C refectory (in private hands), the prior's lodge, and the 15C *Tour St-Jean*. The parish church has an aisleless nave roofed with timber, its choir and transepts with barrel vaults.—1km upstream on the r. bank, at *Truyes*, is a handsome Romanesque belfry; 5km N.E., the *Tour des Brandons*, a 12C cylindrical keep.

The main road climbs out of the valley, but the more attractive riverside road, passing several restored 15C châteaux and manors, may be followed through *Courçay*, with an 11C church, and *Azay-sur-Indre*, meeting again some 15km S.E., 6km from Loches.

LOCHES (7000 Lochois) is an interesting and picturesque old town surrounding a steep hill circled by defensive walls, both ends of the enceinte being dominated by the remains of its fortress, a good view of which may be obtained from the public gardens at *Beaulieu*, on the r. bank of the Indre, here forming several arms. Its history is that of its castle; its most famous native was Alfred de Vigny (1797–1863).

From the *Pl. de la Marne*, at the N. end of the hill, an alley leads S. to the Rue St-Antoine, in which No. 23 is the Renaissance *Hôtel Nau*; the *Tour St-Antoine* (16C) is surmounted by a cupola restored in the 19C. Parallel to the S. is the Grande Rue, leading E. to the *Porte des Cordeliers, with turrets and carved 15C windows; No. 5 is a Renaissance house.—To the W. is the *Hôtel de Ville* (1543; restored), and the *Porte Picoys*, a 15C gate with Renaissance details.

The Grande Rue is continued by the Rue du Château, in which Nos 10, 12, and 14 are remarkable.

The ****Castle**, one of the most impressive medieval strongholds of France, occupies the summit of a fortified escarpment, within which a distinct quarter of the town has grown.

The original 6C castle was acquired in 879 by Foulques le Roux, Count of Anjou, whose descendant, Geoffrey IV, was Henry II's father. John ceded it to Philippe Auguste, but Richard I, on his return from captivity, took it by storm (1194). In 1205, after a year's siege, the French king recaptured it, and Loches became a royal residence. Charles VII used to retire here with Agnès Sorel.

In 1536 James V of Scotland and Madeleine of France were married here. After her escape from Blois in Feb. 1619 Marie de Médicis made for Loches, where the Duc d'Éperon, the governor, equipped her with the means of reaching Angoulême. It had a sinister reputation as a state prison, particularly during the reign of Louis XI.

From the *Porte Royale*, flanked by 12C towers, and an adjacent museum of local antiquities, the Rue Lansyer ascends to ***St-Ours**, consecrated in 965 but dating mainly from the 12C. Two of its four 'steeples' are formed by spires over the central and W. towers, while the other two are hollow octagonal pyramids over the two square bays of the nave.

These were constructed under the direction of Thomas Pactius (d. 1168), a prior, who called them '*dubes*'. The vaulted porch was added in the mid 12C, beneath which stands a circular Gallo-Roman altar used as a stoup. The archivolts of the

The tomb of Agnès Sorel in the Logis du Roi.

main portal, a fine early 12C work, are sculptured with fabulous monsters and other figures. The N. aisle was altered in the 14-15C; the S. is a mid 19C reconstruction.

Interior. The base of the W. tower, said to date from the late 10C, forms a kind of vestibule divided by low arches from the nave, whose two bays are separated by a plain pointed arch. At the crossing, the responds which support the arches abutting the nave are elaborately corbelled in two stages; the crypt contains a curious contemporary mural painting.

A short distance to the N. is the entrance to the ***Logis du Roi**, its terraces commanding views over the steeply-pitched roofs of the old houses clustered below. The early 15C l. wing, with its turrets and battlements, contrasts with the more richly decorated Louis-XII wing. A spiral staircase ascends to the diminutive *Oratoire d'Anne de Bretagne*, with its ermine decoration, and to the chamber in which Charles de Lorraine was imprisoned in 1589; among the paintings here are an anon. triptych of the School of Jean Fouquet (1485), and a portrait of Agnès Sorel, the shapely mistress of Charles VII, born in the neighbourhood, and who died at Jumièges in 1450.

Her **Tomb*, violated during the Revolution, was transferred here from St-Ours, after being pieced together in 1809. She is represented by a statue of white limestone reclining on a black marble base, her head guarded by kneeling angels, her feet resting on two lambs.—In the *Salle de Jeanne d'Arc* Charles VII interviewed Joan in June 1429; Fouquet's portrait of the king is a copy of the original in the Louvre.

Repassing St-Ours, we approach the ***Donjon**, standing within its own ward at the S. end of the escarpment, and protecting its weakest side, near the adjacent plateau. Inside the enclosure is the *Keep* proper, a fine example of 11-12C military architecture, consisting of two unequal rectangular towers, the larger of which, supported by semicircular buttresses, is 42m high. Forming the W. defences of the keep is the *Tour Ronde* (or *Neuve*), said to have been constructed by Louis XI for the reception of his prisoners, where the more distinguished were provided with spacious rooms and handsome fireplaces; others contain instruments of torture.

In a domed chamber in this tower was suspended one of the infamous cages, in which Card. Le Balue is believed to have been mewed up by Louis for 11 years. They were 2.5m wide and as high as a man 'et un pied de plus', according to Comines, who was confined in one at Plessis by Charles VIII.

The real dungeons were in a 15C building called *Le Martelet*, whose upper storeys have disappeared. Here is shown the cell occupied for eight years by Ludovico Sforza, who covered the walls with drawings and inscriptions, but in consequence of his deprivation died on being set free in 1508. Below is the dungeon where the bishops of Autun and Le Puy were incarcerated by François I in 1523–24, together with their fellow-conspirator St-Vallier, father of Diane de Poitiers.

The exit leads down to the 13C **S. Front* of the enceinte, flanked by three huge towers, which instead of being semicircular in plan, come to a point in front, perhaps the earliest example of a modification which in the 15C led to the system of fortifying with bastions instead of flanking towers. The walk round the outside of the walls, which takes c. 30 minutes, is recommended.

Another view of the fortress as a whole may be obtained from the *Côteau de Vignemont*, to the S.E., on which stands the desecrated chapel of an old hospital.—About 2km S. is the square *Tour de Mauvière* (14C).

On the E. bank of the Indre is **Beaulieu**, with a Romanesque *Abbey*

Church built by Fulk Nerra in 1008–12, who was buried here in 1040. It was later remodelled, and partly destroyed by the English in 1412; the N. wall of the nave and 12C *Belfry* crowned by an octagonal stone spire survive, together with relics of its apse. The whole was rebuilt in the early 15C, and since restored. Note the allegorical reliefs carved on the gable of the N. transept.—To the N. is the 12C tower of the church of *St-Laurent*. The 15C *Prior's House* has a curious exterior pulpit, while the *Mairie* opposite occupies an 18C dependency.

LOCHES TO CHÂTELLERAULT (53km). The D31 leads S.W., at 10km passing N. of *Esves-le-Moutier*, its 9th and 11C church and two towers being relics of a fortified priory, to (8km) *Ligueil*, with a 12-15C church and several 14-15C houses.—6km N.W. is the impressive 15C *Château de Grillemont*, flanked by three huge cylindrical towers; and 10km W., the 15C *Château de Bagneaux*.

A DETOUR may be made from Ligueil to *Ferrière-Larçon*, 7.5km S.E., with an imposing 11-13C *Church*, thence turning W. down the Brignon valley past *Paulmy* (burial-place of the Argenson family), beyond which are the ruins of the *Château du Châtellier*, a huge 12-13C stronghold, once the property of François La Noue, the Calvinist. The moated enceinte, with drawbridge and portcullis, enclosed a 16C wing (now a farm) and 14C cylindrical keep.—The main road may be regained at *Descartes*, 13km S.W. of *Ligueil* (see Rte 56), 9.5km beyond which we meet the N10 14km N. of *Châtellerault*.

LOCHES TO CHÂTEAUROUX VIA MONTRÉSOR AND LEVROUX (53km). The D760 leads 6.5km E. to the *Pyramide des Chartreuse*, and 3km beyond, in the *Forêt des Loches*, the *Chartreuse du Liget* (adm. on application), where the ruins of the 12C church and part of an 18C cloister may be seen. It was founded by Henry II in expiation of the death of Becket, as was the *Chapel*, 1km S., containing late 12C frescoes.—We shortly pass (l.) *La Corroirie*, another dependency, with a machicolated tower and a Romanesque chapel.—6.5km. **Montrésor**, a village on the Indrois, with a 17C market-hall, and *Castle* on a detached rocky spur, founded c. 1005. It was replaced by the late 15C château of the family of Imbert de Bastarnay (d. 1523) the lieutenant of Louis XI, whose restored *Tomb*, and that of his wife and son, is in the Renaissance *Church* (cons. 1532).—We pass (l. at 2km) the ruins of a 15-18C abbey before traversing *Villeloin*, to approach *Nouans-les-Fontaines*, where the 13C church, with notable sexpartite vaulting, contains a fine Deposition by Jean Fouquet or his School.—The D760 continues hence to *Valençay* (see Rte 53), 23km E., via *Luçay-le-Mâle*, with a 15C castle.

The D81 turns S.E. from Nouans to (7km) *Écueillé*, and is continued by the D8, which after 14km passes 3km N. of the abbey of *N.-D.-du-Landais* (?) and 6km beyond, N. of an '*allée couverte*' and stone circle, to enter (6km) **Levroux**. Roman *Gabbetum*, it was invitingly renamed *Leprosum* in the Middle Ages by a mayor who had been miraculously cured of that disease. The beautiful 13C *Church of St-Sylvain* is built on the ruins of a Gallo-Roman palace. Of its three incomplete towers, that S. of the choir is Romanesque. The sexpartite vaulting of the nave in conjunction with the barrel-vaulting of the aisles is remarkable, while the ribs of the apse-vault are supported by statues of saints. Note also the 15C organ-case and the 16C stalls.—Adjacent is a curious wooden shelter for pilgrims to Santiago.—*Bourges-le-Château* lies 9km N.E.; see Rte 50.—At 8km we pass 3km E. of *Villegongis*, with a moated 16C château ascribed to Pierre Nepveu of Chambord.—12km. **Châteauroux**.

Driving S.E. from Loches on the N143, *Perrusson*, with a Romanesque church, is traversed, and 11.5km beyond we pass (r.) *Bridoré*, its 15C church with an interesting crypt, and dominated by a ruined 15C castle retaining some unusual features.—10.5km. *Châtillon-sur-Indre*, a quaint little town with an 11C church and *Castle*, whose remains consist of a cylindrical keep and a gabled and turreted 15C building supported by thick walls on the valley side.

CHÂTILLON TO LE BLANC (43km). The D975 leads S.W. to (17km) **Azay-le-Ferron**, where a charming Renaissance *Château in a large park preserves a tower of 1496 abutting a Louis-XIII wing, adjoined by a pavilion in the style of François-I, on the far side of which is a smaller classical pavilion. Parts of the building date from the 13C. It contains some well-furnished rooms, particularly of the Empire and Restoration period.—For *Preuilly*, 12km W., see Rte 56.—Although the main road continues directly to *Le Blanc* (26km S.; see Rte 51), it may also be approached by bearing r. to *Tournon-St-Martin*, on the Creuse, which we skirt via *Fontgombault* (see Rte 51), or alternatively by traversing the **Brenne**, a clayey plain with innumberable little pools and meres recalling the Sologne, which lies to the S.E.

An interesting road is that leading due E. to (6km) *Paulnay*, with a Romanesque church, and *Mézières-en-Brenne*, 6km further S.E., with a 14C *Church containing a beautifully sculptured porch and an elaborate Renaissance chapel of 1522–44. The main road may be regained some 16km S.W., or by continuing S. on minor roads through the meres through *Rosnay*, 3.5km N.W. of which is the strikingly placed 13C castle of *Le Bouchet*.

8km. *Clion*, just N. of which is the 15C *Château de l'Île-Savary.*—7km. A l.-hand turning leads 3km to *Palluau-sur-Indre*, commanded by its imposing feudal *Castle* (restored), with a sculptured 16C gateway, and tower named in honour of Philippe Auguste's recapture of the place from the English in 1188.—More interesting than its church is that at *St-Genou*, 3km S.E., one of the purest examples of Romanesque in Berry, originally forming part of an abbey founded in the 9C over the tomb of the first bishop of Cahors, who died here. The original monastery was nearer the N143, where a *'Lanterne des Morts'* may be seen.

9km. **Buzançais**, a small market-town astride the Indre, has a market-hall occupying the desecrated church of St-Honoré, but is otherwise of slight interest.

At *Argy*, 6km N., is a 15-16C château; in the cemetery at *Pellevoisin*, 5km beyond, lies Georges Bernanos (1888–1948).—At *St-Lactencin*, 6km E., the church has a Romanesque tower similar to that at *Déols* (near Châteauroux).

The N143 traverses (11km) *Villedieu-sur-Indre*, with a mutilated 12C church, to enter **Châteauroux** 13km beyond; see Rte 51.

56   Tours to Poitiers

104km (64 miles). N10. 35km *Ste-Maure-de-Touraine*—35km **Châtellerault**—34km **Poitiers**.

Maps: IGN 26, (25), 34, or 106. M 232.

The A10 motorway runs parallel, and to the W. of the N10, providing a rapid route direct to Poitiers.

For **Tours**, see Rte 54.

12.5km. *Montbazon*, at a crossing of the Indre, grew up around the 10C donjon built by Fulk Nerra; the remains of the present castle consists of a massive square 11-12C *Keep (surmounted by an incongruous image added in 1866), and the ruins of double ramparts with corner towers.

2km N.E. is the *Château de Couzières*, home of the dukes of Montbazon since the 16C, and rebuilt in the early 17C, where in Sept. 1619 took place the interview between Marie de Médicis and her son Louis XIII, which resulted in the ratification of the Treaty of Angoulême and effected a momentary reconciliation between them.

MONTBAZON TO AZAY-LE-RIDEAU (23km). The D17 follows the verdant l. bank of the Indre to the W., passing below the motorway and railway; not far N. of the latter is the *Château de Candé*, where in 1937 took place the morganatic marriage of Edward, Duke of Windsor (1894–1972). The road passes several minor châteaux and manors before reaching (15km) *Saché*, an attractive village with the château owned by Balzac from 1829–48, and described by him in 'Le Lys dans la Vallée'; it contains souvenirs and his room as furnished in his time. The sculptor of 'mobiles', Alexander Calder, was a later resident of the village.—7.5km. *La Chapelle-St-Blaise*; on the far bank of the river here, among the trees, lies **Azay-le-Rideau**, and its château; see Rte 57A.—**Chinon** is 20km further S.W.

15.5km. *Ste-Catherine-de-Fierbois* (l.) has a beautiful Flamboyant *Church containing a carved wooden altar and 15C Entombment.

It stands on the site of a chapel founded in 732 by Charles Martel, who is said to have deposited his sword here after his victory over the Moors at Poitiers. Almost 700 years later, its position behind the altar having been revealed to her in a vision, Joan of Arc came in 1429 to collect the weapon, marked with five crosses, which she proceeded to wield to effect!

Opposite the church is the *Maison du Dauphin* (1515), and an old *Hospice* founded c. 1400 by Marshal Boucicaut; to the S.E., besides the remains of his castle, is the *Château de Comacre* (1845).

6.5km. **Ste-Maure-de-Touraine**, on a plateau honeycombed with marl-pits, is noted for its goats' milk cheese; it owes its name to the discovery here of the tombs of SS Maura and Britta in the 5C; it had previously been known as *Arciacum*. The 12C trouvère Benoît de Ste-Maure was a native. The over-restored 12C church covers a Romanesque crypt. Of the *Castle*, within the rampart walls of which stands the church, the most conspicuous remains are a 15C building adjoining a 14C tower. There is also a 17C *Market-hall*.

STE-MAURE TO CHINON (34km). Of the two alternative roads, the most direct, the D760, is first described. It leads due W. to (15km) *L'Île-Bouchard*, birthplace of André Duchesne (1584–1680), the 'Father of French History', with 12C *St-Gilles*; on the l. bank is *St-Maurice* (14-15C), with a good steeple; the ruined priory of *St-Léonard*, further S., preserves Romanesque details.—3.5km. **Tavant** has a church of c. 1124, with vaulted nave, cupola, and apsidal choir, containing remarkable mural paintings both in the choir (13C) and in the *Crypt* (early 12C). Continuing W., we pass the churches of *Sazilly*, and (r.) *Rivière*, both of interest (the latter with an 11C choir above its crypt, and restored 11-15C paintings in its nave), to reach the turning for (13.5km) **Chinon**; see Rte 57A.

The minor road leads N.W. from Ste-Maure, descending to Manse valley past the 15C *Château de Brou* to (8km) *St-Épain*, with a notable 12C church with 16C additions, and a 15C gateway.—The D21 continues W. through (5km) *Crissay-sur-Manse*, a charming village with a Flamboyant church and remains of a 15C castle.—Passing (r.) *Avon-les-Roches*, with a 12C church, the road runs parallel to the Vienne via *Panzoult* (where in Rabelais's 'Gargantua and Pantagruel', Panurge went to consult the Sibyl).—10km. *Cravant-les-Côteaux*, just N. of which is a partly 9C church at *Le Vieux-Bourg*.—**Chinon** is 9km further W.

The road S. from Ste-Maure shortly passes (r.) several megalithic monuments, as at 7km near *Maillé*, a village rebuilt since its destruction by the Germans in 1944, where 124 of its inhabitants were killed, N.W. of which are the ruins of the *Château d'Argenson*, cradle of that family, and 3km beyond this turning, *La Celle-St-Avant*.

LA CELLE-ST-AVANT TO ST-SAVIN (63km), OR VIA FONTGOMBAULT TO LE BLANC. The D750 forks l. to (9km) *Descartes*, a village taking its name from René Descartes (1596–1650), who was born here and baptised in the interesting 12C church of *St-Georges*. It was also the birthplace of the novelist René Boylesve (1867–1926).—The main road continues down the charming valley of the Creuse, at 10.5km passing near (r.) *La Guerche-sur-Creuse*, with a grimly turreted 15C castle built by Charles VII for his mistress Antoinette de Maignelais, Vicomtesse de Villequier, to reach the crossroads at *La Revaudière*, 12km beyond; see below.

An alternative road is the D24 turning l. 3km S. of Descartes to (8.5km) **Le Grand-Pressigny**, at the foot of a hill crowned by its castle, with a well-preserved 12C keep, a partly ruined enceinte with turrets (14-15C), and a wing of c. 1550 flanked by a slender octagonal tower, and containing a *Prehistoric Museum*, with an important collection of neolithic flint weapons, which were manufactured here in quantity. The road continues S.E. to (13.5km) *Preuilly-sur-Claise*, with a *Mairie* and other mansions of the 16-17Cs. The ruined castle and collégiale (12th and 15C) above the village are adjoined by a modern château, while *St-Pierre*, originally part of an abbey founded in 1001, is an imposing building too drastically restored in the 19C; the rich arcading above the windows should be noted.—*Azay-le-Ferron*, (see Rte 55), lies 12km E.—From Preuilly we turn S.W. past (r.) the 17-18C moated *Château de Boussay*, preserving its 15C towers and a Renaissance tomb-chapel in its church, to (10km) *La Revaudière*.

3.5km S.E. of this village, at *Yzeures-sur-Creuse*, the church stands on the site of a Gallo-Roman temple; sculptured fragments are preserved in an adjoining garden.—2.5km. S.W. is **La Roche-Posay**, a picturesque little town on a rugged slope above the l. bank of the Creuse, just below its confluence with the Gartempe, and noted for its mineral springs, discovered in 1573. It preserves remains of its 12th and 14C ramparts, and a machicolated gateway gives access to the main street. The 14-16C church, with a Romanesque belfry, contains the tomb of a bishop of Poitiers (d.1650), while the square 12C *Tower* in the town centre commands a fine view.—The D5 continues S.E. to (12km) **Angles-sur-l'Anglin**, a delightfully sited old village with a 12C church tower, and a ruined *Castle* (12-15C) in the valley below. Angles was the birthplace of Card. Le Balue (1421–91; cf. *Loches*). Magdalenian rock paintings have been discovered in a cavern to the S.—From Angles one may continue S.E. via *Fontgombault* to (17.5km) *Le Blanc*, or 17km S. to *St-Savin*, for which see Rte 51.

From La Celle, the N10 continues S. through (6km) *Les Ormes*, with another château of the Argenson family, still containing the canvases by Lenfant of battles of the War of the Austrian Succession viewed by Arthur Young when visiting the place in 1787.—10km S.W., at *Marmande*, are the imposing ruins of a 14C castle with a keep over 40m high.—11km. *Ingrandes-sur-Vienne*, with a 12C church, is traversed.

8km. **CHÂTELLERAULT** (36,900 Chatelleraudais), the ancient *Castellum Airaldi*, named after an early viscount of Poitou, and reputed for its manufacture of cutlery, which dates from the 14C; later the manufacture of small-arms contributed to its prosperity, and in 1829 an arsenal was established here.

In 1549 Henri II bestowed the duchy of Châtelherault on James Hamilton, 2nd Earl of Arran and Regent of Scotland, in order to induce him to promote the marriage between his ward, the infant Queen Mary, and the Dauphin François. By failure of male issue, the duchy was forfeited to the Crown, although later claimed and the title borne by the Duke of Hamilton, a descendant of the Regent in the female line. It was recreated in favour of the 11th Duke by Napoleon III, a relative of whom he had married, although the Duke of Abercorn's claim is better founded, being based on descent in the male line from the youngest son of the Regent Arran.

The composer Clément Janequin (c. 1480–c. 1558) was born here.

The wide tree-lined Blvd Blossac in the centre divides the older town from its modern suburbs, parallel to and W. of which is the Rue de

Bourbon, near the N. and S. ends of which respectively, stand *St-Jean-Baptiste* (15-16C), and *St-Jacques* (12-13C), both heavily restored in the 19C, when the latter was provided with a neo-Poitevin-Romanesque facade. At No. 126 Rue de Bourbon (N. end) is the town house of the Descartes family, where the philosopher spent his boyhood.

To the W. of the central point in this street is the *Castle* of the Harcourts (1423) housing a small local *Museum*. Further S. in the Rue de Sully, Nos 12 and 14 are of interest, the latter, known as the *Hôtel de Sully*, being a work of Charles Androuet Du Cerceau (1600). To the W., spanning the Vienne, is the *Pont Henri-IV*, begun in 1572 and completed by Du Cerceau in 1609, flanked by two sturdy towers on the W. bank.—Further S. on this far bank, the buildings of the old arms manufactory have been converted to accommodate a *Musée de l'Automobile et de la Technique*.

10km due W. is the huge *Château de Scorbé-Clairvaux* (late 15th-17C), to the N. of which is a hilltop tower of an earlier castle.

CHÂTELLERAULT TO CHAUVIGNY (30km). The D749 leads S. along the E. bank of the Vienne (although most of its villages are sited on the W. bank), shortly traversing *Ozon*, where a Romanesque Templar commandery contains frescoes.—16km. *Bonneuil-Matours*, with an 11-12C church and where Roman remains have been found. A road leads hence through the *Forêt de Moulière* to Poitiers.—8.5km. *La Voûte*, to the N.W. of which, on the far bank, stands the imposing *Château de Touffou*, with a 12C keep, Renaissance buildings, and two 15C towers with mural decorations. There are several old manors and minor châteaux in the neighbourhood, while at adjacent *Bonnes* are two Romanesque churches, one disused.—5.5km. *Chauvigny*; see Rte 51.

Immediately S. of Châtellerault we cross the Vienne and skirt the W. bank of the Clain, at 9km passing on the far bank the site of *Vieux-Poitiers*, with a Roman wall, apparently part of a theatre, and an inscribed menhir; *Moussais-la-Bataille*, a short distance further S., is supposed to be named after Charles Martel's victory over the Moors in 732 (see below).—5km. *La Tricherie*, with the near-by 12C keep of *Beaumont*.—3km. To the l. is the restored *Château de Dissay*, built largely by Pierre d'Amboise (1481–1505), and reconstructed in the 18C; the Gothic chapel preserves an oratory decorated with 16C murals.

5km. On the far bank of the Clain is the 15-17C *Château de Vayres*, with its remarkable pigeon-cote.—The main road continues past (l.) *Chasseneuil*, which disputes with Chasseneuil near Agen the succession of *Cassinogilum*, a residence of Charlemagne, where Louis le Débonnaire was born in 778.—The valley narrows between cave-riddled cliffs as *Poitiers*, also by-passed to the W., is approached.

POITIERS (82,900 Pictaviens, but also known as Poitevins—of Poitou), the ancient capital of *Poitou* and préfecture of the *Vienne*, is a rapidly growing city (52,000 inhab. in 1954), which has long outgrown its original naturally strong site on a hill overlooking a bend of the Clain, and its tributary, the Boivre. Modern industrial suburbs to the S. and E. are served by a ring road, beyond which, to the S.E., are new University buildings. The area near the station suffered from air raids during the Second World War, and certain parts of the city centre have more recently been the scene of town-planning forays. It does not entirely deserve Young's condemnation: 'one of the worst built towns I have seen in France; very large and irregular, but containing scarcely anything worthy of notice, except the cathedral. . .'. Its Romanesque churches, among a few other

buildings, are of interest, and the town, in general too often by-
passed by travellers hurrying south, deserves exploration; its student population adds to its animation, and its 'Chabichou' cheese is
excellent.

The capital of the Pictones or Pictavi, called by the Romans *Limonum*, had St
Hilary (a native of the place; d. 368) as its first bishop. It was later conquered by
the Visigoths, and became a residence of their kings, one of whom, Alaric II, was
defeated and killed by Clovis the Frank in 507 at *Voulon*, 3km S. (not, as
sometimes stated, at *Vouillé*, 17km N.W.). In 732 Charles Martel decisively
repulsed the Moorish incursion under Abderrahman 'al-Gāfiqī' in a battle
fought, it is believed, at *Moussais*; see above.

Poitou passed to the English Crown on the marriage of Henry II with Eleanor
of Aquitaine, who often lived at Poitiers, and granted a communal charter to the
town in 1199. Philippe Auguste regained Poitou, but after the Black Prince's victory in 1356, fought some 9km S.E., it was again made over to England by the
Treaty of Brétigny. In 1369–72 Du Guesclin reconquered the province and
restored it finally to France.

Charles VII transferred the Parlement de Paris to Poitiers, where it remained
from 1423 to 1436; in 1431 he founded the university, at which Francis Bacon
studied briefly. During the Religious Wars it sheltered many Protestants, including Calvin in 1534, and was subjected to the violence of both parties, in
1569 withstanding a seven-week siege conducted by the Huguenots under Coligny. At the Bourbon restoration, as a result of the discovery of the Thouars and
Saumur conspiracy, Gén. Berton and his principal confederates were executed
at Poitiers (17 Oct. 1822).

Few natives have become famous. Guillaume Bouchet (c. 1513–93), a local
bookseller, was the author of curious conversations entitled 'Serées', published
in 1584–98, and the rhetorical poet Jean Bouchet (1476–c. 1557) was a friend
of Rabelais. Here in 1579 was discovered—on the breast of Catherine Des
Roches—the famous flea (La puce de Mme Des Roches), subject of a celebrated
collection of verses composed by the literary coterie entertained at the home of
Catherine and her mother, Madeleine Des Roches.

Entering the town from the N., one is directed round the *Pl. Jean-de-
Berry*, in which—and immediately to the N.E.—are the slight remains
of the castle built in 1388 by Jean de Berry, and follow the main
boulevard S., halfway along which is the *Railway Station* (r.). A turning to the l., opposite, ascends steeply into the old town, and a sharp
r.-hand bend brings one to the *Préfecture*, from which the Rue Victor-
Hugo leads due E. to the central *Pl. du Maréchal-Leclerc*, after passing (r.) the old *Collège de la Grand' Maison* and the *Hôtel de Chièvres*
(Museum of decorative art and projected). On the E. side of the Place
is the 19C *Hôtel de Ville*, with the S.I., on the staircase of which is a
mural by Puvis de Chavannes.

The Rue Gambatta (now part of a pedestrian precinct) leads from
its N.W. corner past *St-Porchaire*, a poor specimen of 16C architecture, retaining a Romanesque W. doorway and late 11C *Tower. It
contains the epitaph of a Scottish writer and partisan of Queen Mary,
Adam Blackwood (1539–1613), who died at Poitiers. Adjacent is the
old *Hôtel de Ville*, with a chapel of 1460.

Further on (r.) is the *Palais de Justice*, which combines with the
more modern building the remains of the palace of the Dukes of
Aquitaine, which faces the adjacent Rue des Cordeliers. These consist of the *Tour Maubergon* (1395), with statues of heroes of romance
surmounting its buttresses, and the *Salle des Pas-Perdus* (apply to
the concierge), a magnificent early 13C hall (48m long and 16m
wide), partly rebuilt by Duc Jean de Berry (d. 1416), brother of
Charles V.

It is covered with a wooden vault, and the walls are arcaded, the arches on one

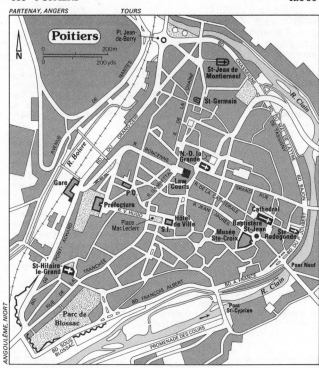

side being round, and on the other, pointed. In the S. gable-wall are three
sculptured fireplaces, above which is a gallery and handsome mullioned windows. Charles VII was proclaimed king here in 1442, and here, seven years later,
Joan of Arc was interrogated on the genuineness of her mission. A spiral stair
gives access to the roof (view). The Tour Maubergon is also entered from here,
preserving a fine aisled hall flanked by four small hexagonal tower-rooms.

The next r.-hand turning (Rue de Regatterie) leads to *N.-D.-la-
Grande*; see below.

The Rue René-Descartes leads N., in which No. 8 is the *Hôtel Fumée*, with a
Gothic facade, beyond which the Rue de la Chaine leads downhill. In the courtyard of No. 24 is the *Hôtel Berthelot* (1529) housing the *Centre d'études
supérieures de Civilisation Médiévale*, with an interesting library of photographs
of Romanesque churches, etc.—To the r. at the bottom of the hill stands **St-Jean
de Montierneuf**, a late 11C Benedictine church, with a lantern above the central
apse added in the 14C. It was much mutilated during the Religious Wars, and is
again under restoration.

To the E. of the Rue de la Chaine is disused *St-Germain* (11C, with a 12C tower
and 15C choir).

N.-D.-la-Grande now stands forlornly beside modern market
buildings, the earlier unity of which with the church having been
almost entirely sacrificed to utility. Its richly sculptured but weather-
worn *W. Front* is composed of three storeys of arcading framed by
clustered pillars supporting the lateral turrets, which, like the central
tower, are crowned by conical spires similar to those at St-Front at
Périgueux.

In the upper storey is a (headless) Christ Triumphant surrounded by the symbols of the Evangelists; the sculptures in the lower storeys depict scriptural subjects from Adam and Eve to the Nativity; in the arches above are rude statues of St Hilary, St Martin, and the Apostles. On the S. side are two porches, one 12C, the other 16C. Traces of the ancient foundations on which the 11C nave and choir are built may be seen at the base of the belfry in the N. arcade.—The piers and the barrel vault of the nave and the groined vaults of the aisles have been sadly defaced by daubs of 1857, the removal of which is long overdue. There are no transepts. In the vaulting of the choir, the capitals of which are notable, appear remains of a 13C fresco. Adjacent is a 16C Entombment.

Almost opposite the W. front are the 17C buildings of the former *Hôtel-Dieu*, with scant remains of the cloister of Notre-Dame, and partly occupied by the *Library*, preserving some MSS of interest, and an incunable printed in Poitiers in 1479.

The Grande Rue descends S.W., passing the *Hôtel des Trois Poissons* (No. 190), the 16-18C *Hôtel d'Aquitaine* (No. 159), and the *Maison des Trois-Clous* (15C; No. 118); Nos 101, 102, 96, and 60 also have features of interest.

Half-way down this street the Rue Émile-Faguet leads r. towards the unfortunately-sited **Cathedral** (1166–1271), to which the upper parts of the two W. bays were added in the 14C; at the time of its consecration (1379) the two dissimilar towers were still unfinished, and have remained so, except for the octagonal storey added to the N. tower c. 1510.

The facade, too broad for its height, is pierced by three doorways, in which the sculptures of the tympana represent the Last Judgement, the Incredulity of St Thomas, and the Coronation of the Virgin. The doors are 14C.

The *Interior* (90m long, and 27m high) is a well-planned structure whose proportions are rendered more imposing by a slight decrease in height and narrowing of the nave towards the choir. In the 3rd N. bay is a 14C labyrinth. The magnificent *Stained-glass* dates from the early 13C, the oldest window (after 1212) being that in the apse depicting the Crucifixion, in which the features of Henry II and Eleanor are discernable. Baroque altars embellish the otherwise forbidding E. wall. The carved *Choir-stalls* (1235–57) are, with those of N.-D.-de-la-Roche (near Chevreuse), the oldest extant in France. The organ-case and pulpit date from 1789. In the sacristy is a curious series of portraits of bishops since the 15C. The undercroft chapel beneath the S. stalls incorporates foundations of an 8th or 9C church.

Walking round the N. side of the cathedral we pass the charming *Porte St-Michel* (14C), with sculptured capitals of scenes of the life of the Virgin, rare at this period, and the square E. facade, and continue downhill to *Ste-Radegonde*, founded c. 560 by Radegunde, wife of Lothair I, who was buried here in 587. In 1099 it became collegiate, and was rebuilt, and has undergone several alterations since. The aisleless nave dates from the 13C; the main portal is 15C; and the tower, with an octagonal top storey, was begun c. 1100. The walled parvis has stone seats suggesting its use as a consistory court.

In the porch (l.) is a 12C Virgin in high relief. The nave contains some good 13C glass, but the 14C paintings in the apse have been disfigured by restoration. Note the capitals in the raised choir. The *Crypt* contains the 8-9C tomb of St Radegunde, a black marble sarcophagus (empty since 1562, when the Huguenots burnt its contents) resting on a 12C table; the statue was a gift of Anne of Austria in gratitude for the recovery of Louis XIV from an illness (1658). The early 13C sacristy, formerly the chapter-house, has a ribbed vault.

A short distance to the S. is the *Pont Neuf* (1778).

Some minutes' walk from its far end, the Rue de la Pierre-Levée forks l., off which is the *Hypogée Martyrium*, a partly subterranean chapel of the 7th or 8C, conjectured to have been that of a Christian cemetery enclosed in the pagan necropolis; three reliefs and traces of an altar may be seen.—At the next l.-hand turning is the *Pierre-Levée*, a broken dolmen beside which—as mentioned by Rabelais—the students of Poitiers used to hold their revels. The new university buildings are conveniently sited no great distance further S.E.

The Rue Jean-Jaurès leads back uphill from the bride to pass (r.) the remains of the abbey of *Ste-Croix*, and circles the **Baptistry of St-Jean**, which although heavily restored since 1934, is one of the oldest Christian monuments in France.

Erected in 356/68 for the purpose of baptism by immersion, with a piscina in the middle, it originally consisted of a rectangular room c. 13m long, but only the lower courses of this building survive. In the 7C the piscina was filled in, and the edifice was heightened and enlarged by the addition of an E. apse and two small lateral apses, incorporating Roman columns. It was damaged by fire in 1018, and the 11C porch was added. 12C paintings of the Apostles and other subjects survive on its walls. The sarcophagi preserved here may be removed to the adjacent museum, together with other antiquities unearthed in the Gallo-Roman and Merovingian cemeteries in the neighbourhood.

In the lane leading back to the cathedral are two rebuilt chapels.

To the S.W. is the attractively designed open-plan building, of 1974, incorporating a central garden, of the **Musée Ste-Croix**, into which various dispersed collections are being progressively installed, including a series of Limoges enamelled croziers, etc.

Among the somewhat miscellaneous works of art exhibited—some placed in a better setting than they deserve—are representative examples of *Boudin*, *Bonnard*, *Guillaumin*, *Vuillard*, *Sisley*, *Lépine*, and *Forain* (Sleeping woman). Among works by local artists, those by *Henri Pailler*, and *Alfred de Curzon* (1820–95) are of interest, together with a series of Portraits by *Jean Valade* (1710–87). Earlier works include several portraits of the Dutch School; a good Flemish Portrait of Fernando of Aragon; Portrait of a Lady (dated 1579) attrib. to *Frans I Pourbus*; *Pieter Potter*, Battle scene; *B.G. Cuyp*, Adoration; *Martin van Valkenborch*, Winter Scene; and a curious series of 17 early-17C Dutch or Flemish paintings of the Life of Christ from the Abbey of Ste-Croix, on part of the site of which the museum is built.

To the S., the Rue St-Pierre-le-Pueiller, continued by the Rue de la Celle, ascends past the *Lycée*, in part a former Jesuit college (1605), with an elegant central pavilion, and a chapel containing good Louis-XIV *boiseries*.

The Rue Puygarreau, opposite the entrance, leads past the Renaissance *Hôtel Jean-Beauce* (1554), behind the Hôtel de Ville, and is continued by the Rue Henri-Oudin, in which No. 9 is the *Hôtel d'Elbène* (1557).

Flanking the gardens of the Lycée, the Rue Magenta leads shortly to the Rue des Arènes, where the remains of a large *Roman Theatre* have been exposed. Just W. of the Rue Magenta is the Rue Carnot, which with its extension, the Rue de la Tranchée, bears S.W.; see below.

The Rue Doyenné leads r., in which is the Renaissance *Doyenné* (1517), in which Rabelais resided, near which we get a good view of the apse of ***St-Hilaire-le-Grande***. Rebuilt in the 11-12C on the site of a Gallo-Roman edifice, it is one of the most interesting buildings in Poitiers, in spite of the fact that the facade (and two bays of the nave, destroyed by the collapse of the bell-tower in 1590), was replaced by a 19C front at the time of its restoration.

The vault over the truncated nave is formed by a series of octagonal cupolas, an arrangement (with the exception of Notre-Dame at Le Puy-en-Velay) which does not occur elsewhere in the case of a church with aisles. A unique feature is the presence of the triple aisles on either side of the nave, one equal to it in height but much narrower, the others lower and wider. Parts of the transepts date from the early 11C; the S. transept contains 17C statues from the Porte de la Tranchée; the N. transept preserves only a fragment of the bell-tower. The sacristy (usually shut) contains some Carolingian *Capitals*. The raised 12C choir with its four radiating chapels is built over the crypt. Faint or restored 11-12C wall-paintings may be seen about the building. The marble lid of the sarcophagus of St Adra, Hilary's daughter, is preserved near the S.W. door.

The street N. of the church leads back to the Rue Victor-Hugo.

S. of the Rue de la Tranchée, which ends in the *Porte de la Tranchée*, pierced through the ramparts on the narrow front between the Clain and the Boivre, is the *Parc de Blossac*, the only large open space in the town, and laid out by the Comte de Blossac, intendant of Poitou, in 1751–84. At its S. angle, where the 12-15C walls are practically intact, the *Tour à l'Oiseau* provides a panoramic view over the Clain valley; the E. corner has been cut into to provide space for the Gare Routière.

For roads from Poitiers to **Limoges**, **Bordeaux**, and **La Rochelle**, see Rtes 69, 70, and 72, respectively; for those to *Bourges*, *Angers*, and *Nantes*, see Rtes 51, 60, and 61, in reverse.

57 Tours to Saumur

A. Via Azay-le-Rideau and Chinon

77km (48 miles). D751. 27km **Azay-le-Rideau**—21km **Chinon**—16.5km *Candes*—1.5km *Montsoreau*. **Fontevraud** is 4.5km S. —12.5km **Saumur**.

Maps: IGN 25, 26, or 106. M 232.

Although the three routes below describe the area between Tours and Saumur, which is particularly rich in châteaux, a compromise route can be taken by driving from Tours to *Villandry*, later crossing the Loire to *Langeais*, and then returning S. to *Azay-le-Rideau* and *Chinon*.
    The note on p 69 should be read first.

For **Tours**, see Rte 54.
    We turn off the N10 c. 1.5km after crossing the Cher, to traverse *Joué-les-Tours*, and later the *Forêt de Villandry* to approach **Azay-le-Rideau**, an attractive village in itself, with a church incorporating a 9C facade embellished with 11C statues, but better known for its beautifully sited ****Château**, ◇ washed on three sides by tree-lined branches of the Indre.

It is a graceful edifice of 1527 built for Gilles Berthelot, the financier, who was involved in the disgrace of Semblançay, and had to abandon his château to François I. Although in appearance it recalls the castles of the 14C, the defensive details—such as the *échauguettes* or corner-turrets—are purely decorative, and the Gothic sculpture everywhere gives place to Italian ornament in the manner of Giròlamo Della Robbia. Purchased by the State in 1905, it now contains a collection of Renaissance furniture, etc.

The entrance facade, with its delicate Renaissance decoration, the salamander and ermine motifs of François and Claude de France, and the elaborate internal pendants of the staircase seen through the open loggias, are impressive.

Visitors are first conducted to the vaulted kitchen. In the *Grand Salon* is a chimneypiece ascribed to Goujon, displaying the salamander device. A number of royal portraits, including one of Gabrielle d'Estrées, after Clouet, embellish other rooms, while among the furniture a *Secretaire* reproducing on ivory six scenes from Callot's 'Grandes Misères de la Guerre' (1633; the same year as the original 18 engravings were produced) is outstanding. Two Beauvais tapestries depicting hunting scenes are notable, among others. The panelled ceiling of the staircase is decorated with medallions of the kings of France, but only those on the second floor are contemporary.

3km N.W., on the Langeais road, is the charming *Château d'Islette* (1526); for *Saché*, 10.5km E., see Rte 56.

Crossing the Indre, we continue S.W. through the *Forêt de Chinon* (52,000 hectares) to (21km) **CHINON** (8900 Chinonais), an ancient and picturesque town on the banks of the Vienne, dominated by the extensive ruins of its castle, and retaining a number of narrow streets and turreted 15-16C houses. Its local 'vin rouge' has long been celebrated, among others by François Rabelais (1484–1553), who was probably born in the neighbouring *gentilhommière* of *La Devinière*; see p 344.

In 1044 Chinon came into the possession of the counts of Anjou, and in the next century passed to Henry II, who died here in 1189. A local legend maintains that Richard I also died here, being brought back mortally wounded from Châlus in the Limousin, in 1199. It was again in French hands in 1205, after an eight-months siege by Philippe Auguste. In 1308 the Grand Master and 140 other Knights Templar were imprisoned here for a year before being sent to Paris to their execution; and in 1321 260 Jews accused of having poisoned the town's water-supply were burnt alive on an island in the Vienne. Philippe de Comines was a governor of Chinon. From 1631 until the Revolution it was a fief of the Richelieu family.

Just E. of the bridge, behind a seated statue of Rabelais on the quay, is *Pl. de l'Hôtel de Ville*, planted with chestnut trees. Hence a narrow lane climbs steeply towards the castle, also approached by road from the Rue du Puy-des-Bancs turning uphill from the Rue J.-J. Rousseau (see below) leading E. from this Place.

The *Castle* consists of three strongholds separated by deep moats and ranged in line from E. to W. on a narrow steep-sided plateau. On the r. are seen the ruins of the *Château de St-Georges*, built by Henry II, passing which, we enter the principal ward or *Château du Milieu* by the 12-14C *Pavillon de l'Horloge*. This central enceinte, on the site of a Roman castrum, commands extensive views over the surrounding countryside, while overlooking the town is the partially restored *Grand-Logis*, where Charles VII first received Joan of Arc on 9 March 1429, when she persuaded him to undertake the relief of Orléans. Beyond a second moat is the *Château du Coudray*, with the fine cylindrical 13C keep. At the S.W. corner is the slender *Tour du Moulin*; the W. curtain wall is the oldest part of the fortress, parts of it dating from 954.

An alternative descent may be followed by diverging r. soon after making our exit. This track climbs down to the *Grand-Carroi*, in the Rue Voltaire, the medieval centre of the town, which has undergone tasteful even if drastic restoration.—Further W. is **St-Maurice**, to the 12C nave of which a S. aisle was added in the 16C; the Romanesque tower is surmounted by a 15C spire. Within, the carved and painted keystones and statuettes at the springing of the vaults should be noticed, while in the pavement near the centre of the nave appears the inscription: 'Henricus II Rex Anglorum aedificam'.—No. 48 was the residence of the lieutenant-governor; No. 81 is the local *Musée*.

The Rue J.-J. Rousseau, on the far side of the main square, is likewise interesting for its old houses; Rabelais occupied a house on the site of No. 15 in the Rue de la Lamproie (r.). Beyond this turning is *St-Étienne*, built in 1480 by Philippe de Comines, whose armorial bearings may be seen on its W. front. At the end of the street stands *St-Mexme*, the 11C facade of which is flanked by two towers, one Romanesque, one 15C.—Some frescoes were uncovered in the nearby chapel of *Ste-Radegonde* in 1964.

Below Chinon, between the Vienne and the Loire, is a triangle of land known as the *Véron*, whose inhabitants claimed descent from the Moors settled here after their army had been defeated at Poitiers in 749.

CHINON TO POITIERS VIA RICHELIEU (75km). We cross the Vienne and past *Rivière* (see Rte 56), shortly forking r. onto the D749 past (l.) the *Château du Rivau* (13-15C) to (14km) **Champigny-sur-Veude**, where the painter Chaïm Soutine (1894–1943) sought refuge from 1940 until his death. Of the 16C château of the Bourbon-Montpensier family—acquired and demolished by Richelieu, jealous for the pre-eminence of his own town (see below)—the main survival is the elegant *Chapelle St-Louis (1499–1543), Renaissance in style, embellished with emblems and escutcheons, and containing fine stained-glass, including family portraits and scenes from the life of Louis IX; the effigy of Henri de Bourbon-Montpensier dates from the early 17C.—3km. To the r. is the 16C *Château de la Pataudière*.

3km. **Richelieu**, an attractive little town, retaining on its W. side some defensive walls, laid out on a regular plan—like the older bastides—and rebuilt in a severely classical style by the Cardinal, whose own sumptuous château (with which he replaced his paternal mansion, but rarely visited) was demolished in 1805. Its park, embellished by a statue of Richelieu brought from Versailles, lies to the S.—The direct road to Poitiers is reached by a r.-hand fork off the D749, passing (l.) at 6.5km the beautiful but over-restored church of *Faye-la-Vineuse* (12C), fortified in the 16C, preserving perhaps the finest *Crypt in Touraine.—17.5km further S. on the D757 is *Lencloître*, its church with a 12C dome and fortified 15C facade.—10km. *Vendeuvre-du-Poitou*, with ruins of the 16C château of Adm. de Bonnivet (demolished 1810–25) and a church with 12C details.—20km. **Poitiers**; see Rte 56.

Crossing the Vienne at Chinon on a bridge with piers dating from the 12C, we turn r. at 2km (retrospective views) and drive N.W.; for an attractive alternative road, see below.—11.5km. *St-Germain-sur-Vienne*, with a 13C church, 2.5km beyond we reach the confluence of the Vienne and Loire at **Candes-St-Martin**, where the *Church (12-14C) has a colonnaded W. front and extraordinary N. porch, with rows of (mutilated) statues, and vaulted from a single monolithic column. Note also the statues, some retaining their original colouring, near the capitals of the interior clustered columns. The fortifications were added in the 15C. The N.E. chapel, with a recumbent effigy of a bishop, is said to cover the spot where St Martin of Tours died in 397.

1.5km. **Montsoreau**, a quaint little town with a 13th and 18C church containing 15C stalls. The *Château* (1455–1520) was in the 16C the property of Jean de Chambes, a persecutor of the Huguenots, who by means of a pretended assignation with his wife, lured Bussy d'Amboise to his death in 1579. It contains a good stair-turret and a '*Musée des Goums*' (Moroccan troops in the French service), illustrating their military exploits, and of Maréchal Lyautey, etc.

For **Fontevraud**, 4.5km S., see Rte 60B.

Fontevraud may also be approached from Chinon by turning l. off the D751
after 5km, and then r. onto the D117. After 1km a lane to the r. leads to *La
Devinière*, a farmhouse where it is generally supposed Rabelais was born
c. 1494.—To the l. of the D117, S. of *Seuilly* (with remains of a Benedictine abbey
where Rabelais was first educated), is the 15C château of *Coudrey* (a residence
of Maeterlinck after 1927, who restored it).—Beyond, on the r., are the ruins of
the château of *Maulevrier*, and further W., past the village of *Lerné*, the château
of *Chavigny* (r.; c. 1600); it was here, in 'Gargantua' that the 'picrocholine' war
took place, Picrochole being 'King' of Lerné!—Immediately W. of Chavigny a
by-road climbs N. through the woods to (7km) *Fontevraud*.

The road continues along the river-bank, passing a number of villages
and dwellings hollowed out in the rock, many of them dating from
the 15-16C, via (4km) *Parnay*, with a part-Romanesque church, and
adjacent *Souzay*, where in the château of *Dampierre* Marguerite
d'Anjou (1429–82), the ambitious queen of Henri VI, died in exile.
 7km. **Saumur**; see Rte 60B.

B.   Via Villandry and Ussé

65km (40 miles). D7. 17.5km **Villandry**—9km *Lignières-de-Touraine*.
Langeais lies 3.5km N.; **Azay-le-Rideau**, 6.5km S.E.—11.5km
Ussé—3.5km **Chinon** lies 10km S.—15km *Candes*—12.5km **Saumur**.

Maps: IGN 25, 26, or 106. M 232.

See first paragraph of Rte 57A.

We turn r. prior to crossing the Cher, and then follow the D7 (with
distant views N.W. towards *Luynes*) through (15km) *Savonnières*,
with a good Romanesque N. door to its church.
 2.5km. **Villandry**, with a *Château* rebuilt by Jean Le Breton after
1537, and until 1639 known as Coulombières. It was radically altered
in the 18C, and was restored before 1936 by the Carvallo family.
The dormers recall the style of the earlier building, while the S.W.
tower (14C) is a relic of an earlier castle.

Of great charm are the terraced ***Gardens**, laid out in the 16C manner with box
hedges (clipped once a year) and fountains. These are best seen from a belvedere
above the E. terrace, below which is an orangery. The terrace themselves are
flanked by lime or linden trees. The formal gardens are arranged to display symbolic designs, and the Vegetable Garden (or *Potager*) is likewise laid out (in nine
squares) with emphasis on its decorative effect.—In the E. wing is exhibited a
small collection of Spanish paintings, some of them of the School of Zurbaran, or
attrib. to Berruguete, and including a little Infanta of the School of Velázquez.
One room contains a restored stalactite *artesonado* ceiling from Toledo, interesting even if out of place.

Beyond the village we pass near the present confluence of the Loire
and Cher, and after 9km reach the crossroads for *Langeais* and
Azay-le-Rideau. Continuing ahead, *Ussé* is approached, better seen
from a minor road skirting the river, reached by forking r. 4km
beyond *Lignières* through *Bréhémont*, the projected site of Rabelais's
Utopian 'Abbaye de Thélème'.
 The **Château d'Ussé**, a romantic-looking white-stone slated pile
between cylindrical towers (effective in floodlighting), stands on a
thickly-wooded slope overlooking the Indre and Loire. It was built
before 1480 by Antoine de Bueil, but was considerably altered in the
16-17C and drastically restored in the 19C. The detached *Chapel*
(1538), with Italianate details, is usually open, and part of the mansion is also shown.

A turning 3.5km further W. leads to Chinon via *Huismes*, with a late 12C church, some 4km S. of which, in the park of the *Château d'Uzage* are the slight remains of the brick *Château de Bonaventure*, built by Charles VIII, and frequented by Louis XI for hunting.

The D7 continues W., later skirting a *Nuclear power-station*, and crossing the Vienne at its confluence with the Loire at *Candes*, for which, and the road on to **Saumur**, see Rte 57A.

C. Via Langeais

65km (40 miles). N152. 10km **Luynes**—14km **Langeais**—21km *Le Port-Boulet*. **Chinon** lies 13km S.E., and *Candes* 8.5km S.W.—20km **Saumur**.

Maps: IGN 25, 26, or 106. M 232.

We skirt the N. bank of the Loire to *Luynes*, 1km r., just prior to which, on a parallel road, is the late 15C *Château de Chatigny*, with chequered towers, built for Jean Quetier, Semblançay's brother-in-law.

 Luynes, known as *Maillé* in the Middle Ages, takes its name (like Albert, in Picardy) from Louis XIII's favourite, Albert de Luynes, who acquired the estate in 1619. Many villages dwellings were hollowed out of the rock; some other houses opposite the church, and the market-hall, are quaint 16C wooden buildings. Steps ascend to the *Castle, defended by heavy cylindrical towers, within which is a graceful late-Gothic and Renaissance edifice (1465), with an addition of 1650.—To the E., below the castle, is the church of a college founded in 1486; 2km N.E. are the remains of a Roman aqueduct.

 6km. To the r. is the mysterious *Pile de Cinq-Mars*, a solid square tower of patterned masonry, 29m high, on a Gallo-Roman base, but erected for no known purpose. At adjacent *Cinq-Mars-la-Pile* are preserved the two towers of its moated castle, the rest of which was razed after the execution of another of Louis XIII's favourites, the Marquis de Cinq-Mars (1620–42), beheaded, with his friend de Thou, for conspiring with the King of Spain against Richelieu.

 Langeais, a pleasant old town with a famous castle, opposite which is a Renaissance house at which Rabelais once stayed, its *Church* with a 4C crypt, and a Romanesque tower and apse.

 The *Château was originally a stronghold of Fulk Nerra, the ruins of whose keep (c. 900; one of the oldest extant in France) surmounts the ridge seperating the Loire from the valley of the Roumer.

It was a Plantagenet fortress in 1154–1216, and was retaken by the English in 1427. The present castle, which retains its stern feudal aspect, was constructed in 1469 for Jean Bourré, minister of Louis XI, and in 1491 the marriage of Charles VIII and Anne of Brittany was celebrated here. It was restored by Jacques Siegfried, who bequeathed it to the Institute de France in 1904.

The exterior walls, approached by a flight of steps and drawbridge, are defended by three huge drum-towers with conical roofs; the inner facade, with its high dormers and stair-turrets, is less forbidding in appearance.

On the ground floor the *Salle des Gardes*, with the only original tiled floor, contains a fireplace by François d'Orléans and two 15C stalls from Arques. Other rooms contain 15-16C tapestries and furniture, some of it of remarkable quality. Observe also a polished silver mirror (15C) and a series of Aubusson tapestries representing heroes in the _Grand Salon_; also one of the Crucifixion, and 'millefleurs' tapestries. On the third floor is the _Chapel_, with an imposing wooden barrel-vault; the covered rampart walk commands impressive plunging views.

Azay-le-Rideau lies 10km S.E. in the Indre valley; see Rte 57A.
 4km. _St-Michel-sur-Loire_, 1km r., preserves a 14C gatehouse.

4km beyond this turning, the D35 forks r. towards _Angers_, after 1.5km passing near the _Château de la Rochecotte_, where Talleyrand often stayed, and 5.5km beyond, by-passing (l.) _Restigné_, with some 10C work in its church.—4.5km. _Bourgueil_, noted for its wine; there is a Cave 2km N.W., with a collection of wine-presses. The church, with an early-Romanesque facade, and elegant 12C choir, is that of the once-famous Benedictine abbey, of which some dependencies survive (13-18C).—A l.-hand turning 16km further W. leads directly to (6km) **Saumur**.

The N152 continues to skirt the Loire, with a good view of the _Château of Ussé_ on its far bank (see Rte 57B), and later of a 'Centrale Nucléaire' opposite (13km) _Le Port-Boulet_.—1.5km. To the r. is the _Château des Réaux_, formerly _Le Plessis-Rideau_, with its moat and chequered towers, rebuilt before 1539 for the Briçonnet family, and later the property of Tallement des Reaux.—7km. A bridge here crosses the Loire just W. of _Montsoreau_; see Rte 57A.—The main road veers N.W. to the transpontine suburb of **Saumur**; see Rte 60B.

58 Saumur to La Rochelle

A. Via Thouars, Parthenay, and Niort

178km (110 miles). N147. 16km **Montreuil-Bellay**—D938. 18km **Thouars**—40km **Parthenay**—D743. 42km **Niort**—N11. 63km **La Rochelle**.

Maps: IGN 25, 33, 39, or 107. M 232, 233.

For **Saumur**, see Rte 60B.
 5km. _Distre_, its church retaining Romanesque details, is traversed, and 11km beyond, _Montreuil-Bellay_; see Rte 60A.
 18km. **Thouars** (11,900 Thouarsais), an ancient fortress whose feudal lords were devoted to the English cause throughout the Hundred Years War, is divided into an old and new town by the _Pl. Lavault_; the former, traversed by the Rue Porte de Paris and Rue La Trémoïlle, occupying a bluff overlooking a bend in the river Thouet. A few paces to the r. of this street (the latter named after the family that controlled the place from the time of Charles VIII) is the former abbey-church of _St-Laon_, with the _Mairie_ in the 17C abbey buildings. The church, partly 12C, including the tower, was largely rebuilt in the 15C, and contains the tomb of Margaret (c. 1425–45), first wife of Louis XI, and daughter of James I of Scotland.
 St-Médard, to the l. further on, has a notable W. front (restored) with a richly sculptured central portal (12C) and a 15C rose-window.—The parallel Rue du Château, with 15-16C houses, leads to the _Château_ (1635), replacing an earlier castle commanding the loop in the river below, crossed to the E. by a 14C _Bridge_. Adjacent to the castle is the *Sainte-Chapelle* (1514).—A lane leading N.E.

from St-Médard passes near the 12-13C *Tour du Prince-du-Galles*, the 15C *Hôtel du Président Tydo*, and through the 13-14C *Porte du Prévôt*, to regain the E. end of the Pl. Lavault.

The Thouet valley is charming, both upstream and down, especially at the *Cirque de Missé*, to the S.E., and the *Gorge du Ligron*, to the W.

An interesting DETOUR may be made with ease from Thouars (taking in *Oiron*, *St-Jouin-de-Marnes*, and *Airvault*), rejoining the main road 25km further S. By following the D759 E., at 5km we pass S. of the château of *Beauvais* (c. 1525), 4km beyond, and fork r. for (3.5km) *Oiron*, a village where the famous Oiron ware (once known as 'faience Henri-Deux', and now rare) was made in a pottery established in 1519 by Hélène Hangest, widow of Artus Gouffier, builder of the château. The church contains monuments of that family, mutilated by the Huguenots in 1568.

The *Château d'Oiron ◇ (1518–49), an imposing Renaissance edifice enlarged in 1667 by the Duc de la Feuillade, was owned by Mme de Montespan from 1698 to 1707, and she was responsible for founding the Hospice in 1703. Adjoining the l. wing is a charming arcaded gallery adorned with medallions of the Twelve Caesars, Mahomet, and other historical personages. In the *Salles des Gardes* are murals illustrating the Aeneid, by Noël Jallier (1549). The 17C ceilings and woodwork of the main buildings are likewise notable, particularly in the *Salle des Fêtes*. Also of interest is the central spiral *Staircase*, the richly decorated *Cabinet des Muses*, and the *Oratory*, its floor tiled with Oiron faience.

8.5km due S. is **St-Jouin-de-Marnes**, where in the 4C a powerful Benedictine abbey was founded at a place called *Ansion*, and later renamed in honour of Jovin, its first abbot. A school of painting was established here by the monks in the 17C, examples of which may be seen here and in St-André at Niort. The *Church, which besides part of a 15C cloister and some 18C dependencies, is all that remains of the monastery, is remarkable for its size (71m long) and for its architectural character.

The facade of c. 1130 is divided by clustered columns into three parts corresponding to the nave and aisles, and is embellished in its upper storey with a group representing the Last Judgement. Although of later date, the apsidal chapels (late 12C) are equally ornate. Only the first three bays of the nave and aisles retain their original barrel vaults, the rest being re-roofed in the 13C with a fantastic and complicated system of vaulting. Note also the splay of the piers. Over the crossing is an octagonal cupola supporting a two-storeyed belfry. The W. bay of the choir is the oldest part of the building (c. 1095).

3km E. lies **Moncontour**, which fell into English hands in 1370, but was retaken by Du Guesclin two years later. At a battle here in 1596 Adm. de Coligny was heavily defeated by Henri III, then Duc d'Anjou. The huge 12C *Keep* was restored in the 15C. The remains of the enceinte and the ruins of a Romanesque chapel may be seen, while the village preserves a Romanesque church and several 15-16C houses.

St-Généroux (6.5km W. of St-Jouin) has a medieval bridge, and a *Church, recently restored, dating in part from the 9C, 7km due S. of which (and 9km S.W. of St-Jouin) is **Airvault**.

The abbey church of *St-Pierre at Airvault, dating from the early 12C, one of the finest Romanesque monuments in Poitou, has recently been restored. The steeple is 13C, at which time the nave and choir were vaulted in the Angevin manner, while the aisles retain their barrel-vaults. Note the statues on either side of the finely carved capitals in the nave. The equestrian statue which once stood at the l. of the entrance (like that at *Melle*, and elsewhere in the region), has long been destroyed. In the N. transept io an abbot's tomb of 1110, and the N. aisle contains a 12C altar-front. Remains of the 15C cloister and 12C chapter-house may be seen in the presbytery gardens.—To the S.W. the Thouet is crossed by a 12C *Bridge*.

5.5km. *St-Loup-Lamairé* was the home of François Arouet, Voltaire's father, the philosopher assuming his name from a neighbouring estate; the town was known as *Voltaire* during the Revolution, and later as *St-Loup-sur-Thouet*. The Louis-XII château preserves a 15C keep, and some 15-17C houses survive.—We rejoin the D938 4.5km S.W., and after 5km pass 3.5km N.E. of the 14C castle of *Tennesus*.

10km. **Parthenay** (11,700 Parthenaisiens), the ancient *Partiniacum* and capital of the *Gâtine*, is a picturesque stronghold built above the valley of the Thouet, which skirts the N. and W. ramparts (12C) of the older town. It was presented in 1425 to the Constable de Richemont (d. 1458), and then passed to Dunois, in whose family it remained until 1641.

The central *Pl. de la Mairie* may be approached from the Blvd de la Mailleraie (the main road) via the Rue Jean-Jaurès; or better, by forking r. just before the bridge N. of the town, and entering by the 13C *Porte-St-Jacques*, thence ascending to the ancient *Rue de la Vaux-St-Jacques*, lined with brick and wooden-beamed 15C houses.

From the Place one may enter the citadel quarter by the *Porte-de-l'Horloge* (1454), beyond which is *Ste-Croix*, with a restored Romanesque nave and aisles and a late 12C choir.—Further N. two capitals and a triple portal remain of the castle chapel of *N.-D.-de-la-Couldre*, beyond which three 13C towers survive of the fortress.—Not far S.E. of the Place is *St-Laurent*, with two partly Romanesque towers, but it was largely rebuilt in 1855.

The D743 bears S.W. through **Parthenay-le-Vieux**, its 12C *Church* with a fine facade in the Poitevin style; note the equestrian statue of a knight hawking to the l. of the entrance.—There is a 11-13C church of some interest of *Secondigny*, 14km W.—The road now crosses the undulating district known as the *Gâtine* (there is another S. of Nemours), where the thickets and sunken roads flanked by hedges were the haunt of the Chouans. After (15km) *Mazières* we descend into the valley of the Sèvre Niotaise, and at 18km pass (r.) the imposing 13C towers of the *Château de Coudrey-Salbart*.—1km. *Echiré*.

A lane leads some 4km W. to the *Château de Mursay*, the home of Agrippa d'Aubigné (1552–1630), the Protestant leader, and of his grand-daughter Françoise, later Marquise de Maintenon (1635–1719), wife of the poet Scarron, and afterwards of Louis XIV.

8km. **Niort**; for which, and for the road hence to **La Rochelle**, 63km S.W., see Rte 72.

B. Via Bressuire and Fontenay-le-Comte

167km (103 miles). D960. 17km *Doué-la-Fontaine*—D69 and D32.
29km *Argentan-Château*—D748. 17km **Bressuire**—D938 ter. 54km
Fontenay-le-Comte—27km *Marans*—N137. 23km **La Rochelle**.

Maps: IGN 25, 33, 39, or 107. M 232, 233.

At 3.5km from **Saumur** (Rte 60B) we fork r. to pass the ruined castle
of *Pocé*, and 13.5km beyond, enter *Doué-la-Fontaine*, which with
contiguous villages is built over ancient quarries, remarkable among
which are those beneath the *Pl. de la Halle*; while another, the so-
called '*Arènes*', long considered to be of Roman origin, was the site
of dramatic performances in the 15-17Cs. It is also known for its
copious springs, forming the source of the Douet, filling two reservoirs excavated in 1764. *St-Pierre* is 15C; the ruins of *St-Denis*, mid
12C. A feudal motte dominates the castle ramparts, while a larger
earthwork protects the town to the S.W.

Hence the D69 continues S., at 11.5km passing 3km E. of the imposing ruined castle of *Passavant*.—17.5km. *Argenton-Château*,
prior to entering which we pass (l.) another ruined château. The charmingly situated village, with an elaborate 12C church doorway,
likewise had a castle, once inhabited by Philippe de Comines, but
destroyed in 1793.

Some 20km further W. are the ruins of the château of *La Durbelière*, birthplace
of the Vendean leader Henri de la Rochejaquelein (1772–94); the family tombs
lie in the adjacent village of *St-Aubin-de-Baubigné*.

17km. **Bressuire** (19,500 Bressuirais) is an ancient town (*Bercorium*)
with an unhappy history. It was burnt in 1214 for adherence to the
Plantagenets, pillaged in 1598 by the Protestants, and burnt again in
1798 by the 'infernal column' of the Republican general, Grinon, for
the first abortive rising in the Vendée had occurred in the region in
Aug. 1791.

The only old building surviving is *Notre-Dame*, with an aisleless
12C nave in the Angevin style and a large aisled 16C choir without
an ambulatory. The remarkable mid 16C belfry, 55m high, modelled
on the towers of the cathedral at Tours, had its cupola added in 1728.
The sculpture of the W. door has been sadly mutilated; the S. doorway is 12C, and within is a sumptuous 17C marble pulpit. Above the
town rises the double ring of ruined walls fortified with 48 towers,
which surrounded the 11-15C *Castle*. The 12C priory church of *St-
Cyprien*, now a barn, is on the other side of the valley.

9km S.E. is the *Château de Clisson*, home of the Vendean Lescure, gutted by
Westermann in 1794; while the manor of *La Baronnière*, the home of Bonchamp,
the ablest of the rebels, was at *La Chapelle-St-Laurent*, 5km further S.W.

BRESSUIRE TO CHANTONNAY (49km). The D960 bis runs W. through
(14.5km) *Cérizay*, burnt by the Germans in 1944, just beyond which (l.) is the
beautiful abbey chapel of *Beau Chêne* (13-15C). Crossing the Sèvre Nantaise,
the road traverses the undulating wooded *Collines Vendéennes*, after 4.5km
passing (l.) the 14-15C castle of *St-Mesmin-la-Ville*, and the *Puy Crapaud* (288m)
prior to entering (10km) **Pouzauges**, a small town with a 12th and 15C church.
To the N. are relics of the outer enceinte and great square keep of its 13C *Castle*;
to the S., at *Pouzauges-les-Vieux*, a 13C church.—At *Réaumur*, some 7km further S., was the ancestral home of the famous physicist.—7km N.W. of
Pouzauges is the hilltop village of *St-Michel-Mont-Mercure*, its name combining

both ancient and more recent patrons, just E. of which at *La Flocellière*, is a noble 13C keep.—Continuing S.W., at 4.5km we pass 3km S. of *Le Boupère*, with a fortified 13th and 15C church of interest, and (after another 10km) 4km N. of the ruins of the *Château de Sigournais* (13C).—8.5km. *Chantonnay*; see Rte 62.

Continuing S.W. from Bressuire, the D938 ter traverses (16km) *La Forêt-sur-Sèvre*, where a mansion of 1810 replaces the house in which Duplessis-Mornay (cf. *Saumur*) died in 1625.—A long ascent brings one to (11km) *St-Pierre-du-Chemin*, with a charming 15C church, and (6km) *La Châtaigneraie*.

Mouilleron-en-Pareds, 9.5km W., was the birthplace of both Georges Clemenceau (1841–1929), and Maréchal de Lattre de Tassigny (1889–1952).

9km. *Vouvant*, a picturesque village preserving the 13C 'Tour Mélusine' of its castle, and a partly restored 12C church with an admirably carved N. front, lies 2km E.

Hence a DETOUR may be made through the *Forêt de Vouvant* via the D31 to *Foussais-Payré*, 9km S.E., where *St-Hilaire* has a magnificently sculptured Romanesque facade.—The main road may be regained by following the D99 W. through *Mervent*, a finely sited village with its castle above the gorge in which the Mère joins the Vendée, both now dammed.

14km (from the Vouvant turning) is **Fontenay-le-Comte** (16,650 inhab.), a curious old town built astride the Vendée, owing its name to the 11C castle erected by the Counts of Poitiers, which in 1372 was gallantly but unsuccessfully defended by the wife of its English governor against Du Guesclin.

Although besieged eight times between 1568 and 1621, Fontenay remained a centre of Protestantism throughout the 16-17Cs, until the ruin brought about by the revocation of the Edict of Nantes, and in 1793 was the scene of two battles in the Vendean rising. It was the birthplace of André Tiraqueau (1480–1558), the jurist and friend of young Rabelais, and Nicolas Rapin, the poet (1535–1608). Georges Simenon, the novelist, lived here during the Occupation.

Roads converge on the *Pl. Viète*, in the upper town, from which the Rue Clemenceau descends to the *Pont Neuf* (1775), to the r. off which a lane leads to the *Château de Terre-Neuve* (1600), built for Rapin, and decorated in the taste of the time with inscriptions and terracotta figures of the Muses; the interior contains chimneypieces and ceilings of interest, some taken from the castle at *Coulonges*. 9km E.—Further down the main street on the r. is the *Hôtel de Ville*, occupying the site of the Franciscan convent of *Puy-St-Martin*, where Rabelais received part of his education.—To the E. of the Pl. Viète is late-Gothic *Notre-Dame*, with a curious N. portal, lofty spire, and Renaissance chapel.

Hence the Rue Pont-aux-Chèvres descends towards the river. There are several 16-17C houses here and in the adjacent *Pl. Belliard*. Lower down (l.) is the *Fontaines de Quatre-Tias* (1542), beyond which (l.) are the insignificant ruins of the castle.—Crossing the *Pont des Sardines*, one may follow the Rue des Loges, preserving a number of old houses, notably No. 85, the late 16C *Maison Millepertuis*, to 16-17C *St-Jean*.

While the main road continues S.W., traversing the *Marais Poitevin* (see p 370) to meet the N137 at (27km) *Marans*, see below, a more interesting DETOUR is that via *Maillezais*.

We follow the N148 S.E. (towards *Niort*), at 11km passing, 1.5km l., *Nieul*, the birthplace of Eleanor 'of Aquitaine' or 'of Guyenne' (1122–1204), queen of France in 1137–52, and of England in

1154–89. Its fine abbey *Church (11-12C; recently restored) retains
its Romanesque vaulting, contemporary cloisters, and chapter-
house.—6km S.W. lies **Maillezais**. N.E. of which are the ruins of a
Benedictine abbey, among which are the impressive remains of a
*Church which served as a cathedral from 1347 to 1648. These in-
clude the 11C narthex, with the stumps of two square towers, the
contemporary N. wall of the nave, and 15C transept. Its 14C
dependencies have been embodied in a farm, and the whole is surrounded by a line of fortifications erected by Agrippa d'Aubigné
when the place was turned into a Protestant stronghold.—The
Romanesque parish church, at the other end of the village, has a
good W. front.—Turning r. at crossroads 4.5km S.W., we regain the
main road 10km W. and turn l. for (14.5km) *Marans*, a small grain
port on the canalised Sèvre Niortaise.

Marans preserves the polygonal steeple of its old church, and
other ruins, and the Mairie contains a collection of locally manufactured faience.—We meet the N11 12km S. and enter **La Rochelle**
11km beyond; see Rte 72.

59 Saumur to Nantes

A. Via Angers

140km (87 miles). N147. 52km **Angers**—N23. 51km *Ancenis*—37km
Nantes.

Maps: IGN 25, 24, or 106. M 232.

The A11 motorway provides a rapid route between Angers and
Nantes, also by-passing the latter to meet the N165.

For **Saumur** itself, and the riverside road hence to **Angers**, via
Cunault; see Rte 60B, in reverse.

Crossing the Loire (retrospective views), we fork l. at 5km, traversing *Longué-Jumelles* 10km beyond, to by-pass (10km) *Beaufort-en-
Vallée* (r.), with a ruined castle of 1346, where Jeanne de Laval, second wife of King René, spent her last years, and a partly 15C church
with a belfry of 1542.

3km. *Moulines*, where a by-road forks r. to (3km) the *Château de
Montgeoffroy* (1775; by Barré), containing a notable collection of furniture, much of it contemporary with the building.

25km. **ANGERS** (141,100 Angevins; 46,600 in 1851; 94,400 in
1946), the ancient capital of the duchy of *Anjou*, and préfecture of
Maine-et-Loire, lies largely on the E. bank of the Maine a short
distance N. of its confluence with the Loire, the riverside dominated
by a massive castle, one of the finest feudal fortresses in France.
Boulevards have replaced the ramparts of the old town, in the centre
of which stands the cathedral, while in the extensive suburbs
flourish electronic industries, textile and rope factories, and slate
quarries (worked since the 9C), etc. It is a great producer of um-
brellas, and a centre for the wines and liqueurs of Anjou, and the surrounding countryside is noted for its market gardens.

Andegavi, the capital of a Gallic tribe, known to the Romans as *Juliomagus*,
became the seat of the powerful counts of Anjou (870–1204), the most famous
of whom was Fulk III (Nerra; 972–1040). His descendant Geoffrey IV (Plan-

tagenet; c. 1100– 51) was the father of Henry II, who thus became overlord of the province, but King John was forced to surrender his Angevin possessions to Philippe Auguste in 1204 after having laid siege to Angers, which remained loyal to his nephew Arthur (comp. 'King John', I and II). The title of count or (after 1360) duke of Anjou was later reserved for connections of the crown of France; the last duke to have any real concern with the city was René (1409– 80), titular king of Naples and Provence, and a native of Angers. In 1470, Prince Edward, son of Henry VI and Marguerite d'Anjou (daughter of René), was betrothed to Anne Neville in the cathedral.

Its university, founded in 1364, was suppressed at the Revolution, and the military academy (among whose pupils were Chatham and, in 1786, Wellington) was removed to Saumur. For a few months in 1793 it was in the hands of the Vendeans; the Terror claimed 200 victims here the following year. In 1801 its population was 33,000. In 1944 it was bombed, causing serious damage, particularly near the station.

Among Angevins are Marbode (1035– 1123), the latin poet; Jean Bodin (1530– 96), the political philosopher; Gilles Ménage (1613– 92), the scholar and philologist Eugène Chevreul (1786– 1889), and Louis-Joseph Proust (1754– 1826), chemists; the sculptor Pierre-Jean David d'Angers (1788– 1856); the artist J.-E. Lenepveu (1819– 98); René Bazin (1853– 1932), the novelist; and the composer Henri Dutilleux (1916–   ).

By far the most imposing building in Angers is the **Castle*, ◊ entered by a drawbridge on its N.E. side, from the Bout-du-Monde. Completed in 1238, this irregular pentagon is flanked by 17 large drum-towers of alternating bands of stone and slate rising sheer from the rock, most of them razed to the level of the curtain-wall by Henri III in 1589. After many years of use as barracks, it was well-restored in the 1950s. The moat, 30m wide and 11m deep, was hewn out of the rock in the late 15C.

The castle contains an outstanding *Museum of Tapestries, dispersed in three buildings, including a low gallery constructed to exhibit the unique *Apocalypse Tapestries, a series of 70 (originally 90) scenes completed in 1380 by Nicolas Bataille (from the cartoons of Henequin de Bruges) for Louis I d'Anjou, brother of Charles V.—Adjoining is the Petit-Château, the gatehouse of a vanished residential palace, abutting which is the early-15C chapel with an Angevin vault. Tapestries displayed here include the Story of St Martin (1460); three Passion Scenes (c. 1500); and Angels with Instruments of the Passion on a background of foliage, etc. (1532).

To the E., beyond gardens, is a range of buildings comprising the Logis du Gouverneur and du Roi, in which, among 16-17C tapestries, are the Stories of St Maurille (1616) and of St Saturninus (1527 and 1649), some beautiful 'verdures' of the 16-18C; the *Concert Champêtre' from the series 'La Dame á la Licorne' (1530), and one of the 'Penthesilia' series (c. 1500).

To the W., and S. of the Pont de la Basse-Chaîne (the successor of a bridge which collapsed in 1850 causing the death of over 200 troops) is a typical 16C Angevin 'logis', known as the Château du Roi de Pologne, now surrounded by lawns, which have replaced an area of derelict old houses between the castle and river.—Uphill is the restored 13-15C Chapelle de l'Esvière, relic of a vanished priory.

Opposite the castle entrance, the Rue Donadieu-du-Puycharric (on the lower side of which are remains of the 3C town wall) leads through an old quarter towards the W. front of the **Cathedral**, from which a gentle but long flight of steps.—the *Montée St-Maurice*—descends to the river. In spite of its unsatisfactory proportions externally, it is an interesting example of late 12th and early 13C architecture.

The 12C doorway in the unusually tall W. front is flanked by four statues, and in the tympanum is Christ surrounded by the symbols of the Evangelists, retaining

traces of their original polychrome, above which is an arcade. The central tower
of the three, an incongruous Renaissance addition of 1540, is surmounted by a
cupola and lantern, and is embellished by eight grotesque statues representing
St Maurice and his fellow martyrs in 16C military costume, which are attrib. to
the Angevin sculptors Jean Giffard and Antoine Desmarais. The slender lateral
towers, of which the N. is 65m high, and the S., 69m, end in tapering stone spires,
restored in 1845.

The well-lit *interior* (91m long, 16m wide, and 26m high) is severe but impressive. The vaults are stilted throughout to give the appearance of domed
bays. The aisleless nave contains a stoup in *verde antico* presented by King
René. The organ, restored c. 1750, is supported by four telamons. Much of the
stained-glass in the windows is contemporary with the building, while the mid
15C rose-windows in the transepts are the work of André Robin, a local craftsman. Standing forlornly behind the altar (1699; canopy of 1757) is a statue of St
Cecilia, by David d'Angers. The *Treasury* ◊ may be visited, and also the adjacent
12C *Salle Synodale* of the *Ancien Évêché*.

Behind the apse is the *Pl. Ste-Croix*, with the 15C *Maison
d'Adam.—The Rue St-Aubin leads S.E., off which a lane turns r. to
the *Logis Barrault* (c. 1487), built by Olivier Barrault, treasurer of
Brittany, and occupied by Marie de Médicis in 1620, and later governors of Anjou, and now housing the **Musée des Beaux-Arts**.

Most of the GROUND FLOOR is devoted to *David d'Angers*, and displays some
of his original sculptures (including a Crucifixion previously in the cathedral),
drawings, and a series of plaques; also a collection of casts of his works, and some
that belonged to him (Lemoyne, Houdon, etc.).—FIRST FLOOR: Medieval antiquities, including good panelling and an imposing lectern; two Nottingham
alabasters; a 16C *Chest, carved with the Dance of Death; five crozier-heads
containing 12-13C Limoges enamels; a late 12C bronze crucifix; a 'Lorraine' or
'Anjou' cross covered with gilt copper and gems; an enamelled pyx; 12C processional cross of repoussé copper over wood; an 11C Virgin in Majesty; the terracotta 'Vierge du Tremblay' (16C); a 12C portrait-head; a late 14C Italian
wooden box inlaid with bone and ivory; and a Madonna and Child by *Sassetta*.

Among the paintings on the SECOND FLOOR are: *Catena*, Male portrait;
anon. 15C Portrait of Agnés Sorel; *anon. French* Adoration of the Magi (1539;
painted for the abbey of Ronceray); *A. Storck*, Seascape; *G.-B. Tiepolo*, Design for
a ceiling; *Greuze*, Mme de Porcin; *Gérard*, Laréveillère-Lépeaux, the revolutionary; *Géricault*, Sketch for the 'Raft of the Medusa'; *Clarkson Stanfield*, View
of Angers; *Ingres*, Studies of Heads; Portraits by *J.-E. Lenepveu*; and representative works by *Boucher, Fragonard, Pater, Lancret*, et al.

To the E. is the *Tour St-Aubin*, 55m high, the belfry of a Benedictine
abbey, to the r. of which the *Préfecture* occupies the restored abbey
buildings, which date in part from the mid 12C, and were completed
in the 16C, to which a facade was added in 1850. On the l. of its courtyard a gallery preserves a Romanesque door and an *Arcade* with a
central doorway of the 12C decorated with curious carvings and
paintings.

Opposite the entrance, the Rue St-Martin leads N., off which is *St
Martin (apply at entrance on r.), of which the late 12C choir and lady-
chapel, and a Carolingian lantern-tower transformed in the 11C into
a belfry, remain; note the alternating brick and stone voussoirs at
the crossing.

Continuing downhill, the *Pl. du Ralliement* is soon reached, with
the *Théâtre*, rebuilt in 1869 after a fire.—From the far corner, the
Rue Lenepveu leads N. past (l.) the *Logis Pincé* (1530; by Jean de
l'Espine), poorly restored in the 19C, containing a miscellaneous collection of art and archaeology (including an Iron Age griffin's head
found in the Loire), drawings, Japanese prints, etc.

The streets to the N. preserve several old houses, such as that on

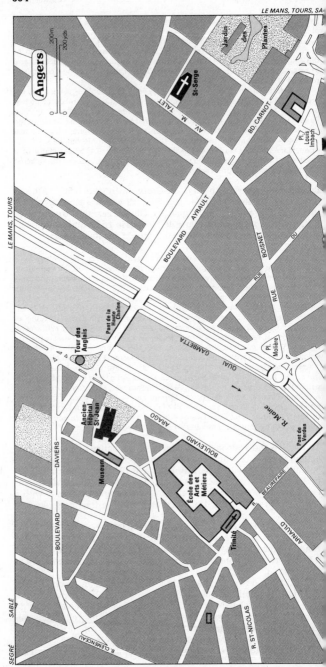

Angers

200m
200yds

Jardin des Plantes

St-Serge

AV. M. TALET

BD. CARNOT

Pl. Louis Imbach

N

LE MANS, TOURS

BOULEVARD AYRAULT

RUE BOISNET

RUE DU

Pont de la Haute Chaîne

Tour des Anglais

QUAI GAMBETTA

Pl. Molière

R. Maine

Pont de Verdun

BOULEVARD DAVIERS

BOULEVARD ARAGO

Ancien-Hôpital St-Jean

Museum

École des Arts et Métiers

BOULEVARD BEAUREPAIRE

R. ARNAULD

Trinité

BOULEVARD

SABLÉ

SEGRÉ

B CLEMENCEAU

R. ST-NICOLAS

the corner of the Rue du Mail, the next cross street, which leads uphill parallel to the Rue David, at No. 38 in which the sculptor was born; opposite is the *Hôtel de Chemellier* (1785). These streets approach the Blvd Bessonneau, in which the *Hôtel de Ville*, in the former *Collége d'Anjou* (1691) faces the pleasant *Jardin du Mail*, while the adjacent *Pl. du Gén. Leclerc* is flanked by the *Palais de Justice* (1883).

Bearing l. at the *Pl. du Pélican*, we follow the Blvd Carnot, passing (r.) the *Jardin des Plantes*, enclosing disused *St-Samson*, with a Romanesque doorway. To the l. are the buildings of the old *Court of Appeal* on its rock foundations, the main entrance to which is in the *Pl. Paul-Imbach*.—The Rue Boreau (r.) leads to **St-Serge**, retaining a beautiful 12C *Choir in the best Angevin style, its 15C nave containing 16C glass.

Some minutes' walk downhill brings one to the *Pont de la Haute-Chaine*, to the r. of which on the far bank is the 13C *Tour des Anglais*. To the l. is the **Hôtel-Dieu** or *Hôpital St-Jean*, founded by Henry II in 1175 and used as a hospital until 1865. The *Salle des Malades* (before 1181), an imposing three-aisled hall of eight bays, is remarkable for its bold proportions, the elegance of its pillars, and the graceful design of its vaulting. It now accommodates ten large symbolic Aubusson tapestries (1957–66) known as 'Le Chant du Monde' by Jean Lurçat (1892–1966). At the far end is the entrance to the *Chapel* and *Cloister*, two sides of which date from c. 1185, to which a third was added by Jean de l'Éspine in 1549.

A lane behind climbs uphill past (r.) a huge three-aisled *Tithe Barn* of unusually elaborate design, altered in the 16C, and restored in 1922; its vaulted cellars contain old wine-presses, etc. —To the l. lie the extensive buildings of the former *Abbaye de Ronceray*, founded by Fulk Nerra, and now partly occupied by the École des Arts et Métiers.—To the W. the Rue de l'Hommeau, preserving two or three 16C houses, leads S. to the Blvd Descazeaux, in which No. 23 is the early Renaissance *Hôtel des Pénitentes*; the adjoining hospice was originally the abbey of *St-Nicolas*. Two 16C houses are preserved in the *Pl. de la Laiterie*, further downhill, flanked to the E. by **La Trinité**, which is united to the dilapidated 11C *Tower* of the abbey church of Ronceray. It is a restored 12C edifice, with a handsome tower by Jean de l'Éspine (1540 on a Romanesque base), and unusual nave-vault. Beside the spiral Renaissance organ-stair, steps descend to the *Crypt*, containing a bronze Virgin (?11C).

Hence the Rue Beaurepaire crosses the low-lying *Quartier de la Doutre* to the *Pont de Verdun*; from the far bank the narrow old Rue Baudière, passing a 16C fountain and (r.) a 13C tower, ascends to regain the Pl. Ste-Croix (by the cathedral apse), from which the Rue Toussaint leads S.W. past 17C abbey buildings, some being restored for secular purposes, to the *Pl. Président-Kennedy*, adjacent to the castle.

For roads from Angers to **Le Mans**, and *Laval* and **Caen**, see Rte 37, and 34 respectively, in reverse; to **Poitiers**, Rte 60.

The N23 leads W., from which, after 8km the D963 forks N.W. via *Candé*, to (63km) *Châteaubriant*; see Rte 39.

8.5km. To the l. is the **Château de Serrant**, a large moated building of three wings with two domed towers, once the property of Anthony Walsh, Comte de Serrant (1702–63), an Irish merchant who furnished Prince Charles Edward with ships for his descent upon

Scotland in 1745; a painting in the library shows the two in conversation. Other rooms contain good tapestries, and in the chapel, by Hardouin-Mansart, is the tomb of the Marquis de Vaubrun (d. 1675), by Coysevox.

We traverse (1.5km) *St-Georges-sur-Loire*, its 17C church once the chapel of an abbey, and 7.5km beyond, *Champtocé*, with ruins of a 13-15C castle.—To the l. at 4.5km lies the riverside village of *In-grandes*, with several 16C houses.—9km. *Varades*; on the opposite bank lies *St-Florent-le-Vieil*; see Rte 59B.

12km. **Ancenis**, with remains of a 15-17C castle, and a statue of Joachim du Bellay (1524–60), a member of the Pléïade, who was in fact born at *Liré*, 3km S., on the far bank of the Loire.—9km. To the l. is *Oudon*. dominated by a handsome late 15C octagonal keep.—At the *Château de la Contrie*, some 6km N., beyond the motorway, near *Couffé*, was born the Vendean leader François Charette (1763–96).—6km. A by-road (l.) leads to the imposing château of *Clermont-sur-Loire* (1631) on a cliff above the river.—7km. An avenue (r.) leads to the *Château de la Seilleraye*, from which Mme de Sévigné dated several letters in 1675 and 1680; it was rebuilt in the 17C on the plans of François Mansart.

14km. **Nantes**; see Rte 61.

B. Via the South Bank of the Loire

151km (94 miles; including crossing to Angers and back). D751.
12km **Cunault**—27.5km *Érigné*. **Angers** lies 8km N.—43km. *St-Florent-le-Vieil*—21.5km *Champtoceaux*—31km. **Nantes**.

Maps: IGN 25, 24, or 106. M 232.

For **Saumur** itself, see Rte 60B.—2km. *St-Hilaire-St-Florent*, with remains of the abbey of *St-Florent-le-Jeune* (see below), notably the church porch and crypt, both 12C; the rest was demolished in 1803. The two parish churches are of slight interest.—On the far bank of the Loire is the *Château de Boumois*, birthplace of Adm. Dupetit-Thouars (1760–98).—6.5km. *Chênehutte*, with a 12C church with a good portal and tower, is traversed, and 2km beyond, *Trèves-Cunault*, with another church of the same date, containing a contemporary porphyry stoup and the tomb of Robert Le Masson (d. 1443); also a keep.

1.5km. **Cunault**, where the 11-13C *Church, its tower surmounted by a short spire, is one of the most remarkable buildings in Anjou. Steps descend into the nave, 72m long, with a striking series of sculptured *capitals*, a 12C marble stoup, 15C murals, and in the S. apse, a 13C carved wood *shrine*.

2.5km. *Gennes*, with two interesting churches incorporating fragments of ancient brickwork (earlier than the 10C), of which the finer is *St-Eusèbe* (11-15C), on the hill, damaged in 1940; *St-Valère* retains a good timbered porch.—About 1km S. is the **Dolmen de la Madeleine*.—The main road continues N.W., at 10km passing S. of the château of *Montsabert*, with three round towers and a square keep.

The riverside road skirts the villages of *Le Thoureil*, with a church of interest; *St-Maur*, with remains of the first Benedictine abbey in France, suppressed at the Revolution, and briefly reoccupied in the 1890s; and *St-Remy-la-Varenne*, with an 11-12C church.

At 15km we meet the road junction from which an easy approach by a new bridge turns N. to (11km) **Angers**; see Rte 59A.

Immediately to the W. is *Érigné*, 1.5km S. of the old town of **Les Ponts-de-Cé**, on an island between the Louet and Loire, which is here spanned by a series of bridges, damaged by demolitions in 1944. Restored *St-Aubin* dates from the 12th and 16Cs; a pentagonal keep survives of a castle frequently occupied by King René.

The Gallic chieftain Dumnacus is said to have been defeated by the Romans in 51 B.C. while crossing the river here. It was always a position of military importance, which often changed hands during the Middle Ages. The facile expulsion of the partisans of Marie de Médicis by the troops of Louis XIII in 1620 is known in French history as the 'Drôlerie des Ponts-de-Cé'.

From Érigné the D751 turns S.W. to (12km) *Rochefort-sur-Loire*, an old town noted for its white wines, with ruins of a feudal castle.

On an island 2.5km N. lies *Béhuard*, where a curious church, on two levels, was built by Louis XI, while on the N. bank of the Loire, the church at *Savennières* dates in part from the 9C, just beyond which are the remains of *La Roche-aux-Moines*, the castle where Philippe Auguste finally defeated King John in 1204.

The road now ascends the so-called *Corniche Angevine*, commanding a splendid view over the Loire; in the valley 3km S. are the 15C *Manoir de la Basse-Guerche*, and the ruins of the 15C castle of *Haute-Guerche*, burnt down during the Vendean war. The Vendean leader Jacques Cathelineau (1759–93) was born and is buried at *Le Pin-en-Mauges*, 16km S.W. of (10km) *Chalonnes-sur-Loire*, which we next traverse, where the river, here divided into four branches, is crossed by a series of suspension bridges. Both churches at Chalonnes date from the 12C.

21km. **St-Florent-le-Vieil**, named after the abbey founded in the 4C by St Florence, was sacked by the Normans in 875, whose monks eventually, in 1025, settled at *St-Florent-le-Jeune*, near Saumur. The village is famous for its part in the Vendée rebellion, and in its church is the tomb (by David d'Angers) of Bonchamp, who died here after the bloody defeat sustained by his army at *Cholet* (17 Oct. 1793), and who, on the point of death, ordered the release of 5000 Republican prisoners.

6km. To the l. is the beautiful early Renaissance **Chapelle de la Bourgonnière*; 2km beyond which, at *Bouzillé*, we pass N. of the Louis-XIII *Château de la Mauvoisinière*, and, 4km further W., traverse *Liré*, with the scanty remains of the château in which Joachim du Bellay was born (cf. *Ancenis*).—9km. *Champtoceaux* was the site of the castle in which Marguerite de Clisson held prisoner Jean V of Brittany in 1424; the Promenade du Champalud, by the church, commands views over the valley.

31km. **Nantes**; see Rte 61.

C. Via Cholet and Clisson

128km (79 miles). D960. 17km *Doué-la Fontaine*—49km **Cholet**—D753 for 17km—N149. 16km **Clisson**—29km **Nantes**.

Maps: IGN 25, 26, or 106. M 67.

For the road to *Doué*, see Rte 58B.—21km. *Vihiers*, 3.5km beyond which we pass (r.) the elegant 15-16C *Château du Coudray-Montbault*, and a ruined priory church (mid 12C).

18km N.W. lies **Chemillé**, a cattle-market, which was the scene of the 'Grand Choc de Chemillé', when on 11 April 1793 the Vendeans defeated the Republicans. In the lower town is Romanesque *St-Pierre* (restored); 3km N.E. is the chapel of *La Sorinière*, containing remarkable 16C wall-paintings.—The main route may be regained 14.5km S.W., passing near the *Puy de la Garde*, which although only 210m high, commands extensive views.

The D960 continues W., after 6km passing (l.) the ruins of the château of *La Roche-des-Aubiers*, one of many in the area despoiled in 1793.—11km. *Nuaillé*, where the Vendean leader La Rochejaquelein was killed in 1794.

At *Maulévrier*, 12km S., a pyramid commemorates the gamekeeper Jean-Nicolas Stofflet (1751–96), leader of the first insurrection, who was taken prisoner in the neighbouring bocage.—Another leader of the revolt, Gigot d'Elbée, lived adjacent to *Beaupréau*, 19km N.W. of Cholet.

Cholet (56,500 Choletais), a flourishing modern town provided with by-passes, has been completely rebuilt since the 1790s, when it was three times sacked and burnt, although on ancient foundations (*Cauletum*; i.e., a cabbage-patch). It preserves the 13C base of a tower of *St-Pierre*, in the *Marché-aux-Moutons*, and part of a bridge over the Moine. It is still an important cattle market, and apart from the manufacture of shoes, it continues to produce linen goods, a survival of the old domestic weaving industry of the *Mauges* district.

10km S.W. lies *Mortagne-sur-Sèvre*, a picturesque village overlooking the river, with a ruined castle dating from the 14C: a 12C church, the S. aisle rebuilt in the 15C; and relics of a convent burnt in 1793.

At 17km W. of Cholet we turn N.W. at the crossroads of *La Colonne*, a monument commemorating the defeat of Kléber's army by the Vendeans in 1793.

3km S.W. is **Tiffauges**, with the extensive ruins of a feudal *Castle, the successor of a Gallo-Roman castrum, and the legendary scene of some of the more repugnant atrocities perpetrated by Gilles de Rais; its most prominent features are the square 12C keep, and cylindrical *Tour du Vidame* (15C).

2km. *Torfou*, 1km N.E. of which is a rocking-stone.—14km. **Clisson**, an old town at the confluence of the Moine and Sèvre, gave its name to a famous family, among whom were the Constable Olivier de Clisson (1336–1407). The Republican army sacked and set light to the place in 1794, but four years later it was rebuilt by the brothers Cacault with assistance of the architect Lemot of Lyon. The ruined *Castle*, dating in part from the 13C, but mostly rebuilt by François II of Brittany c. 1470, included four courtyards, in the last of which was a well (filled in; a pine-tree indicates the site) into which some 30 refugees were cast during the sack. Both rivers are crossed by old bridges, and near the castle is an old market-house. On the E. bank stands *La Trinité* (12-13C; restored).

7.5km. *Le Pallet*, noted for its white Muscadet wine, was the birthplace of Abélard (1079–1142), and—traditionally—of his son Astrolabe, 8km beyond which the road veers W.—3km N.E. is the Louis-XII *Château de Goulaine*, surrounded by vineyards.—13km. **Nantes**; see Rte 61.

60 Angers to Poitiers

A. Via Montreuil-Bellay and Loudun

132km (82 miles). D748. 18km *Brissac-Quincé*—D761. 23km *Doué-la-Fontaine*—12km *Montreuil-Bellay*—N147. 24km *Loudun*—27km *Mirabeau*—28km **Poitiers**.

Maps: IGN 25, 34, or 106. M 232.

From **Angers** (Rte 59A) we may follow the old road through *Les-Ponts-de-Cé* (see Rte 59B) or cross the Loire by the new bridge further E., shortly bearing l. to (18km) *Brissac-Quincé*, famous for its *Castle, the seat of the ducal family of Brissac since 1611.

Of the feudal fortress built for the Brézé family on 11C foundations, only the 14C towers survive, the rest dating from the reconstruction carried out by Jacques d'Angluze in 1620 for the opportunist Marshal Charles de Cossé (d. 1621), the first duke, who opened the gates of Paris to Henri IV in 1594. Notable are the main front with the five classic orders superimposed; and within, the carved wooden ceilings, furniture, and tapestries, the family portrait gallery, and chapel, with a statue by David d'Angers.

The road continues S.E., roughly parallel to the *Côteaux du Layon*, a range of hills to the W. extending from beyond *Beaulieu-sur-Layon*, surrounded by vineyards, to Doué.—At 11.5km a road leads 7.5km S.W. to *Martigné-Briand*, with conspicuous ruins of a 16C castle burnt in 1793, when the Vendeans under Bonchamp and La Rochejaquelein were defeated near by.

11.5km. *Doué-la-Fontaine* (see Rte 58B), 6km beyond which we pass 2km S. of the ruined Tironensian abbey of *Asnières*, preserving the choir and transepts of a beautiful 12-13C church, the abbot's chapel (14C), and later dependencies, including a 17C dovecot, etc.

6km. **Montreuil-Bellay**, a picturesque old town approached by an old bridge over the Thouet, still partly surrounded by 13C walls, and retaining three town gates, among them the *Porte St-Jean* (S.W.). The *Castle, dry-moated on three sides, is one of the finest in Anjou.

Within the outer enceinte are three ranges of buildings: the 13C *Châtelet* or *Château Vieux*, through which we enter; the 15C *Château Neuf*, incorporating an octagonal staircase-turret with a remarkable heraldic keystone; and the *Petit Château* (also 15C), which includes four separate dwellings, each with its own stair. These were the houses of the canons who served the adjoining castle-chapel, which is now the parish church. The kitchen recalls that at Fontevraud. Note the two towers near the entrance, surmounted by gabled dormer windows (lucernes à gables); the little oratory decorated with 15C frescoes is also of interest.

On the river bank below the castle are the 12-13C ruins of *St-Pierre*, and other dependencies of a Benedictine priory.

7.5km. due W. is *Le Puy-Notre-Dame*, a hilltop village with several 16C houses, and 13C priory-church with a 15C steeple. Abutting its S. side are four Gothic chambers, one retaining remarkable vaulting. It contains 16C stalls, and one of several 'Girdles of the Virgin' extant, brought back from the Holy Land by credulous Crusaders; this particular relic, on account of its professed power of alleviating the pains of childbirth, was taken with great ceremony to Anne of Austria before the birth of Louis XIV.

The N147 leads S.E., after 11km passing near a series of dolmens,

before entering (13km) **Loudun** (8400 Loudunois), a decayed old
town surrounded by boulevards marking its original enceinte, which
is said to have contained a population of 20,000 in the Middle Ages;
it still retains many quaint old houses and 17-18C mansions in its narrow streets.

The majority of its inhabitants had embraced the reformed faith, and it never
recovered from the blow dealt to its prosperity by the revocation of the Edict of
Nantes. Some fifty years earlier, in 1634, and the curé Urbain Grandier was here
burnt alive on a charge of subjecting some Ursuline nuns to demoniac posses-
sion, as described in Huxley's 'The Devils of Loudun'. It was the birthplace of
Scévole de Sainte-Marthe (1536–1623), a poet praised by Ronsard; and
Théophraste Renaudot (1586–1653), the physician who in 1631 founded the
'Gazette de France', the first newspaper printed in France.

In the town centre, near the *Hôtel de Ville*, is the restored Gothic
church of *St-Pierre-du-Marché*, with a 15C steeple and Renaissance
portal. To the S. is the *Pl. Ste-Croix*, with arcaded houses; the market-
hall occupied the former 11C church, although its choir is
intact.—To the W. of the Hôtel de Ville is the keep of the castle
demolished by Richelieu (view), whence one may descend W. to *St-
Hilaire-du-Martray*, with a row of chapels united to form an aisle. Adjoining is the surviving relic of Loudun's walls, the *Porte du Martray*.

For *Richelieu*, 19km due E., and *Oiron*, 14.5km W., see Rtes 57A and B, respectively.

The N147 continues S., at 5.5km passing 2km E. of the imposing
ruins of a moated castle at *St-Cassien*, before traversing the *Forêt des
Cévolles*, to approach (21.5km) *Mirebeau*, with traces of its walls and
castle, built on a limestone rock riddles with subterranean dwellings.
Here Arthur of Brittany was taken prisoner by King John in 1202,
shortly after to disappear from human ken at Rouen.

At 13km we by-pass *Neuville-de-Poitou*, and 7km beyond (l.) the
château of *Auxances* (1474) overlooking the river, and shortly after
pass below the A10 to enter (8km) **Poitiers**; see Rte 56.

B.   Via Saumur and Fontevraud

137km (85 miles). D952. 31km *Les Rosiers*—15km **Saumur**
(preferably approached by crossing the Loire at Les Rosiers, and
following the l. bank)—D947. 11km *Montsoreau* (1.5km beyond
which is *Candes*)—D147. 4.5km **Fontevraud**—20.5km *Loudun*
—N147. 27km *Mirabeau*—28km **Poitiers.**

Maps: IGN 25, 34, or 106. M 232.

At 10km we reach the Loire, and skirt its r. embankment to (21km)
Les Rosiers, where the Renaissance steeple is sometimes ascribed to
Jean de l'Éspine, and here cross the river to *Gennes*; for the road
hence via *Cunault* to *Saumur*, see Rte 58B, in reverse.

SAUMUR (34,000 Saumurois) is an interesting old town, well sited
on a tongue of land between the Loire and the Thouet, and overlooked by the imposing mass of its castle, which has long commanded the
bridgehead here. The surrounding district is noted for its white
wines.

It came into possession of Henry II as part of the dowry of Eleanor of Aquitaine,
but remained in French hands after its capture by Philippe Auguste. The gover-

nor of the town under Henri IV was Duplessis-Mornay, the 'Huguenot Pope', when it became a headquarters of Protestantism, and Andrew Marvell was among the many English here in 1656. It was ruined by the revocation of the Edict of Nantes in 1685. In June 1793 La Rochejaquelein's Vendeans captured the place, but it was regained by Republican troops within three weeks.

In 1763 the riding-school of the Carabiniers de Monsieur was established here, to which the Cavalry School owes its origin, which brought back some measure of prosperity. On 19-21 June 1940 its cadets held up a German force more than ten times its strength, at the cost of heavy casualties and much damage to the town. Since the war the cavalry have largely given way to the 'Armée Blindée'.

It is a curious fact that Saumur, the stronghold of Protestantism, should have practically a monopoly in France in the (declining) manufacture of rosaries, together with Ambert, in the Forez.

Among natives are the learned Mme Dacier (1651–1720), translator of Homer; and the financier Joseph Foullon (1715–89), whose cynical remark: 'if the people cannot find bread, let them eat hay', caused him not merely to swallow his words, but to be hung by the Paris mob with a handful of hay in his mouth.

The centre of animation is the *Pl. de la Bilange*, just S. of the *Pont Cessart*. On the quay behind the *Théâtre* is the turreted **Hôtel de Ville* (partly 16C), which defended an earlier bridgehead, from the courtyard of which 13C *St-Jean* may be visited.

On the island suburb opposite is the restored *Maison de la Reine de Sicile*, the late Gothic manor of Yolande of Aragón, queen of Louis II of Anjou and the Two Sicilies, and mother of King René.

A turning further E. of the town hall leads shortly to *St-Pierre*, partly 12C, with a good Romanesque door in its S. transept; the N. porch is Renaissance, and the W. front dates from 1674. The interior likewise contains features of Renaissance decoration, 15C choir-stalls, and 16C tapestries.

In streets to the S.W. are several 15-16C houses, and at the far end of the Rue des Païnes, the 16C *Tour Grainetière*, part of the ramparts.

Hence the Rue du Petit-Mail and Av. du Dr Peton ascend to the **Castle*, an impressive battlemented fortress with four angle towers, displaying the transition from the purely military to the more domestic architecture of the Renaissance. Although probably founded in the 10C, no part is older than the 13C. It illustrates September in the 'Très Riches Heures' of the Duc de Berri. After a century of use as a powder-magazine and barracks, the castle was acquired by the municipality in 1906, and houses the town museums.

A turreted barbican provides access to the central courtyard, in which is a well 50m deep. The N.W. wing no longer exists; the S.W. wing has been restored. A spiral stair in the N.W. wing ascends to the **Musée**, displaying several curious tapestries (of hairy men; children gardening, etc.); Limoges enamels; a priest at prayer (alabaster; 14C); St Catherine (oak), and other carved groups; ecclesiastical vestments; furniture, etc. The good *Ceramic collection*, mainly Rouen ware, also included examples from Nevers, Mennesy, Moustiers, Marseille, Sceaux, and Strasbourg.—The SECOND FLOOR is devoted to an *Equestrian Museum*, with all manner of harness, bits, stirrups, etc., together with the skeleton of 'Flying Fox', winner of the Derby in 1899, and English sporting prints.

Regaining the Av. du Dr Peton, we turn l. along the Rue Duruy to **N.-D.-de-Nantilly**, a fine 12C building with a large Flamboyant S. aisle added by Louis XI. The five barrel-vaulted bays of the nave are supported by lofty pillars with historiated capitals.

On the 2nd pillar on the S. is a Renaissance relief of St John preaching in the desert; on the 3rd is the epitaph composed by King

René for his nurse; on the 4th is an enamelled and damascened 13C crozier found in the tomb of Gilles de Tyr, privy seal to Louis IX.—In the S. aisle, the keystone displays the arms of Louis XI and his wife, Margaret of Scotland. The transepts date from the 15C.

Just N.W. of the central Place is *St-Nicolas*, with a 13C nave.—Further W., in the Rue Beaurepaire, are the buildings of the *Cavalry School* (1768), N. of which is a *Tank Museum*.

Some 1.5km S., beyond the Thouet, are a dolmen, a menhir, and an '*allée couverte*' known as the 'Dolmen de Bagneux'.

For roads hence to *Thouars* and *Parthenay*, and to *Fontenay-le-Comte*, see Rtes 58A and B, respectively; for *Cholet*, Rte 59C.

On quitting Saumur, we pass on its E. outskirts, *N.-D.-des-Ardilliers* (1534), enlarged by Richelieu, and with a dome added by Mme de Montespan in 1695.—For the road to *Montsoreau*, where we turn S., and *Candes*, see Rte 57A.

  15.5km. **Fontevraud** (also spelt *Fontevrault*), a village famous for its ***Abbey**, ◇ the burial-place of the early Plantagenet kings of England.

In 1099 Robert d'Arbrissel founded two communities, one for men and one for women, and at his death this mixed community—which as such, provided scope for scandal—was ruled by Pétronille de Chemillé, the first of a long line of abbesses. During the English occupation of Anjou it was used as a royal burial-place, and subsequently the title of abbess was sought after by ladies of the highest rank, until after 700 years of prosperity, it fell on evil days. In 1793 the monks' convent was largely destroyed, and in 1804 the remaining dependencies were converted into a penitentiary, which it continued to be until 1963; indeed it is still partially a prison, the inmates commendably occupying themselves with the continuing restoration of the abbey, work on which started in 1910.

Once a group is formed, visitors are conducted to the *Church, the tower of which dates from the 13C; the upper part of the facade is a 15C reconstruction. Its magnificent interior proportions are well seen owing to the absence of furniture. Consecrated in 1119, it was altered in 1160, when the aisleless nave—which later served as a dormitory for the convicts, being divided into four floors by the Philistine Republican authorities—was roofed with four domes on pendentives, supported by massive pillars with historiated capitals, while a fifth dome, without pendentives, covered the crossing. The early-13C choir and ambulatory are particularly impressive.

In the S. transept lie the four *Statues from the Plantagenet tombs (spoilt by later painting), placed on plinths. Three of them are of stone; the largest, and the most ancient effigy of any English king, is that of *Henry II* (1133–39). Beside it are effigies of his wife, *Eleanor of Aquitaine* (1122–1204), and their son *Richard I* ('Coeur-de-Lion'; 1157–99). The fourth statue (of wood) represents *Isabelle d'Angoulême* (d. 1246), wife of King John, who ended her days as a nun here. The remains of the first three were only discovered in 1910, in a vault against the N.W. pier of the crossing, which bears traces of baroque decoration.

An adjacent door leads to the *Great Cloister*, with three mid 16C walks; that on the N. side is slightly earlier, and displays the cyphers of Louise and Renée de Bourbon. The *Chapter-house* has an overcharged doorway and mutilated 16C wall-paintings, to which later portraits of abbesses were added. Off the S. walk opens the 16C *Refectory* (like the nave divided into floors; under restoration); the cloister of *St-Benoît* is likewise under restoration, as is *St-Lazare*, further S.

Abutting the refectory is the pyramidal ***Tour d'Évrault** (early 12C), in fact the *Kitchen*, with its numerous chimneys, which served the several monastic

The 12C Tour d'Évrault, or kitchen-tower at Fontevraud

houses on the site. Octagonal in plan, and in appearance similar to that at Glastonbury, it had an apse opening off each side (three have disappeared), and becomes a square higher up, culminating in a smaller lantern-crowned octagon.—Before leaving one should walk round to the N. side of the church for the exterior view.

The *Parish Church*, partly surrounded by wooden galleries on clumsy pillars, has a fine Angevin vault and chancel arch, and a gilded altar of 1621 formerly in the abbey church.

10km. *Bournand*, its church with a Romanesque facade, lies 1km l., 3km N.E. of which is the *'allée couverte'* of *Pierre-Folle*—6km. We pass, 2km to the E. the ruined *Château de la Tour du Bois Gourmand*, on approaching *Loudun*, for which, and the road beyond, see Rte 60A.

61 Nantes

NANTES (247,000 Nantais; 73,900 in 1801; 133,000 in 1901), préfecture of the *Loire-Atlantique*, is a thriving industrial city and commercial port at the confluence of the Erdre and Loire, which is navigable to this point by large vessels. Nantes was originally situated on the l. bank of the Erdre, but spread to the r. bank in the 18C; during the 19C and since, its extensive suburbs covered both banks of the Loire, a branch of which, forming the *Île Feydeau* and *Île de la Gloriette*, has recently been filled in. Other 'improvements' such as diverting the Erdre into a subterranean canal beneath the Cours St-André and St-Pierre, have transformed the town, in which much rebuilding has taken place since the war. It has a cathedral and castle among several other buildings of interest, and its museums contain valuable collections which deserve a visit, while its Muscadet and Gros Plant should be sampled.

Cordovicum, the capital of the Gallic *Namnetes*, was the probable predecessor of the Roman *Portus Namnetum*, evangelised in the 3C by St Clair, where SS Donatian and Rogatian were later martyred. It was in continual dispute between Bretons and Normans until in 937 Alain Barbe-Torte (Wrybeard) established Breton supremacy. Pierre de Dreux, created Duc de Bretagne by Philippe Auguste, made Nantes his capital, and in 1214 defended it against King John. Jean IV de Montfort died here in 1399, and Jean V in 1442.

Gilles de Rais, or Retz, a Marshal of France (and by some considered the original of 'Bluebeard'), and the debaucher and murderer of some 100 boys, was hanged and burned here in 1440 after confessing his crimes, Duc François II (d. 1488) was a great benefactor of the town; his daughter Anne (who married Charles VIII of France) was born here in 1477. Mercoeur, governor from 1582, held the castle for the Catholic League, but the town opened its gates to Henri IV in 1598, who signed here the famous *Edict of Nantes*, which until its contemptible revocation by Louis XIV in 1685, was the charter of Huguenot liberties.

The shipowners (*armateurs*) and corsairs of Nantes grew wealthy in the 18C, largely through the slave trade carried on with the West Indies. It welcomed the Revolution, but did not escape the excesses of the Terror, when Carrier, sent here in 1793 by the Committee of Public Safety, instituted the macabre 'Noyades' or 'Republican marriages', in which the victims, stripped naked and bound in pairs, were crowded into barges that were then scuttled in mid river.

Charette, the Vendean leader, was executed in the Pl. Viarme in 1796. In 1832 the Duchesse de Berri (1798– 1870) was arrested here after a foolish attempt to stir up another rising in the Vendée against Louis-Philippe. Much damage was caused by air raids during 1943– 44, and again by German demolitions prior to the entry of American troops on 12 Aug. 1944.

Among Nantais were Charles Errard (1606– 89), joint founder with Colbert of the French Academy in Rome; Germain Boffrand (1667– 1754), and Mathurin Crucy (1749– 1826), architects; Gén. Cambronne (1770– 1842), famous for his defiant 'Mot'; Gén. de Lamoricière (1806– 65), who captured Abd-el-Kader in 1847; Jules Verne (1828– 1905); Pierre Waldeck-Rousseau (1846– 1904), the statesman; and Aristide Briand (1862– 1932).

John Knox, taken prisoner by the French at the surrender of St Andrew's castle in 1547, was held at Nantes as a galley slave for some months. Turner was painting here in 1828.

A main thoroughfare follows the line of the filled-in branch of the Loire, and is dominated to the N. by the ***Castle**, overlooking the Cours John-Kennedy and *Pl. de la Duchesse-Anne*. This deeply moated stronghold, founded in the 13C, was rebuilt on its present plan by Duc Françoise II c. 1465; additions were made by Mercoeur in 1592. Much of the N. side was destroyed by the explosion of a magazine in 1800. The entrance front is to the W., where the *Tour* *des Jacobins* and *Tours du-Pied-de-Biche* and *de-la-Boulangerie* together form a gatehouse.

This residence of Duc François and his daughter Anne has been visited by almost every French king since Louis XI. Mme de Sévigné stayed here in 1675. It was a prison for Fouquet in 1661, and (briefly) for the Duchess of Berri in 1832; the Card. de Retz escaped from it in 1654.

In the inner court is a *Well-head* surmounted by a ducal crown in hammered iron, adjacent to which is the *Tour de la Couronne-d'Or*, with elegant loggias and a good stair-vault; it communicates with the *Grand Gouvernement* (r.; above the castle entrance), built in the 16-17C, and the imposing *Grand Logis*, with late-Gothic dormers.

The former accommodates the ***Musée d'Art Populaire**, an important collection of Breton coifs and costumes, furniture—note the bed-cupboards (*Lit demi-clos*)—and utensils of all kinds, arranged topographically.

On the S. side is the Renaissance *Petit Gouvernement*, and to the N.E. (behind the Musée de Salorges, and better seen from the exterior), the *Tour du Fer-à-Cheval*, and some excavated fragments of the *Château de la Tour-Neuve*, the 13C fortress. The ***Musée de Salorges** concentrates on the naval and industrial history of Nantes, and contains an attractively displayed collection of ship models, a Chart of the Loire (1765), a huge Maquette of the town (1905), a good representative selection of the faïence de Croissic (16-17C), and a display of Nantes *toile de Jouy*, together with original printing-blocks, etc.

The Rue Mathelin-Rodier (in which at No. 3, the *Maison de Guígny*, the Duchesse de Berri was found ignominiously concealed in a secret recess behind a third-floor fireplace) climbs N. to the *Pl. St-Pierre*, and the **Cathedral**. Begun in 1434 by Guillaume de Dommartin, and continued by Mathelin Rodier, it was not completed until 1893.

The *Choir*, part of this late building (from 1849) was damaged in 1944; on 28 Jan. 1972 it was more severely injured by fire. Outwardly it is undistinguished, with two rather stumpy W. towers, the decoration of which was never completed. The W. front has some badly weathered sculptures of the Last Judgement over the central portal.

More imposing is the *Interior*, with its shafts, unadorned by capitals, soaring directly to the vaulting, while a good triforium runs above the arches. The recently cleaned *Nave*, mainly 16C, retains some 15C works of art; note the stair to the l. of the entrance, the statues to either side of the main portal, and the graceful Flamboyant doorways at the ends of the aisles. The modern chandeliers are an unfortunate addition.

The transepts have been remodelled several times, and the crossing may be a survival of the 12C Romanesque predecessor of this building. Michel Colombe's *Tomb of Duc François II and his second wife, Marguerite de Foix, completed in 1507, is a masterpiece of French Renaissance sculpture. It was commissioned by their daughter, Anne, whose heart was for some time also contained in it, together with the ashes of the duke's first wife, Marguerite de Bretagne. Originally in a Carmelite church, it was moved here in 1817 after being violated during the Revolution, when the remains of the Constable de Richemont were enclosed in it.

The effigies rest on a black marble slab supported by angels, with a lion and greyhound at their feet; they are guarded by figures of Justice, Strength (in armour), Moderation (holding a bit), and Prudence (with the face of a young woman, with that of an old man looking in the reverse direction); in the upper row of niches are statuettes of apostles and saints, and in the lower. mourners.

Immediately S. of the cathedral, in the Impasse St-Laurent, is *La*

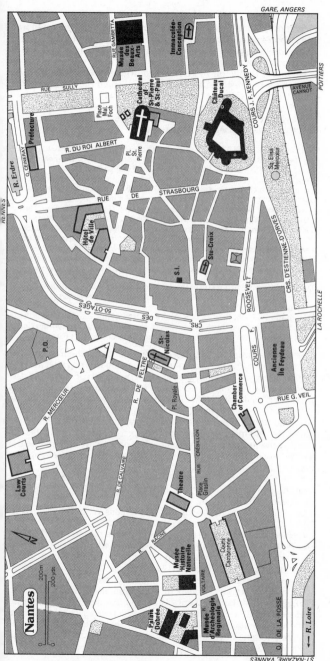

GARE, ANGERS

POITIERS

LA ROCHELLE

ST-NAZAIRE, VANNES

Immaculée-
Conception

Château
Ducal

Ste Elise
Mercœur

AVENUE
CARNOT

COURS J. F. KENNEDY

Musée
des
Beaux-
Arts

RUE GAMBETTA

RUE SULLY

Cathedral
of
St-Pierre
& St-Paul

Place
Mal.
Foch

Préfecture

Q. CEINERAY

R. DU ROI ALBERT

Pl.
St.
Pierre

RUE DE STRASBOURG

Hôtel
de Ville

Ste-Croix

S.I.

CRS. D'ESTIENNE D'ORVES

R. ERDRE

RENNES

P.O.

DES 50-OTAGES

CRS DES

St-
Nicolas

R. DE FELTRE

Pl. Royale

COURS F. ROOSEVELT

COURS F.

Ancienne
Ile Feydeau

RUE G. VEIL

R. MERCŒUR

Chamber
of
Commerce

Law
Courts

R. DE CALVAIRE

Theatre

RUE CRÉBILLON

Place
Graslin

R. RACINE

Cours
Cambronne

N

200 m
200 yds

Nantes

Musée
Histoire
Naturelle

Palais
Dobrée

Musée
d'Archéologie
Régionale

R. VOLTAIRE

Q. DE LA FOSSE

← R. Loire

Psallette, a 15C building housing a collection of religious art.—To the
N. stands the late-Gothic *Porte St-Pierre*, formerly incorporated into
the bishop's palace, and containing a small museum of local history;
in the adjoining gardens are remains of the *Gallo-Roman Wall*, and of
the baptistry of *St-Jean* (?11C).

Beyond is the *Pl. du Maréchal-Foch* (with a statue of Louis XVI),
flanked by two restored 18C mansions.—Behind the cathedral apse
is the tree-lined Cours St-Pierre and Rue Henri-IV, which descends to
the Pl. de la Duchesse-Anne. To the r. off this street (beyond the *Archives* in the 17C *Chapelle de l'Oratoire*), the Rue Clemenceau leads
shortly to the *Musée des Beaux-Arts.

Notable on the GROUND FLOOR are: *Sano di Pietro*, St Francis of Assisi receiv-
ing the stigmata; *Perugino*, SS Sebastian and Bernardin de Feltre; *Borgognone*,
Scenes from the life of St Benedict; *Bronzino*, Male portrait; *Moroni*, Contessa
Vertova.—FIRST FLOOR: among a somewhat miscellaneous collection, are
Daubigny, Landscape; *Prosper Barbot* (1798–1878), Breton Calvary, etc; *Elie
Delaunay* (1828–91), Portraits; *B. Koekkoek*, Skating scene; *Carle Vernet*, A
storm; *Lancret*, Dog-cart, and La Camargo dancing; *Georges de la Tour*, Hurdy-
gurdy player, Angel appearing to St Joseph, and The Denial of Peter; *Pierre
Claez*, Still life; *attrib. Govaert Flinck*, Girl with a bouquet; *Van der Meulen*, Siege
of Luxembourg; *Largillière*, Portrait of the Nantes 'armateur' Delaselle; *Guardi*,
Assembly of Venetian grandees, and Doge's banquet; *Hüber*, Voltaire at Ferney;
Courbet, Winnowing; *Ingres*, Mme de Sénonnes; and Landscapes by *Corot*,
Théodore Rousseau, and *Boudin*. Also a small collection of modern works.

The Rue Clemenceau goes on to the *Jardin des Plantes*, while in the parallel Rue
Malherbe (to the S.) is the church of the *Immaculée Conception* (1496), with
sculptured keystones.

From the Pl. Foch, the Cours St-André leads N. to the quays of the Erdre; a
l.-hand turning off the Cours passes the *Préfecture* in the old *Chambre des Comp-
tes* of 1777, whence the Rue Roi-Albert leads back to the Pl. St-Pierre.

The Rue Maréchal-Leclerc descends E. from the cathedral, crossing
the transverse Rue de Strasbourg, and passing (r.) the *Hôtel de Ville*
in the early 17C *Hôtel Derval*, with a portal of 1814. In the
neighbouring Rues de la Commune and St-Jean are the 17C *Hôtel
Rosmadec*, and 15C *Hôtel St-Aignan*.—Just beyond the Hôtel de
Ville, a lane leads l. to the *Pl. du Change*, with the S.I. accommodated
in an old house; there are several others, in the adjacent Rue de la
Barillerie, and in streets further S., the oldest quarter of Nantes. To
the E. is the *Pl. du Pilori* (also approached directly from the cathedral
by the Rue de Verdun). To the S. is 17C *Ste-Croix*, its tower containing the old town bell.

To the W. lies the Cours des 50-Otages (commemorating hostages
shot in 1941), built over the original course of the Erdre, and
dominated to the N.E. by the modern *Tour Bretagne*. From the far
side of this boulevard the Rue d'Orléans leads W. to the *Pl. Royale*,
laid out in 1790, but largely rebuilt since 1943, whence the Rue
Crébillon ascends past (l.) the arcaded *Passage Pommeraye* (1843) to
the *Pl. Graslin* (named after fermier-général who laid out this new
quarter of the town to Mathurin Crucy's plan in the 1780s). Crucy
likewise designed the **Théâtre** (1788), adorned with statues of eight
Muses—the ninth is at the Bourse. It much impressed Arthur Young,
who visited Nantes the year of its inauguration, who thought it
perhaps twice as large as Drury Lane, and five times as magnificent.

Hence the Rue Voltaire continues W., passing (r.) the *Natural
History Museum*, just beyond which is the *Musée Dobrée*, the
building designed by Viollet-le-Duc and opened in 1894 for Thomas
Dobrée (1820–95), who bequeathed his treasures to the city.

Among the principal items are the 13C cloisonné enamel Shrine of St Calminus, from Tulle; nine 15C Nottingham alabasters, evidently from one large altar-piece; a painted stone altar from Guenrouet; an illuminated MS of the 'Mémoires' of Philippe de Comines; a Flemish St Anne and the Virgin (15C); late 15C statues of SS Adrian and Matthew from the Église des Carmes; good examples of armour (including a Roman legionary's helmet), and a collection of carved beams, etc. from the old town.

On the FIRST FLOOR is the furniture collection, together with further paintings, including views of Nantes by *Antoine Henon* (c. 1720–89) and *Laubert Doomer* (1624–1700), and a plan of Bordeaux in tiles, dated 1756.—Rooms on the SECOND FLOOR are devoted to the Vendean Wars, and relics of the 'noyades' (see above), including buckles, etc. dredged from the Loire.—A subterranean gallery, with a collection of pewter, leads from the ground floor to an *Extension*. On the floors above are the archaeological collections: Gallo-Roman figurines, pottery, glass, jewellery, and metalwork, etc.

The separate *Manoir de Jean V* houses ethnological collections, including sections devoted to Egyptian and Etruscan art, and Greek pottery.

Immediately S.W. of the Pl. Graslin is the *Cours Cambronne*, designed by Crucy, lined with 18C houses, passing which, we may make our way downhill to the Allée de la Bourse; the neo-classical *Bourse*, likewise by Crucy, but rebuilt since its W. end was destroyed in 1944.

Hence the Quai de la Fosse leads W. along the river bank (here the Bras de la Madeleine), retaining several 18C houses of the Nantes 'armateurs' (including Nos 10, 17, and 86), towards the industrial suburb of *Chantenay*. A new bridge (1975) crosses to the *Île de la Prairie-au-Duc*, with its shipyards, etc., which is connected to the S. bank or Bras de Pirmil by the *Pont de Pirmil*, and further E., the *Pont Clemenceau*; between the two, on the far bank, stands *St-Jacques* (12-15C).

The Cours Franklin-Roosevelt, leading E. from the Bourse, passes (r.) the former *Île Feydeau*, retaining a number of mansions built between 1730 and 1760, to regain the *Castle*.

62 Nantes to La Rochelle

A. Via La Roche-sur-Yonne and Luçon

148km (92 miles). D937. 65km **La Roche-sur-Yonne**—D746. 32km **Luçon**—D949. 5km—N137. 46km **La Rochelle**.

Maps: IGN 32, 39, or 107. M 232, 233.

6km S. of **Nantes** (Rte 61), we fork r. and traverse the wooded *Bocage Vendéen*, at 25km by-passing *Rocheservière*, where the last Vendean rising of 1815 was crushed by Gén. Lamarque.—19km. *Belleville-sur-Vie*, where Charette shot 300 Republican prisoners in 1795 to avenge the Quiberon massacre; the following year he was wounded and captured at the château of *La Chabotterie*, 11km N.E.

13km. **La Roche-sur-Yonne** (48,200 Yonnais), préfecture of the *Vendée*, which apart from its importance as a road junction, is of very slight interest: little has changed since Murray designated it as 'about the dullest town in France', with its 'mesquin and meagre' houses.—In the central Pl. *Napoléon* is a bronze equestrian statue of the emperor; on its E. side stands a 'Classical' *Church*.

The small medieval town was almost destroyed by Republican troops in 1794, and a decade later, Napoleon, in an attempt to show his authority in the heart of the disaffected Vendée, laid out a new town on a regular plan, which was called *Napoléon* until rechristened *Bourbon-Vendée* at the Restoration; Napoleon III re-named it *Napoléon-Vendée*, and it was not until 1871 that it re-assumed its original name.

6km W. lie the ruins of the 13C abbey of *Fontenelles*, some 4km S.W. of which, at *Les Clouzeaux*, the Republican Gén. Haxo was defeated and killed by Charette's Vendeans in 1794. The N160 leads hence to *Les Sables-d'Olonne*, 36km from La Roche; see Rte 62B.

The D746 bears S.E. through (22km) *Mareuil-sur-Lay*, with a partly Romanesque church and a feudal keep.—10km. **Luçon** (9500 Luçonnais) retains its little *Cathedral*, replacing a 12C abbey church, the gable of which is preserved in the N. transept. The aisles and nave are 13C; the choir 14C, and the classical facade of c. 1700 is surmounted by an openwork spire, 85m high. The stalls and high altar date from the 18C; on the S. side is the so-called pulpit 'of Richelieu' (bishop here in 1607–24), with Renaissance paintings.—To the S., the *Bishop's Palace* encloses an Italianate 16C cloister; near the Hôtel de Ville is a house built for Richelieu in 1612, who converted it into a seminary.

LUÇON TO L'AIGUILLON-SUR-MER (21km). The D746 leads S. roughly parallel to a canal traversing the *Marais Poitevin*, much of it reclaimed from the sea in the 17C (cf. Rte 72), at 8km passing *Traize*, formerly an island, beyond which is a strange series of mounds formed of conglomerate oyster-shells, almost certainly deposited by man.—7km. *St-Michel-en-l'Herm* (i.e. 'in eremo', in the desert), with its whitewashed houses, occupies another islet. Adjacent to the buildings of the former *Abbey* (by Leduc de Toscane; 1700) are some 14C ruins, a reminder of the destruction of this 7C foundation by the Huguenots. An altar in the style of Michel Colombe survives in the parish church.—6km. *L'Aiguillon*, a small port at the mouth of the Lay, beyond which, on a narrow sand-bar, is the resort of *La Faute*. The *Anse d'Aiguillon*, a rather muddy bay to the S.E., is all that remains of the former *Gulf of Poitou*.

LUÇON TO LA ROCHELLE VIA THE D50 (41.5km). This minor road leads S. across the marshes to (20km) *Pont du Brault*, a swing bridge across the canalised *Sèvre Niortaise*, 2km beyond which we may turn r. by (7km) *Esnandes*, with a fortified 12th-15C *Church*. The village is the centre of mussel-fishing on this coast, shellfish being collected from rows of posts ('*bouchots*') in flat-bottomed boats ('*acons*'), an adaptation of a system said to have been introduced by a shipwrecked Irish sailor in 1235. The road continues S. past oyster-beds and (r.) *Marsilly* and *Nieul-sur-Mer* (now 3km from the sea), both with churches preserving features of interest, to *La Rochelle*.

The main road (N137) is gained 5km due E. of Luçon at *Les Quatre Chemins*, which crosses the *Marais Poitevin* (cf. Rte 72), at 12km traversing *Chaillé*, an 'island' in the marshes, to *Marans*, 11.5km beyond, for which see the last paragraphs of Rte 58B.—23km. **La Rochelle**; see Rte 72.

B. Via Fromentine and Les Sables-d'Olonne

218km (135 miles). D937. 10km D178. 4.5km—D262. 8km *St-Philbert-de-Grand-Lieu*—D117. 15.5km *Machecoul*—D64 and 59. 14km *Bouin*—D758. 8km *Beauvoir-sur-Mer*, for the **Île de Noirmoutier** D22. 9km **Fromentine**—D38. 12km *St-Jean-de-Monts* —47km **Les Sables d'Olonne**—D949. 49km **Luçon**—5km N137. 46km **La Rochelle**.

Maps: IGN 32, 39, or 107. M 232, 233. The Îles de Noirmoutier and d'Yeu are covered in detail on IGN 502 and 503, respectively.

For the area between *Nantes* and *Pornic*, see the last paragraphs of Rte 46. The D751 and D758 drive directly to *Bouin* via (40km) *Bourgneuf-en-Retz*, a decayed port with a small local museum.

22.5km. *St-Philbert-de-Grand-Lieu*, some 4km S.E. of the *Lac de Grand-Lieu* (7000 hectares), has a church, remodelled in the 17C, preserving in its nave and transepts the important remains of a Carolingian edifice (9C); the ancient crypt was the temporary resting-place of the body of St Philibert on his way from Noirmoutier (see below) to Tournus.

15.5km. *Machecoul*, retaining a few old houses, and the remains of a stronghold of Gilles de Rais, was where the Vendean rising started in 1793, whose leader, Charette, lived in the manor of *Fonteclose*, 10.5km S. on the road to *Challans*, a poultry and agricultural market-town 8.5km further S.—The Protestant leader François de la Noüe (1531–91) was probably born at the manor of *La Noüe-Briord*, near *Fresnay*, 5km N.W., which was the property of his mother's family.

The road leads W. over the *Marais Breton*, a wide expanse of salt-marshes criss-crossed with tidal canals known as '*étiers*', to (14km) *Bouin*, on an 'island', where we turn S.W. to *Beauvoir-sur-Mer*, now 3.5km inland, with a church retaining some Romanesque features.

To the W. is the causeway known as *Le Gois*, practical for cars at low tide (there are three refuges for travellers overtaken by the rapidly rising tide here), crossing the 5km-wide strait to the Île de Noirmoutier, also—since 1971—approached by a toll-bridge from the small resort of *Fromentine*, 9km S.W. of Beauvoir.

The narrow **Île de Noirmoutier**, approx. 20km long, is largely composed of dunes and salt-marshes, and its name is derived from *Heri Monasterium*, a Benedictine monastery founded by St Philibert c. 680, and pillaged by Normans in the 9C. The Dutch under Tromp made a landing here in 1676.

From the bridge, the island is traversed by road to (17km) *Noirmoutier-en-l'Île*, where Vendean leader D'Elbée was captured and shot. The 15C *Castle*, a dependency of the ancient abbey, consists of a square keep with corner-turrets; the neighbouring *Church* preserves some Romanesque parts, the 11C crypt containing the empty tomb of St Philibert (cf. Jumièges), whose remains, removed to protect them from the Norman raids, are now at Tournus in Burgundy. On the N. coast are the ruins of the *Abbaye de la Blanche*; to the N.E., the small resort of *Le Bois de la Chaise*; to the N.W., the sardine-port of *L'Herbaudière*.

Fromentine is the ferry terminus for the **Île d'Yeu**, lying 17km out to sea, consisting of a granite rock 9.5km long, and 3-4km wide, largely populated by fishermen. It is more akin to Belle-Île than to the alluvial islands of Noirmoutier, Ré, and Oléron, a relationship emphasised by the number of place-names beginning with the Breton prefix 'ker'. On its N.E. coast is the main village and harbour of *Port-Joinville* (which in 1846 changed its name from *Port-Breton* to flatter the third son of Louis-Philippe). Marshal Pétain (1856–1951) was confined from 1945, until shortly before his death, in the *Porte de Pierre-Levée* and is buried in the local cemetery. On the rocky S.W. coast are the ruins of the 11C *Vieux-Château*, altered in the 14-15Cs; to the E. of which is the picturesque *Port de la Meule*.

The D38 follows the afforested coast S. from Fromentine past several small resorts to (30km) *St-Gilles-Croix-de-Vie*, 18km E. of which are the ruins of the *Château d'Apremont* (1535).—5.5km. The *Château de Beaumarchais* (c.1600) is 3.5km E. and 3km beyond is the 12C church of *La Chaize-Giraud*, with a good Poitevin facade.—7.5km *St-Nicolas-de-Brem*, with a partly ruined Romanesque church of interest, beyond which the road traverses a track of wooded dunes, skirting salt-marshes, to (11km) *Olonne-sur-Mer*, 2km E. of which is the 18C *Château de la Pierre-Levée*, with a menhir in its park.

5km. **Les Sables d'Olonne** (16,700 inhab.), a popular family resort, which has succeeded what was in the 17C a flourishing small port, the older fishermen's quarter of *La Chaume* lying to the W. of the harbour, retaining relics of a 14C fort erected during the English occupation. To the N. are salt-pans, the remnants of a lagoon. To the E. extends a curving beach of fine sand, skirted by promenades, ending in a line of cliffs. The father of the American naturalist J. J. Audubon (1785–1851) was a ship's captain from Les Sables. In the town centre is *N.-D.-de-Bon-Port* (1646) with three mutilated Renaissance doorways; further E. is the restored *Abbaye Ste-Croix* (16-17C), now housing a local museum.

13km. *Talmont-St-Hilaire*, once a port on an arm of the sea which washed the foot of the ruined *Castle (15-16C, with an 11C keep), abutted by a late-10C church tower.

TALMONT TO L'AIGUILLON-SUR-MER (35.5km). The D21 forks r. to (7km) *Jard-sur-Mer*, with a Romanesque church, 2.5km W. of which is the ruined abbey of *Lieu-Dieu*, founded by Richard I in 1196.—2km. *St-Vincent-sur-Jard*, where Clemenceau spent his last summers, is traversed as we turn S.E. past reafforested dunes through (16km) *La Tranche-sur-Mer*, a modest resort rebuilt since its destruction in 1944, to approach (10.5km) *L'Aiguillon* (see Rte 62A), with a view S. towards the *Île de Ré*; see Rte 72.

The main road drives due E. from Talmont past (l.) a 16C château, beyond (10km) *Avrillé* passing several dolmens and other megaliths.

6km. At *Moutiers-les-Mauxfaits*, 4.5km N., is a good Romanesque church. That at *Angles*, 6km S., has a Romanesque crypt and a curious figure of a bear surmounts its W. gable; at *Moricq*, 2km E. of Angles, is a castellated tower and a smaller tower perhaps of Roman origin.

6km. *St-Cyr-en-Talmondais*; the adjacent château of *Le Court-d'Aron* contains collections of medieval antiquities, etc., while the church at *Curzon*, 2km S.E., has an 11C crypt.—14km. **Luçon**, for which, and the road, beyond, see Rte 62A.

C.   Via Chantonnay

146km (90 miles). N137. 73km *Chantonnay*—27km *Les Quatre-Chemins*—46km **La Rochelle**.

Maps: IGN 32, 33, 39, or 107. M 232, 233.

19km. *Aigrefeuille*, 10km E. of which lies *Clisson*; see Rte 59C.
    The road now traverses the *Bocage Vendéen*, through (13km) *Montaigu*, to reach the cross-roads of *Les Quatres Chemins*, 25km beyond.

Some 7.5km E. lie the ruins of the abbey of *La Grainetière*, where the Abbé Prévost is believed to have written 'Manon Lescaut'; the cloister and chapter-house, now part of a farm, are striking.—8.5km S.W., at *Les Essarts*, is a pictures-que ruined château, and church with an 11C crypt.

15km. *Chantonnay*, the scene of a battle in 1793, when D'Elbée's Vendeans defeated a force of 6000 Republicans. For the area to the E., see Rte 58B.

At 11.5km we pass (r.) the 16C *Château de l'Aubraie*, and 7.5km beyond, the 17C château of *Ste-Hermine*, once the property of Philippe Dangeau (1638–1720), the memoirist, amidst the ruins of an older castle.

The N148 leads 22km S.E. to *Fontenay-le-Comte* (see Rte 58B), via (10km) *Pouillé*, 3.5km N.E. of which is *L'Hermenault*, preserving a 15C tower of the castle of the bishops of Maillezais.

8.5km. *Ste-Gemme-la-Plaine*, the scene of the overwhelming defeat of the Vendeans in 1793. The 13C church contains a fine 15C credence-table; the adjacent *Château de la Popelinière* dates from c. 1570.—2km. *Les Quatre-Chemins*, 5km E. of **Luçon**. For the road hence, see Rte 62A.

VI LIMOUSIN; CHARENTES; PÉRIGORD

The **Limousin** (now the departments of the *Haute-Vienne* and *Corrèze*, with their préfectures at *Limoges* and *Tulle*), part of Eleanor of Aquitaine's dowry, passed into English hands until reconquered by Charles VII. To its N.E. stood **Marche** (now the *Creuse*; préfecture *Guéret*), bequeathed by Guy de Lusignan to Philippe le Bel in 1308, later passing by marriage to the Armagnac family, but reunited with the crown in 1472. To the S.W. stood the districts of **Quercy**, and *Rouergue*, the former now comprising the *Lot*, with *Cahors* its préfecture, and *Tarn et Garonne*, with *Montauban* its préfecture, and forming for some decades part of the Plantagenet dominions after the treaty of Xaintes (1259). The **Rouergue** (now represented by the *Aveyron*; préfecture *Rodez*) lay further to the S.E. The whole area was scourged by the Religious Wars, Cahors and Rodez being reactionary strongholds of Catholicism, while Montauban stood for reform.

Readers of Cyril Connolly's 'The Unquiet Grave' will remember what he called 'The Magic Circle', his preferred area of France, but of course he was evoking the pre-war period, before it was invaded by secondary residents. The circumference of this circle, centred on the Cahors, were the towns of Tulle, Aurillac, Espalion, Castres, Auch, Tonneins, and Bergerac.

To the W. was **Angoumois** (capital *Angoulême;* now the **Charentes**), claimed by John in the name of his wife Isabelle d'Angoulême, but which was only acknowledged English territory from the treaty of Brétigny (1360) to 1371, when it became a fief of the dukes of Berry, bring united to the crown in the person of François I, who was count of Angoulême. Further W. were **Aunis et Saintonge** (now *Deux-Sevres*—préfecture *Niort*—and *Charente-Maritimes*, in which *Saintes* was of importance in Roman times), also united to France at the same time. *La Rochelle* was the last important bastion of Protestantism during the Religious Wars.

Abutting Limousin to the S. is the present department of the *Dordogne*, with *Périgueux* its préfecture, and also known as **Périgord**, the northern-most part of **Aquitaine**. To the S. and S.W. are the old districts of *Agenais*, and *Bordelais* respectively (with *Agen* and *Bordeaux* their capitals). The huge province, also known from the mid 12C as **Guyenne**, a corruption of *Aquitania*, the Roman province, was with *Gascony* (see Section VII) the centre of the English sphere of influence in France during the 12-15C. The prehistoric importance of the Dordogne valley, with its caves, particularly those of *Les Eyzies* and *Lascaux*, need hardly be emphasised.

63 Châteauroux to Limoges

125km (77 miles). N20. 31km **Argenton-sur-Creuse**—47km *La Croisière*—47km **Limoges**.

Maps: IGN 35, 34, 41, or 107. M 238, 233.

The road leads S.W. from **Châteauroux** (Rte 51), traversing flat wooded country through (15km) *Lothiers* where the N151 forks r.; see Rte 51.—7.5km. *Tendu*, to the S.E. of which, in the Bouzanne valley rise the medieval keeps of *Prunget* and *Mazières*.

7.5km. **Argenton-sur-Creuse** (6100 inhab.), an old cloth-making town replacing Gallo-Roman *Argentomagus* (under excavation) on the site of *St-Marcel* (2km N.W.), its Romanesque and Gothic church with an 11C crypt.

Argenton itself is of slight interest, except for the picturesque view of galleried houses overlooking the Creuse, which flooded the town in 1845, crossed to the S. by the *Vieux Pont*. There are slight remains of a castle on the W. bank, the view of which is spoilt by a disfiguring image surmounting the chapel of *N.-D.-des-Bancs*.

Hence an attractive DETOUR may be made to the *Barrage d'Éguzon*, by following the r. bank of the Creuse to the S.W. via (13.5km) *Gargilesse*, described by George Sand in 'Promenade autour d'un Village', with a 12C church and castle ruins.—A further 7km brings one to the ruined castle of *Châteaubrun*, with a 13C keep, the scene of the same author's 'Péché de Monsieur Antoine'. At the far end of the *Lac de Chambon* formed by the dam, rise the towers of the 13C fortress of *Crozant, dominating the confluence of the Creuse and Sédelle, which superseded a residence of Charlemagne and Louis le Débonnaire.—From *Éguzon* itself, S.W. of Châteaubrun, one may regain the N20 further W., 17.5km. S. of Argenton.

8.5km W. of this crossroad lies **St-Benoît-de-Sault**, where on a promontory to the S. is the well-sited medieval village, once walled, with a priory church founded in the 11C, from which one may regain the main road 11km S.W.

21km. 9km S.E. lies **La Souterraine** (5850 inhab.), built on the site of the Gallo-Roman *Villa Sosterranea*, its old centre dominated by a remarkable 12C *Church of a local type, the first bay of which supports a 13C tower, while the next four perfectly illustrate the development of the Gothic vaulting system. The portal is notable, with scalloped jambs like those at Moissac, and the corbels and capitals throughout are worth inspecting. The crypt communicates with a Gallo-Roman cella.—Adjacent is a 14C gate; another is a short walk S.W. of the church.—3km S.E. stands the huge cylindrical keep of *Bridiers* (14-15C) on the site of the oppidum of *Breith*.—10km N.E. is the château of *St-Germain-Beaupré*, to which Mlle de Montpensier was exiled in 1652.—The N20 may be regained 9.5km S.W. of La Souterraine, at *La Croisière*.

9km. *La Croisière*, beyond which we enter some very beautiful country of chestnut woods and lakes in the neighbourhood of the *Monts d'Ambazac*, passing near (l.) the 14-16C *Château de Fromental*.—8km. *Châteauponsac*, 7.5km W., has a number of 15C houses, and an old bridge over the Gartempe, restored in 1609.

Uranium mines are being exploited at *Bessines*, some opencast, which we soon traverse, and likewise at (16.5km) *La Crouzille*.

At *Ambasac*, 7km S.E. of the latter, the church preserves treasures from *Grand-mont* (slight remains of which lie 6km N.), an abbey founded in 1124 by St Stephen of Muret, including an enamelled reliquary brought from Cologne in 1181 and a dalmatic, the gift of the Empress Matilda.—At *Compreignac*, 6km W., is a fortified church of the local type (12th and 15C).

20km. **LIMOGES** (144,100 Limougeauds; 41,600 in 1851; 107,600 in 1946; Limousins designates the inhabitants of the province), préfecture of the *Haute-Vienne*, stands on rising ground above the Vienne, and although it has expanded very considerably in recent decades, it preserves a number of interesting streets in its old centre which have been the object of restoration, and an imposing cathedral. It has long been famous for its enamels and porcelain, and its growth as an industrial centre has received further impetus with the discovery of uranium in the area (see above).

The capital of the Gallic Lemovices was a short distance downstream, while Roman *Augustoritum* occupied both banks of the Vienne near the Pont St-Martial. The area known as the *Cité* originated as a refuge from the barbarian invasions, while the *Ville* grew up in the 10C round the tomb of St Martial, the apostle of the Limousin, and both were encircled with their own ramparts (as at Périgueux). In 1370, led by its bishop (who had been a personal friend of the Black Prince), Limoges revolted against his overlordship, and infuriated by this treachery the Prince assaulted the town and massacred 3000 citizens. Its medieval history is bound up largely with its fame as a centre of goldsmiths' work and of the minting of coins, an industry said to have been founded by St Eligius (St Eloi; born in the neighbourhood in 588), the patron of goldsmiths and a craftsman at the court of Clothair II and Dagobert I. The manufacture of Limoges enamels, which reached its zenith in the 16C, had disappeared by the end of the 18C (although revived in 1875), but from 1768, following the discovery of kaolin at St-Yrieix (c. 40km S.), the prosperity of the town was maintained by the manufacture of porcelain, and thanks to the able administration of Turgot during the year 1762–74, the Revolution left it almost undisturbed. It suffered from ravaging fires in 1790 and 1864.

Limoges has given its name to the '*limousine*', a shepherd's cloak entirely covering the body, a term extended to describe a saloon car; and to '*limousinage*', a coarse masonry of small stones set in mortar. During the First World War the slang term '*Limogé*' applied to generals who had 'received an appointment at the Base'.

Among the better known artists in enamel were those of the Limosin family, particularly Léonard I (c. 1505– -c. 1577), and the Pénicauds (Nardon or Léonard; c. 1470– c. 1540, also Jean I, II, and III, and Pierre); also Pierre Raymond, Pierre Courteys, and the Laudins, and the Nouailhers, in the 17-18Cs.

Other eminent natives were the humanist Jean Dorat (1502–88); the Chancellor d'Aguesseau (1668–1751); Étienne de Silhouette (1709–67), briefly controller-general of Finances, and translator of Pope, whose name became famous as designating outline drawings; Pierre Vergniaud (1752–93), the Girondist; Marshal Jourdan (1762–1833); Marshal Bugeaud (1784–1849); Sadi Carnot (1837–94) the politician; Auguste Renoir (1841–1919), who only passed his infancy there; and Suzanne Valadon (1867–1938).

Enquiry should be made to the S.I., Blvd de Fleurus, leading S.W. from the Pl. Jourdan, with regard to visiting porcelain factories, and enamel workshops, etc.

The *Pl. Jourdan* lies slightly N. of the site of the ramparts of both Ville and Cité (see above). From its S.E. corner one may follow the Rues du Maupas and Neuve-St-Étienne (passing a restored area to the r.) to the **Cathedral**, occupying the centre of the old Cité.

It was begun in 1273, and clumsily strengthened in the late 14C, replacing an earlier basilica of which only the base of the slender Gothic *Tower remains. Its spire was destroyed by lightning. The *Choir* (1273–1327) was built in the purest Gothic style, and the S.

transept is a late 14C continuation; the N. transept and two E. bays of the nave are Flamboyant (1458–99). The N. transeptal front, dating from 1517–30, is a fine example of late Gothic decoration, with doors depicting scenes from the lives of SS Stephen and Martial. The three W. bays of the nave were only added in 1876.

Interior. At this W. end is the Renaissance *Rood-Screen* (1535) with keystones representing the Virtues, and medallions of the Labours of Hercules. Most of the glass dates from the 16C, except that in the upper range at the E. end, which is 15C. In the *Ambulatory* are the tombs of Card. Raynaud de la Porte (d. 1316), the mausoleum of Bp Jean de Langeac (d. 1541), with *Bas-reliefs* illustrating the Apocalypse (after Dürer), and the mutilated tomb of Bp Bernard Brun (d. 1350), with statuettes and reliefs, including one of St Valerie bringing her head to St Martial. The chapels retain good stone tracery, and some 19C paintwork still remains. The *Sacristy* preserves enamels, etc.

The former *Bishop's Palace* (1766–87), briefly the residence of Lord Macartney when prisoner in France in 1779, and visited by Arthur Young in the year of its completion, who considered the garden 'the finest object to be seen at Limoges, for it commands a landscape hardly to be equalled for beauty', now houses the *Municipal Museum*.

It consists of four main sections: *Archaeology*, including a 2C fresco discovered in the Rue Vigne-de-Fer in the 1960s, and other objects unearthed in the vicinity of Limoges, together with several Romanesque capitals and heads from the

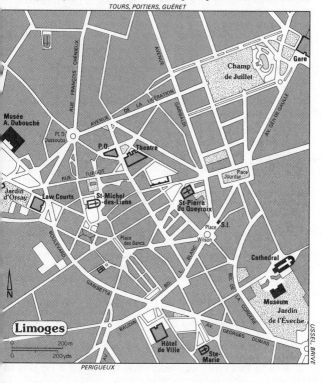

former cathedral; *Egyptian Antiquities*, including a fine Mummy, and Mask from a sarcophagus of the Graeco-Roman period, etc.; *Limoges* *Enamels, among them examples by the Limosin and Pénicaud families (see above)—regrettably 30 objects from the collection were stolen on New Year's Eve, 1982, and have not yet been recovered; and *Paintings*, among them works by *Nattier*, *Renoir* (Portrait of Mme Le Coeur; 1866), and *Suzanne Valadon*, etc. Some furniture is also on display.

A maquette of Limoges in the 16C may be seen in the *Orangerie*.

The terraced *Gardens* overlook the Vienne, crossed (l.) by the 13C *Pont St-Étienne*, reached by a steep lane descending from the cathedral apse.

From its W. front we approach the Av. Georges-Dumas, continued to the W. beyond the Hôtel de Ville, by the Blvd Gambetta.

To the S. stands *Ste-Marie*, with a 13C doorway, whence the Rue du Pont St-Martial leads down to the 13C *Bridge*, on Roman foundations.

Off the N. side of the Blvd Gambetta is *St-Aurélien* (1475, with a 17C tower and facade), the chapel of the butchers, whose influential corporation was founded in the 10C, and whose stalls still line the adjacent Rue de la Boucherie, one of several characteristic lanes in the area under restoration. From its N. end we approach the Pl. d'Aine, overlooked by the *Palace de Justice*, steps behind which ascend to the *Jardin d'Orsay*, in which are relics of a *Roman Arena* uncovered during excavations in 1966 on this highest point of the town. It dated from the 1C, and could hold 20,000 spectators, the dimensions of the amphitheatre being 136 by 116m, and its arena 68 by 48m.

To the N. of the adjacent Place stands the ***Musée National Adrien-Dubouché**—named after the curator (d. 1881) who formed the basis of this extensive collection of porcelain and chinaware. Among the more remarkable pieces are several from the Gasnault and Jacquemart collections.

The GROUND FLOOR is at present devoted to temporary exhibitions. FIRST FLOOR (plan available at the entrance): to the r. of the vestibule, containing Chinese porcelain, are cases displaying an outstanding selection of Hispano-moresque and Talavera ware; majolica; faience from Nevers, Delft, Moustiers, Rouen, Sinceny, Lille, St-Cloud, Marseille, Sceaux, and Limoges itself, together with examples from other European countries.—To the l. is another wing, on the r.-hand side of which are examples of '*porcelaine tendre*' (without kaolin) from St-Cloud, Chantilly, Mennecy, Vincennes, etc.; and also from Worcester, and Capodimonte; on the l. are examples of '*porcelaine dure*' from Dresden (Saxe), Meissen, Limoges, and Paris, together with several cabinets devoted to German porcelains in particular. A section at the far end displays *Glass*.

On regaining the Pl. d'Aine, from its N.E. corner we approach **St-Michel-des-Lions** (14-15C), with a lofty tower of 1373, whose restored spire is topped by a fretted copper ball. On either side of the door in the tower are the two 12C stone lions which gave the church its name. The interior is remarkable for its slender pillars, leaning out of true, and its 15C glass; it also contains the reliquary of St Martial's head.

From just S. of the church the narrow Rue du Clocher, together with the Rues du Temple and Consulat, further S. (the latter leading from the picturesque *Pl. des Bancs*), lead N.E. to the transverse Rue Jean-Jaurés.

The former street is continued by the Rue St-Martial, traversing the site of the nave of the former abbey of *St-Martial*, passing (l.) the entrance to its **Crypt** (uncovered while excavating a car-park in

1966), parts of which date from the 4C, and containing the sarcophagi of that saint and St Valerie, among others; also a 9C mosaic. It is normally only on view from July-Sept., but enquiry should be made at the S.I. of Municipal Museum about admission at other times.

Further E., to the r. of the Rue Porte-Tourny, stands **St-Pierre-du-Queyroix**, largely rebuilt in 1534, although the tower and parts of the facade exhibit 13C workmanship. It is remarkable in having three aisles on the S. side of the nave, and only two on the N., the low vault being sustained by massive cylindrical pillars. At the end of the inner S. aisle is a restored window (Death and the Coronation of the Virgin) by Jean Pénicaud I (1510); the choir-stalls date from 1513.

The Pl. Jourdan lies a short distance to the E., from which the Cours Jourdan leads N. to the extensive *Champ de Juillet*, facing the E. end of which is the *Railway-station*, with its copper dome, and clock-tower.

64 Limoges to Toulouse via Brive and Cahors

306km (190 miles). N20. 56km **Uzerche**—35km **Brive-la-Gaillarde**—37km **Souillac**—66km **Cahors**—39km *Caussade*—22km **Montauban**—51km **Toulouse**.

Maps: IGN 41, 48, 57, 64, or 110, and 113 or 114. M 233, 239, 235.

LIMOGES TO BRIVE VIA ST-YRIEIX (103km). After 5.5km we fork r. off the N20 onto the D704 to (6.5km) *Le Vigen*, with a 12C church, just W. of which is **Solignac**, its **Church* (1143), formerly crowned by three towers, but a remarkable example of Romanesque Périgordine architecture. The exterior has a blind N. arcade with grotesque capitals, and a heavy 12-13C porch, the basement of a vanished belfry. The roof consists of four cupolas (originally five; the S. transept has been re-vaulted), two of which cover the wide nave, and are supported by curious pilaster-capitals and consoles. It ends on each side in a small staircase communicating with the galleries above the transeptal arches, which are themselves connected by a gallery across the choir-arch. The apse is lined with 15C stalls, and on the r. of the altar an old painting shows the church before it was despoiled of its towers. The conventual buildings, long occupied by a porcelain-factory, were the first workshop for the production of Limoges enamels, founded by Eloi in 631 (see Limoges; Rte 63).—3km E. of Le Vigen is the double ruin of the castle of *Chalusset* (12-13C).—18km. *La Roche-l'Abeille* (l.) was the scene of Coligny's victory over the Catholic armies of the Duc d'Anjou and Filippo Strozzi (1569), when Henri of Navarre (later Henri IV), then aged 16, bore arms for the first time.

11.5km. **St-Yrieix-la-Perche** (8000 Arédiens), the centre of the china-clay (or kaolin) quarries used for the potteries of Sèvres and Limoges, grew around the abbey founded in the 6C by St Aridius or Yrieix, chancellor of Theodebert of Austrasia. The abbey is now represented by the **Moûtier* (or Minster), 13C except for its 12C narthex and choir walls. Note the curious arrangement of the nave buttresses. To the S. is the Romanesque *Tour du Plot* (1243).—*Le Chalard*, 7km N.W., has a notable priory church and other 12C buildings.—Some 8km S.W. of the latter stands the fine late 14C castle of *Jumilhac-le-Grand*.

The D704 continues to a junction 20.5km S., where the D705 leads 6.5km S.W. to *Excideuil*, with remains of a castle of the Talleyrand-Périgord family, with two 14C towers, and Renaissance chapel, etc. Excideuil was the birthplace of the troubadour Guiraut de Borneil.—After 11.5km, to the l. of the D704, on an abrupt hill above the confluence of two streams, stands the splendid **Chateau de Hautefort*, rebuilt in the 16-17C, and restored after a fire in 1968. It once belonged to the troubadour Bertrand de Born (c. 1140 – c. 1215), who was buried at the ruined abbey of *Dalon*, at *Ste-Trie*, 6km N.E., as was the troubadour Bernard de Ventadour.—6km W. of the main road lies *Tourtoirac*, a ruinous fortified village.—15.5km further S. the Brive-Périgueux road is met at *Bastignac*; see Rte 94.

Turning E. from St-Yrieix, we pass at 11km the château of *Bonneval* (12-15C; restored), birthplace of Germain de Bonneval, who died defending François I at Marignano (1515), and of Alexandre Bonneval Pasha (1675–1747), a general in the service of Sultan Achmed III.—The road soon veers S. through (12km) *Lubersac*, with a curious sculptured apse to its church, and 6km beyond, *Pompadour*, with a 15-17C château, never occupied by the famous Marquise, and a stud-farm.—*Arnac*, 2km N.W., has a Romanesque church of interest; there are ruins of a castle and old houses at *Ségur-le-Château*, 6km beyond.—*Beyssac*, 3km S.E., was the birthplace of Pope Innocent IV (d. 1362; cf. Villeneuve-lès-Avignon).—17km. *St-Bonnet-la-Rivière* has a round 12C church, later altered.—6km. *Objat*, E. of which is the charming village of *Le Saillant*, with a Gothic bridge and a manor at which Mirabeau used to stay with his sister, the Marquise du Saillant.—*St Robert*, 14.5km W. of Objat, is another characteristic old village.—19.5km. **Brive**; see below.

Quitting **Limoges** (Rte 63), we follow the N20 S.E. to (36km) *Fombelaux*, 4km N.E. of which, at *St-Germain-les-Belles*, is a fortified church of 1376.—The road climbs past (7.5km) *Masseret* (Views; with Mont Gargan to to the N.E.) before descending into the Vézères valley.

14.5km. **Uzerche** is an ancient town of Gallo-Roman foundation (*Uzerca*), picturesquely sited on a loop of the Vézère, and preserving several turreted 15-16C mansions. It was the birthplace of the troubadour Gaucelin Faidit (fl. 1185–1230); and Alexis Boyer (1757–1833), Napoleon's surgeon; and here c. 1780 Mme de Genlis retired for a time. The road ascends past (r.) the *Château Pontier* to the *Pl. Marie-Colein*, from which the narrow main street of the old town leads N. through the 14C *Porte Bécharie* to *St-Pierre* (11-12C, except for the W. bay and S.W. tower, 13th and 15C respectively), with an admirable **Belfry*, and 11C crypt remarkable for the rudeness of its vaults. Note the pestle and mortar insignia on the 15C *Maison Eyssartier*, once a pharmacy, in the adjacent square (views).

UZERCHE TO TULLE AND AURILLAC (115km). The N120 forks l. 2km S., via (15km) *Seilhac* and (8km) *Naves*, the church of which contains a notable 18C altarpiece, before climbing down to (6km) *Tulle*; see Rte 94.—For the road hence to *Figeac*, see below.—We ascend S.E. through (4km) *Laguenne*, with a 12C church, and beyond the watershed, descend to (26km) **Argentat**, attractively sited on the r. bank of the Dordogne, and preserving a number of quaint old houses overlooked by its square church tower.—The road follows the valley of the Maronne for a short while, before climbing to the (12km) *Sexcles*, whence a lane leads c. 8km N.W. to the picturesque ruins of the **Tours de Merle*.—The N120 soon veers E. above the *Gorges de la Clère*, reached by a lane bearing r. after 13km to *Laroquebrou* (6.5km S.E.), with a ruined castle, bridge of 1281, mairie of 1340, and an ornate Gothic church (14-15C), whence the main road may be regained further E.—We continue some distance above the reservoir to *St Étienne-Cantalès*, with a view ahead of the *Monts du Cantal*, to (29km) **Aurillac**; see Rte 95.

TULLE TO FIGEAC (103km). The D940 climbs S., crossing a lonely plateau before descending into the Dordogne valley at (44km) *Beaulieu-sur-Dordogne*, a large village of old houses, whose splendid Benedictine **Church* (12-13C) retains a remarkable tympanum of the Last Supper, the prototype of that at St-Denis, Paris. The 12C Chapter-house serves as a sacristy; a silver repoussé 12C Virgin may be seen. The poet and musician Eustorg de Beaulieu (c. 1495–1552) was born here, and in the neighbourhood, was Gén. Marbot (1782–1845).—7.5km. *Bretenoux*, a bastide of 1277, near the confluence of the Dordogne and Cère, to the S.W. of which it is commanded by the restored 11C *Château de Castelnau*, ◇

strengthened in the 14-15C, with a keep 62m high. It contains good Beauvais and Aubusson tapestries, etc. and the ramparts provide plunging views.—For the road to *Martel*, 25km W., see Rte 65.—Crossing a ridge to the E., we descend to (8.5km) **St-Céré**, a small town on the Bave, to the N. of which rises the two *Tours de St-Laurent* (12th and 15C). The poet François Maynard (1582–1646) was buried in *Ste-Spérie*, in the old centre; Marshal Canrobert (1809–95) was born here.—2km to the W. is the *Château de Montal* (1534), restored after its sculptural features had been dispersed in the late 19C, and reassembled.—Some 5km further W. on a spur stands *Loubressac*, a village preserving part of its medieval fortifications, and its château (15C; rebuilt 17C).—From just W. of Montal, the D673 climbs steeply past the stalactite *Grotte de Presque*, and (r.) the *Gorge d'Autoire*, a chasm in the causse, with a waterfall, towards (14km) the turning for the *Gouffre de Padirac*; see Rte 65.—The main road ascends S. from St-Céré, between the *Causse de Gramat* (r.) and the wooded *Ségala*, with its deep valleys, to (24km) *Lacapelle-Marival*, with a 13th-17C château, 3km to the S.W. of which we meet the N140 at *Le Bourg*, and turn l. for (18km) **Figeac**; see Rte 65.

From Uzerche, the N20 climbs out of the valley, at 2km passing a turning (r.) for (5km) *Vigeois*, with an interesting Romanesque abbey church, and medieval bridge.

18km. A new road forks r. for (17km) *Brive*; the old road continues S. via *Donzenac*, where the 18C church preserves the early 14C belfry of its predecessor.

10km. **Brive-la-Gaillarde** (54,000 Brivois or Brivistes), a prosperous industrial town largely on the S. bank of the Corrèze, is an important road and rail junction. It is also a centre for market-gardening and fruit, and nut, production.

Of importance prior to the Roman invasion, it was evangelised by St Martial in the 5C. In the Middle Ages it acquired its suffix from the courage of its citizens when feuding with their neighbours, particularly the seigneurs of Turenne and Malemort. It was the birthplace of the unscrupulous Card. Dubois (1656–1723), minister of the Regent Orléans; and Marshal Brune (1763–1815). Its pâtés de foie gras truffées are reputed.

The *Pont-Cardinal* crosses the river to approach the old centre, whose formerly 'stinking streets' so disgusted Young, now encircled by boulevards, in which the main streets converge on *St-Martin*, a church which has suffered repeated alteration since the 12C. Its lofty nave was rebuilt in 1310; its tower added in 1896. The pillars of the nave and the arrangement of the side-aisles are remarkable; the capitals of the choir and transepts are of some interest.—To the S. is a turreted 16C mansion.—Hence the Rue du Dr-Massénat leads E. to the *Musée Rupin*, with somewhat miscellaneous collections, local history and archaeology, and paintings, etc.—A short distance S. of the museum is the *Hôtel de Labenche* (16C), with an attractive arcaded courtyard.

For the road W. to **Périgueux**, see Rte 94; likewise—in the reverse direction—for *Clermont-Ferrand*, to the N.E. For the road to *Martel*, *Figeac*, and **Albi**, see Rte 65.

In the district immediately S.E. of Brive are several places of interest, among them, approached by the D38, are (13km) *Noailhac*, with a fortified 15C church, and *Collonges-la-Rouge*, 7.5km beyond, a red-sandstone village preserving several old mansions and a Romanesque church with a notable *Tympanum, the belfry of which is one of the oldest in the Limousin; two rampart gates survive.

Climbing S. from Brive, the N20 shortly passes (l.) the artificial *Grottes de St-Antoine*, and the more extensive *Grottes de Lamouroux*, further S.—8km. *Noailles* (l.) has a 12-13C church and restored castle from which the ducal family took its title.

1.5km. *Jugeals Nazareth*, 4.5km E., founded and named by Raymond I of Turenne on his return from the First Crusade, preserves remains of a commandery of the Templars and of a lazar house, both of that epoch.—4.5km beyond lies the medieval village of *Turenne*, built in the shadow of the ruined stronghold of its seigneurs, most famous of whom was Henri de la Tour d'Auvergne, the 'Grand Turenne' (1611–75), first the ally and then the opponent of the Grand Condé. It preserves two keeps, the 15C *Tour de César*, and the *Tour du Trésor* (14C).

The N20 continues S.; just beyond (9.5km) *Cressenac*, the N140 diverges l.; see Rte 65.

16.5km. **Souillac**, in the Dordogne valley, is a somewhat scruffy little town, but preserves a 15C tower and a remarkable *Abbey Church, a fine example of the local type of 12C architecture, which stands a few paces to the r. of the main street.

The doorway at the W. end of the nave is embellished by a mutilated statue of Isaiah and an extraordinary column—originally the central pillar of the door—of intertwined dragons, and the sacrifice of Isaac. The aisleless nave is covered by three huge domes (similar to those in the cathedrals of Cahors, Périgueux, and Angoulême); the owl will be noted among the apse capitals.

For the road down the valley to *Bergerac*, see Rte 74, in reverse; for the valley immediately to the E., see Rte 65.

The N20 climbs S. onto the plateau above the Dordogne (views).

19.5km. The D673 leads 13km S.W. to *Gourdon*, on its hill crowned by *St-Pierre* (1304–1415; with a good rose-window), the old centre being surrounded by boulevards. It was the birthplace of J.-B. Cavaignac (1763–1829), the 'Conventionnel'. The Rue du Majou, with its gateway, and the *Église des Cordeliers* (1278) will be noted.—3km N. are the *Grottes de Curgnac*, one preserving paintings.—The road from Gourdon continues S.W. to (51km) *Fumel*, and *Villeneuve-sur-Lot*, 25km beyond; see p 394.

After 20.5km, where the road reaches a height of 423m, a l.-hand turning leads 7.5km to *Labastide-Murat* (previously *Fortunière*), birthplace of Joachim Murat (1767–1815), king of Naples and son of an innkeeper; 5km N.W. stands the *Château de Vaillac* (14-16C). The N20 gradually descends from the *Causse de Gramat* towards the valley of the Lot, passing (l.) after 15.5km, the ruins of the *Château de Roussillon*.

12km. **CAHORS** (20,800 Cadurciens or Cahorsins), préfecture of the *Lot* (pron. Lott), and the capital of the province of *Quercy*, occupies a peninsula surrounded on three sides by the river, crossed to the W. by the Pont Valentre, one of the finest medieval bridges extant, while on the E. side of the town, with the cathedral, are several old houses and characteristic streets in the process of restoration.

Divona, capital of the Gallic Cadurci, was reputed in the time of Juvenal for its linen cloth (*cadurcum*). With the disintegration of the Empire it was occupied by the Visigoths (471), and was briefly in Moorish hands in the mid 8C (cf. Poitiers). Quercy was part of the dowry of Eleanor of Aquitaine, and Thomas Becket was appointed governor by Henry II in 1159–60. In the 16C it was a Catholic stronghold, and rebelled against Henri (of Navarre), who sacked the place in 1580.

Here were born Jacques d'Euse (or Duèze; 1244–1334), who as John XXII was from 1316 the second pope at Avignon; in 1331 he founded its university, which until its suppression in 1751 rivalled Toulouse; Clément Marot (c. 1496–1544); and Olivier de Magny (1530–61), poets; and Léon Gambetta (1838–82), the republican statesman.

Entering the town from the N., traffic is directed to the r. and then l.

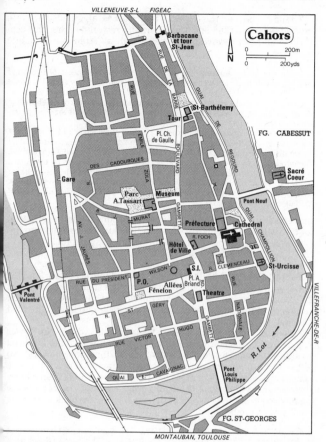

on reaching the *Barbacane*, a 15C gate in the 14C ramparts stretching across the neck of the peninsula, to the E. of which is the *Tour St-Jean*, overlooking the Lot. To the W. of the *Pl. Thiers* is the *Porte de Diane*, an archway of a Roman bath; beyond its N.E. corner is the tall *Tour du Jean XXII*, part of an unfinished project, and adjacent *St-Barthélemy* (14C), with an older tower. The Blvd Gambetta, the main thoroughfare (originally Les Fossés, separating the old town from the new), leads S. past (r.) the *Palais de Justice*, behind which, in the old *Bishop's Palace*, is the *Museum*, with archaeological collections and a few paintings. The boulevard passes the Rue du Président-Wilson (see below) to reach the central *Pl. Aristide-Briand*, to the W. of which is the Allées Fénelon.

To the S. of the Place the boulevard descends past the *Théâtre* to the *Pont Louis-Philippe* (1838); to the E. lies the old town of narrow lanes preserving several mansions of interest, and the whole area is being restored and tidied up. At the far end of the Rue Clemenceau stands *St-Urcisse* (12-13C).

To the N., beyond the *Halles*, is the *Cathedral, founded in 1119, altered between 1285 and 1500, partially restored earlier this century, and now receiving the more radical attention its fabric deserves.

Its most remarkable features are the nave roof, which consists of two huge cupolas, whose drums are well seem from outside, and the finely carved *N. portal* (c. 1190), with decorated blind arcades on either side of the porch and beneath it. On the tympanum is Christ ascending, surrounded by two rows of reliefs, below which are the Apostles, vigorously sculptured; the W. door is an echo of the same motif.

Seventeen steps descend into the nave. The first dome bears a 14C painting of the Apostles, and the Stoning of Stephen; in the 2nd N. chapel is the tomb of Bp Sicard de Montaigue (d. 1300). In the *Choir* are wall-paintings of 1315; and the Flamboyant doorway between the apse-chapels will be noted. To the S. is a *Cloister* of 1500, preserving a spiral-staircase at its N.E. corner; the main pillar at the N.W. corner retains a statue; off the E. walk is the Gothic *Chapter-house*. A passage admits to a garden commanding a view of the Renaissance sculpture of the adjacent *Archdeaconry*.

Immediately N.W. is the 17C *Préfecture*. Turning r. past the N. portal (of the cathedral; see above) we reach the Quai Champollion, to the r. in which is the *Maison Henri-IV* or *de Roaldès* (late 15C); to the l., the ugly *Pont Neuf*, where stood a 14C bridge.—On the far bank stands *Sacré-Coeur* (15C) and the ruins of a Jacobin church.

To the N.W. of the bridge are relics of the *Collège Pélegri*, founded 1364, with a 15C tower containing a fine spiral-staircase; and further N. the remains of the *Château du Roi*, mainly 14C, once the residence of the Seneschal of Quercy. Ascending to the W. the Blvd Gambetta is regained.

The Rue du Président-Wilson leads W., in which No. 9 was Gambetta's birthplace, passing the 17C brick tower of the *Lycée* (l.) to end at the superb *Pont Valentré, with its three lofty towers, two with machicolations, and six arches spanning the Lot. It is a remarkable monument of medieval architecture (1308), even if over-restored in 1878 by Paul Gout *sans goût*. The bases of its piers are pointed, to break the current of the stream. The far bank provides a fine view of the bridge.

CAHORS TO VILLENEUVE-SUR-LOT (75km). The main road (D911) forks l. just N. of Cahors to (25.5km) *Castelfranc* (a 13C bastide), at 7km passing the château of *Mercuès*, once a palace of bishops, part medieval, part Renaissance.—The more interesting road (D8) turns r. at the far end of the Pont Valentré, following the valley of the Lot to (19km) *Luzech*, on a neck of a meander of the river, an old village preserving a 13C keep, N. of which rise the ruins of the Roman oppidum of *L'Impernal*, formerly a Neolithic site.—Continuing on the S. bank, we traverse *Albas*, and at 8km cross to *Castelfranc* (see above), there turning l., with a view across the river of the 15C *Château d'Anglars. Prayssac*, birthplace of Marshal Bessières (1768–1813), is traversed, and 7.5km beyond, *Puy-l'Évêque*, with some old mansions, and the keep of a castle of the bishops of Cahors.—The church at *Martignac*, 3km N., preserves 15C wall-paintings.—15km. *Condat*.

By turning r. up the side valley and then l., we approach (7km) the *Château de Bonaguil* (1480), one of the most impressive ruined strongholds in France, and one of the first built to resist canon, constructed on the site of an earlier castle. The cylindrical *Grosse Tour*, 35m high, commands a wide view.

The D911 traverses the industrial town of *Fumel*, 2km W. of Condat, and then adjacent *Monsempron-Libos*, overlooked by its Romanesque church, beyond which the valley widens.—17km. *St-Sylvestre-sur-Lot*, on the far bank of which stands *Penne-d'Agenais*, with remains of its ancient fortifications, including the *Porte Ricard*, built by Coeur-de-Lion, and two other gates.—8km. **Villeneuve-sur-Lot**, where we meet the N21; see Rte 66.

For the road up the Lot to *Figeac*, see pp 388-89, in reverse.

CAHORS TO MOISSAC (60km). The D653 turns r. 3km S. of Cahors for (21.5km) *Montcuq* (pron. Moncook), with a tall keep, 12.5km beyond which is *Lauzerte*, hill-top bastide of character. The D2 crosses two ridges before descending to (23km) *Moissac*; see Rte 76.—An alternative route is the next turning off the N20, the D659, via (20km) *Castelnau-de-Montratier*, fortified, and preserving its quaint arcaded place.

The N20 traverses the *Causse de Limogne*, at 24km passing (3km r.) *Montpezat-de-Quercy*, with old houses over arcades, and a church of 1334 with a rich treasury and 16C Flemish tapestries depicting the life of St Martin.—2km N. stands the isolated church of *Saux*, containing 14-15C frescoes.

12.5km. *Caussade*, a centre of straw-hat manufacture earlier this century, with a fine 15C belfry.—12.5km N.E. lies *Puylaroque*, a bastide built on a commanding site, sacked in 1209 during the Albigensian crusade.—For the road between Caussade and *Villefranche-de-Rouergue*, see Rte 65.

CAUSSADE TO ALBI (72km). The most direct route is that following the D964 S.E. via (12km) *Montricoux*, on the Aveyron, and *Bruniquel* (see Rte 65), there turning S., skirting the *Forêt de la Grésigne*, a hilly tract of beech and hornbeam woods, containing a number of megalithic monuments, to (9km) *Puycelci*, a picturesquely sited village, with ten towers of its ramparts extant, which resisted a siege under Guy de Montfort in 1213, together with several old houses, and (13km) *Castelnau-de-Montmirail*, also fortified, to approach (12km) *Gaillac* (see Rte 65), where we turn E. onto the N88. After 11km the Tarn is crossed, and **Albi** lies 11km beyond; see Rte 89.

An alternative road (74km) is that via *Cordes*, approached by following the D926 N.E. past (7km) *Septfonds*, a bastide of 1271, and forking r. to (12km) *St-Antonin-Noble-Val* (see Rte 65), there skirting the Aveyron to the E. for 13km before turning onto the D600 for (17km) *Cordes*, 25km N.W. of Albi; see Rte 65.

The N20 veers S.W. from Caussade, at 7km. traversing *Réalville*, a bastide of 1310, with its arcaded square, shortly beyond crossing the Aveyron.

15km. **MONTAUBAN** (53,100 Montalbanais), the dusty provincial préfecture of the *Tarn-et-Garonne*, stands on the high E. bank of the Tarn, its old red brick buildings providing 'many good houses without forming handsome streets', to quote Arthur Young.

It owes its origin and name to the union of the bastide of Montauban (founded 1144) with the settlement which had grown up round the abbey of Montauriol (c. 820). It suffered severely during the Albigensian persecutions, and in the 16C was a stronghold of Protestantism, being established in 1570 by the treaty of St-Germain as one of the four cities allotted to the Huguenots for freedom of worship. It withstood a siege by Charles de Luynes in 1621 and surrendered voluntarily in 1629 to Richelieu after the fall of La Rochelle, but despite the infliction on the Protestant inhabitants of the iniquitous *'dragonnades'*, when troops were billeted on them with instructions to behave with the utmost brutality, a high proportion of its citizens remained staunch supporters of Reform. Its lower lying districts were much damaged by floods in 1930.

Among its natives were Jean-Auguste-Dominique Ingres (1780–1867), and the sculptor Antoine Bourdelle (1861–1929); while the Republican president of Spain, Manuel Azaña (1880–1939), died here in exile.

A number of roads converge on the *Pl. Bourdelle*, from which the fine *Pont Vieux* of seven arches (1316) spans the Tarn. The square is overlooked to the W. by an imposing brick edifice of 1659, preserving considerable remains of a 14C episcopal castle, and is now occupied by the ***Musée Ingres**, notable for the collection of over 4000 drawings it contains, bequeathed by the artist, and displayed in rotation.

The FIRST FLOOR contains numerous representative works by Ingres, notable among which are Portraits of the enigmatic Mme Gonse; of Belvèze-Foulon; of J.-F. Gilibert; of Lorenzo Bartolini, the sculptor; and of his father, Jean-Joseph-Marie Ingres (1754–1814), several of whose own paintings are shown. Also Roger delivering Angélique (a reduced version of that in the Louvre); the Song of Ossian, etc.—SECOND FLOOR: *anon.* Young woman and mirror (16C French); *Jordaens*, various studies; *Nanteuil*, Male portrait; *Frans Franken le Vieux*, Ball scene; attrib. *Ribera*, St Jerome; attrib. *van Honthorst*, Singing by candelight; *Momper*, Village under snow; *Duplessis*, Portrait of Louis XVI; *Verdussen*, Army on the march, and Siege of Valenciennes.The GROUND FLOOR is devoted to sculptures by *Bourdelle*.—Stairs descend to the BASEMENT, with good brick vaulting, and containing local and archaeological collections, as does the sub-Basement, known as the *Black Prince's Chamber*, a large vaulted hall of 1369 containing two 15C fireplaces; the bronze figurines (mostly found at the neighbouring Roman settlement of *Cosa-Hispalia*), and a curious column, will be noted.

To the N.E. of the Place stands *St-Jacques* (14-15C), a brick building in the Gothic Toulousaine style, with an octagonal tower.—A street immediately to its N. leads r. into the *Pl. Nationale* (17C), surrounded by a brick arcade with a gateway at each corner, turning S. from which we gain the Rue de la République, leading E. to the Pl. Maréchal-Foch. From its S.W. corner a street leads back past the large but uninspired classical *Cathedral* (1692–1739), containing the Vow of Louis XIII by Ingres.—From behind the building a lane leads down to the *Jardin des Plantes*, through which the little river Tescou runs into the Tarn. Hence we may regain the Pl. Bourdelle, just N. of which is a *Natural History Museum*.

MONTAUBAN TO AUCH (86km). The D928 bears S.W., crossing the A61 motorway to (12km) *Montech* (see Rte 76) and then both the N113 and the Garonne.—14.5km. *Larrazet*, with a 13th and 15C church and a château of 1500, 3.5km N. of which is the brick-built *Château de Terride*, of the same date.—We ascend the Gimone valley to (10km) *Beaumont-de-Lomagne*, a bastide preserving its central arcaded Place, a late 15C wooden *Halle*, and a 14C church with an octagonal belfry; it was the birthplace of Pierre de Fermat (c. 1595–1665), the mathematician.—The church at *Bonillac* (c. 13km S.E.) preserves an important treasury, largely of objects from the Cistercian abbey of Grandselve.—20km. *Mauvezin*, a bastide with a huge arcaded Place, a stone-columned *Market-hall*, and 13C *Belfry*.—*Cologne*, 9km due E., is another attractive bastide, its 15C houses under restoration, and with a *Halle* of the same period.—For *Gimont* (13km S. of Mauvezin), see Rte 84.—The D928 continues S.W. to meet the N124 at (14km) *Aubiet*, where we turn r., after 4.5km with a view (r.) of the 18C *Château* of the Duc de Montesquiou Fezensac at *Marsan*, and some 9km beyond, descend from the ridge into the Gers valley, with the cathedral of **Auch** dominating its far bank; see Rte 84.

The N20 drives S. from Montauban, briefly skirting the l. bank of the Tarn to meet the N113 after 22km, there running parallel to the Garonne for (29km) **Toulouse**; see Rte 86. It may be preferable to join the motorway 11km from Montauban. See also the last section of Rte 76.

65 Brive to Albi via Figeac

200km (124 miles). N20. 20km N140. 13km *Martel*—16km
Rocamadour lies 4km S.W.—8km *Gramat*—35km **Figeac**—D922.
37km **Villefranche-de-Rouergue**—17km *Najac* lies 7km S.W.—16km
Laguépie—13km **Cordes**—D600. 25km **Albi**.

Maps: IGN 48, 57, 64, or 110, 111, 114. M 239, 235.

For **Brive**, see Rte 64.—We fork l. 20km S. of Brive across the *Causse de Martel*, a centre of truffle cultivation, to (13km) **Martel**, a charming little town, preserving a number of old buildings, where in 1183 died Henry Plantagenet, the eldest son of Henry II. To the E. of the main road is the *Market-hall*, near which is the *Hôtel de la Raymondie* (14-16C), under restoration; and further S., a large 15C *Church* with a 12C doorway, an impressive belfry of 1513 and a fortified apse. It contains some early 16C glass, but the interior deserves restoration.

The *Puy d'Issolud*, some 8km E., was probably the site of *Uxellodunum*, the last stronghold of the Gauls after the fall of Alesia; it fell to Caesar in 59 B.C. only after he had diverted its water supply.

MARTEL TO SOUILLAC. The direct D703 leads S.W. (14.5km), but the more attractive if slightly longer road is that along the Dordogne valley, to which the N140 descends past (l.) the château of *Mirandol*, with a Renaissance stair, and a good view of the *Cirque de Monvalent*, on the far bank, its cliffs rising 200m from the valley floor.—We may follow the N. bank past *Gluges*, with a disused semi-subterranean 12C church of interest, to (5km) *Creysse*, an old village with a Romanesque church of unusual plan, with twin apses and a large vaulted hall on the N. side, originally part of the castle.—After c. 5km we skirt the far bank to *Lacave*, with a series of stalactite caverns containing small lakes, later passing the picturesque châteaux of *La Belcastel* on its rocky spur, and *La Treyne* (17C), and re-cross the Dordogne to turn N.W. to *Souillac*; see Rte 64. The N20 may also be reached c. 14km S.W. by a lane leading up a side valley from La Belcastel to *Calès*.
   A minor road turns l. below the Cirque de Monvalent to (10km) *Carennac*, an old village where Fénelon wrote 'Télémaque'; its priory church (12th and 15C) preserves a part Romanesque and part Gothic cloister.

The N140 climbs to the *Causse de Gramat*, a typical limestone plateau (cf. Rte 102) riddled with pot-holes, at 16km (from Martel) reaching crossroads.

The r.-hand turning leads 4km to *L'Hospitalet*, with a fortified gate, providing a plunging view into the narrow Alzou valley, in which, below an abrupt cliff, nestles the commercialised village of **Rocamadour**, to which we may descend (3.5km), although there are many who would prefer the distant view, the closer merely provoking disillusion. Celebrated in medieval times as a goal of pilgrimage, but for no intelligible reason, it was well promoted and visited by sundry saints and credulous monarchs, as it still is visited, particularly by unsophisticated Bretons, etc. In the long, and usually congested, village street, are four gateways. Some two-thirds of the way along a flight of steps ascends to the fortified *Palace of the Bishops of Tulle*, and beyond a courtyard is the *Crypte de St-Amadour* (1160), surmounted by the basilica of *St-Sauveur*. A tunnel leads to a terrace (views), while at a higher level, reached by more steps, are other chapels 'restored' out of all recognition (as has been the château on the summit) or built in a bogus Romanesque style, two of which preserve relics of 13C frescoes.—The main Brive-Cahors road may be reached c. 20km. W., via *Calès*.
   The l.-hand turning at the Rocamadour crossroads leads 9km E. to *Padirac*, 2.5km N. of which is the '**Gouffre de Padirac**', a huge pot-hole, 114m wide and 246m deep, a veritable tourist trap. The descent by lifts and staircases, and the

exploration of the electrically lit galleries with their stalagmites and stalactites, and of the subterranean river by boat, may be made, usually in the company of crowds, which occupies 1½ hours. It was discovered by the speleologists E.A. Martel and G. Gaupillat in 1889, and has been much commercialised since.—The road goes on to (14km) *St-Céré*; see p 381.

Continuing S. from the Rocamadour crossroads, we shortly pass (l.) the *Gouffre du Saut de la Pucelle*, one of several pot-holes, '*avens*' or '*igues*' scattered over the causse, to (5km) *Gramat*, and 13.5km beyond, *Rudelle*, with a curious fortified church of the 13C.—3km. *Le Bourg*, 2km beyond which a r.-hand turning leads 5km to *Assier*, with a ruined Renaissance *Château and church, both built by Galiot de Genouillac (1466–1546), Grand Master of Artillery to François I, whose exploits are depicted on the exterior frieze of the church; the upper part of his tomb shows him standing beside a cannon.

The main road continues S.E., later descending to (16km) **Figeac** (10,500 Figeaçois), a quaint old town in the valley of the Célé, preserving a number of 13-14C houses in its narrow lanes. It was the birthplace of Jean-François Champollion (1790–1832), the Egyptologist.

A short distance N.E. of the *Pont Gambetta* stands *St-Sauveur, Romanesque in origin, and altered in the 13C (S. triforium) and 17C (N. side and nave vault), while its W. front dates from 1825.—From its N. side a lane leads and then climbs to hill-top *N.-D.-du-Puy*, another much-altered Romanesque church, originally with double aisles; the triple apse and crypt date from the 12C: the W. front from the 14C.—Another lane descends S.W. to the triangular *Pl. Champollion*, and continuing S.W. we reach the restored late 13C *Hôtel de la Monnaie* in the *Pl. Louis-Vival*, now housing the S.I. and a small museum of local interest.

FIGEAC TO RODEZ (65km). The main road (N140) via *Decazeville* is first described, although that unattractive industrial town is better avoided. We climb steeply onto a narrow ridge between the Célé and the Lot.—5km. *Capdenac-le-Haut*, a charming little village on a promontory, with remains of 13-14C ramparts and of a castle which belonged to Sully, lies to the l.—We descend to the modern settlement of *Capdenac-Gare*, on the far bank of the Lot, from which the D944 leads S.E. via (21km) *Montbazens*—passing some 6km E. of *Peyrasse-le-Roc*, a curious decayed town with a ruined church and ramparts—to meet the Villefranche-Rodez road 8.5km beyond, and 31km from Rodez.—The main road skirts the r. bank of the Lot for c. 12.5km to *La Rocque-Bouillac*. Just beyond this village a l.-hand turning (D627) continues to ascend the Lot valley to the E. to (c. 25km) the *Pont de Coursavy*, 6.5km N.W. of *Conques*; see p 518.—The N140 bears S.E. shortly traversing (7.5km) **Decazeville** (9200 inhab.), strung out along the valley, which grew around the foundries established by Duc Decazes in 1830 in the Aveyron coalfield: surface coal has been mined since the 9C at *Aubin*, 4km S. (with a curious 12-15C church). The opera-singer Emma Calvé (1862–1942) was born at Decazeville.—After (5km) *Firmi* we quit the coalfield and after (14km) *Valady* commence to climb up to the bleak *Causse de Comtal*, reaching **Rodez** 18km beyond, dominated by its cathedral tower; see Rte 95.

FIGEAC TO CAHORS. There are several routes: The main road (D653; 69km) leading W. over the *Causse de Gramat*, eventually descending into the valley of the Vers below (47km) the well-preserved Gaulish oppidum of *Mursens*.—At (7.5km) *Vers*, we meet the Lot and turn r., following its r. bank, passing at *Laroque-des-Arcs* a château preserving its 13C tower, to (14.5km) *Cahors*; see Rte 64.

An alternative and more attractive road is the D41, turning l. off the former after c. 6km to follow the meanderings of the Célé via *Espagnac-Ste-Eulalie*, with a 13-17C priory church, to (33km) *Marcilhac*, with a 12th and 15C abbey church with a 9C doorway. 1.5km N.W., approached by a steep lane, is the stalactite

Grotte Bellevue.—15km. *Cabrerets*, with a ruined cliff-top stronghold, a 15C château, and in the adjacent valley of the Sagne, the *Grotte de Pech-Merle*, with prehistoric wall-paintings.—After 4.5km we enter the Lot valley at *Conduché*, just below *St-Cirq-Lapopie*, high up on the far bank (see below), where we turn r. to follow the river to (28.5km) *Cahors*.

A third road is reached by following the D19 S.W. from Figeac to (25km) *Cajarc*, whose ramparts were destroyed by Louis XIII, there turning r. along the Lot valley, skirting either bank past *Calvignac*, a rock-perched village (S. bank) and the huge 13-16C castle of *Cénevières*, and further W., ***St-Cirq-Lapopie**, picturesquely sited on a height above the valley, and not yet too spoilt (although to be avoided in the season). A belvedere to the W. provides a good view of the Lot, the far bank of which may be regained at *Bouziès*, just W. of *Conduché*; see above.

The D922 climbs S. over the dividing ridge between the Célé and the Lot, at 8km crossing the latter by the *Pont de la Madeleine*.

From the far bank, the r.-hand turning leads to (c. 8km) a bridge crossing back to *Larroque-Toirac*, with a tall tower to its castle, and adjacent *St-Pierre-Toirac*, with a fortified 12C church.—Hence the valley may be followed to *Cajarc*, see above.

We mount rapidly onto the causse, at 17km traversing *Villeneuve-d'Aveyron*, its church with a Romanesque apse at one end, and a Gothic apse at the other, later descending into the Aveyron valley.

11km. **Villefranche-de-Rouergue** (13,900 inhab.), the nucleus of which is a good example of a bastide, this one being re-founded on the r. bank of the river by Alphonse de Poitiers, Count of Toulouse, in 1252. On the E. side of the arcaded central *Place* stands *Notre-Dame*, commenced in the mid 13C, finished in 1581, and flanked by a robust W. tower. To the S. of the town a hospital occupies the dependencies of a 15-16C Carthusian monastery.

VILLEFRANCHE TO MONTAUBAN VIA CAUSSADE (73km). The D926 climbs N.W., and after 5km forks l., after a further 5km passing (r.) the former Cistercian abbey church of *Locdieu*, with three cloister galleries, much restored in the mid 19C when the adjacent château was built.—Traversing part of the *Causse de Limogne*, we approach (10km) *St-Martin*, 8km S. of which—first passing the 16C château of *Cornusson*—is the 13C Cistercian abbey-church of *Beaulieu-en-Rouergue*, ◊ founded in 1144, which with its dependencies, has recently been restored, and is in use as an Arts Centre.—9km. *Caylus*, with its Grande Rue lined with 14-15C houses, a church and ruined castle of the 14C, and a large covered Market.—*Lacapelle-Livron*, 3km N., was a commandery of the Templars.—12km. S., reached by following the Bonnette valley, lies *St-Antonin*; see below.—The main road continues to (15km) *Septfonds*, a bastide of 1271, and 7km beyond meets the N20 at *Caussade*, 22km from Montauban; see Rte 64; but see below for an alternative route.

From Villefranche the D922 climbs above the valley of the Aveyron.—At 17km a r.-hand turning leads 7km to ***Najac**, an attractive slate-roofed village perched on a steep hillside, at the foot of which is the 13C church, above which, on a bold cliff, the ruined castle (1110; altered 1252).—A lane hence leads across the river and S.W. to *Varen*; see below.—The main road is regained at *La Croix Grande*, 7km S.E., 6.5km S. of the turning off, and later descends to (9.5km) *Laguépie*, sacked by Simon de Montfort in 1212, at the confluence of the Viaur and Aveyron.

LAGUÉPIE TO MONTAUBAN (74km). We follow the Aveyron valley to the W. via (8km) *Varen*, a quaint village with a 12C church and 14-15C keep.—16km. **St-Antonin-Noble-Val** (r.), a medieval town sufficiently important not to be laid waste by de Montfort in 1212, and thus preserving a valuable example of early

12C domestic architecture, formerly the town hall, and restored by Viollet-le-Duc. The figures of Solomon and of Adam and Eve, on the first floor, are skilfully carved.—Recrossing the gorge, we shortly circle to the S. to (15km) *Penne*, an old fortified village with considerable remains of its 13-14C castle, which stands on the edge of a precipitous cliff.—6.5km. *Bruniquel* is another rock-perched village, with an 11-12C castle, in which Raymond VI of Toulouse shut himself up in 1211 before delivering it to his brother Baldwyn. (It is said, by Gregory of Tours, to have been founded by Brunehaut, wife of Sigebert, king of Austrasia, and known as *Brunichildis Castrum*.)—5.5km. *Montricoux*, with a 13C church and ruined castle, lies to the r., as we bear away from the river via (8.5km) *Nègrepelisse*, to *Montauban*, 16km beyond; see Rte 64.

The road from Laguépie climbs steeply out of the valley before descending into that of the Cérou, with a view ahead of (13km) **Cordes**. Founded in 1222 by Raymond VII of Toulouse, and named *Corua* after Andalusian Cordoba, it is one of the most interesting of the bastides of Languedoc extant, and as such is somewhat spoilt by 'tourist blight'; nevertheless it deserves the detour. The town stands on the summit of a conical hill, riddled with excavations used as grain-stores in times of siege, for it long remained a Cathar centre, even as late as 1233 lynching two inquisitors sent to examine them. Three lines of ramparts may be distinguished, although only the second is very noticeable. The Rue Droite traverses the whole length of the upper town from the *Porte des Ormeaux*, and is lined by a number of 14C mansions, including the so-called *Maison du Grande-Fauconnier*. In a parallel street to the N. is *St-Michel*, with a 13C apse and 14C tower, and a nave (1460–85) in the style of Albi cathedral.

The D600 leads 25km S.E. to **Albi**, a good view of which it commands on the descent into the Tarn valley; see Rte 89.

66   Limoges to Agen, via Périgueux and Bergerac

237km (147 miles). N21. 35km *Châlus*—66km **Périgueux**—47km **Bergerac**. **Marmande** lies 58km S.W.—60km **Villeneuve-sur-Lot**—29km **Agen**.

Maps: IGN 41, 48, 47, 56, or 110. M 233, 235.

The N21 from **Limoges** (Rte 63) follows the N. bank of the Vienne, crossing the river at (13.5km) *Aixe-sur-Vienne*, there ascending S.W. to (21.5km) **Châlus**, with two 12C castles; it was when besieging that on the far bank of the Tardoire, occasioned by a petty dispute over treasure-trove, that Richard I, 'Coeur-de-Lion', was mortally wounded by a bolt from a cross-bow, dying shortly after at Chinon, where he was carried (1199).—The 12-15C château of *Montbrun* is 8km S.W.

29km. *Thiviers*, with a 12C church restored in the 15C, behind which is an old fortified house, and the 15-18C *Château de Vaucocour*.—The 16C *Château de Laxion* at *Corgnac*, 6km S.E., is of interest.

St-Jean-de-Côle lies 8km W., with an interesting 11C church, once domed and formerly the chapel of an Augustinian priory, preserving parts of a Renaissance cloister, and the imposing *Château de la Marthonie* (15-18C). The road goes on to *Brantôme*, 19km S.W.; see Rte 71.

At (24km) *Sarliac* we reach the river Isle, and veer S.W. past the strik-

ing *Château de Rognac*, and l., on a height, the *Château de Caussade*
(15-16C), with an octagonal enceinte.

  15km. **PÉRIGUEUX** (35,400 Pétrocoriens or Périgourdins), préfecture of the Dordogne, and ancient capital of the *Périgord*, stands
largely on the r. bank of the Isle, the medieval nucleus on a hill
around the cathedral, while to the W. the *Cité* occupies the site of the
Gallo-Roman town. Tasteful restoration of dilapidated buildings has
taken place during recent years, particularly between the Pl. Montaigne and the river, which has done much to improve the general
appearance of the town, long famous for its truffles and pâté de foie
gras.

It was an important centre of prehistoric settlements; the hill of *Ecorneboeuf*, on
the l. bank, being occupied both by neolithic man and by the Gallic Petrocorii.
This was superseded by Roman *Vesunna*, where the Cité now stands, which by
the 4C was the see of a bishop. The abbey of St-Front was founded after the 5C
on a neighbouring height, and the two districts remained at loggerheads until
united by the threat of English invasion in the 13C, who held the place briefly
from 1356. It was in Huguenot hands in 1575–81, and was garrisoned by Condé
during the Fronde, in 1651, since when its history has been comparatively
uneventful. Among its natives were Gén. Daumesnil (1776–1832), and the
writer Léon Bloy (1846–1917).

From the r. bank of the Isle it is convenient to turn up the Cours
Tourny, flanked by the Allées de Tourny, overlooked by the *Préfec-
ture*; the Allées are extended by the *Pl. Montaigne*, dominated by the
Palais de Justice, of 1839.

On the S. side of the Cours is the **Musée du Périgord**, largely devoted to archaeological and ethnographical collections, which occupy its E. wing, together
with a Gallo-Roman section containing several bronzes, mosaics, and glass of interest. The adjacent courtyard contains a lapidary collection, while the chapel to
the S., a relic of the Augustinian convent formerly on this site, preserves ter-

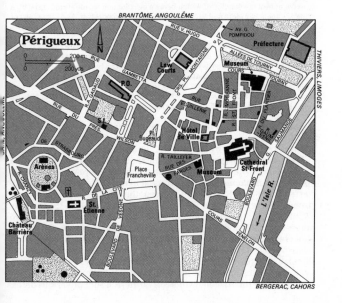

racotta figures from Thiviers, and a somewhat miscellaneous range of local antiquities. The Art Gallery is of little moment, although notable are the Portrait of
Fénelon by *F. Bailleul*, and The Siege of Namur, by *Martin 'des Batailles'*.

Although the Rue St-Front leads directly to the cathedral, this is
preferably approached by the Rue Limogeanne, parallel to the W., in
and off which are several Renaissance houses preserving elements of
interest, among them Nos 3 and 5, and the inner doorway of No. 12;
the *Maison Tenant* (17 Rue Éguillerie), to the r.; and the *Hôtel de St-
Astier* (2 Rue de la Miséricorde), to the l., with a Renaissance stairway; another may be seen at No. 1 Rue de la Sagesse, in which Nos 3
and 11 are notable.

Beyond a small market square, we reach the 18C *Hôtel de VIIIe*,
once the home of François Joseph Lagrange-Chancel (1677–1758),
a dramatist and satirical poet.—A few paces to the S.W. brings on the
Pl. de la Clautre and the cathedral.

*St-Front which succeeded St-Étienne (see below) as the cathedral
in 1669, is certainly one of the more curious ecclesiastical edifices in
France; which makes it the more unfortunate that the 19C 'restorations' of Abadie (later responsible for the erection of the 'Sacre-
Coeur' at Paris), Brugère, and Boeswillwald, were tolerated, with
which it lost much of its character, and gained nothing.

The present church is on the plan of a Greek cross, similar to that of St Mark's at
Venice, with five magnificent domes, one over the crossing, and one over each
arm, but there the resemblance ends. The domes of St-Front, with the pendentives resting on twelve square attached piers of colossal size, are quite unlike the
Byzantine domes of St Mark's, and traces of a sixth dome on the W. side of the
tower indicate that the usual Latin cross plan was the original intention. It was
probably erected in 1125–50 to succeed the earlier abbey-church founded in
the 6C, rebuilt in 984–1047, but largely destroyed by fire in 1120, relics of
which may be seen. The primitive facade possibly dates in part from the 6C.

The 60m-high *Tower* is a reconstruction by Abadie, and consists of two
massive cubes, the smaller of which bears a circular colonnade surmounted by a
conical cupola; six piers had to be strengthened to support this. The upper part of
the original belfry may be seen in the adjacent *Cloister*, an amalgam of styles
from the 12C on.

The massive simplicity of the interior is impressive, with its walls decorated
with plain blind arcading. In the W. arm are two chambers, known as *Confessions* (10-11C), and another is under Abadie's apse. The high altar of 1762 comes
from the chartreuse de Vauclaire, and the pulpit is likewise well carved. There is
little else to say. As Freda White succinctly put it: '. . . looking at St Front. . . one
imagines that M. Abadie is employed carrying the stones of his good intentions
to build the walls of hell. This is a supreme example of how not to restore'.

A short distance N. of the apse is the 15C *Hôtel Gamenson* (7 Rue de
la Constitution); while the Rue Daumesnil descends to the river,
overlooked to the l. by several 16C houses.

From just W. of the Pl. de la Clautre, the Rue des Farges, with a
small *Military Museum*, and in which Nos 4-6 are remarkable, leads
to the *Tour Mataguerre*, reconstructed in the 15C, a relic of the ramparts of the Puy-St-Front.—Crossing the *Pl. Francheville*, we approach in the Rue de la Cité the former cathedral of *St-Étienne.
Mutilated by the Huguenots in 1577, only two of its cupolas have
survived (1120; and the larger, over the choir, of 1150). On the N.
side of the street is a chapel of 1521, sole relic of the Bishop's Palace
destrroyed in 1544.—From the *Pl. de la Cité* the **Tour de Vesone**, the
circular cella of a temple of Vesunna, tutelary deity of the Roman city, is seen at the end of the Rue Romaine (S.). A short walk to the W.
brings one to the so-called *Château Barrière*, a ruin of various dates;

the tall round tower is 10C; the body of the castle is 12C with 16C windows; at its N. end is the Roman *Porte Normande*.

Turning N.E. we reach the *Arènes*, an elliptical garden and the site of the Roman Amphitheatre, of which only a few detached rubble arches are visible, having been used as a quarry after 1644, but it is at present the object of excavation.—We may return to the centre from its E. side (Rue des Gladiateurs) to the Av. du Aquitaine (with the S.I.), where, turning r., the Pl. Montaigne is regained.

For the road from Périgueux to *Bordeaux*, see Rte 67; for *Brive* and *Clermont Ferrand*, Rte 94, in reverse; and for the road from *Angoulême* to *Cahors* via *Périgueux* and *Sarlat*, Rte 71.

After crossing the *Pont Neuf*, commanding perhaps the best view of St-Front, we turn r., climbing out of the valley and traversing undulating wooded country for some 40km before descending into the valley of the Caudau, and (7km) Bergerac, on the Dordogne.

Bergerac (27,700 Bergeracois), an important centre of the wine trade, was a Protestant stronghold in the 16C, and the Peace of Bergerac (1577) was an abortive attempt to end the Religious Wars. Much has been done in recent years to restore the older town, which preserves some picturesque corners.

It was the birthplace of the introspective philosopher Maine de Biran (1766–1824); the celebrated Savinien Cyrano de Bergerac (1619–55), the duellist author, and long-nosed hero of Rostand's play (1897), although descended from an old family of Périgord, lived and died in Paris; they had an estate called Bergerac in the valley of the Chevreuse.

The r.-hand fork as we enter from the N. traverses the *Pl. de la République* and descends the Rue Neuve d'Argenson, with (l.) the *Hôtel de Ville*, which contains a local museum and also the *Musée de Tabac*, describing the interesting history and influence of that weed: there is an experimental tobacco institute near Bergerac. To the W. of this street are the characteristic lanes of the older town, in which one may visit the vaulted cellars of the former *Couvent des Récollets* (12-17C), and several other tastefully restored buildings of minor interest.

For the road from *Bordeaux* to *Souillac* via Bergerac, see Rte 74, likewise for thee sub-route from Bergerac to *Cahors* via *Monpazier*. For roads from Bergerac to **Bayonne**, see Rte 79.

The N21 bears S.E. on crossing the Dordogne, shortly passing the E. end of the *Monbazillac* vineyards (see Rte 79).

10.5km. The l.-hand fork offers an interesting ALTERNATIVE ROAD TO VILLENEUVE-SUR-LOT via (8km) *Issigeac*, once walled, with a good Renaissance church, while the mairie occupies the buildings of an abbey where Fénelon once lived.—7km E. stands the restored *Château de Bardon* (15-16C).—16km. *Villeréal*, a bastide of 1265, with its wooden-pillared Market-hall, 'cornières' (see below), and fortified church in excellent preservation.—*Monpazier* lies 15km E.; see Rte 74.—13km. *Monflanquin*, a well-sited and picturesque hilltop bastide founded by Alphonse de Poitiers in 1269, with a 14-15C church, the terrace behind which provides a good view to the S.E., with the keep of *Bonaguil* in the distance; see p 384.—17km. *Villeneuve*; see below.

After 16.5km the main road traverses *Castillonnès*, an over-restored bastide of 1260, 3km W. of which are the ruins of *Cahuzac*, visited by Rabelais in the 1520s, and where La Rochefoucauld wrote some of his 'Maximes' in 1653–57; *La Roche-Guyon*, N.W. of Paris, also claims that honour.—14km. *Cancon*, a pleasant village, beyond which the road becomes hillier, with good views E., before descending into the valley at (19km) **Villeneuve-sur-Lot** (23,700 Villeneuvois), which has grown up round a bastide founded in 1264 by Alphonse de Poitiers, brother of Louis IX. Its dried plums are reputed.

The old town is entered by the *Porte de Paris* (13-15C); the central *Place* is surrounded by arcades, locally called '*cornières*'. Adjoining is a brick-built church of 1937 preserving 14-15C glass from its predecessor. The *Pont Vieux* (13C; altered in the 17C) crosses the Lot, bordered by old houses, to reach the *Porte de Pujols*, resembling the Porte de Paris.—*Pujols*, a decayed walled village, 3km S.W., is best approached by the old Roman road which enters through an arch in the church-tower.

10km N.W. (via the D242) is *Casseneuil*, with a fine 12C church, and the birthplace of Louis le Débonnaire (778–840), eldest son of Charlemagne.—9.5km W. of Villeneuve on the D911, lies *Ste-Livrade-sur-Lot*, with a 14C church tower. The road continues to (27km) *Tonneins*, on the N113; see Rte 76.—For the road from Villeneuve up the valley of the Lot to *Cahors*, see Rte 64, in reverse.

The N21 leads S. across the plateau between the Lot and the Garonne.—At 4km a l.-hand turning leads c. 10km S.E. to to *Hautefage*, where the hexagonal belfry remains of a Renaissance palace of the bishops of Agen.—26km. **Agen**; see Rte 80.

67 Périgueux to Bordeaux

121km (75 miles). N89. 35km *Mussidan*—17km *Montpon-Ménestrol*—38km **Libourne**—31km **Bordeaux**.

Maps: IGN 47, or 110. M 75.

For **Périgueux**, see Rte 66.

PÉRIGUEUX TO LIBOURNE VIA RIBÉRAC (105km). This alternative route follows the D710, turning l. off the Angoulême road (D939) leading N.W.—Almost immediately we pass (r.) *Chancelade*; see Rte 71.—The D710 climbs over a ridge, entering the valley of the Dronne at (24km) *Tocane-St-Apre*. *Montagrier*, and *Grand-Brassac* (2.5km N., and 3.5km beyond) have churches of interest.—2.5km S. of Tocane is the 16-18C *Château de Fayolle*.—We drive due W., with a view (l.) of the 12C keep of *Vernode*, and later (r.) the 18C *Château de la Rigale*, preserving a Gallo-Roman tower, to (14km) **Ribérac**, of slight interest in itself, but the birthplace of the troubadour Arnaut Daniel (1180–1210). It is the local centre for the large British expatriate population of the region.—Among the villages in the district, *Lusignac*, c. 10km N.W., is one of the more attractive.—From Ribérac the D5 leads W. across the undulating plateau of the *Double* via (20km) *St-Aulaye*, a bastide of 1288 with a 12C church, to *La Roche-Chalais*, 12km beyond; see below.

A more interesting DETOUR is that following the D20 along the valley to (17km) **Aubeterre-sur-Dronne**, with two Romanesque churches; *St-Jean*, hollowed in the rock and containing a curious two-storeyed monument with mutilated statutes (added later) of Marshal de Lussan (d. c. 1620) and his wife, and a baptistry; its cemetery has been in use from the 6-7C. At a higher level is *St-Jacques*, wtih a richly-carved 11C facade.—11km W. is *Chalais*, its church with a Romanesque facade, and with a large château of various dates of the Talleyrand family.—The 12C church at *Rioux-Martin*, 4km S.W., is of interest.—Hence we turn l., and descend the valley via (15km) *La Roche-Chalais*, to (18km) *Coutras* (pron. *Coutra*) a one-street town with a partly rebuilt 15C church, and the well-

head surviving of its Renaissance château, demolished in 1730. It was the scene
of Henri of Navarre's victory over the troops of Henri III in 1587.—*Guîtres*, 6km
W., has a church of various periods since the 12C, with interesting
details.—*Libourne* (see below) is entered 17km S.W. of Coutras, passing en route
St-Denis-de-Pile, its church with a crenellated belfry.

The N89 descends the valley of the Isle, following the S. bank, at
14km passing S. of *St-Astier*, with a large domed 12C church with
16C alterations, 2km W. of which is the 15C *Château de Puy-Ferrat*.

7km. The large Renaissance *Château de Mellet* (1530) lies to the r.,
9km beyond which we traverse *Sourzac*, with an 11-12C church and
ruined 14C castle, and 2km beyond, *Mussidan*.—5km S.E., in the
valley of the Crempse, is the Renaissance château of *Montréal*, with
13C fortifications.

17km. *Montpon-Ménesterol*, of interest for the collection of organs
in the vicinity restored under the auspices of Francis Chapelet.—The
D9 drives S.W. hence passing near (l.) the ruined hilltop castle of *Gur-
son* (14C) and (14km) *Montpeyroux*, with a fine Romanesque church,
to approach the château of *Montaigne*; see Rte 74.

17.5km. *St-Médard-de-Guizières*, 4km S. of which is the church of
*Petit-Palais, with a remarkable Romanesque facade.—The main
road shortly veers S.W. to (20.5km) **Libourne** (23,300 inhab.), a dull
town, the old centre of which, at the confluence of the Isle and Dordogne, is a regularly built bastide founded in 1270 by Edward I when
Prince of Wales. A castle was then built by Roger de Leybourne,
seneschal of Gascony, who gave the town name. Here in 1366
the Black Prince signed a treaty with Pedro the Cruel of Castile and
Carlos II of Navarre. It has long been a commercial centre for the
vineyards of the area and previously for those of Bergerac, likewise
for the salt trade with Souillac. Its only relics of interest are the *Porte
de l'Horloge*, a gateway of the 14C ramparts on the quay, and the arcaded *Grande-Place*, with its restored 15C Hôtel de Ville, incorporating a small museum. To the S.E. of the town, beyond the
railway bridge, is the 12C *Chapelle de Condat*.

2km W., on the r. bank of the Dordogne, lies *Fronsac*, an old town dominated by
the *Tertre de Fronsac*, on which stood a celebrated stronghold of Charlemagne,
commanding a good view of the valley, especially interesting when the tidal
'bore' is ascending the river.
  For *St-Émilion*, 6.5km E., see Rte 74.

We cross the Dordogne by a bridge built during the First Empire,
after c. 7km passing S. of *Vayres*, ancient *Varatedum*, with a 13C
and Renaissance château. The road traverses the peninsula of Entre
Deux Mers to approach the E. outskirts of **Bordeaux**, the centre of
which we reach at 24km; see Rte 75.

68 Limoges to Angoulême and Saintes

173km (107 miles). N141. 30km **St-Junien**—51km *La
Rochefoucauld*—22km **Angoulême**—44km **Cognac**—26km **Saintes**.

Maps: IGN 41, 40, or 107 or 110. M 233.

We drive W. from **Limoges** (Rte 63), after 14km passing the r.-hand
turning for *Oradour-sur-Glane*, 8km N.W.; see Rte 69.
  17.5km. **St-Junien** (11,200 inhab.), a glove-making and tanning
town of some charm, has a 13C bridge across the Vienne, at one end

of which is a 15C chapel. The *Church, largely 12C, is a fine example of Limousin Romanesque, notable for its vaulting. The E. part of the choir and parts of the transepts were rebuilt in 1230; the cupola over the crossing has been restored. Within may be seen the well-sculptured 12C *Tomb of the 5C hermit, St Junian, and some good capitals, among other features; and a 13C limoges enamel shrine is kept in the presbytery.

Hence we may make a DETOUR via **Rochechouart**, 11km S.W., standing on a commanding height at the confluence of the Graine with the Vayres. The *Castle, rebuilt under Louis XII, contains some curious wall-paintings; the tower to the l. of the entrance is part of a 13C edifice.—The main road may be regained 10km N.W. via _Chassenon_, preserving a few remains of Gallo-Roman _Cassionomagus_.

The N141 continues W. from St-Junien, at 9km passing (r.) the imposing château of _Rochebrune_ (11th and 16C), once the home of Blaise de Montluc, and traversing (5km) _Chabanais_, partly destroyed by the Germans in 1944, where we cross the Vienne.—_Confolens_, see Rte 69, lies 18km N.W. of Rochebrune.—We shortly pass (r.) _Exideuil_, with a priory church of 1200 and 16C château, and veer S.W. through (24km) _Chasseneuil_ with a _Memorial to the Resistance_.—There is a Lanterne des Morts and 12C church at _Cellefrouin_, 8.5km N.W.—11km. **La Rochefoucauld.**

The town is famous for its _Castle_, founded by Foucauld in the 11C on the banks of the Tardoire, rebuilt in 1527, and now little more than a ruin, having been allowed to crumble from neglect by the descendants of François, Duc de la Rochfoucauld (1613–80), author of the celebrated 'Maximes', although some tardy attempt has been made to stay its further deterioration by securing the foundations.—_St-Pierre_ has a good 13C steeple; disused _St-Florent_ (11C) lies on the river bank, which may be followed to _Rancogne_, a charming village 5km S.

An ALTERNATIVE ROUTE HENCE TO ANGOULÊME may be followed by driving S.W. to (9.5km) _Pranzac_, with a Renaissance church and Lanterne des Morts, there turning W.—S.E. at the next cross-roads are the stalactite _Grottes du Quéroy._—Continuing due W., we shortly reach _Touvre_, with a fortified Romanesque church, and the neighbouring _Source de la Touvre_, with its waterfalls, unfortunately spoilt by a fish-hatchery. Adjacent _Magnac-sur-Touvre_ has a 12C church, beyond which we approach _Angoulême._

The main road traverses the forest of _La Braconne_ to (15.5km) _Ruelle_, with a naval ordnance factory founded in 1750 (now manufacturing missiles), beyond which we cross the Touvre and shortly enter (6.5km) **Angoulême;** see Rte 70. A by-pass is under construction, bearing r. just prior to Ruelle.

Beyond Angoulême the N141 continues due W., at 5km passing (l.), on the Charente, the domed 12C church of _Fléac._—After c. 15km _Blassac_ lies 4km S., its notable 13C abbey church with good 18C woodwork, an older *Tower, and 15-17C additions. Near by is a memorial pyramid on the battlefield of Jarnac (1569), in which Louis I de Condé, uncle of Henri IV, was treacherously killed.

At (8km) **Jarnac**, with the cognac warehouses of such establishments of Messrs Hine, Bisquit-Dubouchés, and Courvoisier, among others, we cross the Charente. The expression 'coup de Jarnac' refers to a duel (1547) in which the Seigneur de Jarnac vanquished his adversary with a backward stroke. Charles Morgan's 'The Voyage' is set here in the 1880s.

4km. _Bourg-Charente_ has a good 11-12C church with a domed vault, beyond which we traverse part of the 'Grande Champagne' de

Cognac, where the best grapes for eau-de-vie are grown, roughly included in the triangle Cognac – Châteauneuf-Charente – Barbizieux; its area is c. 11,000 hectares; approx. 8 per cent of the total delimited area.

2km S. of the main road stands the 11C church of *Gensac-la-Pallue*, with good sculptures on its arcade, four domes, and a 13C choir.—Some 5km to the N.W., on the N. bank of the river is the fortified farm of *Garde-Épée*, and hidden in the woods, the ruins of the church of **Chatres*, a relic of an Augustinian abbey founded in 1077.

8km. **COGNAC** (21,000 Cognaçais), centre of the brandy trade of the Charente, was the birthplace of François I (1494 – 1547), and Octavien de Saint-Gelais (1466 – 1502), the poet-bishop of Angoulême, and father of the more famous Mellin.

Roads converge on the *Pl. François I*, with the S.I. to the W.—The Rue d'Angoulême leads to *St-Léger*, Romanesque in origin, but much altered, with a rose-window breaking the design of the W. front, and an upper storey added to the tower in the 18C.—A short distance to the E. is the **Museum**, with a section devoted to the manufacture of cognac, and the making of casks, etc., and a collection of Faïence de Cognac.

Among the paintings are a charming early 16C *Flemish* Adam and Eve; another of the same subject by *Frans Floris*; *Jan Metsys*, Lot and his daughters; *Scipio Pulzone*, Female portrait; 16C *German*, Old man and young woman; *anon. English* Portrait of Robert Dudley, Earl of Leicester; and characteristic works by *Lepine, Harpignies, Alfred Smith*, and *John-Lewis Brown*. The four terracotta female sphinxes by the entrance will not be overlooked.

Adjacent is the *Hôtel de Ville*, attractively sited in its park.

Between the church and river is a warren of alleys leading to the *Chais* or brandy warehouses of Messrs Hennessy, and Otard, best seen from the adjoining quay. Between the two is the 15C *Porte St-Jacques*, the latter company being established in the 13-16C *Château* (in which François I was born) since 1795. The *Chais Martell* is a few minutes' walk to the S.W. Apart from the last-named, most of the other great names—Rémy-Martin, Augier, Hine, Delamain, et al, are now swallowed up by international companies. Each traveller will have his preference, and most houses, here and at Jarnac, may be visited. *Hennessy's*, founded in 1765 by Captain Richard Hennessy, will hospitably conduct visitors round their cellars, and will explain the processes of distillation, etc.; they have also set up a *Cooperage Museum (tonnellerie)* of some interest, for the maturing of the spirits in casks of Tronçais or Limousin oak is very relevant. Further information may be found in Cyril Ray's 'Cognac'. Just S. of the town are the huge St-Gobain glass works, which may be visited.

At *Lonzac*, 17.5km S., is an interesting Renaissance church, erected in 1530 by Galiot de Genoulliac as a mausoleum for his wife (cf. Assier).
To the r. of the D731 4.5km N.W., is *Cherves*, with a Romanesque church, and remains of a Roman road leading W. to Saintes; adjacent is the château of *Chênel* (1610).—3.5km to the l. of the road 8.5km beyond, are the ruins of the Benedictine abbey of *Fontdouce*, preserving a notable chapter-house.—The N141 may be reached 8km to the S.W.

From Cognac we continue W., at 6.5km a l.-hand turning offering an alternative riverside road to (20.5km) Saintes, the district round which suffered from serious flooding in Dec. 1982.

SAINTES (27,500 Saintais), ancient and somewhat somnolent capital of the *Saintonge*, lies on both banks of the Charante, preserving several Roman remains and Romanesque churches of interest.

Formerly written *Xaintes*, it was in Roman times an important centre, and capital of the Gaulish Santones, but the Roman name—*Mediolanum*—was superceded by that of the tribe. It flourished under the dukes of Aquitaine, and passed with that duchy to England. Louis IX inflicted a decisive defeat here on Henry III in 1242, and in 1259 the latter's claim to the duchy of Normandy was abandoned, as confirmed by the Treaty of Xaintes. It was ceded to England by the Treaty of Brétigny (1360), but fell to Du Guesclin in 1371.

Bernard Palissy produced his earliest enamel-ware here in 1542. It was the birthplace of Dr Joseph-Ignace Guillotin (1738–1814), who proposed that beheading was a rapid and sure way of death, although he did not personally invent the machine named after him.

On the E. bank of the Charente stands the so-called *Arc de Germanicus*, a Roman votive arch erected in honour of Tiberius and Drusus Germanicus, which stood on the Roman bridge until the latter was demolished in 1845. A few paces to the S. is the *Musée Archéologique*, housing in an old pottery an interesting collection of Roman antiquities, much of it built into the 5C ramparts, discovered when they were razed in the 19C, and mostly dating from the 1-3Cs A.D.—The street opposite the arch leads E. to *St-Pallais* (12-13C), adjacent to which stands the *Abbaye aux Dames (11-12C), with a typical facade of the Saintonge region, and a notable square tower bearing a conical cupola. Its domes were destroyed by a fire in 1648. One or two curious capitals remain. The sacristy occupies a 15C chapel, and two bays of a cloister survive on the S. side, but the abbey buildings were in military hands for over a century, until 1924, and that so much has survived is remarkable. Mlle de Tonnay-Charente, later Mme de Montespan, received part of her education here.

One may regain the W. bank by a footbridge to reach **St-Pierre**, the cathedral until the Revolution, with new buildings adjacent to its apse.

Little remains of the Romanesque church of Bp Pierre de Confolens (1117–27) except the much-altered transepts. The present nave is an inadequate building of 1585, necessitated by the damage wrought by the Huguenots in 1568. The brick vault was lowered in the 18C, giving an impression of clumsiness. More interesting are those parts remaining of a reconstruction in the mid 15C, including the W. doorway, tower, and side-chapels. The elaborate spiral-staircase in the S.W. corner, and the gutted organ-case will be noted. The choir has been cleaned, and restoration continues. To the S. are six bays of a 13C cloister.

Not far to the N. are the museums (see below), the 16C *Hôtel Brémond d'Ars*, and a Flamboyant window of 1445 in the Rue des Jacobins.

The Rue Clemenceau leads S. past the *Sous-Préfecture* and *Hôtel de Ville*, and (l.) the *Hôtel d'Argenson*, beyond which is the *Musée Dupuy-Mestreau*, a collection of local antiquities accommodated in the 18C *Hôtel Monconséil*.

From the adjacent *Pl. Blair* (to the N. of which the Hospital occupies the site of the Roman Capitol) we may follow the Rues Barthonnière and St-François to approach ***St-Eutrope**, dedicated to the first bishop of Saintes, consecrated in 1096. It lost its nave in 1803, and the original choir takes it place; the present choir and tall tower are 15C additions. The transepts preserve some good capitals.—Of interest is the *Crypt, entered from the street to the N., altered in the

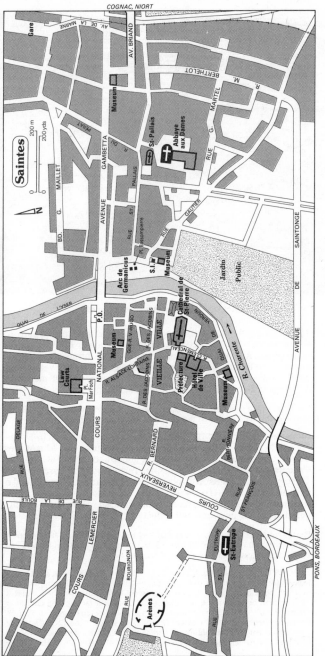

COGNAC, NIORT

Saintes

0 — 200 m
0 — 200 yds

Gare

AV. DE LA MARNE

AV. BRIAND

R. M. MARTEL

R. BERTHELOT

Museum

St-Pallais

Abbaye aux Dames

RUE G. MARTEL

R. DU PÉRAT

AVENUE GAMBETTA

BD. G. MAILLET

RUE ST. PALLAIS

RUE GAUTIER

RUE Pt. Bassompierre

Arc de Germanicus

S.I.

Museum

Cathédral de St-Pierre

AVENUE DE SAINTONGE

Jardin Public

QUAI DE LYSER

P.O.

Museum

GDE R. V.-HUGO

R. DES JACOBINS

VIEILLE

R. ALSACE LORRAINE

Law Courts

Pl. Mar Foch

COURS NATIONAL

R. DES JACOBINS

VIEILLE

Préfecture

Hôtel de Ville

R. G. CLEMENCEAU

QUAI DE VERDUN

R. Charente

Museum

RUE A. DELAGE

RUE DE LA BOULE

LEMERCIER

R. BERNARD

R. BERTONNIER

RUE REVERSEAUX

COURS

RUE ST-FRANÇOIS

COURS BOURIGNON

RUE

St-Eutrope

RUE ST. EUTROPE

Arènes

PONS, BORDEAUX

ROYAN

POITIERS, ROCHEFORT

The salt-marshes of Marennes, seen from the air

15C, but remarkable for its size. It contains the tomb of the patron, rediscovered when the site was cleared of debris in 1843.

Hence the Rue des Arènes and a path to the l. brings us to the remains of the Roman *Amphitheatre*, constructed in a small valley, and which appears to date from the late 1st or early 2C. It measures 126m by 102m, with an arena of 64m by 39m.

There are remains of Roman baths, or *Thermes*, some distance N. of the Cours National, the main tree-lined thoroughfare descending to the river.

From its S. side leads the Rue Alsace-Lorraine, off which (l.) the *Présidial* (1605), in the Rue Victor-Hugo, houses the **Musée des Beaux-Arts**. Among the few works of importance are a 15C Catalan Crucifixion; *Brueghel de Velours*, La Terre; *Paul Bril*, Pyramus and Thisbe; *De Troy*, Louis XIV receiving the Persian ambassador; and a portrait by *Rigaud*.—To the W., is the *Échevinage*, preserving 18C features and a 16C tower, recently modernised to house the 19-20C paintings of the museum, and collections of Sèvres porcelain.

For the roads to *St-Jean d'Angély* and *La Rochelle*, see Rtes 70 and 73 respectively, in reverse; for *Bordeaux*, Rte 70. The A10 motorway between Poitiers and Bordeaux now runs immediately W. of Saintes.

SAINTES TO ROYAN (37km). The D150 leads W. across the A10, and shortly forks l.; for the r.-hand fork to *Marennes*, see below.—13.5km. *Pisany*, 5km S.E. of which, at *Rétaud*, is an 11C church of interest, with a 15C tower, while that at *Rioux*, 5km beyond, has a remarkable 12C apse and facade. The church at *Thaims*, 7km W. of the latter, is built on the site of a Roman temple.—5.5km. *St-Romain-de-Benet* has a 12C church, 4km N.W. of which is the 12C *Church* of the former Augustinian abbey of *Sablonceau*, its dependencies now farm buildings, but which may be visited.—To the S. of St-Romain is the *Pile de*

Pirelonge, of Roman construction, while a mound to the r. of the main road further W. is presumably a Roman camp.—7km. *Saujon*, birthplace of Émile
Gaboriau (1823–73), the creator of 'Monsieur Lecoq', the precursor of 'Sherlock
Holmes'.—5km. *Médis*, the church of which has an admirable sculptured facade
(12C), is traversed as we approach (6km) **Royan**; see Rte 73.

SAINTES TO (40km) MARENNES, for the *Île d'Oléron*. By following the r.-hand
fork W. of Saintes we pass (14.5km) *Corme-Royal* (r.), its church with a good
Romanesque facade, and 2.5km beyond, *Balanzac*, with a late 16C château,
which lies 3km N. of *Sablonceau* (see above).—5km. *Cadeuil*, where we reach the
Rochefort-Royan crossroad (see Rte 73). 3km further (r.) is the church of *St-
Sornin*, with interesting archaic capitals, beyond which rises the great 12C keep
of *Broue*.—6km. *St-Just-Luzac* (r.) has a good 15-16C church on the edge of salt-
marshes, while to the W. lie the extensive oyster-parks of **Marennes**, the town of
which gives its name to a well-known breed of green oysters. It preserves several
Renaissance houses, and a tall 14C steeple, a notable landmark in this low-lying
area, damaged by shell-fire in 1944.—For the *Presqu'île d'Avert*, to the W., see
Rte 73; likewise for *Brouage*, 6.5km N.E., and the *Île d'Oléron*.

69 Poitiers to Limoges

A. Via Bellac

119km (74 miles). N147. 36km *Lussac-les-Châteaux*—42km
Bellac—41km **Limoges**.

Maps: IGN 34, 40, 41, or 107. M 233.

At 7km S.E. of **Poitiers** (Rte 56) a r.-hand fork leads c. 2.5km to the
farm of *Maupertuis*, now called *La Cardinierie*, near which was
fought the battle of 1356 (cf. Poitiers), 1.5km to the S. of which is the
fortified abbey-church of *Nouaillé-Maupertuis* (12C), with a crypt
recently cleared, and a choir rebuilt in the 17C, the whole surrounded by a 13C wall.—We regain the main road via *Nieuil-l'Espoir*, at
Fleuré.

11.5km. *Fleuré*.—7km E. lies *Morthemer*, with a fine late 12C
church and a splendid feudal *Castle (12-14C; restored), where Sir
John Chandos (c. 1320–70), seneschal of Poitou, died (see below).

10.5km. *Civaux*, 4km N.E., has a 12C church with an earlier apse,
and curious old cemetery. On the far bank of the Vienne is an imposing 12-13C tower, whence we may regain the road a short distance
to the S.

6km. To the S. on the l. bank of the Vienne is the cenotaph of
Chandos, who fell mortally wounded near by.—We cross the river to
(2km) *Lussac-les-Châteaux*, whence the N147 continues directly S.E.
to (42km) *Bellac*, but the more interesting road is that taking in
Montmorillon and Dorat, an additional 11.5km.

The D727 leads E. to (12km) **Montmorillon** (7500 inhab.), on both banks of the
Gartempe. On the r. bank is 19C *St-Martial*, with a 12C belfry. *Notre-Dame*, on
the l. bank, has an aisleless nave in the Angevin style of 1300, Romanesque
transepts and apse, and wall-paintings of c. 1200 in the crypt. Further up the
hillside is the old *Maison-Dieu des Augustins*. Its chapel, Romanesque *St-Laurent*,
is remarkable for the frieze depicting the Childhood of Christ on its W. front. La
Hire (1390–1443), Joan of Arc's companion-at-arms, was originally buried
here.—To the S. is the curious *Octagone* (1180), a two-storeyed sepulchral
chapel, with four contemporary statues.

The D54 leads S.E. to (29.5km) **Le Dorat**, noted for its macaroons and its Romanesque *Church* (1088–1130), with a massive W. tower. The gilded angel (13C) on the elegant central spire (late 12C)—'lou dorat'—is said to give the town its name. The well-proportioned interior contains an 11C monolithic font (now a stoup), the relics of SS. Israel and Theobald, and a crypt of interest.—Part of the town *Walls* (1429), with the curious *Porte Bergère*, still survives.—The D675 leads 12km S. to *Bellac*.

Bellac (5500 Bellacquais or Bellachons), birthplace of Jean Giraudoux (1882–1944), the author and playwright, a small town on the Vincou, contains several 15C houses, while its Hotel de Ville is in the 16C *Château des Barthou de Montbas*. The church has two parallel naves, one 12C, the other 14C, and preserves a 12C enamel casket.—Hence we follow the N147 and ascend the valley of the Glayeulle, to the W. of which the *Monts de Blond*, a group of typical Limousin hills, rise to 515m.—41km. **Limoges**: see Rte 63.

B.   Via Gençay and Confolens

128km (79 miles). D741. 25km *Gençay*—33km D948.—14km *Confolens*—D82. 34km **Oradour-sur-Glane**—22km **Limoges**.

Maps: IGN 34, 40, 41, or 107. M 233.

The D741 leads S., shortly passing (r.) *St-Benoît*, the 11-12C church and chapter-house of an abbey founded in the 7C, and continues S., at 5km passing 3.5km E. of *Ligugé*; see Rte 70.—5km. *Roches-Prémarie-Andillé*, with a 14C keep, 3km S. of which, at *Villedieu-du-Clain*, is a Romanesque church with a remarkable doorway.

12km. *Gençay*, a small market-town, preserves the ruins of a 13C castle; to the S.W. is the *Château de la Roche-Gençay*, with a partly Renaissance facade. On the far bank of the river stands 12C *St-Maurice-la-Clouère*, containing 14C murals.

The road now ascends the valley of the Clouère, at 16km passing (l.) *Usson-du-Poitou*, with a church of 1091, and a 15C château adjacent.—6km. *St-Martin-d'Ars*, with a Renaissance château, and 3km beyond (l.) the former *Abbaye de la Réau* (12-13C), a romantic ruin converted into a château.

The next r.-hand turning leads 12km S.W. to *Charroux*; see Rte 70. 9.5km. *Pressac*.

A DETOUR may be made to the E. via (7km) *Availles-Limouzine*, there following the far bank of the Vienne to the S., passing the *Château de Serres*, with a 15C keep, where Mme de Montespan retired after her disgrace. Beyond is the château of *Fayolle* (late 15C), and the picturesque ruins of that at *St-Germain-de-Confolens*. On an island here is a curious dolmen, altered in the 11C to form an oratory.

14.5km. **Confolens**, an ancient town astride the Vienne, here crossed by a 15C bridge, with a ruined castle and 15C church on its r. bank, and 11C *St-Bartélemy* on the l.—The D948 leads S.E. to (27km) *Rochebrune*; see Rte 68.

We turn due E. to (9.5km) *Lesterps*, the church of which has a splendid 12C belfry.—14km. *Montemart*, 7km N., has a ruined castle, the cradle of a famous family.—To the N.E. rises the *Monts de Blond*; see above.—10.5km. **Oradour-sur-Glane*, ◊ where on 10 June 1944 German S.S. troops rounded up and massacred its 643 inhabitants, burning alive the women and children in its church, and shooting the men. The martyred village has been left as it stood after this notoriously savage reprisal, although tastefully tidied up. Rusting cars remain in situ, and smaller personal effects are pathetically displayed in a subterranean vault: the whole is a moving monument to the horrors of war, which will always be remembered by those who visit it.

After 8km we reach the N141 14km W. of **Limoges**; see Rte 63.

70 Poitiers to Bordeaux

A. Via Angoulême

256km (159 miles). N10. 49km *Les Maisons-Blanches*—12km **Ruffec**—44km **Angoulême**—33km **Barbezieux**—58km A10 autoroute—27km **Bordeaux.**

Maps: IGN 34, 40, 47, 46, or 107, 110. M 233.

The N10 leads S.W. from **Poitiers** (Rte 56), shortly passing, to the l. of the road, the *Arcs de Parigné*, remains of a 1-2C Roman aqueduct, 6km beyond which is an entrance to the A10 motorway.

2km beyond this turning the N11 bears S.E. to *Lusignan*, there dividing for *Niort* and *La Rochelle*, and for *St-Jean-d'Angély* and *Saintes*: see Rtes 72 and 70B, respectively.

12km. *Vivonne* (l.) has a 12th and 16C church and a ruined castle of the same date, the ancestral home of Catherine de Vivonne (1588–1665), Marquise de Rambouillet ('Arthénice', most distinguished of the 'Précieuses').

Vivonne may also be approached from Poitiers by a minor road (D4) forking l. off the N10 and leading down the valley of the Clain via *Ligugé*, famous for its abbey founded by St Martin in 361, and many times rebuilt. Rabelais was there in 1524–27, and J.-K. Huysman spent a period as an oblate there (1899–1901). The present church, of c. 1600 (restored since 1853) is occupied by Benedictines (male visitors admitted).—Further S. we pass (r.) the Renaissance château of *Aigne*, to regain the main route.

5km E. of Vivonne, at *Château-Larcher*, is a church with a 12C tower and a 'lanterne des morts' in its graveyard, and slight remains of its castle.

9.5km. It was probably at *Voulon*, 4km E., that Clovis defeated Alaric II at the so-called 'Battle of Vouillé' in 507.

6km. To the r. are the remains of the Cistercian abbey of *Valende* (13C), and beyond (l.) *Couhé*, with its 17C Market-house.

19km. *Les Maisons-Blanches* crossroads.

9km. E. lies **Civray**, mainly on the r. bank of the Charente. *St-Nicolas*, with its central tower, has an elaborate 12C facade preserving a mutilated equestrian statue (cf. Melle, Parthenay-le-Vieux, etc.); the tower, and apse are also notable, while the octagonal crossing in the interior, with its grotesques, and a butt of wine, etc., are also of interest; while the process of removing its 19C paint has commenced.—11km further E. is **Charroux** with a 16C covered market, and town gate. Its centre is dominated by the curious *Tour Octogone* (1096) of its *abbey-church*, ◊ other relics of which are a late 12C doorway, and a 15C chapter-house, now displaying 13C statuettes from the main portal.—From Civray the main road may be regained at Ruffec.

12km. **Ruffec**, also by-passed, has a late-Gothic church with a notable 12C *Facade.*

At *Courcôme*, 7.5km S.W., is an interesting 11-12C church with an imposing tower and naive capitals; while 7km S.E. is a fine château at *Verteuil-sur-Charente*, of 1459, where in 1787 Young 'found everything that travellers could wish in a hospitable mansion'; a previous guest had been the Emperor Charles V, who was here entertained by Anne de Polignac, widow of François II de La Rochefoucauld.

16km. To the W. are several dolmens; 2km E. lies *Lichères*, with a good Poitevin Romanesque church, with a sculptured tympanum and apse of interest.—10.5km. At *St-Amant-de-Boixe*, 5km W., is a notable abbey-church, begun in the 10C and altered in the 15th, perserving part of a cloister.—There is a ruined keep overlooking the Charente further S.W. It was in this vicinity that Théodebert, son of Chilperic, was killed in a battle between the Neustrians and Austrasians in 575.

11.5km. The Angoulême by-pass leads r.—We shortly cross the Touvre.

6km. **ANGOULÊME** (50,150 Angoumoisins), préfecture of the *Charente* and capital of the old province of *Angoumois*, stands on an abrupt hill overlooking the confluence of the Charente and the Anguienne; at least the older town does, which is all that is of any interest.

Gallo-Roman *Iculisma*, or *Ecolismensium* later *Engolisma*, was evangelised by St Ausonius in the 3C. Here in 1200 Isabelle d'Angoulême (1186–1246) married King John of England. It was hotly contested during the Hundred Years' War, but the English were finally expelled in 1373. The Angoumois was held by the House of Orléans until the accession of François d'Orléans, Count of Angoulême, as François I (1515). The town suffered greatly during the Religious Wars (1568–86), and slightly from bombing in 1944.

Among its natives were Mellin de Saint-Gellais (1487/91–1558), the poet; Marguerite de Valois or d'Angoulême (1494-1549), sister of François I and queen of Navarre, authoress of the 'Heptameron'; Guez de Balzac (1594–1654), a perfector of French prose (who in 1624 retired to his estate to spend the remaining years of his life 'in an affectation of antique wisdom'); he was buried in the Chapelle des Cordeliers of the Hôtel-Dieu here; the engineer-Marquis René de Montalembert (1714–1800), founder of the arsenal of Ruelle (cf.; 6km N.E.); and Charles-Augustin de Coulomb (1736–1806), the engineer and physicist. Balzac frequently visited the town in the early 1830s.

It was long well-known for its paper-mills, which produced, among others, a fine writing-paper known as 'anglais'.

The ascent into the upper town is not exactly simple, and one must follow signals with care. A direct approach to the cathedral may be made by turning abruptly l. just S. of the ramparts and following the Av. du Président-Wilson.

The **Cathedral** is a curious edifice more impressive from a distance than at close quarters. It was begun in the 11C after its predecessor had been burned in 981, and largely rebuilt in the early 12C; the damage inflicted on it during the religious wars was repaired in 1634 but it also suffered at the Revolution, when the label 'Temple de la Raison' was added to the facade. The damage caused by Paul Abadie in 1866–75 was far more serious; indeed he destroyed rather than restored most of the original work, including the 6C crypt. Certain sculptured *Groups on the facade are original; others he mutilated by restoration, or replaced. He also added towers to this W. facade. The *N. Tower, 59m high, was rebuilt, but its original sculptures were broken up; the corresponding S. tower had been demolished in 1568. The interior has similarities with St-Front at Périgueux (cf.; likewise savaged by Abadie), but here the three cupolas of the nave are greater in diameter, and the central octagonal lantern (1638) is

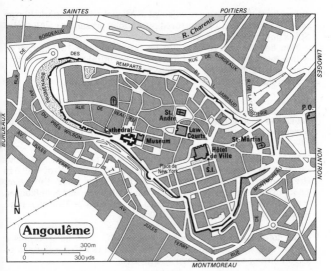

raised on a drum supported by coupled columns, as is that of the N.
transept. On the N. side of the nave are the tombs of 11-12C bishops.

Immediately behind the cathedral is the former *Bishop's Palace*
(almost entirely rebuilt in the 15C), in which the municipal *Museum*
is installed, a somewhat miscellaneous collection, notably of African
sculpture. (The *Musée de la Société Archéologique* is to be found at
the junction of the Rampart de l'Est and the Rue de Montmoreau.)

Further E., facing the *Pl. F.-Louvel*, is the *Palais de Justice* (1826),
just N. of which is *St-André*, with a 12C tower and 15C nave, while to
the S.E. is the *Hôtel de Ville* (1865; by Abadie), occupying the site of
the historic castle of the Counts of Angoulême, and incorporating
two of its towers (1300, and late 15C), described earlier in the 19C as
'distinguished by its 3 picturesque feudal towers, and tall donjon,
now converted into a prison, and surmounted by the telegraph'.—A
short distance N., No. 15 in the Rue de la Cloche-Verte is the *Hôtel
St-Simon*, with a Renaissance courtyard of 1540.

Perhaps the best that Angoulême now has to offer—before its local
authorities raze them—are its rampart walks, particularly the Promenade de Beaulieu, although the views they command are not what
they were. This may be approached by traversing the Rue de
Beaulieu (leading W. from the Pl. F.-Louvel) in which No. 79 is a mansion of 1783, and off which the Rue Vauban leads to the *Pl. du
Minage*, in the vicinity there are one or two other house of interest
(in the Rues de Turenne and du Soleil).

For the road from Angoulême to *Saintes*, see Rte 68; to *Périgueux*, Rte 71.

ANGOULÊME TO CHALAIS (42km). The D674 leads S., at 19km passing 2km W.
of *Charmant*, its church with a fine 12C apse, and 5km beyond, 2km E. of the
restored 11-12C abbey church of *Puypéroux*, prior to entering (8km)
Montmoreau-St-Cybard, with an over-restored 12C church dominated by its 15C
château which preserves a Romansque chapel.—16km. *Chalais*; see the first part
of Rte 67.

The N10 leads S.W., passing (first r.-hand turning after the by-pass enters from the r.) a road to adjacent *St-Michel*, with a remarkable octagonal church of 1137 (restored by Abadie) preserving a *Relief of St-Michael and the Dragon.

3km beyond this turning lies *La Couronne*, the 12C church of which has a curious central tower; the beautiful ruins of an abbey church of 1200 may be seen close by.

5km. *Roullet-St-Estèphe*, with a restored 12C church.

The Romanesque churches at *Mouthiers-sur-Boëme* (6km E.), *Claix* (4.5km S.), and *Plassac-Rouffiac, S. of the latter, have features of interest.—8km W. of Roullet lies *Châteauneuf-sur-Charente*, its church retaining a remarkable 12C facade. Romanesque nave, and Gothic choir, whence one may regain the N10 7km S.E. by the D10.

7.5km. *Blanzac*, 10km S.E. (which may also be approached from Plassac; see above), has a 13C church of interest, 2km N. of which is the manor of *Maine-Giraud*, where De Vigny spent the years 1850–53 nursing his invalid wife Lydia Bunbury.—3km S. of Blanzac is a Templar's chapel preserving late 12C frescoes.—The main road may be regained at *Barbezieux*, 16km W.

13.4km. **Barbezieux** (5400 Barbeziliens), a pleasant town with a good hotel, has an 11C church, whose 18C front incorporates a Gothic doorway, and on a hill to the W., the relics of a château of 1453 housing a local museum and theatre.

20.5km. *Montguyon*, 12km S. (l.-hand fork) preserves the imposing ruins of a 12-15C castle, with a cylindrical keep.

The road now traverses somewhat monotonous wooded 'landes', and then vineyards to (38km) the A10 motorway, which may be entered just prior to *St-André-de-Cubzac*, with a partly 11C church. To the N. of the town stands the *Château de Bouilh* (1787; by Louis).—To the l. of the Libourne road (D670; leading S.E.), the church of *Lalande-de-Fronsac* has a remarkable 12C tympanum.

The motorway crosses the Dordogne on a bridge completed in 1974 just S. of Eiffel's bridge (1883; 1046m) and the railway bridge of 1889, by Gérard, beyond which we cross the tongue of land between that river and the Garonne—the wine-growing district of *Entre-Deux-Mers*—with a view ahead of Bordeaux as we approach it. The A10 bears W. and crosses the Garonne by the *Pont d'Aquitaine* (1967), 1767m long and 53m above water-level; the old main road veers S.W., descending to and traversing the suburb of *La Bastide* before crossing the river by the *Pont de Pierre*; see p 427. Further S. is the new *Pont-St-Jean*, and Eiffel's railway bridge of 1860.—For **Bordeaux**, see Rte 75.

B. Via St-Jean-d'Angély and Saintes

242km (150 miles). N11. 19km *Lusignan*—D150. 31km *Melle*—D950. 28km *Aulnay*—17km **St-Jean-d'Angély**—N150. 27km **Saintes**—N137. 22km *Pons*—24km *Mirambeau*—21km *Blay* lies 9km S.W. —23km *St-André-de-Cubzac* turning, where we enter the A10 motorway for (27km) **Bordeaux**.

Maps: IGN 34, 33, 40, 46, or 107, 110. M 233.

The A10 motorway now provides a rapid route from Poitiers to Bordeaux, passing close to Niort and just W. of Saintes. It is recommended as an approach to Bordeaux from adjacent to St-André-de-Cubzac.

At 8km from **Poitiers** (Rte 56) we fork r. off the N10, and after 1km pass (r.) *Fontaine-le-Comte*, with a large 12C abbey church.

17km. **Lusignan**, an ancient hilltop town built within a loop of the Vonne, has a 12C *Church with a crypt beneath its apse, and vaults and a S. porch of the 15C. Little remains of the castle erected overnight by the watersprite Mélusine, the legendary foundress of the illustrious family of Lusignan (cf. Fougères), but a pleasant promenade has been laid out on its site.

For the road from Lusignan to *Niort* and *La Rochelle*, see Rte 72.

16km. *Chenay*, with a good 12C *Doorway* to its church.

9km. **Melle** (r.) drives its name from the Latin *Metallum*, and with argentiferous lead mines in the vicinity, it was the seat of an important mint in the Middle Ages (cf. Niort). It has three fine Romanesque

The W. front of St-Hilaire, Melle

churches: in the valley, the 12C priory church of ***St-Hilaire**, consisting of an aisled nave and a multiple apse, with apsed transepts and central tower, has close affinities with Airvault (see Rte 58A). The arcaded W. front, the rich design of the N. front with an equestrian statue (traditionally of Constantine), and the sculptures of the S. portal, which seems to have been originally a tomb-niche, are noteworthy. Among the capitals, those of a boar-hunt, and of a centaur and stag, are outstanding.

Behind the former church of *St-Savinien* (11C), long used as a gaol but still preserving its charming tower, a street leads to the sham-Gothic Palais de Justice, incorporating two 15C towers.—*St-Pierre* (12C), further N., is remarkable for the simplicity of its W. front and the ornate design on the exterior of its three apses. The S. doorway, above which is a mutilated relief of Christ surrounded by angels, admits to the aisled nave with its fine capitals, including one showing the entombment of St Hilary.

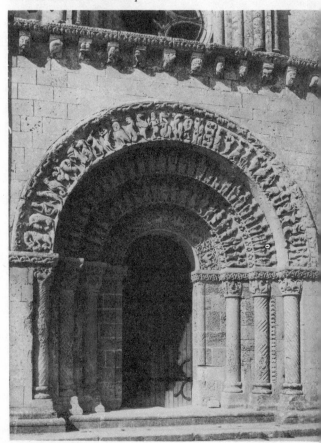

The S. doorway at Aulnay

At *Celles-sur-Belle*, 7km N.W., is an Abbey Church preserving a Romanesque doorway, but otherwise rebuilt in the Gothic style c. 1670 by Leduc de Toscane.

5km. To the l. is seen the *Tour de Melzéard*, a relic of a 15C castle.

5km. At *Javarzay*, 12km S.E., is a castle of 1515 of the Rochechouart family, and a 12C priory church, its choir (also 1515) larger than its nave.

9km. We skirt the *Forêt d'Aulnay*, and after 9km reach **Aulnay**, a village possessing perhaps the finest Romanesque *Church in Saintonge*, standing back from the road and still surrounded by its cypress-shaded churchyard. The sculptural decoration of the W. *Front* and *S. Doorway* repay detailed examination.

The former displays (l.) the crucifixion of St Peter, and (r.) Christ in Majesty, and (centre) virgins, knights, and signs of the zodiac, etc.; the niche above lacks its equestrian statue. The archivolts of the S. entrance are decorated with animals and monsters, and armed Virtues trampling Vices; note the squatting and kneeling supporters. The apse window is also vividly decorated. The interior is remarkable for its historiated *Capitals*, particularly those of the 2nd and 4th pillar on the r., and the acrobats on the 2nd l.; Samson being shorn, N.W. of the crossing, with its ribbed cupola; wrestlers; Cain and Abel; and the well-known small-eared elephants, with its inscription (at the junction of the S. aisle and transept).

7.5km N.W. is the imposing Renaissance château of *Dampierre-sur-Boutonne*.—The church at *Nauillé-sur-Boutonne*, 7.5km W. of Aulnay, is also remarkable.—The remains of the abbey-church of *Marestay*, 18km S., on the direct road to *Cognac*, are notable.

At 14km we meet the D939 and turn r. for (3km) **St-Jean-d'Angély** (9500 inhab.), a busy market town still retaining a number of attractive old houses, famous as one of the strongholds of Protestantism in France. The wealthy Benedictine abbey here was completely destroyed by the Huguenots in 1568, and its citizens were not finally subdued until 1621, when Louis XIII took the town and razed its fortifications. Henri I de Condé died here in 1588, and here his posthumous son, Henri II (1588–1649), father of the Grande Condé, was born. The local tipple, the '*pino de Charente*', should be sampled.

A short distance S. of the *Hôtel de Ville* in the main Place is the market, and just beyond, the *Tour de l'Horloge*, the 16C town belfry, passing beneath which we soon reach the Renaissance *Fontaine du Pilori* (1546), transferred here in 1819 from the château of Brizambourg (15km S.). Hence a narrow lane leads N. to the *Lycée*, installed in the remnants of the 13-14C *Abbey* and its 17-18C reconstruction, including a classical church commenced in 1741 but never finished. Its monumental buttresses remain, known as 'les Tours', dominating this part of the town. Further S. is a small *Museum*, containing the first car to cross the Sahara (1922), and local antiquities.

At *Varaize*, 8.5km E., is a notable 13C church.

ST-JEAN TO ROCHEFORT (39km). We cross the Boutonne just S. of the town and turn r. onto the D739, and shortly cross the motorway.—18km. *Tonnay-Boutonne*, on a hill overlooking the marshes, preserves a noble gateway of its medieval walls. After 13km we meet the N137 and by-pass (l.) *Tonnay-Charente*, a small river-port where the hospital occupies what is left of the château of the Rochechouart family, the birthplace of Mme de Montespan (1641–1707).—8km. *Rochefort*; see Rte 73.

From St-Jean, we follow the N150, at 8km passing some 7.5km E. of **Fenioux** (near the motorway), with a charming 12C *Church*, with a remarkable spire and sculptured porch, and *Lanterne des Morts.*—Further S. is the *Chaussée de St-James*, a Roman causeway restored in the 14th and 17C, which was held by the English during a skirmish here in 1242, when their force was defeated by Louis IX. The more famous *Battle of Taillebourg* took place in 808, when Charlemagne defeated an incursion of Moors from Spain. The imposing but battered castle lies nearer the Charente, some 9km further S.W.

16km. To the W. lies *Le Douhet*, with a restored 17C château, beyond which are the remains of a Roman aqueduct.

10km. **Saintes**; see Rte 68.—Hence the N137 bears S.E. to (21km) **Pons** (pron. Pon), a picturesque old town on the Seugne, with a fine feudal *Castle (12C keep; 15-17C buildings occupied by the mairie), and in its S. suburbs, the priory chapel of *St-Vivien (11C facade), beyond which a 12C bridge, across the main road, connects the hospital with the former church of *St-Martin.* To the W. are the ruins of the château of *St-Maury*, birthplace of Agrippa d'Aubigné (1552–1630), the Protestant poet and grandfather of Mme de Maintenon, while to the E. is the charming Renaissance *Château d'Usson*.

There are several churches of interest not far E. of Pons, which may be taken in on a brief detour, among them *Échebrune*, 7km E., and *Chadénac*, 4km S. of the latter, with a remarkable W. Front. Hence we continue S.W. via (4km) *Marignac*, with an interesting priory church; 10km further S. lies *Jonzac*, with a fine 13-14C *Castle*, now traversed by a street, and occupied by the mairie. The facade and apse of the rebuilt church are original Romanesque.—The main road may be regained 12km S.W.

12.5km. *Plassac*, with the huge *Château de Dampierre* (1772; by Victor Louis), and 3km beyond (l.) the abbey-church of *Tenaille*, its dependencies now a farm; the château dates from 1830.—7.5km. *Mirambeau*, where the road from Royan to Bordeaux joins our route (see Rte 73), beyond which we cross the motorway and veer towards the Gironde to (23km) *Pontet*, where the main road forks l., and 8km beyond turns l. for (18km) the entrance to the A10 just N. of *St-André-de-Cubzac*, 27km from **Bordeaux**: see the latter part of Rte 70A.

An alternative route from Pontet follows the r.-hand fork to (9km) **Blaye**, an ancient wine-growing town, the Roman castrum of *Blavia* on the *Promontorium Santorium*. This was replaced by a castle in 769, erected by the sons of Clotaire II, in which the paladin Roland was buried after his death at Roncevaux in 778. A new fortress was built in 1140, in which the troubadour Jaufré Rudel was born, which in turn was sacrificed to Vauban's *Citadel* (1685), in which the Duchess de Berri was imprisoned in 1832. A ferry crosses the Gironde to *Lamarque*.

Hence we follow the river bank through *Bayon*, with a Romanesque church, to (14km) *Bourg* (pron. Bourk), an old town, the terrace of which provides a good view of the confluence of the Dordogne with the Garonne, which here form the Gironde (and also of extensive oil-refineries).—We pass (l.) after 6km the rock-shelter of *Pair-non-Pair*, with its Aurignacian drawings, and 6km beyond, reach *St-André-de-Cubzac*; see the latter part of Rte 70A.

71 Angoulême to Cahors, via Périgueux, and Sarlat

224km (139 miles). D939. 58km **Brantôme**—27km **Périgueux**—N89 for 11km, then D710 for 13.5km, there following the D47 for 20.5km **Les Eyzies**—21km **Sarlat**—D704. 26km *Gourdon*—12km N20. 35km **Cahors**.

Maps: IGN 40, 47, 48, 57, or 110. M 233, 235.

The road leads S.E.—later traversing a well-wooded countryside—past (7.5km) the 14-17C *Château de la Tranchade*, 2km S. of which is the interesting Romanesque church of *Dirac*.—At *Marthon*, 16km due E., are a ruined 12C castle, and an unfinished 16C château.

10.5km. *Villebois-Lavalette*, 7km S., a well-sited fortified village, previously an oppidum, preserves its 13C *Market-house*, from which we may regain the main road 8km E.

11km. *La Rochebeaucourt*, with relics of its 14C castle, its traversed, and 9km beyond, *Mareuil*, with a 14-15C château, under restoration.—5km. *Vieux-Mareuil*, with a Perigord Romanesque church of three domes, although 13C, with 14C additions.—11km. The late 16C *Château de Richemont* lies 2km l., containing the tomb of Pierre de Brantôme (see below) in its chapel.

4km. **Brantôme**, delightfully sited on an island in the Dronne, is famous as being the residence of Pierre de Bourdeilles, Abbé and Seigneur de Brantôme (1535–1614), the chronicler of 16C military and court life, entertaining if/or because scandalous, published posthumously in 1665–66. It contains several interesting buildings, including the *Porte St-Roch*, adjoining a riverside pavilion of c. 1530, and a curious 16C bridge built with an elbow. The abbey-*Church*, over-restored, has a separate **Belfry*. It was originally domed in the Perigord manner, but was revaulted in the Angevin style in the 13C; the cloister gallery is 115C; 18C dependencies accommodate the mairie, etc. A few old houses (12-16C), and a market-hall in a disused church of 1516, may also be seen.

1km E., on the Thiviers road, is the *Pierre-Levée* dolmen, and c. 12km N.E., the early 16C château of *Puyguilhem*, beyond which is the stalactite *Grottes de Villars*.

A worth-while DETOUR is that to **Bourdeilles**, 7km S.W., reached by a minor road skirting the meandering Dronne, crossed by a 14C bridge, with its two **Castles* surrounded by a double enceinte. Within the inner ring of ramparts stands the 14C fortress, overhanging the river, and separated from the town by a natural ravine and artificial trench. The polygonal keep, 34m high, commands a good view. Jacquette de Montbron erected a 16C château adjacent to the feudal stronghold, in which to entertain Catherine de Médicis, who never came. It contains some imposing rooms, some retaining their painted beams, restored and embellished with remarkably good Renaissance furniture, much of it Spanish, collected by M. Robert Santiard and his widow, who bequeathed it to the Department. Notable are a chair carved with the Tree of Jessé; a late 16C Beauvais tapestry of the Rape of Helen, and another of François I hunting; a carved Entombment (16C Rhenish); a 16C coffer, and powder-flasks, etc. Brantôme (see above), brother-in-law of the foundress, was probably born at Bourdeilles, and frequently paid visits to the château.—The restored 12C church and 15C bailiff's house may also be seen.—The main road may be regained 6km E., although good map-readers will work their way S. to the ancient priory of *Merlande* (see below).

10km. *Château-l'Évêqué* takes its name from a former castle of the bishops of Périgueux (15-16C).—*Agonac*, 7km N.E., has a 12C keep and a late 11C church domed in the Périgord style.

6km. *Chancelade* (r.) has an abbey church with a doorway and tower dating from 1120; the elaborate vault with armorial keystones was added in 1629; murals survive in the choir. Adjacent is the Romanesque chapel of *St-Jean*.

A lane ascends c. 5km hence to the picturesquely sited priory-church of *Merlande* (12C), preserving capitals of interest, and some dependencies.

5km. **Périgueux**; see Rte 66. Quitting the town, we shortly bear S.E., following the railway, at 11km forking r., and after a further 13.5km turn l.; the D710 leads S. to (16.5km). *Le Bugue*; see Rte 74.

After c. 16km several stalactite caves are passed, before crossing the Vézère and entering (5km) **Les Eyzies-de-Tayac**, a small town too often crowded with excursion coaches, which sprang into prominence with the discoveries of Lartet and Christy in 1862, when large deposits of chipped flints and prehistoric bone-carvings were found in the neighbourhood. The shelter of *Cro-Magnon*, where the skulls of the cave-dwelling race were found in 1868, and the *Grotte des Eyzies*, where depictions of reindeer were first seen in 1863, may not be visited, but for the layman a very good idea of the importance and extent of the finds may be gained by a visit to the *Musée National de Préhistoire* (closed Tues.) recently re-formed, standing below the overhanging cliffs to the E. of the town centre.

We follow the D47 E. from Les Eyzies, shortly passing (r.) the *Grotte de Font-de-Gaume*, and further upstream, the *Grotte de Combarelles*, both containing representations of animals, the former with paintings, the latter with incised engravings.

At the next fork, the l.-hand road leads up the valley of the Beune to reach the *Abri du Cap-Blanc*, with its frieze of sculptured horses and other animals (Magdalenian). The little cave of *La Grèze*, in a side valley on the l., just prior to the former, contains incised bisons. Above Cap-Blanc is the ruined 12C castle of *Commarque*, with the 16C château of *Laussel* on the other bank beyond, near which was found the 'Venus of Laussel' (now at St-Germain-en-Laye), a female figure in low relief of the Aurignacian period.

The r.-hand fork, which we follow, passes successively the châteaux of *Beyssac*, *du Roc* (18C), and *de Puymartin*, before descending to (21km) *Sarlat*, a small town which has rapidly extended and scattered over the surrounding area within recent decades, an apparently uncontrolled development which detracts considerably from its charms.

Sarlat-la-Canéda (10,600 Sarladais), the old centre of which still retains a large number of fine stone buildings—many still being restored—has not lost too much of its character with commercialisation. It grew up round a Benedictine abbey founded in the 8C, and between 1317 and 1790 was the seat of a bishop. It was the birthplace of Étienne de la Boétie (1530–63), chiefly remembered as being a colleague of Montaigne, who wrote his essay 'On Friendship' in his memory. 156 civilians from the district were killed here in reprisals in 1944.

Slight remain of its walls may be seen to the S.W. of the old town through which La Traverse (Rue de la République) was pierced from N. to S. in 1842. While most of the edifices of importance lie to the E of this main artery, time should be taken to explore the town as a whole, particularly its less frequented alleys.

Among the more remarkable mansions is the *Hôtel Plamon* (14C), approached from the N. by taking the first l.-hand turning off the Traverse. Beyond this is the disused 14C church of *Ste-Marie*, and (l.) the *Hôtel de Ville* (17C). Continuing S., we pass (r.) the *Hôtel de Maleville* (S.I. on ground floor). The Rue de la Liberté leads ahead to the Pl. du Peyrou, with (r.) the *Maison de La Boétie* (c. 1525), opposite which is the former bishop's palace. The abbey-church of *St-Sacerdos* (later the cathedral) was entirely rebuilt in the 16-17C, except for the 12C tower and porch. The interior is of slight interest. Continuing S. we reach the *Pl. de la Grande Rigaudie.*—To the W. are relics of the walls; by passing through the second gateway, we may traverse the W. side of the enceinte by threading its lanes, many of which bring one back to the main street.

The D704 descends to (7km) *Carsac*, with an 11th and 16C church, in the Dordogne valley (see Rte 74), where we cross the river.

A l.-hand turning on the far bank leads 6km to the 15-16C *Château de Fénelon*, birthplace of François de Salignac de la Mothe Fénelon (1651–1715), the author of 'Télémaque' and other works, and archbishop of Cambrai.

17km. *Gourdon* (see Rte 64), 12km beyond which we meet the N20, and turn r. for (35km) **Cahors**; see Rte 64.

72   Poitiers to Niort and La Rochelle

139km (86 miles). N10. 8km—N11. 19km *Lusignan*—26km *St-Maixent*—23km **Niort**—23.5km *Mauze*—40km **La Rochelle**.

Maps: IGN 34, 35, 40, 32, or 107. M 233. The Île de Ré is covered in detail in IGN 504.

The A10 motorway provides a rapid route to Niort, which may be by-passed to the S., the N11 being gained some 15km S.W. of Niort.

For **Poitiers**, see Rte 56.

POITIERS TO ST-MAIXENT VIA SANXAY (52.5km). The D6 leads W. (gained by crossing the railway immediately S. of the station), skirting the N. side of the Boivre valley, at 14km passing the ruins of the *Abbaye du Pin* (l.), founded in 1120, 2km beyond which a lane leads to *Montreuil-Bonnin*, where the imposing ruined castle is attrib. to Richard I.—6.5km. *Lavausseau*, where a school occupies an commandery of the Knights Templar, 2km beyond which we turn l. for (8.5km) **Sanxay**, famous for its **Roman remains* excavated in 1881–82 by Père de La Croix. These lie c. 1.5km W. in a loop of the Yonne, N. of the Ménigoute road. They consist of the substructures of an octagonal temple, the ruins of baths, and beyond the river, the remains of a theatre with a capacity of 8000 spectators. The absence of any trace of fortifications might indicate that it was the site of a villa or large country-house with dependencies, comparable to those of Tivoli. The buildings, dating from the 1st of 2C, were destroyed by fire in the early 5C.—3km to the N. of Sanxay are the interesting remains of the châteaux of *Forzon* and *Marconnay.*—Continuing W. from Sanxay, we pass (3.5km) *Ménigoute*, with an attractive late-Gothic church (14-15C), a disused church with a 12C doorway, and above the village, a Gothic chapel of 1530.—At *Coutières*, 4.5km further W., we turn l. past (2.5km l.) the extensive ruins of the *Abbaye des Chateliers* (12-13C), founded in 1110 and overlooking a lake.—11km S.W. lies *St-Maixent*; see below.

For the road to *Lusignan*; see Rte 70.—At *Jazeneuil*, 6km N.W., is an 11C church.

26km. **St-Maixent-l'École** was given part of its name by St Maxentius of Agde (d. 515), who with St Léger, Bp of Autun (d. 678), ruled an ancient abbey here, entirely destroyed by the Huguenots; of the church of *St-Maixent* only the porch and nave walls (12C), part of the transepts and choir, with a 13C rose-window, and the 15C tower surmounting the W. porch, survived; the rest dates from a rebuilding in the Gothic style (1682) by Leduc de Toscane. In the 12C crypt are the desecrated tombs of early abbots.—The 7C crypt of the former church of *St-Léger* may also be seen. The site of the castle is occupied by an infantry training school. A native was Col Denfert-Rochereau (1823–78), defender of Belfort in 1870–71.

We now follow the valley of the *Sèvre-Niortaise* to (23km) **NIORT** (60,200 Niortais), préfecture of the *Deux-Sèvres*, built on the gently sloping bank of the river, here divided into several branches by islets. Among its older industries is that of leather-dressing, and the manufacture of angelica.

The castle, founded by Henry II, passed finally to France after Du Guesclin's assault in 1372. During the Religious Wars, despite its favourable attitude towards the Huguenots, it was sacked by the Protestants in 1588. On 2 July 1815 Napoleon spent his last night on the French mainland in a house on the N. side of the Pl. de la Brèche.

From the N.W. side of the central *Pl. de la Brèche*, the Rue Ricard, continued by the Rue Victor-Hugo, leads towards the river, passing near (r.) the *Old Hôtel de Ville*, a Renaissance mansion of 1535 by Mathurin Berthomé, surmounted by a restored belfry, its upper part dating from the 17C. It now houses the *Musée du Pilori*, a miscellaneous collection of antiquities, the most interesting treasure of which is a complete collection of coins from the Carolingian mint at *Melle* (28km S.E.). At the back of the courtyard of No. 13 Rue Victor-Hugo is the 15-16C *Maison de Candie*. Beyond, to the W. of the market-hall, rise the two 12C towers of the *Donjon* of the Counts of Poitiers, joined by a 15C building altered in the 18C, now containing a small regional museum with good collections of local costumes, etc.

The Rues du Pont and St-André lead N. from the market-place to *St-André*, devastated by the Huguenots and reconstructed in the mid 19C, and 'disgraced by terrible stained glass'. At No. 5 in the former street, the *Hôtel de Chaumont* was the probable birthplace of Françoise d'Aubigné, her father being held prisoner in the Donjon at the time; see *Château de Mursay*, p 348.

The Rue Thiers leads S.W. from the market to the new *Hôtel de Ville*, beyond which is *Notre-Dame* (1491–1540), a Gothic work by Berthomé; to the S.E. of the town hall is the *Musée des Beaux-Arts*, containing tapestries, ivories, and enamels, etc., and a series of curious 14C painted panels from the château of *La Mothe-St-Héraye* (11km S.E. of St-Maixent) among other works of art. Hence the Rue St-Jean—off which runs the Rue Petit-St-Jean—in both of which several old houses survive, leads back to the Rue Victor-Hugo.

NIORT TO ST-JEAN D'ANGÉLY (44km). The N150 drives due S., at 14km crossing the A10, later skirting (l.) the *Forêt de Chizé*, and passing (14km) the 14C castle-keep of *Villeneuve-la-Comtesse*, 16km beyond which lies *St-Jean*; see Rte 70B.

Fontenay-le-Comte lies 29km N.W. of Niort on the N148, at 11km passing (l.) *Benet*, its church with a rich Romanesque facade, and 6km beyond, passes between (r.) *Nieul-sur-l'Autise* and *Maillezais*; see Rte 58B.

From Niort we follow the N11 S.W., leaving to the r. part of the

Marais Poitevin, an extensive tract of fen-like country reclaimed from the sea in the 17C, largely by the skill of engineers imported from Holland by Henri IV. A good approach is via *Magné*, 7km due W. of Niort, with a Renaissance church doorway by Berthomé, beyond which is the typical whitewashed marshland village of *Coulon-Sansais*.

10km. *Frontenay-Rohan-Rohan*, an ancient stronghold of the Rohan family, has a church once fortified, restored in the 15C, but preserving a tower and some good capitals of the 12C.—13.5km. *Mauzé-sur-le-Mignon* (also by-passed) was the birthplace of René Caillié (1799– 1838), the first European to visit Timbuctoo and return alive (1828); the church has a lofty Romanesque nave.

At the château of *Olbreuse*, 6km W. of Mauzé was born (in 1638) Eléonore Desmier, mother of Sophia Dorothea. In 1682 the latter married her cousin who, as George I, became king of England.

MAUZÉ TO LA ROCHELLE VIA SURGÈRES (46km). This alternative route follows the D911 just S.W. of Mauzé to (10.5km) **Surgères** (6500 inhab.), where the walls of the 14-16C castle now form the boundary of a pleasant garden in which stands the *Hôtel de Ville*, connected by an elegant Renaissance portico with the grass-grown parvis in front of the 12C *Church*. This preserves its magnificent * W. *Front*, restored, with seven arches at ground level, the three on either side of the central door each containing sculptured tympana. Above are two equestrian figures. The curious central tower was never completed. The disappointing effect of the nave is due to a 16C restoration.—For *Rochefort*, 26km S.W., see Rte 73.—The D939 leads due W., at 16km passing S. of *Aigrefeuille-d'Aunis*, with a restored 12-14C church and remains of a nunnery.

The N11 leads W. from Mauzé through (7km) *La Laigne*, with a Romanesque church, and the *Forêt de Benon*, later veering S.W. to approach *La Rochelle*.

LA ROCHELLE (78,200 Rochelais), the capital of the old province of *Aunis*, and préfecture of the *Charente-Maritime*, is an old-established seaport on a shallow gulf facing the Basque Roads, with a picturesque harbour; preserving numerous arcaded streets and ancient buildings, it retains its characteristic old centre, and as a redoubt for the principles of Protestantism, its history is of no less interest.

With the destruction of Châtelaillon in 1127 (see Rte 73) it grew in importance, being in English hands from 1152–1224 and again in 1360–72, and during the following two centuries was one of the greatest maritime cities of France, the Rochelais being among the first to trade with America. Royal attempts in the 16C to deprive its citizens of their independence resulted in a riot, and they eagerly accepted the doctrines of reform. An unsuccessful siege by the Catholic party in 1573 resulted in the grant of complete liberty of worship to the Calvinists, but by 1627 the bigoted Richelieu once more invested the town and cut off supplies by sea with the construction of a 'digue' across the harbour mouth. Two relief expeditions sent out by Charles I failed in their object, the first (July-Oct. 1627) from the incompetence of Buckingham, the second on account of Buckingham's assassination (23 Aug. 1628) at Portsmouth. On 28 Oct. 1628, despite the courage of Jean Guiton, the mayor, the garrison, reduced by famine, were forced to surrender, and the fortifications, except for what remains, were levelled.

The revocation of the Edict of Nantes (1685) and the cession of Canada to England (1763) further impoverished the town, and the harbour, obstructed by the remains of Richelieu's digue, became silted up. In 1891 a new deep-water harbour was opened at La Pallice. In the Second World War La Rochelle escaped serious damage, although the Germans shot the 75-year-old mayor. In 1945 their garrison prepared to hold out, although the place was invested by the French, but on 7 May, deluded by a false radio announcement of the general surrender

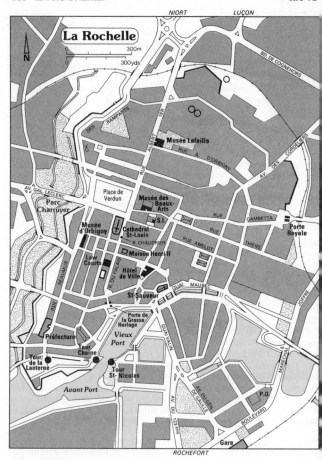

ROCHEFORT

of Germany, their commander handed over the town to the civil authorities
before the threatened bombardment commenced.

Among its natives were Tallemant des Réaux (1619–90), 'frondeur' and writer
of memoirs; René-Antoine Frechault de Réaumur (1683–1757), the physicist;
Billaud-Varenne (1756–1819), the revolutionary; and Eugène Fromentin
(1820–76), the artist and critic. Jean-Paul Sartre was educated at the lycée here
in 1917–19. The 'Four Sergeants of La Rochelle' were members of the garrison
executed in 1822 on a charge of conspiracy against Charles X.

For details of vedettes to the *Îles de Ré, d'Aix,* and *d'Oléron,* enquire at the S.I.
in the Pl. de Verdun; likewise regarding boats for hire, etc.

A complex series of ring-roads surrounds the town, and visitors are
directed into the centre from the N. After briefly following the remaining line of ramparts, flanked to the W. by the *Parc Charruyer,*
we reach the large *Pl. de Verdun.* On its S. side is the **Cathedral**, a
classical building of 1742–84, designed by Jacques Gabriel, but not
finished until 1862. It preserves the square 15C tower of the
demolished church of St-Barthélemy. The interior, of slight interest,

is decorated with frescoes, and a chapel off the l. aisle contains some quaint 17-18C ex-voto paintings.

A new **Museum** has been installed at No. 10 Rue Fleuriau, to the E., the restored 18C residence of an *armateur* with interests in the plantations of Santo Domingo, and devoted to French maritime commerce with the New World. Among several sections are those concerning sugar plantations, French influence in Canada, and Louisiana, etc. Notable are the 'Inca' wallpapers by Dufour and Leroy of 1826, among many other objects.

The Rue Chaudrier, continued further downhill by the picturesque Rue du Palais, is the main thoroughfare of the old town, much of it with arcades known as 'porches', a characteristic of several streets leading off it. A few paces to the l., in the Rue des Augustins, is the so-called *Maison Henri-Deux* built in 1555 by Hughes de Pontard of Champdeniers, a charming two-storeyed loggia with a square staircase-tower. The 'C' in the monogram 'HC' which occurs on the coffered ceilings has been incorrectly interpreted as being a crescent, and the building accordingly named (after her emblem), the 'House of Diane de Poitiers'.

Behind the cathedral, the Rue Aufrédy leads W. to the **Musée d'Orbigny-Bernon** (2 Rue St-Côme), with an interesting collection of local art and archaeology, including Gallo-Roman remains from Châtelaillon.

Notable are the old Pharmacy transferred here from the near-by hospice; a comprehensive collection of La Rochelle ware (1750–70), showing Oriental influence; maps and plans of the town, including *Callot*'s engraving of its Siege, and of the siege of the Île de Ré (1629), and a Panorama by Adrien van der Kabel (1631–1705). Among the paintings are a copy of *Joseph Vernet*'s View of La Rochelle, and *Robert Lefèvre*'s Portrait of the Duchesse d'Angoulême. On the Second Floor are an Oriental Collection, and bygones.

Returning to the Rue du Palais by the next street to the S., we pass the *Hôtel du Médecin Venette*, a 17C mansion decorated with busts of famous physicians (now the *Justice de Paix*); there are some good 18C houses in the Rue Pernelle, which we next cross.—Turning r. in the main street, the *Palais de Justice* (1789; with a few Henri-IV survivals), is passed, and beyond, the **Bourse* (1785), with a charming courtyard and notable back door.

From the *Pl. des Petits-Bancs* the 13C *Porte de la Grosse-Horloge* provides an approach to the Cours Wilson, flanking the ***Vieux Port**, with a picturesque view the two towers guarding its entrance. At the end of the promenade is the *Tour de la Chaine* ◇ (1375), whence a chain, closing the harbour at night and in times of war, used to stretch across to the Tour St-Nicolas; Rabelais jocularly suggested that it was originally one of those forged to restrain the exuberance of young Pantagruel! The *Tour St-Nicolas* (1384), with a double spiral staircase and well vaulted apartments, including an oratory, may be visited, its tower commanding, a panoramic **View* of the town and harbour, and at low tide, the *digue* built by Richelieu (see above). The tower is approached from the far side of the Vieux Port, passing the yacht harbour to the l., and stands on a small promontory on which is the fishermen's quarter.

To the W. of the Tour de la Chaine the Rue Sur-les-Murs runs along the top of the old curtain wall to the quaint-looking *Tour de la Lanterne* (1468), a cylindrical tower with a Flamboyant spire and lantern-turret that once served as a lighthouse.—A short distance to the N. is the *Préfecture*, in a 17C mansion.

Retracing our steps to the *Porte de la Grosse Horloge*, we may follow the lively Quai Duperré to the bridge over the mouth of the canal which connects Marans with the sea. To the N. stands *St-Sauveur*, rebuilt in 1669 and after 1718, but preserving a 15C tower.—An alley N. of its apse leads to the *Protestant Church* (rebuilt 1708; with a collection of documents relative to the local history of the cult).

The Rue St-Sauveur leads shortly to a small square, to the N. of which is the **Hôtel de Ville**, which although founded in 1289, dates mainly from the 16-17C; its courtyard is entered by a doorway pierced in a 15C wall with overhanging battlements, at either end of which is a slender cylindrical turret. Opposite the entrance is the principal facade (1606). On the ground floor is a rather heavy arcade with coupled columns; this is surmounted by eight lofty columns of the composite order framing allegorical figures, and above are dormers of various styles. On the l. is a Renaissance pavilion (after 1540) with a statue of Henri IV in enamelled faïence (replacing the original figure of 1612). The interior contains a number of historical souvenirs of the town and its famous siege.—The S.E. facade, fronting the Rue des Gentilshommes, has a rather pompous doorway of 1607, by which, at the end of the term of their office (which secured for them the rank of 'Gentilshommes'), the magistrates left the Hôtel de Ville.

Hence we may follow the Rue St-Yon, or preferably the Rue des Merciers (parallel to the E.; another arcaded street of old houses, in which Nos 3, 5, 8, and 17 are good examples of the 16C style), to the *Pl. du Maché*, with a remarkable slate-banded house. From the N.E. corner of the square the Rue Gambetta leads E. to the *Porte Royale* (17C); from the N.W. corner we reach the *Fontaine du Pilori* (1711; rebuilt 1822), from which the arcaded Rue du Minage leads back to the Pl. de Verdun.

This may also be approached from the W. side of the Pl. du Marché via the Rue Gargoulleau, on the N. side of which, in the former bishop's palace (1777) is the **Musée des Beaux-Arts**, a somewhat miscellaneous collection including *Le Sueur*, Adoration; St Christopher carrying Christ (15C Dutch); *Delatour*, pastel Portrait of a man in blue; Marine views and Landscapes by *Fromentin*, *Corot*, and *Paul Bril*, and a View of La Rochelle by *E. Pinel* (1804–84), etc.

The Rue Albert-Ier leads N. from the Pl. de Verdun to (r.) the *Jardin des Plantes* and the *Muséum Lafaille, a good natural history collection housed in an 18C mansion, and retaining some 18C cabinets. An extension is accommodated in the building opposite, devoted to ethnology; those sections on Sao and Tchad civilisations and on Oceania are of particular interest.

For roads from La Rochelle to *Nantes*, and *Saumur*, see Rtes 62, and 58, in reverse; for *Rochefort* and the *Île d'Oléron*, see Rte 73.

LA ROCHELLE TO THE ÎLE DE RÉ. The Av. Gén. Leclerc leads from the S.W. of the Pl. de Verdun through suburbs to (5km W.) *La Pallice*, the port being largely rebuilt since 1944, although the late 19C installations were only slightly damaged; the mole, over 1km long, was completed in 1951. Hence a regular car-ferry leaves for the **Île de Ré**, lying immediately to the W., a flat sandy island 90km², in area, with a high population for its size (28km long, and between 3 and 5km wide).

It was in the intermittent possession of the English until 1457, and in 1627 withstood an attack by the English fleet under Buckingham (see above), and it is suggested that a relic of the English occupation is the name 'quiche-notte' (kiss-not) of the wide sun-bonnets worn by its women!

From *Sablanceaux* we follow the main road N.W., passing (4km) the ruined

Abbaye des Châteliers and (3.5km) *La Flotte,* with a curious 15C church.—4km. *St-Martin-de-Ré,* the main town, preserves its fortifications, by Vauban (c. 1680), almost intact, including two typical gateways and a citadel (now a prison). The fortified church, largely rebuilt since the Anglo-Dutch bombardment of 1692, contains the tombs of the Baron de Chantal, father of Mme de Sévigné, and other soldiers who fell in the English assault of 1627. To the S., in the *Pl. de la République,* is the 17C *Hôtel des Cadets-Gentilshommes de la Marine,* now the *Hôtel de Ville;* to the E. of the old port is the *Hôtel de Clerjotte,* previously the arsenal, in a 16C convent building, and now housing the *Musée Cognacq,* a local and regional collection.—Beyond the isthmus of *Le Martray,* only 60m wide, is an area of salt-marshes and abandoned windmills, to the W. of which, in the village of *Ars-en-Ré,* is a Renaissance house and an interesting 12-15C church, whose spire has been slightly inclined since it was struck by lightning in 1840.—Beyond is the *Phare des Baleines,* a lighthouse of 1854 near its 17C predecessor.

73 La Rochelle to Bordeaux via Rochefort, and Royan; the Île d'Oléron

171.5km (106 miles). N137. 30km *Rochefort*—D733. 8km *Marennes,* for the **Île d'Oléron,** lies 15km S.W.—32km **Royan.** Ferry to the *Pointe de Grave*—N215 (or D1). 38.5km *Lesparre-Médoc*—63km **Bordeaux.** Detours, or the exploration of the Île d'Oléron, will of course add to the total figure. Those wishing to drive rapidly from Rochefort to Bordeaux may join the A10 motorway 37km S.E., near *Saintes;* see below.

Maps: IGN 39, 46, or 107, 110. M 233. The *Île d'Oléron* is covered in detail on IGN 505.

The N137 drives S.E. from **La Rochelle** (Rte 72), at 11km passing the resort of *Châtelaillon,* bearing the name of the old capital of Aunis, which was swallowed up by the sea in the 14C after its destruction in 1127 by the Duc d'Angoulême.

10km. *Fouras,* 5km W., at the mouth of the Charente, preserves a tree-shaded shore, but the receding tide uncovers a wide expanse of mud, which although unsightly, is odourless. At the S. end of the main beach is a 15C keep surrounded by outworks (17C); beneath it is the *Port Sud,* from which Napoleon was carried out to a boat of the French frigate 'Saale', which conveyed him to the offshore island of Aix (8 July 1815).

On the **Île d'Aix** (pron. 'dé'), lying in the Pertuis d'Antioche, the strait between the Îles de Ré and d'Oléron, less than 2km² in area, is the *Maison de l'Empereur,* with a small collection of Napoleonic relics. It was his brief residence before embarking on the 15 July 1815 on board the 'Bellerophon', which was waiting in the adjacent Basque Roads to prevent his anticipated escape to America. Hence he was conveyed to Portsmouth and then in the 'Northumberland' to St Helena.

In 1809 the 'Rade des Basques' was the scene of Lord Cochran's attempt to destroy the blockaded French fleet by fireships. His stratagem, partly successful, forced the French ships ashore, but they were saved from destruction by the incompetent dilatoriness of his commander, Lord Gambier.

9km S.E. of the turning for Fouras, lies **Rochefort** (27,700 inhab.), a town of little interest, lying on a loop of the Charente.

It was developed by Henri IV, and laid out on a regular plan by Colbert in 1666 to serve as a military port and arsenal, and was strong enough to dissuade Adm. Tromp from attacking it from 1674. It defied the British fleet five times between 1696 and 1809. In 1940 it was bombed by the Germans, and much damage was done to the harbour and arsenal in 1944. It most distinguished native is the novelist Julien Viaud, better known as 'Pierre Loti' (1850–1923).

The road from La Rochelle, on entering the town, crosses a tree-planted esplanade on the site of its fortifications, which had been progessively demolished. The disused Romanesque church (the *Vieille Paroisse*) of the village that preceded Colbert's foundation is in the Av. Rochambeau, S. of the esplanade; to the N. is the *Maritime Hospital* of 1788.

To the E., in the centre of the old town, is the *Pl. Colbert*, flanked by *St-Louis* (1839), adorned with an arch bearing figures of the Charente and the Atlantic. The Rue Pierre-Loti leads S. from this square, in which No. 141 is the *Maison de Loti*, with relics of the author. At the corner of the next street is the municipal *Museum*, containing a somewhat miscellaneous collection, including Polynesian masks, etc.

A short distance E. of the Place stands the *Hôtel de la Marine* (1771), the naval headquarters (no adm.), where Napoleon stopped briefly on his journey from Niort to Fouras (see above). To the S., beyond the *Porte de Soleil*, is the 17C *Hôtel de Cheusses*, formerly the Commissariat de Marine, accommodating a *Naval Museum*, with ships' models, figure-heads, charts, etc., and documents relative to the history of the arsenal; also a casket (presented by the British Admiralty) of the timbers of the 'Implacable' (sunk in 1949), launched at Rochefort as the 'Duguay-Trouin' in 1800. The buildings of the old arsenal, further S.E., and the warehouses on the quay of the commercial harbour (1671–93) to the N., and the *Dockyard* (no adm.) are largely in private hands and are much reduced in importance.

ROCHEFORT TO SAINTES (37km). The N137 leads E., shortly circling round *Tonnay-Charente*, where a hospital occupies what is left of a château of the Rochechouart family, the birthplace of Mme de Montespan (1641–1707).—*St-Jean-d'Angély* lies 31km E.; see Rte 70B.—At 20km there is a 12-13C church and other remains of a Benedictine abbey at *Pont-l'Abbé-d'Arnault*, 4.5km S.W.—6.5km. To the l. is the **Château de la Roche-Courbon*, described by Loti as 'the Sleeping Beauty's castle'. The main buildings, including the detached keep, are 15C, although modernised since and restored; the Louis-XIV decoration of the so-called 'Salle de Bains' (1662) is noteworthy; the **Gardens* likewise.—Some 8km further E. are the châteaux of *Crazannes* (15-18C), and *Panloy* (18C).—At 11km we reach the A10; **Saintes** lies 3.5km beyond; see Rte 68.

The D733 leads due S. from Rochefort, at 4.5km passing W. of *Échillais*, with an elaborate but worn Romanesque W. front to its church. It continues S. skirting the salt-marshes, and with a view of the 12C keep at *Broue* (r.) to (18km) *Cadeuil* (see last paragraphs of Rte 68), and *Royan*, 17.5km beyond: see below.

A more interesting route is that turning r. at 3.5km immediately after crossing the Charente to traverse *Soubise* and (8km) *Moëze*, its church with a fine openwork spire and *Cross* of 1563.—6km. **Brouage**, once an important port, but now a decayed village, preserving its **Ramparts* of 1640, which, although restored, are almost perfect examples of pre-Vauban fortifications. The coats-of-arms and cardinals' hats which embellish them are a reminder that this was Richelieu's base of operations against La Rochelle in 1628. The 16-17C church was restored by the people of Quebec in honour of their founder, Samuel de Champlain (1567–1635), a native of Brouage.

In 1658 Mazarin exiled to this remote stronghold his niece Marie Mancini, with whom Louis XIV had fallen passionately in love, until the 'Spanish Marriage' with Maria-Teresa had been consummated. While returning from St-Jean-de-Luz to Paris with his bride, the king made a special detour to Brouage from St-Jean-d'Angély simply to pass the night in the room that Marie Mancini had recently occupied!

12.5km. *Marennes*; see last paragraphs of Rte 68.

The **Île d'Oléron**, the largest of the islands lying off this coast of France (c. 173km²; 30km long, and 6km wide), with a population largely occupied in agricultural and vinicultural pursuits, and in the cultivation of oysters, lies to the N.W., since 1966 reached by a viaduct over 3km long (toll) spanning the *Pertus de Maumusson*, and passing near the *Fort du Chapus*, built by Louvois.

Like the rest of the neighbouring country, Oléron passed to England as part of Eleanor of Aquitaine's dowry; the 'Rôles d'Oléron', a maritime code established by her, have been the basis of all subsequent French naval statutes. The island reverted to France in 1370, and since 1577 has been largely Protestant. Augustin Courtauld (1660–1706), founder of the English Huguenot family of goldsmiths and silk-weavers, was born at St-Pierre d'Oléron, and emigrated to London after 1685.

To the W., on crossing the strait, lies the resort of *St-Trojan-les-Bains*, backed by extensive pine-woods, beyond which is the Grande Plage, a vast expanse of sand exposed to the Atlantic, and continued to the N. by the Plage de Vert-Bois, both being reached by by-roads forking l. at the far end of the bridge.—Bearing r., we enter *Le Château-d'Oléron*, the main town, with 17C fortifications ruined in 1945, and a pretty Renaissance fountain.—5.5km beyond, a r.-hand fork leads to (7km) *Boyardville*, the port-of-call for boats from La Rochelle.—To the N.W. are the wooded dunes of *Les Saumonards*.

5.5km (r.) *St-Pierre-d'Oléron* has a 13C *'lanterne des morts'*, crowned by an 18C pyramid, in its market-place. Pierre Loti (cf. Rochefort) is buried in the garden of a house he owned here.—There is a beach at *La Cotinière*, 3km S.W.—5km. *St-Georges-d'Oléron*, E. of the road, has a church retaining Romanesque features; 3km to the W. are the dunes of 'du Domino'.—7km further N. lies *St-Denis-d'Oléron*, with another partly Romanesque church, 3km beyond which, at the N.W. extremity of the island, is the *Chassiron lighthouse* (1836), while off-shore is seen the *Tour d'Antioche*, marking a dangerous reef.

From crossroads just N.W. of Marennes, one may turn S.W., to cross its oyster-parks irrigated by the Seudre, on the S. bank of which lies *La Tremblade*; turning r. through (7.5km) *Ronce-le-Bains*, we may circle the afforested *Presqu'Île d'Avert* to (15km) the powerful *Phare de la Coubre*.

To the S. one can discern the *Phare de Cordouan* on its isolated rock, guarding the mouth of the Gironde; the first known lighthouse was erected by the Black Prince in 1371, while Louis de Foix (a pupil of Herrera, architect of the Escorial) was responsible for the lower part of the present building (1584–1610); the upper storeys were added by Teulère in 1789.

19.5km **Royan** (18,100 inhab.), a well-situated Atlantic resort at the neck of the Gironde estuary opposite the *Pointe de Gave* (a bridge to which is projected) has been largely reconstructed since its virtual destruction by bombing between Sept. 1944 and April 1945, when it was occupied by a pocket of German troops. Its main attractions are a series of sandy bays in its vicinity, its cliff walks, and the pine *Forêt de la Coubre* traversed on approaching it from the N.W., skirted by dunes. There is a small Romanesque church at *Vaux-sur-Mer*, 3km N.W.

Contiguous to the S. of Royan is the resort of *St-Georges-de-Didonne*, 12km S.E. of which, on a cliff overlooking the estuary, is the 12C church of *Ste-Radeonde* at

Talmont, a short distance beyond which is the *Moulin du Fâ*, erected on the site
of the Roman temple of the town of *Tamnum*.—8.5km N.E. of Talmont lies
Cozes, 24km E. of which is *Pons*, and 33km S.E. of which is *Mirambeau*, both just
beyond the A10 motorway; see Rte 70B.

Regular ferries cross from Royan to the *Pointe de Grave*, the N. extremity of the **Médoc peninsula**, on the far bank of the Gironde,
here 5km wide, 4km S. of which is *Verdon-sur-Mer*, developed in the
1920s as a foreport for Bordeaux, but wrecked by the Germans in
1944.—6km. *Soulac-sur-Mer*, a small resort to the W., was the ancient port of *Noviomagus*, buried by shifting sands in the 6C, a relic
of which is *N.-D.-de-la-Fin-des-Terres* (11-12C), itself buried in 1744
but exhumed in 1859, and restored. It was here that Talbot's army
disembarked in 1452 in a vain attempt to hold Guyenne for England.

SOULAC TO ARÈS (90km). The D101, continued by the D3, leads S. towards the
Bassin d'Arcachon, traversing pine forests most of the way, from which several
roads turn W. to approach the sandy coast, passing near the *Lacs d'Hourtin, de
Carcans*, and *de Lacanau*.—2.5km prior to Arès, the D106 turns S.W. to (22km)
Cap-Ferret, a small resort on a narrow tongue of land opposite *Pyla-sur-Mér*, contiguous with Arcachon; see Rte 77. The high dunes of Pilat are better seen from
the headland of Cap Ferret, 4km beyond.—*Arès* itself lies 48km W. of
Bordeaux.—*Arcachon* may be approached by circling the E. shore of its Bassin
(38km); but see Rte 77.

The main road leads S.E. via (13km) *St-Vivien*, where the old church
was destroyed in the fighting of April 1945, when a German garrison
isolated here was forced to surrender to French troops.—17km.
Lesparre-Médoc, with a 14C donjon. The direct road continues S.E.
to (63km) Bordeaux, traversing the **Médoc peninsula**, the flat
triangle of land between the Gironde and the Atlantic. Its vineyards
occupy the central tract between the marshy meadows along the
estuary and the '*pignadas*' or pine forests further W., marking the
beginning of *Les Landes* (see Rte 77) which extend as far as the sand-
dunes flanking the ocean.

The more interesting riverside road (D2) forks l. at Lesparre, at
10.5km passing (l.) *Vertheuil*, where the Premonstratensian abbey
*Church (12C, with a 15C vault) is the finest in the Médoc.—We pass
(r.) *Château Lafite*, and *Château Mouton-Rothschild* (with a Wine
Museum) before reaching (9.5km) *Pauillac*, N. of which, near *St-
Estèphe*, are oil-refineries and steel-works, while on the opposite
bank of the Gironde a Centrale nucléaire is under construction.
Other '*crus*' in the area are Pinchon-Longueville, Pontet-Canet,
Château-Montrose, Calon-Ségur, Cos d'Estournel, and Lynch-Bages,
etc.—3km. The vineyard of *Château-Latour* is passed on the l., and
1km beyond, *St-Julien-Beychevelle*, known for the wines of Gruaud-
Larose and Léoville.—At 2km we pass the *Château de Beychevelle*
(rebuilt 1757), and 5.5km beyond pass W. of *Fort Médoc* (1689; by
Vauban; restored), facing *Blaye*, on the far bank (see Rte 70B).—4km.
Some 6km S.W. lies *Moulis*, the Romanesque church of which has a
richly ornamented apse.—7.5km. *Château-Margaux*, celebrated for
its vineyards, among others in the vicinity, such as *Cantenac* and
Rauzac.—At 16.5km we pass (l.) the ruins of the 14-16C *Château de
Duras* at *Blanquefort*, just prior to reaching the ring-road circling
Bordeaux.

For **Bordeaux**, see Rte 75.

74   Bordeaux to Bergerac and Souillac

195km (121 miles). N89. 31km **Libourne**—D670. 6.5km **St-Émilion** lies 2km N.—D936. 11.5km *Castillon-la-Bataille*—21km **Ste-Foy-la-Grande**—22km **Bergerac**—D660, etc. 19km *Pont de Couze*—20km *La Buisson-de-Cadouin*—26km *Beynac*. **Sarlat** lies 10.5km N.E.—8km *Port de Domme*—9km *Carsac*—21km **Souillac**.

Maps: IGN 47, 48, or 110. M 233, 234, 235.

One may follow either the N89 from **Bordeaux** (Rte 75) to **Libourne** (see the latter part of Rte 67, in reverse), or alternatively we may take the D936 crossing the *Entre Deux Mers* further S., after 15km passing (r.) the road to *Créon* (see Rte 76), and 5.5km beyond (l.) the *Château du Grand-Puch* (14C).—7.5km. To the r. are the ruins of the 14-16C castle of *Curton*, with a 32m-high tower, beyond which we descend into the Dordogne valley, crossing the river at (6km) *Branne*.—4km. St-Émilion lies 6km N.

ST-ÉMILION, famous for its wines (and those of Pomerol, a short distance to the N.W.), is a curious old town standing on a steep hill 5.5km S.E. of Libourne. The moated town walls survive to a remarkable extent, at the N. end of which is the upper *Porte Bourgeoise*, to the W. of which are remains of the Dominican church of c. 1300. To the E. are relics of the *Palais Cardinal* (13C). On the N.W. side is the 12C *Collegiate Church* (under restoration), with two domed bays, and a late 13C choir. The N. door is regrettably mutilated. To the S. is a beautiful 13C cloister.—Further S.W. is the *Porte St-Martin*, leading to the conspicuous *Château du Roi*, built for Louis VIII in 1225.

S. of the cloister is a small square overlooked by a 13C *Belfry* with a 15C spire, below which, approached by descending further to the E., facing the central *Pl. du Marché*, is the remarkable subterranean *Église Monolithe, said to have been hewn out of the cliff by disciples of St Emilion, who in the 8C lived in the adjoining hermitage, now surmounted by a 12C chapel.—A lane leading N.E. ascends through the *Porte de la Cadène* towards the ruins of a Franciscan Convent* (15-17C), with relics of a cloister, some distance beyond which survives the *Porte Brunet*.

We regain the Dordogne at *Castillon-la-Bataille*, so called as being the scene of the final defeat of the English in Guyenne, and of the death of the Earl of Shrewsbury (1388–1453), Shakespeare's 'Old John Talbot' (Henry VI, 1), 'who was so renowned in France that no man in that kingdom dared to encounter him in single combat'.—There is an interesting Romanesque church at *Pujols*, 7km S.

5km. A l.-hand turning leads 2.5km to the **Château de Montaigne**, rebuilt after a fire in 1885. Only one separate tower survives of the former château (14-16C), once the home of Michel de Montaigne (1533–92), where—when adm. is conceded by the present proprietor—one may visit the chapel, bedroom, and round library so minutely described in the 'Essais' (III, 3), with its three windows and five shelves of books in view of the writing-table. None of the furniture is original, and only the faded inscriptions on its beams recall its august author. It is now a sad place.

The main road continues E. to (4km) *Montcaret* (l.).

A little Romanesque church here (with 4th, 6th, and 11C capitals) stands in the midst of the excavated foundations of a large Roman Bath of the 4C, used as a church and burial-ground since the 6C. Some fine mosaic floors have been exposed, notably in a hall with hypocausts and sculptural and architectural remains. The adjacent *Museum* ◊ preserves smaller objects found on the site, including 1-6C ceramics, Visigothic bronzes (including an enamelled pectoral cross, and buckle embellished with silver niello).

Gensac, 6.5km S., preserves several old houses and a ruined château.

12km. **Ste-Foy-la-Grande**, where we cross the Dordogne, a mid 13C bastide, preserves its grid of streets, in which a few timber-framed houses survive. It was a Protestant stronghold in the 16C, and was the birthplace of Paul Broca (1824–80), the surgeon, and the geographer and early Communist Élisée Reclus (1830–1905).

22km. **Bergerac** (see Rte 66), where we re-cross the river, skirting its narrow N. bank to (19km) the *Pont de Couze*, to the S.W. of which is the *Château de Lanquais* (14C and Renaissance).

PONT DE COUZE TO FUMEL, VIA MONPAZIER (56.5km). The D660 turns S.E. up the valley past (6km) the 15-16C château of *Bannes*, 2km beyond which we fork r.—The l.-hand fork leads to (3.5km) *St-Avit-Sénieur*, with a Benedictine abbey-church (12-13C).—*Molières*, 3.5km N. of St-Avit, is a decayed but characteristic late 13C bastide, once with a castle, preserving a 12C church.—2km. *Beaumont*, another 13C bastide, but better preserved, and a small town of some charm, has a fortified church of 1272 with four towers.

The road veers S.E., passing some 4km W. of the Romanesque church of *Ste-Croix*, and the village of *Montferrand-du-Périgord*, beyond, to (16km) ***Monpazier***, an excellent example of a bastide, founded in 1285 by Edward I, with an arcaded Place of great character, but lacking fortifications.—Hence we turn S.W. for 5km and then l. through the woods to (4km) **Biron**, with a conspicuous *Château* of various dates since the 11C, part of which was destroyed by De Montfort in 1214. The chapel (1515) has been restored.—The road goes on via (4km) *Lacapelle-Biron*, birthplace of the potter Bernard Palissy (1510–90), to (6km) *Gavaudun*, a curious old village near the foot of a striking gorge, with tall towers of a ruined castle impressively perched on a cliff, and the half-ruined Romanesque church of *Laurenque*.—At the next T-junction we turn l. (*Monflanquin*—see Rte 66—lies 10.5km W.), descending to and crossing the D710 after 6.5km.—By turning l. at the next junction we may approach the *Château de Bonaguil*, 5km N.E. (see p 384), or make our way down into the valley of the Lot at *Condat*—just E. of *Fumel*.—For the road hence to **Cahors**, see p 384.

Continuing E. from the Pont de Couze, we traverse (3km) *Lalinde*, a bastide of 1267, probably founded on the site of the Gallo-Roman settlement of *Diolindum*, beyond which the thickly wooded circumjacent hills close in on the Dordogne, spoilt by the erection of a power-station at (6km) *Calès*.—Here one may cross to the N. bank and *Trémolat*, with an 11C *Church*, and follow the river to *Le Bugue*; see below.—The main road leads E. to (9km) *Le Buisson*, 6km S.W. of which is the remarkable *Church* of **Cadouin** (1154), with its splendid Flamboyant *Cloister*.

LE BUISSON TO LES EYZIES AND MONTIGNAC: the Vézère valley (44.5km). We turn N. across the Dordogne to (10km) *Le Bugue*, on the far bank of the Vézère, and there turn r. towards (10km) **Les Eyzies**; see Rte 71. Most of the prehistoric caverns which may be visited lie further N. on this road beyond the turning across the river into the town, among them the *Gorge d'Enfer*, the *Grotte du Grand-Roc* (stalactites), and the *Laugerie Basse* and *Haute*, etc.—To the l. on the far bank is the 11-12C fortified church of *Tayac*.—E. of Les Eyzies we fork l. off the Sarlat road through *Tursac* (with its massive belfry), where, on the far bank of the Vézère, was found the rock shelter of *La Madeleine*, the site of the first discoveries of the late Palaeolithic age, now called Magdalenian.—9.5km. *Le Moustier*, on the far bank, also with a Romanesque church, is the site of the early Palaeolithic shelter which gave its name to the Mousterian Age. On the S. bank rises the cliff of *La Roque-St-Christophe*, riddled with caves and bearing the remains of a medieval stronghold. The road traverses *St-Léon*, with a restored Romanesque church, and the châteaux *de la Salle* and that of neighbouring *Clérans* (15C; restored). It continues up the valley with its frowning limestone cliffs, which formed such convenient shelters for prehistoric man, and passes the 16C châteaux of *Belcayre* and *Losse*.

15km. *Montignac*, retaining some old riverside houses and commanded by its feudal castle, sprang into prominence after 1948, when the adjacent prehistoric site of **Lascaux** was made accessible to the public; unfortunately it has been closed since 1963 as its remarkable cave-paintings were showing signs of deterioration caused by the humidity generated by the breath of tourists. A concrete 'bunker', which is a replica of the main cave, and containing accurate reproductions of its more important painted sections, was inaugurated in the summer of 1983, the entrance of which is 200m distant from the original site.

The cave, c. 2.5km S.E. of the village, was discovered by accident in 1940 by some boys whose dog had fallen into a hole which proved to be its entrance. Its vivid paintings (in iron and manganese oxide pigments), and incised drawings, cover the walls and roof of the two main halls and a connecting passage (apart from other sections of the cave), and depict bison, bulls, cows, horses, and deer, etc., and for the most part they were assigned by the Abbé Breuil to the late Aurignacian period (c. 20,000 B.C.), and are thus earlier than the equally famous Magdalenian paintings at Altamira in N. Spain (c. 12,000 B.C.). Their remarkable state of preservation *was* due to the dryness of the atmosphere and to the covering of calcite which had formed through the ages, amounting to a coating of transparent varnish.

A road from Montignac circles E., and then S. to (26.5km) *Sarlat*; see Rte 71.—After 3km a l.-hand fork off this road ascends to (5km) *St-Amand-de-Coly*, with a fine 12C fortified church.

The main road continues N.E. up the Vézère valley to *Condat*, and 1km beyond meets the N89 26.5km W. of **Brive**; see Rtes 64 and 94.

From Le Buisson we follow the l. bank of the Dordogne to the S.E. and (7km) *Siorac*.

SIORAC TO CAHORS VIA VILLEFRANCHE-DU-PÉRIGORD (67km). The D710 climbs S. past (5.5km) *Belves*, with a 15C belfry and characteristic old houses, etc.—*Monpazier* (see above) lies 16km S.W.—At 18.5km we turn l. onto the D660 (c. 12km S. stands the castle of *Bonaguil*; see p 384).—5km. *Villefranche-du-Périgord*, a bastide of 1261 commanding the Lémance valley, 6km N.E. of which, at *Besse*, a Romanesque church preserves a fine portal; while c. 10km S.W. down the valley is the curious fortified church of *St-Front*.—The road continues S.E. via *Goujounac* to meet the D911 at (21.5km) *Rostassac*, which we follow E. to (19km) *Cahors*; see Rte 64.—7.5km N.E. of this junction, in the Vert valley, lies *Catus*, with a good 11-14C church and ruined priory; while c. 6km N. of Rostassac stands the *Château de Crabillier*.

At Siorac we cross the Dordogne and follow its N. bank via (8.5km) *St-Cyprien*, with a former priory church, and the *Château de Fage* (under restoration since burned by the Germans in 1944), N.E. of which is that of *La Roque* (early 16C).—The road veers S.E., with a good view up the valley, almost every height on either side of which being here crowned with a castle, or ruin.

12.5km. **Beynac** preserves a splendid although dilapidated *Castle (13-16C), while on the far bank stand the late 15C château of *Les Milandes* (once owned by Josephine Baker), and the picturesque manor of *Fayrac* (15-16C).—Just beyond the latter rise the ruins of *Castelnaud* (12-14C), with a keep added by the English in the 15C.

Just beyond Beynac, a l.-hand turning ascends to **Sarlat**, 9.5km N.E.; see Rte 71.—Skirting a meander of the river, and passing *La Roque-Gageac*, picturesquely huddled against the cliff, with a fortified church and the manor of *Tarde*, we approach (8km) *Pont-de-Domme.*—On the far bank lies *Cénac*, with the fine priory church of *St-Junien* (c. 1130), with an apse of interest and good historiated capitals.

A l.-hand turning climbs steeply to ***Domme**, a well-sited bastide of 1281, with well-preserved ramparts and three gates, reconstructed *Halles*, and a terrace commanding a good plunging view over the valley, to which we may descend further E., crossing to *Vitrac*, the river-port of Sarlat, or at *Groléjac*, on the Sarlat-Gourdon road; see Rte 71.

From Pont-de-Domme the main road, keeping to the N. bank, traverses *Vitrac*, and passes the medieval castle of *Montfort* (r.), many times rebuilt, beyond which we may reach the main road from Sarlat at (9km) *Carsac.*—For the road hence to (21km) *Souillac*, see p 413; for Souillac itself, Rte 64; for the valley beyond, Rte 65.

75 Bordeaux

BORDEAUX (211,200 Bordelais; 91,000 in 1801; 130,900 in 1851), préfecture of the *Gironde*, and capital of the old province of *Guyenne*, stands on the l. bank of the Garonne some 25km S. of its confluence with the Dordogne—there forming the Gironde—and approx. 100km from the Atlantic. The river here, here over 500m broad, and making a sweeping curve, forms a harbour below the town to accommodate vessels engaged in the export of 'Bordeaux' wines, still its most important trade, although in recent decades its manufactures and industries have been much diversified.

Parts of the old centre, at least, were laid out in the grand 18C manner, and the river frontage is imposing from a distance, but considering its size and commercial importance, it contains few buildings of great interest. It was long a difficult place to traverse, but the system of ring-roads recently constructed promises to ease the flow of traffic.

A flourishing town since the Roman occupation, as *Burdigala* (capital of the Bituriges Vivisci) it was the metropolis of the province of *Aquitania Secunda.* It materially prospered during the English occupation of Guyenne (1154–1453), and was a favourite residence of the Black Prince, who held his court here in 1356–71, while his eldest son (later Richard II) was born here in 1367. Charles VII briefly captured the place, in 1451, but unwisely attempted to restrict the civic liberties accorded to the Bordelais by the English, who were later welcomed back with open arms; but the battle of Castillon in 1453 virtually ended the English domination.

Louis XI, unlike his father, encouraged the citizens by establishing the Parlement of Guyenne, and founding a University, but subsequent monarchs were less far-sighted, and in 1548 the Bordelais rebelled against the 'gabelle' or salt-tax. Montaigne was mayor of Bordeaux in 1581–85. The Bordelais were the chief supporters of the Fronde insurrection in the 17C, when the city withstood a memorable siege by the troops of Mazarin and Louis XIV. The 18C saw a great expansion of its commerce; and governors and intendants appointed by the crown, especially Aubert de Tourny, spent large sums on its embellishment. In 1787 the Parlement was banished to Libourne as a punishment for having failed to ratify the edict establishing provincial assemblies at the expense of the States General. At the Revolution Bordeaux was distinguished by its more moderate counsels, and its representatives formed the nucleus of the Girondist party. It was 'liberated' by Allied troops commanded by Beresford in March 1814, during the closing weeks of the Peninsular War, welcomed by Mayor Lynch.

In 1870–71, and in 1914, the seat of government was transferred from Paris to Bordeaux, and in June 1917 the first American troops to participate in the War landed at Bassens, a short distance down river. In the Second World War, after the fall of France on 13 June 1940, the French government likewise moved to Bordeaux, but two weeks later was superseded by the 'Vichy' government. It was bombed by the Germans on the 18-20th of that month, and by the Allies in May 1943; it was liberated on 28 Aug. 1944.

Among famous Bordelais were the Latin poet Ausonius (c. 310–95); Romain de Sèze (1748–1828), Louis XVI's advocate; the chemist Joseph Black (1728–99); the artists Carle Vernet (1758–1835), Narcisse Diaz de la Pena (1807–79), John-Lewis Brown (1829–90), Odilon Redon (1832–82), Adrien Dauzats (1808–68), Albert Marquet (1875–1947), and André Lhote (1885–1962); among musicians, the conductors Lamoureux (1834–99), and Colonne (1838–1910), the singer Garat (1764–1823), Jacques Thibaut (1880–1954), the violinist, and Henri Sauguet (1901–   ), the composer; and among writers, Jacques Rivière (1886–1925), François Mauriac (1885–1970), and Jean Anouilh (1910–   ).

Simon Stock, first Prior General of the Carmelites, died here in 1265 (whence his relics were removed in 1951 to his birthplace at Aylesford in Kent); and Francisco de Goya (1746–1828) died here in exile. The composer Clément Janequin lived here during the period 1505–31; and George Buchanan (1506–82), when professor at Bordeaux, had Montaigne among his pupils.

The **Pont de Pierre**, 501m long, an impressive structure of 17 arches (1810–21 by Deschamps and Billaudel; enlarged in 1954) crosses the Garonne from the suburb of *La Bastide* on the r. bank, and commands a wide view up and down the river.

It is advisable to turn r. along the Quai de la Douane to the *Esplanade* or *Place des Quinconces*, normally providing ample parking space, which may also be approached from the *Pont d'Aquitaine* (1967) spanning the river further N. The area between the Pont de Pierre and the Place is described below.

This extensive tree-lined promenade was laid out in 1818–28 on the site of the *Château Trompette*, a citadel erected by Charles VII to dominate and control the discontented citizens in the 1450s. At its E. end stand the two *Colonnes rostrales* (1829), while in the centre of its semicircular W. end stands the supererogatory *Monument des Girondins* (1895; see above).

Turning S., the short Cours du 30-Juillet passes the S.I. and *Maison du Vin*, where information with regard to visiting wine-cellars may be obtained. We now reach the central *Pl. de la Comédie*, on the E. side of which is the ***Grand-Théâtre**, a monumental building by Victor Louis (1773–80), one of the finest extant of its type, with statues of Muses and Graces or Goddesses surmounting its colonnade. Above the vestibule is a concert-hall, while the staircase ascends to the circular auditorium, scene of the National Assembly of 1871. It was erected on the site of ruins of a Roman temple razed in 1680.

Hence the broad Allées de Tourny leads N.W. to the busy *Pl. Tourny*, in the centre of which stands a statue of Aubert de Tourny (1690–1760), Intendant from 1743–57, who was responsible for much of the 18C town-planning. Beyond, the Rue Fondaudège con-

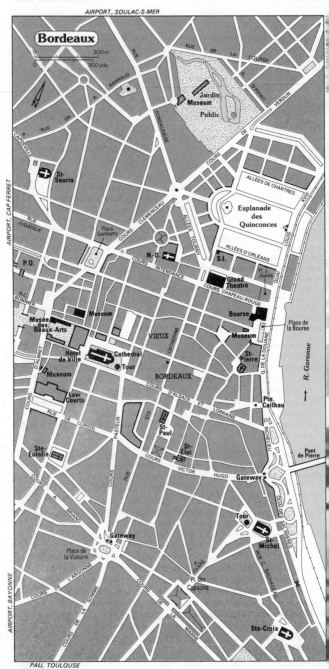

tinues N.W., just to the r. of which lie *Public Gardens* laid out by
Tourny as a promenade, but altered in 1858, with a *Natural History
Museum* in the 18C *Hôtel Lisleferme*, and botanical library.—To the
l. of the street, after a few minutes' walk, is the so-called **Palais
Gallien**, the neglected ruins of a 3C Roman amphitheatre, of which
several arches and sections of wall, constructed of bands of stone
and brick, remain standing, although much damaged at the Revolution. Hence the Rue Dr. A. Barraud leads S.W. to *St-Seurin* (see
below).

From the N.W. corner of the Pl. de la Comédie a street leads W. to
Notre-Dame (1684–1707; recently cleaned), formerly the chapel of
the adjoining Jacobin or Dominican convent, which now contains a
Musée Lapidaire and *Library.*

The latter conserves c. 400,000 volumes, including the 1588 edition of Montaigne's 'Essays' annotated and corrected by the author, and among 3500 MSS.
the 'Histoire Romaine' by Tite-Live or rather Titus Livy (1359; with 109 illustrations), three MS volumes of Montesquieu's 'Pensées', and 450 of his letters, etc.
  Behind the building is the circular *Marché des Grandes-Hommes*, better
demolished.

The Cours de l'Intendance (in which, at No. 57, Goya died in 1828)
leads W. from the Pl. de la Comédie to end at the ***Place Gambetta**
(formerly the *Pl. Dauphine*), a good example of Louis-Quinze architecture, with its ranges of masks, in the centre of which a
guillotine executed over 300 citizens during the Terror; it now contains gardens, which would be more in keeping if formal. At its S.E.
corner is the *Porte Dijeaux* (1748).

Medieval Bordeaux lay within the quadrangle immediately to the S., the outer
limits of which were the Bourse (N.E.), the Pl. Gambetta (N.W.), the Pl. Rohan (by
the cathedral; S.W.), and the Pl. du Palais (S.E.); see below.

From the N.W. corner of the Pl. Gambetta, the Rue Judáique leads
W., off which (r.), beyond the *Pl. des Martyrs de la Résistance*
(previously the *Allées d'Amour*), a paleo-Christian site, stands ***St-
Seurin**, mainly 12-14C, although the W. porch, masked by a sham
Romanesque facade (1831) dates from the 11C. The S. door, beneath
a 16C porch, is an elaborate work of the 13C; the Romanesque
towers received their upper storeys in the 16th (S.) and 18Cs.

The interior, some of whose pillars were cased in stone in 1698, is somewhat
heavy in effect. The bronze font dates from 1659. In the S. transept is the tomb of
Bp du Sault of Dax (d. 1623). The Choir contains some good 16C stalls and a
stone bishop's throne (15C), opposite which are 14C alabaster panels depicting
the legendary history of the church. In a 15C choir-chapel are carvings of the
Life of the Virgin. The early 11C *Crypt* contains Roman columns, 6C sarcophagi,
and several tombs, including the 17C cenotaph of St Fort.

Regaining the Rue Judáique, which we cross, we may follow the Rue
St-Sernin, continued by the Cours d'Albret. To the W. of their junc-
tion rises the modern *Quartier Meriadeck*, containing the new
Préfecture, beyond which is the extensive *Chartreuse Cemetery*.
  To the E., facing the 16C *Hôtels de Poissac* and *Pierlot*, are the two
galleries housing the **Musée d'Aquitaine** (S.), and the **Musée des
Beaux-Arts**, between which are the colourful *Jardins de la Mairie*.

The former contains extensive collections of archaeological and antiquarian interest. Among the more important individual items are the Golden torque from
Tayrac (3-2C B.C.); a three-headed God (2C); a late 2C bronze Statue of Hercules;

the so-called 'Vénus à la corne' from Laussel (20,000 B.C.); several statues of saints, mostly early 16C, found in 1971 when excavating an underground car-park adjacent to the Jacobin Convent (see above).—It is expected that the contents of the museum will be moved shortly to the former university faculty buildings at No. 20 Cours Pasteur, S. of the cathedral; see below.

Among the more interesting paintings in the Art Gallery are: *Perugino*, Virgin and Child between SS Jerome and Augustine; *Veronese*, Holy Family; *Van Dyck*, Marie de Médicis; *Rubens*, Martyrdoms of St George, and of St Just; *Mignard*, Duc d'Orléans; *De Troy*, An Abbé des Feuillants; *Nattier*, Henrietta, daughter of Louis XV; *Delatour*, pastel Portrait of Gravelot, and of Mlle Courrégeolles, by *Perronneau*; *Gilbert Stuart*, Mrs Arden; *Reynolds*, Baron Rokeby; *Raeburn*, Portrait of a writer; *Terbruggen*, Lute-player; *Delacroix*, Greece at Missolonghi; *Gros*, Embarkation of the Duchesse d'Angoulême at Pauillac; *Isabey*, Burning of the steamer 'Austria'; *Boldini*, Portrait of Señora Madrazo-Fortuny; also several characteristic paintings by *John-Lewis Brown, Marquet, Matisse, Lhote, Odilon Redon*, et al. Among sculptures are works by *Bernini, Lemoyne, Houdon*, and *Rodin*, among others.

Following the Rue Montbaxon, we may turn l. into the Rue Bouffard, where the 18C *Hôtel de Lalande*, at No. 39, is occupied by the *Musée des Arts Décoratifs, re-opened in 1983 after reorganisation, displaying important collections of furniture; ceramics and glass; ironwork and arms; enamels and bronzes; miniatures (many by Dagoty); silver, and objets d'art; and several paintings, including a Portrait of the Marquis de Tourny, by *Allais*; View of Bordeaux in 1804, by *Pierre Lacour*; and a bust of Montesquieu, by *Lemoyne*; also a terracotta bust of 'Young America' from the house of Nicolas Fenwick, the first U.S. consul at Bordeaux, etc.

To the S. is the *Hôtel de Ville*, built in 1782 for the Abp de Rohan, conveniently near to the cathedral, to the E. of which is the *Musée Jean-Moulin*, devoted to the Resistance.

The **Cathedral of St André** has suffered the attentions of Abadie (cf. Angoulême and Périgueux), who gratuitously destroyed its cloister. The W. front, with its large buttress, and which once abutted the ramparts, is of slight interest, but the transeptal fronts are good examples of 15C work, especially on the N., with its twin spires, with its bas-reliefs of the Last Supper and Ascension.

The *Porte Royale*, on the N. side of the nave, is embellished with 13C statues, but it is in need of cleaning, as is most of the building; a start has been made in the interior of the S. transept, and below the *Organ*, where two reliefs (Resurrection, and Descent into Limbo) from the destroyed rood-screen of 1531 are preserved. The most striking feature of the interior is the contrast between the lofty choir and the aisleless nave, begun in the 12C, a plain transitional structure remarkable for its breadth. The huge *Choir*, with ambulatory and transepts, not completed until the 15C, was begun under Bp Bertrand de Got (1300–5), later Pope Clement V, and is one of the most complete examples known of 'Rayonnant' Gothic, corresponding in inspiration to the English Decorated style. The sanctuary contains good ironwork and misericords; the ambulatory, an early 16C group of the Virgin and St Anne, and the tomb of Antoine de Noailles (d. 1562), governor of Bordeaux, among other items. The *Treasury* preserves a Crucifixion by Jordaens, among other paintings, and the usual cult objects.

To the S.E. of the cathedral apse (the broken glass in which has been stuffed with newspapers) rises the *Tour Pey-Berland* (after 1440), a belfry which survived demolition in 1793, and later used as a shot-tower, to which an ugly gilt image was added in 1863 to its rebuilt spire.

The area to the S.W. is of slight interest. Further S., near the Cours d'Albret, is the so-called *Tour des Anglais*, a relic of the *Fort du Hâ* (1456), beyond which is the *Palais de Justice* of 1846. Facing this is the facade of the *Hôpital St-André*

(1829; founded 1390), opposite the E. side of which is *Ste-Eulalie*, exhibiting every stage of Bordeaux Gothic from the 12-16Cs.

A short distance S. of the Tour Pey-Berland is the University faculty building (20 Cours Pasteur) in which is the *Tomb of Montaigne* (d. 1592; mayor of Bordeaux in 1581–86), with his effigy in armour, brought here from the vanished church of the Feuillants. The *Musée d'Aquitaine* (see above) is to be transferred here.

   Hence the Cours Victor-Hugo, laid out in 1708 as a promenade on the site of a moat, leads E., shortly crossing the long transverse Rue Ste-Catherine, one of the principal shopping streets (pedestrian in part), leading N. to the *Pl. de la Comédie*, and S. to the *Pl. de la Victoire*, dominated by the *Porte d'Aquitaine* of 1755.—Continuing E., we pass (l.) a market (N. of which stands *St-Paul*, of 1676), and then the *Grosse-Cloche*, a belfry above a gateway, a relic of the 15C Hôtel de Ville, abutted by 16C *St-Eloi*.

   Before reaching the end of the street, and the *Porte de Bourgogne* (1755), we fork r. along the Rue des Faures to the splendid hexagonal ***Tour St-Michel** (1492), with a 12-sided spire (109m high; restored 1865), being cleaned. Its vault preserves 70 cadavers moved hence in 1510 from a neighbouring cemetery.—The church of *St-Michel* (14-16C), in need of restoration, has had its glass, shattered in 1940, replaced by work by Max Ingrand. It contains an elaborate pulpit of 1753, a 17C Spanish painting of St Francis, an early 15C Flemish Annunciation, and several sculptured groups, etc.

   Hence the Rue Camille-Sauvegeau leads through a poor area to **Ste-Croix* (12-13C), the church of what was once the richest abbey in Bordeaux, with a remarkable **Facade*, freely 'restored' by Abadie, who added the N. tower and an incongruous equestrian statue of St George. The Romanesque capitals in the interior and the tiled floor of the N. transept are of interest.

Between the church and the river, here crossed by the *Pont St-Jean* (1965), stands the new *Centre* or *Conservatoire André-Malraux*.

From just N.E. of St-Michel, we may follow the quays past the *Pont de Pierre* (see p 427) and (l.; off the Quai Richelieu) the machicolated *Porte Cailhau* (1495), with pointed roofs.

It was also known as the *Porte du Palais*, a former gate (of 1309) having been the entrance to the palace of the dukes of Aquitaine and later of English kings. The present gate was erected as a triumphal arch in honour of Charles VIII's victory of Fornovo.

From the adjacent *Pl. du Palais* we may turn N. through an area in the process of being restored, following the Rue des Argentiers to *St-Pierre*, partly 15C, and then N.W. to the characteristic *Pl. du Parlement*. From its N.E. corner the ***Place de la Bourse** is approached, designed by Gabriel in 1738–55, and recently restored. Between the *Douane* (1738) to the S., and the *Bourse* (opened 1749) stands the *Musée de Marine*, with a good collection of ships' models, including the huge 'Louis le Grande', navigational instruments, charts, and other objects of maritime interest.

From the *Pl. Jean-Jaurès*, N. of the Bourse, we may turn W. along the Cours du Chapeau-Rouge to regain the Pl. de la Comédie, or continue N. to the Esplanade des Quinconces.

Of interest in the immediate environs are the huge '*chais*' or warehouses of the Bordeaux wine-merchants facing the Quais des Chartrons and de Bacalan, N. of the Esplanade des Quinconces. The vineyard of *Haut-Brion* is the nearest '*grand cru*' to Bordeaux, just N. of the N250 leading S.W. to the suburb of *Pessac*, S. of which is the *Domaine Universitaire*, and beyond which is the *Établissement Monétaire*. Here since 1973 the French Mint has been established (previously in the Hôtel des Monnaies in Paris); for times of admission, enquire at the S.I.—In the suburb of *Bègles*, S. of the city, is the *Musée Bonnal-Renaulac*, devoted to vintage cars; while due W. lies the airport of *Mérignac*.

For roads from Bordeaux through the Médoc to the *Pointe de Grave*, for *Saintes* or *Angoulême*, and for *Périgueux*, see Rtes 73, 70, and 67, in reverse; for **Bergerac, Toulouse, Pau**, and **Bayonne**, see Rtes 74, 76, 78, and 77 respectively.

VII AQUITAINE; PAYS BASQUE; PYRENEES; WESTERN LANGUEDOC

Aquitaine, that part of Gaul which lay between the Garonne and the Pyrenees, was not finally conquered by the Romans until 28 B.C. The original province was later considerably extended to include most of the country S. and E. of the Loire, and named *Aquitaine Tertia* or *Novempopulania*. It is asserted that Honorious presented it to Ataulph the Visigoth, but by c. 507 it was under the control of Clovis the Frank, who passed the kingdom to his son Clodomir. It was laid waste by the Burgundians, and the city of Convena (below St Bertrand-de-Comminges) was destroyed in 585. In the 7C the Vascones, crossing from N. Spain, invaded the S.W. corner of the country, which later became known as *Gascony*. A halt was put to their incursions by Dagobert in 663, although sporadic fighting continued until they sided with Charles Martel to combat the Moorish threat in the early 8C.

Louis le Débonnaire, the infant son of Charlemagne, was crowned king of Aquitaine, but with the inevitable division of power the various scions of the royal family were soon squabbling, Pepin II, Louis's grandson, revolting against Charles le Chauve. The latter rewarded his supporter Ranulph of Poitiers with the lordship of Aquitaine in c. 855, whose successor, Guillaume I, le Pieux (the Pious) of Auvergne, became duke in 886. Succeeding dukes increased their hold on the area, and by 1086 Guillaume IX was as much a menace to the kingdom as the Count of Toulouse. In 1152 his grand-daughter and heiress, Eleanor, married Henry II of England, bringing in her dowry the whole province of *Guyenne* (as it was known from the mid 12C, being a corruption of Aquitania), together with Gascony, Limousin, and Poitou, so that the king of England, already the inheritor of Normandy, Anjou, Touraine, Maine, and Saintonge, was virtually master of the whole of W. France.

The local winegrowers and shippers, supported by their English governors at Bordeaux, were reluctant to hazard their fortunes under a French ascendancy, but further inland anarchy was widespread, particularly near the frontier with Languedoc, further E., wasted by the Albigensian crusade. In an endeavour to counteract this state of affairs both the English and French founded a large number of *bastides* or fortified settlements, usually laid out on a grid plan around a central arcaded square. With the attainder of John, the English rapidly lost a high proportion of their continental territories, but in 1259 Louis IX, by the treaty of Xaintes (Saintes) confirmed Henry III's possession of Guyenne and Gascony from the Charentes to the Pyrenees. Up to 1360 the Black Prince was virtually king of this huge area, governing with moderation, but during the following century the French continued to encroach. The English were defeated in battle at Castillon, near St-Émilion, in 1453, and Bordeaux, with some misgivings, found themselves under the French yoke. With the accession of Henri IV the province flourished, but although many of its most industrious citizens were driven into exile with the revocation of the Edict of Nantes in 1685, the general misgovernment of the 18C was less felt here than in some other parts of France, largely due to the wise administration of such men as Turgot, Tourny, and Étigny, and the Revolution was likewise less savage in its reaction, the party of the Gironde standing for moderation in reform.

E. of the deserted Landes lay Gascony, extending N. from the foot of the western Pyrenees, roughly commensurate with the Roman province of Novempopulania (see below), the country of the nine peoples of Eauze, Auch, Bazas, Tarbes, Dax, Lectoure, Labourd (the diocese of Bayonne), Béarn, and Comminge. The rebellious ducal house of Armagnac, based on Auch and Lectoure, and then headed by megalomaniac Jean V, was in 1472 object of Louis XI's attention, who seized Lectoure, killed the duke, and confiscated his territories. The political party of the Armagnacs, the rivals of the Burgundians during the reigns of Charles VI and VII, had little to do with the province, the name being taken from their leader, Duc Bernard VII of Armagnac.

This S.W. corner of France was again the scene of fighting during the last months of the Peninsular War, when Wellington's forces pressed back Soult's army from near Bayonne through Orthez, St-Sever, Aire, Maubourguet and Vic-en-Bigorre; then N.E. towards Lombez, reaching the Garonne late in March 1814. Attempts were made to cross the river from Seysses, to the S.W. of Toulouse, but the main crossing was made from Grenade, to the N.W., on 4 April, Toulouse itself being approached from the N., between the Garonne and the Hers; see Rte 86.

The history of the **Pyrenees** has been governed largely by geographical considerations. With the disintegration of Roman Aquitania, several independent counties sprang up along its foothills, among them *Béarn*, from 820, which later passed by marriage into the hands of the families of Moncade, Foix, and Grailly, and finally, owing to the marriage of Catherine de Grailly-Foix, Queen of Navarre with Jean d'Albret in 1482, it passed to France in 1589. Also now included in the department of the *Pyrénées-Atlantique* (until recently known as the Basses-Pyrénées; préfecture *Pau*) is one of the six *'mérindades'* or bailiwicks of the ancient kingdom of **Navarre**, its capital being St-Jean-Pied-du-Port. Berengaria, daughter of Sancho VI of Navarre, married Richard I, 'Coeur-de-lion' in 1191 (in Limassol, Cyprus). The crowns of France and Navarre had been united in 1316 in the person of Louis X, son of Philippe le Bel and Jeanne de Navarre, but under Jeanne II, daughter of Charles IV, Navarre became independent. Her descendant, Eleanor, married Gaston de Foix, thus uniting Navarre with Foix and Béarn (1479), but on the marriage of Catherine, their granddaughter, to Jean d'Albret, who had fallen under the Papal ban, the rest of Navarre was annexed by Fernando the Catholic (1512), that part on the N. flank of the range being all that remained with the French crown on Henri of Navarre's accession to the throne. For the **Pays Basque**, see p 462.

The central Pyrenean valleys, nominally subject to the counts of Bigorre, Couserans, and Cominge (themselves vassals of Guyenne) had early shown its independence, and even in 1097 a document signed by Bernard II of Bigorre confirms the inhabitants of the Lavedan valley in their ancient *'fors'* or customs, and similar constitutions applied in several other valleys, but the only one to retain its independence was Andorra, partly because of its inaccessibility, the road through it not being completed until 1931. Further E. was the *County of Foix*, now roughly represented by the department of the *Ariège*, long ruled by a family among whose members were Gaston III (1331–91), called 'Phoebus' from his golden hair, who as Count of Béarn defied the English, and Gaston, Duc de Nemours (1489–1512), who died at Ravenna, leading the French armies in an Italian campaign; the latter's cousin, Odet de Foix, Viscount de Lautrec (1485–1528) died of plague at the siege of Naples.

N. of the County of Foix lay the ancient dominions of the counts of Toulouse, usually known as **Languedoc**, a name which first seems to have been applied to the province when it became royal property in 1270, to signify the country where 'oc' was used as a particle of assent in contrast to the 'oïl' or 'oui' of northern France; see also *Provence*, Section XII. The later name of 'Occitania' is a fanciful coinage on the analogy of 'Aquitania'. Its three western departments are *Haute-Garonne* (préfecture, *Toulouse*), *Tarn* (préfecture, *Albi*), bordering on the old districts of Quercy and Rouergue (see Section VI), and the *Aude* (préfecture, *Carcassonne*). Present-day *Hérault* partly represents *Bas-Languedoc*; see Section VIII.

The Roman province of *Gallia Narbonensis* was formed out of territory conquered from the Gauls c. 125 B.C. In A.D. 381 the province was divided, *Narbonensis Secunda* having its capital at *Aix*, while *Narbonne* remained the centre of *Narbonensis Prima*, approximating in extent to Languedoc. In 419 Honorius presented the territory to Ataulph the Visigoth, under whose successors it received the name of *Septimania*, from the seven cities of Nîmes, Uzès, Maguelone, Lodève, Agde, Béziers, and Toulouse; Carcassone and Elne were later added to this territory. It was overrun by the Moors in 714, but retaken after their defeat at Poitiers in 732, and Charlemagne founded the Marquisate of Gothia and the County of Toulouse in 778. In 865 Charles le Chauve made the Corbières the separation between Septimania and *Catalonia*, thus adding *Roussillon* to the Spanish march; this was not recovered by France until 1659, at the Treaty of the Pyrenees.

In 936 Raymond III Pons, of Toulouse, annexed the marquisate and the county, and the dynasty flourished, particularly under Raymond IV (d. 1105), until the start of the Albigensian crusade in 1208, in which Raymond VI (1194–1216) protected the Cathars not so much from religious motives as from a sense that he was engaged in a struggle to survive being crushed between the centralising powers of Paris, the expanding Spanish march, and the predatory Papacy. He lost, little expecting the ferocity with which the Christian 'crusade'—ostensibly against the 'heretics'—was fought, and a civilisation, even if in decline, was virtually obliterated. With the death of Jeanne, heiress of Raymond VII, and wife of Alphonse de Poitiers, Louis IX's brother, the province passed to the crown. But the innate enmity between South and North only slumbered, breaking out with renewed fury during the Religious Wars of the 16C, the South fighting for Reform against the official religion of the Court, and although pacified by the Edict of Nantes, the storm broke out again after its Revocation in 1685 in the Camisard insurrection (1702).

Languedoc extended N., and W. of the Rhône, and its sub-divisions included the *Velay*, the bishopric of *Le Puy* (now the *Haute-Loire*); the *Gévaudun*, and the *Vivarais*, now the *Lozère* and the *Ardèche*, and ruled by the bishops of Mende and Viviers respectively; see also Section VIII.

76 Bordeaux to Toulouse via Agen

205km (155 miles). D10. 35km *Cadillac*—12km *St-Macaire*—N113. 17km *La Réole*—19km **Marmande**.—17km *Tonneins*—41km **Agen**—43km **Moissac**—8km *Castelsarrasin*. **Montauban** lies 21km E. —At 29km we join the N20 for (29km) **Toulouse**. For the N113 to Langon, on the l. bank of the Garonne, see Rte 78.

Maps: IGN 46, 56, 57, 63, 64, or 110 and 114. M 234, 235.

The A61 motorway, or 'autoroute des deux-mers' now provides a rapid route from Bordeaux direct to Toulouse, with exits near several of the more important towns.

BORDEAUX TO LA RÉOLE (62.5km). This alternative route, traversing the vineyards of Entre Deux Mers, is followed by the D916 from the transpontine suburb of *La Bastide*, after 15km forking r. onto the D671.—9km. *Créon*, a somewhat mutilated bastide of 1315, 3km S. of which, *St-Genes* has a good 12C church portal.—3km E. of Créon are the imposing ruins of the abbey-church of *La Sauve-Majeur* ◊ (1079–1231), dominated by its octagonal tower, preserving a number of remarkable *Capitals*, among them the Beheading of the Baptist; Samson and the lion, and about to be shorn; Daniel in the lions' den; Adam and Eve; sirens; fabulous beasts, etc.—11C *St-Pierre*, near by, has four life-size statues in niches on its E. end, and contains 13C wall-paintings.—22.5km. *Sauveterre-de-Guyenne*, a bastide of 1281, preserving its 'cornières' and four gateways.—11km to the N. is the ruined 14C castle of *Rauzan*; 7.5km N.E., the abbey-church of *Blasimon* (12-13C), with a notable portal.—The D670 leads S. to (14km) *La Réole*; see below.

Crossing to the r. bank of the Garonne at **Bordeaux** (Rte 75), we turn S.E. on the D10, at 26km traversing *Langoiran*, beyond which are the ruins of a 14C castle.—At *Capian*, 5km N.E., Anatole France frequently stayed with Mme Arman de Caillavet at the turn of the century.—5km. *Rions* (r.) retains some of its ramparts and a 14C gatetower.—4km. **Cadillac**, a bastide of 1280, preserves ramparts on its S. and E. sides and two gates, and a long derelict Épernon château of 1598–1620 (under restoration).

5km N.E. is the ruined 13C castle of *Benauges*.—2km. *Loupiac*, where some mosaics found in the ruins of a Roman villa suggest that it might have been the rural retreat of the poet Ausonius after the assassination of the Emperor Gratian in 383. Both Loupiac and adjacent *Ste-Croix-du-Mont* are noted for their white wines. Towards the N.E. corner of the cemetery at (6.5km) *Verdelais*, to the l. of the D10, (opposite the church) is the plain *Tomb of Henri de Toulouse-Lautrec* (1864–1901; who died in the château of *Malromé* at *St-André-du-Bois*, 6.5km N.E. of St-Macaire).

2.5km. *Langon* lies on the far bank of the Garonne; see Rte 78.—We turn l. to **St-Macaire**, a very ancient town, preserving a 13C *Gateway, and the restored *Place du Marcadieu* a few steps N.E. of its 12-13C priory-church of *St-Sauveur near the river, with relics of a cloister. The dark interior contains some overpainted murals in the apse.

17km. **La Réole** is a curious old town overlooking the Garonne. In the centre is the *Old Hôtel de Ville* (12-14C), the basement of which served as a market. Little remains of its castle built by Richard I. Adjoining the buildings of the former abbey (*Regula*) which gave the town its name, and which are now municipal offices, stands widenaved *St-Pierre (13C, with a modern tower); note the grotesque masks on its apse.

The Faucher twins (1759–1815), called 'Les Jumeaux de La Réole', served as generals under Napoleon and were unjustly shot for treason at Bordeaux.

The D668 leads N.E. past (9km) the *Château de Guilleragues* (r.), and 14km beyond, the imposingly sited *Château de Duras* (12th and 16-17C), under restoration, and preserving Renaissance features of interest.

19km. **Marmande** (17,800 inhab.), although a busy town, is of slight interest other than for an expressive 17C Entombment in its 13-15C church, on the S. side of which are remains of a Renaissance cloister providing a view over the Garonne.—For the road from **Bergerac** through Marmande to **Bayonne**, see Rte 79.

10km. *Fauguerolles.* At *Le Mas d'Agenais*, 4.5km S.W., on the far bank of the Garonne, a number of Roman antiquities have been discovered (now in the museum at Agen), while the church contains a Crucifixion of 1631, discovered in 1960, ascribed to Rembrandt.

8km. *Tonneins.*—The D911 leads S.E. to (7km) *Clairac*, birthplace of Théophile de Viau (1590–1626), who despite his Huguenot upbringing, was condemned to death for his licentious verse, and saved only at the intervention of the Duchesse de Montmorency. It then continues E. to (29km) *Villeneuve-sur-Lot*; see Rte 66.

At 10km the mouth of the Lot is crossed just above its confluence with the Garonne at *Aiguillon*, once two rival towns, and a bastide after 1296, and with a ducal château partly rebuilt in 1765, but unfinished when visited by Arthur Young in 1787.—10km beyond, *Port-Ste-Marie* is traversed, retaining a few quaint 15-16C streets, as does *Clermont-Dessous*, to the E., an over-restored fortified village on a commanding height above the river.

20km. **Agen**; see Rte 80, and for roads to the S., and S.W.

AGEN TO CASTELSARRASIN VIA AUVILLAR (53km). A slightly complicated route, crossing and re-crossing the motorway, but traversing several villages of interest above the l. bank of the Garonne, which is crossed 7.5km S.E. of Agen (Layrac road), just beyond which we turn l. for *Caudecoste*, with a charming rustic market-place, and (11.5km) *Dunes*, a bastide of 1263/6, with a stone *Halles* and cornières.—Hence turn N.E. to (4.5km) *Donzac*, with a 14C tower known as the 'Château des Anglais', and follow the D12 S.E. to (9km) **Auvillar**, a hill-top village preserving an old gate-tower (restored), a curious triangular *Place de la Halle*, a 12-15C church, and ruins of its castle.—The road continues E. to (20.5km) *Castelsarrasin*, 8km S. of *Moissac*; see p 438.

The N113 leads S.E. from Agen.

At 9km the D16 turns l. up the valley of the Séoune past (7.5km) *Puymirol*, a hill-top bastide of 1246 of some character, and 10km beyond, *St-Maurin*, a curious village built amongst the extensive ruins of a Benedictine abbey founded in the late 11C.—10km further E. is *Brassac*, with a 13-16C château, whence we may regain the main route by turning S. via *Castelsagrat*, a bastide of 1255/62, preserving its cornières, and with a 14C church.

17km. *Valence-d'Agen*, a relic of a bastide of 1279, preserves three sides of its Place, and some old houses may be noted in the side streets.—*Auvillar* (see above), is seen above the far bank of the Garonne, while on an island site between the river and the Canal Lateral, the nuclear power-station of *Golfech* is under construction.

17km. **MOISSAC** (11,400 Moissagais), on the W. outskirts of which we pass (l.) 10C *St-Martin*, built of *'petit appareil'*, on the site of Roman baths. It is a dull place on the N. bank of the Tarn just E. of its confluence with the Garonne, famous however for the abbey-church of **St-Pierre** at the N. end of the town. Its history is largely that of the abbey, which was sacked when Moissac was besieged by Simon de Montfort in Aug. 1212. It was retaken by Raymond VII in 1222, and in 1234 the Inquisition burned 210 heretics there.

The present *Church* is a clumsy 15C brick edifice incorporating remains of the 11-12C abbey church. A curious *Porch* of 1140 covers the famous ***Portal** of c. 1115, which was moved here from the W. front in the 13C. On the side walls are vividly depicted (l.) the story of Dives and Lazarus; the punishments of pride and luxury at the Last Judgement, etc.; to the r. the Annunciation, Adoration of the Magi, and Flight into Egypt, etc. On either side of the curiously scalloped door-frame are angular Byzantine-type sculptures of (l.) St Peter, and (r.) Isaiah. The centre pier, decorated by a series of fantastic lions, supports a lintel of classical rosettes, above which are the elders of the Apocalypse, while in the centre of the tympanum is Christ enthroned, accompanied by the symbols of the evangelists and two elongated angels.

The biliously restored interior preserves 16C groups of the Flight into Egypt, and Entombment, and a 15C Virgin with SS John and Mary Magdalen. The choir-

Sculpture in the portal at Moissac

screen and altarpiece are Renaissance work. On the N. side of the nave is a Romanesque Christ; the mid 17C Organs were presented by Mazarin. The Carolingian apse has been recently uncovered.

The *Cloisters—once threatened with destruction during the construction of the adjacent railway line—entered to the N. of the church, were completed in 1100, although the arches were altered in the 13C, and the roof has been subsequently lowered. The marble columns supporting the 76 arches are alternately double and single, and at each corner and in the middle of each walk are square piers. The capitals, strongly Byzantine in character, depict scriptural scenes and bear explanatory notes in Latin. The upper part of each capital is a hard grey stone, well preserving their incisive carving; the lower section is whiter and worn. The figure on the central pier of one gallery is that of Abbot Durand de Bredon, Bp of Toulouse, largely responsible for the work, and who consecrated the church in 1053, although it was finished during the time of Abbot Ansquitil. A lapidary collection is seen adjacent.

A small regional museum has been installed in a dependency of the abbey to the E. of the church.

The D927 circles to the N.E., at 14km passing the bastide of *Lafrançaise*, and crossing the Aveyron at its confluence with the Tarn, enters (17km) **Montauban**; see Rte 64.—The D999 continues E. up the valley of the Tescou, and later passes *Gaillac* to (72km) **Albi**; see Rte 89.

From Moissac, we turn S. across the Tarn to (8km) **Castelsarrasin** (12,100 Castelsarrazinois), with a large brick late 12C church, and in the former Carmelite church, N.W. of the central Place, the tomb of Antoine de Lamothe-Cadillac, founder of Detroit, born in 1658 at *St-Nicolas-de-la-Grave*, on the far bank of the Garonne.

6.5km S., likewise on the far bank, are the ruins of the abbey of *Belleperche*, founded in 1143.—8km beyond lies *Larrazet*; see the sub-route at the end of Rte 64.

3km. The D958 leads directly to **Montauban**, 18km E; see Rte 64.

10km. *Montech*, 1.5km E., preserves a good 15C brick belfry.—At 16km we meet the N20 from Montauban.

The next r.-hand turning leads 8km across the Garonne to **Grenade**, a bastide founded in 1290, with a 16C *Halles* and large Gothic church with a tall brick belfry. It was the birthplace of Marshal Pérignon (1754–1818). Hence we may follow the l. bank of the river to (17km) *Blagnac*, and the airport of **Toulouse**, entering the city from the N.W.

3km. *Pompignan*, with the 18C château of the poet-Marquis, Jean-Jacques Lefranc de Pompignan (b. 1709, in Montauban), who died here in 1784.

The N20 continues S.E. parallel to the Canal Lateral. It was near here that on 5 April 1814 Wellington, with 19,000 men, including cavalry and artillery, crossed the Garonne by a pontoon bridge prior to the Battle of Toulouse.

26km. **Toulouse**, the N. suburbs of which we traverse some kilometres previously; see Rte 86.

77 Bordeaux to Bayonne

A.   Via the N10

172km (107 miles). N10. 41km *Belin-Béliet*—12.5km *Le Muret*
—22.5km *Labouheyre*—43km *Castets*—23km *St-Geours-de-*
Maremne—7km *St-Vincent-de-Tyrosse*—25km **Bayonne.**

Maps: IGN 46, 55, 62, or 110, 113. M 234.

Work has recently been completed on this road whereby all villages
have been by-passed between Belin-Béliet and St-Geours-de-
Maremne. A new motorway (A63) has been constructed from
Bordeaux, circling to the W. of this route and joining it 6km S. of
Belin; while from 1km N. of St-Geours the continuation of the
motorway may be joined, avoiding six villages between there and
Bayonne. The motorway is slightly longer, but the S. half is recom-
mended, particularly in summer, and by travellers driving direct to
Spain.

There is little of interest to be seen on this route, which is merely a fast road
traversing the monotonous pine-forests of **Les Landes**. These cover
c. 14,000km² within a rough triangle, its S. limit being a line from *Capbreton* (N.
of Bayonne) to near *Nérac* (30km W. of Agen), and its N.E. limit being a line
hence to the W. suburbs of Bordeaux, and beyond to *Soulac*, near the mouth of
the Gironde (see latter part of Rte 73), while it is bounded by the Atlantic coast to
the W. Never at any time fertile, that this vast sandy tract was stabilised was
largely due to the efforts of the engineer Nicolas Brémontier (1738–1809), who
in 1788 started the long-term project of fixing the wind-blown dunes, which
were inexorably encroaching on and liable to overrun the plain, by planting
marram grass, and pines. The 1855 work continued under François Cham-
brelent, who drained large areas and extended the pine plantations. Its timber
and resin are important industrially, although numbers of sheep are still supported on poor pasturage in some districts. On the seaward side several land-
locked lagoons remain, while characteristic of the region are its low timber-
framed houses. Parts of the forest were ravaged by fire—which still is a
hazard—in the 1940s; a number of small resorts have been developed along the
coast, and since the mid 1950s petroleum deposits near *Parentis-en-Born*, among
several other sites, have been exploited. At the same time a large area in the centre of the Landes was designated a nature reserve.

On crossing the new road circling the W. side of Bordeaux (last
paragraph of Rte 75) we pass the slight remains of the 13C priory of
Gayac, and traverse *La House*, before entering the pine forests, and
meet the new A63 6km S. of *Belin-Béliet*.

6.5km. The road by-passes (r.) *Le Muret*.—Hence the N134 bears l.
through the forest, traversing half-a-dozen small villages, to **Mont-
de-Marsan**, 67.5km S.E.; see Rte 79.

10.5km. *Liposthey*, 16km W. of which is *Parentis-en-Born*; see Rte
77B.—12km *Labouheyre* is bypassed.—*Mimizan* lies 27km to the
W.; see Rte 77B.

19km. *Morcenx*, an important centre for the products of the
Landes, with sawmills, etc., lies 8km E.—23km. *Castets*, whence the
D947 leads 18km S.E. to **Dax**; see Rte 79.—12km. *Magescq*, with a
13C church, later fortified.

10km. The A63 bears to the S.W.—After 1km, at *St-Geours-de-
Maremne*, with a conspicuous church, the N10 likewise turns r., the
route being joined here by the road from Dax.—7km. *St-Vincent-de-
Tyrosse*, and *Benesse-Maremne*, 6.5km beyond, are traversed.—*Capbreton* (see Rte 77B) lies 8.5km W. of the latter.

The forested areas become thinner as the road undulates on approaching (18.5km) **Bayonne**; see Rte 81.

B. Via the Coast

A slow route, taking in a number of resorts among the lagoons and sand-dunes skirting the Atlantic shore, and through pine-forests which anchor them: see *Les Landes*, above. The area to the N., between the *Bassin d'Arcachon* and the *Pointe de Grave* is covered in the latter part of Rte 73. Not every Plage need be visited, and many of them may be approached directly and more conveniently from the N10; see above.

Total distance, 223km (138 miles). N250. 60km **Arcachon** (also approached direct by a branch of the A63 motorway; see Rte 77A)—28km *Biscarrosse-Plage*—9km *Biscarrosse*—D652. 9km *Parentis-en-Born*—24km *Mimizan*, whose Plage is 6km W.—66km *Vieux-Boucau*—17km *Hossegor*—3km *Capbreton*—18km **Bayonne**, also approached by the A63, which may be joined 3km E. of Capbreton.

39km. *Facture*, from which the D3 turns N.W. through several villages on the S. bank of the *Bassin d'Arcachon*, fed by the river Leyre, and bordered by oyster-parks.—15km. *La Teste* (l.) was the ancient capital of the *Pays de Buch*, whose overlords bore the title of 'captal'. The Captal de Buch of Froissart's 'Chronicle' was Jean de Grailly (d. 1376), a strong supporter of the English.

Arcachon (13,700 inhab.), a popular resort on the sandy shore of its 'bassin', has thrived since its connection by rail with Bordeaux in the 1850s, even if described by Augustus Hare as having 'nothing to enjoy and nothing to admire'. From the contiguous resorts of *Le Moulleau* (frequented by Gabriele d'Annunzio between 1910–15) and *Pyla-sur-Mer*, facing Cap Ferret on the far side of the sound (see Rte 73), we turn S., and shortly pass the *Dune du Pilat*, at over 100m, the highest sand-hill in France. Hence the road skirts the coast to *Biscarrosse-Plage*, where we turn inland, the area between here and Mimizan Plage being a restricted 'Military Zone'.—*Biscarrosse* itself, with a 15C church and 16C château, lies between the *Étang de Cazaux et de Sanguinet* (N.) and the *Étang de Biscarrosse et de Parentis*, the latter with a flying-boat base, and oil-derricks, etc.—9km. *Parentis-en-Born*, the main drilling centre of the recently developed area, where we turn S. to *Mimizan*, passing (r.) the small *Étang d'Aureilhan*.

Mimizan itself was an important port during the Middle Ages, but overwhelmed by sand in the 18C, it retains little of its antiquity except the mutilated portal of its 12C church, part of a Benedictine abbey.—*Mimizan-Plage*, 6km W., at the mouth of the Courant de Mimizan, has a good sandy beach.

From Mimizan we bear S. on the D652, some 5-7m parallel to the coast, from which byroads lead to several small resorts, to (52km) *Léon*, S.E. of its Étang, from which one may visit—traversing the Courant d'Huchet, with its thickly wooded banks, by boat—the tiny resort of *Huchet* (also approached by roads).

The road now veers towards the coast at (14km) *Vieux-Boucau*, named after the 'old mouth' of the Adour (see below).—8km to the E., on its Étang, is *Soustons*, before which the road turn S., after c. 11km reaching the *Lac d'Hossegor*, a relic of the old channel of the Adour.

Hossegor and adjacent *Capbreton* are popular family resorts, the latter once an important harbour, until the end of the 14C, when the mouth of the Adour shifted from here to Vieux-Boucau after a tempest blocked its old course with a sand-dune. It survived to some extent until in 1579 the citizens of Bayonne cut a canal through a strip of dune separating the river from the sea further W., thus shortening its course once and for all. The only trace of antiquity at Capbreton is an old tower near its church. The Canadian island of Cap Breton takes its name from the mariners of this port, who first landed there in the early 16C. The vineyards along the shore here produce a good 'vin de sable'.

At *Labenne*, 5km S., we join the N10, and 13km beyond, enter **Bayonne**; see Rte 81.

78 Bordeaux to Pau

194km (120 miles). N113. 47km **Langon**—D932. 15km **Bazas**—46km *Roquefort*—D934. 37km **Aire-sur-l'Adour**—N134. 49km **Pau**.

Maps: IGN 56, 62, 63, or 110, 113; also 274. M 234.

The A61 motorway provides a rapid route to *Langon*, but it is hardly worth taking for such a short distance.

The N113 drives S.E. from **Bordeaux** (Rte 75) parallel to the A61 to (18km) *La Prade*, some 3km S.W. of which is the wide-moated *Château de Labrède*, with a 13C keep and 15C chapel, a favourite residence of Charles de Secondat, Baron de la Brède et de Montesquieu (1689–1755), preserving mementoes of the author of 'Lettres persanes', 'Esprit des Lois', etc.'

The road traverses the wine-growing district of Graves, while further to the S.E., beyond (17km) *Cérons*, is the region of the Sauternes, the most prestigious of which comes from the *Château d'Yquem* (17-18C), some 7km W. of Langon. We enter this town 11km beyond Cérons, after skirting the Garonne and traversing (4km) *Barsac*, with a curious 18C church, also noted for its white wine, and *Preignac*, with its ruined castle.

Langon (6300 inhab.) is itself of slight interest; for *St-Macaire*, 2.5km N.E., on the far bank of the river, see Rte 77.

Turning S., at 8km a r.-hand turning leads 3km to the 14C *Château de Roquetaillade*, just beyond which one may turn l. to (7km) *Uzeste*, with a beautiful collegiate *Church* (under restoration), containing the mutilated tomb of Pope Clement V (c. 1264–1314), who endowed the church, and the effigy of the Captal de Buch, Jean de Grailly (d. 1376; see La Teste); the pope was born 5km further W., at *Villandraut*, with the massive ruins of a 14C moated castle.—The D932 may be regained at *Bazas*, 9km E. of Uzeste, and 7km beyond our turning-off.

BAZAS, the former capital of the Vasates, one of the chief towns of Novempopulania, and a bishopric from the 5C, was also long an important staging post for travellers crossing the Landes from Bordeaux to Bayonne and Spain.

From the main crossroads just W. of the old centre the Rue Fondespan leads to the triangular *Place de la Cathédral*, and market place, partly arcaded, with a late Gothic house on its N. side, dominated by *St-Jean-Baptiste*, a cathedral until 1790. It was begun in 1233 and rebuilt in 1576–1635 after the Religious Wars; the belfry has a Romanesque base. Its three *Romanesque Portals* are remarkable, even if only retaining part of their original sculpture; above is a rose-window.

To the N. of the apse is the 13C *Porte du Gisquet*, the finest relic of its ramparts, while to the E. are the Allées Clémenceau, overlooking the Beuve valley. Several old houses may be seen in Quartier St-Martin, S. of the Rue Fondespan.

BAZAS TO AUCH (125km). The D655 leads S.E. through the woods, at 16km passing (l.) the 15-16C *Château de Grignols*, to (14km) *Casteljaloux*; see Rte 79.—10km *Fargues-sur-Ourbise*, with a Gothic church and fortified cemetery, is traversed, and 4km beyond, a by-road (D141) leads 4.5km E. to the 12C castle of *Xaintrailles*, rebuilt in the mid 15C for Jean de Xaintrailles (c. 1400–61), companion-in-arms of Joan of Arc and La Hire. The road goes on to (5km) *Vianne*, a bastide of 1284, on the Baïse, preserving its ramparts, two towers, and four gates, and a Romanesque church.—Hence one may regain the main route at (4km S.W.) *Barbaste*, with a fortified mill (14C; restored).—*Durance*, 11.5km W., a charming relic of a bastide of 1320, has remains of a 13C castle known as that of Henri IV.

The D930 leads S.E. from Barbaste to (6km) **Nérac** (7300 inhab.), an important stronghold of the princes of Béarn, where Marguerite of Navarre, Jeanne d'Albret, and Marguerite de Valois (wife of Henri IV) held court, and where the former offered a refuge to such Protestants as Calvin, Beza, and Marot. It retains few old buildings apart from a 16C wing of the *Château*, now occupied by a *Musée*. St-Nicolas, designed by Louis, dates from 1780. On the E. side of the Baïse lies the faubourg of *Petit-Nérac*, retaining more of a 16C aspect, S. of which extends the Promenade de la Garenne, laid out by Antoine de Bourbon, and possibly the scene of 'Love's Labour Lost'.—Continuing up the valley, at 8km we pass 5km W. of the bastide of *Francescas*, and then by-pass (l.) *Moncrabeau*, whose inhabitants formerly vaunted themselves the most boastful of the Gascons, to reach (14km) **Condom**; see Rte 80, and likewise for the villages of interest to the W. of this road.—We continue S., at 8km passing (r.) the abbey of **Flaran*, with a beautiful 12C church, chapter-house, and cloister.—The ruins of the 14-16C castle of *Tauzia* lie 2km E.—18km. 3km E., at **Lavardens**, is a huge ruined early 17C **Château*.—Regaining the main road we continue S., at (4km) *St-Lary* passing near (r.) a Gallo-Roman Tower, one of several in the area, and 7km beyond, meet the N124 prior to turning E. for (7km) *Auch*; see Rte 80.

From Bazas, the D932 drives S. through the pine-forests of the *Landes* (see Rte 77) to (46km) **Roquefort**, once the capital of the *Pays de Marsan*, where in 1371 John of Gaunt and Edmund of York married the two daughters of Pedro the Cruel of Castile. The 13C church has a fortified Romanesque apse, and there are remains of other fortifications.

At *Sarbazan*, 2km S.E., is a Romanesque church and relics of a Roman villa.—*Labrit*, 20km N.W., formerly *Albret*, was the capital of the duchy created in 1556 for Antoine de Bourbon, husband of Jean d'Albret, and father of Henri IV.—22km S.W. lies *Mont-de-Marsan*; see Rte 79.

ROQUEFORT TO AUCH (98km). The D626 leads S.E. to (11km) *St-Justin* (see Rte 79), and 4.5km beyond, passes *Labastide-d'Armagnac*, a charming little bastide of c. 1283, its church with a good W. door.—11km. *Cazaubon*, just beyond which (l.) lies the small spa of *Barbotan-les-Thermes*, preserving a 16C gate, and an 11-16C church.—18km. **Eauze**, on a height above the Gélise, ancient *Elusa*, was the capital of the Roman province of *Novempopulania* or *Aquitaine Tertia*, which extended from the Garonne to the Pyrenees, some relics of which have been built into the partly brick-built church (c. 1500). It succeeded the Celtiberian oppidum of *Lesberous*, 3km N.—Hence the D626 continues S.E. across country to (24km) *Vic-Fezensac*, with a mutilated church of 1090, later fortified, and restored in 1616.—N124.—At *Roquebrune*, 4.5km S. of the main road, are remains of a 3C temple.—8km. To the l. is the 12-14C castle of *Her-*

rebouc.—4km. The picturesque fortified village of **Biran* stands on a height 3km to the S., whence one may regain the main road further E.—There are several Gallo-Roman towers to the l. of the N124, at 5km beyond the Biran turning.—13km. **Auch**; see Rte 80.

The D934 drives due S. from Roquefort, at 8km crossing the D933, and 8km beyond by-passing (r.) *Villeneuve-de-Marsan*, with a 12C church containing restored wall-paintings of 1529, and a 17C tower.—2km S.E. is the *Château de Ravignan*.

21km. **Aire-sur-l'Adour** (7200 inhab.), an old town and see of a bishop from c. 500 (transferred to Dax in 1933), its *Cathedral*, mainly 12C, with a nave vaulted in the 15C, and with 17-18C alterations, but spoilt by repellent paintwork. The former Bishop's Palace, now the *Hôtel de Ville*, and containing part of a Gallo-Roman pavement, dates in part from the 12C. In the S.W. suburb of *La Mas* (off the Pau road), is brick *Ste-Quitterie* (13th and 16C), its Romanesque crypt containing a fine 5C **Sarcophagus.*—6km N.W. is the ancient Premonstratensian abbey of *St-Jean-de-la-Castelle*, founded in 1160.—The D2 turns W. off the Pau road to approach (13km) the insignificant spa of *Eugénie-les-Bains*, where Michel Guérard, promoter of the 'nouvelle cuisine française' has his fashionable restaurant, which has caused its temporary revival.—There is not much to see at *St-Loubouer*, once walled, some 6km further W.

AIRE TO TARBES (69km). The D935 drives S.E., at 15km turning r. to cross the Adour, traversing *Riscle* to (13km) *Laloncage*, to the S.E. and S.W. of which, respectively, are the fortified Romanesque church of *Mazères*, and the 15C church and ruined 12C keep of *Castelnau-Rivière-Basse*; there is an interesting church at *Madiran*, 5km beyond the latter.—15km. *Maubourguet*, its church partly Romanesque, lies 15km E. of *Lembeye*, with a fine 15C church and feudal tower.—9km. *Vic-en-Bigorre* (see Rte 84B), 17km beyond which we enter **Tarbes**; see Rte 84A.

From Aire, the N134 continues S., later crossing several ridges.

49km. **PAU** (85,800 inhab.), préfecture of the *Pyrénées-Atlantiques*, and once the capital of *Béarn*, well-sited on a ridge overlooking the Gave de Pau, has grown rapidly in recent decades since the discovery of natural gas at *Lacq*, but some of the buildings thrown up since then have not improved its appearance. In the 19C, and until 1939, it was much frequented by the English as a centre of excursions into the Pyrenees, and its sunny winter climate made it an ideal resort for valetudinarians. Its museum should not be overlooked.

Its name is probably derived from the Roman settlement called *Castellum Palli* rather than from the three stakes or '*pals*' (Béarnais, *paou*) which figure in the city arms. It grew up round the 11C castle which in 1389 was rebuilt by Gaston Phoebus, and in the 15C became the principal residence of the lords of Béarn, one of whom, Henri d'Albret, in 1527 married Marguerite 'de Navarre' (1492–1549). In her train came Italian artists and the leading spirits of the French Reformation (cf. Nérac). She was the author both of religious verses and of the collection of 72 gallant tales known as the 'Heptaméron', which was posthumously published. Her daughter, Jeanne d'Albret (1528–72) was converted to Protestantism, which, by persecuting Catholics, she enforced throughout her kingdom. In 1553 Henri, son of Jeanne and Antoine de Bourbon, was born in Pau. He married Marguerite de Valois, daughter of Henri II, in 1572, and in 1600, after his divorce from her, Marie de Médicis. In 1589 he became king of France as Henri IV 'of Navarre' for political reasons abjuring his faith in 1593, and granting toleration to Protestants in 1598 by the Edict of Nantes. He appointed his sister Catherine as governor of Béarn, but his successors ruled through intendants-general, and the importance of Pau declined.

The discovery of its mild winter climate led to an influx of English visitors soon after the termination of the Peninsular War, who at first settled in the area just N.E. of the Pl. Royale, and a Protestant church was built in the Rue des Cordeliers. In 1825, Alfred de Vigny, stationed with his regiment at Pau, married one of them, Lydia Bunbury. The number of permanent residents fluctuated during the following decades, and at a later date the colony congregated in the district immediately N. of the present Palais de Justice. In the 1860s 3000 of the population of 21,000 were British. Liszt gave two recitals here in 1844; regular fox-hunts were established. The decline set in during the mid 1880s, but Pau continues to retain a small British colony. A detailed description of this period may be read in either Joseph Duloum's 'Les Anglais dans les Pyrénées' (1970), or the more recent 'Pau; Ville Anglais', by M. Tucoo-Chalaa.

F.M. Lord Alanbrooke (1883–1963), born at Bagnères-de-Bigorre, spent much of his childhood at Pau, where his father Sir Victor Brooke, a great naturalist, was a pillar of the sporting set. Among natives of Pau were Marshals Jean de Gassion (1609–47), military tutor of Gustavus Adolphus, and Jean-Baptiste Bernadotte (1763–1844), who became King Charles XIV of Sweden in 1818, and from whom the present dynasty is descended.

From the *Pl. Gramont*, just N. of the château, the Rue Bordenave-d'Avère leads S. to the Rue Maréchal-Joffré, which with the Rue Henri-IV, further S., and its continuation, are the main thoroughfares of the older town. From the W. end of the former a bridge approaches the entrance arcade of the disfigured **Château**.

Little remains of Gaston Phoebus's construction except the massive brick keep at its S.E. corner. The N.E. *Tour de Montauzer* (Monte-Oiseau, so-called because the ladders by which it was entered could be removed in case of siege) was rebuilt in the 16C. After two centuries of neglect, the rest of the exterior was largely reconstructed in dubious taste by Louis-Philippe and Napoleon III. The central courtyard retains some of its Renaissance ornament.

Visitors are conducted through a series of rooms on the GROUND FLOOR, the most interesting of which are the *Kitchen*, containing a maquette of Pau of

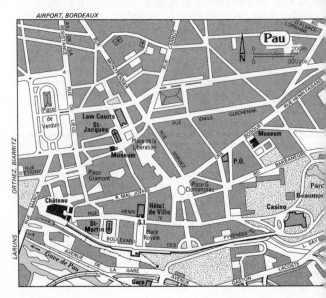

c. 1830, and *Dining-Room*, with its huge table and early 16C Gobelin tapestry copies of the famous Flemish 'Chasse de Maximilien' series. The Gobelin tapestries with a red background displayed on the SECOND FLOOR are also notable, as are the 'Mois arabesque' of c. 1680 in another gallery. Portraits of Henri IV of the Schools of Quesnel, and Pourbus, and an anon. one of Jeanne d'Albret, together with Henri IV's backgammon board inlaid with ivory and mother-of-pearl, are among the few individual items of consequence to be seen; too much of the furniture and decoration is in the mid 19C 'Troubadour style'. Abd-el-Kader, Emir of Algiers, was interned here in 1849.

On the THIRD FLOOR, which may be visited directly by ascending the main staircase, is the **Musée Béarnais**, containing local archaeological, and natural history collections, together with collections of utensils, implements, costume, furniture, and musical instruments, prints, etc.

Turning r. on making our exit, we shortly pass the tower of the old *Palais du Parlement de Navarre* before reaching the much-extolled *Boulevard des Pyrénées*, commanding—in clear weather—a distant *Panorama* of the range. Conspicuous are the double peak of the *Pic du Midi d'Ossau* (2885m; 50km due S.); the *Pique-Longue du Vignemale* (3298m; 61km S.E., above the church of Céles, and the highest mountain in sight); and away to the l., the steep mass of the Bigorre mountains (*Pic du Midi de Bigorre*; 2877m).

Passing (l.) 19C *St-Martin*, the *Pl. Royale* is gained, below which a funicular descends to the *Railway Station*. There is a plan to restore the area to the S.W. of this point to improve the pedestrian ascent from the station towards the castle. The Boulevard continues E. to the *Parc Beaumont*.—At the N. end of the Pl. Royale stands the *Hôtel de Ville* (and S.I.), whence the Rue St-Louis regains the Rue Maréchal-Joffré.

From this point the Rue des Cordelliers leads N. to the *Pl. de la Liberation*, dominated by 19C *St-Jacques* and the *Palais de Justice*, while immediately to the W., at 8 Rue Tran, is the *Musée Bernadotte*, containing numerous mementoes of the marshal and his wife Désirée.

A short distance behind the Palais de Justice is the area once inhabited by the British community, crossed by the Rue Montpensier, off which the Rue (Patrick) O'Quin leads to *St-Andrew* (1880).

The Rue Maréchal-Joffre leads E. to the central but undistinguished *Pl. Clémenceau*, on the S. side of which are the two modern towers of the so-called *Palais des Pyrénées*, already crumbling, but, as Stendhal had already remarked of another building when passing through the town in 1838, 'the city fathers. . . deserve the highest decoration for nonperception of the beautiful'!

Some few minutes' walk E. from the N.E. corner of the square brings one to the **Musée des Beaux-Arts*, the contents of which are among the more interesting things to be seen in Pau.

It contains a comparatively small but well-catalogued collection of paintings. Among the most notable are: *El Greco*, St Francis; *Juan de Juanes*, Procession on Mt Gargano; *Ribera*, St Jerome; *Alonso Rodriguez*, Supper at Emmaus; *Zurbarán*, Felipe de Guimaran; *Luca Giordano*, Philosopher; *Brueghel de Velours*, Entry into the Ark; *Frans II Franken*, Golgotha; *Pieter Neefs, the Younger*, Interior of Antwerp Cathedral; *Rubens*, The Last Judgement, and two canvases from the History of Achilles series; *Nicolas Berchem*, The Return of Tobias; *Bart. van der Helst*, Female portrait; *Romney*, Portrait of an Adolescent; *Wilkie*, Self-portrait 1840); *Louise Abbema*, Lunch in the conservatory; *Gaston Balande*, Improvisation; *J.-A. Bard*, Piazza Mazaniello, Naples; *Boudin*, View of Antwerp, and The Port of Bordeaux; *J.B. Labbé* (known as *Butay*; Pau, 1759–1853), View of Pau and the Gave; *Degas*, The Cotton Exchange, New Orleans (1873); *Claude*

Lefebvre, Portrait of Colbert; *Laurent Fauchier*, Man with a lute; *Lépine*, Landscape; *François Gerard*, L'Amour et Psyché (a copy by *La Caze*); *Alex. Millin du Perreux*, The château at Pau; *Berthe Morisot*, Pasie sewing; Pyrenean landscapes by *Doré*, *Paul Huet*, and *Victor Gallos*; *La Caze*, Self-portrait, c. 1843; *Largillière*, Mlle de Barral as Diana; *Nattier*, Mme Henriette as a Vestal; *Edmé Jean Pigal*, Portrait of Mme Bail; *Rigaud*, Male portrait; *Hubert Robert*, The cascades at Tivoli; *Théodore Rousseau*, The Pyrenees seen from Ustaritz; *De Troy*, Mme de Miramion; *Horace Vernet*, Judith and Holophernes; *Henri Zo*, The patio; *Benjamin Constant*, The Shereefs; and *Alfred Smith*, The Place de la Concorde, Paris.

The museum mounts some good temporary exhibitions, among the most remarkable being that entitled 'Les Pyrénées Romantiques' (1979), in which numerous paintings and water-colours from its reserves and other collections were displayed, among the former being examples of the work of *Eugène Deveria*, *Pierre Gorse*, *Harpignies*, *Julien Jacottet*, *Auguste-Ignace Melling* *William Oliver*, and *Henri de Trinqueti*, apart from the above-mentioned. Among the pioneers of Pyrenean artists were *Archibald Robertson*, whose View of Luz was painted in 1772, and *George Barret, the Elder*.

For roads from Pau to **Bayonne**, via *Orthez*, and via *Oloron*, see Rte 83A and 83B respectively; from Pau to *St-Jean-de-Luz*, via *Oloron* and *St-Jean-Pied-de-Port*, Rte 2: all these in reverse. For the road from Pau to **Toulouse**, via *Auch*, see Rte 84B for that via *Tarbes* and *St-Gaudens*, and for the Pyrenees S. of Tarbes, see Rte 84A.

PAU TO (37km) LARUNS AND THE COL DU PORTALET (29km beyond). The N134 is followed to (8km) *Gan* (see p 466), where we fork l. onto the D934.—Beyond (18km) *Louvie-Juzon* the road enters the *Vallée d'Ossau*, passing (l.) the ruined *Château Gélos*, and traversing (3.5km) *Bielle*, the ancient capital of this independent valley, preserving several 15-16C houses, and a church with an unexpected northern Flamboyant door (15C).—On the E. side of the valley are the marble-quarries of *Louvie-Soubiron*, which provided material for the statues in the Pl. de la Concorde, and on the Madeleine, Paris.—We pass (l.) *Béost*, with a restored 12C church, just prior to entering (7.5km) **Laruns**, almost encircled by mountains. For the road hence to *Eaux-Bonnes* and *Argelès-Gazost*; see below.

The *Gorges du Hourat* are threaded to approach (6km) **Eaux-Chaudes** (656m formerly *Aiguescaudes*—ad aquas calidas), a small spa and Customs-post. After crossing the *Pont de l'Enfer* one may ascend to *Gabas* (1020m), 8km further up the valley, with a 15C church, and the centre for mountain excursions in the area, among them the *Pic du Midi d'Ossau* (2884m), to the S.W.—To the E. a cable-railway ascends in summer towards the *Pic de la Sagatte* (2031m), from the upper station of which a miniature railway runs along the N. slope of *Le Lurien* (2826m) to the *Lac d'Artouste* (1989m), from which the ascent of the *Balaïtous* (3146m; on the frontier to the S.E.) may be made.—From Gabas the road continues to climb round the flank of the *Pic Lavigne* (2018m), skirting (l.) the *Lac de Fabrège*, beyond which rises *Le Lurien* (see above), and soon the pyramid of the *Pic de Midi d'Ossau* rises majestically on the r. After 15km the *Col du Portalet* (1794m; French Customs) is reached, providing a splendid retrospective view.—Spanish Customs are at *El Formigal*, 7km below to the S.E., overlooked by the pyramidal *Peña Foradada* (2285m), 4km beyond which is *Sallent*, in the wild valley of the Rio Gallego, to the E. of which rises the *Picos del Infierno* (3076m) for which see *Blue Guide Spain*.

LARUNS TO ARGELÈS-GAZOST (48km). The D918 climbs S.E. to (6km) **Eaux-Bonnes** (750m), a little spa at the mouth of a side valley, the virtue of whose sulphurous waters was established by the cure of Béarnais troops wounded a Pavia in 1525. There are some delightful cascades in the vicinity, and it is a base for several ascents.—8km up the valley lies *Gourette* (1400m), a winter-sport centre, to the S.W. of which rises the *Pic de Gers* (2613m); to the S., the *Géougue d'Arre* (2619m); and to the S.E., the *Grand Gabizos* (2692m).—The narrow mountain road climbs round to the N.W. to the *Col d'Aubisque* (1709m; views). After 10km—partly 'en corniche'—we reach the *Col du Souler* (1450m), from which point a road descends to *Nay*, 32km N.—The main road descends steeply to (8km) *Arrens* (878m), with a 15C church and a crenellated churchyard wall. The *Vallée d'Arrens* ascends S.W. towards (9.5km) *Aste*, on the border of the *Parc National des Pyrénées*, from which ascents to the surrounding peaks may be made

among them, to the S., the *Balaïtous* (3146m).—The road (N618) improves as we
descend above the *Gave d'Azun* through (3km) *Aucun*, with a Romanesque
church on the plan of a Greek cross, and (6km) *Arras-en-Lavedan*, dominated by
the ruined stronghold of *Castelnau-d'Azun*, 3km beyond which **Argèles-Gazost**
is entered; see the sub-route Pau to *Cauterets* and *Luz-St-Sauveur* of Rte 84A.

79 Bergerac to Bayonne

251km (156 miles). D933. 58km **Marmande**—23km *Casteljaloux*
—73km **Mont-de-Marsan**—N124. 50km **Dax**—15km N10. 32km
Bayonne.

Maps: IGN 56, 62, or 110, 113. M 234.

The D933 leads due S. from **Bergerac** (Rte 66), at 6.5km climbing
towards the vineyards of *Monbazillac*, its *Château* (c. 1550) 2km l. of
the road. We shortly pass the old mill of *Malfourat* (view), and at 3km
leave the 15-16C château of *Bridoire* to our l.

15km. **Eymet**, a bastide of 1271, with a charming central Place a
short distance to the r. off the main road.—*Lauzun*, 6.5km S.E., with a
large Gothic church with an 11C tower, and 15-17C château, gave its
name to the Duc de Lauzun (1632–1723), a notable figure at the
court of Louis XIV, lover of 'la Grande Mademoiselle', and commander of the French contingent at the Boyne.—5km. *Le Sauvetat-
du-Dropt*, to the r., was the birthplace of Jean Claude (1619–87), the
Protestant opponent of Bossuet in a famous controversy.—5km.
Miramont-de-Guyenne, a bastide of 1278, preserving part of its cornières, is traversed before the road veers W. to (23km) **Marmande**;
see Rte 76.

The Garonne, the Canal Lateral, and the A61 motorway are crossed.—23km **Casteljaloux**, a bastide on the edge of the pine-forest of
Les Landes (see Rte 77A), preserves several old timber-framed
houses with projecting storeys, the best of which is that known as 'de
Xaintrailles' or 'de Jeanne Albret'; the mairie is housed in part of an
old convent of the Cordeliers.

9km E. (via the D261) stands the ruined Romanesque church of *St-Sabin*, preserving good historiated capitals, etc.: see also the sub-route Bazas–Auch in Rte 78.

The D933 now traverses the E. side of the Landes, gradually circling
to the W. to (48km) *St-Justin*, a small bastide of 1280, of which a few
relics survive; see also the sub-route Roquefort–Auch in Rte 78.

24km. **Mont-de-Marsan** (30,900 Montois), préfecture of the
Landes, founded in 1133, but now of very slight interest, lies at the
confluence of the Douze and Midou, here forming the Midouze. It
was once an important staging-post for travellers crossing the
Landes from Bazas, but its main activities, apart from administering
the department, are cow-baiting, a traditional Landais entertainment, and horse-racing. The church of *St-Pierre-du-Mont*, 2km S.W.,
preserves a Romanesque apse. A by-pass is under construction.

14.5km S.E. lies *Grenade*, a bastide on the Adour, with an arcaded *Market-place*,
and church typical of the area, 14km beyond which is *Eugénie-les-Bains*; see
p 443.

MONT-DE-MARSAN TO (54km) ORTHEZ, AND ST-JEAN-PIED-DE-PORT,
71km beyond. This sub-route follows part of one of the pilgrimage roads which
converged further S.W. before crossing the Pyrenees at Roncesvalles. The D933
bears S.W., crossing the Adour at (15km) **St-Sever**, once known as *Cap-de-*

Gascogne from its prominent situation, commanding a wide view over the valley and the forests of the Landes to the N. It was the birthplace of Gén. Lamarque (1770–1832), who in 1808 captured English-occupied Capri. The *Church, rebuilt in the 12C, was a Benedictine foundation of the 10C, although altered in the 17C (central apse, etc.). It retains remarkable Romanesque features, notably the small apses flanking the main apse, several capitals, and its N. doorway. The *Hôtel de Ville* occupies 17C conventual buildings. The *Cornmarket* behind is part of the church and cloister of a 17C Jacobin convent.—Hence the road undulates across the *Chalosse* towards (12km) *Hagetmau*, where Wellington briefly lodged after the battle of Orthez, preserving in the 12C *Crypt of the vanished abbey-church of *St-Girons* some good capitals; this is approached by turning r. off the main road immediately on entering the town from the N.—The D933 continues S.W. over the hills before descending to (25km) **Orthez**; see Rte 83A.

The road goes on via (16km) *Salies-de-Béarn*, to (11km) *Sauveterre-de-Béarn* and then through (12km) *St-Palais* to *St-Jean-Pied-de-Port*, 31km beyond; for which see Rtes 82 and 83.

The N124 leads W. from Mont-de-Marsan to (27km) *Tartas*, with remains of a castle, and a wood-pulp factory, c. 4km beyond which a lane to the r. leads 5km to *Lesgor*, with a massive late 13C fortified church.—After 15km we pass (r.) the so-called *Berceau de St-Vincent-de-Paul*, where the founder of the Lazarists and Filles de la Charité was born in 1576.

4km. **DAX** (19,700 Dacquois), together with *St-Paul-lès-Dax* (9100 inhab.; on the N. bank of the Adour), is of slight interest apart from its hot springs and mud baths, and the church of **St-Paul**, a short distance S.W. of the N124 crossroad, which it is preferable to visit first, for the remarkable sculptured *Frieze representing the Last Supper on its apse, mostly of the 11C, but incorporating earlier fragments.

Part of the frieze on the apse of St-Paul-lès-Dax

Dax occupies to the site of the capital of the Gallic *Tarbelli*, and its thermal springs were known to the Romans as *Aquae Tarbellicae* (or *Aquae Augustae*). In the 10-11C Acqs or Dacqs, whose first bishop was St Vincent (c. 250), had counts of its own, but their territory was later added by Richard I to his possessions in Gascony, and under English rule it was granted numerous privileges. It did not become part of the French kingdom until 1451.

J.-Ch. Borda (1733–99), the astronomer; and Roger Ducos (1754–1816), consul with Napoleon and Siéyès in 1799, were born here. Maurice Utrillo died here in 1955.

To the l. on the far bank of the river is the *Parc Théodore-Denis*, flanked by remains of Gallo-Roman ramparts, largely demolished in 1856, and parts of the enceinte are also seen from the *Pl. des Salines*, further to the S.E.—W. of the latter stands the cathedral of *Notre-Dame*, an unremarkable building in the classical style (1656–1719), replacing a 13C English Gothic church demolished as unsafe, the old N. door of which has been incorporated into the N. transept.—The Rue Gambetta leads to late 19C *St-Vincent-de-Xaintes*, in the S.W. suburb, containing a Gallo-Roman mosaic discovered beneath the foundations of a previous church on its site.—The Rue Cazade leads N. from the cathedral apse to the Esplanade Gén.-de-Gaulle, with the curious ***Fontaine-Chaude**, a large steaming tank, where hot waters have gushed for centuries, and long used for washing linen.

15km beyond Dax, at *St-Geours-de-Maremne*, we meet the N10 from Bordeaux, which leads S.W. to (32km) **Bayonne**; see Rte 81; alternatively, one may join the A63 motorway, 1 km N. of *St-Geours*; see also the last part of Rte 77B.

80 Agen to Auch and Bagnères-de-Luchon

185km (115 miles). N21. 36km **Lectour**—11km **Fleurance**—24km **Auch**—D929. 63km *Lannemezan* crossroads—N117. *Montrejeau* —N125. 8km **St-Bernard-de-Comminges** lies 2km W.—30km **Bagnères-de-Luchon**.

Maps: IGN 56, 63, 70, or 113. M 235, 234.

AGEN (32,900 Agenais), préfecture of *Lot-et-Garonne*, stands on the r. bank of the Garonne (crossed to the N. by the Aqueduct of the Canal Lateral), near the foot of the steep wooded slopes of the *Côteau de l'Ermitage*, site of a Gallic oppidum. It is noted for its *pruneaux fourré* (stuffed plums), and is a centre of market-gardening.

Ancient *Aginnum*, the capital of the Nitiobriges, was captured by the Frankish king Clovis in 506. In 1152, with the rest of Aquitaine, it passed to Henry of Anjou, later Henry II of England, but in 1196 his daughter Joan brought the Agenais as dowry to Raymond VI of Toulouse. From 1271 the district was nominally part of the kingdom of France, but Agen was re-occupied by the English in 1360 and was not definitively united to the French crown until 1444.

Here in 303 was martyred St Foy (Faith; cf. Conques) and St Caprasius, both natives of the place. Julius Caesar Scaliger (1484–1558), the enemy of Erasmus, having come from Italy in the train of Bp Marcantonio della Rovere (1525), settled down and married at Agen, where he was visited by Bandello, and where his son Joseph Justus Scaliger (1540–1609) was born. Other natives were the naturalists Étienne de Lacépède (1756–1825), and Bory de Saint-Vincent (1780–1846); and the dialect poet called Jasmin (Jacques Boë; 1798–1864). Gérard de Nerval visited his father Gérard Labrunie, a doctor here, during the years 1834–53.

The central network of narrow lanes of old Agen is intersected from W. to E. from the *Pl. Jasmin* (traversed by the N113) by the Blvd de la République, and from the railway station (at the N. end of the town) by the Blvd Président-Carnot, leading S.—N.W. of their intersection stands the *Cathedral* (St Caprais; replacing St-Étienne, destroyed at the Revolution). The best part is the apse which, with the transepts was built in the 12C. Although its W. door is good, the 15-16C nave with its 19C murals, is ineffective. Noteworthy are the capitals of the main piers of the crossing and the corbels in the W. corner of the N transept.—The *Chapter-house*, to the N., has a Romanesque facade and preserves an early Christian sarcophagus.—To the W., masked by later buildings, rises the 14C *Tour du Chapelet*, a survival of the town walls.

To the S.W. of the cathedral, the massively arcaded, but mutilated Rue Cornières leads to the Blvd de la République, crossing which we follow the Rue Garonne to the *Pl. de l'Hôtel de Ville*, with the *Théâtre*; the 17C *Hôtel de Ville*, and **Musée**, the latter occupying a group of Renaissance mansions: the *Hôtel d'Estrades*, birthplace of Maréchal d'Estrades (1607–86); the *Hôtel de Vaurs*, and the *Hôtel de Jean Vergès* (1575).

The Museum contains a number of prehistoric and Gallo-Roman antiquities, including the remarkable *Venus du Mas d'Agenais*, discovered in 1876, of the 1C A.D., probably a copy from a Greek original; notable also a large bronze Minotaur, by F.-X. Lalanne (1970). Among the ceramic collections are examples of the local faïence de Moncaut (18C); note the marble relief of a girl, attrib. to Mino da Fiesole. Among the paintings an *anon.* Portrait of Cinq Mars; *Courbet* Portrait of Charles Fourier; a rare Self-portrait by *Goya* (1783), and his sketch for an Equestrian portrait of Fernando VII, The Ascent of Montgolfier's balloon etc., also claimed by some to be by Eugénio Lucas; School of Corneille de Lyon Male portrait; *Philippe de Champaigne*, Male portrait; The Procession, and Mass for the churching of women, by *Lucas*; *Drouais*, Mme du Barry, and Mme Sophie and representative works by *Corot*, (L'Étang de Ville-d'Avray), de Troy, Nattier Watteau, Greuze, Sisley, and Picabia, among others. Note the Renaissance sculpture in the interior courtyards, and elegant spiral staircase.

N.-D.-du-Bourg, just E. of this Place, has a 13C brick bell-gable in the Tolosan style; *N.-D.-des-Jacobins*, to the W., is a good example of 13C Dominican construction. Some distance N. of the latter, in the Ruelle Scaliger, is the 12C apse and 16C tower of *St-Hilaire*, with a modern facade.—Near the *Préfecture*, some distance S., the site of a large Roman amphitheatre has been recently discovered.

For roads from Agen to *Bergerac* and *Périgueux*, and for *Bordeaux*, see Rtes 66 and 76, respectively, in reverse, and also Rte 76 for the road S.E. to *Montauban* and *Toulouse*.

AGEN TO CONDOM AND AIRE-SUR-L'ADOUR (102km). On crossing the Garonne the D931 leads S.W., at 9km passing (r.) the 13C château of *Estillac* reconstructed c. 1570, where Blaise de Monluc (1502–77) wrote his 'Commentaires', and died. 2.5km beyond is *Aubiac*, its 12C church preserving a notable choir and lantern-tower.—At *Moirax*, 5km E., is an interesting 11-12C *Church* with remarkable 17C choir-stalls.—4km. *Laplume*, ancient capital of the *Pays de Brulhois*, has a stunted octagonal belfry over the porch of its 16C church, 5km beyond which we traverse *Lamontjoie*, a bastide of 1299, as the winding but picturesque road continues S.W.—At 5.5km a l.-hand turning leads 7km S. to *La Romieu*, whose 14C church has a beautiful cloister. Hence we may regain the route 8km W.

14km. **Condom** (7800 inhab.), on the river Baïse, the centre of the brandy trade of Armagnac, and see of a bishop from 1317–1790, possesses a good *Cathedral* (1506–31), with a remarkable organ of 1605, and to the N., a 16C cloister inside the *Hôtel de Ville*. Outside the cathedral is a 13C tower, and further N., the 18C *Évêché*, to the W. of which is the *Musée de l'Armagnac*. Several 17-18C mansions survive in the town.

For the road hence to **Auch**, see p 442.—The D931 continues S.W. to (29km) *Eauze*, but a more interesting road is the D15 leading due W., at 5km passing (l.) *Larressingle, a well-preserved fortified village of the 13C, with ruins of an episcopal castle, with a church within its keep.—Beyond (2.5km) the 17-18C *Château de Beaumont* (l.) turn r. for (6.5km) *Fourcès, a charming bastide of 1279/86, with 41 houses surrounding its circular *Place*, approached by a little bridge over the Lauzoue stream; to the S.E. is a small château.—Turning S.W., we follow the D29 through (5km) *Montréal, another well-sited bastide of 1255, preserving its arcaded market-place, sections of its ramparts, a fortified gate, and church of 1300; there are relics of a Gallo-Roman villa 1.5km S.W., at *Séviac*.—From Montréal one may regain the D931 just prior to (14.5km) *Eauze* (see p 442), passing en route *Lamothe*, with a 14C tower.—Continuing S.W., the road traverses (9km) *Manciet*, with a fine brick tower, and (9km) *Nogaro*, with a curiously debased 11C church, of which four arches of a cloister survive, 20km beyond which lies **Aire-sur-l'Adour**; see Rte 78.

The N21 and D17 converge 9km S. at *Layrac*, whose massive 12C church has a nine-bayed apse, on the floor of which is an 11C mosaic, and a notable choir.

At (8km) *Astaffort* we climb out of the valley of the Gers onto a ridge, traversing (8km) *Ste-Mère*, a fortified village with a well-sited castle, later bearing S.W. to (11km) **Lectoure**, on a promontory overlooking the valley.

It was a bishop's see until 1790, and the capital of the country of Armagnac from 1325. *St-Gervais-St-Protais*, the former cathedral, with a fine belfry of 1488, is partly 13C, but was largely rebuilt in the 15-17Cs. The adjoining *Évêché* (16th and 18C) is now occupied by the *Hôtel de Ville*, and *Museum*, in which is an extraordinary collection of 34 taurobolium altars (2-4C) discovered in 1540 when reconstructing the cathedral choir. Of lesser interest are *St-Esprit* (15-16C), the ruins of the castle of the counts, and the Gothic *Fontaine Houndélie* or *Diane*, on the S. side of the town. Marshal Lannes (1769–1809), once a dyer's apprentice, was born here.

10km E. is the château of *Gramont ◊ (13th and 16C), 6km S. of which is the charming hill-top bastide of *St-Clar, of 1289.—At *Terraube*, 8 km S.W., is a 17 C château and other fortifications.

From Lectoure we descend and cross to the l. bank of the Gers to (11km) **Fleurance**, a bastide of 1274, preserving its arcaded central *Place*, with a later market hall. The imposing 14C church, with a fine octagonal tower, contains good 16C glass by Arnaud de Moles in its choir and other features of interest. Several ancient houses survive in the side streets.

The N21 continues S. up the valley to (24km) **AUCH** (25,500 Auscitains), préfecture of the *Gers*, an attractive old town standing mainly above the steep W. bank of the river, although more modern quarters lie on the E. side of the valley. Its cathedral, containing outstanding Renaissance glass and woodcarving, is one of the more remarkable in the S. half of France.

Ancient *Elimberri*, which flourished under the Gallo-Roman Auscii, has been the seat of an archbishop since the destruction of Eauze in the 8C, and was once capital of Gascony. Among its natives were Adm. Villaret de Joyeuse (1750–1812), defeated by Howe off Ushant in 1794 ('the glorious First of June'); and of Jean Laborde (1806–78), explorer of Madagascar. It is noted for its Armagnac brandy and sparkling wines.

Adjacent to the main crossroads of the upper town, the *Pl. de la Liberation*, is the Rue de la République, on the N. side of which, at the entrance of the attractive Rue Dessolles, is a restored 15C house and the S.I. Hence one obtains a good view of the impressive Renaissance W. Front of the *****Cathedral of Ste-Marie**, preceded by a classical porch closed by an 18C grille. This facade masks what is basically a late-Gothic edifice (1489–1592), replacing a 13C building, burnt in 1483, itself succeeding a previous church. The two *Towers*, 44m high, were only completed in 1678.

At the W. end of the nave is a fine organ of 1694, by Jean de Joyeuse (c. 1635–98), restored in the 1950s; another smaller instrument (1860), by Cavaillé-Coll, is seen above the choir-screen of 1671. Except in the apse, few of the chapels are of interest, although the 2nd S. chapel contains the tomb of Antoine Mégret d'Étigny (see below), and the 4th a carved and gilt Nativity. The stained-glass *****Windows** are throughout notable, particularly those in the apse, which are ascribed to Arnaud de Moles (1513), depicting colossal figures of the prophets, apostles, and sibyls, etc. in an architectural framework. A chapel in the apse preserves a 16C marble Entombment.

The *Choir* may be entered from its S. side (fee), in which 67 of the 113 oak *****Stalls**, early 16C, have their backs carved in high relief with some scriptural or allegorical personage, and the pilasters between the seats bear statuettes, the whole being surmounted by an elaborately carved canopy. Neither should the misericords be overlooked. The sacristan will also unlock the *Crypt*, in which the 7C marble sarcophagus of St Léothade is of interest.

To the S. of the cathedral is the umbrageous *Pl. Salinis*, overlooked by a slender 14C tower, from which a monumental staircase of 234 steps (1866) descends towards the river.

To the N. of the cathedral, where the 18C *Archbishop's Palace* accommodates the *Préfecture*, a lane leads downhill to the **Musée**, tastefully installed since 1979 in a former Jacobin convent.

It displays collections of ceramics (including faïence d'Auch, manufactured since 1757) and furniture, a Gascon kitchen, and a room devoted to Charles de Batz (c. 1613–73), otherwise d'Artagnan, hero of 'The Three Musketeers' (1844; by Dumas *père*), who was born at the *Manoir de Castelmore* or *Castelmaure* (some 40km W. of Auch). The basement contains archaeological collections, a 2C sarcophagus; Gallo-Roman votive altars; epitaphs, including one in Hebrew (Merovingian period); Roman sculpture; and parts of Pomeian style frescoes from the Gallo-Roman villa of *Roquelaure* (A.D. 50-70).

Some of the narrow lanes further downhill, still known as *pousterles* (from the low Latin *posterula*), lead to posterns in the city wall.

Immediately W. of the Pl. de la Liberation stands the *Hôtel de Ville* of 1777 preserving a small theatre; to the N.W. a flight of steps ascends to the Allées or Cours d'Étigny with a statue of Mégret d'Étigny (1720–67), intendant of Guyenne and a benefactor of Auch. At the far end stands the *Palais de Justice* (1860).—To the N., the Rue Gambetta leads past (l.) the restored *Halle aux Grains*.

For the road to **Toulouse**, see Rte 84B; or that to **Pau** and **Tarbes**, Rte 84B in reverse; for the area N.W., see pp 442 and 451.

Of interest to the W., approached via the D943, forking l. after 5km, are (11km beyond) *Barran*, a bastide of some character, and *Montesquiou* (13km beyond), with a fortified gate and the ruins of the 13th and 16C castle in which Marshal Montesquiou (1645–1725) was born. 5.5km beyond lies *Bassoues*, a small bastide preserving a tall 14C keep.

The D929 forks l. just S. of Auch, following the Gers valley through the bastides of *Pavie*, and (26km) *Masseube*, 16km E. of which, ap-

Some of the early 16C stalls in the cathedral of Auch

proached by the D27, is *Simorre*; see p 475.—At (16km) *Carrole*,
Castelnau-Magnoac lies 1.5km r.; see below. After 12km the road
ascends to the *Plateau de Lannemezan*, and 10k beyond, reaches the
crossroad for *Lannemezan*, 2.5km W.; see Rte 84A.

THE LANNEMEZAN CROSSROADS TO ARREAU AND ST-LARY (39km). The
D929 continues S., at 5.5km traversing *La Barthe-de-Neste*. This village was the
main town of the *Vallée de Neste*, which with the *Vallée d'Aure*, which we next
ascend, and those of the *Barousse* (the Ourse valley to the E.), and the *Magnoac*
(upper Gers valley, to the N.), made up the *Pays des Quatre-Vallées*, an independent community under the suzerainty of the kings of Aragón, and after 1398, of
the counts of Armagnac. In 1475 they attached themselves voluntarily to the
crown of France, with the condition that they should always be directly under
the king's command. The capital of the Pays was *Castelnau-Magnoac* (see
above).

14km. *Sarrancolin*, a marble-quarrying village, with remains of fortificatiòns,
preserves a 13C Limoges enamel reliquary in its 12C church.—7km **Arreau**

(704m), the ancient capital of the valley, stands at the confluence of several small rivers. Its 15-16C church retains the Romanesque door of a previous building, and in the main street opposite the *Halle*, with its wooden pillars, is a good 16C house; another is adjacent to the *Chapelle St-Exupère*, on the quay of the Neste de Louron.—At *Jézeau*, 2km E., the 12C church contains curious 16C frescoes.

For the road hence to **Luchon**, see below.

From Arreau we follow the W. bank of the Neste d'Aure through (2km) *Cadéac*, with a 12C tower and church retaining 11C features.—At *Gouaux*, 3km S.E., the church preserves 16C murals.—8.5km. *Bourisp*, its church with an 11C tower and a remarkable painting in its porch representing the Seven Deadly Sins (1592).—To the r. at *Vielle-Aure* is a 12C church.—1.5km. **St-Lary-Soulan** (817m), a small winter-sports and mountaineering centre, with a Romanesque crypt to its church and an 11C chapel.—*Espiaube*, 8.5km W., is also being exploited.—The valley narrows.—3.5km. To the l. opens the wooded *Vallée du Rioumajou*, in part traversed by road, with the peaks of *Lustou* (3023m) and *Batoua* (3034m) rising to the S.E.—5.5km. *Fabian*, from which the D929 climbs N.W. to the *Lac d'Orédon*, there dividing to approach the *Barrage de Cap-de-Long*, to the S.W. of which rises *Pic Long* (3192m), and to the *Lac d'Aumar*, in the *Massif de Néouvielle*.—The D118 climbs W. from Fabian to (4km) *Le Plan d'Aragnuoet*, to the W. of which lie the ski-slopes of *Piau-Engaly*, and ascends S. (D173) to French Customs, shortly beyond which we plunge into the *Tunnel de Bielsa* (3km long), making our exit in Spain, and 10km beyond (first passing Customs) pass *Bielsa*, to the W. of which is the *Parador Nacional Monte Perdido*; see *Blue Guide Spain*.

ARREAU TO BAGNÈRES-DE-LUCHON (32km). The D618 ascends the valley of the Neste de Louron to the S.E. through *Bordères-Louron*, with relics of a 12C castle, 3.5km beyond which the r.-hand fork leads through (6.5km) *Loudervielle*, passing the old keep of *Génos*, to a point 10km further up the Louron valley, dominated to the S. by the *Pic Schrader* (3174m), and to the W. by the *Pic de Lustou* (3023m), while to the S.E. lies the mountain-encircled *Lac de Caillauas*.—The main road forks l., climbing the valley side and turning E. to (9.5km) the *Col de Peyresourde* (1569m), providing a good prospect of the mountains of Luchon. On the descent into the *Vallée de Larboust*, we pass (r.) the chapel of *St-Pé-de-la-Moraine*, partly constructed of Roman materials, and traverse *Cazeaux*, where the church contains restored 15C wall-paintings.—For the road ascending S. towards the *Lac d'Oô*, see p 457.—2.5km. *St-Aventin*, its *Church with a 12C porch with capitals depicting the life of that saint, a Romanesque stoup, and 12C ironwork.—5.5km. **Luchon**; see below.

At the Lannemezan crossroads we turn l., following the N117 to (14km) *Montréjeau* (beyond which it forks l. for *St-Gaudens*; see Rte 84A), and fork r. onto the N125.—At 6km the road divides: the old main road turning r.; the new D33 following the E. bank of the Garonne through (13km) *Fronsac*, with a ruined tower, just beyond which, at *Chaum*, one may regain the W. bank.—For the road to *St-Béat* and *Viella*, see p 457. For the road from Fronsac to *St-Giron*, see Rte 90 in reverse.

The r.-hand turning approaches a fortified hill dominated by the cathedral of **ST-BERTRAND-DE-COMMINGES**, but one should first turn l. by the modern church of **Valcabrère** to visit *St-Just-St-Pastor*, the cathedral of the see of Comminges until the 11C. The churchyard is entered through a 12C arch. The restored church (c. 1100) has a remarkable late 12C N. Portal, with statues of the patron saints (l.) and SS Helen and Stephen (?; r.), and sculptured capitals and tympanum. Within a numerous re-used columns and other antique fragments built into the structure, taken from the neighbouring Roman town (see below). Behind the altar is a 14C tomb-shrine.

Regaining the road, we shortly approach a crossroad, by which are the main extant relics of the Gallo-Roman city.

Distant view of St-Bertrand-de-Comminges

It was founded in 72 B.C. as *Lugdunum Convenarum* by Iberians driven across
the Pyrenees by Pompey's army, which gave its name to the surrounding *Pays
de Comminges*, more correctly written *Cominge*. This was destroyed by Vandals
in 408/9, and its inhabitants moved to the more defensible hill-top fortress, but
this was sacked by the Burgundians in 585/7, and the site remained deserted until Bertrand de l'Isle-Jourdain, bishop in 1075–1123, began building his
cathedral, much enriched by Bp Bertrand de Got (1295–99), later Pope Clement
V.

Excavations in the 'Ville Basse' have uncovered (r.) late 3C *Thermae*,
and further S., the substructures of a forum, temple, and more baths;
and to the l. of the road, a basilica or market. S. of the crossroad are
the foundations of a 4C Christian basilica.

Ascending the hill (515m) we pass (l.) the slight remains of a Roman
Theatre, before reaching the ramparts—medieval on Gallo-Roman
foundations—and enter the *Porte Cabirole*, one of its three gates, and
pass several 15-16C houses. A Roman imperial trophy of the 2C
found in the forum, a 5C Christian sarcophagus, and a mosaic, etc.,
may be seen in a former chapel to the l. of the small square facing the
W. front of the cathedral; to the r. is the *Hôtel de Ville* and S.I.

The *Cathedral* itself, perhaps the finest church *in* the Pyrenees,
has a stumpy W. tower surmounted by a belfry protected by wooden
hoardings. The Romanesque narthex (1140) is entered by a curiously
carved portal, in the tympanum of which is depicted the Adoration
of the Magi. Beyond the first bay the church is a Gothic building of
1304–50, without aisles.

To the l., curiously built across a corner, is an elaborately carved pulpit and
organ-loft (mid 16C), sustained by five columns; the instrument was last restored
in 1975. A *Rood-screen*, and rails, now divides the choir from the nave, to enter
which one must leave the church and turn l., first traversing the partly rebuilt

Cloisters (fee), one walk providing a pleasant belvedere overlooking the valley; but only one arcade is 15C. The statues of the Evangelists, back-to-back, in the W. walk, are curiously primitive in design. The *Choir-stalls*, and bishop's throne, carved in the 1530s at the expense of Bp Jean de Mauléon, are among the finest of their period in France, and are ascribed to Toulousian sculptors. Steps ascend to a S. chapel containing 16C tapestries. Behind the high altar is a repainted retable (mid 16C), below which is the shrine of St Bertrand (15C). On the N. side of the Ambulatory, with glass of 1539, are the tombs of Bp Bertrand de Miramont (d. 1258), and beyond, the *Tomb* of Bp Hughes de Châtillon (d. 1352), dating from 1450, but with a statue of c. 1375.

From the crossroads just below St-Bertrand one may regain the N125 some 4km S.E. After c. 10km the valley widens to form the charming *Vallée de Luchon*, encircled by wooded hills, beyond which rises a line of peaks, mostly from 2500–3000m high.

8km. **LUCHON** (officially *Bagnères-de-Luchon*; 630m) still perhaps the most fashionable of the Pyrenean resorts, is an attractive and lively town, and now within each reach of the winter-sporting centre of *Superbagnères* (see below).

Excavations have revealed that the Romans had a bathing resort at its sulphurous and radioactive springs, connected by road with *Lugdunum Convenarum* (St-Bertrand); but with their departure the springs were disued until c. 1759, when Mégret d'Étigny, Intendant of Guyenne, visited the valley, and appreciating its properties, commenced the construction of a new road there from Montrejeau (completed in 1763), and laid out new promenades, for the village itself had been largely destroyed by fire in 1723. It was visited by Arthur Young in 1787; and James Erskine Murray, among a number of other English visitors in the 1830s and 40s, was enthusiastic in its praise, although the editor of Murray's Hand-Book preferred Bagnères-de-Bigorre, at least its accommodation, although conceding that the main tree-lined avenue protected the pedestrian from the sun, and allowed him at the same time to enjoy the view of the mountains closing the upper end of the valley. Its first bath-house was erected in 1815, but was burnt down in 1841; its original casino opened in 1880.

The old village clusters around *Notre-Dame*, a 19C edifice preserving a 16C doorway from its predecessor. To the S. extends the Allées d'Étigny, with the S.I. in an 18C mansion (No. 18), with a small local museum above. At the S. end is the *Établissement Thermal*, beyond which is the *Parc de Quinconces*.

LUCHON TO SUPERBAGNÈRES (19km). From this park, we follow the D125 S. for 5.5km, passing (l.) the old tower of *Castelvieil*, to the *Pont de Ravi.*—Hence the *Vallée de la Pique* leads S.E., its upper end blocked by a landslide. Beyond stands the ransacked *Hospice de France*, to the S. of which rises the *Pic de Sauvegarde* (2448m). Just to the E. is the *Port de Vénasque* (2448m), an opening in the frontier ridge commanding a fine view of the Spanish *Val de Vénasque* and the *Monts Maudits*.—From the bridge we turn W. on the D46 up the *Vallée du Lys*, at (4km) *Bordes-du-Lys* commencing a steep zigzag ascent to (9.5km) **Superbagnères** (1804m), a popular resort providing superb views, to the W. of which rises the *Pic de Céciré* (2403m).—Beyond Bordes, the valley widens, providing a view of the *Cirque des Crabioules*, with the Lys falling in headlong cascades from the foot of its glacier, the lowest fall being the *Cascade d'Enfer*. To the S. rises the *Pic de Maupas* (3109m), to the W. of which is the *Pic de Crabioules* (3116m), behind which is the *Pic Perdiguère* (3222m), and further W., the *Pic Lézat* (3107m). S, of the latter, in Spain, rises the *Pic des Posets* (3371m), the second highest of the Pyrenean peaks, while to the S.E. is the highest summit, also in Spain, the *Pic de Néthou* or *d'Anêto* (3404m), part of the *Maladetta* massif, the *Monts Maudits*, the 'accursed mountains', so-named from their utterly barren appearance.

LUCHON TO THE COL DE PEYRESOURDE (14.5km), FOR ARREAU. The D168 climbs N.W. At 4.5km the D51 forks r. up the *Vallée d'Oueil*, passing (r.) the

tower of *Castel Blancat*, and several village churches. Rising above the head of
the valley is *Mont Né* (2147m), just S. of which is the *Port de Pierrefite* (1885m;
view).—The main road (D618) traverses (1km) *St-Aventin*, and 1km beyond,
Castillon-de-Larboust, a stronghold of the counts of Cominge, from which a
mountain road bears l. to reach the torrent of Astau at (3km) *Oô*, whose church
has a Romanesque apse. Hence one may ascend the *Val d'Oô* to (4km) the
Granges d'Astau, beyond which, passing (r.) the cascade known as the
'Chevelure de la Madeleine' in the *Val d'Esquierry*, noted for its flora, is the *Lac
d'Oô*, in a wild mountain basin, fed by a waterfall; regrettably the exigencies of
electric power have marred the scene. To the W. rises the *Pic de Hourgade*
(2964m); to the S. the *Pic des Spijoles* (3065m).—Continuing to climb past
Castillon, *Cazeaux* is traversed (see p 454), beyond which a l.-hand turning
ascends c. 7km to the ski-centre of *Les Agudes*.—5km. Above this turning we
reach the *Col de Peyresourde* (1569m; view); **Arreau** lies 17.5km below in the
Vallée d'Aure, to the N.W.; see p. 454.

LUCHON TO BOSOST (18km). Driving S.E. from Luchon on the D618 via the
suburb of *St-Mamet*, with a 16C church, we pass French Customs and (r.) the
Tour de Castleviel, and start the steep ascent up the wooded *Vallon de Burbe* to
(9.5km) the *Col du Portillon* (1293m), marking the frontier, before descending,
later in zigzags, to (8.5km) *Bosost* (Spanish Customs), in the upper Garonne
valley; see below.
  From *Chaum* (18km N. of Luchon), the N125 leads S.E. to the frontier post
(French Customs) at (13km) *Fos*, and on to (5km) **St-Béat**, once of strategic importance, but its 14C castle on a terrace above the village has been marred by mid
19C additions. The 12C church is a relic of a priory. Its white marble quarries
furnished material for the fountains at Versailles, and—it is claimed—Trajan's
Column at Rome. It was the birthplace of Gén. Gallieni (1849–1916). To the N. it
is overlooked by the *Pic de Gers* (1785m), while to the S.W. the mountains rise up
to the *Pic de Bacanère* (2193m).
  The Garonne and frontier are crossed at *Pont-du-Roy*, 3km S. of Fos, 5km S. of
which, at *Lés*, are Spanish Customs. Hence the N230 enters the *Val d'Aran*, the
upper basin of the river, which although on the N. side of the watershed, and inaccessible from Spain by road until 1925, has remained Spanish owing to an
omission in the Treaty of Corbeil (1255) perpetuated in the Treaty of the
Pyrenees (1659). *Viella* lies 16km S.E., for which see *Blue Guide Spain*.

81 Bayonne to Behobie (for San Sebastian or Pamplona)

32km (20 miles), direct. N10. 4km **Biarritz** lies 3km W.— 14km **St-
Jean-de-Luz**—11km *Behobie*.

Maps: IGN 9, or 113. M 234.

The A63 motorway (33km), first crossing the Adour and then the Nive, is recommended in the summer for those wishing to get rapidly to Spain, as the road between Bayonne and St-Jean-de-Luz is likely to get congested. The main object of
note seen as it winds through the Pyrenean foothills, apart from occasional
glimpses of the sea, is the conspicuous mountain of *La Rhune* (900m), the key of
Soult's position in Oct.–Nov. 1813, scaled by Wellington's forces from the far
side before pressing the French back towards Bayonne; see also Rte 82. The
motorway passes French and Spanish Customs prior to crossing the Bidassoa into Spain, and may be followed to San Sebastian and beyond to Bilbao.

BAYONNE (43,000 Bayonnais) stands at the confluence of the Nive
and the broader Adour some 6km inland from the Atlantic. Arthur
Young considered it 'by far the prettiest town' he had (yet) seen in
France, although F.A. Fischer, passing through a decade later, felt
otherwise, even if it had 'several tolerably fine edifices'. Its position
on the main carriage-way to Spain, and the only fortress of conse-

quence in the S.W. corner of the country, has influenced its history,
and although it is on the N. edge of the Basque-speaking area it is still
the main town of the French *Pays Basque*. It is reputed for its hams;
for Izarra, a local liqueur; marzipan, and chocolate: the latter two
manufactures having been introduced by the Jewish community
after their expulsion from Spain in the late 15C. The Musée Bonnat
contains impressive collections.

Roman *Lapurdum* was the main port of *Novempopulania*, and its name survives
in the old Basque province of *Labourd*. The present name first appears as *Baiona*
in the 12C. It prospered while under English rule, from 1154 until 1451, when it
surrendered to Dunois. Edmund, Earl of Lancaster, known as 'Crouchback'
(1245–96) died here. It was granted privileges in 1215, and its shipbuilding,
whaling, and deep sea fisheries flourished, although the port later silted up and
trade declined, but it was not until 1578 that Louis de Foix re-diverted the Adour.
Its improved defences resisted a Spanish siege in 1523, and here in 1526 François
I, on his release from captivity in Madrid, denounced the treaty which the
Emperor Charles V had imposed on him. In 1565 Charles IX, with his mother
Catherine de Médicis, here met his sister Elisabeth (married to Philip II) to plan
the eradication of Protestantism. By 1757 Bayonne and St-Jean-de-Luz between
them were responsible for arming 45 privateers, and in 1784 it became a free
port.
  In 1808 Carlos IV (accompanied by his son Fernando, and Godoy), under
pressure from Napoleon, surrendered the Spanish throne to Joseph Bonaparte at
the neighbouring Château de Marrac. In Dec. 1813 Bayonne, long blockaded by
the British Navy, but strongly defended by Vauban's fortifications, was invested
by Wellington and Gen. Hill after Soult's defeat at St-Pierre, S.E. of the town (in
which the Allies suffered 1775 casualties, and the French some 3300), and after
the Adour had been crossed near its mouth by a bridge of boats. Gen. Hope surrounded the place after a minor action at *St-Étienne*, but the garrison of c. 17,000
under Thouvenot held out for another four months, when on 14 April 1814, *after*
the governor had been informed of Napoleon's abdication, an inexcusable,
sanguinary, and unsuccessful sortie was made, in which Hope was wounded and
Gen. Hay killed. The port again thrives, the river mouth being protected by a
long breakwater.
  Among its natives were Duvergier de Hauranne (1581–1643), one of the
founders of Jansenism; Francisco Cabarrús (1752–1810), and Jacques Laffitte
(1767–1844), financiers; Augustin Chaho (1812–58), the romantic writer on
Basque subjects; and the artist Léon Bonnat (1833–1922). The bayonet is said to
have been invented here by its armourers in the 16-17C.

In the town centre, immediately W. of the confluence of the rivers
and the *Pont Mayou*, stands the arcaded building housing the *Hôtel
de Ville, Théâtre* (c. 1840), and S.I. Hence the Rue Thiers leads S.,
shortly passing (r.) the *Château-Vieux* (12th and 15C; on Roman
foundations), now in military hands, towards the **Cathedral**
(1213–15C; on the site of a Roman temple). The interior is more imposing than the exterior, the stone of which is friable. The spires, by
Boeswillwald, were completed in 1878. Some 15-16C glass is preserved, and the three leopards of the arms of England may be seen on a
keystone of the nave-vault. There is a good 14C doorway in the
Sacristy, and the organ is notable. The *Cloister* of three walks
deserves another restoration.
  Hence a lane leads W. to a rampart walk, beyond which gardens
have been laid out.—From the N. transept one may return to the centre either via the Rue de la Monnaie and the partially arcaded Rue
Pont-Neuf, with its *confiseries*, or the Rue Argenterie, further E., the
latter soon descending to the Nive (here crossed by five bridges),
with a pleasant view of the old houses on its far bank, among which is
the *Musée Basque.

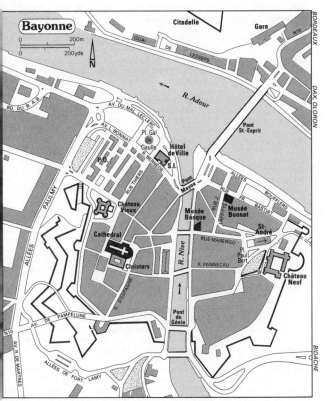

This 17C building has since 1922 accommodated a series of ethnographical collections which give a good general idea of life in the Basque provinces (both
Spanish and French, although understandably slanted towards the latter) during
recent centuries. Here are arranged a Basque kitchen, and bedroom; Basque
costumes, and furniture, and sections devoted to the local manufacture of
espadrilles or *alpargatas* (rope-soled shoes), *makhilas* (a defensive stick), and
chocolate; a stable and barn, together with agricultural implements such as the
two-pronged *layas* (for turning the earth on steep hillsides); fishing equipment,
including flat-bottomed boats, and a section descriptive of the whaling industry
and Newfoundland cod-fisheries. A collection of discoidal tombstones may be
seen, and rooms devoted to the game of *pelota*, Basque dances, Pastorales,
musical instruments, and archaeology. Another part is concerned more
specifically with Bayonne itself, including its Jewish community, with a view of
the city in 1612 and a plan of the district in 1638. Also on display are several
engravings and portraits of the Peninsular and Carlist War periods; a painting of
the château of Marrac before it was burnt in 1825, and a bust of the Rev. Wentworth Webster (cf. St-Jean-de-Luz, and Sare).—Adjacent premises have been acquired, and it is expected that the museum, which also contains important Basque archives and a library, will be extended and reformed before long.

The Rue Marengo leads E. towards the *Château-Neuf* (1489).—The
first l.-hand turning off this street approaches (r.) the ***Musée Bonnat**, entirely reformed in 1979, and its building of 1899 renovated.
Its collections—including over 2000 drawings—remarkable for their

range and quality, were largely acquired by Léon Bonnat and bequeathed by him to his native town.

It is advisable, in order to view the paintings in chronological sequence, to ascend to the SECOND FLOOR where, well displayed and labelled in an open-plan setting, are: **RI** Italian Primitives, including *Matteo di Giovanni*, Virgin and Child; *Piero della Francesca*, Head of Christ; *Master of the Chevalier de Montesa* (?Rodrigo de Osona; late 15C), Adoration of the Magi; *anon.* St Martin parting his cloak (late 15C Valencian); *School of Botticelli*, Virgin and Child with a pomegranate; *School of Isembrandt*, Virgin and Child. Note also the ivories, and 12C Limoges enamel plaque, and the late 15C painted and gilt Italian chest.—**R2** (l.) a rotunda devoted to 15 works by *Rubens*.—**R3** *Corneille de Lyon*, two Portraits; *Guido Reni*, Coronation of the Virgin; attrib. *Poussin*, Nymph and Satyr; *El Greco*, Card. Quiroga, and The Duke of Benavente; attrib. *Murillo*, Daniel in the lions' den; *Van Dyck*, Sketches for various works, including a study of a Man with a sheaf of arrows (an executioner of St Sebastian); *Second School of Fontainebleau*, Scene from Comedy; *Vouet*, Roman Charity; *Ribera*, Woman in despair; attrib. *Herrera*, Monk; *Teniers the younger*, The Alchemist; *A. van der Hecke*, Philosopher; *Lépicié*, Male portrait.—**R4** English School. *Thomas Phillips*, Portrait of Bonaparte (1802); *Hoppner*, Female head; *Lawrence*, Portraits of J.H. Fuseli, and Karl Maria von Weber; and Male and Female portraits; *Raeburn*, An aging man; *Reynolds*, Col Tarleton; *Constable*, Hampstead Heath; also *Goya*, Self-portrait (? copy), Portrait of the 10th Duke of Osuna, and Sketch for the Last Communion of San José de Calasanz.—**R6** *Ingres*, Charles X, Portrait of a youth, Mme Devauçay, Bather's back (1807), Female hands, Francesca da Rimini and Paolo Malatesta; *Girodet-Trioson*, Male portrait, Napoleon I, and Duroc; *David*, Sketch for 'Le Serment des Horaces'; *N.-A. Taunay*, Benediction of the flock; *Madrazo*, Portrait of Baron de Weiswseiller, and of his wife.

FIRST FLOOR. On the landing, a collection of Medals.—**R7** is devoted to bronze sculptures by *Barye*.—**R8** Representative works by *Géricault, Horace Vernet, Meissonier, Delacroix, Isabey, Harpignies, Daubigny, Alex.-E. Fragonard* (son of the more famous artist), The death-bed of the Duc de Berry; *Henner*, Portrait of young Bonnat; *Léon Cogniet*, Père Enfantin; and works by *Enrique Mélida* (1838–90; Bonnat's brother-in-law).—**R9** is devoted to works by *Léon Bonnat*, including Portraits of his sister (Mme Mélida), of Charles Sarvy (his uncle) 'en chasseur', of Louis Arias, a Self-portrait aged 17, Landscapes, and copies and studies of well-known masterpieces.—**R10** (landing) *Puvis de Chavannes*, Landscape entitled 'Doux Pays', given to Bonnat in 1882; *Degas*, Portraits of Albert Mélida, and of Bonnat (1862).—**R11** Works by *Boudin, Jongkind, Lebourg, Guillaumin*, and *Ernest Laurent*, and among sculptures, *Rodin*, Caryatid.—In an adjoining room are Municipal Acquisitions, of lesser quality, among them *Lucas*, Three half-figures; and *Achille Zo*, Portrait of his child.

GROUND FLOOR. Round a patio (with its plastic palm) are displayed full-length society Portraits by *Bonnat*, including those of Mme Stern, of Mme Édouard Kann, of Mme Albert Cahen d'Anvers, Mme Bishoffsheim, of Countess Potocka, and of Barye; also *Paul Dubois*, Bust of Bonnat aged 55, and *Vincenzo Gemito*, Bust of Verdi.

The BASEMENT contains a small but important collection of Antiquities, among them bronze, basalt, and stone figurines, and amulets, from Egypt; and among the Greek and Roman antiquities, a number of bronze and marble statuettes, heads, and busts, terracotta statuettes, Greek vases, and Roman glass, etc.

Several rooms are devoted to temporary exhibitions, many of them displaying selections of drawings from the collection, which range from sketches by old masters (including Leonardo da Vinci and Dürer) to those of Bonnat and most of his contemporaries. Application should be made in advance to the curator of the *Cabinet des Dessins* by those wishing to study specific artists, etc.—The building also houses an art library, and small cinema.

From a point a short distance N.W., the *Pont St-Esprit* crosses the Adour, here dominated by Vauban's redoubtable *Citadel* (1679).—To the l. on the far bank is *St-Esprit*, with a late 15C carved wooden group of the Flight into Egypt. Behind the church is the *Railway Station*, and nearby, the *Synagogue*.

An interesting excursion is that to the **Cimetière des Anglais**, reached by

ascending the Bordeaux road hence for c. 2km, then turning l. along the Rue de
Barrat (signposted), at the end of which (apply at cottage for key) a path leads
shortly to the walled cemetery, in which lie several officers of the Coldstream
Guards, among others, who fell in the sortie from Bayonne. It was visited by
Queen Victoria in 1889. There is another small cemetery containing graves of
Scots Guards c. 1km further S.W.

The motorway crosses the battlefield of *St-Pierre*; see above.

The N10, straight but undulating, drives S.W., passing the r.-hand
fork for Biarritz, the Airport (l.) and (r.) the *Lake of Mouriscot*, before
being rejoined by the road from Biarritz.

BIARRITZ (26,600 Biarrots) is still a popular resort, with its bracing
climate and great Biscay rollers, its long promenades, rocky coves,
and sandy beaches, however crowded in summer.

Long an insignificant fishing-port, it is claimed that its later prosperity began in
1838, when exiled Carlists patronised it, but in fact Edmund Wheatley, camping
nearby with Wellington's army, had already referred to it in his Diary (Feb.
1814) as 'a watering place on the sea shore', as did Gleig, who appears to have
enjoyed his visits to the ladies there, caught between two camps! Stendhal dined
extremely well there, for three francs (April, 1838), but its growth as a winter
residence was almost entirely due to British valetudinarians. Its climate had been
praised by several British doctors (among them Dr Bennet, who had already put
Menton on the map); by 1865 there were some 200 residents, which doubled in
the next four years; by 1861 the first Anglican church was built; in 1872 the first
British Club was founded, and the first golf-links laid out in 1888.
    It was described in the *Hand-Book* of 1843 as 'a group of white-washed lodging-
houses, cafés, inns, traiteurs, cottages, etc., and generally of a humble
character', where 'French ladies and gentlemen "en costume des bains", con-
sume hours in aquatic promenades. The ladies may be seen floating about like
mermaids, being supported on bladders or corks, and over-shadowed by broad-
brimmed hats', but 'Beyond its sea-bathing, its rocks, and its view. . . must be the
dullest place on earth. . .'. Eugénie de Montijo, who had spent her childhood
summers there, began building her imperial villa in 1855 (described at the time
by Adolphe Joanne as more like a college or barracks than a château), which
after a fire in 1903 was reconstructed to become the present *Hôtel Palais*.
Bismarck visited Napoleon III here in Oct. 1865 to obtain French neutrality prior
to attacking Austria. Queen Victoria visited the place in 1889, as did Gladstone
on three occasions in the 1890s, and the frequent sojourns of Edward VII and
later the Duke of Windsor attracted a raffish British clientèle. Here in 1906
Alfonso XIII of Spain was betrothed to Ena of Battenberg. Bernard Shaw went
there in 1910, and Kipling in 1925, while Walter Starkie recorded his disillusion-
ment. It was again the residence of Spanish Basque exiles after 1937. Adm.
d'Albarade (1743–1819), who started his career as a privateer, was born here;
Pablo Sarasate (1844–1908), died here.

The beaches are divided by a rocky peninsula, or *Plateau de
l'Altalaye*, on which stands the *Musée de la Mer*, with an aquarium,
and sections devoted to local history. etc.—To the S. is the *Plage de
Port-Vieux*, and beyond another promontory, the *Plage de la Côte
des Basques*.—To the N., beyond the tiny *Port des Pêcheurs*, is the
Grande Plage, overlooked by two casinos, which continues as far as
the *Pointe St-Martin*, with its lighthouse. Beyond this is the *Plage de
la Chambre d'Amour*, where two lovers were said to have been
drowned by the swiftly rising tide.—No. 18, Rue Peyroloubilh, on
the S. side of the peninsula, is dated 1632.

The main road descends through *Bidart*, with a 16C church, skirting its beach, and then turns inland behind *Guéthary*, another small
resort, before briefly running parallel to the motorway and descending into St-Jean-de-Luz.

Although tainted by cosmopolitan Biarritz, at Bayonne we are on the threshold of the **Pays Basques**, the country of the original inhabitants of both slopes of the W. Pyrenees. The intensely individual Basques, enterprising, and materialistic, are a race of unknown origin occupying seven provinces, four in adjoining Spain, and in France *Labourd*, on the coast, *Soule*, and *Basse-Navarre*, now making up the department of the *Pyrénées-Atlantiques*. They total c. 1,500,000, of which some 250,000 live in France, where they are more occupied with agriculture than their industrious and independent Spanish cousins, with whom they have much sympathy in their long struggle against the centralising policies of Castile. Indeed there has been considerable friction and recrimination between the frontier authorities as members of the militant Spanish Basque extremist group known as ETA (Euskadi Ta Azkatasuna, or Freedom for the Basques), after seeking political asylum in French territory, have made it a base from which to carry out their subversive activities in Spain.

They are a tall and handsome race, and their language (Euskara) is distinct from most other European tongues. Their costume is now only represented by their beret or *boina* and rope-soled shoes. Their domestic architecture is individual, their houses or farms, usually white-washed, or of stone, have wide-gabled roofs with doors and shutters often painted dark green or maroon; while even in the smallest villages, usually abutting the church-yard—some preserving their characteristic discoidal tombstones—one will see an open court with one high wall, the ubiquitous *frontón*, where their ball-game of *pelota* (*pelote* in French) is played. It resembles fives, utilising in one of its forms a large basket-work glove, or *chistera*. Rodney Gallop's 'Book of the Basques' is still the best description in English of the area and people, etc.

ST-JEAN-DE-LUZ (*Donibane* in Basque; 12,900 inhab.), on the N. bank of the Nivelle, and until the growth of Hendaye, the nearest town of consequence to the Spanish frontier, is a clean and attractive fishing-port and summer resort, preserving numerous old Basque houses, while its sheltered bay provides safer bathing than elsewhere on the coast.

It was an important port during the English occupation (1152–1451), and among its sea-faring activities were whaling and cod-fishing as far afield as Newfoundland (which Basque mariners claim to have discovered in 1372), and privateering: 'Its inhabitants are very bellicose, especially at sea', wrote a Spanish author in 1559. Their ships formed the greater part of the force which relieved the English blockade of La Rochelle in 1627. It was sacked by the Spanish in 1558, and occupied by them for some months in 1635–36. On 9 June 1660, the marriage of Louis XIV and the infanta María Teresa was solemnised here. With the transference of the Newfoundland fishing rights to Britain in 1713 its prosperity languished, although it later became an important centre for tunny, sardine and anchovy fisheries. During the Revolutionary period it was known as *Chauvin-le-Dragon*. From Dec. 1813 to Feb. 1814 it was Wellington's H.Q., bad weather and the state of the roads making the movement of troops and guns impossible, although it did not appear to interfere with the Duke's fox-hunting!

As a watering-place it was preferred by many English to the sophisticated pleasures of Biarritz, and from 1869–82 the community had a permanent chaplain in the Basque scholar, the Rev. Wentworth Webster (cf. Sare). George Gissing (1857–1903) died here of pneumonia, having caught a chill at St-Jean-Pied-de-Port (cf.). Rodney Gallop resided here in the 1920s, while studying Basque folklore.

The *Pl. Louis-XIV*, near the river bank, is the main centre of animation, on the S.W. side of which is the *Château Lohobiague* (1635), in which the young king resided for a month prior to his marriage, with the *Hôtel de Ville* of 1657 adjacent. María Teresa lodged in the turreted *Maison de l'Enfante*, of red brick and stone, on the quay to the N.W. Wellington's H.Q. was the nearby *Maison Grangabaita* (2 Rue Mazarin), beyond which steps ascend to the Digue-Promenade overlooking the curving beach, and providing a view across the bay towards Socoa; see below. The Rue Gambetta, the main artery of the old town, leads E. from the Place, on the N. side of which is the typical Basque church of **St-Jean-Baptiste** (13C), but rebuilt after a fire in 1558. It is entered by a 15C door; the main portal was ridiculously walled up after the royal wedding. The wide-vaulted nave surrounded on three sides with wooden galleries (reserved for the men; the women sit below), the 17C organ-case, and the gilt retable, will be noted.—From the E. end of the street, the tree-lined Blvd Thiers leads to the N. end of the Plage.

For the road hence to *Cambo* and *St-Jean-Pied-de-Port*, see Rte 82.

The N10 leads across the Nivelle, on the far bank of which lies **Ciboure** (6200 inhab.). At No. 12 in the quay bearing his name, which skirts the harbour, was born Maurice Ravel (1875–1937).

CIBOURE TO HENDAYE BY THE COAST (16km). D912 traverses *Socoa*, with a small harbour and 17C fort, semaphore tower, and lighthouse, and follows the indented coast, with several relics of German fortifications, and views ahead towards Spanish *Fuenterrabía*, descending to the Blvd de la Mer of *Hendaye-Plage*, with its long sandy beach, where Winston Churchill had a brief holiday in July 1945. Here we turn l., skirting the Baie de Chingoudy to reach **Hendaye-Ville** (together 11,100 inhab.). It was across the wide estuary of the Bidassoa here that Wellington's troops waded by an unsuspected ford, enabling them to turn the strongly defended French right flank (7 Oct. 1813). Pierre Loti (1850–1923) died here. The *Railway Station*—the rail from Paris reached here in 1860—was the scene of fruitless negotiations between Hitler and Franco on 23 Oct. 1940. The *International Bridge* here crosses the Bidassoa into Spain (French and Spanish Customs), the first town in which is *Irun*; see *Blue Guide Spain*.

Those intending to cross into Spain at *Béhobie*, 2km inland, where the motor-way to San Sebastian may be entered, will pass on neutral ground in the river bed the unprepossessing **Île des Faisans**, where negotiations between Louis XIV and Philip IV put an end to hostilities between their nations in the Thirty Years' War (1659). Velázquez contracted a fever here when fitting up the conference salon, from which he later died. Earlier international meetings had taken place here between Louis XI and Enrique IV of Castile in 1468, and in 1615 between Isabelle, daughter of Henri IV, destined to be the wife of Philip IV, and the latter's sister Ana (of Austria), who was on her way to Paris to marry Louis XIII.

Soon after quitting *Ciboure* we pass (r.) the 17C *Château d'Urtubie*, where in a previous castle was signed a frontier agreement in 1513, before by-passing (r.) *Urrugne*, once fortified and of importance, but damaged in 1813. It preserves its 15-16C church, on the clock of which is the oft-quoted inscription 'Vulnerant omnes, ultima necat'. We get a good view to the S.E. of *La Rhune* (see p 464), commanding the W. end of the Pyrenees, before curving r. for the long descent to *Béhobie*. *Hendaye-Ville* (see above) lies 2km to the r.

Here we cross the Bidassoa, marking the frontier, with French and Spanish Customs. The r.-hand turning leads to *Irun* (also by-passed) and follows the old road to (22km) **San Sebastian**; the l.-hand turning winds up the Bidassoa valley to the *Puerto de Velate*, and on to (87km) **Pamplona**. The A1 motorway (*autopista* in Spanish) may also be joined here, avoiding much traffic between the border and San Sebastian. For the Spanish Basque country, including Navarre—Las Provincias Vascongadas, see *Blue Guide Spain*.

A minor road skirts the N. bank of the Bidassoa from Béhobie to *Biriatou*, a village overlooking the river, from which the ascent of *Choldocogagna* (479m) may be made, part of a range of hills vainly fortified by Soult when—despite massive counter-attacks—attempting to stem Wellington's passage of the lower Bidassoa and inexorable advance into France during the autumn of 1813.

82 St-Jean-de-Luz to Pau, via St-Jean-Pied-de-Port and Oloron-Ste-Marie

178km (110 miles). D918. 13km *St-Pée-sur-Nivelle*—18km **Cambo**
—34km **St-Jean-Pied-de-Port**—40km *Mauléon-Licharre*—13km
Tardets-Sorholus—13km *Aramits*—D919. 14km **Oloron-Ste-Marie**—N134. 33km **Pau.**

Maps: IGN 69 or 113. M 234.

ST-JEAN TO CAMBO VIA SARE. An attractive, slightly longer, and more hilly alternative to the main road is that turning r. off the D918 at 6km through *Ascain*, a characteristic Basque village, where in the *Hôtel de la Rhune* Loti wrote 'Ramuntcho' (1896). The church with its stumpy tower and interior galleries is typical of the region; its vicar was burnt at the stake at the instance of Pierre de Lancre for celebrating the Black Mass in the early 17C; the old mill here was constructed on the site of one built in 1302.—The D4 climbs to (3.5km) the *Col de St-Ignace*, on the N.E. flank of **La Rhune** (900m), to which a rack-and-pinion railway ascends regularly. The summit commands a wide view. The S. side was scaled by Wellington's troops in the autumn of 1813. In the hill-girt valley beyond rises the village of **Sare**, with the galleried church of *St-Martin*, and a *Marie* of 1693. Pierre Axular, curé of Sare, buried here in 1556, was the compiler of an important collection of Basque proverbs, etc., published in 1643. The village was fought over by Spanish troops commanded by Sir John Downie in Nov. 1813. The Rev. Wentworth Webster (1828–1907), the Basque scholar, retired here, living in a house called 'Bechienea', where he died (cf. St-Jean-Luz).—A minor road climbs S. over the *Col de Lizarrieta*, known for the netting of pigeons in Oct., descending to Echalar in Spain, passing near the *Grottes de Sare*.—The D4 continues E., after 9km reaching the border-crossing of *Dancharia* (or *Dancharinea*; Customs), from which the N121 climbs S. over the *Puerto de Otxondo* (570m) to *Elizondo* in the Baztan valley, and *Pamplona*; see *Blue Guide Spain*.—Turning onto the D20, we shortly traverse *Ainhoa*, another attractive Basque village, and regain the main route 5.5km further N.E., just before entering *Espelette*.

The D918 follows the N. bank of the Nivelle from **St-Jean-de-Luz** (Rte 81) to (13km) *St-Pée-sur-Nivelle*, with a large 17C retable in its church, just S. of which (l.) is a ruined 16C château and tower-house of 1403. It bears S.E., at 12km traversing the pleasant village of *Espelette*, with a tower-house, and 5.5km beyond, enters leafy **Cambo-les-Bains**, now more of a village for convalescents than a spa.—*Hasparren* (see Rte 83A) lies 10km N.E.—2km N.W. are the gardens of the *Villa Arnaga*, built in a 'Basque style' for Edmond Rostand (1868–1918), and as conspicuous as Cyrano's nose.

From Cambo the road leads S.E. past (r.) *Itxassou*, an old village famous for its cherries, S. of which is the *Pas du Roland*, a defile said to have been cut in the mountain by the sword of the paladin (not to be confused with the similarly cleft *Brèche de Roland*, near Gavarnie), beyond which a road ascends to the summit of *Arsamendi* (926m).—Beyond (8.5km) *Louhossoa*, its massive church tower with an exterior stair (1674), we follow the E. bank of the Nive, passing (r.) *Bidarray*, with a medieval bridge, and (13.5km) *Ossès*, with a curious red and white octagonal tower.

1.5km. The D948 leads S.W. to (8km) *St-Étienne-de-Baïgorry*, in the valley of the Aldudes, with the 16C *Château d'Echau* and medieval bridge. The local wines of *Irouléguy* are reputed. Hence one may climb W. into Spain by the *Col d'Ispéguy* (672m) to *Ariscun* and *Elizondo*; or S.W. via the *Collado de Urquiaga* (890m) to *Zubiri*, on the road to Pamplona. Gallop mentions that at one time the locals in this bottleneck-valley refused to change their clocks during French 'Summer-time'!

Crossing the Nive, the road follows the valley to (11km) **St-Jean-Pied-de-Port**, so-called from its position at the foot of the pass or 'port' of Roncesvalles.

Founded by Garcia IV of Navarre in the 11C, it has only belonged to France since the Treaty of the Pyrenees (1659), and until the Revolution it was the capital of *French Navarre*. Hence in July 1813 Soult attempted to relieve Pamplona, but was forced back into France by his defeat at Sorauren. George Gissing convalesced here, completing 'Will Warburton' and starting 'Veranilda' before moving to St-Jean-de-Luz, where he died in 1903.

It lies on both banks of the Nive near its confluence with the Laurhibar, the lower town being defended by ramparts of 1668, with additions by Vauban, whence the narrow Rue de la Citadelle, flanked by 16-17C houses, ascends to the *Porte St-Jacques*, part of the 15C defences. The *Citadel* also dates from 1668. The *Porte d'Espagne*, by the church, provides an attractive view of old houses overlooking the Nive.—At *Uhart-Cize*, just W. of the town, the church preserves a good 14C choir.

The D933 leads S.W. parallel to the Petit-Nive, to (8km) *Arnéguy* (Customs). Crossing the river, we enter Spain (C135), and start to climb up the narrowing *Val Carlos* to (16km) the *Puerto de Ibañeta* (1057m), just beyond which lies the hamlet of *Roncesvalles*, on the Pamplona road; see *Blue Guide Spain*. It was in this pass that the rearguard of Charlemagne's army, retreating from Pamplona and led by Roland, was in 778 cut off and overwhelmed with rocks hurled down by hairy Basques on the crags above. Louis le Débonnaire, in 810, preserved his army from a like fate by forcing the wives and children of the peasantry to accompany him through the defile. The Black Prince led his troops this way in Feb. 1367 to the battle of *Nájera* or *Navarrete*; while in 1813 Clausel and Reille were sufficiently delayed here by Sir Lowry Cole's forces to enable reinforcements to be brought up by Wellington before the battle of *Sorauren*, just N. of Pamplona.

From St-Jean we turn E. through *St-Jean-le-Vieux*, its church with a Romanesque doorway (some 20km S.E. of which is the ancient *Forêt d'Iraty*), shortly after passing (r.) the over-restored 12C *Château d'Harispe*.—16km. The D933 continues N.E. to (15km) *St-Palais*, and *Sauveterre-de-Béarn*, 12km beyond; see Rte 83B.—The D918 turns r., climbing to the *Col d'Osquich*, above which to the S.E. is the *Chapelle St-Antoine*, providing good views, before descending past (r.) *Ordiarp*, with a pretty little church, to (24km) **Mauléon-Licharre** (8500 inhab.), the ancient capital of the viscounty of Soule, ceded to the Black Prince in 1261, and reconquered by the Comte de Foix in 1449. It now manufactures *espadrilles* (rope-soled shoes). The Renaissance *Hôtel d'Andurain* stands in the town centre, overlooked by the ruins of its 15C castle. It was the birthplace of the poet Jean de Sponde (1557–95) and Arnaud d'Oyhenart (1592–1667), compiler of 'Proverbes basques'.

The D24 leads E. to (30km) *Oloron*, meeting the Bayonne-Oloron road some 4km beyond (13km) *L'Hôpital-St-Blaise*, once a pilgrimage hospice on the road to Compostela. Its curious 12C church has a central octagonal spire.

We now pass out of the Basque country into *Béarn*: the architecture changes, slate rooves being more noticeable. The D918 leads S. along the valley of the Saison through (3.5km) *Gotein*, the church with a three-gabled belfry, symbolising the Trinity, one of several in this district, passing (at 7.5km) *Trois-Villes*, with a mansion of

1653.—2km. *Tardets-Sorholus*, a pleasant village, 1.5km beyond which a road junction is reached.

The D26 leads S. along the upper valley of the Saison past (l. at 13km) the deep *Gorges d'Holcarté*, to (15.5km) *Larrau* (French Customs).—The road beyond climbs to (12km) the frontier at the *Port de Larrau* (1573m), overlooked to the N.W. by the *Pic d'Orhy* (2017m; view), before descending to *Ochagavia* in Spain.

At 8km S. of this turning the D113 forks l., threading the defile of the *Uhaïtxa* to (11km) *Ste-Engrâce*, with a notable Romanesque church. About 3km prior to reaching the hamlet, a track on the r. leads to the impressive *Gorges de Kakouetta*, preferably visited in late summer. The waters emerging here may be connected to an underground river in the *Gouffre de la Pierre-St-Martin*, c. 8km E., where in 1953 pot-holers reached a depth of 728m.

From Tardets we continue E. to (27km) Oloron via (13km) *Aramits*, whose name was assumed by Aramis in Dumas *père's* 'The Three Musketeers'.—1km before the village the D918 forks r. via *Arette* (from which the unfrequented D132 turns S. to cross to *Isaba* in Spain via the *Col de la Pierre-St-Martin*; 1760m; see above).—We meet the N134 10km E. at *Asasp*, on the Gave d'Aspe 8km.S. of *Oloron*. For **Oloron** itself, and the road S. to the *Col de Somport*, see Rte 83B.

Beyond Oloron, the N134 leads E. (off which at 7km the D918 forks r. to *Louvie-Juzon* in the *Vallée d'Osseau*, 14km beyond), climbing to *Belair* (views) before bearing N.E. to *Gan*, preserving a Gothic gateway and some Renaissance houses, beyond which we approach *Jurançon*, reputed for its wine, on the S. bank of the *Gave de Pau*, with **Pau** itself on the higher N. bank; see Rte 78.

83 Bayonne to Pau

A. Via Orthez

107km (66 miles). N117. 36km *Peyrehorade*—16km *Puyoô*. **Salies-de-Béarn** lies 8.5km S.—14km **Orthez**—16km *Lacq*—25km *Pau*.

Maps: IGN 69, or 113. M 234.

Parts of the A64 motorway have been opened between the two towns, which when completed will provide a rapid route.

The N117 climbs N.E. from **Bayonne** (see Rte 81), traversing undulating country, after c. 27km crossing the Adour, 9km beyond which **Peyrehorade** is a large village overlooked by ruins of the 13C *Château de Aspremont*, replacing an earlier fortress, and burned down in 1567. Near the bridge over the Gave is the 16C *Château de Montréal*.

To the W. on the S. bank of the river lies the characteristic bastide of *Hastingues*, founded 1289/1303, and named in honour of Lord Hastings, Lieutenant of Guyenne, while 2km S.W. of the bridge is the restored Romanesque *Church* of the former priory of *Arthous*, with remarkable sculpture on its apse; mosaics and other antiquities may be seen.—For *Bidache*, 7km S., see Rte 83B.—The D29, skirting the N. bank of the river, leads 4km E. to **Sorde**, with an *Abbey Church* (12-13C; nave rebuilt) containing in its choir a remarkable mosaic, probably from an adjacent Gallo-Roman villa. The N. door and apsidal capitals have good grotesque capitals.—The road goes on via *Carresse* to (14km) *Salies-de-Béarn*; see below.

16km. *Puyoô*, on the Gave de Pau, on the far bank of which, at *Bellocq*, is a ruined 14C castle, a residence of Jeanne d'Albret when taking the waters at Salies in 1568.

Salies-de-Béarn, 7km further S., in the valley of the Saleys, has been famous since the 11C for its saline waters, and the older town of tortuous lanes preserves several quaint riverside houses once owned by the salt shareholders. The salt is still put to commercial use, but at *Oraàs*, to the S.W., on the *Gave d'Oloron. Sauveterre* (see Rte 83B) lies 9km S. of Salies, whence one may regain the main route 9km N.E.

14km. **Orthez**, (11,500 inhab.), now by-passed to the S. by a section of the A64, was the capital of *Béarn* from 1198–1464, and is noteworthy principally for its 13-14C **Bridge* over the Gave, defended by a gate-tower, somewhat spoilt by a restoration in 1873. It is best approached by the Rue Bourg-Vieux, just W. of the central *Pl. d'Armes*. Also in this street of old houses is the so-called *Maison de Jeanne-d'Albret* (No. 39), from which the Rue de l'Horloge (note No. 15) and its continuation lead up to the *Tour Moncade* (1242).

Jambons 'de Bayonne' are one of the main products of the district. It was a stronghold of Gaston Phoebus, count of Foix and Béarn (1331–91), who led here a life of crime, murdering his brother and his only legitimate son, who had been falsely accused of poisoning him. In spite of his excesses, he was a patron of art and literature, and was visited by Froissart in 1388. The town was sacked in 1569 after its capture by Protestants, and suffered in the subsequent plague. A more momentous battle took place on the hills between Orthez and St-Boes, c. 7km, N.W., on 27 Feb. 1814, when Wellington (who was here slightly wounded, for the first time in the Peninsular War) defeated Soult, who was forced to retreat N.E. A monument 3.5km N. of the town marks the spot where Gén. Foy received his fourteenth wound.—About 2km S. of St-Boes is the site of a Roman camp, fought over during the battle.

For the road to Mont-de-Marsan, 52km N.E., see Rte 79. Navarrenx lies 22km S. (see Rte 83B), and some will prefer this attractive but longer alternative road to Pau via Oloron.—L'Hôpital d'Orion, 9km S.W., has a Gothic church built on the plan of a Greek cross.

The N117 bears S.E., skirting an area above a huge field of natural gas discovered in 1949, and since exploited, as is only too evident from the rigs, petro-chemical factories, and other installations which have been erected during the last three decades on both sides of (16km) *Lacq*, 6km to the S. of which is the 'new town' of *Mourenx* (9000 inhab). The district has also experienced earthquakes.—8km S.E. of the latter lies *Monein*, with a 15C Gothic church and 16C belfry-keep. The composer Henri Duparc lived here for some years prior to 1896.

From Lacq the main road continues S.E., after 18.5km passing (l.) on a ridge, **Lescar** (5900 inhab.), said to be the Gallo-Roman *Beneharnum*, from which the province of Béarn was named. It preserves a 12C **Cathedral*, restored in the early 17C after the nave and belfry had collapsed, but containing good capitals (and some copies by Boeswillwald), and in the choir two mosaics (c. 1125; including a wooden-legged archer) and Renaissance stalls. Here are buried twelve members of the royal house of Navarre, among them Queen Marguerite (1492–1549; see p 443). The exterior of the apse is also of interest. Adjoining are the ruins of the brick-built *Fort de l'Esquirette* (14C), with a 12C gateway.

Here one may enter **Pau** from the N., or by regaining the main road, from the N.W.; see Rte 78.

B. Via Sauveterre-de-Béarn and Oloron-Ste-Marie

127km (79 miles). D936. 32km *Bidache*—23km *Sauveterre*—19km **Navarrenx** lies 2km N.E.—20km **Oloron**—N134. 33km **Pau.**

Maps: IGN 69, or 113; also 273-4. M 234.

Leaving Bayonne by the Allées Boufflers (S. bank of the Adour), at 3.5km a road junction is reached, the r.-hand fork providing an alternative approach to (21km) *Hasparren* (see below) by the Route impériale des Cimes.

Forking 1. the D936 shortly passes the *Croix de Mougerre*, where Col Bunbury bungled and retired during the *Battle of St-Pierre* on 13 Dec. 1813; see Rte 81.

11.5km. Hence an alternative road (D21; c. 52km) is that turning r. here via Hasparren and St-Palais.—11km. *Hasparren*, (5600 inhab.) a small shoe-manufacturing town, where over the church door is a 4C inscription relating to the origin of the province of *Novempopulania* (see p 442); it was the birthplace of the great pelota player 'Gaskoina' (Jean Erratchun; 1817–59), and here from 1920 lived the poet and novelist Francis Jammes (1868–1938).—The D10 leads E., off which at 3.5km the D251 turns r., shortly passing the ruins (r.) of the *Château de Belzunce*, where in 1450 a treaty between Labourd and England was signed.—3km beyond are the prehistoric *Grottes d'Isturuts* and the stalactite coverns of the *Grottes d'Oxocelhaya*.—On reaching the D14, turn l. for (15km) *Garris*, an attractive little village, where we turn downhill to (2.5km) *St-Palais* in the valley of the Bidouze and Joyeuse, a busy place, before 1620 the capital of French Navarre, later superceded by St-Jean-Pied-de-Port.—*Sauveterre* lies 12km N.E.

The main route follows the D936 E. through *Briscous*, 6km S. of which lies *Labastide-Clairence*, a characteristic village built on a regular plan in the early 14C, the older church of which has a Romanesque portal.—12km. *Bidache*, on the Bidouze, retains the well-sited ruins of a castle of the Ducs de Gramont (15C, with Renaissance additions). *Peyrehorade* (see Rte 83A) lies 9km N.E.—11.5km. *Labastide-Villefranche*, with a ruined 14C keep, 2.5km beyond which is *Escos*, on the *Gave d'Oloron*, the l. bank of which we follow to the S.E.

9km. **Sauveterre-de-Béarn**, 2km N., is a quaint little town with fragmentary ramparts, and one arch and a gateway of the 14C bridge E. of the present bridge. Higher in the town, near its Mairie, is a terrace commanding a charming vista, the ruins of a 13C keep, and the 13C church—part Romanesque; part Gothic—of little interest internally.—*Salies-de-Béarn* (see Rte 83A) lies 11km N.—*Athos*, a hamlet 2.5km N.W. recalls Dumas's musketeer.

A very pleasant minor road (D27) follows the N. bank of the Gave, passing through the attractive hamlets of *Laàs*, with its château, *Audaux*, and *Bugnein*, before reaching Navarrenx, also approached via the D936. ***Navarrenx**, an old town, has ramparts rebuilt on a modern plan c. 1540 for Henri d'Albret by the Veronese architect Fabrici Siciliano; they later received attention from Vauban.—7.5km *L'Hôpital-St-Blaise* (see Rte 82) lies 4.5km W.

12.5km. **OLORON-STE-MARIE** (12,200 inhab.) is an ancient feudal stronghold originally on a hill between the Gave d'Aspe and the Gave d'Ossau, but the later settlements on either bank have since merged.

Iluro, of Gallo-Roman foundation, was the capital of Béarn from 1194–1464, and a bishopric until 1790. It was also an important staging-point for pilgrims to Compostela crossing the Pyrenees by the Somport pass. It is now a busy slate-roofed agricultural centre and market, and has some industry, including the manufacture of chocolate.

The main building of interest is the former cathedral of *Ste-Marie, with its massive square tower, conspicuous on a hill S.W. of the centre, near to which roads from the W. converge.

The tower serves as an entrance porch, protecting the finely sculptured *W. *Doorway* of Pyrenean marble (12C), with a Deposition in the tympanum, in the archivolts above which daily activities are depicted together with a series representing the Apocalypse. To the r. is an equestrian statue of Gaston IV of Béarn, who built the church on his return from the Crusades. To the l. is a man being devoured by a monster, etc.; note the two chained Saracens supporting the central pillar. The interior is likewise remarkable, although dark, but minuteries light up the various carved and gilded altarpieces (18C), carved plaques, the painted *Choir* (early 14C) and its glass, and the bishop's bust in the apse, etc. The pulpit and organ-loft of 1650 are also notable.—A 13C tower of the *Bishop's Palace* is incorporated in the hospice to the S. of the church.

By descending a street S.W. of the apse, crossing the Gave d'Aspe, and turning r., we approach, via the *Pl. St-Pierre*, with old houses, the early church of *Ste-Croix*, erected in 1080 by Centulle IV, viscount of Béarn, and Amatus, bishop of Oloron. The side-vaults in the Auvergnat style, the capitals, and the side portal are interesting, but its most curious feature is the dome over the crossing, added in the 13C.—A terrace to the W. provides a good view of the Pyrenees.—From the N. side of the church one may descend through lanes to the central *Pl. Mendiondou*, thence crossing to the E. side of the Gave d'Ossau, with the Market-place, S.I., etc.

For the road hence (N134) to (33km) **Pau**, see Rte 82.

OLORON TO THE SOMPORT (55km). The road across the frontier may be impassable between Nov. and May. The N134 leads S. along the W. bank of the Gave d'Aspe, shortly entering the *Vallée d'Aspe*, a mountain vale which has long been one of the main arteries of traffic across the Pyrenees, once traversed by a Roman road from *Beneharnum* (Lescar) to *Caesaraugusta* (Zaragoza). After threading the defile of *Escot* we traverse (18km) *Sarrance*, with an octagonal church tower and unusual coventual cloisters, both 17C.—6.5km. *Bedous*, once noted for its yew-tree vessels, called 'herrades', 2.5km beyond which is *Accous*, the old capital of the medieval valley-republic.—3.5km. *Lescun*, superbly sited within a cirque of mountains, lies 5.5km up to the S.W. Near here a 'battle' took place in Sept. 1794, when an incursion of Spanish troops was forced back across the frontier by volunteers and peasants. To the W. rises the **Pic d'Anie** (2504m), the most westerly of the great Pyrenean summits, which may be ascended from Lescun.

The main road bears slightly S.E., passing (l.) a fort before reaching (10.5km) *Urdos* (French Customs), beyond which we enter the *Parc National des Pyrénées*, and climb steeply; below us the railway plunges into the *Somport Tunnel*, almost 8km long, opened in 1928.—14km. *Col du Somport* (1632m; views; and the Spanish Customs on the frontier). To the W. rises the peak of *Visaurin* (2668m). It was by this Roman *Summus Portus* that the greater part of Abderrahman al Gāfaqī's Moors crossed into France in 732; cf. Poitiers. Just beyond the pass are the ruins of a hospice built in 1108 by Gaston VI of Béarn for Compostelan pilgrims, and *Candanchu*, a winter-sporting centre.—13.5km below the col is *Canfranc*, and 23km further S., following the valley of the Rio Aragón, overlooked (l.) by the peak of *Collarada* (2886m), lies **Jaca**, for which see *Blue Guide Spain*.

84 Pau to Toulouse

A. Via Tarbes and St-Gaudens

195km (121 miles). N117. **Tarbes**—35km *Lannemezan*—16km
Montréjeau—14km **St-Gaudens**—18km *St-Martory* crossroads—51km
Muret—21km **Toulouse**.

Maps: IGN 70, 71, 64, or 113, also 275-6. M 234, 235.

The A64 motorway is under construction N. of and parallel to the
N117.

For **Pau**, see Rte 78.

PAU TO LOURDES VIA THE D937 (41km). Following the N. bank of the Gave de
Pau, the road traverses a number of villages of slight interest (mainly because so
many of their slate-roofed houses, built at r.-angles to the road, face E.) until
(17.5km), where one may cross the river to **Nay**, a regularly built small town
with a 15C Gothic church, and at the S.W. corner of the main square, the
Renaissance 'Maison de Jeanne-d'Albret'. The actor Laurence Olivier's
ancestors were a Protestant family which emigrated hence.—The main road continues S.E. through *Coarraze*, with the rebuilt château in which Henri IV was
brought up *'à la paysanne'*. Crossing the Gave, after *Lestelle-Bétharram* is a 17C
pilgrimage-church replacing an older building destroyed during the Religious
Wars, and a *Bridge* of 1687. Not far beyond, a lane to the r. leads to the stalactite
Grottes de Bétharram, through which flows a subterranean stream. The road now
veers E. skirting the N. bank of the Gave, at *St-Pé-de-Bigorre* passing remains of a
Benedictine abbey founded in 1089 by Sanche Guillaume, Duc de
Gascogne.—About 7km beyond, a l.-hand fork enables one to circumvent the
centre of *Lourdes* (see below), the basilica of which is passed to the r.

The N117 drives straight to (17km) *Soumoulou*, providing several
good views S. towards the Pyrenees, and again after 15km, before
reaching a sharp descending elbow in the road.—7km **Tarbes**; see p
471.

SOUMOULOU TO LOURDES (24km). The D940, later by-passing *Pontacq*, with a
14C church, provides both a faster road from Pau to Lourdes, and also enables
one to by-pass the latter town, if the main target is the Pyrenean valleys.
    Lourdes (17,600 inhab.) was once known as 'the key to the valley of Lavedan',
its grim-looking but once picturesquely sited fortress dominating what the
1840s Murray's *Hand-book* described as a town 'of narrow dirty streets and
shabby houses'. The scene has changed. In 1858 an illiterate 14-year-old peasant
girl, Bernadette Soubirous, claimed that she had witnessed visions of the Virgin
in the *Grotte de Massabielle*, adjacent to the Gave de Pau, since when it has seen
a phenomenal growth with the commercialisation of the cult: a whole 'Cité
Religieuse' has sprung up on the W. bank of the river, and hundreds of
thousands of devout Catholics, a high proportion of them incurably ill, physically or mentally, flock there each year in the hope of a cure from its miraculous
waters. It has not improved since Hilaire Belloc, at the turn of the century, condemned it as 'detestable in its accommodation, and to make it the more
detestable there is that admixture of the supernatural which is invariably accompanied by detestable earthly adjuncts'.
    Non-Catholics will be appalled by what they will see at Lourdes, most of which
is an affront to any instinct of veneration, and would do well to avoid the place
entirely. It is unpleasantly crowded during the summer, and on the occasions of
frequent parades there organised by the ecclesiastical authorities. Beware
pickpockets (particularly during torchlight processions), and the professional activities of touts and others preying on the credulity of ingenuous pilgrims: but
thus it has always been.
    Until the 17C the history of Lourdes was of its castle, which resisted Simon de

Montfort in 1216, and from 1360 to 1406 was an English stronghold. It later became a state prison, in which Lord Elgin was briefly incarcerated while passing through France from Constantinople in 1804. It was used as barracks in 1828–56. The authenticity of the visions of Mlle Soubirous (1844–79) being accepted by the diocesan, and the miracle being confirmed by the papal authorities, a feast day was appointed on the anniversary of the first apparition. Bernadette died a nun at Nevers, was beautified in 1925, and canonised in 1933. Lourdes had a reputation for its manufacture of linen, and chocolate.

The *Castle* may be approached by a rough ramp from its N.E. side, by steep flights of steps from the S.E., and from the E. by a lift (fee; for here, as everywhere else in the town, 'where every trifle may be turned into money, money will be expected for every trifle'). The present building is mainly 17-18C, but preserves the 14C keep and the *Tour de Garnabie* of the medieval ramparts, which provide a view W. towards the Basilica (see below).

Since 1922 it has contained a *Musée Pyrénéen*, with a sequence of rooms fitted up to illustrate the domestic life of earlier inhabitants of the range, together with collections of fauna, etc., souvenirs of mountaineers—including Charles Packe (1826–96), and Henry Russell (1834–1909)—and a Library of Pyreneica, in which are preserved the library of the early alpinist Ramond de Charbonnières (cf. Bagnères-de-Bigorre), and an extensive collection of prints, paintings, and drawings—among them original sketches by 'Gavarni'—and albums of lithographs, most French and English. Regrettably the museum is too often crowded by the overflow from the streets below who have wandered in assuming it is part of the general exhibition. There is a strong move to transfer the Library and collections of art to other accommodation in Pau or Tarbes, where they may be studied in tranquility.

The two main bazaar-like streets leading from the town centre towards and across the river are almost entirely devoted to the sale of religious souvenirs and trinkets of the most tawdry description. The more northerly Blvd de la Grotte—where at No. 87 one can see, for a price, a waxwork reproduction of da Vinci's 'Last Supper'!—is the most direct approach to the Esplanade des Processions, to the S. of which a huge subterranean concrete-bunker-like vault has been built. Ahead, at ground level, is the *Church of the Rosary* (1889; in a pseudo-Byzantine style), on either side of which curved ramps rise to a platform from which one may enter the *Crypt* and ascend to the *Basilica*, with its lofty spire, erected in 1876 in a grotesque 13C style by Hippolyte Durand, the interior being meretriciously decorated and adorned with indescribable ex-votos: the whole a sight to be seen to be believed. The chastening experience may be rounded off by running the gauntlet of the Av. B.-Soubirous (bearing S.E.) and the Rue Grotte, which leads back to the Pl. Peyremale in the town centre.

To the S.E. rises the *Pic du Jer* (948m), and to the S.W., *Le Béout*, their summits commanding views of the Pyrenees.

LOURDES TO BAGNÉRES-DE-BIGORRE (22km). The D937 drives E. through (4km) *Arcizac*, overlooked by the ruined *Château des Angles*, and bears N.E., after c. 8km providing a wide view to the S., before descending to meet the D935 from Tarbes to *Bagnères-de-Bigorre*, 11km to the r.; see p 474.

The N21 leads 19km N.E. to *Tarbes*, for which, and for the Pyrenean valleys to the S., see below

Tarbes (54,100 inhab.), préfecture of the *Hautes-Pyrénées*, lying largely on the W. bank of the Adour, is a town of very slight interest, and unfortunately not yet provided with a by-pass.

The capital of the Tarbelli was occupied by the English between 1360 and 1406, and in the Religious Wars suffered severely at the hands of Montgomery (1569). In 1592 the district was devastated by the Leaguers. A skirmish took place near by in 1814 during the French retreat from Orthez to Toulouse. It was the birthplace of Bertrand Barère (1755–1841), the Conventionnel; S.-G. Chevalier, better known as 'Gavarni' (1804–66), the artist and caricaturist; Théophile Gautier (1811–72); and Marshal Foch (1851–1929).

The *Pl. de Verdun* lies at the town centre, a short distance W. of which is the ungraceful *Cathedral*, of brick, stone, and rolled pebbles; it has a Romanesque apse, and a Gothic cupola over the crossing. To the S.W. of the Place are the *Haras*, or national stud-farm. To the N. is the *Jardin Massey*, in the S.E. of which has been re-erected part of an early 15C Gothic cloister from St-Sever-St-Rustan, c. 18km N.E. of Tarbes. Further N. is the *Musée*, containing a somewhat pedestrian collection of paintings, a section devoted to the archaeology of the High Pyrenees, and on the floor above, the *Musée des Hussards et du Cheval tarbais.*

TARBES TO LUZ-ST-SAUVEUR (50km), AND CAUTERETS. The N21 leads S.W. past (r.) the Airport, and at 18km by-passes *Lourdes* (see above), to enter the upper valley of the Gave de Pau, the centre of the medieval *Pays de Lavédan*, or *Sept-Vallées*, a series of semi-independent mountain republics of which the most important were those of St-Savin, and Barèges. From the 10-15C they were under the very nominal suzerainty of a viscount whose seats were at *Castelloubon* (c. 9km S.E. of Lourdes) and *Beaucens* (see below).—11km. *Vidalos*, with a 13C keep (l.) is traversed prior to (4km) **Argelès-Gazost** (463m), a spa near the confluence of the Gave d'Azun and Gave de Pau. At the N. end of the town is the *Château de Vieuzac*, once the home of Barère (cf. Tarbes); to the S. is the *Château d'Ourout*; the older town, 'destitute of a good inn' 140 years ago, lies to the W., clustered around the *Tour Mendaigne.*—For the mountain road hence to *Eaux-Bonnes*, see p 446, in reverse.—The main road goes on the (6.5km) *Pierrefitte-Nestalas*, along the valley floor, but the more interesting r.-hand fork on leaving the town ascends the side of the valley to (3km) **St-Savin** (580m), a pleasant village commanding a good view over the valley and across to *Beaucens*, with its ruined 12C *Castle, with two rings of ramparts. The *Abbey-Church* of St-Savin, one of the finest in the Pyrenees, is a fortress-like edifice with a 14C tower topped by a conical spire. Note the covered wall-walk. The W. portal is worn. The abbey is said to have been founded by Charlemagne on the ruins of the Roman *Palatium AEmilianum*, and re-founded by Raymond I of Bigorre in 945 after its destruction by marauders a century earlier. Remarkable are the 12C stoup; the 18 Catalan 15C paintings on wood illustrating the life of St Savinus (a Spanish hermit who lived on this site), and his tomb, now serving as an altar; the original canopy of the high altar (14C); the octagonal crossing; the organ-case of 1557; and 13C Gothic Christ. The well-vaulted *Chapter-house* (12C) may be visited, while the cloisters are under restoration.—Some 2km N.W. at *Arcizans-Avant* is the ruined *Château du Prince-Noir* (15C).

We continue S. through chestnut woods before descending to (3km) **Pierrefitte-Nestalas**, the railway terminus, with rather nasty factories. Murray had remarked that its population 'seem to live by begging, much to the travellers' annoyance'!

PIERREFITTE TO CAUTERETS (9km). Hence the N21C climbs r. through contiguous *Soulom*, with a curious belfry to its fortified church, and threads a thickly wooded narrow gorge high above the tumbling Gave de Cauterets to approach *Cauterets*. As the valley widens we get a fine view ahead of the fir-clad *Pic de Péguère* (2316m). To the W. of the town rises *Moun Né* (2724m). **Cauterets** (932m), lying in a trough-like valley, and built on both banks of the Gave, is not so abounding as it once was, with 'agents, guides, horse-jobbers, and itinerant merchants ... who beset the traveller the moment he sets foot within it'. The qualities of its waters have been known since at least the 10C, but it was not until the 16C that the place was resorted to with any frequency, among others—in the 19C—by Chateaubriand (who met a young girl there 'au bord du gave'), Baudelaire, Heine, Hugo and Juliette Drouet, George Sand (accompanied), et al.—For the ordinary traveller the attraction of Cauterets lies in the easy accessibility of some of the finest country in the Pyrenees, and for the excursions which may be made in its vicinity.—To the r. on entering the town is the useful Centre d'Information du Parc (National des Pyrénées), opposite which is the lower station for the Téléphérique ascending to 1850m near the *Cirque du Lys*. The 'classic' excursion (and therefore apt to get crowded) is that to the *Pont d'Espagne* (1496m), 8km S.W., passing several cascades, and leaving on our l. the track up the *Vallée de Latour*, on the E. side of which rises the *Pic d'Ardiden* (2988m). Hence one may ascend with ease to the *Lac de Gaube*, a charming mountain tarn (in which, in 1832, William and Sarah Pattison, on honeymoon, were drowned when boating), commanded to the S. by the mighty **Vignemale**, whose crevassed glacier is well seen, although the highest summit (3298m; the highest of the Pyrenees *in* France) is concealed by the W. slope of the valley.—From S.W. of the Pont d'Espagne a track ascends to the *Refuge Wallon*, S.W. of which rises the *Grande Fache* (3005m); to the E. of the latter is the *Port du Marcadau* (2541m), beyond which lies the *Balneario de Panticosa* in Spain (1639m).

From Pierrefitte-Nestalas (1km S. of which a l.-hand turning leads via adjacent *Villelongue* to the ruined abbey of *St-Orens*, c. 3km E.) we thread the *Gorge de Luz*, beyond which the valley widens, and poplar-shaded meadows are traversed, passing (l.) just before reaching (17km) Luz itself, the very ancient church at *Sère.*—**Luz-St-Sauveur** (711m) is charmingly sited near the confluence of the Gave de Bastan, which flows through the village, and the Gave de Gavarnie, on the W. bank of which is the old spa of *St-Sauveur (-les-Bains)*. The *Church at Luz is a curious fortified building erected by the knights of St-John of Jerusalem in the 12-13C, to which battlements were added in the 16C, and it is surrounded by a crenellated rampart with several lines of loopholes. On the N. side is a tower connecting the edifice with the ramparts, below which is the 12C portal; another tower adjoins the apse.—Overlooking the village to the N. is the ruined 14-15C *Château de Ste-Marie*.

LUZ TO GAVARNIE (20km); coach traffic in summer is apt to mar its tranquility. One may either follow the main road through *St-Sauveur*, with a view S.E. of the *Massif de Néouville* (rising to 3091m at *Pic Néouville* and to 3192m at *Pic Long*, further S.), and cross the *Pont Napoléon* (commemorating a visit by Napoleon III), or fork l. on leaving Luz onto a better road providing a view of St-Sauveur across the valley. To the E. rises the *Pic de Bergons* (2062m), easily ascended for the view from near the church at Luz.—From St-Sauveur a mountain road (D12) climbs in zigzags to the N.W. towards the *Col de Riou* (1949m; view) and the *Soum des Aulhères*.—After traversing rocky gorges, at 3km the *Piméné* (2031m) comes into view ahead, with to its r. *Marboré* (3248m). *Monte Perdido (Mont Perdu*; 3355m) rises further S., in Spain.—8.5km. **Gèdre** (1011m), a village at the confluence of the Gaves de Gavarnie and de Héas, beyond which is the *Cirque de Troumouse*; see below.—A mountain road to the r. just beyond Gèdre climbs in steep zigzags to the high-lying *Plateau de Saugué* (1640m), commanding magnificent mountain scenery, and a fine view S. towards the Cirque de Garvanie.—The main road climbs past (r.) cascades and traverses the stony *Chaos de Couméliе*, beyond which the summits of the wall of the Cirque de Gavarnie come into view. The valley narrows slightly with the so-called *Pain de Sucre* on the l., beyond which it widens. The entrance of the *Vallée d'Ossoue* is on the r.; at its head rises **Vignemale** (3298m). Bearing S., for the first time the whole expanse of the ***Cirque de Gavarnie** comes into view. From the village (1357m) 'of guides and muleteers', one which Belloc described in 1909 as 'hideously overrun', a track (3km) continues S., passing the grave of the Pyrenean geographer Franz Schrader (1844–1924), to approach the *Hôtel de Cirque*, commanding one of the finest views. The cirque is a colossal amphitheatre, c. 3km in diameter, whose vertical walls rise in three terraces to a height of c. 1700m. The almost horizontal line of the summit (c. 2700m) is broken by some half dozen peaks. At the E. end is the *Pic d'Astazou* (3012m), then come the four summits of the **Marboré**—the *Pic* (3248m), the *Épaule*, *Tour*, and *Casque*; to the W. are the notches of the *Brèche de Roland* (2807m), a cleft c. 100m deep and 40-60m wide in a rock wall 24m thick, said to have been hewn by the paladin with one blow of his sword Durandal (cf. Pas de Roland). Further W., in front of *Le Taillon* (3144m) stands the *Sarradets*.—Hence we may approach the *Grande Cascade, a waterfall 442m high, by which the waters of a glacier hurl themselves to the base of the precipice. When the snows are melting there is a single fall; after July there are two. At the foot of the fall (keep away from the walls of the Cirque to avoid falling stones) the torrent tunnels through masses of hardened snow, which form the 'Ponts de Neige'.—From the village of *Gavarnie* a mountain road ascends in zigzags to the S.W. up the winter-sporting *Vallée de Espécières*, between two mountain ridges and overlooked to the l. by the *Pic de Tantes* (2322m; views) to (13km) the *Port de Gavarnie* (or *de Bouchero*; 2270m) on the Spanish frontier.

GÈDRE TO THE CIRQUE DE TROUMOUSE (15km). A steep and narrow mountain road ascends to the S.E. along the Gave de Héas. The valley soon widens, and to the S.W. is the *Cirque d'Estaubé*, at the head of which is the *Pic de Pinède* (2860m), with *Monte Perdido* (3355m) beyond. We continue to climb S.E. past an early 18C chapel, and enter the ***Cirque de Troumouse**, a wild amphitheatre of mountains, with the *Pic de Troumouse* (3085m) to the S.E., the *Pic de la Munia* (3133m) further S., and the *Pic de Gerbats* (2904m) to the N.

LUZ TO BARÈGES (7km). The N618 climbs the side valley of the Bastan, overlooked to the N. by the *Soum de Nère* (2394m), ascended from (3km) *Sers*, shortly traversed, before the road ascends more steelply to (4km) **Barèges** (1219m), a mountaineering and winter-sporting centre, and spa, which first came into vogue after the visit there of Mme de Maintenon and the 7-year-old Duc de Maine (to whom she was governess) in 1677. It was popular with the English, particularly after Dr Meigham in 1742 published 'A Treatise of the Nature and Powers of Barege's Baths and Waters (Wherein Their superior Effects in the Cure of Gun-shot Wounds, with all their Complications of investerate Ulcers, Caries's of the Bones, Fistula's, Contractions of the Nerves and Tendons; of Schirrus's, Anchiloses's, and all Kinds of indurated Tumours, besides many other Distempers, both external and internal, are clearly demonstrated and confirmed by PRACTICAL OBSERVATIONS . . . etc.' It was also the subject of an engraving by Archibald Robertson in 1787. It preserves an 18C military hospital. The road continues up the desolate valley to (11km) the *Col du Tourmalet* (2115m), the last section being very steep. The fine road hence and the *Pic du Midi de Bigorre* is described in the sub-route. Ste-Marie to Arreau; see below.

TARBES TO BARÈGES VIA BAGNÈRES-DE-BIGORRE (60km). The D955 leads due S., after 8.5km traversing *Pouzac*, whose 15C church is surrounded by ramparts, the bell-tower of which is in the middle of the village.—2.5km. **Bagnères-de-Bigorre** (682m; 9850 inhab.), an old established resort, which 'contains little worthy of notice, but it is much frequented by company on accounts of its waters' to quote Arthur Young. It continued to be patronised by the English in the mid 19C; F.M. Lord Alanbrooke was born there in 1883. Belloc was particularly scathing about the place, or at least its accommodations, observing that 'the rule holds here, as everywhere, that where rich people, especially cosmopolitans, colonials, nomads, and the rest, come into a little place, they destroy most things except the things that they themselves desire. And the things that they themselves desire are execrable to the rest of mankind'.

To the E. of the central *Pl. Lafayette* (S.I.) stands *St-Vincent* (14-15C), with five tiers of arches on its facade; immediately to the S. are the umbrageous Allées des Coustous; from the S.W. corner the Rue Victor-Hugo leads S. past (r.) the Rue de l'Horloge, with the 15C *Tour des Jacobins*. We pass some disfigured Renaissance houses before turning r. into the Rue des Thermes, where beyond the market are relics of the cloister of *St-Jean*. At the end of this street are the *Grands Thermes*, in which is preserved the Pyrenean *Librarie Ramond*, named after the geologist and mountaineer Louis-François Ramond de Charbonnières (1755–1827), author of 'Observations faites dans les Pyrénées' (1789), etc. Adjacent is the *Musée Salies*, containing a few pictures of interest, beyond which are the *Néothermes*, and *Casino*. Between the two bathing establishments are laid out attractive and colourful gardens.—For the road hence to *St-Bertrand-de-Comminges*; see below.

Driving S. parallel to the W. bank of the Adour, at 3.5km the *Château de Médous* is passed (r.), adjoining which are the *Grottes de Médous*, a series of stalactite caverns discovered in 1948, traversed by an underground river. On the far bank of the Adour lies *Asté*, with a 16C church; to the W. rises the *Monné* (1259m).—3.5km. *Beaudéan*, birthplace of Dominique Larrey (1766–1842), surgeon-general of the 'Grand-Armée', has a curious 16C church tower.—Hence a road climbs S.W. up the *Vallée de Lesponne* to (10km) *Chiroulet* (1062m), N. of which rises the *Pic de Montaigu* (2339m); to the S.E., the *Pic due Midi de Bigorre* (2865m; see below); and to the S. a bridle-path ascends to the *Lac Bleu* (1944m), a beautiful sheet of blue water in a frame of yellow rock.—1km. *Campan* has another curious mountain church, with a gilt and white altarpiece, and plain bench-pews. Note also the covered market and other 16C buildings. Here is a S.I. and post for mountain guides.—6.5km. *Ste-Marie-de-Campan*.

STE-MARIE TO ARREAU (26km). The N618 forks l. On the slopes towards the *Pic de l'Arbizon* (2831m) is the *Camp Bataillé*, the legendary scene of a defeat of the Bigourdan Gauls by the proconsul Messala in 27 B.C.—8km. *Espiadet*, which furnished marble columns for the Grand Trianon, the Paris Opéra, and the Royal Palace at Potsdam.—The road climbs steeply to (5km) the *Col d'Aspin* (1489m) before descending in zigzags to (13km) **Arreau**, in the *Vallée d'Aure*; see Rte 80.

The N618 continues to climb, circling to the S.W. through (5km) *Gripp*, and making a wide turn to the S. past the *Cascades du Garet* before ascending to (8km) *La Mongie* (1800m), a recent winter-sports development which has hardly improved the otherwise unspoilt and splendid mountain scenery. We have a fine view of the *Pic du Midi de Bigorre* on our r. in climbing still higher to (4km) the **Col de Tourmalet** (2115m), the highest main-road pass in the Pyrenees. The **Pic du Midi** (2865m) is the most accessible of the major Pyrenean heights, the summit of which may now be ascended by a toll-road (5.5km). Just below the peak is the *Observatory* (1881), beyond which the N. face falls away in tremendous precipices towards the *Lac de Peyrelade*. The panoramic **Views* of the range are unsurpassed.—The road descends from the col to the W. in a series of very steep zigzags. The upper Bastan valley is desolate, only improving as we approach (11km) **Barèges**; see above.

BAGNÈRES-DE-BIGORRE TO ST-BERTRAND-DE-COMMINGES (c. 45km). The D938 climbs N.E. (good retrospective views) past (16km) the remains of the abbey of *Escaladieu*, with a 12C church, and (2.5km) the ruined 14C castle of *Mauvezin*, in which a museum of local history and folklore has been installed.—4.5km. *Capvern*, in the valley to the N.W. of which lies the spa of *Capvern-les-Bains*. The N117 may be joined just to the N., 6km S.W. of *Lannemezan*, but the D938 continues S.E. via (7km) *La Barthe-de-Neste* (see Rte 80), and skirts the N. bank of the Neste to *St-Laurent-de-Neste* and *Montréjeau*. By crossing the river at St-Laurent and following its S. bank past the stalactite *Grottes de Gargas*, **St-Bertrand** is approached (see Rte 80), 17km S.W. of *St-Gaudens*; see below.

From **Tarbes** (see p 471) the N117 turns S.E., soon climbing steeply, via (17.5km) *Tournay*, birthplace of the poet Francis Jammes (1868–1938), before ascending to the *Plateau de Lannemezan*, on which several tributaries of the Garonne have their source.—11km. The r.-hand turning here leads to (7km) *La Barthe-de-Neste*, and the road S. to *Arreau* and *St-Lary*; see Rte 80.—Bearing N.E., at 6km *Lannemezan* (585m) is traversed, and 3km beyond, the Lannemezan crossroad (D929 from *Auch*); see Rte 80. The views S. towards the Pyrenees are frequently very fine.

LANNEMEZAN TO TOULOUSE VIA LOMBEZ (113km). This alternative road (D17) leads N.E. to (24.5km) *Blajan*, off which we turn r. after 7.5km via *Lécussan* to (8km) *St-Plancard*, just beyond which (l.) is the 11C chapel of *St-Jean-des-Vignes* (key at last house on l.), built on the site of a Gallo-Roman sanctuary, preserving contemporary wall-paintings.—5.5km beyond, after passing the ruined 13C castle of *Larroque*, one may fork r. for (2km) *Montmaurin*, where the town hall contains a small archaeological collection. In the valley 1.5km S.E. is a Gallo-Roman villa (1C A.D.). A lane (D9D), leading N.E. from the road threads the *Gorges de la Save*, in a cave of which the calipigian ivory statue known as the 'Venus of Lespugue', of the Aurignacian period, was found (now at St-Germain-en-Laye).—The main road may be regained a short distance N.W. at *Blajan*, whence we turn r. for (6km) *Rebirechioulet*, there following the valley of the Save N.E. to (17km) *L'Isle-en-Dodon*, with a brick church preserving its fortified apse (14C) and octagonal belfry (16C).—After 6.5km the D632 is reached.—**Simorre**, an attractive village with a re-restored fortified brick *Church* (1304), with good glass and other features, including carved oak stalls and Pieta, an interesting crossing, and 15C Catalan Crucifixion, lies 8km N.W. across the hills.—7.5km r. at this junction is **Lombez**, a crumbling old town with a 14C brick church once a cathedral, with a fine octagonal tower, where Bp Colonna was visited by Petrarch in 1330.—Hence the undulating road is followed through (25km) *St-Lys*, and 15km beyond enters the W. suburbs of **Toulouse**; see Rte 86.

11.5km. **Montréjeau** (468m), above the confluence of the Neste with the Garonne, commands a wide view of the Pyrenees, 14km beyond which lies **St-Gaudens** (12,200 inhab.), once described as an 'old and gloomy town', and the ancient capital of the *Nébouzan*. It should have a good view S., but this is often obscured by the pall of smoke from a factory. Its 11-12C *Church*, mutilated by Montgomery in 1569, with a Romanesque tower and chapter-house, and Flamboyant portal, preserves some good capitals. St Raymond (1090–1163), founder of the Spanish military order of Calatrava, was born here. There are several natural gas installations in the vicinity.

The N117 continues due E., providing good views S., and after 9km of the striking ruins of the *Château de Montespan* (13-16C).—At 3km the Garonne is crossed, and the road for St-Girons turns r.; see Rte 85.—2km N. of this junction lies *St-Martory*, with a *Bridge* of 1727, and a Romanesque door to its church.

The road bears N.E., crossing the Salat, and passing (r.) the 12C ruins of *Roquefort*. To the l. as the Garonne is re-crossed at *Boussens* is the principal plant in the district for the extraction of natural gas.—The road circles N. of *Martres-Tolosane*, with a good 13C octagonal steeple of the local style, where a Roman villa was uncovered in the 1890s.—A ruined castle of the bishops of Cominges, with a Gothic doorway, may be seen at *Alan*, 8.5km N.W.

The valley of the Garonne now widens.—A r.-hand turning some 13km beyond Martres-Tolosane leads 4km to *St-Julien*, where one may cross the river to (5km) **Rieux**, preserving several old buildings, including its former *cathedral* (1440), sadly mutilated in the 16th and 18Cs, but retaining its original brick tower, also a 16-18C *Bishop's Palace*, and a 17C *Bridge* across the Arize.

6km further S.E. on the D627 lies *Montesquieu-Volvestre*, with a quaint fortified *Church* (14C), and 16C *Market-hall*.—There is another good church (12th and 16C) at *Daumazan*, 10km further S.E.; 4km S.W. of the latter, at *Montbrun Bocage*, the church preserves 16C murals. The main road may be regained 9km N. of Rieux, beyond *Carbonne*.

Approx. 30km beyond the above turning for St-Julien is **Muret** (also by passed), the old capital of the county of *Cominge*, the walled centre of which lay between the Garonne and its tributory, the Louge. On the bank of the former was the important market-place. The old church (rebuilt) has a 14C tower.

The battlefield of Sept. 1213, in which Simon de Montfort dispersed the troops of Pedro II of Aragón, himself killed in the *mêlée*, stood to the N. It was the birthplace of the opera-composer Nicolas Dalayrac (1753–1809); Marshal Niel (1802–69), a hero of the Crimea; and Clément Ader (1841–1925), a pioneer of telephony and aeronautics.

After 8km we join the N20 from Pamiers, and shortly enter the S.W. outskirts of **Toulouse**; see Rte 86.

B. Via Morlaàs, Mirande, and Auch

181km (112 miles). D943. 11km Morlaàs—D7. 30km Vic-en-
Bigorre—D943. 8km Rabastens-de-Bigorre—N21. 15km Miélan
—14km Mirande—25km **Auch**—N124. 26km Gimont—.
52km **Toulouse**.

Maps: IGN 63, 64, or 113; also 412. M 234, 235.

Morlaàs, the capital of Béarn until the 12C, preserves interesting
relics in the church of *Ste-Foy, founded in 1089, largely ruined by
Jeanne d'Albret during her crusade of reform; its apse and narthex,
with its restored portal, richly sculptured in the Byzantine manner, is
mainly original.

After 2km the D7 is followed to the N.E., at 18.5km passing 6km N.
of the imposing 14C brick castle of Montaner, with a 36m high keep,
from which the main road may be regained to the N.E., passing a
Gallo-Roman oppidum at St-Lézer.

9.5km. Vic-en-Bigorre, just N.E. of which is the village of Artagnan,
which belonged to the family of Charles de Batz (c. 1613–73), killed
at Maastricht, who became the hero of Dumas père's 'The Three
Musketeers'.—8km. Rabastens-de-Bigorre, a bastide with an adjacent
canal said to have been dug at the instance of Alaric II.—5km.
Villecomptal-sur-Arros, 6.5km S. of which lies St-Sever-de-Rustan,
once famous for its Benedictine abbey (cf. Tarbes).—The road climbs
to (4km) the Puntous de Laguian (320m), a fine view-point.

4km. Tillac, a quaint old village, lies 6km N.—At (2km) Miélan, on
a ridge between the valleys of the Boues and Osse, we turn N.E. to
(9km) Mirande, a bastide founded in 1285 on the W. bank of the
Grande-Baise, with a 15C church tower curiously supported by an
arch and buttress spanning the street.—25km. **Auch**; see Rte 80.

The N124 ascends and follows a ridge to (16km) Aubiet, in the Ar-
rats valley (see the sub-route on p 386).—8km. **Gimont**, in the centre
of which is a huge wooden Market-hall built astride its steep main
street. A bastide of 1265, it was originally named Francheville; its
church of 1506, with an octagonal brick belfry, contains a notable
16C triptych.—A short distance S. on the W. bank of the river
Gimone, are the 12-17C ruins of a Cistercian abbey founded in 1145.

19km. L'Isle-Jourdain, on the Save, the birthplace of Bertrand de
Comminges (cf. St-Bertrand), preserving parts of two market places,
is traversed before crossing a ridge, after 19km passing (l.) Pibrac, the
birthplace of Germaine Cousin, a shepherdess unaccountably
canonised in 1867, with a château of c. 1540. We shortly reach the
outer suburbs and (l.) the Airport of Toulouse-Blagnac, to enter
Toulouse itself; see Rte 86.

85 St-Gaudens to Foix and Perpignan

224km (139 miles). N117. 18km—D117. 28km St-Girons—44km
Foix—N20. 7km—D117. 20km Lavelanet—35km **Quillan**—74km
Perpignan.

Maps: IGN 71, 72, or 113, 114. M 235.

At 16km N.E. of **St. Gaudens** (see latter part of Rte 84A) fork r., and
3km beyond, turn r. through Montsaunès, with a 12C brick
Templars' church.—At 4km we pass (l.) the small spa of Salies-du-

Salat, overlooked by a ruined castle of the counts of Cominge.—Traversing *Mane*, the valley of the Salat is ascended for 22km, before turning l. across a restored 13C bridge, on the r. of which is a tower of 1120, to **St-Lizier**. The ancient *Lugdunum Consoranorum*, and long the ecclesiastical capital of the *Couserans*, is now little more than a picturesque village. The former *Cathedral*, whose N. portal and 14C octagonal tower are masterpieces of brickwork in the Tolosan style, contains Roman masonry in its apse. The E. end of the two apsidal chapels of the transepts are 12C work. Of similar date is the charming *Cloister*, although the wooden upper storey was added in the 15C. The effigy of Bp Auger dates from 1303.—The former *Archevêché* is now an asylum; it also incorporates part of the old ramparts, and a 14C chapel containing 17-18C woodwork. Several old houses, some restored, survive in the upper town near the church, many built over arcades.

A lane leads 2km E. to *Montjoie*, a hamlet containing a diminutive 14C bastide whose walls are almost filled by a church surmounted by a fantastic turreted belfry.

2km. **St-Girons**, pleasantly sited at the confluence of the Lez and the Baup with the Salat, is of slight interest. On the E. bank of the Salat are the churches of *St-Girons*, with a 14C steeple, and a short distance S.E., that of *St-Valier*, with a crenellated wall-belfry and Romanesque door.

For the road to *Mas d'Azil*, *Pamiers*, and **Carcassonne**, see Rte 90 in reverse.

ST-GIRONS TO TARASCON-SUR-ARIÈGE (58km). This partly mountainous road (D618) bears round the S. side of the *Massif de Larize*, first passing the cigarette-paper factory of (4km) *La Moulasse*, and 3km beyond, the ruined 14C keep of *Lacourt* (l.), before threading the *Gorges de Ribaouto* and after 6km bearing l.

The r.-hand turning leads to (20km) *Aulus* via (3.5km) *Vic*, whose church has three Romanesque apses and a painted 16C ceiling, and adjacent *Oust* (501m) the main village in the valley.—7km beyond is the hamlet of *Ercé*, where performing bears were once trained.—8.5km. *Aulus-les-Bains* (762m), a small spa (since 1854), but famous for its ferruginous waters in Roman times, beyond which a mountain road winds across country to *Vicdessos*; see Rte 87.—The *Pic de Cayzardets* (1412m), N. of Aulus, commands a fine view.

1.5km S.W. of Oust lies *Seix*, with some curious woodcarvings in its church.—Hence the D3 leads S. past (5km) the ruins of the *Château de la Garde* to (5.5km) *Couflens* and to the hamlet of *Salau*, 4km beyond. At the head of the valley rises *Mont Rouch* (2858m), while a track climbs S.W. to the *Port de Salau* (2087m), descending into the Spanish valley of the *Noguera Pallerésa*.

The D618 ascends the valley of the Arac through (12km) *Biert*, facing the curiously shaped *Rocher de Queire*, and beyond (l.) the ruined *Château d'Amoun* enters (3km) *Massat*, the civil capital of the *Couserans*, with a 17C church with an ogee gable and 14C steeple. The road climbs N.E. to (6km) the *Col des Caougnous* (947m).

A very steep mountain road climbs 3.5km N. to the *Col de Péguère* (1375m) just above which rises the *Tour Lafont*, commanding one of the finest *views* in the Pyrenees.—Hence the D17 leads N.E. to (27.5km) *Foix* via (8.5km) the *Col des Marrous* (900m; views), beyond which the Arget valley is descended past (10km) *Serres*, birthplace of Joseph Lakanal (1762–1845), the educationalist.

The D618 continues to climb, the *Pic de Fonfrède* (1617m) conspicuous to the N.—6km. *Col de Port* (1249m), overlooked to the S. by the *Pic d'Estibat* (1663m; views). We now descend in zigzags to (9.5km) *Saurat*, with a long main street of 18C houses and a picturesque Place. Beyond are (l.) the ruined *Tour Montorgueil*, and (r.) a ruined castle. Near adjacent *Bédeilhac* are some prehistoric caves.—The Ariège valley is entered at **Tarascon**; see Rte 87.

From St-Girons, we ascend the pastoral valley of the Baup. At 8.5km the D119 bears 14km N.E. to the *Grotte de Mas d'Azil*; see Rte 90.—9.5km. *Castelnau-Durban*, with a ruined 13-15C castle and red marble quarries, 3.5km beyond which a l.-hand turning leads to (2.5km) *Durban*, past which in the trees is another massive ruined fortress (12-15C).—5.5km. *Bastide-de-Sérou*, a quaint old town, is traversed, and soon after the road climbs to the *Col de Bouich* (599m) overlooking the valley of the Arget, with the *Massif de l'Arize* to the S., rising to 1716m, and then descends rapidly into the Ariège valley (several attractive panoramas), there turning E. again, with a sudden view of the castle-crowned rock of *Foix*, for which see Rte 87.

The N20 is followed to the S. for 7km, there turning l. onto the D117, which ascends the Baure valley parallel to a ridge of hills to (11.5km) *Nalzen*, with a view towards the strikingly sited ruin of *Roquefixade* (l.).

At 4.5km turn r.; the road ahead leads to (4km) **Lavelanet**, a small industrial town of slight interest (19km S. of *Mirepoix*; see Rte 90), 8km E. of which the main road is regained after making the recommended DETOUR (22.5km) to Montségur.

This is approached by turning l. on meeting the D9 in the adjacent valley, and bearing round to the S.E. After 4.5km we climb l. and in 2km have a fine view ahead of the dome-shaped hill surmounted by the extensive ruins of the castle of *Montségur, well worth the stiff climb for the view from its summit (1261m).

Montségur, built 1204, was the Cathar stronghold where Esclarmonde, sister of Count Raymond-Roger of Foix, held court, and where Guilabert de Castres retreated in 1209. In 1232 it was further fortified, and was almost the last fortress left to the Albigensians. Raymond VII was forced to raise a siege in 1241, but in May 1243 it was again besieged by an army commanded by Hugh d'Arcis. It only capitulated on 2 March 1244. Some 200 who refused to abjure their errors were collected together within a stockade below the castle on the 16th, and were consumed on a huge pyre. Although it was not the last Cathar refuge to fall—*Queribus* (see below) held out until 1255—its surrender and the subsequent immolation of this nucleus precipitated the virtual extinction of the heretical cult; cf. p 498.

On descending past the village of *Montségur* the Lasset valley is traversed, at the head of which rises the *Pic de St-Barthélemy* (2348m); passing below the commanding peak, we bear away to the E. through *Fougax-et-Barrineuf* (7km S. of which is the deep *Gorges de la Frau*), regaining the D117 at *Bélesta*, to the S. of which lies its extensive forest.

The road ascends to (8km) the *Col de la Babourade* (655m; views) before descending to (3km) *Puivert*, commanded by its ruined castle, and climbs again to (11.5km) the *Col du Portel* (601m), where we cross the watershed between the Atlantic and Mediterranean, and commence the final steep descent to (4.5km) *Quillan*. From the col, providing extensive views to the N.E. over the *Corbières*, the D613 leads S.W. to *Ax-les-Thermes*; see Rte 87.

Quillan, a flourishing small market and manufacturing town (plastics, hats, and shoes), and trading in timber and figs, although an important crossroads, is of slight interest in itself. The *Hôtel de Ville* occupies an attractive 18C mansion, but the ruins of its medieval castle are of no moment. For the road hence to **Carcassonne**, 51km N., see Rte 89 in reverse.

Bearing S., the *Défilé de Pierre-Lys*, caused by the river Aude cutting through limestone cliffs, is traversed. The first of four tunnels is called the 'Trou du Curé' in memory of the Abbé Armand (1742–1823), of St-Martin-Lys, at the head of the gorge, who initiated the construction of the road.—At 10km the D107 for Ax-les-Thermes via the Reventy valley bears r., and 1km beyond, the D118 turns S. through *Axat* to (57km) *Mont-Louis*; see Rte 89.

The D117 turns due E., after 3.5km commencing a gradual descent between wooded hills through (2.5km) *Lapradelle*, passing (r.) the ruined 13C castle of *Puilaurens*.—6km. *Caudiès*, 2km S. of which is the castle of *Fenouillet* (which gave its name to the 'pays' of *Fenouillèdes*, a part of Languedoc now included in the *Pyrénées-Orientales*). The valley widens. To the N. rises the *Pic de Bugarach* (1230m).—11km. *St-Paul-de-Fenouillet*, the main village of the district.

Hence an interesting short DETOUR may be made by following a narrow by-road climbing N., and threading the *Gorges de Galamus* to (9.5km) *Cubières*, 9.5km E. of which (by the D14) lies *Rouffiac-des-Corbières*, overlooked to the S. by the splendid ruin of *Peyrepertuse*, the largest and most complete example in the area of a frontier fortress between France and Roussillon, dating from the 13-16C, and easily approached from *Duilhac*, 4km S.E.—The main route may be regained by continuing S.E. on the D14 to (4km) *Cucugnan*, there climbing S. to (2km) the *Grau de Maury*, a pass in this range of hills (view), just E. of which rises the 13C keep of *Quéribus* (restored), a Cathar retreat which held out until 1255.—5km below in the valley lies *Maury*.

8km. *Maury*, not far beyond which we obtain a distant view (r.) of the *Canigou*.

8km. A l.-hand turning leads through vineyards to (7km) **Tautavel**, overlooked to the S.E. by a conspicuous medieval tower, near which, in the huge cavern of the *Caune de l'Arago*, the oldest human skull in Europe (c. 450,000 years old) was found in 1971 by M.H. de Lumley. A visit to the well-displayed small *Museum* in the village is of considerable interest, not only to the professional archaeologist.—One may regain the main road by turning W. to the D611, and then l. for 6km.—The r.-hand turning leads N. to (13km) *Tuchan*, in the heart of the *Corbières*, and the market town for its 'Fitou' wines, overlooked to the E. by the ruined *Château d'Aguilar* (late 12C). The road continues N. through the Corbières via (17.5km) *Durban*, also with a ruined castle, towards *Narbonne*.

2km. *Estagel*, on the river Agly, was the birthplace of the astronomer François Arago (1786–1853).—Hence the D612 climbs S. over a ridge of hills to (14km) *Millas*; see Rte 147.—12.5km. *Espira-de-l'Agly* has a late 12C church with twin apses and polychrome marble decoration.—To the E. lies *Rivesaltes*; see Rte 146.—The D117 turns S.E. towards the airport of **Perpignan**, and crossing the B9 motorway, enters its N. outskirts; see Rte 146.

86 Toulouse

TOULOUSE (354,300 Toulousains; 50,200 in 1801; 149,800 in 1901), the ancient, animated, and dusty capital of Languedoc, préfecture of the *Haute-Garonne*, and the fourth town in France, is a rapidly expanding commercial metropolis situated on a dull plain traversed by the Garonne, on the W. bank of which stands the sun-burnt rose-brick nucleus, characteristically surrounded by boulevards. Although, to quote an earlier Hand-Book, 'It is far from being a handsome city . . . and neither public or private buildings are distinguished by special architectural beauty', some—such as Romanesque St-

Sernin—are of considerable interest, and it contains an important museum. Among its specialities are violets, plain or crystalised, and pâtes-truffés.

A stronghold of the Volcae Tectosages, ancient *Tolosa* was of slight importance, when compared to Narbonne, but was famous for its sacred pool, which in 106 B.C. the consul Caepio drained, appropriating the coins and other offerings which it contained, an act of sacrilege to which his subsequent defeat by Gallic tribes was attributed. Slight remains of its amphitheatre survival. it was evangelised by St Saturninus (Sernin), who in 257 suffered martyrdom by being tied to the tail of a wild bull.

From 419-507 it was the Visigothic capital. They were succeeded by the Franks in 628, Dagobert creating the kingdom of Southern Aquitaine for his brother Charibert, who established his court here. In 778 an independent countship was founded by Chorson, succeeded in 790 by 'William Short-nose' of Orange, the hero of sundry 'chansons de geste'. Under Raymond IV (1093–1105), who endeavoured to consolidate his domain (which then consisted of 13 recalcitrant counties, stretching as far E. as Savoy), it reached its greatest extent. He also led the First Crusade to Jerusalem, in 1096. Raymond V (1148–94) was able to preserve Toulouse from his predatory neighbour Henry II of England, who had recently acquired Aquitaine by marriage, but further E. his territories were ravaged by unruly vassals, and the ensuing anarchy was propitious for the growth of heresy. Raymond V was also a patron of troubadours, although they flourished mainly in minor courts. One of them, Folquet de Marseille, rabid opponent of heresy, became bishop of Toulouse, and a fierce antagonist of his son, Raymond VI (1194–1222), under whom the county suffered all the horrors of the Albigensian crusade.

Toulouse itself was besieged in vain by Simon de Montfort (whose son became Earl of Leicester) in 1211, who was killed during another attempt to take the heavily defended town in 1218. In 1229, at the Treaty of Paris, Raymond VII (d.1249) relinquished the struggle, marrying his daughter Jeanne to Alphonse de Poitiers, brother of Louis IX, and on her death in 1271 the county became the royal province of *Languedoc*. A university had been established here in 1299 as part of a scheme to combat heresy, while the Dominican-dominated Inquisition, ruthlessly active in the eradication of Catharism in the diocese, was only officially suspended in 1279, although the Parlement founded in 1302 was later notorious in its severity towards heretics. The university was later associated with Dolet, Bodin, and Scaliger, while it was probably attended by Montaigne, whose maternal grandparents lived here. In 1317 its bishop was appointed archbishop. In 1619 the free-thinking philosopher Lucilio Vanini was burnt to death here after having his tongue cut out, and as late as 1762 Jean Calas, a Protestant accused of having murdered his son to prevent his conversion to Catholicism, was broken on the wheel; his subsequent rehabilitation was due to the persistence of Voltaire's pleading. Some thousands of Huguenots perished here in the troubles of the 1560s, and hundreds more on St Bartholomew's Day (1572).

Here in 1323 a college 'du gai savoir' was founded, it is said, by seven troubadours, for the purpose of encouraging literary talent, and the annual *Jeaux Floraux* (so-called from the golden violet and silver marigold and eglantine distributed as prizes) was later revived by the legendary Dame Clémence Isaure. The Academy still attempts to preserve the *langue d'Oc* (cf. Hôtel d'Assezat).

Sterne spent a year here from July 1762, for the sake of his health, renting an elegant house with a courtyard and two acres of garden for £30 a year; he had previously written to his wife to bring out a copper tea-kettle, as there were no such things in France. His daughter Lydia later married a certain M. de Medalle. In 1764 Adam Smith (then bear-leading the young Duke of Buccleuch) started to compose his 'Wealth of Nations' to pass the time in Toulouse.

On 10 April 1814 the last battle of the 'Peninsular War' was fought here (commemorated by an obelisk), when Wellington commenced a concentric attack on Toulouse from the N. (the news of Napoleon's abdication not having yet reached the strongly fortified town), and only after Beresford's assault of the Calvinet ridge (or Mont Rave, just S. of the Albi road, and between the Canal du Midi and the river Hers) was Soult forced to abandon the place rather than get cut off. He slipped away to the S.E., but not before inflicting heavy losses on the British.

Numerous Spaniards sought exile here during the Civil War, while since the Second World War much capital has been expended on developing Toulouse as a centre of the electronics industry and of aircraft research and construction, the airport of *Blagnac*, just to the N.W., being used by the French 'Concorde' on her early test flights. Its student population has also grown very considerably in recent decades.

Among illustrious natives were Nicolas Bachelier (c. 1485–1557), sculptor and architect; Jacques Cujas (1522–90), jurist-consul; Guy du Faur de Pibrac (1529–84), moralist and advocate of religious toleration; Pierre de Fermat (c. 1595–1665), mathematician and inventor of the integral calculus; and the artists Antoine and François de Troy (1608–84, and 1645–1730, respectively).

Almost everything of interest in Toulouse lies within the inner ring of boulevards and on the E. bank of the Garonne. Those entering the centre from the W. will cross the *Pont St-Michel*, off which (r.) a road admits to what remains of the island *Parc Toulousain* encroached on by a *Palais des Congrès, Cité Universitaire*, etc. The bridge replaced another which succeeded a suspension bridge swept away in the flood of June 1875 (in which 300 people lost their lives), which also destroyed the old bridge of St-Pierre, further N.

The wide Allées Jules-Guesde is shortly reached, on the S. side of which is *St-Exupère* (17-18C), near the site of the Château Narbonnais, a rambling fort of Roman origin and an important bone of contention in early 13C sieges; adjacent is the *Natural History Museum* (also containing prehistoric collections from the caverns of the Ariège), behind which is the *Jardin des Plantes*. On the l. is the *Jardin Royal*, and ahead the *Grand Rond*, on which roads from the S.E. converge. Circling to the N., one may follow the Allées Forain-Verdier, the first main l.-hand turning off which leads to the cathedral of *St-Étienne* (see below); those wishing to visit St-Sernin first will continue to circle towards the church, near which, or below the *Pl. du Capitole*, parking may be found. Those entering the city from the N. (N20) or Albi (N88) will find that both these roads converge on St-Sernin.

*Brick-built *St-Sernin** is, since the destruction of Cluny, the largest Romanesque building in France, and although some will prefer small stone churches, it is indeed imposing. A good view may be obtained from the N.E., where the semicircle of apsidal chapels leads the eye up the octagonal tower of five storeys, diminishing in size, crowned by a short spire (?15C). The three lower tiers of arches, with round heads, date from the early 13C; the upper two, with angular heads, from after 1250. The twin doorways of the S. transept (*Porte des Comtes* or *des Filhols*) have historiated capitals, while in an adjoining niche are sarcophagi. One may enter by the *Porte Miégeville* (c. 1120) on the S. side of the nave, above which is a tympanum representing the Ascension. This is preceded by a Renaissance gateway of 1525.

The basilica was begun between 1075–80, and the choir consecrated by Urban II in 1096, by which time St Raymond Gayrard had commenced the nave and transepts. This continued into the 13C, when it was decided to extend the nave to the W., but the facade with its two stumps of towers and arcade was never completed. The four piers at the crossing were strengthened to support the tower, but since 1271—except for a number of minor restorations and some suspect exterior alterations made since 1855—it has been practically unaltered architecturally.

Its plan is almost exactly reproduced in the great cathedral of Santiago de Compostela, in Spain, started c. 1075, the dimensions of which are smaller. The double-aisled interior, although spacious, is dark. It is 115m long and 64m across the transepts; the nave is 32.50m wide, and 21m high. The cradle-vaulted Nave is supported by plain angular piers with engaged columns. From the *N. Transept*, preserving murals, a 12C fresco, and good capitals, one may enter (fee) the *Ambulatory*, where on the wall supporting the choir, beyond the entrance to the crypt, is a series of marble *Reliefs*, among them a beardless Christ surrounded

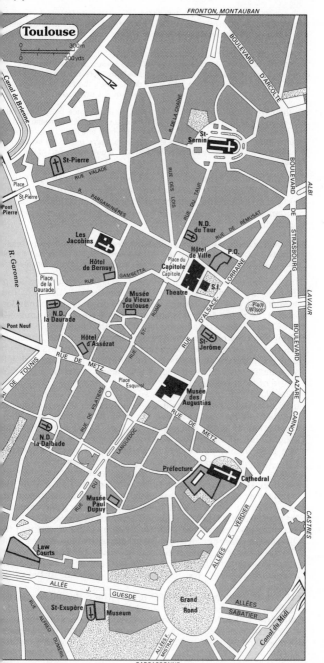

FRONTON, MONTAUBAN

Toulouse

0 ————— 300 m
0 ————— 300 yds

Canal de Brienne

St-Pierre

RUE VALADE

Place St-Pierre

Pont Pierre

R. PARGAMINIÈRES

R. Garonne

Les Jacobins

Hôtel de Bernuy

RUE　GAMBETTA

Place de la Daurade

N.D. la Daurade

Pont Neuf

Hôtel d'Assézat

RUE DE METZ

QAI DE TOUNIS

RUE DE FILATIERS

Place Esquirol

RUE DE METZ

N.D. la Dalbade

RUE DU LANGUEDOC

Musée Paul Dupuy

Law Courts

ALLÉE J. GUESDE

RUE ALFRED DUMERIL

St-Exupère

Museum

R. DE LA CHAINE

R. DES LOIS

RUE DU TAUR

St-Sernin

N.D. du Taur

RUE DE RÉMUSAT

Place du Capitole

Capitole

Hôtel de Ville

P.O.

Théatre

S.I.

RUE D'ALSACE

Musée du Vieux-Toulouse

RUE ST-ROME

St-Jérôme

Musée des Augustins

Préfecture

Cathedral

ALLÉES F. VERDIER

Grand Rond

ALLÉES SABATIER

Canal du Midi

BOULEVARD D'ARCOLE

BOULEVARD DE STRASBOURG

LAVAUR

BOULEVARD LAZARE CARNOT

Place Wilson

CASTRES

ALLÉES F. MISTRAL

CARCASSONNE

ALBI

by symbols of the Evangelists, a late 11C work in the Byzantine style; hanging from the vault is a votive model (1528) of the fortified church.—Steps descend to the restored *Crypt*, containing several shrines and reliquaries, tastefully distributed.

The *Choir* preserves good Renaissance stalls (1670), and behind the altar (a stone table of the 6C, decorated in the 11C, and consecrated by Urban II) is the tomb of St Saturninus (1746) resting on bronze bulls. Note also the corbels of the choir. In the *S. Transept*, facing the Porte des Comtes, the two feet protruding from a pillar (r.) formed the base of a depiction of St Christopher.

To the N.W. is the facade of the 18C *Hôtel du Barry*, once belonging to the brother-in-law of the countess, and visited by Arthur Young, who remarked that 'By some transaction, favourable to anecdote, which enabled him to draw her [Jeanne Bécu] from obscurity, and afterwards to marry her to his brother, he contrived to make a pretty considerable fortune'. It now forms part of the *Lycée St-Sernin.*

To the S.W. is the *Musée St-Raymond*, occupying a building (1510) of the old Collège St-Raymond, a successor (in 1403) of the hospital founded in the late 11C by its patron. It is at present (1983) closed for reorganisation, but will probably house additional archaeological collections.

The street opposite the W. front of St-Sernin leads past (r.) university faculty buildings (to the N. of which is the *Cité Administratif*, on the site of the old Arsenal), and remains of *St-Pierre*, with Romanesque details, to the *Pont St-Pierre*.

The Rue St-Sernin leads S., No. 69 in which is the gate of the *Collège d'Esquile*, by Nicolas Bachelier (1556); on the l. is the 12C *Tour Morand* and part of a former Carmelite convent, the foundation stone of the richly decorated chapel of which was laid by Louis XIII in 1622; at the same time he also laid that of the church of St-Jerome S.E. of the Capitole.—In the Rue du Périgord (l.) is the *Municipal Library*, with an important collection of incunables and MSS.—Continuing down the street, we pass (l.) *N.-D.-du-Taur* (14C; named after St Saturninus's bull), its bell-gable with six angular arches, a common feature of local architecture.

The *Place du Capitole* is dominated by the *Hôtel de Ville* (here called the **Capitole**, being named after the magistrates—capitouls or capitularii— who long governed the city). Its W. front is an Ionic composition of brick and white stone of 1760, which Stendhal thought 'the ugliest building you could imagine, but the rest of the town is so shabby that this huge structure ... is quite a pleasant sight'. The interior courtyard dates from 1606, preserving a door of 1546 by Bachelier. It was here that the Duc de Montmorency was executed in 1632. On 12 April 1814, and for some days after, the Capitole was the scene of great festivity on hearing that peace had been declared; Lord Wellington was received with great applause. The rear facade is late 19C, adjacent to which in the *Sq. Charles-de-Gaulle* stands the restored **Tour du Donjon** (1529), containing the S.I.—For the *Église des Jacobins*, a short distance to the W.; see p 48see p 48.

To the E. of the Capitole is the oval *Pl. Wilson*, beyond which is the shopping precinct of the *Pl. Occitane.*—Further S. is the *Pl. St-Georges*, from which the Rue Boulbonne leads S.E. to the *Pl. St-Étienne.*

On its W. side (with the *Préfecture* to the S. in the former archbishop's palace of 1715) stands the curiously unbalanced **Cathedral**, which, to quote Augustus Hare, was indeed 'greatly abused for its want of regularity, which is carried out even in the details the rose-window ... of its W. front not being in line with the portal

.. below it; but the artist will find a great picturesqueness in the conflicting lines of the interior'.

'he nave was begun in the 11C, and altered in 1211, when its piers were removed, and a vault, unusually wide for the period, was flung across from wall to wall. 'he rose-window dates from 1230. In 1272 Bp Bertrand de l'Isle decided on a new blan on a different axis, but any hope of completing this ambitious work was ater abandoned, although by 1445 a triforium had been added to the choir and a V. doorway built. An oblong tower was later erected, and the 'nave' and choir aults unsymmetrically connected, while in 1609, after a fire, the choir vault vas restored; but it was not until the 1920s that its N. wall was cleared of abuting buildings and a doorway added, similar in style to the W. entrance.

The incongruous interior contains worn tapestries, four of which (the life of St tephen) date from 1533. The choir, probably by the same architect as that of Narbonne, shows the propensity of 13C builders in the Midi towards the Flamoyant style. The Organ-case dates from 1614. The glass of the apse is by Jean nd Arnaud de Moles (1612), possibly of the family of the glass-painters of Auch; hose in the 4th and 8th chapels from the S. date from the 15C. At the S. entrance to the Sanctuary are statues of Antoine de l'Estang (d. 1617), and a Virgin and Child by Arthur Legoust (1625); the corresponding figures on the N. side, of 760, represent Pierre de la Porte (d. 1523), and St Augustine.

The Rue Croix-Baragnon leads W. from the square (in which some ave seen Spanish influence, the word 'barragana' meaning a conubine, usually of the celibate clergy), in which are preserved some f the oldest houses in Toulouse, among them No. 15 (13-14C), and No. 19, the Gothic *Hôtel Bonnefoy*; No. 41 is the 18C *Hôtel de Puivert*.

To the r. on meeting the Rue du Languedoc at the *Pl. Rouaix* is the *Chamber of Commerce* in the 18C *Hôtel de Fumel*, a few steps N. of which is the intersection of the Rue de Metz with the transverse Rue d'Alsace-Lorraine, both driven through the old centre in the late 9C. The ***Musée des Augustines** (founded in 1795), occupying a uilding designed by the ubiquitous Viollet-le-Duc, and those of an Augustinian priory, two 14C cloisters of which are preserved, stands t the N.E. side of this junction, and contains important collections of omanesque and medieval sculpture, and paintings. Its brick belfry vas practically destroyed in 1550. The main entrance is in the Rue e Metz.

The *Great Cloister*, with coupled columns, contains huge gargoyles from the uurch of the Cordeliers, etc. In the Sacristy, Chapter-house, and chapel on its E. de, with remarkable Flamboyant windows of early date (1377), are the collecons of sculpture, including an Angel playing an organ (15C); N.-D.-de-Grâce aid 15C); St Paul (14C), from the Chapelle de Rieux; an alabaster Virgin and hild; the Tomb of a knight (c. 1292), and other funerary effigies, including that f Jean Tissandier; two women with a lion and ram (from St-Sernin); keystones, c. The display is continued in the *Church*, containing a charming early 16C one Virgin, and terracotta statues from St-Sernin. Among the paintings are an *non*. Miracle of St Anthony of Toulouse (an Albigensian is converted at the ght of an ass which knelt before the Host, neglecting its feed); History of the aptist (early 16C Dutch); a late 15C Deposition; *Van Dyck*, Crucifixion; *Rubens*, hrist between the thieves (the central figure only being completed); *Nicolas* urnier, Virgin and Child, Deposition, and Entombment; and works by *Vouet*, uvenet, et al.—The *Little Cloister*, to the N.W., dates from 1626.

From the S.W. corner of the larger cloister one ascends to a room displaying a ne ***Collection of capitals** from the cloister of La Daurade, from St-Étienne, and -Sernin, and Paleo-Christian sarcophagi (5-8C), while in a passage below are exmples of epigraphy, including some Jewish inscriptions.—On the FIRST LOOR, to the W. of the cloister, are the main picture galleries, some on two vels, containing: *Jean Chalette* (1581 – 1644), Portrait of a Canon (1623); *anon.* ortrait of Descartes; *De Troy*, Pierre Goudouli, the poet; *Philippe de Cham-*

paigne, Louis XIII conferring the Order of the Holy Ghost (1663); allegorical
paintings by *Antoine Rivalz* (Toulouse, 1667–1735), *Subleyras*, and pupils
Oudry, Louis XIV stag-hunting; *Rigaud*, the Marquis de Grosbois; *Largillière*
Self-portrait; *G.-J. Roques* (Toulouse, 1754–1847), Self-portrait, Portrait of his
mother, and Death of Marat; *Vigée-Lebrun*, the Baronne de Crussol; *Gros*, Por
trait of his wife; *Gérard*, Portrait of Gros, aged 20; *Ingres*, Sébastien Desmarets
Antoinette-Cécile-Hortense Haudebourg-Lescot (1784–1845), Two Merveill
euses; *Solimena*, Female portrait; *Mirevelt*, Male portrait; *Beschey*, Fish-market
and Game-market; *W. de Poorter*, Lucrecia; and works by *Momper II, Frans
Franken, Guardi, Caneletto,* and *Toulouse-Lautrec*; also several Nottingham
alabasters.

Immediately to the W. is the *Pl. Esquirol*, whence the pedestrian Rue
des Changes and its continuation, the Rue St-Rome, lead back to the
Pl. du Capitole, both containing several 16-17C houses preserving
architectural features of interest, to the W. of which is the
dilapidated *Musée du Vieux-Toulouse*, installed in the late 16C *Hôtel
d'Antoine du May*.

For the area S. of the Pl. Esquirol, see below.

The Rue de Metz leads W. past (r.) the **Hôtel d'Assézat* (1558; or
the plans of Bachelier, with an upper storey added in the 17C). In
1896 the mansion was bequeathed to the learned societies of
Toulouse, among which was the Académie des Jeaux Floraux (see
p 481), whose seat it is.

Further W. is the *Pont Neuf* (1544–1626), which crosses the Garonne to the
suburb of *St-Cyprien*, where stands the *Hôtel-Dieu St-Jacques* (founded 1258
with 17-18C buildings); *St-Nicolas*, preserving 15C statues; and to the N., the
Hospice St-Joseph de la Grave, its chapel with a brick dome completed in 1830

Turning N. along the E. bank of the river we shortly reach the *Pl. de
la Daurade*, whence an older Pont Neuf used to cross the Garonne
from the Capitole. The adjacent 18C *Church* stands on the site of a
Gallo-Roman basilica containing the golden mosaics (dorata), from
which it derived its name.

The Rue Jean-Suau leads E., continued by the Rue Gambetta, on
the l. of which is the **Hôtel Bernuy* (1530), the first court of which
contains good Renaissance work.—The Rue Lakanal turns l. to ap
proach the ***Église des Jacobins**, with its graceful octagonal tower
(1230–94).

It was used as an artillery regiment's barracks in the early 19C, and divided into
storeys, with stables below, and its thorough restoration was only completed
and the floor paved, in 1965. It is remarkable for its single row of seven column
(22m high), and beautiful fan vaulting at the E. end. The painted imitation of
brickwork is unfortunate. The rose-windows on the W. wall retain 14C glass; the
rest is by Max Ingrand. Below the modern altar are relics of Thomas Aquinus
previously in St-Sernin. The reconstructed *Cloister* (1310), Chapter-house, an
Chapelle St-Antonin (1340; with remains of contemporary frescoes) may also b
visited.

From just N., the Rue Romiguières leads back to the Pl. due Capitole
Further N. is the 15C *Collège de Foix*, and the 14C *Tower* of the
former *Église des Cordeliers*, burnt down in 1871, not surprisingly, a
it was used as a hay-barn.

There are several buildings of interest in the area S. of the Pl. Es
quirol, among them, at No. 36 Rue du Languedoc, the *Hôtel de
Béringuier-Maynier* (or *du Vieux-Raisin*; 1573), with a charming
courtyard, while No. 16 is the *Hôtel de la Belle Paul*
(15-16C).—From the former, the Rue Ozenne leads S.E., in which

No. 8 is the *Hôtel de Guillermy*, and No. 9, the *Hôtel Tournoer* or *l'Aussargues*, both 16C.

To the l., at 13 Rue de la Pleau, is the **Musée Paul Dupuy**, occupying the 17C *Hôtel Bessón* (at present closed), but containing a collection of regional applied art, etc., including 18C faïence from local factories, a pharmacy from the former Jesuit College (1632), collections of tools and utensils illustrating domestic and rural life in Languedoc; old maps and prints, and drawings by local artists.

The Rue Ozenne ends at the Allées Jules Guesde; see p 482.

Some distance S.E. of the Grand Rond, at 43 Rue des Martyrs-de-la-Resistance, is the *Musée Labit*, containing Middle and Far Eastern collections, including ceramics and sculpture, bronzes, costumes, and drawings of interest to the orientalist.

By turning r. on reaching the Allées, which leads W. towards the *Pont St-Michel* (1962), we approach the *Pl. du Parliament*, on the N.E. side of which is the *Palais de Justice* (1847), facing the *Pl. du Salins*, where the Inquisition used to celebrate their autos-da-fe.—Nos 21 and 47 in the adjacent Rue Pharaon are of interest.

The Rue de la Fonderie leads N., continued by the Rue de la Dalbade, with several old mansions, among them the *Hôtel Felzins or Molinier (No. 22), with two courtyards of 1556; and No. 25 (l.), with an elaborate facade of 1615, is the *Maison de Pierre*, a rare example of stone-building in old Toulouse, with a courtyard by Bachelier (1545). Note also Nos 29, 32, and 37. Wide-vaulted *N.-D.-de-la-Dalbade* (1503 – 42), restored since its brick tower collapsed in 1926, preserves a remarkable Renaissance portal by Mérigon Bailhan. The Rue de Metz is regained a short distance N.

Relics of its *Roman Amphitheatre* may be seen to the N.W. of the city, to the E. of the D2 before it crosses the river Touch.—The scanty remains of the Gallic oppidum of *Vieille-Toulouse* lie some 11km S., approached by the D4 skirting the E. bank of the Garonne, and the D95.

For roads from Toulouse to *Agen* and *Bordeaux*, and to *Montauban, Cahors*, and *Limoges*, see Rtes 76, and 64, respectively, in reverse; for *Auch* and *Pau*, Rtes 84B and A, in reverse; for **Foix**, Rte 87; for **Carcassonne** and *Castres*, Rtes 88A and B; for *Albi*, Rte 89, in reverse.

87 Toulouse to Foix and Bourg-Madame

180km (112 miles). N20. 33km *Auterive*—31km **Pamiers**—19km **Foix**—16km *Tarascon-sur-Ariège*—26km **Ax-les-Thermes**—55km **Bourg-Madame**.

Maps: IGN 64, 71, or 114. M 235.

The A64 motorway likewise drives S.W. from the city (see Rte 86), to join the N20 (from which the N117 bears r. after 12km; see Rte 84A) on the r. bank of the Garonne near its confluence with the Ariège, the course of which the route follows.—10km. *Vernet-Venerque*, on the far bank, preserves a Romanesque church of slight interest.—11km. *Auterive*.

9km.—2km l. on the E. bank of the Ariège lies *Cintegabelle*, with a 12-14C church, 2km S.E. of which are the relics of the abbey of *Boulbonne* (reconstructed in the 18C), while c. 3km N.E., approached by the D25, is the restored brick *Pigeonnier of Bouyssou*.—8km further E., at *Montgeard*, a bastide are a fortified 16C church, and ruined castle.

10km. *Saverdun*, where we cross the river, was the birthplace of Jacques Fournier, later Pope Benedict XII (1334–42).—9.5km. To the right is the ruined castle of *Bonnac*, beyond which the Pyrenees come into view ahead.

5.5km. **PAMIERS** (15,100 Appaméans), the largest town in the Ariège, is not its most attractive: in some respects it has little changed since it was visited by Arthur Young in 1787, who condemned it as 'ugly, stinking, and ill built'.

The lordship of Pamiers was a frequent bone of contention between the Count of Foix and the Abbot of St Antonin; it was often the place of debate or conference during the Albigensian crusade; the Statute of 1212 strengthening Simon de Montfort's control over Languedoc was promulgated here; and here in 1231 Guillaume Bélibaste, the last Prefect to be lured into the hands of the Inquisition was burned. It suffered from plague in 1553. The abbey of St-Antonin (S. of the town) was destroyed in 1586, and most of its other medieval churches were gravely mutilated by the Huguenots. It was sacked by Condé in 1628.

Pamiers was the birthplace of Gabriel Fauré (1845–1924), and of Théophile Delcassé (1852–1920), principal author of the 'Entente Cordiale' of 1904.

Just N.E. of the undistinguished *Pl. de la République* stands *N.-D.-du Camp* (16C), preserving a broad brick facade of the 14C and Romanesque portal; N. of its apse is the ruined *Tour des Cordeliers* of 1512.—From the W. end of the Place one turns S. to approach the brick-built *Cathedral*, retaining its 14C octagonal tower but restored in a mock medieval Tolosan style in the late 17C; it contains a contemporary organ.—The *Lycée* at which Fauré taught has been incorporated in a modern building to the N.E.—To the N.W. is the *Hôtel de Ville*, and beyond, an old town gate.—To the S.W. is the umbrageous *Butte du Castella* (or *Castelas*), site of the medieval castle overlooking the Ariège, and providing a view of the Pyrenees.

Mirepoix (see Rte 90) lies 23km E.—Continuing S., at 9.5km *Varilhes* is traversed, and the ridge of the *Montagnes du Plantaurel* or *Petites-Pyrénées* are crossed by threading a defile.—4km. *St-Jean-de-Verges*, with a 12C church.

5.5km. **FOIX** (380m; 10,100 Fuxéens), préfecture of the Ariège, standing at the confluence of that river with the Arget, is—with the exception of the imposing silhouette of its three-towered castle—an unremarkable town, although pleasantly sited.

It grew up in the 10C round an abbey built over the grave of St Volusian (an archbishop of Tours), exiled by the Arian Alaric II, and martyred at Varilhes c. 497. Bernard Roger, Viscount of Carcassone, built the castle in 1012, and his son Roger assumed the title of Count of Foix. In 1272 Roger Bernard III was forced to acknowledge the suzerainty of Philippe le Hardi, but in 1280 united his house to Béarn by marriage with Marguerite, the heiress of that county, so that Foix became the direct property of the crown on the accession of Henri IV.

The Ariège is crossed to approach the central Allées de Villote. A lane to the r. on the far side of the bridge leads shortly to *St-Volusien*, a wide-aisled 14C building with an older porch, behind which is the *Préfecture* in a 17C mansion, the gardens of which occupy the angle between the rivers.

From the W. end of the Allées the Rue St-James, extended by the Rue du Rocher, leads up to a small square adjacent to the *Palais de Justice*. Hence a steeply climbing rough path ascends to the **Castle** entirely dominating the town. It only surrendered to Philippe le Hardi after his threat to blow up its foundations. Its main features are the slender N. tower (12C), connected by a vaulted hall to the square 14C central tower, beyond which rises a cylindrical 15C tower. Long used as a prison, it now contains a departmental museum 'of which the guide knows how to make the most', to quote the succinct phrase of Henry Myhill. Tours are conducted, and much time can be wasted waiting to enter.

The D1 leads c. 6km N.W. to the underground river of *Labouiche*, with stalactite formations, parts of which may be traversed by boat.
  For the road to *St-Girons*, and *Quillan*, see Rte 85.

On quitting Foix, the road follows the E. bank of the Ariège, shortly passing the conical hill known as the *Pain du Sucre* (l.), just beyond which, at 7km, the D117 turns l.—4.5km. *Mercus*, whose church has notable dog-tooth ornament.—Ahead, at the far end of the valley rises the *Pic des trois Seigneurs* (2119m). The road curves l. to (4.5m) **Tarascon-sur-Ariège** (474m), with electro-metallurgical works, at the mouth of the Vicdessos valley. It has two conspicuous towers, one belonging to its old castle, the other the 15C belfry of *St-Michel's*; the church of *La Daurade* has a 16C door, while on the spur commanding the junction of the two valleys is Romanesque *N.-D.de-Sabart.*

TARASCON TO AUZAT (16km). The D8 leads S.W. to (4km) *Niaux*, N.E. of which is the ***Grotte de Niaux**, ◇ a remarkable prehistoric cavern containing unusually well-preserved drawings of animals of the Magdalenian period (c. 20,000 B.C.) in a huge chamber some distance from its entrance.—10km. *Vicdessos*, a mountain village with an old castle and 13C belfry, and abandoned iron-mines in the vicinity, is connected by a mountain road with *Aulus-les-Bains* in the valley of the Garbet to the W. From the adjacent village of *Auzat*, with hydro-electrical works, several ascents may be made, among them the *Pic de Montclam* (3078m), and the **Pic d'Estats** (3145m) to the S.W., the latter the highest peak in the Pyrenees E. of the Maladetta. From the far end of the mountain-encircled valley a number of high-lying bridle-passes lead W. into Spain or E. into Andorra.

Beyond Tarascon the N20 bears S.E. through a defile, passing (l.) *Ussat-les-Bains*, and (r.) the *Grottes de Lombrives*, a huge cavern connected with that of Niaux (see above; enquire at the S.I. in Ussat), in which it is said some hundreds of Albigensians were walled-in to starve to death in the early 13C. After (10.5km) *Les Cabannes* the valley expands. To the E. rises the *Pic de St-Barthélemy*; see below.

7km. At *Unac*, on the far side of the valley, is a Romanesque church, whence a mountain road ascends past *Lordat*, with its ruined 13-15C *Castle. At *Axiat*, just to the N., is another Romanesque church. The road continues to climb N.E. from Lordat towards (12km) the *Col de Trimouns*, with talc mines not far E. of the *Pic Soularac* (2368m) and adjacent *Pic de St-Barthélemy* (2348m), both of which may be ascended from here, and which overlooked the site of *Montségur*, some distance further N.E.; see Rte 85.

8.5km. **Ax-les-Thermes** (720m), a sulphurous spa of ancient origin (ad Aquas) situated at the confluence of the Lauze and the Oriège with the Ariège, and a centre for excursions into the surrounding mountains, and for skiing (on the *plateaux de Bonascre* and *du Saquet* to the S.W., beyond which rises the *Tute de l'Ours*, 2255m). Ax was the birthplace of François Mansart (1598–1666). The *Bassin des Ladres* in the Pl. du Breilh has remains of a bathing-pool of a hospital founded here in 1260. *St-Vincent*, to the N., is mainly 17C.

For the road from Ax to *Quillan* and *Axat*, see Rte 89.

The N20 ascends due S. along the narrowing valley of the Ariège through (8.5km) *Mérens-les-Vals*, with the ruins of a Romanesque church to the S.E., burned in 1811 by Spanish Miquelets (armed frontier guards more often engaged in brigandage).—9.5km *L'Hospitalet* (1436m; Customs post), overlooked to the W. by the *Pic de la Cabanette* (2818m), and to the E. by *Pic Pédrous* (2842m). The road begins to zigzag up towards the *Col de Puymorens* (1915m), before which the N22 diverges r. towards *Andorra*.

After 6km the latter road reaches the frontier at the *Pas de la Case* (2091m; French Customs), near the *Étang de Font-Nègre*, the source of the Ariège, beyond which it zigzags up to (4km) the **Port d'Envalira** (2407m), the highest road-pass across the Pyrenees, providing spectacular views, before descending as steeply to (7.5km) *Soldeu* (1826m), the first and highest village in **Andorra**, the capital of which, *Andorra la Vella*, lies 18.5km S.W. at 1029m, and only 20km N. of *Seo de Urgel* in Spain. Independent Andorra, although preserving some wild romantic mountain scenery in its isolated upper valleys, now subsists on a particularly obnoxious form of tourism, the streets of its unattractive boom-towns below being lined with hotels, garages, and shops supplying everything from souvenirs to untaxed luxury goods. For its history, and description, see *Blue Guide Spain*.

At the Col de Puymorens the watershed is crossed, and the road descends the Mediterranean slope of the *Cerdagne*. To the E. is the **Pic Carlit** (2921m), the highest of the Eastern Pyrenean peaks within France, the summit of which may be ascended from *Porté-Puymorens*, at the foot of the col. Threading the defile of *La Faou* we bear S.E. below *Puig Pédros* (or *de Campcardos*; 2905m), marking the Spanish frontier to the S.W., and shortly pass the two *Tours de Carol* (13C) before descending to *Latour-de-Carol* (1248m), the last French station on the international railway, and the junction of the line to **Font-Romeu**. This resort, c. 15km N.E., is approached by road from *Ur*, 5km beyond Latour-de-Carol, for which, and for **Bourg-Madame** (3.5km S. of Ur), see Rte 147; likewise for the Spanish enclave of *Llivia*.

88 Toulouse to Béziers

A. Via Carcassonne and Narbonne

174km (108 miles). N113. 55km **Castelnaudary**—37km **Carcassonne**—55km **Narbonne**—N9. 27km **Béziers**.

Maps: IGN 64, 72, or 114; also 310. M 235, 240.

The A61 motorway runs more or less parallel to the N113, providing rapid access to the principal towns en route.

Driving S.E. from **Toulouse** (Rte 86), the road runs close to and parallel to the **Canal du Midi** for much of the way.

This canal was constructed in 1666–81 largely at the expense of Paul Riquet of Béziers (1604–80), and connects the Garonne with the Mediterranean. It starts at the Bassin de l'Embouchure, just below Toulouse, and descends through 46 locks to end in the Étang de Thau near Agde, a distance of c. 240km. It was prolonged in the 19C towards Bordeaux by the Canal Latéral de la Garonne, built to avoid difficult reaches of the river, and extended E. by the Canal des Étangs to meet the Rhône at Beaucaire.

The canal is crossed at 21km, just beyond which (l.) *Bazièg*e, and (6km) *Villenouvelle*, possess fortified belfries of a type peculiar to the district, the best example of which is at *Villefranche-de-Lauragais* (6km beyond), above the façade of its 14C brick church.

7km. *Avignonet-Lauragais*, with remains of its walls, the conspicuous hill-top church of which preserves a graceful 16C spire, was the site of the assassination of four inquisitors in May 1242 by a group of knights from Montségur, led by Pierre-Roger de Mirepoix, an action to some extent precipitating the final attack on the Cathar stronghold the following year.—We cross the *Col de Naurouze* (190m) 3km beyond, where an obelisk marks the point where the Canal du Midi crosses the watershed. Soult and Wellington signed the armistice after the Battle of Toulouse in the neighbouring *Maison de l'Ingénieur* (April 1814).—At *Montmaur*, 6km N., is an imposing medieval castle, while at *Les Cassés*, 5km beyond, 50 Cathars were burned alive by Simon de Montfort, when found hidden in a tower.—*Labastide d'Anjou*, founded in 1370 by Louis d'Anjou, brother of Charles V, is by-passed prior to entering (12km) **Castelnaudary** (11,400 Castelnaudariens or Chauriens), which may also be by-passed, where 14C *St-Michel* has a street running beneath its tower.

The town was taken by Simon de Montfort in 1211, and resisted a siege by Raymond VI. Amaury, Montfort's son, was knighted here, but in 1220 it held out for some months when in turn besieged by Amaury. Here in 1235, when making a tour of the Toulousain, the inquisitors were met by a conspiracy of silence. In 1632 Henri de Montmorency was captured here before being put to death at Toulouse. It was the birthplace of Pierre de Castelnau (cf. St-Gilles). Its 'cassoulets' are reputed.

Of more interest is the *Cathedral of **St-Papoul**, 8km N.E., with a Romanesque choir rebuilt in the 14C, containing the tomb of Bp François de Donadieu (d. 1626). On the S. side is a cloister, with remains of a chapter-house.—The road goes on to (14km) *Saissac*, with ruins of a 14C castle, at the foot of the *Montagne Noire*, a granitic mass of thickly forested hills.
    The D623 leads S.E. from Castlenaudary to (19km) the crossroads below *Fanjeaux*, and *Limoux*, 23km beyond; see Rtes 90 and 89 respectively.
    The D33 runs parallel to and S. of the main road through (9km) *Pexiora*, with an imposing square church tower, and (7.5km) *Bram*, with a 17C château, where Simon de Montfort blinded the whole garrison but one, when he captured the place.

The N113 continues S.E. from Castelnaudary, with views N. towards the *Montagne Noire* (see above) through (20km) *Alzonne*, 6km N. of which are the ruins of the Cistercian abbey of *Villelongue*, founded in 1150.—The road from Saissac (see above) comes in from the l. just prior to (8km) *Pezens*, with a 14C church, 4km beyond which we pass (l.) the 16C château of *Pennautier*, where De Montfort had his base camp c. 1210, and shortly after enter Carcassonne from the N.W.
    CARCASSONNE (42,450 inhab.), préfecture of the *Aude*, is famous for its medieval fortified *Cité*—which some have said looks its best when seen from the motorway—rising to the S.E. of the modern town, the hexagonal centre of which retains the regular plan of a bastide, which lies between the river Aude and the Canal du Midi.

Gallic *Carcasso* was occupied by the Visigoths in the 5-8C, and rose to prominence in the 12C under its viscounts, the Trencavels. In August 1209, when taken by Albigensian crusaders led by Arnald-Amaury, Abbot of Citeaux, Raymond-Roger VI was captured (and soon after died), the viscountcy, was offered to Simon de Montfort. After the latter's death in 1218, Raymond-Roger's son, Raymond-Roger VII Trencavel, recovered his estates, but was dispossessed of them in 1229. The *Ville Basse* was laid out after 1247, but in 1355 this was burnt to the ground by the Black Prince, thwarted in his attempt to take the strengthened citadel. The ramparts were allowed to fall into decay after 1659, when Roussillon was annexed to France, for Perpignan replaced it as a frontier fortress. Its demolition for building stone was averted by Mérimée, who from 1834 was Inspector-general of Historical Monuments, and by the appeals of J.O. Cros-Mayreville (1810–76), a local archaeologist. Its all-too-thorough restoration was commenced in 1855 by Viollet-le-Duc, and continued by Boeswillwald after 1879, since when its walls and towers have mellowed with time.

It was the birthplace of Philippe Fabre d'Eglantine (1755–94; guillotined), the poet and inventor of the names in the Republican calendar.

Two bastions of the Ville Basse may be seen in the Blvd Barbés, on the S. side of the old town of narrow streets, which may be entered through the *Porte des Jacobins* (1778) or beside adjacent *St-Michel* (14C), with a good rose-window. Further N., beyond the central *Pl. Carnot*, stands *St-Vincent*, larger and slightly later in date, with a wide nave and tall 16C octagonal tower. To the E. is the *Sq. Gambetta*, on the W. side of which is the S.I. and *Museum*, with a small collection of paintings, including several by the Surrealists, etc.

Hence one may cross either the *Pont Neuf* (1846), providing a view of the 13C *Pont Vieux* and of the Cité, or the latter bridge, to approach the main E. entrance (the *Porte Narbonnaise*) to the **Cité**, near which are car-parks.—A recommended alternative, on crossing the Pont Vieux, is to turn sharp r. and follow the Rue de la Barbacane to *St-Gimer*. Hence one may climb a path dominated by the *Château Comptal* to enter the fortified enceinte—comprising some 50 towers altogether—by the *Porte d'Aude*. One first traverses part of the Lices between the two rows of ramparts, astride which, further S., stands the 13C *Tour Carrée de l'Évêqué*. The *Château* ◇ itself, of c. 1125, but greatly altered since, largely used as barracks for a century prior to 1926, and now containing a small lapidary museum, is separated from the rest of the town by a dry moat. Excavations have established that it occupies the site of a Gallo-Roman castellum, while most of the towers of the inner ramparts have Roman or Visigothic foundations. Those on the S.W. side, notable for their projecting beaks, were added by Philippe le Hardi in 1285; the other ramparts are mainly due to Louis IX (1270). The inner towers to the N.E. have been re-roofed with tiles, the slate used to roof other turrets being one major error in Viollet-le-Duc's reconstruction; another is his conical pepper-pot roofs rather than the much flatter southern type, an expensive error being corrected.

Of more interest is *St-Nazaire*, ◇ further S., one of the finest churches in the Midi, the transeptal turrets and Romanesque W. tower of which are noteworthy. The plain Romanesque nave of 1095 is abutted by a graceful Gothic choir of c. 1300.

The interior is remarkable for its 14-16C glass, particularly in the transeptal roses, and on the S. side a stone relief depicts one of the 13C sieges of Carcassonne. In the S. transept is the tombstone of Simon de Montfort, who was later translated to Montfort l'Amaury (cf.); several bishop's tombs are notable, as is the 17C organ-case; the organ itself is under repair.

One may follow lanes to the N.E., mostly disfigured by souvenir shops, to reach the *Porte Narbonnaise*, with its two towers guarded

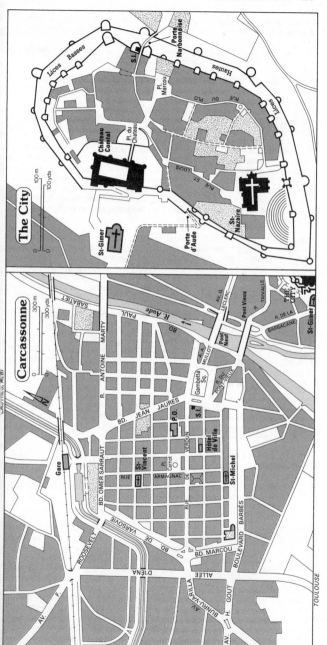

The City

Lices Basses

Ponte Narbonaise

S.I.

Pl. Marcou

Hautes

RUE DU PLO

Lices

Château Comtal

Pl. du Château

RUE ST-LOUIS

SINUS

St-Gimer

Porte d'Aude

St-Nazaire

100 m / 100 yds

Carcassonne

300 m / 300 yds

R. ANTOINE MARTY

SABATIER

BD. PAUL

R. AUDE

AV. G. LECLERC

Pont Vieux

R. TRIVALLE

THE CITY

R. DE LA BARBACANE

St-Gimer

AV. A. MULLOT

Pont Neuf

Gambetta Sq.

R. DU PECH

BD. JEAN JAURÈS

P.O.

S.I.

VERDUN

Hôtel de Ville

BD. OMER SARRAUT

Gare

St-Vincent

RUE

Pl. Carnot

ARMAGNAC

RUE DE

St-Michel

BD. DE VARSOVIE

ROOSEVELT

BOULEVARD BARBÈS

AV. F.

D'IÉNA

ALLÉE

BD. MARCOU

AV. BUNAU-VARILLA

AV. H. GOUT

TOULOUSE

TOULOUSE

TOULOUSE, AIRPORT, FOIX

TOULOUSE, ALBI

by a double barbican. Immediately to the N. is the huge *Tour de Trésor*, which has no communication with the rampart-walk.

For the road N. to *Castres* and **Albi**, and S. to *Quillan* and beyond, see Rte 89; for that to *Mirepoix, Pamiers, St-Girons*, and **Luchon**, see Rte 90.

CARCASSONNE TO BÉZIERS VIA CAPESTANG (76km). The D610 forks l. 6km E. of Carcassonne, crossing the Aude and Canal du Midi.—22.5km. *Rieux-Minervois*, 8.5km N.W., has a round 11C church.—4.5km. *Homps*.—**Minerve**, 11.5km N., on the far side of a ridge, is a curiously sited fortified village overlooking the confluence of the Cesse and the Briant. An Albigensian stronghold, it was bombarded by De Montfort in 1209, and 140 heretics were burned after the place surrendered. The main road may be regained 15km to the S.E., near *Cabezac*, and 14km beyond Homps.—8km. *La Croisade*, 4km N. of which is the interesting 10-11C church of *Ste-Marie* at *Quarante*, in which the shells on the crossing will be noted—7km. *Capestang*, with an imposing but un-finished 13-14C church, only the huge apse and choir of which were completed, just beyond which a r.-hand turning leads via *Poilhès* to the Oppidum of *Enserune*; see Rte 145.—The main road traverses (8km) *Montady*, with its curious concentric *Étang*, better seen from Ensérune, shortly beyond comman-ding a view ahead of (7km) **Béziers**.

CARCASSONNE TO ST-PONS (65km). Driving N.W., after 5km we turn r. onto the D620, passing (l.) *Conques-sur-Orbiel*, with relics of its castle and a Gothic church, to (15.5km) *Caunes-Minervois*, an old village with notable remains of a Benedictine abbey, beyond which the wooded gorge of *Argent-Double* is thread-ed, by which the *Montagne Noire* is crossed to (7km) *Citou*, with a ruined castle. Climbing round below the *Roc de Peyremaux* (1008m), the road bears N.E. over minor passes to reach the N112 at *Courniou*, 5km W. of **St-Pons**; see Rte 88B.

The N113 drives E. from Carcassonne, with a good view of the Cité, and after 7km follows the S. bank of the Aude, with the ridge known as the *Montagne d'Alaric* to the S., on which stand the ruins of the 11-12C *Château de Miramont*.—28km. *Lézignan-Corbières*, by-passed, preserves a few old houses.—At 16km the D613 leads r. to (9km) the abbey of **Fontfroide**; see Rte 146, likewise for **Narbonne**, 5km beyond this turning.

From Narbonne the N9 leads N.E. via (7km) *Coursan*, with a Gothic church, where the Aude is crossed, 9.5km beyond which a l.-hand turning leads up to the oppidum of **Enserune** on a ridge to the N.W., for which and for **Béziers**, 10.5km further N.E., see Rte 145.

B.   Via Castres and St-Pons

173km (107 miles). N126. 71km **Castres**—N112. 16km **Mazamet** lies 2km S.—35km **St-Pons**—51km **Béziers**.

Maps: IGN 64, 65, or 114; also 310. M 235, 240.

TOULOUSE TO CASTRES VIA LAVAUR (76km). This alternative route follows the D112 N.E. over several ridges through (21km) *Verfeil*, where in 1145 its an-ticlerical inhabitants humiliated St Bernard by walking out of the church when he began to speak, and hammering on doors to silence his sermon in the street.—16km. **Lavaur** (8300 Vauréens), ancient *Vaurum*, on the Agout, the seat of a bishopric from 1318 until the Revolution. Its fortress made a heroic resistance to Simon de Montfort in 1211, for which its châtelain was thrown into a well and lapidated, while her brother and 90 knights were massacred; some 3-400 heretics were merely burned alive. In the New Year of 1213 a council of bishops here refused to restore to Pedro II of Aragón the lands which De Mont-fort had expropriated; the following September Pedro was killed at Muret. Com-te Emmanuel de Las Casas (1766–1842), author of 'Reminiscences of St Helena', was born here. Brick *St-Alain* (13th—early 16C), the chapel on the S. side of which contains a door of its predecessor destroyed in 1211, was the former cathedral, and has two dissimilar towers. The interior has been disfigured by 19C paintwork. *St-Francis* dates from the 14-15C.—The road leads up the valley of the Agout, passing (l.) the bastides of *Viterbe* and *Damiatte*, bearing the names of famous medieval fortresses, to (15km) *Guitalens*. At 3.5km we pass near (l.) *Cuq*, with a 13C castle, and N. of *Vielmur-sur-Agout*, with an 18C church and other dependencies of a Benedictine abbey founded in 1038, and 9.5km beyond, enter **Castres**; see below.

The N126 leads E. across a series of low hills and valleys to (38km) *Cuq-Toulza*, 7km S. of which is *Montgey*. There in 1211 a German contingent of Albigensian crusaders was ambushed and massacred, and De Montfort burnt it to the ground in retaliation.—11km. **Puylaurens**, once a Cathar centre, was the birthplace of Guillaume de Puylaurens (c. 1210–95), a chronicler of the Albigensian Crusade, and in the 17-18C was famous for its Protestant Academy which flourished under Pierre Bayle and his disciples.

14km S. lies *Revel*, a bastide of 1332, with an old wooden *Market-hall* in its central square, 3km S.E. of which is the *Bassin de St-Ferréol*, the principal reservoir for the Canal du Midi; see first section of Rte 88A.—5.5km E. of Revel lies *Sorèze*, an old village, and site of an abbey founded by Pepin le Bref in 758, of which little remains, and since 1854 of the more famous Dominican Collège in the 17C buildings of a Benedictine abbey founded as a counterblast to Puylaurens (see above). Lacordaire was its principal until 1861.—At *En Calcut*, 7.5km N.E. of Sorèze, are two Benedictine establishments of 1895–1936.—At *St-Félix-Lauragais*, 9.5km W. of Revel, are a 14C church, and castle.

9km. *Soual*, where the N126 veers N.E. to (13km) Castres, and the D621 continues E. via (13km) *Labruguière*, with a tall 14C belfry and 13C castle, to *Mazamet*, 11km beyond; see below.

   Castres (46,900 Castraits), a busy textile town, and long a cloth-working centre, is built largely on the W. bank of the swiftly flowing Agout.

It was the ancient *Castra Albiensium*, the site of a Benedictine abbey from 673–1317, and seat of a bishop from 1317–1790, although a Protestant stronghold from 1595–1678. Here in Sept. 1209 took place the first public burning of Albigensian heretics, under the personal supervision of Simon de Montfort. It was the birthplace of the savant André Dacier (1651–1722); Paul Rapin (1661–1729), the historian; Lord Ligonier (1680–1770), the British Field-marshal, a Huguenot refugee; and the socialist statesman Jean Jaurès (1850–1914).

In the town centre is *St-Benoit* (1678–1718), once the cathedral, to the S. of which is the former *Bishop's Palace* (1666), designed by Jules Hardouin Mansart, incorporating the Romanesque belfry of the ancient abbey. It is now occupied by the *Mairie* and the ***Musée Goya** (on the First Floor).

The collection, of particular interest for the study of Spanish art, and assembled by the painter Marcel Briguiboul (1837–92), presures four important works by Goya. The 17-18C Salle des États Diocésians contains a Portrait of Lord Ligonier by *Saura*, and his bust by L.-F. Roubillac; and an ivory helmet made for George II of England by David Lemarchand. Other rooms display: *Rodrigo de Osona the Younger*, Death of St Martin; *Aléjo Fernández*, Adoration of the Magi; *Morales*, Christ bound; *Borassa*, Flagellation; *Garcia de Benabarre*, Adoration of the Kings; *Murillo*, Virgin and Child with a rosary; works by *Valdes Leal*; *Ribera*, Mitred abbot, and Hercules resting; *Velázquez* and *Del Mazo*, Portrait of Philip IV; *Bayeu*, Man with a red waistcoat; *De Crayer*, Equestrian portrait of the Marquis de Leganez; *Claudio Coello*, Girl with green ribbons; *Melendez*, Still life; and *Fortuny*, Bulls.
   Among works by *Goya* are: Self-portrait wearing spectacles (c. 1793); Portrait

of Francisco del Mazo (c. 1820); Portrait of Mathias Allué (c. 1780); The Junta of the Philippines (c. 1814); and sets of his engravings. Also *Eugenio Lucas y Padilla*, The Diligence, Extreme Unction, The Fusillade, Bull-fighting scenes, and Witches' Sabbath, etc. Among more modern paintings are works by *Berruete*, *Zubiaurre*, and *Javier Bueno*, and *Zuloaga*, Portrait of Maurice Barrès.

To the S. are formal gardens laid out by Le Nôtre, while several 16-17C houses may be seen in the quarter N. of the Rue Émile-Zola, among them the *Hôtel Nayrac*. Further W. is the *Lycée Jean-Jaurès*, incorporating a 13C tower and cloister of a Franciscan convent. Dilapidated balconied houses overlook the river.

For the road to **Albi**, 42km N., see Rte 89.

CASTRES TO PÉZENAS VIA LACAUNE (131km). The longer alternative minor road via *Vabre* is first described.—The D89 leads N.E. for 5km, turning r. along the Agout valley to *Burlats*, with a 12C church (under restoration) and house of the same period. Crossing the river, we turn l. and climb r. onto the *Sidobre plateau*, partly wooded, and covered with granite boulders; also characteristic of the landscape are the smaller valleys clogged with chaotic runs of boulders, or 'rivières de rochers'; also rocking-stones, among other curious formations. One may regain the main route beyond the quarry-village of *Lacrouzette* by driving S.E. past the *Lac du Merle*, or by continuing E. past the chaos of *Las Hortès*, later turning l. across the Agout through *Vabre*. Thence the Gijou valley is followed via *Lacaze*, where the imposing ruined 12C castle was added to in the 17C, the road later passing, through *Viane*, a centre of Portestantism since the 16C, with the ruins of the older town above, and veering S.E. for *Lacaune*.

The main route follows the D622, likewise traversing the *Sidobre*. Beyond (8km) *La Fontasse* there are 'rivières de rochers' at no great distance on either side of the road. Several rocking-stones are later passed, the most remarkable being the *Sept Faux*.—At 9km a l.-hand turning leads down into the valley of the Agout to the impressive ruins of the castle of *Ferrières*, whence one may regain the road at slate-roofed Brassac.—6.5km. *Brassac*, with ruined ramparts and castle, lies on the Agout, here crossed by two bridges, one Gothic.

Hence several minor road cross the *Parc Natural du Haut Languedoc*, among them one leading S.E. via *Anglès* to *St-Pons*; a more northerly one, above the r. bank of the Agout, skirts the reservoirs of *La Raviège to La Salvetat-sur-Agout*, and then that of *Laouzas*, to regain the main road at *Murat*; see below.

The D622 climbs N.E. and at 14.5km crosses the *Col de la Bassine* (885m) in the bleak *Monts de Lacaune*, descending to **Lacaune**, 8.5km beyond, an old town on the Gijou, later a minor spa, the diuretic properties of its waters being emphasised by a quaint fountain of 1399. Adjacent is the château of *Calmels*.—The road continues E., passing (r.) the *Roc de Montalet* (1259m), just E. of the slightly higher *Montgrand*, and traverses the villages of *Murat-sur-Vèbre* and (26km) *La Croix-de-Mounis*.—12km. *St-Gervais-sur-Mare*, 12km beyond which we meet the D908 at *Hérépean*, between Lamalou and Bédarieux (see below).—Continuing S.E., a ridge of hills is crossed, and after 9km we turn l. to follow the D13 via *Gabian*, once fortified, and *Roujan* (see p 497), to (25km) **Pézenas**; see Rte 145.

From Castres, the N112 bears S.E., at 16km. skirting **Mazamet** (13,300 Mazamétains), a small industrial town with wool-spinning and leather-dressing establishments, built in the valley after the destruction by De Montfort in 1212 of *Hautpoul*, overlooking it to the S.—For the road hence to **Carcassonne**, see Rte 89.

The valley of the Thoré is followed to the E., with the wooded *Montagne Noire* rising to the S., now in part the *Parc Regional du Haut Languedoc*, to (9.5km) *St-Amans-Soult*, birthplace of Marshal Soult (1769–1851), long Wellington's principal adversary in the Peninsular War, his tomb is outside the S. wall of the church.

8km. *Lacabarède*, home of the Protestant martyr Jean Calas (1698–1762; cf. Toulouse).—Beyond (6km) *Labastide-Rouairoux* the watershed between the Atlantic and the Mediterranean is crossed at the *Col de Fenille*, and the road descends to (6.5km) *Courniou*, with the stalactite *Grotte de la Devèze*, discovered during the construction of the railway in 1886.

5km. **St-Pons**, a small town in a hill-girt basin, retains its fortified *Cathedral*, founded c. 1200 but mutilated by the Huguenots. It was altered in 1450, and again in 1716, when a façade was constructed on the site of the former choir. The original façade, at the other end, preserves its double portal. The finest capitals are in the Sacristy, originally the entrance-porch.—Below the battlemented *Tour de la Gascagne* is the *Grotte du Jaur*, the principal source of the river Jaur.

ST-PONS TO CLERMONT-L'HERAULT (74km), for *Montpellier*, 41km beyond. The D908 follows the valley of the Jaur to the N.E., to the N. of which rise the *Monts de l'Espinouse* (1000–1100m) to (18km) *Olargues*, on an abrupt bend in the river, crossed by a beautiful 12C bridge.—5km. *Mons-la-Trivallel* (l.), near the confluence of the Jaur with the larger Orb, is a convenient point from which to explore the *Gorges d'Héric*, the most striking of the ravines which cut into the S. flank of the *Plateau de Caroux*, the detached E. spur of the Espinouse, broken by cliffs and gullies of gneiss. To the S. are the gorges of the Orb.—We shortly pass (l.) *Colombières*, with its feudal castle, beyond which are more gorges, to (11km) *Le Poujol*, an old fortified village.—2km. *Lamalou-les-Bains*, to the N. in the Cévenol valley of the Bitoulet, is a small pleasantly sited spa.—3km. *Villemagne*, 3km N., preserves the 14C choir of its abbey-church, a disused 13C church, an old *Hôtel des Monnaies*, and other relics of its medieval importance.—At (5km) **Bédarieux**, a small industrial town, with a 16C bridge, is *St-Alexandre*, rebuilt in 1650.—*Lodève* lies 29km to the N.E., approached by the D35; see Rte 101.—**Pézenas** lies 34km to the S.E., approached by the D909 and D13 via (10km) *Faugères*, with an ancient gateway, (10km) *Gabian*, another old town, and (3km) *Roujan*, where the Gothic church has a tall square tower and a curious baptistry.

Crossing the Orb, we drive E. from Bédarieux through wooded country.—At 18.5km a short DETOUR may be made by turning l. to *Salasc*, and then r. through the *Cirque de Mourèze*, a wild dolomitic chaos of limestone boulders amid which the village of *Mourèze*, with its tiny Romanesque church, lies concealed; the main route may be regained 6.5km E. of the turning-off.—At (1.5km) *Villeneuvette* (l.) a government factory of army cloth was established by Colbert in 1677 in a walled village entered through an arch bearing the inscription 'Honneur au Travail'; and which has been compared to a labour camp!—3.5km. **Clermont-l'Hérault**; see Rte 101A; likewise for the road hence via *Gignac*, to *Montpellier*.—*Pézenas* lies 21km S.

Just E. of St-Pons the N112 climbs S.E. to (9km) the *Col de Rodomouls* (562m) and threads the *Défilé de l'Ilouvre*, descending to (14km) *St-Chinian*, beyond which extends a vine-covered plain.—12km. *Puisserguier*, the castle of which was burnt and its garrison thrown into its moat by Giraud de Pépieux in 1209, a Cathar supporter.—16km. **Béziers**; see Rte 145.

89 Albi to Carcassonne and Quillan

158km (98 miles). N112. 42km **Castres**—16km **Mazamet**—D118. 49km **Carcassonne**—24km **Limoux**—27km **Quillan**.

Maps: IGN 64, 71, 72, or 114; also 310. M 235.

ALBI (48,300 Albigeois), a small industrial centre, and the préfecture of the *Tarn*, the banks of which it straddles, retains in its characteristic old centre one of the most startlingly original buildings of the Middle Ages, its cathedral. Also of interest is the Musée Toulouse-Lautrec. The city's name evokes the tragedy of the

Albigensian Crusade, although it was itself a relatively minor centre of the dualist heresy, but there were sufficient numbers of Cathars in the S. half of the diocese for it to be applied indiscriminately to all the heretics of the Midi.

Although *Albiga* or *Civitas Albigensium* was the capital of the Gallo-Roman Albigenses, the town took no very prominent part in history until late in the 12C. In some respects allied to Manichaeism, the heresy known as Albigensian was in fact little more than part of the first wave of rebellion against the corruption of the Church of Rome: there had been numerous other similar heretical disturbances in such places as Liège, Cologne, and Rheims in the mid 12C, and fugitives from the church moved S., many settling in Languedoc, where some lesser nobles protected them. *Lombers*, some 16km S. of Albi, became a Cathar centre, where one of the first major (verbal) confrontations took place in 1165, and in the dispute the orthodox dignatories were worsened. Military force was first used to suppress the heresy at *Lavaur* in 1181, but it was not until 1208, after the murder of Peter of Castelnau, the papal legate, on the banks of the Petit Rhône near *St-Gilles*, that the crusade started in earnest.

Under Arnald-Amaury, Abbot of Citeaux, and the elder Simon de Montfort, the whole of Languedoc was devastated in a series of the most sanguinary campaigns in medieval history, followed in 1229 by the institution of an Inquisition. For details of the doctrines, and a fuller history, see Jonathan Sumption's 'The Albigensian Crusade' (1978). The *Verrerie Ouvrière* founded in 1896 in the transpontine Faubourg de la Madeleine, was one of the earliest examples of a factory managed by its employees.

Albi was the birthplace of the navigator and explorer Jean-François de La Pérouse (1741–88), massacred by the natives of the New Hebrides; and the artist Henri de Toulouse-Lautrec (1864–1901). On retiring from politics, Card. de Bernis was archbishop here from 1764–91.

The town is dominated by the towering mass of its red-brick ****Cathedral** (Ste-Cécile), which rises more like a fortress than a church from the surrounding streets, an impression strengthened by its square W. tower (octagonal in its upper storeys), 78m high, with its loophole windows and corner turrets. The flank of the building, without transepts, where tall windows alternate with small semi-circular buttresses, seems even more grim in contrast with the elaborate decoration of the S. entrance.

Begun by Bp Bernard de Castanet in 1277 (who is said to have revived a form of Inquisition in order to extort money from its long-suspect citizens for its construction), the main body was finished by 1392, although its consecration did not take place until 1480, under Bp Louis I d'Amboise, who was responsible also for the inception of the choir and rood-screen. Louis II d'Amboise (1502–11) began the S. porch and summoned Italian artists (probably from Bologna) to decorate the interior. The tower was also completed in his time. It was restored in the late 19C, when a parapet and further towers were added, but the latter were later removed, leaving those which were there originally.

Passing through an early 15C stone gateway guarded by a brick tower, a long flight of steps along the side of the edifice is climbed to reach the richly carved Flamboyant porch or **Baldaquin* (early 16C), with three arched openings. The dark *Interior* consists of one huge apsidal hall, 18m wide and 28m high, surrounded by chapels of two storeys, which, together with the vault, is covered with frescoes on an azure background (see below). The *High Altar* has stood at the W. end since 1823. In the 3rd chapel on the N. side is a Sienese polyptych of 1345. The **Rood Screen*, which lost much of its statuary in 1794, extends across the whole width of the church; above its central door stand the Virgin and St John, with Adam and Eve below, and at the back is a charming statue of St Cecilia, a figure nearly repeated among the other less saintly females, such as Esther and Judith, which are likewise notable on the **Choir Screen* (fee), the sculpture of which is of the later Burgundian school, and may be compared with contemporary work at *Brou* (see Rte 128). Over the side entrances stand Constantine and Charlemagne. The whole is framed in a profusion of delicate carving, in-

cluding 72 niches with infant angels behind the plain wooden stalls, above which
are pinnacled canopies. The upper windows of the apse contain 14C glass,
restored.

Of the *Frescoes*, some of which have been badly restored, perhaps the most
interesting series depicts the legend of Constantine and Helena (N. side of choir).
On walls invisible from the floor the artists have amused themselves by painting
grotesques. The W. wall is decorated with a huge *Last Judgement*, French work
of c. 1490, the central section of which was unfortunately destroyed by the in-
sertion of a chapel in 1693. The organ dates from 1736.

Between the cathedral and the Tarn stands the **Palais de la Berbie**, a
rambling red brick château-fort of the late 13C with a massive
square keep, the residence of an archbishop requiring protection
from the citizens he had abused. It was altered in the 17-18C by Abp
de Bernis, among others, used to more sophisticated comforts in the

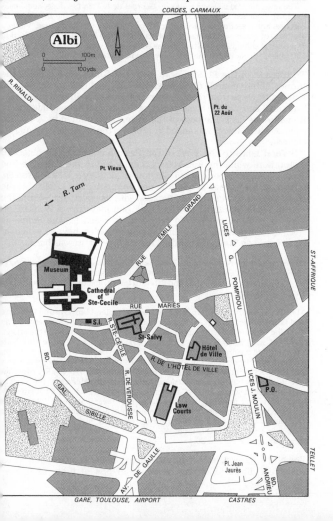

presence of Mme de Pompadour, and was later the *Préfecture*. Part of it now houses the ***Musée Toulouse-Lautrec**.

The subsidiary fortifications were completed in the 14-15Cs and formerly connected the palace to the cathedral. They are now surrounded by gardens, and afford a good view of the river, spanned by the *Pont Vieux* (much altered since it was built in 1035), and further upstream, the *Pont du 22-Aout* (the date of Albi's liberation in 1944), themselves providing a view of the old town.

A series of rooms in the museum is devoted to the paintings, drawings, lithographs, and posters of Toulouse-Lautrec, notable among which are his early 'Gunner saddling his mount' (1879), 'Carmen la rousse', Portraits of Berthe Bady, of his Mother, of Dr Tapié de Céleyran (his cousin, who donated numeous canvases to the museum), Mlle Lucie Bellanger, of Jane Avril, of Miss Dolly, of Yvette Guilbert, of 'La Goulue', 'Au salon de la rue des Moulins', and numerous other examples of his work, including 'L'Examen de Médecine', his last painting (1901).

The museum also displays works by *Georges de la Tour* (SS. Jude, and James the less), *Boucher, Guardi,* and *Vernet; Greuze's* Portrait of the Comte de La Pérouse, and a section devoted to works by *Bonnard, Utrillo, Matisse, Vuillard* (Portraits of Toulouse—Lautrec, and of his mother and father), et al. A collection of medieval antiquities, a suite of rooms embellished with 17C frescoes, and the 13C chapel, decorated in the 17C, may also be visited.

To the S.E. of the *Pl. Ste-Cécile* (with the S.I. on its S. side) is the former abbey church of **St-Salvi** (10-12C), abutted by shops, and entered by steps from the Rue Mariès. It was later altered internally. The small apses in the transepts, the N. door, and nave windows, are Romanesque, as is the base of the tower, surmounted by a 13C arcade. A watch-tower was added in 1385. To the S. are relics of its 13C cloister.

Several lanes to the S.W. of the Place have been the object of restoration, while the Rue Mariès is extended to the E. by the Rue Timbal, preserving one or two old houses, notably (r.) the *Maison Enjalbert*, at the corner of the Rue des Pénitents, and l. (No. 14) the *Hôtel Reynès* or *Maison des Viguiers*, with its courtyard.—From the *Pl. du Vigan*, bordered by the Lices, one may turn S.W. through gardens laid out on the old ramparts, to reach (r.) the *Palais de Justice*, incorporating a rebuilt Carmelite cloister, beyond which, at No. 14 Rue de Toulouse-Lautrec, the crippled artist was born.

At *Lescure*, on the N. bank of the Tarn, 3km N.E., is the Romanesque cemetery-chapel of *St-Michel*, with a remarkable sculptured doorway.

For roads from Albi to *Figeac* and **Brive**, to *Rodez*, and to **Millau**, see Rtes 65, 100, and 102, all in reverse.

ALBI TO TOULOUSE (76km). The N88 leads W., after 11km crossing the Tarn, to (11km) **Gaillac** (10,700 Gaillacois), a flourishing brick-built town noted for its sparkling white wine. In the older nucleus stands *St-Pierre*, and nearer the bridge, *St-Michel*, with a Romanesque choir and nave, but disfigured in the 19C; both have fortified towers. Near the former is the *Hôtel de Pierre de Brens* (c. 1500) with an earlier tower, and S. of the central *Pl. Thiers* is the *Hôtel d'Yversen*, with a late 16C door.—For the road hence to *Montauban* (50km W.), see Rte 64.—The N88 leads S.W. through (9km) *Lisle-sur-Tarn*, originally *Montégut*, 12C bastide with an arcaded square and 14C church.—After 4km the 14-18C Château of *St Géry*, with good furniture, is passed (l.) before traversing (4km) *Rabastens*, a brick-built town dominated by the fortress-tower of *Notre-Dame* (13-14C).—6km. The Tarn is crossed at its confluence with the Agout, just S.E. of which, at *St Sulpice*, is a restored 14C church. We continue S.W. over a series of ridges, to (32km) **Toulouse**; see Rte 86.

The N112 drives S. from Albi, at 14.5km passing *Lombers*, 3km W., a well-sited village, once the residence of one of the four Cathar

bishops of the Midi, and in 1165 the scene of an important doctrinal
confrontation between the Albigensians and the bishop of Lodève;
see p 498.

5.5km. *Réalmont*, a bastide with a 16C church, is traversed, 10km
S.W. of which lies *Lautrec*, an old fortress with a 15-17C church and
fragmentary ramparts, which gave its name to a viscounty held at
one time by Odet de Foix (1485–1528), who fought at Ravenna and
Pavia, and died at the siege of Naples.

15km S.E. of Réalmont is the ruined 12C castle of *Montredon-Labessonnié*, 2km
S.W. of which is the *Château de Castelfranc*, whence one may regain the main
road at Castres via *Roquecourbe*, on the Agout.

For **Castres**, 22km from Réalmont, and *Mazamet*, 16km beyond, see
Rte 88B.

Just as the main road mounts S. from Mazamet, a l.-hand turning
climbs 14km S.E. to the *Pic de Nore* (1210m), the highest point of the
Montagne Noire, in clear weather providing a distant view of the
Pyrenees.—The D118 ascends its N. slope to (14km) *Les Martys*,
where an alternative road to (31km) *Carcassonne* turns l. via
Miraval-Cabardès (home of the troubadour Raimon de Miraval), and
Mas-Cabardès, in a narrow defile, and the four ruined *Castles of
Lastours (les Tours de Cabaret)*, which were never taken by assault
but were delivered to De Montfort in 1211 by Pierre-Roger de
Cabaret in exchange for a safe-conduct. *Conques-sur-Orbie* (see Rte
88A) is by-passed 8km N.E. of Carcassonne.

The less interesting main road from Les Martys follows the valley
of the Dure for c. 9km, before bearing S.E. to (24km) **Carcassonne**;
see Rte 88A.—For the road hence to *Mirepoix*, see Rte 90.

AN ALTERNATIVE ROAD FROM CARCASSONNE TO LIMOUX is that turning
l. on its S. outskirts, following the E. bank of the Aude to (16.5km) **St-Hilaire**,
with an interesting Romanesque and Gothic *Church*, spoilt by recent accretions,
adjoined by a small 14C cloister, and containing the 11C sarcophagus of St
Hilary, bishop of Carcassonne, and some good capitals and corbels.—Hence we
climb over the hills, passing the 14-15C chapel of *N.-D. de Marseille* near *Pieusse*,
a Cathar base in 1223, on the descent to *Limoux*.

The D118 bears S.W., following the W. bank of the Aude, here flowing through low vine-covered hills, to (24km) **Limoux** (10,900
Limouxins), the capital of the county of *Razès* after Rennes-le-
Château was sacked by Aragonese troops in 1170 (see below), noted
for its 'touron' and sparkling wine ('blanquette'). Near the arcaded
Place is *St-Martin* (12-16C), with a good 14C tower and spire. Many of
its narrow streets contain carved wooden house-fronts of some antiquity; note also the 15C bridge.

The road shortly enters the defile of the *Étroit d'Alet*, and at 8km
passes (l.) the small spa of *Alet-les-Bains*, with a ruined cathedral,
destroyed by the Huguenots in 1577. Adjoining is a 14-15C church,
and in the old town are some 13C and Renaissance houses of interest.—The road crosses to the E. bank of the Aude and approaches
(7km) *Couiza*, with the 16C château of the Ducs de Joyeuse.

3.5km to the S.E. on a castle-crowned hill stands *Rennes-le-Château*, probably
the ancient *Rhedae*, the Visigothic capital of the Pays du Razès; in the valley to
the N.E. are the ruins of the castle of *Coustausse*.

12km. **Quillan**; see Rte 85.

QUILLAN TO AX-LES-THERMES (53km). The D117 climbs steeply W. for 4.5km, off which the D613 forks l., traversing the *Plateau de Sault* to (10.5km) *Belcaire* (1002m), beyond which the road narrows as we cross the *Col de 7 Frères* (1253m), some 3km beyond which a lane leads l. to (2km) *Montaillou*, with its ruined castle, and the subject of Leroy Ladurie's detailed study of the years 1294–1324. *Montségur* (see Rte 85) lies c. 11km N.W.—as the crow flies. The *Col de Marmare* (1361m) is next crossed, then the *Col de Chioula* (1431m) prior to descending in zigzags below (l.) the *Roc de l'Orri d'Ignaux* (1724m), to **Ax-les-Thermes**; see Rte 87.

An alternative road is that turning r. 10km S.E. of Quillan, ascending the valley of the Reventy, and threading a succession of defiles.

QUILLAN TO (68km) MONT-LOUIS AND FONT-ROMEU, 9km beyond. Having threaded the *Défilé de Pierre-Lys* (see Rte 85), at 11km we turn r., still on the D118, through *Axat*, and wind through the narrower *Gorges de St-Georges* (spoilt by hydro-electricity works) and the *Gorges de l'Aude*, to (20.5km) the tiny spa of *Usson-les-Bains*, overlooked by a ruined castle on a rocky spur.

A mountain road forks l. 3.5km S. of Axat, climbing through the hills to (18.5km) the *Col de Jau* (1513m), beyond which it descends the Castellane valley to (25.5km) *Prades*; see Rte 147.

8km S. of Usson, approached by a parallel valley to the W., lies *Quérigut* (1205m), the ancient capital of the hilly *Pays de Donézan*, also with a ruined castle, from which one may regain the main route 8km beyond.

The D118 now bears S.E., passing other small spas to (17km) *Puyvalador*, overlooking a reservoir, which with *Fontrabiouse*, 2.5km W., have little Romanesque churches built of the local granite.—5km. *Formiguères*, the main town of the *Capcir*, one of the coldest inhabited districts of France, a mountain-girt plain to the W. of which rises the *Pic Peric* (2810m).—*Les Angles*, 5km S.W., is a winter-sports centre, above which rises the *Roc d'Aude*, to the W. of which is the *Lac des Bouillouses*.—We bears S., shortly skirting (r.) the *Lac de Matemale* as we climb to the *Col de la Quillane* (1714m), descending towards the Têt valley via (12km) *La Llagonne*, the church of which contains a 12C carved Christ, to adjacent **Mont-Louis**, for which, and for **Font-Romeu**, 9km W., see Rte 147.

90   Carcassonne to St-Girons

129km (80 miles). D119. 18.5km *Montréal*—11km *Fanjeaux*—17.5km **Mirepoix**—23km **Pamiers**—22km *Pailhès*—13km *Le Mas-d'Azil* —24km **St-Girons**.

Maps: IGN 71, or 114. M 235.

Driving due W. from Carcassonne (Rte 88A), at 18.5km **Montréal**, a fortress of importance during the time of the Albigensian Crusade, is traversed, its conspicuous church preserves a good Gothic portal. Here in April 1207 took place a theological disputation between the fanatic Dominic de Guzman (later canonised) and Guilabert de Castres, the heretic bishop of Toulouse.

7.5km beyond, at the crossroads below Fanjeaux, is a modern monastery on the site of one founded for Cathar women reconverted to orthodoxy. **Fanjeaux**, its 13C church built on the ruins of a temple of Jupiter (Fanum Jovis), another Cathar stronghold, is perched on a ridge to the S.W., and commands extensive views.—The road bears S.W., providing after 10km a good view, in clear weather, of the Pyrenees ahead, before descending into the valley of the Hers, which is crossed at Mirepoix by a bridge building in 1787, when Arthur Young passed that way.

The centre of **Mirepoix**, a bastide, preserves a charming square of late 13-15C houses built over arcades, at the S.W. corner of which is the *Hôtel de Ville*. To the S. is the former *Cathedral*, rebuilt in

1497–1537 by Bp Philippe de Lévis, with a fine spire; the interior is
spoilt by 19C restorations and embellishments, but the span of the
nave is remarkable. As the road turns W. towards Pamiers, the 14C
Port d'Avail is passed. Mirepoix was the birthplace of Marshal
Clausel (1772–1842).—At *Lagarde*, 7.5km S.E., is an imposing ruined castle.

An alternative to the main road—regained after 13km—is that following the N.
bank of the river, where at *Vals*, a very ancient settlement, is a curious rock-
built church with a Carolingian crypt, 11C apse, and 12C murals, etc.

At 16km the D12 forks l. for **Foix**, 17.5km S.W.; the D119 leads r. for
(6.5km) **Pamiers**; see Rte 87.

Hence the road bears N.W., following the W. bank of the Ariège
and after 4km turns abruptly S.W. through (5.5km) *Escosse*, 7.5km
N.W. of which is the once-fortified village of *St-Martin-
d'Oydes.*—12.5km. *Pailhès*, with a ruined 13-16C castle, beyond
which we traverse (7.5km) *Sabarat*, and (5.5km) **Le Mas-d'Azil**, a 13C
bastide known for its devotion to the Portestant cause. Just beyond
is the celebrated *Grotte or tunnel in a limestone ridge worn by the
river Arize. The side caverns, which may be entered from the main
tunnel (420m long), through which the road likewise passes, contained remarkable prehistoric remains, among them the famous
sculptured horse's head now at St-Germain-en-Laye. The site served
also as a refuge for early Christians, Albigensians, and in 1625,
Huguenots. The vault of the S. entrance is remarkable.

The D117 is joined some 14km beyond, where we turn r. for
(8.5km) **St-Girons**; see Rte 85, and for the road N.W. to gain the
N127.

ST-GIRONS TO LUCHON (80km), a slow and mountainous cross-country road
(D618), leads S.W. up the Lez valley through *Aubert*, noted for its white-veined
black marble, and (5km) *Moulis*, with two castles, one ruined, and adjacent
Luzenac, where the church has a Romanesque doorway and belfry.—7km.
Audressein.

1km S. lies *Castillon-en-Couserans*, commanding the upper valleys of the Lez,
where a curious chapel to the E. is all that remains of its feudal stronghold.—2km
further S. is *Les Bordes*, with an 11C church, at the mouth of the *Vallée de
Bethmale* (S.E.); to the S. rises the tower-like crest of the *Pic du Midi de Bordes*
(1762m), while 8.5km S.W. is *Sentein* (732m), 'capital' of the *Vallée de Biros*, with
a 12C church encircled by remains of its fortified enclosure. The road ends 5km
beyond at *Eylie*, with a power-station, and plant for treating the ores of
neighbouring lead and zinc mines. Further S.W. are the *Grottes de la Cigalère*
and the *Gouffre Martel*. The *Pic de Maubermé* (2880m) rises to the S. of Eylie, and
the *Mail de Bulard* (2750m) to the S.E.

From Audressein we ascend the Bellongue valley, in which runs the river
Bouigane, to (7km) *Orgibet*, with an old church tower, 11km beyond which is the
Col de Portet-d'Aspet (1069m), overlooked to the N. by the *Pic de Paloumère*
(1608m). Descending steeply into the adjacent valley, we turn N.W., with the *Pic
de Cagire* (1912m) rising to the l., and ascend to (12km) the *Col de Buret* (599m),
beyond which the village of *Juzet-d'Izaut* is traversed.—At 9km the wooded *Col
des Ares* (797m) is crossed before descending past (5km) *Antichan-de-Frontignes*,
just N. of which, at *St-Pé-d'Ardet*, the 12C church contains 15C wall-
paintings.—A further 4km brings one down to *Fronsac*, with its tower, 2km S. of
which is *Chaum*; see Rte 80, likewise for **Luchon**, 18km S.W.

VIII MASSIF CENTRAL; BERRI; AUVERGNE; CÉVENNES

On approaching the *Massif Central* from the Orléanais, **Berri** is traversed, now forming the departments of the *Cher* and the *Indre*. It was purchased by Philippe I in 1100 and made a royal duchy; its last duke, Charles Ferdinand (1778–1820), the younger son of Charles X, was assassinated in Paris. The country and manners of the Berrichons is well described in the novels of George Sand. To the E. and S.E. are the small provinces of the **Nivernais** (capital *Nevers*) and **Bourbonnais** (capital *Moulins*).

The mountainous central province of **Auvergne**, now consisting of the *Puy-de-Dôme*, and *Cantal*, and parts of the *Haute-Loire*, takes its name from the Gallic tribe of the Arverni, whose stronghold of Gergovia, near Clermont-Ferrand, was the headquarters of Vercingetorix in his campaign against Julius Casear in 53 B.C. Bounded on the S. by the wilderness of the Cévennes (see below), and most easily approached by the valley of the Allier, it has shared the history of France proper longer than any of the other southern provinces. As early as 1121 Louis VI sent an expedition into Auvergne, and its conquest was completed by Philippe Auguste in 1190. The feudal subdivision of the province prevented it from playing a leading part in medieval history. *Riom*, the capital of a royal duchy, and *Montferrand*, headquarters of the counts and later of the Dauphins of Auvergne, kept a jealous watch over each other's rising power, and the bishops of Clermont and St-Flour were careful to divide their favours. In 1610 the province was wholly united to the crown by the cession of the rights of Marguerite de Valois, divorced wife of Henri IV. Although it included the fertile *Limagne*, or plain of the Allier, Auvergne is pre-eminently the country of the volcanic *'puys'*, whose conical shapes are so characteristic of the landscape. The Romanesque churches with their heavy circular arches and their decoration of polychrome masonry are proof of the former ecclesiastical importance of the province, when Urban II preached the First Crusade at Clermont, and the fame of the abbey of La Chaise-Dieu was at its height.

The **Cévennes**, a huge mass of igneous and limestone mountains, form the backbone of central France. Their steep S. and E. margin follows a long curve from Lyon to Carcassonne, overlooking the Rhône valley and the Mediterranean basin. To the N. and W. the descent is more gradual, and it is cut into by the upper valleys of the Loire, Dore, Allier, Lot, and Tarn. Geologically speaking, it extends W. to the Causses (see Rte 102) and the Montaigne Noire, and N. into the Monts d'Auvergne, the Montagne de la Madeleine, and the Lyonnais hills. But the Cévennes proper, centering round the old 'pays' of La Cévenne, between the sources of the Allier and the Gard, extend for about 130km from the foothills of Mont Aigoual, about Le Vigan, to the narrow col separating the Lignon and Eyrieux valleys, S. of the *Vivarais*, and are comprised within the old bishoprics of *Gévaudun* and *Velay*. The highest of the summits are the pointed Mont Mézenc (1753m) and Gerbier de Joncs (1551m) to the N., the rounded Pic de Finiels (1699m) on the Mont Lozère ridge in the centre, and the widespreading Aigoual (1565m) in the S. The average height of the main ridge is about 1100m.

Owing to the extent of their foothills on the N., and the steepness of their slopes on the S., communications are not too easy, although several roads radiating from Nîmes, Clermont, Montélimar, etc. afford access to the heart of the region. The only towns of any consequence on its verges are Le Puy in the N., Mende on the W., and Alès to the S. The Cévenois have frequently shown their independence, particularly in matters of religion. As early as the 13C the persecuted Albigeois found a refuge here, and later its mountain valleys were peopled by fugitive Waldensians from Lyon. Attempts to impose conformity after the Revocation of the Edict of Nantes provoked the insurrection of the *Camisards* (as they were called from the blouse—the old Provencal *camisa*, a shirt—they wore over their clothes) in 1702. They were at first successful—forcing the Comte de Broglie to retreat within the walls of Nîmes—but Pierre Laporte, called Roland (1640–1704), their leader, was killed in a surprise attack at Castelnau by the troops of Marshal Villars, and Jean Cavalier (1681–1740), his lieutenant, was suborned after being induced to parley with Villars at Nîmes in 1704. All assurances of toleration were repudiated, and Nicolas Lamoignon de Basville (1648–1720), Intendant of Languedoc from 1685–1718, systematically persecuted the Camisards. Those not slaughtered or burned (together with their villages), were deported or languished in prison for years. Cavalier entered the British service, fighting in Spain and rising to the rank of major-general. He ended his days as governor of Jersey; he died and was buried in Chelsea. The district came to more general notice in England after the publication of Robert Louis Stevenson's 'Travels with a Donkey in the Cévennes', a description of his hazardous journey on foot (with Modestine) from Le Monastier to St-Jean-du-Gard in 1878; see also 'The Cévennes Journal' (Edinburgh, 1978).

91   Bourges to Brive-le-Gaillarde

283km (176 miles). N144. 18km *Levet*—D940. 53km *La Châtre* —55km **Guéret**—33km *Bourganeuf*—30km **Eymoutiers**— 32km *Treignac*—27km *Seilhac*—D44. 35km *Brive*.

Maps: IGN 35, 41, 48, or 106, 111. M 238, 239.

For **Bourges**, see Rte 48.

Immediately beyond (18km) *Levet* we fork r. to (11km) *Châteauneuf-sur-Cher*, with a château of many periods, largely rebuilt in the 16C on the site of a medieval fortress.—17km. *Lignières*, where Calvin preached Protestantism while still a student at Bourges, has a château of 1657 and a 12C church altered in the 16C.

25km **La Châtre**, overlooking the Indre, preserves some old houses and tanneries, and humpbacked bridges, and the *Tour de la Prison* is a relic of its castle, containing a museum devoted to George Sand and the Vallée Noire (see p 509), together with an ornithological collection.—6km N.W. stands the 13C château of *Sarzay*, with four pepperpot towers.

For *Nohant*, 6km N., see Rte 93A; and for the road to Aubusson.—The road now veers S. to (55km) **Guéret** (16,600 Guérétois), préfecture of the *Creuse*, and ancient capital of the province of *La Marche*. It preserves little of its past except the *Hôtel des Moneyroux* (15-16C), W. of the town centre; further S. is the *Musée*, with miscellaneous collections, among which are some Limoges enamels and Aubusson tapestries. As the author of 'Fastness of France' observed, 'if you want to ask the way to Guéret, it is worth remembering that the "G" is hard and the "u" silent. But I, at least, would be more interested in asking the way out of it'.—For the road hence to *Aubusson*, see Rte 93B.—24.5km S.W. of Guéret by the D914, beneath the *Puy du Goth* (546m) stands the Romanesque abbey-church of *Bénévent, of unusual plan.

The D940 climbs S. through the *Forêt de Chabrières* and winds through hilly and well-wooded country to (35km) **Bourganeuf**, standing above the pleasant valley of the Taurion, preserving the *Tour de Zimzim* (1484), part of an ancient priory of the Knights of Malta, which takes its name from a suspect story that it was built by Pierre d'Aubusson, grand master of the Order, to serve as a prison for Djem, brother of sultan Bajazet II. The *Tour Lastic* (1430) also survives, together with a 12th and 15C church.

BOURGANEUF TO LIMOGES (49km). The D941 leads to (28km) **St-Léonard-de-Noblat** (5300 Miaulétous!), a picturesque old town containing several medieval houses and a beautiful *Church* (11-12C) with a W. front added in the 13C. The *Tower, the finest in the Limousin, raises its five graceful storeys above the N.

porch; between it and the N. transept is a curious round chapel, restored, and probably a baptistry. The 12C choir, somewhat disfigured by a restoration of 1603, contains late 15C stalls and the relics of St Léonard (d. c. 559), a nobleman of the court of Clovis converted by St Remy. In the first ambulatory chapel on the S. are 14-15C reliefs.—L.-J. Gay-Lussac (1778–1850), the discoverer of boron, was born here.—5km to the S.E. are the ruins of the 12C priory of *Artige*; 22.5km W. is **Limoges**; see Rte 63.

The D940 continues S. across heathy and wooded country to (20km) *Peyrat-le-Château*, 6km E. of which is the extensive reservoir-*Lac de Vassivière*.—10km. *Eymoutiers*, an old town with a church retaining a Romanesque nave and 15C choir.

AN ALTERNATIVE ROAD hence (D30, and later D3) leads 50km S. past (r.) *Mont Gargan* (731m) to *Uzerche* (see Rte 64), 35km N. of Brive.

Our route ascends S.E. onto the W. side of the granitic *Plateau de Millevaches*, the source of several rivers and springs (*batz* in Celtic, from which its name has been distorted). The valley of the Vézère is descended to (32km) *Treignac*, an ancient little town in which several 15C houses survive, beyond which we continue S., with the *Monédières* hills to the l. rising to 910m, to meet at 27km the road from Uzerche (17km N.W.) to *Tulle*, 14km S. (see Rte 94).—Turning r. and then l. at *Seilhac*, the D44 bears S.W. across country, later descending to (34km) **Brive**; see Rte 64.

92   Bourges to Clermont-Ferrand

183km (113 miles). N144. 44km **St-Amand-Montrond**—48km **Montluçon**—76km **Riom**—N9. 15km **Clermont-Ferrand**.

Maps: IGN 35, 42, or 108, 111. M 238, 239.

For **Bourges**, see Rte 48.

BOURGES TO ST-PIERRE-LE-MOÛTIER (51km), FOR MOULINS. The N76 leads S.E., at 9.5km passing 3km N.E. of the former abbey of *Plaimpied*, on the far bank of the Cher, founded in 1082. The church, showing the influence of Auvergnat Romanesque, preserves some interesting capitals, particularly in the crypt.—14.5km. *Dun-sur-Auron*, 5.5km S.W., with relics of its fortifications, including a 16C gate-tower, has a mutilated Romanesque church altered in the 15C.—7.5km N.E. of this turning stands the huge château of *Jussy-Champagne* (1590–1650), and a 12C church with an arcaded W. front.—The N76 traverses (10.5km) *Blet*, with remains of a Roman aqueduct, a Romanesque church, and a partly 15C château. At adjacent *Charly* the Poitevin Romanesque church contains 12-13C frescoes in its apse.—At *Chalivoy-Milon*, 5km S.W., is another Romanesque church of interest, 2.5km beyond which is the turreted castle of *Yssertieux*; 4km beyond is the castle of *Bannegon*, which gallantly held out against the Catholics in 1568.—9km. To the r. lies *Sagonne*, with a 12-15C church and the ruins of a château acquired by the architect Jules Hardouin-Mansart in 1698, together with the title; the keep dates from the 14-15C.—7.5km. *Sancoins* (also by-passed) preserves several old houses and remains of ramparts, 8.5km beyond which we cross the Allier, to enter (7.5km) *St-Pierre-le-Moûtier*, 31km N.W. of *Moulins*; see Rte 96.—There is a 12C castle, with 17C additions, at *Grossouvre*, 6km N. of Sancoins.

BOURGES TO NEVERS (69km). The D976 leads E., before veering S.E. through (21km) *Avord*, its church preserving a fine Romanesque doorway, to (14km) *Nérondes*, some 13km N.E. of which are the remains of the Cistercian abbey of *Fontmorigny* (13th and 18C).—12km *La Guerche-sur-l'Aubois*, 5km S.W. of which, at *Germigny-l'Exempt*, is a Romanesque church with a charming 13C

tower and doorway, while just beyond La Guerche is the 12th and 15C church of
Le Gravier.—9km. *Cuffy*, 2km N., has a Romanesque church and ruined castle,
while *Apremont*, 5km S., has an imposing 15-17C château.—We pass the
aqueduct carrying the Loire Canal over the Allier, and 8km beyond meet the N7
just S. of **Nevers**; see Rte 96.

The road leads due S. to (18km) *Levet*, 6km. E. of which is the ruined
castle of *Bois-Sir-Amé*, once the home of Agnès Sorel.—At 17.5km
Bruère-Allichamps, above the Cher, is traversed, preserving sections
of its ramparts.

At **La Celle**, 1km E., is a remarkable Romanesque *Church*, deserving restoration; 5km beyond is the well-furnished *****Château de
Meillant**, built for Charles d'Amboise in 1510, with a richly
decorated octagonal staircase-turret.

To the r. of the main road just S. of Bruère lies the former Cistercian *****Abbey of Noirlac**, ◊ restored since 1949, having been used as
a china factory in the 19C, and later as an orphanage. The austere
church was begun in 1150; the cloister, which had been much
mutilated, dates from the 13-15Cs. The refectory and other
dependencies may also be visited.

8.5km. **St-Amand-Montrond**, a prosperous dairying centre of
12,800 inhab., and a hub of resistance in 1943–44, which suffered
severe reprisals before its liberation, preserves the fine portal of its
12C church in the old town; a 'new' town grew up around the wooded *Butte de Montrond*, nearer the Cher, on which are relics of its castle. The town was once of importance, and the Grand Condé passed
his infancy there. Its fortifications were razed after the siege of 1652.

At 4.5km we pass (r.) *Drevant*, a small village with a Romanesque
chapel now a house, and remains of the theatre, forum, and other
buildings of Roman *Derventum.*—After another 4.5km *Ainay-le-
Vieil* lies 2km W., with a fine Renaissance château and medieval
postern-gate.

5km. To the E. lies the oak *Forêt de Tronçais*, containing many
magnificent trees, which has long supplied wood for the manufacture of casks for the maturing of Cognac.

5km. *Meaulne*, a village which gave its name to Alain-Fournier's
'Le Grand Meaulnes' (1913). The author spent his childhood years
(1891–1901) at *Épineuil-le-Fleuriel*, 5.5km S.W., the 'St-Agathe' of
the novel, which has a small museum.

A by-road (D157) from Meaulne leads S.E. along the valley of the Aumance, a
favourite haunt of the painter Harpignies, in which stands the 18C *Château du
Creux*, to (8km) *Chasteloy*, where the 12C church contains 15C wall-paintings,
and *Herisson*, with its striking ruined castle.

The main road continues S., at 8km passing 1.5km E. of *Vallon-en-
Sully*, with a good 12C church tower, and 4.5km beyond, passing
near the 16C château of *Nassigny* (r.).

18km. **Montluçon** (51,800 Montluçonnais), an industrial town with
founderies, chemical and rubber works, and damaged by bombing in
1940–44, preserves on a low hill near the r. bank of the Cher its ancient centre, dominated by its 15-16C **Château**. This now contains a
good *Museum* of folklore including a remarkable collection of
hurdy-gurdies. Neither of the two churches—*Notre-Dame* (15C) to
the N.E., and *St-Pierre* (partly 12C), to the W. of the last—is
remarkable. It was the birthplace of the composer André Messager
(1853–1929).

MONTLUÇON TO AUBUSSON, USSEL, AND MAURIAC (167km). The main

road (N145) leads S.W. to (34km) *Gouzon*, with a 13C church, and (10km)
Chénérailles, where a church of the same date has a fine tomb of 1300; the
Château de Orgnat, 3km N.W., conserves some Aubusson tapestries.—Veering
S. past (14km) the early 15C château of *St-Maixant* (l.), *Aubusson* is reached 5km
beyond; see below.

An alternative road is the D993, further E., traversing (25km) *Chambon-sur-
Voueize*, with the remarkable Romanesque church of *Ste-Valérie* (11-12C), with
two towers, one at the W. end, the other above the E. bay of the nave, preceding
the crossing, which bears a low lantern.—5km E. lies *Évaux-les-Bains*, a small
spa, the *Thermes* of which served as a political prison during the Vichy régime,
and Édouard Herriot was confined here in 1942. Only the 11C tower and porch
of the church survived a fire in the same year. We continue S.W., at 19.5km
passing near the 16-17C *Château de Mazeau* (r.), and l. the ruins of the abbey of
Bonlieu, founded in 1110.—20km. **Aubusson**; see Rte 93B.

The D982 continues S. through **Felletin**, a carpet-making town, where Graham
Sutherland's tapestry for Coventry cathedral was woven, since 1912 a centre of
the diamond-cutting industry, and the birthplace of Philippe Quinault
(1635 – 88), the librettist and collaborator of Lully. *Ste-Valérie*, rebuilt in the 15C,
has a fine belfry, while there is a notable *'lanterne des morts'* in the
cemetery.—The road continues to ascend the upper Creuse valley to (20km) the
Col de Massoubre (828m)—to the S.W. of which rises the *Signal d'Audouze*
(953m)—beyond which we bear S.E. to (28km) **Ussel**; see Rte 94.—The D982
traverses (21km) *Neuvic*, commanding a view of the Monts Dore and
Cantal.—9km S.E. is *Sérandon*, with a 12C church.—The road descends rapidly into the Dordogne gorge, which is crossed by the *Pont de St-Projet*, beyond which it
bears S.E. to (14.4km) **Mauriac**; see Rte 95.

The N144 leads S.E. from Montluçon to (9km) *Néris-les-Bains*, a small
spa reputed since the days of Augustus, and three piscinas and remains of a theatre have been exposed of Roman *Neriomagus*. Some
antiquities are preserved in the *Museum* by the Thermes. The parish
church, mainly 11-12C, contains masonry perhaps of the 6C; while
since 1966 a Merovingian necropolis has been excavated in its
vicinity.

6km to the E. is the colliery and ironworking town of *Commentry*.

6km. A minor road forks r. towards (10km) the imposing ruins of the abbey of
Bellaigue, founded by St Bernard in 1137, 6km W. of which is the 15C château of
Marcillat. The main road may be regained to the E.

The N144 traverses the *Combraille*, a district of wooded hills near
the crest of which stands (12km) *Montaigut*, 12km beyond which the
small colliery town of *St-Éloy-les-Mines* is entered.—10.5km. To the
r. lies *Menat*, where the 12C *Abbey-church* has notable sculptured
capitals.—At 2.5km we cross the Sioule beside a medieval bridge.

Hence the D915 turns N.E., traversing the granite defile of the *Gorges de
Chouvigny* to (17km) *Ébreuil*; see Rte 100. To the S., the D109 ascends the rocky
valley below the ruins of *Château-Rocher* to (10km) *Châteauneuf-les-Bains*, a
small spa, just N. of which, at *Ayat*, was born Gén. Desaix (1768–1800, at
Marengo).—From *St-Gervais-d'Auvergne*, 7km to the W., a minor road runs S.W.
to (26.5km) *Pontaumur* (see Rte 93B), passing near a reservoir and the 470m long
railway *Viaduc des Frades* (1908), the loftiest in France, spanning the Sioule at a
height of 132m.

The main road passes (r.) *St-Hilaire-la-Croix*, with a late 12C church
with a good S. portal, before traversing (23km) *Combronde*, and (l.)
the *Château de Davayat* (early 17C), to the S. of which is a notable
menhir.—7km. **Châtel-Guyon**, 3.5km W., a spa since 1817, owes its
name to a castle built in 1195 by Guy II of Auvergne, to the W. of
which is the 16C *Château de Chazeron*, where Gén. Gamelin was imprisoned by the Vichy government in 1940–41.

5km. **Riom**, for which, and for the road S. to (15km) **Clermont-Ferrand**, see Rte 100.

93 Châteauroux to Clermont-Ferrand

A. Via Montluçon

189km (117 miles). D943. 30km *Nohant*—6km *La Châtre*—62km **Montluçon**—N144. 76km **Riom**—N9. 15km **Clermont-Ferrand**.

Maps: IGN 35, 42, or 111. M 238, 239.

The D943 leads S.E. from **Châteauroux** (Rte 51) to (14km) *Ardentes*, with a Romanesque church preserving primitive capitals, while that of *St-Martin* at Vic, 14km beyond, contains a series of 12C frescoes discovered in 1849 by George Sand and Mérimée.

2km. **Nohant**, with the château which Aurore Dupin, Baroness Dudevant (1804–76), better known by her *nom de plume* of 'George Sand' (at first 'Jules Sand', after her liason with Jules Sandeau), made her occasional refuge, and died. The *House* ◇ contains numerous survenirs of the authoress, who often visited the place with her lovers and friends, among them Chopin, Liszt, Delacroix, Balzac, Flaubert, Gautier, and Dumas *fils*. Many of her novels describe the district. Her tomb is in the adjacent courtyard.

6km. **La Châtre**; see Rte 91.

LA CHÂTRE TO GOUZON (c. 56km), FOR AUBUSSON. At 8km S., turn l. past the *Tour Gazeau* (cf. George Sand's 'Mauprat') to (6.5km) *Ste-Sévère*, with a 13C keep. Thence follow the D917 S.E. to (21.5km) *Boussac*, with a strikingly placed 15-16C château, and old houses. The D997 bears S., and E. of the hill of *Pierres-Jaumâtres*, with its curious rock-formations, and *Toulx-Ste-Croix*, a village on the site of a Gallic oppidum (655m; view), whose church has a massive detached belfry. The road continues S. to *Gouzon*; see Rte 92.

We now turn S.E., at 9km passing near (r.) *La Motte-Feuilly*, with a château once belonging to Charlotte d'Albret (d. 1514), wife of Caesar Borgia, Duc de Valentinois, and a church containing her marble *Tomb, by Martin Claustre. (The château is now a home for deaf children; enquire at the café for the key to the church.)—9km. *Châteaumeillant*, ancient *Mediolanum*, where Romanesque *St-Genès* has seven small apses, and the *Hôtel de Ville* occupies an 11C church of similar plan. The 16C château now houses the Gendarmerie. A small archaeological collection may be visited.—12km N.E. is the former Romanesque abbey-church of *Puyfférand*.

At (11.5km) *Culan*, with wisteria in its main street, dominated by its fine 13-15C castle, recently restored, the valley of the Arnon is crossed.—There is an attractive gentilhommière at *St-Christophe-le-Chaudry*, 4.5km N.; some 6km S.W., on either side of the D977, lie the ruins of the château of *Roche-Guillebault*, and of the *Abbaye des Pierres*, founded in 1149.

9km. To the l. is the 12C priory-church of *St-Désiré*.—11.5km. *Huriel*, 6km S., has a 12C church and a massive keep of the same date.—12km. *Montluçon*, for which, and for the road beyond to **Riom** and **Clermont-Ferrand**, see Rte 92.

B. Via Guéret and Aubusson

220km (136 miles). D990. 48km *Aigurande*—D6. 36km **Guéret**—
D942. 42km **Aubusson**—D941. 94km **Clermont-Ferrand**.

Maps: IGN 35, 41, 42, or 111. M 238, 239.

Quitting **Châteauroux** (Rte 51), the *Forêt de Châteauroux* is traversed, to (26km) crossroads, 2.5km E. of which is the remarkable
*Church of **Neuvy-St-Sépulchre**, consisting of a rotunda (1042; partly restored by Viollet-le-Duc in 1850), with a 12C upper part, attached to which is another 11C church with nave and aisles, vaulted in
the 12C.

To the N. of the road, 6km further E., are the relics of the Cistercian abbey of
Varennes, founded in 1155, and now a farm.

Continuing S., at 6km *Cluis* is traversed, with a 12-13C church, N.E.
of which are the ruins of the château 'des Demoiselles de Montpensier'.—15.5km. *Aigurande*, with a 13C church, beyond which the
minor winding D6 is followed to the S.E., after c. 12km passing near
(r.) *Malval*, with a ruined 15C castle, and a church partly 12C, later
joining the D940 12.5km N. of **Guéret**; see Rte 91.
    The D942 turns S.E. past (r.) the *Puy de Gaudy*, a hill on which
stood the Gallic oppidum whose inhabitants founded Guéret, to
(20km) *Ahun*, on a height above the Creuse, with a partly 12C
church containing 17C woodwork, more of which may be seen at adjacent *Moûtier-d'Ahun*, with a partly ruined *Church of a Benedictine abbey, with a 12C choir and 15C vault, and 17C boiseries.
    22km. **Aubusson**, on the Creuse, the Roman station of
Albuconium, with a population of 6200, has since the 15C been
famous for its Carpet and Tapestry Works, which may be visited,
where Savonnerie carpets, and Gobelins and Beauvais tapestries are
woven on hand-looms. The *Maison du Vieux Tapissier* illustrates the
history of tapestry. Pierre d'Aubusson, Grand Master of the Knights
of St John, the defender of Rhodes against the Turks in 1479, was
born here. Several 16C houses, and fragments of its castle
survive.—*Bellegarde-en-Marche*, 13km N.E., once a centre of carpet-
making, preserves two towers of its walls.
    The D941 leads E. towards the *Puy de Dôme*, at 17km passing 7km
N. of *Crocq*, with remains of a massive 12C castle, and in its church a
15C painted altarpiece.—30km. *Pontaumur*; for the road N.E. to
Manzat and *Riom*, see p 508.
    23km. **Pontgibaud**, on the Sioule, is dominated by its restored cas-
tle, rebuilt in 1200 and 1450. The high altar in its church comes from
the Chartreuse de Pont-Ste-Marie, the ruins of which lie in a gorge
c. 12km N. via *Montfermy*, with its Romanesque church. The town
also preserves a gate and part of its fortifications.—Some 2km S. is
the curious *Camp* or *Cité des Chazaloux*, of indeterminate date, surrounded by a wall.

Just E. of Pontgibaud, the D941 turns l. through an interesting, volcanic district
to (26km) *Riom*, passing between the *Puy de Tressous* (l.; 983m) and the *Puy de
Louchadière* (1198m), and then between the *Puy de Jumes* (r.; 1161m) and the
Puy de la Nugère (987m), with its double crater.—At 14km a r.-hand turning
winds down to (16km) **Clermont**; the road continues N.E. to (4km) *Volvic*, and
Riom; see Rte 100.

The main road from Pontgibaud shortly bears S.E., skirting (r.) the

enormous lava-flow or 'cheïre' of the *Puy de Côme* (1253m), passing
(l.) the *Puy Chopine* (1181m), and then between the *Puy de Goules*
(l.), N. of which rises the *Grand Sarcoui* (1147m), craterless, like the
Puy de Dôme, and (r.) the *Puy de Pariou* (1209m), with an unusually
deep crater. The villages of *La Fontaine du Berger* and *Orcines* are
traversed to reach (16km) the T-junction at *La Baraques*.—The *Puy
de Dôme* rears up to the W.; see p 546.—Turning l. we descend rapidly into **Clermont-Ferrand**; see Rte 100.

94 Clermont-Ferrand to Brive and Périgueux

248km (154 miles). D941A and N89. 43km *Ussel*—60km
Tulle—29km **Brive**—73km **Périgueux**.

Maps: IGN 49,48, or 111, 110. M 239, 233.

For the roads W. from **Clermont-Ferrand** (Rte 100) to the junction
just S. of *Laqueuille*, see Rte 95. Here we turn r. past (12km) the *Puy
de Préchonnet* (948m; view) to (3km) *Bourg-Lastic*, with a small 12C
church, and flourspar mines, some distance beyond which the N89
veers S.W. to (28.5km) **Ussel** (12,300 inhab.), a dull and isolated town
containing several 15-16C houses, the best of which is the turreted
Hôtel des Ducs de Ventadour, at the N. end of the old nucleus. In the
Pl. Voltaire, to the l. as we make our exit, stands a Roman eagle,
found in the 18C on the site of a Gallo-Roman oppidum S. of the
town.

9km. *St-Angel*, with a 12C priory-church altered in the 15-16Cs.

8km N.W. lies *Meymac*, with the remarkable 12C church of its Benedictine abbey, parts of which have been rebuilt. A curious old *Cross*, a 15C door, and
covered *Market* are also preserved.—To the N. extends the *Plateau de
Millevaches*; see p 506. One may regain the main road 8km S.

15km. *Soudeilles* (r.) has a notable 12th and 15C church.—5km
Égletons, 6km E. of which lie the ruins of the castle of *Ventadour*, the
cradle of a ducal family, who later moved to Ussel, among whom Eble
II composed verses, but which has become famous because the
troubadour Bernard de Ventadour (c. 1150–80; variously spelt,
sometimes Bernart de Ventadorn), born here, took the name.

4.5km. *Rosiers*, 2.5km E. of which is the castle of *Maumont*, where
Pierre Roger de Beaufort and his nephew Roger were born, who
became popes Clement VI and Gregory XI respectively.

13km. *Corrèze*, 4km N., preserves some 15-16C houses, and remains of fortifications.—We pass between two small lakes, among
the many expenses of still water in this wild and heathy
district.—5km. *Gimel*, 2km S.E., with a church containing the 12C
Limoges-enamelled shrine of St Stephen and other treasures. Nearby
are the waterfalls of the *Montane*, where the river plunges into a
chasm.

The road descends into the Corrèze valley to approach (9.5km)
TULLE (20,600 Tullistes), préfecture of the *Corrèze*, the upper town
of which, at its N.E. end, around the cathedral, is a maze of narrow
alleys and steps.

It grew up round a manastery founded in the 7C or earlier, which since 1317 has
been the seat of a bishop. In 1369 it repulsed an English attack, and in 1577

likewise held Turenne at bay, but in 1585 he returned and sacked the place. The day after its liberation in June 1944, the S.S. re-entered Tulle and hung 99 citizens from their balconies, as a parting shot. it was the birthplace of Gén. Nivelle (1856–1924). The fabric called '*tulle*', more exactly 'point de Tulle', was first made here.

The **Cathedral** is an early Gothic building of c. 1190, whose choir and transepts were destroyed in 1796. The 12-13C *Tower is surmounted by a graceful 14C spire. To the S. are two remaining galleries of its 13C cloister, with ogival vaulting and pierced spandrels. The two-bayed chapter-house is of the same period. Here are an archaeological collection and other miscellaneous exhibits.

Opposite the W. end of the cathedral is the early 16C *Maison de Loyac*, while there are several other buildings of interest in the lanes ascending N., and in the Rue de la Barrière leading S.W. from the wider Av. Gén. de Gaulle. — To the N.E., facing the Quai Baluze, is the round church of *St-Pierre* (17C).

The church at *Naves*, 6km N. on the Uzérche road, contains a remarkable 18C altarpiece. — For the roads S.E. to *Aurillac*, and S. to *Figeac*, see Rte 64.

Continuing down the valley of the Corrèze, at 17km the D130 leads l. to (3.5km) **Aubazines**, formerly *Obasine*, famous for its *Abbey Church* of 1176, one of the more remarkable in the Limousin.

Three bays of the nave were pulled down in 1731; the three remaining bays ascend by steps to the crossing, crowned by an octagonal tower. The N. transept with some 13C grisaille glass, contains a 12C cupboard, fragmentary murals o 1466, and the monks' night-stair; the S. transept preserves the 13C *Tomb of S Stephen of Obasine*, founder of the church in 1135. The choir contains stalls o 1719 with interesting misericords.—The lower storey of its dependencies date from the 12C, the upper floors from the 17C.

In the gorge to the E. are the romantic ruins of the 13C abbey of *Coiroux* above Aubazines rises the *Puy de Pauliac* (524m; views), on which is a cromlech

10km. *Malemort*, with remains of a 12C castle, is on the outskirts o **Brive-la-Gaillarde**; see Rte 64.—The N89 briefly follows the valley of the Vézère to (11km) *Larche*.

Just beyond the village the D60 climbs S.W. to (41.5km) *Sarlat* (see Rte 71), via (7km) *Chavagnac*, with a Romanesque church and 13C keep, and (16km) *Salignac-Fénelon*, with a 12C château, with later additions.

9.5km. *Terrasson-la-Villedieu*, with some good stone houses, a 15C church, and 12C bridge, is traversed before reaching (6km) Le Lardin-St-Lazare. For the road descending the Vézère valley to (11km) *Montignac* and beyond, see Rtes 74, in reverse, and 71.

We ascend a tributary valley, after 6km passing (l.) the late 18C château of *Rastignac*, restored since set alight by the Germans in 1944. The road traverses wooded country to meet the Périgueux Cahors road (see Rte 71) after 30km, where it veers N.W. to (11km) **Périgueux**; see Rte 66.

95 Clermont-Ferrand to Rodez via Mauriac, Aurillac, and Conques

275km (171 miles). N89. 23km *Randanne*—15km *Massagette*—16km D922—5km *St-Sauves-d'Auvergne*. **La Bourboule** lies 5km S.E.— 37km *Bort-les-Orgues*—30km **Mauriac**—16km **Salers** lies 6.5km E.—43km **Aurillac**—D920. 18km, there forking r. onto the D601 for 28km—D901. 6.5km **Conques**—37.5km **Rodez**.

Maps: IGN 42, 49, 58, or 111; also 261, and 263. M 239, 235.

For **Clermont-Ferrand**, see Rte 100.

Alternative routes from Clermont to the La Bourboule crossroad are first described.

VIA ORCIVAL (46km). The D941A ascends 9km W. to the crossroads E. of the *Puy de Dôme* (see Rte 100, p 546), there bearing S.W. to (10km) *Les Quatre Routes*, where the N89 is crossed, descending into the valley and forking l. past (r.) the château of *Cordès* (15th and 17C), with attractive gardens, to (8km) **Orcival**. Its 12C *Church is a fine example of Auvergnat Romanesque, and its central tower, capitals, and the plan of the apse (beneath which is a crypt) are all remarkable. The main route is regained at *Rochefort-Montagne*, 3km W., and 15km N.E. of the La Bourboule crossroads.

VIA ST-NECTAIRE (78.5km). The D978 forks r. off the N9 18.5km S. of Clermont (see Rte 100) past (l.) *La Sauvetat*, with a 14C keep of the Knights of St John, and through *Plauzat*, with its old church and castle, to (10km) *Champeix* (pron. Champé) on the *Couze de Chambon*, dominated by its ruined castle, demolished in 1635 on Richelieu's orders. — Some 10km S.W. is the old village of *Saurier*, beyond which are the *Gorges de Courgoul*. — Shortly beyond Champeix the ruins of the fortress of *Montaigut-le-Blanc* are passed, and at (6.5km) *Rivalet* we bear r.

RIVALET TO BORT-LES-ORGUES VIA BESSE AND CONDAT (75.5km). The l.-hand fork ascends past the artificial *Grottes de Jonas* to (15.5km) *Besse-St-Anastaise* (or *en-Chandesse*; 1050m), an old hill village preserving fragments of ramparts, several 15-16C houses, and *St-André* (9-12C, with a choir of 1551) with some quaintly carved capitals.—*Super-Besse*, 7km W., is a winter-sporting development, with ski-lifts, etc., on the S.W. flank of the *Puy de Sancy* (1885m). The main road may be regained at *Murol*, 11km N. of Besse. There is a similar church to that at Besse at *Compains*, c. 10km S. of Besse.

Continuing W. past (l.) *Lac Pavin*, overlooked by the well-preserved crater of the *Puy de Montchal* (1411m), we bear l., passing (r.) *Lac Chauvet*, to (17km) *Égliseneuve-d'Entraigues*, with an interesting Romanesque church, beyond which the valley of the Rhue is descended to (11km) *Condat*, a small resort (some 3km S. of which are the ruins of the Cistercian abbey of *Féniers*), there turning W. to traverse the *Gorges de la Rhue* to (32km) *Bort-les-Orgues*; see below.

CONDAT TO MAURIAC (55km). The D678 leads W through St-Amandin before bearing S. to (18km) *Riom-ès-Montagnes*, an old cheese-making town with an interesting Romanesque church.—Hence a road continues S. towards the *Puy Mary* (see p 549) after c. 6km passing (r.) the ruins of the castle of *Apchon*, to *Cheylade*, with a richly adorned 12C church.—The main road turns W. from Riom, shortly passing a r.-hand turning for *Menet*, with a Romanesque church overlooking its lake, and bears S.W. past the château of *Total-Haut* to cross the summit level and reach (14km) *Trizac*, with a Romanesque church and old houses. The road descends the valley of the Mars through *Moussages*, with a view N. of the 15C Château de *Valans* near *Auzers*, to reach the D922 just prior to *Mauriac*; see below.

The D996 from Rivalet at 6.5km reaches the small spa of **St-Nectaire**, noted both for its cheese, and for its remarkable Auvergnat Romanesque *Church, dominating the upper village to the r. Although the towers date from 1875, the narthex, with its foliated capitals, is original, while within is a fine series of historiated capitals, naively but admirably carved; its treasury contains several 12C objects.—The summit of the *Puy de Mazeyres* (914m) to the E. provides a good view.—5km. *Murol*, a small resort with a well-sited ruined castle (mainly 14-15C), is overlooked to the S.E. by the *Puy de Bessolles* (1057m), 1km beyond which we pass (l.) *Lac Chambon*, not a volcanic crater but formed by a quaternary lava-flow which dammed the valley of the Couze. The village of *Chambon* has a 12C church, beyond which the road commences to climb steeply, with striking views of the Auvergnat mountains as it zigzags up to the *Co.*

A plunging view of the church of St-Nectaire

de la Croix-Morand (1401m), overlooked (l.) by the Puy de la Tache (1636m). The road from Randanne (see below) is shortly met as we skirt the slope of the Puy du Barbier (1729m) before descending to **Le Mont-Dore** (1050m), a flourishing spa (since c. 1797) and winter-sports centre lying in the narrow upland valley of the Dordogne, with the Puy de Cliergue to the W. (1667m), and the **Puy de Sancy** (1885m; the highest summit of the Monts d'Auvergne) closing the view to the S.

An interesting walk, providing immense panoramic views, may be made by ascending the Pic du Capucin (1465m), immediately S.E. of the town, and circling round the huge cirque past the Puy de Sancy to the Puy Ferrand, Puy de Cacadogne, and the Roc du Cuzeau (1724m), thence descending to Le Mont-Dore near the Grande Cascade; but this is only one of the many mountain excursions which may be made in the area.

The road leads N.W. out of the valley, shortly descending to (7km) **La Bourboule** (852m), its sister spa, delightfully sited and with a more equitable climate. The Dordogne flows through the centre of the town, partially flanked by gardens.

To the N. stands the old village of Murat-le-Quaire, from which a road ascends to the Banne d'Ordanche (1513m; views) to the N.E.; to the S. of La Bourboule the ascent may be made to the Plateau de Charlannes by a road circling up further W., S.W. of which is the strikingly placed village of La Tour-d'Auvergne: see below.

The D922 is reached 5km W. of La Bourboule, at St-Sauves-d'Auvergne. An excursion may be made further W. to the Gorges d'Avèze, a defile lower down the Dordogne.

THE MAIN ROAD (N89) climbs S. from Clermont through the suburban village of Beaumont, with 12th and 15C churches, beyond which rises Montrognon (699m), with its 13C tower, one of the many conical 'puys' characteristic of Auvergne. Ceyrat, with its gorge to the S.W., is traversed, to the E. of which lies the Plateau de Gergovie; see Rte 100. The road climbs W. to cross the Cheires Hautes, an ancient lava-flow, to the S. of which are the Lac de la Cassière and the larger Lac d'Aydat, thus formed, and traversing the Col de la Ventouse, at 25km reaches the Randanne crossroads.

AN ALTERNATIVE ROUTE is that turning l. onto the D983, which later commands some outstanding *Views to the N. towards the Puy de Dôme and into the valley to the N.E., in which stands Orcival (see above). To the l. we pass the Lac de Servière, a crater-lake, before climbing through the Col de Guéry, passing (r.) the two huge volcanic dykes of Roche Sanadoire and Roche Tuilière facing the head of the valley. The Lac de Guéry is skirted, beyond which we meet the D996 from St-Nectaire, and circle down to (26.5km) Le Mont-Dore; see above.

The N89 continues N.W. past (7km) Les Quatre Routes (see above), with the Puy de Dôme rising to the N.E., and with Orcival in the valley to the S.W. The descent continues through (8km) Massagettes, where we veer S. through (6km) Rochefort-Montagne and (9km) La-queuille, 1km beyond which the N89 turns r. for Ussel and Tulle; see Rte 94.—5km. St-Sauves-d'Auvergne.—La Bourboule lies 5km up the Dordogne valley to the E.

4km. The village of La Tour d'Auvergne (990m), of whose castle nothing remains, but which was the cradle of a famous family, lies 2.5km to the S.E.—Beyond (5km) Tauves the road crosses a stony moraine-plateau to (21km) Lanobre (l.), with a little Romanesque church, and 2km W., the romantically sited and turreted **Château de Vals* (15C), overlooking the huge reservoir of the Dordogne, dammed by the *Barrage de Bort* (1954), which is shortly reached.

3.5km. The r.-hand fork leads across the dam itself, from which the main road may be regained; it also approaches the remarkable cliff of basalt columns resembling organ-pipes, which gives **Bort-les-Orgues** its name. It was the birthplace of Jean-François Marmontel (1723–99), but is of slight interest in itself. The 12C church has been over-restored. The 'orgues' are seen across the valley after the town is traversed.—There is a ruined 14C castle at *Madic*, 2km W.

3km. *Saignes*, with a 12C church, lies 3km S.E., overlooked by a ruined castle further S.—Beyond, to the E. rises *Chastel-Merlhac* on the site of *Castrum Meroliacense*, taken by Thierry I in 532.—At *Ydes*, 2km W. of Saignes, the 12C church has an exterior of interest.

The D922 next crosses an area of isolated coalfields, passing (r.) the ruins of the *Château de Charlus*, and (10.5km) *Vendes*, on the Sumène.—The 15C château of *Auzers*, overlooking the valley of the Marlhioux, is 12.5km S.E.—The road climbs in a wide curve onto the Cantal plateau, to enter (14.5km) **Mauriac** (722m), an ancient town, once noted for its horses and mules, and taken by the English in 1367.

The most important building is *N.-D.-des-Miracles*, founded in the 12C, the W. door of which has remarkable although mutilated sculptures; it contains a Romanesque font and 17-18C altar-screens. By the S. door is a 14th or 15C 'lanterne des morts'.—Beyond the S.W. corner of the square is the *Collège* at which Marmontel was a pupil, with a Renaissance doorway; adjacent is the 16C *Hôtel d'Orcet*, incorporating a 12C tympanum.

At *Brageac* (c. 5km S.W., as the crow flies, but only approached circuitously via *Ally*, 11km S.) is a 12C church and ruined abbey, well-sited above the gorge of the Auze.—Just E. of Ally is the 18C *Château de la Vigne*.

MAURIAC TO THE PUY MARY (c. 40km); the upper road may be impassable between Oct. and mid-June. The D678 leads N.E. to (9km) *Pons*, where we cross the Mars and turn r. along the valley past (5km) the restored 17C château of *Chanterelle*, ascending the thickly wooded *Vallée du Falgoux* to (14km) the village of *Le Falgoux*.—5.5km beyond we meet the D680 and turn l., skirting the *Cirque du Falgoux* to (5.5km) the *Col de Peyrol* (1582m), between the *Puy de la Toute* (1709m) to the N., and the **Puy Mary** (1787m), surpassed in height but not in beauty of outline by the **Plomb du Cantal** (1855m) to the S.E. (see p 549), and commanding quite as good a view. A safe but steep path ascends to the summit.—The road beyond the Col descends E. to (23km) *Murat*; see Rte 100.—The r.-hand fork leads S. over the *Col de Redondel* into the upper valley of the Mandailles; see p. 549.—The return journey may be made by following the D680 to the N.W., later skirting the N. side of the Maronne valley via (20.5km) *Salers*; see below, regaining the main route 16.5km S. of Mauriac.

From Mauriac the road undulates S., after 7km commanding a view of the *Cascade de Salins*, meeting crossroads in 9km.

Salers (951m), 6.5km E., an austere old town on a commanding site, prettied up, and preserving two 15C gateways and ramains of ramparts, with its main *Place* surrounded by grey stone mansions (15-16C), some turreted. To the N.E. is the late 15C church with a 12C porch, containing a painted stone Entombment of 1495; to the S., an Esplanade overlooks the Maronne valley. One may regain the main road by climbing down E. from the Place into the valley, there turning W. past the 15C château of *Palemont*.

4km. *St-Martin-Valmeroux*, a quaint old town with several 15-16C ouses, is commanded by an old castle, beyond which the D922 veers W. again before turning S.E. past (7km) *St-Chamant*, with an 8C château preserving its 14C keep; the church contains 15C woodwork, as does that at *St-Cernin*, to the r. of the road further S.

8km. The *Château d'Anjony* stands in the valley of the Doire 5km l., with its four 15C towers, and containing rooms of interest, and some 15C frescoes.—To the W. of the D922 is the *Château de Rageaud*.

21.5km **AURILLAC** (631m; 33,200 Aurillacois), the ancient capital of the *Haut Auvergne* and préfecture of the *Cantal*, has been much modernised. It has important cattle and cheese markets, and is a centre of the France umbrella trade.

Gallo-Roman *Aureliacum* was the birthplace of St Gerald (856-909), who founded an abbey here in which Gerbert (later Pope Sylvester II; d.1103) was a monk; likewise of the historian Piganiol de la Force (1669–1753), and Président Paul Doumer (1857–1932).

Few of its buildings are of great moment. *N.-D.-des-Neiges* (16C) stands at the S. corner of the central Place, from the opposite side of which the Rue Duclaux leads N.E., passing (l.) the Rue Vermenouze, in which is the *Hôtel de Noailles* and other mansions preserving Renaissance features. The *Maison Consulaire* (16C; restored), further N.E., houses a museum of regional interest, beyond which the Rue du Collège leads to a small square, to the N. of which rises the 11C keep of the *Château St-Étienne*, containing a 'Volcanic Museum', with specific reference to the geology of the region. To the S.E. of the Square stands *St-Géraud*, with a mid 17C Gothic choir and transepts and a later nave, built on the site of the ancient abbey, with a tower added in 1868; relics of the medieval edifice may be seen in the 15C chapels at the E. end. The adjacent Place preserves a house with Romanesque arcading, and an old fountain-basin. In the 'Bâtiment de l'Horloge', some distance S. of Notre-Dame, are collections of art and archaeology.

For the N120 to *Argentat*, see Rte 64; for the N122 leading N.E. to *Murat*, see Rte 100.

AURILLAC TO FIGEAC (67km). A minor and attractive alternative road (D17) turns l. off the sub-route 3km from Aurillac, to regain it just prior to Maurs.—The N122 leads S.W. to (11km) *Sansac*, with a graceful Gothic church, shortly after which the Cère is crossed, beyond which several minor roads leads r. towards the huge but picturesque reservoir formed by the *Barrage de St-Étienne-Cantalès*. The N122 later bears S. to descend into the Rance valley and (34km) *Maurs*, notable for its chestnut trees and the 14C nave and 15C doorway of its church, which contains the naive bust-reliquary of St Césaire (13C).—Some 5km N., beyond *St-Hilaire*, is the château of *Bessonnies*, where Marshal Ney was arrested in 1815, prior to his judicial murder in Paris.—We continue down the valley, with a view across to the 15C château of *Trioulou*, to (7.5km) *Bagnac*, where a medieval bridge crosses the Célé below its confluence with the Rance.—14.5km. **Figeac**; see Rte 65.

AURILLAC TO LAGUIOLE (82km). At *Arpajon*, 4km S., turn l. onto the D990 through *Carlat*, at the foot of a basalt rock, which from the 9C to 1604 bore the castle of the viscounts of Carlat, razed to the ground by Henri IV.—At 25km the château of *Cropières*, birthplace of the Duchesse de Fontanges (1661–81), a favourite of Louis XIV, lies to the N. Here we turn S. through (2km) *Raulhac*, 2km beyond which passing (r.) the Renaissance château of *Messilhac* prior to entering (5.5km) *Mur-de-Barrez*, an old town with a 12C church and massive *Tour de l'Horloge*.—Hence the D904 leads 30km S. to *Entraygues*.—The D900 continues S.E. past (l.) the *Barrage de Sarrans*, in the upper gorge of the Truyère, through (19.5km) *Ste-Geneviève-sur-Argence*, a small summer resort, to cross the Plateau de la Viadène to (23km) *Laguiole*; see Rte 100.

AURILLAC TO ESPALION (76km). The D920 leads S.E., crossing the Cère beyond (4km) *Arpajon* before winding across the hills to (18km) *Lafeuillade*; see below.—13km. *Montsalvy*, with an Augustinian priory church (12th and 15C) and old gateways at either end of its main street. The *Puy de l'Arbre* (825m), to the N.E., commands panoramic views. The road descends, with views of the Lot and Truyère valleys, to (14km) **Entraygues**, with a castle built by Henri II, Comte de Rodez, in 1278, splendidly situated at the confluence of the two rivers (the latter spanned by a medieval bridge). Several old houses survive in the Rues Basse and Droite.

A road descends the Lot to (21km) the *Pont de Coursavy* (see below), passing the charming village of *Vieillevie*, with a little 16C château.—The *Barrage de Couesque*, damming the Truyère c. 8km N. of Entraygues, is impressive.—A direct cross-country but minor road (D904) climbs S.W. from Entraygues, with good retrospective views, via (21km) *Villecomtal*, on the Dourdou, with old houses and fortifications for which Henri de Rodez (see above) was responsible

The D920 threads the Gorges of the Lot to the S.E. to (17km) *Estaing*, where the river is crossed by a 13C bridge. The massive 15-16C castle was once the seat of a famous family: it was Tristan d'Estaing who saved the life of Philippe-Auguste at Bouvines in 1244.—10km. **Espalion**; see Rte 100, where we climb S.W. to (32km) **Rodez**.

From Aurillac the D920 is followed S.E., to (22km) *Lafeuillade*, there forking r. onto the D601, which winds across country before descending into the Lot valley at (28km) the *Pont de Coursavy*, beyond which the valley of the Dourdou is ascended.

6.5km. **Conques**, a picturesque hillside village, once an important staging-post on a pilgrimage road to Compostela, was the seat of one of the most powerful abbeys in France, founded in the 8C. Besides the abbey church, it preserves three of its 12C gates, and some (restored) 14C houses.

The ****Church of Ste-Foy**, begun c. 1050 by Abbot Odolric, is one of the most remarkable edifices in Languedoc after St-Sernin at Toulouse. Perhaps its most notable feature is the **Tympanum* of the W. Door, a vivid representation of the Last Judgement (c. 1135) preserving traces of its original colouring. The W. Towers, reconstructed in the 19C after the building had been 'discovered' by Mérimée in 1837, are notable, as are the niches containing the sarcophagi of abbots.

The lofty nave is lit through a triforium of twin arches, which are continued round the transepts and choir, except at the ends of the transepts, where they are replaced by a cornice. In the S. transept are 15C wall-paintings; others survive in the Sacristy. Almost all the capitals are notable; the glass is not. The vault of the towers reveals the 14C reconstruction. The sanctuary is separated from the three-apsed ambulatory by nine 12C wrought-iron grilles, forged—it is said—from the fetters of prisoners released at the intercession of St Faith (Foi), a girl who suffered martyrdom for her faith at Agen in 303.

To the S., one line of arches of the 12C cloister now serve as windows for the **Museum and Treasury*, an exceptionally fine collection of French goldsmiths' work from the 9th to 16C, the most famous object in which is a *Reliquary-statue of Ste Foy* (85mm high; 10C, with later additions), a curiously hideous idol, upright in its throne, as if sitting on a carbuncle. The wooden statue is encrusted with silver gilt and studded with precious stones, antique cameos, and enamels of varying dates. The head, with its staring eyes, preserving the child-saint's skull, dates from the 5C. Otherwise, the oldest piece in the treasury is a golden reliquary presented by Pepin of Aquitaine (9C).—The abbey is at present used by Premonstratensian monks.

The road ascends the narrowing valley of the Dourdou, with attrac-

The reliquary-statue of Ste-Foy, in the Treasury at Conques

tive retrospective views, to (11.5km) *Nauviale*, below which are the picturesque ruins of the château of *Belcaire*. Crossing the river, we continue through (7.5km) *Marcillac-Vallon*, with old houses and a 14-15C church, and (3.5km) *St-Austremoine*, with an 11-13C church with good capitals, to (3.5km) *Salles-la-Source*, taking its name from a copious spring that tumbles in cascades into a rocky amphitheatre.

12km. **RODEZ** (26,300 Ruthénois), former capital of the *Rouergue*, and préfecture of the *Aveyron*, stands on a steep escarpment some 120m above the river Aveyron and at an altitude of 630m; its winter climate is severe.

Segodunum, capital of a Gaullish tribe allied with the Arverni, was colonised by the Romans and renamed *Ruthena*. Its medieval history was one long struggle between its bishops and the courts of Rouergue, the two factions going so far as to erect a double wall between the episcopal Cité and the feudal Bourg, whose names survive in the two main squares of the old town. It remained orthodox during the Religious Wars of the 13th and 16Cs. It was briefly in English hands

(1360–68), and later Bp Bertrand de Cardaillac, suspected of anglophile sym
pathies (for he was an ex-chancellor of the Black Prince) was expelled by th
citizens. The 14C *Tour des Anglais*, E. of the Cathedral, recalls the occupation. I
August 1944, the day before the German evacuation, 32 hostages were shot a
Ste-Radegonde, to the E. of the town (with a 13C fortified church).

Most main roads converge on the *Pl. des Armes*, overlooked by th
red-sandstone **Cathedral of Notre-Dame**, begun in the Norther
Gothic style in 1277 and only completed in 1562. The severe W
Front has a fortress-like appearance, although above the Flamboyan
rose-window is a Renaissance gable. The Flamboyant S. doorway i
striking, but lost its statuary during the Revolution. Mor
remarkable is the beautifully proportioned and richly-decorated *N.I
Tower (87m high), its plain lower late 14C storeys surmounted b
three octagonal upper tiers (1526) built during Bp Françoi
d'Estaing's incumbency by Antoine Salvan, a local architect. Th
unusual statues at the bases of the octagonal corner-turrets will b
noted.

The plain but impressive interior (170m long; 36m wide) is notable for i
quatrefoil-shaped pillars with ring capitals. In the N. transept is the gutte
organ-loft of 1631. Below the W. window is a heavy 16C stone gallery extendin
to the N. aisle; in the S. aisle is a painted stone Entombment depicting figure
dressed in the height of 1530 fashion. The S. Transept contains a profusel
decorated rood-screen (15C) by Bertrand de Chalençon, sensibly moved her
from the choir in 1872. The choir-stalls of 1482 are by André Sulpice. The Am
bulatory preserves two marble sarcophagi of bishops (5-6C), and in the chapels
tomb of other bishops, including that of Raymond d'Aigrefeuille (d. 1361); othe
notworthy objects are a 10C altar-table; a Renaissance doorway, perhaps b
Nicolas Bachelier; a Renaissance Noli Me Tangere; and an earlier Pietà, etc.

Opposite the N. entrance is the *Bishop's Palace* (15-17C; restored), t
the E. of which is the *Pl. de la Cité*, providing a view of the cathedra
tower. Some characteristic old lanes to the S. and E. of the apse con
tain Renaissance houses, among them the *Maison Molinier* (near S
door). The Rue Neuve leads S., passing between the *Préfecture* (r.
and nearby *Hôtel de Ville*, and *Library*, to approach the *Pl. du Bourg
where several 16C houses survive, including the *Maison de la An
nonciade*. Near its S.W. corner is the *Hôtel d'Armagnac*, while fur
ther S. is *St-Amans*, whose 18C exterior conceals a 12C nave
(restored); it contains 17C tapestries and 18C stalls.

Near the N.E. corner of the Pl. du Bourg is the *Musée Fenaille*, in
Renaissance mansion. Notable amongst its collections of antiquities
furniture, and sculpture, is a 16C polychrome Virgin, Gallo-Roma
pottery of local manufacture, and a Roman bronze vizor.

The Rue Ste-Catherine leads to a boulevard, with view-points at both N. and S
ends, and the *Musée des Beaux-Arts*, containing sculpture by Denys Puec
(1854–1942; born in the neighbourhood), among others, and a miscellaneou
collection of paintings.

For the road from *St-Flour* to **Albi** via Rodez, see Rte 100.

96 Nemours to Moulins

211km (131 miles). N7. 33km **Montargis**—25.5km *Le Poteau*. **Gien**
lies 13.5km S.W.—16km *Briare*—31km *Cosne-sur-Loire*—28km **La
Charité-sur-Loire**—24km **Nevers**—23km *St-Pierre-le-Moûtier*—31km
Moulins.

Maps: IGN 27, 36, or 108. M 237, 238.

For the road between *Nemours* and *Montargis*, see Rte 48.

AN ALTERNATIVE ROAD TO BONNY-SUR-LOIRE (10km beyond *Briare*) is the
D93, forking S.E. just S. of Montargis, which after 15.5km passes the ruins of the
Gallo-Roman Amphitheatre of *Chenevière*, and 6.5km beyond, enters *Châtillon-
Coligny*, the cradle of the family of which Adm. de Coligny (1519–72), born
there and buried in the château park, was the most eminent member. The
16-sided castle keep dates from the 12C. The road continues through *Rogny*,
with its abandoned sluice-gates, to (19km) *Bléneau*, which gave its name to
Turenne's victory over Condé in 1652, which saved the court, then at Gien. In
the choir of the late 12C church is a fresco of 1480.—For *St-Fargeau*, 12km further S.E., see Rte 119. From Bléneau we turn S.W. on the D64 to (20km) *Bonny*.

For the road from Montargis to *Le Poteau*, see Rte 48. Here fork l., at
3km passing (l.) the 15-16C château of *La Bussière*, with an *Angling
Museum*, and 13km beyond, by-passing *Briare*; see Rte 49.—10km.
Bonny-sur-Loire, and (5km) *Neuvy*, are respectively by-passed and
traversed, before reaching (14km) *Cosne-sur-Loire*, once a medieval
fortress. Early 15C *St-Jacques* has a massive square tower; *St-Agnan*,
with a richly sculptured W. door, has good capitals on the exterior of
its Romanesque apse.

Near *St-Père*, 3km E., its 16C church preserving contemporary glass, is the partly
Romanesque *Commanderie de Villemoison*.—At *Donzy*, some 15km further E.,
is the almost impregnable keep of its barons, a 12-14C church, and the ruins of a
Benedictine priory.
   9km N.W., on the far bank, is *Léré*, its Romanesque crypt containing 13C
murals.

8km. A new bridge crosses the Loire to *St-Satur*, 6km W.; for the road
hence via *Sancerre* to **Bourges**, see Rte 119.—7km. *Pouilly-sur-Loire*,
by-passed, is known for its white wines, 13km beyond which we
enter **La Charité-sur-Loire** (6400 inhab.), an ancient town preserving
relics of its 11C walls and three towers of its ruined castle. It derives
its name from a monastery founded in the 8C. The place was besieged in vain by Joan of Arc in 1429, and suffered severely in the
religious wars of the 16C. Just E. of its *Bridge* (1763), built slightly
askew, stands the abbey-church of *Ste-Croix-Notre-Dame (11-12C).
It was poorly restored in 1695, but retains an octagonal Romanesque
tower over the crossing, and ambulatory (with fluted pillars similar
to those at Autun), choir, transepts, and capitals of interest, although
deserving a further restoration. On the site of the nave is a small
square in some houses of which have been incorporated fragments
of the vanished aisles. A vaulted passage leads to 17-18C dependencies.
   Bourges lies 50km W. on the N151, see Rte 119.—The road shortly
bears away from the Loire through (13km) *Pougues-les-Eaux*, an old
spa, 3km to the S. of which lies *Garchizy*, its 12C church with an octagonal tower, beyond which rise the foundries of *Fourchambault*.
   11km. **NEVERS** (44,800 Nivernais), the grey-roofed préfecture of
the *Nièvre*, pleasantly sited at the confluence of the Nièvre (here in a

partly covered channel) and the Loire, just E. of the confluence of the latter with the Allier.

Nevers, one of several stations called *Noviodunum* by the Romans, became the seat of a bishop under Clovis, and later the capital of the hilly *Nivernais*, one of whose counts, Pierre de Courtenay, erected its walls in 1194. The countship was held by several eminent families, including the dukes of Burgundy and the house of Clèves. François I made it a duchy, which in 1565 passed to the Gonzagas of Mantua (Luigi Gonzaga introducing the manufacture of faïence, for which the town became famous). In 1659 it passed to Card. Mazarin, who bequeathed it to his nephew Mancini, in whose family it remained until the Revolution. The carpenter-poet Adam Billaut (1602–62), a protégé of Richelieu, was born here, as was the author and diplomat Baron de Bourgoing (1748–1811). Bernadette Soubirous (1844–79), the visionary of Lourdes, retired to the convent of St-Gildard here in 1866, where she died, and was buried. The town is noted for its nougatine.

From the S.E. corner of the central *Pl.Carnot*, with a park to the N., a street ascends between the *Hôtel de Ville* (r.), behind which are vestiges of de Courtenay's 12C castle, and (l.) the former **Palais Ducal**, begun c. 1475 and modified in the mid 16C in the Renaissance taste, partly by the Gonzagas. The graceful middle tower is decorated with restored low reliefs depicting the traditional history of the house of Clèves; the flanking towers and octagonal turrets are likewise noteworthy.

To the S.W. rises the **Cathedral**, which like that at Besançon, has an apse at each end, and is formed by the joining of a Gothic to the Romanesque church, oriented E. and W. respectively.

Indifferently restored in 1864, it is still interesting in that it represents every period of medieval French architecture, although of the original structure, begun c. 1028, only the W. apse and transept remain, the nave and E. end having been replaced by a second church after a fire in 1211. The side aisles, graceful S. portal, and ornate *Tower* (of 1528 on a 14C base; some of its statues replaced by copies) were 15-16C additions. The N. portal, of c. 1280, is in a pure Gothic style. It retains some good gargoyles, and the wild boar high above the W. apse will be noted.

The nave has a well-carved triforium with trefoil arches resting on caryatids. The W. apse preserves a 12-13C fresco; in the crypt below is a 16C Entombment. A flamboyant doorway in the S. transepts leads to an openwork staircase surmounted by a group of St Michael and the dragon. Most of the altar-pieces are mutilated; the choir preserves 18C stalls.

The former *Bishop's Palace*, to the S., dates from 1786.—The Rue des Jacobins leads W., off which the Rue St-Genest turns l. past relics of its Romanesque church, and a *Ceramic museum* of interest, to the riverside *Pl. Mossé* (near which are vestiges of the Romanesque abbey-church of *St-Sauveur*, which collapsed in 1838). Turning r., one may walk through gardens overlooked by a stretch of town Wall, passing first the *Tour Goguin*, to re-enter the old enceinte by the *Porte du Croux* (1398), preceded by a barbican. It contains an archaeological collection.

The Rue St-Martin leads E. from the Pl. Carnot, passing (l.) the Italianate Baroque facade of the *Chapelle Ste-Marie* (1639), to the *Pl. St-Sébastien*, overlooked by a *Belfry*, partly 15C. By turning l. up the pedestrian Rue du Commerce, and then r., the Rue Creuse is crossed to approach *St-Étienne, the church of an old Cluniac priory, a remarkable Romanesque edifice of 1063–97, with several characteristics of the Auvergnat style such as the small galleries, and the apse with three chapels, while the windows beneath the vaulting of the nave are Burgundian in inspiration. Only the bases of its three

towers remain; a Gothic cloister abuts it. The interior may be
described as sombre.

Just beyond the N. end of the Rue Creuse is *St-Pierre* (1612), and the
Porte de Paris, an arch of 1746 commemorating the battle of
Fontenoy (cf.p 643), with a florid inscription by Voltaire. Adjacent is
the *Préfecture*.—One may regain the Pl. Carnot by following the Rue
du Rampart to the S.W.

NEVERS TO AUTUN (103km). The D978 leads due E. across the *Côtes du Nivernais* via (31km) *Rouy*, with a Romanesque church, 10.5km N. of which is *St-
Saulge*, with a 16C church and older crypt, and 3km W. of the latter, *Jailly*, with
a Romanesque church with a 15C painted tympanum.—10km beyond Rouy lies
Châtillon-en-Bazois, with a 16-17C château, and the hilly *Parc du Morvan* is
entered prior to traversing (25km) *Château-Chinon*. The road continues to wind
through the broken and thickly forested countryside, at (10km) *Arleuf*, passing
10km from *Anost*, to the N.E., in the heart of the Morvan, once the home of the
'Galvachers', the carriers of the district whose picturesque ox-carts were
characteristic.—We later bear S.E. into the basin of the Arroux, on the S. side of
which stands **Autun**, dominated by its cathedral; see Rte 120.

NEVERS TO PARAY-LE-MONIAL (112km). The N81 follows the r. bank of the
Loire through *Imphy*, with foundries, and *Béard*, with a 12C church, to (23km)
Decize, a small manufacturing town 7.5km S. of industrial *La Machine*, surrounded by forests. Decize was the birthplace of Louis-Antoine de Saint-Just
(1767–94), the revolutionary. *St-Aré* has a 12C choir and 7C crypt containing
the tomb of its patron, a bishop of Nevers (d. 558); on an adjacent hill is the ruin-
ed 15-17C castle and the former *Couvent des Minimes* (17C).—35km. **Bourbon-
Lancy**, a small spa 3km E., preserves some old houses and town gates, and the
secularised church of *St-Nazaire* (11-12C), now a museum. The road traverses
St-Aubin-sur-Loire, with a château of the 16C and 1780, and bears S.E. to (20km)
Digoin and *Paray-le-Monial*, 12km beyond; see Rte 97; and likewise for the road
S. to **Roanne** and the several churches of interest near it.

10km S.E. of Nevers is the château of *Chevenon* (14C; restored), and a 12-15C
church.

The N7 leads S., at 12km passing 3km W. of *St-Parize-le-Châtel*, with
a 12C church, relic of an abbey founded by St Patrick in the 6C, with
a remarkable *Crypt.—7.5km *St-Pierre-le-Moutier*, once fortified, and
at the junction of a road from Bourges, is named after a Benedictine
monastery taken from the English by Joan of Arc in 1429; 12C *St-
Pierre* contains some good sculpture.—19km. The remains of the 16C
château of *Le Riau* lie 2km E.

12km. **MOULINS** (25,500 Moulinois), ancient capital of the *Bourbonnais*, and préfecture of the *Allier*, stands on the r. bank of the
river Allier, here crossed by the *Pont Régemortes* (1763), one of the
more important crossing-points from Occupied France into that administered by the Vichy regime. It is a thriving agricultural centre
and market town, and preserves several old houses in the cathedral
quarter.

Its prosperity was founded in the 14C, when Louis I de Bourbon erected a castle
here, and here in 1548 the marriage of Antoine de Bourbon and Jeanne d'Albret
(parents of Henri IV) was celebrated. It was badly damaged by the explosion of its
arsenal in Feb. 1918. Lord Clarendon composed much of his 'History of the
Great Rebellion' at Moulins (cf. Rouen). The melancholy scene of Maria in
Sterne's 'Sentimental Journey' occurred here. It was the birthplace of Marshal
Villars (1653–1734); the Duke of Berwick (1670–1734; natural son of James II
and Arabella Churchill); Henri Baude (c. 1430–c. 96), satirical poet; Adm. d'Orvilliers (1708–92); and the poet Théodore de Banville (1823–91).

The Rue de Paris enters the old centre, passing (r.) the *Lycée Banville*, in buildings of a former convent, the 17C chapel of which con-

tains the *Tomb of Henri*, last duke of Montmorency (1595–1632), erected by his widow, the Princess Orsini (Mme Félicie des Ursins) from the designs of François Anguier, Regnaudin, and Poissant. Enquire first at the S.I. in the *Pl. Hotel de Ville* about Adm.

To the l. is the *Palais de Justice* in a 17C Jesuit college; while No. 7 in the street is the 16C *Hôtel Laferronays*, beyond which opens the Cours Anatole-France, and a short distance S. rises the **Cathedral**, with a remarkable Flamboyant choir of 1468–1507; the nave is 19C. The unusual arrangement of the E. end gives a curious exterior effect, the low chevet of the ambulatory being rectangular, and that of the sanctuary being polygonal. The window-tracery, the openwork gallery encircling the roof, and the N. door (note man with bear), are features of interest.

The 15-16C *Windows* of the Choir (restored after the explosion of 1918) display portraits and armorial bearings. The figure of a corpse being devoured by worms will be observed in the S. ambulatory; also a late 15C Entombment. The Sacristy contains the 15C *Triptych 'of the Maitre de Moulins'* (Jean Hey), representing the Virgin and Child surrounded by angels, with Pierre II de Bourbon (1439–1503) and his wife Anne de Beaujeu, the donors (cf. Beaujeu); the side-panels are by another artists. Also notable is a triptych by Joos van Cleve.

Facing its W. entrance is the *Tour Malcoiffé* (14C), a relic of the ducal castle, N. of which is the Renaissance *Pavillon d'Anne de Beaujeu*, now containing a *Museum*, with an archaeological section, collections of arms, ceramics, and paintings, including some of the German School.

The Rue Ancien-Palais leads S.E. past a 16C mansion in which is a *Museum* of folklore and local history, to a *Belfry* of 1455, its upper part damaged by fire in 1655, with a restored gallery and Jacquemart.

The *Hôtel de Ville*, opposite, contains the *Library*, preserving among its treasures the *Souvigny Bible* (12C) with a binding adorned with wrought copper, and containing numerous historiated initials and minatures of Byzantine inspiration; it was used at the Council of Constance in 1415 to verify the proposed textual emendations of John Huss.

Several 15-16C houses may be seen in the Rue d'Allier, a few paces to the S., leading W. to the central *Pl. d'Allier*.—In the suburb of *Yzeure*, 2km E., is a good Romanesque church, with 14-15C additions.

MOULINS TO MONTLUÇON VIA SOUVIGNY (67.5km). The N145 leads W. to (12km) **Souvigny**, an ancient town where *St-Pierre*, the church of a former Cluniac priory, largely 11-12C, contains the mutilated tombs of Louis III de Bourbon (d. 1410) and Charles I (d. 1456), with their respective wives, Anne d'Auvergne and Agnès de Bourgogne. Also remarkable in its interior are the arcade along the N. wall; the foliage along the main ridge of the nave vault; the painted panels in the S. aisle, off which is one walk of a 15C cloister; and in the apse, the carving of an archer and mermaid, etc.—A lapidary collection may be seen in a chapel to the N. of the church, which includes a remarkable octagonal column carved with scenes representing the months (12C). There are several attractive old houses in the village, notably that near the apse.—The main road goes on past (9km) *Meillers* (l.), with an imposing Romanesque church, via (21.5km) *Cosne-d'Allier*, to **Montluçon**, 25 km beyond (see Rte 92), but the more interesting alternative is that via **St-Menoux** (6km N.W. of Souvigny), with a notable *Church* (11-15C), a relic of a Benedictine abbey, its choir containing remarkable capitals, ribbon-decoration, and the saint's tomb. The D953 later veers S.W. via (9km) **Bourbon-l'Archambault**, a spa famous since Roman times, when as *Aquae Borvonis* it was extolled by Vitruvius. It was the capital of the Bourbonnais from the time of Archambault I (13C) until succeeded by Moulins. Its baths flourished again in the late 17C, when they were taken by Louis XIV, bringing in his train Mme de Sévigné, Boileau, and Henrietta of England

(daughter of Charles I), which Mme de Montespan spent her last years here,
where she died in 1707. The *Logis du Roi*, a 17C pump-room, was built by Gaston
d'Orléans, and parts of the 13C ducal castle, and the rebuilt 12C church still survive at opposite ends of the town.—The road continues through (13km) *Ygrande*,
also with a 12C church, to regain the main route at *Cosne-d'Allier*, 13km beyond.

For roads from Moulins to **Mâcon** (via *Paray-le-Monial*, and *Cluny*); to **Roanne**
(for *Lyon* or *St-Étienne*); for **Montélimar** via *Vichy* and *Le Puy*; and for **Albi**, via
Clermont-Ferrand, *St-Flour*, and *Rodez*, see Rtes 97, 98, 99, and 100, respectively.

97 Moulins to Mâcon via Paray-le-Monial and Cluny

146km (91 miles), including the detour to **Cluny**. D12. 31km
Dompierre-sur-Besbre—N19. 25.5km *Digoin*—12km **Paray-le-
Monial**—N79. 49.5km. **Cluny** lies 5km N.—18km **Mâcon**.

Maps: IGN 43 or 108. M 238, 243.

The D12 forks r. in *Yzeure*, a suburb of **Moulins** (Rte 96), and
traverses a district dotted with small lakes to (31km) *Dompierre-sur-
Besbre*, 4km N.E. of which is the former Trappist monastery of *Sept-
Fonds* (18C), founded in 1132; 6km to the S.W. are the châteaux of
Toury (late 15C) and *Beauvoir* (13-15C).

The road approaches the Loire and veers S.E. to (25.5km) *Digoin*,a
junction of roads and three canels, one of which is carried across the
Loire in an aqueduct of 16 arches.—12km. **Paray-le-Monial**, a town
of 11,300 inhab. in the valley of the Bourbince, preserves an impressive Romanesque church, and although a place of pilgrimage
since 1873, is not as obviously corrupted as some other such centres.

Surnamed 'le Monial' from its numerous medieval monasteries, it only acquired
notoriety during the reign of Louis XIV, when Marguerite-Marie Alacoque
(1647–90), a visitandine nun, professed to see visions, which inspired the cult of
the Sacred Heart of Jesus, a revival of which followed her beatification in 1864.

Overlooking the river stands *Notre-Dame (since 1875 called by
some the 'Basilica du Sacré-Coeur'), a striking example of 12C
Burgundian Romanesque, revealing the direct influence of Cluny.
The narthex at the W. end, surmounted by two dissimilar spired
towers, probably dates from an earlier (11C) structure, but the octagonal tower over the crossing is a restoration of 1860. The ambulatory, from which three chapels radiate, contains eight
monolithic columns, while traces of classical influence are apparent
in the capitals and other ornamentation. The semi-dome of the apse
contains a 15C fresco of Christ in Majesty, uncovered in 1935.

The Rue de la Visitation leads N., to the r. at the far end of which is
the *Musée du Hiéron*, preserving a fine tympanum from Anzy-le-Duc
(see below), paintings by *Van Steenwick*; *Giaquinto's* St Philip Neri in
extasy; and a section devoted to the Eucharistic cult, etc.—To the W.
is the *Hôtel de Ville* in a Renaissance mansion of 1528, its facade
embellished with sculpture; opposite rises the square *Tour St-Nicolas*,
a survival from a former church. Hence the Rue Victor-Hugo leads
back to the river.

PARAY-LE-MONIAL TO ROANNE (53km; considerably longer if all the churches of interest along the r. bank of the Loire are visited). Amongst the latter are
(15km) *Montceaux-l'Étoile* (l. off the D982), with a relief of the Ascension in its

tympanum; **Anzy-le-Duc** (4km S.), a striking Cluniac abbey-church with an octagonal tower, good capitals, but a mutilated portal; hence we regain the main road N. of *Marcigny*, with the 15C *Tour du Moulin*, 5km E. of which, at **Semur-en-Brionnais**, is a Romanesque *Church*, one of the types of Mâconnais architecture (12C), with a richly sculptured W. door, and also with an octagonal tower, near which is a 9C keep.—5km further S.E., at *St-Julien-de-Jonzy*, the mid 12C church preserves a remarkable portal, although the sculpture of the Last Supper is mutilated.—The *Château de Chamrod*, birthplace of Mme du Deffand (1697–1780), stood near *St-Bonnet-de-Cray*, just to the S.—Hence the main road is regained to the S.W. at *Iguerande*, with an 11-12C church.—At 6km S. a l.-hand turning leads 5.5km to *Charlieu*: *Roanne* (see Rte 98) lies 13.5km S. of this junction, 5km to the W. of which, at *La Bénisson-Dieu*, are the picturesque ruins of a Cistercian abbey founded by St Bernard.

Charlieu, (Charliandins), preserving several interesting old houses, grew up around a Benedictine *Abbey* (founded in 872), of which important ruins remain at the W. end of the town. The square to the N. is overlooked by two medieval towers, opposite that to the W. is the mutilated sculptured *Portal* of the 12C narthex of three bays, a masterpiece of Burgundian Romanesque, virtually all that remains of the huge 11C church. Foundations of 9-10C predecessors lie under the site of the choir. Entrance may be gained to view three mutilated walks of the late 15C cloister, in the E. walk of which are six arches of an 11C cloister, off which open a chapter-house and chapel; to the S. is the 16C abbot's house.—A few minutes' walk to the W. brings one to the irregularly shaped *Cloître des Cordeliers*, with early 15C capitals, all that remains of a Franciscan monastery 'removed' to the U.S.A.

From Paray-le-Monial we drive E. through (13km) *Charolles*, an ancient town with ruins of a castle of its counts, with 14C towers. The *Charollais* is reputed for its breed of cattle.

CHAROLLES TO LYON (109km). The D985 leads S., at 17km passing (l.) the 17C château of *Drée*, to (3km) *La Clayette* (pron. La Clette), with its restored 14C castle overlooking a lake, to the S.E. of which rises the *Montagne de Dun* (709m; views); 8km to the N.E. is *Bois-Ste-Marie*, with a fine Romanesque church.—13km. *Chauffailles*.—13km. *Les Écharmeaux*, well-sited on its col (718m) on the main ridge of the thickly wooded *Monts du Beaujolais*, with its highest point, the *Massif of St-Rigaud* (1009m) to the N.E.

The D37 leads 28km E. hence to *Belleville*, on the N6, via (5km) *Chenelette*, overlooked (r.) by the *Tourvéon* (953m), and 11km beyond, *Beaujeu*, the earliest capital of the Beaujolais, with a church of 1134 and vestiges of a castle dismantled by Richelieu. Anne of Beaujeu (1462–1522), daughter of Louis XI and the skilful regent of France during the minority of her brother Charles VIII, was the wife of Pierre II, lord of Beaujeu and duke of Bourbon.

The D485 descends the charming valley of the Azergues to (25km) *Chamelet*, once fortified, with a 13C church, and 5km beyond, *Ternand* (r.), with more imposing fortifications, and an ancient church with some Carolingian capitals built over a remarkable crypt.—*Oingt* (3km E.) preserves picturesque remains.—5km. *Chessy*, also formerly walled, with a Flamboyant church and vestiges of a castle of the abbots of Savigny, has an abandoned copper-mine which belonged to Jacques Coeur.—Adjacent *Châtillon* has ruins of a 12-16C castle with a two-storeyed chapel containing the tomb of Geoffroy de Balsac (d. 1510).—We shortly meet the N9 prior to entering **Lyon**; see Rte 129.

At 13km E. of Charolles the road passes between (r.) *Mont Botey* (561m) and the *Butte de Suin*, to the N.E., regaining the older road at 20.5km, and passing 9km S. of the 16C *Château of Chaumont-la-Guiche*.—Some 5km S. of this junction stands the *Château of Lamartine*, a favourite residence of Alphonse de Lamartine (1790–1869), buried in the adjacent church of *St-Point*.

The l.-hand turning here leads 5km N. to **Cluny**, an ancient town in the Grosne valley, once famous for its Benedictine abbey, the relics of which still dominate the place.

Founded in 910 under Guillaume I, duc de Guienne, by St Berno and enlarged by his successor St Odo (926), who introduced the reformed rule of St Benedict, the monastery became in the 11-12C the influential base of an Order with some 300 dependent houses; among its abbots were St Odilio (962-1048) and Peter the Venerable (1092-1156), who gave sanctuary to Abélard, and among its members were popes Gregory VII, Urban II, and Paschal II. The vast and splendid buildings—particularly the third church as conceived by Hugues de Semur (the high altar of which was consecrated in 1095 by Urban II)—profoundly influenced the development of the Burgundian Romanesque school of architecture. In 1245 Louis IX and Innoccent IV met here to discuss the future of Frederick II, who had been deposed at the Council of Lyon. But with increasing wealth came decreasing intellectual influence, and its abbots became merely royal appointees 'in commendam', among whom were four members of the house of Guise, Richelieu, the Prince de Conti, Mazarin, and the Card. de Bouillon. It suffered severely during the Religious Wars and was suppressed in 1790, the church being progressively demolished for its stone between 1798–1812.

It was the birthplace of the painter Pierre-Paul Prud'hon (1758–1823).

To the E. of the central *Pl. de l'Abbaye* is the restored facade of the 14C *Palace of Pope Gelasius II*, behind which is a large cloister surrounded by 18C buildings. Before viewing the remains of the church, it is recommended to walk W. along the Rue Kenneth J. Conant (named after the American scholar, who from 1928 devoted years studying the architectural history of Cluny), which is on the site of its original nave. The *Hôtel Bourgogne* stands on the site of the N. aisle, while the W. towers were in alignment with the *Hôtel de Ville* (further N.), completed in 1518 for Jacques d'Amboise (who also built the *Hôtel de Cluny* in Paris) adjacent to the 15C *Abbot's Palace*. The *Musée Ochier* contains sculptures and other relics from the monastery, a maquette of 1855 and plans showing its original extant, etc. Further N. is the *Tour Fabry*, of 1347.

The somewhat disappointing remains of the ***Abbey Church** ◊ (1086–1131) may be visited by escorted groups (except Tues.). Skirting the cloisters of the 18C dependencies (at present occupied by an engineering school), we enter the *S. Transept* (33m to the vaulting), which with fragments of the apse, the octagonal *Clocher de l'Eau-Bénite* (62m high; under restoration), and a smaller square tower, is vitually all that now survives of what was the largest church in Christendom until the erection of St Peter's in Rome. The interior was 177m long, and its choir contained 225 stalls.

One is also shown the *Gothic Chapelle de Bourbon* (1456). A short distance to the S.E. in the former gardens is the 13C *Farinier, an impressive chestnut-vaulted granary adjoining the *Tour du Moulin*, containing Conant's model of the abbey-church, and other objects descriptive of the building, while in the vaulted basement (the windows of which were later enlarged), with additional lapidary collections, a stream ran which drove its machinery. To the N.W. of the enceinte (incorporating a national *haras* or stud farm) is the *Tour Ronde*.

Other buildings of interest are the *Tour des Fromages*, S. of the Pl. de l'Abbaye, opposite which is *Notre-Dame*, 13C Burgundian, with good rose-windows in its transepts. Further S., to the r. of the main street, is the *Hôtel-Dieu*, its chapels preserving fragments of a sumptuous but uncompleted tomb of the Card. de Bouillon (1643–1715); to the E. is *St-Marcel*, with a Romanesque tower and heavy spire.

For the road from *Autun*, and *Beaune*, to Cluny, see Rtes 120 and 127 respectively.

Regaining the main route 5km S., we pass (l.) the feudal château of *Berzé-le-Châtel*, once the seat of the oldest barony of the Mâconnaise, and shortly beyond, l., of the road, **Berzé-la-Ville**, where the *Chapelle des Moins* (in 1947 presented to the State by Joan Evans, its previous owner) preserves remarkable 11-12C *Frescoes* of Byzantine inspiration.

To the r., further S.E., is *Milly-Lamartine*, where the poet spent part of his childhood; another of his residences was the château of *Montceau*, to the r. beyond *La Roche-Vineuse*.—*Prissé* is shortly passed to the r., just S. of which Abélard spent two years in the priory of *Chevigné*, now a farm.

S.W. of the latter rises the precipitous *Roche de Solutré* (495m), below which extensive deposites of bones have been found, confirming the existence here of a prehistoric horse-hunting tribe. Although excavations began in 1866, it was not until 1922 that human skeletons of an earlier period were discovered, together with Bronze Age ceramics: see the museum at Mâcon.

The main road descends into the Saône valley, crossing the A6, to enter **Mâcon**; see Rte 127; likewise for the road to *Bourg-en-Bresse*, 34km further E.

98 Moulins to Roanne for Lyon, or St-Étienne

184km (114 miles). N7. 30km *Varennes-sur-Allier*—20km *Lapalisse*—48km **Roanne**—86km **Lyon**. The N82 forks r. 10km S. of Roanne for (68km) **St-Étienne**.

Maps: IGN 43, 50, or 111, 112. M 238, 239, 244.

From **Moulins** (Rte 96) the valley fo the Allier is ascended some distance E. of the river to *Varennes* (see Rte 99), just beyond which the road to **Vichy** forks l.—11km. *St-Gérand-le-Puy* has a 16C château and an 11C church with later murals, 3km N. of which are the ruins of the 14C castle of *Montaigu*.

9.5km. **Lapalisse**, an ancient seignory, is overlooked by a 16C *Château*, with a 'salon doré', and an earlier chapel containing the mutilated tombs of Jacques de Chabannes (d. 1453) and his wife.—The road ascends and traverses the N. end of the *Montes de Madeleine*, providing several panoramic views, via *Châteaumorand* to (24km) *La Pacaudière*, 2km W. of which is the walled village of *Le Crozet*, with a 12C drum tower.

4km. *Changy* (just W. of which is an attractive yellow stone château).

5km S. lies **Ambierle**, the ancient oppidum of the Ambluarètes, preserving its town gate, a separte *Belfry*, and a Flamboyant *Church* with a characteristic Burgundian multi-coloured roof, and unusual figures on its buttresses. Steps descends into the yellow stone nave with notable capitals (vineyard scenes; rosettes, etc.), retaining good glass, and carved 15C stalls; also a 15C Flemish triptych.—*St-Haon-le-Châtel* (pron. St-Han), 5km beyond, preserves several relics of its many-towered walls, just beyond which we may turn E. to (12km) *Roanne*, passing (l.) the *Château de Boisy* (14th and 16C), once a residence of Jacques Coeur.—2.5km S. of this turning is *St-André-d'Apchon*, with a 15-16C castle, and 12th and 16C church, with notable glass.

21km (from Changy) is **Roanne** (49,600 inhab.), an industrial town and river-port, with manufacturers based on cotton-weaving, on the l. bank of the Loire at its highest navigable point. A garrison town and arsenal, it resisted an Austrian attack in 1814, but, apart from its gastronomic reputation, it has little to recommend it, and it is suggested that the by-pass is used. Even in 1890 it was condemned as 'an ugly, smoky manufacturing town'. In the centre is rebuilt *St-Étienne*, the *Keep* of its 14-16C castle, and a short distance S., a *Museum* containing a good archaeological collection and Gallo-Roman antiquities. Nearer the river is the old waterman's chapel of *St-Nicolas*.

A minor road leads S. along the l. bank, here descending through a gorge (to be dammed) to the old villages of *Villerest* and *St-Maurice-sur-Loire*, with its ruined castle.

Charlieu lies 19km N.E.; see Rte 97.

9km. The road for **St-Étienne** forks r.; see below.

We bear E., ascending and crossing the *Monts du Lyonnais*, at 13.5km passing near (r.) the 16-18C château of *l'Aubépin*, with its pepper-pot towers, soon after reaching a height of 760m, before descending to (20.5km) *Tarare* (10,900 inhab.), a centre of cotton industries and their synthetic substitutes, lying in the narrow valley of the Turdine.—We pass (l.) the well-sited yellow stone château of *Bully* (14C and Renaissance) before entering (18km) *L'Arbresle*, with a 13-15C church retaining good glass, remains of walls and an 11C castle of the abbots of *Savigny*, the ruins of the once important Benedictine abbey of which lie 4km S.W. L'Arbresle (2km S. of which is a Dominican convent built by Le Corbusier in 1959) was the birthplace of Barthélemy Thimonnier (1793–1856/9), inventor of perhaps the first form of sewing-machine (c. 1830).

20km. **Lyon**; see Rte 129, preferably having first studied the general town-plan in the Michelin Red Guide, the approaches being somewhat complicated.

The r.-hand fork 9km S. of Roanne after 16km passes 2km W. of *St-Marcel-de-Félines*, where the picturesque turreted and moated late 16C château contains remarkable 17C decoration.—At (6km) *Balbigny* we meet the Loire at the N. extremity of the *Forez* plain, the basin of an ancient lake.—*Néronde*, 6km N.E., with remains of fortifications, was the birthplace of Père Cotton (d. 1621), the confessor of Henri IV and Louis XIII.

9km. *Feurs*—by-passed to the W.—with a 15C church with a rebuilt facade, was Roman *Forum Segusiavorum*, on the main road from Lyon to Clermont-Ferrand, and the original capital of the Forez.—For *La Bastie d'Urfé*, c. 12km W., see p. 532; *Montbrison* lies 23km to the S.W.

11km. *Montrond-les-Bains*, a small spa, preserves ruins of a 14-16C castle, 3km beyond which a by-road (l.) leads to *St-Galmier*, known for its mineral waters. The upper town contains several old houses and a 15-16C church with a 16C polyptych. Hence one may regain the main road at *Veauche*, 10km S. of Montrond.

4km. *Andrézieux-Bouthéon* lies 2km W.; see below. Here we meet the motorway, which the N82 follows in parallel for 8km through an industrial district. A l.-hand turning then leads E. to (14km) *St-Chamond*; see Rte 139. The main road veers S. across the motorway to enter—and after 6km reach the centre of—*St-Étienne*. The stretch of railway in this valley is the oldest in France, constructed by Marc Séguin, a native of Annonay (see below), and opened for goods traffic in 1827, and for passengers in 1832. (The Stockton-Darlington line had been in operation since 1825).

ANDRÉZIEUX TO LA CHAISE-DIEU (70km). The D498 crosses the Montbrison road N.W. of *St-Just* (cf.) and climbs S.W. into the *Monts du Forez* and (25km) *St-Bonnet-le-Château*, with several 15-16C houses, a 15C and Renaissance collegiate *Church*, a *Hospice Chapel* containing Louis-XIV decoration, and commanding a wide panorama.—At 5km the *Estivareilles Bridge*, possible of Roman construction, is crossed, and *Usson-en-Forez*, with relics of its ramparts and castle, is traversed 8km beyond, 5km S. of which stands *St-Pol-de-Chalenton*, with a 15C castle and three medieval gates.—13km. *Craponne-sur-Arzon* has an interesting church (16C, with a 13C belfry). The main road continues S. to meet after 14km that from La Chaise-Dieu some 25.5km N. of *Le Puy*. We fork r., and after 13km turn r. for (8km) **La Chaise-Dieu**; see Rte 99.

ST-ÉTIENNE (206,700 Stéphanois; 16,300 in 1801), the centre of an important but unattractive industrial and colliery area (the second largest in France), and since 1856 the préfecture of the *Loire*, is strung out on either side of a long main street running N.-S.; it has a propitiatory museum.

As early as the 12C the surface beds of coal were used by the smiths of the Forez, but it was not until the 15C that it became an industrial centre, when the manufacture of ribbons was introduced by Gayotti of Bologna, and in the 16C the production of firearms was commenced. The 19C saw an immense development in coal-mining and the manufacture of steel, the first steel-works having been founded in 1815 by an Englishman named Jackson. The production of bicycles (introduced in 1886 by Duncan, from the firm of Rudge) and motorcars, glass, chocolate, and dyeing, are likewise industries which have contributed to its prosperity. Its population in 1831 was 33,000; in 1901, 146,000. The town suffered from bombing in 1944.

It was the birthplace of Claude Fauriel (1772–1844), the author and critic; Jules Janin (1804–74), the novelist and critic; and the composer Jules Massenet (1842–1912).

A short distance S.W. of the main crossroads of the town centre stands Gothic *St-Étienne* (14C; with a 15C doorway); some minutes' walk to the S. brings one to the **Musée d'Art et d'Industrie**, adjacent to which is a model mine-shaft.

On the GROUND FLOOR are early bicycles and spinning and weaving machines, models of those producing *passementerie* (ribbons, braids, and trimmings, etc.), and a collection of 'stevenographs' (named after Thomas Stevens). To the l. of the entrance is a natural history section. Others are devoted to *Arms and armour, some manufactured locally, and *Paintings*.

Notable are: *School of Anthony Mor*, Portrait of Elizabeth de Valois; *Louis Brea*, Christ and the apostles; *anon.* 17C Flemish Female portrait; *P. Fontana*, Crucifixion; *Van der Heck*, Gravedigger; *Nicolas Berchem*, SS Paul and Barnabas; The Flight into Egypt (*17C Flemish*); *W.-C. Heda*, Still Life; *Oudry*, Dog and puppies; *Pillement*, Chinoiserie; *Le Brun*, Entry into Jerusalem; *Georges Rouget*, Mme Ranchon; *Boilly*, Family scene; *Courbet*, Pastoral scene (an early work); *Eugenio Lucas*, Attack on the diligence; and more modern works. Also a collection of alabasters from Malines.

ST-ÉTIENNE TO LE PUY (88km). From the S. end of the town we fork r. on the N88 through the suburban coal-mining towns of *La Ricamarie* and *Le Chambon-Feugerolles*, to the S.E. of which rises its 11-14C castle, to (12km.) **Firminy** (24,400 Apelous), an old industrial centre (coal and steel), 3km to the N. W. of which, at *Cornillon*, overlooking the gorges of the Loire, the 12-15C church stands within the ramparts of its 14-16C castle.—17km. *Monistrol-sur-Loire*, with a curiously constructed church with a Romanesque nave, and the two huge towers of a castle of the bishops of Velay.

Hence an attractive minor road follows the l. bank of the Loire, at 5.5km passing near the fine 15C château of *Rochebaron* (to the N.W.; view), later traversing (17.5km) *Retournac*, with a Romanesque church restored in the 15C, and 5km beyond, *Chamalières-sur-Loire*, overlooking its deep gorge, where the remarkable 11-12C priory church preserves a 12C external altar-tomb, wall-paintings, a Romanesque stoup and remains of its cloister. The road soon turns S., following the curve of the river, through (18km) *Lavoûte-sur-Loire*, with a Romanesque church, W. of which, on a commanding site, is the château of *Lavoûte-Polignac* (13C; rebuilt 1634)—After 9km, beyond the winding *Gorge de Peyredeyre*, **Le Puy** is entered.

The main road from Monistrol climbs S.W. above the valley of the Lignon to (21km) **Yssingeaux** (860m; 6,700 inhab.), on the plateau of Megal, volcanic *Mont Megal* itself (1436m) rising to the S. The Italianate *Hôtel de Ville* occupies a machicolated wing of a castle built in 1490 for Jean de Bourbon, Bp of Le Puy.—Hence we ascend (views) across the *Col du Pertuis* (1026m) before climbing down through basaltic hills and passing (r.) the ruins of the castle of *Lardeyrol* to (29km) *Le Puy*; see Rte 99.

ST-ÉTIENNE TO (43km) ANNONAY AND THE RHÔNE, 13km beyond. The N82, bearing S.E., shortly commences to climb steeply through the *Parc Natural du Pilat* to the *Col de la République* (1127m) and (28km) *Bourg-Argental*, a small silk-weaving town, preserving an 11C church porch.—Hence roads lead N. towards the summit of **Mont Pilat**, the *Crest de la Perdrix* (1432m), and further E., the *Crest de l'Oeillon* (1370m), both providing extensive panoramic *Views*, particularly of the French Alps, from Mont Blanc to Mont Ventoux.—9km. The r.-hand fork leads into (6km) *Annonay*, which is by-passed by the N82, leading ahead to (6km) crossroads N.E. of the town.

Annonay itself (20,000 Annonéens), an ancient and flourishing industrial town (with paper-mills, tanneries, and textile factories), capital of the *Haut-Vivarais*, stands astride a hilly site in the valley of the Déûme and Cance (on a ridge between which stood its castle), and is of slight interest, although the old centre of breakneck cobbled alleys and vaults preserves occasional relics of its past. It was the birthplace of the brothers Montgolfier, Joseph (1740–1810) and Étienne (1745–99), whose first balloon ascent was made here in 1783; their nephew Marc Séguin (1786–1875), the engineer (cf. St-Étienne); Comte François Boissy d'Anglas (1756–1826), the revolutionary, although buried here, was born at St-Jean Chambre, S. of Lamastre.—We regain the N82 4km N.E. and turn r. to reach the Rhône at *Andance*.—**Tournon** lies 22km to the S.; see Rte 139.

For roads from St-Étienne to **Lyon**, *see sub-route on p 759, in reverse.*

99   Moulins to Montélimar via Vichy and Le Puy

344km (213 miles). N7. 30km *Varennes-sur-Allier*. N209. 27km **Vichy**—D906. 36km **Thiers**—44km **Ambert**—33km **La Chaise-Dieu**—42km **Le Puy**—N88. 33km *Pradelles*—N102. 58km **Aubenas**—41km **Montélimar**.

Maps: IGN 43, 50, 52, 59 or 111, 112. M 238, 239, 940.

The Lyon road is followed from **Moulins** (Rte 96), running parallel to and E. of the Allier, after traversing (30km) *Varennes*, near which is the keep of the *Château de Gayette* (15-17C). Just beyond we fork r. through (10km) *Billy*, with an ivy-covered ruined castle, and the railway-junction of *St-Germain-des-Fosses*, with a Romanesque chapel and church, to enter (9km) *Cusset*. Preserving a few interesting houses and relics of fortifications, it is now continuous with *Vichy*, 3km S.W., being part of what is known as the 'agglomération *Vichyssoise'*.

VICHY (30,600 inhab.), long the most famous and fashionable spa in France, stands on the r. bank of the broad Allier, bordered by an umbrageous park, but being almost entirely late 19C and early 20C in construction and devoted to the requirements of invalids seeking both distractions and the benefit of its much exploited waters, it offers little of interest to the healthy.

Its springs, known as *Aquae Calidae* to the Romans, were never entirely forgotten during the Middle Ages, and began to be revisited in the early 17C. In 1676–77 Mme de Sévigné came here for a cure, and it was patronised by the aunts of Louis XIV and by the Duchesse d'Angoulême. Its vogue increased after the frequent visits of Napoleon III from 1861 onwards. 'Here are no inns; every one lives in boarding houses; of these there are 6 or 8 . . . in none is the accommodation first-rate', wrote Murray in the 1840s, although by then it was a frequented watering-place, and troops of donkeys were kept for guests making excursions. It has been estimated that it had 575 visitors in 1833, which rose steadily to 2543 in 1840, reaching c. 20,000 in 1860, and approaching 100,000 in 1890.

Vichy was the seat of Pétain's cowed government in 1940 to Aug. 1944, that senile marshal's official residence being the *Pavillon Sévigné*, while cabinet meetings (attended by Laval, Darlan, et al) were held at the *Hôtel du Parc*, until their departure for Sigmaringen. It was the birthplace of Valéry Larbaud (1881–1957).

The main centre of animation is the triangular *Parc des Sources*, with the *Hall des Sources* at its N. end, beyond which is the *Grand Établissement Thermal*. The park, with its avenues of planes and chestnuts, is provided with covered walks along each side. At its S. end is the *Casino*, much extended since its erection in 1865, and providing the usual facilities.

S. of the part lies what remains of the older centre, with the restored *Tour de l'Horloge* of its 15C castle; to the E. of the tower is *St-Blaise*, enveloped in a monstrous modern basilica, the interior of which contains some glass of interest and the 12C head of a 'black Virgin' re-christened 'N.-D.-des-Malades'.—To the W. is the *Pavillon Sévigné*, while a short distance to the S. is the 16C *Maison du Bailliage*, containing a small *Museum* of old prints of Vichy, of Bourbonnais folklore, and Gallo-Roman pottery.—To the S.E., nearer the riverside, is the *Source* and *Parc des Celestines*, the site of a convent of which only one small building remains.

From the transpontine suburb of *Bellerive* (with its intermittent spring) two roads lead S.W. to (c. 38km) *Riom*, via *Effiat* and *Aigueperse*, and—further S.—via *Thuret*; see Rte 100.

Châtel-Montagne, 22.5km E. of Vichy on the D25, is an ancient town among the little-visited *Monts de la Madeleine*, with a remarkable 12C *Church* preceded by a notable two-storeyed narthex, beyond which the road winds through the hills to (c. 23km) *Ambierle*, near the Roanne roads; see Rte 98.

VICHY TO ST-ÉTIENNE, VIA MONTBRISON (134km). From Cusset the D995 is followed, ascending the picturesque Sichon valley to (23km) *Ferrières-sur-Sichon*, passing (l.) the ruined castle of *Montgilbert* and the commanding spur of *Roc St-Vincent*, to (14km) *St-Priest-Laprugne* (with uranium mines), some 6km N.E. of which rises the *Pierres du Jour* (1165m), the highest summit of the *Monts de la Madeleine*; to the S.W. in the *Bois-Noirs* rises the *Puy de Montoncel* (1287m). Continuing S.E. on the D493, at 11km *St-Just-en-Chevalet*, with its old castle commanding a fine view, is traversed.—Some 7km to the S. (beyond the motorway under construction between Clermont-Ferrand and St-Étienne) is the ruined hilltop fortress of *Château d'Urfé* (12-14C), cradle of a distinguished family (see below).—18km. *St-Germain-Laval*, 5km E. of which is *Pommiers*, with a 12C church with 15C wall-paintings, an old bridge over the Aix, and other traces of its former importance. We turn S. to (12km) *Boën*, with a late 18C bridge over the Lignon, and an Italianate château of 1786.—To the S.W. is the well-sited *Château de Couzan*, with a restored Romanesque chapel.—7km to the E., just S of the Feurs road, stands the *Château de la Bastie d'Urfé*, where Honoré d'Urfé wrote part of the novel 'L'Astrée' during 1610–27. Restored since 1951, it is well worth the detour. The ramp and loggia, shell grotto, its chapel in its original state with a well carved marble altar, fine chimney-pieces, Aubusson and Bruges tapestries, and the portrait of Louise d'Urfé (1693), will be noted.—To the S. is an isolated volcanic hill bearing the 12-15C priory church of *Montverdun.*—Regaining the main road (D8) we pass near (l.) the 14-16C château of *Chalain-d'Uzore* before reaching (12km from Boën) **Champdieu**, which preserves a partly fortified 12C priory *Church, abutted by its quadrangle of dependencies (12-16C).

5km. **Montbrison** (13,650 Montbrisonnais), an attractive old town, which succeeded Feurs as the capital of the counts of Forez and was the departmental capital of the Loire in 1801– 56. It is the birthplace of the composer and conductor Pierre Boulez (1925–   ). To the N.E. of its circle of tree-lined boulevards is the castle-hill, to the W. of which the *Palais de Justice* occupies the buildings of a Visitandine convent. Hence the Rue du Marché leads S. from 19C *St-Pierre* to cross the Vizézy stream, lined with old houses and crossed by several hump-backed bridges, to collegiate **N.-D.-d'Espérance,* a plain but imposing edifice with a spacious nave, founded early in the 13C but not completed until c. 1500. The central doorway of the W. front is good 15C work with a 13-14C Virgin in its tympanum. On the l. of the choir is the tomb of Count Guy IV of Forez (d. 1239), its founder. The ancient Crucifix is notable; the organ is under restoration.—Behind the church is the *Diane ('decania' or deanery), a 14C hall decorated with contemporary heraldic paintings, the exterior of which was savagely restored by Viollet-le-Duc in 1866.—Immediately S. of Montbrison is *Moingt,* possibly Roman *Aquae Segetae,* with a 14C chapel, and within the enciente of a 13C castle of which a tower remains, a Romanesque church.

The road bears S.E., past (r.) the partly ruined priory church of *St-Romain-le-Puy,* and (15.5km) *Sury-le-Comtal,* with a square late Gothic church tower, 7km beyond which *St-Rambert-sur-Loire* is traversed, connected with *St-Just* by a bridge over that young river. The former preserves a curious *Church (11-12C) with two towers, one of each period, and in its W. front are incorporated Roman inscriptions and early Romanesque carvings. Relics of its priory include an 11C chimneypiece, 14C frescoes, and a 16C gateway.—4km S. stands the old castle of *Essalois,* overlooking defiles of the Loire, now dammed.—We now approach (11km) **St-Étienne** (see Rte 98) which may be partially by-passed by the motorway.

From Vichy the D906 drives S. below (l.) the *Côte St-Armand,* shortly traversing (8.5km) *St-Yorre,* 5km. E. of which stands the 13-14C château of *Busset.*

7.5km. A by-road (l.) leads through *Ris,* with an ancient church of some interest, to (6km) *Châteldon,* with several 15-16C houses, and a castle. it was the birthplace of Pierre Laval (1883– 1945), the 'maquignon' minister of the collaborating État français in 1942– 44.

The main road continues S., later passing below the Clermont-Ferrand—Lyon motorway, to enter the upper end of (20km) Thiers, a surprisingly attractive industrial town.

THIERS (436m.; pron. Tear; 16,800 Thiernois), or rather its riverside faubourg of *Moûtier,* was the *Tigernum Castrum* mentioned by Gregory of Tours in 531. It is a curiously sited and interesting old place steeply perched on a hillside overlooking the Durolle, a 'Sheffield' on a smaller scale, manufacturing cutlery of every description, including 'Toledo' blades.

The centre of the upper town is the *Pl. de la Mutualité,* just W. of which is a *Museum* devoted to local history and industry, from which steep lanes descend to the middle town, most of its shops glittering with knives, scissors, and cutlery in general. Hence the narrow Rue du Bourg continues downhill into the lower town past (r.) the fine half-timbered *Maison du Pirou* (15C), to the E. of which is the *Maison des Sept Péchés Capitaux,* with quaintly carved beam-ends. On a slight eminence further S. stands ***St-Genès**, a 12C building much altered in the 13-14C, and recently restored. The exterior of the S. transept preserves its original decoration of 1120. The nave floor has been raised. Note the fragmentary mosaics from a 6C church on this site, the domed vault over the crossing, and the Renaissance apse of the N. transept.—The Rue de la Coutellerie, continuing the descent, is lined with more old houses, among them the *Maison de l'Homme des Bois* (No. 21). The Rue du 4-Sept. goes on to plain 15C *St-Jean*, whose cemetery commands a plunging view over the valley.

The main street descends in zig-zags to the valley floor, where we cross the Durolle and turn r. A short distance to the l. is the mutilated abbey-church of *Moûtier* (11-12C) with good capitals, the gateway to which is now a dwelling.

THIERS TO BOËN (49km), for *Montbrison*. The D89 leads E. and then S.E., traversing the *Monts du Forez*, at first keeping high over the valley, and through several minor cutlery-making towns, to (14km) *Cabreloche*, N. of which rise the wooded *Bois-Noirs* and the *Puy de Montoncel* (1287m), where it bears S.E. to (10km) *Noirétable*, 4km N. of which is the fortified village of *Cervières*. The road then descends the Anzon valley to (19km) *L'Hôpital-sous-Rochefort*, with a good 12-16C church, and overlooked (r.) by the ruined castle of *St-Laurent-Rochefort*.—8km. *Boën*; see p 532.

THIERS TO CLERMONT-FERRAND (40km). Although the motorway is faster, we follow the N89 W. to (16km) *Lezoux*, an important ceramic centre in Gallo-Roman times (with a small museum in its mairie), and a 15C belfry, 6km S. of which stands the château of *Ravel*, in English hands from 1377, and rebuilt in the 17-18C.—The church at *Moissat-Bas*, 3km W., preserves the 13C Reliquary of St-Lomer.—12km. *Pont-du-Château*, on the Allier, contains several old houses, a fortified church (13C), and 17C château, now the mairie.—14km **Clermont-Ferrand**; see Rte 100.

Turning l. 5km W. of Thiers, the D906 is followed through (5km) *Néronde*, with a Romanesque church, to the S.W. of which is the 19C *Château de Aulteribe* ◊, on the site of a feudal castle, containing some furniture and paintings of interest.—Before entering (5km) *Courpière*, the 15C *Château de la Barge* and (r.) the 15C *Manoir de Bélime*, possibly Chateaubriand's 'Tour du More', may be seen on the far bank of the Dore. Courpière itself has a Romanesque church fortified in the 15C, with an Entombment of the latter date.—The road becomes more picturesque as it threads the valley between (r.) the *Monts du Livradois* and the *Monts du Forez*.—5km. *Augerolles*, 5km E., at a height of 1160m, preserves a 14C church with a Romanesque choir dated 980.—11km *Olliergues*, which retains several 15-16C houses, is traversed, 4km beyond which a l.-hand fork (D40) climbs 16km E. to the *Col du Béat*, from which a road now ascends to the *Pierre sur Haute* (1634m), the highest peak of the Forez, providing extensive panoramic views.

Further on the valley expands into the narrow hill-girt plan of the *Livradois*, and we enter (19km) **Ambert** (535m; 8000 inhab.), birthplace of Emmanuel Chabrier (1842–93), and famous for the manufacture of hand-made paper (from the 16C), cheese, and rosaries (cf. Saumur), a curious combination. Conspicuous in the town centre is late Gothic *St-Jean* (1471–1516), whose square tower has a Renaissance upper storey; its gargoyles and other details, together with the S. doorway, are notable. The *Hôtel de Ville*, to the S.E., is circular in plan.—Some 5.5km E., in the *Val de Laga*, are two old paper-mills of the many once in production, one—the *Moulin Richard-de-Bas*—containing a small museum.

The Dore is crossed and the road turns up the valley, overlooked to the r. by *N.-D.-de-Mons* (1218m), the loftiest summit of the *Monts du Livradois*.—11km. *Marsac-en-Livradois* has a disused 12C church and 15C parish church, 5km beyond which *Arlanc* is traversed, with a mutilated Romanesque church enlarged in the 16C.—At 4km a lane leads 5km to *St-Sauveur-la-Sagne*, with a 12-15C church built on a curious promontory over the Gorge of the Dore.

The road now climbs steeply out of the valley by a series of hairpin bends, with good retrospective views, traversing beech and oak woods to reach a bleak plateau before entering (12km) **La Chaise-Dieu** (1082m), a quaint village owing its origin to the Benedictine monastery of *Casa Dei* founded here in 1044 by St Robert, a canon of Brioude.

The church of ***St-Robert**, the successor of the original abbey-church, was begun by Abbot Pierre-Roger de Beaufort (later Pope Clement VI) in 1343, and completed by his nephew, Gregory XI (Roger de Beaufort) in 1378. Apart from its architectural interest, it is notable as standing at a higher level above the sea than any other historic building in France.

The edifice is in the plain heavy Gothic style of the Southern French type, the master of works being Hugues de Morel, of Languedoc. Most of the conventual dependencies, sacked by the Huguenots in 1562, were destroyed by fire in 1695, and their rebuilding was never finished. After 1518 it was always in the hands of commendatory abbots, among whom were Charles d'Orléans, Richelieu, Mazarin, and Card. Édouard de Rohan, exiled here in 1786 after the affair of the Diamond Necklace.

The W. facade is flanked by square towers joined by an arcade. The bare *Nave* is disproportionately wide and low (over 73m in length, 24m wide, and 18m high), interrupted by a rood-screen added in the 15C and bearing a rood of 1603. The massive organ-loft of 1683 will be noted. The key-stones of the vault bear the arms of Clement VI and Gregory XI. In the S. aisle is the tomb of Abbot Renaud de Montclar (d. 1346), and in the N. aisle are two other 14C tombs, said to cover the remains of Nicolas-Roger de Beaufort (uncle of Clement VI), and of Edith (d. 1075), the widow of Edward the Confessor, who spent her last days here.

On the wall of the choir in this aisle are three restored tempera paintings (15C) of a Dance of Death. In the *Choir* are the black and white marble **Tomb of Clement VI* (d. 1352); the canopy and statuettes were destroyed in 1562. The 144 ***Stalls**, surrounded by a frieze of vine-leaves, were presented by Abbot André de Chanac (1378– 1420); above them are Arras **Tapestries*, presented in 1518 by Jacques de Sénectaire, the last resident abbot, each panel of which depicts a New Testament scene flanked by the Old Testament event said to predict it. Opening off the apse are five radiating chapels and the *Tour Clémentine*, a square keep joined diagonally by de Chanac, it erected by the *Cloister*, likewise of c. 1400, adjoin the S. side of the church, to the E. of which is a large court containing the so-called *Salle de l'Écho*.

After 6km a road junction is reached. The main road continues S.E. to (21km) *St-Paulien*, also approached by the more interesting D13 forking r., which passes (r.) the *Lac de Malaguet* amid forests, and (9km) the gallows-shaped ruins of the castle of *Allègre* beneath (l.) *Mont Bar* (1175m), an extinct volcano with an almost circular crater. Just before regaining the D906 it passes (r.) the *Château de la Rochelambert*, a late Gothic building (1575), described by George Sand in 'Jean de la Roche'.

St-Paulein (795m), ancient *Ruessio*, capital of the Vellavi, was until the mid 6C the seat of the bishop of Velay, and preserves a fine Romanesque *Church* with an unusually wide nave, main apse, and four subsidiary apses.—After 4km we meet the N102 from Brioude and veer S.W. (views), passing (l.) the château of Polignac (see below)

and then (r.) the basalt '*Orgues d'Espaly*', after which the remarkable
*View of Le Puy with its volcanic pinnacles is suddenly unfolded
before us on descending to the city. To the r. rises a rock crowned by
an atrocious ferro-concrete church and statue of St Joseph, where
formerly stood the castle in which the infant Charles VII, despoiled
of his dominions, was hailed as King of France by a few faithful supporters.

The ruins of the *Castle of Polignac*, standing on a huge square block of basalt,
accessible from one side only, except by a small postern, are all that remains of
the stronghold of that famous family. The huge keep (1385) was restored in
1897. There is a Romanesque church of interest in the village.

LE PUY (en-Velay; 26,000 Ponots), the high-lying préfecture of the
Haute-Loire (630m), is one of the most curiously-sited towns in
France, set amongst a denticulated landscape of volcanic cones
thrown up during the convulsions of the quaternary period. The old
town clustered around the cathedral retains some attractive and
characteristic corners, but the modern town is undistinguished. Its
main industry in the past, apart from imposing on pilgrims, was the
manufacture of lace; its local specialities are lentils and verveine liqueurs.

Its name is derived from the Roman name of the hill, *Podium Aniciense*, on
which it stands, where a temple of Jupiter was replaced by a church in which a
blackened image of the Virgin of unknown provenance attracted medieval
pilgrims including miscellaneous popes and crowned heads. Later its count-
bishops were engaged in crushing the Protestant tendencies of its populace, but
in spite of savage persecutions, numbers survived, flourishing especially in the
neighbourhood of Yssingeaux. Among its natives were the 13C troubadour
Peire Cardenal; Louis XIV's minister, the Card. de Polignac (1661–1742); the
writer Jules Vallès (1833–85), and Marshal Fayolle (1858–1928), commander
of French forces in Italy in 1917–18. Simon Weil taught philosophy at the Lycée
in 1931–32.
    Prior to 1914 some 70,000 women in the town and surrounding villages were
occupied in producing 'Dentelles du Puy', a silk-thread lace, or the cotton-thread
'Dentelles de Craponne', but this has now largely given way to mechanical
methods of manufacture.

On entering from the N.W., the Borne is crossed to reach (l.) *St-
Laurent*, a large 14-15C building preserving the tomb of Bertrand du
Guesclin (d. 1380; cf. p 539), containing his entrails only. The
chapter-house of the old Dominican convent is notable.
    The street to the r. approaches the *Rocher d'Aiguilhe*, a vertical
outcrop of volcanic breccia 80m high, surmounted by a chapel. At its
foot is the octagonal 12C *Chapel of St-Clair* (or, inexplicably, the
'Temple de Diane'), perhaps built by the Templars, from which 267
steps (fee) ascend to *St-Martin-d'Aiguilhe*, a 10C cratory to which an
elliptical ambulatory was added at the end of the 11C. its capitals and
the trefoiled doorway are admirable examples of Romanesque
sculpture, and its bell-tower may have been the model for that of the
cathedral.
    A path leads hence towards the cathedral, which is perhaps better
approached from St-Laurent by the Av. de la Cathedrale, leading l.
from the S. end of the contiguous Blvd Carnot (before reaching the
Tour Pannessac, sole remnant of its medieval walls) to the small Pl.
des Tables, with a 15C fountain. Hence there is a steep climb to the
foot of the cathedral steps, on the l. of which are the late Gothic
Hôtel-Dieu (with two Romanesque doorways with fine capitals), and
abutting the N. side of the cathedral, the *Machicoulis*, a curious

edifice which formed part of the defence-works of the bishop's palace.

A flight of steps continues to ascend to the triple porch of the polychromed facade of the *Cathedral, which rises high above, its rows of arches surmounted by three low gables. The stairway formerly led up past the *Porte Dorée* to the nave floor.

Turning r., we enter by the S. transeptal doorway. The interior is spacious and plain, but is not improved by its lamps. The choir and transepts and the two E. bays of the nave date from the 17C; the remainder from the 12-13Cs. Each bay is surmounted by a domical eight-sided vault, oblong in plan; the cupola over the crossing is modern. On the high altar is a copy of the original image of the Virgin burned in 1794. Note the ex-voto of the Pest of 1629, by Jean Solvian. The N. transept is embellished with wall-paintings, both in the E. chapel (13C) and W. (12C): light adjacent. The *Sacristy*, beyond the S. transept, preserves the 9C Bible of Theodulphus, inscribed partly on purple parchment, among other treasures.

Hence one may visit the *Pl. du For* and the *Porche du For*, a good example of late Romanesque work, remarkable in having the lowest order of the arch on each side completely detached from the main arch except at three points. From the adjacent terrace, steps descend to the Rue Card. du Polignac (see below), but one should first turn behind the detached bell-tower (1887), a reconstruction of the 12C original, to the *Porche St-Jean* and *Baptistry*, with an antique font and columns. To the l. is the entrance to the *Cloister* ◊ (11-12C; shut Tues.), its particoloured arches surmounted by a mosaic of polychromed stonework and a cornice of grotesque heads. Its capitals, and 12C iron grille, are notable. A collection of ecclesiastical art may be seen in the vaulted hall of the *Mâchicoulis*, decorated with late 15C wall-paintings. The *Chapel des Morts* preserves a 13C fresco, and a room above contains a Romanesque chimneypiece.

On turning l. after making our exit, we pass (l.) the *Chapel des Pénitents* (1584; restored in the 18C), with a ceiling of painted panels, and may follow a stepped path to the foot of the *Rocher Corneille*, providing a panoramic view of Le Puy from a platform, above which rises a colossal and supererogatory image, cast in 1860 from the metal of 213 cannon taken at Sebastopol at the instance of Mgr de Morlhon, who is unlikely to be canonised for his pains.

Regaining the Porche St-Jean, we may turn E. through the *Porte St-Georges* to the Rue Card. du Polignac, preserving several 17-18C mansions, whence descending through a maze of alleys and steps to the triangular *Pl. du Martouret*, flanked by the 18C *Hôtel de Ville*, a short distance to the N.E. of which stands the Jesuit church of *St-François-Régis* (1607; by Martellange). The Rue Pannessac leads back to the Tour Pannessac from the *Pl. du Pot*, with a 15C fountain, behind the Hôtel de Ville (as do the Rues Chênebouterie and Raphael to the *Pl. des Tables*), while the short Rue Porte-Aiguière leads S. to the spacious *Pl. du Breuil*. Beyond this extend gardens, at the far end of which is the **Musée Crozatier**, with a number of French and Dutch portraits, among them one by Rigaud of Marlborough (?); a lapidary collection, and others, principally lace.

LE PUY TO VALENCE (113km). The D15 leads S.E. and then E. to (20km) *St-Julien-Chapteuil*, with its gabled church of Romanesque origin, and birthplace of 'Jules Romains' (Louis Farigoule; 1885– 1972), beyond which are its castle ruins. To the N.E. is *Mont Meygal* (1436m), providing panoramic views over the volcanic landscape. Some distance to the S. rises *Mont Mezenc* (1753m).—18km. *Les Baraques* (1216m), beyond which we descend through the *Monts du Vivarais* to (14km) *St-Agreve*, a small summer resort named after a martyred bishop of Velay, the castle hill of which commands extensive views.—Hence the D120 descends S.W. via (16km) *St-Martin-de-Valamas*, to the N. E. of which is the imposing ruin of the castle of *Rochebonne*, to (9km) *Le Cheylard*, beyond which the *Gorges de l'Eyrieux* (crossed by the ancient *Pont de Chervil*) are traversed, to (29km) *Les Ollières*, 20km W. of *La Voult-sur-Rhône*; see Rte 139.—The main road continues to wind through the hills, with a view (l.) down the valley of the Doux towards the *Château de Rochebloine*, later traversing the fortified village of *Désaignes*, to (21km) *Lamastre*, at the junction of three rivers, with remains of its castle.—5km S. is the 13-17C *Château de Maisonseule*.—A roads leads N.E. past (l.) the picturesque old village of *Boucieu-le-Roi* to (35km) *Tournon*, threading the *Gorges du Doux*; the main road continues E. via the *Col des Fans* (754m; views) before descending to (36km) *St-Péray*, perched 200m above which, to the r., are the ruins of the fortress of *Crussol*, commanding panoramic views. Hence the Rhône is crossed to (4km) **Valence**; see Rte 139A.

LE PUY TO AUBENAS VIA LE MONASTIER (108km), a lonely cross-country drive across the *Monts du Vivarais*. The N88 is followed N.E., off which we shortly fork r. onto the D15, and again r. to follow the D535 to (21km) **Le Monastier-sur-Gazeille**, a large village, where in Sept. 1878 R. L. Stevenson, staying at Mme Morel's hotel, first met Modestine and began his mountain tramp across the Cévennes. The *Church of the 7C abbey which gave the place its name is a Romanesque building of the 11-12C with a multicoloured facade. The vault and apse are 15C, and the corbels in the nave are remarkable, while one of the S. aisle chapels preserves 16C decoration. The *Mairie* occupies part of the abbey and a cloister walk of 1754; the *Abbot's Castle* of black basalt also remains.—The D535 is followed for a further 5.5km.

The D631 turns l. to ascend the barren Gazeille valley to (c. 10km) *Les Estables*, at the base of **Mont Mézenc** (1753m), the highest peak of the Cévennes, of irregular shape although of volcanic origin, and which falls away much more steeply to the E. The *Views* hence are varied and extensive: to the N. rises *Mont Mégal*, and far to the N.W. and W., respectively, the *Puy de Dôme*, and *Plom du Cantal*; while immediately to the S. is the *Gerbier de Jonc*, with *Mont Lozère* in the distance. The prospect to the E. is less desolate, where the ravines and 'sucs' of the *Boutières* fall abruptly away towards the Rhône, and behind their dark shapes are seen — in reasonably good weather—the distant peaks of the French Alps, from Mont Buet in Savoy to Mont Ventoux.—A track leads S. past the ruins of the *Chartreuse de Bonnefoy* to the Gerbier de Jonc, but it is preferable to return to the main road, which we follow via (14km) *Le Béage*, 8km S.W. of which is the deep crater-like *Lac d'Issarlès*, where troglodite habitations have been found, and (4km) *Les Jalades*.—The l.-hand fork here approaches, 7.5km N.E., the regular cone or 'suc' of the **Gerbier de Jonc** (1551m), providing a view almost as fine as from Mont Mézenc.—From Les Jalades one follows the D536 S., circling round the *Suc de Bauzon* (1471m) before descending the Fontolière valley via *Montpezat* to (40km) the *Château de Ventadour* on the N102 (see below), and (13km) *Aubenas*.

The N88 leads S. from Le Puy, climbing slowly, and providing views towards the E. as we approach (7km) *Les Baraques*, 5km S.E. of which is the well-sited 12C church of *Solignac-sur-Loire*, with its 'multiple' belfry, overlooking the young river.—4km. A 4.-hand fork leads 6km to *Cayres*, and the deep crater-lake of *Bouchet*, from whence one may regain the main route at Costaros.

8km. *Costaros*, 8km S.E. of which, *Arlempdes*, with its castle-crowned crag, commands a romantic view of the upper Loire valley.—3km. *Landos*, with a Romanesque church, lies 2km S.W.—At 11km a road junction is reached just N. of *Pradelles*, where the N102 forks l.; see below.

PRADELLES TO MENDE (59km). The N88 bears r. past *Pradelles* (where the inn, kept by the three sisters Pichots was—according to Young—one of the worst he had met with in France: 'Contraction, poverty, dirt, and darkness'), once a fortified town, and containing old houses and on arcaded market-place, and descends to (9km) **Langogne** (912m), the old town of which preserves five rampart towers and the *Tour de l'Horloge*, a medieval gateway, an 11-13C church with a 15C facade, and some early 17C houses.—To the W. lies the huge new reservoir of *Naussac*.

LANGOGNE TO VILLEFORT (50km). The D906 follows the railway along the upper valley of the Allier past (12.5km) *Luc*, with a 12C castle on which a huge Virgin has been superimposed, to (8km) *La Bastide-Puylaurent*.—The Trappist monastery of *N.-D.-des-Neiges*, founded in 1850, lies c. 3km E., where Stevenson and Modestine were hospitably received in 1878. Charles de Foucauld (1853–1916), the apostle of the Sahara, served as a monk here in 1890–1901; its white wine, 'Fleurs de Neiges', should be sampled.—The D4 continues E. via (4.5km) *St-Laurent-les-Bains*, later following the *Corniche du Vivaraise*, before descending to (37.5km) *Lablachère*; see Rte 142B.—The road crosses the main ridge and descends via the fortified village of *La Garde-Guérin*, on a commanding site overlooking a reservoir, to (29.5km) **Villefort**, a pleasant centre for excursions into the Lozère range to the W. It was the birthplace of Odilon Barrot (1791–1873), a prime mover in the overthrow of Louis Philippe. See also Rte 101B.

From Langogne we continue S.W. to (21km) *L'Habitarelle*, with a monument marking the site of the camp where Du Guesclin died in 1380. On a hill to the N. is *Châteauneuf-de-Randon*, the last town he captured from the Enqlish, now a cattle-market; see also p 548. The high-lying *Causse de Montbel* is crossed before descending into the upper valley of the Lot, which we follow downstream to (29km) *Mende*; see Rte 101B.

The main route (N102) after 8.5km passes the *Auberge de Peire-Beille*. a lonely upland inn notorious c. 1800 for the cut-throat exploits of its landlord.—The D16 leads l. hence to (18.5km) the *Lac d'Issarlès* (see above), passing *La Chapelle-Graillouse*, with a curious belfry.—The road descends before mounting again to (9.5km) the watershed *Col de la Chavade* (1266m), just N.E. of which is the source of the Ardèche, the l. bank of the imposing valley of which is descended in steep curves, traversing *Mayres*, an old village with a ruined castle, before reaching (20.5km) **Thueyts** (462m), pleasantly situated in one of the most striking reaches of the Ardèche, on the far bank of which is a remarkable basalt terrace, approached by the *Pont du Diable*.—The crater of *La Gravenne* (846m) lies to the N.

Neyrac-les-Bains, a small spa of ancient origin, the waters of which were in the Middle Ages reputed to cure leprosy, is passed to the r.; beyond (l.) is the ruined castle of *Ventadour*. After 6.5km the Ardèche is crossed, and after 8km the spa of *Vals-les-Bains*, on both banks of the Volane, whose waters, (containing a high proportion of bicarbonate of soda) have been known since the early 17C, is seen in a narrow valley to the N., c. 2km E. of which are the stalactite *Grottes de Lautaret*.

The D578 leads up the Volane valley through chestnut woods and a basalt defile, to (10km) *Pont de l'Huile*, past *Antraigues*, whose church tower was once part of a castle.—15km beyond lies *Mézilhac*, whence a road climbs W. to (13.5km) the *Gerbier de Jonc*; see above.

To the r. of the main road stands *Mercuer*, with an 11C church with a four-arched belfry of local type.—The unattractive industrial district of *Labégude* is traversed before forking r. and entering the upper town of (5km) **Aubenas** (13,100 Albenassiens), well-sited on a steep hill commanding the Ardèche valley, the busy capital of the *Bas-Vivarais*, and once an important Protestant centre and silk depot. It was also the centre of a bloodily supressed peasants' revolt in 1670.

We pass (r.) a conspicuous 18C dome, a relic of the Benedictine convent of *St-Benoît*, founded by the wife of Marshal d'Ornano

(1581–1626), and now containing their tombs, and then the 13-16C *Castle* (occupied by administrative offices) before reaching the *Pl. de l'Airette* (views), where we turn r. The Grand Rue of the older centre preserves one or two 17C houses. Restored *St-Laurent* has a good 15C tower and early 17C boiseries transferred here from a Jesuit chapel demolished c. 1900. The marrons glacés of Aubenas are succulent.

For the road from Valence to **Montpellier** via Aubenas and Alès, see Rte 142B.

AUBENAS TO BOURG-ST-ANDÉOL VIA VALLON (64km). The D579 leads S. to (10.5km) *Vogüé*, an old village beneath an abrupt bluff; its 16C château is the home of the family of Vogüé. From its station, 2km beyond, a track climbs onto a plateau and to the little church of *Sauveplantade* (9C).—1km S. of the station a minor road forks l. directly S. across the plateau to (16km) *Vallon* (see below), off which a track soon leads l. to the deserted village of *Rochecolombe*, with the original stronghold of the Vogüés.—The main road continues S., passing (r.) the finely-placed village of *Balazuc*, to (11.5km) *Ruoms*, an old fortified town with a Romanesque church; see also Rte 142B. The family of Daudet's mother once lived at the neighbouring *Mas de la Vignasse*, preserving souvenirs of the author.—We turn l. 2km S. of Ruoms; the r.-hand turning continues S.W. to meet the D104 10km S. of *Lablachère*.—7km. *Vallon-Pont-d'Arc*, with its *Mairie* occupying a Louis-XIII château, commands views of medieval ruins on either side of the Ardèche gorge. Hence the D4 leads E. across the lonely and scrubby *Plateau des Gras* to (30km) **Bourg-St-Andéol** (see Rte 142A), passing, just beyond the solitary hamlet of *St-Remèze*, a turning for the *Aven de Marzal*, a stalactite cavern now conveniently approached. It was first discovered by Martel in 1892, and rediscovered in 1949; its name is that of a murdered gamekeeper flung into the pit in 1812. A minor road goes on hence through an area rich in megalithic monuments, to *St-Marcel d'Ardèche*, or alternatively by a road further S. following the meandering course of the river; see below.—The *Aven d'Orgnac*, one of the finest and largest stalactite caverns in France, discovered in 1935 and noteworthy for the colour of its formations and for the fantastic shapes caused by an earthquake in the Tertiary epoch, may be approached by crossing the Ardèche at Vallon, and following a minor road via *Labastide-de-Virac*.

From Vallon a road leads S.E. via the limestone *Gorges de l'Ardèche*, the more remarkable features of which are the natural bridge of *Pont d'Arc*, and nearby, on the far bank, the *Grotte d'Ebbo*, containing Aurignacian drawings discovered in 1946. The road also commands several fine view-points. A turning to the l. some halfway down the gorge approaches the *Aven de Marzal* (see above) and emerges at *St-Martin d'Ardèche*, 10km N.W. of *Pont-St-Esprit*; see Rte 142A.

The road descends through the lower town of Aubenas to cross the Ardèche, steeply climbing the far bank to (16km) *Villeneuve-de-Berg*, a stronghold established by Philippe le Hardi in 1283, and the birthplace of Olivier de Serres (1539–1619), who introduced the mulberry into France. His residence, at *Pradel*, 5km N., was visited by Arthur Young, who considered him 'the great parent of French agriculture'. The road circles to the E., with the plateau du Coiron rising ahead, and after 11km reaches a junction, the r.-hand fork of which leads along the Escoutay valley to *Viviers*, 15.5km beyond (see Rte 142A) via (2km) **Alba**, now a mere village, which was once *Alba Augusta*, capital of the Helvii, but few traces of its ancient importance survive. Some antique fragments have been built into the walls of houses, and above the ruined priory of *St-Martin* are traces of a circus; the turreted castle is 15C.

The main road forks l. to reach the Rhône at (11km) *Le Teil* (see Rte 142A), where the river and its deviation are crossed, to enter **Montélimar**, 6km E.; see Rte 141A.

100 Moulins to Albi via Clermont-Ferrand, St-Flour, and Rodez

400km (248 miles). N9. 81km **Riom**—15km **Clermont-Ferrand**
—35km **Issoire**—19km *Lempdes*—52km **St-Flour**—D921. 89km
Espalion—29km **Rodez**—N88. 78km **Albi**

Maps: IGN 42, 49, 58, or 111, 114. M 238, 239, 235.

We cross the Allier at **Moulins** (Rte 96) and turn l., following the W.
side of the valley to (9km) *Chemilly*, with a Romanesque church.

4.5km S.W., at *Besson*, is another Romanesque Church, to the N.W., and W.
respectively of which are the restored châteaux of *Ritz*, and that of '*Vieux-Bostz*
(15-16C), while 2km S. is the fine 14C castle of *Fourchaud*.

9.5km. *Châtel-de-Neuvre*, with a well-sited Romanesque church
dominating the Allier, is traversed as the road continues S. to
(12.5km) *St-Pourçain-sur-Sioule*, with a large **Abbey-church* exhibiting most architectural styles from the 12-18Cs; its wines are
reputed.

At *Saulcet*, 3km N.W., is an imposing belfry, and another rises at *Verneuil-en-
Bourbonnais*, 2.5km beyond, also with a ruined château.

A DETOUR may be made via *Châtelle*, 14km S.W., with ruins of a 11C castle,
once a residence of the dukes of Bourbon, now incorporating a Benedictine convent; *St-Vincent* is partly 12C.—There is another church of the same date with an
octagonal 14C tower at *Bellenaves*, 7.5km further S.W., turning S. from which,
via *Vicq* (3km N.W. of which, at *Veauce*, is a 12C church and restored 15C
château), we reach (10km) **Ebreuil**, where **St-Léger* has a tower over its porch, a
Romanesque nave, and fine early Gothic choir, behind the high altar of which is
the 15C shrine of its patron.—*Gannat* lies 10km E.

The D6 forks l. 5km S. of St-Pourcain to (28km) **Vichy** (see Rte 99) via
the remains of the 12C abbey of *St-Gilbert-de-Neuffonts* and the *Forêt
de Marcenat*.

16km. *Janzat* (with 15C murals in its church) and *Charroux*, further N.W., preserving part of its walls and a 12-13C church, lie to the
r. of the road.—5km. **Gannat**, with remains of a 12-14C château (r.;
restored), preserves in its museum a richly bound Carolingian
Gospel, and l. in the town centre, *Ste-Croix*, with a 12C ambulatory,
13C nave, and 17C choir. Jacques de Chabannes de la Palice, marshal of France (c. 1470– 1525, at Pavia) may have been born here.

As (9km) **Algueperse** is approached, the church of Montpensier is
passed (l.) on a hill formerly crowned by one of the strongest castles
in Auvergne, where Louis VIII died in 1226. It was destroyed by
Richelieu in 1633. The town was the capital of the old duchy of
Montpensier, of which 'La Grande Mademoiselle', Louise d'Orléans
(1627– 93), was perhaps the most famous to hold the title. It was the
birthplace of the humanist Chancellor Michel de l'Hospital
(1505/6– 73). The 13C **Choir* of *Notre-Dame*, on the r. of which is a
curious two-storeyed mortuary chapel of 1515, and the *Ste-Chapelle*
(1475; the rose-window of which has been stolen), built by Louis I de
Bourbon, Count of Montpensier, are notable.

To the W. of the town is the well-sited *Château de la Roche* (1525); 5km to the
N.E. is the *Château d'Effiat*, demesne of the Marquis d'Effiat (1581– 1632), the
ambassador who arranged the marriage of Charles I of England to Henrietta

Maria, and whose son was the Marquis de Cinq-Mars (1620–42), beheaded at Lyon with his friend De Thou for conspiring with Philip IV of Spain against Richelieu.—Further N.E. are the 16C château of *Denone* and the 12C church of *Boizat*.—There is an attractive 11-12C priory church at *Thuret*, 8km S.W. of Aigueperse.

The peaks or 'puys' of Auvergne come into view to the S.W. on approaching (16km) **RIOM** (18,900 Riomois), an ancient town (*Ricomagus*) damaged by earthquake in the 13C, once the capital of the Duchy of Auvergne, and still the judicial capital of the region. it retains several stately but sombre Renaissance mansions (built of Volvic lava) within the old town encircled by an oval of boulevards, but nothing remains of the Château of Jean de Berry, in which that duke married Jeanne d'Armagnac in 1359, and the poet Charles d'Orléans married Bonne d'Armagnac in 1410.

Riom was the birthplace of the Jansenist Antoine Arnauld (1612–94). Here took place the 'procés de Riom' of 1942, in which the Vichy government attempted to incriminate ministers of the Third Republic, among them Édouard Daladier, Paul Reynaud, Léon Blum, and Gén. Gamelin. In 1943 Marshal Lattre de Tassigny (1889–1952), held captive by the Germans, made a daring escape hence.

From the *Pl. de la Fédération* (S. of which is an 18C gateway and 17C fountain) one may turn E. past *St-Amable*, begun in 1120 but since much altered, the central tower being a 19C reconstruction. The W. facade is of 1747, but the transepts are mainly original, while the choir is 13C.—Just N. of the central Carrefour des Taules, at No. 12 Rue de l'Horloge, stands the *Hôtel Guimoneau*, with a fine courtyard, opposite which is a 15-16C clock-tower; the courtyards of Nos 7 and 19 are likewise noteworthy, and also the facade of No. 4.—Some distance S., in the Rue du Commerce, is 15C *N.-D. du Marthuret*, with a Flamboyant facade, preserving in a S. chapel a sculptured Virgin and Child with a bird (14C).—Regaining the central junction, one may follow the street to the E. past (r.) the arcaded *Maison des Consuls* (1531), and (l.) the *Hôtel de Ville*. Further E. is the *Musée Mandet* in a mansion of 1680, containing an uninspiring collection of paintings, and fragments of sculpture from *Mozac*; see below.—At the end of the street opposite is a *Regional Museum*, E. of which is the *Palais de Justice*, rebuilt 1830, preserving some Beauvais tapestries, and of the original 14C edifice, the *Ste-Chapelle*, with three good early 15C stained-glass windows in its apse.

From opposite the W. gate (see above) the Av. du Commandant Madeline leads 1.5km to the suburb of **Mozac**, with a remarkable Benedictine *Abbey-church* (12C), containing some outstanding capitals, and the Shrine of St Calminus, Limoges work of 1168.

At *Marsat*, 2km S.W., the 11-12C church preserves a 12C Black Virgin; *Volvic*, further W. (7km from Riom) has been known since the 13C for its quarries in the dark grey lava-stream of La Nugère seen in so many buildings in the region. Its church (nave rebuilt) has an 11C choir and 12C transepts. To the N. is the romantically poised *Château de Tournoel* (12-16C), providing panoramic views.—The road (D941) may be continued from Volvic to (18km) *Pontgibaud*; see Rte 93B.—For *Châtelguyon*, 5km N.W. of Riom, see Rte 92.

The D224 leads 9.5km E. from Riom to *Ennezat*, a small town in the Limagne depression, with a beautiful *Church* with a 12C nave preceded by a narthex, and a 14C choir; *Maringues*, 9.5km beyond, with abandoned tanneries on the banks of the Morge, has a 12th and 16C church.

From Riom, the N9 leads S., shortly passing near (r.) the square keep of *Châteaugay* (16C), beyond which the landscape is dominated by the imposing mass of the *Puy de Dôme* (see below), before entering the industrial outskirts of Clermont-Ferrand, largely occupied by the Michelin Tyre Co.; see below.

Some 11km from Riom the Tiretaine is crossed, where it is recommended to fork r. into **Montferrand**, what is first an unprepossessing suburb, but which preserves in its old centre an interesting series of ancient **Mansions*, some restored, once the residence of its long-vanished aristocracy. The town, pillaged by the English in 1388, was administratively united with Clermont only in 1731. Just S.E. of the central junction (Les Taules) stands *Notre-Dame* (1298–16C), notable for its flamboyant W. front and carved altarpieces (17C), built on the site of a chapel of a stronghold of the counts of Auvergne, which stood further E. on what is now the *Pl. Marcel-Sembat*. Immediately S. of the church are the *Maison de l'Eléphant* (late 12C), among others of interest, including No. 4 Rue Montorcier; while at the N.E. angle of Les Taules is the half-timbered *Maison de l'Apothicaire* (15C). Further W., in the Rue de la Rocade, Nos 29 and 36 are of interest, and 11, 13, 18 (*Hôtel de Lignat*), 20, and 28 (*Hôtel Fontfreyde*) in the Rue Jules Guesde, leading S. from the junction, are likewise notable. By following this latter street we reach the *Pl. de la Fontaine*, and turn r., following the Av. de la République, to approach Clermont itself.

CLERMONT-FERRAND (151,100 Clermontois; 24,500 in 1801; 102,600 in 1901), préfecture of the *Puy-de-Dome*, and an important industrial centre, lies at 400m altitude at the S.W. end of the Limagne, surrounded by volcanic *buttes* on three sides, the most conspicuous of which, to the W. is the Puy de Dôme itself. The old Auvergnat city, on a hill clustering around the cathedral, is surrounded by a modern town of slight interest, the principal manufacture of which is heavy rubber goods, particularly motor-tyres.

The Gaulish centre of Auvergne was at *Gergovia* (see below), but the Roman settlement, *Augustonemetum*, on the site of Clermont, grew to such importance that in the 4C it was called *Civitas Arvernorum*. In 1095 the prelates of France assembled at the Council of Clermont, at which Peter the Hermit preached the First Crusade. its bishops were always at odds with the counts of Auvergne, and obtained virtual mastery of the place with the intervention of Louis VI. It later became capital of the province, and in 1731, with the absorption of Montferrand (see above) assumed the title of Clermont-Ferrand. Arthur Young referred to it as 'one of the worst built, dirtiest, and most stinking places' he had met with. Its university was founded in 1854.

A small factory for making rubber had been established there in 1832 by Aristide Barbier and Édouard Daubrée, whose wife was a niece of Charles Macintosh (1766–1843), who had patented the invention of waterproof fabrics in 1823. Mme Daubrée would amuse her children by making rubber balls as she had seen her uncle make them; and under Édouard and André Michelin, grandsons of Barbier, the business expanded rapidly. Since the last decade of the 19C the town has remained the hub of the pneumatic empire, where inflated and bouncing M. Bibendum spins his elastic web. ('Bibendum' was a figure invented in 1907 by the gastronome Maurice Sailland—'Curnonsky'; 1862–1956.)

The most illustrious native of Clermont was Blaise Pascal (1623–62); in 1648 he caused barometric experiments to be undertaken on the Puy de Dôme to verify those he was making in Paris. Others include Gregory of Tours c. 538–94), the historian; the troubadour Pierre d'Auvergne (c. 1130); the Abbé Jacques Delille (1738–1813), a poetaster and translator of Milton; Chamfort (1741–94), the moralist; George Onslow (c. 1783–1853), the composer; and Pierre Teilhard de Chardin (1881–1955), at the nearby château of Sarcenat. Vercingetorix, hero of Gallic independence, was probably born in the vicinity. Among bishops of Clermont were the satirical Sidonius Apollinaris (c. 460), and J.-B. Massillon (d. 1742).

The monuments of Clermont-Ferrand are few, and may be best approached from the *Pl. de la Poterne* (embellished by a Renaissance fountain erected by Bp Jacques d'Amboise in 1515) on the N. side of the old centre, adjacent to the *Hôtel de Ville*. It is perhaps convenient to visit first *N.-D.-du-Port*, a few minutes' walk to the E. down the Rue du Port, preserving several old houses, among them Nos 21 and 38.

N.-D.-du-Port (12C), replacing a 7C building, and with the addition of two 19C towers in tolerable imitation of the originals destroyed in 1793, is an interesting structure. Notable is its apse, with four radiating chapels, and typical black-and-white patterning; the sculptures of the S. door, although mutilated, are remarkable, as are the historiated capitals of the choir, and the interior vaulting of the cupola. In the crypt is a mid 18C copy of a Romanesque 'Black' Virgin.

On returning up the street, one may turn l. along the Rue Pascal, passing No. 4, the former *Hôtel de Chazerat*, with an oval 18C courtyard, to reach the *Pl. de la Victoire* (where a statue of Urban II commemorates the First Crusade), and the S. side of the *Cathedral*, built of the ubiquitous dark grey Volvic lava, and the finest, if sombre, Gothic edifice in Auvergne. The exterior is not striking, except for the N. transeptal doorway, which has good but mutilated sculptures, and is surmounted by a watch-tower.

The present structure was begun in 1248 on the site of a Romanesque church whose crypt survives, with contemporary murals. The choir was completed in 1287, but the building of the transepts and nave continued into the 14C; while the two W. bays, with the W. front and spire, were added in 1855 by Viollet-le-Duc.

The double-aisled nave is noteworthy for the slenderness of its piers, made possible by the strength of the Volvic stone. The triforium is well designed. The rose-windows of the transepts describe a circle within a square. The *Choir* is distinguished by fine 13C glass in its chapels; also notable are paintings of the Legend of SS Crepin and Crépinien, and an altar made up from a 6C sarcophagus. In the Chapel of St-George are 13C frescoes and a battle-scene; in the Lady Chapel, a Romanesque Virgin and Child.

From the W. front one may descend the Rue des Gras or the parallel Rue des Chaussetiers to the S., in which No. 3 is the *Maison Savaron* of 1513. In the former we pass (r.) the *Maison des Architects* (1560) before reaching the Av. des États-Unis. To the S. is the spacious *Pl. de Jaude*, the main centre of animation of the town, on the W. side of which is *St-Pierre-les-Minimes* (1630), with 18C woodwork in its choir.

Ascending to the E., the *Préfecture* is reached, from the S.E. corner of which the Rue St-Esprit is followed to gain the N. end of the Rue Ballainvilliers. This leads S. to the *Jardins Lecoq* and University buildings. To the l. is the **Musée Bargoin**, containing important prehistoric and Gallo-Roman collections; Gothic and Romanesque sculptures; Limoges enamels; medieval antiquities; and paintings.

Notable are its series of bronze figurines, some from the Temple of Mercury or the Puy de Dôme; the wood-sculptured ex-votos discovered in 1968 at the Source des Rochers at Chamalieres; and the collection of glass cinerary urns. Among the few paintings of note are: *School of Corneille de Lyon*, Portrait of Jean d'Albon; *Th. Rombouts*, The Dentist; *Boucher,*, Washerwomen; *J. Duplessis*, Portrait of A.-L.Thomas; and *Philippe de Champaigne*, Vincent Voiture.

To the E. is the *Library*, and *Musée Lecoq*, with ethnological, geological, and natural history collections.—Beyond the *Lycée Blaise Pascal* (at which Bergson taught in 1883– 88), at the N. end of the

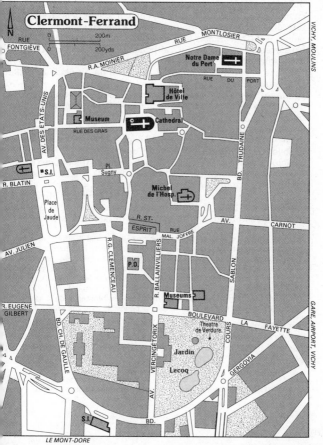

LE MONT-DORE

Rue Ballainvilliers, stands Flamboyant *St-Gènes*, whence by threading lanes to the N. one may regain the cathedral.

For roads hence to *Bourges* and *Montluçon*, and to *Aubusson*, see Rtes 92 and 93, in reverse; for *Brive*, Rte 94; for *Mont-Dore*, *Mauriac*, and *Aurillac*, Rte 95; and *Thiers*, Rte 99; for *Ambert*, see below.

THE EXCURSION TO ROYAT AND THE PUY DE DÔME (c. 30km there and back) may be made by following the D68 W. from the Pl. de Jaude, shortly traversing the industrial suburb of *Chamalières*, with note-printing works of the Banque de France, and an 11-12C church disfigured in the 17C, preserving in its narthex two antique columns with 10C capitals. The road ascends steeply to (3.5km) the spa of **Royat**, whose warm springs were known to the Romans, but which were not commercialised until 1823. The *Établissement Thermal* and *Casino* lie in gardens flanking the Tiretaine; N. of the former are remains of Roman baths, while N.E. of the casino is the so-called *Grotte du Chien*, where powerful emanations of carbon dioxide rise high enough above ground level to asphyxiate a dog, although a standing man may still breathe freely, but the proof is no longer put into practice to amuse tourists. In the old village, higher up the valley, is the remarkable fortified church of *St-Léger (11-12C), with battlements added in the 13C, although most of those surviving, and the tower, are 19C restorations.

To the S. rise the summits of the *Puys de Montaudou* (589m), *Gravenoire* (822m), and further S.W., *Charade* (904m).—The D68 continues W. via the village of *Fontanas* towards the imposing butte of the *Puy de Dôme, the highest and most famous summit in this extinct volcanic chain, rising to 1416m, and ascended by a toll road (cars and motorcycles only), which makes a bold clockwise spiral up the mountainside at a gradient of 12 degrees: pedestrians are obliged to follow a track further S. to the *Col de Ceyssat* (1078m), thence climbing a zigzag path of Gallo-Roman origin up the wooded slope to the summit. Some may prefer to view the peak from a distance, for the top is clattered by an observatory, radio mast, and souvenir shops, etc., apart from the foundations of a *Temple of Mercury*, excavated since 1873, to the S. of which its dependencies appear to have been extended to form a series of terraces and steps.

This Puy, a rounded mass of porous trachyte called 'domite', differs from most of the other puys in having no crater, its volcanic mass having hardened at once after having been thrust up, and has thus retained its shape almost perfectly. The *Views is commands are extensive. In the foreground are fifty or more of the characteristic crater-like puys interspersed with greyish lava-flows. To the S. and S.E. are the Cantal and Velay mountains; to the E. lie Clermont and the Limagne backed by the hills of Livradois and Forez, and the Montagne de la Madeleine, and in clear weather Mont Blanc is said to be visible over the Monts du Forez.

The descent on foot may be made by the N.E. slope to see the *Petit Puy de Dôme*, which has two craters, one a very regular and typical example, called the *Nid de la Poule*. The descent from the valley between the two puys is obvious.

An alternative return by road to Clermont may be made by following the main road (D941A) via *La Baraque*, built on a lava flow descending from the *Puy de*

Looking towards the Puy de Dôme

Pariou, providing a notable retrospective view of the great dome-shaped mountain.—For other excursions in the vicinity, see pp 513 and 515.

CLERMONT-FERRAND TO AMBERT VIA BILLOM (77km). The N9 is followed for 6km and then the D212 turning l. via *Cournon-d'Auvergne*, with a 12C church, beyond which the Allier is crossed.—3km. *Chauriat*, 6km N.E., preserves an Auvergnat Romanesque church of some interest, part of a priory founded in 1015.—There is an imposing ruined castle of 1170 at *Busseol*, c. 4km S. of the road.—To the l., on approaching (10km) **Billom**, are the ruins of a 12-13C castle. The town, of ancient foundation and once famous for its ecclesiastical schools, preserves several half-timbered 15-16C houses around centrally sited *St-Cerneuf*, dating mainly from the 13C. Its apsidal chapels contain good 17C woodwork, and the tomb of Aycelin de Montaigue (d. 1318), founder of the Collège de Montaigue in Paris; round the sanctuary is a Romanesque grille.—On the E. side of the town is *St-Loup* (14-15C), with a graceful tower.—There is a very early Romanesque church at *Glaine*, 6km N.E.—5km S. are the ruins of the castle of *Montmorin* (with a small museum).—From Billom we follow the D997 across the *Monts du Livradois*, after 9km passing (l.) the imposing ruins of the episcopal castle of *Mauzun* (view), and 9km beyond, the unusual Romanesque church of *St-Dier*. After 5km the *Château de Martinanches* (15th and 19C, on 11C foundations) is passed, and at 5km the D996 is followed to (12km) *St-Amant-Roche-Savine*, with a 15C church, and castle ruins 2km S.—After 8km the road descends (views) into the valley of the Dore to (4km) **Ambert**; see Rte 99.

On quitting Clermont-Ferrand, the N9 is regained by following the Blvd La Fayette S.E.—After 10km the road is overlooked (r.) by the *Plateau de Gergovie*, a mass of deeply scarped basalt.

This was the site of the Gaullish oppidum of *Gergovia*, where Julius Caesar met his first reverse at the hands of Vercingetorix, and narrowly escaped capture (53 B.C.), but practically no trace of the settlement remains above ground. Since 1933 there has been much academic discussion as to whether the battle took place here or just N. of Clermont on the *Plateau de Chanturge*, also the site of a Gallic fortress.

Orcet is passed on the l., the birthplace of Georges Couthon (1756–94), one of the most ruthless instruments of the Terror, although partially paralysed.—The next r.-hand turning leads 6km S.W. to *St-Saturnin*, with a notable 12C church and 15C château.—For the roads to *St-Nectaire*, see Rte 95.—The N9 shortly passes between *Las Sauvetat* (r.) and later *Montpeyroux* (l.), both once fortified, the former retaining a 14C keep of the Knights of St John, the latter a fine cylindrical keep, before entering (24.5km) *Coudes*, on the Allier.

6km N.E. lies *Vic-le-Comte*, a little old town with a curious *Ste-Chapelle*, built in 1510 for the Duke of Albany (John Stewart, regent of Scotland during the minority of James V), who bore the title of Comte d'Auvergne. It is a remarkable type of the transition from Gothic to Renaissance architecture and contains a wide balustraded gallery with statues of the Apostles, and contemporary glass and sculptured altarpieces. A gateway of the castle of the counts of Auvergne and other buildings have also been preserved.

Above the valley to the l. are the ruins of the castle of *Buron*.—The bank of the Allier is briefly followed before veering S. to (11km) **Issoire** (15,400 Issoiriens), Gallo-Roman *Iciodorum*. As a stronghold of Protestantism it was practically destroyed in 1577 by the Duc d'Alençon, and a pillar erected on its site bore the grim inscription: 'ici fut Issoire'. Card. Duprat (1464–1535), Chancellor of François I, was born here.

The *Abbey-church* of St-Austremoine (Strymonius), on the E. side

of the town centre, is a remarkable specimen of 12C Auvergnat architecture, resembling N.-D.-du-Port at Clermont-Ferrand in plan,
except for the unusual addition of a square E. end. Note the signs of
the Zodiac on the exterior of the apse chapels. The façade and
towers are inoffensive 19C reconstructions, but the interior is spoilt
by hideous paint-work of 1859 in the nave. Note also the 15C mural
of the Last Judgement to the r. of the entrance, and a restored capital
of the Last Supper; the crypt should be visited.

Some 9km E. via *Parentignat*, with a Louis-XIV château, lies *Usson*, near which
are the remains of a castle (destroyed 1634) in which Queen Marguerite occupied herself in writing and gallantry when exiled from Court in 1585–1605.
The church dates from the 12-15C.—*Sauxillanges*, with a 12C church, lies
c. 5km N.E., and 9km further N. is *Manglieu*, its remarkable *Church having a
Romanesque narthex and choir, and 12C doorway.
    The D999A leads S.E. from Issoire across the unfrequented *Montes du
Livradois* via *St-Germain-l'Herm* to (57km) *La Chaise-Dieu*; see Rte 99.

10km. **St-Germain-Lembron**, 5km. N.W. of which is the restored
Renaissance château of *Villeneuve* ◊, preserving several 15C
frescoes.—5km to the N.E. is *Nonette*, with an 11-14C church of interest and the ruins of one of the oldest castles in Auvergne.
    9km. *Lempdes*, where we turn r.

LEMPDES TO BRIOUDE AND LE PUY (74km). The N102 leads S.E., at 4km passing 6km S.W. of *Auzon*, once fortified, and with a church preserving a 12C porch
and good capitals.—10km. **Brioude** (7,900 Brivadois), an old market-town of interest for its spring salmon, and the *Church of St-Julien*, erected on the site of its
patron's martyrdom. The W. front and the towers are mid 19C, but the S. porch,
with its old doors, the N. porch and ambulatory, with its five radiating chapels
are admirable examples of early 13C work. The narthex and the five W. bays of
the nave date from c. 1170; in the chapel above the narthex are remains of
13-14C murals; in a chapel in the S. aisle is a wooden altarpiece by Vaneau
(1693).—From (4km) *Vieille-Brioude*, with a ruined priory church, a by-road leads
S. along the gorge of the Allier to *Langeac* (see below) via (19km) *Lavoûte-
Chilhac*, with an interesting church.—The main road at 8km by-passes (l.)
Lavaudieu, with a good 12C *Church containing contemporary wall-paintings
and a charming cloister among other dependencies of a Benedictine abbey;
there is a ruined 15C castle at adjacent *Domeyrat*, also with a small Romanesque
church.
    At 7km the D56 forks r. to (13km) **Langeac**, a pleasantly sited small town with
a 15C church, lying on the main cross-country road between St-Flour and Le Puy
(51km W., and 42km E., respectively). On the latter road lie *Vissac*, with a
Romanesque church and ruined castle, and *Siaugues*, picturesquely placed
beneath the ruins of the castle of *St-Romain*, to the S. of which rises *La Durande*
(1299m).
    Hence the lonely D585, continued by the D985, crosses the E. flank of the
Monts de la Margeride to (66km) *Châteauneuf-de-Randon* 29km N.E. of Mende,
passing through (5km) *Chanteuges*, where a Romanesque church occupies a
commanding site. Just beyond Chanteuges we leave to the l. the wild *Gorges of
the upper Allier, and *Pébrac*, 5km S.W., with its 11C Abbey-church and later
relics of a monastery, and climb S. to (16km) *Saugues* (960m), to the W. of which
rises *Mont Mouchet* (1465m; see below). The 13C *Tour des Anglais*, and the
curious *Tombeau du Général Anglais* in the cemetery recall the campaign of Du
Guesclin against these outposts of the English occupation of Languedoc.—The
road goes on through (24km) *Grandrieu*, with a 13C church, below the wildest
part of the range, reaching *Châteauneuf* 17km, beyond; see Rte 99. It was this
district, near the once vast *Forêt de Mercoire*, that was terrorised by the so-called
'Bête du Gévaudan' during the 1760s, but which was probably more than one of
the 679 wolves killed in the Gévaudan during the period May 1761—Feb. 1770
and which in the years 1763–65 had claimed 92 human victims.
    At the Langeac crossroads, the N102 forks l., by-passing (l.) at 7km the unat-
tractive château of *Chavaniac-Lafayette*, birthplace of Marie-Joseph Môtier

Marquis de La Fayette (1757–1834), a partisan of liberty in France and America, and so, commercialised.—10km. *Fix-St-Geneys* stands on the main ridge of the *Velay hills*, beyond which, with wide views, we descend to meet, at 15km, the D906 from Vichy, and turn r., shortly enjoying the panorama of **Le Puy** in its basin; see Rte 99.

From *Lempdes* the N9 threads the *Gorges de l'Alagnon*, following the E. bank of the river, and shortly passes the ruins of the 14C castle of *Léotoing*, commanding extensive views.—15km. **Blesle** (r.), an ancient town retaining a section of its walls and an imposing 13C *Keep*; the 11-12C church of a Benedictine nunnery replaces the parish church destroyed in 1793 except for its 14C belfry.—7km. *Massiac*.

MASSIAC TO AURILLAC VIA MURAT (86km). The N122 leads S.W. up the Alagnon valley to (35km) *Murat* (917m), a sombre looking town of steep streets, a centre of Cantal cheese production, and of the Resistance in the early 1940s. 15C *N.-D.-des-Oliviers* contains a 'Black' Virgin (said to have been brought back from Palestine by Louis IX). For the road hence to *Salers* and *Mauriac*, see Rte 95.—To the N.W., the town is dominated by the basalt columns of the *Rocher de Bonnevie*, while the hamlet of *Bredons*, to the S., built on the extremity of a volcanic dyke, is worth a visit for the curious altarpiece of gilded wood bearing two Trees of Jesse (1616) in its church of 1074.—There is a Romanesque church at *Dienne*, 9km N.W.—The road continues to climb from Murat through gorges to (11.5km) *Le Lioran* (1153m), a resort for the exploration of the Cantal mountains and for winter-sporting (at *Super-Lioran*).

The **Plomb du Cantal** (1855m), to the S., the highest point in the range, is no more than a slight elevation on the lip of an enormous disintegrated crater, and may be claimbed with ease; the views from the summit are extensive. To the N.W. rises the **Puy Mary** (1787m), approached by the *Col de Rombière*, near the head of the Mandailles valley. To the W., in the centre of this broken rim of mountains, rises the conical peak of *Puy Griou* (1694m). The road crosses the watershed by a tunnel and descends the valley of the Cère, threading the *Pas de Campaing* and the *Pas de la Cère*, between which we traverse (12km) *Thiézac*, in an open vale, known for its 'fromage bleu'.—6.5km. *Vic-sur-Cère*, a small sheltered resort and spa, and the ancient capital of the viscounty of Carladès. It preserves several interesting mansions, notably the 15C *Maison des Princes de Monaco* (that family bearing the title 'Vicomte de Carlat' from a castle c. 12km S. as the crow flies). To the S.E. rises the *Rocher des Pendus* (views).—We pass the 16C château of *Pesteils* (r.) in which Cocteau's 'L'Éternel Retour' was filmed in 1943, with a 14C keep, among other châteaux, before turning N.W. to (20km) *Aurillac*; see Rte 95.

From Massiac the road climbs S. to follow a ridge, providing occasional views, to the *Col de la Fageole* (1104m), before crossing the featureless basaltic upland *Plateau de la Planèze* to approach (30km) St-Flour.

ST-FLOUR (881m; 9,100 Sanflorains), or at least the ancient town, is remarkably sited on a precipitous basalt bluff some 100m above the confluence of two streams, approached from the main crossroads to the E. by the Av. de Verdun, which ascends from the S., later climbing past the so-called 'Orgues basaltiques' to the tree-lined but wind-swept Allées Pompidou. From the N.E. corner of this promenade the Rues du Collège and Rue du Breuil (note No. 8) lead near a dissaffected 14-15C church to the bleak little Pl. des Armes, on the N. side of which is the Renaissance *Maison Consulaire*.

The square is dominated by the **Cathedral** (the most loftily sited in France), a dark squat building with two square W. towers. The present edifice, begun in 1396 on the plans of Maitre Hugues, mastermason of Jean de Berry, and dedicated to St Florus (d. 370), replaced the basilica of St Odilo consecrated in 1095. The double-aisled in-

terior is plain to the point of baldness; the piers are without capitals.
A 12C Christ in the N. aisle and a 15C Pietà, carved from lava, are
notable.

Behind the apse is a terrace (view); abutting the cathedral is the
18C bishop's palace, now the *Hôtel de Ville*, containing also a
Museum of regional interest, with a notable archaeological section.
The Rue Marchande (note Nos 15 and 31) leads back through the
sombre old town, in which few architectural relics are preserved,
among them the Gothic *Porte des Roches*, on the S. side (approached
from the lower town by the ramshackle Rue du Thuile), to regain the
Allées. Jacques-Paul Migne (1800–75), the erudite editor of Patristic
writings, was born at St-Flour.

There is a restored château beside the *Cascade de Basborie*, 5km N.W., S. of
which, on the D926, is the old church and fortress-tower of *Roffiac*.

For the roads from St-Flour to **Montpellier** via *Millau* and *Lodève*, and via
Mende and *Florac*, see Rtes 101A and B, respectively.

The D921 leads S.W.—At 8.5km *Villedieu*, with a beautiful unfinished church of 1366, lies 2.5km S.E., some 5km beyond which, at
Alleuze, near a reservoir, is the ruined stronghold of Aymerigot Mar-
chez, terror of the Haute Auvergne in the 14C.

3.5km. *Les Ternes* (in the vicinity of which are several tumuli),
beyond which a fine wooded descent brings us to the *Pont de
Lanau, on the Truyère, before reaching (21km) *Chaudes-Aigues* ('ad
calidas aquas'; Caldaguès), a small spa in the Remontalou valley,
whose hot springs (rising to 180° Fahr., or 82° Celsius) were anciently piped to many of the houses by an ingenious system of conduits.

CHAUDES-AIGUES TO MARVEJOLS (57km). The D13 leads S. into the high-
lying basaltic *Aubrac plateau*, by-passing (l. at 13km) *La Chaldette*, a diminutive
spa, to (10km) *St-Urcize*, with a remarkable church with a 12C apse and 13-14C
nave, some 4km S.E. of which is *Nasbinals*, with a little 12C church and important cattle fairs.—Hence the D900 is followed to the S.E. for 30km, shortly passing the cavern and waterfall of *Déroc*, to join the N9 just N. of *Marvejols*; see Rte
101A.

32km. *Laguiole* (pron. Layole; 1004m), with a well-sited 16C church
is the cheese-making mountain capital of the Aubrac. It is also
known for its cutlery. Its castle was taken and burnt by the English in
1338.

The village of *Aubrac* itself is some 20km S.E., also noted for its cattle-market
and preserving a Romanesque church and the medieval buildings of a hospice
which once sheltered travellers crossing that bleak upland.

The D921 descends past (l. at 20km.) the *Tour de Masse* (1453), all
that remains of the Cistercian abbey of *Bonneval* (founded 1147)
suppressed in 1789 and replaced by a 20C Trappist convent, 4km
beyond which the Lot valley is reached at *Espalion*.

Espalion stands mainly on the S. bank of the river, overlooked by
the ruined castle of *Calmont d'Olt*. It preserves a 13C *Bridge*, which
makes an attractive group with a turreted *Château* of 1572 (containing a folk museum) and other old riverside houses and tanneries. The
15C church is dissaffected. Of interest is the original parish church
or *Église de Perse, c. 1km S.E., a charming and well-preserved
building erected in the 11-12C on the spot where St Hilarion is said to
have been beheaded by the Moors in the 9C. The rude relief over the
doorway, inspired by that of Conques, and the row of grotesque carvings outside the apse, are noteworthy, while the arcaded belfry

The château and bridge of Espalion

may be compared with that of *St-Urcize* (see above).—For *Estaing*, 10km W., see Rte 95; for *St-Cóme d'Olt*, 4km E., Rte 102.

The D920 climbs up the S. side of the Lot valley to (10km) *Bozouls*, a curious village built on both sides of the steep gorge of the Dourdou—the '*trou de Bozouls*'—with an interesting Romanesque church standing on a promontory on the r. bank.—Traversing the barren *Causse du Comtal*, we have a view of **Rodez** ahead, dominated by the tower of its cathedral; see Rte 95.

Hence the N88 leads due S., crossing the Aveyron and ascending to (8km) a T-junction, where we meet the D911, and turn r. After another 11km it veers l.; at *Vors*, to the N.E. of this turning, commences the Gallo-Roman aqueduct which fed Rodez.

The l.-hand turning lead E. and then S.E. to (63km) *Millau* (see Rte 101A), traversing the barren granitic plateau of *Levézou*, passing N. of the reservoir of *Pareloup*, and the old village of *Salles-Curan*.

15km. *Villefranche-de-Rouergue* (see Rte 65) lies 9km to the N.W., some 5km S.W. of which, in the valley of the Lézert, is the ruined château of *Villelongue*, H.Q. in 1944 of André Malraux (then 'Col Berger').—3km S. of this turning is the 19C *Château du Bosc*, where Toulouse-Lautrec passed much of his infancy, and which preserves early souvenirs of his painting.

After 6km a r.-hand fork leads 9km to *Pampelonne*, a bastide named after Pamplona in Navarre, overlooked by the ruined château of *Thuriès*, commanding a view of the Viaur gorge and reservoir.—The N88 descends to cross the valley to (7km) *Tanus*, with a view (l.) of the impressive *Viaduc du Viaur* (1902), 460m long and 120m above the valley floor, with a central span of 220m.

The road veers W. to (16km) **Carmaux** (12,200 Carmousins), an industrial town in the centre of a coalfield, with important glassworks.

The D91 leads W. hence to (23km) **Cordes** (see Rte 65) via (7km)

Monestiès, with a church of 1550 and rebuilt chapel containing a remarkable Entombment of 1490.—The main road leads S. towards the Tarn, providing a good view of (16km) **Albi** on its approach, for which see Rte 89.

101 St-Flour to Montpellier

A. Via Millau and Lodève (for Pézenas and Beziers)

256km (159 miles). N9. 35km *St-Chély-d'Apcher*—33km **Marvejols**—42km *Sévérac-le-Château*—32km **Millau**—61km **Lodève**—24km *Gignac*—N109. 30km **Montpellier**.

Maps: IGN 49, 58, 65, or 111, 114; also 354. M 239, 240.

The N9 turns due E. from *St-Flour* (see Rte 100) before bearing S.E.

At 6.5km the D4 leads c. 20km E. into the *Monts de la Margeride* towards a summit of the range—here thickly wooded—*Mont Mouchet* (1465m). Here stands the *National Monument to the Maquis de France*, on the scene of one of their more important combats, in which c. 1000 were killed of some 15,000 partisans dispersed throughout the area.

The road goes on (as the D589) to (24km) *Saugues* (see Rte 100) and *Monistrol-d'Allier*, 16km beyond, to the N. of which rise the ruins of the château of *Rochegude*, commanding a spectacular view over the lava and gneiss crags of the upper Allier. The road leads N.E. out of the gorge to (16.5km) *Bains*, with a Romanesque church, and **Le Puy**, 11.5km further E.; see Rte 99.

The N9 climbs down to cross the Truyère at 5.5km, with a good view of the railway *Viaduc de Garabit*, constructed by Eiffel from the plans of Boyer in 1884, which spans the ravine in a great arch; its total length is 564m.

From the S. bank the D13 leads S.W. to the *Belvedere du Cheylé*, overlooking the *Barrage de Granval*.

23km. *St-Chély-d'Apcher*, by-passed, a chilly upland town (1000m), once fortified, and besieged by the English in 1362, 2km S. of which the N106 forks S.E. to (46km) *Mende*; see Rte 101B.

We bear r. through (8km) *Aumont-Aubrac*, whence the D987 leads 23km S.W. to *Nasbinals*; see Rte 100.—The village of *Javols*, 6.5km S.E., was ancient *Anderitum*, capital of the Gabales, and Gallo-Roman *Gabalum*, where several Roman antiquities have been discovered.

12km. The well-furnished *Château de la Beaume* (17-18C) is 4.5km to the W., standing at 1116m.—The road descends into the valley of the Colagne at (11km) **Marvejols**, a market-town for the cattle of the Aubrac, and an ancient fortress (651m; 6,000 inhab.), preserving three gates, and some 17C houses.—Hence the N108 bears S.E. to (20.5km) *Balsièges*, 7.5km W. of Mende; see Rte 101B.

4km. *Chirac*, with two curious old churches, beyond which *La Monastir-Pin-Moriès* is traversed, named after the monastery at which Urban V took the habit, but only the 11C church remains.—At 5km the N88 is joined in the Lot valley, the wooded banks of which are followed for 11km.

At the junction here, the D988 turns r. towards **Rodez**; see Rte 102.—From *Banassac* (with Roman potteries; see below), on the far bank of the Lot, which is now crossed, the D998 leads 28.5km S.E. across the *Causse de Sauveterre* to the *Gorge of the Tarn* (dangerous descent) and *Ste-Enemie*; see Rte 102.—2km E. of Banassac lies *La Canourgue*, with several old houses and an 11-14C church, just S. of which the D46 forks r. to cross the Causse to the *Point Sublime*, 17km due S.; see Rte 102.

The improved road climbs S.W. to (22km) *Sévérac-le-Château* (750m), an old town overlooked by a huge castle altered in the 17C. The Maquis fought a battle here in 1944.—For the road W. to *Rodez*, see Rte 102.

The Aveyron is crossed near its source, and traversing a ridge, we climb down to a tributary of the Tarn, met at (25km) *Aguessac*, where its r. bank is followed to *Millau*, 7km S.; its gorge is described in Rte 102.

Millau (22,300 Millavois), an animated town dominated by its circumjacent causses (*Noir* to the E., and *du Larsac* to the S.), at the confluence of the Tarn and the Dourbie, is an important entre of communication for this anfracturous region.

Traces of the ancient industry of *Aemilianum Castrum* are found in the Roman pottery works of *La Graufesenque*, in the Dourbie valley, the productions of which, with those of Banassac, were widely exported. In more recent centuries Millau has been famous for its tanneries and the manufacture of gloves, and for the ewes'-milk cheese of nearby Roquefort. Although born at Decazeville, the singer Emma Calvé (1862–1942) lived much of her life here; the entomologist J.-H. Fabre (1823–1915) was born at *St-Léons*, 18km to the N.W.

Roads converge on the semi-circular *Pl. du Manarous*, S. of which is the older town, dominated by a square 14C *Belfry*, octagonal above, with a tall thin stair-turret, to the E. of which is the partially arcaded *Pl. Foch* (with a small museum devoted to archaeology and gloves). In the corner of the square stands *Notre-Dame* (Romanesque and 14C), with an octagonal tower, 12C below and 17C above. Further S. is the *Eglise des Penitents*, with an altarpiece by Gaspard de Crayer. A 15C mill stands near the *Pont Lerouge*, adjacent to which are two arches of its 12C predecessor.

For the road hence to **Rodez**, and for the Tarn Gorges, see Rte 102.

MILLAU TO MONT AIGOUAL VIA MEYRUEIS (79km). We drive N. and at 7km Aguessac fork r., following the r. bank of the Tarn to (14km) *Le Rozier*, with the *Causse Noir* on our r., the *Causse de Sauveterre* to the N., and ahead the *Rocher de Capluc*, the S.W. promontory of the *Causse Méjean*. For a description of the most imposing reach of the *Tarn Gorge*—between Le Rozier and Ste-Enimie—see Rte 102 in reverse.—Crossing the Tarn, the N. bank of the Jonte is skirted, which also flows through a cañon to (21km) *Meyrueis*, where the valley expands.—A minor road climbing N. onto the Causse Noir from Meyrueis approaches (8.5km) the *Grotte de Dargilan*, an impressive stalactite cavern; the Ste-Enimie road (D986) ascends N.W. to approach (11km) *Aven Armand*; see Rte 102.

Meyrueis, a largely Protestant village, is admirably sited at the confluence of the Bétuzon with the Jonte, with barren causses to the N. and S.W., and the green foothills of Mont Aigoual to the S.E.; it preserves two of its old gates and a battlemented belfry, and is overlooked by a chapel-crowned rock. Its local 'bleu d'Auvergne' resembles Roquefort cheese, but is made with cows' milk.—The circuit of the *Causse Méjean* may be continued hence by following the D996 N.E. to (11.5km) the *Col de Perjuret* (1028m; cf.) and descending into the Tarnon valley via *Les Vanels* to (25km) *Florac*; see Rte 101B.

From Meyrueis we climb S. past the château of *Roquedols* (16-17C), and at 6km

fork l. and l. again in 3.5km for the *Col de Montjardin* (1005m), beyond whic
continuing E. along the upper slope of the Bonheur valley before descending
(10km.) crossroads near (r.) *Camprieu*, and the subterranean river of *Bramabio*
which here flows beneath the limestone causse, emerging from a dee
fissure.—Continuing S.E. beyond the *Col de Faubel* (1285m) another crossroa
is reached at 7.5km just prior to the village of *L'Espérou*, 10km N.E. of whi
rises *Mont Aigoual*; see p 558.

MILLAU TO GANGES VIA NANT AND LE VIGAN (91km). The D991 is follo
ed to the E., crossing the Tarn and skirting the r. bank of the Dourbie, betwee
the cliffs of the *Causse Noir* (l.), and the *Causse du Larzac*, which later flo
through a narrow gorge, to (14km) *La Roque-Ste-Marguerite*, its church once t
chapel of the now ruined castle.

An alternative but recommended longer road is that taking in *Montpellier-
Vieux*; this, the D110, turns l. off the latter immediately E. of Millau and climbs
steep zigzags to the top of the *Causse Noir*. At 16km a r.-hand turning lea
shortly to the entrance of *Montpellier-le-Vieux (fee for essential guide-pla
an extraordinary wilderness of dolomitic rocks, in places overgrown with den
vegetation, the exploration of the limestone labyrinth of which may be reduce
to the shorter scramble, which takes approx. one hour.—We reach crossroa
4km further E. and turn r. to descend past the *Roques Altes* (l.) to *La Roque-S
Marguerite*.

We shortly cross to the far bank, and follow the valley past (l.) the perch
hamlet of *St-Véran*, with a ruined castle, to (13km) *Cantobre*, on its bold pr
motory.—A minor road ascends the narrow valley of the Trèvezel to the E., a
(10.5km) *Trèves*, later threading a gorge before reaching (16km) *Bramabiau*, a
the road to *Mont Aigoual*; see Rte 101B.—5km. *Nant*, with a good 16C monas
church, is traversed, as we veer E. up the valley to (7km) *St-Jean-du-Bruel*, a lar
village at the foot of the granitic gorge of the Dourbie; a r.-hand fork just S.
Nant is an alternative approach to *La Couvertoirade* (see below), some 15k
S.—Hence a minor road climbs N.E. to (6.5km) the *Col de la Pierre-Planté*, a
forks r., winding E. above the valley via the village of *Dourbies* to (21km) t
crossroads just prior to *L'Espérou*; see Rte 101B.—At St-Jean we turn S., a
after 7km, E., below the *Montagnes de Lingas*, to (27km) **Le Vigan** (Viganais),
well-sited if unprepossessing town, the ancient *Avanticum*, and birthplace of t
Chevalier d'Assas (1733–60), killed at Clostercamp. *St-Pierre*, rebuilt in 1901,
shaded by huge plane trees; the Gothic *Bridge* spanning the Arre has an impo

Part of the wilderness of Montpellier-le-Vieux.

ng central arch; while a small *Musée Cénevol* may be visited.—The main road
continues E. to (7km) the *Pont d'Hérault*, there following the river S. to (11km)
Ganges; see Rte 101B.

LE VIGAN TO THE CIRQUE DE NAVACELLES. The excursion may be made
by driving S. via *Montdardier*, with a feudal castle restored by Viollet-le-Duc, to
(20km) *Madières*, on the Vis, there turning r. to *St-Maurice*, and r. again to approach the **Cirque*, the finest site overlooking the gorge of the Vis, 400m
below.—Regaining St-Maurice, one may either follow the D25 N.E. along the
Gorges of the Vis to (26km) *Ganges*, or S.W. to meet the N9 N. of (25km) *Lodève*;
see below.

Leaving Millau the N9 ascends to the huge *Causse du Larzac*, with
good plunging views over the Tarn and Dourbie valleys, and across
to the *Causse Noir*, and traverses the dry plateau strewn with rocky
hillocks, passing (l.) a military training ground, the presence of which
has been the subject of controversy in recent years, to (19km) *La
Cavalerie*. This village, together with *Ste-Eulalie-de-Cernon*, 4km
S.W., with relics of fortifications, were commanderies of the
Templars of La Couvertoirade.—5km. *L'Hospitalet-du-Larzac*, 3km
beyond which the D7 leads E. to (42.5km) *Le Vigan*; see above.

8km. **La Couvertoirade* lies 4km to the l., an almost complete example of a 12-14C fortified village, once a Templar stronghold, and
later of the Hospitallers. Although long depopulated, it is again inhabited.—The main road may be regained by driving S.

Beyond (6km) *Le Caylar*, with an old clock-tower, the road
descends, after 5km penetrating the rocky **Pas de l'Escalette*—the
name recalling the ladders by which the descent had once to be
made—bringing us abruptly from the causse out onto the flank of the
Lergue valley. The 17C château of *Pégairolles* (r.) is passed as the
road continues downhill to (14km) Lodève.

Lodève (8,600 Lodévois), an old cloth-working town at the con-
fluences of the Lergue with the Soulondres, takes its name from
Luteva, once one of the chief towns of Septimania. It was the birthplace of Card. Fleury (1653–1743), tutor and minister of Louis
XV, and of the composer Georges Auric (1899–   ).

The former cathedral of **St-Fulcran* was dedicated to a bishop of
Lodève (d. 1006); the present building, partly fortified, dates from
the 13-14C, and has a fine square tower. In a chapel on the S. side is
the tomb of Bp Plantavit (d. 1651), near which is the only surviving
cloister-walk (15-17C). The organ and its loft date from 1753.—The
adjacent 18C bishop's palace is now partly the *Hôtel de Ville*. Several
old houses are preserved, while a picturesque hump-backed *Bridge*
crosses the Soulondres to the S. At the E. end of the town stands the
medieval *Tour de Montalangue*.

The interesting remains of the priory of *St-Michel-de-Grandmont*, founded in the
12C, lie 6km E.

LODÈVE TO BÉDARIEUX (29km). The D35 leads W. over a ridge of hills, at
Lunas passing 4km S. of a ruined 12-13C abbey at *Joncels*. On meeting the river
Orb, we follow its valley to the S. through a small coalfield, at *La Tour-sur-Orb*
passing (r.) the ancient village of *Boussagues*; for *Bédarieux*, see Rte 88B.

The N9 now veers S.E. through (7km) *Cartels*, to the N. of which is an
area under exploitation for its uranium deposits; to the S. is the reservoir of *Salagou*.—After 8km a road junction is reached; the l.-hand
fork (N109) leads E. through (9km) *Gignac*, with a fine 18C *Bridge*, to
Montpellier, 30km beyond; see Rte 144.—On the W. outskirts of the
latter is the 12-14C church of *Celleneuve*.

The r.-head turning leads S. to skirt (5km) **Clermont-l'Hérault**, with
an imposing fortified church (*St-Paul*; 1276–1368), and over-looked
by its ruined castle, beyond which the N9 continues S. to (21km)
Pézenas, and **Béziers**, 23km further S.W.; see Rte 145.

B.   Via Mende, Florac, and Alès
(for Nîmes or Avignon)

265km (164 miles). N9. 35km *St-Chély-d'Apcher*—N106. 48km
Mende—7.5km *Balsièges*—32km **Florac**—69km **Alès**. **Avignon**
and **Nîmes** lie 71km and 45km further S.E., respectively.—N110
42.5km *Sommières*—27km **Montpellier**.

Maps: IGN 49, 50, 58, 59, 66, or 111, 114; also 265, and 354.
M 239, 240.

For the road to *St-Chély*, see Rte 101A, 2km beyond which we bear
across the bleak granite upland of *Gévaudan* (see p 548), through
(13.5km) *Serverette*, with a ruined medieval fort, and (8km) *S.
Amans*, to the E. of which rises *Mont Randon* (1551m), the highest
of the *Monts de la Margeride*. The road commences the descent into
the valley of the Lot, reaching the river at (22km) **Mende**; see Rte
102.

MENDE TO VILLEFORT (60km). The N88 is followed to the E. for 9.5km, then
turning r. onto the D901, continuing to skirt the bank of the upper Lot t
(11.5km) *Bagnols-les-Bains*, a small spa amid pinewoods (also approached from
Lanuejols; see below). The road ascends below the N. flank of *Mont Lozère* t
(9km) *Le Bleymard*.—Hence a mountain road, much improved since Stevenson
passed that way in 1878, climbs S. past zinc mines to the *Col de Finiels*, providing
extensive mountain views. To the W. rises the *Pic des Finiels* (1699m), the
highest of the granite range from which the headwaters of the Tarn, Lot, and
Gard descend. Its E. summit, the *Roc Malpertus*, rises to 1680m.—Continuing E
the road shortly crosses the *Col des Tribes* (1131m) on the main ridge of the
Cévennes, and descends the steep valley fo the Altier to (30km) *Villefort*, after
skirting its reservoir; see p. 539.—Hence one may climb E., traversing a ridge
and descending S. of the gorge of the Chassezac through chestnut woods t
(24km) *Les Vans*; see Rte 142B. Alternatively, the D906 may be followed to the
S. past (18km) *Génolhac* into the valley of the Luèch; see below.

Leaving Mende, the N88 descends the Lot valley to (7.5km)
Balsièges, overlooked to the S. by the cliffs of the *Causse d'
Sauveterre*.

For the road hence to *Ste-Enimie* and the *Gorges du Tarn*, see Rte 102.

We follow the N106 S.E., off which at 4.5km a minor road ascends
up the Nize valley to (7km) *Lanuéjols*, with a Romanesque church
and a Roman mausoleum of the 3C (?).
    The road climbs to (11.5km) the *Col de Montmirat* (1046m; views
between the *Causse de Sauveterre* (r.) and the ridge of *Mont Lozère*
further E., rising to 1699m; see above. We descend in zigzags past (r
Ispagnac, in a fruitful valley, where Merle lowered his canon in an
attempt to control the district, and adjacent *Quézac*, with a 14C
church and a *Bridge* of 1365, to reach the Tarn a short distance
before (17km) **Florac**, on the Tarnon. Now little more than a large
village, it was a Protestant centre during the Camisard wars, and is a
well-placed base from which to explore the *Parc National des Cévennes* and the *Tarn Gorges*. Its castle preserves two round towers o

1703, and the *Convent of the Presentation* (1583), a fine doorway.

FLORAC TO ALÈS VIA LE PONT-DE-MONTVERT (84km). The D998 climbs E.
from the *Pont de Tarn* (just N.) up the upper valley of that river to (21km) *Le Pont-de-Montvert*, N. of which rises *Mont Lozère* and the Col de Finiels; see above.
The village was a seat of discontented protestantism in the Cévennes which
broke out into the Camisard insurrection in 1702 with the murder of the Abbé
du Chayla, a local priest.—At *Grizac*, a hamlet to the S.W., was born Urban V
(1309–70). The road later descends the valley of the Luëch, leaving *Génolhac*
(see above) to the l. before climbing S.W. past (r.) the ruins of the *Château de
Portes* and veering S. to *Alès*.
   For other alternatives to the main road, see below.

The N106 leads S.E. up the Mimente valley, dominated to the N.E. by
the *Montagne du Bougès* (1421m), crossing the main ridge of the
Cévennes at (23km) the *Col de Jalcreste*, and descending through the
Protestant village of *Le Collet-de-Dèze* to (33km) *La Grand'Combe*,
the centre of an unattractive colliery district, 13km beyond which
Alès is entered.
   Alès (44,300 Alésiens), a dreary but prosperous industrial town on
a bend of the Gardon, with important chemical works (a by-product
of the adjacent coal basin), is also a centre for the silk trade. Here
Pasteur studied the diseases of silkworms in 1866–68; it was the birth-place of the chemist J.-B. Dumas (1800–84). The *Cathedral*, the W.
front of which dates from the 12C, preceded by a porch bearing a
heavy Gothic tower, was rebuilt in the 18C. To the N. is the *Hôtel de
Ville* (1732), to the W. of which, in gardens of *Le Bosquet*, stands *Fort
Vauban*, replacing a medieval castle. There is a small *Museum* in the
Parc du Colombier, some distance to the N.E.

The D981 leads 33km S.E. (forking l. off the Nîmes road; see below) to *Uzès* and
the *Pont du Gard*, 17km beyond, for which see Rte 143. **Avignon** lies 22km fur-ther E.

ALÈS TO NÎMES (45km). The N106 descends the l. bank of the Gardon d'Alès,
which flows through the rich plain of the Gardonnenque, beyond *Vézonobres* (l.)
meeting the Gardon d'Anduze to form the Gard, which is crossed at 15km before
Boucoiran, with relics of 12C fortifications, is traversed.—*Moussac* (l.), 8km
beyond, preserves a medieval keep, 2km N.E. of which is the 15-17C château of
Castelnau, where the Camisard leader Rolland was in 1704 surprised and killed
(cf. Anduze).—Descending through the 'mazets' of the stony Garrigues, we fork
r. on approaching Nîmes, passing near the *Tour Magne*; for **Nîmes** itself, see Rte
143.

The N110 drives S. from Alès, at 5km passing a r.-hand turning for
Anduze, 13km S.W.; see below.
   After 3km *Ribaute* lies to the S.W., near which, at *La Mas Roux*
was born Jean Cavalier (1680–1740; died at Chelsea), the Camisard
leader.
   35km. **Sommières**, a picturesque small town on the Vidourle,
preserving an arch of a Roman bridge, parts of its fortifications, and a
ruined castle.—At *Villevieille*, to the N.E., is a large 16-17C *Château*
on 12C foundations. Lawrence Durrell has lived in the congenial
vicinity of Sommières since 1957.
   Hence the road veers S.W. over the Garrigues to (15km) *Castries*,
over-looked by an imposing *Château* (1560–1650) standing in a
park containing an aqueduct constructed by Riquet; the 11C church
preserves some historiated capitals.—*Assas*, 8km N.W., also has a
small Romanesque church, and a well-sited château of 1758.—3km

beyond Castries we meet the N113, and turn r. for (9km) **Montpellier**; see Rte 144.

FLORAC TO ST-JEAN-DU-GARD AND ANDUZE (67.5km). The D9, which follows the *Corniche des Cévennes*, bears S. up the Tarnon valley, with the *Causse Méjean* on the r., after 5.5km forking l. and climbing past a ruined Templar keep to the ridge—with a view S. towards *Mont Aigoual* (1565m), among other wide views on either side—which is followed to (30km) *St-Roman-de-Tousque*.—Hence the D20 descends S. through broken country to (43.5km) *Ganges*, via *L'Estréchure* and the *Col de l'Asclie*; see below.—18km beyond St-Roman we climb down to **St-Jean-du-Gard**, a typical Cévenol village, with an old bridge over one of the numerous Gardons which unite to form the Gard. It was the last stage of Stevenson's walk across the Cévennes and the scene of his final parting with Modestine; and it was near here in June 1944 that a German regiment capitulated to Marceau Lapierre, a local schoolmaster and Resistance leader, and his maquisards.—14km. *Anduze*, a decayed old town of narrow streets, standing at the mouth of a deep gorge. The church, the *Tour de l'Horloge*, and a fort built by Vauban are picturesquely grouped round a square at the entrance to the town.—The *Parc* or *'Bambuseraie' de Prafrance*, off the road N. to (3.5km) *Générargues*, is noted for its exotic vegetation, including giant bamboos, while 4.5km N.W. of that hamlet is the *Mas Soubeyran*, with the *Musée du Désert*, commemorating in this farmhouse of Pierre Laport (or Rolland; 1675–1704), a leader of the Camisards Revolt, the Protestant reaction to the revocation of the Edict of Nantes in 1685, and their subsequent persecution, particularly in this area. Over 100 ministers were executed, and 5000 Huguenots were sent to the galleys, while the women were imprisoned in the Tour de Constance at Aigues-Mortes (cf.).—The *Grotte de Trabuc*, c. 2km N., is the largest in the Cévennes, inhabited since Neolithic times to the days of the Camisards.—*Alès* lies 18km N.E. of Anduze; and the N110 to Montpellier may be reached 14km S.E.; see above.

FLORAC TO ST-JEAN-DU-GARD VIA BARRE-DES-CÉVENNES (50.5km). At a point 11.5km along the previous sub-route, a l.-hand turning leads to (3.5km) *Barre-des-Cévennes*, with traces of 17C fortifications, c. 8km E. of which, on the *Plan de Fontmort*, is a monument commemorating Louis XVI's Edict of Tolerance (1787), which put an end to the tribulations of the Protestants. The road later descends S.E. along the *Vallée Française*, a Camisard base, past (l.) *St-Germain-de-Calberte* to rejoin the D9 at (35.5km) *St-Jean*: see above.

FLORAC TO MONTPELLIER VIA GANGES (133km). The D907 leads S. to (15km) *Les Vanels*, and continues to climb (r. on the D996) to (8.5km) the *Col de Perjuret* (1028m).—The tumbled masses of rocks named *Nîmes-le-Vieux* lie near the S.E. edge of the *Causse Méjean*, c. 4km N.; *Meyrueis* (see p 553) is 11.5km W.—We turn l. onto the D18 to approach (15.5km) **Mont Aigoual** (1565m). The granite summit is the southernmost of the great peaks of the Cévennes, and commands one of the widest views in France. On clear days—which unfortunately are not that frequent—it is possible to discern at the same time the Maladetta in the Pyrenees, and Mont Blanc, some 650km (or 400 miles) apart, and to the S.E. the curve of the Mediterranean coast beyond Montpellier. The meteorological *Observatory* was built in 1889 on the plans of Georges Fabre, who was also responsible for the afforestation of the surrounding slopes.—The descent of the upper Hérault valley may be made to *L'Espérou*, c. 10km S.W. (see below), passing the *Col de Prat-Peirot* and *Col de la Serreyrède* (1299m), and the source of the Hérault. This road has long been an important transhumance route, known as the 'Grande Draille'.—The D986 climbs down the flank of the *Montagne de l'Espérou* in zigzags to (21km) *Valleraugue*, a pleasantly sited village beyond which we follow the river to (16km) *Pont d'Hérault*, 11km N. of *Ganges*.—An alternative descent S. from *L'Espérou*, a good centre from which to explore the massif, is the D48, first crossing (6km) the *Col du Minier* (1264m view), separating the Tarn basin from that of the Hérault, and climbing down in long zigzags round a spur of *Montagne d'Aulas* (1417m) to (23km) *Le Vigan*, 7km W. of Pont d'Hérault.—**Ganges**, ancient *Aganticum*, a busy little textile town and minor hub of communications, is of slight interest in itself, and nothing remains of its once famous castle.—For roads hence to *Nîmes* and *Pézenas*, see below.—The D986 continues S., at 6km passing (l.) the fairy *Grotte 'des Demoiselles'*, an 'aven' discovered in 1770, and made more accessible in 1931, whose stalagmitic forms have suggested the much-publicised name.—We cross a ridge to (15km) *St-Martin-de-Londres*, a characteristic old village of arcaded streets, with a good Romanesque *Priory-church and its dependencies.—A road leads E. hence towards Sommières between the *Montagne d'Hortus* (l.) and the conspicuous *Pic St-Loup* (658m; view), near which stands the ruin of the castle of *Vivioures*, a drawing of which served as the frontispiece to Freda White's 'West of the Rhône'.—From St-Martin we veer S.E. to (25km) **Montpellier**; see Rte 144.

GANGES TO NÎMES (64km) The D999 leads E. to (13km) *St-Hippolyte-du-Fort*, a former stronghold of protestantism, with several 17-18C houses, which lies beneath its ruined castle, from which a road circles N.E. to (22km) *Anduze*; see above.—9km. *Sauve*, a curious old fortified place, with the ruined château of *Roquevaire*, once a summer residence of the bishops of Maguelone.—6km *Quissac*, another old town, with a long bridge over the Vidourle, 4km N. of which is the château where the fabulist J.-P. Claris de Florian (1755–94) was born.—After 12km we cross the N110 11km N. of *Sommières*, and traverse the Garrigues to **Nîmes**, 24km further E.; see Rte 143.

GANGES TO PÉZENAS VIA ST-GUILHEM-LE-DÉSERT (72.5km). The D4 leads S. via (7.5km) *Brissac*, with a partly 12C church and castle (rebuilt in 1524), from which a minor road ascends the valley of the Buèges.—We follow that of the Hérault, shortly passing (l.) *St-Étienne-d'Issensac*, with a medieval bridge and Romanesque church, before climbing away from the river through the wild Garrigues. The river is regained after a steep descent shortly before reaching (11km) **St-Guilhem-le-Désert**. It is preferable to leave one's car at the riverside end of the village (which can become crowded), and walk up the side-valley of the Verdus to the older village hidden in the gorge below a precipitous rock crowned by a ruined castle. it grew up round the Benedictine abbey of *Gellone*, founded by William 'Short Nose', Duke of Aquitaine, and ancestor of the Princes of Orange, who retired and died here in 812 and was later canonised. The *Abbey-church, facing a picturesque square, was consecrated in 1076, and preserves several features of interest, including the so-called altar of St-Guilhem, and the 10C crypt uncovered in 1962. The organ (1790) is under restoration; the 18C altar is out of place. Fragments remain of its cloister, which now embellishes the Cloisters Museum in New York. The apse is notable, with its belvedere; the belfry is 16C—One may regain the river by traversing a long lane flanked by medieval houses and the ruins of *St-Laurent*.—We shortly emerge from the narrow valley of the Hérault at the *Pont de Diable* (11C; since widened) crossing the river by a new bridge.—*Aniane*, shortly passed, owes its origin to a monastery which rose beside the hermitage of St Benedict of Aniane (750–821), a reformer of medieval monasticism; it was entirely rebuilt in the 17-18C.—5km. *Gignac*, for which and the road hence to **Montpellier**, 30km E., see the last section of Rte 101A.—**Pézenas** lies 27km S. on the D32; see Rte 145.

102 Mende to Albi via the Gorges du Tarn and Millau

195km (121 miles). N88. 7.5km—D986. 20.5km *Ste-Enimie*—D907B. 35km *Le Rozier*—D907 and N9. 21km **Millau**—D992 and D999. 31km *St-Affrique*—32km *St-Sernin-sur-Rance*—48km **Albi**.

Maps: IGN 58, 65, 64, or 111, 114; also 354. M 240, 235.

The **Causses** cover a roughly semicircular tract of land between the Lot valley on the N., the main ridge of the Cévennes on the E. and S., and the road from Marvejols to Millau on the W.; see Rte 101A. They were originally a vast plateau of Jurassic limestone inclining gradually towards the W. In the course of ages, the rivers descending from the Cévennes have eaten their way through the porous rock, cutting channels with perpendicular sides and dividing the plateau into several smaller areas, barren and deserted, known as Causses from the local form 'cau' of the French *chaux*, lime.

Most characteristic of these is the *Causse Méjean*, between the Tarn, the Tarnon, and the Jonte, a limestone table 600-1200m above sea-level. Almost waterless, it is sparsely populated by Caussenards and sheep. Such water that falls filters down to the river through pot-holes or 'avens', several containing stalactite formations of great beauty. To the N. of the Causse Méjean is the *Causse de Sauveterre*, prolonged westwards by the *Causse de Séverac*, while to the S. are the *Causse Noir* and the huge *Causse de Larsac*.

In striking contrast to their barrenness is the fertility of the valleys intersecting them, the most remarkable being the *Gorge of the Tarn*, which like that of the Verdon in Provence, is among the finest natural curiosities in France. Here the river has cut a passage between the Causse Méjean and the Causse Sauveterre some 60km long, 400–500m deep, and 1350–1800m wide, on whose vertiginous walls vegetation grows wherever it finds a foothold.

Among other curiosities which may be included with ease when exploring the area are the rocky chaos of *Montpellier-le-Vieux*, the *Aven Armand*, the *Grotte de Dargilan*, and the subterranean river of *Bramabiau*, etc.

MENDE (731m; 12,100 Mendois), préfecture of the *Lozère*, and once capital of the *Gévaudan*, stands on a terrace above the Lot and beneath the steep wall of the *Causse de Mende*, to the S.

It is said to have been built around the tomb of St Privatus, an early bishop martyred by the Vandals, whose hermitage, a partially rock-hewn chapel, lies S. of the town. Apart from having been occupied and sacked by Merle and his Huguenots in 1579–80, its history has been comparatively uneventful. Henri Bourrillon (1891–45), its mayor and a Resistance leader, died in captivity.

From the N. bank we cross the Lot and follow the Allée Piencourt to the *Pl. Charles de Gaulle*, immediately E. of the old centre, where a circle of boulevards replaces the old walls. The *Tour des Pénitants* is almost the only relic of these, which we pass (r.) off the Blvd du Soubeyran (S.W. of the Place). The next r.-hand turning approaches the **Cathedral**, begun by Urban V (Guillaume de Grimoard; c. 1309–70) in 1365.

Severely damaged by the Huguenots, it was partly reconstructed in 1599–1620, while its W. porch was rebuilt in 1900 in a 15C style. The W. front is pierced by a fine rose-window flanked by two towers; the N. tower, erected by Bp François de la Rovère, is a splendid example of the latest Gothic with Renaissance motives, crowned by a crocketed spire (84m), embellished with sculpture.

The late-Gothic nave is in the simplest style, without capitals, and has ten chapels on each side. The choir preserves stalls of 1692, while below the clerestory hang Aubusson tapestries of 1706. The crypt contains the tomb of St Privatus.

To the N. stands the *Préfecture*, behind which the Rue Notre-Dame leads through a quarter of characteristic old houses to the *Pl. Th.-Roussel*, whence the Blvd des Capucins descends to the *Pont N.-D.-de-Peyrenc*, a steep and narrow 14C bridge over the Lot.—There is a small *Museum*, devoted to archaeology and local bygones, a few minutes' walk W. of the cathedral.

The N88, leading W., descends the green valley of the Lot to (7.5km) *Balsièges* to follow the river past *Barjac*, beneath the *Causse de Changefège* (r.) and *Charnac*, dominated by its massive tower, below the steep red cliffs of the *Causse de Sauveterre* (l.) to meet the N9 after 25km; see Rte 101A and immediately below. For the N106 from Balsièges to (32km) *Florac*, and beyond, see Rte 101B.

From a junction 11km S. after meeting the N9, the D988 forks r. to (24km) *St-Geniez-d'Olt*, an old-fashioned town famous for its strawberries, beyond which the road bears away from the Lot onto the *Causse de Sévérac* to (25km) *Bozouls*; see Rte 100.—At 8.5km beyond St-Geniez, the D6 forks r. to regain the river at (13km) *St-Côme-d'Olt*, an old village with a 15C church surrounded by medieval and Renaissance houses, 4km W. of which is **Espalion**; see Rte 100.

Another cross-country road (N88) leads W. from *Sévérac-le-Château* (22km further S.W. on the N9) to (49km) *Rodez*, after 31km passing (r.) the imposing 14C castle of *Montrozier* and descending the valley of the Aveyron. For **Rodez**, see Rte 95.

The shortest road to the ***Gorges of the Tarn*** climbs up the steep N. edge of the *Causse de Sauveterre* from Balsièges, later traversing the wretched hamlet after which the plateau is named. The ravine of *Le Bac* is later descended, with a view ahead of the cliffs of the *Causse Méjean*, to (21km) **Ste-Enimie**, a village standing on an abrupt bend of the Tarn, the central arch of its 17C bridge being carried away by a flood in 1900, the high-water mark being indicated by a plaque in the church. At a higher level stands a Romanesque chapter-house of a convent founded in the 6C by Enimie, a Merovingian princess, possibly a daughter of Lothaire II, who was cured of leprosy in the *Fontaine de Burle*; her hermitage lies some 20 minutes to the W.

The longer ALTERNATIVE ROUTE to Ste-Enimie is that turning r. off the Florac road after 26.5km for *Ispagnac*, with a rebuilt Romanesque church, to (5.5km) *Molines*, at the start of the Tarn gorge proper. On the far bank lies *Quézac*, approached by a 14C bridge, and with a 14C church; Urban V was responsible for the building of both.—Passing below the château of *Rocheblave* (r. ;16C), overlooked by 12C ruins, the next bridge reached spans the Tarn to (l.) *Montbrun*, and r., the strange hamlet of *Castelbuc*, huddled below the frowning cliffs of the *Causse Méjean*. A short distance W. of the bridge is the 16C château of *Charbonnières*.—Traversing *Prades*, we reach, 16km from Molines, *Ste-Enimie*; see above.

STE-ENIMIE TO MEYRUEIS (29km). Crossing the Tarn, the D986 ascends the l. bank to the *Cirque de St-Chély*, with the village far below it, and the *Col de Coperlac*, crossing the cheerless *Causse Méjean*.—At 19.5km a r.-hand turning leads in 1.5km to the ***Aven Armand***, the finest of the underground caverns of the Cévennes, discovered in 1897 by Louis Armand, an assistant of E.A. Martel, and opened to the public in 1927. An artificial sloping tunnel approaches the great chamber at the foot of the original shaft, in which rises the extraordinary 'Forêt Vierge', a forest of stalagmites of every shape and size, skilfully illuminated. The largest stalagmite is 30m high.—Regaining the main road, we continue S.E., shortly commencing the descent into the *Gorges de la Jonte*, to reach (9.5km) Meyrueis; see Rte 101B.

Ste-Enimie stands at the head of the navigable reach of the gorge, although the classic descent of the river by a flat-bottomed boat to the Cirque des Baumes usually starts at *La Malène*, where full information may be obtained of facilities available.

The road skirting the Tarn keeps to the r. bank, threading several short tunnels, although there are a number of bridges across the ravine, as at *St-Chély* below its Cirque, with a little Romanesque church. A sharp bend brings one to the *Cirque de Pougnadoires*, and the 15C *Château de la Caze* (now a luxury hotel); beyond, on the far bank, is the ruined 12C castle of *Haute Rive*.

13.5km. **La Malène**, an historic crossing-point of the gorge, although the roads ascending to the Causses are precipitous. By climbing S. one may gain that to Meyrueis described above, and to the N. one may approach the Point Sublime; see below. A monument in the Romanesque church commemorates 39 villagers who were shot by the Terrorists in 1793.—The finest stretch of the gorge is now entered, where the Tarn flows through the *Détroit* between towering vertical cliffs, beyond which the imposing *Cirque des Baumes* is reached. The river now veers S. through the *Pas de Souci*, a chaos of limestone blocks which have fallen from the circumjacent heights, and we enter the hamlet of (11.5km) *Les Vignes*.

Hence a steep zigzag road climbs up the side of the gorge to the *Causse Sauveterre*, where by following the road to the r., the *Point Sublime* is approached, at a height of 861m, and c. 420m (1380ft) above the river.—From *Le Massegros*, to the W., one may continue W. to (9km) *Sévérac-le-Château*, or turn S. to (17km) *Boyne*, 16km from Millau.

From Les Vignes, the final stretch of the cañon is followed, on each side of which rise curious dolomitic rocks, later passing (l.) the huge detached *Pic de Cinglegros* and (r.) the *Cirque de St-Marcellin*, and skirting a reach of rapids, the road enters (10km) *Le Rozier*.—The main road hence continues to follow the r. bank of the Tarn via *Boyne* to meet the N9 after 14km, and 7km N. of **Millau**; see Rte 101A.

For the road up the Jonte to *Meyrueis*, see p 553; an alternative road from LE ROZIER TO MILLAU is the D29, climbing in zigzags to the quaint village of *Peyreleau* on the *Causse Noir*, and descending to *La Roque-Ste-Marguerite* in the Dourbie valley.—At 7km a l.-hand fork leads to several scattered hamlets on the larger E. section of the Causse, and just beyond, a r.-hand turning leads to (4km) the entrance to the limestone wilderness known as *Montpellier-le-Vieux*; see p 554. Hence the D110 continues W., later descending steeply to *Millau*.

A minor road from Millau continues to follow the meandering Tarn to (24km W.) *St-Rome-de-Tarn*, 15km N. of St-Affrique, while the main road (D992) follows the l. bank before veering S. up the valley of the Cernon through *St-Georges-de-Luzençon*, retaining remains of walls built by the Templars, and several old houses.

21km **Roquefort-sur-Soulzon** lies on a height 3km E., a village famous for its ewes'-milk cheese, which ripens in caverns in the limestone cliff against which the place clings.

The skins of the lambs—taken almost at birth from their dams, whose milk is reserved for this cheese-production—go to the glove-makers of Millau; the sheeps' wool to the cloth-mills of Lodève. An explanation of the various interesting processes of Roquefort production (and a view of the 'caves') is provided by the 'Société', who organise a conducted *Tour of their establishment.

10km. **St-Affrique** (9,200 inhab.), with a 15C bridge, a town of slight interest in itself, was the birthplace of Gén. Castelnau (1851–1944).

A road leads S. to (14km) *St-Félix-de-Sorgues*, between the old fortified village of *St-Jean-et-St-Paul*, c. 6km N., and the 12C church and ruins of the Cistercian abbey of *Sylvanès*, c. 6km S.—From the latter a minor road continues S. up the valley of the Dourdon to (27km) *La Croix-sur-Mouris*; see Rte 88B.—At crossroads beyond *Fayet* (5km S. of Sylvanès) one may turn r. via (7.5km) *Camarès*, with a beautiful Gothic bridge, to regain the main road at *St-Pierre*, 12.5km further N.W.

4km. *Vabres-l'Abbaye*, a decayed cathedral town (from 1317–1790), is traversed, and then (12km) *St-Pierre*, 2 km beyond which the l.-hand turning leads via (9km) *Belmont-sur-Rance*, with an early 16C church, 19.5km beyond; see Rte 88B.

14km. *St-Sernin-sur-Rance*, a village preserving several 15-16C houses and a 15C church, beyond which we climb over a ridge to (22km) *Alban*.

A minor road (D53) leads 11.5km N. to the Tarn, which one may follow W. to

(14km) *Ambialet*, a strange village occupying the isthmus of a meander, the neck of which is only 25m wide; in the centre stands 11C *N.-D.-de-l'Oder*. The main road may be regained further W., the valley being later disfigured by a foundry.

12km. *Villefranche-d'Albigeois*, a bastide of 1239, is traversed as we approach **Albi**, 17km W., dominated by its brick cathedral; see Rte 89.

IX   FLANDERS; CHAMPAGNE; ALSACE-LORRAINE; FRANCHE-COMTÉ

For **Flanders**, see introduction to Section I. The old province of **Champagne** (campania, 'the plain-country'), with *Troyes* as its capital, extended N. from Burgundy to the Ardennes and the Belgian border, and from the Île de France to Lorraine. It became an independent countship at the break-up of the *Vermandois* (c. 943). Jeanne, daughter of Henri III, the last count (who was also king of Navarre), in 1284 married Philippe le Bel, it was formally united to France in 1361. The area to the N. and E. of Reims was overrun by the Germans during the First World War, and between here and Verdun, on the Meuse further E. in contiguous Lorraine, took place most of the fighting on the French, and later American, fronts.

Lorraine (*Lotharingia*; in German, *Lothringen*), was originally the Austrasian domain allotted to Lothair by the treaty of Verdun in 843. From 1048 until 1736 it was ruled by hereditary dukes. Charles le Téméraire of Burgundy was killed in 1477 when attempting to seize their capital, *Nancy*. Sons of René II (d. 1504), named after his grandfather René of Anjou, became the first Duc de Guise, and Jean, Card. of Lorraine, respectively. Owing to them French and Catholic influence was for some time paramount. The duchy was occupied by France at the end of the Thirty Years' War, when the treaty of Westphalia (1648) confirmed their possession of the 'Three Bishoprics' of *Toul, Verdun*, and *Metz*. The duchy was revived under Duc Leopold Joseph in 1697, and was re-occupied by French troops during the War of the Polish Succession (1733–35). Stanislas Leczinski (d. 1766), the ex-king of Poland, and father-in-law to Louis XV, was given a life interest in the duchy, while the reigning duke was consoled with Tuscany. In 1871, after the Franco-Prussian War, the N. part of the province, including Metz and Thionville, was annexed by the Germans, and it was not returned to France until after the end of the First World War, then forming the department of the *Moselle*.

To the E., Lorraine is abutted by **Alsace** (*Alsatia*; in German, *Elsass*), named from the river Ill, which flows through its fertile plain, which since 1919 has been divided into the departments of *Bas-Rhin* and *Haute-Rhin*, with *Strasbourg* and *Colmar* their respective préfectures. It has long been disputed territory, the Gauls claiming the Rhine as their natural frontier, and the Teutons the heights of the *Vosges*. Although originally Frankish, it was largely Germanised after the 10C, and when the French regained it between 1648–97, Louis XIV ruled in conjunction with the Catholics who were then in the political ascendency. its bonds with France were strengthened during the Revolutionary period. In 1827–30, Benjamin Constant was Deputé for Alsace. Although a high proportion of its inhabitants were German speaking, the Prussian annexation of 1871 was in general greatly resented, although, as always, there was a proportion of collaborators or sympathisers, most of whom made themselves scarce when it was returned to France by the treaty of Versailles. The whole area suffered considerably during the winter of 1944–45. Strasbourg itself has grown in importance in recent decades, as being the site of the Conseil de l'Europe (Since 1949) and the European Parliament. The *Territoire de Belfort*, to the S. of Alsace, remained a French possession at 1871.

To the S.W. of Alsace, and S. of Lorraine, lies the **Franche-Comté**, originally a fief of Burgundy, with *Dôle* as its capital, acquiring the title of the 'free countship' during an attempt to throw off the yoke of Lothaire. Frederick Barbarossa bestowed it on his third son, Otto, in 1185, and made *Besançon* a free imperial city. The countship passed for a time to the Emperor Charles V, but in 1668 it was overrun by Condé in a fortnight, and in 1674 became a French province.

The '**Spanish Road**', the military corridor from Lombardy to Luxembourg and the Low Countries, used by the Spanish Army of Flanders during the late 16th and the first half of the 17C, passed through Savoy and the Franche-Comté, and was regularly used for both the movement and supply of troops. The *Col de Mont Cenis* formed the most practical pass over the Alps. Henc the route St-Jean-de-Maurienne—Chambéry—Belley—St-Rambert—and Poncin was followed to the border of the Franche-Comté, crossed N.W. of Nantua. Another route, from the *Col du Petit St-Bernard* ran through Aime to Annecy, crossing the frontier S. of St-Claude.

The road hence was in fact a series of 3-4 main routes, in the S. part often interweaving, which converged on Champagnole and Lons-le-Saunier respectively.

The easternmost then followed a line Pontarlier — Baume-les-Dames — Lure — Remiremont — Baccarat — Falquemont — Sierck, crossing Lorraine, but by-passing the bishopric of Metz. The westernmost road followed the line Dôle — Gray — Pont-sur-Saône — Monthureux — Mirecourt — Toul — Étain — Longuyon. The central roads from Champagnole, or N. of Lons, traversed Ornans, Besançon, and Vesoul; and across country further W. via Rans and Gy to converge at St-Loup (12km N.W. of Luxeuil). A branch veered W. to Mirecourt; another to Remiremont, and thence via Épinal and Charmes, there turning N.E. towards Lunéville, before by-passing Nancy, to Pont-à-Mousson. It would then turn W. up the valley of the Rupt de Mad before climbing N. to Conflans, there dividing for either Thionville or Longwy.

The subject is studied in detail in Geoffrey Parker's 'The Army of Flanders and the Spanish Road, 1567–1659'.

103　St-Quentin to Troyes

A.　Via Soissons and Sézanne

209km (130 miles). D1. 60km **Soissons**—41km **Château-Thierry** —24km *Montmirail*—RD373 24km *Sézanne*—35km N19. 25km **Troyes**.

Maps: IGN 4, 9, 22, or 103; also 408. M 236, 237.

For **St-Quentin**, see Rte 3. The D1 leads S., at 26km passing between the industrial towns of *Tergnier* (l.), and *Chauny*, the former entered on the second day of the great German offensive of March 1918, the marshes of the Oise to the E. and S.E. having been made passable to the enemy by weeks of dry weather. Crossing the Oise, the road skirts the *Forêt de Coucy-Basse* and passes below (17km) **Coucy**, with its ruined castle; see Rte 5.—17km **Soissons**; see Rte 17, and *Blue Guide Paris and Environs*, which describes in detail the road S. to **Château-Thierry** (see also Rte 18), and S.E. through *Montmirail* and *Sézanne*; see also Rte 19.

From Sézanne, the RD373 continue S.E. to (18km) *Anglure*, beyond which the Seine is reached at (13km) *Méry-sur-Seine*. Crossing the river we turn l. on meeting the N19 4km beyond.

At 19km *Barberey-St-Sulpice* (l.) is passed, with a 16C château and 12th and 16C church, 6km beyond which **Troyes** is entered; see Rte 122.

B.　Via Laon, Reims, and Épernay

222km (138 miles). N44. 46km **Reims**—N51. 27km **Épernay**—RD51. 44km *Sézanne*—RD373. 35km—N19. 25km **Troyes**.

Maps: IGN 4, 9, 22, or 103. M 236, 237.

For the road from St-Quentin to **Reims**, see the latter part of Rte 3; for **Laon**, and **Reims**, Rtes 105, and 106, respectively.

The N51 leads S. from Reims towards the *Montagne de Reims*, with

Vendage in the valley of the Marne.

its woods and vineyards, which provided a natural bastion during the
defence of the city during the First World War. Ludendorff's attacks
of 15-17 July 1918 briefly gained a footing on its lower slopes, but
British troops restored the line on the 23-28th. The ascent commands
good retrospective views. Traversing its plateau, we reach *Bellevue*
and descend in sweeping curves towards (27km) *Épernay*, with impressive views over the neat champagne vineyards.

To the E., on the descent, lies **Hautevilliers**, its church, with a Romanesque
facade, being a survival of the 7C Benedictine abbey in which Dom Pérignon
(1683–1715) is said to have discovered the subtle art of making champagne in
its sparkling form. The interior preserves paintings of the Life of St Helen, etc.,
well-carved boiseries, and the tomb of Dom Pérignon.

Épernay (28,900 Sparnaciens), Merovingian *Sparnacum*, which had a
turbulent history in the Middle Ages, has since the early 18C
established itself as the centre of the champagne trade, where in
1789 Arthur Young 'solaced' himself with a bottle of excellent *vin
mousseux* for 40 sous and drank prosperity to *true* liberty in France.
Its most famous native was Jean-Remy Moët (1758–1841).

The wines grown here are distinguished as 'Vins de la Rivière' from the 'Vins de
la Montagne' produced near Reims. For a detailed history of the area and the
manufacture of champagne, one cannot do better than acquire 'Champagne: the
Wine, the Land, and the People', by Patrick Forbes.

There is little to see in the town except the champagne cellars, mostly situated in the Av. de Champagne, leading E. off the central *Pl. de
la République*. A *Museum*, on the N. side of this avenue opposite
Caves Mercier contains sections on champagne, on Épernay ware,
and local archaeology, etc.
    Dominating the avenue is the establishment of *Moët & Chandon*
(founded 1743, and now the largest house), whose cellars may be
visited, preferably by appointment in advance, when the complicated processes of production are outlined. The chalky rock on
which the town stands is riddled by labyrinths of galleries, the Caves
of Moët & Chandon—with their ramifications—alone extending
some 28km in total length, and at any one time containing

45-50,000,000 bottles. Among other firms devoted to the making of
champagne in Épernay are *Perrier-Jouët, Pol Roger*, and *Bollinger* (at
adjacent *Ay*); but see also **Reims**, Rte 106.

The RD51 bears S.W., leaving the *Côtes des Blancs* to the E., and
traverses the *Forêt de la Chamoye* to (18km) *Montmort-Lucy*, with an
11-15C church and a brick *Château* flanked by four towers, built by
Jeanne de Hangest in 1580.—At 6km the road from Montmirail to
Chalons is crossed (see Rte 107), and 2km beyond, *Baye*, with a
12-13C church and earlier crypt; the restored château was rebuilt in
the 17C, but preserves medieval towers and a 13C chapel. Marion
Delorme was born here c. 1611.—2km E., at *Andecy*, are remains of
a Cistercian abbey founded in 1136, but rebuilt in the 18C.

The road shortly passes (l.) the W. limit of the *Marshes of St-Gond*
(see p 585); c. 2km. to the W. are relics of the abbey of *Reclus*
(1140).—We continue S., leaving some 3km to the E. a monument to
the battle of the Marne, before entering (18km) *Sézanne*; see Rte 19,
and *Blue Guide Paris and Environs*.—For the road hence to **Troyes**,
see Rte 103A.

From crossroads S.E. of the town one may continue S.W., skirting the *Forêt de la
Traconne* (r.) to (22km) *Villenauxe-la-Grande*, the restored 14-15C church of
which preserves a good 13C choir.—*Nogent-sur-Seine* lies 14km beyond (see Rte
122), and **Provins** 20km due W.; see *Blue Guide Paris and Environs*, and Rte 20.

104 Cambrai to Verdun via Charleville-Mézières

216km (134 miles). N43. 54km *La Capelle*—69km **Charleville-Mézières**—A203. 22km **Sedan**—D964. 80km **Verdun**.

Maps: IGN 4, 5, 10, or 101; also 416. M 236, 241.

CAMBRAI (36,600 Cambrésiens), formerly a fortress on the r. bank
of the canalised Scheldt, is an industrial town of slight interest since
its devastation in 1918, when the Germans left it heavily mined, so
that the British entry was followed by explosions and fires which
wrecked it centre; and it suffered again in 1944.

Roman *Camaracum*, and later capital of the Cambrésis, was dominated by its
bishops, from whom its citizens succeeded in extorting a charter in 1227. Baptiste Cambray, a 13C weaver, was the alleged inventor of a fine linen known in
English as 'cambric' and called 'batiste' by the French. Cambrai was hotly contested in the wars of François I, Henri II, and Louis XIV, who added it to France in
1677. The short-lived League of Cambrai (1508) united Pope Julius II, the
Emperor Maximilian I, Louis XII, and Fernando of Aragón against the Venetians;
and in 1529 the Peace of Cambrai was signed here by Louise of Savoy (mother of
François I) and Margaret of Austria (aunt of Charles V), on behalf of these
monarchs. In 1559 it became the seat of an archbishopric, of which the most
distinguished encumbent was Fénelon (1651–1715) from 1695, succeeded a few
years later by the unscrupulous Card. Dubois (1656–1723).

It surrendered to Wellington in 1815, to the Prussians in 1870, and was occupied by Von Kluck in Aug. 1914, in 1916 being Prince Rupprecht of Bavaria's
H.Q. It was briefly threatened by Gen. Byng's thrust of Nov. 1917, but was not
recaptured until 9 Oct. 1918. It was again occupied by the Germans from May
1940 until 3 Sept. 1944.

Among its natives were Gén. Dumouriez (1739–1823); Louis Blériot
(1872–1936), the aviator; the brother sculptors Gaspard and Barthélemy Marsy
(1624–81 and 1628–74 respectively); and was once the residence of the

chronicler Monstrelet (d. 1453). The composer Guillaume Dufay died here in 1474.

In the centre of the old town is the *Pl. Fénelon*, adjacent to *St-Géry*, the restored 18C successor of a church founded in 520 by St Vaast. It contains a Renaissance rood loft and panelling of 1740, and an Entombment by Rubens.

Some distance N., near the exterior boulevard, are bastions of the 13C *Château de Selles*.—E. of the church is the undistinguished *Pl. Aristide-Briand* (Previously the Pl. d'Armes) and the *Hôtel de Ville* (1873; rebuilt), its belfry containing jacquemart figures of 1510. A short distance N. is the *Porte Notre-Dame* (1623); to the S.E. are gardens adjacent to Vauban's *Citadel*.

The Av. de la Victoire leads S. from the Hôtel de Ville to the *Pl. St-Sépulcre*, on the corner of which is a house of 1595, and to the S.E., the *Cathedral*, an 18C edifice twice rebuilt, preserving Fénelon's Tomb, by David d'Angers. (Fénelon's cathedral, a 12-13C structure, was destroyed at the Revolution.)—Further S. is the *Porte de Paris* (1390).—On the W. side of the Place is the facade of the chapel of the *Grand Séminaire*, an Italianate building of 1695 now containing a collection of ecclesiastical art. Hence a street leads W. to the *Musée Municipal*, just beyond which one may turn r. to regain the Pl. Fénelon.

For the road S. to (39km) **St-Quentin**, see Rte 3.

The N43 leads S.E. at 14.5km passing (r.) the textile town of *Caudry*.

Just beyond, to the S., took place the battle of 26 Aug. 1914, in which Smith-Dorrien's three divisions, retiring from Mons to the Marne in the face of Von Kluck's seven divisions supported by an overwhelming weight of artillery, fought a brief rearguard action before continuing their retreat. They lost c. 8000 men and 36 guns in this action, which however stayed the pursuit, and the Germans changed their plan of driving directly towards Paris.

9.5km. **Le Cateau** (-*Cambrésis*) owes its name and origin to a former castle of the bishops of Cambrai. Treaties of peace, disadvantageous to France and only partly fulfilled, were signed here in 1559 with England and Spain. Its fortifications were dismantled in 1642. It was Wellington's H.Q. when he entered France in 1815. Both Marshal Mortier (1768–1835) and Henri Matisse (1869–1954) were born here.

The Renaissance *Hôtel de Ville*, with a belfry of 1705, contains a small museum partially devoted to Matisse. The *Church* is 17C, while in a park stands the former *Bishop's Palace* (17-18C).

8km. *Catillon*, on the Sambre à Oise Canal, the passage of which was forced by Rowlinson's Fourth Army a week before the Armistice, is traversed, and 2.5km beyond, the *Chapeau-Rouge* crossroads; see Rte 1.—9km. *Le Nouvion-en-Thiérache* and its forest are traversed.—10km. *La Capelle*; see Rte 105.

LA CAPELLE TO REIMS (88km). The N2 leads S. to (17km) *Vervins*, and then the D966 is followed S.E. to (20km) *Moncornet*; for both see Rte 105. The road continues S. over uninteresting country to cross the Aisne after 30km.—*Asfeld*, 9km N.E., with a curious brick church of 1683, was raised to a marquisate in 1730 for Marshal d'Asfeld, a commander in the War of the Spanish Succession.—The Roman road drives due S., at 10km passing (l.) *Bourgogne*, an ancient moated village with a rebuilt 12-14C church, and (r.) the fortified hill of *Brimont*, a fort since Roman times, and which for four years from Sept. 1914 commanded Reims with its guns.—10km. **Reims**; see Rte 106.

Continuing E. from La Capelle, at 6km *Fourmies*, an industrial town, lies some 7.5km to the N.; *Wimy*, 3.5km S., preserves a fortified 15C church.—7km. **Hirson** (11,800 Hirsonnais), a manufacturing town on the Oise and an important railway junction, is of little interest, but at *St-Michel*, 4km E., is an imposing 12-16C *Church and the extensive 18C dependencies of a former abbey, founded in 944 for Irish Benedictines, and restored since a fire in 1971; the organ of 1714 is notable.

The Belgian frontier (Customs) lies 10km N.E. of Hirson, 15km beyond which lies *Chimay*, for which see *Blue Guide Belgium*.

The N43 continues S.E. and then E., after 15.5km passing 6km S. of *Signy-le-Petit*, with a fortified church of 1645 and an early 17C château—9.5km *Rocroi* lies 12km N.E., on the watershed separating the basins of the Oise and the Meuse.

Here, 2km S.W. of the small town, took place the young Condé's great victory over the Spaniards (19 May, 1643). **Rocroi** itself was fortified with pentagonal ramparts by Vauban, which are largely preserved. It sustained a month's siege in 1815, and in 1871 fell to the Prussians after a bombardment.—The Belgian frontier lies 6km N., and *Revin* (see Rte 105) 12km E.—The main road may be regained 9.5km S. after passing near (l.) *Bourg-Fidèle*, founded for Huguenots in 1566 by Antoine de Croy, but depopulated after the revocation of the Edict of Nantes.

We meet this road from Rocroi after 10km, and shortly traverse a region of slate-quarries.—7km. To the l. lies *Renwez*, with an interesting 15C church, just E. of which are the massive ruins of the 15-16C castle of *Montcornet*.

12km. **Charleville-Mézières**; see Rte 106.

The N64 leads S.E., off which a new road turns E. directly to *Sedan*.—Continuing on the former road, at (9km) *Flize*, we pass 4km N. of *Élan*, with a 14th and 17C church and the ruins of a Cistercian abbey founded in 1148, the first abbot of which was St Roger.—8km. **Donchery** (l.) has a church damaged in 1940.

It was the Prussian H.Q. during the battle of Sedan in 1870; see below. Here Von Moltke and Gén. Wimpffen met on 1 Sept., but failed to come to terms. Napoleon III's interview with the King of Prussia took place next day at the nearby *Château de Bellevue*, where the capitulation was signed, after which the French army was detained on the peninsula of Iges, to the N.E. The Germans forced a crossing of the Meuse near here on 7 Nov. 1914, the l. bank of which was gained by the vanguard of the 1st American Army on 7 Nov. 1918.

5km **Sedan** (24,500 Sedanais), an ancient fortress, and modern manufacturing town, lies at the foot of wooded hills rising above the r. bank of the Meuse. On a slope to the E. of the river stands the huge *Château Fort* (15-17C), on the site of an 8-9C necropolis, now containing a small military museum.

It was long the capital of a principality belonging to the dukes of Bouillon, and in the 16-17C its cloth trade, largely in the hands of Huguenots, prospered. In 1642 it was forfeited to Louis XIII as the penalty for the conspiracy against Richelieu of the reigning duke, an elder brother of Marshal Turenne (1611– 75), who was born there. Pierre Bayle, author of the 'Dictionnaire historique et critique' (1695– 97), was professor of philosophy at the Protestant Academy here from 1671, until that institution was closed down a decade later, when he went to Holland. On 1 Sept. 1870 an entire French army of c. 87,000 men under Marshal MacMahon (accompanied by Napoleon III) was here surrounded by the Prussians, and being unable to break the encircling cordon, were compelled to surrender. It was seriously damaged by the Germans in 1940, and has since been rebuilt.

If there is any connection between this town and the early 17C origin of the 'Sedan'-chair, it is obscure. Marshal Macdonald (1765–1840), son of a Scottish Jacobite, was born here.

Some 16km N.E., in the wooded gorges of the *Forest of the Ardennes*, just beyond the frontier, lies the town and fortress of *Bouillon*; see *Blue Guide Belgium*.

3.5km *Bazeilles*, which stood on the extreme r. of the French position during the disastrous battle, preserves a late 18C château, and the heroically defended cabaret known as 'À la Dernière Cartouche', the subject of De Neuville's famous painting.

SEDAN TO METZ VIA LONGUYON (138km). From a road junction 4.5km E. of Bazeilles, the N43 continues ahead, between 8-15km from the Belgian frontier, to (12km) *Carignan*, a small industrial town, formerly known as *Yvois*, and with remains of its 16C fortifications, but renamed in 1661 when Louis XIV made it a duchy for a son of the Prince of Carignan; both the town and its 15-16C church have been restored since seriously damaged in 1940.—20km **Avioth**, 3km N.E., has a remarkable Gothic *Church*, begun before 1328 and completed about a century later, with two towers and two well-sculptured portals, and retaining some 14C glass and sculptures of interest; adjacent is an unusual hexagonal chapel, the *Recevresse*, with an openwork spire (15C).—4km. **Montmèdy** (Mons Medius), on an isolated spur between two valleys, fortified by Vauban, was formerly the seat of a countship captured by Turenne in 1656. It fell to the Prussians in 1870 after two days of bombardment, and to German howitzers in 1914. The railway here, the main lateral communication of the German front, came under American fire in Nov. 1918, and the last shots of the war were fired in the neighbourhood. For the road hence to *Verdun*, see below—12km. **Marville**, an ancient village of some character, with a 13-15C church, containing a notable organ-case; the *Chapelle St-Hilaire*, to the N.; and several 16-17C houses.—13km. **Longuyon** (7,000 inhab.), at the confluence of the Chiers and the Crusne, with a partly 13C church.—Near *Fermont*, 8km N.E. via the D174, one may visit a restored stretch of the *Maginot Line*.

At the road junction 4.5km E. of Bazeilles, we turn r. for (9km) *Mouzon*, ancient *Mosomagus*, on an island in the Meuse, damaged in 1940, but preserving a striking 13C church, formerly collegiate, with two towers. The road shortly crosses a ridge, with a view S.W. towards *Beaumont-en-Argonne*, scene of Gén. de Failly's defeat by the Saxons in 1870, and of further fighting in 1914, 1918, and 1940.—16.5km. **Stenay**, Gallo-Roman *Satanacum*, where Dagobert II was assassinated in 678, was an ancient frontier fortress, and H.Q. of the German Crown Prince during 18 months of the First World War; it suffered some damage in the Second, but retains some 17-18C houses and an 18C church.

13km. *Dun-sur-Meuse*, on its hill, overlooks the river, the crossing of which was forced by the Americans in early Nov. 1918, bringing weeks of static warfare to an end.—On the far bank, to the N., lies *Mont-devant-Sassey*, its church with a Romanesque crypt.

The main road continues S.E. along the E. bank of the Meuse towards the battlefield of 1916–18 and (33km) **Verdun**; see Rte 117.

An ALTERNATIVE ROAD may be followed, some distance W. of the river, which passes near the American cemetery of *Romagne-sous-Montfaucon* (over 21,000 graves) and the monument on the *Butte de Montfaucon*, the ridge of which was long a German observation post in 1916, and which did not fall to the Americans until 27 Sept. 1918. The strong *Kriemhilde Line* ran E. and W. in this region. We then pass the monument on *Côte 304*, and that of *Le Morte-Homme*, before turning E. to reach the road on the W. bank of the winding Meuse 11km from *Verdun*.

For an alternative route from Longuyon to Metz, see below.—The N43 soon bears S.E., after 25km passing just E. of the iron-mining town of *Piennes*, 15km beyond which is **Briey**, the centre of an important basin of iron-mines, with remains of a castle in the upper town, and a 15C church with good gargoyles.—One may join the motorway a short distance beyond, or cross it, to enter **Metz** after 30km; see Rte 111.

LONGUYON TO METZ VIA LONGWY AND THIONVILLE (89km). The N18 leads N.E., at 14km passing N. of the Renaissance château of *Cons-la-Grandville*, remodelled in the 18C.—4km. **Longwy** (17,500 Longoviciens), an industrial town dominated to the N. by the old fortress and *St-Dagobert* (1690), several times bombarded. It was conceded to France at the Treaty of Nijmegen (1678), and fortified by Vauban, but fell to the Prussians in 1792, although recovered after Valmy. It was captured by the Prussians in 1815, in 1870, in 1914, when it capitulated to the German Crown Prince (who styled himself 'the victor of Longwy'), and again in 1940.—3km to the N. is the steel-working town of *Mont-St-Martin*, on its hill, with a Romanesque church of Germanic character, with a good rose-window and low reliefs of interest. Immediately beyond is the Belgian frontier, and 16km N., the town of *Arlon*; to the N.E. is the frontier with *Luxembourg*, its capital 31km from Longwy; see *Blue Guide Belgium and Luxembourg*.—Driving S.E., at 20km the Verdun—Luxembourg road is crossed at *Aumetz*, and 5km beyond, we fork l., with extensive views later, for (16km) **Thionville** (41,400 Thionvillois), an ancient fortress and now the metallurgical capital of Lorraine, lying on the W. bank of the canalised Moselle. It was originally called *Theodonis Villa*, and was a favourite residence of Charlemagne. It has endured many sieges, notably in 1643, when it was wrested from the Spaniards by Condé, and in 1814–15, when it was held for Napoleon by Gén. Hugo. Near the bridge is the *Hôtel de Ville* (1695); the *Tour aux Puces*, relic of a castle of the counts of Luxembourg, containing a small museum; and the arcaded *Pl. du Marché*; while on the far bank beyond the railway are remains of its fortifications.—The city of **Luxembourg** lies 32km due N.

The N153 leads N.E. along the r. bank of the Moselle to (18km) *Sierck*, a small spa dominated by a ruined castle of the dukes of Lorraine, first mentioned in 1065, 3km beyond which is the German frontier, just S. of which, and 6km to the E., is the ruined 15C castle of *Mensberg*, in which Marlborough stayed in 1705.—*Trier* lies 50km N.E. of the border.

The D918 leads E. from Thionville to (32km) *Bouzonville*, an ancient town, which, with its restored church, was damaged in 1940 and 1944.—*Saarlouis*, in Germany, lies 21km further E.; it was the birthplace of Marshal Ney (1769–1815) at which period it was part of France.

The roads leading S. from Thionville to Metz run through unattractive industrial districts, and it is advisable to take the A31 motorway, which may be entered just S. or S.E. of the town; for **Metz**, see Rte 111.

MONTMÉDY TO VERDUN (48km). We turn off the N43 after 7km, and in 4km pass 4km E. of *Louppy-sur-Loison*, a picturesque village with a Renaissance château and the ruins of an ancient castle surrounding its church.—11km. *Damvillers*, with remains of fortifications, and a 15C church, is traversed, 7km beyond which we turn r. to cross the *Côtes de Meuse* to meet the D964 4.5km N. of **Verdun**; see Rte 107.

105 Soissons to Laon and Maubeuge (for Brussels)

123km (76 miles). N2. 35km **Laon**—37km *Vervins*—33km *Avesnes*—18km *Maubeuge*.

Maps: IGN 9, 4, 5, or 101. M 237, 236.

For **Soissons**, *Blue Guide Paris and Environs*, or Rte 17. On quitting the town the road by-passes *Crouy*, giving its name to the plateau from which German guns commanded Soissons for three years dur-

ing the First World War, to reach (11.5km) the mill of *Laffaux*, 3.5km
beyond which is the W. extremity of the *'Chemin-des-Dames'*,
traversing a ridge to the r., which is honeycombed with quarries.

This *'Ladies' Road'* was constructed for the journeys of the daughters of Louis
XV between Compiègne and the Château de la Bove, in the upper valley of the
Ailette. The ridge was assailed by Haig's Corps during the *First battle of the Aisne*
(1914), when on 13-14 Sept. the river crossings were forced, but on the 18th the
attempt to carry the German positions by frontal assault was abandoned, and
after three weeks the British were relieved by French reserves, and moved to
the Flanders front. The French gained a footing on the central section of the
ridge during Nivelle's unsuccessful offensive (17-20 April, 1917), and secured
the E. heights that May. The *Battle of Malmaison* (17-23 Oct.; named after a fort)
gave Pétain's army possession of the W. terminal of the ridge, and the Germans
fell back upon the Ailette. On 27 May 1918 Von Bulow's army made a surprise
attack in overwhelming force, pushing the Allies back across the Aisne (*Second
battle of the Aisne*), claiming 45,000 prisoners as they advanced again on the
Marne. The ridge was only finally regained by Mangin and Guillaumat that October.

7km. *Urcel*, with a restored Romanesque church.

3km. A r.-hand turning provides an alternative approach to *Laon*
via the villages of *Nouvion-le-Vineux* (S.E. of which are the ruins of a
12-13C castle of the bishops of Laon), *Presle*, *Vorges*, and *Bruyères*,
all with churches of some interest.

At 5km we reach the N44 (see Rte 3) by-passing *Laon*, on a commanding ridge ahead, to which we ascend by continuing ahead
through *Semilly*, climbing steeply to the upper walled town, entered
near (r.) the ruined *Porte de Soissons* and a leaning 13C tower.

LAON (pron. long, without emphasising the g; 29,100 Laonnois),
the préfecture of the *Aisne*, is a splendidly sited and characteristic
old town built along a solitary hill with several spurs, rising abruptly
c. 100m above the surrounding plain, the summit of which is crowned by its great cathedral.

Laon (*Laudunum*) was fortified by the Romans. In 497 its bishopric was founded
by St Remigius of Reims, and later Carolingian kings made it their capital, a
palace being maintained there until the reign of Philippe Auguste, although the
bishops themselves (ranking among the twelve ecclesiastical peers of France)
were its actual rulers, and the commune was only emancipated after several
revolts, notably in 1111, when Bp Gaudry was assassinated and his palace and
cathedral burnt down. It was besieged at various times during the Hundred
Years' War.
Blücher defended it successfully against Napoleon in 1814, and after Waterloo
it was briefly the rallying point of the latter's defeated army. On 9 Sept. after its
capitulation had been signed, a French sapper blew up the powder-magazine of
the citadel at the cost of his and 500 other lives, both French and German. It was
in no position to resist Von Kluck's vanguard on 30 Aug. 1914, and was only
retaken, by Mangin's army, on 13 Oct. 1918. Both St-Martin, the Hôtel-Dieu, and
the area around the station in the lower town to the N., were badly damaged by
bombing prior to its liberation on 30 Aug. 1944.
Among its natives were St Remi (439–533), bishop of Reims; Louis IV
(d'Outremer; 921–54); Lothaire (941–86); Louis V ('le Fainéant'; the sluggard;
957–87); Anselm of Laon, the theologian (d. 1117); the 15C artist Enguerrand
Charanton, or Quarton; the 17C artist brothers Antoine, Louis, and Mathieu Le
Nain; the Jesuit missionary Jacques Marquette (1637–75), who explored the
Mississippi valley; Marshal Sérurier (1742–1819); and 'Champfleury' (Jules
Husson; 1821–89), the author.

At the W. end of the upper town stands restored **St-Martin**, a
massively-buttressed Transitional building (1150), which is a relic of
a famous Benedictine abbey at which Anselm and Abélard taught.

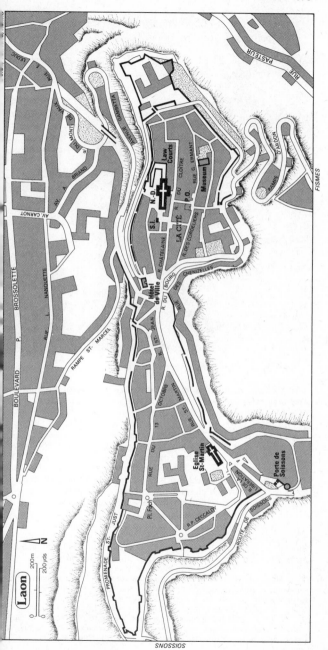

Laon

FISMES

RUE PASTEUR

RUE LEDUC

RUE E. PAUL

AV. CARNOT

RUE DU MONT

AVENUE GAMBETTA

AV. A. BRIAND

Law Courts

R. DU CLOITRE

RUE G. ERMANT

Museum

P.O.

N.-D.

S.I.

LA CITÉ

R. DESCORDELIERS

R. CHATELAINE

RAMPE D'ARDON

BROSSOLETTE

P. BROSSOLETTE

RUE L. NANOUETTE

BOULEVARD

RAMPE ST.-MARCEL

Hôtel de Ville

R. DU BOURG

RUE DES CHENIZELLES

R. ST.-JEAN

RUE ST.-MARTIN

R. OCTOBRE

13

RUE DU

PROMENADE ST.-JUST

Pl. Foch

Eglise St-Martin

R.P. CECCALDI

R. DE LA LIBERATION

ROUTE DE SOISSONS

Porte de Soissons

N

200m

200yds

SNOSSIOS

The W. towers of the cathedral at Laon

Two 13C towers are unusually placed at the junction of the transepts and nave, while on the principal portal of its 13-14C facade is a relief of St Martin dividing his cloak. Beneath the organ-loft are effigies of a lord of Pierrepont and a lady of Coucy (13-14C), while a Renaissance screen of 1540 is also notable.

The Rue St-Martin, No. 1 in which is an attractive early 16C house, leads E. towards the *Library*, containing MSS and autographs of interest, to reach the central *Pl. du Gén. Leclerc*, with the *Hôtel de Ville* and *Théâtre* (once a church, with a 17C front). To the S. an archway leads to the steep and picturesque Rue des Chenizelles.

Both the Rue Sérurier, in which are several old houses, or the more southerly Rue Châtelaine, approach the ****Cathedral**, a 12-13C building noted for the purity of its style and for its noble proportions, which replaced an earlier church destroyed in 1111. It was begun by Bp Gautier de Mortagne (1155–74), completed in 1230, and restored after 1852. The see was suppressed at the Revolution.

It was designed to have seven towers, only four of which were completed, while the single spire, crowning the tower above the facade, was destroyed at the Revolution. From the upper stages of the W. towers project figures of colossal oxen, perhaps representing the beasts which traditionally dragged the stone for the cathedral up the hill of their own accord. The restored *Facade, although over-elaborate, preserves admirable proportions in its cavernous arches and portals. Among the sculptures are figures representing the liberal arts; note the hippopotamus gargoyle.

Interior. Its dimensions are 118m in length by 30.65m in width at the transepts, with a height of 24m. At the E. and W. ends are rose-windows, the former with good glass; the latter masked by the early 18C organ, the work of a Premonstratensian monk. The broad and luminous *Nave*, with eleven bays, is noteworthy for the elegant grouping of its pillars, with sheaves of annulated columns branching upwards from their capitals. Beneath the triforium are galleries. The pulpit (1681) and the churchwardens' pews are notable.

The aisles are flanked by chapels added at the close of the 13C, in 1574 enclosed by a Renaissance screen. Above the central crossing is a lantern, while the N. transept contains a good rose-window, and the S. a 12C font. The deep *Choir* (1225), enclosed by early 18C grilles, was at first apsidal, but now terminates in a straight E. wall (c. 1230) with three fine lancet windows.

The restoration of buildings is taking place to the S.W. of the cathedral, and also of its cloister, where, overlooking the Rue du Cloître, is a mutilated statue holding a sundial.

A short distance to the S.E., at 32 Rue Georges-Ermant, is the *Museum*, with archaeological collection of some interest. In its garden is a *Templar chapel*, an octagonal building with an apse of 1134 and an upper part of the 14C.—To the N.E. is the former *Bishop's Palace*, now the *Palais de Justice*, which may be visited; while the *Citadel* at the W. end of the plateau—commanding wide views—now accommodates the *Cité Administrative*.

The more interesting descent is to the S. from the central square, passing the *Préfecture* (with a view across the 'Cuve St-Vincent' to the *Arsenal* on a spur to the S.W.) to the 13C *Porte d'Ardon*, beyond which the road climbs down in zigzags to meet the by-pass, where we turn l.

LAON TO ROCROI (80km). From the roundabout just E. of the town, the D977 is followed through marshy country to the N.E. via (12km) *Liesse*, where the church (1380–15C) was once a goal of pilgrimage, 2.5km S. of which is the Renaissance château of *Marchais*, belonging to the puppet Prince of Monaco. The road continues through (13km) *Clermont-les-Fermes*, once seven monastic farms with a walled enceinte, 7km beyond which *Montcornet*, with a 13C church later fortified, is traversed, just N.W. of which, at *Chaourse*, is a 11-15C church containing a 16C *Entombment*.—7km. *Rozoy-sur-Serre*, with a fortified 12-16C church containing numerous tombstones of the period.—10km. *Brunehamel*, with ruins of a 16C castle, 3km beyond which, the relics of the Cistercian abbey of *Bonnefontaine*, founded in 1154, with 18C dependencies, lie to the E.—5km. *Rumigny*, with a partly 16C château, 12km beyond which we reach the N43 at the *Mon Idée* crossroads.—12km N.E. is *Rocroi*; see Rte 104.

From just E. of Laon the N2 is followed past (23km) *Marle* (r.), with a late 12C church, a *Mairie* with a 17C facade, and remains of a 13C castle. There are several village churches of interest to the r. of the road, notable among them that of *Burelles*.—14km **Vervins**, an ancient town (1C *Verbinum*), former capital of the hilly *Pays de Thiérache*, with a 13-16C church, partly fortified, and 18C *Mairie*. Here was signed the treaty of 2 May 1598 in which Philip II of Spain and the Duke of Savoy recognised Henri IV as king of France.—The D963 leads 19km N.E. to *Hirson*; see Rte 104.

The N2 continues N., at (8km) *Étréaupont* passing c. 4km W. of the remains of the Cistercian abbey of *Foigny*, founded in 1121.—9km. *La Capelle*, where we cross the N43 (see Rte 104), was the point at which the German plenipotentiaries on their way to sue for an Armistice crossed the French lines on 7 Nov. 1918. They presented themselves at *Rethondes*, near Compiègne, the following day, and the Armistice was signed on the 11th; see *Blue Guide Paris and Environs*.

Hence the dull road leads due N. through (16km) **Avesnes-sur-Helpe**, once fortified, where *St-Nicolas*, rebuilt in the 16C, with a 13C choir and good bell-tower, has fine brick vaulting with stone ribs. It was the advance H.Q. of Hindenburg and Ludendorff during the critical struggles of 1918, and was captured by British forces three days before the Armistice.

A road leads E. up the valley of the Helpe to (14km) *Liessies*, and the adjacent *Château de la Motte*, which incorporates vestiges of a Benedictine abbey founded in the 7C; elegant chapels of 1739 stand at the four exits of the village.—7km N. lies *Solre-le-Château*, its picturesque 15C church with a leaning spire.

At 18km (after passing industrial *Hautmont* to the l., with its blast-furnaces and rolling-mills) **Maubeuge** (36,200 Maubeugeois), is entered, an industrial town and former fortress on the Sambre, which has been virtually rebuilt since its destruction by German incendiaries in 1940. It retains stretches of ramparts, and—N. of the undistinguished central Place—the *Porte de Mons* (1685), but very little else of interest.

Originating in a monastery and nunnery founded by St Aldegonda (7C), *Malbodium* later became the capital of *Hainault*, and was assigned to France by the Treaty of Nijmegen in 1678. It was fortified by Vauban at the command of Louis XIV, who won his spurs here under Turenne in the siege of 1655. In 1793 Jourdan' victory at *Wattignies* (10km S.E.) raised the siege undertaken by the Prince of Coburg. It was vainly besieged by the Duke of Saxe-Weimar in 1814, but fell the following year after a stout resistance. It was invested by Von Kluck's army on 23 Aug. 1914, its garrison of 35,000 being forced to capitulate on 7 Sept., and became an important German base until re-entered by British troops on 9 Nov. 1918. Its most famous native was the Flemish artist Jan Gossaert, or Mabuse (1465–1533).

The town is surrounded by a series of outlying forts, one of which is passed (l.) on approaching the Belgian border 8km N. (Customs), 12km beyond which is *Mons*: see *Blue Guide Belgium*.

For the road from Maubeuge to *Valenciennes* via *Bavay*, 14km W., see Rte 1.

106 Château-Thierry to Reims and Charleville-Mézières

143km (89 miles). N3. 23km *Dormans*—RD380. 38km **Reims**—N51. 39km **Rethel**—43km **Charleville-Mézières**.

Maps: IGN 9, 10, 5, or 103, 101. M 237, 241.

The A4 motorway, entered 5km. N., provides a rapid route as far as Reims.

For **Château-Thierry**, see *Blue Guide Paris and Environs*, or Rte 18.

We cross the Marne, and turn l. onto the N3, skirting the l. bank of the river to (9km) *Crézancy*.

4km to the S. lies *St-Eugène*, its 12-13C church with a remarkable portal of the Last Judgement; at *Condé-en-Brie*, 2.5km beyond, is a 12C castle, which in 1518 passed to Louis de Bourbon, who took the name Condé. The château was remodelled in the 17-18C, and contains some well-furnished rooms decorated by Servandoni, and Oudry.—For *Orbais*, 10km further S.E., see Rte 107.

The main road circles to the N.E. to (14km) *Dormans*, with a restored 12-14C church, 17C château with older towers, and modern

Chapelle de la Reconnaissance, a monument to the battles of the Marne (view).

It was the scene of the final German attempt to break through the Allied front on 15-16 July 1918, when eight of Von Boehn's divisions forced the crossing, only to retire to the N. bank four days later. The place was again damaged during the German advance in June 1940. Dormans was the birthplace of the architect Claude-Nicolas Ledoux (1736–1806).

DORMANS TO CHÂLONS-SUR-MARNE (59km). The N3 forks r. 2km E. to skirt the river, with vine-covered slopes on the far bank, and a district of woods and lakes extending to the S., at 16.5km passing S. of *Damery*, with a 12-16C church, and the birthplace of the tragic actress Adrienne Lecouvreur (1692–1730).—6.5km. **Épernay**; see Rte 103B. The road traverses (4km) *Chouilly*, with an 11C church, 2km beyond passing the l.-hand turning for *Mareuil-sur-Ay*, 2.5km N., with highly esteemed vineyards, a 12C church, and a château once owned by Marshal Lannes.—*Avenay-Val-d'Or* (2.5km further N.), has a Flamboyant facade to its church, which contains a 16C organ and paintings from the Abbaye du Breuil, a Benedictine foundation of 660, destroyed at the Revolution.—The N3 now traverses the flat plain of Champagne, through (6.5km) *Athis*, with a 17C château, and *Jâlons*, with an 11-12C church of interest, to approach (19.5km) **Châlons**; see Rte 107.

The RD380 crosses the Marne and climbs N.E. through hilly country between the Tardenois plateau and the *Montagne de Reims* (E.), at 37km. entering Reims itself.

REIMS (pron. Răns; anglicised as **Rheims**; 182,000 Rémois; 45,000 in 1851; 108,400 in 1901), once a thriving textile manufacturing town, was devastated during the 1914–18 War, and its industries have been much diversified since the Second World War, but it is still—with Épernay—one of the main centres of champagne production, and is partly surrounded by vine-clad hills. The old town is still dominated by its venerable cathedral, which suffered comparatively little damage, considering the bombardments it has experienced.

Durocortorum, the capital of the Remi, the least bellicose of the Belgian tribes, was Christianised in the 3C, and although ravaged by the Vandals and by Attila, never ceased to be of importance. From the period of the Frankish conquests its history has been largely bound up with that of its church; see below. Edward III was repulsed in 1359 while marching on Reims with the intention of having himself crowned king of France, and it was not until 1420 that it fell into the hands of Henry V. The English were expelled nine years later, and Charles VII was crowned in the cathedral under a standard held by Joan of Arc.

Card. Charles of Lorraine founded the university in 1547, and due to its English college, the town became a focus of English recusancy during the reign of Elizabeth I and James I. In 1694 the earliest French newspaper, the 'Gazette de France', was printed here. Marmont won a battle against the Allies on 13 March 1814 in the vicinity, but this was the last smile of Fortune on the Emperor. In 1870 it was occupied by the Prussians. Here in Aug. 1909 took place the first aviation meeting ever held. On 4 Sept. 1914 it was again occupied by the Germans, and sacked, but they retired on the 12th in the face of D'Esperey's advance, and during the next four years it lay in the centre of the battle zone, being subjected to sporadic bombardment, during which time its extensive wine-cellars proved invaluable protection for those citizens who remained, but its civilians were evacuated at Easter 1917, when over 25,000 shells fell there in a week. The capture of the almost-obliterated city was the immediate objective of Ludendorff's 'Friedensturm' of 15 July 1918, but it held fast, a menace to the German's flank march, and was only disengaged by the Allied advance of 2-9 Oct. In clearing the ruins some relics of the Roman city were discovered beneath crumbling houses near the Hôtel de Ville. It was estimated that hardly 2000 of 14,000 houses remained standing; another 5000 were destroyed during the Second World War. On 7 May 1945 the German unconditional surrender was signed in a room of a Technical College here, where Gen. Eisenhower had established his G.H.Q.

Among famous natives were Jean-Baptiste Colbert (1619– 83); Gilles Gobelin, the 16C weaver of tapestries, and other members of his family; Jean-Baptiste de la Salle (1651– 1719), founder of the Frères des Écoles Chrétiennes; Robert Nantheuil (1630– 78), the designer and engraver; Marshal Drouet d'Erlon (1765– 1844); and the poet Paul Fort (1872– 1960).

Its biscuits and pain d'épice are reputed.

Information about visiting Champagne cellars may be obtained from the S.I. in the Blvd de la Paix, N.E. of the cathedral.

Several roads coverge on the W. side of the town, N. of the Canal de l'Aisne à la Marne, with its port, and the small river Vesle, and convenient parking may be found in the Blvd Gén. Leclerc or Blvd Foch, its N. extension, between the Railway Station and the old centre. Both these wide promenades were laid out in the reign of Louis XV.

From between the two, the *Pl. Drouet d'Erlon* leads S. to (l.) *St Jacques* (13C), containing modern glass designed by Maria-Helena Vieira da Silva, just beyond which we turn l. along the Rue de Vesle to the *Théâtre* and *Palais de justice* (the latter preserving in its interior court part of the 18C facade of the *Hôtel-Dieu* previously on this site).

Turning r. down a short street between these two buildings, the W. front of the ***Cathedral** is reached, which suffering irreparably in many details, is still a fine example of French Gothic, remarkable for its unity of style and wealth of decoration.

The archbishopric was founded by St Sixtus (c. 290), but the earliest building on this site was erected in the early 5C. Here Clovis was baptised by St Remigius in 496, and here from 1180 (Philippe Auguste) to Charles X in 1825, the kings of France, with certain exceptions, were crowned. Guillaume de Machault, the composer and poet, was a canon of the cathedral in the mid 14C. Its predecessor was destroyed by a fire in 1210, which devastated the town, and the present edifice was begun the following year from the designs of Jean d'Orbais, and continued by Jean Le Loup, Gaucher de Reims, Bernard de Soissons, and Robert de Coucy (d. 1311). The W. front was commenced in 1241 and the W. towers were completed in 1430. The rose-window and the apsidal spire were destroyed in the bombardments of 1914– 18, and havoc was caused on the S.W. side in particular, but numerous sculptures were saved by protective measures, and most of the treasures it contained, including its tapestries, were preserved. It was closed for restoration until Oct. 1937, but the work of repair has continued since.

The ***West Front** is enriched by a wealth of sculpture, a proportion of them replicas of the originals, which tends to blur the architectural line. The central doorway of the deeply recessed triple portal is dedicated to the Virgin, and included groups of the Annunciation and Visitation (r.) and Purification (l.); in the gable is her Coronation. The lintel of the door was unhappily planed flat in 179? and received a banal inscription. The r.-hand doorway, flanked by statues of prophets, is surmounted by a mutilated Last Judgement; the l.-hand doorway likewise damaged, is dedicated to the Passion, and here, immediately to the l. is the restored figure of the 'Sourire de Reims', a smiling angel which was decapitated. Note also the arras-like carving just above the pavement at this entrance.

Above the rose-window is David challenging Goliath, and on either side are Saul, Solomon, and the apostles. Still higher, between the towers, is a group of the baptism of Clovis, the centrepiece of a gallery consisting of a line of colossal statues of kings of France. The ***Towers**, which end in openwork turrets, were several times struck by shells, and the pierced staircase of the S. tower was partially destroyed.

The harmonious N. facade is noteworthy for the triple portal (undergoing cleaning and restoration) in which the central doorway is beautifully but soberly decorated with statues of bishops; on the tympanum are histories of SS Nicasius and Remigius. The so-called ***Porte de l'Enfer** has striking reliefs of the Last

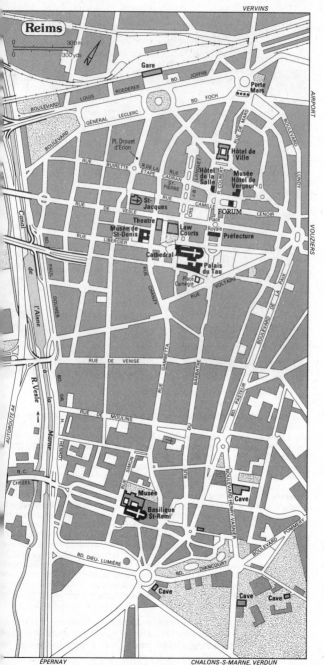

VERVINS

Reims

0 _____ 300 m
0 _____ 300 yds

Gare

BD. JOFFRE

Porte
Mars

LOUIS   ROEDERER

BD. FOCH

BOULEVARD

GÉNÉRAL   LECLERC

RUE DE MARS

BOULEVARD

AIRPORT

BOULEVARD

Pl. Drouet
d'Erlon

RUE   BUIRETTE

R. DE LA
ÉTAPE

RUE
CADRAN
ST-
PIERRE

RUE

COLBERT

R. COLBERT

Hôtel de
Ville

Hôtel
de la
Salle

Musée
Hôtel de
Vergeur

LUNDY

St-
Jacques

RUE

J-B.

CAMILLE

CRS.

FORUM

LENOIR

VOUZIERS

RUE   DE   VESLE

Theatre

Musée de
St-Denis

Law
Courts

Place
Royale

Préfecture

RUE

LIBERGIER

BD.

PAUL

DOUMER

Cathedral

Palais
du Tau

Place
Carnegie

RUE   CHANZY

RUE   VOLTAIRE

BOULEVARD   DE   LA   PAIX

Canal   de   l'Aisne

RUE   DE   VENISE

RUE   GAMBETTA

RUE   BARBATRE

BD.

DR.

H.

RUE   DE   MOULINS

BD. PASTEUR

AUTOROUTE A 4

à   la

R. Veste

Marne

RUE

HENRIOT

R.C.

CHEZEL

RUE   SIMON

Musée

Basilique
St-Remi

RUE   DU

Cave

BOULEVARD   HENRY   VASNIER

BD.   DIEU- LUMIÈRE

BD.   DIANCOURT

Cave

POMMIER

BOULEVARD

Cave

Cave

ÉPERNAY

CHALONS-S-MARNE, VERDUN

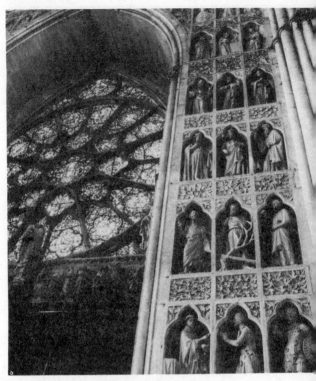

Looking W. from the nave at Reims

Judgement and a 13C 'Beau Dieu', which was decapitated by a shell. The relie
above the r.-hand doorway is a Romanesque relic of the earlier cathedral. Above
the 13C apse, with its pinnacled flying buttresses, stood the elegant 15C 'Ange
Spire' of wood and lead which was destroyed together with the roof in the fire o
19 Sept. 1914. The much-damaged S. facade has a 16C gable.

Interior. The cathedral is 149m long, 61m wide at the transepts, and the nave
vaulting is 38m high. The W. end of the *Nave*, which contains ten bays, the firs
four of which are slightly later than the others, is decorated by numerou
Statues (13C; deserving illumination), among which the Knight's Communio
in the lowest row on the r. of the central doorway will be noted, together with
sculptured groups on the lintels. The great rose-window was the work of Bernar
de Soissons. The pillar-capitals are in most cases carved with foliage, but note the
Vintage Scene on the 6th pillar on the r. The 18C Pulpit was built by Blondel o
Reims. The Gothic Organ-loft, with a case of 1647, stands in the N. transept
below another rose-window. The glass in the S. transept is old glass re-used. I
the *Lady Chapel* is stained-glass designed by Chagall. On the walls hang severa
Flemish tapestries depicting the Life of the Virgin presented by Abp Robert de
Lenoncourt in 1530. Part of the vaulting in the long *Choir* fell upon the high altar
in 1917. The *Ambulatory*, with its radiating chapels, is surmounted by a 13C
clerestory, while an arcaded triforium extends round the entire building.

Immediately to the S. is the rebuilt former *Archbishop's Palace*, o
Palais du Tau, ◇ originally 17C, although relics of its Salle de Tau
date from 1497, and the chapel from 1235. It now houses an in

teresting collection of mutilated statuary from the cathedral, including—at the head of the staircase—the Coronation of the Virgin, removed from the central gable of the W. front.

Among tapestries here displayed are Scenes from the Life of Clovis (Tournai; c. 1440), presented to the cathedral by Card. de Lorraine in 1573; and an early 17C depiction of the Song of Songs, from Hauteville. The rebuilt *Salle de Tau* contains hangings designed by Hittorf for Charles X, while in the adjacent room are his coronation mantles and those of the Duc d'Angoulême, together with Gérard's Portrait of the former wearing his. The *Treasury* preserves the Ivory Comb of St Bernard; a fine late 12C chalice; the Reliquary of the Resurrection (2nd half of 15C); and the boat-shaped Reliquary of St Ursula (1505), among other cult objects used at the coronation masses of French kings, etc.

To the S.E. is the *Carnegie Library* (1930), a municipal library rebuilt at the expense of that philanthropist.

A short distance S.W. of the cathedral stands the **Musée St-Denis**, installed in the 18C buildings which were originally part of the abbey of St-Denis, on the GROUND FLOOR of which are miscellaneous portraits, and a *Ceramic collection*, etc.

FIRST FLOOR. Distributed throughout a series of rooms are items of furniture, while notable among the works of art are *Portrait-drawings by both *Cranach the Elder* (1472–1553) and *Younger* (1515–86), and by *Berthel Bruyn*, among others; a series of early 15C paintings on cloth of Scenes from the Passion; *Le Nain brothers*, several Peasant Scenes (and copies), and Venus at the forge of *Vulcan*; *Jordaens*, Satyr; *Govaert Flink*, Female portrait; *P. Mignard*, Charles Maurice, and Michel Le Tellier; *Philippe de Champaigne*. The Children of Hubert de Montmort; *Laurent La Hyre*, Sacrifice of Abraham; *anon*. Portrait of Colbert; *Poussin*, Landscapes; *P. van Mol*, Deposition; *Boucher*, Odalesque; *L.-M. van Loo*, The Duchesse d'Orléans; *Roslin*, Mgr de la Roche-Aimond; *David's* copy of the Death of Marat; *anon*. View of the Abbaye de St-André, Villeneuve-lès-Avignon; 25 Landscapes by *Corot*, and 11 by *Lépine*; and examples of the art of *Renoir*, *Bonington*, *Daubigny*, *Gauguin*, *Géricault*, *Jongkind*, *Boudin*, *Th. Rousseau*, *Millet*, *Monet*, *Courbet*, *Sisley*, *Daumier*, *Bonnard*, *Dufy*, *Marquet*, *Matisse*, *Vieira da Silva*, *Foujita*, *Pissarro*, *Delacroix*, *Vuillard* (Forain in his studio), et al., and several bronzes by *Barye*.

For the church of *St-Remi*, just over 1km S.E.; see below.

From the cathedral apse, one may turn N. past the *Sous-Préfecture* to the restored *Pl. Royale*, a severe but not unhandsome square laid out by Legendre in 1758, but burnt out in 1918, leaving only its facades. In the centre a statue of Louis XV by Cartellier (1818) replaces the original monument by Pigalle (1755), destroyed at the Revolution.—Colbert was born in a house which stood on the site of No. 13 Rue Cérès, adjacent, while No. 30 is the 18 *Hôtel Ponsardin*.

The *Pl. du Forum* is shortly reached, the emplacement of the Roman forum, where the imposing vaulted **Cryptoporticus** has been uncovered. It may be visited by applying to the adjacent **Musée Le Vergeur**, installed in a rebuilt mansion, and largely devoted to Old Reims (conducted tour).

In the garden one is shown a Renaissance facade and other relics of buildings here re-erected, while a Gothic room has also been incorporated into the edifice. Some good furniture (including a rare Louis-XV bath), and collections of Meissen, Saxe, Wedgwood, and porcelain de Paris, are displayed, left to the city by Hugues Krafft, together with several watercolours of Reims by *Émile Auger*, a gouache by *J.-P. Martin le Jeune* of a Cavalcade passing the Cathedral, and complete sets of *Dürer's* engravings of the 'Apocalypse' and 'The Great Passion', among others; also a maquette of the cathedral.

In the adjacent Rue Tambour stands the Gothic *Hôtel des Comtes de*

Champagne (restored), while further W., in the Rue de l'Arbalète, i
the Renaissance *Hôtel de la Salle*, with its courtyard.—A short
distance N. of the latter stands the *Hôtel de Ville*, the restored facade
of which, by Jean Bonhomme (1636), is a good example of Louis-XII
architecture. The rest was reduced to a shell by a conflagration ii
which its library of 100,000 volumes perished.

A short walk further N. brings one to the ***Porte de Mars**, a Roman
triumphal arch dating from the beginning of the 3C. Under the cen
tral archway the months of the year are represented; and under the
side arches appear Romulus and Remus suckled by the she-wolf; and
Jupiter and Leda.

Hence the Rue du Champ-de-Mars leads r. to the Caves of *Champagnes Mumm*
and the Chapel of *N.-D.-de-la-Paix*, decorated after his conversion to Catholicism
by Léonard-Tsugouharu Foujita (Tokio, 1886–1968), who is buried there.

The Av. de Laon leads N. from the *Pl. de la République*, just beyond the Porte
de Mars, from which the first l.-hand turning after crossing the railway leads to
No. 10 Rue President-Roosevelt, where in the '*Salle de Guerre*' the German
capitulation was signed in 1945; see above.

The Rue Chanzy, continued by the Rue Gambetta, leads S.E. from
the *Musée St-Denis* (see above) to the former *Jesuit College*
(1617–78), with an imposing Library, refectory, and kitchens, and
the adjacent church of *St-Maurice* (16C; restored 19C).

A short distance further S. is the former Benedictine abbey of *St
Remi* (12-18C), long used as a hospital, and now containing a small
collection of arms and armour; it is planned to accommodate the
city's archaeological collections in the building, including the
Cenotaph of the consul Jovinus (d. 370), an early Christian convert

Abutting it is the large abbey-church of ***St-Remi** (11C), the oldest
church in Reims, which succeeded the Chapel of St-Christopher
erected in the cemetery in which St Remigius was buried in 533. Its
principal facade, between two slim Romanesque towers (the S. one is
11C), and weatherworn S. facade (16C) survived the worst of the
bombardments. In the spacious interior, the Romanesque capitals of
its restored 12C choir, with its five radiating chapels, are notable, as
is the Entombment off the S. transept. Behind the altar is the
reconstructed mausoleum of St Remigius (1847), embellished with
16C statues.

S.E. of its apse is the round *Pl. des Droits-de-l'Homme*, near which are several
Champagne Caves, among them those of *Veuve Clicquot-Ponsardin*; those o
Taittinger are slightly to the N. of the Place, in part occupying the cellars and
crypt of the former abbey of *St-Nicaise*. To the E. of the latter and N.E. of the
Place is the *Butte St-Nicaise*, part of the old town ramparts, commanding a view
of the city; and N.W. of the adjacent *Rond-Point-Gén. Gouraud*, are the Caves o
Piper-Heidsieck; to the E., those of *Pommery*; and further E., of *Ruinart*, in Gallo
Roman quarries. All have several kilometres of galleries tunnelled in the ol
chalk quarries, which provided shelter during bombardments. A visit to one
Cave at least—if not those of neighbouring *Épernay* (see Rte 103B)—will give an
insight into the wine-trade of Reims, and the processes of manufacturing cham
pagne.

N.E. of the Rond-Point is the suburb known as the *Foyer Rémois*, laid out after
1918, in the centre of which is *St-Nicaise*, containing murals by Maurice Denis
and glass by Lalique.

For roads from Reims to **Laon**, **Soissons**, and **Vervins**, see Rtes 3, 5, and 104
respectively, in reverse; for *Épernay* and **Troyes**, Rte 103B, and for **Châlons** and
Dijon, Rte 109.

REIMS TO STE-MENEHOULD (73km). The RD31 leads S.E. past (r.) the *Parc Pommery*, to cross the notorious sector of the battlefield known as the *Butte de Tir* (from an old rifle-range), and at 8.5km passes (r.) the immense chalky mine-craters surrounding the *Fort de la Pomelle*, with a museum of militaria. This key position changed hands more than once, and was never far removed from the front line of 1914–18.—After 1.5km we fork l. along what was a Roman road to approach (l.) the *Moronvilliers hills*, a range memorable for the battles of April–May 1917, when Gén. Degoutte's army advanced here.—At 7km another Roman road leads off to the r.—13km. 4.5km to the S. stands a small *Russian memorial Church* and cemetery, where are buried Russian soldiers who fought for France in both world wars, and civilians.—Regaining the main road, we continue E. to (12km) *Suippes*, to the N. of which stretch of road took place Joffre's offensive of 25-29 Sept. 1915, when the German third position was momentarily breached, while further to the E. is the field of the American advance of Oct. 1918.—20km *Valmy*; see Rte 107.—3km beyond we meet the N3, and turn l. for (8km) *Ste-Menehould*; see Rte 107.

REIMS TO MONTMÉDY (117km) The RD380 leads N.E., at 22km crossing the Suippe, and 17km beyond, traverses *Machault*, birthplace of the influential composer Guillaume de Machault (c. 1300–77).—7km. *Mazagran*.—**Attigny**, ancient *Attiniacum*, lies 11km N., once a residence of Carolingian kings, preserving a partly Renaissance *Hôtel de Ville* and a 15-17C church, both restored since serious damage in the First World War.—9km. *Vouziers*, in the valley of the Aisne, the birthplace of Hippolyte Taine (1828–93), has a 16C church retaining a beautiful Renaissance triple portal.—Hence the D977 leads N.E. to (47km) *Sedan*, at 26km passing (r.) a 17C moated château, a relic of the *Chartreuse du Mont-Dieu*, founded in 1130 but destroyed at the Revolution.—The D946 continues E. from Vouziers, off which at 6km a r.-hand forks leads to (11km) *Grand-pré*, the centre of severe fighting in the latter part of Oct. 1918, during the American advance through the *Forêt d'Argonne*, further S.—For *Varennes*, 22km to the S.E., see Rte 107.—16km **Buzancy**, an ancient fortress, captured on 2 Nov. 1918, preserves a 13-16C church, while the *Château de la Cour* was owned by Gén. Chanzy (1823–83). The road shortly traverses *Nouart*, his birthplace, and later descends through hills into the Meuse valley at (20km) *Stenay*; see Rte 104; likewise for **Montmédy**, 16.5km beyond another ridge.

The N51 is followed N.E., at first the line of a Roman road, off which we veer l. to traverse (7.5km) *Witry-lès-Reims*, an ancient but rebuilt village, 1.5km S.E. of which is a fort occupied by the Germans from Sept. 1914 until 6 Oct. 1918.—*Lavannes* (r.), with a late 12C church, is shortly by-passed, and later the shallow depression formed by the valleys of the Suippe and Retourne in the otherwise dull chalk plateau of 'Champagne Pouilleuse' is traversed, to approach (43.5km) *Rethel*.

Rethel (9,100 Rethelois), a town of Roman origin, afterwards the seat of a duchy, and a fortress situated above the r. bank of the Aisne, is largely rebuilt, having suffered considerable damage in both world wars. *St-Nicolas* consists of two buildings, one of the 13C formerly attached to a monastery, and one of the 15-16C, with a noteworthy portal of 1510 and detached tower of 1650.

Jacques Boucher de Perthes (1788–1858), author and archaeologist, and the publisher Louis Hachette (1800–64) were born here; Verlaine taught at the former college in 1877–79, where the actor Louis Jouvet (1887–1951) was later a pupil. Robert de Sorbon (1201–74), founder of the Sorbonne at Paris, was born in the village of *Sorbon*, some 3km N.; while Gerson (Jean Le Charlier; 1363–1429), the famous chancellor of the University of Paris, was born near Barby, 4km W.

The road now turns N.E. through (7.5km) *Novy-Chevrières*, with a priory church rebuilt in the 17C, and traverses an undulating fruit-growing district, at (20km) *Poix-Terron* descending into the valley of the Vence to enter that of the Meuse.

15km. **CHARLEVILLE-MÉZIÈRES** (61,600 Carolomaceriens)
préfecture of the *Ardennes*, is an 'agglomeration' of two distinct
towns which have merged. The older fortress of Mézières, on a narrow neck of the Meuse which here makes an inverted S-bend, lies to
the S. of the more recent commercial town of Charleville, which has
grown up inside the upper loop of the river.

Mézières owes its medieval growth to successive immigrations of Liégois. It was
besieged in 1521 by the Imperial troops of the Duc de Nassau and Franz de Sick-
ingen ('Raub Ritter'), but was successfully defended by Bayard's garrison. In
1570 Charles IX and Elisabeth of Austria were married here. *Charleville* is named after Duc Charles de Gonzaga (1580–1637), who founded it in 1606 on the
site of *Arches* (*Arca Remorum*). In 1815 Mézières held up an army of 20,000 Prussians for 42 days, and it was three times invested in 1870, and only capitulated
after a bombardment, in Jan. 1871. Its fortifications were dismantled after 1886.
Both towns were occupied by the German in Aug. 1914, and Charleville became
the H.Q. of the Crown Prince. They were fired on by German artillery on the
morning of Armistice Day (11 Nov. 1918), and were again damaged in 1940. The
most famous native of Charleville is Arthur Rimbaud (1854–91), who is buried
in the cemetery here, although he died at Marseille.

Relics of Vauban's *Citadel* in **Mézières** may be seen near the *Préfecture*, on an island site now occupied by the *Cité Administrative*, to the
E. of the main road crossing the town, the isthmus here being only
300m wide. To the W. rises late Gothic *N.-D. d'Espérance*
(1499–1566), with a Renaissance tower, scarred by successive bombardments. Further W. are two 16C towers overlooking a moat
formed by an arm of the Meuse.

Crossing to **Charleville**, if driving we turn r. beyond a railway
bridge, and some distance beyond, l. up the Rue du Petit-Bois, to gain
the central ***Pl. Ducal** (126m by 90m), laid out by Clément (or Louis)
Métezeau after 1608, and similar in style to the Pl. des Vosges in
Paris, likewise with a line of adjoining brick and stone mansions built
over arcades.—Rimbaud's birthplace was No. 14 Rue Thiers, a prolongation of the Rue de la République, leading S. — To the N. in the
Vieux Moulin on the river bank is installed the *Musée Ardennes*, also
devoted to Rimbaud, who lived—when not escaping from
home—from 1869–75 at No. 7 in the quay named after him, where
he composed 'Le Bateau ivre'.

CHARLEVILLE-MÉZIÈRES TO GIVET (55km), for *Namur*, 51km beyond. The
D988 ascends N.W. through the W. edge of the *Forest of the Ardennes* (the
Roman *Arduenna Silva*) to (23km) *Revin* (see below), which may also be approached by the longer D1 turning r. just N. of Charleville. The D1 skirts the l.
bank of the Meuse, winding through its valley, the steep banks of which are
thickly wooded to the water's edge when not occupied by iron-works and quarries. It passes some picturesque rock formations, but is somewhat monotonous,
traversing (21km) **Monthermé**, whence the narrow valley of the Semois, to the
E., may be explored, for the upper valley of which see *Blue Guide Belgium*; also
for the *Battle of the Ardennes*, otherwise known as 'the Battle of the Bulge',
Hitler's 'last fling' (Dec. 1944–Jan. 1945), in which Von Rundstedt's forces
reached a point some 15km E. of Givet. Monthermé, and most of the villages
traversed are characterised by their slate-roofed '*corons*' or workers'
dwellings.—17km. *Revin*, a small industrial town on a double loop of the river,
has a church of 1706 with contemporary boiseries, and the so-called '*Maison
Espagnole*', a 16C half-timbered house; hence a road climbs up the *Vallée de*
Misère to *Rocroi*, 12km W.; see Rte 104.—*Mont Malgrétout* (416m), to the E.,
gives its name to a novel by George Sand.—Beyond (9km) *Fumay*, with slate
quarries, we skirt the Belgian frontier, to by-pass (l. at 13km) *Molhain*, whose
18C church preserves the 10C crypt of its predecessor, and good Louis-XV
plasterwork.—2km. *Hierges*, with three towers of a 16C castle burnt in 1793, is

passed, and beyond, to the r. in a meander of the Meuse, is a Franco-Belge nuclear power-station.

8km. **Givet**, the gloomy frontier-town of 7,700 inhab., an obsolete fortress, lies at the end of a projection of French territory into Belgium, to the W. of which is the citadel of *Charlemont*, built by Charles V and completed by Vauban. (It was from Givet that Marryat's Peter Simple and his friend O'Brien made their ingenious escape.) The church of *St-Hilaire*, designed by Vauban (1682), is surmounted by a bizarre slated belfry, which excited the raillery of Victor Hugo. On the r. bank is *Notre-Dame* (1729), with contemporary boiseries. The composer Étienne-Nicolas Méhul (1763–1817) was born here.—Hence one may cross the frontier (Customs) to (8km) *Hastière*, and *Dinant*, 13km beyond; **Namur** lies 26km further N., for which see *Blue Guide Belgium*.

107   Montmirail to Metz

216km (134 miles). RD33. 64km **Châlons-sur-Marne**—N3. 42km **Ste-Menehould**—45km **Verdun**—D903. 65km **Metz**.

Maps: IGN 9, 10, 11, or 103, 104; also 311 and 416. M 237, 241.

The Autoroute de l'Est (A4) provides a rapid route from just N. of Chalons to Metz.

For *Montmirail*, see *Blue Guide Paris and Environs*, or Rte 18.

Hence we drive E.—6km. At *Orbais* (10km N.E., on the direct road to *Épernay*, 24km beyond) are the remains of a remarkable *Abbey-church of 1180–1210.—7km. *Fromentières*, its church containing a late 15C carved retable of the School of Nuremberg, is traversed prior to crossing the RD51 (see Rte 103B) at *Champaubert*, where on 11 Feb. 1814 Napoleon beat a Russian force under Gen. Alsuflew.—6km. *Étoges*, with a 17C château, 10km beyond which *Mont Aimé* is passed to the r., with the subterranean ruins of a medieval castle of the last counts of Champagne (views; with the *Marsh of St-Gond* to the S.W.).

1km. *Vertus*, 3.5km N., ancient *Vertudis*, and birthplace of the poet Eustache Deschamps (1340–1410), has a good 12C church reconstructed after damage in 1940, with a crypt of unusual design.—The main road veers N.E. across the Champagne plain.

28km. **CHÂLONS-SUR-MARNE** (54,400 Châlonnais), préfecture of the *Marne*, a centre of the wine trade, and an important road centre and military headquarters ('the Aldershot of France'), is bleakly sited on the r. bank of its river, but possesses several churches of interest.

The capital of the Catalauni became an episcopal see in the 3C, and under its bishops (who from the 12C ranked among the twelve peers of France) it enjoyed long period of prosperity. At the *Battle of Châlons* (451), fought on the *Catalaunian Fields*, the plain between here and Troyes, perhaps nearer the latter, Attila and his Huns were decisively defeated by the Gallo-Romans aided by the Franks and Visigoths. The woollen cloth manufactured here is referred to by Chaucer as 'chalouns', and by Swift as 'shalloons'. In 1147 St Bernard preached the crusade here in the presence of Pope Eugenius VI and Louis VII. Margaret Stuart c. 1424–45), the maligned daughter of James I, and first wife of the Dauphin, later Louis XI, died here. It was repeatedly attacked by the English in the 15C. Although occupied by the Germans in Aug. 1914, it was retaken by Foch on 11 Sept. Ludendorff considered it the principal objective of the fruitless German attack of 15 July 1918. It was damaged by the Germans in June 1940. it was the birthplace in 1749 of Nicolas Appert, 'père de la conserve', one of the first to investigate the problems of conservation of vegetables, etc.

entering the town by the northernmost of the two bridges, of 1771, across the Marne and a canal, we reach (r.) the **Cathedral**, mainly 13C, with an incongruous classical W. front added in 1634; its Romanesque N. tower is a relic of the 12C church. The nave, with an open triforium, was used to store fodder, and served as strables during the Revolutionary period. The high altar of 1686 by J. Hardouin-Mansart is modelled on that at St Peter's, Rome. Some of its glass is noteworthy, but apart from its N. transept, the building is otherwise unexceptional.

Continuing along the Rue de la Marne, the *Pl. du Maréchal Foch* is reached, on the S. side of which, entered from the Rue des Lombards, stands *St-Alpin*, a venerable building of 1136, preserving its main portal and most of its nave in its original form. The choir and towers are 15C; the S. transept and side portals are Renaissance; the glass in the S. aisle is 16C.

From behind the *Hôtel de Ville* (c. 1771) on the E. side of the Square, the *Museum* may be visited, containing miscellaneous archaeological, and dusty natural history collections; and among paintings, Landscapes by *Joos II de Momper*; *Perronneau*, Portrait of Jacques Cazotte (1719–92; author of 'Le Diable amoureux'): *J.-B. Liénard*, Female portrait; *Daubigny*, Park and château of St. Cloud; and works by *Courbet*, etc.

To the N. is the most imposing building in Châlons, **N.-D.-en-Vaux*, formerly collegiate, with its conspicuous spires. It was rebuilt in the 12C and retains the facade and S. portal of that epoch, the latter with a porch added in 1469. Of the four towers, that nearest the bridge retains its 13-14C leaden spire; its companion is a rebuilding, part of the restoration of 1852–70 by Lassus. The aisles preserve good 16C glass, and capitals of interest. Adjacent is the reconstructed Cloister ◊.

Some distance to the N.E. and S.E. respectively are *St-Loup* (15C), and *St-Jean Baptiste*, with a Romanesque nave and elaborate baptistry of c. 150v, both partially reconstructed in the late 19C.—To the S. of Notre-Dame the Rue Prieur-de-le-Marne leads to the unfinished *Porte Ste-Croix*, erected in 1770 for the passage of Marie Antoinette through Châlons, passing (r.) the *Préfecture*, in which Louis XVI and his family were briefly lodged on their ignominious return from Varennes in 1791. By turning r. just beyond the latter we may make our way back towards the cathedral by traversing the park known as *Le Jard*.

For roads from Châlons to **Troyes** and to *St-Dizier* and **Dijon**, see Rte 109.

The N3 leads N.E. to (6.5km) **L'Épine**, with a very fine buff-coloured Gothic **Church* of 1410–1600, attributed to Guichard Antoine, surmounted by two delicate openwork spires of unequal height. The transepts of this cathedral in miniature are flanked by polygonal turrets, and the apse is formed by five radiating chapels of c. 1520. The triple portal of the facade is richly sculptured, with spirited gargoyles. It contains a good carved Deposition, and organ, but nasty glass. The same architect was responsible for the nave capitals of *St Martin* at *Courtisol*, 4km distant, approached by forking r. at L'Épine.

8.5km. *Bar-le-Duc*, see Rte 108, lies 55km S.E. via (31km) *Nettancourt*, where Pétain had his H.Q. in June-Oct. 1916.—Just W. of *La Cheppe*, 8km N.W., on the Roman road to Reims, is the so-called *Attila's Camp*, an oval entrenchment, probably a Roman or perhaps Gallic oppidum.

The N3 continues N.E., at 15km passing 3km S. of **Valmy**, where on 20 Sept. 1792 Kellermann defeated the Prussians under the Duke of Brunswick, a battle in which Goethe, then in the Prussian camp entered the firing line to test the excitement of battle-fever. It was the first notable success of the Revolutionary army.

The A4 motorway is crossed and at 10km **Ste-Menehould** (pron. Menould; 5800 Menehildiens) is entered. The older town, known as the 'Château', occupies a rocky height overlooking the Aisne; the Gothic *Church* of 1280–1350 is of the local type. In the lower town is the *Hôtel de Ville* (1730) and restored *Maison de Poste*, where on 21 June 1791 Louis XVI and Marie Antoinette, on their attempted flight from France, were recognised by Drouet, the postmaster of Varennes (see below). Its pigs' trotters are reputed.

An ancient fortress, it has been repeatedly besieged, and was briefly occupied and sacked by the Germans in their attempt to encircle Verdun in Sept. 1916, and then became a French H.Q. during the years of static trench warfare on the Argonne front, a wooded plateau here forming a natural boundary between Champagne and Lorraine, to the E., where a line of rocky bluffs overlooks the wide plain of the Barre. The German Crown Prince hammered away for 16 months at the French lines without making much impression, and it was not until 26 Sept. 1918 that a surprise attack by the U.S. Army, between here and the Meuse, being protected on the r. by that river, and by the simultaneous advance of Gouraud's 4th French Army in E. Champagne, pushed the Germans back. The hills around *Montfaucon*, to the N. of *Clermont* (see below) were gained, and 8000 prisoners taken within hours, but German resistance did not weaken until the close of October. The 2nd U.S. Army had meanwhile advanced E. of the Meuse; the 1st Army steadily forced their way through the defences of the *Kriemhilde* system, and by 7 Nov. had reached the Meuse opposite Sedan; on the 11 Nov., just before the Armistice took effect, the important crossing at *Stenay* (see Rte 104) had been secured. 22 American divisions, numbering 630,000 men, were engaged in this battle; their casualties totalled 119,000. Nearly 20,000 prisoners were captured, and 847 guns.

Adalbert von Chamisso (1781–1838) was born near *Ante*, some 12km S., during the Revolution emigrating and becoming a Prussian citizen.

The road now traverses the wooded hills of the Argonne to (9km) *Les Islettes*, 8km N. of which is the 14C abbey-church of *Lachalade*, to enter (6km) *Clermont-en-Argonne*, situated on the slopes of a ridge (308m; views) near which during the 1914–18 war were installed two batteries, one commanded by Commandant Lebrun, the other by Lieut. Truman, who by a curious coincidence later became presidents of the French and American Republics, respectively. Its church retains two Renaissance portals, and the neighbouring chapel of *Ste-Anne*, a good 16C Entombment.

Varennes, 15km N., is the village where on 21 June 1791 Louis XVI and his entourage were arrested on their flight from the Tuileries. It contains a small museum, partly devoted to mine-warfare. Varennes stood some 3km behind the German front, and fell to the Americans on 26 Sept. 1918, the *Forêt de Hesse*, to the E., having given cover to Gen. Pershing's secret concentration earlier in the month. There are numerous war memorials in the vicinity, including the pillar on the *Butte de Montfaucon*, 10km N.E., and that on the *Butte de Vauquois*, 4km S.E., with its barbed-wire entanglements still visible; the D38 leads E. beyond the latter through *Avocourt* to *Côte 304*, *Esnes*, and the *Morte-Homme*, to *Verdun*.

The main road makes a circle to the N. before descending into the valley of the Meuse and entering (30km) **VERDUN** (24,100 Verdunois), an ancient fortress town, and an episcopal see since the 3C. Standing some 60km W. of Metz, which it faced after the debacle of 1871, it formed a bulwark of French defences, and it was after this that its forts and batteries were constructed. These crowned most of the surrounding hills, and certainly were more effective than the later Maginot Line. Its defence was one of the exploits of the

1914–18 War deemed 'heroic'; the fact that a million men were killed in the vicinity is conveniently scouted by the advocates of such decimating wars and their supporters.

Ancient *Virodunum* gave its name to the treaty of 843, which divided the empire of Charlemagne among his three grandsons, and laid the foundations of several states of modern Europe. To Charles le Chauve was assigned France; to Ludwig the Bavarian, Germany; and to Lothair, Italy and Lotharingia (in which Verdun was included). It later became one of the 'Three Bishoprics' (with Toul and Metz), which were united to France in 1352. In 1792, in defiance of its commandant Beaurepaire, who killed himself, it opened its gates to the Prussians, a pusillanimous action punished by the Revolutionary government by the execution of 35 citizens, including 14 women. Many British civilians were interned here during the Napoleonic wars. It was occupied by the Germans in 1870–73. Verdun was invested in Aug.-Sept. 1914, when it was defended by Gén. Sarrail and later formed the pivot of Joffre's manoeuvre in the battle of the Marne, and then remained in a salient. The *Battle of Verdun* began with Falkenhayn's offensive (21 Feb. 1916), bringing the Germans within 5km, in which a series of mass attacks was met by an equally desparate resistance: 'Ils ne passeront pas'. The casualties of the attackers numbered 300,000; those of the defenders, commanded by Pétain and Nivelle, hardly less. The siege of the shattered town was largely raised by the Franco-British assault on the Somme (1 July 1916) and the attacks of Mangin (24 Oct. and 15 Dec.), and Guillaumat recovered ground on both banks of the Meuse (20 Aug. 1917), but it was not entirely freed until Pershing's advance after the *Battle of St-Mihiel* (12 Sept. 1918), which opened the road to Metz. The task of clearing the battlefield was undertaken by the Society of Friends. Some 400,000 Frenchmen alone died here, 300,000 buried in unknown graves. It was comparatively slightly damaged in 1940, and 1944.

On approaching the town from the W., the huge *Citadel* is first passed (l.), on the site of the abbey of St-Vanne (founded 952). The surviving tower, used as a wireless station during the war, was a favourite target of German heavy artillery, but its thick walls—laid out by Vauban—and its deep vaults, in which several important conferences took place, afforded safe shelter. Several other gateways survive from earlier ramparts, including the *Porte Châtel* (W. of the cathedral), and the massive 17C *Porte Chaussée*, defending one of the main bridges.

From the latter, the short Rue Chaussée is followed. To the r., in the Rue St-Paul, are the *Palais de Justice* and *Sous-Préfecture*, established in the 18C buildings of the former abbey of St-Paul, beyond which is the drawbridge of *St-Paul* (1877), with a memorial by Rodin adjacent.—The Rue St-Pierre leads W. to the *Pl. Maginot*, where we climb l. up the Rue Belle-Vierge, in which (l.) is the **Museum** in the *Hôtel de la Princerie*, rebuilt in 1525 but retaining an earlier cloister.

The Archaeological section is of interest, with Gallo-Roman ceramics, etc., and a finely carved ivory Comb (12C); other rooms are devoted to arms and armour, and militaria; furniture and firebacks; sculpture; 'dragée'; etc., and a collection of tombstones is displayed in the courtyard.

The street leads to the nondescript **Cathedral**, Rhenish in character, which preserves some Romanesque portions at its E. end. The nave and transepts were remodelled in the 18C, when the present towers were added. The roof has been restored since its destruction in 1917. The crypt contains new capitals depicting military themes; the baldachin over the high altar is like that at Châlons. Adjacent is a small Gothic cloister, and the former *Bishop's Palace* (by Robert de Cotte).

Retracting our steps, by turning r. prior to the museum, one may descend past a colossal *Victory Monument* to gain the Rue Mazel, leading to another bridge over the Meuse, a short distance along the far bank of which stands the restored *Hôtel de Ville* (1623).

The **Battlefields of Verdun** extend in a semicircle to the N. of the town, on either side of the re-afforested heights through which flows the Meuse. At least eight villages were wiped off the map, and the only landmarks not obliterated are the concrete forts, well-signposted, and for most visitors to the area, a brief view of one of the most famous will be sufficient to give them a good general impression of the conditions in which the sanguinary contest was fought. It is recommended that either the **Fort de Vaux**, or that of **Douaumont** (7.5km and 8km to the N.E.) are visited, both conveniently approached by by-roads leading off the N3. On the road between the two is a (dead) *Lion Memorial*, and a *Memorial* and **Museum** devoted to the battle; while near the latter fort is the *Ossuaire de Douaumont*, a strange edifice dominated by a rocket-like tower, containing the bones of 100,000 men; another 15,000 lie in the adjacent cemetery. The casements and subterranean galleries of the forts, dripping with moisture, and the retractable gun-emplacements with their steel cupolas, should be seen, and a sombre hush seems still to lie over the whole area, however green and peaceful it may now appear, two-thirds of a century later.—The N.W. part of the battlefield, the monument of *Le Morte-Homme*, and *Côte 304* may be approached by the road skirting the W. bank of the Meuse; see the latter part of Rte 104.

For the road from Verdun to **Langres**; see Rte 110.

The N3 continues E., traversing the *Côtes de Meuse*, a long narrow range of wooded hills which line the E. bank of the river, separating it from the plain of the Woëvre, and the Briey basin, along which heights a series of forts was built in echelon from Verdun to Toul.

The Woëvre, a rolling fertile district interspersed with small lakes and streams for the most part tributaries of the Orne, which in turn flows into the Moselle, was the scene of constant artillery duels during 1914– 18, but the Germans failed to break through, although in 1916 they advanced as far as the foothills of the *Côtes de Meuse*.

VERDUN TO LUXEMBOURG (85km). The N3 is followed to the E. to (20km) *Étain*, there forking l., and after 7km r. onto the D106.—2.5km N.W. of this junction lies *Senon*, near which is a Gallo-Roman oppidum; the village has a restored church of 1536 of interest.—The road continues N.E. through an increasingly industrial district to the frontier at (42km) *Audun-le-Tiche* (Customs), an ironworking town as is *Esch-sur-Alzette*, across the border. For **Luxembourg** itself, 23km beyond, see *Blue Guide to Belgium and Luxembourg.*

Quitting Verdun, we follow the D903 S.E., after 16km crossing the A4 motorway.—25km. *Mars-la-Tour*. Between this village and *Gravelotte*, 11km E., with *Rezonville* as its centre, took place the inconclusive battle of 16 Aug. 1870, the field of which extended 10km N. to *St-Privat*.

In this conflict some 188,300 Germans, with 732 guns, were engaged, commanded by Prince Frederick Charles of Prussia and Von Moltke, against 112,800 French, with 500 guns, commanded by Marshal Bazaine, supported by Canrobert and Bourbaki. The Prussians lost over 20,000 men, the French at least 12,000, an incomplete and approximate figure.

The road now descends into the valley of the Moselle, passing the ancient fortified village of *Rozérieulles*, with a 15C church, to enter the W. suburbs of (14km) **Metz**; see Rte 111.

108   Sézanne to Nancy

182km (113 miles). N4. 65km **Vitry-le-François**—29km **St-Dizier**
N35. 24km **Bar-le-Duc**—N135. 15km *Ligny-en-Barrois*—N4.
26km **Toul**—23km **Nancy**.

Maps: IGN 21, 22, 23, or 103, 104; also 311, and 414. M 237,
241.

For *Sézanne*, see *Blue Guide Paris and Environs*, or Rte 19. Hence the
N4 leads due E. across the chalk plateau where the fiercest fighting
of the *Battle of the Marne* (7-9 Sept. 1914) took place, passing 4-5km
N. of *Gaye*, with a 13-16C church; *Pleurs*, Foch's H.Q. in early Sept.
1914, with an imposing 12C nave to its church; and *Corroy*, with a
church of 1070– 16C, to (21km) *Fère-Champenois* (also by-passed),
with a 13C church tower, ravaged by fires in 1756 (and 1940), briefly
defended against the Allies by Marmont and Mortier on 25 March
1814, and occupied on the 8-9 Sept. 1914 by the Germans.—The D5
bears N.E. to (36km) *Châlons-sur-Marne*; see Rte 107.

The N77 is crossed 18km further E. and 14km beyond, *Coole*, on a
Roman road, is traversed, 8km S. of which lies *Sompuis*, birthplace of
the   statesman   and   philosopher   Pierre-Paul   Royer-Collard
(1763– 1845).

14km. **Vitry-le-François** (18,800 Vitryats), designed on a regular
plan by the Bolognese engineer Marino, was laid out in 1545 by
François I to replace Vitry-en-Perthois (see below). The fortress,
dismantled in the late 19C, was Joffre's H.Q. in the early weeks of
the First World War, being retaken after the Battle of the Marne. It
was considerably damaged in the Second World War. In the town
centre is the *Pl. des Armes*, and *Notre-Dame*, begun in 1629. Here the
Marne-Rhine, and Marne-Saône canals meet the Canal Latéral of the
Marne.

Vitry-en-Perthois, or *Vitry-'le Brulé'*, 4km N.E., is notorious for the burning of its
church, in which 1300 citizens perished, by Louis VII in 1142, and it was partly in
expiation of this crime that he undertook the Second Crusade. It was sacked in
1420 by Jean de Luxembourg, and razed by Charles V in 1544. Its church retains
elements of the original building, with Renaissance additions.

20km. *Perthes*, an important centre during the Merovingian period,
has a 13C church, 3km S.E. of which is the 12C church of *Ambrières*,
rebuilt on a different site in 1935 owing to subsidence.

11km. **St-Dizier** (37,400 inhab.; sometimes designated 'Bragards', a
contraction of 'braves gars'), a flourishing industrial centre better
by-passed, and formerly a fortress, the siege of which in 1544
delayed the Emperor Charles V's march on Paris with his Spaniards.
It was ravaged by fire in 1775, after which *Notre-Dame*, with a 15C
facade, was reconstructed; *St-Martin de Gigny*, further E., has a 13C
portal.—There is a Veteran car museum in the vicinity of St-Dizier, at
Villiers-en-Lieu.

10km due N., in its forest, lie the remains of the *Abbaye de Trois-Fontaines*, with
the ruins of its 12C church, and several 18C dependencies.—5km beyond, at
Cheminon, is a 13-16C church, and relics of an abbey founded in 1100.

The N4 continues E. to (32km) *Ligny-en-Barrois* (see below), but the
more interesting route, which we follow, is the N25 turning N.E.
over the hills to (24km) *Bar-le-Duc*, the older part of which is ap-

proached by forking r. prior to descending into the valley.

BAR-LE-DUC (20,000 Barisiens), préfecture of the *Meuse*, and once the capital of the ancient duchy of *Bar*, comprises the *Ville-Haute* on the plateau to the S.E., commanding the *Ville-Basse*, astride the Or-nain in a narrow valley between vine-covered hills.

It was an important transport base during the 1914–18 war, being connected to Verdun by the so-called 'Voie Sacrée' (see below), and was attacked in early air-raids. Bar was the birthplace of Duc François de Guise (1519–63); Marshal Oudinot (1767–1847); Marshal Exelmans (1775–1852); and President Raymond Poincaré (1860–1934). James Stuart, 'the Old Pretender', retired here after the Treaty of Utrecht (1713), and thence made his unsuccessful descent on Scotland in 1715. It impressed Edmund Gosse, who visited the place in 1891. Its redcur-rant confiture is reputed.

At the upper end of the Ville Haute is the *Pl. St-Pierre*, with its substantial 15-18C houses, and 14C *Church*, which contains in its S. transept the **Tomb of René de Chalon*, Prince of Orange (killed at the siege of St-Dizier in 1544), surmounted, according to his wish, by a remarkable if gruesome sculpture of a decomposing corpse, carved by Ligier Richier, and known as 'Le Squelette'.—The Rue des Ducs-de-Bar descends past the *Pl. de la Fontaine* and the 14C *Tour de l'Horloge* to an esplanade (views) and the ducal *Château* (13C; remodelled in the 18C) now housing the **Museum**, including an ar-chaeological collection of interest, arms and armour, and paintings.

The Rue du Baile circles down to the lower town past (l.) the *Col-lège Gilles-de-Trèves* (1575) to (r.) the *Hôtel de Ville*, once the residence of Oudinot.—Some distance N. on the far bank of the river stands *Notre-Dame* (13-15C), with an 18C facade and tower. The pic-turesque mid 14C bridge near by was destroyed in 1944, and replac-ed.

Revigny, 17km N.W., with a 15-16C Gothic church, was the birthplace of André Maginot (1877–1932), the War Minister who sunk millions of francs of concrete along the Franco-German frontier in constructing what he considered would be an impregnable line of defence, which was merely side-stepped by the Germans in 1940.

BAR-LE-DUC TO VERDUN (43km). The N35, which is followed, here known as the 'Voie Sacrée', was the main channel of communication with Verdun (together with the railway constructed in 1916–18), for the transport of troops and supplies, and for the evacuation of the wounded during the interminable battles. During the spring of 1916 more than 2000 lorries shuttled along the road in each direction, with repairing units working day and night. It is embellished with special kilometric stones.—At 22km *Rembercourt-Sommaisne* lies 6km W., its church with a Gothic and Renaissance facade, restored, and a French military cemetery containing 12,000 killed at the battle of *La Vaux-Marie* (3km N.) in Sept. 1914.—From *Souilly*, 14km further N. on the N35, Pétain and Nivelle directed the defence of Verdun in 1916. It was also Pershing's H.Q. in 1918.—8km beyond, the A4 is crossed, and **Verdun** is entered 12km N.E.; see Rte 107.

The N135 is followed from Bar, leading S.E. to (16km) *Ligny-en-Barrois*, to regain the N4. **Ligny**, with manufacturers of optical in-struments, has a 12-17C *Church* in which lies the famous Marshal de Luxembourg (1628–95), a relic of whose ancestral castle is seen in the 15C *Tour Valéran*.

At 11.5km the l.-hand fork (D958) leads 12.5km to *Commercy* (see Rte 110) and continues across the rolling and wooded countryside of the *Parc Naturel de Lorraine* to *Pont-à-Mousson*, 40km further N.E.; see Rte 112.

The D984 is crossed at (12.5km) *Void*, ancient *Novigentum*, birth-place of Nicolas Cugnit (1725–1804), inventor of the first steam-carriage (1771). The district is also noted for its cream cheeses.—*Écrouves*, overlooked by a Romanesque church of c. 1200, is traversed at 19km.

4km. **TOUL** (17,800 Toulois), on the l. bank of the Moselle, ancient *Tullum*, and once a first-class fortress, was one of the 'Three Bishoprics' (with Verdun and Metz).

It was occupied by France in 1552 and the union was confirmed at the Treaty of Westphalia (1648). It capitulated in 1870, but was not seriously threatened in 1914–18 except by air raids and long-range bombardment. In 1918 it became an American Red Cross base. It suffered in 1940, when part of the former bishop's palace was destroyed and the cathedral damaged, and again in 1944. Toul was the birthplace of Marshal Gouvion-Saint-Cyr (1764–1830), and of Adm. de Rigny (1788–1835), who commanded French ships at Navarino (1827), where Codrington was the senior admiral. Hilaire Belloc did his military service here in 1891.

Towards the E. of the old fortified enciente stands **St-Étienne**, the former cathedral, with a late 15C Flamboyant *façade (its statues destroyed at the Revolution) between two towers 66m in height. The choir and transepts are 13C; the nave 14-15C; to the latter were added two Renaissance chapels in 1580, both near the transepts. The building, the crossing of which is under restoration, has no triforium or apse, but preserves some good glass (13-16C); the choir is unexceptional; the organ modern. Steps descend to the late 13C cloisters.

To the N. is the former 18C *Bishop's Palace*, restored to serve as the *Hôtel de Ville*.—In the town centre, by the *Pl. du Marché*, is *St-Gengoult* (13C), with Flamboyant cloisters.

Blénod-lès-Toul, 8km S.W., has a Gothic church of 1512 with original stained-glass.

The N4 now ascends to a plateau between the valleys of the Meurthe and Moselle, and runs due E. parallel to the A33, through the *Forêt de Haye*, later descending into (23km) **Nancy**; see Rte 113.

109 Reims to Dijon

282km (175 miles). N44. 44km **Châlons-sur-Marne**—32km *Vitry-le-François*—N4. 29km **St-Dizier**—N67. 31km *Joinville*—43km **Chaumont**—N19. 35km **Langres**—N74. 68km **Dijon**.

Maps: IGN 10, 22, 29, or 104, 108. M 241, 243.

An ALTERNATIVE ROUTE is that from Reims to *Troyes* (Rte 103B) or Châlons to *Troyes* (see below), thence continuing on Rte 122.

A motorway is under construction, bearing off the A4 between Reims and Châlons, which will drive S. to Troyes, and then run S. of the N19 towards Langres, meeting the N74 between Langres and Dijon.

The N44 drives S.E. from **Reims** (Rte 106), at 10km by-passing (l.) *Sillery*, famous for its champagne, and (l.) *Prunay*, reached in the final German offensive (15 July 1918), and crosses the Vesle and the Canal de l'Aisne à Marne to run parallel to the A4. To the S.W. rises the *Montagne de Reims*, on which stood the armoured observation-post 'du Sinai', from which Gén. Gouraud planned his offensive in 1918.—13km. To the E. is the military *Camp de Mourmelon*, established by Napoleon III in 1857. At 9km the motorway is cross-ed, which bears off to the E., and **Châlons-sur-Marne** is entered 8km beyond; see Rte 107.

CHÂLONS TO TROYES (77km). The N77 leads S.W., shortly forking l. to traverse the Champagne Sèche, and at 28km crossing the N4, beyond which, to the E., is the military *Camp de Mailly*.—*21.5km*. *Lhuître*, 8km E., preserves a large 12-14C church with good capitals and 16C glass.—*1.5km*. *Arcis-sur-Aube* (ancient Arciaca), the birthplace of Georges-Jacques Danton (1759– 94); 15-16C *St-Étienne*, damaged in 1940, preserves a good portal; the *Hôtel de Ville* occupies a 17C château. Here on 20-21 March 1814 Napoleon, with 14,000 men, held at bay Schwarzenberg's army of 90,000 (who set fire to the town), before retiring.—*26km*. *Pont-Ste-Marie* has a late Gothic and Renaissance church of in-terest, as is that at *Ste-Maure*, 4km N.W., likewise with glass attrib. to Linard Gontier.—*2km*. **Troyes**; see Rte 122.

Quitting Châlons, the N44 continues S.E., at 20km by-passing (5km S.E.) *St-Amand-sur-Fion*, with a good 12-14C church, and veers S. to (13km) *Vitry-le-François*; see Rte 108.

VITRY TO BAR-SUR-AUBE (66km). The RD396 leads S. to (22.5km) *Margerie-Harcourt*, with an early 13C church.—4km. The churches at *Chavanges* (5km E.) and *Lentilles*, 4km beyond, the latter half-timbered, are notable.—*7.5km*. *Rosnay l'Hôpital* preserves a huge 12C crypt below its church.—8km. **Brienne-le-Château** had a military school (suppressed in 1790) at which Napoleon studied from 1779– 84, leaving it at the age of 15. Near here, thirty years later (29 Jan. 1814), the Emperor gained a partial success over Blücher. To Brienne, severely damaged by his artillery, Napoleon left a legacy of a million francs, of which 400,000 were eventually paid off by Napoleon III in 1854. It was again seriously damaged in June 1940. Bourrienne, Pichegru, and Davoust were also cadets here. The late-Gothic *Church* has some good Renaissance glass; the *Château*, by Fontaine, dates from 1778; the reconstructed *Halles* from the 13C.—Relics of the 12C *Abbaye de Basse-Fontaine* lie 2.5km S.W.—The road now veers S.E. through *La Rothière*, scene of Napoleon's battle, to meet the N19, which is followed up the valley of the Aube to (24km) **Bar-sur-Aube**; see Rte 122.

From Vitry the N4 is followed S.E. to (29km) **St-Dizier**; see Rte 108.

ST-DIZIER TO BAR-SUR-AUBE (55km). The D384 leads S.W. past (9km) the ex-tensive *Lac du Der-Chantecoq* to (15km) *Montier-en-Der*, deriving its name from a monastery founded in 672 in the *Forêt le Der* by St Berchaire. The abbey-church, with a nave and aisles of 992, the choir of a local 13C type, was largely destroyed in June 1940, together with the village, but both have been well restored.—Ad-jacent *Ceffonds* has a 12-16C church with a Romanesque belfry and 16C glass, just beyond which the l.-hand fork leads to (13km) *Soulaines-Dhuys*, with a Flam-boyant and Renaissance church, and continues S., later descending into the valley at (18km) **Bar-sur-Aube**; see Rte 122.

ST-DIZIER TO COLOMBEY-LES-DEUX-ÉGLISES (56km). The D2 shortly forks l. off the D384 to (18km) **Wassy-sur-Blaise**, a small iron-working town. Here on Sunday 1 March 1562 an accident precipitated or at least was a contributing cause of the wars of religion, when the Duc de Guise, the governor, was atten-ding mass. He was disturbed by the psalm-singing of a Protestant congregation in a neighbouring barn, and in the ensuing quarrel was struck by a stone; 60 Pro-testants were forthwith massacred. It was sacked by the Leaguers in 1591. *Notre-Dame* (11-16C), which is some details recalls the cathedral of Langres, has a fine central tower and two sets of transepts; the W. portal (13C) is much mutilated. The *Hôtel de Ville* (1775) preserves a remarkable early 19C astronomical clock.—Continuing S., at 16km *Doulevant-le-Château* is traversed, and 5km beyond, *Cirey-sur-Blaise*, where the 17-18C château was the property of the Marquise du Châtelet (1709– 49), the 'belle Emilie' of Voltaire, who fitted it up for himself and his temperamental hostess, and made it his headquarters from

1734–49.—At 7km we turn r. to approach (9km) *Colombey-les-Deux-Églises* (see Rte 122), or alternatively, continue up the valley to meet the N19 after 13km, some 18km N.W. of *Chaumont*; see below.

From St-Dizier the l. bank of the Marne and Canal de la Marne à la Saône is followed to (31km) **Joinville**, birthplace of Jean, Sire de Joinville (1224–1317), the chronicler, and friend of Louis IX, and also associated with the family of Guise, who obtained the lordship in the 16C.

Here, on 31 Dec. 1584 a secret treaty was signed, in which the Leaguers and Philip II of Spain agreed to exclude Henri of Navarre from the succession to the throne, and thus added political bitterness to the religious animosity then agitating France. The Château in which this took place was sold to Philippe-Égalité d'Orléans at the Revolution and demolished. The title Prince de Joinville was borne by the third son (d. 1900) of Louis-Philippe.

To the N. of the town, in its park, stands the *Château du Grand-Jardin* (1546), built by Duc Claude I de Lorraine (first Duc de Guise) for his wife Antoinette de Bourbon. Two alabaster statues from the tomb of the former (1496–1550), by Domenique Florentin of Troyes, may be seen in the *Hôtel de Ville*. *Notre-Dame* preserves a 13C W. portal, and Renaissance S. portal; the *Hôpital Ste-Croix* and the *Chapelle Ste-Anne* contain relics of the Guise family.

JOINVILLE TO NEUFCHÂTEAU VIA GRAND (c. 51km). The D427 leads S.E. through *Poissons*, its church of 1528 with an attractive portal, and some 4km beyond (19km) *Germay* we fork l. to (8km) **Grand**, the successor of Gallo-Roman *Granum*, destroyed in the 5C, and itself sacked in 1585. It possessed an amphitheatre holding 20,000, and a mosaic pavement has been uncovered. Smaller objects may be seen in the local museum; excavations continue.—Bearing S.E., the main road is regained. Turning l. on reaching the N74 *Neufchâteau* is entered 10km N.E.; see Rte 110.

The N67 continues S. from Joinville, at 10km passing near (l.) *Jonjeaux*, with a 12C abbey church and 17C château.—13km. *Vignory*, with a *Church of 1049 preserving good sculpture; a ruined castle, and several old houses.

11km. **CHAUMONT** (*en-Bassigny*; 29,600 Chaumontais), préfecture of the *Haute-Marne*, but still 'a dull town' as described by Murray, stands on an abrupt and desolate plateau above the confluence of the Suize and the Marne. Unfortunately it has not yet been provided with a by-pass, although its long *Railway Viaduct*, 50m high, is imposing.

Chaumont (*Calvus Mons*), in turn the seat of the counts of Bassigny and of Champagne, was later a fortress. Here, on 1 March 1814, was concluded the treaty by which England, Austria, Russia, and Prussia formed an alliance against Napoleon. From 6 Sept. 1917 it was Gen. Pershing's G.H.Q. It was bombed in 1940, and in May 1944. The sculptor Edmé Bouchardon (1698–1762) was born here.

From the *Sq. du Boulingrin*, at the N. end of the older centre, the Rue Victoire de la Marne leads S. towards the *Hôtel de Ville* of 1790. The Rue St-Jean turns W. off this street to *St-Jean-Baptiste*, a 13-16C building with two towers and richly sculptured side portals. Its scruffy interior contains a pulpit carved by Jean-Baptiste, the father of Bouchardon, and a striking Entombment of 1471. The keystones in the choir, and organ-case, are notable.

The Rue du Palais leads W. to the *Palais de Justice*, on the site of the castle of the counts, of which the square 11-12C *Tour*

Hautefeuille survives, adjacent to which is a small basement *Museum* containing Gallo-Roman collections, and other miscellaneous exhibits.

CHAUMONT TO LUXEUIL (113km). The D417 leads E. and then veers S.E., at 19.5km passing 3.5km N. of *Nogent-en-Bassigny*, devoted to the manufacture of cutlery and surgical instruments, to meet (10.5km) the D74, where by turning r., and after 2km l., we approach (21km) *Bourbonne-les-Bains*, Roman *Aquae Borvonis*, a small spa with an early 13C church with a rebuilt tower, remains of a 15C castle, and an 18C *Military Hospital*.—The road traverses (3km) *Villars-St-Marcellin*, with a late 12C church, and 10km beyond, *Jonvelle*, near which a 2C Gallo-Roman villa was discovered in 1968.—11.5km. *Demangeville*, with castle ruins, is passed as the D417 continues E. to (27km) *Luxeuil-les-Bains*; see Rte 112.

The N19 continues S.E. from Chaumont along the upper valley of the Marne to (35km) **Langres**, on a height ahead, its walls rearing up above the road as we skirt its W. side to enter the town from the S.; see Rte 117.
    The N74 drives due S. through the *Citadel* of 1882.

3.5km. The D428 leads 23.5km S.W. past the *Haut-du-Sec* (516m), the highest point of the forested plateau of Langres, to *Auberive*; see Rte 122.—10km S.E. of this turning is the château of *Pailly*, a fine Renaissance building, with an earlier keep, etc.

8km. *Longeau* (see Rte 117), 11.5km beyond which *Montsaugeon*, on its hill, is by-passed (l.), its church with an 11C choir, good glass, and 17C boiseries.

A DETOUR may be made hence to the S. via adjacent *Isômes*, its 12C church with a square tower and octagonal spire of Burgundian type, *Cusey*, with castle ruins, and the high-lying village of *Sacquenay*, to (19km) **Fontaine-Française**, with a château of 1755, where Mme de Saint-Julien was hostess to Voltaire, Rousseau, Mme de Staël, and Mme Récamier. It was a French fief within the duchy of Burgundy, hence its name, and was the scene of a victory by Henri IV over the Leaguers in 1595.—The detour may be continued via the miniature château of *Beaumont-sur-Vingeanne* (c. 1724), the 15-17C *Château de Rosière*, some 5km N.E. of the latter, and *Mirabeau*, a decayed little town, once walled, with a 13-14C church of interest.—9km N.E. lies **Bèze**, birthplace of Dom Clément (1714–93), the historian, while Chanoine Kir, curé from 1910–24, produced the drink named after him. it was formerly dependent on an abbey, founded in the 7C, of which two towers remain; its monks used to cultivate the vineyard of Bèze at Chambertin (cf.) as early as 630. In the square is a facade of the 13C, while to the N. is the copious *Source of the Bèze*, giving instant birth to a river.—Hence one may work S.W. to (10km) *Beire-le-Châtel*, with a feudal castle, and 4km further S., *Arcelot*, with a château of 1761, to reach the D70 3km beyond, and 12km E. of *Dijon*.

17.5km. *Til-Châtel* has a striking Romanesque fortified *Church* with decorated pillar-capitals.—At *Lux*, 3.5km S.E., is an early 16C château; *Bèze* lies 5.5km beyond; see above.
    5.5km. Both *Gémeaux* (r.) and *Pichanges* (S.E.) have fortified churches.—13km. To the r. lie the white stone-quarries of *Asnières-lès-Dijon*.—**Dijon** itself lies 6.5km further S.; see Rte 123.

110   Verdun to Langres

164km (102 miles). D964. 53km *Commercy*—D964 and D164.
42km **Neufchâteau**—D74. 69km **Langres**.

Maps: IGN 10, 11, 23, 29, or 104; also 311. M 241.

For **Verdun**, see Rte 107. Hence the r. bank of the Meuse is followed,
at 7km passing below the A4 motorway, to (9km) *Génicourt-sur-
Meuse*. Its early 16C church has a fortified belfry, and contains
sculptures attrib. to Ligier Richier.

8km. To the l. stand the ruins of the *Fort de Troyon*, whose
resistance saved Verdun from encirclement in Sept. 1914.—A cliff is
skirted on entering (11km) **St-Mihiel** (5,600 Sammiellois), built on the
slopes of the *Côte de Meuse*, famous for the American victory of
Sept. 1918.

The town derives its name from a Benedictine abbey founded in 709, to which
was attached a celebrated school. Ligier Richier (1506–67), the sculptor, was
born here, and his descendants Gérard (1564–1600), Jean, Joseph, and Jacob
(16-17C) form the St-Mihiel school of sculptors, which flourished here. Nicolas
Cordier (1564–1612), whose sculptures are mainly in Rome, was a native, as
was Jean Bérain (1640–1711), the designer, and head of another distinguished
artistic family.

The capture of the town (including the bridge and station on the far bank) and
its adjacent forts by Von Strantz in Sept. 1914 made it the tip of a large wedge
penetrating the French front, severing their rail communications in this sector.
The front hence then ran N. to a point between *Les Éparges* and *Fresnes-en-
Woëvre*, and from just S. of St-Mihiel through *Aspremont*, and from there approx.
following the road E. to a point just N. of *Pont-à-Mousson*. In the *Battle of St-
Mihiel* (12-13 Sept. 1918), Pershing's 1st U.S. Army, with French Colonial troops,
attacked the flanks of this salient and reduced it, capturing 16,000 prisoners and
443 guns, and liberating an extensive area.

In the town centre stands 17C *St-Michel*, classical in style, with
medieval survivals, and containing a Swooning Virgin supported by
St John, by Ligier Richier, and a noteworthy organ-case.—Adjacent
are the 17-18C dependencies of the former abbey, much damaged in
1918, containing the *Library* of Card. de Retz, who wrote a large part
of his 'Memoires' here; also a small museum.—A short distance to the
E. stands *St-Étienne*, a 13-18C edifice in which florid Gothic
predominates, containing a remarkable *Entombment by Ligier
Richier, and an organ-loft of 1681.—Several Renaissance and 17-18C
houses also survive in streets to the N.W.

An EXCURSION may be made with ease via the D901 to *Vigneulles-lès-
Hattonchâtel*, 17km N.E., which was the point of juncture of the American forces
which destroyed the salient.—2km N. is the restored hill-top church of *Hattonchâtel*, containing a carved stone retable of 1523. The neighbouring château
(1927) is an attempt to reproduce its 15C predecessor dismantled in 1634. The
views are good.—Hence one may follow a forest road 11km N.W. along the
ridge, where a monument commemorates Lieut. Alain-Fournier (1886–22 Sept.
1914; author of 'Le Grand Meaulnes'), who was killed in action on this sector of
the front.—From Hattonchâtel one may turn due S. to visit (c. 16km) the *Butte de
Montsec*, surmounted by the circular colonnade of the *American Memorial*
(views over the reservoir of the Étang de Madine to the N.). Hence, via *Aspremont* and *Gironville*, one may regain the main route at (21km) *Commercy*; see
below.

Quitting St-Mihiel, the ruins of the *Fort du Camp-des-Romains* (l.) are
passed, erected on the site of a Roman camp and Gallic oppidum,

defended to the last by its French garrison in Sept. 1914. The forests
to the E. and N.E. were riddled with German defensive works.

18km. **Commercy** (8,000 Commerciens), a small industrial town
noted for its 'madeleines'. Its *Château* (1708), in which Voltaire and
the Marquise de Châtelet stayed as guests of King Stanislas of Poland
(cf. Nancy) has been restored since being burnt out in 1944.

The N4 is crossed 9km S.; *Toul* lies 23km to the E.; see Rte 108.

11km. *Vaucouleurs*, formerly a small fortress, of which some
towers remain on either side of the main street on the N. side of the
town, was the birthplace of Mme du Barry (1743–93).

Here in May 1428 Joan of Arc revealed to Robert de Baudricourt, the governor,
the message which her 'voices' had conveyed to her. On her second interview,
she prevailed upon him to present her to the Dauphin at Chinon, and here she
was equipped and provided with an escort of six men-at-arms by the inhabitants.

To the r. of the 18C church in the town centre, steps ascend to the *Chapelle
Castrale* (rebuilt in 1929 over a late 13C crypt), where Joan spent long hours
before the altar of N.-D.-des-Voûtes. Near by are relics of Baudricourt's castle,
and the *Porte de France*, from which in Feb. 1429 Joan set out on her momentous
journey.

Continuing up the valley of the Meuse, at 5km *Sepvigny* (l.), with a
14C fortified church, is by-passed to approach (20km) **Domrémy-la-
Pucelle**, where Jeanne d'Arc (1412–31; La Pucelle, the Maiden) was
born, with her oft-restored *Cottage* and a museum adjacent devoted
to her cult, while 2km to the S.W. a *Basilica* (1881) marks the site of
the *Bois Chénu*, where she first heard 'voices' urging her to drive the
English from France, etc. The village was exempted from taxation by
Charles VII, and remained immune until the Revolution.

Continuing S. we pass (l.) *Mont Julien*, said to have been used by
Julian the Apostate as a place of execution for criminals, and at 5km
traverse *Coussey*, with a 12-15C church, beyond which (r.) is the
hillside château of *Bourlémont* (13-16C) with a 19C keep.—*Grand*
(see p 594) lies c. 15km W.

6km. **Neufchâteau** (9,100 Neufchâtellois or Néocastriens) lies
above the confluence of the Meuse and the Mouzon, and is named
after a 'castellum', later a feudal castle, but little remains of its ancient fortifications. *St-Cristophe* (12-15C), N.E. of the bridge, contains a florid Gothic baptismal chapel and 17C boiseries. Turning N.
and then r. past the *Hôtel de Ville* in a Renaissance mansion formerly
belonging to the princesses of Lorraine, the *Pl. Jeanne-d'Arc*, with
17-18C houses, is crossed to 13C *St-Nicolas*, with a curious crypt
with double naves, and in the S. transept a group of the Anointing of
Christ; the organ-case is of 1695.

NEUFCHÂTEAU TO ÉPINAL VIA VITTEL (74km). The D164 leads S. up the
valley of the Mouzon, and then veers S.E. past (r. at 15km) *Beaufremont*, with a
ruined 12C castle, through (6.5km) *Bulgnéville*, where René I, later René of
Sicily, was taken prisoner in 1413 by his rival for the duchy of Lorraine, Count
Antoine de Vaudémont.—At *Saudaucourt*, 6km N., is a fortified 15C church and
17C château.—7.5km. **Contrexéville** (*Contre Aquas Villa*), 1km S., a small spa
made fashionable by king Stanislas, where a Russian chapel contains the tombs
of the Grand Duchess Wladimir and her son the Grand Duke Boris (d. 1920 and
1943, respectively); the parish church of 1779 preserves an 11C tower.—The
D164 leads S.E. via (15km) *Relanges*, with a Romanesque church of interest, to
Darney (4km beyond), with a *Hôtel de Ville* of 1725, in which a *Franco-
Czechoslovak Museum* commemorates the proclamation there by Poincaré of
the 'independence' of that country (30 June 1918).—From the Contrexéville
crossroads we continue E. to (5.5km) **Vittel** (6,400 Vittellois), now the most
flourishing spa in the region, whose waters were first exploited commercially in

1845. The *Établissement* lies in a park to the N., near which is the *Casino*, originally designed by Garnier, but entirely reconstructed in 1930, and the *Palais des Congrès* (1970); the bottling plant to the W. may be visited.—8.5km. The church at *Esley*, 2.5km S., preserves an interesting crypt.—The road continues E., by-passing (l.) at 19.5km *Dompaire*, beyond which is a monument commemorating Gén. Leclerc's division, which fought here in Sept. 1944.—19km. **Épinal**; see Rte 112.

NEUFCHÂTEAU TO CHAUMONT (56km). The 74 leads S.W., traversing the watershed separating the Meuse and Marne basins, to (34km) *Andelot-Blancheville*, where a treaty was concluded in 587 between Gontran de Bourgogne and Childebert of Austrasia, in which historians have detected a germ of the feudal system. It is dominated by the hill of *Montéclair*, surmounted by the ruins of a castle on the site of a Roman castrum. The church is 12C.—The road veers S., leaving to the N.W. the former abbey of *Sept-Fontaines*, founded in 1123, to (22km) *Chaumont*; see Rte 109.

NEUFCHÂTEAU TO BOURBONNE-LES-BAINS (53km). The D1 shortly forks l. to (11.5km) *Pompierre*, the church of which preserves a good Romanesque portal, beyond which (l.) stands the ruined hill-top fortress of *La Mothe*. Roman remains have been discovered at *Nijon*, 3km S.W. of the latter, suggesting it was the site of *Noviodunum* or *Noviomagus*.—14km. *Lamarche*, once a fortress, was the birthplace of Marshal Victor, Duc de Belluno (1764– 1841), and has a 12-13C church.—Continuing S.E., the road passes near (6km E.) the Benedictine convent of *Morizecourt* and the ruins of the *Abbaye de Flabémont*, founded 1132.—6km. *Isches*, with a church of interest, lies 2km E.—9km. *Bourbonne-les-Bains*; see p 595.

By turning S.W. from Lamarche along the D429, after 10km we pass 2.5km S. of the ruined abbey of *Morimond*, founded in 1115 by St Stephen, and afterwards one of the four 'daughters' of Citeaux (cf.).—After 10km, by turning r., and after 5km, l., the D74 is met 22km N.E. of *Langres*.

The D74 leads S. from Neufchâteau, skirting (26km) *Huilliécourt*, once fortified; *Vroncourt-la-Côte*, to the r. 2km beyond, was the birthplace of Louise Michel (1830– 1903), the revolutionary.—6km *Clefmont*, with a 9-11C priory.—2.5km. *Choiseul*, 6km E., was the cradle of that illustrious family.—At 7.5km we meet the D417 and after 14km pass (r.) the *Reservoir de Charmes* to approach **Langres** on its height 10km beyond; see Rte 117.

111 Metz to Strasbourg

A. Via St-Avold and Saverne

157km (97 miles). N3. 43km *St-Avold*—N56 and 61. 64km **Phalsbourg**—N4. 11km **Saverne**—39km **Strasbourg**.

Maps: IGN 11, 12, or 104; also 311. M 242

The A32 and A34 motorways may be followed by those requiring a rapid approach to Strasbourg.

METZ (118,500 Messins; 57,700 in 1851; 70,100 in 1946), préfecture of the *Moselle*, and long one of the most formidable fortresses in W. Europe, surrounded by a double ring of detached forts, is a lively town standing at the confluence of the Seille and Moselle, which flows to the W. of its centre, forming several islands linked by bridges, which gives it a character of its own. A quarter of narrow irregular streets surrounds its impressive cathedral, while its museum is also of particular interest.

Divodorum was the capital of the Mediomatrices, and Caesar described it as one of the oldest towns in Gaul. The Romans fortified it, and supplied the place with water by an imposing aqueduct, but it was sacked by the Huns in 451. On the death of Clovis it became the Austrasian capital (*Mettis*), and after the treaty of Verdun (843) that of Lotharingia or Lorraine. In the 10C Metz fell to Heinrich I of Germany ('the Fowler'), and in the 12C it became a free imperial town, and defended its liberties against both the bishops and dukes of Lorraine. In 1522 it passed to the French, and under the Due de Guise it successfully held out against the Emperor Charles V. Their possession was confirmed at the Peace of Westphalia (1648), and Metz, the capital of the 'Three Bishoprics' (with Toul and Verdun) remained in French hands for the next 223 years. It resisted two sieges in 1814–15, and the fortress preserved its title 'La Pucelle' until 1870, when Bazaine ignominiously surrendered it to the Prussians (27 Oct.), with 179,000 men, 6000 officers, and 1600 guns, after a feeble resistance of ten weeks. By the Treaty of Frankfurt, Metz, together with a large part of Lorraine, was annexed to Germany, which made it the principal bulwark of its W. frontier. From it, a crushing blow was aimed at the French advancing S.E. of the town in Aug. 1914, and a front of static trench-warfare was stabilised a few kilometres S.W. of its outer defences. Its forts were bombarded in 1915 and again in the closing weeks of the war, and after the American victory at St-Mihiel a great offensive was mounted to outflank it, but the Armistice intervened. Pétain's forces entered the Porte Serpenoise on 19 Nov. 1918, by which time—after 47 years of occupation, about half the population were German-speaking. It suffered from bombing in 1944, and most of its bridges were destroyed prior to its liberation on 19 Nov; its forts held out until 13 Dec.

Among natives were Marshal Fabert (1599–1662); Théodore de Neuholz (c. 1690–1756), King of Corsica; J.-B. Leprince (1733–81), the artist; the Comte de Custine (1740–93); Paul Verlaine (1844–96); the composers Ambroise Thomas (1811–96), and Gabriel Pierné (1863–1937); Gén. Kellermann (1770–1835); Pierre-Louis Roederer (1754–1835), politician and economist; Pierre-Louis de Lacretelle (1751–1824), politician and publicist; and the symbolist poet Gustave Kahn (1859–1936).

Rabelais lived here in 1546–7; Bossuet was for some time a dean of the chapter of Metz; and in 1776 Lafayette set out hence on his mission to America.

Convenient parking may be found below the *Esplanade* adjacent to the central *Pl. de la République*. To the S.W. of this square is the *Caserne du Génie*, built by the French in 1840, beyond which is the *Porte Serpenoise*, a mid 19C reconstruction of an older gateway, standing on the site of the S. ramparts of old Metz, now replaced by boulevards, the slate-roofed *Tour Camoufle* of which (1437) survives in a small square to the S.E.

To the W. of the Esplanade stands brick-built ***St-Pierre-aux-Nonnains**, under restoration or reconstruction, one of the oldest churches extant in France, part of an early 7C foundation on the site of a Roman basilica of c. 310.—A short distance further S. is a late 12C octagonal *Templar Church*; both buildings were previously engulfed by the mid 16C *Citadel*, dismantled in 1802.

The Esplanade itself commands a view over the Moselle valley and its islands below.—To the N. it is flanked by the imposing *Palais de Justice*, built in 1776 on the site of a mansion erected by Richard de la Pole (d. 1525), son of the 2nd Duke of Suffolk, and Elisabeth, Edward IV's sister, exiled from England as a pretender to the throne.

The Rue des Clercs leads N. to the *Pl. des Armes*, dominated by the ***Cathedral of St-Étienne**, a fine late Gothic edifice of blackened ochre-coloured stone, characterised by its height, lightness, and the development of window-space.

Erected in the mid 13th-16C on the site of the circular church of N.-D.-la-Ronde, it is essentially the work of the architect Pierre Perrat (d. 1440), although the nave dates from 1332, and the choir from 1510. Its W. front was unfortunately

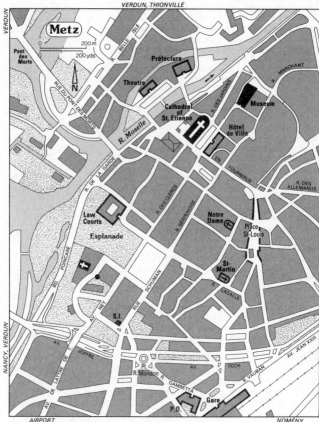

marred by Blondel's classical porch of 1764, demolished a century later to make way for the present portal in the Gothic taste (1903). Among statues here, that of Daniel was carved with the features of Wilhelm II, which caused later merriment, until his moustache was shaved off by the Germans in 1940.

It is notable for its wealth of flying buttresses, separating the great pointed windows, while above rises the *Tour de la Mutte* (88m), containing a bell of 1605. On its N.W. side is the *Tour du Chapitre* (1468), the portal below which contains reliefs of the Stoning of Stephen, and St Clement and the 'Graouly' (a fearsome dragon which terrorised Metz until captured and drowned by the saint; it is mentioned by Rabelais).

The cathedral is entered by the *Portal de la Vierge* (S.E. corner). The *Interior* is 123m long, 31m wide, and 42m high; indeed the unusual height of the clerestory arrests attention, being the highest in France after Beauvais and Amiens. A beautiful triforium runs round the entire church, the stained-glass of which is notable, particularly the rose at the W. end, designed by Hermann of Munster (d. 1392). Most of the monuments were destroyed at the Revolution. The nave incorporates part of the earlier church, the raised choir of which has become a side-chapel in the S. aisle; the foliated capitals and the bold slender pillars likewise belonged to the earlier building. The porphyry basin in the side aisle, once used as a font, is of Roman origin.

The transepts and raised open *Choir* are remarkable for their *Glass, the work of Valentine Bousch of Strasbourg (d. 1541) and (in the W. transept), some designed by Chagall. To the E. are remains of the old organ; the modern one is unprepossessing. The high altar was designed by Viollet-le-Duc. The large *Crypt* (fee), reproducing the plan of the apse, contains some unexceptional 'treasures' which survived the Revolution, but is of slight interest.

On the E. side of the square stands the *Hôtel de Ville*, erected by Blondel in 1766–81, once the rendez-vous of that bastion of French culture, the Academy of Metz, founded by Belle-Isle in 1760.

Passing this, the entrance to the ***Musée d'Art et d'Histoire'** is approached a short distance to the N., in the former convent-church of the *Petits-Carmes*, in the basement of which are Roman baths, discovered in the 1930s. The collections were entirely reformed in 1980, being partly exhibited in a series of dark but well-lit rooms and passages. The objects are seen to great advantage even if some perhaps do not merit the ingenuity shown in their display.

The *Archaeological section* contains several sepulchral monuments of interest; a well-carved banquet scene; tombs from a necropolis S. of Metz, and some leaden sarcophagi; an octagonal altar; note the baby owl on one cippus; part of a temple of Mithra from Sarrebourg; mosaics and relics of murals; examples of metalwork; terra sigilata; ceramics; and a damascened buckler, etc. Remarkable are the Visigothic stonecarvings from St-Pierre-aux-Nonnais (see above), and lintels; and part of a frieze from Arles (early 5C); also a bronze equestrian statue of Charlemagne. A series of Gothic window-carvings is notable.

The covered *Grange* or *Grenier de Chèvremont* of 1457 is traversed, in which a number of medieval wood and stone sculptures are displayed; note also the painted ceiling panels, floor tiles, fireplaces and firebacks, and Jewish tombstones.

A Renaissance staircase ascends to the **Musée des Beaux-Arts**. Notable are a 16C German Deposition, attrib. to *Hans Schüchlin*; a Dormition of the Virgin, attrib. to *Jan Polak*; *Van Mandyn*, St Christopher; Portraits by *Daniel Dumoustier*, *Jan van Bylert*, *Paul Moreelse*, *J.C. Cuyp*, and a good *anon.* 17C Male portrait; *Luca Giordano*, Plato; *School of Largillière*, Portrait of J. Hardouin-Mansart; *Claude Lefebvre*, Portrait of N.E. Olivier; *Nattier*, Portrait of a young female artist; *J.-F. Duplessis*, The Princesse de Lamballe; *Rigaud*, Card. Fleury; *J.-B. Leprince*, Scène champêtre; *Greuze*, Comte d'Angiviller; *Joseph Vernet*, Port of Marseille in 1754; *Gustave Moreau*, Equality before Death; and examples of the art of *Delacroix*.

Other sections are devoted to utensils and furniture; ceramics, including 'grès alsacienne de Betschdorf', and others of local manufacture, etc. A small collection of Militaria may be seen in the attic.

A short distance N.E. is mid 13C *Ste-Ségolène*, almost entirely rebuilt in the late 19C, near which is the *Hôtel St-Livier* (12C, and Gothic).—Further S. is the **Pl. St-Louis*, the W. side of which, with its tall houses built over arcades, is characteristic.

Some distance to the E. is *Ste-Eucaire* (12-15C; restored), and beyond, the *Porte des Allemands*, a restored gateway of a 13-15C castle, near which stood a medieval guest-house of the Teutonic knights.—S. of the latter stands *St-Maximin* (12-13C); while to the W. of the Pl. St-Louis are the churches of *Notre-Dame* (1665–1740), and to the S.W., *St-Martin*, preserving its 13C nave.

From the W. side of the cathedral one may descend to approach an island in the Moselle, where the *Pl. de la Comédie* is flanked by the restored *Théâtre* of 1738; to the N. is the 18C *Préfecture*, restored after a fire in 1803.—Crossing an arm of the river behind the latter and turning l., we reach *St-Vincent* (1248–1376), with a Renaissance facade and mid 18C restorations.—Further W. are the ruins of the late 19C Protestant garrison church; to the N. is *St-Clément* (1693), Gothic is spite of its late date.—S.W. of the former is the *Pont des*

Morts of 13 arches over the Moselle. By turning l. along the Rue du Pont des Morts, crossing another arm of the river, and turning r. uphill, one may regain the Palais de Justice and the Esplanade.

Quitting Metz, the N3 leads E., S. of and parallel to the A32 motorway to (43km) **St-Avold** (17,000 inhab.), 8km N. of which is the extensive industrial complex of *Carling-Merlebach*, the road to which shortly passes (r.) the *American Cemetery of Lorraine* (16,000 dead in the fighting of 1944–45).

ST-AVOLD TO SAARBRÜCKEN (25km). The N3 bears N.E. via (6km) *Hombourg-Haut*, with a handsome Gothic church, once collegiate, and relics of the town's former fortifications, to traverse industrial *Forbach* and *Stiring-Wendel* (French and German Customs), to the E. of which, on the heights of *Spicheren*, was fought the first engagement of the Franco-Prussian War (Aug. 1870).

The N56 leads E.—At 6km the D910 forks l.; see Rte 111B.

Forking r., after 13km the N74 is crossed at *Puttelange*, and 10km further S.E. we turn r. at *Sarralbe*, an ancient town with important salt-mines, and once a fief of the bishops of Metz.—9km. *Sarre-Union*.

A by-road (D8 and D919) turns E. to traverse the *Parc Naturel des Vosges du Nord* (see p 608) to (35km) *Ingwiller*, 3.5km prior to which a l.-hand turning leads 4km up to the feudal castle of *Lichtenberg* (views).—From Ingwiller one may join the D421 via (7km) *Bouxwiller*, once fortified, or continue E. to (25km) **Haguenau**; see Rte 111B.

The N61 leads S.E. from Sarre-Union to (26km) *Phalsbourg*, for which, and the road beyond via *Saverne* to **Strasbourg**, see Rte 114A.

B.   Via St-Avold, Bitche, Wissembourg, and Haguenau

211km (131 miles). N3. 43km *St-Avold*—D910. 27km **Sarreguemines**—N62. 34km *Bitche*—D35 and D3. 47km **Wissembourg**—D263B and D263. 32km **Haguenau**—N63. 28km **Strasbourg**.

Maps: IGN 11, 12, or 104; also 311. M 242.

From the junction 6km E. of *St-Avold* the D910 leads 21km E. to **Sarreguemines** (25,200 Sarregueminois), an industrial frontier town at the confluence of the Sarre and Blies, with ceramic factories, etc.—There is a striking Transitional church at *Zetting*, on the Sarre 7km E.

Immediately E. of the town we fork r. onto the N62 and traverse pleasant country to (34km) **Bitche** (7,800 inhab.), fortified by Vauban in 1679, the citadel of which, with a garrison of 300, held the enemy at bay throughout the Franco-Prussian War. It was the birthplace of Gén. Bizot (1795–1855), killed at Sebastopol.

BITCHE TO HAGUENAU (40km). The N62 turns S.E. through the *Parc Naturel des Vosges du Nord* (see p 608) passing (l.) the ruins of the castles of *Falkenstein*, and (l.) *Wasenbourg*, on their heights, before by-passing (23km) *Niederbronn-les-Bains*, to approach *Haguenau*, 27km beyond; see below.

The D35 winds through the wooded hills of the northern Vosges, later passing the ruins of the castles of *Lutzelhardt*, *Wasigenstein*,

Obersteinbach, and *Froensbourg*. At 29km a l.-hand turning leads shortly to the castle of **Fleckenstein* (13C; destroyed in 1680).—3.5km. *Lembach*.

Hence the D27 leads 24km S. to Haguenau via (9km) *Woerth*, just W. of which took place the sanguinary *Battle of Froeschwiller* (5 Aug. 1870), in which Mac-Mahon's army was defeated by a superior force of Prussians. Each side suffered serious losses—between 10, 500– 11,000 killed and wounded—but some 9000 French prisoners were taken in addition.

From Lembach the D3 climbs E. to cross the wooded *Col du Pigeonnier* (432m) before descending to (14.5km) **Wissembourg** (7,300 inhab.), an attractive and ancient frontier town on the Lauter (Customs), which grew up round a Benedictine abbey of the 7C, and which became a free imperial city in 1255.

Two memorable battles were fought here: in 1793, when the 'Weissenburg Lines' were forced in turn by the Allies and the French; and in 1870, when the destruction of part of MacMahon's army, commanded by Gén. Douay (who was killed), opened the door for the Prussian invasion. It also suffered some damage in the Second World War.

To the W. of the old centre stands the abbey-church of *St-Pierre-et-St-Paul*, a fine Gothic edifice with an octagonal tower flanked by graceful turrets, and a Romanesque tower. It contains some interesting frescoes, 13-15C glass, and relics of its cloister.—The adjacent *Sous-Préfecture* is in a building of 1784, while in the parallel street to the S. is the *Hôpital Stanislas*, residence from 1720 of the exiled king of Poland (cf. Nancy), who here received the Duc d'Antin, sent by Louis XV to request his daughter Marie Leczinska's hand is marriage (1725). On the N. side of the town, near the Promenade des Ramparts, is the small *Musée Westercamp*, in a house of 1599.

WISSEMBOURG TO STRASBOURG VIA LAUTERBOURG (81km). The D3 continues E., skirting the frontier—to the N. of which extends the *Bienwald*—to (19km) *Lauterbourg*, at the N.E. corner of France, near the confluence of the Lauter and the Rhine.—**Karlsruhe** lies some 20km N.E. on the r. bank of the Rhine.—Here the N63 leads S.W. to (13km) *Seltz*, Roman *Saletio*, later a country seat of the Frankish kings.—Some 14km beyond, *Sessenheim* is by-passed, first visited by Goethe in 1770, where he met Frederike Brion.—The road continues S.W., roughly parallel to the Rhine, traversing industrial districts as it approaches the outskirts of (35km) **Strasbourg**.

The D263B leads S. from Wissembourg, at 3.5km passing a l.-hand turning for **Oberseebach*, a charming little Alsatian village, from which one may regain the main road to the S.W., on the far side of which lies *Hunspach*, similar in character.

The road shortly traverses the extensive *Forêt de Haguenau* to enter **Haguenau** itself (29,700 Haguenoviens), a busy commercial town, its fortifications being reduced in 1677 and entirely dismantled in 1871. It suffered serious damage before its liberation in 1945. Here in 1193 Richard I, Coeur-de-Lion, when a prisoner of the Emperor Heinrich VI, appeared before a Diet convened at the old palace of Frederick Barbarossa, which has disappeared. The place was visited by Longfellow c. 1830, who wrote 'The Cobbler of Haguenau'.

At the N. end of the town stands *St-Nicolas* (13-15C), containing a stone Entombment in high relief of 1420; *St-Georges*, to the W. of the central *Pl. d'Armes*, was originally built in 1137 by the Emperor Conrad II. Two local museums lie a short distance to the S.E.

Bischwiller, 8km S.E. of Haguenau, of slight interest in itself, derives its name from a 12C residence of the bishops of Strasbourg; in 1673 it was encircled by a double line of walls, demolished in 1706.

The main road leads S.W. through (11km) *Brumath* at approach **Strasbourg,** 17km further S.; see Rte 115.

112 Metz to Besançon, via Nancy and Épinal

254km (157 miles). N57. 29km **Pont-à-Mousson**—28km **Nancy** —69km **Épinal**—25km **Remiremont**—32km **Luxeuil**—28km **Vesoul**—43km **Besançon**.

Maps: IGN 11, 23, 30, or 104, 109; also 311. M 242, 243.

The A31 motorway provides a rapid route to a point some 10km S. of Nancy, which it by-passes to the W.

For **Metz**, see Rte 111A.

METZ TO NANCY VIA NOMÉNY (58km). The D913 drives due S., passing several old forts on approaching (13.5km) *Verny*, 4km S.W. of which, at *Sillegny*, is a 13-14C church with frescoes of 1540, which survived the severe fighting in its vicinity in 1944.—14.5km. *Nomény* likewise was badly damaged, and its church was reconstructed after being destroyed in 1914. It was the birthplace of Louise de Vaudémont (1553–1601; wife of Henri III), and of the Duc de Mercoeur (1558–1602).—The road makes a swing to the E. and then bears S., after 20km passing (l.) the *Grand-Mont d'Armance* (410m; views) before entering (10 km) **Nancy**.

The N57 bears S.W., parallel to the Moselle, passing under the A31 and at 10km the *Roman Aqueduct* or *Arches de Jouy.—Pagny-sur-Moselle*, on the far bank, is later passed, dominated by the ruined 13C castle of *Prény*, with a pentagonal keep, once a residence of the dukes of Lorraine.

19km. **Pont-à-Mousson** (15,700 Mussipontains), an industrial town on both banks of the Moselle, dates from the 9C.

It was the birthplace of Margaret d'Anjou (1430–82), wife of Henry VI of England, and of Marshal Duroc (1772–1813), who died on the field of Bautzen. It was occupied by the Germans in Aug. 1914, and retaken by the French that Sept., but it was never more than 5km from the firing-line. It was seriously damaged in Sept. 1944.

On the E. bank., N. of the bridge, are the imposing buildings of the ***Couvent des Prémontrés** (1609; reconstructed in 1711), restored since set alight in 1944, to accommodate a Cultural Centre.

Opposite the bridge-head stands *St-Martin*, with two dissimilar towers, containing a late 15C Entombment. On the N. side of the *Pl. Duroc*, on the l. bank, is the *Hôtel de Ville* (1788; by Richard Mique), behind which is *St-Laurent*, of various dates, containing a Christ bearing the Cross, perhaps by Ligier Richier, a 16C triptych, and 15C Pietà.—On the W. side of the square stand the restored late 16C 'House of the Seven Deadly Sins', together with another arcaded mansion preserving a Renaissance turret.

To the S.E. rises a conical hill once crowned by a Roman camp (*Mussum*) and later by a fortified village with a 13C castle, a French viewpoint during the First World War; to the N.W. is the *Bois-le-Prêtre*, bitterly contested in 1914–15.

The road now skirts the l. bank of the Moselle, traversing the industrial district of *Blénod*, with its 'centrale thermique', to (7km) *Dieulouard*, taking its name from its ancient castle of 'Dieu-la-Garde', with a 15C church with a curous sub-choir. On an island to the N.E. stood the Roman station of *Scarpone*, where Jovinus defeated the Alemanni in 366, beyond which rises *Mont Ste-Geneviève*, where the German advance on Nancy was checked on 7 Sept. 1914.

12km. *Pompey*, an industrial town, whose furnaces provided the girders for the Eiffel Tower, has a 14C church and ruins of a chapel on the spot where St Eucarius, bishop of Toul, and 2000 Christians are said to have been martyred in 362; the saint's tomb lies in the 13C church of *Liverdun*, picturesquely sited on a promontory 5.5km W.—Adjacent *Frouard* and *Champigneulles*, famous for its beer, are traversed, to enter the N. suburbs of (9km) **Nancy**; see Rte 113.

NANCY TO NEUFCHÂTEAU (59km). The D974 leads S.W., traversing industrial *Neuves-Maisons*, to cross the Moselle at (12km) *Pont-St-Vincent*, with a gateway of 1567, a 16C church, and several 15-16C houses.—2km. *Bainville-sur-Madon*, with the family home of Jacques Callot (cf. Nancy), beyond which we veer W. through woods before turning S.W. again, at 37.5km by-passing (r.) *Soulosse*, Gallo-Roman *Solicia*, entering **Neufchâteau** 7.5km beyond; see Rte 110.

The N57 leads S. from Nancy, at 8km passing (l.)—after crossing the A33 motorway—the imposing *Château de Fléville* (1533), built on the site of an earlier fortress, and after 6.5km reaches the *Pont de Flavigny* over the Moselle.

AN ALTERNATIVE ROUTE VIA MIRECOURT TO ÉPINAL (66.5km). The D913 here forks r.—At (14km) *Tantonville*, the attractive ***Château of Haroué** lies 3.5km E., built in 1720 by Boffrand for the Prince de Beauvau-Craon on the site of the former castle in which Marshal Bassompierre (1579–1646) was born. Surrounded by a carp-filled moat, it contains furniture, Gobelins tapestries, and paintings of interest, including portraits by Van Loo, Gérard, Rigaud, etc.—Jean-François de Saint-Lambert (1716–1803) was born at adjacent *Affracourt*.—*Vézelise*, 5km W. of this junction, was the capital of the countship of *Vaudémont*, and has a late 15C church containing good glass, a *Halles* of 1599, and several 16-18C houses.—6.5km S.W. of Vézelise lies *Thorey-Lyautey*, where Marshal Lyautey (1854–1934) died in his château, which preserves mementoes of his campaigns.—The main road may be regained by turning E. below the horseshoe ridge of *La Colline Inspirée* (541m), so-called in the novel by Maurice Barrès (1913). At its N. end is an image-crowned tower (views) and the basilica of *N.-D.-de-Sion*, rebuilt in 1741 and enlarged in 1853, replacing a 10C church on this Gallo-Roman site of *Semita* or *Seuntun*.—At the S.W. end of the ridge is *Vaudémont* ('Mount of Woden'), with the ruins of an 11C castle of the counts.—19.5km. (S. of Tantonville), **Mirecourt** (8,500 Mircurtiens), ancient *Mercuri Curtis*, derives its name from the Gallo-Roman cult. The manufacture of musical instruments has long flourished here, and more so since 1970 when a national school 'de lutherie' (stringed instruments) was established. The *Halles* date from 1617; the *Hôtel de Ville* preserves a Renaissance portal; the 13-16C church is clumsy.—*Vittel* (see Rte 110) lies 23km S.W.—Forking S.E. and at 14km traversing *Dompaire*, the D166 veers E. to enter **Épinal** 19km beyond; see below.

The N57 leads S.E., following the valley of the Moselle through *Flavigny*, preserving a 15C chapel and 12C tower of a Benedictine convent, to (15.5km) *Bayon*—a small wine-growing village on the far bank—where on 24 Aug. 1914 Dubail and Castelnau checked the German invasion from the E.

14km. **Charmes** (5,500 Carpiniens or Charmésiens), a small industrial town on the l. bank of the Moselle, which suffered severely in 1944, when set alight by the retreating Germans. Maurice Barrès

(1862– 1923; see above) was born and is buried here, while *Chamagne*, 4.5km N. on the r. bank, was the birthplace of Claude Gellée (or Lorrain; 1600– 82), the landscape painter. The late 15C *Church* at Charmes was damaged in 1944, but contains sculptures of interest, while the so-called *Maison des Loups* (16C), which once belonged to Bassompierre, is near by. On a hill to the S. stands a *Monument 'de la Victoire de Lorraine'*.

CHARMES TO ST-DIÉ (59km). The D32 follows the r. bank of the river for 5.5km before veering E. at *Portieux*, with glass-works founded in 1705, to (24.5km) *Rambervillers*, in the high valley of the Mortagne, a former stronghold of the bishops of Metz. Here 200 National Guardsmen made a stand against 2000 Prussians in 1870. The *Hôtel de Ville* (1581) has a quaint inscription.—At *Autrey*, 7km S.E., is the Renaissance church of a former Augustinian abbey, from which one may regain the main route to the N.E.—The D32 continues E., traversing forests, and from the *Col du Haut du Bois* (470m) descends to meet at 23km the N59 6km N.W. of *St-Dié*; see Rte 114B.

At 10km. S. of Charmes, *Châtel-sur-Moselle*, on the far bank, is passed, an ancient little town, damaged in 1944, preserving remains of its fortifications and a 15C church with a graceful spire.

15km. **ÉPINAL** (41,000 Spinaliens), préfecture of the *Vosges* (see below), lies on both banks of the Moselle and on the island site formed by the river here, and was once a first-class fortress. It is attractively situated in the centre of a thickly forested district, and although savaged in the last war, preserves much of its character.

Épinal (*Spinalium*) grew up around a church founded in 980 by Thierry I, bishop of Metz, whose successors ruled the town until 1444. It then passed to Charles VII, and in 1466 to the duchy of Lorraine, which was incorporated in France three centuries later. The chapter of Noble Ladies of Épinal, members of which had to show sixteen quarterings, owned no superior but the Pope (cf. Remiremont). It fell to the Prussians in 1870, after which war its detached forts were linked with those of Toul and Belfort. It was damaged in June 1940, by bombing in May 1944, and by deliberate destruction by the Germans when retreating in that Sept.

It was long noted for the manufacture of popular images and figures ('imagerie') and was the birthplace of the sociologist Émile Durkheim (1858– 1917), and H. Daniel-Rops (1901– 65), the Catholic historian.

Among gardens at the S. prow of the island stands the ***Musée departmental des Vosges et musée international de l'Imagerie**, of more interest than many.

The GROUND FLOOR is devoted to local *Archaeological collections*, funerary steles, Gallo-Roman and medieval sculpture, and the tomb of De Lenoncourt and his wife (1363); also a section of furniture and handicraft. Among the paintings on the FIRST FLOOR are: *Nicolas Bellot*, Perspective view of Épinal in 1626; *Rembrandt*, Female portrait (1661); *Paul Bril*, two Landscapes; *anon. 17C Flemish* Skirmish in woods; *Georges de la Tour*, Job mocked by his wife, and The hurdy-gurdy player; *Van Cleeve*, Holy Family; *anon. late 16C*, Woman with lapdog; *Van Goyen*, Landscape; *Brueghel de Velours*, Winter, and Summer; *Van Balen*, Diana; *Louis Vigée*, Portrait of the Marquis de Boisbaudon; *Chinnery* (?), Young Girl; *J. Heinsius*, Portraits of a Lady, and Gentleman; *Bonington*, Male portrait; attrib. *Cosway*, Miss Fitzherbert; and examples of the art of *Panini, Guardi, Largillière, Carmontelle, J.-B. Leprince, Boilly, Drouais, J.-B. Mallet, Boucher, Watteau, Hubert Robert, Claude Joseph Vernet, Vestier, Joseph Boze, L.-N. de Lespinasse*, and *Picasso*.

Also collections of ***Stained-glass** (1543) from the abbey of Autrey; tobacco-pipes; arms; and faïences d'Épinal (1759– 1840). A separate section is devoted to **Imagerie**, which is subject to periodic re-arrangement, with extensive and well-

THEODOLINA, Reine des Amazones.

An example of the 'imagerie' of Épinal

displayed collections of wood-blocks, naive paintings on glass, paperweights, icons, and a variety of folk art.

Crossing to the r. or E. bank, the *Préfecture* is passed (r.) and the second l.-hand turning leads to ***St-Maurice**, a curious mixture of white and red sandstone, Romanesque and Gothic (11-14C), 'built anyhow, in twenty styles' as Belloc remarked. It preserves an original transept with striking exterior turrets, and the 14C pentagonal apse and Romanesque tower at the W. end are noteworthy. The deep N. portal, or 'des Bourgeois' (the 'citizens' porch') to distinguish it from that of the Noble Ladies (see above), opening onto the cloister to the S., is the main entrance; the interior contains several good carvings and paintings.

From the apse one may turn E. to ascend to the *Parc du Château*, with castle ruins, commanding a good view over the town.—To the N., beyond the island, is the *Library* (W. bank), with some illuminated MSS and incunables of interest; while one may cross to the E. bank to visit the manufactury of *Imagerie Pellerin*, founded in 1796 by J. C. Pellerin (1756–1836), with perpetuates the tradition. (Some 17 million prints were produced here during the Second Empire alone.)

The department is named after the mountain range of the **Vosges** (the Roman *Sylva Vosagus*; and the German *Wasgenwald*), consisting of a long granite and sandstone massif separated from the Jura by the Belfort gap, extending thence to the neighbourhood of Bingen, on the Rhine, its total length being some 275km, and its greatest width (at the two extremities) 65-70km. Geologically a continuation of the Black Forest, it presents its main escarpment to the Rhine, sloping more gently to the W. The granite *Hautes-Vosges* extend from Belfort to the valley of the Bruche, S.W. of Strasbourg; thence the sandstone *Basse-Vosges* continue the range to Saverne, beyond which the N. *Vosges*, covered with heath and brushwood, extends to the Rhine in Germany. The highest of the summits, the *Grand Ballon (de Guebwiller*, 1424m) and *Le Hohneck* (1362m) are in the S. part of the range, which from 1871 to 1918 formed the boundary between France and Germany, and which during the First World War constituted the 'extreme right' of the Allied line. The are characterised by splendid pine forests on their lower slopes, above which are open pastures. The rainfall is heavy (130–150cm), mainly in spring. On the E. side the vine ripens even at the height of 400m. Hilaire Belloc describes a journey on foot through the Hautes-Vosges in 'Path to Rome'.

ÉPINAL TO ST-DIÉ (50km). The N420 leads N.E. to (15km) *Girecourt-sur Durbion*, there turning E. to (12km) *Bruyères*, a small industrial town and former fortress, sited among wooded hills and seriously damaged in 1944. It was the birthplace of the artist and designer Jean Lurçat (1892–1966).—*Champ-le-Duc*, 2km S., possesses an archaic Romanesque church of some interest, whence the D423 leads due S.E. up the narrow *Valley des Granges* to (23km) *Gerardmer*; see below.—The N420 turns N.E. again up a wooded valley, later passing a *Monument to the Resistance* at the *Col de Haut-Jacques* (606m) before descending into the valley of the Meurthe and (25km) **St-Dié**; see Rte 114B.

The D434 leads direct to *Plombières*, 29km due S. (see below), but we follow the N57 up the valley, at 11.5km traversing **Arches**, with a famous paper-mill, founded in 1469, which produced when Beaumarchais was its proprietor (from 1779) the paper for the two Kehl editions of the works of Voltaire; it now manufacturers de luxe papers and special limited makings.

Further on, to the l, rises the *Tête des Cuveaux* (783m; views).—11.5km. *St-Nabord*, above which is the moraine of the former glacier of the Moselle. The N57 bears r. 2km beyond.—2km to the l. lies **Remiremont** (10,900 Romarimontains), a small industrial town among wooded hills below the confluence of the Moselle and the Moselotte, and a centre of communications in the S. Vosges.

It grew round a monastery and Benedictine nunnery founded by St Romaric (Romery) in the 7C. The latter was afterwards replaced by a chapter of noble canonesses (Dames de Remiremont), numbering fifty, who were admitted only after giving proof of two centuries of unblemished noble ancestry on both sides (cf. Épinal, and Baume-les-Dames, etc). These canonesses held the title of countess, and several times took the field, notably in the 'War of the Escutcheons' (or 'des Panonceaux'; 1566). In later centuries the vows of the order were temporary, and although for some time protected by the dukes of Lorraine, it was suppressed at the Revolution. The town, which has suffered from fires at various dates, is noted for its trout and its gingerbread-nuts, known as 'chanoinesses'. It was the home of Denys in Charles Reade's 'The Cloister and the Hearth'.

To the S. of the arcaded Grande Rue (or Rue Charles de Gaulle), in which No. 70 houses a small *Museum*, stands the former *Abbey-Church*, with a granite tower of 1800 surmounted by a bulbous spire. The curious 10-11C crypt beneath the choir has pillars with cubical capitals, and several tombs and incriptions, but the buildings are otherwise of slight interest. Adjacent is the former *Abbesses' Palace*, rebuilt in 1752, now tenanted by local government offices, *Hôtel de Ville*, etc. Another small *Museum* devoted to the Dames and local history is a few minutes' walk to the W., at 12 Rue Gén.-Humbert.

To the N.E., above the suburb of *St-Étienne*, on *St-Mont* (809m) are the ruins of the 7C monastery, the *Pont des Fées*, bridging a Gallo-Roman ditch, the *Pierre Kerlinkin* (a red sandstone monolith), and other antiquities.

REMIREMONT TO COLMAR VIA GÉRARDMER AND THE COL DE LA SCHLUCHT (80km). The D417 leads N.E. to the junction at (8km) *Le Syndicat*, where the D43 turns r. for *Cornimont*; see below.—The l.-hand turning ascends the valley of the Cleurie to (10km) *Le Tholy* (in the valley to the N.W. of which falls the *Cascade de Tendon*), and veers E. to skirt the N. shore of the *Lac de Gérardmer* (views) for the whole of its length to (10km) **Gérardmer** itself (665m; *pron.* Gérarmé; 9,600 Géromois), noted for its cheeses ('Géromés'). Its name is derived from Gérard d'Alsace, first Duc de Lorraine, who built a keep here in 1070. The climate is bracing but chilly, but although it is a flourishing and beautifully sited summer and winter resort, the town itself has lost much of its character since deliberately devastated and burnt by the Germans on their retreat (Nov. 1944), since when it has been rebuilt on a new plan.

It is also approached from Le Syndicat (see above) by a road circling to the S. via *Vagney*, once a fief of the abbey and chapter of Remiremont, and with silver-mines worked in the 13C, beyond which the road ascends the wooded valley to (19km) *Cornimont*, a small industrial town, damaged in 1944, over-looked by the *Grand Ventron* (1204m) to the E., where Charlemagne is said to have hunted the aurochs (a wild ox long extinct) and the bear; the last of the latter in the area was killed in 1709.—The road turns N. to (6.5km) *La Bresse*, a small resort (638m) rebuilt since its destruction in 1944.—The D34 climbs N.E. to (17.5km) the *Col de la Schlucht* (see below); the D486 ascends to the *Col de Grosse Pierre* (953m) before descending to (14km) *Gérardmer*; see above.

From Gérardmer we ascend the valley of the Vologne to (3km) *Saut-des-Cuves*, where the road for *St-Dié*, 27km N., turns l., and shortly pass the charming *Lac de Longemer*, overlooked by the *Roche du Diable*, and the smaller *Lac de Retournemer*.—At 10km the road from La Bresse (see above) is met 2km prior to reaching the **Col de la Schlucht* (1139m; views), the highest point of the route, which until the restoration of Alsace to France by the Treaty of Versailles was the frontier post. To the S. rises **Le Hohneck** (1362m), the rounded grassy summit of which is the highest point of the main ridge of the *Vosges* (see above), and commands a wide **View* of the whole chain from the Ballon d'Alsace to the S. to the Donon to the N.—To the E. lies Alsace, and the Black Forest beyond the Rhine; to the S.E., in the distance, beyond the Grand Ballon, rise the Alps (rarely seen in summer); to the S. is the chain of the Jura.—The pass is intersected by the *Routes des Crêtes*, constructed by French engineers during the First World War, which leads S. over the *Col du Herrenberg* (1186m) to (22km) *Le Markstein* and 7km beyond, to the Grand Ballon, from which one may descend the Lauch valley to *Guebwiller*; see Rte 116B.—The same ridge road leads N. to (21.5km) the *Col du Bonhomme*, on the St-Dié – Colmar road, and beyond to meet the N59 at *Ste-Marie-aux-Mines*; see Rte 114B.—The Col de la Schlucht and other suitable slopes are frequented for winter sports.

From the pass the D417 descends the E. side of the range in zigzags to (18km) **Munster**, a cheese-making town at the confluence of two arms of the Fecht, owing its name to a Benedictine abbey founded here in 634 by Oswald, a disciple of St Gregory, and suppressed in 1790. It became a free imperial city and later a republican community and Protestant stronghold. In 1915 the French worked their way down the slopes from the Schlucht towards Munster, which remained in German hands and was sporadically bombarded. The *Hôtel de Ville*, although dating from 1550, is much restored.—To the N. it is over-looked by the ski resort of *Horodberg*; to the S. rises the *Petit Ballon* (1267m).—The road descends the valley past (r. at 5km) *Soultzbach*, a village known for its table-waters (discovered in 1603) and for its 'bains des fous', said to cure hysteria.—5km. To the r. stand the ruins of the castle of *Pflixbourg*, a Hohenstaufen foundation, just beyond which the l.-hand fork enters *Turkheim*; see Rte 116B).—The main road

veers r. through *Wintzenheim*, there meeting the N83 (Routes des Vins; see R●
116B) 4km W. of **Colmar**; see Rte 116A.

REMIREMONT TO THANN AND MULHOUSE (82km). The N66 leads S.E. u●
the narrowing valley of the upper Moselle, near the head of which the *Ballo●
d'Alsace* rises 'like a wall at the end of a lane' to quote Belloc, at 12km traversin●
Rupt, a small industrial town, as is *Le Thillot* 11km beyond, and climbs to (6km) *S●
Maurice-sur-Moselle*, a station on the Roman road from Metz to Basle.—To th●
S.W. rises the *Ballon de Servance* (1216m; views).

From St-Maurice a narrow road climbs steeply S., with good retrospectiv●
views, passing (r.) at *La Jumenterie*, the ruins of a stud-farm established in 16●
by the Duc de Lorraine, to (9.5km) near the summit of the **Ballon d'Alsac●**
(1247m; *Views, including the whole range of the Vosges, the Black Forest, an●
the Jura, and—in clear weather, rare in summer—the Alps). The word 'ballo●
derives from 'bolong' or 'bois long' of Alsatian patois, recalling the age when th●
Sylva Vosagus covered all these heights; the summit is now a green expanse ●
mountain pasture.

Hence a mountain road zigzags S. to (16.5km) *Giromagny*, 12km N. of *Belfo●
see Rte 118.—A short distance below the summit another road turns l. (th●
'Route Joffre', constructed during the 1914–18 war), descending past the *L●
d'Alfeld* and down the valley of the Doller to (21.5km) *Masevaux*, which grew u●
round an abbey founded in 720. The abbey became a chapter of noble ladie●
where Catherine of Russia received part of her education (?); little survives of th●
buildings and town walls.—The D466 continues E. to (10km) the *Anspac●
crossroads*, 17km W. of Mulhouse; see Rte 118.

The road from St-Maurice circles to the N.E., ascending through the resort ●
Bussang and near the source of the Moselle to (8.5km) the *Col de Bussan●*
(731m), between the *Tête du Rouge-Gazon* (S.; 1232m) and, to the N., the *Pit Dr●
mont* (1222m), and beyond, the *Grand Ventron* (1204m), formin*g* part of the rid●
which was once the frontier; here descends the *Grand Ballon*. The road descends i●
to the valley of the Thur by steep zigzags, later traversing the small industri●
towns of *Husseren-Wesserling*, *St-Amarin* and (18.5km) *Willer-sur-Thur*, from whic●
a road ascends to the summit of the **Grand Ballon**, or *Ballon de Guebwiller*, th●
highest mountain in the Vosges (1424m). It rises from a spur on the E. of the pri●
cipal chain, and may also be reached from the valley leading W. from Gue●
willer; see Rte 116B.

5km after traversing *Bitschwiller-lès-Thann*, **Thann** (7,800 Thannois), an i●
dustrial town on the Thur, is entered. It is overlooked from the N. by the ruins ●
the feudal castle of *Engelbourg*, one of whose cylindrical towers was blown up ●
1674 by Turenne, and lies on its side like a barrel. Thann became the French a●
ministrative centre of 'reconquered Alsace' after Aug. 1914, after which it w●
sporadically bombarded. It was the birthplace of Ernst Robert Curti●
(1886–1956), the francophile German scholar and author of 'Europea●
Literature and the Latin Middle Ages', among other works. The great collegi●
church of *St-Thiébaut*, restored after the slight damage it sustained in bo●
wars, dates largely from 1380–1516, when its delicate openwork spire (71●
high) was completed. The richly-sculptured W. portal is specially remarkabl●
although in need of cleaning, while the elegant interior contains notable 15●
glass and (repaired) choir-stalls.—A small *Museum* has been installed in the 16●
Halle-au-blé on the riverside to the N.; to the N.E. a tower of its fortifications su●
vives.

The road continues S.E. to (5km) crossroads 2km S. of *Cernay* (see Rte 116●
and 6km N. of the Anspach crossroads, and traverses the dull *Ochsenfeld* (cham●
des boeufs), probably the field of battle between Caesar and Ariovistus in 5●
B.C., and fought over several times since; lastly in Jan. 1945.– Later forking ●
the road enters **Mulhouse** 16km beyond; see Rte 118.

Regaining the N57 just W. of Remiremont, and turning l. up th●
valley of the Augronne, at 14km **Plombières-les-Bains** is entered.

Interest in this famous spa—known to the Romans, relics of whose occupatio●
may be seen—was revived after several centuries. Montaigne visited the place ●
1580, and among others who took its radio-active waters were Richelie●
Stanislas of Poland, Voltaire, Beaumarchais, the Empress Josephine (in whos●

presence Robert Fulton is said to have first sailed his steam-boat, in 1802), De
Musset, Lamartine, Baudelaire, Delacroix, Berlioz, and Napoleon III, to whom its
later development is chiefly due; here he negotiated with Cavour for the cession
of Savoy and Nice to France in 1858.

Beyond the church we pass in succession the *Bain Stanislas* (1736;
previously belonging to the Dames of Remiremont); the *Maison des
Arcades* (1760; erected for the visit of the daughters of Louis XV;
cf. 'Chemin des Dames'); the *Bain Romain* (described by Montaigne
in his 'Journal de voyage en Italie'), beyond which are other
establishments, and the *Casino*, etc.

The road crosses a ridge, descending to (11km) *Fougerolles* (also
by-passed), a small town manufacturing kirsch, and 9km beyond, the
ancient town and spa of **Luxeuil-les-Bains** (10,500 Luxoviens), in the
valley of the Breuchin, at the foot of wooded hills, to the S. of which
is an air base.

Of Celtic origin, it also preserves remains of Roman baths. In 585/90 the Irish
monk Columbanus founded a monastery here (see below), which became one of
the most notable in Gaul, and its abbots were later princes of the Holy Roman
Empire (one of Charlemagne's illegitimate sons had been made abbot); the community was dissolved at the Revolution after some centuries of decadence.

The *Établissement* lies at the N. end of the town, threaded by the
main street, in which (r.) is the *Hôtel du Card. Jouffroy*, built by Jean
le Jouffroy (1412–73), a counsellor of Louis XI, who was born at
Luxeuil; it was in 1831–35 the residence of the historian Augustin
Thierry, who, blind from 1832, here dictated to his wife his 'Récits
des Temps mérovingiens'. Opposite is the *Hôtel des Echevins*, a
crenellated tower with a Flamboyant Gothic loggia of c. 1440, housing a small *Museum*.

Further S. is the arcaded *Maison de François-I*, named after an abbot, and resembling the Granvelle Palace at Besançon; Granvelle
had also once been abbot of Luxeuil. Near-by stands *St-Pierre*
(13-14C), formerly the abbey-church, with a tower of 1527, choir-
stalls of 1545, and an elaborate 17C organ-loft. To the S. is part of a
Gothic cloister; the apse was rebuilt in 1860.—The former *abbot's
palace* (16-18C) is now the *Hôtel de Ville*; to the N. is the *Maison du
Bailli* (1473).

Columbanus had earlier founded the abbey of *Anagratis* (c. 575) at *Annegray*,
where slight ruins may be discerned S. of *Faucogny*, with a 12-14C chapel, 15km
. of *Luxeuil*, in the valley of the Breuchin, in a district of little lakes among
woods.

LUXEUIL TO BELFORT (50km). The D64 leads due S. to (18km) **Lure**, also by-
passed, on the Ognon, which grew round an abbey founded c. 610 by an Irish
disciple of Columbanus; the abbey buildings were rebuilt in 1770–89, partly
under the direction of J.-B Kléber, (1753–1800) an architect before he became a
soldier. They now accommodate the *Sous-Préfecture*.—12km. **Ronchamp**, a small
industrial town, 3km above which stands the eccentrically designed chapel of
N.-D.-du-Haut (by Le Corbusier; 1955), replacing one destroyed in the fighting of
1944, and serving as a war memorial; admirers of the architect will be
impressed.—The road now veers S.E. past (l.) the reservoir of *Champagney*, and
later the *Montagne de Salbert*, with its fort, to approach (21km) **Belfort**; see Rte
18.

The N57 veers S.W. to (27km) **Vesoul** (20,300 Vésouliens), a former
fortress below the isolated conical hill of *La Motte*, and the préfecture of the *Haute-Saône*, but a town of slight interest. A short
distance N.W. of the central *Pl. de la République* stands *St-Georges*

(1745), in the classical idiom, containing some 16C sculptures. There
are several old houses in its vicinity, among them the late 15C *Hôtel
Thomassin*, to the W.—The municipal *Museum* has recently been in
stalled in former convent buildings in the Rue des Ursulines.

VESOUL TO BELFORT (66km). The D9 leads S.E. past the curious crater-like
Gouffre du Frais Puits and (13km) the ruins of the 12-16C château of *Vallerois-le
Bois*, and 13km beyond, traverses *Villersexel*, site of the battle between Gén
Bourbaki and the Prussians (9 Jan. 1871), in which the château was destroyed
The French lost 1390 men; the Prussians 579.—28km. *Héricourt*, for which, an
the road on to (12km) *Belfort*, see Rte 118.

Quitting Vesoul, at 10km the Renaissance château of *Filain* (c. 1550
lies 4km E., containing imposing sculptured chimney-pieces an
other features of interest.—14km. *Rioz*, 5km S.E. of which stands th
18C château of *Bellevaux*, once the residence of Gén. Pichegru, wit
relics of a Cistercian abbey adjacent.—11km. *Voray-sur-l'Ognor*
with a large church rebuilt in 1770 on the plan of a Greek cross, i
passed as **Besançon**, 8km beyond, is approached; see Rte 124.

113 Nancy

NANCY (99,300 Nancéiens), the historic capital of *Lorraine*, an
préfecture of *Meurthe-et-Moselle*, lies in the broad valley of th
Meurthe at the foot of wooded hills. Part of a flourishing industria
conurbation, and a garrison town, it preserves an attractive centre o
18C buildings laid out on a rectangular plan in the vicinity of the im
posing Pl. Stanislas, and museums of interest.

Originally a castle (*Castrum Nanceium*) of the dukes of Lorraine, it was the
capital in the 12C. In an attempt to wrest the duchy from René II, Charles l
Téméraire of Burgundy was killed at its gates in 1477. The town was improve
under Duc Charles III (1545– 1608) and Leopold (1690– 1729), but owes its mai
embellishments to Stanislas Leczinski (1677– 1766), ex-king of Poland, who wa
consoled for the loss of his throne (1736) by becoming in 1738 Duc de Lorrain
for life. Under Stanislas, who was the father-in-law of Louis XV (cf. Wissem
bourg), Nancy became the seat of a brilliant court attracting many distinguishe
artists, and on his death the duchy passed to France. In 1801 its population wa
29,700; in 1851, 45,100.

In 1870 it was held to ransom by the Prussians, and after 1871 profited by th
immigration of many Alsatians and Lorrainers. In Aug.-Sept. 1914 the German
gained some heights to the E., and approached its N. outskirts, but the Bavarian
(attacking in the presence of the Kaiser) failed to capture the place, and wer
driven back by Castelnau's offensive. it was, however, bombarded and bombe
and its communications with Paris were hampered by the German possession o
the railway line at St-Mihiel. It escaped damage in the Second World War.

Nancy was the birthplace of Jacques Callot (1592– 1635), and Israel Sylvestr
(1621– 91), engravers; the architect Richard Mique (1728– 94); Claude Miche
or 'Clodion' (1738– 1814), the sculptor; J.-B. Isabey (1767– 1855); Émile Gall
(1846– 1904), the designer of glass and furniture; the Duc de Choiseu
(1719– 85); Gén. Hugo (1773– 1828), father of Victor Hugo; Gén. Droue
(1774– 1847); Eugène Schneider (1805– 75), the industrialist; Edmond de Gon
court (1822– 96); and Marshal Lyautey (1854– 1934).

Its macaroons and 'bergamottes' (a sugered candy) are reputed.

Convenient parking may be found in the *Pl. Carnot*, the lower part o
the long Cours Léopold. From the S.E. corner of this square one ma
turn S., and then l. into the Rue Stanislas; some distance to the r.
the Doric *Porte Stanislas* (1764). The street descends gently to th

Place Stanislas, the great pride of Nancy, and certainly a striking if somewhat ornate example of 18C town planning, laid out by Stanislas in 1752–60, and enclosed by buildings of uniform design by Emmanuel Héré (1705–63), a pupil of Boffrand.

At its N.E. corner is the *Théâtre*; the S. side is flanked by the **Hôtel de Ville**, with its Corinthian pilasters; to the N.W. is the present *Musée des Beaux-Arts* (see below). In the centre is a bronze statue of Stanislas by Georges Jacquot (1831), replacing one of Louis XV. At the N.E. and N.W. angles are two monumental fountains with leaden statues of Neptune and Amphitrite and their allegorical retinue, by Barthélemy Guibal of Nîmes. The wrought-iron and gilded *Railings* surrounding these, and elsewhere in the square, together with most of the balconies, are the work of the native artist Jean Lamour (d. 1771), who also made the balustrade of the Hôtel de Ville staircase.

A short distance E. of the Place is the small *Pl. d'Alliance*, with its fountain, erected by Stanislas to commemorate the treaty between the houses of Bourbon and Austria in 1756.—Further E. is a *Botanical Garden*, and zoological museum and aquarium (entrance in the Rue Ste-Catherine, leading back to the Pl. Stanislas).

From the S.E. corner of the Place the Rue Maurice-Barrès leads to the *Cathedral*, a dull edifice of 1703–42, designed by Giovanni Betto, modified by Hardouin-Mansart, and completed by Boffrand, who added the towers. Its sombre interior contains good boiseries and ironwork, the latter by Jean Lamour and Jean Maire.

The **Musée des Beaux-Arts**, is under reorganisation.

At present it contains on the GROUND FLOOR representative works by *Orthon Friesz, Dufy, Vlaminck, Vuillard, Utrillo, Manguin,* and *Suzanne Valadon*; and

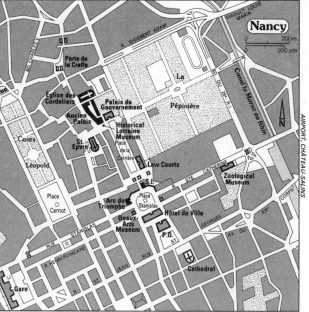

among individual paintings of merit: *H. Haudebourt-Lescot*, Self-portrait; *Manet*
Female portrait; *Modigliani*, two Female portraits; *Isabey*, View of Dieppe
Delacroix, Death of Charles le Téméraire at Nancy; and *Matisse*, Portrait of
Marguerite Matisse.

FIRST FLOOR: *Claude Lorrain*, small Pestoral scene; *Falconet*, Self-portrait
and Portrait of his wife (?); Portraits by *Tocque*, and *Largillière*; *Bibiena*, two Ar
chitectural scenes; *Restout*, Boffrand, the architect; *De Troy*, Repose of Diana
Boucher, Aurora and Cephalus; *Girodet*, Portraits of Stanislas Leczinski, and of
Prince Charles-Alexandre de Lorraine; *Gustave Lundberg*, Gén. Wittinghof
Philippe de Champagne, Charity; *Poussin*, Entry into Jersualem; *Jean Garnier*
Louis XIV: *Caravaggio*, Annunciation; *Ribera*, Baptism of Christ; *Momper*
Muleteers, and Village fête; *Ruisdael*, Landscapes; an *anon.* Flemish Kermesse
De Crayer, The Pest in Milan; *Gisbert Lytens*, Winter; *Pourbus*, Male portrait
anon. Marriage of St Catherine (17C Dutch); *Lucas van Leyden*, Passion scene
Jan Lievens, Expiration of Christ; *Bramantino*, St Lucy; *Perugino*, Virgin and
Child with angels; *G.P. Ricci*, Saviour of the world.

Facing the Hôtel de Ville, the short Rue Héré leads to the *Porte*
Royale, a triumphal arch erected in honour of Louis XV in 1752
Beyond extends the 293m-long tree-planted *Pl. de la Carrière*, a 16C
tourney-ground of the dukes, entirely transformed by Stanislas. On
the W. side is the *Palais de Justice* (1751; by Boffrand); at the far end
a decorative hemicycle completes the architectural plan by connec
ting the houses on either side with the former *Palais du Gouverne*
ment (1753; by Mique).—To the E. of this Place extends the large
Square Pepinière, laid out in 1765, in which stands a statue of
Claude Lorrain by Rodin.

Parallel to the W. is the Grande-Rue, with several 16-17C man
sions, to the l. of which is *St-Epvre* (1872), occupying the site of its
predecessor of 1451, from whose tower 100 Burgundian officers
were hanged in 1477 in revenge for the death of the Duc de
Lorraine's chamberlain.

On the r., further on, adjoining the Palais du Gouvernement, is the
former **Ducal Palace**, a florid Gothic edifice begun by René II
c. 1495, and continued by his son Antoine (1508–44), whose
equestrian statue surmounts the *Gateway, known as the 'Porterie'
built by Mansuy Gauvain in 1512. The surviving wing, restored after
a fire in 1871, contains the *Musée Historique Lorrain, one of the
most interesting provincial collections of its kind in France.

The GROUND FLOOR is devoted to medieval collections; sculpture (including
16C Christ on the Mount of Olives); arms and armour; jewellery; and in
separate wing across the courtyard (in which some Jewish tombstones are
displayed), archaeology, including some good Gallo-Roman figurines.

The FIRST FLOOR contains numerous portraits, illuminations and early
printed books, and documents relative to the duchy, among the former being
those of Philippe de Gueldre, wife of René II; several portraits by *Claude Deruet*
Jacques Bellange, Portrait of Nicolas Fournier, ducal physician, and his wife
anon. Portrait of Didier Pariset, an ennobled valet-de-chambre; *Georges de la
Tour*, Woman with a flea, and Death of St Alexis; and portraits of cardinals of Lor
rain. Also several carved wooden groups, and a set of five tapestries (Tournai
c. 1525), by Nicolas de la Chesnaye.

Outstanding are the engravings of *Jacques Callot*, including numerous
original copper plates; among those displayed are the 'Grand Misère de la
Guerre' (c. 1633), and 'Petit Misère'; the Siege of La Rochelle; the Siege of Breda
and the Siege of the Île de Ré. Also notable are engravings by *Claude Deruet*
(c. 1588–1660), and *Charles Mellin* (1597–1649), both born in Nancy; Views of
Nancy by *J.-B. Claudot*, and *Richard Mique*; *F. Dumont*, Portrait of Girardet
(1709–78), born at Luneville; and a portrait of St-Lambert (1716–1803), born at
Affracourt; a Plan of Nancy of 1754; furniture; scientific instruments; watches
etc.

The SECOND FLOOR contains a Jewish section; furniture and fabrics; wax figurines, etc.; others are devoted to the Revolution and Empire, with portraits, souvenirs, and armour, etc.

Other sections are at present under reorganisation, and a collection of folk-art is to be opened adjacent; see below.

The ***Eglise des Cordeliers**, next door, was built by René II in 1480–87 to commemorate the deliverance of Nancy in 1477, where after the Revolution were collected together the scattered tombs of the dukes of Lorraine.

It contains the tombs of Card. de Vaudémont (d. 1587); Antoine de Vaudémont (d. 1447) and his wife (d. 1476); that of Jacques Callot; the Tomb-statue of Philippa de Gueldra (d. 1547), second wife of René II, by Ligier Richier; and the elaborately decorated tomb of René (d. 1509). The octagonal Chapelle Ronde, with its compartmented cupola, the ducal burial chapel from 1607, preserves several sculptures and sarcophagi of note.

A short distance further N. is the massive *Porte de la Craffe* (1436), beyond which is the *Porte de la Citadelle* (1598), with a statue of Charles III and bas-reliefs by Florent Drouin.—The Rue de la Craffe leads W. to the *Porte Désilles*, at the N. end of the *Cours Léopold*, erected in 1785 in honour of the birth of the Dauphin, son of Louis XVI, and of the alliance between France and the United States.

The Rue St-Dizier leads S. from the Rue Stanislas, crossing the so-called Point-Centrale (where the Rue St-Jean divides from the Rue St-Georges) to the *Porte St-Nicolas*, an early 17C gateway (restored), beyond which is the *Pl. des Vosges*.

Hence the long Av. des Strasbourg continues S.E. to **N.-D.-de-Bonsecours**, built for Stanislas in 1741 on the site of a chapel erected in 1484 in memory of the defeat of Charles le Téméraire. Its interior, decorated in an Italian Renaissance style, contains the tombs of Stanislas (d. 1766; by L.-C. Vassé) and his wife Catherine Opalinska (d. 1757; by N.-S. Adam); a tablet covers the heart of their daughter Marie Leczinska (1703–68), queen of Louis XV; it also preserves an image of the Virgin by Mansuy Gauvain (1505).

The second turning to the r. further S.E. leads to the ***Musée de Fer** (Av. du Gén. de Gaulle, *Jarville*), founded in 1967 and devoted to the history of metallurgy, not only of interest to the technically minded, with numerous models of machines, early locomotives, automobiles, etc.

From the Porte Stanislas (see above), the rue Raymond-Poincaré leads W., off which the Rue St-Lambert turns S. to approach the **Musée de l'École de Nancy**, with furniture of the turn of the century designed by Gallé, among others, and also glass, ceramics, paintings, and sculpture of the period.

114 Nancy to Strasbourg

A. Via Lunéville and Saverne

149km (92 miles). N4. 30km **Lunéville**—53km *Sarrebourg*—16km **Phalsbourg**—11km **Saverne**—39km **Strasbourg**.

Maps: IGN 12, 23, or 104; also 311. M 242.

The motorway may be joined just W. of Phalsbourg, driving direct to Strasbourg.

Driving S.E., *N.-D.-de-Bon-Secours* (see above) is shortly passed (r.), and after 5km, on the far bank of the Meurthe, the former *Chartreuse de Bosserville* (1666–1721), under restoration.

7km. **St-Nicolas-de-Port**, an industrial town (devastated by the Swedes in 1635), is dominated by the lofty towers of its imposing early 16C *Church, still under restoration since damaged in 1940, with a nave of cathedral-like proportions (97m long, and 32m high).

Crossing the river, after 16km we enter **Lunéville** (23,200 Lunévillois), a garrison town remarkable for the huge palace built by Duc Léopold of Lorraine in 1702–14, standing on a plateau above the Vezouze. It was completed by Stanislas Leczinski (cf. Nancy), who died here in 1766.

The Treaty of Lunéville (1801) gave the left bank of the Rhine to France. It was the birthplace of the artist Jean Girardet (1709–78); Gén. Haxo (1774–1838); and the physician Ernest Bichat (1845–1905). Georges de la Tour lived here from 1620 until his death in 1652; Mme du Châtelet (1706–49) died here giving birth to a child whose father was Saint-Lambert, and is buried in the church of St-Jacques; Émile Erckmann (cf. Phalsbourg, below) passed his last years and died here in 1899.

The ***Château**, imposing in size, is the work of Germain Boffrand; its wings flanking the *Cour d'Honneur* now house local government offices, having long been inhabited by cavalry and pigeons. The **Museum**, also accommodated here, contains sections devoted to Cavalry; **Collections of Lunéville faïence*; several portraits of interest; and a display of the calligraphy of Jean-Joseph Bernard. The chapel may be seen from the museum.—To the E. extends the *Parc des Bosquets*, slowly recovering from years of neglect.

A few minutes' walk to the S. brings one to Baroque **St-Jacques** (1745; by Boffrand and Héré), under restoration. its facade is surmounted by a huge clock between two towers; it contains a monumental urn preserving the entrails of Stanislas; the plain black marble tomb of Mme du Châtelet (see above); some good 18C boiseries, and a organ-loft of 1751 by Héré.

For the road S.E. to *St-Dié*, see Rte 114B.

The N4 continues E. up the valley of the Vezouze, later circling to the N.E. through (29km) *Blâmont*, an ancient town with ruins of a castle burned in 1636, and the birthplace of the composer Florent Schmitt (1870–1958), 10km to the E. of which, at *Cirey-sur-Vezouze*, a famous mirror-manufactury was established in 1801.

At (16km) *Heming*, where the Marne-Rhine Canal is crossed, the D955 comes in from the N.W.; see Rte 114C.—8km. **Sarrebourg** (15,100 inhab.), the Gallo-Roman *Pons Saravi*, on the river Sarre, and the birthplace of Gén. Mangin (1866–1925), was entered by Dubail's army on 18 Aug. 1914, but four days later they were forced to retreat on Nancy after the 15th Corps had been routed E. of Morhange; see Rte 114C. A small *Museum* is installed at 13 Av. de France.—To the N.W. of the town is the *Cimetière national des Prisonniers*, with the graves of over 14,000 French prisoners-of-war who died in captivity during the First World War.

Hesse, 5km S., has a late 12C church, a relic of a Benedictine priory, 5km E. of which, at *Vallerysthal*, are glass-works founded in 1707.—At *Fénétrange*, 15km N., are the remains of its fortifications, a 13C and Renaissance château, and a 15C church containing the tomb of Henri de Fénétrange (d. 1335).

16km. **Phalsbourg**, ceded to France in 1661, and fortified by Vauban in 1680, relics of which are its town gates, held out for four months against the Prussians in 1870.

It was the birthplace of miscellaneous generals. Marshal Mouton, Comte de Lobeau (1770–1838) was the most eminent, of whom Napoleon said 'Mon Mouton est un lion'. Also born here was Émile Erckmann (1822–99), author, with Alexandre Chatrain, of novels of Alsatian life.

Lutzelbourg, 4.5km S., lies on the Zorn, overlooked by the ruins of a 12C castle, from which a road threading its wooded gorge offers an alternative approach to *Saverne*.

11km. **Saverne** (10,500 Savernois), pleasantly situated on the Zorn and Marne-Rhine Canal, was the *Tres Tabernae* of several early chronicles.

Under the Carolingians it was a fief of the bishops of Metz, but those of Strasbourg held it from the 13C until the Revolution. In 1525 it was seized by the 'Rustauds' in a peasant rebellion. It suffered severely in the Thirty Years' War, and its fortifications were razed in 1677. At *Dietwiller*, 8km E., took place the 'Zabern Incident' of autumn 1913 between civilians and the Prussian garrison, which lead to a domestic crisis in Germany during the months prior to the outbreak of war.

The *Château* (1780) is an imposing edifice of red sandstone, replacing its predecessor, the country seat of bishops, destroyed by fire in 1779. It was built at the cost of Card. Édouard de Rohan, implicated in the 'Diamond Necklace' scandal, and was somewhat mutilated during its use as barracks between 1870-1944.—The *Parish Church* (12-15C) lies to the S. E., while to the S.W., off the Grand' Rue opposite the château, is the cloister of the *Récollets* (1303).

5km N. stands the Romanesque church of the Benedictine abbey of *St-Jean-Saverne*, on a wooded height; 5km S. lie the ruins of the castle of *Haut-Barr* (1170), with a pentagonal keep, the surviving ramparts of which provide attractive views.

Neuwiller-les-Saverne, 12km N., overlooked by the ruins of the castle of *Herrenstein*, had a Benedictine abbey founded in 723, and was long fortified. Romanesque and Gothic *St-Pierre-et-St-Paul* (restored in the mid 19C by Boeswillwald) preserves a double-storeyed choir-chapel of the Carolingian period. In the cemetery of *St-Adelphe* is the tomb of Marshal Clarke (1765–1818), Napoleon's Minister of War from 1807.—*Bouxwiller*, 7km E. of Neuwiller, likewise once fortified, has a restored *Hôtel de Ville* of 1659 and several characteristic old houses.

The D421 leads due E. from Saverne to (36km) *Haguenau*; see Rte 111B.

From Saverne, the N4 turns S., at 6km by-passing (r.) **Marmoutier**, preservinging an *Abbey-church (founded c. 600 by a disciple of St Columbanus), with an interesting facade (c. 1150) in the Lombardic style, its central tower flanked by two octagonal turrets. It contains a restored Silbermann organ of 1710.

4km. *Romanswiller*, 1.5km r., has a 15-16C Jewish cemetery. —4km. *Wasselonne*, with relics of a feudal castle destroyed by the troops of the Elector of Brandenburg in 1674. The stone for Strasbourg cathedral was quarried in the vicinity.—3km. The r.-hand fork leads S. via *Avolsheim*, the church of which preserves a 10-11C crossing, to (9km) *Molsheim*; see Rte 116B.—Bearing l. and traversing a somewhat uninteresting plain, **Strasbourg** is entered at 22km; see Rte 115.

The Lombardic facade of the church at Marmoutier, c. 1150

B.   Via Lunéville, St-Dié, and Sélestat

168km (104 miles). N4. 30km **Lunéville**—N59. 25km *Baccarat* —25km **St-Dié**—43km. **Sélestat**—N83. 45km **Strasbourg**.

Maps: IGN 23, 31, 12, or 104. M 242.

For the road to *Lunéville*, a by-pass to which is under construction see Rte 114A.—The N59 leads S.E. up the broad valley of the Meur the, skirting (l.) the *Forêt de Mondon*, to (25km) **Baccarat** (5,400 in hab.), famous for its glass-works founded in 1764 and revive c. 1816, with a glass museum, etc.

9km. *Raon-l'Étape*, damaged in 1914 and 1944, is traversed.

A minor road leads N.E. up the *Vallée des Celles* to (28km) the *Col du Donon* overlooked by the isolated and imposing peak of *Le Donon* (1009m), twice recap tured by the French at the outset of the 1914–18 war, from which the main roa may be regained at (10km) *Schirmeck*; see below.

4.5km. The D420 leads E. to (2.5km) industrial *Moyenmoutier*, with the church (rebuilt 1766) of a famous abbey founded in the 12C.

Senones, 5.5km beyond, beautifully situated in an amphitheatre of wooded hill was the capital of the independent principality of *Salm-Salm* between 1751–9 The buildings of the Romanesque abbey founded in 662, and the château of the princes, are put to commercial use; the church contains the tomb of Dom Calme (1672–1757), to whom Voltaire paid a month's visit in 1754. The road ascends the *Col de Hantz* (636m) before descending to (16.5km) *St-Blaise-la-Roche*; se

1.5km. To the r. lies *Étival-Clairefontaine*, with an abbey-church of
1146, restored since damaged in 1944.—11.5km. **ST-DIÉ** (24,800
Déodatiens), a small cathedral town on the Meurthe, surrounded by
wooded hills, has suffered twice from ravaging fires; in 1757, and
again in 1944.

It takes its name from St Deodatus (7C), founder of a monastery which later
became a celebrated chapter of canons. Here in 1507 the former collegiate
printing-press issued the 'Cosmographiae Introductio', a geographical work in
which for the first time the name of America (after Amerigo Vespucci) was suggested for the New World. St-Dié was bombarded by the Germans in 1914–15,
and deliberately destroyed by them on their retreat in Nov. 1944, since when it
has been largely rebuilt in a contemporary style. It was the birthplace of the
statesman Jules Ferry (1832–93).

At the N. end of the central Rue Thiers steps ascend to the dull red
sandstone **Cathedral**, with a Romanesque nave, 13-14C choir and
aisles, and an 18C portal flanked by two towers. To the N. are three
walks of the late Gothic Cloister, beyond which is Romanesque *N.-D.
de-Galilée*.—Near the cathedral is the *Museum*, and further E. the
Library, the latter with important collections of MSS and incunables,
together with an example of the 'Cosmographiae'; see above. In the
former are several objects from the Celtic camp of *Bure*, N. of the
town.

ST-DIÉ TO COLMAR (56km). The N415 leads S., from which, at 12km the D8
turns r. for *Gérardmer*, 18km beyond; see Rte 112.—The main road bears E.
through (3.5km) *Fraize*, a small industrial town, to climb to (10.5km) the *Col du
Bonhomme* (949m; views), descending thence from the transverse *Route des
Crêtes* (see p 609) below (l.) the peak of *Le Brézouard* (1228m) to (18.5km)
Kaysersberg (see Rte 116B), 11.5km N.W. of *Colmar*; see Rte 116A.

ST-DIÉ TO STRASBOURG VIA SCHIRMECK AND MOLSHEIM (89km). The
N159, continued by the N420, circles N.E. to climb the *Col de Saales* (556m) and
descends into the *Vallée de la Bruche*, passing (r.) the peak of *Le Climont* (966m),
and (28km) traversing *St-Blaise-la-Roche*. There was some fighting to the W. of
this road in the summer and autumn of 1914, and again in 1944; *Saales* itself was
bombarded in both wars.—8km. At *Struthof*, 8km E., are the sad remains of a German concentration-camp, with a monument to the deported adjacent to a
cemetery in which the are the 1120 graves of a total of c. 10,000 who perished
there.—3km. *Schirmeck*, dominated to the N.E. by *Le Donon* (1009m), beyond
which we veer E.
  At 12km **Niederhaslach** lies 2km N., which grew up around a monastery
founded by St Florent, an Irishman, in the 7C. The restored *Abbey-church*,
begun in 1274 and completed in 1316 under the direction of Jakob Erwin
(d. 1330; son of the architect of Strasbourg cathedral), who is buried here, contains 14C glass depicting episodes in the life of St Florent, and 18C stalls. The
road continues N.W. to the ruins of the castle of *Nideck* and the neighbouring
waterfall.
  The next r.-hand turning leads 5km to the ruined medieval stronghold of
Guirbaden.—13km. *Mutzig*, birthplace of Antoine Alphonse Chassepot
(1833–1905), inventor of the musket named after him, is traversed, 3km beyond
which *Molsheim* is entered, or by-passed to the S.—**Molsheim** (7,000 inhab.), an
ancient town below the vine-clad foothills of the Vosges, preserves considerable
remains of its fortifications, particularly on its W. and E. sides. To the S. is a
gateway of 1412 leading to the *Metzig* or *Hôtel de Ville* (1525); to the S.E. stands
the large *Church* (1619; by Christophe Wamser), founded for a college of
Jesuits.—Here we may follow by-roads through (3.5km) *Dachstein*, once fortified, which fell to Turenne in 1674, to *Strasbourg*, or join the N420 2km S. to approach **Strasbourg** 24km to the N.E.; see Rte 115. The latter road shortly
traverses *Altorf*, with a Romanesque church of a Benedictine abbey founded in

From St-Dié the N59 circles to the N.E.

At 6.5km it bears r. to climb to the *Col de Ste-Marie*, overlooked by the *Roc du Haute de Faîte*, before descending to (17km) **Ste-Marie-aux Mines**; the N159 continues N.E., at 4km turning r. to traverse the range by a tunnel, the E. exit of which is just N. of Ste-Marie.

This industrial town owes its earlier prosperity to lead and copper mines which were worked from the 9C until they gave out in the 18C. During this period it belonged partly to the dukes of Lorraine, and partly to the Alsatian lords of Ribeaupierre, whose territories were separated by the Lièpvrette which flows through the town; hence the proverb that 'dough kneaded in Alsace was baked in Lorraine'. The Alsatian dwellers on the r. bank embraced Protestantism and spoke German; the Lorrainers remained French-speaking Catholics.

The N59 descends the valley through (8km) *Lièpvre*, just beyond which a r.-hand turning ascends to the castle of *Haute-Koenigsburg*; see Rte 116B.—We continue E., passing (l.) below the ruins of the castle of *Frankenbourg*, traditionally founded by Clovis.—9.5km. *Châtenois*, ancient *Castinetum*, with a Romanesque belfry adjacent to its church of 1760, is traversed, 4.5km beyond which **Sélestat** is entered, for which and for the road to **Strasbourg**, 45km N.E., see Rtes 116A and 115.

C. Via Vic-sur-Seille and Sarrebourg

140km (87 miles). N74. 22.5km—D 38. *Vic-sur-Seille* lies just N. of the road at 3.5km—2.5km *Moyenvic*—D955. 34km *Heming*—N4. 8km *Sarrebourg*—66km **Strasbourg**.

Maps: IGN 11, 12, or 104. M 242.

The N74 leads N.E., at 9km passing S. of the *Grand-Mont d'Armance* (see Rte 112), on the S.W. flank of which is *Laitre-sous-Amance*, with a Romanesque church, to (11.5km) *Moncel*, the old frontier station, which stood just within the French lines. In the region of Moncel all was in readiness for the great Franco-American advance to outflank Metz, just before the signing of the Armistace in Nov. 1918.—9km. *Vic-sur-Seille* (l.), an old town in a fertile valley known for its wine, has a 15-16C church and the elaborately decorated *Maison de la Monnaie* of 1456 (restored). It was the birthplace of Georges de la Tour (1593–1652). The 'Briquetage de la Seille' in this region, apparently designed to strengthen the marshy banks of the river, or for the evaporation of salt, is supposed to be Roman work, or earlier.—2.5km. *Moyenvic*, 34km S.E. of which we meet the N4 at *Heming*, for which, and the road beyond, see Rte 114A.

From a junction 5.5km E. of Moncel, the N74 bears N.E. to (5km) *Château-Salins*, severely damaged in 1944, owing its name to an old castle and salt-mines dating from 1330.—18km further N.E. lies *Morhange*, an ancient town with a restored 15C church. It was just E. of this point that the French offensive movement of Aug. 1914 was brought to a halt by a crushing blow delivered against their left flank on the 20th from German forces based on Metz, which resulted in the rout of the 15th Corps and a general retreat on Nancy.

From Moyenvic, the D38 continues N.E. past (3.5km) *Marsal*, fortified since Gallo-Roman times, finally in the 17C, with a Romanesque church restored since 1944, to (8.5km) *Dieuze*, ancient *Duosa Villa*, birthplace of Edmond About (1828–85), the journalist, and of the composer Gustave Charpentier

(1860–1956). It was the site of a rearguard action by Polish troops in 1940, when it was seriously damaged.—The road goes on to (24km) *Fénétrange* (see Rte 114A), at 12km passing 7km S. of *Munster-en-Lorraine*, with a notable 13-15C church, mutilated by the Swedes in 1637, and later restored; the towers and facade were designed by Viollet-le-Duc, and have been restored since 1944.

115 Strasbourg

STRASBOURG (252,300 Strasbourgeois; 49,100 in 1801; 151,000 in 1901), the old capital of Alsace, préfecture of the *Bas-Rhin*, site of the Conseil de l'Europe and the European Parliament. It is a thriving city of much attraction, with a remarkable cathedral, and several museums, the old centre of which is surrounded by branches of the Ill, while canals surround the inner suburbs. To the E. is the riverport on the l. bank of the Rhine, while to the W. rise the rounded summits of the Vosges.

It originated in a Celtic fishing-village fortified by the Romans (*Argentoratum*), which although it escaped the depredations of the Allemanni (due to their defeat by the emperor Julian in 357), was overrun in the 5C by Teuton invaders. It was later named *Strataburgum* from its position near the main road between Gaul and Germany. Here in 842 the 'Strassburg oaths' were sworn by Charles le Chauve in a German dialect, and by Ludwig the Bavarian in an early form of French, when addressing the other's followers. Lothair, their brother, gained Alsace by the subsequent Treaty of Verdun, but it reverted to Ludwig and remained nominally a part of the Holy Roman Empire until the Treaty of Westphalia (1648), although in fact an independent city ruled by its bishops and after 1332 largely by a guild of citizens who impressed upon it a very democratic character, one reason why several leaders of the Reformation settled here in the 16C. Its university was founded in 1566, endowed with new privileges in 1621, and suppressed between the Revolution and 1872.

In 1681 it was siezed by Louis XIV, assisted by the Catholic faction, who struck a medal commemorating the event, bearing the legend 'Clausa Germanis Gallia' (Gaul closed to the Germans), the annexation being confirmed by the Treaty of Ryswyck in 1697, but it forfeited its privileges at the Revolution, becoming merely another provincial capital. Louis Napoleon made an ineffectual attempt to gain power here in 1836. Strasbourg surrendered to the Prussians on 27 Sept. 1870 after a seven week siege and a destructive bombardment, and the following year it was, with the whole of Alsace (with the exception of the Territoire de Belfort), joined to Germany by the Treaty of Frankfurt, and remained the seat of government of Alsace-Lorraine (Elsass-Lothringen) until its liberation on 22 Nov. 1918. During the Occupation (1940–44) its citizens, many of whom took refuge in the centre and S.W. of France, suffered the vindictive attentions of the Germans until its second liberation on 23 Nov. of the latter year, prior to which it experienced severe damage by bombing, also remaining under fire from German artillery for almost five months.

It was the birthplace of Gottfried de Strasbourg (d. c. 1210), author of the epic poem 'Tristan und Isolde'; Sébastien Brant (1458–1521), the humanist; Johann Andreas Silbermann (1712–83; whose father, Andreas, died here in 1734), the organ-builder; Marshal Kellermann (1735–1820); Gén. Kléber (1753–1800); Louis-François Ramond de Charbonnière (1755–1827), the geologist and mountaineer; the artist-general Louis-François Lejeune (1775–1848); Gustave Doré (1832–83); the architect Émile Boeswillwald (1815–86); and the sculptor Jean Hans Arp (1886–1966).

Gutenberg worked here with Peter Schöffer between 1434–44 in perfecting his printing press. Samuel Prout visited it c. 1824; Longfellow in 1851; and Ruskin in 1852.

The description of the city is divided into three sections: that to the

E. of the central Pl. Gutenberg; that to the W.; and the area to the
N.E. of the central island site.

A.   The Cathedral, and Château des Rohans, etc.

In the centre of the *Pl. Gutenberg* is a statue of the famous printer, by
David d'Angers, to the W. of which is the **Chamber of Commerce**
(1585; the former *Hôtel de Ville*), with mullioned windows, and housing also the S.I.

Here, on the evening of 21 July 1789 Arthur Young, passing through
Strasbourg, saw for himself a dramatic pre-Revolutionary scene: 'the mob were
breaking the windows with stones . . . Perceiving that their numbers not only increased, but that they grew bolder and bolder every moment, I thought it worth
staying to see what it would end in, and clambered on to the roof of low stalls opposite the building against which their malice was directed . . . Perceiving the
troops would not attack them, except in words and menaces, they grew more
violent, and furiously attempted to beat the door to pieces with iron crows, placing ladders to the windows. In about a quarter of an hour, which gave time for
the assembled magistrates to escape by a back door, they burst all open, and
entered like a torrent with a universal shout of the spectators. From that minute
a shower of casements, sashes, shutters, chairs, tables, sofas, books, papers, pictures, etc., rained incessantly from all the windows of the house . . . which was
then succeeded by tiles, skirting boards, bannisters, frame-work, and every part
of the building that force could detach. The troops, both horse and foot, were
quiet spectators.'

To the N., the Rue des Grandes-Arcades leads shortly to the *Pl.
Kléber* (see below), the street marking the S.W. side of the Roman
castrum, the N.W. limit of which was the Pl. Broglie.
    From the S.E. corner of the square the short Rue Mercière, preserv-
ing several timbered and gabled houses, leads directly to the *Pl. de la
Cathédrale* and the splendid red sandstone W. front of the
**Cathedral, above which soars its single spire.

The earliest church erected on this site by Clovis (496) was rebuilt by
Charlemagne, but it was sacked in 1002, and struck by lightning in 1007. Of its
successor, started a decade later by Bp Wernher, only part of the crypt survives.
A Romanesque edifice was then begun, but in 1253–75 the nave was
reconstructed in the French Gothic style, and the W. facade was commenced in
1277, the masterpiece of Erwin of Steinbach (d. 1318), buried here, whose son
Jakob continued the work until 1339. Ulrich of Ensingen, the architect of Ulm
cathedral, built the octagonal tower, and its crocketed spire was completed in
1439 by Johann Hültz of Cologne.
    The W. *facade* (still under restoration) is remarkable for its tracery and for the
multitude of statues with which it is embellished. Its central portal contains prophets and a late 13C depiction of the Life of Christ in the tympanum, above
which is a double gable on which gambol 14 lion cubs (see below), two supporting a mid 19C statue of the Virgin and Child. The r. side portal is flanked by
Wise and Foolish Virgins (several beautiful heads), but all the portals were
mutilated at the Revolution, and contain numerous replicas. In the intervening
buttresses are equestrian statues of Merovingian, Carolingian, and later kings,
while above the pinnacles of the central gable is the delicately carved *Rose-
window*, surmounted by a gallery of Apostles. The original plan provided for
twin towers of equal height, rising from the second storey, but eventually the
two unfinished towers were joined by the existing platform on the third storey,
above which was raised the N. tower, exaggerated in height in accordance with
the Gothic principle of verticalism; the dizzy but beautiful *Spire*, decorated with
statuary and flanked by four turrets with winding stairways, consists of a six-

storeyed openwork pyramid rising to a height of 142m.

Both sides of the building are flanked by 18C screens. On the N. side projects the Flamboyant *Chap. St-Laurent*, masking the N. porch; the tympanums of the Romanesque S. portal, with twin doors, date from c. 1230, above which are a clock, and two rose-windows. Over the crossing is a stumpy tower of 1878.

The *Interior* is 110m long and 32m high, consisting of little more than a vast and dimly lighted nave, in which the general harmony of the proportions is enhanced by the beauty of the window tracery and the quality of the *Stained-glass*. The triforium is open. The *Nave* contains a carved stone *Pulpit* by Johann Hammerer (1486), and an organ-case of 1385 containing an *Organ* of 1740 by J. Andreas Silbermann. The N. aisle contains some 12-13C glass, but most of it, here and in the S. aisle, is later. The N. transept preserves a 15C *Font* by Jodoque Dotzinger of Wurms; the vaulting in the S. transept is supported by the so-called *Angels' Pillar* (1230), supporting a series of statues under canopies. Here too is an *Astronomical Clock* (1842; in action at noon daily), its mechanism replacing that of the clock of 1571, constructed by Conrad Dasipodius, which had so fascinated Thomas Coryate in 1608, and which remained in use until 1789. The raised *Choir*, adjacent to which are 16C retables, is surmounted by an octagonal cupola; to the N. and S. respectively of the shallow apse, with glass by Max Ingrand, are the chapels of St-Jean-Baptiste, with the Gothic tomb of Bp Conrad de Lichtenberg (d. 1299), and of St-André, partly Romanesque, containing tombs of other bishops.—Steps on either side of the choir descend to the restored early 11C crypt.

For the area N. of the cathedral; see below.

Abutting it to the E. is the *Lycée Fustel de Coulanges*, in a former Jesuit college (1757), by Massol, also the architect of the adjacent **Palais de Rohan** (1742; on the plans of Robert de Cotte), so-named because four 18C bishops were members of the Rohan family. It housed the university briefly in the 1870s, and later several museums. It has been restored after bomb damage in 1944, and its collections are under reorganisation.

The **Musée des Beaux-Arts** contains several works of interest on the FIRST FLOOR, among them: *anon.* Portrait of a youth (16C; N. Italian); *Piero di Cosimo,* Virgin and Child with the Baptist; *Botticelli,* Virgin and Child and angels; *Cima da Conegliano,* St Sebastian, and St Roch; *Lorenzo di Credi,* Virgin and Child; *School of Caravaggio,* Lobster merchant; *Domenico Tiepolo,* The Virgin appearing to SS. Laurence and Francis-de-Paul; *Pietro Novelli,* SS. Peter and Paul; *Paolo Domenico Finoglia,* Saint praying; *Jean de Boulogne,* Tavern scene with fiddler; *Goya,* Portrait of Bernardo Iriate (1797); *Zurbaran,* St Ursula; *El Greco,* Mater dolorosa; *Martin Drolling the elder,* Portrait of Adeone Drolling; *Michel-Martin Drolling,* Portrait of Marie-Ange Jaubert; *Vernet,* Bathers in a grotto; *H. Robert,* Temptation of St Antony; *Simon Vouet,* Lot and his daughters; *Oudry,* Still life with musical instruments; and characteristic works by *Lancret, Toqué,* and *Largillière.*

The GROUND FLOOR (where there is a *Chapel*) contains Portraits and souvenirs of the Rohan family in an imposing white and gilt room; ceramic collections: *Sèvres, Lunéville, Niderviller, Frankenthal, Haguenau,* and Strasbourg ware (the latter established by Paul Hannong c. 1721); Gobelin tapestries (1705); and *Largillière's* 'La Belle Strasbourgeoise'. The *Library* contains an important collection of prints and drawings, etc. The *Museum of Decorative Art* is still in the process of reorganisation.

The BASEMENT accommodates the *Archaeological collections,* including numerous funerary steles; a peasant couple from Oberhaslach (3C); examples of the art of the Hallstatt culture; ceramics, bronze statuettes, glass, terracotta figures; fibulas, etc.; and the silver and bronze Baldenheim helmet (7C), etc.

Immediately to the W. is an interesting building with a crenellated gable over its Gothic wing of 1347, and a late 16C German Renaissance wing by Hans Thomann Ulhberger, its richly decorated gable surmounted by an armed figure. It was the residence of the cathedral architects, and the whole edifice, restored since 1944, with

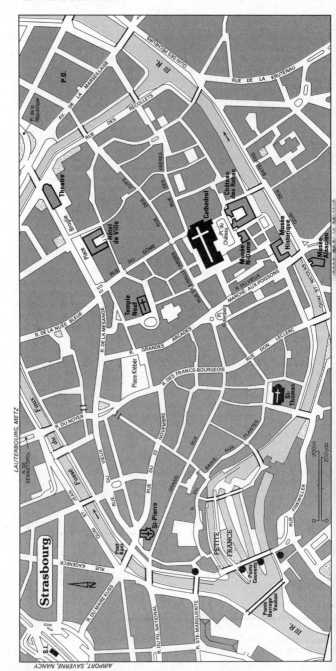

a fine spiral staircase in its courtyard, now houses the notable
*Musée de l'Oeuvre Notre-Dame.

Its 40-odd rooms are devoted to medieval and Renaissance collections, including
several original statues from the cathedral, outstanding among which are The
Church, and The Synagogue (1240); glass from its Romanesque predecessor; a
curious lintel carved with a Christ in Majesty (mid 12C); the original gable of
lion-cubs from the central doorway of the cathedral; capitals from the cloister of
Eschau, etc. The Treasury contains a good collection of goldsmiths' work,
ivories, and ecclesiastical ornaments, etc.; tapestries depicting the Life of St
Odile (c. 1450), and medieval furniture, including a Table for calculating
workers' wages. Among paintings are: *Conrad Witz*, The Magdalen and St
Catherine; *Hans Baldung Grien*, Virgin and Child, and parts of a retable of 1530;
Martin Schongauer, Annunciation, Death of the Virgin; SS. George and Matthew; and two Male portraits; *Cranach*, Portrait of a youth; *B. Hopffer*, Return
from the chase (1655); *Sebastian Stoskopff* (Strasbourg, 1597–1657), The Senses,
and Elements (still lives); and *Albrecht Kauw* (1621–81), The poultry-seller. **R10**
preserves drawings of the cathedral (13-15C) produced by its master masons.

A short distance to the S. best approached by a lane leading to the Ill,
providing a view of the S. facade of the Palais Rohan, and close to the
Pl. du Marché-aux-Cochons-de-Lait, is the former '*Grande Boucherie*'
(1587), housing the **Musée Historique**.

The collection includes a variety of documents and objects relating to the
history of Strasbourg, including a large Maquette of the city (1727, at 1:600); early photographs; old views and prints; furniture; arms and armour, and militaria in
general, including a collection of lead soldiers, etc; and mechanical toys from the
period 1820–1914 donated by the artist Toni Ungerer, (Strasbourg, 1931–).
Immediately to the W., is the *Ancienne Douane*, dating from 1356, but
reconstructed since its destruction in 1944, housing the **Musée d'Art moderne.**
Notable are *Renoir*, Portrait of young Marie Lecoeur (c. 1870); *Degas*, Design for
a ball at the Prussian court (c. 1879); *J.-É. Blanche*, Mme Langweil; *W.A. Bouger-
eau*, Virgin consolatrice; *Vuillard*, Around the lamp; *Gauguin*, Still life; *Burne-
Jones*, Sketches for glass windows; *Jacques Cachot* (Strasbourg, 1885–1955),
Self-portrait; *Utrillo*, Ruined abbey; and characteristic examples of the art of
*Monet, Sisley, Henri Martin, Lébourg, Pissarro, Signac, Carrière, Klimt, Bakst,
Dufy, Ernst, Klee*, and *F.-R. Carabin* (Saverne, 1862–1932). Also sculptures and
paintings by *Jean Arp; Henry Moore*, Mother and child; *Bourdelle*, Bust of
Beethoven; and glass by the Ott brothers of Strasbourg (c. 1900).

Crossing the adjacent *Pont du Corbeau*, from which criminals were
once hurled into the Ill, to the l. on the far bank is the old *Hôtel du
Corbeau*, a hostelry with a quaint courtyard in which Turenne lodged in 1647 and Frederick the Great in 1740; to the r. (23-5 Quai St-
Nicolas) is the ***Musée Alsacien**, with a charming galleried courtyard.

It contains a remarkable collection of Alsatian furniture, much of it painted, and
some displayed as rooms of the period; iron or tiled stoves (*poêles*); chests, and
chair-backs; butter-churns, and other wood-carvings (such as butter-moulds);
carved masks for wheat or flour-containers; household untensils; pottery, tiles,
and fabrics; wrought-iron signs; a Jewish section, with ritual objects; costumes
at present closed), etc. A room is devoted to souvenirs of Pastor Jean-Frédéric
Oberlin (1740–1826), the teacher and philanthropist, and minister at
Waldersbach from 1767. The forge to the l. of the entrance, and the farm implements in the courtyards will also be noted.

Recrossing the river, one may follow the Rue du Vieux-Marché-aux-
Poissons (in which Goethe lodged as a student in 1771; No. 36, now
selling hot dogs), to regain the *Pl. Gutenberg*.

Immediately N.W. of the W. front of the cathedral is the restored late 16C *Maison Kammerzel*, one of several half-timbered houses in the vicinity, another being the *'Pharmacie du Cerf'*.

Hence the Rue de Frères leads E. past the cathedral to the *Pl. St-Étienne*, with a house of 1598, and its 13C *Church*, largely rebuilt since the nave was destroyed in 1944. The Rue Arc-en-Ciel leads N. to the Rue de Parchemin.—To the S. beyond the Ill, stands *St-Guillaume*, founded in 1300, and a Protestant church since 1534.

The more interesting Rue des Hallebardes, continued by the Rue des Juifs, leads E., parallel to and N. of the Rue des Frères, to the Rue du Parchemin. Here one may turn l. along the Rue Brullée (where Jews said to have poisoned the city's wells were burnt in 1348), passing (r.) the *Préfecture*, and (l.) the *Bishop's Palace*. Further on (r.) is the *Hôtel de Ville* (by Massol in 1736, but rebuilt 1840), just prior to which a r.-hand turning leads shortly to the *Pl. Broglie* (pron. Breuil), laid out in 1740 by Marshal de Broglie, then governor of Alsace. Here, in the house (No. 2) of Frédéric Dietrich, the mayor, Rouget de Lisle first sung the Marseillaise (25 April, 1792). At its E. end is the *Théâtre*, rebuilt after a fire in 1870.

For the district to the N.E.; see below.

From the W. end of the Place, the Rue de la Nuée-Bleue leads N.W. to the Protestant church of *St-Pierre-le-Jeune*, founded in 1031 although probably originating in a 7C Irish monastery, containing a handsome rood-screen and font, and Silbermann organ, and with a simple cloister partly rebuilt in the 14C.

The Pl. Kléber may be reached a short distance to the S.

B. W. Strasbourg

The *Pl. Kléber*, the main square of the old town (previously 'des Carmes-Déchaux', 'des Cordeliers', 'Paradeplatz', etc.) is embellished by a statue of Gén. Kléber—Stabbed in Cairo by a Moslem fanatic—by P. Grass (1840). Its N. side is flanked by the *Aubette* (1771 by Blondel; rebuilt after 1870, when it was bombarded and set alight).

From its S.W. corner one may follow the Rue du 22 Novembre to **St-Pierre-le-Vieux**, with a 15C spire, a Protestant nave and Catholic choir (since 1681), the latter part rebuilt earlier this century. it contains some paintings of c. 1500 of interest. It derives its name from the 5C church which once stood on this site.

Hence the *Pont Kuss* crosses the canal to the N.W. towards the *Railway Station*.—Skirting the near bank to the l., and following the Quai Turkheim, the *Tour du Bourreau* (12-14C), the first of four towers, is reached, the restored relics of fortifications, two of which rise from islands in the Ill, in a district known as *'Petite France'*. By crossing the **Ponts Couverts**, and turning r. on the S. bank, one may approach the *Barrage Vauban*, providing a splendid *View of its four-square 14C towers.

On regaining the N. bank, turn r. through a picturesque area of old Strasbourg, where many timbered houses have been tastefully restored. The Rue du Bain au Plantes traverses a small place, with a view of the old sluice-gates, and mill-race, and is continued E. by the Rue des Dentelles, to approach **St-Thomas** (1270–1330), with Romanesque and Gothic towers, a Protestant church containing the theatrical **Tomb of Marshal Saxe* (1696–1750), by Pigalle, com-

pleted in 1777, and saved from destruction during the Revolution
because—it is said—it was covered in hay when the building was converted into a fodder store. Here also is the tomb of Martin Bucer
(cf. Sélestat), and a carved sarcophagus of the 9C. On the Silbermann
organ here (1740), Albert Schweitzer inaugurated in 1908 a tradition
of concerts commemorating the death of J. S. Bach (28 July 1750).

From the adjacent Place the Rue des Serruriers leads back to the *Pl.
Gutenberg*.

N.E. STRASBOURG; preferably visited by car. From the Théâtre (see above), a
bridge spans the canal of the Fossé du Faux Rempart to the *Pl. de la République*,
flanked to the W. by the *Palais du Rhin* (1889), and to the E. by the *Library*.—Further E. are the notable art nouveau *Municipal Baths*, by J.C. Ott (1908).

The Av. de la Paix leads N.E. to the *Pl. de Bordeaux*, to the N. of which is the
new *Palais de la Musique et des Congrès* (1975). From the S.E. corner of the latter
square the Rue Ohmacht leads across two arms of the Ill to the Allée de la
Robertsau, where turning l. we approach the *Palais du Conseil del'Europe* (1977),
to the N.E. of which is the smaller *Palais des Droits de l'Homme* (1966); to the W.
the *Assemblée Européene*.

To the S.E. of this group of buildings is the *Orangerie*, rebuilt since a destructive fire in 1968.

The Allée leads S.W. to the *Pl. de l'Université*, to the S.E. of which are several
faculty buildings, and some distance further S.E., remains of Vauban's *Citadel*
(1685).

Main roads converge to the S.E. of the city, above the river-port installations,
to cross the Rhine by the *Pont de l'Europe* (1960; French and German Customs),
on the far bank of which is *Kehl*, fortified by Vauban in 1683, where in 1780
Beaumarchais set up a printing-press from which several forbidden books, including Voltaire (purchasing Baskerville type for the occasion) and Rousseau,
were issued; cf. Arches.—**Freiburg** lies 82km S.; **Baden-Baden** lies 40km N.E.

For roads from Strasbourg to *Nancy*, and *St-Dié*, see Rtes 114A, and B; for
Metz, 111A, and for *Wissembourg*, 111B: all these in reverse; for roads S. to *Colmar* and *Mulhouse*, direct or via the 'Routes des Vins', see Rtes 116A and B.

116 Strasbourg to Mulhouse

A. Via Sélestat and Colmar

108km (67 miles). N83. 45km **Sélestat**—22km **Colmar**—N422.
41km; **Mulhouse**.

Maps: IGN 12, 31, or 104. M 242.

The N83 drives S. and shortly forks r. through industrial suburbs,
later traversing tobacco plantations prior to by-passing (l.), at 21km,
Erstein, once fortified, and reaching (7km) *Benfeld*, mentioned as a
'villa' of the bishops of Strasbourg as early as 765. Its arcaded *Hôtel
de Ville* (1531) had a curious turret added in 1619. Over the main dial
of the clock is a wooden bust of the traitor Stubehanzel, who was
bribed to betray the town to the Bavarians in 1331.—The hamlet of
Ehl, to the N.E., is believed to occupy the site of the Roman settlement of *Hellelum* or *Helvetum*.

The Vosges foothills are approached, many summits crowned with
ruined castles (see Rte 116B), and at 10km **Ebermünster** (formerly
Aprimonasterium, 'the monastery of the wild boar') is passed to the l.
It was the seat of a famous abbey, later Benedictine, said to have
been founded in 667 by Duc Adalric of Alsace, father of St Odile.
The present church (1727; by Peter Thumb) with three towers of

bulbous shape, contains good furniture and carvings, and an organ
of 1732 by André Silbermann.

7km. **SÉLESTAT** (15,500 Sélestatdiens), an ancient town on the Ill,
retains its irregularly-built centre long pent up within its fortifications, of which only the *Tour des Sorcières*, at its N.E. corner, and the
massive early 14C *Tour de l'Horloge*, facing the Rue de Prés. Poincaré, survive.

An early residence of Frankish kings, *Schlestadt* became a free Imperial city in
the 13C, and played its part in the wars that disturbed the region. It was captured
in the Thirty Years' War (1632), but held out against the Allies in 1814–15. Its
celebrated academy, at which Erasmus is said to have been a student in 1515,
was founded in the 15C, and exerted considerable influence on the revival of
learning in Alsace.

Here was born the reformer Martin Bucer (1491–1551; cf. St-Thomas
church, Strasbourg), who sought refuge in England at the invitation of Cranmer
and in 1549 became professor of divinity at Cambridge, where he died.

A short distance W. of the Tour des Sorcières stands Gothic *St*
Georges (13-15C), restored in the mid 19C, with a graceful tower
and containing good 16C glass in its choir. To the S. is ***Ste-Foy**, one
of the finest Romanesque buildings in Alsace, erected as a priory
church in the late 12C, replacing its predecessor built by Princess
Hildegarde of Hohenstaufen and her two sons. The two W. tower
date from 1889, but the central polygonal tower, with arcades on
each face, is original; note also the apse. The interior, although
somewhat heavy, is impressive, with arcades supported by Romanesque columns with cubical capitals.

To the W. of the former church is the ***Bibliothèque Humaniste**,
with an important and interesting collection of early printed books
and incunables, a selection of which, together with MSS, etc., is on
display. Many of them formed the library of Beat Bild (Beatus
Rhenatus; 1485–1547), the friend of Erasmus. A number of antiquities, sculptures, and a collection of faïence are also to be
seen.—Among several old buildings, the former *Arsenal Ste-Barbe*
and the *Maison de Stephan Ziegler* (c. 1538), in the Rue de Verdun,
further W., are notable.

The N83 runs parallel to the 'Route des Vins' (see Rte 116B), on a
height further W. of which stands the castle of *Haut-Koenigsbourg*,
traversing (10km) *Guémar* (Roman *Herbarium*), and by-passes (3km)
Ostheim, rebuilt after its destruction in 1945, to enter (9km) *Colmar*.

COLMAR (63,800 Colmariens), préfecture of the *Haut-Rhin*,
situated on the plain of Alsace near the foothills of the Vosges, is a
characteristic Alsatian town through which the Lauch flows. Its old
centre preserves a surprising number of picturesque painted and
half-timbered houses, and its museum contains several outstanding
works of art, which makes its somewhat too tourist-conscious.

Its origin is obscure, but a farm of the Frankish kings established here in the 8C
was called *Columbaria*. It was made a free imperial city in 1226. In 1474 it was
vainly besieged by Charles le Téméraire, but in 1632 fell to the Swedes during
the Thirty Years' War, and in 1635 was taken under French 'protection'. Louis
XIV later razed its ramparts. Voltaire, who visited Colmar in 1753, later described it as 'half German, half French, and totally Iroquois'! It was held for Napoleon
in 1814–15, and its sympathies during the 19C remained French. It was the centre of a German 'pocket of resistance' during the winter of 1944–45, when
several villages in the neighbourhood were destroyed, although Colmar itself
suffered only slightly. it was liberated by Gén. Lattre de Tassigny, assisted by
American troops, on 2 Feb. 1945, when 27,000 Germans were captured
together with 70 tanks and 50 guns.

The late 12C church of Ste-Foy, Sélestat

Amongst its natives were probably Martin Schongauer (c. 1420–91), also claimed by Augsburg; the German fabulist Theophilus Pfeffel (1736–1809); Gén. Rapp (1771–1821); Adm. Bruat (1796–1855); Auguste Bartholdi (1834–1904), sculptor of the 'Lion of Belfort', and the 'Statue of Liberty' in New York harbour; and Jean-Jacques Waltz (known as 'Hansi'; 1873–1951), the artist and caricaturist.

Just N.W. of the centre of the old town stands the ****Musée d'Unterlinden**, attractively installed in buildings surrounding the cloister of the former Dominican convent, founded in the 13C, and once an historic centre of German mysticism.

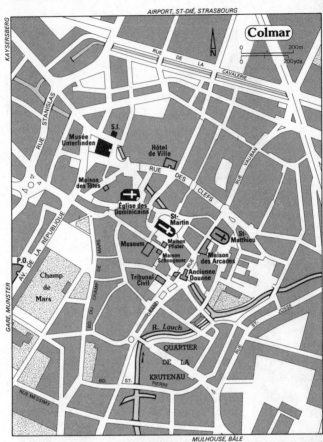

To the l. of the entrance-hall are several German primitives, including *Martin
Schongauer*, Adoration of the Magi; *anon.* Martyrdom of St Ursula (early 16C);
Gaspard Isenmann, Christ on the Mount of Olives, part of an altarpiece of 1565;
anon. St Martin exorcising; *Holbein the Elder*, Female portrait.—From the
cloister walk we enter the 13C *Chapel*, in which is displayed the *Isenheim
Altarpiece* (1516), by *Mathias Gothardt Nithardt*, better known as *Mathias
Grünewald* (c. 1455–1528), the sculptured parts of the retable carved c. 1490 by
Nicolas de Haguenau. It was this altarpiece which inspired Hindemith to compose his symphony 'Mathias der Mahler'. The altarpiece displays, when closed,
the Crucifixion, with the swooning Virgin supported by St John, below which is
Mary Magdalen, and to the r. the Baptist pointing to Christ on the cross; to the l.
of the central panel is St Sebastian; to the r. is St Anthony; while below is the Entombment.—On opening, the l.-hand panel displays the Annunciation; the
r.-hand panel, the Resurrection; and in the centre, the Virgin and Child (r.), with
angel musicians. A further opening displays the sculptured section, with St Anthony enthroned in the centre, on either side of which stand SS Augustine and St
Jerome, with a predella of Christ and the Apostles, by *Desiderius* or *Sébastien
Beichel*. To the l. is Grünewald's painting of St Anthony being visited by St Paul
the hermit; to the l. is the Temptation of St Anthony.

Also in the Chapel are several panels from the retable of the Dominican
Church, by the *School of Schongauer* (c. 1480); engravings by *Schongauer*; the

Bergheim predella (1460), depicting St George and the Dragon; a Massacre of the Innocents; a Martyrdom of St Bartholomew; a diptych of St Catherine and St Laurence; and the Tomb of Ulrich de Huss (d. 1344).

Notable in the following rooms are the carved Triptych de Bergheim (1517); a series of capitals from Alspach; and the Tomb of Jean de Kayserberg (1482).—Adjacent is a section devoted to *Alsatian Wines*, and temporary exhibitions.

FIRST FLOOR. It is worth while entering the gallery of the Chapel for another distant view of the Grünewald altarpiece.—Continuing in a clockwise direction, one traverses a series of rooms containing local costumes and furniture; toys, and moulds; ironwork; pewter; arms and armour; ceramics; stoves; musical instruments; and sections devoted to local history and traditions; the Napoleonic period, etc.—The basement accommodates archaeological collections, a Gallo-Roman mosaic (3-4C), and exhibitions of contemporary art, etc.

On making our exit, it is convenient to turn r. along the Rue des Têtes, passing a gabled house of 1608 which gives the street its name, and then l. along the Rue des Boulangers, to reach the S. facade of the **Dominican Church** (13-15C), long used as a corn-market. The interior contains—while *St-Martin*, its usual home, is under restoration—the altarpiece by Schongauer of The Virgin in a bower of roses (1473).

Continuing E., we turn r. past the W. front of **St-Martin** (commonly called the *Cathedral*), a striking basilica of 1237–1366, replacing a 10C church. The campanile was added to the S. tower after a fire in 1572. The *Portal St-Nicolas*, on the S. side, is noteworthy for the expressions of its grotesques, and for the statue (l.) of Master Humbert (1245–1300), architect of the nave, with his square and drawing-board. The interior contains good 14-15C glass. The octagonal choir (1366; by Guillaume de Marbourg), containing good stalls, is surrounded by an ambulatory, unique in Alsace; the Silbermann organ dates from 1770.

To the S. stands the old *Corps-de-Garde* (1575) and the *Maison Pfister* (1537), with its exterior murals. In the adjacent Rue des Marchands is Bartholdi's birthplace, with a small *Museum*.

Hence one may continue downhill through a district preserving numerous half-timbered houses, among them the *Maison du Pélerin* (1571), to the *Pl. de l'Ancienne-Douane* or *Koïfhuss* (1480–17C), long used as the Hôtel de Ville. To the S. is the attractive **Quartier de la Krutenau**, an area known as 'Petite Venice' for the picturesque riverside views it provides, approached by the Rue des Tanneurs or the Rue St-Jean, the latter passing (r.) the pink *Law-courts* (1771), and several Renaissance houses.

Turning N. along the Grand' Rue, we pass (l.) The Renaissance *Maison des Arcades* (1609), behind which is the former *Hospital*, a classical 18C building. Further N. stands **St-Matthieu**, once a Franciscan church, and now a Protestant temple, containing good 14-15C glass, including a Crucifixion attrib. To Pierre d'Andlau, and an early Silbermann organ.—Turning l. along the Rue des Clefs, the late 18C *Hôtel de Ville* is passed (r.) before regaining the Pl. Unterlinden.

To the S.W. is the *Pl. Rapp*, the *Champ des Mars*, and the *Préfecture*.

The main road continues due S. via (25km) *Ensisheim*, an old town preserving a *Hôtel de Ville* of 1540, to enter **Mulhouse** 14km beyond (see Rte 118), but an interesting DETOUR may be made via **Neuf-Brisach**, 18km S.E. of Colmar, a fortress built by Vauban in 1699–1708 to guard the river-crossing 5km further E.

(Customs).—**Freiburg** lies 20km E. of the Rhine.—*Ensisheim* (see above) may be gained 20km S.W. of Neuf-Brisach.

B. Via Obernai, Ribeauvillé, and Riquewihr, to Guebwiller (taking in Colmar)

141.5km (88 miles). B35 and N422. 33km **Obernai**—7km *Barr*—D35. **Ribeauvillé**—D1B. 4.5km **Riquewihr**—11km **Kaysersberg**—11km **Turkheim**—5.5km **Colmar**—D83. 15km **Rouffach**—10.5km **Guebwiller**—D430. 23km **Mulhouse**.

The distance will be considerably longer if more detours—such as the recommended one to **Haut-Koenigsburg**—are included, while the route may be extended to take in **Thann**, an additional 37km.

Maps: IGN 12, 31, or 104. M 242.

The road leads S.W. from **Strasbourg**, at 9.5km traversing *Entzheim*, to the N. of which Turenne fought an indecisive battle against the Imperialists in 1674.

At 13.5km *Krautergersheim*, in the cemetery of which lies Lili Schönemann, once betrothed to Goethe, lies to the l., and 3km beyond, we turn r. to (3km) **Obernai** (9,400 Obernois), a picturesque town and ancient residence of the dukes of Alsace. It was once fortified, and has a restored *Hôtel de Ville* of 1523, behind which is a 13-16C *Belfry*, a relic of a chapel demolished in 1873. To the N. rises *St-Pierre-et-St-Paul*, in the Gothic taste of 1873.

Rosheim, 5km N.W., is a convenient place from which one may follow the so-called 'Route des Vins'. It preserves, in the main street, the 12C *Maison des Païens*, possibly the oldest surviving example of civil architecture in Alsace. Restored *St-Pierre-et-St-Paul* (late 12C) retaining its Lombardic decoration and some sculpture of interest, has a later tower. Three of the ancient *Town Gates* also survive.

The road turns S.W. through picturesque *Boersch* to (5.5km) *Ottrott* (r.) producing a good red wine, overlooked by the feudal ruins of *Lutzelbourg*, and *Ratsamhausen*.

Hence a by-road ascends to (11km) **Ste-Odile** (764m; view), site of a convent founded in the 7C by Odile, the patron of Alsace, born blind at Obernai but who miraculously received sight at her baptism. Abandoned after a fire in 1546, it was re-occupied in the 17C by Premonstratensians, who remained there until the Revolution. It was re-opened in 1853. The church of 1687 and adjacent chapels are devoted to her cult.—Of more interest is the **Mur Païen**, a prehistoric or Celtic work composed of huge blocks of unhewn stone piled up to form a wall over 10km long and in some places 3m high. The best preserved section is the N. end, near the ruins of the castle of *Dreystein*, almost due W. of Ste-Odile.—To the S.E. are the ruins of the castle of *Landsberg*.

7km S. of the Ottrott crossroads lies *Barr*, an ancient town of tanneries with a Renaissance *Hôtel de Ville* and small *Museum*.

We bear S.W. to (5km) **Andlau**, with a remarkable restored *Romanesque church* (9-11C), a relic of a famous convent for noble ladies founded in the 9C by Richarda, the repudiated wife of Charles le Gros, with a *Frieze* round the lower part of the tower, and in the porch some notable sculptures, one on the lintel depicting Adam and Eve.

8km. *Dambach*, a picturesque walled village, preserving several characteristic old houses, is traversed, and 5km beyond, *Scherwiller*, site of Duc Antoine de Lorraine's victory which crushed the rebellion of the 'Rustauds' (cf. Saverne) in 1525.—3km. *Châtenois* (see Rte 114B), 4.5km E. of which lies **Sélestat**; see Rte 116A.—2km. *Kintzheim*, with ruins of a 14C castle.

Hence it is convenient to make the DETOUR to (8km) the *Castle of **Haut-Koenigsburg**, ◇ crowning an abrupt promontory (757m) dominating the plain below, and one of the most splendid and picturesque fortresses in Alsace.

The main fabric was constructed by Count Oswald de Thierstein (1480), although the keep dates from the 12C. In 1899 the ruins were presented by Sélestat to the Kaiser, who had them restored with German thoroughness at the public expense. The interior contains heterogeneous collections of furniture, etc., and a maquette of the castle prior to its restoration. It served as the background to Jean Renoir's film 'La Grande Illusion' (1937).

The main route may be regained 4km S. of Kintzheim at *St-Hippolyte*, ancient *Audoldivillare*, sacked by the Swedes in 1633, where we turn r. for (3.5km) *Bergheim*, and 4km S.W., **Ribeauvillé**, a long straggling village of considerable charm, known for its white wines, situated in the valley of the Strengbach and overlooked from the N. by the ruined castle of *St-Ulrich, among others in the neighbourhood belonging to the Ribeaupierre family.

To the r. near the S. end of the Grand-Rue stands the *Pfifferhaus*, said to be the old headquarters of the itinerant musicians of Alsace. Further up the street stands the late 13C *Tour des Bouchers*, a relic of its former ramparts; beyond which (r.) is the parish church (1282–1473), its organ of 1708 under restoration.—At *Hunawihr* (r.; between Ribeauvillé and Riquewihr) is a curious fortified church and cemetery (14-15C).

4.5km. **Riquewihr**, an ancient and partly-walled village, lying at the foot of the vine-covered slopes of the Vosges, preserves numerous old houses, many converted to commercial use, and to the l. of the E. entrance, the *Château* of 1539 containing an *Alsatian Postal Museum*. The upper end of the Grande Rue is dominated by the *Dolder*, a 13C gate-tower, beyond which is an outer gate, the *Obertor* (1500). Unfortunately the place can be uncomfortably crowded with trippers during weekends and in the summer.

The road skirts the village of *Beblenheim*, noted for its wines, *Mittelwihr*, and *Bennwihr*, the latter two rebuilt since their destruction in 1945, and at 5km. we turn r. through *Sigolsheim* (likewise rebuilt), its restored church of c. 1200 with a portal of interest, and *Kintzheim*, preserving its ramparts and several old houses.

6km. **Kayserberg**, a picturesque and historic town on the river Weiss, with a ruined castle acquired in 1226 by Heinrich VII, son of the Emperor Frederick II Hohenstaufen. In 1293 it became a free Imperial city. In 1636 it was sacked by the Swedes, and damaged in 1945. It was the birthplace of Albert Schweitzer (1875–1965). The German Renaissance *Hôtel de Ville* (1604), and adjacent *Church* (12-15C), with naive Romanesque sculpture in its portal and a carved and gilt retable of 1518, are of interest. The valley is dominated to the N.W. by *Le Brézouard* (1228m); see Rte 114B.

Hence we drive S.E. through *Ammerschwihr* to (11km) **Colmar**; see Rte 116A, or alternatively turn r. after 7km past (r.) *Niedermorschwihr* to (2.5km) **Turkheim**, another picturesque old town preserving three of its gates, and noted for its white wine. Near here, in 1675, Turenne gained one of his victories over the Imperialists. To

Landscape near Turkheim

the W. rises the *Grand Honnack* (976m); to the S.W. is the castle of *Pflixbourg*; see Rte 112.

Driving S.E. through (3km) Wintzenheim, Wettolsheim is shortly by-passed (r.), where in 1784–87 Alfieri lived with the Countess of Albany, his 'good angel'.—To the r. is *Eguisheim*, once fortified, above which rises the ruined towers of 11-12C strongholds destroyed in 1466, erected by the family of Eguisheim, one of whose members was Pope Leo IX (1048–54).—The road continues S. through (7km) *Hattstatt*, another ancient village with an 11-15C church, restored, 2km S.W. of which lies *Gueberschwihr*, with its Romanesque tower.

6.5km. **Rouffach**, an ancient and once fortified town, was the birthplace of Marshal Lefebvre (1755–1820), a miller's son who became Duc de Dantzig, and whose wife was the original of Sardou's 'Madame Sans-Gêne' (1893). To the r. of the main street is a Franciscan church of 1280–1300; to the E. stands *Notre-Dame* (11-14C), with an octagonal belfry; it contains several Romanesqu details, particularly in the choir. Nearby are several characteristic gabled houses, notable among which is the old *Hôtel de Ville* (1575).

The attractive village of *Westhalten* lies 3km W.—At 4.5km we fork S.W. past *Issenheim*, with relics of a cloister of the old Antonites convent for which Grünewald's magnificent retable (now in the museum at Colmar) was painted.

3.5km. **Guebwiller** (11,100 Guebwillerois), a small industrial town on the r. bank of the Lauch, is known for its wines. Near the S. end of the Rue de la République stands *Notre-Dame* (1766), an imposing red sandstone building with rounded transepts, containing a Baroque altar. At the N. end of the street is *St-Léger*, with two dissimilar Romanesque towers and a rebuilt octagonal tower over the crossing. The three figures in the tympanum of the portal, and the gable above, are of interest. To the E. of the main street is the former Dominican church, now housing a small museum.

3km N.W. lies *Buhl*, just prior to which a l.-hand turning leads 3km to **Murbach**, with the important remains of the Romanesque *Church (10-11C), whose abbots were princes of the celebrated abbey founded by St Pirmin in 727, whose abbots were princes of the Holy Roman Empire, and none but members of noble families were admitted as monks; it was secularised in 1764. What survives are the choir, and transepts, surmounted by two towers, while the curious flat apse is of particular interest.

At *Lautenbach*, 3km beyond Buhl, is a fine Romanesque church with a remarkable porch, well-carved capitals, and a pulpit and organ-loft which rank among the best works of the 17C Rhenish school.—The road continues to (17km) *Le Markstein*; see Rte 112.—To the N. of the valley rises *Le Petit Ballon* (1267m); to the S. the *Grand Ballon* (1424m), both commanding extensive views; see p 610.

The D430 leads 23km S.E. to **Mulhouse**; see Rte 118. Travellers wishing to visit *Thann* first should turn l. at (3km) *Soultz*, and continue S. below the *Vieil Armand* (956m) or *Hartmannswillerkopf*, an important artillery position which changed hands repeatedly, but remained in French hands from 1915–18, to (12km) *Cernay*, there turning r. for **Thann**; see Rte 112. Cernay itself, with remains of its ancient fortifications, was considerably damaged in both world wars.—The direct Thann-Mulhouse road lies 2km S., and 6km beyond is the Aspach junction. *Altkirch* lies 19km S.E., and **Belfort** 27km S.W.; for both see Rte 118.

117 Langres to Besançon and Pontarlier, for Lausanne

158km (98 miles). N74. 11km *Longeau*—D67. 43km **Gray**—46km **Besançon**—N57. 58km *Pontarlier*.

Maps: IGN 29, 30, 38, or 104, 109. M 243.

LANGRES (11,400 Langrois), an ancient cathedral town and fortress, finely placed on a spur of a plateau (466m) in a strategic position between the valleys of the Marne and Bonnelle, is almost entirely surrounded by its partially restored medieval ramparts, providing a succession of remarkable views, the circuit of which is recommended.

Andematunum was the capital of the Lingones, allies of Caesar in Gaul, one of whose chiefs was Sabinus, who attempted to establish a Gallic empire after Nero's death in 71 A.D. St Benignus founded a church here in the 2C, followed by St Sénateur, its first bishop (early 3C). In 301 the Germans were decisively defeated under its walls, but in 407 it was devastated by another wave of invaders. During the feudal period it was an ecclesiastical countship, and from the 12-18C its bishops were peers of France.

Its most famous native was Denis Diderot (1713–84), the philosopher and encyclopaedist, whose father worked in the cutlery trade, for which Langres and its neighbourhood was noted. Others include Jacques Gillot (c. 1590), a contributor to the 'Satire Ménippée'; the artist Claude Gillot (1673–1722), and Claude Godart d'Aucourt (1716–95), farmer-general and pamphleteer.

From the *Pl. des États-Unis* one enters the walled town from the S. by the reconstructed *Porte des Moulins* (1647), just E. of which is an area under excavation. The first r.-hand turning beyond the gate leads to the *Tour St-Fergeux* (1472). The main Rue Diderot leads past (r.) the *Théâtre* (once a chapel, in which Bossuet was ordained), and a few paces l., Gothic *St-Martin* (13C), with a belfry of 1745 and other 18C additions, including the portal. The carved *Crucifixion (16C) above the high altar is attrib. of François Gentil of Troyes; a painting of a

Martyrdom near the entrance, by Richard Tassel includes a view of mid 17C Langres.

The *Pl. Diderot* contains a statue by Bartholdi (1885) of Diderot, born at No.6 in the square, just beyond which is the *Pl. Jeanne-Mance*, named after a local woman (1606–73) who founded the Hôtel-Dieu in Montreal (Canada).

To the r. rises the incongruous classical W. front (1768; by Davilliers) of the **Cathedral of St-Mammès**, above which are two heavy towers. The interior of the building (1141–96) is well-proportioned but gloomy.

The pulpit and organ-case come from the abbey of Morimond. In the N. aisle is the striking *Chapelle de Ste-Croix* (1549); on the S. side are the mutilated remains of a cloister. In the transepts are 16C tapestries depicting the Life of St Mammès, etc., and good rose-windows. An ambulatory and radiating chapels were added to the original choir in the 14C; the arches between the choir and transepts are notable; the eight monolithic columns beneath the triforium, with their fantastic capitals, are said (traditionally) to have come from a temple of Jupiter; the tile pavement, of Rouen manufacture, is by Masseot Abaquesne (c. 1542). A Romanesque doorway leads to the Chapelle des Reliques.

In the street opposite the cathedral is the *Musée St-Didier* (in a former 12-13C church; and once 'degraded as a receptacle for fire-engines'), now housing archaeological collections, mainly Gallo-Roman funerary stellae, statues, and bronzes; also several carved capitals and 14-16C tombs. The picture-gallery contains *Seghers*, Roman Charity, paintings by the *Tassel* family, and a tiger's head by *Delacroix*.

In the Rue Card. Morlot, further W., is a well-restored Renaissance house.—Turning r., the *Hôtel de Ville* is approached, dating from 1778. In the adjacent *Pl. de Verdun* stands the *Musée du Breuil de St-Germain*, installed in a Renaissance mansion, containing a variety of objets d'art, etc., including ceramics from Apré, and paintings by *Van Loo* of Diderot (1767); of *Racine*, by *De Troy*; and *Ranc*, Diana. Sections are devoted to Diderot, Claude Gillot, etc.

To the W. is the *Porte de l'Hôtel de Ville*, and further S. is a walled-up Gallo-Roman gate, one of the four earlier entrances to Langres.

Travellers pressed for time should make their exit through the former and turn l., following the outside of the ramparts, to re-enter at the *Porte Neuve*, shortly passing (r.) the *Tours de Navarre et d'Orval*, the most imposing fortification (1519), with an interior vaulted ramp, to regain the Porte des Moulins.

LANGRES TO BELFORT (138km). The N19 leads E., traversing attractive country and at 10km passing 3km S. of *Celsoy*, its 14C church containing the fine tomb of Guibert, the physician of Jean II, Charles V, and Charles VI.—14km. *Fayl-la-Foret* or *Fayl-Billot*, where a national school of basket-ware has been established, and 6km beyond, we enter the *Franche-Comté*.—31km. *Pont-sur-Saône*, with its 18C bridge, 15km N.E. of which lies *Faverney*, with a 12-15C church of a Benedictine abbey founded in 722, with remains of 18C dependencies.—12km. *Vesoul* (see Rte 112), whence one may follow either the main road through *Lure* (30km N.W.) to *Belfort*, or the more southerly D9; see Rte 112.

The N74 leads due S., traversing the *Citadel* of Langres, of 1882, to (11km) *Longeau*, where we fork l. off the Dijon road (see Rte 109) to (24km) *Champlitte*, preserving relics of its walls of 1538 and a church of 1525 with a tall belfry; the *Hôtel de Ville* was once the château of Toulongeon (1748–1812), a historian of the Revolution, who was born here; it now accommodates a *Folklore Museum*.—9.5km *Oyrières*, with several ruins of its past importance, is traversed.

10.5km. **Gray** (8,300 Graylois), on the Saône, crossed by a handsome 17C bridge of 14 arches, is an old town preserving in its centre a *Church* begun in 1478 but since mutilated, a much restored *Hôtel de Ville* (1568) with red granite columns, and a 17C *Château* entered through the medieval gateway of its predecessor, and now housing a *Museum* devoted to local archaeological finds, and painting including several good pastels, among them works by Pierre-Paul Prud'hon.

To the N.E. of Gray are several places of interest, including Membrey (22km on the N70), with slight Roman remains, 7km E. of which at *Ray-sur-Saône* is a château rebuilt in the 17-18C; and 4km S., at *Seveux* (ancient *Segobodium*), the church contains the tomb of Otho de la Roche (c. 1225), the crusading knight who became 'sire' of Athens in 1205 and founded a ducal line of Latin princes from whom, Gibbon remarks, 'Boccace, Chaucer, and Shakespeare have borrowed their Theseus, Duke of Athens'.—There is a cloister and other relics of the 12C *Abbaye de Corneux* 6.5km E. of Gray; and 18km S.W., the attractive château of *Talmay* (1762).

The D475 leads S., and E. of *Montseugny*, with a sculptured church porch and ruins of a castle of the Knights of Malta, to (19km) *Pesmes*, with a 12-16C church containing a fine Renaissance chapel and other details of interest.—7km beyond lie the extensive ruins of the castle of *Montmirey*, destroyed in 1477, and 17km further S. is *Dôle*; see Rte 126.

The D67 drives S.E. to (23.5km) *Marnay*, preserving relics of fortifications and old houses.—Some 8km N.E. is the restored 13C castle of *Pin* and the neighbouring 18C château of *Moncley*.—13.5km. *Pouilley-les-Vignes*, with the ruins of a 14C castle, is traversed as we approach, 8km beyond, **Besançon**; see Rte 124.

The direct road to *Pontarlier* (N57), although 2km shorter, and faster, is less interesting than the D67, which forks r. off it after 9km, first skirting the l. bank of the Doubs before climbing to cross a tract of high wooded country and descending into the valley of the Loue.

16km. **Ornans**, an attractively sited small industrial town, was the birthplace of Nicolas Perrenot de Granvelle (1486–1550; cf. Besançon), and Gustave Courbet (1819–77), who is also buried there. The *Grand-Pont* commands picturesque views of the old houses flanking the river, on the S. bank of which to the l. is a small *Museum* devoted to Courbet. To the r. is the 15C *Hôtel de Grospain*, beyond which is the 16C church.—In a valley to the W. lie the ruins of the château of *St-Denis*, and at 9km that of *Cléron* (14C; restored).

Leaving Ornans, the road continues to ascend the valley of the Loue via *Montgesoye*, *Vuillafans*, and (11km) *Lods* (prin. Lo), to (13km) *Mouthier-Haute-Pierre*, with a church of 1512 and relics of a priory. We now ascend the *Gorges de Nouailles* through pine forests to meet the N57 after 7km. Just prior to this junction a r.-hand road leads 4km to *Ouhans*, where another r.-hand turning approaches the *Source of the Loue*, where the river bursts forth from a cavern at the end of a cirque.—The main road traverses a plateau to (14km) **Pontarlier** (18,800 Pontissaliens), taking its name from *Pons Ariolicae*, a bridge over the Doubs. Here in 1871 the French Army of the East under Bourbaki made its last stand against the Prussians before retreating into Switzerland. *St-Bénigne*, to the S. of the main street, has a Flamboyant portal, but its facade was reconstructed after a fire in 1736, which ravaged the town.

14km N.E., on the D437, lies **Montbenoît**, its remarkable 13-16C *Abbey-church* with a small cloister. it contains good stalls and misericords of 1527—note the two women pulling each others' hair, and Samson and Delilah. The pulpit, and the knights on horseback above the entrance, will be noticed.—17km further N.E., beyond a defile of the Doubs, lies *Morteau*, with a 13-18C priory church. The waterfall of *Saut-du-Doubs* may be approached via *Villars-le-Lac*, 6km E., close to the Swiss frontier.

Beyond Pontarlier the *Cluse de Pontarlier* is threaded to (4km) the **Fort de Joux** (r.), where in the old fortress, in 1775, the younger Mirabeau was imprisoned by a 'lettre de cachet' obtained by his father. He escaped the following year, accompanied by Mme Thérèse de Monnier. The negro patriot of San Domingo, Toussaint Louverture (1743–1803) died a prisoner here. Gén. Dupont was held here after his capitulation at Baylen, in Spain, in 1808. The fort was blown up in 1877.

Here the road divides: the l.-hand turning leading to (7km) the Swiss frontier (Customs) to approach **Neuchâtel**, on its lake, 42km beyond. The N57 continues S., passing near (r.) the *Lac de St-Point*, the largest in the Jura, beyond which is the *Lac de Remoray*, and *Malbuisson*, 9km S.W., among other small ski resorts on the shore of the first, to reach the frontier (and Customs) after 19km, below (r.) *Le Morand* (1419m) and *Le Mont-d'Or* (1460m).—44km **Lausanne**.

118   Besançon to Mulhouse

132km (82 miles). N83. 29km *Baume-les-Dames*—26km *L'Isle sur-le-Doubs*—34km **Belfort**—27km N466. 17km **Mulhouse**.

Maps: IGN 30, 31, or 109, 104. M 243.

The A36 motorway provides a rapid route from just N. of Besançon to Belfort and Mulhouse.

For **Besançon**, see Rte 124. The road leads N.E. along the bank of the Doubs to (18km) *Roulans*, with a ruined 13C castle and a chapel-crowned hill, 11km beyond which is **Baume-les-Dames**, originally *Baume-les-Nonnes*, after its Benedictine abbey founded in 763, which became a chapter of noble ladies entitled to 16 quarterings (cf. Épinal, and Remiremont). The church contains a Pietà of 1549; the domed abbey church, long used as a corn-exchange, is much dilapidated. The Marquis de Jouffroy made his first attempts to use steam power for navigation near Baume, in 1776.

The Doubs is crossed at (15km) *Clerval*, with a ruined castle, and a château of the 13th and 18Cs, and several 16C houses, to be recrossed at (11km) *L'Isle-sur-le-Doubs*. To the S. extends the long ridge of the *Montagne du Lomont*, rising to 840m.

L'ISLE-SUR-LE-DOUBS TO BELFORT VIA MONTBÉLIARD (42km). After 2km the N463 forks r. to follow the Doubs to (21km.) **Montbéliard** (33,400 inhab.), an industrial town manufacturing Peugeot cars, bicycles, etc., once a fortress, and commanded by its castle, rebuilt in 1751, retaining towers of 1425 and 1594. Its last countess married the Tsar Paul I in 1776. From 1397 until 1793 it was a fief of the house of Württemberg, under which it acquired its predominant Protestant character. Near here in Jan. 1871 took place the battle of Héricourt (see below); more fighting was seen during Sept.-Nov. 1944. The Peugeot family agreed to allow their factory at *Sochaux* to be sabotaged during the war, an example *not* followed by the Michelin family at Clermont-Ferrand. It was the birthplace of the naturalist Georges Cuvier (1769–1832).—At the W. end of the old centre is the 16C *Halles*, a short distance N.E. of which is the *Pl. St-Martin*, with the *Hôtel de Ville* of 1770, a *Protestant Temple* (1605), and the Renaissance *Maison des Princes*, now a bank. On an adjacent wall the Editor took note of a graffiti, in

English, which read 'This is the city of the Dead'.

At *Mandeure*, c. 15km S., Roman *Epomanduodorum*, are relics of a large Roman theatre, 142m is diameter,—which would suggest it was once a place of considerable importance. *St-Hippolyte*, a small town 21.5km further S., with a 14C church, situated at the confluence of the Doubs and the Dessoubres, was the birthplace of the artist Jacques Courtois, 'Le Bourguignon' (1621 – 76).

Traversing an industrial area, we bear N.E. from Montbéliard to (19km) *Belfort*; see below.

The N83 forks l. to (20km) *Héricourt*, retaining a tower of its old castle, which gave its name to the battles of Jan. 1871, when Bourbaki attempted unsuccessfully to raise the siege of Belfort, which is entered 12km N.E.

BELFORT (52,700 Belfortains; only 8,400 prior to 1870), an industrial and garrison town on the Savoureuse, of slight interest to the tourist, commands the Trouée de Belfort or 'Belfort Gap', between the Vosges and the Jura, and was long a first-class fortress. It is now the préfecture of the *Territoire de Belfort*, a relic of the department of the Haut-Rhin which remained to France after the German annexation of 1871.

Named 'Bel-fort' from its citadel, it was a stronghold from the 13C, enduring several sieges when under Austrian domination between 1350 – 1648. In 1813 – 14 it resisted the Austrians for 113 days, and during the Hundred Days of 1815 it was held for Napoleon. The heroic defence of Belfort in 1870 – 71 under Col Denfert-Rochereau was one of the few 'glorious' episodes of the Franco-Prussian War. The garrison marched out with all the honours of war at the end of the fighting, having withstood German attacks for 103 days. It successfully defended the 'Gap' in 1914, and was a base for operations on the Alsatian front. It was liberated on 22 Nov. 1944 after the fort of *Salbert*, to the N.W., had been taken, but suffered some damage in the process.

In the centre of the five-sided old town, on the W. bank of the river, is the *Pl. d'Armes*, on the E. side of which rises the impressive red sandstone church of **St-Christophe**, built in 1727 – 50 in the Greco-Roman style, and restored since damaged in 1870 – 71. The stone is well-carved, and the orgaⁿ case is notable.

From behind the *Hôtel de Ville* of 1784, to the S., we get a good view of the famous **Lion de Belfort*, carved by Bartholdi below the rock-face of the citadel, to commemorate its defence, and which despite its size (22m by 11m) is masterly in expression. In the *Château* are installed archaeological and historical collections, and some 18-20C paintings.—To the N.E. of the old centre is the *Porte de Brisach*, built by Vauban, together with part of the fortifications.

BELFORT TO BASLE (65km). The D419 leads E. through (22km) *Retzwiller* and (5km) *Ballersdorf*, to (7km) **Altkirch**, on the r. bank of the Ill, which grew up round a priory and became the chief town of the old German *Sundgau*; its small regional museum contains portraits by J.-J. Henner (1829 – 1905), born at *Bernwiller*, 10km N.W.—The main road continues E. via (24km) *Hésingue* for **Basle**, 7km beyond (Customs).—An attractive detour through the Sundgau may be made by turning S. to (13km) *Feldbach*, with a restored Romanesque church of archaeological interest, and (9km) *Ferrette*, an ancient little town with ruined castles (views), seat of the counts of Pfirt. From the latter the D473 leads past (l.) relics of the monastery of *Luppach*, to gain the main road at Hésingue, 25km N.E.

Delle, 22km S.E. of Belfort, with a church of 1573 and 1709, is the frontier town (Customs) on the road to (14km) *Porrentruy* and *Belémont*, 29km beyond, between **Basle** and **Berne**.

Quitting Belfort, the N83 leads 27km N.E. to a road junction 9km S.E. of *Thann*. For the road N.—the 'Route des Vins', see Rte 116B, in reverse. Turning r. and crossing the motorway (an alternative direct route between Belfort and Mulhouse), the D466 leads E. to (17km) *Mulhouse*.

MULHOUSE (pron. Mooloose; 113,800 Mulhousiens; 6,600 in 1801; 89,100 in 1901), a busy heavy industrial and textile conurbation, the old centre of which lies between the Rhone-Rhin Canal and the river Ill, here canalised, contains museums of interest, and is an important hub of communications.

Mühle Haus, or mill-house, after being ruled in turn by the bishops of Strasbourg (11-12C) and by the House of Austria (1261), became a free Imperial city under the emperor Wenceslas (1397). Its citizens constituted a 'bourgeoisie fermée', which several times defended the town against the bellicose nobles of Alsace. In 1648, when the Treaty of Westphalia gave the greater part of Alsace to France, the little republic of Mulhouse was added to the Swiss Confederation, with which it had already made an alliance; but in 1798 it voluntarily rejoined France. In 1871 it was annexed by Germany, but was treated as occupied enemy territory by the Germans during the 1914–18 war; and likewise from June 1940 until Nov. 1944 it suffered privation, and was bombed by the Allies prior to its liberation. Among its natives were the physicist Jean-Henry Lambert (1728–77), Godefroy Engelmann (1788–1839), the lithographer and chromolithographer; and Alfred Dreyfus (1859–1935), of the 'Affaire'. In 1848 Adolphe Braun (1811–77) established his print-publishing firm here, its reproductions ubiquitous throughout France.

The central *Pl. de la Réunion* is overlooked by the *Temple St-Étienne* (1866), containing 14C glass and 17C stalls from its predecessor, demolished in 1858.

To the E. is the **Hôtel de Ville**, the most notable relic of old Mulhouse, a two-storeyed building of 1552 covered with curious mural paintings of 1698, several times restored; lastly in 1968, in which year the *Musée Historique was moved here. There is an external covered stairway, and the style throughout is a blend of Gothic with the German Renaissance.

The collections include archaeology of the area and of the Hallstatt Culture; furniture, among which is a remarkable marquetry 'dressoir' (16C); arms and armour; costume; glass and ceramics, including a faïence stove or 'poële' (18C); prints, and paintings, among them the Retable of Rheinfelden (15C); and the imposing Council Chamber, among others with painted ceilings, may be visited.

A lane immediately S. leads shortly to the **Musée des Beaux-Arts**, in need of reform, but including several paintings of interest.

Among them are: *School of Cranach*, Woman with a child; *Ruisdael*, Landscape; *Brueghel le jeune*, Skating scene; *Teniers*, Interior; *Van Dyck*, Female portrait; *Jouvenet*, Self-portrait; *Lawrence*, Sketch for a female portrait; *Martin Drolling*, Old man; *J.-É. Blanche*, Maurice de Rothschild; characteristic works by *Boudin, Monticelli*, *Henner*, *A. Ingenbleek*, and *Léon Lehmann* (1873–1953), and watercolours by *Henri Zuber*.
  Some distance to the W., installed in the *Chapelle St-Jean*, that of the old commandery of the Knights of St John of Jerusalem, is a lapidary collection.

Of great interest and importance is the *Musée de l'Impression sur étoffes**, a few minutes' walk S.E. of the Hôtel de Ville, beyond the *Pl. de la République*, approached by the Rue Poincaré. This remarkable and well-displayed collection itself makes a visit to Mulhouse rewarding. The whole process and history of printing on cotton, for which the town is famous, is graphically described, with numerous rich and colourful examples of materials from the late 18C, when the manufacture of printed fabrics was established here, in 1746, by

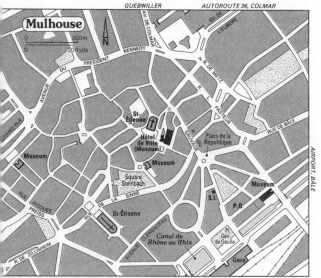

Jean-Jacques Schmaltzer (1721–97), Samuel Koechlin (1719–76), and Jean-Henri Dollfus (1724–1802).

The collection includes examples of the work of Christophe-Philippe Oberkampf 1738–1815), manufacturer of 'toiles de Jouy' from 1760; Batik, and a variety of Oriental forms, etc., apart from fabrics from other parts of Europe. The museum also contains a number of costumes, working models of printing machines, a comprehensive reference section, and—in addition—reimpressions of a variety of handkerchiefs and headscarfs of historical interest may be purchased on the premises.

To the S.E. of the centre is a *Zoo* and *Botanical Garden*; c. 3km to the W. is a *Railway Museum*, with a collection of French locomotives from the year 1844. Also of interest is the collection of 600 veteran cars in the *Musée de l'Automobile*, assembled since 1960 by the Swiss industrialists Fritz and Hans Schlumpf.

MULHOUSE TO BASLE (34km). The N666 leads S.E. through (7km) *Habsheim*, with a *Hôtel de Ville* of 1578, then parallel to the motorway, which is crossed at 4km for (8km) *St-Louis*, the frontier town (Customs), just E. of which lies *Hunıngue* (Hunzinger), a former fortress, which was bravely defended in 1799 and 815.—A further 5km brings one to the centre of **Basle** (*Bâle*, or *Basel*).

MULHOUSE TO MÜLLHEIM, FOR (54KM) FREIBURG. The D39 is followed to the N.E. across the *Forêt de la Hardi*.—At 15km a by-road forks r. for (4km) **Ottmarsheim**, with a curious octagonal church (mid 11C), restored, a replica in miniature of the palatine chapel of Aix-la-Chapelle, modelled on San Vitale, Ravenna.—To the S.E. are hydro-electrical works.—Regaining the main road, we turn r.—11km N. is the nuclear power-station of *Fessenheim*.—The Rhine is crossed (Customs) to *Neuenburg* and *Müllheim*, 5km E.—**Freiburg** lies 29km N.E.; **Basle** 35km S., both also connected by autobahn skirting the E. bank of the river.

X BURGUNDY; JURA

What is now known as **Burgundy** (Fr. Bourgogne) comprises only the depart
ments of *Yonne*, *Côte-d'Or*, *Saône-et-Loire*, and *Ain*. The powerful medieva
duchy, with its capital at Dijon, covered a considerably larger area, although its
frontiers fluctuated over the centuries. The name appears first with the advent
of the Burgundii or Burgundiones, who in the 5C established a kingdom between
the Aar and the Rhône, afterwards absorbed in the Frankish empire. This re
emerged in the 9C, and in c. 900 its territory was extended S. to unite with the
short-lived kingdom of Arles. It later became a fief of the French crown, and in
1363 it fell to Philippe le Hardi (1342– 1404), who acquired Flanders and Artois
(see Section I), and also the Franche-Comté, by marriage. Philippe le Bon
(1396– 1467) added Hainault, Brabant, Limburg, and Holland to the duchy; but
the ambition of his son Charles le Téméraire (1433– 77) to establish a great
Gallo-Belgium kingdom foundered at his death at Nancy, and the duchy
reverted to the French, while his other possessions passed by the marriage of his
daughter Mary (d. 1482) to the Archduke Maximilian of Austria, who in 1494
was elected Holy Roman Emperor. During the wars of the 15C the Burgundian
faction supported Henry V against Charles VI, and more or less represented the
popular party as opposed to the 'aristocratic' Armagnacs. The successes of Joan
of Arc (who the Burgundians captured at Soissons and sold to the English) later
induced Philippe le Bon to unite his interest with those of France (1453).

The **Jura** (Juria, 'a forest') is a curving mountain chain some 240km long and
40-80km wide, forming the frontier between France and Switzerland, separated
from the Vosges by the Belfort gap, but linked with the Savoy Alps. It was the
'Mons Jura' of Caesar's 'Commentaries', dividing the Sequani from the Helvetii
Sloping on the French side in a series of plateaux, with pine forests and high
pastures, it forms a rocky wall on the Swiss side, where its highest ridge, facing
the Alps, falls away to the lakes of Bienne, Neuchâtel, and Léman. The 'Jurassic
system' (clay and limestone) derives its name from the range, which is deeply
furrowed by characteristic gorges or 'cluses', formed by volcanic fracture. It
surface has been likened to a sieve, and its interior mass to a sponge; to this
porous nature are due its numerous caverns, underground rivers, and copious
springs.

Its main summits in France are the *Crêt de la Niege* (1718m) and *Le Recule*
(1717m), overlooking the frontier W. of Geneva; those in Switzerland are *Mon*
Tendre (1680m) and *La Dôle* (1678m), N.W. of Lac Léman. The main ridge is
crossed by the *Cols de St-Cergue* and *La Faucille*—N.E. and S.W. respectively o
La Dôle—which afford splendid views of the Alps.

Its main rivers are the Doubs and Ain, and the range contains several pictures
que lakes. Rock salt is mined, and it produces much Gruyère cheese. Its climate
is rainy in spring, but fairly dry in summer.

119 Troyes to Bourges

226km (140 miles). N77. 49km *St-Florentin*—11km *Pontigny*
—20km **Auxerre**—N151. 43km **Clamecy**—52km **La
Charité-sur-Loire**—51km **Bourges.**

Maps: IGN 22, 28, 27, or 103, 108. M 237, 238.

For an alternative road via *Sens*, and *Gien*, see below.

For **Troyes**, see Rte 122. The N77 leads S. past (r. at 14km) *Bouilly*
with a 16-18C church containing a stone retable of 1556 and a 16C
statue of St Margaret, among others.—14km. *Auxon* and *Ervy-le*
Châtel (*Arviacum*; 9.5km S.), the latter once fortified, possess
church of interest, as does *Neuvy-Sautour*, 13km S.W. of the former
and l. of the N77.

7km. *St-Florentin* (see Rte 121), beyond which one turns due S. to

(11km) **Pontigny**, site of a famous Cistercian *Abbey* (1114), the second of the 'daughters' of Citeaux, itself the 'mother' of 34 abbeys and priories in France, and intimately connected with several archbishops of Canterbury.

Becket fled here from Henry II in 1164, and remained until Henry's threat to expel the Cistercians from England compelled his retirement to Sens in 1166. From 1200 until c. 1213 it was the residence of Stephen Langton during his struggle with John, who rightly refused to recognise his primacy; on his way here in 1240 died Edmund Rich, protesting against the intrusions of Henry III.

The monastery was destroyed at the Revolution, but the *Church* remains, an imposing if severe edifice in the Burgundian Gothic style, 108m long, erected by Thibaut de Champagne in 1150 and completed within 20 years, except for the 13C choir. In the ambulatory is the tomb of Hugues de Macon, the first abbot, and the Baroque shrine of St Edme (Edmund Rich).

20km. Auxerre; see Rte 120.

AUXERRE TO BOURGES VIA ST-FARGEAU AND SANCERRE (139km). The D965 leads S.W. through (24km) *Toucy*, birthplace of Pierre Larousse (1817–75), the lexographer, with a 15C church incorporating two towers of a castle of the bishops of Auxerre.—10.5km S., at *Fontenoy*, previously *Fontanet*, an obelisk commemorates the victory of 841 of Ludwig the Bavarian and Charles le Chauve over Lothair, which led to the treaty of Verdun (cf. Verdun).—21km **St-Fargeau**, on the Loing, has an imposing 13C *Castle* with five large towers and an elliptical keep, which once belonged to Jacques Coeur and was restored by Mlle de Montpensier. The *Church*, of the same date, preserves two good 16C windows, while the *Tour de l'Horloge* is late 15C. The town was the medieval capital of the marshy and wooded region of the *Puisaye*, in the heart of which, 1km S.E., lies *St-Sauveur*, birthplace of the author Gabrielle Colette (1873–1954), with a 17C château retaining an ancient keep.

The D18 leads S. from St-Fargeau to (13km) *St-Amand-en-Puisaye* (see Rte 49), whence the D955 is followed S.W. to meet the N7 N. of (19km) *Cosne-sur-Loire*; see Rte 96.—Crossing the river, the l. bank is followed to *St-Satur* and (14km) **Sancerre**, a hilltop town which was a Huguenot stronghold and earned the title of 'Little Rochelle' but was forced to capitulate in 1573 after a siege of eight months, and its walls were razed. In the park of its château is the 15C *Tour des Fiefs*, the only relic of the old castle, while in the town is a Romanesque abbey gateway.—A r.-hand turning beyond Sancerre leads 15.5km N.W. to *Jars*, with a notable Renaissance church.—18km. The 13-15C *Château de Maupas* lies 4.5km W.—7km. *Les Aix-d'Angillon*, with a good Romanesque church choir, is traversed prior to meeting the N151 E. of (20km) **Bourges**; see Rte 48.

From Auxerre the N151 leads due S. through (9km) *Gy-l'Évêque*, with the 12C belfry of its ruined church, to (14km) *Courson-les-Carrières*, 10km S.W. of which, on the edge of the *Collines de la Puisaye*, lies *Druyes-les-Belles-Fontaines*, with the ruins of a 12-14C castle, a 14C gateway, and Romanesque church.—The *Forêt de Frétoy* is traversed to (10km) *Coulonges-sur-Yonne*, with a 17C bridge, and remains of the 13C *Tour de la Comtesse Mahaut.*—10km E. lies *Châtel-Censoir*; see Rte 120.

Continuing S., with a view (r.) of the spire of *Surgy*, we enter (9km) **Clamecy** (5300 Clamecycois), well sited at the confluence of the Yonne and Beuvron, owing its picturesque appearance largely to the steep and narrow lanes of the old town with their quaint turreted and gabled houses.

First mentioned in the 9C, it flourished owing to the custom of 'flottage', originated by Charles Lecomte of Châtel-Censoir in 1547, of floating down great rafts of timber to Paris, a practice which almost disappeared after the building of the Canal du Nivernais in 1834. The local life in the 16C is described in 'Colas Breugnon' by Romain Rolland (1866–1944), who was born here, while Daudet's

'La Belle Nivernaise' gives an account of the bargeman's life on the canal.

The town is entered by the *Pont de Bethléem* from the Faubourg de
Bethléem, its name being explained by a curious history.

On his expulsion by Saladin in 1188, the Bishop of Bethlehem transferred his see
to the Hospital de Panthenor, founded in 1147 at the gate of Clamecy by the
counts of Nevers; and this strange little bishopric, with jurisdiction over the
hospital alone, survived until the Revolution. The title of Bishop of Bethlehem *in
partibus* has since 1840 been borne by the Abbot of St-Maurice, in Switzerland.

Part of the 12C chapel of the bishop's palace still survives near the
bridge, although enveloped in an ugly 20C construction. Crossing
the Yonne, and circling to the N.W., the Rue du Collège is reached,
beyond which stands *St-Martin* (13-15C), with an elaborate Flamboyant facade and well-proportioned 16C tower. The carved doors
are well preserved, but in the interior the nave piers are supported
by a disproportionate rood-loft, one of Viollet-le-Duc's devices;
fragments of its predecessor of 1525 are preserved, together with
some 16C glass, a figure of St Roche, a St Genevieve by Simart, and a
carved altar-frontal, together with an unusual rectangular ambulatory.—The *Hôtel de Ville*, opposite, stands above the vaulted
cellars of an old castle of the counts of Nevers.

The D951 leads E. through an attractive hilly district to (23km) **Vézelay** (see Rte
120), providing a charming view of the hill-top town on its approach.

CLAMECY TO CORBIGNY (30km). By turning r. off the Vézelay road after 8km
one may follow the D985 S.E.—At 7km *Metz-le-Comte*, with a 13-15C church, is
2.5km N.E. (views), and *Tannay* 2.5km S.W., with the fine collegiate church of *St-
Léger* (13-16C) and other medieval buildings.—6km. To the l. lies the former abbey of *Réconfort*, a nunnery founded by Countess Mahaut of Nevers in
1235.—Once-fortified *Montceau-le-Comte* is shortly traversed, to enter (9km)
Corbigny, a small cattle-market town on the Auguison, with Flamboyant *St-
Seine* (1537) erected on the ruins of an earlier church, and the 17-18C dependencies of its ancient abbey.—6km E. lies *Cervon*, with an 11-12C church with a
good Romanesque portal; and 5km S. is the château of *Marcilly*.

CORBIGNY TO PRÉMERY (32km). The D977B leads S.W. via (3.5km) *Chitry-les-
Mines*, so-called after silver mines exploited in the 16C; Jules Renard
(1864–1910), author of 'Poil de Carotte', lived much of his life here and was
Maire. It retains its 16-18C château.—13.5km. *St-Révérien*, with a remarkable
12C priory church containing curious Romanesque capitals and 16C
frescoes—15km. *Prémery*; see below.

From Clamecy we continue S.W. to (16km) *Varzy* (ancient *Var-
ciacum*) with several old houses, and *St-Pierre* (1350), with transepta-
towers and an elaborate apse, containing a triptych of the Legend of
St Eugenia (1535).

VARZY TO NEVERS (53km). The D877 forks l., passing r. at 18km the 16C
château of *Giry* to reach (6km) **Prémery**, amid the Nivernais hills, with a good
13-14C *Church*, preserving a carved stone Pietà and the tomb of Canon Ap-
peleine (d. 1466), whose house, known as the *Maison du Saint*, stands close by;
the old castle of the bishops of Nevers has a 14C gateway.—The valley of the
Nièvre d'Arzembouy is descended to (15km) *Guérigny*, with forges manufacturing naval equipment, and an 18C château, 5km beyond which the 16-18C
Château des Bordes, with four towers of 1486, is passed to the l.—9km. **Nevers**,
see Rte 96.

From Varzy, the N151 continues S.W. through the *Forêt d'Arcy*, in
which, 7km to the N.W., is the impressive 17C château of *Menou*,
some 4km to the N.E. of which is the Renaissance *Manoir de Cor-*

belin, once the residence of Claude de Saumaise.—Traversing the *Côtes du Nivernais*, we descend to (36km) **La Charité-sur-Loire**; see Rte 96. Crossing the Loire, the road leads almost due W. throught (8km) *Sancergues*, its beautiful church with a Romanesque choir and 13C nave, and 32km beyond, *Maubranches*, with (r.) a 15C castle and the remains of a camp occupied by Vercingetorix during his siege of Avaricum.—10km. **Bourges**; see Rte 48.

An ALTERNATIVE ROUTE is that VIA SENS AND GIEN (220km). For the road between Troyes and (65km) *Sens*, see the first section of Rte 120, in reverse. For **Sens** itself, see *Blue Guide Paris and Environs*, or Rte 21.—Hence the N60 climbs S.W. onto the wall-watered plateau of the Gâtinais to (22km) *Courtenay*, where a mansion of 1774 replaces the feudal castle of the Sires of Courtenay, descendants of Pierre, 7th son of Louis VI, le Gros; three members of the family were successively emperors of Constantinople in 1216–61.—We shortly fork l. onto the D37 for (17km) *Châteaurenard*, on the Ouanne, named after the 10C fortress of Renard, Count of Sens, now in ruins; its 11-13C chapel is the parish church. In one of its towers, Anquetil, curé from 1766–92, wrote part of his 'History of France'. On the river bank is the *Château de la Motte*, rebuilt in 1609 for Louise, daughter of Adm. de Coligny, and second wife of William of Orange.—15km. *Châtillon-Coligny* (see Rte 96), 9km W. of which we meet the N7 just N. of the D940 bearing r. to **Gien**, for which, and the road beyond, see Rte 48.

120 Sens to Chalon-sur-Saône via Auxerre, Vézelay, Avallon, and Autun

257km (160 miles). N6. 30km **Joigny**—27km **Auxerre**—42km D951. 10km **Vézelay**—D9571. 15km **Avallon**—N6. 39km **Saulieu**. Hence the N6 continues directly S.E. to (85km) **Chalon**. The D980 turns at Saulieu for (41km) **Autun**—D978. 53km **Chalon-sur-Saône**.

Maps: IGN 21, 28, 36, 37, or 108; also 306. M 237, 238, 243.

The A6 motorway is a rapid direct route from Paris, and for those driving S.E. from Avallon provides an alternative approach to Dijon, or Beaune, 27km N. of Chalon.

For **Sens**, see *Blue Guide Paris and Environs*, or Rte 21.

SENS TO TROYES (65km). The N60 leads E. to (23km) *Villeneuve-l'Archevêque*, founded in 1163 by an archbishop of Sens, with an interesting 12-16C church.—Some 15km N. are several dolmens.—5km. *Rigny-le-Ferron*, 3km S., has a 12-16C church, and *Bérulle*, 4km beyond, gave its name to Card. de Bérulle (1575–1629), who introduced the Carmelite Order and the Congregation of the Oratory into France.—At 3.5km we pass (r.) the 15-17C château of *St-Benoist-sur-Vanne*, and 4.5km beyond, *Villemaur-sur-Vanne*, with remains of fortifications, some old houses, and a 13-16C church with a square slate-covered belfry and carved rood-screen of 1521.—*Aix-en-Othe*, 4km S., once of importance, has a Renaissance choir in its church.—27km. **Troyes**; see Rte 122.

From Sens the valley of the Yonne is ascended, the r. bank being followed, later passing (l.) the 17C château of *Passy*, to (13km) **Villeneuve-sur-Yonne**, by-passed by the N6, founded in 1163 and preserving at each end of its main street two Gothic *Gates*; sections of its ramparts, including a cylindrical keep to the N.E., also survive, together with a long bridge, partly 13C. *Notre-Dame*, commenced in 1240, shows influences of the Burgundian and Champagne schools; almost opposite is the 18C *Maison des Sept-Têtes*.

5km. The *Château de la Grand Palteau*, 2km E., belonged to the Chevalier de St-Mars, the gaoler of the 'Man in the Iron Mask', who was confined here in 1698.—3km. *St-Julien-du-Sault*, on the far bank of the Yonne, has some 15-16C houses, and good glass in its church. To the S. is the ruined château of *Vauguillain*.—The road now veers S.E. to (9km) **Joigny** (10,500 Joviniens), probably Roman in origin, and once the seat of a powerful line of counts. It resisted an English attack in 1429, but suffered from bombing in 1940.

From the bridge a street ascends to a medieval gateway, passing several characteristic old houses. On the hillside to the r. stands *St-Jean*, rebuilt in the 16C and enlarged in the mid 19C, with a tomb of a 13C countess of Joigny, and a 15C Entombment attrib. to Mathieu Laignel.—The adjacent *Château-Neuf* dates from 1550–1613, while further E. is *St-André* (12-17C), with a Renaissance portal and 16C glass.—*St-Thibault* (1490–1530), to the W., with a later tower, contains various works of art of doubtful attribution, and a choir built on the skew.

6km E. lies *St-Cydroine*, with a late 11C church of a Cluniac priory with an octagonal tower, erected near the tomb of a local 3-4C saint, just E. of which commences the *Canal de Bourgogne* (1775–1834) uniting the Yonne with the Saône.

17.5km. *Appoigny*, with a fine 13-16C church, is traversed, 7km N.E. of which is *Siegnelay*, with a good church-tower of 1560. For **Pontigny**, 10km further E., see Rte 119.—After 3.5km the A6 is crossed and the N. suburbs of (6km) Auxerre entered.

AUXERRE (pron. Ausserre; 41,200 inhab.), préfecture of the Yonne, lies on two low hills overlooking the river, and is the centre of a wine-growing region, the white of *Chablis* being well known. A horseshoe of boulevards has replaced the walls of the old town, which with the Yonne separated it from its suburbs.

Roman *Autricus* or *Autissiodurum*, a town of the Senones, became the seat of a bishop in the 3C, and later a scholastic centre. It was fortified in the 12C by Pierre de Courtenay, afterwards emperor of Constantinople, and was several times invested in the 14-15Cs (and pillaged by the English under Robert Knowles in 1358), and was united to the French crown in 1476. Here in the mid 18C Thicknesse left his daughters in a well-endowed convent to perfect their French; and here in 1815 Napoleon reviewed the troops of Marshal Ney sent to bar his progress.

Among natives were St Germanus (its bishop; 390–448), sent to Wales to combat the Pelagian heresy, and who defeated the heathen Picts and Scots near Mold in 430; the scholar and lexographer J.-B. de la Curne de Sainte-Palaye (1697–1781); the physicist J.-B. J. Fourier (1763–1830); and Paul Bert (1833–86), the politician. The humanist and translator of Plutarch, Jacques Amyot (1513–93), was a Bp of Auxerre; Restif de la Breton resided here in 1751–53 and 1759–61, as apprentice to the printer Fournier.

A convenient point from which to visit the town is the Quai near the S.I., from which the Rue Sous-Murs ascends steeply to the Rue Joubert. A short distance to the l. is the mutilated Renaissance *Porte de St-Père*, beyond which stands *St-Pierre*, mainly 1575–1672, with a Renaissance facade and Burgundian tower.—By turning r. and then l. up the Rue Fecauderie, one of several streets now a pedestrian precinct, a triangular Place is traversed, flanked by the *Hôtel de Ville* and a number of characteristic gabled houses. Beyond, to the W., rises the *Tour de l'Horloge*, a gateway dating from 1483 surmounted by a clock of 1672 and rebuilt spire.

A short distance to the S.W. stands *St-Eusèbe*, with a Romanesque tower, 15C spire, and Renaissance choir. To the N.W. of the church is the *Musée Leblanc-Duvernoy* in an 18C mansion, with collections of Beauvais tapestries, furniture, porcelain, and paintings, etc.—Turning E., the 14C *Hôtel du Cerf-Volant* is passed (l.) in the *Pl. Robillard*, as we approach *St-Étienne.*—To the N. in the Rue de Paris, Nos 59, 67, and 83 (which belonged to the architect Soufflot) are of interest, while No. 98 was a Visitandine chapel (1714), now containing a lapidary collection.

   St-Étienne, the former cathedral—the bishopric was merged with Sens at the Revolution—was founded c. 400, but dates in its present form from 1515–43, although never completed.

The W. front, lacking its S. tower, was mutilated during the religious wars of the 16C, but its three portals preserve some 14C sculpture, while the central tympanum represents the Last Judgement. The later transeptal portals show the Stoning of Stephen (S.), and the Life of St Germanus. The *Nave* has a rose-window of 1573; that in the N. transept has fine stained-glass of 1528. Some chapels preserve traces of frescoes. The **Choir* is an admirable example of early Gothic, and the capitals in the ambulatory and the design of the Lady Chapel are noteworthy. On the l. of the altar is a bust of Jacques Amyot. The panel painting of the Stoning of Stephen in the N. ambulatory is attrib. to Félix Chrestien, a canon. The five-aisled *Crypt* of the earlier church (1030), with early 12C frescoes, may be seen on application to the sacristan.

A short distance opposite the N. portal, a r.-hand turning descends below an arch, beyond which turn l.—To the r. is the 13C *Bishop's Palace*, with later additions, now the *Préfecture*, its Romanesque exterior arcades facing the river.—The Rue Cochois climbs towards the old *Abbey of St-Germain*, founded by that saint, to which students flocked in the 9C, but little remains except its 18C buildings, a fragment of the 14C precinct wall, and a 12C dormitory.

   The disused ***Church of St-Germain**, rebuilt in the 13-15Cs, was partly ruined in the religious wars, and the 14C nave was almost entirely destroyed in 1810, so that the splendid Burgundian *Clocher de St-Jean* (49m high with its stone spire) stands separate from the rest of the edifice. The transepts and choir are 13C. The statue of the saint on the gable of the S. transept will be noticed, while the N. transept has a 15C rose-window. The whole building, including the 17C cloister preserving some Romanesque arcades, is in the process of restoration.

   Of particular interest is the **Crypt*, constructed in the 9C by Count Conrad, uncle of Charles le Chauve, and remodelled in the 11C. Below the choir are two superimposed circular chapels, while in the inner crypt are seen Carolingian frescoes of 858, the earliest extant in France, the tomb of St Germanus, two Merovingian tombs, and the remains of earlier martyrs and later bishops.

   By returning downhill and descending steps (l.) near the so-called *Maison 'du Coche d'Eau'* (16C) the river-bank is regained not far N. of the S.I.

For the road from Auxerre to *Clamecy* for *Bourges*, see Rte 119.

   19km E. lies *Chablis*, a small town famous for its white wines, but damaged in 1940, with paintings ascribed to Mignard and Philippe de Champaigne in *St-Martin* (completed c. 1275).

The N6 crosses the Yonne, and after bearing S.E. for 4km veers S.—A l.-hand fork leads to (4km) *St-Bris-le-Vineux*, its 13C church with a Renaissance choir, 5km N.E. of which is the fortified church of *Chitry*.

   7km. To the r. lies *Escolives-Ste-Camille*, with Gallo-Roman remains and a Burgundian Romanesque church.—2km. *Irancy*, 4km E., noted for its wines, was the birthplace of Germain Soufflot (1713–81), architect of the Panthéon in Paris. It has a 12-16C church.—*Coulanges-la-Vineuse*, 3.5km W., has a church of 1742 in the Doric style, by Servandoni.

3km. A r.-hand fork ascends the valley of the Yonne past (5km) the ruins of the abbey of *Crisenon*, founded in the 11C, opposite which lies *Prégilbert*, with a 13C church, and neighbouring *Ste-Pallaye*, with a 12-15C church above a crypt preserving the 5C sarcophagus of its patron.—8km. *Mailly-le-Château*, a very ancient fortified place on a cliff overlooking the Yonne, was the home of the three 'Sisters of Mailly', successively favourites of Louis XV, the youngest of whom was the ambitious Duchesse de Châteauroux (1717–44). The 12C church has 14-15C chapels and a 16C tower. Below is a 15C bridge with its chapel, which is crossed to follow the far bank to (8.5km) *Châtel-Censoir*, where the former collegiate church of *St-Potentien* (11th and 16C), has an interesting portal and primitive Romanesque ambulatory with huge sculptured capitals.—16km S.E., beyond the *Forêt de Champornot*, lies *Vézelay*, see below.—The road continues W. via the 14-16C *Château de Faulin*, to meet the N151 at (10km) *Coulanges-sur-Yonne*; see Rte 119.

3.5km **Cravant**, with some ancient houses and a fine bridge over the Yonne, was the site of a battle in 1423 in which the English and Burgundian troops of the Marshal de Chastellux defeated the French under the Constable James Stuart. Of its fortifications only the *Tour de l'Horloge* (1387) and fragments of walls remain; two 18C archways have replaced medieval gates; the *Church*, with a 15C nave and tower of 1551, has a Renaissance choir surrounded by eleven elaborately decorated chapels.

5km. *Vermenton* has a 12-13C church with two towers, but its Romanesque portal is mutilated.—2km. To the W. is the two-aisled 13C refectory of the Cistercian abbey of *Reigny*.

Near *Sacy*, 8km E., was born Nicolas Restif 'de la Bretonne' (after the name of the farm; 1734–1806), author of 'Monsieur Nicolas', and numerous other works.

7km. *Arcy-sur-Cure*, to the S.E. of which are the stalactite *Grottes d'Arcy*, and those of *St-Moré*, once both animal and human habitations.—To the W. of (5km) *Voutenay* are the remains of the Gallo-Roman fortress of *Cora* on the Via Agrippa between Lyon and Boulogne.

4km. *Avallon* lies 10km S.E., but the Detour should be first made to (10km) **VÉZELAY**, a small fortified hill-top village, approached by turning r. It was the birthplace of Théodore de Bèze (1519–1605), the humanist, and here died Romain Rolland (Clamecy, 1868–1944).

The main street mounts from the *Porte du Barle* past (r.) secularised *St-Étienne*, a 15C house, and the 17C *Tour de l'Horloge* to reach the abbey-church of **La Madeleine*, reconstructed between 1840–61 by Viollet-le-Duc after earlier mutilations. Its length is 120m, comprising a large narthex and a long nave of c. 1130, and earlier choir and transepts.

Once called *Vidiliacus* or *Virziliacus*, the Benedictine abbey of Vézelay was founded in 864, and flourished after what purported to be the relics of Mary Magdalen were translated hither from St-Maximin in Provence (cf.), but prosperity embittered relationships between the monks and the jealous peasantry, and in 1105/6 Abbot Artaud was murdered and the monastery set alight. In 1137 the citizens, abetted by Guillaume de Nevers, obtained the abolition of mortmain, but some of them were condemned to death when the town was placed under papal interdict in 1154, and the abbots regained their ascendency.

here in 1146 St Bernard preached the Second Crusade; from hence, in 1168, Thomas Becket further exasperated Henry II by his intransigent complaints; here in 1190 Richard I and Philippe Auguste met en route for the Third Crusade.

The discovery c. 1280 that the relics still remained at St-Maximin gave its prosperity a rude shock from which it never recovered; pilgrimages diminished; and the place later suffered severely at the hands of the Huguenots, while in the 17-18Cs the abbots (with the possible exception of Berthier in 1759–69) behaved with such repugnance that the Vézaliens were heartily relieved at their extinction at the Revolution.

The central tympanum of the *Narthex* represents the Last Judgement, and the life of Lazarus and his sisters; it is crowned by an incongruous 13C gable. The three doors of the nave are more elaborate, but despite the medieval disproportions and stiff attitudes of the figures, and the awkwardness of their draperies, it is a striking example of early Romanesque art. The sculptures of the side portals depict the lives of Lazarus, the Baptist, and the Magdalen.

The early quadripartite vault of the *Nave* (18m high) is notable for the alternate bands of light and dark stone in the voussoirs, and its historiated *Capitals. The *Choir*, with vaults 22m high, contributed considerably to the development of Burgundian Gothic architecture, but only one of its transeptal towers remains. The *Crypt* contains 12 columns with square capitals, four of which date from the 9C. Above the 13C Chapter-house to the S., is a vaulted hall, once the granary.

To the E. of the church extends a terrace commanding attractive views, while to the N.W. an exterior boulevard passes the *Porte Ste-*

A capital from the nave at Vézelay

Croix and the massive 16C *Porte-Neuve*, its towers ornamented b
bosses.

From Vézelay we turn E., descending to (2km) *St-Père*, where th
13C church preserves a tower decorated with statues, but the na
thex was restored by Viollet-le-Duc; an earlier church (*St-Pierr*
10–11C) lies further S. Adjacent to the former is a small a
chaeological *Museum* of artefacts found at *Les Fontaines Salées*, t
the S.E.

Further S., at *Pierre-Perthuis*, are old bridges, and relics of a fortress whee
Philippe Auguste convoked an assembly of barons in 1189.—6km further S. li
Bazoches, with a 13C castle, once the property of Sebastién Le Prestre, Maréch
de Vauban (1633–1707), the military engineer, who was buried in the 12
church; what remained of his heart was removed to the Invalides in Paris
1809. He was born at St-Léger-Vauban, some 20km due E., and took his title fro
the *Château de Vauban*, 3km S. of Bazoches.

Continuing E. from St-Père, we traverse (10km) *Pontaubert*, with
late 12C church of the Hospitallers, 1.5km N.W. of which, at *Vau*
de-Lugny, with its château, the church contains a large 16C mura
Nearby are remains of the Roman temple of *Montmarte*.

3km. **Avallon** (9,200 inhab.), Roman *Aballo*, principal town of th
N. Morvan, a mountainous and sparcely populated district, is fine
sited on a spur overlooking the Cousin. From the E. end of the Pr
menade des Terreaux one may enter the walled enceinte, preservir
several old houses, and in the main street, the *Hôtel de Condé*, with
Renaissance tower and 17C gateway, the *Ursuline Convent* of 162
and tall spired *Porte de l'Horloge* (from 1450). To the W. is a sma
Museum; to the S. stands *St-Lazare* (1106), with a battered Romane
que facade, and some interesting capitals. Under the choir is a 4
crypt.—Further S. is the Promenade de la Petite Porte (view:
whence one may explore the exterior of the ramparts, and their e
tant towers.

Chastellux-sur-Cure (pron. Chatelu), 14km due S., has a bridge of 1573 and
restored 13C *Castle; off this road another forks S.E. via *Marrault*, with a 18
château, to (19km) *Quarré-le-Tombes*, deriving its unusual name from the quan
ty of tombs surrounding its 15C church, once said to have been over 2000.

Driving E. from Avallon, we pass (l.) at 3.5km near the ruins of th
priory of *St-Jean-des-Bonshommes*, founded in 1210, and short
veer S.E.

Some 8.5km further N.E., beyond the motorway, lies *Montréal*, a hill-top villag
where a fine early Gothic church (1145) has carved choir-stalls of 1526 and
15C alabaster retable; 4km beyond is the 13C château of *Thizy*. At *Annoux*, 8k
further N., was born Marshal Davout (1770–1823).

6.5km. The D954 leads 25km E. to **Semur-en-Auxois** via (5kr
Ragny, with a 12th and 17C château, and 1km beyond, *Savigny-e*
Terreplaine, with a 12C church and 16C belfry.—6.5km further
lies *Époisses*, with a château of 1560 built on the site of a 12C castl
and often visited by Mme de Sévigné.—Some 8km N.E. is the abbe
of *Moutiers-St-Jean*, mostly a 17C rebuilding of a 14C abbey founde
in 425.—*Semur* lies 12.5km E. of Époisses; see Rte 121.

4.5km. *Ste-Magnance* contains in its church the 12C tomb of
Magnantia, one of the Roman ladies who escorted the body of
Germanus from Ravenna in 448 (cf. Auxerre).

At 7.5km we fork r. via (4km) *La Roche-en-Brenil*, with a moate castle once occupied by Montalembert (1810–70), later traversing plantations of Christmas trees.

The l.-hand fork (D70) leads E. via (13km) *Précy-sous-Thil*, with a ruined collegiate church and 9-14C castle (under restoration) on a hill further E., probably a Gallo-Roman oppidum.—*Vitteaux* (see Rte 121) lies 18km beyond.

12km. Saulieu, an ancient town which in 179 was the scene of the martyrdom of Andocius Thyrsus and Felix, whose tombs became a focus of pilgimage. It has long had a reputation as a gastronomic halting-place.

The *Tour d'Auxois*, on the S.W. side of the enceinte, is the sole relic of its defences. *St-Andoche, the church of an abbey founded in the 8C, is a good example of Burgundian Romanesque (late 11C), although the choir was destroyed by the English in 1359, and tastelessly reconstructed in 1704. The W. front, with a doorway restored by Viollet-le-Duc, has two square towers, one of which is capped by a cupola in 1594. The capitals of the nave are noteworthy, while the 5C sarcophagus of St Andocius, in the choir, combines both pagan and Christian symbols in its ornamentation. The stalls date from the 14C.—The adjacent *Museum* contains works by François Pompon (1855–1933), the animal sculptor, born here, and buried a short distance to the S.E. in the churchyard of *St-Saturnin*, which dates in part from the 11C; some Gallo-Roman tombs may also be seen.

SAULIEU TO CHALON-SUR-SAÔNE (85km). The N6 continues S.E.—AT 4.5km the D977B forks l. via (5.5km) *Thoisy-la-Berchère*, with an interesting castle, and 3km S. of (4.5km) *Mont-St-Jean*, with ancient houses, a castle keep, and an 11-15C church with a crypt.—10km further E. is *Chailly-sur-Armançon*, with a mid 16C château, and 5.5km beyond lies *Pouilly-en-Auxois*, with an interesting 14-15C church containing a 16C Entombment.—**Dijon** is 43km further E. on the motorway; see the latter part of Rte 121, and Rte 123.

23.5km **Arnay-le-Duc**, an old town famous for the battle of 1570 in which Coligny's Protestants overwhelmed twice the number of Catholics, and in which Henri of Navarre, aged 16, first bore arms; it was also the birthplace of Bonaventure des Périers (1510–44), author of the satirical 'Cymbalum Mundi' (1538). It contains a 15-16C church, restored in 1752; an ancient priory-gate; 15C tower; and the former *Manoir de Sully*,—17km. *Cussy-la-Colonne*, 1km l., preserves a Roman commemorative column 11.5m high.—The château of *Corabeuf* (16C, with an earlier keep) lies to the r. of the N6.—At 10km we meet the crossroads at La Rochepot (see p 685) 16km S.W. of *Beaune*, and 12km from *Chagny*, for which, and for the road on to (17km) **Chalon**, see Rte 127.

From Saulieu we turn S. onto the D980, skirting the *Morvan*, to (41km) **AUTUN** (122,200 Autunois), finely sited on the N.W. slopes of the *Signal de Montjeu* (643m), domianted by its remarkable cathedral, and also preserving considerable Roman remains.

Roman *Augustodunum*, having supplanted *Bibracte*, once had the reputation of being the most learned city in Gaul ('soror et aemula Romae'). It was later scourged by sporadic barbarian invasions, and the modern town only just fills the extension of its ancient walls, once with some 55 towers. In the middle ages its powerful bishops dominated the place, which later declined again, and has only recently revived with the establishment of light industries. The original grid of Roman streets are hardly anywhere followed by later building: the Rue de Paris, and the lower half of the Rue de la Grille, and the Rue de la Jambe de Bois are among the few on Roman foundations.

Among its natives were the martyr St Symphorien (d. 179), and Nicolas Rolin (1376–1461), chancellor of Philippe le Bon of Burgundy; while Talleyrand was appointed to the see of Autun in 1789 at his father's dying request to Louis XVI.

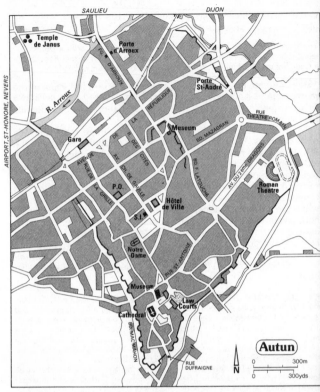

One of the two remaining Roman gates, the more elegant **Porte d'Arroux** or *Porta Senonica* (Sens Gate), 17m high and 19m wide, with two main arches flanked by smaller openings for foot passengers, and with an upper gallery supported by Corinthian pilasters, is traversed after crossing the river Arroux.—From the N. side of this stream a path leads N.W. to the so-called *Temple of Janus*, probably an isolated defence work.

We turn r. on meeting the Av. de la République, beyond which the Rue de Paris leads through the *Quartier Marchaux*, partly encircled by subsidiary walls during the middle ages, surrounding the 12C chapel of *St-Nicolas*, beyond which is the 15C *Tour de Marchaux*.—Bearing l. off the former avenue, the Av. Charles de Gaulle is ascended to the central *Champ des Mars* (S.I.), on the N. side of which is the *Hôtel de Ville* and *Library*, preserving several interesting MSS. On the S.W. side of the square is the *Collège*, founded in 1709, which numbered among its pupils Napoleon, Joseph, and Lucien Bonaparte, and Lazare Carnot. Adjoining is *Notre-Dame* (1763).

The narrow Rue St-Saule and its continuations climb to the *Pl. St-Louis*, dominated by the cathedral, and adorned by the *Fontaine St-Lazare* (1543). As early as the 10C the monks at Autun laid claim to the bones of Lazarus, which relics invited pilgrims.

The ****Cathedral of St-Lazare**, dating from 1120–78 and consecrated by Innocent II in 1132, was reconstructed by Card. Rolin, Bp of Autun from 1436–83, who added the side chapels and central tower with its superb stone spire (77m high) after the collapse of the Romanesque tower. Extending the whole width of the W. front is a two-storeyed *Narthex* flanked by towers partly rebuilt in 1873, protecting the admirably carved W. doors, to which steps steeply mount.

The angular **Last Judgement* of 1135, by Gislebertus, in the tympanum, was plastered over between 1766 and 1834 in consequence of Voltaire's scoffs at the style of its sculpture, and so escaped the fury of the revolutionary iconoclasts. The head of Christ, long decapitated, was found in the Musée Rolin (see below) and replaced in 1948.

Interior. The barrel-vaulted *Nave* of seven vaulted bays carried on pointed arches, with its fluted pilasters (copied from those of the Ponte d'Arroux), fine ***Capitals** (which deserve close attention), and triforium, is very simple yet noble in effect. In the N. aisle the 1st chapel contains a 16C altarpiece; in the 3rd is the Martyrdom of St Symphorien, by Ingres; the 4th preserves a 16C Jesse window. In the N. transept is a Renaissance staircase. The small *Choir*, spoilt by modern glass, has no ambulatory. To the r. of the altar are the kneeling marble statues of Pierre Jeannin (d. 1623), finance minister of Henri IV, and his wife.—Steps ascend to the *Salle Capitulaire*, in which is a collection of historiated capitals, etc. from the church. A 15C tribune supports the organ. The modern pulpit is a lapse in taste in what is otherwise a satisfying building.

The *Tour des Ursulines*, at the S. extremity of the town, where several houses have been restored, is the sole relic of the *Château de Rivault*, to the E. of which the Roman *Aqueduc de Montjeu* entered the town; further N.E. is the picturesque *Porte de Breuil*; see below.—To the N.E. of the cathedral stands the former *Bishop's*

The Last Judgement in the narthex of St-Lazare, Autun

Palace, now the *Palais de Justice*, partly 13C but much restored, while at No. 3 in the Rue des Bancs (by which we ascended) is the **Musée Rolin**.

This small but well-arranged museum contains a good collection of Gallo-Roman stellae, and a 3C sarcophagus from Arles; collections of Roman and Gallo-Roman bronzes, together with a gilt bronze parade helmet; ex-votos, jewellery, mosaics, pottery, and statuary. Off the interior courtyard—providing a view of the old circular prison, adjacent—are further rooms preserving an unusual reclining Temptation of Eve, attrib. to Gislebertus, from the N. door of the cathedral; a head of Christ 'of St Odon'; a well-carved long-tailed sheep; and relics from the tomb of St Lazarus. Rooms devoted to the Gothic period contains a charming Magdalen (late 15C); a triptych of the Last Supper (1515); the *Nativity of Card. Rolin*, attrib. to the Master of Moulins (Jean Hey); the polychromed stone Virgin of Autun (late 15C; note the swaddled child); St Catherine, attrib. to Juan de la Huerta; two early Adorations of the Magi (Antwerp School), and a statue of the Baptist (patron of Card. Rolin). Another room is devoted to the oppidum and bronze-working centre of *Bibracte*, 25km to the W. of Autun, on Mont Beuvray (see below), and the excavations carried out there by Gabriel Bulliot and his successors. Also of interest is the Plan of Autun of 1591 by Evrard Bredin, and a Last Supper by Pieter Coeck d'Alost. Among more modern canvases, the Siege of Malakoff by *Horace Vernet*, and a collection of works by *Maurice Denis* (1870–1943) are notable.

Descending to the N.E., we pass (r.) the 17C *Grand-Séminaire* to reach the Promenade des Marbres, probably named from a vanished gateway. Just beyond its S. end stood a temple of Apollo. To the r. is the old *Cavalry School* (1669). From the N.E. corner of the promenade one may visit (r.) the slight remains—cleared since 1931—of a *Roman Theatre*, once the largest in Gaul, with a diameter of 149m (cf. Vienne, 115m). An *Amphitheatre* stood slightly to the N., its site crossed by the main avenue descending into the valley, with its small lake.

From the N. side of the promenade, the Rue de la Croix Verte descends to the **Porte St-André** (14.5m high and 20m wide), formerly the *Porta Lingonensis* or Langres gate, which like the Porte d'Arroux, has two main arches flanked by smaller openings, but its arcaded gallery is supported by Ionic pilasters.

Good views of the *Walls* can be obtained from roads approaching the town from the S.

Near the village of *Couhard*, some 20 minutes, walk to the S.E. from the *Porte de Breuil*, is the conspicuous *Pierre de Couhard*, a partly ruined pyramid of Roman masonry, 27m high, probably a tomb.

A longer excursion (by car) is that to **Mont Beuvray**, approached by turning r. off the N81 3km W. of Autun, shortly after passing the 15C château of *Monthelon*, where in 1602–09 Francis de Sales was a frequent visitor.—17km. *St-Léger-sous-Beuvray*, dominated to the W. by *Mont Beuvray* 821m), its summit once the site of *Bibracte*, the flourishing capital of the Aedui, of which little remains above ground. Some of the antiquities excavated there are to be seen in the *Musée Rolin* (see above), but most are in the museum at St-Germain-en-Laye.—To the N.W. rises *Mont Prénelay* (855m), and further N., the *Bois du Roi* (901m), the two highest summits of the *Morvan*.

AUTUN TO DIGOIN (68km). We fork l. off the N81 11km S.W. onto the D994, shortly passing (l.) the ruins of the 15C *Château de Chazeu*, built by Nicolas Rolin, and later the home of Bussy-Rabutin.—26km. *Toulon-sur-Arroux*, ancient *Télonum*, with a fine 16C bridge, 12km beyond which *Gueugnon*, an industrial town with forges founded in 1721 by the Marquis de Latour-Maubourg, is bypassed to the r.—16km *Digoin*, 12km W. of *Paray-le-Monial*; see Rte 97.

AUTUN TO CLUNY (85km). The N80 climbs S.E. through the *Forêt de Planoise*, before descending into the valley of the Mesvrin, and ascending to (27km) crossroads 4km W. of **Le Creusot** (32,300 Creusotins), an important industrial town owing its prosperity to the famous *Schneider Ironworks*, founded in 1836 by the brothers Adolphe (d. 1845) and Eugène Schneider (1805–75). It was here in 1838 that the first locomotive was constructed in France, while during the First World War enormous quantities of arms were produced, including large numbers of 75-mm guns. The town was severely damaged by bombing in 1942–43, since when its factories have been much modernised. Travellers with an interest in industrial archaeology should apply to the *Château de la Verrerie* for detailed information concerning the *Écomusée* of Le Creusot and Montceau-les-Mines.—We fork r. (views) and at (14km) *Blanzy* cross the N70 N.E. of **Montceau-les-Mines** (26,950 inhab.), part of the industrial complex of the Dheune valley, traversed by the Canal du Centre.—The D980 now veers S.E., climbing to (9km) *Gourdon*, with an 11C church; it was near here that the gold 'Treasure of Gourdon' (now in the Cabinet des Médailles, Bibliothèque Nationale) was discovered in 1845.—3km. To the l. lies *Mont-St-Vincent* (603m), with a 12C church, and providing extensive views.—The road continues S.E. across ranges of hills before descending to (32km) **Cluny**; see Rte 97.

For the road from Autun to *Beaune*, in reverse, see Rte 127.

From Autun, the D978 leads E. and then S.E. to (25km) *Couches*, once an iron-mining town, with a 13C church, 15C castle, and other old buildings.—Some 6km N.E. is the camp of *Rome-Château* (545m; views), 2km N.W. of which is the fine 13C church of *St-Gervais-sur-Couches*.—The road descends into the valley of the Dheune and climbs up the far side of the hills of the Chalonnaise, before entering the Saône valley and (28km) **Chalon-sur-Saône** itself; see Rte 127.

121 Sens to Dijon

197km (122 miles). N60. 11km—D905. 34km *St-Florentin*—28km **Tonnerre**—46km **Montbard**—33km *Vitteaux*—19km N6. 26km **Dijon**.

Maps: IGN 21, 28, 29, or 108. M 237, 241, 243.

The A6 motorway provides a rapid route from Paris to Dijon, leading S.E. some 30km W. of the road described.

For **Sens**, see *Blue Guide Paris and Environs*, or Rte 21.

The N60 leads E., after 11km turning S.E. to (8km) *Cerisiers*, with a 12C church and 13C Templar tomb.—*Dixmont*, 9km S.W., has an interesting 13C church.—Part of the *Forêt d'Othe* is traversed and the road descends into the valley of the Armançon, there turning l. for (26km) **St-Florentin**, Gallo-Roman *Castrodunum*. Of the Renaissance *Church*, restored in 1862, only the choir and transepts remain, containing good glass, a rood-loft of 1600, and a well-carved but mutilated Entombment of 1548.—For *Pontigny*, 11.5km S., see Rte 120.

The valley is followed to the S.E., passing at 24km near the remains—on the far bank—of a castle built in 1540 by Jean Stuart, captain of François I's Scots Guard.—4km. We turn r. for **Tonnerre** (6,200 Tonnerois), Gallo-Roman *Tornodorum*, birthplace of the Chevalier d'Éon (1728–1810), who spent most of his life as a transvestite spy. A Roman road leads N.W., but the most interesting building in the otherwise dull town is the *Hospital*, founded in 1293 by Marguerite de Bourgogne (d. 1308; queen of Sicily, and wife of Charles d'Anjou), which incorporates the timber-roofed *Salle des*

Malades. Here is the tomb, by Girardon, of the Marquis de Louvois (1639–91), war minister of Louis XIV, who purchased the countship of Tonnerre in 1684; also an Entombment of 1453. A small museum has been installed adjacent.

To the S. is the *Hôtel d'Uzès* (1533), and beyond stands *Notre-Dame* (13-16C). Its later W. front has a carved portal and tower of 1628.—A lane opposite climbs to *St-Pierre*, largely Renaissance, with a choir of 1351, and a notable S. portal.—A short distance beyond is the so-called *Fosse Dionne*, a spring serving as a roofed wash-house.—1km S.E. are remains of the 11-12C abbey of *St-Michel* (now a hotel), founded in 980 by Miles, the first count of Tonnerre.

22km due S., off the road to *Avallon* (approached by the D86) lies the charming village of **Noyers**, with a fine 15C church, Renaissance houses, and considerable remains of ancient fortifications; and 22km beyond, *Montréal*; see Rte 120.

The road turns E. At 3km a l.-hand fork leads 5.5km to **Tanlay**, with a notable Renaissance *Château ◇ in a spacious park. The oldest part was begun in 1559 by François d'Andelot, brother of Adm. de Coligny, while beyond a bridge is the *Grand-Château* (1648), built for Particelli d'Emery, finance minister under Mazarin, from designs by Le Muet (1591–1669). It was a meeting-place during the wars of religion between the Prince de Condé and Coligny. At the far end of the part are ruins of the 12-15C abbey of *Quincy*, with 13C cellars.

The main road may be regained 4.5km S., there turning l. for (10km) **Ancy-le-Franc**, with its Renaissance *Château, designed by Serlio in 1546 and purchased by Louvois (cf. Tonnerre) in 1684. In the Galerie de Pharsale are frescoes attrib. to Nicolo dell'Abbate, and in the Chambre des Arts are oval paintings ascribed to Primaticcio (or his pupils).

Crossing the Canal de Bourgogne, and river, its l. bank is followed, re-crossing at 17km for *Rougemont*, with a good 13C church, and 3km beyond, *Buffon*, with the neighbouring ***Grande Forge**, built in 1768 by the naturalist, and recently the object of restoration.

6km **Montbard** (7,900 Montbardois), a small industrial town, with slight remains of its old centre on either side of the bridge over the Brenne, to the W. of which rises the *Château*, an important feudal stronghold, where Anne de Bourgogne and the Duke of Bedford were married in 1423. It was acquired by the Comte de Buffon (1707–88), but only the outer wall, the 13C keep, and two towers survived his demolitions. His collaborator, Daubenton (1716–1800) was born in Montbard, where Gén. Junot, Duc d'Abrantès (1771–1813), committed suicide.

MONTBARD TO SAULIEU (47km). Turning l. onto the D980 just W. of the town, after 5km the ruins are passed of the 14-17C château of *Montfort*, destroyed at the Revolution, to reach (13km) **Semur-en-Auxois**, a charming town, picturesquely sited above a loop of the Armançon, the neck of which is guarded by four huge drum towers, relics of a fortress. Roman *Sinemurum* was the capital of the district of Auxois (cf. Alesia), united to the duchy of Burgundy by Robert I c. 1060, who founded the collegiate church. It suffered at the hands of Louis XI for its allegiance to Burgundy in 1478, and its castle was largely dismantled in 1602, having afforded sanctuary to the Leaguers. It was the birthplace of the scholarly Claude de Saumaise (1588–1653), whose Latin defence of Charles I (composed in 1649 at the request of Charles II) incited a reply by Milton.—From the 15C *Porte Sauvigny*, at the E. end of the old centre, *Notre-Dame (1230) is approached, a striking example of Burgundian architecture, even if restored by Viollet-le-Duc in the mid 19C. The sculptures of the W. front (14-15C), with its towers, are mutilated, but those of the *Porte des Bleds*, on the N. side, are untouched. The octagonal central tower and spire rises to 58m. The narrow nave, unusually high in proportion to its width, is flanked (l.) by a series of chapels containing a delicately carved Entombment of 1490, and relics of glass provided by the town guilds (butchers, and drapers). The ciborium covered with sculpted pinnacles will be noted, while in the ambulatory is a painted Tree of Jesse under a late 15C canopy. The *Choir* is surrounded by an arcade of stilted arches supported by heavy pillars, and by a well-proportioned triforium gallery, embellished by sculptures. The keystone of the apse vault is carved with the Coronation of the Virgin.—To the S.E. is a small *Museum*.—One may explore the silent streets and secluded 18C mansions further W., to the Promenade des Ramparts, providing plunging views over the valley.—9km S.W. is the 13C castle of *Bourbilly*, once the property of Mme de Sévigné.—The D980 continues S. from Semur, at 8km crossing the A6 motorway, to *Précy-sous-Thil*, 5km beyond, to reach **Saulieu** 16km further S.; see Rte 120.—One may also regain the D905 at *Vitteaux*, 23km S.E. of Semur, passing near *St-Thibaut*, 7km W. of Vitteaux, where the church of 1297, of which the choir and fine 13C portal remain, contains the reliquary of that saint (d. 1247).

From Montbard we continue E.

At 3km a l.-hand turning leads 3km to the *Abbaye de Fontenay, founded in 1118 by Evrard, Bp of Norwich. It is a good example of Cistercian building, converted into a paper factory in the early 19C, and well restored earlier this century by members of the Aynard family, who allow regimented groups to visit it at specific hours. The *Church* (1147) is in a Transitional style, but the cloisters and chapter-house are of the plainest Romanesque.

Regaining the road, the valley is followed to (11km) *Les Laumes*.

The l.-hand turning leads 6km to the N.E., where to the r. stands the *Château de Bussy-Rabutin ◇. It was rebuilt in 1649 by Roger, Count of Bussy-Rabutin (1618–93), a cousin of Mme de Sévigné, who was banished from court for his scandalous but diverting 'Histoire Amoureuse des Gaules' (1665).

He spent his years of exile in decorating his home with historical portraits and allegorical paintings, one satirising the inconstancy of his mistress, Mme de Monglat. The *Salon des Grands Hommes de Guerre* contains 65 portraits of 4-17C warriors, mainly copies; the *Chambre Sévigné*, 26 of women (many of them royal mistresses), among them Mme de la Sablière and Mme de Maintenon, by *Mignard*, Elizabeth Charlotte d'Orléans, by *Coypel*, and Mme de Sévigné and her daughter Mme de Grignan. The *Tour Dorée* contains portraits above the pillars of Isabelle de Montmorency and Louise de la Châtre, by *Mignard*; Lucie de Tourville, by *Juste*; and Roger de Rabutin and Isabelle de Monglat, by *Le Brun*, many of them here and elsewhere with inscriptions or epigrams by Bussy-Rabutin.

Junot (cf. Montbard) was born at *Bussy-le-Grand*, to the N.E., with a fine Romanesque church.—By continuing N.E. we reach the N71 (see Rte 122) just beyond (12km) *Baigneux-les-Juifs*.

Returning towards Les Laumes, one may climb S. to the site of **Alesia** on the flank of *Mont Auxois* (407m), where an oppidum is said to have been the scene of the siege and final defeat of Vercingetorix (in 52 B.C., who died in captivity at Rome six years later), commemorated by a colossal statue erected in 1863. In the adjacent village of *Alise-Ste-Reine* (named after a virgin-martyr of 252) are museums containing a variety of objects excavated since 1861 on or near the site of the Gallo-Roman town, and the adjacent Merovingian basilica, etc.—5km S.E. lies *Flavigny-sur-Ozerain*, an ancient walled town, well sited on a spur, preserving remains of an abbey founded in the 8C, and a 13-15C church containing 15C choir-stalls and a 16C rood-loft.—Hence one may descend to the W. to regain the main road 4km S. of Les Laumes, and 11.5km E. of *Semur-en-Auxois*; see above.

Continuing S., the restored châteaux of *Villiers* (1554) and *Posanges* (mid 15C) are passed before reaching (15km) *Vitteaux* where the church contains a 15C organ-loft.

The road now ascends the valley of the Brenne to the S.E., at 10km passing (r.) the 15-16C *Château de Groisbois* and a reservoir, and 6km beyond, reaches a road junction 3km before meeting the H6.

The r.-hand turning leads S.W. to (7.5km) *Commarin*, with relics of its fortress and 4km beyond, the ancient village of *Châteauneuf*, with its 12-15C *Castle*. ◇ —3.5km further S., on the far side of the A6, lies *Ste-Sabine*, with a remarkable 13-14C church.

We follow the H6 to the E. along the valley of the Ouche, skirting the Canal de Bourgogne, passing N. of the 18C *Château de Montculot*, owned by Lamartine's uncle, the abbé, and later pass below *Mont Afrique* (600m) to enter the W. suburbs of (26km) **Dijon**; see Rte 123.

122 Provins to Troyes and Dijon

226km (140 miles). N19. 18km *Nogent-sur-Seine*—56km **Troyes**—N71. 33km **Bar-sur-Seine**—35km **Châtillon-sur-Seine**—84km **Dijon**.

Maps: IGN 21, 22, 29, or 103, 108. M 237, 241, 243.

Driving S.E. from **Provins** (for which see *Blue Guide Paris and Environs*, or Rte 20) the road descends through a ridge of hills into the Seine valley to enter (18km) **Nogent-sur-Seine**, with two 17C bridges, and late-Gothic *St-Laurent*, with a florid N. portal and N.W. tower (1522; 52m high) surmounted by an openwork lantern representing the gridiron of that saint's martyrdom.

6km S.W. is the 18C château of *La Motte-Tilly* ◇; and 5km S.E., on the direct road to Troyes (D442), a château stands near the site of the *Abbaye du Paraclet*, founded by Abélard in 1123 for Héloïse, its first abbess, who died here in 1164. The relics of the unfortunate pair (his having been brought here from St-Marcel; cf.) remained in its crypt until their tomb was destroyed in 1792, when they were removed to Nogent, and in 1817 to Père-Lachaise in Paris.

The N19 continues due E. to (18km) *Romilly* (16,300 Romillons), an industrial town of slight interest, some 4km N.W. of which stood the abbey of *Sellières*, where in 1778 the body of Voltaire was hurridly buried by his nephew, the Abbé Mignot, having been refused burial in Paris. The remains were transferred hence to the Panthéon in 1791.—*Marcilly-sur-Seine*, 7km N. of Romilly, preserves several 18C mansions and the ruins of the 18C château of *Galliffet*.

13km. *La Belle-Étoile*, junction for the road from Soissons and Sézanne; see Rte 103.—The road continues S.E. parallel to the l. bank of the Seine, at 13km passing (l.) *Payns*, where Hugues de Payns (or de Paganis; 1070–1136), founder of the Order of the Knights Templar in 1118, was born.—6km. To the E. lies *Barberey*, with a 16C château and 12-16C church, 2.5km beyond which is the Renaissance church of *Ste-Maure*, with glass attrib. to Linard Gontier (cf. Troyes) and the 9C sarcophagus of its patron.

6km. **TROYES** (64,800 Troyens), préfecture of the *Aube*, with an old centre of considerable charm and character, lies on a loop of the

Seine, and is divided into two parts by the Canal de la Haute Seine, here partly covered, and the W. half is surrounded by boulevards replacing its walls. Much work has been done in recent years to restored its many medieval half-timbered houses, while of unusual interest is the newly established Museum of Implements. Its andouillettes have been reputed for centuries.

Roman *Augustobona*, capital of the Tricassi, was long ruled by its bishops, the most famous of whom was St Loup or Lupus (426–79), who saved it from being sacked by Attila, but from the 9C until its formal union with France during the reign of Philippe VI (1328–50), it was the capital of the counts of Champagne, who encouraged the celebrated fairs which are said to have standardised 'Troy weight'. A Talmudic school was established here towards the end of the 11C. It took sides with the Burgundians after Agincourt; and the Treaty of Troyes (May 1420) assigned the hand of Catherine, daughter of Charles VI of France, to Henry V, together with the succession to the French throne in defiance of the Salic Law. Nine years later it opened its gates to Joan of Arc.

From c. 1480–1635 it flourished as an artistic centre, notably in the field of sculpture. Among sculptors were Jean Gailde, Nicolas Cordonnier, Nicolas Haslin, Jacques Bachot, Jacques Juliot, François Gentil, and the Italian 'Dominique Florentin'. In 1524 it was devastated by a ravaging fire, but revived. Under Henri IV it is said to have had a population of c. 60,000, but with the revocation of the Edict of Nantes many of its industrious Huguenot citizens left, although the manufacture of bonnets and hats expanded. By 1801 its population had shrunk to 23,900. Its suburbs were damaged by bombs in June 1940; several locomotives were destroyed by the SOE agent Ben Cowburn in July 1943, and the town was liberated on 25 Aug. 1944.

Among famous Troyens were Chrétien de Troyes (1135–83), one of the great literary figures of his time; Jacques Pantaléon (1185–1264), a shoemaker's son, afterwards Pope Urban IV; Jean Juvernal des Ursins (1388–1473), the chronicler; Jean Passerat (1534–1602), the satirist; the artist Jean Chalette (1581–1643); François Girardon (1628–1715), and Pierre Simart (1809–57), sculptors; Nicholas Mignard (1608–68), and his brother artist Pierre (1612–95); and Édouard Herriot (1872–1957), the statesman.

From the Quai des Comtes de Champagne or Quai Dampierre to the N., between the two older parts of the town, one may conveniently make one's way S. and turn l. along the Rue de la Cité towards the cathedral. This street traverses the Gallo-Roman town, passing (r.) the *Hôtel-Dieu*, with its fine wrought-iron railing of 1759, an 18C chapel, and a ***Pharmacy** of the period. Ahead is the *Pl. St-Pierre*.

The ***Cathedral** is a remarkable edifice in which every period of Gothic architecture is represented, but a certain deficiency in height will be noticed, owing probably to the unsure foundations of its island site.

Begun in 1208 by Bp Hervée, its choir and part of the transepts were completed by 1314, but the nave was still unfinished when the building was consecrated in 1429 in the presence of Charles VII and Joan of Arc. among later architects working on it were Jeançon Granache, Martin Cambiges, and Jean de Soissons, but work was retarded by subsidence, and the solitary W. tower was not finished until 1640.

The Flamboyant W. front is characterised by open fleurs-de-lys forming friezes above the three portals, but most of its statues and bas-reliefs were destroyed at the Revolution. The Renaissance tower, with its double lanterns, is 67m high. The building is 114m long, 51m wide, and only 29m high exclusive of the vaulting. The wealth of *Stained-glass of all periods is immediately apparent, although showing anomalies of restoration, and the perspectives are good.

In the *Nave* the large rose (Christ and the Apostles) was painted by J. Soudain in 1547; in the 4th chapel of the N. aisle is **The Mystic Wine-press*, by Linard Gontier (1625); the rose-windows in the transepts are also noteworthy. In the 1st chapel in the S. aisle is a terracotta group of the Baptism of St Augustin, attrib. to

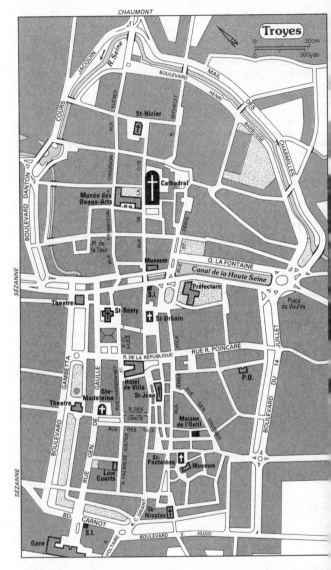

François Gentil (1549). The restored *Organ* of 1737, made for Clairvaux, wa moved here in 1809.

The *Choir* has been entirely rebuilt, and its windows and arches presen several inconsistencies. The rich *Treasury* may be visited on application to the sacristan.

Adjacent, in the former *Bishop's Palace*, is the new **Musée d'Ar Moderne**, containing some 350 paintings and other works of art largely by 20C French artists, left to Troyes by Pierre Lévy, a local industrialist.

These include paintings etc. by Daumier, Seurat, Van Dongen, Dufy, Derain, Braque, Vlaminck, and Nicolas de Stael; also glass by Maurice Marinot, and a collection of African art and sculpture.

Immediately N.W. of the cathedral is the 18C building (all that survives of an abbey erected over the tomb of St Lupus), now accommodating the **Musée des Beaux-Arts**, and the *Library*. The latter contains a number of illuminated MSS, and c. 700 incunables, while the older reading-room preserves 32 stained-glass windows by Linard Gontier and his school brought from the old Hôtel de l'Arquebuse.

The GROUND FLOOR of the museum contains *Ornithological* and *Archaeological* collections, the latter including the Treasure of Pouan (5C); a bronze statue of Apollo (2-3C), unearthed in 1818 at Vaupoisson, and other Gallo-Roman and Merovingian artefacts, etc.

On the FIRST FLOOR are paintings, and a small collection of Limoges enamels. Notable are an *anon.* mid 18C Portrait of a man with a snuffbox; *Cornelis van Haarlem*, Old man and serpent; *B. Spranger*, Venus; *Bergerat*, Musicians; *Jacques de Létin* (Troyes, 1597–1661), Self-portrait, and other works; *Lubin Baugin*, Infancy of Jupiter; works by *Jean Tassel*; *Pierre Mignard*, Portrait of Anne of Austria; *H. Janssens*, Return of the Prodigal; *Brueghel de Velours*, L'Age d'Or; *Hondekoeter*, Birds; *J.D. de Heem*, Still-lives; characteristic works by *Watteau, Boucher, H. Robert, Joseph Vernet, Greuze,* and *Desportes*; *P. J. Grosley*, several busts; *Roslin*, Dr Nicolas Carteron; *Vigée-Lebrun*, The Countess of Baussencourt as Ceres; *B. Bellotto*, Views of the ruins of Dresden (c. 1766); Portraits by *Thomas Hudson, Gros, L. David,* and *Natoire*; attrib. *Richard Wilson*, Landscape; *J.-L. Laneuville*, Portrait of Danton's mother; *J. L. Boilly*, The Mesgriny family; *Prud'hon*, Nude bakc; collections fo furniture and tapestries, etc.

A short distance behind the cathedral apse stands *St-Nizier*, a late Gothic and Renaissance edifice with a good triple portal of 1574 in the Italian style, and other earlier porches. It retains good glass and an Entombment of the School of Troyes.

Returning S.W. we cross the quays to early Flamboyant **St-Urbain*, begun in 1262 by Urbain IV on the site of his father's shop, but never finished; the facade was added in 1875–1905. The graceful arrangement of the gabled windows will be noticed.

To the S.E. is the *Pl. de la Liberation*; to the N.W. stands Gothic **St-Rémi**, with a belfry of 1386 and elegant spire. The apse windows preserve their 15C grilles, and the vaulting at this end is noteworthy. The bronze Christ above the high altar is by Girardon.

A short distance to the S. stands the *Hôtel de Ville* of 1624–70, the Minerva on the facade of which was originally a figure of Liberty, erected in 1793.—Adjoining is the *Maison Consulaire* of 1594.

To the S. stands 14-16C **St-Jean**, in which Henry V and Catherine de France were married on 2 June 1420, but the exterior has been heavily buttressed and much mutilated; the belfry collapsed in 1911. The interior contains a Visitation of 1515, and a high altar sculptured by Girardon; the Baptism is by Pierre Mignard, while some of the 16C glass is by Linard Gontier.

To the N. is the Rue de Champeaux, with several old mansions, among them the *Hôtel des Ursins* (1520), at the corner of the transverse Rue Paillot-de-Montabert, parallel to which (W.) is the narrow *Rue des Chats*, also retaining several gabled houses. Near its N. end, in the Rue Charbonnet, stands the *Hôtel de Marisy* (1545; restored), with a charming corner-turret, and a contemporary grille on its ground-floor window.

The corner turret of the Hotel de Marisy, Troyes

A short distance N. is **Ste-Madeleine**, with its Renaissance tower (under restoration). It was originally planned in the form of a Greek Cross (early 13C), but in 1495–1508 remodelled by the architect and sculptor Jean Gailde (Giovanni Gualdo). The Stone *Rood-loft* within, of three Flamboyant arches surmounted by a stone parapet, is his masterpiece. The statue of St Martha, by the S.W. pillar of the crossing, is a fine example of the Troyes School; the Choir contains some notable 16C glass.

Retracing our footsteps S., we approach, in the Rue de la Trinidad, several old houses preserving interesting details, outstanding among which is the ***Hôtel Jean de Mauroy**, a chequered brick and stone (*damier champenois*) half-timbered building of c. 1550, scrupulously restored to house the fascinating ***Museum of Implements**. Established by an association of craftsmen known as the 'Compagnons du Devoir', it preserves a well-displayed collection of woodworking tools, perhaps the most comprehensive of its kind, and also tools and instruments used by masons, leatherworkers, and smiths, and contains a specialised library devoted to such crafts.

In the Rue de Turenne, parallel to the W., stands **St-Pantaléon**, a striking edifice of 1508–50, with a wooden roof of 1675. It contains numerous works of art, many saved from other churches at the Revolution, but is somewhat neglected.

The pillars are embellished by a double row of statues, including St James, a seated Virgin, St Nicolas, and Faith and Charity (by Dominique Florentin). The 16C windows in grisaille in the S. aisle are attrib. to Jean Macadré; and the bronze panels of the pulpit are by Simart. The Calvary in a chapel off the S. aisle, with quaint figures in a gallery, and a coloured group (St Crispin) in the adjoining chapel, include figures by Gentil.

Opposite is the Renaissance *Hôtel de Vauluisant*, flanked by turrets, and containing an **Historical Museum** of interest, displaying numerous examples of the sculpture of the Troyes School, and among paintings, the early 16C Virgin with a red cloak; a Triptych of the Passion (1569) from destroyed St-Gilles; and a Jewish scene (second half of the 16C); also a collection of early views, architectural prints, and maps of Troyes, etc.—A section (the *Musée de la Bonneterie*) is devoted to the manufacture of hosiery in the district during the last three centuries, together with looms, and a display of stockings, bonnets, and other articles of clothing of this period.

To the W., beyond the *Pl. Jean-Jaurès*, stands Renaissance **St-Nicolas**, with a mid-19C facade added when the adjoining ramparts were demolished. The N. portal and *Choir* are Gothic; in the S. portal are statues by Gentil (1553). The interior is characterised by its vaulted gallery, in which is a Scourging of Christ, attrib. to Gentil; several other sculptures, and the windows in grisaille, are notable.

There are several churches of interest in the suburbs of Troyes, among them *St-Savine* (1km W.), 16C, rich in glass and carvings; *St-Martin-lès-Vignes* (2km N.W.), with glass by Gontier; *St-André-les-Vergers* (2.5km S.W.), with a Flamboyant facade; *Les Noës* (beyond Ste-Savine), with Louis-XIII portals; and *Pont-Ste-Marie*, 3km N.E., late Gothic and Renaissance, with good 16C glass.

For roads from Troyes to *Soissons* and **St-Quentin**, or **Reims**, see Rte 103 in reverse; for **Auxerre** and **Bourges**, Rte 119; for *Sens*, Rte 120, in reverse.

TROYES TO CHAUMONT (95km). The N19 leads E., shortly skirting the S. edge of the *Parc Naturel* of the *Forêt d'Orient*, at 19km passing just N. of *Montiéramey*, relics of a Benedictine abbey founded in 837, with a 12-16C church and 17C dependencies.—To the N. lies the extensive *Lac de la Forêt d'Orient* (2,300 hectares), on the S. bank of which stands the 12-16C church of *Mesnil-St-Père*.—13km. *Vendeuvre-sur-Barse*, with a 16-17C château on the site of a 12C castle, and a largely rebuilt church preserving a beautiful N. portal of 1510.—21km. **Bar-sur-Aube** (7,100 Baralbins or Barsuraubois), an attractively sited small town preserving several half-timbered houses, originating in a Gallo-Roman oppidum on a height to the S., near which took place a battle in Jan. 1814, when the Prince of Schwarzenberg checked Marshal Mortier. It was the birthplace of the late 12C poet Bertrand de Bar; and Alexandre Du Sommerard (1771–1842), the archaeologist and founder of the Musée de Cluny in Paris. The town is bisected by the Rue Nationale, on the N. side of which is *St-Pierre*, late 12C, with quaint wooden exterior galleries (15-16C), while within is a Romanesque triforium, partly walled up, and the floor is considerably lower than ground level. It contains some good statues. The organ is from Remiremont; the high altar from Clairvaux (see below). *St-Maclou*, to the S. (12-15C), retains Romanesque N. and S. portals and a square Gothic tower. (The Chapel on the bridge marking the spot where Charles VII caused the rebellious Bastard of Bourbon to be sewn up in a sack and thrown into the river, in 1440, was destroyed in 1940).

A r.-hand fork just E. of Bar leads 14km to **Clairvaux**, where, amidst forests, the once famous Cistercian abbey (*Clara Vallis*), founded in 1115 by St Bernard, was in 1808 degraded to house a convict prison, in which Prince Kropotkin was confirmed for three years in the 1880s. Parts of the former church and a vaulted cellar, both 12C, are incorporated in the huge 18C dependencies.—The N19 continues E. past a supererogatory memorial in the shape of a Cross of Lorraine, to (15km) **Colombey-les-Deux-Églises**, where in his country residence, 'La Boisserie', Gén. Charles de Gaulle (1890–1970) died. He is buried in the village cemetery, the church of which has a charming apse and pendant keystones.—The road veers S.E. to (27km) *Chaumont*; see Rte 109.

From Troyes, the N71 ascends the Seine valley to the S.E. past (8.5km) *Buchères*, whose inhabitants were massacred by the Germans and the village burnt during their retreat in Aug. 1944.

The r.-hand turning here leads S. via (3km) *Isle-Aumont*, with a double-naved church, and an extensive necropolis excavated in 1942–61, to (17.5km) *Chaource*, Carolingian *Cadusia*, which preserves several old houses, and a Gothic and Renaissance church rich in sculptures, including an Entombment of 1515.

The main road continues S.E., at 10.5km passing N. of *Rumilly-lès-Vaudes*, with an early 16C manor, and a church of the same period containing glass in part attrib. to Linard Gontier, and a painted retable of 1533.—More good glass may be seen in the churches of *Chappes*, N. of the N71, and *Fouchères*, further S.E.

14km. **Bar-sur-Seine**, an old town, the birthplace of Joanna of Navarre, Countess of Champagne, whose marriage with Philippe le Bel in 1286 led to the union of Champagne with France. *St-Étienne* (1505–1628) contains some remarkable glass (some in grisaille) and interesting Renaissance bas-reliefs of the Lives of the Virgin, and of St Stephen.

4km. A. r.-hand turning leads to (14km) *Les Riceys*, three villages, once fortified, each with Renaissance churches, and 7km beyond, *Molesmes*, with the ruins of a famous 11C Benedictine abbey, 3km S. of which stood the Gallo-Roman town of *Vertillum*.

The main road traverses (4km) *Neuville-sur-Seine*, birthplace of Paul de Chomédy (d. 1676), Sieur de Maisonneuve, the founder of Montreal in 1642, to reach (12km) *Mussy-sur-Seine*, with a collegiate church (13-15C) containing the *Tomb of Guillaume de Mussy and his wife* (late 13C), and several other sculptures.

15km. **Châtillon-sur-Seine** (8,000 Châtillonnais), pleasantly sited on two arms of the river, is an old faudal town in a region dotted with walled 'bourgades'. Here in Feb. 1814 an Allied Congress offered Napoleon the throne of France with its borders as before the Revolution, a proposal rejected by the Emperor. It was the birthplace of Marshal Marmont (1774–1852), Duke of Ragusa. It was briefly Joffre's H.Q. in Sept. 1914, and in June 1940 some destruction was caused here by bombing.

St-Vorles, to the S.E. of the town, begun in 991, has a 12C central tower and a heavy 17C belfry at its W. end, and contains an ancient crypt. Behind are remains of its 13C castle, and the tomb of Marmont.—Near the main road is a small *Museum*, preserving the *Treasure of Vix* (a village 6km N.W.), discovered in 1953 in a 6C tomb; also an Entombment of 11 figures (1527).—The D988 leads S.W. to (35km) *Montbard*; see Rte 121.

CHÂTILLON TO IS-SUR-TILLE (71km). The D928 leads E. into the valley of the Ource, bearing S.E. At (13km) *Vanvey*, we turn l. across the river; the road ahead leading 9km to the ruined Cistercian abbey of *Val-des-Choux* (founded

193), reformed in the 17C, and an occasional 'retreat' of Louis XIII and Louis XIV.—6.5km. *Voulaines*, with a feudal tower, to the S.W. of which is a fortified quarry with subterranean works, believed to be of Gallic origin.—5km. *Lugny* (l.), with a former Carthusian monastery, founded in the 12C, and later a tile factory, is passed, and 3.5km beyond, *Recey*, its restored Romanesque church containing objects from the monastery.—20km E. lies *Auberive*, with a Cistercian abbey, at which St Bernard of Clairvaux was the first abbot in 1135; its grille is the work of Jean Lamour of Nancy. The D428 leads E. past *Haut-de-Sec* (516m), the highest point of the forested plateau of Langres, to meet the N74 just S. of *Langres*.—The D959 turns S. at Recey, at 22.5km passing the 17-18C château of *Grancey-le-Château-Neuvelle*, also with ruins of a feudal castle.—20.5km. *Is-sur-Tille*, 5km E. of *Til-Châtel* (see Rte 109), and 24km N. of *Dijon*, approaching which, at 16km passing 2.5km E. of *Messigny*, with a 14C church and old houses.

The road turns S., following the upper valley of the Seine and skirting (l.) the *Forêt de Châtillon*, passing a monument commemorating the junction of Free French Forces under Leclerc (from Normandy) with those of Lattre de Tassigny (from Provence) on 9 Sept. 1944.

32.5km. *Baigneux-les-Juifs*, lies 3km S.W., so-called from its Jewish colony in the 13-14C.

17km. At the *Source of the Seine*, 2km W., a number of wooden ex-voto statues, among other artefacts, were discovered in 1963. They are displayed in the Musée Archéologique, Dijon.

8km. *St-Seine-l'Abbaye* owes its name to a Benedictine abbey founded in the 6C by St Seine (Sequanus); its church (13C, with later additions) contains 16C paintings of the saint's life, and 18C stalls.

We cross (10.5km) the Val Suzon, and after 11km by-pass (r.) *Talant*, with an interesting church of 1212 (views), and l., *Fontaine-ès-Dijon*, birthplace of St Bernard (1091–1153), with a 15C church, near which stood the castle of Tescelin le Roux, the saint's father.—4.5km. **Dijon**; see Rte 123.

123 Dijon

DIJON (145,600 inhab.; 21,000 in 1801, 77,300 in 1901), préfecture of the *Côte d'Or*, and once the capital of the Duchy of Burgundy, is situated at the confluence of the Ouche with the Suzon and the Canal de Bourgogne. It is a busy commercial and industrial town, an important railway junction, and the centre of the Burgundy wine trade. It is also the gastronomic capital of the region, and its gingerbread, *cassis* (a blackcurrent liqueur), and mustard—its name whimsically connected with Philippe le Hardi's motto 'moult me tarde'—are reputed. It preserved a number of important buildings, and well-restored medieval houses, while the Musée des Beaux-Arts contains one of the better collections outside Paris: indeed its old centre remains one of the most attractive and interesting of French provincial capitals.

Dijon (Divio or *Castrum Divionense*) is said to have been first fortified by Aurelian in c. 273, and converted to Christianity by a 2C martyr, St Benignus, in whose honour an abbey was founded in c. 525. This capital of the early Burgundian kingdom, which became under Robert I a powerful Valois duchy, was destroyed by fire in 1137. It was rebuilt and fortified by Duc Hugues II. Under Philippe le Hardi (the Bold; 1342–1404), Jean sans Peur (the Fearless; 1371–1419), and Philippe le Bon (the Good; 1396–1467), the splendours of the Burgundian court reached their height, but the death of Charles le Téméraire (the Bold; 1433–76, at the Battle of Nancy) left the Valois dukes without a male heir, and Louis XI, who, in spite of the protestations of the states of Burgundy,

seized the province, set up a 'parlement' at Dijon, and re-fortified the place.
Although it survived a siege by 30,000 Swiss, Germans, and Francs-Comtois in
1513, it opened its gates to Henri IV in 1595. From 1631 until the Revolution it
was governed by the princes of Condé, and enjoyed a second period of prosperity. The enlightened Academy of Dijon was founded in 1740, and a decade later
'crowned' Rousseau's essay on the morality of the Arts and Sciences. It resisted
the Prussians in 1870, with the help of Garibaldi's corps of volunteers, but later
capitulated, and suffered occupation, after which eight detatched forts were
built for its future defence. The railway station and some 700 houses were
destroyed in 1944.

It was the birthplace of Jacques-Bénigne Bossuet (1627–1704); Crébillon the
Elder (1674–1762), the dramatist; Jean-Philippe Rameau (1683–1764), the composer; Maret, Duc de Bassano (1763–1839); Jean Dubois (1626–94), Claude
Ramey (1751–1838), and François Rude (1784–1855), sculptors; Philippe Quan-
tin (d. 1636), J.-F.-G. Colson (1733–1803), Claude Hoin (1750–1817), artists;
and the engraver Alphonse Legros (1837–1911); présidents Jean Bouhier
(1673–1746), and Charles de Brosses (1709–77); Gustave Eiffel (1832–1923),
the engineer; Alexis Piron (1689–1773), the comic poet; and Adolphe Joanne
(1813–81), the first reliable compiler of French topographical guides. St Bernard
(1091–1153) was born at neighbouring *Fontaine-lés-Dijon*.

Claus Sluter (d. 1406), and his nephew Claus de Werve (d. 1439) spent the
greater part of their lives in Dijon, while Buffon spent some years of his youth at
No. 34 in the street named after him.

Several roads converge on the tree-shaded *Square* and *Pl. Darcy* (S.I.)
not far W. of the city centre, facing which is the *Porte Guillaume*
(1788), erected to flatter Condé, the governor of Burgundy, near the
beginning of the Rue de la Liberté, the main thoroughfare, leading
directly to the Pl. de la Libération; see below.

The Rue du Dr-Maret leads S. from the Porte Guillaume to the
Cathedral, a good example of Burgundian Gothic, the late 13C successor of a Romanesque basilica commenced in 1001, the apse of
which existed until 1791, which in turn replaced the earlier abbey.
Its parti-coloured glazed tiled roof is characteristic of the region; its
tall timber spire was restored in 1896. The W. door retains fragments
of a 12C entrance, but the relief in the tympanum of the Stoning of
Stephen is 18C.

Interior. Among tombs in the nave are those of the kneeling Président Legouz de
la Berchére (d. 1631) and his wife, and in the S. aisle that of Jean de Berbisey, and
the tombstone of King Ladislas of Poland (d. 1388). The Organ of 1743 is by Karl
Joseph Riepp. The *Crypt*, entered from the passage leading to the sacristy, filled in 1791, but excavated and restored c. 1858, appears to be the original crypt
of the first abbey church (6-10C), and contains the remains of the tomb of S
Benignus. It is circular in plan, and off it open three semicircular chapels. Some
capitals were either added or recarved in the 12C.

Immediately N. of the cathedral, approached through gardens, is a
wing of the 12C dependencies, including the splendidly vaulted
Dormitory, 70m long. Here is installed the **Musée Archéologique**,
displaying a Head of Christ, by Claus Sluter (1400), and a curious
painted stone Holy Family, with Mary suckling the Child in a recumbent position, with Joseph looking on (15C).

On the FIRST FLOOR, together with prehistoric collections, are examples of
bronze Gallo-Roman statuettes; a gold Merovingian bracelet from La Rochepot
(discovered in 1970); and two huge carved heads from Chorey, etc.—In the Crypt
is an interesting collection of stellae, bronze, and wooden ex-votos from the
Source of the Seine, including the goddess Sequana on a duck-billed boat, and
another bronze boat; also artefacts from the Roman temple of Crain, and other
objects from the castrum of Dijon, the cemetery of which was centred on the

cathedral, while the fortified enclosure was centred on the present Palace de Justice, further E.

To the S. of the cathedral apse stands disused *St-Philibert* (12C), once used as cavalry stables and as a salt store, which caused substantial damage to the structure. It retains a Romanesque side portal and a Flamboyant tower and spire; its restoration is projected.

Continuing E., the *Pl. Bossuet* is shortly reached, with (No. 4), the *Hôtel de Brosses*, among other 17C mansions. Here also stands mutilated *St-Jean* (15C), with two towers flanking its apse. Bossuet, who was born at No. 10 in the Place, was baptised here. It is now used for theatrical performances.

One may bear N. along the Rue Bossuet to regain the Rue de la Liberté (note the Renaissance turret on the *Hôtel Millière*), and turn r. to reach (l.) the picturesque *Pl. François-Rude*, with its bronze fountain-figure of a vintager, by Girard, and half-timbered houses.

Hence it is recommended that one continues E. along the pedestrian precinct of the Rue des Forges, passing (l.; No. 52) the *Hôtel Morel-Sauvegrain* (1435), the *Hôtel Aubriot*, and No. 38, the *Hôtel Maillard* (or *Milsand*; 1561), and just beyond, in a characteristic courtyard, the *Hôtel Chambellan* (No. 34; 1490), with offices of the S.I. on the 1st floor. The spiral staircase should be ascended to the top to see its palm-vaulting.

We now reach (r.) the N. side of the former **Palais des Ducs**, later the *Logis du Roi*, and now forming, with the *Palais des États*, the *Hôtel de Ville*. A passage leads to the *Cour de Flore*, on the S. side of which is the imposing internal *Escalier Gabriel*, ascending to the *Salle des États*. A few paces to the E. lies the *Pl. des Ducs de Bourgogne*, from the S.W. corner of which another passage approaches the *Cour d'Honneur*, facing the *Pl. de la Liberation*; see below. Here is the entrance to the *Tour de Philippe le Bon* (1446), which may be ascended for the view on occasions (apply to the concierge; also to view the *Chapelle des Élus*).

Erected on Roman foundations, and later extended, the old palace was abandoned after the death of Charles le Téméraire, and then rebuilt by the States of Burgundy from 1682. The wings enclosing the main courtyard were designed by Hardouin-Mansart, but the extreme W. wing was not completed until 1787, and the Palais des Beaux-Arts, to the E., dates only from 1852. In the N.E. corner of the *Cour du Bar*, with the charming *Escalier de Bellegarde* (1620) is a tower in which René d'Anjou, Duc de Bar, was imprisoned in 1431.

To approach the main entrance of the museum from the Rue des Forges, pass the 16C turret of the *Hôtel de Berbis* on the E. side of the *Pl. des Ducs*, and turn r. into the *Pl. de la Ste-Chapelle* (recording the site of the Ducal Chapel demolished on 1804), flanked (l.) by the *Théâtre* (1810–28).

The ***Musée des Beaux-Arts***, founded in 1783, contains one the richest collections in provincial France.

To the l. of the entrance vestibule is a series of rooms containing collections of sculpture, including works by *Jean Dubois*, *Lemoyne*, and *Rude*; a retable attrib. to *Jean Damotte*; Burgundian Virgins; prophets, by *Claus Sluter* (from the Chartreuse). Beyond is the well-vaulted *Kitchen (1445) of the palace.

To the r. of the entrance, and l. of the staircase, is the vaulted *Salle de la Ste-Chapelle* (14C), containing relics from a chapel destroyed in the 14C, and a 13C altar-frontal; the crown of Philippe le Hardi 1404); the crozier of Robert, founder of Citeaux (1098), and the tasse' or porringer of St Bernard of Clairvaux, etc.

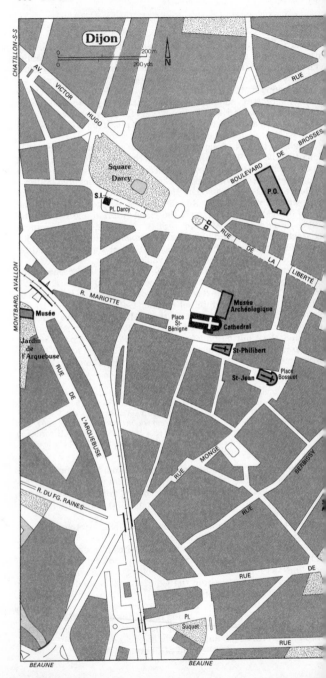

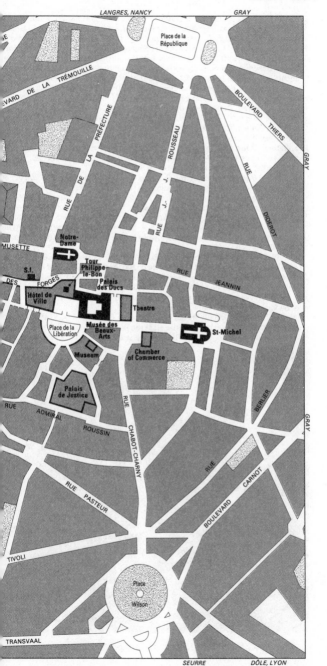

LANGRES, NANCY   GRAY

Place de la République

BOULEVARD DE LA TRÉMOUILLE

BOULEVARD THIERS

GRAY

RUE DE LA PRÉFECTURE

ROUSSEAU

RUE J.-J.-

RUE J.-

RUE DIDEROT

MUSETTE

Notre-Dame

Tour Philippe le-Bon

S.I.

DES   FORGES

Palais des Ducs

RUE   JEANNIN

Hôtel de Ville

Théâtre

Place de la Libération

Musée des Beaux-Arts

St-Michel

Museum

Chamber of Commerce

Palais de Justice

BERLIER

RUE   GRAY

RUE   ADMIRAL   ROUSSIN

RUE   CHABOT-CHARNY

RUE   CARNOT

RUE   PASTEUR

BOULEVARD   CARNOT

TIVOLI

Place Wilson

TRANSVAAL

SEURRE   DÔLE, LYON

FIRST FLOOR. **R1** (r.) *Ferrari*, St Jerome; *Machiavelli*, Coronation of the Virgin; *Giovanni di Francesco*, St Antony presenting a pilgrim to Santiago; *Gaddi*, Adoration of the Magi; *Lorenzetti*, Triptych of the Virgin and child; *Bartolo di Freddi*, Adoration of the Magi; *School of Fontainebleau*, Lady at her toilet; *Bart. Veneto*, male portrait; *Lorenzo Lotto*, Female portrait.—**R2** Carved furniture; ivories; cloisonné; Limoges enamels; a 12C Byzantine reliquary cross; and the scabbard of Philippe le Bon.—**R3** (German) *Master of 1521*, Presentation of the Virgin; *Master of the Passion of Darmstadt*, SS Dorothy and Catherine; *anon.* Swiss Nativity of c. 1460; and a naive Adoration of the Magi; the Swiss *Master á l'oeillet de Baden*, Retables of the Passion, and of the Visitation, SS Jerome, Augustine, Gregory, and Ambrose (15C); *Schongauer*, Annunciation; *S. German* Crucifixion (late 15C); SS Stephen, Blaise, the Baptist, and Peter (Swiss; 1450); SS Jerome, and Christopher (Swiss; 1416); attrib. *Wolgemut*, St John the Evangelist.—Stairs lead to a room containing carved wood statues, some gilt, from the Malines workshop; a Swabian St Catherine of Alexandria (15C); a German St Barbe; and others of the Antwerp School.

R4 *Conrad Witz*, St Augustin, the Emperor Augustus and the Sibyl; *Gallego*, St Augustin; and a Consecration of St Augustin (15C Aragonese).—**R5** *Bassano*, Entrance of the animals into the Arc; *Jean Tassel*, Tobais and the Angel, The Stoning of Stephen, Presentation, and Adoration of the Magi, and other works; *Veronese*, Moses in the bullrushes; *Rubens*, Entry into Jerusalem, and Washing of the feet; *Titian*, Virgin and Child with St Agnes and the Baptist; *Guido Reni*, Adam and Eve; *Batoni*, Cleopatra showing Antony a bust of Caesar; *Guardi*, View of Prato.

R6 (*Salles des Gardes*), an imposing hall rebuilt after a fire in 1502, displays the *Tomb of Jean sans Peur and Marguerite de Bavière**, commissioned in 1443, by *Juan de la Huerta* (an Aragonese) and completed in 1470 by *Antoine Le Moiturier*; and the *Tomb of Philippe le Hardi**, by *Jean de Marville*, *Claus Sluter*, and *Claus de Werve*, with architectural ornament by *Jacques de Baerze*. They may be viewed from the adjacent gallery of 1548.

The two tombs, originally in the Chartreuse de Champmol (see below), were disjoined but not broken up or mutilated at the Revolution, and their restoration was completed in 1827. That of Philippe le Hardi lies on a black marble plinth.

The tomb of Jean sans Peur and Marguerite de Bavière

ach side consists of an arcade surmounted by an openwork gallery and sup-orted by richly decorated pilasters, beneath which are 40 statuettes represen-ing the ducal household and monks of various orders, while above is the recum-ent figure of the duke, with two angels supporting his helmet and a dormant on at his feet.—That of Jean sans Peur and his wife is similar in conception, also urrounded by a procession of hooded mourners or '*pleurants*', and attended by our angels and two lions, an excess of ornamentation which detracts from the eneral effect when compared with the former.

Note also the Chimneypiece by *Jean Dangers*; the tapestry of the Siege of Di-on of 1513; and the Retable of the Passion (1393) by *Jacques de Baerze*, and gilt y *Melchior Broederlan*, originally in the Chartreuse; and the Retable of St ieorge, among others; a painting of the Presentation in the Temple, attrib. to ean *de Maisoncelles*; and a Portrait of Philippe le Bon (*School of Van de Veyden*).

R7 *Tierry Bouts*, The Crown of Thorns; *after Albert Bouts*, St Jerome penitent; doration of the Magi (Antwerp School); *Patinir*, Magdalen penitent (?), and oldier sleeping on guard; *Master de Flemalle*, Adoration of the Shepherds :. 1430); *Isenbrandt*, Magdalen reading; *Ambrose Benson*, the Baptist presenting donor; attrib. *Lancelot Blondel*, panels of the Legend of St Bertin (c. 1450); a mall *anon.* Flemish St Jerome; *School of Bosch*, St Christopher; *Master of St* iudule, St Catherine and the philosophers; *anon.* Burgundian, St Peter and Malchius (c. 1520).

Traversing a landing, **R8** is entered, displaying *Largillière*, Antoine-Bernard iouhier, Président of the Burgundian Parliament; *Greuze*, Abbé L. Gougeuot;)uentin Delatour, pastel Self-portrait; *Caffieri*, Busts of Alexis Piron, and of .ameau; *Coysevox*, Bust of Louis XIV; and busts by *Claude-François* Attiret.—Another room containing more sculpture is crossed to reach **R10**, evoted to portraits by *Colson*, including that of The artist's Father; *Joseph* Vernet, The Tiber and Mount Aventin; *Nattier*, Marie Leczinska; *Natoire*, Abp .-J. Languet de Gergy; *Rigaud*, Portraits of the sculptors Coysevox, and Girar-on; *Tocqué*, M. Doyen; attrib. *Mignard*, Self-portrait; *Jean Tassel*, Catherine de Montholon.—In the following rooms are works by *Brouwer*, *Van Ostade*, and Vouwerman; *Hals*, Male portrait; *Pieter Verelst*, Female portrait; *Brueghel de Velours*, The Château de Mariemont; *Léonard Defrance de Liège*, The Shield of Minerva; and *Van Balen*, Diana the huntress.

Regaining the landing, one may ascend past pastel portraits by *Claude Hoin*, including one of his Brother; and *Robert Tournières*, Musicians.—Rooms on the iECOND FLOOR contain collections of Ceramics and Glass, including some Moustiers, Strasbourg, Rouen, and Delft ware; Oriental porcelain, etc., and ireek pottery. The small collection of modern paintings is of slight interest.)ther collections, such as those of arms and armour, are sporadically on view.

)n making our exit, we may bear r., and r. again, to reach the **Pl. de a Liberation** (previously the Pl. d'Armes), a handsome semicircular pace enclosed by arcades crowned with balustrades, facing the S. acade of the palace, and built in 1686 from the designs of Martin de Noinville.

The Rue Bouhier leads S. from the hemicycle to the **Palais de ustice**, with a picturesque facade, the peristyle of which is the work f Hugues Brouhée (1574). Certain rooms, some with good ceilings, nay be visited on application to the concierge at No. 8 Rue du Palais. This street leads S.E. to the *Municipal Library* (5 Rue de-l'École-de-)roit), partly accommodated in the former *Collège de Godrans*, reserving several bibliographical curiosities. The vaulted *Chapel*, y *Martellange* (1610), is now a reading-room.—In the Rue Vauban, urther to the W., is the *Hôtel Bouhier de Savigny* (No. 12), and op-osite, the *Petit Hôtel Bouhier* (1618, with a balcony of 1786); No. 21, he *Hôtel Legouz de Gerland*, is perhaps by Noinville.

rom behind the Palais de Justice, the Rue Hernoux leads to the *Pl. des Cor-eliers*, a few minutes' walk S.W. of which, passing the 17C *Carmelite chapel* destined to house another museum), in the Rue Ste-Anne, the copper cupola of

Ste-Anne (1709) is conspicuous. This former church accommodates the *Musé d'Art Sacre*, of specialist interest, containing ecclesiastical silver and vestments a late 12C carved Virgin; and a 17C carved wood St Paul (recently preserved b bombarding it with gamma rays at Grenoble), among other works.

The narrow Rue des Bons Enfants leads S.W. from the Pl. de la Libera tion, No. 4 in which is the **Musée Magnin**, installed in the 17C *Hôte Lantin*.

Here, in a succession of rooms surrounding a charming courtyard, are shown th extensive collections of Maurice Magnin, who in the 19C assembled some 190 miscellaneous works of art, mostly small in size and of slight importance, bu characterising the taste of one provincial amateur. Much of the original fur niture remains in place. Among the more notable canvases are (ground floor *Bart. van der Helst*, Woman reading; *Mengs*, Self-portrait; and an *anon.* Floren tine Courtesan. On the first floor are representative works by *Bourdon, Le Nair Le Sueur, Vouet, Drolling, Géricault, Gros, Isabey*, and *Corot*, among others.

Continuing along this lane, we see opposite, in the Rue Chabot Char ny, a medieval *Gate*.

This latter street (in which note Nos 18, 32, 43-5, and 62) leads some distance to the circular *Pl. du President Wilson*, beyond which the wide Course du Gén. d Gaulle, an avenue of limes, continues S. for c. 1.6km towards the *Parc de la Co ombière* (33 hectares), laid out on a design of Le Nôtre in c. 1680 for the Princ de Condé.

On the E. side of the *Pl. du Théâtre* stands the former church of *S Étienne*, once the cathedral. Rebuilt in the 15-17C, it still preserve Romanesque elements. It stood on the edge of the *castrum* of Dijon and having previously been used as a covered market, has been we converted as offices of the *Chambre de Commerce*.

To the N.E. in the Rue Vaillant, No. 4 is the *Hôtel Lory* (1790), op posite which is the *Musée Rude* (occupying the N. transept of S Étienne) containing representative works, or copies of them, by th native sculptor.—The street is dominated to the E. by **St-Miche** begun in 1499 and consecrated in 1529, notable for its Renaissanc front of 1661, although in general style it is Gothic.

Of the three deep-set portals of the W. front, one (S.) has sculptures in it vaulting arranged concentrically in the usual Gothic manner; on the two other the subjects are divided into panels. The bas-relief of the Last Judgement in th central tympanum is by Nicolas de la Court. The two heavily buttressed tower are divided into four storeys, the windows of each being framed in a classica order.—Some of the interior capitals, and the organ-case of 1599, previously i the Ducal Chapel, are notable.

Hence the Rue Vannerie leads N., shortly crossing the Rue Jeannin in the former of which stands the 18C *Hôtel Chartraire de Montign* (No. 39, containing the so-called Escalier d'Independance, of 1783) while Nos 35, 41, and 66 also have features of interest.—Turning along the Rue Jeannin we pass (l.) opposite the *Hôtel Guillaume o* 1621, containing the Archives Departmental, and occupying th 15C *Hôtel de Ville* (rebuilt 1708; Mozart is said to have given a con cert here in 1776), before reaching the Rue Verrerier. This latte street, partly a pedestrian precinct, preserves several quaint ol houses, such as No. 29, of 1664, as does likewise the Rue Chaudron nerie, just to the N., No. 28 in which is the *Maison des Cariatide* (1603).—Further N. is a Renaissance clock-tower, a relic of S Nicolas, destroyed in 1792.

The Rue Chouette leads W., in which (r.) is the *Hôtel de Vogué* (No

; 1614); note the inner side of its porch. No. 10 is also of interest, almost opposite which, on the exterior of the N. side of the church of Notre-Dame, is carved the little owl which gives the street its name.

From the *Pl. Notre-Dame*, the Rue de la Préfecture leads N., in which Nos 39 and 40 (*Hôtel de Dampierre*; c. 1780) are passed before reaching the *Préfecture* (No. 17) in a mid 18C mansion.

Notre-Dame is a remarkable monument of the early 13C Burgundian style. The * W. Front* has a deep triple porch, above which are two arcaded galleries separated by three broad friezes, each richly decorated with human and animal grotesques, an arrangement unique in Gothic architecture, and which is described in Huysman's 'L'Oblat'. The S. corner-turret supports a *Jacquemart Clock* attrib. to Jacques Marques, a Flemish craftsman, and carried off from Courtrai in 1382 by Philippe le Hardi, possibly at the suggestion of Froissart. The tower above the crossing was rebuilt with modifications in the late 19C.—The delicate colonnettes in the interior, some curiously placed on plinths, are remarkable, and also the corbels above the ambulatory; some 13th and 16C glass will be noted, while a 12C 'Black Virgin' stands in a chapel to the r. of the choir.

Hence one may follow the Rue Musette to regain (l.) the Pl. Rude and Rue de la Liberté.

About 1km W. of the Pl. Darcy once stood the *Chartreuse de Champmol*, on a site occupied since 1843 by an asylum, which may be approached directly via the Rues des Perrières.

Founded in 1383 as a burial-place for the ducal house, it was lavishly decorated, but few relics remain of the buildings, torn down in 1793, except the portal of the church, with its statues of Philippe le Hardi and of Marguerite of Flanders, attrib. to Sluter.

Admission should be requested to view the major memorial of its past magnificence, namely the *Well of Moses (Puits de Moïse)*, originally forming the base of a Calvary. The head of the Christ is preserved in the Archaeological Museum. The rest is the work of Claus Sluter (1395–1406) and his assistants. The hexagonal pedestal rising from the well is surrounded by statues of Moses, David, Jeremiah, Zachariah, Daniel, and Isaiah, remarkable for their characterisation. Above are figures of angels. The whole was once coloured and gilt.

Some distance beyond the Chartreuse is the artificial *Lake* formed in the valley of the Ouche in 1964.—The return to the centre may be made by following the Av. Albert-Ier, which passes (r.) the entrance to the Promenade de l'Arquebuse, with a *Natural History Museum* and a good *Botanical Garden*.—Hence, by turning under the railway bridge, one ascends the Blvd. de Sévigné to regain the Pl. Darcy.

124 Besançon

BESANÇON (119,700 Bisontins; 30,000 in 1801; 55,400 in 1901), former capital of the *Franche-Comté*, and préfecture of the *Doubs*, is an ancient fortress and lively modern industrial town, the old centre of which is almost surrounded by a horseshoe meander of the Doubs. It is a town of considerable character, and its museum is particularly fine.

Vesontio, a stronghold of the Sequani, was protected by Galba and made a Roman colony by Marcus Aurelius. Frederick Barbarossa gave it the privilege of a free Imperial city; while under the Austro-Spanish domination (1477–1674) it flourished largely owing to the influence of the Granvelle family at the courts of

Charles V and Philip II. It was taken after a 27-day siege by Louis XIV in 1668 who transferred the Parlement here from Dôle in 1676, and in 1691, the university. Its watch-making industry was established by Swiss political refugees c. 1793. Previously fortified by Vauban, it resisted Austrian attacks in 1814–15; in 1944 the retreating Germans destroyed four of its bridges.

Among natives were Card. Antoine de Granvelle (1517–86); Charles Nodier (1780–1844); Victor Hugo (1802–85); Charles Fourier (1772–1837), and Pierre-Joseph Proudhon (1809–65), the socialist writers; Marshal Moncey (1754–1842); the composer Claude Goudimel (c. 1510–73); the sculptor J.-B. Clésinger (1814–83); and Auguste and Louis Lumière (1862–1954, and 1864–1948 respectively), pioneers of cinematography.

The Grand-Rue traverses the city from N.W. to S.E., from the *Pont de Battant* to the *Cathedral*. Just E. off its N. end is the *Pl. de la Revolution*, with the remarkable *Musée des Beaux-Arts*, one of the richest provincial museums in France, originally intended as a corn market, and recently remodelled and reformed, the floors being connected by a series of ramps, the descent of which may be made after taking the lift to the upper floor.

Among the more important works are: *Goya* (attrib. to; and also to Eugénie Lucas), The Cannibals; *Bonington*, two Marine views; *Constable*, The Mill, and The black cloud; *Lawrence*, The Duchess of Sussex, and Duc A.-E. de Richelieu; *Courbet*, The sleepwalker, Self-portrait, and Peasants of Flagey; *Ingres*, Portrait of an architect; *Géricault*, Head of an Oriental; *David*, three Portraits; *Bonnat*, Jean Gigoux; works by *Daubigny*, and *Diaz de la Pena*.

Hortense Haudebourg-Lescot, Portrait of the architect (of this building) Pierre Adrien Pâris (1747–1819); works by *Guardi*, *Hubert Robert*, and *Pillement*; nine Chinoiseries by *Boucher*; *Oudry*, Self-portrait; *Coypel*, Self-portrait with his daughter; and *Largillière*, Mme Titon du Tillet.

Paintings attrib. to *Philippe de Champaigne*; studio of *Georges de la Tour*, St Joseph; *Zurbaran*, Flight into Egypt, and attrib. to the same artist, a Still-Life.—Portraits of Georges Besson, by *Matisse*, and *Bonnard*; *Marquet*, Two friends (nudes); *Renoir*, Adèle Besson.

Giuseppe Recco, Dead fish; *Guarino*, St Sebastian; *Giordano*, The four Sciences; *Ribera*, St Jerome, and St Peter; *Cranach*, Lucrecia, Diana, and Courtesan and old man; and attrib. *to his School*, Adam and Eve; *Brueghel de Velours*, Terrestial Paradise; *Van Uden*, Landscape; *Van der Vliet*, Church interior; *P.-J. Codde*, Soldier and woman; *G. Terbosch*, Young woman; *W.C. Heda*, Still-life; attrib. *Paul de Vos*, Young seals; *E. van de Velde the Elder*, Cavaliers in a forest; *Van Dyck*, Head of a bearded man; *Frans Franken*, Passage of the Jordan and Red Sea; *Gerard David*, Portrait; attrib. *Van Cleeve*, Virgin and Child; *Patiner*, Flight into Egypt; attrib. *Dirk Jacobsz*, Young woman; *Van Orley*, N.-D. des Sept Douleurs; *Van de Weyden*, Virgin and Child; *Bernardino Licinio*, The black cap.

Tintoretto, Senator and family, and Male portrait; Knight and Lady (15C *Ferrara School*); after *Gaetano Pulzone*, Antoine de Granvelle; *Antonio Moro*, Portraits of Jeanne Lullier and Simon Renard; *Titian*, Nicolas Perrenot de Granvelle; *anon.* Portrait of Erick de Brunswick, commander of Alba's German troops; *Martin des Batailles*, Sieges of Besançon (in 1674), and of Dôle (1636), and a Plan of Besançon; *F. van de Meulan*, Siege of Besançon; View of Besançon in 1691; *anon.* Portrait of Antoine de Choiseul, Abp of Besançon; *Largillière*, Family of Bontin de Diencourt; and a section devoted to P.-J. Proudhon, and Charles Fourier.

Other extensive sections are concerned with the Horological industry together with a *Collection of watch-cases*; Ceramics and Glass; Egyptian, Roman, and Greek antiquities, including a fine mosaic of a Charioteer; Medieval and Ecclesiastical collections, including four statues of saints holding their heads, etc.; and several tapestries of interest.

In the *Basement* are *Archaelogical collections*, including a bronze bull with three horns (1C; from Avrigney), and bronze figurines, many unearthed in Besançon, including a bust of Caesar.

Application should be made for admission to the Lapidary collections housed in the 14C church of *St-Paul*, some minutes' walk to the E., which contain Merovingian sarcophagi, etc.

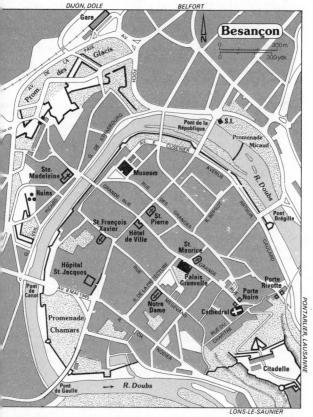

st N. of the museum is a *Protestant Church*, formerly that of a hospital (13C).

*ll*owing the Grand Rue, in which are several imposing mansions, *e* pass (l.) *St-Pierre* (18C), containing modern copper Stations of the *ross*; and opposite, the curiously mottled 16C **Hôtel de Ville**, *hind* which is the rebuilt *Palais de Justice*.

To the r. in this street is the **Palais Granvelle**, with angels on its *cade*, begun in 1535 by Nicolas Perrenot de Granvelle *486* – 1550), chancellor of the Emperor Charles V, and father of the *rdinal*. It now accommodates an interesting *Historical Museum*, *rtly* devoted to Charles V, and containing a series of Bruges *pestries*, and collections of coins and medals.

In the street opposite is *St-Maurice* (1712), and the *Library* (found-*1694*), containing important collections of MSS and incunables.

No. 40 in the Grand Rue was the birthplace of Victor Hugo, while *most* opposite were born the brothers Lumière. Beyond (l.) is the *r. Castan*, with several columns and other remains of a Roman *eatre*, and of a *Baptistry* erected on its site, an underground reser-*ir*, and relics of the basilica of St-Étienne, destroyed in 1676.—Op-*site* is the former *Archbishop's Palace* (18C).

The street passes beneath the **Porte Noir**, a remarkably well-preserved Roman gateway, 10m high, said to date from the A tonine period and still covered· with allegorical and milita sculptures.

The **Cathedral**, in a somewhat cramped site, has been rebuilt various styles since the original 4C structure was replaced. Most the dull exterior dates from the 18C, and like that at Nevers, it h apses at both ends, that at the W. enclosing the choir.

In the E. apse is the marble tomb, carved at Bruges in 1543, of Abbot Fer Carondelet (1473–1528), an ambassador to Rome and a friend of Raphael a Erasmus. The painting above is attrib. to *Sebastian del Piombo*; over the altar i Resurrection by *C. van Loo*, flanked by scenes of the Passion by *Natoire* and Troy.—The Gothic vaulting of the nave (13C) rests upon Romanesque arches a pillars; the stone pulpit is 15C. The S. aisle is flanked by a series of chapels various periods, the baptistry containing the *Rose de St-Jean*, a circular mark slab of the time of Constantine.—On the wall of the N. aisle is a Virgin and Ch with saints by Fra Bartolomeo, with a portrait (r.) of the donor, Fer Carondelet.—Opposite the N. portal is an *Astronomical Clock* ◇ (1860), b Vérité de Beauvais.

A winding road ascends hence to the **Citadel**, built by Vauban on t site of the Roman citadel, guarding the isthmus of the loop with which the city stands, below the Rhône-Rhin Canal runs through tunnel. Here may be visited several museums, the most interestin concerned with folk art, and traditional agriculture.

To the E. of the cathedral, as we descend, is the *Porte Rivotte*, pa of the 16C defences.—Retracing our steps to the Palais Granvell one may turn l., passing (l.) *Notre-Dame*, with a Renaissance port and bell-tower, and some 11C pillars, to approach the *Préfecture*, buildings of 1771.—Turning r., we reach the *Pl. St-Jacques*, adjace to which is the Promenade Chamars, the Roman Camp Martius.—To the N.E. is the *Hôpital St-Jacques*, with good wroug iron grilles of 1703.—Before regaining the Grand Rue the 17C Jesu church of *St-François-Xavier* is passed in a street to the l. its rered contains a Presentation in the Temple attrib. to *Pietro di Pietri*.

Near the far end of the *Pont de Battant*, near which are remains of a Rom bridge, is 18C *Ste-Madeleine*, retaining the jacquemart of an earlier Romanesq building. A short distance to the W. are relics of a Roman arena, and the mo conspicuous *Ramparts* thrown up by Vauban.

For roads from Besançon to *Mulhouse*, see Rte 118; from *Langres* to Besanç and *Pontarlier*, see Rte 117; for *Épinal*, and *Nancy*, see Rte 112; and for *Dôle* a *Dijon*, see Rte 126, both in reverse. For the road to *Lons-le-Saunier, Bourg-Bresse*, and **Lyon**, see below.

125 Besançon to Lyon

210km (130 miles). N83. 49km **Arbois**—10km **Poligny** lies 1kr. l.—28km **Lons-le-Saunier**—61km **Bourg-en-Bresse**—62km **Lyo**

Maps: IGN 37, 44, or 109. M 243, 244.

Driving S.W. from **Besançon**, (see Rte 124), the windings of t Doubs are followed for c. 9km before the road bears away, with view N.W. of the ruins of the castle of *Montferrand* (13-16C), to en the valley of the Loue, with the ruins of the castle of *Chenecey* to t r.

12km. *Quingey.*—A r.-hand fork leads 12km to **Arc-et-Sénans**; see
tte 126.—We veer S., parallel to the hills of the Jura, to (26km)
Arbois, an attractive old wine-growing town, retaining two towers of
ts walls, on the N. outskirts of which is the paternal house of Pasteur
cf. Dôle), who spent his youth here; a small museum may be visited.
The emperor Maximilian I established an armoury here under
Francesco de Merate of Milan. Arbois was the birthplace of Gén.
Pichegru (1761–1804). From the *Pl. de la Liberté* the main street is
followed, with the *Hôtel de Ville* and *Wine Museum*, before crossing
he little river Cuisance. To the r. stands *St-Just*, with a yellow stone
Belfry (16C) and a frieze of grapes carved over its entrance.

11km. **Poligny**; see Rte 126.

3.5km. *St-Lothian*, 1.5km l., has a partly 12C church preserving
sculptures of interest, and a Romanesque crypt.

14km. Both *Château-Chalon*, 5.5km E., and *Arly*, 2km W., have
ruined castles in their picturesque villages.

ome 6km S. of the former are the remains of the monastery of **Baume-les-
Messieurs**, founded by St Colomba in the 6C, of which St Berno (cf. Cluny), and
he 17C adventurer Jean de Watteville, were abbots. The 12-16C *Abbey-
hurch contains an Entombment surrounded by statues (St Paul is by the School
f Claus Sluter), a painted reredos, and several tombs of interest (15C and
ter).—Slightly further S. are the stalactite caves of the *Grottes de Baume*, and
scades, whence one may turn W. for Lons-le-Saunier.

A r.-hand turning as we near (10.5km) Lons-le-Saunier leads shortly
o the 13C *Château du Pin*, with a huge keep.

LONS-LE-SAUNIER (21,900 Lédoniens), préfecture of the *Jura*, and
thermal station since Roman times (*Ledo Salinarius*), is pleasantly
ited on the Vallière among vine-covered hills. it was the birthplace
f Rouget de Lisle (1760–1836), who in 1792 composed at
trasbourg the 'Marseillaise'; and here on 14 March 1815 Marshal
Ney announced his defection to Napoleon.

To the S.E. of the main crossroads are the *Établissement Thermal*,
a park, whence we turn W. through the *Pl. du 11-Novembre*, N. of
hich is the *Église des Cordeliers* (14-15C), with 18C boiseries. Fur-
er W. is the charming arcaded *Rue du Commerce*, just to the N. of
hich is the **Museum**, with archaeological collections, mainly from
e Lacs de Clairvaux and de Chalain, including a dug-out canoe of
terest.

mong paintings are *Brueghel*, Massacre of the Innocents; attrib. to *Ribera*,
lenus; attrib. to *Heinsius*, Portrait of Laplace; an *anon.* Dutch Portrait of a
anish woman; *Delacroix*, Norman fishermen; and *Courbet*, The Château de
hillon.

o the W. is the 18C *Hospital*, with a fine iron grille, and noteworthy
dispensary.—Turning S., we reach the *Pl. de la Liberté*, with an old
lock-tower; a short distance further S. is *St-Désiré*, with an 11C crypt
ontaining the sarcophagus of its patron, bishop of Besançon
l. c. 415).

ONS-LE-SAUNIER TO ST-LAURENT-EN GRANDVAUX (48km). The N78 leads
E. up the valley of the Vallière through (4km) *Conliège*, with a church of 1393,
ter enlarged, and past the *Creux de Ravigny*, a cave-riddled cirque of
iffs.—13km. To the N., on a ridge of the Jura, are the ruins of the 13C castle of
eauregard, dismantled in 1668.—We cross the Ain at (4km) the *Saut de la
aisse*, and 5km beyond, reach *Clairvaux*. A keep and chapel survive of its cas-
e, while *St-Nithier* contains good paintings and 15C stalls. Traces of lake-
wellings have been found adjacent.—10km. *Bonlieu*, beyond which, to the S., is

another charming lake, where relics of a Carthusian monastery founded in 1277 were burned in 1944.—4km. To the N. lies the *Lac de la Motte*; to the N.W. the *Cascades du Hérisson*.—The road winds S.E. onto the plateau of *Grandvau* to (10km) *St-Laurent*; for the road beyond, see Rte 126.

An ALTERNATIVE ROAD is the D39, turning off the D471 E. of Lons to (23.5km) *Doucier*, just S. of the beautiful *Lac de Chalain*, with a horseshoe of rocks at its head and submerged remains of a pile-built village.—To the S.E. are the *Lacs du Chambly* and *du Val*, which are skirted before reaching (after 13.5km) the N78 10km N.W. of *St-Laurent*.

LONS-LE-SAUNIER TO ST-CLAUDE (61km). The D52 leads S.E., at 8km passing (r.) *St-Maur*, with a Romanesque and 14C church containing a reliquary of the saint; above the village is a fine view-point.—We pass (r.) after another 8km the conspicuous ruins of the castle of *Présilly*, on approaching (4km) *Orgelet*, an ancient town, whose castle was destroyed in 1595, with a 13-16C church containing Renaissance choir-stalls, and a hospital dating from 1292, often restored.—Turning E., at 4km *La Tour-du-Meix*, with a ruined castle of the abbots of St-Claude, is traversed, near the so-called *Mur des Sarrasins*, a dry-stone fortification of unknown origin, and the dammed Ain is crossed at the *Pont de l'Pile*; the *Barrage de Vouglans* lies at the S. end of the gorge, in which the *Chartreuse of N.-D.-de-Vaucluse*, founded 1139, has been submerged.—The road later veers S.E., away from the reservoir through (16km) *Moirans-en-Montagne*, and 2km beyond, with a view of the gorge of the Bienne to the S., passes *Villards-d'Héria* (l.), where remains of an aqueduct recall a vanished Gallo-Roman town traditionally known as *Ville d'Antre*.—Winding through the hills, at 7.5km *St-Romain-de-Roche* is passed to the r., commanding a plunging view of the Bienne, with a 14C church and ruins of a priory, originally a nunnery under the name of Balma, where in 460 St Romanus was buried.—The road descends through *Lavans*, just N. of which is *St-Lupicin* (where St Lupicinus founded a priory in 445), known as Lauconne until the 12C, with a Romanesque church.—6.5km. The river is crossed, and we turn l. for (6.5km) **St-Claude**; see Rte 126, and for the road beyond.

For the road from Lons-le-Saunier to *Chalon-sur-Saône* (or *Tournus*), see Rte 127.

Quitting Lons, the road turns W., and after 2km forks l. away from *Montmorot*, with its salt-mines, and skirts the outlying spurs of the Jura through (22km) *Cuiseaux*, preserving two towers of its enceinte.

Some 12km across country to the S.E. are the remains of the abbey-church of *Gigny*, founded by St Berno in 893, whose monks were among the first to go to Cluny, together with those from Baume-les-Messieurs (see above).

At 7.5km *St-Amour* is by-passed to the r., deriving its name from S. Amaturus, a martyr of the Theban Legion, whose remains were brought here in the 6C; it was the birthplace of Guillaume de St Amour (d. 1272), the 'incorruptable' theologian and rector of the University of Paris.

6km. *Coligny*, which gave its name to the family of which Adm. Gaspard de Coligny (1517 – 72) was the most famous member, where important Gallo-Roman artefacts have been found.

23km. **Bourg-en-Bresse**, and **Brou**; see Rte 128.

The road bears S.W. away from the Jura, traversing the *Plateau de Dombes*, a wide plain studded with numerous shallow lakes and small hills (*poèpes*), and ending in the abrupt escarpment of the Rhône valley to the S.

At 5km a l.-hand fork (D22) leads due S. via *Chalamont* to (30km) *Meximieux* and *Pérouges*; see Rte 130.

9km. *St-Paul-de-Varax* has a Romanesque church with an arcaded W. front and an 11C porch surmounted by a carved frieze; a bas-relief on the S. porch represents an abbot and a faun. The brick-built château is 15C.

At 7km *Châtillon-sur-Chalaronne* lies 13km N.W., a market-town of the Dombes, with an old castle-gate and 15C church of which St Vincent de Paul was curé in 1617–18.

7km. *Villars-les-Dombes* retains the motte or 'poèpe' and scanty ruins of its 11C castle, once the seat of a powerful lordship, but dismantled by Marshal Biron in 1595. The 14-15C church preserves good tombstones.

34km **Lyon**; see Rte 129.

26 Dijon to Geneva via Dôle, and Poligny

196km (122 miles). N5. 32km **Auxonne**—16km. **Dôle**—17km. The D472 leads via **Salins** to *Pontarlier*, 69km E.—19km **Poligny**—24km *Champagnole*—22km. *St-Laurent-en-Grandvaux*—22km *La Cure*—27km *Gex*—17km **Geneva**.

Maps: IGN 29, 37, 38, 44, or 109. M 243.

Driving S.E. from **Dijon** (Rte 123), at 11.5km the road passes 3km N. of *Rouvres-en-Plaine*, where the 13-14C church contains three sculptures of the School of Claus Sluter, to (20.5km) **Auxonne** (pron. Aussonne; 7,900 inhab.), a dismantled fortress town attractively situated on the l. bank of the Saône, where in 1788–89 young Lieut. Napoleon Bonaparte was quartered. *Notre-Dame (1309–60), on the site of an earlier Romanesque church of which one tower survives, has a portal of 1516 adorned with well-sculptured figures of prophets, and a tower and spire of the same period, 70m high. The interior is characteristic Burgundian Gothic. The former *Arsenal* (1674) is now a market; the Renaissance château, barracks.

Veering S. past (l.) *Mont Roland*, at 16km **Dôle** is entered, an ancient town of 28,000 Dôlois, once capital of the Franche-Comté, and pleasantly sited above the r. bank of the Doubs and the Rhône-Rhin Canal.

Probably a Gallo-Roman stronghold, it became the earliest capital of the counts of Burgundy, and in the 12C the castle was enlarged by Frederick Barbarossa. A university was established here in 1423, but Charles d'Amboise, who seized it for Louis XI in 1479, virtually razed the place to the ground. Its walls were reerected by the Emperor Charles V in 1540–61, and in 1636 it successfully resisted a long siege by Condé. its fortifications were dismantled by Louis XIV, who transferred the parlement and university to Besançon.

Among Dôlois were Gén. Malet (1755–1812), who plotted Napoleon's overthrow; and Louis Pasteur (1822–95), the scientist.

On the E. side of the Av. de Paris is the wide Cours Georges-Clemenceau, at the far end of which is the *Théâtre*, and just beyond, in the Rue du Collège-de-l'Arc, is a *College* founded by the Jesuits in 1582, until recently containing a collection of paintings, including Le Brun, Siege of Dôle; P.-D. *Martin*, Sieges of Besançon and Gray, and other canvases of doubtful attribution, but these, and the archaeological collection in the former chapel, with a Renaissance porch, are in the process of being transferred to a new site in an 18C edifice at the S. end of the Rue d'Arènes.

The Rue Boyvin, turning r. off the Rue du Collège, in which ar
one or two 18C mansions, leads towards **Notre-Dame**, a Gothi
edifice begun in 1509, with a tall belfry, and showing some scars o
the siege of 1636, but of slight interest.—By following the narro
Rue du Parlement S., and turning l., we gain the Rue Pasteur (onc
the Rue des Tanneurs), in which No. 43 was the birthplace of th
scientist, with a museum devoted to him.

Retracing our steps, we may descend to the river for the view
overlooked to the N.W. by the *Hôtel-Dieu* (1613–83; now th
Hôpital Pasteur), and ascend the Grande Rue to the *Pl. 8 Mai 194*
there turning l. along the Rue des Arènes. The *Pl. aux Fleurs* is shor
ly passed, and (No. 28; r.) the old *Hôtel de Ville*, with a facade o
1609, and the *Tour de Vergy* in its court. No. 32 is the former *Unive
sity*, while further along the street, almost opposite No. 36 (16C)
the entrance to the *Palais de Justice*, occupying the old Francisca
convent, one of the few buildings that escaped the destruction o
1479.

Leading N. from the street at this point is the Rue du Mont Roland
in which (r.) is the 17C *Hôtel de Froissard*, and (l.) the forme
Carmelite Convent, both with good iron grilles, beyond which th
Théâtre is regained.

DÔLE TO BESANÇON (46km). Although the A36 motorway, entered N. of t
town, provides a rapid route, the N73 is equally direct, ascending the r. bank
the Doubs, on the far bank of which lies the extensive *Forêt de Chaux*. At (22k
Dampierre the striking Romanesque church of *Courtefontaine* lies 6k
S.E.—24km **Besançon**; see Rte 124.

10km. S. of Dôle, the r.-hand fork continues S. to meet the N83 afte
25km, 17km N. of **Lons-le-Saunier**; see Rte 125.—The N5 veers l. to
junction 8km S.E., there bearing r. to by-pass *Mont-sours-Vaudre*
the birthplace of the politician Jules Grévy (1807–91), 1km l.

The Director's House, Arc-et-Sénans

MONT-SOUS-VAUDREY TO PONTARLIER (69km). We follow the D472.—At
12.5km the l.-hand turning leads 5km to **Arch-et-Senans**, a small village preserving one of the great architectural curiosities of France, the *Saline Royale, constructed by Claude-Nicolas Ledoux in 1775–79. Ledoux (1736–1806) had been
appointed inspector of salt-works thanks to the influence of Mme du Barry, and
selected this site adjacent to the forest of Chaux. Wood was essential to heat the
water from the saline springs conducted there in conduits to be evaporated in a
long 'bâtiment de graduation', this being the usual method of the time. The
woods in the neighbourhood of *Salins*—see below—had already been depleted.
Ledoux was only able to complete part of his ambitious design for an 'ideal
town', but what remains is a remarkable achievement: eleven buildings, seven of
them ranged in a semicircle facing the central Director's mansion on its
diameter, on either side of which rose two huge evaporation workshops. With
the salt content of the spring decreasing, and more economical methods of extraction being discovered, the factory declined, and by the end of the 19C the
buildings were abandoned and derelict, and later were in part deliberately
destroyed. The works were taken over by the Department of Doubs in 1927, and
have since been restored; since 1972 they have accommodated the Fondation
Claude Nicolas Ledoux, an organisation researching into a variety of future
perspectives.

From the *Entrance wing*, with its peristyle of six baseless Tuscan columns, we
traverse a rusticated archway, from either side of which appear stalactites
representing petrified water; similar decoration suggesting salinity may be seen
on the exterior walls, etc. On either side are a series of pavilions for carpenters,
coopers, farriers, cartwrights, clerks, etc., that on the l. of the entrance now containing an interesting explanatory exhibition on salt extraction, and of the work
of Ledoux. The impressive temple portico of the *Director's house* has six great
banded Tuscan columns, and behind this administrative building are the *Stables*.
The huge vaulted buildings on either side, 81m long, and 28m wide, are now used for congresses, and concerts, etc.

Regaining the main road, one continues S.E., crossing the N83 to ascend the
valley of the Furieuse below (l.) *Mont Poupet* (850m) to (13km) **Salins-les-Bains**, a
small spa deriving its name from its salt-mines and brine-wells, which may be
visited. Under Louis XI the Parlement of Franche-Comté met at Salins
(1477–93). It was the birthplace of Victor Considérant (1808–93), the political
theorist. Several towers of its 15C ramparts survive, while dismantled forts
crown heights to the E. and W. At the N. end of the town, which was partly
destroyed by a fire in 1825, 13-17C *St-Maurice* contains a wooden equestrian
statue of the saint in Louis-XII costume. The 18C *Hôtel de Ville* incorporates a
chapel of 1639, while *St-Anatoile*, on the hillside to the S.E., is an ill-restored
Romanesque building, its portal set between two flamboyant chapels.—The road
turns E. through *Cernans*, with a 12th and 15C church, at 14km passing S. of the
picturesque *Source of the Lison*, gushing from a cavern, and traverses an arid
plateau flanked by forests before reaching (28km) *Pontarlier*, see Rte 117.

The N5 leads S.E. to (19km) **Poligny**, a wine-growing town of
character, where E. of the Grande Rue stands *St-Hippolyte* (1429),
containing several fine statues of the Burgundian School, among
them a 16C Pietà (N. chapel).—**Arbois** (see Rte 125) lies 11km N.E.
   The road now climbs the *Culée de Vaux*, passing at *Vaux-sur-
Poligny* a restored 13C priory church, and traverses the *Forêt de
Poligny* before descending into the upper glen of the Ain at (25km)
Champagnole, a small town with sawmills, etc., rebuilt after a fire in
1798.

Some 17km to the N.E., after threading the *Cluse d'Entreportes* to the r. of the
D471, lies *Mièges*, with a noteworthy 13-16C priory church with a belfry of
1707; while neighbouring *Nozeroy*, a quaint old walled town with a ruined 13C
castle and 16C church, was the birthplace of Gilbert Cousin (1506–67),
secretary to Erasmus.

From Champagnole we continue S., following the railway, at 12km passing (l.) *La Chaux-des-Crotenay*, with a ruined 13C castle and 15C church, and near (r.) the *Lacs de Maclu*, to (10km) *St-Laurent-en-Grandvaux*, a small cheese-making town rebuilt with galvanised roofs after a ravaging fire in 1867.—The lake-side ruins of the abbey of *Grandvaux*, founded in 523 and re-established in 1172, lies 6km S.W.—A road goes on, crossing a ridge above the *Gorges de la Bienne*, to (23.5km) *St-Claude*; see Rte 130.

The N5 now crosses a ridge covered by the *Forêt de Mont Noir* to (12km). **Morez** (7,000 Moreziens) in the limestone gorge of the Bienne, a prosperous little town devoted to the manufacture of spectacles since 1796, and cheese.—Continuing to traverse the ridges of the Jura through *Les Rousses*, with its ski-slopes, at 10km the frontier village of *La Cure* (Customs) is reached.

Nyon, on *Lac Léman*, lies 22km S.E. via *St-Cergue*.

The main road bears S.W., overlooked (l.) by *La Dôle* (1678m) in Switzerland, and climbs to (13km) the *Col de la Faucille* (1820m; see p 706), descending thence to (14km) *Gex*.

Ferney-Voltaire lies 10km S.E. (see Rte 130), and **Geneva** 7km beyond.

127 Dijon to Lyon

193km (120 miles). N74. 39km **Beaune**—16km N6—17km **Chalon-sur-Saône**—27km **Tournus**—30km **Mâcon**—31km **Villefranche-sur-Saône**—33km **Lyon**.

Maps: IGN 37, 43, 44, or 109. M 243, 244.

The A37 continued by the A6 motorway provides a rapid direct road, from which exits may be made to the main towns en route.

For **Dijon**, see Rte 123.

The N74 leads S., skirting the vine-clad hills of the *Côte d'Or*, at 12.5km passing (r.) *Gevrey-Chambertin*, with a 13-16C church and ruins of a 13C castle, where begins the famous '*Côte de Nuits*', which produces the vintages of Chambertin and Clos de Bèze.

5.5km. *Vougeot*, with the vineyards of Clos-Vougeot, cultivated by the monks of Citeaux from the 12C until the Revolution. Part of the château of 1551 remains, together with an old wine-cellar, the 'Vendangeoire de Citeaux', containing 13C wine-presses.—*Vosne-Romanée* is shortly passed, likewise celebrated for its *Romanée-Conti, Richebourg*, etc.—5km. *Nuits-St-Georges*, a small vinous town, noted for its Clos-St-Georges, etc., has a late Romanesque church showing the persistence of the Romanesque tradition in Burgundy, and a monument commemorating the indecisive *Battle of Nuits* (18 Dec. 1870).

13km due E. lies **Citeaux** (Cistercium), now more of interest for its history than for the relics of the famous abbey, the remaining buildings being largely 18C, but they include a disused 12C chapel, a 15C structure with a glazed brick front, a vaulted hall, and remnants of a Gothic cloister.

The Cistercian Order, founded in 1098 by St Albéric, St Robert of Molesme and St Stephen Harding (born at Sherborne; d. 1134), owed much of its importance to the zeal of St Bernard, who settled here with his brothers in 1114, and helped to found the four 'daughter' abbeys of La Ferté, Pontigny, Morimond, and Clairvaux, becoming abbot of the last in 1115. From these sprang many Cister cian communities, so that within a century the order embraced over 1000 monasteries in Europe and Palestine. The original rule was inspired by that of St Benedict, but it developed with more austerity. It was twice reformed (in the 16th and 18Cs), but the abbey of Citeaux was suppressed in 1790. After a short-lived attempt to found a 'phalanstère' on the lines advocated by Fourier (1840), an agricultural colony was established here in 1846 by the Abbé Rey, which prospered until 1888, a decade after which the Cistercians re-congregated here.

Continuing S., we shortly reach the outlying vineyards of the *Côte de Beaune*, and after 16km, after crossing the A6 motorway, enter Beaune itself.

BEAUNE (21,100 inhab.), an ancient town of some charm, still preserving most of its walls, and surrounded by vineyards, now lying close to an important junction of autoroutes, retains its reputation as a gastronomic centre.

Roman *Belina* or *Belnocastrum* was later the capital of the *Beaunois*, and regarded by the dukes of Burgundy as the third city of their duchy. it was a stronghold of the League during the religious wars, against the will of its citizens, who petitioned Henri IV for the destruction of the castle and fortifications, only partially effected in 1602. It was the birthplace of Gaspard Monge (1746–1818), the physicist, and the artist Félix Ziem (1821–1911).

Entering the town from the N. we pass (l.) *St-Nicolas* (12-14C), retaining its original porch and 12C doorway, before reaching the *Porte St-Nicolas*, a triumphal arch of 1761, where we bear r. to circle the medieval enceinte, shortly passing a bastion of the town-walls. The old town may be entered at this point, or the circuit may be continued, at first parallel to the river Bouzaise, to its E. side, where two 15C towers survive of the castle.

Opposite the S.I., abutting the restored covered market close to the S. walls, stands the famous **Hôtel-Dieu*, a building largely constructed of wood, the earliest part of which (1443) preserves the Flemish Gothic character imparted to it by its architect Jehan Wisecrère.

The hospital was founded by Nicolas Rolin, Philippe le Bon's chancellor, and his wife Guigone de Salins, and its administration was committed to nuns of the order of the Saint-Esprit, established in Malines, whose rule, usages, and costume (white in summer; blue in winter, with a Flemish head-dress) were long retained by the 'soeurs hospitalières'. It is now an old people's home. Guided tours take place at fixed hours.

The entrance is protected by a bold and graceful arcaded penthouse, from which the main courtyard is reached, surrounded (except for the 17C Salle St-Louis) by buildings of 1443, until 1948 devoted to their original use, which with its galleries, dormer windows rising from the steeply pitched parti-coloured glazed-tiled roof, with their leaden ornaments and gilded vanes, presents a picturesque scene. One is conducted through the *Grande Salle des Malades* (72m long) under the same polychrome timber roof as the *Chapel* (with copies of its original glass), from which it is separated by a wooden screen adorned with statuettes; the *Kitchen, Dispensary* (containing old faïence, Nevers ware of 1782, pewter, and other utensils); and eventually to the **Polyptych of the Last Judgement* by Roger van der Weyden, which hung in the chapel for which it was commissioned until 1793.

On the r. of the central panel of Christ, presiding, and the archangel Michael weighing souls, are seen the Virgin and six apostles, with the standing figures of Nicolas Rolin, Philippe le Bon, Bp (later Card.) Jean Rolin, the chancellor's son,

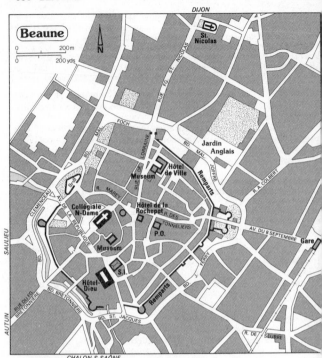

DIJON

CHALON-S-SAÔNE

and Pope Eugenius IV; and l., the Baptist and six apostles, with Guigone de Salins (almost hidden), the duchess of Burgundy, and Philipote Rolin, the chancellor's daughter, who died in the hospital. Above are panels of angels carrying the instruments of the Passion, and below (r.) are the naked figures of the damned, and (l.) the blessed.

Here, on each 3rd Sun. of Nov., the Hospice holds an auction of wine from its vineyards, and the Confrérie des Chevaliers du Tastevin hold their banquets.

The Rue Monge and Rue Carnot lead N. to the small *Pl. Monge*, on the E. side of which is the Gothic front of the *Hôtel de la Rochepot* (1552), with Renaissance courtyards. Opposite is the 15C *Belfry* (with a small museam) of the former Hôtel de Ville.

The Rue de la Lorraine, leading N., with two 16C houses, passes (r.) the chapel of 1645 of the *Hospice de la Charité*, to approach (r.) the *Hôtel de Ville*, occupying the former Ursuline convent (1697). A small *Museum* is installed here, containing rooms devoted to local history and archaeology, paintings (including works by Ziem), and 'chromophotography', invented by E.-J. Marey (1830–1904), born in Beaune.

From the W. side of the Place we turn l. to approach the apse of the former collegiate church of **Notre-Dame**, typical of the Cluniac architecture of the period (12-13C), with a large main porch with its three 13C doorways and their 15C doors. The central tower is Gothic. By the S. transept are relics of a 13C cloister, and a chapel. The fine 15C tapestries of scenes from the Life of the Virgin in the choir, the windows in grisaille by Didron, and the carving of the altarpieces, etc. will be noted. A pleasant view may be obtained from the Impasse Notre-Dame, just E. of the porch.

The next lane to the E. (de l'Enfer) leads to the **Hôtel des Ducs** (15-16C) in which two floors accommodate an interesting Burgundian ***Wine Museum**. Adjacent is a 14C press house or 'Cuverie', in which are 18-19C wine-presses.

Turning l. on making our exit, we reach the Av. de la République, a few paces W. of the *Pl. de la Halle*.

BEAUNE TO AUTUN (48km). The D973 shortly forks r. off the N74, traversing the vineyards of *Pommard*, and *Volnay*, after 15km passing (r.) the **Château de La Rochepot* (11-14C; restored), birthplace of Philippe Pot (1428– 94), Grand Seneschal of Burgundy and Burgundian ambassador to London, whose tomb is now in the Louvre. The church is 12-13C. There are two dolmens on high ground opposite.—The road passes under the N6 to (5km) *Nolay*, birthplace of Lazare Carnot (1753– 1823), member of the Convention, with a 14C timbered *Market-hall*.—7.5km. *Saisy* (l.) has a good 13C church-tower and choir.—4.5km. The r.-hand fork leads 4km N.W., by-passing (r.) *Épinac-les-Mines*, with collieries first worked in 1755, and a 15C castle built for Nicolas Rolin, to the *Château de Sully* (with a courtyard pronounced by Mme de Sévigné as the most beautiful in France), which dates from 1570. It was the birthplace of Marshal MacMahon (1808– 93).—Not far S. of the main road are the ruins of the priory of *Val-St-Benoît*.—10km. *Curgy*, 1km r., has an 11C church.—We shortly get a view of **Autun** (see Rte 120), 6km ahead, with *Mont Beuvray* and the *Morvan hills* in the background.

The N74 continues S.W., passing (r.) the vineyards of *Meursault*, whose 14-16C church has a good belfry and spire, and those of *Montrachet*, to (16km) **Chagny**, a small industrial town possessing an arcaded *Hôtel de Ville* and a priory church with a Romanesque nave and aisles, and 12C tower.

In 1365 Chagny became the headquarters of predatory bands of discharged mercenaries known as the 'Grandes Compagnies' or 'Écorcheurs' (flayers), who were persuaded by De Guesclin, in return for a large bribe and papal absolution for their crimes, to transfer their activities to Spain, where they fought against Pedro the Cruel, at that time an ally of England.

The road now veers S.E., crossing the Canal du Centre and the A6 before entering (17km) **CHALON-SUR-SAÔNE**, a thriving industrial town of 58,000 Chalonnais, largely on the r. bank of the river, with a characteristic old centre.

Ancient *Cabillonum* was a residence of the Burgundian kings in the 6C; its bishopric, suppressed at the Revolution, dated from the 4C. The poet Pontus de Thyard (1521– 1605) was bishop here from 1578. It was the birthplace of Baron Vivant Denon (1747– 1825), the archaeologist and diplomat, and Joseph Nicéphore Niepce (1755– 1833), the pioneer of photography.

From the central *Pl. del'Obelisque* (1790; commemorating the opening of the Canal du Centre), passing the circular market (to the E. of which is the *Neptune Fountain* of 1744 in the *Pl. de Beaune*), we traverse the Rue Gén.-Leclerc to reach (r.) the *Pl. de l'Hotel de Ville*.

On its N. side is the ***Musée Denon**, recently reorganised, and containing important collections of archaeology and art.

Notable are a Merovingian sarcophagus, the funerary stellae, Gallo-Roman bronze figurines, and a 1C sculpture of a gladiator and lion; also a fine bronze helmet.

Among paintings are a Self-portrait by *Denon*; *Robert Lefèvre, Fouché; Philippe de Champaigne*, Président Jean Perrault, and A. Girard; *Mierevelt*, Elizabeth of Bohemia; *Strozzi*, Virgin and child; *Leandro da Ponte*, View of Venice in 1623; *Englebrecht*, Kiss of Judas; an *anon*. Deposition (French; 1516); Female portrait

(Flemish; 1609); *Géricault*, Portrait of a negro; canvases by *Solimena, Paul Potter*, and *Wouverman*; Views of Chalon; also a good collection of furniture, including several examples in walnut 'de Sennecey'.

Opposite is *St-Pierre* (late 17C; restored).—Continuing S. via the Rue du Port-Villiers to the river bank, and turning., the *Musée Niepce* is reached, devoted to the early photographic apparatus of Niepce, and examples of his work, heliogravures, etc., and also that of members of his family.

On the island site opposite, is the 15C *Tour du Doyenne*, re-erected here in 1928 from its earlier position near the cathedral. Adjacent is the **Hospital**, founded in the 16C, but its refectory is no longer open to the public.

Skirting the Saône, crossed by the *Pont St-Laurent*, with its obelisks, inspired by the bridge of 1780 destroyed in 1944, we approach (l.) an area under restoration at the S. end of the Grande Rue, in which are several old houses. Close by is *St-Vincent*, the former cathedral, a 12-15C building with a choir and apse in the 13C Burgundian style; its W. front was rebuilt in 1827–51. Adjacent is a Gothic cloister.

CHALON TO LONS-LE-SAUNIER (64km). Crossing the Saône, the D978 is followed through (3km) *St-Marcel* (ancient *Ubiliacus*), with the 12C church of a Cluniac priory in which Abélard died in 1142.—The road turns S.E. across the *Plaine de la Bresse*, with its characteristic long low half-timbered barns, to (34km) **Louhans**, a prosperous little market-town of 6,900 inhab. on the Seille, known for its poultry, with a picturesque arcaded *Grande Rue* lined with 17-18C houses, a church of 1491, and to the E., the *Pharmacy* of its *Hôtel-Dieu* of 1767, preserving good 16C lustre-ware.—At *Ste-Croix*, 6km S., the 15C church contains contemporary glass and several d'Artagnan tombs, including that of the wife of the famous musketeer.·-The road continues E., at c. 14km passing the once-fortified brick château of *Beaurepaire*, to (13km) **Lons-le-Saunier**; see Rte 125.

Skirting the r. bank of the Saône to the S.W., at 6km *St-Loup-de-Varenne*, with the tomb of Niepce (see above) is passed to the l., 2km beyond which a r.-hand turning leads over the motorway (running parallel to the W.) to (6km) *La Ferté*, with the ruins of the former abbey, one of the four 'daughters of Citeaux', founded in 1113 and destroyed in 1570.

9km. *Sennecey-le-Grand*, with an 11-15C church.—To the W. are the churches of *St-Martin-de-Laives* (11C), and *St-Julien* (12-15C, with good frescoes); near-by is the 12-16C *Château de Ruffey*.

Passing (l.) the 10C chapel of *St-Laurent* at its N. end, we enter (10km) **TOURNUS** (pron. Tournu; 7,300 Turnusiens), an interesting old riverside town, mentioned in 177 under the name *Trenorchium*. Its most famous native was Jean-Baptiste Greuze (1725–1805).

The charming enceinte lies to the E. of the main road, retaining several old towers, and surrounding the Benedictine abbey founded in the 7th or 8C at the tomb of St Valerian. The abbey-church of *St-Philibert*, still with monastic dependencies, is one of the most remarkable examples of Romanesque in Burgundy, and presents an almost unique instance of three separate churches superimposed.

The crypt dates from the 9C; the main church has a 10C narthex, nave, and apse-chapels, and a 12C choir; while the church of *St-Michel*, above the narthex, is also 10C. Of the two completed towers the smaller is 10C and antedates the other by two centuries. The *Chapter-house* is dated 1239, and the *Abbot's lodge*, further E., is late 15C.

The plain and massive *Nave*, entered through a low narthex of three bays, is remarkable for its transverse barrel-vaulting. The choir is separated from the ambulatory by an arcade of great delicacy in contrast to the huge round piers of the nave. The glass is unfortunate. The apse chapel contains the reliquary of St Philibert (cf.). Four of the double row of columns in the *Crypt* are said to be of Roman origin. On the ceiling of the S. chapel is a 12C fresco. From above the castellated narthex of the upper church we get a fine view of the nave, while a stair leads to a terrace providing a view of the sculptures on the tower. The 12C refectory and cellars may also be seen.

To the N. is a *Museum* of local interest; a few paces to the S., beyond deconsecrated *St-Valerian*, is another *Museum* devoted to Greuze, and other collections.—Hence the Rue de la République leads S. to *La Madeleine* (12th and 15C), while to the W. of the street is the 18C *Hôtel de Ville*, from which the Rue de l'Hôpital leads uphill past the *Hôtel-Dieu*, preserving its *Pharmacy*, to regain the main road.

For the road from Tournus to **Bourg-en-Bresse** and beyond, see Rte 128.

TOURNUS TO CLUNY (37km). The D14 is followed over the hills to the S.W. to (12km) **Brancion*, a charming little village dominated by a partially restored *Castle* (10th and 14C), retaining its tiny 15C *Market-hall*, and a 12C *Church* containing 14C frescoes.—7km. *Chapaize*, with a remarkable 11C belfry, beyond which the valley of the Grosne is entered at (4.5km) *Cormatin*, with two wings of a sumptuously furnished Renaissance *Château* (1600), containing some paintings of interest.—Some 8km N. lie the ruins of the castle of *Sercy*, while neighbouring *St-Gengoux-le-National* preserves a 12-15C church.—Turning S. from Cormatin, we by-pass (r.) *Ameugny*, with an 11C church, and (5km) *Taizé*, with a gutted Romanesque church and new buildings erected around an ecumenical centre established in 1940 by Roger Schutz as a Protestant monastic community, but popular with Christian youths in general.—8km. **Cluny** (see the latter part of Rte 97), 5km beyond which is the N79.

4km. A r.-hand fork leads across the motorway to the Romanesque churches of *Farges* and adjacent *Uchizy*; the inhabitants of the latter (Chizerots) are believed to have descended from a colony of Arabs.—8km. *Pont-de-Vaux*, beyond the far bank of the Saône, was the birthplace of Gén. Joubert (1769–99), killed at the battle of Novi.

17km **MÂCON** (39,900 Mâconnais), the old capital of the Mâconnais, and préfecture of the *Saône-et-Loire*, is the centre of the wine trade (including those of Pouilly and Viré, in addition to the local red), but is of slight interest in itself, although once of importance as *Castrum Matisconense*. It was the birthplace of Alphonse Lamartine (1790–1869).

At the N. end of the riverside quay, among colourful gardens, is the *Maison des Vins*. The first turning S. of the bridge leads to the small *Pl. aux Herbes*, where there is an attractive Renaissance house, beyond which (turning l. and then r.) is the old church of *St-Vincent* (12-15C), largely ruined, containing naive sculptures in its mutilated tympanum, and architectural fragments in its interior.—A short distance to the W. is the *Musée Municipal des Ursulines*, installed in a 17C convent, with archaeological collections, including artefacts from *Solutré*, 8km W. (see p 528); an effigy of Dorothea of Poitiers, canoness of Mons (d. 1382); and somewhat miscellaneous collections of paintings and drawings, etc.

For *Cluny*, 23km N.W., see the latter part of Rte 97.

MACON TO BOURG-EN-BRESSE (34km). We cross the old 12-arched *Bridge* (reconstructed in part in 1843) to transpontine *St-Laurent*, and follow the N79 to the E.—6.5km. *St-André-de-Bâgé*, 1.5km N., has a late 11C church built in a very pure style by the monks of Tournus, with a fine octagonal belfry. Neighbouring *Bâgé-le-Châtel*, still partly walled, was the seat of a medieval lordship.—*Pont-de-*

Veyle, 4.5km S. of the crossroad, preserves a 13C gateway surmounted by a 16C belfry, the ancestral mansion (rebuilt in the 18C) of the Lesdiguières family, and other old buildings.—Continuing E., we pass near (l.) characteristic examples of the farms of Bresse, and enter at 22.5km **Bourg-en-Bresse** itself; see Rte 128.

Quitting Mâcon, one descends the valley of the Saône, with the plain of Bresse to the l., and the hills of the Mâconnais merging with those of the Beaujolais to the r., shortly passing under the motorway and following it S. to (30km) *Belleville*, formerly a walled bastide, and with a Romanesque church of 1179, and now a busy vinous town devoted to the marketing of Beaujolais. For the country to the W., see p 526.

  14.5km. **Villefranche-sur-Saône**, the former capital of the Beaujolais, is an industrial and commercial town of 29,100 inhab., sometimes known as 'Caladois' from the 'Calade', an open flagged space that existed near the church, and a favourite rendezvous. Half-way down the long Rue Nationale (E. of the main road), in which are several old houses, stands (l.) *N.-D.-des-Marais*, with a Flamboyant facade and a narrow and elaborately vaulted nave.

10km to the W. is the splendid feudal castle of *Montmelas*, enclosed by a double curtain wall, while c. 5km to the N. of the latter is the 12C priory church of *Salles-Arbuissonnas*.

Continuing S., at 4km the 16-17C château of *La Fontaine* is passed to the r., and 2km beyond, *Anse*, with an 11C castle.

ANSE TO LYON VIA TRÉVOUX (31km). The Saône is crossed to (5km) **Trévoux**, the capital of the Dombes in the 11-16C, which later became an appanage of Mlle de Montpensier. The Jews, who introduced the goldsmith's art here, were much favoured until the 15C, while a famous press, controlled by the Jesuits, printed the 'Journal de Trévoux' and 'Dictionnaire de Trévoux' here during the years 1801–30, when they transferred to Paris. Three towers of its *Castle* remain, while in the hall of the 17C *Palais de Justice* assembled the Parlement of the Dombes.—The road skirts the l. bank of the river and later traverses (10km) *Neuville-sur-Saône*, and several suburbs, including *Rochetaillée*, with its museum of veteran cars, before entering *Lyon* itself.

The l.-hand fork immediately S. of Anse leads 21km to *Neuville*; the N6 continues S., passing (r.) *Chazay-d'Azergues*, with two gateways of its old walls, just before crossing under and then over the motorway, later traversing its N.W. suburbs before reaching the centre of (25km) **Lyon**; see Rte 129.

128   Tournus to Bourg-en-Bresse and Chambéry

166km (103 miles). D975. 54km **Bourg-en-Bresse**, and *Brou*—N75. 31km *Ambérieu*—N504. 45km *Belley*—36km **Chambéry**.

Maps: IGN 44, 51, or 109, 112. M 243, 244.

For **Tournus**, see Rte 127. On crossing the Saône by the *old* bridge (with retrospective views) one may either turn r. just beyond *Lacrost* to make a short cut to *Romenay*, or follow the main road E. to (7km) *Cuisery*, formerly the seat of a lordship, with a triptych of 1520 in its church.—*Louhans* (see Rte 127) lies 21km N.E.

  Forking r. just beyond Cuisery, the D975 drives S.E. across the *Plaine de Bresse* to (10km) *Romenay*, preserving two 14C gateways, and several old houses in its Grand'Rue.—The road traverses a number of villages, some with attractive half-timbered farms characteristic of the region, among them (19.5km) *Montrevel-en-Bresse*, with an 18C château.

16.5km **BOURG-EN-BRESSE** (pron. Bourk; 43,700 Bressans, or Bourgeois), the flourishing préfecture of the *Ain*, an important railway and road junction, and busy market-town (especially for its 'poulets') has little attraction in itself, but is mainly visited for the remarkable late Gothic church at *Brou*, on its S.E. outskirts.

It was made the capital of Bresse in the 15C by the dukes (afterwards princes) of Savoy, who made it their main residence in the following century. It passed definitively to France in 1601. Briefly—in 1659–61—the Cour Souverain of Bresse, which sat here, replaced the Parlement of Dijon, suppressed by Louis XIV.

Among its natives were Jerome Lalande (1732–1807), the astronomer; Edgar Quinet (1807–75, at *Certines*, 8km S.), the historian; and Gén. Debeny (1864–1943).

In the town centre is the *Cours de Verdun*, to the N.W. of which lie the Promenade du Bastion, from which the Rue du Palais leads S., at the end of which is the late 15C *Maison des Gorrevod*; another of the same date may be seen in the Rue Gambetta, to the E. of the last. Adjacent is *Notre-Dame*, a transitional building, started in 1505, with a Renaissance facade and Gothic pentagonal apse. Notable in the interior are the huge pillars at the W. end of the nave, the 16C stalls with their grotesque corner-pieces, the Louis-XIV pulpit, and the 16C glass in a chapel of the N. aisle.

A few paces to the S.E. commences the Blvd de Brou, which is followed for 1km to the ****Church of Brou**, ◇ one of the finest examples of the architecture of its period in France, and containing no less remarkable tombs and stalls, etc.

The village of *Brovium* possessed a priory church in the 12C, but the present edifice was erected regardless of expense in 1506–32 by Margaret of Austria in memory of her husband Philibert le Beau, duke of Savoy, and in fulfilment of a vow made by her mother-in-law, Margaret de Bourbon, to commemorate the recovery from an hunting accident of her husband Philippe: it is thus doubly a monument of conjugal devotion. Jehan Perréal, the first architect, was superseded by Van Boghen, assisted by Conrad Meyt, the sculptor. It is said to have been filled with straw during the Revolution, and thus preserved as a utility. It was restored in 1901. Matthew Arnold's early poem on Brou places it 'Mid the Savoy mountain valleys', within a morning's ride of Chambéry!, either a topographical blunder or poetic license.

Exterior. The W. front is rather heavy, and certain details are unfortunate, such as the arrangement of the buttresses and the quartering of the rose-window above the aisles. Among the statues, St Nicolas de Tolentin, on the central pillar of the porch, and the St Andrew (a replica of one destroyed by lightning in 1889) will be noted; while in the tympanum is an Ecce Homo between Margaret of Austria and Philibert, both presented by their patron saints.—The statuette of St Margaret in the N. portal is also remarkable.

Interior. On the r. in the nave is a marble stoup on which is carved the motto of Margaret of Austria: 'Fortune, infortune, fort une' ('In fortune or misfortune one woman is strong'), a device frequently recurring in the decoration of the church. The **Rood-loft*, carved with foliage, along the entire length of which run the initials P.M. (Philibert and Margaret), and various princely emblems, obstructs the general perspective. On the r. of it is the epitaph of Claude de Challant.

The *Chœr*, with its finely carved Flamboyant doors, contains 74 oak **Stalls*, attrib. to Pierre Terrasson, a local artist, and are almost unrivalled in France for the beauty of their panels, grotesque misericords, and rich fretwork (although those at Auch and Albi spring to mind). The *Stained-glass windows* in the apse represent Christ appearing to the Virgin after the Resurrection, with Philibert and Margaret supported by their patron saints; above are heraldic devices.

The *Tomb of Margaret of Bourbon* (d. 1483), on the S. side of the choir, like its two companion tombs, is over-elaborate, but remarkable for the beauty of detail. Her face is turned towards her son; the greyhound at her feet, and the expressive figures of the mourners (cf. Dijon) will be noticed.

In the middle is the magnificent *Tomb of Philibert le Beau* (d. 1504), the upper part of which shows the duke as in life, his head turned towards his wife, and his joined hands towards his mother; his left foot rests on a lion; beneath is his effigy in death, guarded by Virtues.

The *Tomb of Margaret of Austria* (d. 1530), even more profusely carved, displays two similar figures of the duchess, with her device.

Adjacent is the Lady Chapel, containing a carved stone reredos in high relief depicting the seven joys of Mary, and at either end, alabaster figures of SS Andrew and Philip. The N. window, copied from a design by Dürer, represents the Assumption, while the frieze above, after an engraving by Titian, represents the Triumph of the Faith. The vaulted roof is blazoned, and the celestial blue above the altar will be noted. The adjoining oratory of Margaret of Austria, with a chimneypiece and lectern of 1532, has an oblique opening to afford a view of the altar. Beyond is the Chapel de Gorrevod (named after one of the duchess's councellors), with a window depicting the Unbelief of Thomas. To the S. of the choir are two symmetrical chapels containing admirable glass, which with that in the S. transept, were executed at Bourg.

Adjacent is the entrance to the former priory buildings, with their restored cloisters and refectory, which now accommodates the **Departmental Museum**.

Among the paintings are a 16C Flemish Legend of St Jerome, a triptych presented by Margaret of Austria to the church of Brou; *Jouvenet*, Esther swooning; *Millet*, Cow-keeper; Portraits by *J.-B. Lallemand*; *Van Orley*, Portrait of Margaret of Austria; *Brueghel de Velours*, Stork hunt; *Hondecoeter*, Pelican; *Largillière*, Portrait of Nericault Destouches. Other sections are devoted to collections of furniture, ceramics, archaeology, and costumes, etc.

BOURG-EN-BRESSE TO NANTUA (41km). The N78 leads E. via (8km) *Ceyzériat*, on the slopes of a picturesque and abrupt W. ridge of the Jura, beyond which we wind through the hills, after 14km crossing the Ain, dammed to the S., and 16km beyond, reach *La Cluse*, 3km W. of *Nantua*, for which see Rte 130.

For the road from *Besançon* and *Lons-le-Saunier* to *Lyon* via Bourg, see Rte 125.

The N75 leads S.E. to (20km) *Pont-d'Ain*, with vestiges of a 15C castle of the dukes of Savoy, rebuilt by the Coligny family in 1590. Here was born Louisa of Savoy (1476–1531), mother of François I; and Philibert le Beau (see above).

At 4km we pass W. of *Ambronay* (see Rte 130), and in 5km reach the road junction just N. of *Ambérieu*.

THE AMBÉRIEU CROSSROADS TO VOIRON (80km), FOR GRENOBLE. The r.-hand fork is followed for 4km, where we turn l., continuing on the N75, which drives 5km S. to a road junction at *Lagnieu*, once fortified.—The r.-hand turning here (D65) leads S.W. past (r.) the *Grottes de la Balme*, with their underground lake, to (23km) *Crémieu*; see Rte 131.

The N75 shortly crosses the Rhône and veers S. to (30km) *Morestel*, with a 16C church and ruined keep.—There is a 14-16C castle at *Serrières*, 13km W., and km N.E., at the *Château de Brangues*, is buried Paul Claudel 1868– 1955).—13km. *Evrieu*, on the N516, just beyond which the A43 motorway is crossed before traversing (7km) *Les Abrets*; see Rte 131.—After 6km we pass near the *Lac de Paladru* (r.), on the far shore of which is *Versars*, the site of an ancient town (Ars), which according to tradition was excommunicated by Alexander III, sacked by Frederick Barbarossa, and afterwards engulfed in the waters by an earthquake. Abbot Thierry, natural son of the latter, founded the Chartreuse of *Silve-Bénite* in 1160, relics of which are 3km further W.—16km *Voiron* (see Rte 132B), 26km S.E. of which lies **Grenoble**.

The main route follows the N504, by-passing (r.) *Ambérieu*, and threads the gorge of the Albarine to traverse (13km) *St-Rambert-en-Bugey*, with its ruined castle, and (7km beyond) *Tenay*, both small industrial towns. The road then enters the *Cluse des Hôpitaux*, another defile in the hilly district of *Bugey*, the ancient capital of which, *Rossillon*, is reached in 14km; it retains a tower of its castle, once a residence of the princes of Savoy.

ROSSILLON TO AIX-LES-BAINS (57km). The D904 turns l. off the N504 after km, and at (4km) *Virieu-le-Grand* passes the ruins of a castle once owned by Honoré d'Urfé, Marquis de Valromey (1568– 1625; cf. La Bastie d'Urfé, Rte 99), who retired here with Diane de Châteaumorand, his sister-in-law.—5km. *Artemare*, at the entrance to the Valromey, 4km to the N. of which, at *Vieu*, on the site of a town of the Sequani, are the slight remains of an aqueduct and pagan temple, etc.—From *Virieu-le-Petit*, 6km N.E. of Artemare, one may ascend the *Grand-Colombie* (1531m), its summit commanding a splendid view of the Alps.—Skirting its foot, we pass (l.) after 8km the restored castle of *Mont-Ferrand* (1316), and cross the Rhône to (6km) *Ruffieux*, there turning r. to reach the N.E. corner of the *Lac du Bourget*, the E. side of which is skirted for 15km to enter **Aix-les-Bains**; see Rte 134A.

The N504 continues S.E. from Rossillon to (13km) **Belley**, a small cathedral town (8,400 Belliciens), a later capital of the *Bugey*, whose cathedral, largely rebuilt in 1864, preserves its original choir of c 413. The *Bishop's Palace* was built by Soufflot in 1775. It was the birthplace of Anthelme Brillat-Savarin (1755– 1826), author of the 'Physiologie du Goût' (1825), while Lamartine received part of his education here, in 1803– 7.

After 8km the road turns l. (meeting the N516) to thread the *Defile of Pierre Châtel* to (3km) *Yenne*, after 9km reaching the W. bank of the *Lac du Bourget*, having traversed a tunnel below the *Dent du Chat* (1390m).—**Aix-les-Bains** lies beyond the far bank, for which, and for **Chambéry** 16km S., see Rte 134A.

XI THE RHÔNE VALLEY; SAVOY; DAUPHINY

The alpine province of **Savoy** (Fr. *Savoie*), with *Chambéry* and *Annecy* its two préfectures, lying S. of Lac Léman, and W. of Mont Blanc, was the cradle of a princely house founded early in the 11C by Humbert 'aux Blanches Mains' ('the white-handed'; d. 1048). His son, Otho, by marriage gained a footing in the Po valley, and Humbert II assumed the title of Prince of Piedmont in 1091. Over the centuries the house extended its territory not only in Italy but also into the Valais and Vaud, in Switzerland, and *Bugey* and *Bresse* in Burgundy. Count Pierre (1263–68), uncle of Eleanor, wife of Henry III, was made Earl of Richmond and built the Savoy Palace in London, while his brother, Boniface, became Abp of Canterbury. Its great days began under Amadeus V (d. 1323), Amadeus VI ('the Green Count'; d. 1383), and 'the Red Count', Amadeus VII (d. 1391). Amadeus VIII (1383–1451) was created Duke of Savoy and Piedmont by the Emperor Sigismund. His abdication in 1434 was followed by a difficult period caused by the Reformation, and Savoy came into conflict with France. By the treaty of Utrecht (1713) Victor Amadeus II (1675–1730), who fought against France in the War of the Austrian Succession (even invading Dauphiny in 1692) was rewarded with the Kingdom of Sicily, exchanged in 1720 for that of Sardinia, of which Savoy now became a part. The Revolution was welcomed, and from 1792–1814 Savoy was occupied by the French, but in 1815 Victor Emmanuel of Sardinia resumed possession. Charles Albert (1831–49), influenced by Cavour, declared war on Austria, precipitating the War of Italian Independence, and on the accession of his son Victor Emmanuel II to the throne, the house of Savoy became completely identified with Italy, and by a treaty following a secret understanding between Napoleon III and Cavour, in 1860 the ancient province of Savoy was ceded to France.

To the S.W. of Savoy extends **Dauphiny** (Fr. *Dauphiné*), likewise alpine in character, now represented by the departments of *Isère*, *Drôme*, and the *Hautes Alpes*, their préfectures being *Grenoble*, *Valence*, and *Gap*, respectively. With the break-up of Bourgogne-Provence, or the Kingdom of Arles (see Section X) in the 11C, the counts of Albon—between Vienne (of importance during the Roman occupation) and Valence—extended their territory, and in the 12C adopted the title of *Dauphins of Viennois*. In 1341 the childless Humbert II (1333–49) sold his possessions to Charles of Valois (later Charles V) on condition that the title should continue to be borne by the heir to the throne of France, and that the privileges of the province should be maintained. In 1422 the counties of *Die* and *Valence* were bequeathed to Charles VI and added to Dauphiny, whose later history consisted mainly in attempting to maintain their liberties against the encroachments of the crown, the three estates meeting at Vizille in 1788 to prepare a remonstrance being a premiss of Revolution.

The title seems originally to have been a personal name (Dalfinus or Delphinus), with no demonstrable connection with 'dolphin', although the nickname assumed by Count Guigues IV (1125–42) and adopted as a patronymic by his successors (appearing on the coat of arms of Guigues V c. 1237) later became recognised as a title of dignity.

Further N., on the W. bank of the Rhône, was the **Lyonnais**, one of the smallest of the old provinces, its capital *Lyon* (ancient *Lugdunum*) being of considerable importance during the Roman period. It included the former lordships of *Forez* (with *Montbrison* as its capital), and *Beaujolais*, both added to the crown under François I.

129 Lyon

LYON, anglicised as **Lyons**, the third largest town of France, a sprawling industrial city of 418,500 Lyonnais, part of an extensive conurbation, and préfecture of the *Rhône*, is sited just N. of the confluence of the Saône and the Rhône, two great rivers which gave it strategic and commercial importance. Its population in 1801 was 109,500, and 177,200 in 1851. It was long famous for its fairs, manufactures of silk, and more recently for its synthetic fibres, metallurgical, and chemical products, while it prides itself as a gastronomic centre. Its museums, particularly those devoted to its Gallo-Roman civilisation, to Printing, and the Decorative Arts, and the Musée des Tissus, live up to their reputation.

The city may be conveniently described in four dissimilar sections: (**A**) *Central Lyon* lies on the narrow peninsula between the two rivers S. of the hill of *Croix-Rousse*, once the island of *Kanabae*, formed by an arm of the Rhône now built over, and likewise joined to more southerly islands after 1770, a project of the Intendant M.-A. Perrache (1726–79), whose name denotes the area S. of the Pl. *Carnot* and Railway Station. The Pl. *Bellecour* lies in the centre of this peninsula, which was once defended by walls across its neck at the Pl. *des Terreaux*. Later defences were constructed further N., where now runs the Blvd de la Croix-Rousse, below which a road-tunnel was pierced in 1952.

This central area was formerly joined by the Pont de Saône (just W. of St-Nizier) to (**B**.) *Vieux Lyon*, on its W. bank, where the Pl. *du Change* stands, huddled below the flank of the steep hill of Fourvière, where many medieval and Renaissance houses, still in the process of radical but tasteful restoration, provide this quarter with a character of its own.

On the plateau of *Fourvière* (**C**.) stood Roman *Lugdunum*, with its Theatre and Odeon, but the site of the Capital has been embellished by an all-too-conspicuous late 19C basilica. The S. part of the Fourvière has likewise been pierced in the interest of traffic.

On the E. bank of the Rhône are the more modern quarters (**D**.) of *Guillotière*, with university buildings on the riverside; the recently rebuilt area of *La Part-Dieu*, dominated by its tower, lies further N., and to the E. of the *Préfecture*; while N. of the latter is the quarter of *Le Brotteaux*, beyond which is the *Parc de la Tête d'Or*. The suburb of *Villeurbanne* extends further to the E.

The Roman colony of *Ludgunum*, preceded by a Greek settlement of 59 B.C., was founded by Lucius Munatius Plancus in 43 B.C. on the plateau of Fourvière. Under Augustus it became the capital of *Gallia Lugdunensis*, a province which included most of the country between the Seine, the Loire, and the present E. frontier of France, and was favoured by Nero, Trajan, and Hadrian. it was converted to Christianity by St Pothinus and the slave St Blandina, who were martyred under Marcus Aurelius in 177. In 197 Septimius Severus set fire to the city in revenge for his rival Albinus espousing the Christian cause, and St Irenaeus became another martyr. A monastery was founded in 440 on the island of *St-Barbe*, to the N.W. of Lyon.

By 478 it had become the capital of the Burgundians, and in 1024 the chief town of the kingdom of Provence. At the end of the 12C it was the cradle of the Waldensian movement, possibly named after Waldo, a native of the city. At the Council of Lyon (1245) Innocent IV, who had fled here from Rome, for the second time excommunicated the Emperor Frederick II Hohenstaufen. Aquinas died on his way to the ecumenical council held here in 1274. A comparatively peaceful history in the Middle Ages, and the introduction from Italy of the manufacture of silk (before 1450), and its patronage by François I, increased the wealth of Lyon. It was famous for its printing establishments during the 16C, carried on by Claude Nourry (publisher of Rabelais in 1532), Sebastian Gryphius, Jean de Tournes, François Juste, and Henri Estienne, who died here in 1598. Here in 1600 Henri IV received his Italian bride, Marie de Médicis, on her way from Marseille.

At the Revolution the city refused to comply with the demands of the Terrorists, and in 1793, after a two month siege and the successful assault of Kellermann, it was delivered to the tender mercies of Couthon and Collot d'Herbois;
some thousands of citizens were summarily executed. The fall of Robespierre
saved the greater part of Lyon from destruction, although large areas had
already been razed. The city prospered again with the introduction of
Jacquard's power-loom in 1801, although during the 19C it was sporadically
rocked with industrial unrest on the part of the 'Canuts' or silk-weavers. In 1843
some hundreds of workers were killed in an insurrection. Serious flooding occured, particularly in 1840.

'No *really* good inn here; the dirt and insects horrible', complained the Hand-
Book in the 1840s, while the appearance of grandeur was 'limited to its quais,
bridges, and noble rivers . . . the two Places de Bellecour and des Terreaux; it is
deficient in fine street, and long open throughfares. The interior is one stack of
lofty houses, penetrated by lanes so excessively narrow and nasty as not to be
traversed without disgust'. Here seethed the silk-weavers . . .' amongst them
very many English, who are in the lowest state of degradation, imbibing, in addition to their own vices, all the corruption of the country to which they have
migrated, without adopting any of the better parts of the French character'.

It was occupied in 1942, but was already a headquarters of the Resistance
movement. Jean Moulin, one of its leaders, unfortunately fell into German
hands here in June 1943. it suffered some bombing, particularly before its liberation on 1 Sept. 1944, when all but one of its bridges were blown up by the
retreating Germans. In 1975 its modern airport of *Satolas* was opened; in 1978 its
métro was inaugurated.

The emperors Claudius (10 B.C. – A.D. 54), Caracalla (188 – 217), and probably
Germanicus (15 B.C. – A.D. 19) were natives of Lugdunum, and Herod Antipas,
tetrarch of Galilee (4 B.C. – A.D. 39) and his wife Herodias, died in exile here,
banished by Caligula. Among famous Lyonnais were Sidonius Apollinaris
(430 – 89), the poet; the bibliophile Jean Grolier (1479 – 1565); Philibert Delorme
(1515 – 77), and Étienne Martellange (1596 – 1641), architects; Maurice Scève
(c. 1510 – c. 64) and Louise Labé (1526 – 66), poets; the engraver Gérard Audran
(1640 – 1703); Antoine Coysevox (1640 – 1720), Nicolas, and Guillaume Coustou
(1658 – 1733, and 1677 – 1746, respectively), Joseph Chinard (1756 – 1813), and
François-Frédéric Lemot (1772 – 1827), sculptors; the artists Jean Pillement
(1728 – 1808), Hippolyte Flandrin (1809 – 64), Ernest Meissonier (1815 – 91), and
Pierre Puvis de Chavannes (1824 – 98); Bernard de Jussieu (1699 – 1777), and his
nephew Antoine-Laurent (1748 – 1836), botanists; Joseph Jacquard
(1752 – 1834), inventor of the power-loom; J.-B. Say (1767 – 1832), the free-
trader; Jeanne-Françoise Bernard, later Mme Récamier (1777 – 1849); Marshal
Suchet (1778 – 1826); André-Marie Ampère (1775 – 1836; born at Neighbouring
Poleymieux), the physicist; Charles Philipon (1800 – 62), the caricaturist and
journalist; Jules Favre (1809 – 80), the politician; and Antoine de Saint-Exupéry
(1900 – 44), author and aviator.

Lyons was visited and described by Thomas Gray on his continental tour with
Horace Walpole in 1739. Silvio Pellico (1788 – 1854), the Italian patriot and
dramatist, lived here in 1806 – 10; Auguste Lumière (1862 – 1954), the pioneer of
cinematography, died here, where his experimental laboratory, founded in
1896, was installed in the Hôtel-Dieu. Édouard Herriot (1872 – 1957), mayor of
Lyons from 1905, also died here.

A. Central Lyon

The spacious tree-planted **Place Bellecour**, laid out in 1617, is the
main centre of animation, with the S.I. towards its S.E. corner.

It is embellished by an equestrian statue of Louis XIV by Lemot (1825), with
figures of the Rhône and Saône from an earlier statue by the brothers Coustou.
The E. and W. sides of the square, destroyed in 1793, were rebuilt in 1800.

From its S.E. corner, in the adjacent *Pl. Antoine-Poncet*, rises the
Tower (1665) of the *Hospice de la Charité*, built by Martellange, the

remainder of which was uncharitably demolished in 1934 to make
way for the *Post Office*.—Hence the Rue de la Charité leads S., on the
r. of which, in the *Hôtel de Lacroix-Laval* (1739; No. 30), is installed
the attractively arranged *Musée des Arts Decoratifs, several individual items in which deserve attention.

Notable among the collections of French furniture, mostly 18C, are individual
pieces by Riesener, and Oeben, and a remarkable clock in the Chinese taste by
Saint-Germain. Among tapestries: Gobelins, Aubusson, and Beauvais, and also
Brussels, are several Flemish examples (including scenes of the exploits of
Vespasian and Titus, and of Anthony and Cleopatra; 15th and 17C respectively);
also wall-papers of interest, among them one with a view of Lyons (1825). Other
collections distributed on the three floors include Ceramics, largely devoted to
Lyons china (16-18C) and Italian faience; champlevé Limoges enamels, and 18C
Goldsmiths' work, mostly with Parisian hallmarks; arms; several notable
sculptures of various periods, and representative examples of drawings in the
collection.

Adjacent (at No. 34) in the *Hôtel de Villeroy* (1734) is the *Musée
Historique des Tissus* founded in 1856, and inaugurated here in
1951. The collection—together with that at Mulhouse—is one of the
most important of its kind, illustrating the development of the weaving of fabrics from the earliest times.

The extensive collections include examples of Coptic, Greco-Roman, Sassanian,
and Byzantine textiles; Moslem work of the Fatamite period; Seljuk tapestries,
and some remarkable Turkish and Persian carpets (16-18C), among them a Persian work depicting Portuges caravels, and a mosque carpet of Chinese inspiration. Other sections are devoted to Oriental silks, brocades, and embroideries;
ecclesiastical vestments, mostly French, Spanish, Italian, and Flemish (13-18Cs);
several early costumes and accessories, etc. Notable are the Italian textiles, including Genoese and Torinese velvets, and Venetian fabrics, and also Paler-
mitan and Hispano-Moresque textiles; also several tapestries (Gobelins, Brussels,
etc.). Other sections are devoted to French textiles, especially to an unrivalled
collection of Lyonnais silks of all periods, including documents relative to the industry. Several materials reproduce designs by Laffite, Philippe de la Salle
(1723–1804), Pannini, and Gaspard Grégoire (1751–1846), among others.

By taking the next turning to the r. (Rue des Ramparts-d'Ainay) we
cross the Rue Victor-Hugo at the *Pl. Ampère*, to approach Romanesque *St-Martin-d'Ainay*, the oldest church in Lyon, all that remains
of the Benedictine abbey established here in the 5-6C. The present
edifice was consecrated by Paschal II in 1107.

The W. tower, with a short spire and triangular corner pyramids (acroteria) is
decorated with worn sculptures and red and white bands of Auvergnat type. The
porch, with late 12C arches, is flanked by two bays of 1830. Over the crossing is
a low square lantern tower.
   The *Nave*, despite 19C restorations, is impressive, with six plain columns,
perhaps of Roman origin, and four columns at the crossing almost certainly from
the altar of Roma and Augustus, which stood on the hill of Croix-Rousse. The
pilasters on the aisle walls and the three apses are adorned with Romanesque
sculpture, while the frescoes on the central apse are by Flandrin (1855). The N.
Chapelle St-Michel was rebuilt in the late 15C; to the S., that of *Ste-Blandine* is
probably an 11C reconstruction of an earlier building, and has a small undercroft. The baptistry (1834) incorporates some 12C capitals.

Return to the Pl. Ampère, from which the pedestrian Rue Victor-
Hugo leads S. to the *Pl. Carnot* (with the Gare Routière and Gare de
Perrache beyond), and N. to regain the *Pl. Bellecour*.
   From the N.E. corner of the latter extend the Rue du Président-
Herriot, and the Rue de la République, the main arteries of this

An example of mid 18C silk-weaving

quarter, and the Rue de la Barre, which leads to the *Pont de la Guillotière* (1957). The previous 12C bridge, built of re-used Roman masonry, withstood German sappers in 1944, only to be dismantled nine years later. It provides a good view of the **Hôtel-Dieu**, a large general hospital of medieval foundation reconstructed in the 17-19C, its long facade (begun in 1741, by Soufflot) surmounted by an imposing dome, rebuilt after fire damage in 1944.

It may be approached by the Rue Bellecordière, turning l. off the Rue de la Barre. Note the collection-box or 'Tronc pour les pauvres malades' (1707) to the l. of the entrance. Rabelais practised medicine here in the 1530s. A *Musée des Hospices*, with a 17C council-room, archives, and pharmacy, and carvings from La Charité, may be visited, together with the chapel (17C, by César Laure, a dyer from Milan); further medical relics may be seen or request.

In the graveyard is buried Narcissa, adopted daughter of the poet Edward Young, brought here from here unconsecrated grave at Montpellier; also a certain Elizabeth Danby (1786). In that year Dr James Smith (President of the Linnaean Society) inspected the hospital, where he was surprised to see each bed—each with a large thick woollen curtain—contained two or three patients, but then 'hospitals must not be made too comfortable as the poor would then be too fond of having recourse to them'. Lyon now has several important hospitals and centres of research into cancer, neuro-surgery, cardiology, etc.

Continuing N., we skirt the *Pl. de la République* and follow the Rue Carnot to the apse of the Franciscan church of *St-Bonaventure* (facing the *Pl. des Cordeliers*), completed in 1471, and with a good rose-window. it was used as a cornmarket in 1792.—Opposite stands the *Bourse* (1860), on the steps of which Président Carnot was assassinated in 1894 by Caserio, an Italian anarchist.

From the W. side of the building, we may turn down the Rue de la Poulaillerie, where in No. 13, the restored late 15C *Hôtel de la Couronne*, is installed the ***Musée de l'Imprimerie*** (*et de la Banque*).

Established by Crédit Lyonnais, much to their credit, it is a museum not only of specialist interest to printers, but to all with an interest in the history of typography. Examples are well displayed in chronological sequence in some 130 show cases, while several presses, including a reconstituted 15C press, and a Stanhope press (early 19C), are also shown. A page of the Gutenberg Bible (1455), and several incunables printed in Lyon, are to be seen, together with numerous examples of the work of other early printers, many of them of historical significance; and likewise more modern works. A section is devoted to the techniques of reproduction of illustrations, from woodcuts and copper-plate engravings (including the original plates of Ménestrier's Plan of Lyon of 1696) and other more complex processes such as lithography, chromolithography, and photolithography, etc.

By turning r. along the Rue du Prés. Herriot, the apse of *St-Nizier* (see below) is passed to the l., to reach the E. side of the *Palais St-Pierre*, a large quadrilateral commenced in an Italianate style in 1659 for the Benedictine convent of St-Pierre.

Its N. facade faces the *Pl. des Terreaux*, in which the Marquis de Cinq-Mars and François de Thou were beheaded in 1642 for their conspiracy against Richelieu.

The E. side of the square is dominated by the main facade of the **Hotêl de Ville**, embellished with an equestrian statue of Henri IV. It was erected in 1655 by Simon Maupin of Lyon, restored in 1702 by Mansart after a fire, and again in 1853 and 1913. An arcade separates its two courtyards, while certain sumptuously furnished rooms may be visited on application. On 28 Sept. 1870 Bakunin escaped from its cellars after failing to stir up an anarchist insurrection here.—Further E., beyond the *Pl. de la Comédie*, stands the *Théâtre* of 1830. For the area further N., see below.

The *Palais St-Pierre* accommodates the **Musée des Beaux-Arts**, which contains several collections, the entrance to which is near the S.E. corner of its courtyard.

Rooms to the r. of the vestibule are devoted to a display of **Sculpture**, including among the *Antique sculpture* an Attic Khore in Ionic chiton and himation from the Acropolis at Athens, where the other half remains; this is the so-called 'Aphrodite of Lyons', once thought to come from Marseille, a false provenance from a Phocaean colony which long misled scholars into believing that the 'archaic smile' is a purely Ionic attribute. Also the 'dieu de Coligny', a bronze Mars of the 2C B.C.; an elaborate Gallo-Roman sarcophagus depicting the Triumph of Bacchus, from the foundations of the church of St-Irénée; and a 4C Christian sarcophagus, in style already Romanesque rather than Roman.

Romanesque, Gothic, and Renaissance: a late 12C Burgundian Virgin; reliefs from Bourges and Vic (Catalonia); an Annunciation, *after Nino Pisano*; a polychromed wood Virgin and St Anne (mid 14C); also examples of Bavarian, Swabian, Burgundian, and Osan work; a relief of the Madonna (mutilated), by *Desiderio da Settignano*; Bust of the Baptist, by *Mino da Fiesole*, etc. Caricature busts by *Daumier* are on display, but the main collections of 19-20C sculpture, contained in the former church of *St-Pierre*, abutting the edifice to the S., is still closed.

Retracing our steps, we ascend the main staircase, its upper walls embellished with allegorical murals by *Puvis de Chavannes*; note also the bust of the artist by *Rodin*. It is preferable to start by making the circuit (anti-clockwise) of the Second Floor before visiting the First Floor, to follow some form of chronological order.

SECOND FLOOR: *Gerard David*, Genealogy of the Virgin; *Albert Bouts*, The crown of thorns; *Master of the Monogram A.H.* (c. 1500), Pentecost, Nativity, Adoration of the Magi, Entry into Jerusalem, Incredulity of Thomas, Presentation, and Washing of the feet; *Isembrandt*, Two donors; *Quentin Matsys*, Virgin and Child; *German Primitives*, including a good Christ bearing the cross, and a Death of the Virgin (late 15C); *Lucas Cranach the elder*, Female portrait; *Van Cleve*, a Gentleman of the Bentivoglio family; *Miereveld*, two Female portraits; *Tintoretto*, Danae; *Brueghel de Velours*, The Elements; *El Greco*, Despoliation; *Ribera*, St Peter; *Van Honthorst*, Concert; and several 17C Italian canvases, notable for their dimensions; *Zurbaran*, St Francis; *Vouet*, Crucifixion *Van Goyen*, Landscape; *Rembrandt*, Stoning of St Stephen; *Van Ceulen*, Female portrait; *Van Berchem*, Landscape; *Jacob van Loo*, 'Le coucher à l'Italienne'; *Van der Helst*, Female portrait; a series of huge canvases by *Rubens, Jouvenet, Le Brun, Jordaens, Le Sueur*, and *Philippe de Champaigne*.

Rubens, Adoration of the Magi; *Van Oost*, The message; *Paul Mignard*, Portrait of Nicolas Mignard; *J.-B. Monnoyer*, Flower-paintings; *Rigaud*, Pierre Drevet, the engraver, and Leonard de Lameth; *Largillière*, Jean Thierry, the sculptor; *Desportes*, Still-lifes; *Lancret*, The duo; *Romney*, Miss Sophie Cumberland; *Lawrence*, a Young girl; attrib. *L. David*, 'La Maraîchère'; *Boilly*, Philippe Égalité; *Delacroix*, Death of Marcus Aurelius; *Géricault*, 'La Folle' *Ingres*, the Duc d'Orléans; *P.-P. Prud'hon*, St-Just, and other portraits; *Fromentin*, Arabs hunting; *William Payne* (1760–1830), water-colour Views near Lyon;, and several works by *Corot*. **R33** (circular) is devoted to numerous paintings by *Monticelli*, including his 'La bal travesti'.

We now follow the W. wing: *Fantin-Latour*, 'La Lecture'; *Carrière*, Puvis de Chavannes; *Daumier*, Two advocates; *Courbet*, Paul Chenevard, and Happy lovers; *Monet*, The Thames at Charing Cross, Spring, and Cliffs at Étretat; *Van Gogh*, Dutch peasants; *Renoir*, Guitar-player, and Coco writing; *Degas*, M. Ruelle, and Dancers in green; *Berthe Morisot*, Young Niçoise; *Manet*, Female portrait; *Gauguin*, Nave nave Mahana; works by *Boudin*, and *Sisley*; *Aman-Jean*, 'L'Amour de soi' (nude in a mirror); *Vuillard*, Landscape, and Portrait of his mother; *Picasso*, 'Le buffet du Catalan'; *Matisse*, Portrait of Demotte; *Gino Severini*, The artist's family; *Vieira da Silva*, Composition; *Foujita*, Self-portrait with cat; and representative works by *Suzanne Valadon, Rouault, Braque, Maurice Marinot, Pascin, Maurice Denis, Vlaminck, Dufy, Bonnard, Derain, Utrillo*, et al. A recent acquisition is *Nicolas Régnier*, Woman at her toilet.

Hence we may descend to the FIRST FLOOR, the S. and E. wings of which are devoted to paintings of Lyonnais artists of varying merit, including *J.-J. de Boissieu* (1736–1810), Portrait of his wife; *Pillement*, Landscapes; *Joseph Vivien* (1657–1734) Portraits; *Michel Grobon* (1770–1853), Views of Lyon, Self-portrait, and other portraits; several works by *Puvis de Chavannes*, and *Hippolyte* and *Paul Flandrin*.

The W. and N. wings are devoted to Egyptian, Coptic, and Oriental collections; Attic pottery; Etruscan bronzes; Roman bronzes and glass; Byzantine and Gothic ivories; Coins and medals (by *Warin*; 1604–72); Limoges enamels; Gothic and Renaissance sculutures; Renaissance furniture and carved plaques, etc.

To the N. of the Pl. des Terreaux rises the hill of **Croix-Rousse**, the slope of which was the original centre of the silk-weaving industry, and the quarter known as *Les Traboules*, where the narrow lanes are connected by an intricate warren of alleys and passages, and the scene of industrial riots in the 19C. On an upper level is the Blvd de la Croix-Rousse at the E. end of which is the *Gros Caillou*, a huge boulder deposited by an ice-age glacier. To the W. is the *Pl. de la Croix-Rousse*, a short distance to the N. of which, at No. 10 Rue d'Ivry, is the *Maison des Canuts*, where one may see silk-looms in action, and buy silk ties and scarves, etc.—From this Place the Montée de la Grande Côte descends near to (r.) the *Jardin des Plantes*, where excavations have unearthed a huge *Amphitheature* (A.D.19) dedicated to C. Julius Rufus, where delegates of the 60 tribes of Gaul assembled each year on federal territory to celebrate the cult of Rome and Augustus.

On turning S. along the W. side of the Palais St-Pierre (Rue Paul-Chevenard), we pass the 12C portal of the former church of *St-Pierre* to reach **St-Nizier** (15C Gothic; under restoration).

Built on the site of an earlier church, which perhaps covered the remains of 2C martyrs, the central portal was added by an imitator of Philibert Delorme in the 16C, while of the two spires, that on the r. dates from 1856. Within, the triforium is a peculiar design, and like the clerestory, has an elaborate balustrade. The bosses, a Virgin carved by Coysevox, and the rose-windows of the transepts, are notable.

Numerous insurgents during the troubles of 1834 were pursued into the church and massacred by the military.

Rather than continuing S., it is preferable to follow the narrow Rue Mercière, further W., preserving several characteristic old houses, to cross the Rue Grenette (leading W. to the Pont Maréchal-Juin; see below). We shortly reach the *Pl. des Jacobins*—just W. of which is the *Pl. des Célestines*, with its *Théâtre* (1880)—a short distance N. of the Pl. Bellecour.

B. Vieux Lyon

Twenty years have now elapsed since the rehabilitation of the historical centre of Lyon—*Vieux Lyon*—began. Its narrow streets, which long popular occupation had made squalid; its quaint courtyards communicating with adjacent alleys by vaulted passages or *'traboules'*, and its characteristic tall houses with their staircase-towers, make it an area of great interest to wander through, and while not every detail can be pointed out, an attempt has been made to indicate some of the more curious objects to be seen. Permission to peruse features not normally visible from the street is usually courteously granted. Unlike so many 'secteurs sauvegardés', this one is very much part of a vital city and not merely a theatrical decor, although picturesque. Its 15-17C buildings, having been stripped of ugly accretions, at cellar level occasionally display Roman or Romanesque foundations, on which Renaissance mansions stand.

It is perhaps most conveniently approached by crossing the *Pont Maréchal-Juin*, providing a view of the Corinthian facade (1835; by L.-P. Baltard, father of the architect of the old Halles in Paris) of the **Palais de Justice**. On reaching the W. bank of the Saône, one may continue W. to the small *Pl. de la Baleine* (with a regional tourist office), to the l. of which is the Rue de Trois-Maries, in which almost every house has a feature of interest, notably Nos 5, and 7, while from No. 2 we may thread a 'traboule' to No. 19 in the parallel Rue St-Jean, the main artery of the district. Here we turn r., past No. 24, the *Maison du Grand-Palais*, its splendid courtyard with an octagonal staircase-tower (and traboule). Ask to see the medieval wall-safe in the adjacent tea-shop.

Continuing N., the *Pl. du Gouvernement* is shortly reached, which was the seat of the governor from the 16C to the mid 18C. The Rue St-Jean is followed to the N. past (r.) Nos 11 (courtyard), 9 (with Flam-

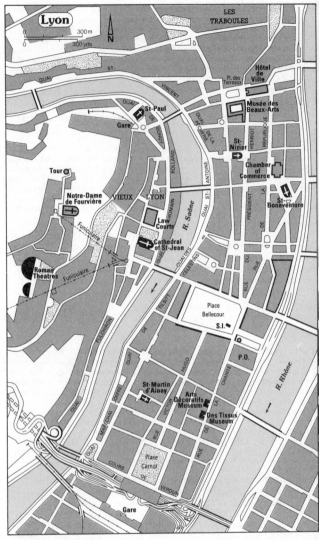

buoyant Gothic sculpture), and 7 with a 15C facade, beyond which is the *Pl. du Change*, in which No. 2 is the *Maison Thomassin* (14C), with a spiral staircase and painted beams. Opposite is the *Loge du Change*, transformed by Soufflot in 1749, and now a Protestant church.

The Rue Lainerie is followed, in which Nos 18, 14 (with a richly sculptured Gothic facade), and 10 (with a spiral stair without a central newel) are of interest, to reach the *Pl. St-Paul*, where at No. 2 lived Laurent Mourguet (b. 1769), creator of the popular puppets

Guignol and Gnafron. Beyond is the collegial church of *St-Paul*, with a 12C nave and choir, defaced 15C W. front, and octagonal tower. Adjacent is a statue commemorating Jean Gerson (1363– 1429), chancellor of the University of Paris, who died in the cloister of St-Paul and was buried in demolished *St-Laurent*, adjoining.

The lower part of the steep Montée St-Barthélemy (S.W. of the Place) provides a good view of the *Maison Henri-IV, or *Hôtel Paterin*, a 16C galleried mansion with an entrance at No. 4 Rue Juiverie, which we now follow S., in which No. 8, the *Hôtel Bullioud* (with a gallery built by Philibert Delorme on his return from Italy in 1536), Nos 10, 20, 21 (containing a vaulted Romanesque chamber and Roman well in its basement), and 23 (showing Florentine influence) are also notable.

We turn l. to regain the Pl. du Change, and then r. to follow the Rue de Gadagne, in which Nos 10, 12, and 14 are notable. The last, refashioned in 1511– 27, divided after 1545, and with its main courtyard restored to its original plan in 1939, now houses the **Musée du Vieux Lyon**, an interesting collection illustrating the history of the city.

Remarkable are a Renaissance chimney-piece, and several Romanesque fragments and Gothic sculptures from St-Pierre-le-Vieux, and the Abbaye de l'Île-Barbe, including an Annunciation from the latter. Other rooms contain Lyonnais furniture, pottery, and portraits, maps and plans, documents and mementoes; paintings of Lyon by *Alexandre Dunouy*, *C. F. Nivard*, and *Michel Grobon*, etc.; a section is devoted to the Compagnonnage. The **Musée de la Marionnette** is housed here, in which only a small part of its extensive collection of puppets is displayed.

The street is continued beyond the *Pl. du Petit Collège* (in which the *Mairie* is installed in a former Jesuit college) by the Rue du Boeuf, containing several mansions of interest, among them Nos 6, and 19, while outstanding is No. 16, which in the 16C belonged to Martin de Troyes, the banker. Its courtyard should be entered for a view of the staircase-tower—the *Tour Rose*—which gives its name to the excellent restaurant now established here, which preserves painted beams in upper rooms.

Mrs Piozzi remarked on the luxuries of the Lyonnais at table, where she counted 'six and thirty dishes when we dined, and twenty-four when we supped. Everything was served up in silver at both places, and all was uniformly magnificent, except the linen, which might have been finer . . .'. And, she added, these 'are merchants, I am told, with whom I have been living'. The quality of the food in Lyon, rather than its quantity and the plate, is now more worthy of comment.

The next corner, where we turn l., is embellished with a sculptured bull which gives the street its name. On meeting the transverse Rue St-Jean (where No. 27, just to the l., has a good Gothic doorway), we follow it to the S. past (l.) the *Palais de Justice*, and No. 37, the *Hôtel du Chamarrier* (1516), with a fine facade and court, in which Mme de Sévigné stayed in 1672– 3 with the brother-in-law of M. de Grignan.

By turning l. down the next lane an area is reached abutting the N. side of the cathedral, which has been recently excavated to reveal the foundations of the 11-12C churches of *St-Étienne*, and *Ste-Croix* (15C), both demolished in 1793, and partly built over the relics of a 4-5C baptistry, remodelled in the 11C.

The ***Cathedral**, the third on this site, was begun between 1165 and 1180. Its elaborate W. front, the latest part of the structure (1308– 1481), mutilated by the Huguenots and Revolutionaries, is again under restoration. It is abutted by the *Manécanterie*, the external wall of which (a fragment of a late 11C cloister) formed part of an early refectory before its restoration in 1394–1419 as the song school. The two W. towers are stumpy and spireless; the more graceful N.E. and S.E. towers are best seen from a distance.

The construction of the church itself covers roughly the years 1175–1275, the choir and four bays of the nave being completed by 1254, when Innocent IV consecrated the high altar. By 1274 it was sufficiently advanced to hold the Great Ecumenical Council of some 1600 ecclesiastics which proclaimed the union of the Greek and Latin churches. Here in 1600 Henri IV married Marie de Médicis.

The *Choir* retains its 13C *Glass, as do the rose-windows of the transepts. In the N. transept is a 14C Astronomical clock. Off the S. aisle is a chapel founded in 1464 by Card. Charles de Bourbon, its sculptural decoration showing remarkable detail of a debased style. Adjacent is the *Treasury*, containing a 9C ivory coffer of Byzantine inspiration, etc.

Continuing S., we reach (r.) the *Gare St-Jean*, from which funiculars ascend the *Fourvière hill* (see below), and turning half-r. just beyond, the Rue Mourguet is ascended to the *Pl de la Trinité*. Hence the Montée du Gourguillon (note No. 2), follows the course of a Roman road which climbed to *Lugdunum*. Hereabouts, arriving from Bordeaux for his coronation as pope in 1305, Clement V is said to have lost an emerald when he fell from his mule. The *Café du Soleil* served as the decor for the *Théâtre Guignol*. Notable in the adjacent Rue St-Georges are Nos 2, 3, 6, and 7, the latter two for their spiral stairs.

Hence one may return to the Gare St-Jean, and follow the Av. Adolphe-Max to the E. past (l.) the former *Archbishop's Palace* (15C, but rebuilt in 1750), until recently housing the municipal library; see below. The *Pont Bonaparte* crosses the Saône to regain the *Pl. Bellecour*, a short distance further E.

C.   Fourvière, and Roman Lyon

The most convenient approach to the summit of the hill of Fourvière (from *Forum vetus*) is by taking the funicular from the Gare St-Jean to *N.-D.-de-Fourvière*, with its four towers. This basilica (1872–96) was erected in fulfilment of a vow made during the Franco-Prussian War, as was the Sacre-Coeur in Paris; both are equally hideous. It is only of interest for the meretricious splendour of its marble and mosaic decoration in a depraved taste which should be seen to be believed. Adjacent is the so-called *Vieille Chapelle* (mid 18C), from a belvedere behind which, c. 175m above the Saône, one may get a good general view over the city.—To the N. is the *Tour Métallique* (1893), a stunted 'Eiffel Tower', since 1954 used for transmitting television.

The Montées de Fourvière leads S. over the site of part of Roman Lugdunum to the entrance of the *Musée de la Civilisation Gallo-Romaine*, inaugurated in 1975. This imaginatively conceived functional structure, for the most part subterranean, is built into the hillside immediately N.E. of the Roman theatres, views of which it commands. Designed by Bernard Zehrfüss, its consists of several superimposed floors connected by lift, and a series of descending steps and ramps. It is devoted largely to Lyon from prehistoric times to the advent of Christianity in Gaul, and aspects of its culture are displayed in some 17 sections.

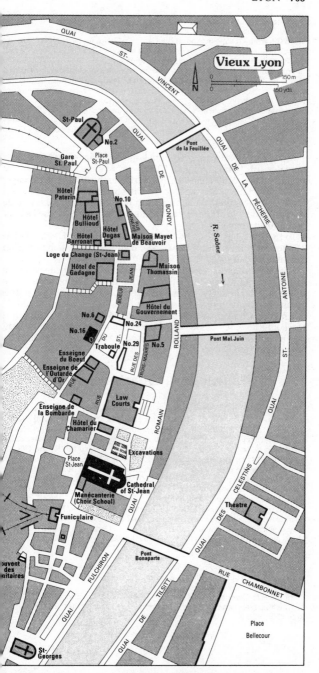

Near the entrance is a maquette of *Lugdunum* in the 2C, together with maps and
plans of the area. Among outstanding objects are a processional or ritual Chariot
(8C B.C.), from La Côte-St-André; the *Claudian Tables* (in fact half only), recording on bronze the concessions made by the Emperor Claudius in A.D. 48, admit-
ting Roman citizens of Gaul to senatorial rights, and unearthed in 1528; a unique
Gaulish Calendar, found at Coligny (Ain), reckoning a lunar year with months of
29 or 30 days, with an intercalary day after every 30 months; several fine
mosaics, including ones decorated with fish, a chariot race, and geometrical
panels, etc.; a bronze brazier, from Vienne; and the usual terracotta objects,
Gallo-Roman glass, figurines, moulds, statues, busts, funerary stellae, etc. A
model of the Theatre demonstrates the system by which the curtain was raised
by counter-weights, etc. The exit may be made close to the theatres themselves
or by taking a lift to the entrance level.

Two **Roman Theatres** survive, the larger (108.5m across, compared
to Arles, of 104m; Orange, 103m; and Vienne, 115m), built by
Augustus, was doubled in size by Hadrian in the 2C to accommodate
10,000 spectators. The smaller, an *Odéon*, once roofed, is less well
preserved, but retains a good mosaic floor. Above are the foundations of a *Temple of Cybele*, and some distance beyond, the remains
of a Roman aqueduct.

To the S.W., beyond *St-Just* and the *Pl. Wernert*, with relics of three
1C Roman tombs, stands *Ste-Irénée*, below which is a 5C crypt on
Roman foundations.

The descent may be made from the upper or intermediate station
of another funicular, the latter not far from the entrance to the
theatres. Alternatively, one may descend on foot by any of the steep
'montées' climbing down the hillside towards the Saône, while the
Chemin de Choulans winds down the slope from the Pl. Wernert to
the *Pont Kitchener*, below which a road tunnel was pierced in 1972,
and near which the 6-7C necropolis of *St-Laurent de Choulans* has
been excavated.

D. Modern Quarters

Crossing to the E. bank of the Rhône by the *Pont Wilson*, one may follow the Rue
Servient past (l.) the *Préfecture du Rhône* (1890) to approach, beyond the Rue
Garibaldi, the recently developed area—on the site of former barracks—known
as *La Part-Dieu* (although some have suggested that other powers have inspired
it). To the N. is the *Auditorium Maurice-Ravel* (1975); to the S., the *Cité Administrative d'État*, and further S., the *Hôtel de la Communauté Urbaine*, both
built to satisfy the pretensions of civil servants. To the E. of these are the *Centre
Commercial Régional*, the *Bibliothèque Municipal* (1972), and the buildings of
Radio France. The whole is dominated by the *Tour de la Part-Dieu*, a cylindrical
erection with a pyramidal roof.

Hence the Rue Tête d'Or leads N. to the extensive *Parc de la Tête d'Or*, laid out
in 1860, with a lake, and rose-gardens. In the *Musée Guimet*, at No. 28 Blvd des
Belges, skirting its S. side, are collections of natural history and related subjects.
On its N. side are a *Palais des Congrès*, and *Parc des Expositions*, site of numerous
commercial fairs.

For roads from Lyon to *Roanne* and *Moulins*; to *Bourg-en-Bresse*, and *Besançon*
and to *Mâcon*, *Tournus*, *Chalon*, *Beaune*, and *Dijon*, see Rtes 98, 125, and 12
respectively, all these in reserve.

For roads to *Nantua* and *Geneva*; for *Grenoble* or *Chambéry*, see Rtes 130, and
131, respectively; and for roads descending the Rhône valley to *Valence*, see
Rtes 139A and B, the latter likewise for the sub-route to *St-Étienne*.

130 Lyon to Évian via Nantua and Bellegarde (for Geneva)

198km (123 miles). N.84. 35km **Pérouges** lies 1km l.—1km *Meximieux*—13km *Ambérieu* is by-passed on the r.—39km *La Cluse*—3km **Nantua**—25km **Bellegarde. Annecy** lies 41km S.E.—N206. 10km *Fort de l'Écluse*—19km *St-Julien* (**Geneva** lies 10km N.E.)—14km **Annemasse**—10km D903.—20km **Thonon**—N5. 9km **Évian.**

Maps: IGN 44, 45, or 109. M 244.

Parts of the A42 motorway are open, providing a rapid exit from Lyon, and are a recommended alternative to the old road between Bellegarde and Annemasse.

Driving N. from central Lyon (see Rte 129), the N84 keeps to the r. or W. bank of the Rhône, traversing an industrial zone to (23km) *Montluel*, with remains of a castle where in 1416 the Emperor Sigismund signed an edict raising Savoy to the status of a duchy.

12km. ***Pérouges**, 1km l., is a picturesque medieval survival, perched on its fortified hill-top, consisting almost entirely of 15-16C flinty houses, some such as the *Hostellerie*, of the 13C. Many have been restored. There is a small museum in the central square, while the circuit of its sombre and long-abandoned cobbled lanes may be made, the occasional background for historical films.

1km. *Meximieux*, distinguished only as the birthplace of Vaugelas (1595–1650), the founder of modern usage in French grammer.—At 3.5km the Ain is crossed, the road passing just N. of the 11C castle of *Chazey-sur-Ain*, which belonged to the Colignys, the dauphins of Viennois, and the counts of Savoy.

At 10km *Ambérieu-en-Bugey* is by-passed (r.), a railway junction of slight interest, overlooked to the N.E. by *Mont Luisandre* (805m), on the flank of which stands the *Château des Allymes* (13-14C).—For the road hence to **Chambéry**, see Rte 128.

The road shortly turns l., and then forks r. through (7km) **Ambronay**, preserving part of its fortifications, and a well-restored 10-15C *Church* of a Benedictine abbey founded in 800; over the central doorway is a Last Judgement (13C), recalling that at Bourges. The interior contains 15C stalls with good misericords, and glass, and the tomb of Abbot Jacques de Mauvoisin (1437); adjoining are a 15C cloister and chapter-house, etc.

At 3.5km we pass near (r.) the restored 13C castle of *Varey*, and after 5km circle to the E. beside the Ain, at 2km passing (l.) *Poncin*, with old gateways and houses, and a 14-17C castle. Several old ruins are passed as the road steeply climbs N.E. below (r.) the *Chaine de l'Avocat* (1014m), and crossing the ridge further N., descends more gradually to (14.5km) the crossroads at *La Cluse*.

The three pillars of a temple at *Izernore*, Roman *Izernodurum*, 6.5km N.W., are of slight interest.

LA CLUSE TO ST-CLAUDE (45km). The D984D leads N.E., by-passing (13km) the industrial town of **Oyonnax** (22,800 inhab.), manufacturing plastics, and at (8km) *Dortan*, enters the wild valley of the Bienne.—24km. **St-Claude** (13,200 San Claudiens), a picturesquely sited mountain town on the slope of *Mont Bayard*, above the confluence of the Bienne and Tacon (crossed by a bold suspension bridge of 1845), is surrounded by the ridges of the Jura range. There are several fine waterfalls in the vicinity.

It is named after a 7C abbot of a monastery founded here in 425, which later
became an independent enclave within the Franche-Comté; it was made a
bishopric in 1742. The enfranchisement of the 'serfs of the Mont-Jura', down-
trodden by autocratic abbots, a cause championed by Voltaire, was not secured
until 1789. It was revaged by fire in 1799, and by a hurricane in 1890. The
Cathedral, sole relic of the abbey, is a plain building of 1340– 1726, with a
classical front, square tower, and five little spires. It contains quaint and
beautiful *Choir-stalls* (1460), carved by Jean de Vitry, on which a variety of subjects are depicted, such as early abbots being lapidated by little demons, a mermaid combining her hair, etc, the details of the misericords are likewise
remarkable. A carved altarpiece of 1533 contains painted panels of the Italian
school.—To the N. is a small *Museum* devoted to the local industries of gem
cutting, and briar pipes.

ST-CLAUDE TO GENEVA (55km). Bearing S. E., we commence to wind up to
and enter the *Gorges du Flumen.*—11km. *Septmoncel*, noted for its cheese, is
traversed, beyond which the road bears r., climbing to *Lajoux*, to the N.E. of
which rises the *Crêt Pela* (1495m), and descending in sweeping curves to (13km)
Mijoux.—We now ascend 6km to meet the N5, and turn r. to climb 2.5km to the
Col de la Faucille (1320m), an important pass in the main ridge of the Jura, providing a fine *View of the Alps on the descent, especially of Mont Blanc, straight
ahead, with Geneva and Lac Léman in the foreground. It was this view which so
impressed Ruskin in 1835 (cf. 'Praeterita'). To the S.W. rise *Mont Rond* (1596m)
and *Colomby-de-Gex* (1689m); the pass itself has ski slopes.—The road descends
in zigzags to (11.5km) **Gex**, once the capital of an independent barony, and
reputed for its cheese, 'bleu de Gex'. The *Pl. Gambetta* commands a good
view.—*Divonne-les-Bains*, 8km N.E., is a small spa on a small lake and a winter
resort abutting the Swiss frontier, beyond which, only 6km S.E., lies *Coppet*, on
the shore of Lac Léman, long the residence of Mme de Staël (1766– 1817).—The
D984C leads S. to (11km) *St-Genis-Pouilly* (Customs), 11km N.W. of Geneva, and
continues S.W., to meet the N206 after 18km, just E. of the *Defile of L'Écluse*; see
below.

The N5 leads S.E. from Gex to (10km) **Ferney-Voltaire** (6,400 inhab.
Customs), a small frontier town in close proximity to the airport of *Geneve*
Cointrin, where in the much-altered *Château* lived Voltaire from 1758– 78, enjoying the social liberty of France together with the political liberty of Geneva.
His bedroom and ante-chamber contain their original furniture, and a *Pastel
portrait of Voltaire by Quentin Delatour, etc. A disused chapel may be seen
with the inscription: 'Deo erexit Voltaire'. In the course of his quarrel with the
republic of Geneve, he set up a rival colony of watchmakers at Ferney; here too
he began his series of polemical protests on behalf of the oppressed (cf. St
Claude).—**Geneva** lies 7km beyond, at the S.W. point of *Lac Léman.*—*An*
nemasse (see below) lies 7km E. of Geneva.

At La Cluse we turn r. and skirt the N. bank of the *Lac de Nantua* to
(3km) **Nantua** itself, situated among limestone hills, rising to the S. to
the wooded heights of *Les Monts d'Ain* (1127m). It originated in a
Benedictine abbey founded in the 7-8C, which was the original
burial-place of Charles le Chauve ('the Bald'; 877). 12C *St-Michel*, at
the S. end of the noisy main street, has a mutilated Romanesque
porch and a curious octagonal lantern-tower over the crossing.

The road, following the railway, continues S.E., shortly turning
N.E. to skirt the *Lac de Sylans*, beyond which it winds through hills
to (20km) *Châtillon-en-Michaille*, on the edge of a rocky terrace
above the confluence of the Semine and the Valserine.—5km
Bellegarde, a small industrial town on the latter river at its confluence with the Rhône, and long a frontier town, is better by-passed
by following the motorway, which circles above it and over the
Rhône by a remarkable viaduct.

BELLEGARDE TO MIJOUX (37km). The D991 leads N., below (r.) the *Crêt d'Eau*
(1621m) to (17km) *Chézery*, where the church of 1648 remains of a former
Benedictine abbey founded in 1140, of which SS Lambert and Roland were ab-

>ots. To the N. rises the *Crêt de Chalam* (1545m), from which Mont Blanc may be
seen above the main ridge of the Jura.—The road continues N.E. below (r.) the
Crêt de la Neige (1718m), the highest peak of the range, deriving its name from a
natural hollow N. of the summit, in which snow lingers long.—*Lélex*, with ski-
slopes, is traversed, beyond which, to the N.E., rise *Colomby-de-Gex* (1689m)
and *Mont-Rond* (1596m).—20km. *Mijoux*; see above.

BELLEGARDE TO ANNECY (41km). The N508 crosses the Rhône and leads
S.E.—At 7km a r.-hand turning leads 7km to the spectacular dam of
Génissiat.—After 5km the next turning leads to (10km) **Seyssel**, an ancient town
on the Rhône, birthplace of François Bonijard (1493–1570), Byron's 'Prisoner of
Chillon', and Philippe de la Salle (1723–1803), the great designer for the silk
fabrics of Lyon.—Further S.W. rises the *Grand-Colombie* (1531m).—At 3.5km
beyond this turning the D910 forks S. to *Aix-les-Bains* via (5km) *Clermont*, with
remains of a sumptuous 16C château, and 16km beyond, **Rumilly**, once the
capital of the *Albanais*, one of the small 'pays' of Savoy, noted for its breed of
cattle. It was besieged in 1630 by Louis XIII, in 1690 by Louis XIV, and in 1742 by
the Spaniards. The belfry of its church dates from the 12C, and there are some
picturesque old houses in the Grande-Rue and its side-streets.
   The road turns E. through *Frangy*, reputed for its white wines, 3km N.E. of
which is *Chaumont*, once an important fortress, and continues S.E. past (6km) the
medieval and Renaissance château of *Sallenôves*, to **Annecy**, 19km beyond; see
Rte 134A.

Quitting Bellegarde, we climb above the r. bank of the Rhône on the
N206, and soon thread the *Defile of l'Écluse*, where the river cuts
through a ridge, beyond which, at 10km, the road to *Gex* turns l.; see
above.—Crossing the Rhône, we bear E., with a view N. towards the
main ridge of the Jura and its highest peak, the **Crêt de la Neige**
1718m); Mont Blanc and other Alpine peaks come into view on the
.—19km. *St-Julien-en-Genevois*.—**Geneva** lies 10km N.E.
   The frontier is skirted below the ridge of *Mont Salève*, and the
motorway is crossed prior to reaching (14km) **Annemasse**, an industrial town of 26,400 inhab., some 3km S. of which lies *Mornex*, a
resort visited by Ruskin, and Wagner, who began both 'Siegfried'
and 'Tristan and Isolde' there.—*La Roche-sur-Foron* lies 16km further
S.E.; see Rte 134A.

ANNEMASSE TO SAMOËNS (44km). The D903 leads E. to (8km) *Bonne*, an old
town preserving several Renaissance houses and a church restored in
580.—From *Findrol*, 2km S., the N205 leads 11km S.E. past *Contamine-sur-Arve*,
with a 13C church, relic of a priory founded in 1083, and beyond to the l., the
ruins of the castle of *Faucigny*, the feudal seat of the barons of the ancient province of *Faucigny*.—The D907 continues E. from Bonne, passing (r.) at 7.5km
near *N.-S. de Peillonne*, the oldest priory in Faucigny, with a restored 12C
church; 6km to the N.E. is the resort of *Bogève*.—4.5km. *St-Jeoire* was the birthplace of Germain Sommeiller (1815–71), engineer of the Mont-Cenis tunnel
1857–80). It has a Romanesque tower later crenellated; to the S. rises *Le Môle*
1863m); to the N. is the entrance of the *Gorges du Risse*.—The fertile basin of
Taninges is shortly entered, below (r.) the *Pointe de Marcelly* (2000m). Just E. of
13km) **Taninges** itself are some 16C buildings of the abbey of *Mélan*, founded in
288 by Béatrix de Faucigny, and under restoration. For the road hence from
Thonon, see below.—The D907 continues up the valley of the Giffre past ski-
slopes (r.) to (11km) **Samoëns**, a well-sited resort, with huge lime-trees in its
market-place, planted in 1438 to commemorate the liberties accorded to the
town by Amadeus VIII of Savoy. The colonnettes of the principal portal of the
16C church are supported by lions.
   6.5km S.E. lies *Sixt*, a village which grew up round an abbey founded in 1144,
of which the church and some dependencies are preserved. it is a good centre
from which the surrounding mountains may be ascended, among them the *Tête
à l'Ane* (2801m) to the S.; *Le Buet* (3099m; S.E.); the *Cheval Blanc* (2831m; E., on
the Swiss frontier), to the N. of which is the ***Cirque du Fer-à-Cheval**, a
precipitous wall rising sheer above the valley, where rises the *Pic de Tenneverge*

(2987m), and further N., *Mont Ruan* (3047m), likewise marking the frontier, wit
their glaciers, snow-peaks, and cascade.

From Annemasse the N206 leads N.E., to the r. of which are th
wooded slopes of the *Voirons*, rising to 1480m.—At 10km the D90
forks r., driving direct to (20km) *Thonon*, passing several château
en route, among them those of *Avully*, *La Rochette*, and (r.) two
Allinges.

The N206 continues ahead to (7km) *Douvaine*, there meeting th
N5 16km S.W. of Thonon.—A pleasant detour may be made by driv
ing ahead at Douvaine to follow the minor road skirting *Lac Léma*
through (8km) **Yvoire**, a 'picturesque' walled village with tw
gateways and an early 14C waterside castle, to regain the N5 9.5km
S.W. of Thonon.

Thonon-les-Bains (28,200 inhab.) is an attractively situated sp
once the capital of the *Chablais*, built on a hill above the S. bank o
Lac Léman, the largest of the Alpine lakes, fed by the Rhône. it wa
the occasional residence of Kropotkin in the 1880s.

In the Grande-Rue is a *Church* of 1429, built above a Romanesqu
crypt, and enlarged in 1689, in which St Francis de Sales preache
the counter-Reformation in the 1590s.—Nearby is the *Musée*, o
local interest, and further N. a Place on which stood a castl
demolished in 1626. Below, at a much lower level, is the harbour an
lake-side suburb of *Rives*.—2km N. of the latter is the *Château d
Ripaille, incorporating four of the seven tall mechicolated roun
towers (c. 1434) which defended a residence of Amadeus VI
(1383–1451), the first count to assume the title of Duke of Savoy i
1516.

He was elected Pope, as Felix V, although not in orders, by the Council of Bâle i
1439, but he abdicated both dukedom and papacy (in 1449). Both he and h
father, Amadeus VII (1360–91; the 'Comte Rouge') died here. The life of in
dulgence that he is reputed to have led gave rise to the expression 'faire ripaill
(to be in clover). The castle was burned by the Swiss in 1589, and until 1793 wa
a Carthusian monastery, for which additional buildings were erected.

For the road from Thonon to *Cluses*; see below.

The N5 skirts the lake—here at its widest (13km)—throug
Amphion-les-Bains, fashionable under the Second Empire when fre
quented by Count Walewski, to (9km) **Évian-les-Bains** (6,100 inhab.
an old and once fortified town, whose watrs have for long been inte
nationally famous, and whose little harbour is the terminus of excu
sions on *Lac Léman*, on the far bank of which lies *Lausanne*. Its co
ourful lake-side gardens are attractive, while 14C *Ste-Marie*, W. o
the *Casino*, has a conspicuous tower.

Some 9km S.W. is the 14C château of *Larringes* (views); in the hills to the S.E., th
small resort of *Bernex* (from which one may ascent the *Dent d'Oche*; 2222m
views), and *Thollon*, overlooked by the *Pic de Mémises* (1677m; views).

The main road continues along the lake-side, traversing several villages, t
(10km) *Meillerie*, a quarry village, and centre of Resistance in 1944, when it wa
damaged by fire. It was the romantic retreat of St-Preux in Rousseau's 'Nouvell
Héloïse' (where St-Preux and Julie sought refuge in a tempest), where in fac
Byron and Shelley were overtaken by a storm in 1816 when visiting the spot, bu
they were able to make the harbour at *St-Gingolph*, 7km further E. on the Swi
border (Customs). A road ascends the French side of the little river Morge
Novel, N.E. of the Dent d'Oche; see above.

Montreux is 23km N.E., and the *Château de Chillon* is at the E. extremity of th
lake. For *Monthey* (22km S.E.), and *Martigny*, 22km beyond, and 42km N.E. o
Chamonix, see Rte 134A.

THONON TO CLUSES (59km). The D902 ascends S.E. up the *Gorges de la Dranse* to (11km) *Bioge*.—The l.-hand turning here leads 16.5km up a side valley to **Abondance**, a village famous for its Augustinian abbey, founded as a priory in 1043, whose restored ,Church, dating from 1314, with a later steeple, is an interesting transitional edifice, with a 15C abbot's throne, and earlier carvings. The *Cloisters* (1354), of which two walks are preserved, contain 15C frescoes. The village, together with the remains of *La Chapelle d'Abondance*, and *Châtel*, 11.5km up the valley, also has ski-slopes.

Continuing S.E. from Bioge, we thread more defiles, where in 1536 a handful of peasants led by Jean de St-Jean-d'Aulps repulsed a Bernese army, and pass (l. at 16km) the remains of the Romanesque church of the abbey of *Ste-Marie-d'Aulps* (de Alpibus), a Benedictine foundation of the 11C, which passed to the Cistercians in 1135, and was largely demolished in 1823.—To the E. rises the *Roc de Tavaneuse* (2156m).—To the l. lies the *Lac de Montriond*.—Continuing to climb S., the resort of *Morzine* is by-passed to the l. prior to crossing the *Col des Gets*, overlooked (r.) by *Mont Chéry* (1827m), with ski slopes, the village of *Les Gets* is said to have been founded in the 14C by a colony of Jews exiled from Florence ('gets' signifying juifs in the local patois).—The road descends steeply through woods to (19.5km) *Taninges* (see above), beyond which it climbs S. over a ridge into the valley of the Arve, and to (10km) *Cluses*; see Rte 134A.

131 Lyon to Bourgoin-Jallieu, for Grenoble or Chambéry

To Grenoble, 107km (66 miles); to Chambéry, 94km (58 miles). N6. 41km *Bourgoin-Jallieu*. Hence the N85, later N75, turns S.E. to (43km) *Moirans*, 23km from **Grenoble**.—The N6 continues E. to (13km) *La Tour-du-Pin*, whence the most convenient approach is the A43 to (40km) **Chambéry**.

Maps: IGN. 51, or 112. M 244.

The A43 motorway provides a rapid direct route to Chambéry, off which the A48 bears S.E. to Grenoble.

Crossing the *Pont de la Guillotière* from central **Lyon** (see Rte 129) the N6 leads S.E. across an uninteresting plain, at 26km passing (l.) the airport of *Lyon-Satolas*, 4km N., after a further 5km reaching the crossroad from Vienne to *Crémieu*, 13km N.E.

Crémieu is a little old town standing at the foot of a semicircle of chalk hills overlooking the Rhône valley, preserving ruins of its fortifications, including two gateways (14th, and 16C), and a 15C hilltop castle. The *Mairie* incorporates the cloister of an Augustinian convent, E. of which is a 15-17C *Church*; a massive 14C covered *Market* is also retained.

3km. *La Verpillière*, S.W. of which are the well-preserved ruins of the castle of *Fallavier*, once belonging to the Prince of Orange, is traversed, 3km beyond which the 15-16C *Château de Monbaly* is passed to the r.—After 4km the textile town of **Bourgoin-Jallieu** (22,950 inhab.) is skirted, with a small museum housed in an early 16C chapel. Rousseau spent six months here in the autumn of 1768 in the company of Thérèse Levasseur. The *Grand-Colombie* may be discerned to the N.E., S. of which rises the *Dent du Chat*; see below.

At *St-Chef*, 5km N.E., is a fine Romanesque church, and remains of an abbey containing 12C wall-paintings.

For the road hence to **Chambéry**, see below.
The N85 bears due S.

At 17km a r.-hand turning leads 7km to **La Côte-St-André**, on the N. edge of the *Plaine de Bièvre*, dominated by a 17C château. The small town was the birthplace of Hector Berlioz (1803–69), whose house, now a museum devoted to the composer, is a short distance S. of the central *Market-hall* (14C). It also contains paintings by J. Jongkind (1822–91), who lived here from 1876, and is buried in the local cemetery.—The main road may be regained at *La Frette*, 8km E.

9km. *La Frette*, beyond which the summits of the *Belledonne massif* come into prominence to the S.E., while to the S. rises the *Vercors massif*.—At 17km *Moirons* (see Rte 132B) is by-passed to the r., before entering (7km) **Voreppe**, situated above the Isère and at the foot of a semi-circle of crags (S.W. outposts of the Grande-Chartreuse massif), down which the Roise falls in a single cascade. it preserves a few 16-17C houses and a 14C church.

A by-road ascends E. to (4km) the old convent of *Chalais*, founded by St-Hugh of Grenoble in 1101, and later a Benedictine abbey; in the 13C the monks moved to Boscodon (cf.), and the place was acquired by the Carthusians, who built the present house in 1640; the church contains 12C sculptures.—To the N.E. rises *La Sure* (1920m), the highest point on the W. side of the range.

The road, now N75, enters the lower part of the *Vallée de Gresivaudan* (see p 712), here dividing the massifs of the *Grande-Chartreuse* (l.) from the *Vercors*, and shortly traverses *St-Egrève*, to the N.E. of which is seen the curious *Aiguille de Quaix*, while the road is overlooked by the formidable hill of *Le Néron* (1298m), as we approach (16km) **Grenoble**; see Rte 133A.

Continuing E. from *Bourgoin-Jallieu*, in 15km **La Tour-du-Pin** (7,000 Turripinois) is entered, once the seat of an important barony, Humbert I being the ancestor of the third and last line of dauphins of Viennois (1282–1349). The *Mairie* is housed in a 17C monastery, while the Rue d'Italie preserves several old houses; the late 19C church contains a *Triptych of the Entombment (c. 1541) attrib. to Georges Penez or Pencz, a pupil of Dürer, a patient in the hospital here, who depicted his own burial on the back of it.

The village of *Dolomieu*, 7km N.E., was the home of Déodat de Dolomieu (1750–1801), discoveror of the nature of the limestone mountains of the Dolomites, which are named after him.
   12km S. of La Tour-du-Pin is the 14C *Château de Virieu* (rebuilt in the 16-18C), 4km beyond which is that of *Pupetière*, rebuilt by Viollet-le-Duc on ancient foundations, where Lamartine wrote 'Le Vallon'; his friend Aymon de Virieu saved him from drowning in a lake further S., beyond the motorway.

The most convenient road from LA TOUR-DU-PIN TO CHAMBÉRY is the A43 motorway, entered just W. of the town, which drives due E., after c. 15km traversing a tunnel, and emerging above the *Lac d'Aiguebelette* before entering (6km) another tunnel piercing the *Montagne de l'Épine* (the southernmost ridge of the Jura) below the *Col d'Épine* (987m). Emerging from the latter we have a view (N.) of the *Lac du Bourget*, with the *Dent du Chat* (1390m) to the l., and circle to the N. to meet (10km) the N504 5km N.W. of **Chambéry**; see Rte 134A.—**Aix-les-Bains** lies beyond the E. side of the lake 10km N. of this junction.

ALTERNATIVE ROUTES FROM LA TOUR-DU-PIN TO CHAMBÉRY diverge N and S. of the motorway.
   The former (N516; 54km) leads E., at 9km crossing the N75 (see Rte 128), and 4km beyond, *Aoste*, of importance in Roman times, preserving relics of their oc-

cupation.—4km. A r.-hand fork ascends the *Col de l'Épine*, but this by-road has been largely superseded by the motorway.—We curve N.E. to approach (l.) the Rhône, which at 22km meet the N504 from Belley (8km N.) to Chambéry.—Turning E., the road traverses the defile of *Pierre-Châtel*, and *Yenne*, overlooked to the S. E. by the *Dent du Chat* (1390m), below which we thread a tunnel, emerging on the W. bank of the *Lac du Bourget* opposite *Aix-les-Bains*; see Rte 134A. (An older road climbs in steep zigzags over the ridge, commanding fine views.) On reaching the lake side, we turn r. near (l.) the restored castle of *Bourdeau*, for (4km) **Le Bourget-du-Lac**, a place of ancient importance, which gives its name to the lake. The *Church* (founded 1030) was rebuilt in the 13C and restored in the 16th and 19C, but preserves its original crypt, and the choir contains sculpture from a 13C rood-screen. Part of a 16C cloister of a Cluniac priory is incorporated in an adjoining house. In the vicinity are the slight remains of the castle of the Counts of Savoy, in which Amadeus V ('the Great'; 1249–1323) and Amadeus VI ('le Comte Vert'; 1334–83) were born.—*Chambéry* lies 12km S.E.; see Rte 134A.

The more southerly route from La Tour-du-Pin (N6) crosses the motorway and at (12km) *Les Abrets*, the N75 (see Rte 128), with a view ahead of the *Montagne de l'Épine* (*Mont Grelle*; 1425m), and to the S.E., the *Grande-Chartreuse massif*.—7km. *Pont-de-Beauvoisin*, with a 15C church on the Savoy side of the Guiers, the 16C bridge over which was destroyed in 1940.—We veer S.E. through (6km) *St-Béron*, whose church was once a chapel of a Benedictine priory.—Hence a road leads N.E. to the charmingly sited *Lac d'Aiguebelette*.—Threading a gorge, we reach (9km) *Les Echelles*, 23km S.W. of *Chambéry*, also a convenient entrance to the massif of the *Grande-Chartreuse*; see Rte 132B.

132 Valence to Chambéry

A. Via Grenoble

154km (95 miles). N532. 18km *Bourg-de-Péage*—18km *Pont-en-Royans* lies 9km E.—61km **Grenoble**—N90. 47km—N6. 10km **Chambéry**.

Between Bourg and Veurey-Voroize it is a more attractive and faster road than that on the far bank of the Isère; see Rte 132B.

Maps: IGN 51, 52, or 112. M 244.

The A41 motorway provides a rapid route between Grenoble and Chambéry.

For **Valence**, and *Bourg-de-Péage*, 18km N.E., see Rte 139A. Here we turn E., with a view across the Isère to *Romans*, and approach the W. wall of the *Vercors massif* (see Rte 133B) at (18km) *St-Nazaire-en-Royans*, a curious old village on the confluence of the Bourne with the Isère, dominated by an ancient aqueduct.—At *Rochechinard*, 2km S., is an imposing ruin of a 14C castle.

For *St-Jean-en-Royans*, 9km S.E., and *Pont-en Royans*, 9km E., both on roads ascending into the Vercors, see Rte 133B.

10km. *St-Marcellin* (see Rte 132B) lies 6km N. on the far bank of the Isère.—Remaining on the l. bank, with its numerous plantations of walnut-trees, one shortly passes the ruined 13C castle of **Beauvoir**, which although partly destroyed on Louis XI's orders in 1476 is still of considerable extent, retaining two gateways of its original enceinte, a square tower, and a high Gothic window of its chapel.

It belonged to the third family of Dauphins, several of whom made it their favourite residence. Humbert II retained it after the cession of Dauphiny to France, and tradition relates that his infant son, whose death led to his abdication, was killed by being accidentally dropped by a nurse from one of its windows.

10km. *Cognin*, which lies at the foot of the deep and striking *Gorges du Nan*, is traversed, beyond which we keep to the narrow bank between the river and the steep slope of the *Vercors*, the bold N. promontory of which is rounded at 23km at the *Bec de l'Echeillon*, rising steeply to *La Buffe* (1623m).—At (4km) *Veurey-Voroize* a bridge crosses the Izère to join the motorway to **Grenoble**, 13km S.E.

Keeping to the l. bank, we shortly pass the *Tour des Templiers* and enter (8km) **Sassenage**, at the mouth of the gorge of the Furon, with the moated early 16C *Château de Béranger* above its l. bank, and a church with an 11C tower, the burial-place of Lesdiguières (whose first wife was Claudia Béranger). Its local cheese, resembling Roquefort, is reputed.—For the road entering the *Vercors massif* hence, see Rte 133B.—7.5km brings one into the centre of **Grenoble**; see Rte 133A.

There are three main roads from Grenoble to **Chambéry**, leading up the valley of *Le Gresivaudan* (also *Graisevaudan*): the A41 motorway, skirting the r. bank of the Izère; the N90, to its W.; and on the far bank, the D523, which is first described. The floor and sides of the valley, up to the crags and forests which line its flanks, are carefully tilled, and the wealth of crops gives it the appearance of a luxuriant garden—'le plus beau jardin du beau pays de France', in the words of Louis XII.

Driving E., at 10.5km industrial *Domène* is traversed, preserving ruins of an 11C priory church, beside which is a 13C chapel with traces of wall-paintings.

To the r. extends the *Chaine de Belladonne*, with its *Pic* (2978m) rising almost due E.; to the N.W. is the *Chartreuse massif* (see Rtes 132B and 133A), with the *Dent de Crolles* (2062m) protruding conspicuously from its E. ridge.

5km. *Lancey*, with a paper-mill and wood-pulp factory founded in 1869 by Aristide Bergès (1833–1904), the hydraulic plant used being the first for producing electricity from water-power, or 'houille blanche' (whilte coal), as the inventor nicknamed it.—At contiguous *Villard-Bonnot* is a round church and the 16C *Château de Vorz* (l., beyond the town), after which we traverse industrial *Brignoud*, above which is the old *Tour de Laval*, and (5.5km) *Froges*.

3.5km E. of the latter is **Les Adrets**, a stronghold of François de Beaumont, baron des Adrets (1513–87), the Huguenot leader, who rallied the whole of Dauphiny to the Protestant cause in revenge—it is said—for an affront offered him by the House of Guise; he died a Roman Catholic.

4.5km. *Tencin*, with the 18C *Château de Monteynard* in its park, on the site of another which belonged to the brilliant Mme de Tencin (1681–1749), a galante renegade nun, the mother of D'Alembert (1717–83), whose father was the Chevalier Le Camus Destouches; her brother was the unprincipled Card. de Tencin (1680–1758). Sainte-Beuve condemned her as 'cupide, rapace, intrigante'.

4.5km. *Goncelin*, with a 13C church tower, from which the D525 forks r. to (10.5km) *Allevard*.

Allevard, still with some characteristic features of a mountain 'bourg', is a small spa attractively situated on the Bréda, whose waters have provided power for old-established metal-works utilising the iron ore mined in the vicinity since the 13C. It is a convenient centre for excursions into the *Belladonne range* to the S.E.—A road climbs S. up the wooded Bréda valley to (17km) *Le Fond de France*, from which ascents may be made into the wild *Massif d'Allevard*, with its lakes, below the *Rocher Blanc*, rising to 2928m, to the S.E., and the *Pic de la Belle Étoile* (2718m), S.W.—From Allevard the main road may be regained at *Pontcharra* by circling round the N. end of the *Brame-Farine*, a ridge to the N.W., turning l. 7km N.—There are ski-slopes at *Le Collet*, on a ridge extending from the Belledonne, on the far side of which, in a wooded valley, approached by a road circling the N. end of the spur, lie the ruins of the *Chartreuse de St-Hugon*, founded by St Hugh of Avalon in 1175; see below.

9km. To the r. stands the 13C *Château Bayard*, birthplace of Pierre de Terrail (c. 1473– 1524), the 'chevalier sans peur et sans reproche', now containing a museum devoted to chivalry.

The Chevalier Bayard covered himself with glory in the wars of Charles VIII, Louis XII, and François I. On one occasion he is said to have defended a bridge over the Garigliano single-handed against 200 Spaniards; and his defence of Mézières in 1521 with a garrison of 1000 against a besieging host of 35,000 placed him among the greatest captains of the age. Twice taken prisoner, he was twice set free without ransom by the admiring enemy. François I received knighthood at his hands. He was mortally wounded in 1524 while defending the French rearguard on the Sesia, not far from Abbaite-grasso in N. Italy, and was buried at Grenoble.

Close to the castle is the hamlet of *Avalon*, where St Hugh, bishop of Lincoln 1186– 1200), was born c. 1135.

1km. *Pontcharra*; a small industrial town.

An approach to the Tarentaise and Maurienne may be made by forking r. and following the D925 N.E. past (8km) *La Rochette* (r.), with a ruined castle and a church with a 16C choir and 15C stalls. It meets the N6 17km beyond; see Rte 135.

Continuing N. we turn l. at (9km) *Montmélian*, for **Chambéry**, 14km N.W.; see Rte 134A.—**Montmélian**, an ancient stronghold of the Counts of Savoy, lies below a hillock (Mons Emilianus) crowned by a ruined fort. This was taken by François I in 1536; in 1600 by Henri IV (who narrowly missed death by a cannon shot); and in 1691, by Catinat, after a 19-month siege.

The N90 leads N.E. from Grenoble, following the W. side of the valley of the *Grésivaudan* roughly parallel to the motorway, forking off the latter soon after crossing the Isère.

The *Dent de Crolles* (2062m) is conspicuous ahead, and the peaks of the *Belledonne ridge* to the E. come into view as we proceed up the valley, flanked to the W. by the E. ridge of the *Massif de la Chartreuse*; see Rtes 132B and 133B. Several villages of slight interest are traversed, approaching at 37km *Fort Barraux* (l.) commanding the passage; to the r. lies *Pontcharra*; see above.

The original fort on this site was built by Charles Emmanuel I of Savoy in full view of a French army commanded by Lesdiguières, who on being rebuked by Henry IV for allowing the work to continue, replied: 'Your Majesty requires a fortress on this side of Savoy to hold in check that of Montmélian: and if the duke is willing to defray the expense, I am willing to undertake its capture. On 31 March 1598 he surprised the place by moonlight, and it became indeed a French bulwark.

We shortly pass (l.) *Bellecombe*, a well-sited hamlet with a ruined priory and castle, lying on the lower slope of *Mont Granier* (1933m), and veer N. to (8km) *Les Marches*, preserving the Gothic gateway of its old castle, and a handsome château, not far N.W. of which is the *Abimes de Myans*, formed by a landslide from the Granier in 1248 which buried 16 villages, and is said to have caused the death of 5000.

Crossing the motorway, at 2km we turn l. on meeting the N6 for **Chambéry**, 10km N.W.; see Rte 134A.

B.   Via Voiron and
the Grande-Chartreuse

124km (77 miles). N532. 18km *Bourg-de-Péage*—**Romans**—N92.
26km *St-Marcellin*—31km *Moirans*—5km **Voiron**—D520. 15km
St-Laurent-du-Pont. **St-Pierre-de-Chartreuse** lies 10km S.E.—8km
Les Echelles—N6. 21km **Chambéry**.

Maps: IGN 51, 52, or 112. M 244.

The N532 is followed to the N.E. to (18km) *Bourg-de-Péage*, then crossing the Isère to *Romans* (see Rte 139A) and turning r., with view of the *Vercors massif* rising abruptly to the E.; see Rte 133B.

At 21km *La Sône* is passed to the r., where stood a silk-mill for which Jacques de Vauvanson invented the endless chain (1771).

7km N.W., via *Chatte*, lies **St-Antoine**, which may be visited for its old *Abbey* founded in the 11C as a shrine for the reputed relics of St Anthony, brought hence from the East, where in 1095 the Order of St Anthony of the East (Antonines) was established, which endured until 1768.

The conventual dependencies, encircled by a wall, date from the 14-17C. The *Church*, although built of soft stone, and much battered in the Wars of Religion, is tolerably well preserved. The present edifice was in construction between the 12C (apse) and the 15C, to which period belongs the unfinished and damaged W front. In the archivolt of the main portal are preserved some statuettes of c. 1464. In the interior, the side chapels are connected by arches added in the 17C, while in the 2nd N. chapel are remains of frescoes attrib. to Robin Favier of Avignon (1450). A series of Aubusson tapestries of 1632 are notable.

5km. **St-Marcellin** (6,900 Marcellinois) preserves a Romanesque belfry, the remains of 13-14C walls, and a ruined 13C castle. The goats' milk cheeses of the neighbourhood are reputed.—10km *Vinay*, which claims with *Tullins*, 14km beyond, to have the richest soil in Dauphiny, are both traversed, the latter a market town known for its walnuts; its church has a fine Romanesque belfry; the chapel of a former *Hôtel-Dieu* (15-16C) contains a 16C triptych.

7km. **Moirans** (r.) where we meet the N75 for **Grenoble**, 23km S.E.—Passing beneath the A48 motorway, at 5km **Voiron** (19,700 inhab.), the ancient oppidum *Voronum*, is entered, a flourishing but undistinguished town manufacturing paper (since 1547), synthetic fibres, and skis. Lying on the Morge, it was not ceded to France by Savoy (in exchange for Faucigny) until 1355, six years after the rest of Dauphiny had been bought. From the central place, the Rue de Sermorens leads N.W. to *St-Pierre*, rebuilt in 1920, retaining two 14C chapels and a Romanesque crypt and tower. Since 1935 Voiron has been the site of the distillery of the Grande-Chartreuse liqueur, which may be visited during weekdays in the Blvd Edgar-Kofler, on the N75 leading S.E.

There are three varieties of liqueurs known as '*Chartreuse*': the *Green*, which is the most ancient and also the strongest; the *Yellow*, which was produced from 840; and the *White*, no longer made, which was manufactured after 1835. The monks used to make an *Elixir*, dating from 1607, when the recipe is said to have been given to them by Marshal d'Estrées, from which Green Chartreuse was evolved. Its basic ingredients are very pure spirits of wine combined with a choice of aromatic plants such as dianthus, balm-mint, and young pine buds etc.

The D520 is followed to the N.E., at (5km) *St-Étienne-de-Crossey* threading a limestone gorge, with a view of the escarpment of the *Grand Sure* ahead, and 10km beyond *St-Laurent-du-Pont* is entered, a small town on the edge of a marshy plain. Its 13C church, rebuilt by Carthusians after a fire in 1855, contains 15C stalls from the Chartreuse de Curière; see below. The hospital erected by the Carthusians in 1898 dominates the place.

ST-LAURENT-DU-PORT TO CHAMBÉRY VIA THE GRANDE CHARTREUSE (48km). This excursion may be made conveniently hence, although the approach to it via St-Pierre-de-Chartreuse is also described in sub-routes from Les Echelles (see below), and Grenoble (see Rte 133A), while the route may also be made in reverse from Chambéry.

The mountain massif of the **Grande-Chartreuse** extends from Grenoble towards Chambéry, and presents a formidable limestone wall averaging 1700–1900m high on its S.E. side overlooking the Isère. it falls away more gently to the N.W., where its slopes are richly wooded (mainly firs, pitchpine, and beech) and is intersected by streams and pastures. At the W. side is another precipitous range. Almost in the middle is a depression in which lies *St-Pierre-de-Chartreuse*, at the meeting of several valleys and at the foot of the principal peaks: the *Chamechaude* (2082m), to the S.; the *Dent de Crolles* (2062m), to the S.E.; and the *Grand-Som* (2026m) to the N.

Since the return of the monks the monastery itself has been closed to visitors, although a propitiatory museum has been set up (see below), which is of interest, but the mountains will always be visited for the wild beauty of their scenery alone; winter sports have also been developed at St-Pierre, Le Sappey, and elsewhere. Among words in local use are 'som' (summit; pron. 'son'), and 'habert', a summer chalet.

The road (D520B), constructed by the monks c. 1510 to bring down timber and charcoal from the forests, follows the l. bank of the Guiers-Mort, leaving on the r. another leading to the *Chartreuse de Curière* (founded c. 1284), with a 15C church and conventual buildings of 1700.—At 2km we pass, at *Fourvoirie* (the 'forata via' of the Carthusians, who pierced a way hence into the wilderness they inhabited), the ruins of the huge distillery (1860) where the Chartreuse liqueurs were made until it was destroyed by a landslide in 1935, after which its manufacture was transferred to Voiron; see above.

On the r. bank of the stream are several small factories, etc., and the '*Entrée du Désert*' (as it is called), beyond which the monks prefer no females to pass. The new road made along the gorge in 1854 is carried up the side of limestone precipices by a series of short tunnels and bridges; at (5.5km) the *Pont St-Pierre* the road to **La Correrie** diverges to the l. (obligatory car park).

This building, formerly the residence of the Père Procureur of the monastery and an infirmary, has since 1957 been tastefully converted into a ***Museum** illustrating the contemplative life of the Carthusians. Its 12C chapel contains paintings depicting the life of St Bruno and a triptych of the *School of Brea*; also to be seen is a pain-

ting of St Bruno at prayer by *Marie Leczinska*, and another by
Jouvenet, a good model of the Monastery, and the alembic in which
the liqueur was made from 1735, etc.

The famous but inhospitable **Monastery of La Grande-Chartreuse**
(no. adm.) may be approached by pedestrians only (c. 1.5km), and is
enclosed by wooded heights and limestone crags, with a few patches
of meadow to redeem the savage character of this traditional
'wilderness'. It is an extensive pile of building, in which 35 monks
live, but owing to repeated conflagrations, very little remains of the
original edifice, the *plan* of which was followed in all later Carthusian monasteries. Externally its tent-like slate roofs, designed to prevent the accumulation of snow, are its most conspicuous features.

Of buildings earlier than the 17C, part of the great cloister (1145–1235), the
Chapelle des Morts (1386), the clock-tower of 1371, refectory, and 15C church
alone survive. The *Chapelle St-Louis* and the kitchens (preserving 12C
fragments) are 18C.

It was founded in 1084 by St Bruno, who was born at Cologne in c. 1035 and
studied theology at Reims and Paris. Embracing the conventual life, he resolved
to retire from the normal world, and with six companions settled in this remote
spot, the haunt of wild beasts, on the recommendation of St Hughes (d. 1106),
bishop of Grenoble. It became in due course the parent monastery for numerous
Chartreux (a name of obscure origin), Certoses, and Charterhouses, among
other Carthusian foundations, but the original cells, built at a higher level, near
the *Chapel of St-Bruno* (replaced by a building of 1640), were swept away by an
avalanche in 1132, although his chapel, because of its site on a rock, was spared.

The first house on the present site was built by Prior Guigues (d. 1137), who
also first committed to writing the ascetic rules of the order, prescribing silence,
abstinence from meat, the exclusion of women, and the residence of the monks
in separate dwellings, etc. In the 13C extensive dependencies were erected,
which after being eight times burned were replaced by the present edifice in
1676. The rigours of the rule had in the meanwhile been relaxed, although it
preserved much of its original spirit, and has never been reformed. Nevertheless
the monastery was stripped of its possessions at the Revolution, and the monks
expelled as drones; they were allowed to return in 1816 and were given certain
concessions with regard to forests and pasture, but their main source of revenue
was the sale of liqueurs.

As a result of the 'Loi des Congrégations' of 1901, the Carthusians, among
other orders, were expelled from France in 1903, and the 'Père Général' moved
his headquarters to Pinerolo and later to Ferneta, near Lucca, in Italy, while the
manufacture of liqueurs was transferred to Tarragona, in Spain. The law was inexplicably revoked in 1940, when the monks returned to their mountain
fastness.

St Hugh of Avalon, bishop of Lincoln (not to be confused with his namesake of
Grenoble; see above), was a monk and bursar of the Chartreuse in 1160–81
before being invited to England by Henry II, where he became head of the Carthusian house at Witham in Somerset. He was canonised in 1220. The refectory
was restored in 1474 by Margaret of York, wife of Charles le Téméraire of
Burgundy, and several English kings have been benefactors of the place, which
was visited by Queen Victoria (although a female) in 1886. Most of the treasures
of the library, scattered at the Revolution, are now at Grenoble.

The *Chartreusette*, to the S.W., may be ascended to for a good general view,
while further up the valley stands *N.-D.-de-Casalibus*, rebuilt c. 1452 on the site
of the original chapel, and restored in 1656 and 1821.

On returning to La Correrie, one may regain the main road 1km E.

3km. **St-Pierre-de-Chartreuse** consists of a group of hamlets near
the meeting of the Guiers-Morts and several mountain streams.

Ascents in the area include the *Grand Som* (2026m), to the N., providing a plunging view of the monastery; the *Charmant Som* (1867m), to the S.W.; and *La Sci-*
(1782m) to the E.—From the hamlet of *Perquelin*, 3km E., the *Dent de Crolle*

(2062m) may be approached via the *Col de Ayes* (1538m) or the *Trou de Glaz*, further E., a curious depression in which is the *Gouffre Berger*, a pothole 1145m deep, connected with the underground channel of the Guiers-Morts and the precipitous E. face of the range.

From St-Pierre-de-Chartreuse, one may continue N. on the D512 via (3.5km) the *Col du Cucheron*, below (l.) the Grand Som, beyond which (r.) opens a gorge overlooked by the ridge known as the *Lances de Malissard*. The road descends to (8.5km) *St-Pierre-d'Entremont*, another centre for excursions into the massif, to the E. of which is the *Cirque de St-Méme*.

Hence the main route may be regained at *Les Echelles*, 12km W., by turning down the *Gorges de Guiers-Vif*, passing below (l.) the old castle of *Entremont*, with which, in the 15C, the Carthusians replaced an older stronghold.

The mountain road may be continued N. through the *Gorges d'Entremont* before climbing to (9.5km) the *Col du Granier* (1134m) below (r.) the limestone plateau, buttressed by cliffs and broken by fissures, of *Mont Granier* (1933m), from which we descend over a series of spurs to (15.5km) **Chambéry**; see Rte 134A.

The D520 continues N. from St-Laurent to (6km) **Les Echelles**, also by-passed to the E., above the confluence of the Guiers-Vif with the Guiers-Mort. The Roman road from Milan to Vienne passed this way. The *Mairie* occupies a commandery of St John of Jerusalem (rebuilt in 1632), founded in 1260 by Beatrice of Savoy, who had a castle here.—The lower of two caverns N.E. of the town is said to have been a hide-out of Mandrin, the 18C 'Robin Hood' of the district.

From Les Echelles one follows the N6, which circles to the E. through the *Tunnel des Echelles*, pierced through a mountain spur on Napoleon's orders in 1804–14 to obviate the inconvenient old road through a gorge, which itself had been improved in 1670 by Charles Emmanuel II.

From the summit level, the road descends the Hyère valley, later passing (r.) the *Cascade de Couz*, to enter (23km) **Chambéry**; see Rte 134A.

133 Grenoble to Die

A. Grenoble and Environs

GRENOBLE (159,500 Grenobloise; 23,500 in 1801; 68,900 in 1901), the old capital of *Dauphiny*, and now the largely modern préfecture of the *Isère*, is a flourishing university town (with some 30,000 students) standing just above the confluence of that river and the Drac. The Grande-Chartreuse massif rises to the N.; the Vercors to the S.W.; and the Belledonne range to the E. The vistas at the end of many streets are thus closed by near or distant mountain peaks, and their proximity offers a welcome escape from the industrial city which is of comparatively slight interest in itself, however bautifully sited. The manufacture of gloves was once its main occupation, but within recent decades it has grown rapidly with diversification, particularly in such fields as metallurgy, electronics, and nuclear studies.

The original Gaulish settlement on the r. bank of the Isère, called *Culoro*, is mentioned in the letters of Plancus to Cicero. It was raised to the rank of town by Gratian in c. 380, becoming *Gracianopolis*, from which Grenoble is derived. It was included in the Burgundian kingdom in the 9C, but by the 12C had come into the possession of the dauphins, who made it their capital, from whom it passed in 1341 to France. It was sacked by the Baron des Adrets in 1562, and after its capture for Henri IV in 1590 was fortified by Lesdiguières.

Even before the outbreak of the French Revolution the attempt of the central government to substitute a new judicial regime for that of the too independent provincial parlement roused the spirit of the Grenobloise, and the 'day of the tiles' (7 June, 1788) is memorable for the defeat of the royalist forces, who were pelted from its roofs. It repulsed an army of 20,000 Austrians in March-April 1814, and openly received Napoleon on his march from the Mediterranean on 7 March 1815, when, in the Emperor's words, he had only 'to knock at the gates' with his snuff-box' to gain admittance. The first Provident Society in France was founded here in 1803. It was occupied by Italian troops in 1942, but remained a hive of Resistance until liberated on 22 Aug. 1944.

Among Grenobloise were Jacques de Vaucanson (1709– 82), the mechanical engineer; the Revolutionary leaders Antoine Barnarve (1761– 93), and Jean-Joseph Mounier (1758– 1806); Casimier Périer (1777– 1832), the politician; the Abbés Mably (1709– 85), and Condillac (1715– 80), brother philosophers; Mme de Tencin (1681– 1749; see p 712); Henri Beyle (better known as Stendhal; 1783– 1842); and the artists Ernest Hébert (1817– 1908), and Henri Fantin-Latour (1836– 1904).

Several main roads converge on the *Pl. Paul-Mistral*, immediately W. of the *Parc Paul-Mistral*, dominated by the plate-glass *Hôtel de Ville* (1967; by Maurice Novarina), just N. of which is the *Jardin Botanique* and *Natural History Museum*, with a valuable mineralogical collection.

The *Library*, in the Blvd Maréchal-Lyautey, to the W. of the Place, displays several important MSS, many from the Grande Chartreuse; MSS by Stendhal; The Vénus de Grenoble (4C B.C.), and the gilt bronze Casque de Vézeronce (6C).

The Rue Haxo leads past the Jardin Botanique to the *Pl. de Verdun*, flanked by the *Préfecture* on the S. side, and the **Musée des Beaux-Arts** on the E., in a building of 1870, parts of which are undergoing modernisation.

On the FIRST FLOOR are *Archaeological collections*, and a section of *Egyptology*, recalling the fact that young Champollion (1790– 1832) lived and worked near Grenoble, with an interesting selection of onshebti, shabtis, funerary steles, pottery, and glass, etc.

The *Picture Galleries* are on the GROUND FLOOR (l. of entrance), notable in which are *Taddeo di Bartolo*, Virgin and Child with saints; a Byzantine St Lucy (13C); *Veronese*, Christ appearing to the Magdalen; *Tintoretto*, Virgin and Child; attrib. to *Tintoretto*, Portrait of V. Bragadino; *Vasari*, Holy Family; *Jacob Richier*, Bust of Lesdiguières, and an *anon.* Portrait of the latter; *Lucas Cranach*, Judith.

Jordaens, Adoration of the Shepherds; *Ribera*, Martyrdom of St Bartholomew; *Rubens*, St Gregory invoking the Holy Spirit; *M. Stomer*, Disciples at Emmaus; *Snyders*, Parroquets; *Zurbaran, Annunciation, Adoration of the Shepherds, Adoration of the Magi, and Circumcision; *Claude Vignon*, Jesus among the doctors; *Philippe de Champaigne*, Louis XIV conferring the Order of the Holy Spirit on the Duc d'Anjou, Crucifixion, and The Baptist in the desert; *Vouet*, Rest on the flight into Egypt; *Claude Lorrain*, Roman Campagna; *Georges de la Tour*, St Jerome; *Rigaud*, Claude de Rouvoy, and the Marshal de Noailles; *Houdon*, terracotta Bust of Barnave; *Largillière*, Jean Pupil de Craponne, and Elisabeth de Beauharnais; *De Troy*, Mother, child, and wet-nurse; *Tournières*, Charles de Beauharnais;, and examples of the work of *Guardi, Canaletto*, and *Desportes*.

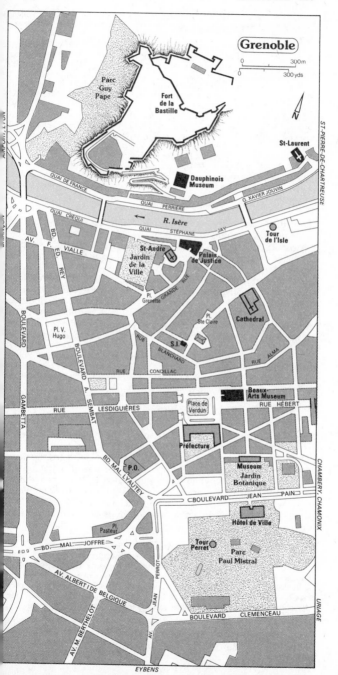

Grenoble

0 — 300m
0 — 300 yds

Parc Guy Pape

Fort de la Bastille

St-Laurent

Dauphinois Museum

QUAI DE FRANCE

QUAI PERRIÈRE

Q. XAVIER JOUVIN

QUAI CRÉQUI

← R. Isère

QUAI STÉPHANE JAY

AV. F. VIALLE

BD. ED. REY

Tour de l'Isle

St-André
Jardin de la Ville

Palais de Justice

Pl. Grenette

GRANDE RUE

BOULEVARD

Pl. V. Hugo

RUE

Pl. Ste Claire

Cathedral

S.I.

BLANCHARD

RUE ALMA

BOULEVARD

RUE CONDILLAC

GAMBETTA

RUE

BOULEVARD A. SEMBAT

LESDIGUIÈRES

Place de Verdun

Beaux-Arts Museum

RUE HÉBERT

Préfecture

BD. MAL LYAUTEY

P.O.

Museum Jardin Botanique

BOULEVARD

JEAN

PAIN

CHAMBERY, CHAMONIX

Pl. Pasteur

BD. MAL. JOFFRE

Tour Perret

Hôtel de Ville

Parc Paul Mistral

AV. ALBERT I DE BELGIQUE

JEAN

PERROT

URIAGE

AV. M. BERTHELOT

AV.

BOULEVARD CLEMENCEAU

EYBENS

ST-PIERRE-DE-CHARTREUSE

Perugino's SS Sebastian and Apollonia, *Brueghel the Elder*, Skaters, and *Van der Meulen*, Louis XIV crossing the Pont Neuf, do not appear to be on view at present.

Among individual canvases in an important collection of 20C paintings, are *Dufy*, 'La dame en rose'; *Picasso*, Infant with doll; *Bonnard*, Woman with a dog, and White interior; *Soutine*, Carcass of an ox; *Chagall*, Midsummer Night's Dream; *Modigliani*, Woman with a white collar; *Derain*, Paul Poiret; *Vuillard*, 'Le dejeuner'; and examples of the work of *Utrillo, Klee, Léger, Robert* and *Sonia Delaunay, Miro, Roger de la Fresnaye, Picabia, Matisse, Camille Bombois*, et al.

FIRST FLOOR. **R1** Works by *Georgette Agutte-Sembat* (1867–1922).—**R2** *Rouault*, Christ and the holy woman; *Signac*, St-Tropez; and works by *Derain, Marquet, Matisse*, and *Van Dongen*.—**R3** *Renoir*, Gabrielle, The milkmaid; *Harpignies*, Autumn; *Boudin*, The port of Antwerp; *Sisley*, View of Montmartre; *Pissarro*, the 'Maison de la Folie' at Éragny; *Monet*, The garden at Giverny; *Doré*, Loch in a storm; and works by *Théodore Rousseau*.—**R4** Paintings by *T. Ravanat* (1812–83), *A. Dubuisson, D. Hahoult, Jean Achard* (1807–84), and *Laurent Guetal*, and other regional artists.—**R5** *Eugène Faure*, Self-portrait, and other portraits; and examples of the art of *Fantin-Latour*, including a Self-portrait of 1859.

Near the entrance, *Picasso*, Woman reading.

From the N. side of the square one may follow the Rue Blanchard (off which is the spacious S.I.; it was in Grenoble that the idea of such tourist offices in France is said to have been initiated; enquiry should be made with regard to admission to the *crypt of St-Laurent*; see below); to the N.W. is the older town.

Off this street turns the pedestrian Rue Lafayette and Grande Rue, the latter extending from the central *Pl. Grenette* to the *Pl. St-André*, passing (r.) the Rue J.-J. Rousseau, at No. 14 in which Stendhal was born, now containing a *'Resistance' Museum*. A museum devoted to the author is installed a short distance N.W., in the old *Hôtel de Ville*, a mansion once the residence of Lesdiguières, behind **St-André**.

This 13C building, considerably restored, retains the tympanum of its W. porch, and its original square belfry surmounted by a spire. Here, in 1622, Lesdiguières abjured Protestantism four years before his death; here also lie the probable remains of Chevalier Bayard (d. 1542; see p. 713).

Further W. lies the *Jardin de la Ville*, embellished by a bronze statue by Jacob Richier (c. 1620) representing Lesdiguières as Hercules, and a terminus of the *Téléférique*, with its globular cabins, to the *Fort de la Bastille*; see below.

The N. side of the *Pl. St-André* is flanked by the **Palais de Justice**, a characteristic example of Dauphinois architecture, occupying the site of the ancient palace of the dauphins, the oldest part, the doorway of the l. wing, dating from c. 1510; the rest of the wing was rebuilt in the 1890s, while the r. wing, apart from the top storey, dates from after 1539. Certain rooms, possessing impressive ceilings, may be visited on application to the concierge, also the chapel, and the First Chamber, containing woodcarvings executed in 1524 by Paul Jude, a Swabian.

Slight relics of a Roman wall and a round tower lie to the N.

A lane leads E. from the E. side of the Palais de Justice towards the *Pl. Notre-Dame*, with the *Tour Clérieux*, and the sham-Romanesque facade (1885) of the **Cathedral**, a heavy building of various styles and periods (under restoration), with an 11C porch and brick tower. It contains (r. of the choir) a gracefully carved Gothic tabernacle or ciborium of 1457, and a high altar in the Italian taste, presented to the Grande Chartreuse in 1576 by the Chartreuse of Pavia.

From the quay just N.E. of the Palais de Justice one may cross the Isère, which in 1219 almost swept the town away, and it was inundated again in 1859. To the E. of the footbridge the river is spanned by the *Pont de la Citadelle*, beyond which, on the S. bank, is the *Tour de l'Île*, part of the fortifications, on the glacis of which, further E., gardens have been laid out.

The Rue St-Laurent (on the site of *Cularo*; see above) leads N.E. to **St-Laurent**, with an 11C choir and *Crypt* of the 6-7C, a rare Merovingian survival, with 28 pillars (some of them in white Parian marble), with curiously carved capitals.—The nearby *Ponte St-Laurent* was built by Vauban.

From the N. bank opposite the footbridge one may ascend N.W. by the *Montée de Chalemont* (with the *Centre d'Archéologie* at No. 11), with views across the river, to the former convent of *Ste-Marie-d'en Haut*, now accommodating round its cloister the attractively laid out **Musée Dauphinoise**. The chapel dates from 1622. It is largely devoted to the traditional arts and crafts of the province, often displaying remarkable specialised temporary exhibitions, and contains an important centre of documentation.

To the N. are the buildings of the *Institutes of Geology* and *Geography*; while above rears the *Fort de la Bastille*, containing a collection of veteran cars, and providing extensive views. It is best approached by the téléférique (see above). The descent may be made through the *Parc Guy-Pape*, on the E. side of the spur, commanded by the former *Fort Robot*, to the *Jardin des Dauphins*, to emerge on the quay by the 17C *Porte de France*, converted into a war memorial.

Excursions from Grenoble

GRENOBLE TO ST-PIERRE-DE-CHARTREUSE (20.5km). The most direct approach (but see below) is by the D512, leading N.E. from the N. bank of the Isère, which shortly commences to climb, passing near the 11C castle of *Bouquéron* to traverse *Corenc*, before reaching (at 9km) the *Col de Vence*, below (r.) *Fort de St-Eynard* (1379m; *view), easily ascended from *Le Sappey*, and a spur of *Mont Rachais* (l.; 1048m).—4km. *Le Sappey-en-Chartreuse* (frequented by the Grenobloise for skiing), immediately N. of which towers the *Chamechaude* (2082m), the highest point in the *Grande-Chartreuse massif*. The summit is reached without difficulty from (4.5km) the *Col de Porte*, on its W. side; the steep S.E. face is for practised climbers only, while on the N. side is a depression traversed by a deep crevasse, and overhung with precipices.—To the W. of the Col rises *La Pinéa* (1773m). From this point a track ascends 4.5km N.W. towards the summit of the *Charmant-Som* (1867m), commanding a view of the Mont-Blanc massif to the N.E., and of the *Monastery of the Grande-Chartreuse* to the N.—The road now descends through the woods to (8km) **St-Pierre-de-Chartreuse**, see Rte 132B. Here we turn l. towards *St-Laurent-du-Pont*, the entrance to the wilderness in which stand *La Correrie* and the monastery of the *Grande-Chartreuse* (r.) being reached after 2.5km.—The return may be made with ease by descending via (8.5km) *St-Laurent*, there turning l. and keeping straight ahead over the *Col de la Placette* to (15.5km) *Voreppe*, 16km N.W. of Grenoble.

An ALTERNATIVE APPROACH is that from *St-Egrève*, 7km N.W. of Grenoble, there climbing r. into the valleys of the Venice and then the *Tenaison*, passing below the *Nerón* or *Neiron* (1301m), a mountain which has claimed many victims, but which is still a favourite practice ground for experienced rock-climbers, providing several difficult ascents.—4.5km. *Proveysieux* commands a good retrospective view up the valley of the Drac, S. of Grenoble.—To the r. we pass *La Pinéa* (1773m) on ascending to (9km) the *Col de la Charmette* (1150m) between (r.) the *Charmant-Som* (1867m) and *La Sure* (1920m) to the W. The road (D105) continues to the *Belvedere des Sangles*, and descends N.W. above the *Gorges du Guiers-Mort*, passing (l.) the *Chartreuse de Curière* before reaching the D520B just prior to entering *St-Laurent-du-Pont*; see Rte 132B. Turning r. here, the ascent can be made past the entrance to the *Grande-Chartreuse* to (9km) **St-Pierre-de-Chartreuse**, the return to Grenoble being made in the reverse direction to that described above.

GRENOBLE TO URIAGE AND CHAMROUSSE. Driving due E., we cross the by-pass and follow the D524, passing (l.) the hill-top ruins of the 14-16C castle of

Gières, and ascend the valley of the Sonnant to (12.5km) *Uriage-les-Bains*, a small sulphur spa and resort lying in a green basin probably once the bed of a lake. Above rises the *Castle*, much mutilated, with a 16C gateway and two cylindrical towers of the 13C.—Hence the circuit via Chamrousse may be made on the D111 by turning N.E. through *St-Martin-d'Uriage*, then climbing E. to the *Col des Seiglières* and traversing woods to (19km) *Le Recoin-Chamrousse*, a splendidly sited resort below the **Croix de Chamrousse** (2257m), easily accessible by foot or by cableway. it provides extensive views: to the N. over the valley of the *Grésivaudan* to the *Grande-Chartreuse* massif; to the N.E. along the *Belledonne* range, with the *Grand Pic* rising to 2978m; E. to *l'Alpe d'Huez* and *les Grandes Rousses*; S.E. towards the *Ecrins*; S. towards the *Taillefer* (2857m), and S.W. towards the *Vercors* massif and *Mont Aiguille* (2086m), etc.—Continuing S. past the resort of *Roche-Béranger*, the road later descends near (8km) the *Col Luitel* and its small lake, to pass the *Maison Forestière de Prémol*, a restored building of the charmingly sited ruins of the *Chartreuse de Prémol*, founded by Béatrix de Montferrat in 1232 and destroyed at the Revolution.—The circuit is completed on returning to (12km) *Uriage*, 9km S.W. of which lies *Vizille*, in the Romanche valley; see Rte 138A.

For roads from Grenoble to *Lyon*, and *Valence*, see Rtes 131, and 132A, respectively, in reverse; and from Grenoble to *Chambéry*, 132A, likewise. For roads to **Briançon**, and **Sisteron**, see Rtes 136, and 138.

B.   From Grenoble to Die; the Vercors

103km (64 miles). N532. 7.5km *Sassenage*—D531. 25km *Villard-de-Lans*—8.5km where the road for (15.5km) *Pont-en-Royans* forks r.—Here fork l. for (14km) *Les Baraques-en-Vercors*—D518. 6km *La Chapelle-en-Vercors* —D178. 10km *Vassieux-en-Vercors*—32km **Die**.

Maps: IGN 52, or 112; also 305, and 226-9. M 244.

The **Vercors**, extending S.W. from Grenoble, until comparatively recently one of the wildest regions of France, and the occasional haunt of bears, is a pastoral and wooded limestone plateau broken up by mountain ridges and deep valleys. Characteristic of the area are the steep gabled roofs of the houses, to protect them from the wind. Owing to its inaccessibility, it became a rallying-ground for resistance to the Germans in 1942–43, and by 1944 some 3-4000 maquisards here constituted a comparatively well-trained nucleus, sporadically harassing enemy communications. In June 1944 the Germans reacted by attacking in force, but it took them two months to clear the area after a campaign of great severity and cruelty, in which 700 French, including 150 civilians, were killed. Regrettably, indeed tragically, although they received some supplies of arms, the relieving forces they were hoping might land on the plateau never arrived, which caused later recrimination. The district is now largely a *Natural Park*.

An ALTERNATIVE to the first part of the main route described is the D106 climbing l. soon after crossing the *Pont du Drac*, through *Seyssinet*, beneath the 18C château of *Beauregard*, to the S. of which, the 11C church of *Seyssins* preserves good capitals, while to the W. is the so-called 'Désert de Jean-Jacques', a depression amid crags and pines where Rousseau is said to have searched for plants during his wanderings in Dauphiny. A little further on rises the *Tour-Sans-Venin*, a ruin since the 13C, providing extensive views. The road continues to climb to *St-Nizier-du-Moucherotte*, burned by the Germans, and now a small resort on the N.W. slope of the *Moucherotte* (1901m; views).—The road continues through *Lans-en-Vercors*, another summer and winter resort, just beyond which it meets the main road from Sassenage.

The N532 leads N.W. from Grenoble to (7.5km) *Sassenage* (see Rte 132A), where we turn l. and climb steeply to traverse a gorge, later entering the upper valley of the Bourne, to (25km) *Villard-de-Lans*, a pleasant resort amid forests. To the E. rises the *Roc de Cornafion* (2049m), on the ridge forming the E. edge of the Vercors, extending S. from the *Moucherotte* to the *Grande Moucherolle* (2284m), to the S.E., and beyond.

The D215C ascends the *Valchevrière*, to the S.W. of Villard, the hamlet of which was destroyed by the Germans, while Stations of the Cross commemorate the inhabitants butchered in 1944.

Descending the valley of the Bourne past (4km) *Les Jarrands*, from which a r.-hand turning leads to the resorts of (5.5km) *Méaundre* and *Autrans*, the road forks l. at a junction 4.5km beyond.

The r.-hand fork (D531) traverses the *Gorges de la Bourne*, passing near the caverns of *Bournillon* (l.) and *Choranche* (r.) to reach (15.5km) **Pont-en-Royans**, the old capital of the *Royans* or *Royannais*, with picturesque houses clinging to cliffs on either side of the defile, here spanned by a single lofty bridge.—*St-Nazaire-en-Royans* lies 9km further down the valley; see Rte 132A.—For the road hence to *Vassieux*, see below.
   The D518 ascends S. from *Pont-en-Royans* to (2km) *Ste-Eulalie-en-Royans*, there turning E., traversing the narrow limestone fissure of the *Petits-Goulets*, through which the Vernaison issues in a small cascade. The road (completed in 1851) continues to ascend to the *Vallée d'Echevis*, and then passes between the perpendicular cliffs of the *Grands-Goulets*, to emerge into the upland plateau of the Vercors proper at (11.5km) *Les Baraques-en-Vercors*; see below.

The l.-hand fork at 11km. traverses **St-Martin-en-Vercors**, where the *Hôtel Breyton* was a headquarters of the Resistance in the Vercors, to (3km) *Les Baraques-en-Vercors*, rebuilt since its destruction in 1944, beyond which the D518 is followed to (6km) *La Chapelle-en-Vercors*, also rebuilt.—Hence the D178 is followed to the S.W., with the extensive *Forêt de Lente* to the W. beyond the *Serre Plume* (1573m), below which we traverse the *Col de Proncel* (1100m) to (10km) rebuilt **Vassieux-en-Vercors**, with a memorial to its population, massacred by the Germans in 1944, who made a parachute landing on the neighbouring plateau, and a *Musée de la Resistance*.—The exposed *Col de Rousset* (1367m) is reached 9km beyond.—This may also be approached from La Chapelle by a more easterly road, passing near the *Grotte de la Luire*, which served as a shelter for wounded maquis, who were shot out of hand by the Germans when captured.—The actual *Col de Rousset* is avoided by a tunnel, beyond which the road descends in zigzags into the valley of the Comane, to meet the D93 just W. of (23km) **Die**; see Rte 140.—*Crest* lies 37km W.; *Aspres-sur Buëch*, on the N75 (see Rte 138B), lies 60km S.E.

ST-NAZAIRE-EN-ROYANS TO VASSIEUX (44km). The D76 circles S.E. through (9km) *St-Jean-en-Royans*, a large village on the Lyonne, with remarkable baroque boiseries in its church, beyond which we climb above (l.) the rocky cirque of the *Combe Laval* to the *Col de la Machine*; a plunging view into the cliff-bound valley is obtained just to the E., with the *Source of the Cholet*, a 'resurgence' of the Brudoir, which disappears into the limestone further S.—The village of *Lente*, surrounded by its extensive forest, is shortly traversed, to reach (19km) a road fork.
   The r.-hand turning (D199) leads 26km W., providing some remarkable views, via the *Col de la Bataille* (1313m), to **Léoncel**, on the S.W. edge of the Vercors massif, 33km E. of Valence. It retains the ruins of a Cistercian abbey founded in 1137, the church of which has a Romanesque nave and aisles.—The D70 descends S. hence to meet the D93 6km E. of Crest, via *Plan-de-Baix*, from which the *Gorges d'Omblèze*, to the N.E. may be visited.
   From this junction, the D76 continues S.E., passing near the *Grotte du Brudoir* (r.), the apparent source of that stream, and later, a track to the ski-slopes and ice-cavern of *Font-d'Urle*, to (16km) *Vassieux*; see above.

134 Chambéry to Chamonix

A. Via Annecy and Bonneville

144km (89 miles). N201. 16km **Aix-les-Bains**—N201. 33km
Annecy—N203. 30km *La Roche-sur-Furon*—7.5km *Bonneville*—
N205. 13.5km *Cluses*—16km *Sallanches*—28km **Chamonix**.

Maps: IGN 53, or 112; for the Mont Blanc massif, see 231-2. M
244.

The A41, continued by the B41 motorway, now provides a rapid
route most of the way.

CHAMBÉRY (54,900 Chambériens), once the capital of the *Duchy of
Savoy*, and now préfecture of the department of *Savoie*, is situated
on the Leysse, here partly canalised, between the massifs of the
Grande-Chartreuse (S.) and the *Bauges* (N.E.). It is an important centre of communications, preserving a number of dignified old streets
of character, and its ancient ducal château. Its vermouth and
chocolate 'Truffes de Chambéry' are reputed.

The rock of *Lémenc*, on the r. bank of the river, takes its name from the Gallo-
Roman settlement of *Lemencum*, but the present town grew up around a castle
founded by Count Thomas I in 1232. Although superseded in the 16C by Turin
as the administrative centre of the extensive domains of the House of Savoy, it
remained the capital of the province until it was united with France in 1860. It
had been several times occupied by the French during the 16-18C, and went
through a period of declining importance, being described by Horace Walpole as
'a little nasty old hole', and 'antique capital of a dismal duchy'. It was, nevertheless, according to Young, 'the winter residence of almost all the nobility of
Savoy'. A sector of the town near the station was destroyed by American bomb-

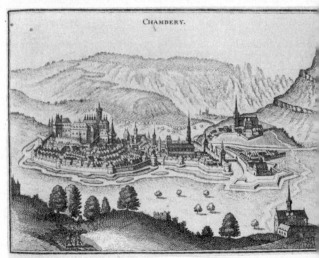

*A 17C engraving of Chambery, with St-Pierre on the hill to
the right*

ing during the Second World War, and several quaint old houses in the Rue St-Antoine were destroyed by a ravaging fire in 1946.

It was the birthplace of Amadeus VII, the 'Comte Rouge' (1360–91; cf. Thonon); Xavier de Maistre (1763–1852, in St Petersbourg), author of the 'Voyage autor de ma Chambre', and his brother Joseph (1753–1821); and the Comte de Boigne (1751–1830), who amassed a fortune in the service of the Rajah Scindia, much of which he left to the town.

Rousseau and Mme de Warens lived together intermittently between 1735 and 1740 in the 'country' villa of *Les Charmettes*, some 2km S.E. (as described in his 'Confessions', book VI), which has been converted into a small museum.

Near the N. end of the Blvd de la Colonne stands the classical church of *Notre-Dame* (1636), S.E. of which is the striking *Fontaine des Eléphants*, a monument in gratitude to De Boigne (see above).

Close by are the *Théâtre*, and the **Cathedral**, a 15-16C building with a much-restored portal of 1506, 19C trompe l'oeil decoration, a 15C wooden Virgin, and the tomb of Antoine Favre (cf. Annecy). The Sacristy contains good Louis-XIII boiseries and a 10C Byzantine diptych. There is a lapidary collection in the 17C cloister.

Opposite is the former *Bishop's Palace*, now housing the **Musée Savoisien**, largely devoted to its history and folk art, with a good collection of local archaeology, particularly finds from the Lac du Bourget, bronze ornaments from burials at St-Jean-de-Belleville; Roman and Samian pottery; a bronze *Caduceus* from Lémenc; and a late-Roman statuette known as the Venus de Detrier.

On the FIRST FLOOR are several paintings of interest, among them *G.-P. Bagetti* (1764–1831), Landscapes; *J. Massotti*, View of the Pl. St-Léger c. 1815; and an *anon.* late 18C View. Also a late 15C Christ at the Gate of Hell, and several Savoyard primitives, among them panels by *Gaspart Masery* (1559), and a Last Supper, by *Godefroy* (1482).

There are several old mansions in the Rue de la Croix-d'Or, a short distance S. of the cathedral, among them Nos 1, 2, 10, 14 (the *Hôtel Costa*, where Rousseau served as music-master), and 15. The **Pl. St-Léger** (in which No. 54 was a town-house occupied by Mme de Warens and Rousseau in 1735), is soon reached. The labyrinth of passages (the 'allées') behind these houses provided access to the ramparts, and several are connected by underground passages.

At the N. end of the Place we meet the imposing Rue de Boigne, divided by the *Pl. d'Octagone*, with handsome arcades ('portiques'), which leads from the Elephant fountain to the *Pl. du Château*. Just N. of this junction is the Rue Juiverie.

The **Château** of the dukes of Savoy, founded in 1232, remodelled in the 14-15C and since enlarged, is still a picturesque and imposing stronghold. The *Préfecture* occupies a heavy wing replacing part burned down in 1743 and again in 1789. The *Chapel*, founded c. 1420, retains fine lancet windows; its main facade of c. 1645 replaces one destroyed by fire in 1532. Lamartine was married here in 1820. A 15C crypt may also be seen.

Passing through the 15C *Portail St-Dominique*, re-erected here from a demolished Dominican convent, we follow the Rue J.-P. Veyrat to the N., where opposite the *Palais de Justice* is the **Musée des Beaux-Arts**, above the *Library*.

Notable are a Holy Family, by the *Ferrara School*; *Battista Dossi*, Euterpe; *Santi di Tito*, Crucifixion, and Portrait of a man and woman; *Ucello*, Portrait of a youth; *Guercino*, Virgin and Child; *Sassoferrato*, Virgin and Child; *anon.* late 16C Italian, Male portrait; *School of Stanzioni*, Magdalene; *Luca Giordano*, Ptolemy; *Solimena*, Deposition; *Jean de Boulogne*, Magdalene; *School of Georges de la*

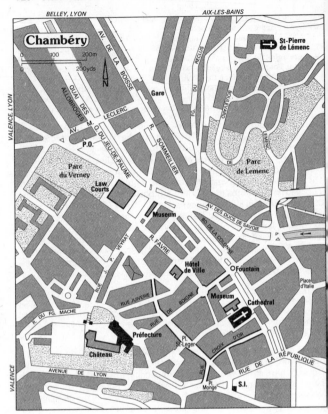

Tour, Blind musicians brawling; *Colson*, Portrait of an ecclesiastic; *Boucher*, Scène galante; *Vigée-Lebrun*, Mont Blanc; *Courbet*, Portrait of Murger; *Joos van Cleve*, Male portrait; *Master of Antwerp of 1518*, Adoration of the Magi; *Bonington*, Sketch; several Dutch and Alsatian Still-lifes; *Louis Watteau*, Cephalus and Pocris, and Mercury and Argus; Portraits of various attributions; a section devoted to Savoyard artists, including works by *J. Massotti* (1765–1842), *P.E. Moreau* (Annecy, 1766-Chambéry, 1839), Portrait of Gén. de Boigne; *Antoine Baud*, Portrait of Lamartine (1840); and *B. Molin*, (Chambéry, 1810–94), Portrait of J. de Maistre.

Also a collection of majolica, and ivories, and an astrolabe of 1565.

From the *Pl. de la Liberation*, further E., the Blvd de Lémenc climbs c. 1km through a park, off which we turn r. to approach ***St-Pierre**, rebuilt in

1445–1513, containing the tomb of De Boigne, and the shrine of St Concord (archbishop of Armagh, who died here in 1176 on his return from Rome); in the churchyard is the grave of Mme de Warens (d. 1762). The *Crypt* incorporates a 6C baptistry with possibly Roman columns, and a 15C extension containing a Deposition. In 1497 Count Philippe II died in a medieval house adjacent to the church.

The road (D991) continues N. direct to *Aix-les-Bains*, but the more attractive lake-side approach is preferable, which skirts the *Lac du Bourget* (see below) for c. 4.5km before circling up to (1.5km) **Aix-les-Bains** (23,500 inhab.), a dull but long fashionable spa, lying on the lower slopes of *Mont Revard* (1537m) and separated from the lake by a ridge.

Its waters were taken by the Allogroges even before the Roman invasions (c. 125 B.C.). The Romans established a thermal station here, its springs being known as *Aquae Gratianea* or *Aquae Domitianae*, but interest in its qualities was not revived until the 16C, and it was not until 1779 that a 'modern' bath-house was built, by Victor Amadeus III, which was later incorporated into the present edifice. Lamartine visited the place in 1816, which together with his romantic attachment to Mme Charles ('Elvire'), or Julie Descherettes, who died the following year, is recorded in his poem 'Le Lac', and his novel 'Raphaël'.

From the main transverse Blvd President-Wilson, the Av. Charles de-Gaulle (opposite the station) ascends E. past gardens and the *Palais de Savoie* (1848, but reconstructed in 1936, and modernised after a fire in 1963), one of the main centres of gaming and socialising. Further E. is the *Hôtel de Ville*, housed in a Renaissance château of 1513, and incorporating the cella of the so-called 'Temple of Diana', and a lapidary collection, including a sun-dial and several stellae with inscriptions describing life in the Gallo-Roman city. Beyond stands the *Arch of Campanus* (3-4C), in a debased Doric style, raised by Lucius Pompeius Campanus to the memory of his family.

Opposite is the *Thermes* (last reconstructed in 1972), founded by Victor Emmanuel II in 1857, which incorporated the 18C bath-house. It was much enlarged in the 1930s, when Lamartine's house was demolished to that end. Relics of the Roman baths were moved to the first floor.

A short distance to the N. is the **Musée du Docteur-Faure**, largely devoted to late 19C-early 20C art, collected by Dr Jean Faure (1862–1942). It includes *Foujita*, Two friends, and Female portrait; *Lebourg*, The port of Rouen; several water-colours by *Pissarro*, and *Victor Vignon*; *Maurice Asselin*, Nude; *Degas*, Mauve dancers, Vase of carnations, and fan, and two sculptures of Dancers; *Marquet*, The Pont-Neuf; *Vuillard*, Reader and bust; *Renoir*, Nude; representative works by *Jongkind*, *Lépine*, *Cezanne*, *Sisley*, *Corot*, *Boudin*, *Monticelli*, and *Fantin-Latour*. Sculptures: *Carpeaux*, Neapolitan fisherboy; *Rodin*, Pallas succube, Fall of Icarus, Rhea, Man walking, and wash drawings; also several small sculptures by *Bourdelle*.

The **Lac du Bourget**, 18km long, and between 1.5km and 3km broad, is the largest lake in France. It has a beach and small harbour, from which excursions commence, and boats may be hired, but it should be noted that even in fine weather it is subject to sudden squalls. Lamartine's rescue of 'Elvire' from a capsized boat was the first episode of their romance.

The promoted excursion is to *Hautecombe*, on the W. bank (but see below), also approached by road by the D48 skirting the E. bank below a ridge of hills. At the N. end, beyond which, to the N.W., rises the *Grand-Colombie* (1531m), is (15km) *Châtillon*, the old castle of which was the cradle of Celestine IV, author of a history of Scotland, who held the papal throne for 17 days in 1241.—Another 11.5km brings one to the well-sited Benedictine monastery (previously Cistercian) of **Hautecombe**, the mausoleum of 43 members of the House of Savoy between the years 1189 and 1502, among them Guillaume (d. 1239), bishop of Valence, Winchester, and Liège; Pierre II (d. 1268), builder of the Savoy palace in London; his brother Boniface (d. 1270), archbishop of Canterbury; Amadeus VI, and Amadeus VII (d. 1383, and 1391 respectively). Unfortunately, the church was virtually rebuilt after 1825 in a debased florid Gothic style, and contains little else but some 250 examples of tasteless statuary.

From Aix, the N201 is followed to the N. to (11km) *Albens*, of some importance in the Roman period, which gave its name to the district; see *Rumilly*, 10km N.; Rte 130.

Here we fork r., following the motorway, at 6km passing (r.) *Alby-sur-Chéran*, with an old arcaded square, to the E. of which rises the ridge of *Le Semnoz*, reaching 1699m at the *Crêt de Châtillon*, providing a fine view over the *Lac d'Annecy*.

16km. **ANNECY** (51,600 Annéciens), préfecture of *Haute-Savoie*, is charmingly situated at the N.W. extremity of its lake, at the foot of a spur of the Semnoz, and overlooked to the E. by *Mont Veyrier* (1291m). Its old centre is intersected by small canals and flower-decked quays; the Canal du Thiou, to the S., conducting the waters of the lake to the river Fier. Its arcaded streets are particularly attractive, and many consider it the pleasantest centre for excursions in Savoy; others prefer Chambéry.

Traces of Gallo-Roman *Boutae* have been found to the N.E. towards *Annecy-le-Vieux*, but Annecy itself, the capital of the counts of Genevois in the 10C, and after 1401 a possession of the dukes of Savoy, was of slight importance until 1535, when it became the seat of a bishop and of various monastic institutions expelled from Geneva at the Reformation. François de Sales was bishop in 1602–22, and here in 1610 his friend Jeanne de Chantal founded the first convent of the Visitation. It was at Annecy in 1728 that Rousseau, at the age of sixteen, found a refuge with Mme de Warens (12 years older), and several passages

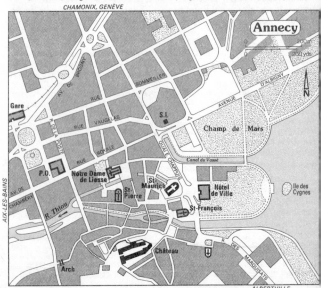

of his 'Confessions' relate to their life here, prior to moving to *Les Charmettes*, near Chambéry.

Among natives were Robert of Geneva, who became antipope at Avignon 1378–84) under the style of Clement VII (one of 'two dogs snarling over a bone', as Wyclif called them); and Eustache Chappuis (d. 1555), an ambassador of the Emperor Charles V, and founder of the Collège Chappuisien (demolished), where François de Sales and Berthollet were pupils. Eugène Sue (1804–57), author of 'Le Juif errant' and other novels, sought refuge here when exiled from France on account of his protest against the coup d'état of 2 Dec. 1851. He died at the *Maison de la Tour* on the lake, and is buried in the cemetery of Annecy.

The Rue Royale, dividing the modern town from the old centre, leads N.E. towards the lake, passing (r.) *N.-D.-de-Liesse*, rebuilt in the classical style in 1851, with the exception of its 16C tower; the adjacent old Hôtel de Ville has a fine 18C facade. The street is continued by the arcaded Rue du Pâquier, in which No. 12 (l.) is the *Maison de Sales* (1688), built by a nephew of François de Sales, decorated by figures representing the Seasons, and later a town house of the kings of Sardinia.

This main artery, a pedestrian precinct at its E. end, is extended past the *Pl. de la Liberation* by the Av. d'Albigny, flanked by the massive *Préfecture* to the N., and to the S. by the riverside esplanade of the Champs-de-Mars.—Hence the *Pont d'Amour* spans a canal to the *Jardins-Public*, to the E. of which is the little *Île des Cygnes*.—To the W. is the *Hôtel de Ville*, with a porticoed inner courtyard.

On the W. side of the *Pl. Hôtel de Ville* rises *St-Maurice 1422–45), originally part of a Dominican convent, with good Flamboyant windows in its distorted apse. On the N. choir wall are a Deposition by Pourbus, and a recently uncovered wall-painting showing the tomb of Philibert de Monthoux, a mid-15C benefactor. On the S. wall is a Holy Family by Jan Kraeck (1577). A 16C mural of the Virgin and Saints, and a carved pulpit of 1715 will be noticed.

To the S. is *St-François*, containing the former tombs of François de Sales and Jeanne de Chantal; see below. It was the chapel of the old convent of the Grande-Visitation, in which Mme de Warens abjured Calvinism in 1726.

Further S., a bridge crosses the *Canal de Thiou*, providing a picturesque view of the **Palais de l'Île**, an ancient and heterogeneous pile which has been successively a chancellory, mint, law-court, and council chamber, and now accommodates temporary exhibitions, and a small lapidary collection.

In the Rue de l'Île, on the S. bank of the canal, No. 1 was the mansion of Mme de Charmoisy, whose correspondence with François de Sales prompted him to compose (in 1609) the 'Introduction to a Devout Life'.—Further W., No. 18 in the arcaded Rue Ste-Claire is the 16C *Hôtel Favre*, where Antoine Favre, author of the 'Code Fabrien', founded the Academie Florimontane under the inspiration of De Sales some 28 years prior to the founding of the Academie Française; he later presented the building to De Sales as an episcopal palace.

To the N., in the Rue J.-J. Rousseau, stands a later *Bishop's Palace* 1785) on the site of Mme de Warens' residence, now inhabited by police. The adjacent **Cathedral** is an uninspired Gothic edifice of 535, in which Rousseau was a chorister. It contains a Deposition attrib. to *Caravaggio*; an Adoration of the Magi, by *Fabrici*; and a Deliverance of St Peter, by *Mazzola*.—No. 13 was the old choir school where Rousseau studied music; No. 15, the *Hôtel Lambert*, was the first residence of De Sales when bishop.

From near the E. end of the Rue-Claire the steep Rue du Château ascends to the **Château**, on a commanding site dominating the old town. The main gateway is late 14C. Notable are the massive square *Tour de la Reine* (12C), the *Tour St-Paul* (1383), *Tour St-Pierre* (1430), and *Tour Perrière* (1445). The edifice has been restored to house the ***Musée du Château**, the entrance to which is in the Renaissance *Logis de Nemours* (l.)

The archaeological section is largely devoted to Gallo-Roman *Boutae*, with a good collection of pottery, and an Etruscan mirror. The FIRST FLOOR contains collections of furniture, lit-clos, coffers, carved woodwork, pewter, and ceramics, etc.; also carved wooden statues, including a fine 15C Virgin and Child, and a St Peter. Also a remarkable series of models showing the timber framework of local styles of houses, etc.—Further rooms are devoted to *Geology* and *Natural History*, with extensive collections of minerals, and fossils.—The splendid *Salle des Fêtes* contains photomurals of old plans of Annecy, Chambéry, Thonon, and Montmélian.

The collection of paintings, mainly of the French School, has not yet been displayed.

Hence a road ascends the *Crêt du Maure* for c. 1km to the *Basilique de la Visitation* (1930), remarkable only for the views it commands, preserving the remains of François de Sales (1567– 1622; canonised 1665), leader of the Roman Catholic revival in Savoy, and Jeanne de Chantal (1572– 1641; canonised 1767), foundress of the order of the Visitation, and grandmother of Mme de Sévigné.

N.E. of the modern town stands *Annecy-le-Vieux*, only of interest for its 11C belfry with twin Romanesque bays.

A short EXCURSION W. of Annecy is that up the limestone *Gorges du Fier*, and to the *Château de Montrottier*, a much-restored building of the 14-16C, containing a miscellaneous collection of antiquities, notable among which are bronze bas-reliefs by Hans and Peter Vischer (1520– 40).

The **Lac d'Annecy**, 14km long, and 3.5km across at its widest point, enclosed by gently sloping orchards and meadows with their background of mountains, is one of the more attractive in the French Alps, although in danger of over-exploitation. For roads skirting either bank; see below. The lake has recently been the object of decontamination and purification.

ANNECY TO UGINE (37km), FOR ALBERTVILLE OR MEGÈVE. The N508 skirts the W. bank of the lake below the shoulder of the *Semnoz* to (14km) **Duingt**, with two castles, one 11C, in ruins; the other rebuilt except for a cylindrical tower, on a peninsula at the narrows of the lake. For the capture of the adjacent hamlet of *Brédanne* by Spanish troops in 1742, the court of Madrid amused Europe by celebrating a 'Te Deum'.—We meet the road following the E. bank some 5km beyond, at *Doussard*.—7km. *Faverges*, a small industrial town in view of the summit of Mont Blanc, named after the copper and iron mines (fabricae) which have existed here since the 12C. Its old castle has been put to commercial use.—Some 6km S. lies the fortress-like abbey of *Tamié*, founded in 1132, rebuilt in the 17C and restored in the 19C by Trappists; its cheese is reputed.—11km. **Ugine**, with electro-metallurgical works, preserves a tower of its castle, destroyed in the 13C. Here the N212 is met 8km N. of *Albertville*; see Rte 134B.

ANNECY TO LA CLUSAZ (32km). The D909 circles the N. end of the lake below *Mont Veyrier* (1291m; cableway to near the summit), commanding a view extending to Lac Léman, Mont Blanc, and the Dauphiny Alps.—5km. *Veyrier-du-Lac*, where we fork l.

The lakeside road continues S. to (15km) *Doussard* via (4km) *Menthon-St Bernard*, the burial-place of the historian Hippolyte Taine (1828– 93); its *Castl* (13-16C) was the birthplace in the 10C of St Bernard of Menthon, the 'apostle of the Alps' and founder of the hospices on the Great and Little St Bernard passes.—3km beyond lies *Talloires*, birthplace of C.L. Berthollet (1742– 1822) he chemist. Most of the former Benedictine abbey is now a hotel, but vestiges of ts 11C church remain. To the S.E. rises the prominent *Tournette* (2351m).

Turning away from the lake, after 11km the *Cemetery de Morette* (r.) is passed, n which the heroes of Glierès lie. The bleak plateau of *Glières*, to the N., was the cene in Feb.-June 1944 of a famous episode of the Resistance, in which 500 men f the maquis were repeatedly attacked by the Germans in increasing force, los-ng over half their number (including the legendary 'Tom'—Lieut. Morel), but ac-ounting for 1000 Germans. The plateau was later re-occupied and supplied by ▶arachute, and became a focus of preparation for the army of iberation.—4.5km. *Thônes*, a small resort known for its 'reblochon' cheese, ▶reserving a church of 1664 with a tower of 1562, and with a small folklore nuseum. Near-by is the manor of *La Tour*, mentioned by Rousseau in his 'Con-▶essions' (Book IV).—8.5km. *St-Jean-de-Sixt*, 3km N.E. of which is *Le Grand-▶ornand*, which with *Chinaillon*, further up the valley, is an important skiiing ▶entre, as is *La Clusaz*, 3km S.E. of St-Jean, on the N.W. slopes of the *Chaîne des* ▶ravis, rising further N.E. to 2752m at the *Pointe-Percée*. The road from La ▶lusaz crosses the *Col des Aravis* to (19km) *Flumet*; see Rte 134B.

▶NNECY TO GENEVA (43km). The N201 leads N., shortly passing (l.) the 13C ▶hâteau of *Monthoux*, to (15km) the *Ponts de la Caille*, where the Usses is cross-▶d by a bridge of 1928 commanding a view of Charles Albert's elegant suspen-ion bridge of 1838, now closed to traffic.—3km. *Cruseilles*, on the S. slope of ▶ooded *Mont Salève*, with the 14-15C *Maison de Fesigny*, and the restored cas-▶le of *Pontverre*.—9km. *Le Châble*, with relics of the 11C *Chartreuse de Pommier*, ▶eyond which we fork l. to (6km) *St-Julien-en-Genevois* (Customs); **Geneva** lies ▶0km N.E.

he N203 bears N. and then N.E. from Annecy, at 14km passing ▶km W. of *Thorens*, birthplace of François de Sales in 1567; in the ▶hâteau are preserved documents, portraits (including paintings by ▶an Dyck), and other mementoes, together with some concerning ▶avour, who was related to the De Sales family by marriage.—Fur-▶her E. is the *Plateau de Glières*; see above.

The road descends to (16km) **La Roche-sur-Foron**, retaining some ▶6C houses in the Rue des Fours, and noted for its tanneries. it was ▶he first town in France to be lit by electricity (1885). Remains of the ▶2C *Château de Saix*, on a rock which gives the town its name, com-▶and a fine view of the Arve valley. Roads lead N. to *Annemasse* ▶nd *Bonne*; see Rte 130.

7.5km **Bonneville** (9,100 inhab.), with a handsome bridge over the ▶rve, here embanked by Charles-Félix, king of Sardinia. To the N.E. ▶ises *Le Môle* (1863m); to the S., the *Pointe d'Andey* (1877m).—The ▶oad continues E., parallel to the motorway to (13.5km) *Cluses*, ▶here in 1848 a National School of Watchmaking was ▶stablished.—After 3km a l.-hand turning ascends to the ski resorts f *Les Carroz-d'Arâches*, and *Flaine*.

The main road veers S., with a view S.E. of *Mont Blanc*.—To the r. ▶ises the *Pointe Percée* (2752m) on approaching (13km) *Sallanches*, ▶ebuilt after a fire in 1840, above which is the small resort of ▶ordon.—Here the N212 forks r. via *Combloux*, another well-sited ▶inter-sporting centre, to (13km) **Mègeve**; see Rte 134B.

The road circles S.E. to (8km) *Le Fayet*, just S.E. of which is **St-▶ervais-les-Bains**, a small summer and winter resort on the Bon-▶ant, in a sheltered position at the mouth of the *Vallée de Montjoie*. ▶rom Le Fayet a tramway ascends to *Le Nid d'Aigle* on the lower ▶lopes of **Mont Blanc**, dominating the mountainscape to the S.E., ris-▶g to 4807m; see below. Closer peaks are those of *Le Prarion* ▶967m), to the E., *Mont d'Arbois* (1827m; S.W.) and *Mont Joly* ▶525m), further S.—8.5km S. in the valley lies *Les Contamines-*

Montjoie, with its ski-slopes. At the head of the valley is the *Col du Bonhomme* (2339m).

Immediately N. of Le Fayet is *Passy*, from which a steep serpentine road ascends to the *Plateau d'Assy*, where *N.-D.-de-Toute-Grâce* (1950; by Novarina) is remarkable only for the quantity of modern art it contains, including a mosaic by Léger, a tapestry by Lurçat, sculpture by Lipchitz, a copper Christ by Germaine Richier, glass designed by Rouault, a baptistry decorated by Chagall, and altars by Bonnard, and Matisse, et al.

The road now ascends on a remarkable series of viaducts including that of *Des Egratz*, 2275m long, round a spur of the Mont Blanc massif, at 11km by-passing (r.) *Les Houches*, another winter resort.—At 7km the N. entrance to the **Mont Blanc Tunnel** lies to the r.

Linking Chamonix with Courmayeur, it is 11,600m long, and was bored between 1957–65. It ascends from 1274m on the French side to 1381m on the Italian, where the Customs houses are grouped, and has a capacity of 450 vehicles an hour (toll).
    Courmayeur (*Cormaggiore* in Italian) lies 5km from the S. exit, and 5km beyond is the road junction of *Pré-St-Didier.*—**Aosta** lies 33km further E., from which the autostrada A5 leads 113km to **Turin**; see *Blue Guide Northern Italy.* The *Col du Petit St-Bernard* lies 23km S.W. of Pré-St-Didier; see Rte 134C.

Chamonix lies 3km N.E. of the entrance, but is also approached by l.-hand fork W. of the tunnel. **Chamonix-Mont-Blanc**, as it is officially styled, once a typical Alpine village (1037m) in an almost inaccessible valley watered by the Arve, is now perhaps the most famous tourist resort at the foot of the Alps. Its resident population is 9,300 Chamoniards, but with some hundreds of thousands of visitors a year, it presents a busy cosmopolitan scene both in summer and winter, while the piercing of the tunnel and construction of motorways approaching each end has caused it to become additionally accessible and important as a resort and stopping place. Its chief characteristic is the number of hotels of all sizes it contains, but all man-made constructions are dwarfed and overshadowed by the mighty mass of *Mont Blanc* looming up to the S.E.

The inscribed stone of Prarion attests that the area was known to the Romans, and in the Middle Ages the valley paid tribute to a powerful Benedictine priory founded here at the end of the 11C. This was burned down in 1758, and in 1786 the inhabitants of the district purchased their freedom.
    Chamonix was 'discovered' in 1741 by a party of English travellers led by William Windham, and it is to his glowing account of its charms that the valley owes the foundation of its popularity. Since 1760, when De Saussure first offered a reward for the ascent of Mont Blanc, the history of Chamonix has been bound up with the mountain; see below. It attracted many distinguished visitors during the early 19C, including Chateaubriand (who disliked the place), Shelley, Byron, Southey, Wordsworth, and Faraday (who praised it highly), while its fame was finally sealed for the English by the approval of Ruskin. Most visitors walked up to the Montenvers, at least, and Huxley has recorded his expedition to the Grands Mulets. Alexandre Stavisky (1886–1934), the swindler, is said to have committed suicide near here, when his hideout was approached by the police.

The town itself is of slight interest, although the main 'Place' is a centre of considerable animation in the mornings when guides and the guided assemble for the day's excursion. Opposite the railway station is a litte *English Church*, besides which are the graves of Capt. Arkwright, and other victims of Mont Blanc; beyond the *Gare du Montenvers* is the *New Cemetery*, in which lie Edward Whymper

1840–1911), the Alpinist; and Louis Lachenal (d. 1955), the conqueror of Annapurna.

Facilities for every variety of winter sport are provided, at a price, and the snow lasts from the middle of December until the beginning of April. Most international contests take place between Christmas and early March. For details, and for general information about excursions and ascents apply to the S.I., just W. of the town centre, near the main church.

A variety of cableways and ski-lifts, etc. ascend to several circumjacent peaks, among them *Le Brévent* (2526m) to the N., and the *Aiguille du Midi* (3842m), almost exactly above the tunnel. A rack-railway ascends from the *Gare de Montenvers* to approach the *Mer de Glace*, a remarkable sweep of glacier.

***Mont Blanc** (4807m), the loftiest of the Alps and the highest peak in Western Europe, is the culminating summit of the great mountain mass which divides the valley of Chamonix from the valley of Courmayeur, and serves as a watershed between the basins of the Rhône and the Po. This huge ridge also forms a partition wall between France and Italy, but its E. slopes are in Switzerland, and the confines of the three countries meet on the summit of *Mont Dolent* (2823m), further to the N.E. On every side it is surrounded by peaks second in importance to the giant itself, and by pointed 'aiguilles', some of which still defy the climbers' skill, and down its slopes stream huge glaciers.

A mention in the earliest charter of Chamonix (1091) of the 'rupes quae vocatur alba' may possibly be the first reference to Mont Blanc, but in the Middle Ages it seems generally to have been known as 'Les Glacières' or 'La Montagne Maudite'. The present name occurs repeadedly in 17-18C writings. Bp Burnet, in 1685, refers to it as 'the hill called Maudit or Cursed, two miles in perpendicular height, and of which one-third is always covered with snow'.

Until 1760 its rocks and glaciers were deserted save by chamois hunters and searchers after crystals, but in that year H.B. de Saussure (1740–99) made his first visit to Chamonix, and was so impressed by the majesty of the mountain that he offered a reward to whoever made the first ascent to the summit. Numerous unsuccessful attemps by local men led to a more organised expedition in 1783 by Marc-Théodore Bourrit, leader of the cathedral choir at Geneva, and Dr Paccard of Chamonix priory. In 1784 the *Bosses* were attained; in July 1786, the *Rochers Rouges*, this time by Jacques Balmat. Finally, on 8 Aug. 1786, Balmat and Paccard reached the summit. De Saussure himself made the ascent on 3 Aug. 1787, six days after which Col Beaufoy made the first English ascent. An accident in 1820, when Dr Hamel and his party were swept away by an avalanche, led to the abandonment of the old route, and in 1827 a new route through the *Corridor* was first successfully made. The first woman to climb Mont Blanc was Mlle Henriette d'Angerville (1838), for although the summit had been attained by Marie Paradis of Chamonix in 1809, she was carried by her companions for a great part of the way! The route usually followed nowadays (via the *Bosses du Dromadaire*) was discovered in 1859 by the Rev. C. Hudson and his party. The first ascent from Courmayeur was made in 1864. The first winter ascent was made on 31 Jan. 1876 by Miss Arabella Straton, who later became Mme Charlet, having married her guide.

The ascent normally occupies two days, and the route from Chamonix is the most frequented and easiest, but guides are essential.

The *View from the summit (when not obscured by cloud), is remarkable rather for its extent than for any feature of individual beauty. The Alps are visible from Dauphiny to the Bernina; the Jura appears like a relief plan, with the plain of the Saône stretching out behind it to the Côte d'Or. The Lombard plain is hidden by intervening ranges, but the line of the Appennines extends S.E. beyond the limit of vision.

CHAMONIX TO MARTIGNY (42km). The N506 ascends N.E. to (8km) *Argentière* (1253m), a well-sited centre for winter sports, and particularly for ascents towards the S., where rise the *Aiguilles Vertes* (4122m), and S.E., where *Mont Dolent* (3823m) rises above the head of the *Glacière d'Argentière*, etc. Other resorts in the area are *Montroc, Tré-le-Champ* and *Le Tour*. Passing the *Col des Montets* (1461m) we enter at 7km the *Vallorcine*, formerly *Valorsine* (*Vallum Ursinum*, the bear's valley), first mentioned in 1264, when the prior of Chamonix undertook to build a church there for a German-speaking colony which had emigrated from the Valais. This and its successors having been swept away by avalanches, the present building is protected by a strong rampart. To the W. rises *Le Buet* (3099m), an easy climb well rewarded by a splendid view of Mont Blanc.—The Swiss frontier (Customs) lies 3km further N.E., whence the road zigzags down to (20.5km) *Martigny*, 44km S.E. of *Ste-Gingolph* on Lac Léman (see Rte 130), and approximately the same distance from **Montreux**.

B.   Via Albertville and Megève

116km (72 miles). N6. 28km—N90. 21km **Albertville**—N212.
9km *Ugine*—23km **Megève**—D909. 11km **St-Gervais**—N205.
24km **Chamonix**.

Maps: IGN 53, or 112. M 244.

The road drives E. from **Chambéry** (Rte 134A) and then S.E. through (6km) *Challes-les-Eaux*, a small spa.

Just beyond, a winding road climbs l. to the high-lying village of *La Thuile*, near a small lake at the S. promontory of the Bauges plateau, with a magnificent view down the Gresivaudan valley towards Grenoble. The main route may be regained just N.E. of Montmélian.

9km. *Montmélian* (see Rte 132A), where we veer N.E. up the Isère valley.

Ahead rises the *Dent d'Arcusaz* (2076m), below which is the conspicuously sited castle of *Miolans*, once belonging to one of the most ancient and powerful families of Savoy. On the extinction of the male line in 1523 it was bought by Duc Charles III and made a state prison; among its prisoners was the Marquis de Sade, in 1773; the keep, dungeons, and 15C chapel, may be visited.

At 13km, below Miolans, the N6 forks r.; see Rte 135.

We continue N.E. traversing the marshy valley between wooded crags. At 21km Albertville lies 2km N.; for the road hence to *Bourg-St-Maurice*, see Rte 134C, and likewise for the route via *Beaufort*.

Albertville (17,500 Albertvillois) is a small industrial town on the Arly just above its confluence with the Isère, and is named in honour of Charles Albert of Sardinia, who founded it in 1835 (and died in 1849 at Oporto, having abdicated after the battle of Novarro).

In striking contrast is **Conflans**, with its steep and narrow lanes, perched on a commanding ridge to the E., approached by the Pont des Adoubes, and a road ascending to a gateway, a relic of its fortifications dismantled by François I in 1536. The *Church*, with crude painting on its facade, was rebuilt in the 18C after a fire in 1632, and restored in 1954, and contains a well-carved pulpit, and a font from the abbey of Tamié. In the main square is the 14C *Maison Rouge*, originally a convent, containing a small collection of bygones. The adjacent terrace commands a view down the valley towards the Grande-Chartreuse massif. The *Tour Sarrasine*, to the W., is said to date from the 11C; while above the village is the 15C *Château Rouge*, a ducal residence. On a height to the E. is the *Fort du Mont*, likewise providing extensive vistas.

At 8km N. of Albertville we turn r., by-passing (l.) *Ugine* (see Rte

134A), and thread the imposing *Gorges de l'Arly* to (13km) *Fumet*, with old galleried houses overlooking the river, and a church with 16C statues.—*La Clusaz* (see Rte 134A) lies 19km N.W. over the *Col de Aravis* (1486m).—*N.-D.-de-Bellecombe*, and *Crest-Voland*, to the S., are ski-resorts, as is *Praz-sur-Arly*—with a view towards *Mont Blanc* to the E. beyond *Mont Joly*—which is traversed en route to (10km) *Megève*, at the head of the valley.

Megève (1113m; 5,400 inhab.), a fashionable and flourishing winter-sports centre, providing all the facilities expected of such resorts, lies on a sunny upland plateau, having grown rapidly in the 1920s around the old village, preserving the round tower of a former Benedictine priory, and a church, mainly 17C, but with a late Gothic apse.

To the S.E. rises *Mont Joly* (2525m), and further E. the view is dominated by *Mont Blanc* (4807m), for which see Rte 134A. Immediately to the E. rises *Mont d'Arbois* (1827m).

A l.-hand fork at 4km leads shortly to *Combloux*; the r.-hand fork turns E., with views N. over the Arve valley, to (7km) *St-Gervais-les-Bains*, and for **Chamonix**, some 25km further E.; see Rte 134A.

C.   Via Albertville, Moûtiers, Bourg-St-Maurice, and Courmayeur

185km (115 miles). N6. 28km—N90. 21km **Albertville**—25km **Moûtiers**—28km *Bourg-St-Maurice*—31km *Col du Petit St-Bernard*—23km *Pré St-Didier*—5km **Courmayeur**—*Mont Blanc tunnel*—24km **Chamonix**.

Maps: IGN 53, or 112; also 235-7. M 244.

For the road from Chambéry to *Albertville*, see Rte 134B.

An ALTERNATIVE but more mountainous route from Albertville to Bourg St-Maurice via *Beaufort* (60km), is described first. The narrow D925 climbs N.E., after following the valley floor.—At 19km a l.-hand turning ascends to the sequestered resort of *Hauteluce*, 7km N.E.—3km to the E. of the junction lies **Beaufort**, a picturesque little resort amid rich pastures and extensive pine forests, and reputed for its cheese. The principal castle of the Beaufort family, twice visited by Henri IV, is probably represented by some ruins at a lower level than the so-called *Châteaux de Beaufort*, to the N.W. (best approached by the Hauteluce road), dating mainly from the 16C, with a tower perhaps 500 years older.—5km S. lies the resort of *Arèches*.—Continuing E., the *Defile of Enreroches* is traversed, and the road zigzags up to the artificial *Lac de Roselend*, the church of which was re-erected above its bank when the hamlet was submerged. The *Cormet de Roselend* (1968m; 'cormet' signifies 'pass') is crossed before descending the W. flank of the *Beaufortin* (rising at *Le Rognais*, to the S. of the pass, to 2999m) via the *Vallée des Chapieux* to *Bourg-St-Maurice*; see below.

The N90 bears S.E. from Albertville up a partially industrialised valley past (8km) the ruins of the castle of *Chantemerle*, and later (13km) passing near (r.) the small spa of *La Léchère-les-Bains*, and—further S.—the resort of *Les Avanchers*.

5km. **Moûtiers**, the old capital of the *Tarentaise*, situated just above the confluence of the Doron de Bozel with the Isère, owes its name to a monastery founded in the 5C. The see of the Tarentaise (*Darentasia*), established at the end of the same century, was made an archbishopric by Charlemagne, and until the Revolution was the metropolitan see of Savoy; it was revived as a bishopric in 1817.

The *Cathedral* is a dull building with a Romanesque choir and crypt, 15C nave, and a porch of 1461, and a handsome episcopal throne (15C). The treasury is unexpectedly rich, and includes some 12C ivories and enamels.—Near-by are the picturesque *Pl. de la Grenette* and Rue du Conchon.

To the S. fan out several valleys at the heads of which rises the *Massif de la Vanoise*. To the S.E. lies the *Vallée de Belleville*, in which are the small resorts of *St-Martin-de-Belleville*, (27km) *Les Menuires*, and *Val Thorens*; S.E. of the latter rises the *Aiguille de Peclet* (3562m).

MOÛTIERS TO PRALOGNAN-LA-VANOISE (28km). The D915 ascends the l bank of the Doron through *Salins-les-Thermes*, a small spa, and then veers S.E. traversing (5.5km) *Brides-les-Bains*, surrounded by steep wooded and vine covered slopes, above which rise the snow-peaks of the Vanoise.—From the latter spa, a road ascends steeply to *Méribel-les-Allues*, as ski-resort and centre for the exploration of the *Massif du Fruit*, which rises to 2736m.—At 5km E. of Brides a r.-hand turning ascends to (13km) **Courchevel**, a flourishing and well equipped complex of ski-resorts, convenient for the ascent of *La Saulire* (2708m) also approached from Méribel, providing fine panoramic views of the *Ecrins* (S.W.), and *Mont Blanc* (N.E.), apart from nearer peaks to the E.—3km. *Bozel*, with an old chapel with exterior frescoes of 1780, a church with a bulbous belfry, and an old tower, is dominated to the N. by *Mont Jovet* (2554m).—We shortly veer S.E., leaving to the l. *Champagny*, birthplace of Pierre de Champagny (1225–76), later Pope Innocent V.—The road continues to ascend, the valley shortly opening out as (14.5km) *Pralognan-la-Vanoise* is approached, surrounded by pine-forests, and a convenient resort for the exploration of the mountains rising to the S. and E., now forming part of the *Parc National de la Vanoise*, several of them between 3400–3600m, while the *Pointe de la Grand Casse*, to the E., reaches 3852m.—To the S.E. rises the *Dôme de Chasseforé* (3586m), in the centre of the great snow-field of *La Vanoise*.

From Moûtiers we turn N.E. up the valley of the *Haute-Tarentaise* noted for its honey and apples, and for a breed of small cattle known as 'tarines'. The *Étroit de Saix* is first threaded, with *Mont Jovet* (2554m) rising to the r., to enter (14km) **Aime**, the ancient *Forum Claudii*, capital of the Centrones, and medieval *Axima*. On an adjacent hill are remains of Roman fortifications, and below the village near the main road, is the Romanesque basilica *St-Martin, one of the finest and best-preserved monuments of Savoy, with rough but attractive decoration on its tower and apse. Of the two crypts, one is perhaps Roman, and was used as a church in the 5C; the other is 9th or 10C.—The parish church contains 17C stalls and two curious frescoes; while there are several medieval towers in and near the village.

A steep road ascends S. to the ski-resort of *La Plagne*, below the N.E. slope of *Mont Jovet*, above which, to the S.E., rises the *Roche de Mio* (2742m).

At 6km a r.-hand turning leads to (9km) *Peisey-Nancroix*, the principal base for the ascent of *Mont Pourri* (3779m) to the S.E., so-called ('rotten') from the crumbling nature of its quartzite. The valley was once famous for its lead mines, discovered in 1714.

7km. **Bourg-St-Maurice** (840m; 6,700 inhab.), the *Bergintrum* of the Antonine Itinerary, and main market-town of the upper valley of the Isère, is attractively sited in a broad vale full of poplars and surrounded by orchards, and beneath the pine-forests on the lower slopes of *Mont Pourri*, above which are the ski-resorts of *Les Arcs*.

'or the road from *Beaufort*, see above; for that to *Val d'Isère* and *Mont-Cenis-Lanslebourg*, see below.

At *Séez*, 3km N.E., are French Customs.—Turning l., we commence the ascent in several sweeping zigzags to (28km) the *Col du Petit St-Bernard* (2188m; 1348m above Bourg-St-Maurice), first passing a monument to St Bernard marking the frontier of 1862–1947, when it was adjusted, and the derelict *Hospice du Petit-St-Bernard* in the grassy saddle of the pass, seriously damaged by an italian attack in 1940.

It was founded by St Bernard of Menthon (cf.) in c. 1000 as the *Hospitale Colum-nae Jovis*, and used to offer free hospitality to poor travellers; in winter, only the rector and two servants, with their St Bernard dogs, used to remain there. It was for 300 years a dependency of the Great St Bernard, on the Italian-Swiss frontier (see *Blue Guide Northern Italy*), but until 1947 was served by the Aosta house of the military and religious order of SS Maurice and Lazarus.

Just beyond the pass—the watershed between the Isère and Dora Báltea—is the re-erected *Colonne de Joux* (Jupiter's Column), a Celtic or Roman monument of cipollino marble, with a statue of St Bernard gratuitously added in 1886; and a little below it is a large iron Age stone burial circle, in which Gaulish and Roman coins have been discovered.—To the N.W. rises the *Lancebranlette* (2928m; commanding wide views), below which lies *Lac Verney*.—Near the italian Customs-post are the remains of a Roman posting-station.

The road descends through *La Thuile* (see *Blue Guide Northern Italy*); beyond a short tunnel we enjoy a sudden view of *Mont Blanc* (l.) before reaching (23km) **Courmayeur**, 5km beyond which is the S. entrance to the *Mont Blanc Tunnel*, for which, and for **Chamonix**, 3km from its far end, see the latter part of Rte 134A.

BOURG-ST-MAURICE TO VAL d'ISÈRE (31km), AND MONT-CENIS-LANSLEBOURG, 49km beyond. The N202 leads S.E. from (3km) *Séez* (with a curious statue embedded in the outside wall of its church), ascending through (9km) *Ste-Foy-Tarentaine*, on a terrace in full view of *Mont Pourri* to the S. (see above); to the N.E. rises the *Testa del Rutor* (3486m), and to the E., the *Pointe l'Archeboc* (3280m), both on the Italian frontier. Continuing up the valley, noted for its honey (and for the female headdress known as the 'frontière' occasionally worn), and with views of several glaciers at its head, after 9km we fork l., by-passing (r.) *Tignes-les-Boisses*, replacing the village of *Tignes*, submerged by the adjacent reservoir (1952) despite the passive resistance of its inhabitants. The new church preserves the 18C altarpiece of the old.—6km to the S.W. is the high-lying resort of *Le Lac de Tignes*, splendidly situated amid mountains encircling its little lake, among which, to the S., rises the *Grande Motte* (3656m), with its glacier. To the E. rises the *Aiguille de la Grande-Sassière* (3747m), commanding a fine view of the Western Alps.—Skirting the reservoir, several tunnels are threaded to reach (7km) **Val d'Isère** (1840m). This once-remote village, dominated by its tall steeple, developed rapidly into an important resort after the opening of the Iseran road in 1937. The most rewarding of the ascents in the vicinity is the *Tsanteleina* (3605m), to the N.E., below which the road turns to climb to (16km) the *Col de l'Iseran* (2770m), normally blocked by snow between mid Oct. and mid June.

The old track across the pass was crossed by the Waldenses in 1689 in the course of the 'Glorieuse Rentrée' to their native Vaudois valleys in Piedmont, from which they had been expelled in 1686. The pass itself commands some fine retrospective views. The descent is fairly steep, with a good view (l.) towards the glaciers at the head of the Arc valley. The road makes a great curve to the W. before climbing down to (14km) *Bonneval-sur-Arc* (1835m), overlooked to the E. by the *Ciamarella* (3676m). The chapel of *N.-D.-des-Graces* (1678) has an ex-voto by J.-B. Clappier, a local artist (1699).—The road continues to descend the valley to the S.W., passing (r.) quarries of serpentine stone known as 'marbre de

Bessans'.—The church at (6km) *Bessans* contains painted and sculptured altarpieces of the local school, and the adjacent chapel has some remarkable early
16C paintings, within and without, partly restored.—To the S.E. rises the *Pointe
de Charbonnel* (3752m).—10km. *Lanslevillard*, largely rebuilt since its destruction by the Germans, preserves paintings of c. 1518 in the *Chapelle
St-Sebastién.*—3km. *Mont-Cenis Lanslebourg*, likewise rebuilt since 1944, is now
a small resort at the foot of the *Col du Mont Cenis*, for which, and for the continuation of the road down the valley, see Rte 135 in reverse.

135 Chambéry to St-Jean-de-Mont-Cenis-Lanslebourg (for Susa, and Turin)

126km (78 miles). N6. 28km *Miolans*—44km **St-Jean-de-
Maurienne**—14km *St-Michel-de-Maurienne*—12km; the entrance
to the *Tunnel de Fréjus* forks l.—5km *Modane*—23km *Mont-
Cenis-Lanslebourg*.

Maps: IGN 53, or 112; also 236, 238, 240. M 244.

For the road from Chambery to the turning below *Miolans*, see Rte
134B. Here we fork r. at the confluence of the Isère and the Arc, and
follow the valley of the latter, circling round the N. extremity of the
Belledonne range, and below *Le Grande Arc* (2482m), to the N.E., to
traverse the *Maurienne*.

The *Basse-Maurienne*, below Modane, where narrow gorges, once fortified,
alternate with wider agricultural basins, is now in part an industrial area, as the
water-power of the Arc and its tributaries has been harnessed, the production of
aluminium and of chemicals being particularly important. The *Haute-Maurienne*
is more pastoral, but its winter-sporting potential has been developed. It was the
scene of bitter fighting in 1944–45, when many villages were burnt by the Germans.

10km. *Aiguebelle*, where the castle of *Charbonnières* was once a fortress of Humbert Albimanus (the White-handed; d. 1048), the first
count of Savoy, it was later besieged by Lesdiguières (1597), sacked
in 1600 by Henri IV and Sully, and finally destroyed in the 18C by
the Spaniards.—At *Randens*, on the far bank, are the ruins of a col
legial church founded in 1267 by Peter d'Aigueblanche (d'Ac
quablanca), bishop of Hereford.

10km. *Épierre*, with iron and copper mines, and ruins of a castle, is
traversed before (14km) *St-Avre* is reached, at the crossroad from the
Col du Glandon (to the S.W.; see Rte 136) to the *Col de la Madeleine*
(N.E.), the latter leading to the valley of the Isère. Adjacent *La Cham
bre* has a church with a curious 17C portal and a 14C cloister.

10km. **St-Jean-de-Maurienne** (10,100 inhab.), the old capital of the
Maurienne and the seat of a bishopric dating from the 6C (merged
with that of Chambéry in 1966), is a small market-town, where in the
Pl. de la Cathedral is an isolated tower, formerly belonging to the
Chapelle Notre-Dame, whose graceful Romanesque portal has also
survived.

The **Cathedral** is mainly 15C, but with a heavy 18C facade. The in
terior has been freely restored.

The nave is 12C, but the aisles and their chapels were added three centurie

ter. The well-carved 15C pulpit will be noted, while in the S. aisle are an altar
d tomb (12C) erected in memory of St Airald, bishop of Maurienne. The 1st
apel in the N. aisle, with its Renaissance doorway, contains the tomb of Oger
e Conflans (d. 1441). The *Choir* is noteworthy for its 15C *Stalls* and contem-
rary bishop's throne; to the l. of the high altar is a remarkable alabaster
borium designed for a reliquary. The restored 6C *Church* (known as the
rypt) under the choir, contains some finely sculptured capitals. The *Cloisters*
te from 1488.

r the road hence to the *Col de la Croix-de-Fer*, to the S.W., see Rte 135.

he roads bear S.E. along the narrowing valley of the Arc, with for-
idable cliffs to the r. on approaching (14km.) **St-Michel-de-**
Maurienne, a small industrial town, above which the older centre is
minated by two 14C towers, while the little Romanesque tower
eside the church is 13C.

-MICHEL TO THE COL DU LAUTARET (41km), FOR BRIANÇON. The D902
mbs steeply, in sweeping curves, to the S., providing good retrospective views,
(11.5km) the *Col du Télégraphe* (1570m), named from an adjacent fort, and
en directly S. to (5km) *Valloire*, a ski-resort in a fertile valley, and possessing a
C church containing elaborate contemporary altarpieces.—The valley gets
ore rugged as we continue to climb, at 17km reaching a tunnel pierced in 1891
low the *Col de Galibier* (2842m). The N. end provides a panorama of the Savoy
ountains and Mont Blanc; from the S. we enjoy a *View of the whole mountain
ass of the *Ecrins* and *Mont Pelvoux* rising beyond the deep valley of the
isane, with one-third of the horizon barred by an array of formidable peaks
d glittering glaciers. At its S. end is a monument to Henri Desgranges
365– 1940), creator of the 'Tour de France' bicycle race, in which the crossing
the Galibier is a crucial test.—The road now descends in wide curves to meet
e N91 at (7.5km) the *Col de Lautaret* (2057m), 28km N.W. of *Briançon*, see Rte
6.

he N6 leads almost due E., between the *Massif de la Vanois* (l.), here
sing to 3407m at the *Pointe de Bouchet*, and *Mont Thabor* (3207m),
the S.

12km. To the r. forks the approach road to the *Tunnel de Fréjus*
980; 12.868km long), pierced in part parallel to the earlier car-
rrier service of the Mont-Cenis railway tunnel below the *Col de*
éjus (2540m). This latter, 13.636km long, was driven through the
nge between 1857– 70. From its S. end we descend the *Bardonec-*
ia valley to meet the main road near *Oulx*, some 16km N.E. of the
l de Montgenèvre, itself 12km from *Briançon*; see Rte
7A.—23km N.E. of Oulx is **Susa**, near the S. side of the *Col du*
ont Cenis, for which see below, and *Blue Guide Northern Italy*.
5km. **Modane**, a frontier town of slight interest, has suffered from
oding of the Arc on several occasions, and was severely damaged
allied bombing in 1943, and by being set alight by the Germans in
44, since when it has been rebuilt, and is now a ski-resort. To the
E. rises the *Aiguille de Scolette* (3508m).

the l. of the road lies *Avrieux*, where the 15C church bears a remarkable ex-
ior *Mural* of the Cardinal Virtues and Seven Deadly Sins (early 18C). It is
lieved that Charles le Chauve died here on his return from Italy in 877.—Adja-
nt *Aussois* is a small ski-resort.

r.-hand turning at (9km) *Bramans* (where Horace Walpole lost his
t spaniel Tory'. which was carried off by a wolf whole being exer-
sed behind his post-chaise) leads shortly to the ruined priory
urch of *St-Pierre d'Extravache* (10-11C), replacing an earlier sanc-
ary.—3km further E. lies the village of *Le Planey*; see below.

8km. *Termignon*, burned by the Germans in 1944, has a churc
containing a notable altarpiece; to the S.E. rises *Mont-Froid* (2819m
and to the W., the *Dent Parrachée* (3684m).

6km. *Mont-Cenis-Lanslebourg*, a small resort overlooked from th
N. by the *Grand Roc Noir* (3583m), is at the foot of the *Col du Mor
Cenis* (2083m; *Moncenisio* in Italian).

This, one of the historic passes of the Alps, was crossed by Pepin le Bref, in 75
Charlemagne (774), and Charles le Chauve (877), and by many other sovereign
with their armies. It is possible that Hannibal crossed the Alps by the *Col*
Clapier, some 10km further S. (2482m), to *Le Planey*; but see p 744. The carriag
road zigzagging up the N. slope was constructed by Napoleon in 1803– 13. Th
Hospice, on the far side (which was founded by Louis le Débonnaire in 825 and e
tensively damaged during the Second World War, when the Italians attacked th
pass but were unable to storm its defences), was submerged by the artificial *L*
du Mont-Cenis, which the road then skirts, below the *Pointe de Ronce* (3612m
and *Mont Lamet* (3504m) to approach (19km) the frontier-post since 1947, ar
French Customs.

The Italian post is a short distance beyond, passed on the descent in zigzags ir
to the valley of the *Dora Riparia* and to (21km) **Susa**, a picturesque little tow
with a *Triumphal Arch* erected in honour of Augustus c. 8 B.C., and a *Cathedr*
dating from 1028, for details of which, and for the road on to **Turin**, 53km E., se
Blue Guide Northern Italy.

For the road up the Arc valley from Lanslebourg to *Bonneval* and the *Col*
l'Iseran, see the last section of Rte 134C, in reverse.

136 Grenoble to Briançon

116km (72 miles). N91. 17km **Vizille**—32km *Le Bourg-*
d'Oisans—28km *La Grave*—11km **Col du Lautaret**—28km
Briançon.

Maps: IGN 54, or 112; also 240, 241, 242, 244. M 244.

For **Grenoble**, see Rte 132A. Rte 138A is followed to **Vizille**.

There we fork l. through an industrial area, with a view ahead
the *Taillefer* (2857m), later veering N.E. below the *Croix*
Chamrousse (2257m); see Rte 133A.

In 1191 a landslide from the N. filled the gorge and formed a huge dam, so th
the Romanche rose and flooded its valley to a height of c. 10m, submergi
several hamlets. In 1219 this barrier burst, the resulting vortex sweepir
downwards, destroying as it went, inundated the plain of Grenoble.

25km. Rochetaillée.

ROCHETAILLÉE TO ST-JEAN-DE-MAURIENNE VIA THE COL DE LA CRO
DE FER (60km). The D526 forks l. up a side valley, with the snow-peaks of t
Grandes-Rousses rising up on the r., at the *Pic l'Etendard* reaching a height
3468m; to the N. are the steep wooded slopes of the *Belledonne* chain, the *Gra*
Pic de Belladonne itself (l.) rising to 2978m.—The road later circles to the E.
thread the gloomy defile of *Maupas*, and mounts to (27km) the *Col du Gland*
(1924m) amid high pastures, with a wealth of Alpine flowers best seen
June.—Hence a road descends N.E. to (10.5km) *St-Colomban-des-Villards*, a sm
winter resort, meeting the N6 11.5km down the valley, some 10km N.W. of
Jean-de-Maurienne; see Rte 135.—We climb E. to (2.5km) the *Col de la Croix*
Fer (2068m), with the *Pointe de l'Ouillon* (2438m) to the l., and descend l
zigzags into the valley of the Arven to (7.5km) *St-Sorlins-d'Arves*, one of seve
ski-resorts in the area.—Continuing down the narrow valley, some distance S
of which rises the *Aiguilles d'Arves* (2510m), the road veers N. by the *Com*
Génin, above a chasm, to thread a series of tunnels, beyond which rocks gi

way to wooded slopes in the lower valley below (l.) *Fontcouverte*, with an interesting 17C church, beyond which we shortly enter (23km from St-Sorlins) **St-Jean-de-Maurienne**; see Rte 135.

Turning S. from Rochetaillée, the road traverses green flats that were once the bed of the lake formed by the dammed Romanche (see above), and at 4.5km the road from the Col d'Ornon (see Rte 138A) joins the N91 2.5km before reaching **Le Bourg-d'Oisans**, a small town long used as a centre for the exploration of the circumjacent mountains.

The *Oisans* is the name given to the basin or valley of the Romanche as far E. as the Col du Lautaret, its ancient inhabitants being the Uceni, but its seems likely that at one time it was colonised by the Saracens, who have left traces in the family and place-names of the district.

The *Prégentil* (1938m) to the W., commands a good view up the valley, and to the S.E., while a mountain road ascends S. to the hamlet of *Villard-Notre-Dame* (views), passing the intermittently worked gold-mine of *La Gardette*.

Just beyond Le Bourg, the D111 ascends steeply in zigzags to the N.E. to (13.5km) **L'Alpe d'Huez** (1860m), a flourishing winter resort, with a cable-way to near *Lac Blanc* and the summit of the *Pic de Lac Blanc* (3327m), in the *Grandes-Rousses* range.

Below its W. flank lies **Lac Blanc**, which may be approached by pedestrians via the *Plateau de Brandes*, with remains of copper and galena mines works by the Romans, who have left a paved track, and then under the dauphins in the 13C; its anthracite mines were closed in 1950 after an avalanche. The medieval *Tour du Prince-Ladre*, and a chapel on the site of a Roman temple may be seen. The path continues over grassy slopes and then rocky terraces (views) to the lake itself, whitened by baryta.

The N91 continues S.E., with the *Pied-Moutet* rising boldly ahead (2338m), to (5km) *Le Clapier*, and turns E.; see below.

LE CLAPIER TO LA BÉRARDE (25km). The valley of the Vénéon, pastoral in its lower reaches, assumes a character of Alpine grandeur as we ascend.—At 4km a track climbs r. towards the deep blue tarn of *Lac Lauvitel*.—A wilderness of boulders which have fallen from the heights to the N. is traversed as the ascent continues and the view changes as some of the high peaks to the N.E. and S. come into sight. The old *Pont du Diable* is crossed to approach (10km) *St-Christophe-en-Oisans*, a famous climbing centre, whose cemetery contains many mountaineering victims.—The route to *La Grave* (see below) is one of the finest glacier excursions in the French Alps.—8km brings us to the hamlet of *Les Étages*, providing some remarkable mountain views.—3km. *La Bérarde* (1738m), where the road stops, lies at the foot of the **Écrins** (4102m), to the E., the highest mountain in the Alps to the S. of Mont Blanc, and second only to Mont Blanc among the mountains of France; to the N. rises **La Meije**, with its three main peaks (3983m). On every hand rise glaciers and snow-peaks, towering above deep Alpine valleys with their crags and torrents. Extensive areas to the E. and S. are now a nature reserve.

From Le Clapier, the road climbs steeply N.E. through the wild *Gorge de l'Infernet* to reach (9km) the *Barrage du Chambon*, its dam completed in 1936.

Here the D213 climbs S. to (12km) *Les Deux-Alpes*, two flourishing ski-resorts situated on an upland plateau. *Pied Moutet* (2338m), to the W., provides splendid views of the *Écrins*, and *Meije*, and the *Mont Blanc* massifs.

Skirting the *Lac du Chambon*, the sombre *Combe de Malaval* is traversed, overhung to the N. by crags, with several waterfalls, passing (r.) the ruined *Hospice de l'Oche*, said to have been founded by

Humbert II of Dauphiny. The valley soon widens, and at 14km **L
Grave** is entered, well-sited on a projecting rock at the foot of th
Meije and in full view of its great glaciers. A frequented mou
taineering centre, it preserves a 14C church, and the 17C cemeter
chapel contains notable vault-paintings.

Perhaps the finest view of the *Meije* (3983m) is gained from the *Oratoire d
Chazalet*, beyond the hamlet of *Les Terrasses*, reached by a path climbing pa
the cemetery, or by a lane turning r. immediately beyond the first tunnel E. of I
Grave. The lower parts of the *Glacier de la Meije* may be safely explored withou
a guide.

A steep ascent brings one in 11km to the **Col du Lautaret** (2057m
the grassy watershed between the valleys of the Romanche and th
Guisane, seen at its best, for its flowers, in mid July. The statio
perhaps grew up around a Roman temple (*altaretum*) on the road t
the Oisans, and another hospice is said to have been founded here b
Humbert II. The Alpine garden and museum of the University c
Grenoble may be visited in summer. A cairn nearby commemorate
Scott of the Antarctic's visit in 1908. To the N.W. rises the *Pic de
Trois-Évêchés* (3118m), named from the fact that its summit was
boundary mark or point of division between the bishoprics c
Maurienne and Grenoble, and the archbishopric of Embrun.—Fe
the road hence to *St-Jean-de-Maurienne* via the *Col du Galibie*
(2642m), 7.5km N., see the sub-route on p 739.

Passing the old *Hospice de la Madeleine*, one of the three mediev
houses of refuge on this road, and later traversing larch forests,
13.5km *Le Monêtier-les-Bains* is reached, owing its name to a forme
Benedictine monastery, and to its sulphur springs. The 15C churc
has a 17C steeple. The *Montagne du Vallon de la Meulette* (2830m
to the N., offers a superb panorama of the *Meije*, *Ecrins*, and *Pelvou*

Together with several of the following villages, it forms part of th
extensive winter-sports complex of **Serre-Chevalier**. Among the
are *Villeneuve-la Salle*, with a handsome church with a 15C porch
and *Chantemerle*, from which cable-cars ascend to the summit of th
Serre Chevalier (2491m), providing a splendid view of the *Aiguille
d'Arves*, the *Pelvoux-Ecrins*, and the mountains of the Briançonnai
and to the N. a road zigzags to (12km) the *Col de Granon* (2413m
likewise commanding fine views.

Beyond *St-Chaffrey* the road provides a good view of (14.5km
Briançon with its picturesque old ramparts.—The r.-hand turning
the rond-point leads to the lower town; the l.-hand ascends to the o
fortress; see below.

137   Briançon to Gap

A.   Briançon and Environs

BRIANÇON (1321m; 11,850 Briançonnais), once a first-class fortre
commanding the passage from Italy into France, stands on the slope
of a height overlooking the confluence of the Durance with th
Guisane, and is an imposing sight from a distance, with its steep an
narrow street of 18C houses climbing upwards to the citadel, and th
whole of the old town is pent up within its walls. Subsidiary fort

crown several circumjacent heights.

The modern town of *Briançon-Ste-Catherine* lies to the S.W., and is both an important crossroads in summer, and a centre for winter-sporting, the neighbouring station of *Serre-Chevalier* (see above) being very close.

Although of ancient foundation—It was the Roman station of *Brigantium* on the road from Mediolanum (Milan) to Vienna (Vienne)—It appears to have been of little more than local significance until 1692, when after its sack by the Sardinians, Vauban was commissioned to rebuild the ramparts. Pope Pius VI was interned here for three months in 1798. In 1815 the garrison of 300 under Gén. Eberlé refused to surrender to the Allies, and maintained a three months' siege by the Austrian army: hence its motto, 'Petite ville et grand renom'. In 1940 its guns silenced the rival fort on the Chaberton. It suffered some damage from German bombardment in 1944–45.

See IGN 244 for its immediate surroundings.

Parking facilities are provided immediately N. of the walled town, near the *Porte Pignerol*, or alternatively one may enter by the *Porte d'Embrun*, at the S.W. corner of the enceinte, approached from the upper end of the Av. de la République, ascending from the lower town. From the former, the narrow **Grande-Rue** leads downhill, with a 'gergouille' or rivulet of water running down its centre. Several houses, many of them Italianate in style, have fine doors.—A r.-hand turning leads shortly to the heavy but not undignified church of *Notre-Dame*, built by Vauban in 1703–18 on a bastion and with an eye to defence.

Further on, to the l., one may follow a lane to a gateway overlooking a bold single-arched *Bridge* overlooking the Durance, built in 1734 on the orders of the Chevalier d'Asfeld (1667–1743), who had been service in Spain, in 1715 becoming director-general of fortifications, and in 1734, a Marshal of France. It is approached by a winding Chemin de Ronde.

At a higher level is the *Citadelle*, replacing an older fort demolished in 1841, now embellished by a supererogatory statue of 'La France', by Bourdelle

BRIANÇON TO MONTGENÈVRE (12km), FOR CESANA AND TURIN. The N94 leads N.E. below (l.) the *Croix-de-Tourlouse*, with its oratory and battery at the S. end of the ridge separating the valley of the Guisane from that of the Clarée, to (3.5km) *La Vachette*.

Hence the N94G forks l. up the latter valley to (11km) *Plampinet*, with a 16C church containing contemporary frescoes and wooden sculpture.—3.5km beyond, a road climbs N.E. over the *Col de l'Echelle* to a minor frontier-post (Customs) to *Bardonecchia*, near the S. entrance of the *Tunnel de Fréjus*; see Rte 35.—The l.-hand fork leads 2.5km to *Névache*, with a church of 1496, preserving good 16C boiseries.—The road goes on for another 9.5km to the *Chalets de aval*, from which *Mont Thabor* (3178m) may be ascended.

From La Vachette, the main road ascends in zigzags to (8.5km) **Montgenèvre**, one of the earliest French winter-sports resorts (1907), established on the approximate site of the hospice founded by the dauphins for the use of pilgrims crossing the *Col de Montgenèvre* (1850m; French Customs), the frontier prior to 1947, which is now a short distance further E., including in French territory the fortress-mountain of the *Chaberton*, to the N. (3136m).

This pass (*Mons Janus*) is one of the oldest, as well as one of the lowest over the main chain of the Alps. It was crossed by the armies of Marius, Augustus, Theodosius, and Charlemagne; and again by Charles VIII and his army, dragging with them 600 cannon. The present road was constructed by Napoleon in 1802–7, over which French armies invaded Italy in 1814 and 1859, and in 1917–18 French reinforcements were sent to the Italian armies over this pass.—A little to the S., and almost from a common source, rise the Dora, which

flows via the Po into the Adriatic, and the Durance, flowing via the Rhône int
the Mediterranean.

At *Clavière* are the Italian Customs, beyond which the road threads a tunnel t
reach (6km) *Cesana-Torinese*, where the main road veers N. down the valley c
the Dora to (24km) **Susa**; see last paragraphs of Rte 135.

An autostrada is under construction between the S. end of the *Tunnel du Fré
jus* (see Rte 135) and **Turin**, with an entrance not far N. of Cesana, for which se
Blue Guide Northern Italy. The r.-hand turning at Cesana leads down the valle
of the Chisone via *Sestrières*, *Fenestrelle*, and *Pinerolo*.

B.   From Briançon to Gap

87km (54 miles). N94. 30km **Mont Dauphin** lies 1km l.—1km
Guillestre lies 4km E.—18km **Embrun**—21km *Chorges*—17km
Gap.

Maps: IGN 54, or 112; also 243-6. M 244, 245.

AN ALTERNATIVE ROUTE VIA THE PARC DU QUEYRAS TO GUILLESTR
(57km) is first described. The D902 ascends the valley of the Cerveyrette, S.E. c
Briançon, commanded by the strategically sited forts on either side, to (11.5kπ
Cervières, of which the 15C church survived when the village was destroyed i
1944.—Turning S., the road zigzags up to (10.5km) the *Col d'Izoard* (2360m), t
the E. of which rises the *Grand Pic de Rochebrune* (3320m). The pass commanc
some splendid views, beyond which we climb down in sweeping loops past (l.) th
jagged orange rocks of the *Casse-Déserte* to *Arvieux*, a small ski-resort with
16C church, to reach (15km) a T-junction.—2km to the l. stands the fort c
Château-Queyras, rebuilt by Vauban, but preserving its medieval keep.

Hence the road continues E. to (3km) *Ville-Vieille*, with a 16C church damage
in the Wars of Religion and restored in 1635. The old village stands in the centr
of the **Queyras** (in patois, 'the huge crag'), a high Alpine valley remarkable fc
its flora, and first inhabited by the Quariates, one of the tribes mentioned on th
triumphal arch of Susa. Commanding several Alpine passes, their successor
('Queyrassins') gained considerable privileges, and the franchises they obtaine
from the dauphins are among the earliest pledges of French liberty. Some Pro
testants took refuge here, and the Reformed faith generally was widespread, bt
the Religious Wars, plague, and the Thirty Years' War ruined the Queyras an
its tributary valleys, and the revocation of the Edict of Nantes precipitate
wholesale emigration. It was invaded by the Austro-Sardinians in 1815, and th
upper   valley   suffered   severely   during   the   German   occupation   i
1944–45.—6km S.E. lies the hamlet of *La Rua*, with some 15C houses and
15-16C church, adjacent to which is the small winter resort of *Molines*; 5kπ
beyond is *St-Véran* (2040m), claiming to be the highest permanently inhabite
village in Europe, a picturesque place of galleried houses, and a 17C church, an
now also a ski-resort.

The main road up the valley continues N.E. from Ville-Vieille through (4.5kπ
Aiguilles, another resort with a small museum containing locally made woode
furniture and utensils, to (4.5km) *Abriès*. The ownership of the *Forêt o
Marassan*, between them, was disputed by the two communes in a lawsuit tha
lasted 446 years (1387–1833). The resort was burned by the Germans in 194
although the Romanesque *Church* (rebuilt in the 16C), with an altar from th
Chartreuse de Durbon, and the *Market-hall* were saved.—The road continues t
(7km) *L'Echalp* (wrecked by an avalanche in 1946 and fire in 1947). A track goe
on to (8km) the *Belvedere du Viso*, commanding a good view of *Monte Vis*
(3841m), rising above its barren foothills beyond the Italian frontier.—To the I
is the *Col de la Traversette*, below which is a tunnel (no longer in use), pierced b
the Marquis de Saluces (Saluzzo) in 1478–80. It has been argued by Gavin d
Beer that this was the pass used by Hannibal when entering Italy in the autum
of 218 B.C.

Turning r. at the above-mentioned T-junction, the road bear S.W. to thread th
Combe du Queyras, one of the more remarkable defiles in the Alps, bounde
by limestone precipices some 200m high and narrowing in places to almost
fissure, through which the Guil winds through a bed of white pebbles intersper

ed with a mosaic of green serpentine and red marble.—To the l. at its S. end a by-
road leads up the side valley of the Cristillan to (8.5km) *Ceillac*, now devoted to
winter-sports.—Traversing several short tunnels we enter (17km) **Guillestre**, a
slate-roofed old town, one of the stations where English prisoners were interned
during the Napoleonic wars. The porch of the 16C church, with its columns supported by lions, recalls that at Embrun, while also characteristic are the open
granaries in the upper floors of some houses, with their cranes.—The N94 is
reached 4km W., just S. of *Mont Dauphin*.—For the continuation of the road S. to
Barcelonnette, see below.

From **Briançon** the N94 leads S.W. along the r. bank of the Durance,
with good retrospective views, past (7km) *Prelles*, where the river is
crossed to *St-Martin-de-Queyrières*, both with 15-16C mural paintings in their churches. Ahead are imposing mountain-scapes.

From the former a road continues along the r. bank before turning round a spur
to (8km) *Les Vigneaux*, its church with wall-paintings of the Seven Deadly Sins
1552), at the entrance to the valley of the Vallouise.—The old village of
Vallouise, 5km N.W., preserves several crooked lanes of sombre chalets and an
interesting early 15C church with a 16C porch and decorated door.—The straggling commune of *Pelvoux* is traversed as the valley of the Gyr is ascended to
8km) *Ailefroide*, a mountaineering centre in summer at the foot of the apparent-
y vertical cliffs of *Mont Pelvoux* (N.W.; 3946m), from which the road continues
he ascent N.W. to (6km) the *Pré de Mme Carle*, at the juncture of the *Glacier
Blanc* (N.) and *Glacier Noir* (W.); beyond the last rises the **Ecrins** (4102m); see Rte
36. It was of this region that Whymper wrote, after his first visit in 1861: 'A
more cheerless and desolate valley it is scarcely possible to imagine. It contains
niles of boulders, débris, stones, sand, and mud; few trees, and they placed so
nigh as to be almost out of sight. Not a soul inhabits it. The mountains are too
teep for the chamois, too inhospitable for the marmot, and too repulsive for the
agle'.

Near Ailefroide is the *Cascade de Claphouse*, and the *Combe de Capescure*, in
vhich is the hollow of *Baume-Chapelue*, where, it is said, the Waldensians were
moked out by Charles VIII's troops in 1488.

8.5km S. of Prelles the N94 passes (r.) industrial *L'Argentière-la-
Bassée*, with a castle ruin and 12C chapel, while above is a 15C
church, on the exterior wall of which is a mural depicting Vice and
Virtue (1516).—To the N., on the road into the Vallouise, are the re-
nains of ramparts known as the *Mur de Vaudois*, built by the men of
Briançon in 1376, not by the Waldensians (see below).

2.5km. The r.-hand turning under the railway, and then l., leads round a spur
he valley of the Biaysse (near the mouth of which is the curious gorge known as
he *Gouffre de Gourfouran*), which was one of the principal refuges of the
Valdensians, who had to submit to frequent persecutions from the Middle Ages
o the 18C; the hamlet of *Dormillouse*, at the head of the valley, overlooked to
he N. by the *Tête de Dormillouse* (3084m), and the *Tête de Vautisse* (3156m), to
he S., was one of their last refuges, before, with the help of Protestants from
yon, the inhabitants emigrated to Algeria.

km. *St-Crépin*, by-passed, on its hillock, has a church of 1454 con-
aining a contemporary stoup.

4km. To the r. rises the walled fortress of **Mont-Dauphin*, the key
o the pass into Italy by the valley of the *Queyras* (see above), which
fter the Sardinian invasion of 1692 was fortified by Vauban, who
onstructed its bastions of rough pink marble hewn near by. A win-
ing ascent leads into the village, with the remains of a large church;
ut the whole site is a remarkable example of military architecture
f the period, at the same time providing extensive mountain
anoramas.

MONT-DAUPHIN TO BARCELONNETTE (53km). We turn l. onto the D902 1km
S. of the fortress to (4km) *Guillestre* (see above), from which a mountain road
zigzags S. to the ski-resort of *Risoul* (1850m). Almost immediately the road commences to climb, later passing the ski-resorts of *St-Marcellin*, *Ste-Marie*, and *Les
Claux* (the three known under the name *Vars*) to the summit at (19km) the *Col de
Vars* (2111m), at its most interesting in June, when Alpine flowers are out. The
high ridge of the Italian frontier is seen ahead on the descent; to the l. is a group
of capped limestone pillars.—8km. *St-Paul*, a small resort.

Hence the upper valley of the Ubaye, leading N.E., may be explored, overlooked
by the formidable cliffs of the *Pic de la Font Sanct* to the N. (3387m), and to the S.,
the rock-peak of the *Aiguille de Chambeyron* (3411m), just E. of the frontier
ridge. The road passes the *Pont du Châtelet* to reach (13.5km) *Maljasset* (or
Maurin), where the church has an inscription recording its destruction by an
avalanche in 1531; the niches in the churchyard wall are for the convenience of
coffins when the ground is frozen. The neighbouring peaks were first explored
in 1879 by W.A.B. Coolidge (1850–1926). Among them, at the head of the
valley, is the *Bric de Rubren* (3340m), on the Italian frontier.
  The road now threads the striking *Pas de la Reyssole* to meet (7km) the D900
(from Barcelonnette to Cuneo), where we turn r. past the *Fort de Tournoux*, and
through (7km) *Jausiers*, to **Barcelonnette**, 8km beyond; see p 751 for this latter
section, in reverse.

3.5km. *St-Clement*, where the road crosses to the r. bank of the
Durance, and follows the river through (7.5km) *Châteauroux*
(*Castrum Rudolphi*) to enter (7km) *Embrun*.

  EMBRUN (870m; 5,800 Embrunais), for centuries a fortress town
is finely situated above the valley on a cliff-girt platform known as
'Le Roc'; with the recent development of the Lac de Serre-Ponçon
and the ski-slopes of Les Orres (see below) it has pretensions to
becoming both a summer and winter resort.

Ebuorodunum, a town of the Caturiges, whose capital was at *Chorges* (see
below), was of considerable importance under Hadrian. The bishopric, founded
c. 360 by St Marcellinus, an African missionary, lasted until the Revolution. In
the Middle Ages Embrun was governed first by its prince-bishops and later by
the dauphins. Louis XI, as dauphin (1440–61) was a devotee of N.-D. d'Embrun
(whose image he wore in his hat), and enriched the cathedral. It was taken by
Lesdiguières in 1585, and in 1692 Victor Amadeus II of Savoy captured it after a
13-day bombardment.
  Among natives were Jean Morel (1511–81), the scholar and friend of
Erasmus; and Henri Arnaud (1641–1721), the Waldensian pastor and soldier.

From the *Pl. St-Marcellin*, at the N. end of the town, the Rue Clovis
Hugues leads through its centre, immediately to the r. off which is a
small square in which the S.I. occupies part of a former convent of
the Cordeliers.—To the l. a few paces beyond is the *Pl. Barthelon*
with one of the many fountains to be seen, and the *Hôtel de Ville*. By
turning l. in the next triangular Place and continuing ahead, the
gardens of the *Pl. de l'Archêvéche* are reached, providing views over
the valley.
  To the W. is the former ***Cathedral***, largely a 12C edifice, with
some fragments of an earlier church (9C). The tower is a replica of
one of the 14C, destroyed by lighning in 1852; the blind arcading
and friezes of the facade date from the 13C. The porch, known as the
Réal, in front of the Romanesque N. portal, has columns supported
by lions and by seated figures. Its design, indeed much of the
building, with its parti-coloured marbles, suggests Italian influence

The interior is plain (black and white); the W. rose contains 15C glass; the organ
was presented by Louis XI. The 18C high altar is flanked by angels said to have
the features of Louis XVI and Marie Antoinette. A 15C painting of the Entomb-

ment, and traces of wall-paintings, will be noticed. The *Treasury* is remarkably rich, containing an important collection of vestments, still preserved in their huge drawers, and other cult objects.

Facing the N. side is the former *Chapter-house* (13C), with the figure of a lion devouring a goat. To the N.E. rises the well-preserved 12C *Tour Brune*.

Quitting Embrun, the road leads S.W., with *Mont St-Guillaume* (2552m) to the r., and crosses the Durance, beyond which a l.-hand turning ascends to (10km) *Les Orres*, with a church of 1501, and skiing facilities, to the E. of which rises the *Grand Parpaillon* (2988m).

4km. *Crots* (previously *Les Crottes*), with a late 14C church, and the 15-16C *Château de Peycomptal.*—2km. The former abbey of *Boscodon* lies 4km S., founded in 1131 by the Cistercian monks of Chalais, but suppressed in 1769; the Romanesque church has been restored.

The road now skirts the N. arm of the artificial *Lac de Serre-Ponçon* (see Rte 138A), which although intended to be of considerable extent, looked as though the plug had been pulled out, when visited by the Editor in 1982.—4km. *Savins-le-Lac*, a new village built in 1962 to replace the old one which was submerged.

SAVINES TO LE LAUZET-SUR-UBAYE (26.5km), FOR BARCELONNETTE OR DIGNE. This road (D954) winds above the S. shore of the lake below the pine forests of the *Pic de Morgan* (2327m), passing the strangely-capped rocks known as the 'Demoiselles Coiffées', and circles the promontory of *Le Sauze*, overlooking what was the confluence of the Durance with the Ubaye. Following the narrowing arm in the latter valley, we cross it to the l. bank and shortly meet the D900B 1.5km from Le Lauzet. For the road hence to *Barcelonnette*, 21km E., see Rte 138A.—At *St-Vincent-les-Forts*, 5.5km W. of this junction, the D900 from Digne joins the road to *Tallard*, for which see also Rte 138A.

ST-VINCENT TO DIGNE (54.5km). The D900 turns S.W., ascending to the *Col St-Jean*, with ski-slopes, and (12.5km) *Selonnet*, occupying the site of a castle of Lesdiguières, one tower of which remains as a belfry, S.W. of which are the ski-slopes of the *Tête Grosse* (2031m).—4km. **Seyne**, a little market-town and summer resort, possesses a 13C *Church* with mutilated sculptures, and the ruins of a castle built under Louis XIV.—The road circles the E. flank of the *Grand Puy* (1761m), with ski-slopes, to the *Col de Maure* (1346m), thence descends past *Le Vernet*, likewise with ski-slopes, to a junction at 10km.—To the E. rises the *Tête de l'Estrop* (2961m), second only to Mont Pelat among the Provençal Alps.

Hence the sequestered D900A leads W., descending the valley of the Bès through the wooded *Clues de Verdaches* and striking limestone gorges of the *Clues de Barles* to (32km) *Digne*.—The D900 turns l. over the *Pont de Verdaches* to cross the *Col de Labouret* (1240m) before descending the narrow valley of the Arigeol, after 13km meeting the Bléone at *La Javie*, there bearing S.W. to (15km) **Digne**; see Rte 153.

At Savines we cross the lake by a 12-arched bridge and skirt the N. bank, shortly rounding a small bay in which an old chapel has been left stranded on an islet, to enter (11km) **Chorges**, which retains few traces of its vanished importance as Roman *Caturigomagus*. The church dates from the 12C, but was rebuilt in 1500 with the exception of a 14C bell-tower. Under the porch is the so-called 'inscription of Nero', more probably of A.D. 300, badly restored and misinterpreted in 1839.

5km. Travellers making direct for *Sisteron* may fork l. via (20km) *Tallard* to join the N75 2km beyond; see Rte 138A.—At 8km this road (D942) passes just S. of *N.-D.-du-Laus*, a church erected after the alleged apparition of the Virgin to a shepherdess in 1664.

12km. **Gap**; see Rte 138A.

138 Grenoble to Sisteron

A. Via Gap

151km (94 miles). N85. 17km **Vizille**—21km *La Mure*—25km *Corps*—40km **Gap**—48km **Sisteron**.

Maps: IGN 54, 60, or 112, 115; also 242-3. M 224, 245.

For **Grenoble**, see Rte 113A.

The N85 drives almost due S. through an industrial district to (8km) *Le Pont-de-Claix*, named from a single-span bridge across the Drac erected by Lesdiguières in 1611 to replace an older bridge swept away in 1219. We cross one of 1875 and fork l. for (9km) *Vizille*.

It may also be approached from Grenoble by the minor D5 via *Eybens*, with a castle built by Christine de Bourbon, duchess of Savoy, a daughter of Henri IV, to the S.E. of which is the 17C château of *Herbeys*, once belonging to the bishops of Grenoble.

Vizille (7,400 Vizillois), a military post since Roman times, and now a small industrial town, is visited for its huge *Château*, ◇ rebuilt in 1620 adjacent to its feudal predecessor by Lesdiguières, a bronze relief of whom, by Jacob Richier, embellishes the proncipal entrance. When 'the old fox of Dauphiny' entertained Louis XIII here in 1623, it accommodated the entire court as well as a strong garrison. A series of furnished rooms may be visited, while its gardens are attractively sited.

In 1720–1840 it belonged to the Casimir-Périer family. On 21 July 1788 the three Estates of Dauphiny, assembling of their own accord in order to express popular discontent, met here to prepare a bold remonstrance, a portend of the Revolution. A serious fire in 1865 destroyed two wings, including the Jeu-de-Paume.

Crossing the Romanche by a bridge of 1753, the N85 mounts the N.E. flank of a ridge, passing (l.) *N.-D.-de-Mésage*, with a 9-10C nave and 11C choir; near-by is *St-Firmin-de-Mésage*, built by the Templars.

From Vizille southwards this road, marked by 'imperial eagle' milestones, formed part of the 'Route Napoléon', that followed—in the reverse direction—by the Emperor on his return from Elba, which culminated in the dramatic encounter at *Laffrey*, which is traversed in 7.5km.

Just S. of this village a bronze equestrian statue of Napoleon by Frémiet over-looks the lake, the scene of his meeting on 7 March 1815 with a battalion despatched by the governor of Grenoble to intercept the Emperor, who, throwing open his coat to show the star of the Legion of Honour, invited the troops to fire; but the soldiers, most of them his own veterans, broke their ranks and crowded around, renewing their allegiance.

A series of lakes on this pastoral upland plateau of Matheysine are skirted to approach (13.5km) *La Mure*, a small industrial town, to the W. of which rises *Le Génépi* (1769m), providing remarkable views from its summit. The women, led by La Cotte-Rouge, the local heroine, played a part in its defence, when in 1580 the Protestant garrison was besieged by the Duc de Mayenne with 12,000 men. A restored *Market-hall* of 1309 and an 18C clock-tower may be seen.

The road descends in zigzags to cross (4km) the *Pont-Haut*, built above two earlier bridges, one Roman; the rocks on one hand are richly coloured, and on the other bank are of dark slate.

The D526 turns l. up the *Valbonnais* to (13km) *Entraigues*, lying at the junction of the narrow valley of the Malsanne to the N., dominated by the *Coiro* (2606m) to the N.W., and forming the W. limit of the *Parc National des Ecrins.*—The latter valley continues N. to (15km) the *Col d'Ornon* (1367m), below a spur of the *Taillefer* (l.; 2857m), to reach the N91 11km beyond, 2.5km N. of *Le Bourg-d'Oisans*; see Rte 136.

    S.W. of Entraigues ascends the *Valjouffrey* to (7.5km) *La Chapelle*, from which one may enter the charming side valley to *Valsenestre*. The road circles the S. side of the *Pic de Valsenestre* (2753m) to (8km) *Le Désert*, whence a path continues to climb, later commanding a view of the N.W. face of the *Pic d'Olan* (3564m).

From the Pont-Haut we mount to the S. by a succession of loops above the Drac valley with its reservoir to reach (21km) *Corps*, an ancient little place overlooking the artificial *Lac du Sautet*, its curved dam completed in 1935.

Hence a minor road ascends to the N.E. to the improbable and unedifying neo-Romanesque basilica of *N.-D.-de-la-Salette*, built to celebrate an alleged apparition of the Virgin to two children in 1846 (pre-dating Lourdes by 12 years); the road does, however, provide an approach to neighbouring *Mont Gargas* (2207m), commanding panoramic mountain views.

CORPS TO VEYNES (44km). After skirting the lake to the W. and crossing the dam, the D537 ascends the valley of the Souloise, with the *Obiou* (2790m) rising to the W., and threads a defile to *St-Disdier* (with a 12C chapel), where a l.-hand turning leads c. 5km to *St-Étienne-en-Dévoluy*, dominated by limestone cliffs riddled with caverns and subterranean streams, and a centre for the exploration of the cirque of mountains rising to the S. to the *Pic du Bure* (2709m).—A good road crosses the ridge at the *Col de Noyer* (1664m) to descend to (20.5km) *St-Bonnet*; see below.—To the S.W. is *Super-Dévoluy*, a winter-sporting development.—Continuing S. from St-Disdier (or circling W. from St-Étienne), we gain the summit at the *Col du Festre* (1441m), and descend the valley of the Béoux, and through the defile of *Potrachon*, to *Veynes*; see Rte 140.

From Corps, the main road passes into the width upper valley of the Drac, shortly swinging to the E., with a view (r.) towards the peaks of the Dévoluy mountains. On the opposite bank of the river is seen the ruined castle of *Lesdiguières*, in the chapel of which are tombs of the family, but that of François de Bonne, duc de Lesdiguières (1543–1626), the famous Constable of France, was removed in 1798 to Gap.

    10km. The l.-hand turning here leads past the ruined castle of *St-Firmin* and up the beautiful valley of the *Valgaudemar*, watered by the Séveraisse, in which *La Chapelle*, 18km E., below the *Pic d'Orlan* (3564m) is a centre for this section of the Ecrins. At the head of the valley rises *Les Bains* (3669m).

    Continuing S., at 16km, *Les Baraques*, we pass (l.) *St-Bonnet*, a small resort preserving the house in which François de Bonne (see above) was born.—Hence a mountain road ascends to *Chaillol*, another ski-resort, at 1600m, below the *Pic Queyrol* (2440m).

    3km. The l.-hand turning here leads up the *Campsaur*, its name probably derived from *Campus Saurus* (Old Fr. 'sor', sorrel-coloured), somewhat sultry in summer, comprising the upper valleys of the Drac. In 1611 part of it was made a duchy for Lesdiguières. Many of the inhabitants are Protestants, descended from the flock of Félix Neff (1798–1829), the Swiss pastor and

philanthropist, who frequently resided at *St-Laurent-du-Cros*, near
which the road passes.

Much of the valley has been developed for winter-sports, including *St-Michel-de-Chaillol*, on its N. slope, and *St-Léger-lès-Manse*, opposite, with *Ancelle* in a side
valley beyond the latter.—The road continues E. via (12km) *Pont-du-Fossé* to a
junction 4km further, where the road on the l. ascends the inhospitable glen of
the Drac-Blanc, or 'de Champoléon', commanded to the W. by *Vieux-Chaillol*
(3163m), which may be climbed without difficulty for the superb views it provides.—This r.-hand fork leads up the more fertile Drac-Noir to (6km) *Orcières*,
which with *Merlette*, at a higher level, provides skiing facilities, and cableways to
the *Sommet Drouvet* (2655m) above.—A direct road to Gap from near the W. end
of the Champsaur leads across the *Col de Manse*, named from the Roman station
of 'Mansio'.

Continuing S., we approach the summit level at (4km) *Col Bayard*
(1248m; views) and descend rapidly to (7km) *Gap*.

   GAP (735m; 32,100 Gapençais), préfecture of the *Hautes-Alpes*, an
important hub of communications, is situated in a tributary valley of
the Durance, but is of slight architectural interest, even within the
older centre, and it can be oppressively hot in summer.

Gallo-Roman *Vapincum* was in the 12C ruled by its prince-bishops, and was
united to Dauphiny in 1512. It changed hands several times during the Religious
Wars, being from 1577 held for four years by Lesdiguières. The Protestant element was always strong, and if suffered severely with the revocation of the Edict
of Nantes. In 1692 it was almost entirely burned by the troops of the Duke of
Savoy. On the evening of 15 March 1815 Gap was the first important town in
France to welcome Napoleon with enthusiasm on his route N. from the coast. It
was the birthplace of Guillaume Farel (1489– 1565), the religious reformer of
French-speaking Switzerland.

A short distance E. of the central *Pl. Ladoucette*, in the Pepinière
gardens, is a departmental *Museum*, containing a somewhat
miscellaneous collection of minor paintings, local collections of
folklore and archaeology (including several important Bronze Age
relics), and the Tomb of Lesdiguières (see above), designed by Jean
Richier in 1604, but executed by Jacob Richier, with four reliefs of
the general's campaigns; also a mural tablet to his wife (d. 1606).
   The Rue Carnot, the main thoroughfare, leads S.W. from the Place,
from the N. side of which several short streets approach the
Cathedral, which although on the site of a 13C building, is an edifice
of 1866– 96 displaying varieties of local marble in its interior.

The *Château de Charance*, 3km N.W., the former residence of bishops, was
notable for the fêtes given there prior to the Revolution by Monseigneur de
Maillé, 'the jolliest priest in France'.
   For the road from Gap to *Briançon*, see Rte 137; for that to *Veynes*, and *Aspres*,
see Rte 140, both these in reverse.

GAP TO BARCELONNETTE (65km). The D900B forks l. off the N85 S.W. of the
town, after 12km turning E. and bearing r. along the Durance valley, skirting (l.)
the *Forêt de Remollon*, the latter an area containing curiously eroded pillars
known as the 'Salle du Bal des Demoiselles Coiffées' (cf. p 747), on the slopes of
Mont Colombis (1733m). At 14km the S.W. corner of the *Lac de Serre-Ponçon* is
reached, passing near its dam, completed in 1960, and above its S. arm. The
reservoir, one of the largest artifical lakes in Europe, was formed by damming
the Durance just below its confluence with the Ubaye, after some decades of
study and exploration. Its purpose was to harness its hydro-electricity potential,
to control the irrigation of extensive infertile regions of the Basse Alpes which
had become depopulated, and to save the plains of lower Provence from summer
drought; but see p 747.
   The road then veers S.E. into the valley of the Ubaye, traversing (20km) *Le*

Lauzet-Ubaye, a small resort with a bridge, possible Roman.—To the r. rise the wooded *Petite Séolane*, beyond which is the *Grande Séolane* (2909m); to the l., a ridge, of which the *Aupillon* (2917m), and further E. above Barcelonnette, the *Grand Bérard* (3048m), are the major peaks.

The valley expands as we approach (19km) **Barcelonnette** (1135m), frequented both as a summer and winter resort. Founded in 1231 by leave of Raymond Bérenger IV, Count of Provence and Barcelona, it was at first called Barcelone, its present diminutive form being adopted some five centuries later. The valley was involved in all the frontier wars of Provence, and the town was defended by Marshal Berwick (1670– 1734; a natural son of James II and Arabella Churchill), who united the Ubaye to France in 1713. During the 19C several of its citizens emigrated to Mexico, where they soon virtually monopolised the textile trade, some later returning to their native valleys with substantial fortunes, with which they built substantial villas. One of its streets was even named after Porfirio Diaz, the Mexican president. It was the birthplace of the politicians Jacques-Antoine Manuel (1775– 1827), and Paul Reynaud (1878– 1966); while at *Faucon*, 2km N.E., was born St John of Matha (1160– 1213), founder of the Order of the Trinitarians.

It preserves a few relics of its past except slight remains of 13-14C ramparts, and on the E. side of the *Pl. Manuel*, the 15C *Tour Cardinalis*, the belfry of a dominican convent, probably built on the site of a Roman tower.—At *St-Pons*, 2km N.W., is an interesting 12th and 15C church.

To the S.W., off the D908, is the ski-resort of *Pra-Loup* (see below); to the S.E., those of *Le Sauze*, and *Super-Sauze*, above the side valley of Enchastrayes.—For the road S. to *St-André-les-Alpes*; see below.

BARCELONNETTE TO THE COL DE LARCHE (32km), FOR CUNEO, 69km beyond. The D900 leads N.E. to (8km) *Jausiers*, a refuge of the Waldensiens in the 15C, until the revocation of the Edict of Nantes forced them to emigrate.—Hence the mountain road via the *Cime de la Bonette* (2860m), 24km S.E., crosses the ridge into the upper valley of the Tinée; see Rte 165.—We enter the narrow and gloomy *Pas de Grégoire* to (5km) *La Condamine-Châtelard*, a village rebuilt since damaged in June 1944, to the W. of which is the resort of *Ste-Anne-la-Condamine*.—The *Fort de Tournoux* (1847; extended after 1870) is passed (l.), beyond which the D902 from Guillestre joins the road; see Rte 137.—After an abrupt bend, we turn due E. and begin the ascent of the Ubayette valley to (10km) *Larche* (French Customs), also with ski-lifts. The Italian frontier (and Customs) is reached 7km beyond, at the *Col de Larche* (1991m), also known as the *Colle della Maddalena*, an easy pass free from snow between mid-May and mid-October, dominated to the N.E. by the *Tête de Moïse* (3104m).

François I passed this way on his invasion of italy in 1515, with 21,000 men and 75 cannon, his vanguard of cavalry descending so rapidly upon the Papal forces that Gen. Colonna, when made prisoner, asked whether the French had come from the clouds. Napoleon decreed that 'the imperial road from Spain to Italy' should be carried over it.—Passing the *Lago della Maddalena*, we descend through (7km) *Argentera*, the first Italian village, and traverse (36km) *Demonte*, meeting the Nice road 18km beyond, at *Borgo San Dalmazzo*, 8km S.W. of **Cuneo** (*Coni*), for which see *Blue Guide Northern Italy*.

BARCELONETTE TO ST-ANDRÉ-LES-ALPES (72km). The D902 bears S.W., off which after 2.5km the D908 turns r.—The D109 shortly climbs r. to (6km) the ski-resort of *Pra-Loup* (1630m); the D902 later bears E. towards the *Col de la Cayolle*; see Rte 165.—We circle a valley to the W., with a view of the *Grande Séolane* (2909m), and commence to climb to (19.5km) the *Col d'Allos* (2240m), before descending in zigzags to (9.5km) *Allos*, a small summr and winter resort at 1425m, beneath (N.) the bare pyramid of the *Roche-Grande* (2410m), and *Mont Pelat* to the N.E., at 3051m, the highest peak of the Provençal Alps, easily ascended from near the charming *Lac d'Allos*, approached by road from the village, which has a little 12C church.—8km after passing (r.) the conspicuous 17C *Fort de Savoie*, we enter **Colmars** (1235m), a diminutive fortress with a narrow main street bordered by tall houses, and with a 16C church. The *Porte de France*, the S. gate of the town, with its sundials, is protected by a barbican; nearby is the old *Fort de France*.—The road continues down the valley to (28km) **St-André-les-Alpes**; see Rte 165.

The main road leading S.W. from **Gap** (N85) at 14km passes 2km S.W. of _Tallard_, with a picturesque ruined *Castle (14-16C; partly restored), and a church (13-16C), with a notable door of 1549.—On reaching the Durance its r. bank is followed, to traverse (12km) _Valenty_, to the W. of which is perched the old fortified village of _Ventavon_, 10km S.W. of which is _Laragne-Montéglin_; see Rte 138B.

The road veers S., with a view ahead of the citadel of Sisteron guarding the narrows as we approach.—22km **Sisteron**; see Rte 154.

B. Via the Col de la Croix-Haute

141km (87 miles). N75. 33km _Monastier-de-Clermont_—34km _Col de la Croix-Haute_—29km _Aspres_—45km **Sisteron**.

Maps: IGN 52, 54, 60, or 112, 115. M 244, 245.

The N75 is followed to the S., at the _Pont-de-Claix_ (see Rte 138A) forking r., and the valley of the Gresse is ascended to (16.5km) _Vif_, with a Romanesque church (restored), and _Mairie_ in the relics of a Romanesque priory.—A by-road forks r. to (3km) _Le Genevrey_, with a well-preserved 11C church.—To the r. is the abrupt ridge of the _Vercors_ massif, most of its peaks rising to 1950–2100m, and to 2284m at the _Grande-Moucherolle_; see Rte 133B.

17km _Le Monastier-de-Clermont_.

From its N. end a by-road ascends to the mountain village of _St-Andéol_, and circling a spur, _Gresse-en-Vercors_, a small resort with a 13C church, beneath the wooded slopes of the massif, the highest summit of which, _Le Grand Veymont_ (2341m) rises to the S.W.—The main road may be regained to the S.E. by a road crossing the _Col de l'Allimas_ (1352m), commanding a fine view of the _Mont Aiguille_ (see below), and descending to _St-Michel-les-Portes_.

2km S. of Monastier a l.-hand turning (D34) leads past (l.) the _Côte Rouge_ (views from its summit), crossing the Ebron by a lofty suspension bridge, to (20km) _Mens_, a village which served as a Protestant refuge after the revocation of the Edict of Nantes, with a Romanesque tower to its church.—Hence a road leads due W. through the wooded upland of the _Trièves_ towards _Mont Aiguille_ to meet the N75 just beyond (14km) _Clelles_, with a Romanesque church.

8km (from Monastier) is _St-Michel-les-Portes_ (r.), from which one may also approach _Gresse_ (see above), and the **Mont Aiguille** (2086m), long named _Mont Inaccessible_.

It was ascended for the first time on 26 June 1492 by Antoine de Ville and ten companions, to satisfy a whim of Charles VIII. Having gained the summit by means of ropes and ladders, they passed six days on the mountain, said mass, and set up crosses. One of the party gave an imaginative account of the marvels they had seen on these virgin heights, including chamois, strange birds and plants, and human footprints. In 1834 Jean Liotard gained the summit alone (without ropes and ladders), discovering no marvels, but only a sloping meadow and what he took to be some remnants of dry walls. After 1877 cables were placed at all difficult points in the gullies and chimneys, thus rendering the mountain accessible to experienced climbers with strong nerves. The ascent of this tower occupies over 4 hours, and affords a varied and interesting rock-climb. The views are extensive, and there is a strange feeling of complete isolation on its summit.

7km. _Clelles_ (l.; see above).—Hence a mountain road leads S.W. over the _Col de Ménée_ to (35km) _Châtillon-en-Diois_; see Rte 140.

16km. A l.-hand turning leads via _Lalley_ to (15km) _Tréminis_, a small summer resort in a pine-clad basin of hills below the slope of the _Grand Ferrand_ (S.E.; 2759m), a limestone mass riddled with pot-holes.

A lateral view of Mont Aiguille

The main road continues to ascend S., passing (r.) the ski-slopes of *Le Jocou* to (4km) the summit-level at the *Col de la Croix-Haute* (1176m), between (r.) the *Montagne de Jocou* (2051m) and the summit of the *Aup* (1796m), beyond which the landscape begins to assume a more southern appearance.

3km. The *Col de Grimone* lies to the r., on the road leading to *Die*; see Rte 140.

11km. *St-Julien-en-Beauchêne*, with a few 17C houses, and a church containing an assumption by Philippe de Champaigne once in the Chartreuse de Durbon (see below), lies at the foot of the *Montagne de Durbonas* (l.; 2086m).

Below its N. flank, reached by a lane hence, is the ruined *Chartreuse*, founded in 1116 as the fourth house of the Carthusian order. Like its parent house, it is situated in a wild and sequestered valley, separated from the outer world by a gorge with a gateway, and shut in to the E. by wooded heights. It is much overgrown, but the walls of the 13C chapel may be distinguished.

The road passes some curious limestone rocks forming a barrier across the valley, and later, fields of lavender.—At 10.5km a l.-hand fork leads to (6.5km) *Veynes*, on the road to *Gap*; see Rte 140.

We circle to the W. and through (4.5km) *Aspres-sur-Buëch*; see Rte 140, and for the road hence via (11km) *Serres*, and (17km) *Laragne-Montégilin*, to Sisteron, 17km beyond. For **Sisteron** itself, see Rte 154.

SERRES TO NYONS (65km). The undulating D994 leads W. below a ridge of hills, on the far side of which, at 12.5km, lies the upland village of *Montmorin*, birthplace of Philis de la Tour-du-Pin-la-Charce (1645–1703), the heroine who is said to have defended the passes of her native valley against Victor Amadeus II of Savoy in 1691–92.—12.5km. *Rosans*, an old village retaining several 15-16C houses and a square 13C tower. To the S. are the hills of the *Baronnies*.—We veer N.W., and following the valley of the Aigues, turn S.W. below the *Montagne d'Angèle* (1529m) to (29.5km) *Curnier*, 6km S.E. of which is the ancient village of *Ste-Jalle* and the 12C church of *N.-D.-de-Beauvert*.—Threading the gorges of the *Trou de Pontias*, we approach (10.5km) *Noyons*; see Rte 141B.—**Vaison-la-Romaine** lies 16km S.; **Orange**, 42km S.W.

For the road from Laragne-Montéglin to *Carpentras* via Séderon and *Sault-de-Vaucluse*, see Rte 153B, in reverse.

139 Lyon to Valence

A. Via Vienne and the E. bank of the Rhône

104km (64km). N7. 27km **Vienne**—44km *St-Vallier*—15km *Taine-l'Hermitage*—18km **Valence**.

Maps: IGN 51, 52, or 112. M 93 or 244.

The A7 motorway provides a rapid route between the main towns.

The N7 traverses industrials districts and uninteresting country immediately S. of **Lyon** (Rte 129), at 14km by-passing *St-Symphorien*.

13km **VIENNE** (29,500 Viennois), the centre of a fruit-growing area, with old-established textile and leather-works, and diversified industries, is—apart from its Roman relics, and the repute in which one restaurant has long been held—a rather dull town. It was once a strategic importance as a crossing of the Rhône, here hemmed in by hills, immediately to the E. rising precipitously.

The chief town of the Allobroges become a Roman colony under the name of *Vienna Senatoria*, and the capital of the province of Gaul. It was referred to by Ausonius and Martial as 'opulent'. Here in 392, probably at the instigation of his Gaulish general Arbogast, Valentinian II was murdered. It later became the capital of the kingdom of Burgundy (413–534), and from 879–1032 of that of the so-called kingdom of Arles. Its archbishops, who from 1119 bore the title of Primate of the Gauls, divided its territory with the dauphins of the Viennois until the accession of Louis IX, when it was absorbed by the province of Dauphiny. At the Council of Vienne (1311–12) Clement V, under pressure from Philippe le Bel, suppressed the Templars. At the Revolution the archiepiscopal see was merged with that of Lyon, and its importance declined. It was the birthplace or seat of several early saints of little moment, and it most famous native is the dramatic poet François Ponsard (1814–67).

From the Quai Jaurès, along which traffic swirls, we turn off just S. of the *old* bridge into the Cours Brillier (S.I.). Hence the Cours Romestang bears N. to the central *Pl. de Miremont*, on the E. side of which is the **Museum**.

Noteworthy are the Roman remains found in the vicinity, among which are an ivory female head; bronze dolphins dredged from the Rhône in 1840, and bronze figurines, and a bronze statue of Julius Pacatianus; Roman coins, glass, terracotta objects, and ceramics, etc. The collection of French porcelain is good.

To the N.E., behind a modern building, are the remains of the *Roman Forum*, including a portico, and a *Temple of Cybele*. The monumental stair which ascended to the theatre is covered by the Rue Victor Hugo, which must be climbed to approach the relics of a **Roman Theatre**, built into the flank of *Mont Pipet*, excavated between 1922–38, and occasionally used in summer. It is 115m in diameter, 2m wider than that at Orange, but is hardly comparable in other respects. To the S. is a small *Odeon* (73m in diameter). On the summit of the hill are the slight remains of the Roman *Citadel* (view).

Descending from the theatre, we pass near the *Porte de l'Ambulance* of 1665, and turn downhill to the W. along the Rue St-André-la-Haut, passing (r.) the Louis-XIV church of that name, to gain the Rue des Orfèvres, there turning r. along the Rue Marchande.

A derelict area of steep stepped lanes lies to the N.E. between this point and the bank of the Gère, with its bridge of 1400, its clustering factories, and its Roman revetment.

Some distance further N. lie the ruins of the 13C *Château de la Bâtie*, on *Mont Salomon*, seen from the quay.

On reaching a small square we turn l. towards the apse of **St-André-le-Bas** (late 9th and 12C; again under restoration), with a good Romanesque tower. Two columns of the chancel are Roman, with capitals from another source. An alley on its N. side leads to the entrance to a small lapidary collection, including a Paleo-Christian sarcophagus, and a Cloister of c. 1125, with worn capitals.

There is a view hence of the ugly overpass on the river-side, masking the modern bridge over the Rhône, which superseded the suspension-bridge (now pedestrian only; crossing to the suburb of *Ste-Colombe*), which itself replaced an earlier bridge swept away in the flood of 1840. On the far bank, between the two bridges, stands a square tower of 1349, built by Philippe VI to defend a Roman bridge (destroyed 1651) crossing what was then the frontier of France.

Also on the far bank, approached by crossing the new bridge and then turning down to the r., lies the Gallo-Roman *Site of St-Romain-en-Gal, in the process of excavation since 1967. Of particular interest are the upturned earthenware vessels in the basement of a room, creating an air pocket. In an adjacent building are displayed a number of artefacts and mosaics found on the site, which has already yielded more splendid mosaics than most other towns in Gaul.

From St-André one may return towards the centre along the Rue des Clercs to the *Pl. du Palais*, on the N. side of which rises the round tower of the *Palais de Justice*, a relic of the Palace of the Dauphins. In the centre of the square stands the **Temple of Augustus and Livia** (c. 41 A.D.) a smaller version of the Maison Carré at Nimes, but less well preserved, consisting of a rectangular cella with a portico of six Corinthan columns in front and five on each side, followed by engaged pilasters. The dedication is known from the disposition of the nail-holes on the front frieze, relics of the original bronze inscrip-

tion during the lifetime of Augustus and of a later one after his
deification.

It was much mutilated during the Middle Ages by having the interstices of its col
umns built up with masonry, and the columns themselves rasped to bring them
level with the walls, in order to convert it into a church. It became a Jacobin club
at the Revolution, and was only restored in 1854– 65. Roman fragments lie scat
tered around the building.

Continuing S., after a short distance we turn r. to reach the N. side of
St-Maurice, the former cathedral, on the exterior wall of which is
12C arcading. Houses abut the apse, and there are no transepts. The
W. front, facing a broad flight of steps descending towards the river
and the old suspension bridge (see above), was begun in the 14C, but
was mutilated by the Protestant troops of the Baron des Adrets in
1562. Its three portals and the lower storey are worth examination.

The central portal (15C), with two curious little twisted columns in the tym
panum, is an admirable example of late Gothic. The upper storeys (1500– 32)
built of inferior stone, have been recently restored.
    The main arcade of the E. pasrt of the nave, with notable capitals, dates from
1107– 40. Note the fluting, as at Autun. The upper part was finished and the
four W. bays added in the 14C, while the choir and apse were completed for the
consecration by Innocent IV in 1251. The central lancet of the W. window bears
the papal tiara and the cardinal's hat in honour of Pope Calixtus II (Abp Guy de
Bourgogne; d. 1124).
    In the N. porch are some 12C statues, and above, a zodiac (?12C), reading from
r. to l., and re-arranged in the 16C to suit the new calendar. Above the adjoining
door and over the S. porch are mutilated 12C sculptured groups. The pretentious
mausoleum of Card. de Montmorin (1713), to the r. of the choir, is by Slodtz.

On descending the steps from the W. front, we may turn l. along the
Rue Boson to approach the former church of **St-Pierre**, rebuilt with
Roman material in the 9-10C on 4-6C foundations. The W. tower was
added in the 12C. It now houses an interesting lapidary collection.

Among the Gallo-Roman fragments, many saved from destruction by M.
Schneyder (1733– 1814), are numerous stellae; a statue of the goddess Tutela, a
2C copy of a Greek original; part of a frienze from the theatre; and a mosaic of
Victorious Athletes uncovered in 1966 from the adjoining Pl. St-Pierre. Also
notable are the tombs of St Léonien (6C, with a 10C epitaph), and of Aymer, Abp
of Embrun (d. 1245).

The Rue Boson continues S. to regain the Cours Brillier, on the far side of which,
in public gardens, a section of the Roman Via Aurelia has been exposed.
    Some 5 minutes' walk along the Cours de Verdun, leading S., a r.-hand turning
approaches the *Aiguille* (probably 4C), a four-faced arch surmounted by an
elongated pyramid, which once adorned the centre of the spina, or longitudinal
wall, of a Roman circus. It was long supposed to be the tomb of Pontius Pilate,
who, according to Eusebius, was banished to Vienne, where he died.—Mme
Point's 'Pyramide' restaurant is adjacent.

VIENNE TO VALENCE VIA ROMANS (87km). An alternative to the dull main
road is the D538, leading S.E., at 22.5km passing E. of the *Château de Bresson*, to
(6.5km) *Beaurepaire*, a small town on the Valloire (a broad glacier-cut valley with
no important river), with a church and several houses of the 15C.—11km
Hauterives, preserving the curious surrealist folly known as 'Le Palais Idéal'
constructed in 1879– 1912 by the local postman, Ferdinand Cheval
(1836– 1924), whose tomb in the cemetery is similarly eccentric.—*Le Grand
Serre*, 6.5km E., preserves its walls, five gateways, and a 13C church.—13km. St-
Donat-sur-l'Herbasse, 6.5km S.W., a wine-growing town, retains ruins of its 12C
castle. It was the scene of particularly repellent German reprisals during 1944.
The collegiate *Church* (12-16C) is noted for its Bach festivals, recitals being per
formed on an organ constructed by C. Schwenkedel on the lines of those of

Silbermann.—14km **Romans-sur-Isère** (33,900 Romanais), an old tanning town,
still largely devoted to the manufacture of footware. Here in 1349 Humbert II,
the last of the independent dauphins, signed the abdication whereby his domains
were resigned to Charles of Valois. In Dec. 1788 an historic meeting of the provincial Estates took place at Romans, summoned by Louis XVI in consequence of
the assembly at Vizille (cf.) that July. In 1982 a mosque, built there for its
Moslem workers, was destroyed prior to its inauguration. To the S. of the old
centre stands the abbey-church of *St-Bernard*, dating from 1140 but radically
restored in 1718, preserving an interesting but sadly mutilated *Portal*; the
polygonal choir (13C), with its three tiers of windows, is of interest; the cloister
was demolished in 1857 to make way for a reconstruction of the riverside
quay.—*A Musée de la Chaussure*, together with other local collections, is housed in the buildings of a 17C convent some minutes' walk to the N.E. See also *E. Le
Roy Ladurie*, 'Carnival at Romans' (in 1579 – 80).

From its transpontine suburb of *Bourg-de-Péage* the road bears S.W. to (18km)
Valence, at 6.5km passing 5.5km S.E. of *Châteauneuf-sur-Isère*, birthplace of St
Hugues (d. 1106) Bp of Grenoble, and a founder of the Carthusian order.—The
road S. may be continued via (16km) *Chabeuil*, a little old town at the foot of the
Vercors range rising to the E. (for which see Rte 133B) to *Crest*, 20km beyond; see
Rte 140.

Quitting Vienne, the main road follows the A7 closely most of the
way, shortly climbing onto a plateau providing a view towards *Mont
Pilat* to the W., before descending to (19km) *Le Péage-de-Roussillon*,
named after a toll-gate set here in the 13C by local lords. In the mid
16C castle at adjacent *Roussillon* Charles IX signed an edict fixing
the 1 January as the commencement of the civil year, in 1564.—3km
S. of the latter, at *Salaise*, the church has a Romanesque choir and
crypt.

Passing (r.) a Rhône-Poulenc factory, we shortly cross the
Grenoble-Annonay road, and traverse (9.5km) *St-Rambert-d'Albon*,
to the S.E. of which a hill-top keep is all that remains of the castle of
the counts of Albon who in the 11C became the dauphins of Viennois. The motorway veers away to the S.E. as (11.5km) *St-Vallier* is
approached, a pottery-making town at the mouth of the Galaure,
with the château of *Chabrillan*, residence of Guillaume, last count of
the Valentinois and brother of Diane de Poitiers.

The road now traverses a defile of the Rhône and passes the ruined
castle of *Serves* to enter (15km) **Tain-l'Hermitage** (5,600 inhab.),
whose famous vineyards are named from a hermit's cell (1425) on
the hillside to the E. of the town. In the main Place stands a
'taurobolium' dating from A.D. 184. The river here was spanned by
an early suspension bridge (1826) by Marc Séguin, until demolished
in 1964. A bridge of 1958 now crosses the Rhône to *Tournon*; see Rte
139B.

The road makes a curve to the E., to a plain on which in 121 B.C.
Quintus Fabius defeated the Allobriges and Arverni, beyond which
the Isère is crossed. The snowy mass of Mont Blanc may occasionally
be distinguished at the head of the valley. On the far bank of the
Rhône stands the castle of *Châteaubourg*, and further S., as Valence
is approached, the ruins of that of *Crussol* are conspicuous; see Rte
139B.

12.5km **VALENCE** (68,200 Valentinois), préfecture of the *Drôme*,
and an important fruit market, occupying a terrace overlooking the
Rhône, facing a precipitous line of cliffs, is of slight interest as far as
remains of its past are concerned: even Stendhal, who visited the
place in 1838, considered it 'a sordid town', and its architecture commonplace. The drawings of Hubert Robert in the museum are
remarkable, however.

The Roman city of *Valentia Julia*, founded 123 B.C., was the last refuge of the usurper Constantine (d. 408), who raised Gaul and Spain against Honorius. Its medieval history, as nominal capital of the duchy of Valentinois, was long involved in a struggle against its bishops, from whom it was partially freed in 1450 by Louis XI. The most famous professor of its university (founded 1452; suppressed 1793) was Scaliger; its most famous pupil, Rabelais. Valence suffered damage in the Protestant uprising of 1562. The title of the duchy was held by Caesar Borgia, and by Diane de Poitiers, and is now hereditary to the Grimaldi family. Napoleon studied at the artillery school here in 1785–86, and returned there in 1791. Pius VI died here in exile in 1799 after being taken prisoner in the Vatican by soldiers of the Directory. It was still surrounded by towers in the early 19C. The N. part of the town was badly damaged by Allied bombing prior to its liberation on 31 Aug. 1944.

The motorway and N7 both skirt the Rhône, spanned here by the *Pont de St-Péray*, rebuilt since its stone predecessor was blown up in 1942, which had replaced a handsome suspension bridge. Adjacent, to the S., is the umbrageous *Parc Jouvet*, above which is the *Champ de Mars* (views towards the ruined castle of *Mont Crussol*).

A narrow street opposite the E. end of the latter leads into the old town of crooked lanes, the first on the l. approaching the **Museum**, installed in the former *Bishop's Palace* (often visited by Mme de Sévigné).

It contains several fine mosaics, including one of Hercules; one from the baptistry, which once abutted the cathedral; and others from Luc-en-Diois, among other collections of Roman antiquities, and notable Romanesque capitals. Remarkable are the series of 95 red chalk *Drawings* (sanguines) executed by *Hubert Robert* in Italy, Rome, and France between 1755–75 (including an interesting one of the Salon of Mme Geoffrin), given to Valence by M. Veyrenc, one of his pupils, in 1835. Among notable paintings are: *Pannini*, Ruins of a pyramid, and of an obelisk; *P. Gysels*, Landscape; *Van Steenwyck*, Deliverance of St Peter; *Valdés Leal*, Christ carrying the cross; *School of Barocci*, Deposition; *Rigaud*, two Portraits of Monseigneur Milon; and representative works by *Horace Vernet, Jules Noël, N. Diaz, Daubigny, Lépine, P.-D. Trouillebert*, et al.

The nearby former **Cathedral** (St-Apollinaire), consecrated by Urban II in 1095 on his way to Clermont, is of the Auvergnat type, the most conspicuous features of which are the apse and the W. porch, with good capitals, but surmounted by an ugly and incongruous tower of 1862, prior to which Stendhal thought the building 'very pretty'. The interior is notable for the narrowess of its aisles and for the height of the slender shafts of the columns abutting the piers facing the nave. The choir was poorly restored in 1730.

Immediately to the E. is a curious monument of the Mistral family known as the *Pendentif* from the shape of its vault, the earliest of its kind in France (1548).—Hence the Rue Pérollerie, with the 16C *Maison Depré-Latour*, leads N. to rebuilt *St-Jean-Baptiste*, preserving its Romanesqe tower. Near the S. end of the Grande-Rue, parallel to the E., is the *Maison des Têtes* (1532), so-called from the worn medallions on its facade; those in the courtyard are better preserved.

For the road from Valence to *Le Puy*, see Rte 99, in reverse; for roads to **Sisteron** via *Die*, see Rte 140; to **Avignon**, and **Montpellier**, Rtes 141 and 142, respectively

B. Via the W. bank of the Rhône

112km (69 miles). N86. 21km *Givors*—12km *St-Roman-en-Gal*,
with **Vienne** on the far bank—30km *Serrières*—31km **Tournon**
—14km *St-Peray*—4km **Valence**.

Maps: IGN 51, 52, or 112. M 93 or 244.

The N86 leads S.W. from the centre of **Lyon** (Rte 129), crossing the
Saône at its confluence with the Rhône, towards (10km) *Brignais*,
now by-passed. Sections of the *Roman Aqueduct* once supplying
Lyon may be seen some distance to the W. of the latter, following a
line from the 76 *Arcs de Chaponost* to *Mornant*, to the S.W., nearly
approached by the D42.

10km. *Givors*, an industrial town at the junction of the Gier with
the Rhône, is crossed.

The Gier valley, to the S.W., is traversed by roads, the A47 motorway, and the
Canal de Givors (1761–89), providing such sights as collieries, glassworks,
founderies, and factories of infinite variety en route, as *Rive-de-Gier*, *Le Grand-
Croix*, and *St-Chamond* are passed, to approach (37km) **St-Étienne**; see Rte 98.

We veer S.E. towards (12km) **Vienne**, first passing under the A7 at *St-
Romain-en-Gal* (see Rte 139A) and the transpontine suburb of *Ste-
Colombe*.

The road now bears S.W. past *Ampuis*, famous for its apricots, to
(11km) *Condrieu*, an ancient place preserving a 15C house opposite
its church, and a ruined castle.—From (6.5km) *Chavanay* a road
ascends via *Pélussin* to the crest of *Mont Pilat* (1370m and 1432m),
also approached by the D503 leading S.W. from (3.5km) *St-Pierre-de-
Boeuf* to (22km) *Bourg-Argental*; see Rte 98.

This latter continues S.W. via (29.5km) *Montfaucon-en-Velay*, and (19km) *Yssingeaux*, to *Le Puy*, 27km beyond; see Rtes 98 and 99.

8km. *Serrières*, a little riverside town, where the Rhône is bridged,
in which *St-Sornin* contains a curious ossuary and folk
museum.—Hence the N82 ascends S.W. to (15km) **Annonay** (see Rte
98), beyond which is the valley of the Cance, and the *Monts du
Vivarais*.

6km. *Champagne* has a unusual 11C church incorporating Roman
capitals and sculptures, 4km beyond which the old town of *Andance*
is traversed, whose 12C church preserves fragments from a Gallo-
Roman temple.

At (6km) *Sarras* the defile of St-Vallier is entered, its S. end guarded
by ruined fortresses.—11km. *Vion*, with a Romanesque church spoilt
by 19C restorations, 3km beyond which, near the church of *St-Jean-
de-Muzols*, is an Roman dedicatory inscription to Trajan by the
Rhône boatmen.

2km. **Tournon** (9,700 inhab.), a pleasant little town with a riverside
promenade. *St-Julien* (14-17C), poorly restored, contains a notable
16C triptych. Adjacent is the imposing *Castle* (16C), much restored
after use as a prison. The eldest son of François I died here aged 19 in
1536, the day young Ronsard arrived to serve him as page.—Further
S. on the quay, with *Tain l'Hermitage* opposite (see Rte 139A) is the
Lycée, occupying the Renaissance buildings of a college founded in
1536 by the Card. de Tournon (1489–1562), where in 1863–66
Mallarmé taught English. Among its pupils were Honoré d'Urfé, and
Pierre Daru, Napoleon's minister.

The D534 ascends S.W. through the *Gorges du Doux* from Tournon to (35km) *Lamastre* (see Rte 99), passing near the quaint old village of *Boucieu-le-Roi*.

On a clear day the *Corniche du Rhône*, approached immediately S.W. of Tournon, provides extensive views, particularly from *St-Romain-de-Lerps*, beyond which we descend to *St-Péray*.

At 8km the restored castle of *Châteaubourg* is passed (l.), and 6km beyond, *St-Péray*, reputed for its wines, is entered. To the S., above the château of *Beauregard* (restored), stand the extensive medieval ruins of that of *Crussol*, commanding a view of Valence, and the *Vercors massif* further E.

4km. **Valence**; see Rte 139A.

XII   EASTERN LANGUEDOC;
ROUSSILLON; PROVENCE

See the latter part of the introduction to Section VI.

Provence, a French province under the *ancien régime*, comprised the departments of the *Bouche-du-Rhône*, the *Vaucluse*, *Var*, and *Alpes de Haute-Provence*. It did not include the papal *Comtat Venaissin* (now part of Vaucluse, to the E. of Avignon), nor the county of *Nice* (now part of *Alpes-Maritime*, in which the anachronistic principality of *Monaco* forms an enclave; cf. Monaco). The term 'Provence' has indicated widely differing areas during its long history. The Roman *provincia* of Gaul, from which its name is derived, included *Languedoc*, and *Dauphiny* also, until the Barbarian invasions restricted it to the region bounded by the Rhône, the Alps, and the Mediterranean. Later *Proenza* was used to denote 'Le Midi' in general, the whole extent of the South of France (below a line describing an irregular curve from the Gironde to Savoy), in which the Provençal language in its various dialects, the Langue d'Oc (see introduction to Section VI) was spoken. Here was composed and sung the literature of the Troubadours (from 'trobar') as distinct from the Trouvères (from 'trouver') of the North; and in this sense also the word was used by the 'Félibres', who promoted the Provençal poetic renaissance in the second half of the 19C. As Peire Vidal wrote in the 12C: 'There is no land to compare with that from the Rhône to Vence, between the sea and the Durance'.

At a very early period Greek (*Phocaean*) colonies were established along the Mediterranean coast, prominent among which were *Marseille* (c. 600 B.C.), and *Glanum* (inland, near St-Remy). In response to requests for assistance in defending these settlements from attacks by local Ligurians, the Romans in 124 B.C. proceeded to conquer the area for themselves. Marius inflicted a severe defeat on the invading Cimbri and Teutons near *Aix* (which later became the Roman capital) in 102 B.C., while the monument erected by Augustus at *La Turbie* in 6 B.C. celebrates their final pacification of this maritime region. Among several Roman settlements which grew in importance in this *provincia* were *Cimiez* (near Nice), *Fréjus*, *Arles*, *Vaison-la-Romaine*, and *Orange*.

This area was later invaded by several waves of Barbarians, but by the 9C *Arles* emerges as the capital of a kingdom of Provence or Arles, which lasted about a century. For c. 90 years prior to their expulsion in 973, the Saracens settled like locusts on the Montagnes des Maures, and ravaged the countryside. In 1246 Provence passed to Charles of Anjou, later king of Sicily and Naples, and ancestor of Joanna of Naples, who in 1348 sold Avignon to Pope Clement VI, and of 'le bon roi' René (1409–80), titular king of Sicily and the last independent count of Provence. With the death of René's chosen successor, who dying without issue had bequeathed his countship on Louis XI, in 1487 Provence was formally united to France. The Parlement established at Aix in 1502 by Louis XII earned its inclusion among the 'scourges of Provence' by its ruthless destruction of 29 Vaudois villages in 1545, and by its general corruption. The other scourges were the violent 'Mistral', which occasionally blows down the Rhône valley, and the river Durance, now tamed. In 1536 the Emperor Charles V briefly invaded Provence in one of his sporadic campaigns against François I. It was again invaded by an Austro-Sardinian army in 1707 during the War of the Spanish Succession; by Napoleon at Golfe Juan (en route to Grenoble), when returning from exile on Elba in 1815; and in 1944 by the allies when liberating the S. of France. *Orange* was annexed in 1713; the *Comtat Venaissin* in 1791; and the *Comté de Nice* in 1860, while a few slight frontier adjustments were made after the second World War.

140 Valence to Sisteron via Die

170km (105 miles). D538A. 28km **Crest**—D93. 37km **Die**—18km
Luc-en-Diois—42km *Aspres*—N75. 11km *Serres*—34km **Sisteron**.

Maps: IGN 52, 60, or 115. M 93, 245.

The road drives S.E. from **Valence** (Rte 139A) to (9.5km) *Beaumont-
lès-Valence*, with remains of walls and an interesting 12C church
with a Protestant nave and Catholic choir.—At 7.5km the road S.
from Romans is met, and 11km beyond **Crest** (pron. 'Cré'; 7,800 inhab.) is entered. This busy little town on the Drôme is overlooked by
a huge 12-15C *Keep* (51m high on the N. side), approached from the
central Place by a labyrinth of rock-hewn stairways, and providing a
fine view from the top. The *Hôtel de Ville*, on the Place, has 16C
doors and preserves a charter on stone of 1188.

The r. bank of the Drôme is followed, traversing (3.5km) *Aouste-
sur-Sye*, once *Augusta*, 2.5km beyond which the D70 leads N. up a
side valley to (9.5km) *Beaufort-sur-Gervanne*, a small fortified hill-
town affording a good approach to the *Vercors massif*; see Rte 133B.

The valley narrows as we skirt the ridge (S.) bounding the *Fôret de
Saou*; see Rte 141B.—9km *Saillans*, an ancient village, lies in a gorge
overhung to the N. by crags, and with *Le Veyou* (1589m) among
other peaks rising to the S.—At 6km a minor road follows the *Gorge
of the Roanne* to the S. to (10.5km) *St-Nazaire-le-Désert*, in a high
wind-swept depopulated region.

The road now makes a large circle to the N., passing (r.) *Vercheny*,
noted for its white sparkling muscatel wine (Clairette de Die), before
crossing the Drôme at (6km) *Pontaix*, picturesquely situated, with a
partly vaulted street running parallel to the river, and ruins of a castle.—3km. *Ste-Croix*, on the far bank, is dominated by the ruined castle of *Quint* (the last possession of the Holy Roman Empire in France),
from which a road ascends the Sure valley to (10km) *St-Julien-en-
Quint*, below the Vercors massif.

The Drôme valley now widens as we turn E., with the cliffs and
forests of the great limestone ridge of the *Glandasse* ahead, rising at
Pié Ferré to 2041m, as we approach (7km) *Die*, the line of its 3C ramparts, now well outside the town on the N., being prominent.

DIE, situated on the Meyrosse near its confluence with the Drôme,
is an ancient walled town on the S. flank of the Vercors massif preserving several relics of its past importance.

Gallo-Roman *Dea Augusta Vocontiorum* was devastated by the Barbarians in
275, after which ramparts were thrown up, judging from the quantity of débris
from wrecked buildings used in their construction. Its ancient bishopric provided
the only representative from Gaul at the Council of Nicaea. Having lapsed in
1276, it was revived between 1687 and 1790. From the advent of Henri IV to the
revocation of the Edict of Nantes in 1685 it was a Protestant stronghold, with a
Protestant Academy between 1598 and 1684. It was the 12C Comtesse de Die
who was passionately envolved with the troubadour Raimbaut d'Orange.

The main street traverses the town from N.W. to S.E., at the former
end of which is a small *Museum* of antiquities; at the latter, near the
present viaduct, is the *Porte St-Marcel*, a Roman triumphal arch, on
the outer side of which a fortified medieval gateway in the Gallo-
Roman ramparts has been built. In the S. part of the walled enceinte
stands the former **Cathedral**, partly demolished in 1570, and
rigorously restored in 1673; it preserves relics of a Romanesque and

Gothic tower, and an 11C porch, with granite columns from a Roman temple and curious capitals on the three arches. Over the W. door is a mutilated 12C Passion, to the r. of which a Roman inscription has been inserted upside down. A side portal has been known as the *Porte Rouge* since the murder there of Bp Humbert in 1222, who had threatened the citizens' freedom. The Renaissance pulpit and late 17C boiseries, etc. will be noted.

The Rue St-Vincent leads S. near a *Protestant temple* (a former Jesuit chapel), opposite which is a Renaissance house; beyond is the former *Bishop's Palace*, now occupied by the *Hôtel de Ville* (its chapel containing a mosaic pavement representing the four rivers of Paradise, apparently from a 7C baptistry); in the outer wall of the adjacent *Tribunal* is a Roman taurobolium.

For the road from Die ascending into the *Vercors* via the *Col de Rousset*; see Rte 133B, in reverse.—1km E. of Die, a l.-hand lane ascends via *Sallières* to (6km) the remains of the Cistercian abbey of *Valcroissant*, founded in 1188, on the W. slope of the Glandasse.

5km. *Pont-de-Quart.*

The D539 turns l. to (8km) *Châtillon-en-Diois*, an ancient fortified village, 4km beyond which a l.-hand lane leads up to *Ménée*, with its ruined castle, to the N.W. of which rises the *Cirque d'Archiane*, a cliff-girt amphitheatre of red-stanined rocks, forming part of the S. edge of the *Vercors massif.*—The main road continues E. through the red-walled *Gorges des Gas*, and the *Col de Grimone* (1318m) to meet the N75 27km beyond; see Rte 138B.

The Drôme is crossed near the *Château de la Salle*, a residence of bishops of Die, and its r. bank is followed to (12km) *Luc-en-Diois*, the ancient *Lucus Augusti*, noted for its lavender, which has yielded a number of antiquarian finds, notably a mosaic in the museum at Valence.

The road now enters a defile of the Drôme, and traverses by a double curve the rocky wilderness of *Le Claps*, the result of a huge double landslide in 1442.—After 10km we turn away from the river to commence the ascent in a series of zigzags to (20km) the *Col de Cabre* (1180m), the 'Caura Mons' of the Itineraries.—17km. *Aspres-sur-Buëch*, lying in a bleak upland basin, a region of ferrugineous springs.

ASPRES TO GAP (29km). The D994A leads S.E., after 4km turning l. onto the D994 for (5km) **Veynes**, an ancient town, Roman *Dovianum*, and later *Vedenetum*, in the centre of which (preserving some old houses in the Rue Sous-le-Barri) the *Mairie* occupies a 16C château, abutted by an earlier gate and tower. It may have been the birthplace of the troubadour Guillaume de Cabestang.—At 6km we pass (l.) *Montmaur*, a village with two castles, the *Château de Terrail* (14C; restored, with a well-preserved armoury), and a ruined 11C fortress at a higher level.—The valley of the Petit-Buëch is followed to the E., with the *Pic de Bure* (2709m) rising to the N., and to the S., the *Pic de Céuze* (2016m), at 7km passing (r.) the château of *Manteyer* (14th and 17C), before commencing the descent to (13km) *Gap*; see Rte 138A.

At Aspres we turn r. onto the N75, after 7km passing near the village of *La Bâtie-Montsaléon* (l.), the 'Mons Seleuci', where Magnentius the Frank was defeated by Constantine II in 353.

4km. **Serres**, a small town on the slope of a rocky spur above the Buëch, has a 12C church and several medieval houses, while the *Mairie* occupies the former mansion of Lesdiguières (16C). On a hill to the N. are a ruined castle (1340) and a 12C Jewish tomb with a Hebrew inscription.

For the road hence to *Nyons*, see Rte 138B.

2km. *Le Bersac* (l.) is noted for its almonds, beyond which lies *Savournon*, with a ruined 12C chapel and castle, and 11C keep, above which rise the *Montagnes d'Aujour* (1834m).

Beyond (9km) *Eyguians*, just W. of which, at *Lagrand*, is a good 12C church, the valley opens to the E., and (6km) *Laragne-Montéglin* is traversed, while ahead the citadel of Sisteron is seen guarding the narrows immediately S. of the confluence of the Buëch and Durance.—11km **Sisteron**; see Rte 154.

141   Valence to Avignon

A.   Via Montélimar, and Orange

125km (77 miles). N7. 18km *Loriol*—23km **Montélimar**—35km **Pont-St-Esprit** lies 4km W.—20km **Orange**—29km **Avignon**.

Maps: IGN 52, 59, or 115. M 93.

The A7 motorway provides a rapid route, from which the main town may be approached with ease.

From **Valence** (see Rte 139A) the N7 runs parallel to and E. of the motorway, at 10km leaving to our l. *Étoile*, with a fine 12C church, to (8km) *Livron*, where the Drôme is crossed, to enter or by-pass (3km) *Loriol*, from which the Rhône is spanned by a bridge to *Le Pouzin* (6km W.); see Rte 142A.

A DETOUR may be made by veering S.E. from Loriol via *Marmande*, with a 12C church, and (15km) *Marsanne*, birthplace of Président Loubet (1838–1929), adjacent to which are the relics of its medieval enceinte.—Turning S.W., we pass near the 16C château of *Condillac* (3km N.W.) before approaching (5km) *Sauzet*, also preserving fortifications, and (2km) *St-Marcel-lès-Sauzet*, with an interesting Provençal Romanesque abbey-church.—Crossing the A7, *Montélimar* is entered 7km beyond.

We shortly cross the A7 (with the ruins of the castle of *Les Tourettes* to the l.) and skirt the Rhône, on the far side of which are the limestone quarries above *Cruas*, and a nuclear-power-station under construction, and the ruins of *Rochemaure* on its basalt rock.

23km. **MONTÉLIMAR** (30,200 Montiliens), Roman *Accusium*, later designated *Mont-Adhémar*, whence its name, although in the mid 19C it was still known as *Montélimart* (when it was still surrounded by ramparts), is reputed for its manufacture of nougat.

The older centre of narrow lanes, preserving several 16-17C houses, is traversed by the Rue Pierre-Julien, running S. from the remaining medieval *Gate* at the Pl. St-Martin, and passes *Ste-Croix* (with its 15C apse) and the market place, to reach the Pl. Marx-Dormoy, named after a former minister of the interior (1888–1941), who was assassinated here by 'miliciens'. On a height to the E. of the centre, overlooking the Roubion, stands and battered *Château des Adhémar*, mainly 14C, with a chapel and relics of an earlier stronghold of the seigneurs de Grignan.

A pleasant road leads along the valley of the Javron to *Dieulefit* (22km E.; see Rte 141B) passing, at 8km, N. of the 13-16C château of *Puygiron*, traversing (8km beyond) *La Bégude-de-Mazenc*, with an 18C château, and 7.5km further E., *Le*

Poët-Laval, a characteristic village perched on a hill overlooking the valley to the N. (well-sited hotel), once a commandery of the Hospitallers.

MONTÉLIMAR TO GRIGNAN AND VAISON-LA-ROMAINE (60km). Not the main road, but a pleasant cross-country road, leads S.E., forking r. off the D4 to (8km) *Allan*, with ruins of its castle (with a Romanesque chapel) and medieval village adjacent, and at 8.5km passes 3km S.W. of the abbey of *N.-D.-d'Aiguebelle*, a Cistercian foundation occupied by Trappists since 1816, and preserving a 12C church and refectory; its liqueurs and confections are reputed.—9.5km. **Grignan**, a small town dominated by the Renaissance *Château* of its counts (1558; restored 1913), where Marie de Rabutin-Chantal, marquise de Sévigné (1626–96), the famous and affectionate mother of the not too appreciative Countess de Grignan, died; here tomb lies in 16C *St-Sauveur*, adjacent. Near the N. end of the town is the 14-17C *Beffroi*; from its S. end a lane leads S.W., to the *Grotte de Rochecourbière*, from which many of Mme de Sévigné's letters are dated.—Continuing S.E. through (4km) *Grillon*, lavender-fields are traversed to (5km) **Valréas**, its old labyrinthine centre surrounded by boulevards. Several old mansions may be found in alleys on its W. side; further E. is the *Chapel des Pénitents-Blancs* and its belfry, beyond which stands *N.-D.-de-Nazareth* (12C, with later additions). To the S. is the 18C *Hôtel de Simiane*, now the *Mairie*, while overlooking the Cours Tivoli, further S., is a ruined 14C tower. The town, known for its cardboard-boxes, is still the centre of the *Tricastin*, a detatched enclave of the department of the Vaucluse.—**Nyons** (see Rte 141B) lies 14km S.E.—We continue S.W. to (9km) *Visan*, there turning l., and on meeting a main road after 4km, turn l. and then r. to cross a ridge to (16km) **Vaison-la-Romaine**; see Rte 141B.

From the S. suburbs of Montélimar a road forks S.W. to (8.5km) *Châteauneuf-du-Rhône*, a fortified village from which a bridge crosses the river to (2.5km) *Viviers*; see Rte 142A.

The main road traverses an area in which in 1944 American forces under Gen. Butler routed the retreating German 19th Army, circling to the E. of a ridge causing the narrows of the Rhône known as the 'Robinet de Donzère'.—Hence, at 11.5km, the main road to *Grignan* (see above), 17km S.E., turns l.—*Donzère* itself is by-passed at 3.5km, standing at the foot of its castle rock, which bears the ruins of a 13-14C stronghold of the bishops of Viviers. The Romanesque church, of a vanished Benedictine priory, has a remarkable apse.

A l.-hand turning leads beyond the motorway, running S. to regain the main route at (23km) *Mondragon*, via Bollène. At 6km *La Garde-Adhémar*, with fine ruined rampart and a Romanesque church with an apse at either end, is passed to the l., 2km E. of which is a ruined Romanesque chapel.—3km. To the r. rises a nuclear power-station.—3km E. lies **St-Paul-Trois-Châteaux**, (6,500 inhab), Roman *Augusta Tricastinorum*, the seat of a bishop from the 2-3C to 1792, whose first bishop, St Restitutus, was probably buried at *St-Restitut*, 3km S.E., under the detached tower of its 12C church. The former cathedral of *St-Paul (12-early 13C) is remarkable for the classical inspiration of its details, the reliefs on the S. Transept, for the elaborate finish of its construction, and for the number and variety of its masons' marks which still survive.—*La Baume-de-Transit*, 9km E., has a Romanesque church preserving three of its original four apses.—Continuing S. parallel to the A7, with the ruined château of *Barry* above us to the l., near a Gallo-Roman oppidum, we enter (8km) *Bollène*, on the Lez, much expanded to house workers at the Donzère-Mondragon sites, in the old centre of which is a disaffected 12-16C church; at *Suze-la-Rousse*, 7km E., is a 14-16C castle.—6km *Mondragon*.

The main road crosses the Donzère-Mondragon Canal de Dérivation (completed 1952), which diverts a great part of the waters of the Rhône from their normal channel, further W., providing electrical power, and facilitating navigation; the locks and power-station lie further S., near *Bollène* (see above).—At 7km *Pierrelatte* (l.) is by-passed, owing its name to the white limestone rock (petra lactea) beneath which its shelters, and we traverse what is now virtually an island caused by the 'aménagement du Rhône' here.

12km. *Pont-St-Esprit* lies 4km to the W.; see Rte 142A.—We re-cross the canal, tunnel beneath the A7, and at 4km pass (l.) *Mondragon*, and 5km beyond, *Mornas*, both places commanded by ruin-ed castles, and bear away from the Rhône, with a view (l.) towards pyramidal *Mont Ventoux* (1909m; see p 770), now the dominating feature of the area.

8km. *Sérignan*, 5km N.E., was the last home of Henri Fabre (1823–1915), the entomologist, known as 'the insects' Homer'.—Crossing the Aygues, at 3km Orange is entered.

ORANGE (27,500 Orangeois), the old centre of which—much shrunk from its original extent—stands between the little river Meyne and the prominent *Colline St-Eutrope*, and is famous for its Roman theatre and triumphal arch.

Gallic *Arausio* was the site of a resounding Roman defeat in 105 B.C., avenged three years later near Aix. It had become an important colony by the time of Augustus, and later suffered severely at the hands of the Alemanni, and the Visigoths (412). The counts of Orange, created by Charlemagne, took the title of prince in the 13C, and the principality, by intermarriage, passed to the House of Nassau, of which William III of England was a member. It was confirmed to William the Silent by the treaty of Cateau-Cambrésis in 1559. In 1622 Maurice of Nassau, using the Roman monuments as his quarry, elaborated its fortifica-tions, but these were razed by Louis XIV in 1660, and the town was formally assigned to the French crown by the treaty of Utrecht (1713). Sir Hans Sloane took his M.D. degree here in 1685 at the university founded in 1365 and sup-pressed in 1790. 378 citizens were guillotined here in the space of three months during the Revolution.

The N7 enters the N. end of the town, first circling the *****Triumphal Arch**, the most remarkable of its kind in France for the wealth of its decoration, commemorating the founding of Arausio as a 'colony' for veterans. Despite traces of an inscription of A.D. 25 naming Tiberius, the arch appears to date from the time of Augustus.

It has three openings with coffered vaulting, and the entablature is upheld by 12 Corinthian columns. Its N.E. and S. faces are adorned with reliefs of naval and military trophies, battle scenes, duels, etc. During the Middle Ages it was bat-tlemented and loopholed as a sort of keep, and known as the Château de l'Arc. It has been much restored since 1825, and its W. face again recently.

On crossing the Meyne by the *Pont de Langes*, we bear r. to the Cours Aristide-Briand, turning l. at its S. end to approach the stark dominating N. wall (4m thick) of the scena of the *****Roman Theatre**, the cavea of which is carved out of the adjoining hill (good view from its summit, on which stood the capital and medieval fortress). Ruins on the r. on entering the theatre represent the *Gymnasium*, and a large temple, its foundations dating to the reign of Hadrian, and perhaps the S. extremity of a *Circus*.

On reaching the auditorium, a hemicycle 103m in diameter, we have a good view of the imposing S. facade of the theatre, almost 37m high, unique in its com-pleteness, although only slight remains of its original facing survive. It has three square doors in the lowest arcade, a blind arcade above, then two rows of sup-ports for posts that held up the velarium, or awning to protect the audience from sun and rain. The colossal statue of Augustus (restored), was placed in a central niche in 1951. These stage-doors admitted the actors to the proscenium. In front of the stage may be seen the trench into which the curtain was lowered (cf. Lyon). The auditorium, of which parts of the five lower rows are preserved, originally held c. 10,000 spectators, and is still used in summer, but during the rest of the year it has a shabby appearance, a lack of pride in the preservation of the place being regrettably evident, in spite of its commercialisation. The whole edifice was filled by tenements until the mid 19C (cf. Arles).

Opposite the entrance is a small *Museum*, containing not only Roman remains, but relics of a cadastral plan of Arausio in the time of Vaspasian, and—unexpectedly—a collection of drawings and paintings by Frank Brangwyn.—An adjacent street leads to the central *Pl. de la République*, just beyond which is the *Hôtel de Ville*, with a belfry of 1671, and ancient but much mutilated *Notre-Dame*, once the cathedral, preserving an unusually wide nave of 1085–1126.

The D975 leads 28km N.E. to **Vaison-la-Romaine**; see Rte 141B.

The D976 leads 11km S.W. to *Roquemaure*, on the far bank of the Rhône (see Rte 142A), 11km N. of **Villeneuve-lès-Avignon**, see Rte 148.—Off this road, 7km from Orange, a by-road forks l. past (r.) the ruins of the *Château de l'Hers* to (6km) *Châteauneuf-du-Pape*, famous for its wines, and with remains of a keep of a papal summer residence, 7km beyond which lies *Sorgues*; see below.

The N7 veers S.E., off which, almost immediately, the D950 forks l. to (23km) **Carpentras** (see Rte 141B), and we skirt the motorway, crossing it to traverse (18km) *Sorgues*, where the Ouvèze is crossed, and after 5km regain the Rhône opposite the *Île de la Barthelasse*, skirting its bank, with a good view of *Fort St-André* at *Villeneuve* ahead, and of the *Rocher des Doms* and *Pont St-Bénézet*, on approaching (6km) **Avignon**; see Rte 148.

B. Via Crest, Dieulefit, Nyons, Vaison-la-Romaine, and Carpentras

164km (102 miles). D538A. 28km **Crest**—D538. 37km *Dieulefit*—31km **Nyons**—16km **Vaison-la-Romaine**—27km *Carpentras*—D942. 24km **Avignon**.

Maps: IGN 52, 59, 60 or 115. M 93, 245.

For the road to *Crest*, see the first section of Rte 140.

Crossing the Drôme and ascending the far side of the valley, at 3km we fork l. over the hills for (6km) *Saou*, an ancient village damaged by the Germans, with a large Romanesque abbey-church, to the E. of which is the **Forêt de Saou*, a large wooded basin surrounded by limestone peaks, those at the far end rising to 1589m.

The valley of the Rubion is followed to (10km) *Bourdeaux*, with a ruined castle, there turning S.W. over a ridge to descend the gorge of the Jabron to (13km) *Dieulefit*, an old centre of Protestantism, known for its potteries.—*La Poët-Laval* lies 6km W.; see Rte 141A.—Climbing S.E. the road turns down the narrow valley of the Lez, passing several ruined towers, to (15km) crossroads 3km E. of *Taulignan*, with remains of fortifications, 7km beyond which lies **Grignan**; see Rte 141A, also for *Valréas*, 8km S.

Turning l. at the junction, the road continues S.E. past (l.) *La Pègue*, where vases of classical Hellenic-type ware have come to light, to (16km) **Nyons** (6,300 Nyonsais), on the Aygues, crossed by a 14C *Bridge* to the E. of the modern one. The place is mentioned by Ptolemy as *Noviomagus*, and was the principal town of an independent district known as the *Baronnais*. Its medieval 'Quartier des

Forts' climbs the hill to the N.E. of the centre, just E. of which is a characteristic Place.

For the road here from *Serres* (65km N.E.), see Rte 138B.

Crossing the river, the D538 turns S.W. through olive-groves and bears away from the valley, with a view of the ridge of *Mont Ventoux* (1909m) to the S.E., before reaching (16km) *Vaison*.

VAISON-LA-ROMAINE (5,900 inhab.), the Roman *Vasio Vocontiorum*, an attractive little market-town (which delighted Stendhal even prior to its excavation), retains extensive remains of the Roman occupation, together with a picturesque medieval quarter.

The flourishing Gallo-Roman city, on the N. bank of the Ouvèze, was ruined by the Barbarian invasions, and its unprotected site, although remaining an ecclessiastical centre, was vitually abandoned in favour of the more defensible hill site on the S. bank, on which, in the 12C, the counts of Toulouse erected a castle. After the 17C the N. bank was repopulated, and since 1907 the Roman site not built over has been progressively excavated, at first by Abbé Joseph Sautel, financed between the years 1924–40 by the philatelist Maurice Burrus. Vaison was an important maquisard centre in 1941–44.

One may obtain a general view from the *Pl. du 11-Novembre*, just N. of the central cross-roads of the new town (S.I.), with areas of excava

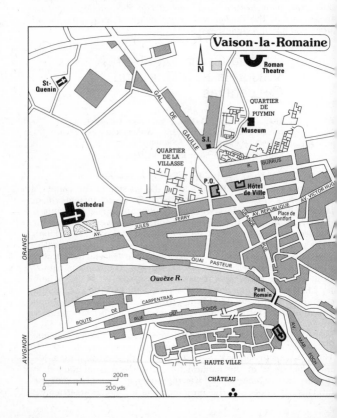

The apse foundations of N.-D.-de Nazareth, Vaison-la-Romaine

on on either side, within the old cathedral further W., and the medieval 'bourg' rising to the S., dominated by its castle.

The entrance to the Roman antiquities of the *Quartier de Puymin* s to the E. of the Place, including the so-called *House of Messii*, and he *Portico of Pompey*. Further up the sloping site is the new **Museum**, containing imperial statues from the theatre (Hadrian; his wife Sabina; and an armoured figure of the 1C); a charming female head; a silver portrait bust; ornaments found in tombs; a tragic mask; ead-piping, etc.; also a cast of the Diadumenos, now in the British Museum.

A tunnel just behind leads to the upper part of the Roman **Theatre**, n the N. slope of the hill, carefully restored, and with part of its upper colonnade replaced in position. Dramatic performances are held ere in summer.

The new excavations of the *Quartier de la Villasse* lie just W. of the lace, where the Post Office building (which should be removed) overs most of the principal *Thermae*. A footpath skirts the S. boundary of this area, passing the archway of the *'Public basilica'*, and the *fouse of the Silver Bust*, etc., to reach a small lane (see below), just eyond which is the apse of ***N.-D.-de-Nazareth**, the former athedral. Note sections of fluted Roman columns serving as a foundation for the square apse, an external frieze, and the relief portrait a Roman funerary stele) built into the E. side of the tower. This Provençal basilica dates from the 11-13C, with traces of 6C work in the wo side apses.

he dark interior contains a hemicycle of seats in the apse, marble Romanesque tars and bishop's throne, the tomb of St Quenin, bishop here in 556–75, and in ne N. aisle, a Gallo-Roman column, near which is the entrance to the restored oister (12C), with good capitals and some piers displaying chevron patterns, nd containing a small lapidary collection.

egaining the lane, we may turn l. to visit the curious chapel of *St-Quenin* (no adm.), the pentagonal apse—triangular outside, with its wo side-apses set askew—being late 12C work, although the decora-

tion derives from antique models. The nave was rebuilt in 1665
Note the Paleo-Christian carving over the entrance.

The Grande Rue leads S. from the Pl. du 11-Novembre, to the E. of
which is the central *Pl. de Montfort*, to the oft-repaired *Roman Bridge*
spanning the Ouvèze, beyond which bearing r. to ascend into the
*Haute-Ville, with its narrow cobbled lanes, retaining several
tastefully restored old houses, and entered by a 14C gateway sur
mounted by a belfry. To the E. stands the mid 15C church, with a
facade of 1776, while alleys lead up towards the somewhat
featureless castle (views). The Hostellerie Le Beffroi here, a 17C
house, is recommended.

The D975 leads 28km S.W. from the N. bank of the river to **Orange** (see Rte
141A), shortly providing striking views of the *Dentelles de Montmirail* to the
S.W.; see below.
    The D977 follows the S. bank to the S.W., crossing the river after 12km, not fa
N. of *Gigondas*, noted for its red wine, to meet the N7 at (15km) *Courthézon*
20km from **Avignon**.

The D938 leads S.E., shortly passing (r.) the ruins of the castle of
Crestet above the picturesque village.—At 3.5km the l.-hand turning
ascends the valley of the Ouvèze via (9km) *Mollans* to *Buis-les
Baronnies*, 9km beyond, a large village in a fruitful hill-encircled
valley.
    6km. *Malaucène*, with a large 14C church in the Romanesque
style, and old belfry. Hence the D974 follows the narrow windswept
ridge of **Mont Ventoux** (the route by which Petrarch made the as
cent in 1336) to the summit, 21km E. (1909m), crowned by an obser
vatory and other installations.

This W. outpost of the Alps commands a *View of the Alps themselves, the
Cévennes, and in the clearest weather, the Pyrenees. At a junction 6km beyond
the summit, the l.-hand turning descends to *Sault-de-Vaucluse* (20km S.E.; see
Rte 153B); by turning r. we continue the circuit through plantations of oaks
olive-groves, vineyards, and orchards, to (16km) *Bédoin*, a village burnt during
the Revolution, and some 180 inhabitants massacred by young Suchet (later
notably murderous Marshal), directed by Maignet, an apostate priest, merely
because a 'tree of liberty' planted there had been sawn through during the
night!—*Carpentras* lies 15km S.W.

Turning S. from Malaucène, we pass (r.) at 6.5km the château of Le
Barroux (1548), with the curiously fretted ridge known as the
Dentelles de Montmirail in the background.—The next l.-hand turn
ing leads shortly to *Caromb*, where the restored church has a late
Romanesque nave, 14C choir, and 15C sculptures.

Beaumes-de-Venise lies some 6km W. of the main road, just beyond which is the
charming little Romanesque church of *N.-D.-d'Aubune*.

11km. CARPENTRAS (25,900 Carpentrassiens), the attractively
situated but dull capital of the *Comtat Venaissin* until the Revolution
and now a flourishing agricultural centre, is famous for its 'bullseyes'
or 'berlingots', and was the birthplace of the artist Joseph-Silfrèd
Duplessis (1725–1802); François-Vincent Raspail (1794–1878), the
chemist and politician, and Édouard Daladier (1884–1970), the
politician.
    On crossing the river Auzon, we ascend towards the Port
d'Orange, all that remains of the mid 14C ramparts built by Innocen
VI, demolished in the late 19C and replaced by a ring of boulevards

The most convenient entrance to the old centre is from the S., by the *Pl. Aristide-Briand*, with parking space in the adjacent Allées des Platanes.—Further S. are the 18C buildings of the *Hôtel-Dieu*, with an interior of interest, including its pharmacy and chapel. In front is a statue of its founder, Card. D'Inguimbert (1687–1757).

The Rue de la République leads N. to the central *Pl. du Gén. de Gaulle*, on the E. side of which stands **St-Siffrein**, the former cathedral, named after a 6C bishop. A late-Gothic edifice (1405–1519), it preserves parts of its Romanesque predecessor on the l. of the choir beyond the vaulted sacristy. In the ogee of the flamboyant S. porch is the 'Boule aux rats', a rat-gnawed globe, of doubtful significance.

N. of the W. front is the former *Bishop's Palace* (1640), now the *Palais de Justice*, retaining some elegantly decorated rooms (adm. on request). In the open courtyard behind this building is a relic of a Roman *Triumphal Arch of the 1C A.D., preserving reliefs of Barbarian captives, their hands bound to trophies.

The Rue d'Inguimbert leads E. towards the *Hôtel de Ville*, almost opposite which is the *Synagogue, the oldest surviving in France, being founded in 1367, and rebuilt in 1743.

From the N.W. corner of the Pl. Gén. de Gaulle, we pass (l.) the Rue du Collège, in which the *Musée Sobirats*, with collections of furniture, etc. is installed in an 18C mansion.

In the Rue des Saintes-Maries, leading r. at the commencement of the Rue de la Porte-de-Monteux, in the former *Chapelle de la Visitation*, is a small lapidary collection.—Following the latter street to the N., we gain the boulevards, where turning l. the important *Bibliothèque Inguimbertine* is reached (containing some 200 incunables, etc.). On the ground floor is a museum of regional interest; adjacent is the *Musée Duplessis*, with a miscellaneous collection of paintings, including portraits by J.-S. Duplessis, and the original portrait of the Abbé de Rance, by Rigaud, etc.

The D974, leading N.E. from the Allées (towards Mont Ventoux) commands a view of an *Aqueduct* of 48 arches crossing the Auzon, completed c. 1730.

Fro the road from Carpentras to *Forcalquier*, see Rte 153B.

CARPENTRAS TO APT (43km). The D4 leads S.E. to (11km) **Venasque**, a hill-top village with a good Romanesque and Gothic church, behind which is a remarkable *Baptistry, a late 6C building in the form of a square with an apse on each side; the low dome is supported by antique columns.—The road climbs to and traverses the *Plateau de Vaucluses*, off which after 3km, a r.-hand turning leads S. to (c. 7km) the abbey of *Senanque*, and *Gordes*; see Rte 153A.—6km. The *Col de Murs* (627m), descending from which, with views across to the *Montagne du Lubéron*, we traverse (5km) *Murs*, birthplace of Louis de Crillon ('brave Crillon'; 1543–1615), with a very restored 16C castle. At 9.5km *Roussillon* lies 2km to the r.; 8km **Apt**; for both see Rte 153A.

CARPENTRAS TO CAVAILLON (27km). The D938 leads S. to (6km) **Pernes-les-Fontaines** (7,000 inhab.), capital of the *Comtat Venaissin* before Carpentras, standing on the Nesque, crossed by a bridge with a chapel, and leading to the *Porte Notre-Dame* (1548). *Notre-Dame* (11-14C) stands further N., while to the S. is one of several fountains which give the town its soubriquet. Ruins of a castle and several rampart towers survive, notably the *Tour Ferrande*, containing 13C wall-paintings; key at the *Hôtel de Ville*, in a 17C mansion. Pernes was the birthplace of *Bp* Fléchier of Nîmes (1632–1710).—11km. The l.-hand turning leads 9km to *Fontaine-de-Vaucluse*; see Rte 153A; likewise for *L'Isle-sur-la-Sorgue*, traversed 1km S.—10km. **Cavaillon**; see Rte 150.

From Carpentras the D942 leads S.W. through (4.5km) *Monteux*, a favourite residence of Clement V, with well-preserved ramparts, and after 5km by-passes (l.) *Althen-des-Paluds*, named after a Persian, Althen, who introduced the cultivation of madder into the Comtat in 1766.—2.5km. *Entraigues*, also with relics of ramparts, is passed. After 4km the A7 is crossed, and **Avignon** is entered 8km beyond; see Rte 148.

142 From Valence to Montpellier

A. Via Pont-St-Esprit, and Nîmes

201km (125 miles). N86. 19km *La Voulte*—6km *Le Pouzin* —35km **Viviers**—14km *Bourg-St-Andéol*—15km **Pont-St-Esprit** —11km **Bagnols-sur-Cèze**. **Avignon** lies 31.5km S.E.—28km *Remoulins*. The **Pont-du-Gard** lies 3km N.W.—21km **Nîmes**—N113. 52km **Montpellier**. The latter part of this route is described in Rte 143.

Maps: IGN 52, 59, 66, or 115, 114. M 93, 240.

From **Valence** (Rte 139A) the Rhône is crossed by the *Pont de St Péray*, with the conspicuous ruins of the 12C castle of *Crusso* ahead.—Veering l. onto the N86, at 6km *Soyons* is traversed, below the rock of the buried oppidum of *Malpas* (5C B.C.), discovered in 1950. Soyons was the birthplace of Gén. Championnet (1762–1800), organiser of the ephemeral Parthenopean Republic a Naples.—*Charmes* is shortly traversed, to the W. of which are the ruins of the fortified priory of *St-Marcel-de-Crussol*.

Crossing the mouth of the Eyrieux, we enter (12km) *La Voulte-sur Rhône* (5,300 inhab.), an ancient town overlooked by its 14-16C château, mutilated by the Germans in 1944 before retreating, commanding a good view up the valley of the Drôme to the E.

6km. *Le Pouzin*, badly damaged in 1944, where the N104 turns S.W. to *Privas*; see Rte 142B.

12km. **Cruas**, whitened by the dust of limestone quarries, preserves an interesting Romanesque *Abbey-church (970), under restoration, with a square W. tower and round E. tower. The crypt beneath the choir dates from the 9C; the choir itself contains a curious 11C mosaic. The nave floor was raised in the 13C, forming second crypt or undercroft.—Above the town stands a turreted keep.

6.5km. *Meysse*, from which a road ascends to the volcanic dyke of the *Coiron*, of which the *Pic de Chenevari* (507m), at the E. end of the ridge, with a basaltic causeway below the summit, dominates the valley above (2.5km) *Rochemaure*, with its cooling towers, Romanesque church, ruined castle, and keeps.

A bridge crosses the Rhône to (5km.) **Montélimar**; see Rte 141A.

4km. *Le Teil*, with disfiguring limestone quarries and cement works, also overlooked by ruins, lies on the direct road between Montelimar and *Aubenas*, 38km to the W.—Immediately W. of the town, at *Mélas*, is an unusual little Romanesque church containing 10C baptistry.

10km. **Viviers**, the episcopal capital of the mountainous *Vivarais* since the 5C, which was probably fixed here after the destruction of Roman *Alba*, 13km N.W.; see last section of Rte 99. The castle

ock, on which stands the Cathedral of St-Vincent, was once the op-
idum of *Vivarium*, below which, to the W., the old town, somewhat
erelict in appearance, huddles.

At the N. end of the main street stands *St-Laurent*, from the apse of
which an alley leads to the 16C *Maison des Chevaliers*, its three
storeys separated by a frieze of medallions.—Hence the so-called
Grand-Rue, with relics of old mansions, leads S.—The **Cathedral**, of
romanesque origin, but several times rebuilt, has a detached belfry.
It was damaged by the Huguenots in 1562, and the nave was re-
aulted in 1757. The vaulting of the apse is 15C. The choir has Flamoyant windows. Three of the 18C Aubusson tapestries that hung
ere were stolen in 1974; the others are not on view.

To the N. is a terrace overlooking the Rhône, from which, turning
., we descend to the *Hôtel de Ville* in the former *Hôtel de Ro-
ueplane*. Across the road is the large *Bishop's Palace* (1732), under
estoration.

The defile or 'Robinet' of Donzère, the 'gate of Provence' (see Rte
41A) is now approached.—The main road veers to the S.W., pass-
ng (r.) the fortified village of *St-Montant* to (14km) *Bourg-St-Andéol*,
he centre of which was seriously damaged by bombing in Aug.
944, in an attempt to destroy the bridge, when the 16C *Hôtel
Nicolaï* was razed except for its tower, but the beautiful Romanesque
Church (early 12C), with the early 3C sarcophagus of its patron,
martyred in 208, survived. Of slighter interest are the 18C *Hôtel des
Comtes de Doise*, the former Palace of the Bishops of Viviers, and
ear the bridge, the *Hospice*, with a chapel and cloister.

To the W. extends the lonely *Plateau des Gras*, abounding in
nderground caverns and Neolithic remains, among them the stalac-
te *Grottes de St-Marcel* in the *Gorges de l'Ardèche* (see also Rte
42B), the S.E. end of which may be conveniently entered at 9km,
ear *St-Martin-d'Ardèche*.—At *St-Marcel d'Ardèche*, just r. of the
oad, was born Card. de Bernis (1715–94).

The river Ardèche is shortly crossed, while to the E. appears *Mont
Ventoux*.

6km. **Pont-St-Esprit** (8,100 inhab.), an old fortified town taking its
ame from a remarkable bridge, 919m long, which here spans one of
he swiftest, though shallowest reaches of the Rhône.

t was begun in 1265 by the Fratres Pontis (a fraternity of bridge-building friars),
ompleted in 1309, and dedicated to the Holy Ghost. Of its original 25 arches 19
emain; two were replaced in 1858 by a metal arch of wider span (and after war
amage, by a suspension bridge); the whole was widened in 1860.

n the town may be noted the 15C *Maison du Roi*, immediately S. of
he bridgehead, with an old fresco of the bridge; the *Citadel*
(1595–1620), largely destroyed in 1944, incorporates remains of a
4C hospital. Following the quays S., we reach *St-Saturnin* (15C), its
djacent terrace providing a good view of the bridge. Hence one may
ontinue S., passing several ancient mansions, including the *Maison
es Chevaliers*. The *Hospice* further S. preserves an old *Pharmacy*.

ravellers wishing to visit **Orange** (20km S.E.) from this bank, should cross the
hône here.

The large 17C *Chartreuse de Valbonne*, preserving its 13C cloister, is in the
ills 10km S.W.

he road now veers away from the river to (11km) **Bagnols-sur-Cèze**
(17,800 inhab.), which has grown considerably in recent decades to

house workers at the neighbouring Atomic Energy Centre of *Mar coule*, its reactors rising above the landscape of vineyards. In the central Place, the *Hôtel de Ville* contains an important ***Museum** o Impressionist paintings collected by Albert André (1869–1954), in cluding representative works by *Renoir, Bonnard, Matisse, Monet Marquet, Vallotton, Van Dongen*, and *Suzanne Valadon*; also an chaeological collections.

The N580 leads S.E. to (31km) **Avignon**, passing (r.) near *Tavel*, giving its name to the light wine of the district, off which, after 12km, a minor road forks l. to (6km) *Rochemaure*, with two towers of its old castle, formerly on an island in the Rhône. Clement V died in 1314 when crossing the river between Rochemaure and Châteauneuf-du-Pape, on the far bank.—A further 11km brings us to **Villeneuve-lès-Avignon**, commanded by *Fort-St-André*; see Rte 148.

The D6 leads 50km W. from Bagnols to *Alès*, at 23km passing 3km S. of *Lussan* with its castle-crowned cliff, from which one may visit the wild **Gorge de l'Aiguillon*, further N.E., known locally as 'Les Concluses', and on higher ground to the N., perhaps the finest menhir in the Midi.

7km. *Laudun*, 4.5km E., has a large 12th and 15C church.

The lonely *Garrigues du Gard* are traversed, with their ilex-woods and at 6.5km a minor road forks r. to (15km) **Uzès**; see Rte 143.

15km. *Remoulins*, for the **Pont du Gard**, 3km N.W. see also Rte 143; likewise for the road to (21km) **Nîmes**, and **Montpellier**, 52km beyond.

B.   Via Aubenas and Alès

213km (132 miles). N86. 19km *La Voulte*—6km *Le Pouzin* —N104. 14km **Privas**—30km **Aubenas**—D104 and then D904. 74km **Alès**—N110. 42km **Sommières**—28km **Montpellier**.

Maps: IGN 52, 59, 66, or 115, 114. M 93, 240.

For the road to *Le Pouzin*, see Rte 142A.

Here we turn S.W. to (14km) **Privas** (10,600 Privadois), préfecture of the *Ardèche*, situated on a ridge between the Ouvèze (crossed by an early 17C bridge), and the Chalaron. Owing to its stubborn adherence to Protestantism it was largely destroyed by Louis XIII and Richelieu in 1629, although a few old houses remain at the N end of the town.—The cardinal resided in the restored château of *Entrevaux*, 5km S.W., during the siege.

· The road climbs to the *Col de l'Escrinet* (787m), overlooked by the *Roc de Gourdon* (1061m), from which the volcanic ridge of the Coiron stretches S.E., and descends through chestnut woods near (r.) the ruins of the 15-16C château of *Boulogne*, with a view ahead of **Aubenas** perched above the valley of the Ardèche; see the latter part of Rte 99.

From Aubenas we drive S.

At 15km a r.-hand turning leads to (4km) *Largentière*, finely placed in the gorge of the Ligne, and commanded by the former castle of the bishops of Viviers (now a hospice). Several old houses and remains of fortifications attest to its medieval importance, largely derived from its silver mines (to the N.), which gave the place its name, and which were worked until the 15C. The 12-15C church has a 19C spire.

1km. The l.-hand turning leads to (8km) *Ruoms* (see Rte 99), in part above a defile of the Ardèche.

7km. *Joyeuse*, an old hill-town, with its *Mairie* occupying the former mansion of the Joyeuse family, who played a conspicuous part in the 16C Religious Wars, 3km beyond which *Lablachère* is entered.

Hence the main road bears l. past (l.) a region noted for its dolmens, end then veers S.W. to (17km) *Les Avelas*, but the more interesting road is that turning r. to (11km) *Les Vans*, with good woodwork in its church, just N. of which, at *Chambonas*, is a Romanesque church and restored medieval castle; and 2.5km S.W., the picturesque village of *Naves*, with a keep and 11C church.—The D901 ascends W. from Les Vans to (24km) *Villefort*; see Rtes 99, and 101B.—Turning E. from Les Vans, the road shortly circles to the S., off which a l.-hand turning leads into the ***Bois de Païolive**, amid a weird labyrinth of distorted rocks on either side of the Chassezac ravine.—The main road is regained at *Les Avelas*, 11km from Les Vans.

At 13km *St-Ambroix* is traversed, standing on the Cèze facing a rocky island crowned by the surviving tower of a castle demolished in 1629; *Bessèges*, some 10km W., is the centre of a small coalfield.—The Auzonnet valley is shortly crossed, also with collieries, and antimony mines, and at 10km the château of *Rousson* (1615) is passed to the l.

9km. **Alès**; see Rte 101B, and for the road hence through *Sommières* to **Montpellier**.

143 Avignon to Montpellier via the Pont du Gard and Nîmes

101km (63 miles). N100. 22km *Remoulins*. The **Pont du Gard** lies 4km N.W., from which the main road is regained after 3km—N86. 20km **Nîmes**—N113. 28km *Lunel*—24km **Montpellier**.

Maps: IGN 66, or 114. M 240.

The A9 motorway, entered W. of Avignon, provides a rapid route.

For the alternative road to Nîmes via *Tarascon*, see Rtes 151B and 150. From *Beaucaire* the stoney plateau of *La Costière* is crossed, producing a heady wine.

From the S.W. corner of **Avignon** (see Rte 148), the Rhône is crossed, and the D976 from Orange is met at 14km.

Just prior to this junction the D108 turns l. for (7km) *St-Armand-Théziers*, with an 11C church, and 4km beyond, *Montfrin*, with a 12C church, from which the main route may be regained at Remoulins.

8km. *Remoulins*, where we meet the N86 from Valence via the Pont-St-Esprit (see Rte 142A), is a dull little town with relics of early fortifications; its *Mairie* occupies a former Romanesque church.

To visit the Pont du Gard, turn r. towards the W. end of the town, to follow the D98 towards *Uzès* (17km N.W.; see below), and after 8km fork l.

The ****Pont du Gard**, one of the finest and loftiest Roman aqueducts extant, bridges the valley of the Gard in three tiers of arches; the first stage of six is 22m high; the second, of eleven—242m in length—is 19m high. Above, a series of smaller arches carries the

A watercolour of the Pont du Gard in 1817

water-canal. It is preferable not to visit it at weekends or at holidays
and it is perhaps best seen early or late in the day.

This immense work was constructed c. 19 B.C. by Agrippa, son-in-law c
Augustus, to conduct the waters of the Eure from the environs of Uzès to Nîmes
the total length of the canal being c. 50km. Its masonry was quarried in the river
bank only a short distance upstream. The N. end has been partially destroyed
and a modern road-bridge has been carried along the downstream side of th
main tier of arches. The water-channel itself (1.22m wide and 1.75m high), partl
covered in by large stone slabs, may be threaded by the adventurous, and thos
not suffering from vertigo may also cross by walking along the roofing slab
themselves.
    From the far end a path leads 1km upstream to the *Château de St-Privat*, partl
Renaissance, with formal gardens.

THE PONT DU GARD TO UZÈS (15km). The D981 leads N.W. past (r.) th
dilapidated late 18C *Château de Castille*, with its picturesque and unorthodo.
colonnades, built by Gabriel Joseph Froment, baron de Castille.—**UZÈS** (7,80
Uzétiens), Roman *Ucetia*, is an ancient and often overlooked town of medieva
appearance above the Alzon valley, which is undergoing rigorous restoration. 1
was the cradle of the ducal family, and amongst its natives were the artist
Nicolas Froment (early 15C), and Pierre Subleyras (1699–1749), although the
latter was actually born at St-Gilles; and Adm. de Bruey (1753–98), killed at th
Battle of the Nile; while in 1661–62 young Racine resided here with his mater
nal uncle (Antoine Sconin; 1608–89), one of the canons. The older enceinte i
surrounded by boulevards on the N. side of which, behind the 18C *Hôtel de Ville*
is the **Duché** or ducal château, opposite the entrance of which is the 14C *Logis d
la Vicomte*, abutted by the principal wing (16C), with a facade attrib. to Philiber

Delorme. The two wings are united by the 12C keep, whose roof and turrets are 19C additions.—To the S. is the square *Tour de l'Horloge*, S.E. of which is the *Tour du Roi*, a 14C relic of a royal residence, while just W. of the former is the *Hôtel Dampmartin*, with a Renaissance courtyard.

A few paces further S.W. is the arcaded *Pl. de la République*, the former Pl. aux Herbes, off the W. side of which is the 17C *Hôtel d'Aigaliers*.—Further S. we pass (l.) *St-Étienne*, with a 13C belfry, and then (l.; 3 Rue Paul-Foussat) a Renaissance doorway to a house once the home of Guillaume de Grimoard, later Pope Urban V.—Continuing E., another Renaissance mansion, *Le Portalet*, is passed at No. 19 (l.) to approach steps ascending to the former cathedral of *St-Théodorit* (1645–60; restored in the 19C), containing a fine 17C organ-case and 18C furniture, and two paintings by Simon de Chalons; it replaced an early cathedral demolished by Bp Jean de Saint-Gelais (c. 1546), who had embraced Protestantism, the only relic of which is the slender cylindrical belfry, 42m high, known as the *Tour Fénestrelle* (12C), unique in France.

To the S. is the so-called Promenade de Racine, on which is a restored pavilion, below which are the old bishop's gardens, extending towards the river, here guarded by a 15C tower. On the N. side of the church is the former *Bishop's Palace* (17C), and to the N.E., the colonnaded *Hôtel de Castille* (late 18C; cf. above). Hence, passing several old mansions in the Rue de Rafin, the Duché is regained, first passing (r.) a primitive *Crypt* of ancient origin (6C, or earlier).—In the Av. Foch, leading S., is the *Museon di Rodo*, a collection of vintage cars (from 1897), motor-cycles (from 1902), velocipides, etc.—The castle of *Montaren*, 4km N.W., is an interesting building of the 12-16Cs.

UZÈS TO NÎMES (25km). The D979 forks S. to (9.5km) the *Pont St-Nicolas*, built c. 1250 across the impressive gorge of the Gardon (which may be descended on foot to the Pont du Gard, or ascended to Dions). The main road continues S. across the stony Garrigues (now partly a military camp) to *Nîmes*; an alternative road, turning r. just short of the bridge, leads to *Dions*, near which is an enormous pot-hole, beyond which, on meeting the N106, turn l. for **Nîmes**.

Regaining the N86 at Remoulins, turn r. through *St-Bonnet*, with a fortified Romanesque church, and continue S.W., twice crossing the A9, to approach (20km) *Nîmes*.

NÎMES (129,900 Nîmois; 38,800 in 1801; 80,600 in 1901), the dusty but prosperous préfecture of the *Gard*, has greatly outgrown its medieval centre, now enclosed within a line of boulevards, which itself was much smaller than the Roman city, the relics of which rival those of Arles. The busy modern town with its huge white cliffs of buildings, impressive from a distance, subsists largely from the wine trade, and numerous other manufacturers, principally textiles (among them silk, and denim, a fabric originally produced here, being a contraction of 'de Nîmes'). But many will agree with Augustus Hare, who remarked: 'There is no beauty in Nimes and, after seeing its Roman antiquities, no one will wish to linger there'.

The Roman colony of *Nemausus*, founded by Augustus, and receiving its water-supply from the Pont du Gard, achieved its greatest prosperity under Antoninus Pius (c. A.D. 150), whose family had lived in the neighbourhood. It was sacked by the Vandals in 407, and in c. 470 the Visigoths built a stronghold in the amphitheatre, and they were succeeded by an invasion of Saracens, expelled by Charles Martel in 737. Unit 1185 it was part of the kingdom of Aquitaine, and then fell into the hands of the counts of Toulouse, in 1299 becoming part of the French kingdom.

The Protestant creed, preached by Pierre de Lavau in 1533, made numerous converts in Nîmes, who later took refuge among the Camisards of the Cévennes. The insurrection of the latter, at first successful, was crushed by the allegedly traitorous submission at Nîmes of its leader, Jean Chevalier, to Marshal Villars 1704), but the Protestant element is still stronger; cf. p 557. Its fortifications were demolished in 1786.

Among its natives were Jean Nicot, who in 1560 introduced tobacco into

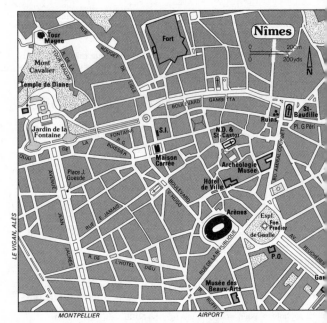

France; the sculptor Barthélemy Guibal (1699– 1757); François Guizot (1787– 1874), the statesman; and Alphonse Daudet (1840– 97; born at No. 2• Blvd Gambetta); the preacher Esprit Fléchier (1632– 1710), born at Pernes, wai bishop here from 1687.

The main open space immediately S.E. of the old town is the Esplanade de Gaulle; at its N.W. corner is the *Palais de Justice* (1838)▪ immediately W. of which is the *Arènes* or **Amphitheatre**, an impos▪ ing relic of the Roman occupation, probably dating from the 1C A.D

The great ellipse (133m by 101m), with its entrance on its W. side is in a very fair state of repair, and unlike that at Arles, preserves it▪ attic storey. There are 34 rows of seats, with room for c. 20,000 spec▪ tators.

Nearly all traces of the Visigothic stronghold, the 11C 'Château des Arènes' and the pulluating hovels which choked it, were removed during the restoratior which began in 1809. As late as 1763, when Smollett visited Nîmes, he observee the citizens carrying away stones for their own buildings. The locals then usec the arena for an entertainment called 'Ferrade', which (according to Murray writing in the 1840s) consisted 'in teasing bulls from the Camargue previous t• branding them ... a poor imitation of a Spanish bull-fight, nearly as cruel without being so exciting, and it has properly been prohibited'. With a reversa of taste, bull-fighting has long been practised here in the summer season although the lowness of the wall of the podium, separating the seats from the arena, would indicate that it was not originally used for the exhibition anc tormenting of wild beasts. The gallery behind the first storey is virtually com plete, and gives a good idea of the massive grandeur of the edifice, constructec with stone from the quarry at *Barutel*, 7km N. on the Alès road.

Some 3 minutes' walk due S. brings one to the **Musée des Beaux-Art**▪ (undergoing re-arrangement), containing a miscellaneous collectior of paintings, including *Bassano*, Suzanna and the Elders; *Rigaud*, Por trait of Charles de Parvillez; *J.-F. Delyen*, Self-portrait, and Portrait of his Mother; and *Zuloaga*, Female portrait; also busts by *Rodin*, *Maillol*, and *Bourdelle*, etc. In the centre of the main hall, a huge Gallo-Roman mosaic discovered near the market-place of Nîmes.

A short distance to the N.W., behind the *Chamber of Commerce*, is a relic of the Roman *Porte d'Espagne*.

From the Amphitheatre, the Blvd Victor-Hugo leads N.W. to the *Pl. de la Comédie*, where (l.) the classicial facade of the *Théâtre* of 1803, burnt out in 1952, faces the ***Maison Carrée**, one of the finest extant Roman temples, marvellously preserved, which Smollett found 'ravishingly beautiful'; it also enchanted Arthur Young, who remarked: 'beyond all comparison the most light, elegant, and pleasing building I ever beheld . . . one perfect whole of symmetry and grace. What an infatuation in modern architects that can overlook the chaste and elegant simplicity of taste manifest in such a work and yet rear such piles of laboured foppery and heaviness as are to be met with in France'.

It was built in the Augustan age, and possibly dedicated to Lucius and Gaius, sons of Agrippa, adopted by Augustus as his heirs: Lucius died aged 19; Gaius was killed in Armenia in A.D. 4 (cf. St Remy; Mausoleum). Its name in patois—'Capduel' (or capitolium)—suggests that it was later assigned to the Capitoline Trinity. It is pseudo-peripteral. having a colonnade which, although it entirely encircles the building, is partly engaged in the walls of the cella. The main entablature and the consoles and cornice above the entrance are of fine workmanship.

Having survived the vicissitudes of being used as fort, private dwelling, warehouse, stable, and Augustinian church, it was restored by Nocolas de Lamoignon, the Intendant, in 1691, and again in the early 19C, and has since 1916 served as a lapidary museum. It is recorded that Colbert wished to transport it piecemeal to Versailles and there re-erect it. It was admired by Jefferson, who had measured drawings of it sent to Virginia in 1787 as a model for the State Capital.

The larger pieces in the collection remain in the courtyard, most noticeable being a pediment from the Jardin de la Fontaine. Examples preserved within the building show less fine workmanship that those at Arles, the Green inspiration being entirely lacking. In the centre is a head of Venus, a marble statue of Apollo, and a bronze head of Apollo (?), both from the Fontaine. Around the cella are 8 sections of the freize of the eagles; to the r. are funerary inscriptions, and the Venus of Nîmes, assembled from 103 fragments found in 1873.

Continuing N. along the Rue Auguste (S.I.), the *Sq. Antonin* is shortly entered, and following the tree-shaded Quai de la Fontaine to the W., the ***Jardin de la Fontaine** is reached, a formal garden laid out in the 18C around the *Source of the Nemausus*, and decorated with statuary. The fountain itself flows out from beneath the rocks of *Mont Cavalier* into a series of basins partly of antique origin, but mainly constructed in 1740 from designs by Le Nôtre.—To the S. extends the wide Av. Jean-Jaurès

The so-called *Temple of Diana* (l.) was probably part of a nymphaeum dedicated to the familiar spirit of the fountain, or an annexe to Roman baths (c. A.D. 117–138), later used as the church of a Benedictine abbey, and now a sad relic. Thicknesse had observed 'various fragments of exquisite workmanship' lying around it in the utmost disorder (probably those now at the Maison Carrée).

Hence paths ascend through the woods to the *Tour Magne*, a Roman tower which antedates the ramparts (16 B.C.), the summit of which commands a view of the city and N. over the *Garrigues*, a range of stony hills covered with scrub-oak.—The descent may be made to the E. via the Rues Stéphane-Mallarmé,

Rouget-de-Lisle, and (l.) d'Albenas, to the *Castellum Divisorium*, the distribution centre for the waters conveyed hence by the Pont du Gard aqueduct, and discovered in 1844. Adjacent is a *Fort* of 1687.—Hence the Sq. Antonin may be regained a short distance S.W.

From behind the Maison Carrée the Rue de l'Horloge leads E. into the medieval city, passing a 16C tower, to approach the *Cathedral* (N.-D. et St-Castor), a mutilated building of various dates displaying on its battered facade a frieze of Romanesque sculpture. The interior is largely a 19C restoration, in which a domed rococo chapel is preserved at the E. end.

The former *Bishop's Palace*, to the S., houses the *Musée du Vieux-Nîmes*, with local furniture, a section devoted to textiles, and another to bull-fighting.—In the Rue St-Castor, on the N. side of the cathedral, is a fine 17C mansion, which is passed on approaching, further E., the *Grand Temple*, a Protestant church of 17C origin flanking the Blvd Amiral-Courbet.—To the N., partly below street level, is the Roman **Porte d'Arles**, or *d'Auguste*, discovered in 1790 during the demolition of the 14C castle which surrounded it. It consists of two large arches, flanked by smaller ones, and is constructed without mortar. A defaced inscription on the frieze records the building of the walls of Nemausus by Augustus.

To the N.E., facing the *Pl. Gabriel-Perí*, stands *St-Baudile* (1867), behind which is the 'Cité Administrative'.—Turning S. along the boulevard to regain the Esplanade de Gaulle, the **Musée Archéologique**, in the buildings of a 17C Jesuit college, is shortly passed (r.).

It contains a good collection of Roman glass; coins; statuary; cinerary urns; Black Etruscan ware, and a Greek crater of 8C B.C.; and the so-called Warrior of Grézan, an example of Provençal sculpture prior to the Roman conquest. Other sections are devoted to *Prehistoric*, and *Natural History* collections.

For roads from Nîmes to *Alès*, see Rte 101B, in reverse; and for Nîmes to **Marseille**, and to **Cavaillon**, Rtes 149, and 150, respectively.

Driving S.W., at 13km *Uchaud* is traversed.—Just prior to the village, the D107 forks r., providing a pleasant alternative road—shortly passing near (r.) the oppidum of *Nages*—via (18km) *Sommières* (see Rte 101B) to **Montpellier**, 28km S.W. on the N110.

3.5km. The D979 forks l. for (20.5km) *Aigues-Mortes*, passing near the mineral springs where Perrier water is bottled, and at 6.5km skirting *Aimargues*, crossed by the road from Arles to Montpellier; see Rte 152B.—Beyond (6km) *St-Laurent-d'Aigouze* the marshes of the Vistre are reached, and 8km beyond, **Aigues-Mortes**; see Rte 152C.

'Continuing S.W. on the N113, at 11.5km **Lunel** (15,700 inhab.), of slight interest, but with a reputation for its muscatel grapes, is traversed, and 11km beyond, *Baillargues*, 4km N. of *Mauguio*, an occasional refuge of Popes during the 11-12C, beyond which lies its lagoon.—4km. *Vendargues*, where we are joined by the N110 from Alès, 9km beyond which **Montpellier** is entered; see Rte 144.

144 Montpellier

MONTPELLIER (201,100 inhab.; 45,800 in 1851; 97,500 in 1954), the prosperous and expanding préfecture of the *Hérault*, and seat of a famous university, lies partly on hills about the W. bank of the Lez, facing the Mediterranean, some 10km to the S.E. The older town, much of its the object of tasteful restoration in recent years, which continues, is a maze of narrow lanes although traversed by several broader streets, and is affectionately known as 'Lou Clapas' ('the heap of stones'). They are flanked by houses dating from the 13th to the early 19C, many preserving splendid courtyards and staircases behind their less distinguished exteriors; and the terraces of the Promenade du Peyrou are an imposing example of 18C taste in town planning. The Musée Fabre and Musée Atger contain important collections of paintings and drawings, respectively.

Montpellier, its name of uncertain origin, appears to have been two separate towns in the 10C: *Montpelliéret* being subject to the bishops of Maguelone, and *Montpellier* to the Guilhems. With the marriage of the heiress of that family in 1204 it passed to the crown of Aragón, from which it was detached in 1262 to form part of the new kingdom of Majorca. In 1292 Montpelliéret was taken by Philippe le Bel, and in 1349 Jaime III of Majorca sold Montpellier to Philippe de Valois, and the two were united.

The medical school, founded prior to 1000, perhaps by Arab or Jewish physicians, was incorporated in 1221, and the University in 1289. Rabelais studied here in 1530, receiving his doctorate in 1537. Its university now has a population of c. 40,000 (including foreign students), of which some 7000 are studying medicine. The bishopric of Maguelone (see Rte 152C) was transferred here in 1536. In the 16-17C Wars of Religion it was a Protestant stronghold, changing hands repeatedly, and of churches only the cathedral escaped destruction. It fell to Louis XIII in 1622, who conducted the siege in person. Although it had no important manufactures in the 18C, it was known for the production of verdigris, silk handkerchiefs, blankets, perfumes, and liqueurs, and later for chemical works, etc.

The reputation of its physicians attracted many distinguished visitors, among them Rousseau, in 1727; Necker and Mme de Staël, in 1785, in which year Charles Bonaparte, Napoleon's father, died here. Sterne, who when travelling with his wife and daughter was taken ill here, stayed in Montpellier from Sept. 1763 until the following Feb.; but Smollett, who spent the first half of Nov. 1763 in the town, had no good opinion of its doctors. Boswell, Thicknesse, Wraxall, and Arthur Young also passed through during the next few years. Indeed Smollett refers to the fact that Montpellier was 'one of the dearest places in the South of France', owing to 'the concourse of English who come hither, and, like simple birds of passage, allow themselves to be plucked by the people of the country', for the French affected to believe that all travellers from England were 'grand seigneurs, immensely rich and incredibly generous; and we are silly enough to encourage this opinion, by submitting quietly to the most ridiculous extortion, as well as by committing acts of the most absurd extravagance'. But at least Sterne found the inhabitants of Montpellier 'sociable, gay, and good tempered'. Stendhal was not so kind when he visited the town in 1838, although he conceded that the Promenade was beautiful. Joseph Conrad spent the winters of 1906 and 1908 here. Richard Aldington (1892–1962) spent some years in retirement here.

Among natives were Jaime I of Aragón ('the Conqueror'; 1208–76), and his son, Jaime II (1243–1311; king of Majorca); St Roch (1295–1327); Jean-Jacques de Cambacérès (1753–1824), Président of the Convention and High Chancellor of the Empire; Auguste Comte (1798–1857), founder of Positivism; A. J. Balard (1802–76), who discovered bromine in 1826; Comte Daru (1767–1829); Aristide Cavaillé-Coll (1811–99), the organ-builder; and the Duchesse d'Abrantès (1784–1838). Among artists, Sébastien Bourdon (1616–71); Jean

Ranc (1674–1735); F.-X. Fabre (1766–1837), and Frédéric Bazille (1841–70); while Robert Delaunay (1885–1941) died here.

The busy hub of this hilly town is the *Pl. de la Comédie*, with the *Théâtre* of 1889 at one end (and S.I.); at the other extends the Esplanade laid out in 1724, flanked by gardens, beyond which is the *Citadel*, erected by Louis XIII in 1624 to keep the rebellious town and its Protestants in check.

From a central point in the Esplanade, the Rue Montpelliéret leads W. In it stands the **Musée Fabre*, installed in the former *Hôtel Massilian* (rebuilt 1775) on the site of the mansion where Molière played before the Prince of Conti in 1654–5.

François-Xavier Fabre, a pupil of David, was in Rome at the outbreak of the Revolution, and remaining there, found favour with the Countess of Albany (widow of the Young Pretender), who on the death in 1803 of her second husband, the poet Alfieri, became Fabre's mistress; on her death in 1824 he inherited not only her valuable collection of pictures and a fine library, but also everything Alfieri had bequeathed to her. These collections he donated to his native city in 1825, which, together with Revolutionary confiscations, was to form the museum which so impressed Stendhal in 1838, later enriched by other donations, and now one of the most important in provincial France.

The museum is in the process of a thorough reorganisation, but the new wing already contains the following paintings: *Ranc*, Woman with a parasol, and Portrait of Nicolas Lamoignon de Basville; *Rubens*, Portrait of Frans Franken the younger; *Van de Temple*, Female portrait; *Sanchez Coello*, A young prince; *Berkheyde*, The cathedral of Haarlem; *Brueghel*, Brawling peasants; *J.-L. David*, Portrait of Alphonse Leroy, his doctor; representative works by *Jan Steen*, and *Teniers the younger*; *Houdon*, Busts of Franklin, Voltaire, and Rousseau; Busts by *Pajou*, and of Pajou, by *Ph. L. Roland*; *Rigaud*, Fontenelle; *Labille-Guiard*, Portrait of J.-M. Vien, the artist; *A. Roslin*, The Grand Duchess Elisabeth Alexievna; *Louis Gauffier*, Portrait of Lady Webster, the future Lady Holland, and of the artist Van Wyck Coklers; *F.-X. Fabre*, Portraits of Antonio Canova, the sculptor, of Dr Henri Fabre, of the Countess of Albany, of Vittorio Alfieri, of Lady Charlemont as Psyche, and of Allen Smith in the Roman Compagna, and Self-portrait; *anon.* Aristotle and Campaspe (late 17C Italian). Landscapes by *E. Castlenau* (1827–94), and *Jean Pillement*, among others; and miscellaneous 20C works.

Rooms on the lower floor still accommodate the following: *Achille Laugé*, Portrait of his wife; *Manet*, Portrait of Antonin Proust; *Frédéric Lottin*, Reminiscence; *Ribera*, *St Mary the Egyptian, and Head of an Apostle; *Oudry*, Still-life with books; *Poussin*, Venus and Adonis; *Sébastien Bourdon*, Portrait of a man with black ribbons at his wrists, and of Adolf Johan de Pflaz, Count Palatine; also a Landscape; *G.-L. Bernini*, Self-portrait of the artist-sculptor, and architect; *Carraci*, Pietà, and Autumn landscape; *Clementi*, Charles Emmanuel III of Sardinia; *Giordano*, Holy Family; *Domenichino*, Card. Jean de Bonsi, Bp of Béziers; *Veronese*, Mystic marriage of Catherine of Alexandria; *Antolinez*, Self-portrait; *Pierre de Campeneer*, Deposition; *Zurbarán*, The angel Gabriel, and St Agatha.

Other rooms contain: *Van Dongen*, Portrait of Mme Fernande Ollivier; *Matisse*, Still-life; *Bazille*, View of Aigues-Mortes, View of Castelnau, The toilette, A negress with peonies, and Self-portrait at the farm of St-Sauveur; *J.A.J. Aved*, The Marquise du Châtel; *J.-L. David*, Portrait of M. de Joubert; *Delacroix*, Algerian woman (a reduced version of that in the Louvre), and Aline, the mulatto; *Courbet*, two Portraits of Alfred Bruyas, Baudelaire reading, The bathers (1853), and Self-portrait, etc.; *Degas*, Luxembourg gardens; *Berthe Morisot*, *Self-portrait; and examples of the work of *Greuze, Corot, Géricault, Ingres, Bonnard*, et al.

Three works by *Bonington*, and *Reynolds*, Infant Samuel praying, are said to be here. Also on view is a collection of Shipibos ceramics, from Peru.

No. 6 in the same street, the *Hôtel de Cabrières-Sabatier-d'Espeyran*, serves as an annexe to the museum, mainly devoted to furniture.

The Rue de la Loge leads from the Théâtre to the *Préfecture*, partly

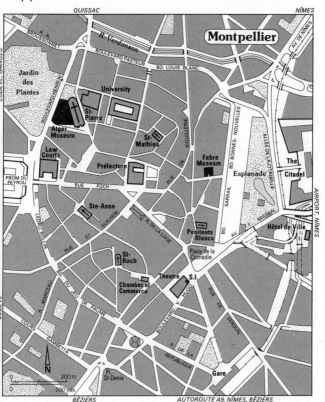

housed in the 17C *Hôtel de Ganges*, and facing the *Fontaine des États* (1772).

The Rue Foch leads W., half way along which a r.-hand turning leads to the 17C *Hôtel de Sarret* (No. 6 Rue de Palais), with a curious 'coquille' or shell-like undercutting of the lower storey. Adjacent is the *Pl. de la Canourgue* and 18C *Hôtel Richier de Belleval*, the former Hôtel de Ville.

The Rue Foch continues past (r.) the *Palais de Justice*, with its Corinthian peristyle (1855), on the site of the ancient palace of the Guilhems. The street ends at the *Porte du Peyrou*, a triumphal arch begun in 1691 by d'Aviler (d. 1701) to honour Louis XIV.

Beyond it is the imposing ***Promenade du Peyrou**, designed by d'Aviler in 1689 and completed by Jean-Antoine Giral assisted by his son-in-law Donnat, and completed in 1776. (*Peyrou* is a dialect form of *pierreux*, stony, the site having previously been bare rock). Behind the equestrian statue of the Sun King (1838), replacing one destroyed at the Revolution, is the *Château d'Eau*, ornamental water-works in the form of a hexagonal pavilion, by Giral, fed by the *Aqueduc de St-Clement* (constructed by Pitot in 1753–66), of 53 arches surmounted by 183 smaller arches, which extends to the W.

The Blvd Henri-IV leads N. from the Promenade, on the l. of which is the *Jardin des Plantes*, the oldest botanical garden in France, founded by Richer de Belleval in 1593.

A tablet in the old town moat within the walls of the Botanical School is said to mark the first (unconsecrated) grave of Narcissa Temple, the adopted daughter of the poet Edward Young, who died in Montpellier in 1730, but who was later buried at Lyon.

On the r. are the buildings of a Benedictine abbey founded by Urban V in 1364, which were used as the *Bishop's Palace* from 1536 to 1791, and from 1795 occupied by the *Faculty of Medicine*, an earlier professor of which was Guillaume Rondelet (1507–66). Apart from Rabelais, among its students were Sir Thomas Browne (c. 1630), and in 1659, Thomas Sydenham (1624–89). Besides a fine library, the building contains, on the first floor, the *Musée Atger, an outstanding collection of some 800 Drawings, largely French and Italian, collected by Xavier Atger (1759–1833), which should on no account be overlooked by the connoisseur.

To the N. of the building is the *Tour des Pins*, a relic of the medieval walls, containing *Archives*, while adjacent to the E. is what Stendhal condemned as a 'ridiculous' **Cathedral**, once the abbey-church. Three of its four towers date from 1364; the fourth was re-erected in 1855, when work started on rebuilding the choir in a neo-Gothic style. An ungainly 15C porch supported by two massive cylindrical pillars admits to the aisleless nave, restored in the 1620s after Protestant depredations in 1567.

In the Rue de l'Université, a short distance E. of the cathedral, is the *Rectorate* of the University, occupying the 18C *Hôtel-Dieu*. The various faculty buildings have been dispersed, most of them to the N. of the old town.

Among the notable 17-18C mansions which one may pass on returning S.E. towards the Pl. de la Comédie are (N. of the Rue de la Loge), the *Hôtel de Beaulac*, and *Hôtel Deydé*; Nos 6 and 8, respectively, in the Rue du Cannau, a short distance N.E. of the *Préfecture*; both are by D'Aviler.—E. of the Préfecture, in the Rue Embouque-d'Or, No. 4 is the *Hôtel de Manse*, with an interesting courtyard; opposite is the *Hôtel de Varennes* (14-18C); while further S., No. 7 is the *Hôtel des Trésoriers de France*, containing the collections of the *Archaeological Society*.

To the S. of the market in the Rue de la Loge are the *Hôtel de Montcalm* (5, Rue Friperie), and *Hôtel de Rodez-Bénavent* (4, Rue Trésoriers-de-la-Bourse).—Further S., in the Grande Rue, is the *Hôtel St-Côme*, by Giral, now the *Chamber of Commerce*, preserving an octagonal anatomy theatre.

The Blvd Victor-Hugo leads S.W. from the Théâtre, at the end of which (r.) is the *Tour Babote*, a rampart tower altered in the 18C to serve as an observatory.—Some distance beyond is *St-Denis* (1702), interesting as an example of church construction by D'Aviler.

There are several villages of some imterest not far W. of Montpellier, among them, approached by the D5, is (6km S.W.) *Lavérune*, with an old castle of the bishops of Montpellier.—*Pignan*, 3km further W., preserves several medieval buildings, and the neighbouring church of *Vignogoul* (2km N. of the latter), dating from 1220, is a curious mixture of Romanesque and Gothic styles.—At *Murviel*, 3km N.W. of Pignan, perhaps Roman *Altimurium*, is a cyclopean wall of pre-Gallic construction.

For roads from Montpellier to *Lodève* and *Millau*, and to *Ganges* or *Alès*, see Rtes 101A and B, respectively; to *St-Pons*, Rte 88B; and to *Nîmes* and *Avignon*,

Rte 143; and to *Arles*, Rtes 152A and B: all these in reverse. For *Béziers* and *Narbonne*, via *Pézenas*, or *Sète*, see Rtes 145A and B.

145 Montpellier to Narbonne

A. Via Pézenas and Béziers

99km (61 miles). N113. 31km *Mèze*—18km **Pézenas**—23km **Béziers**—27km **Narbonne**.

Maps: IGN 65, 72, or 114. M 240.

The A9 motorway provides a rapid route between Montpellier and Narbonne, with convenient exits to Pézenas, and Béziers.

The N113 drives S.W. from **Montpellier** (Rte 144) parallel to the N. flank of the *Montagne de la Gardiole*, and later skirts the *Bassin de Thau*, to (31km) *Mèze*, a small lake-side port with cooperage works, there turning abruptly inland to (12km) *Montagnac*, with a fine 14C belfry and the medieval *Tour Constance*.

7.5km to the E. are the 13-14C church (containing a congregation of huge wine casks) and cloister of the former Cistercian abbey of **Valmagne**, below the limestone pinnacles known as the 'Dentelles de Valmagne'.

6km. **PÉZENAS** (7,800 Piscénois; after the Roman colony here named *Piscenae*), is a charming old stone-built town, once noted for its wool and brandy, and later for its elegant social life under the governorship of Montmorency and Conti, the homogenous centre of which has little altered since its most splendid era (1456–1700), when it was the seat of the Estates of Languedoc.

It is a centre of the Hérault wine-growing region, and was long famed for its 'eau-de-vie' market. In 1650 Molière (and his company) played here during a session of the Estates, and he visited the town on several occasions prior to 1657, gaining inspiration for several of his early plays, although 'Les Précieuses ridicules' was not first performed until 1659, in Paris. The reputed 'petits-pâtes' of Pézenas are said to have been introduced in 1754 by Lord Clive, when he stayed at the *Château de Larsac*, c. 2km N.W.

From the *Pl. du 14 Juillet* one may conveniently enter the old town — between here and the Cours Jean-Jaurès further W. — via the Rue François-Oustrin, on the r. of which is the *Hôtel de Lacoste* (15-17C), with an attractive courtyard and staircase. On our l. as we enter the central *Pl. Gambetta* (previously the Pl. du Marche au Bled) is the S.I., in the *Maison du Barbier Gély*, where Molière put up. The 'Amis de Pézenas' have shown some initiative by producing a plan of the protected area—a maze of narrow lanes—and suggesting a numbered route (arrowed, with explanatory plaques) to be followed, but almost the whole may be explored with pleasure.

Among the many interesting houses, with their courtyards (usually so marked), the following may be mentioned: the *Tribunal de Commerce* (or Maison Consulaire; 16-18C) stands opposite, to the r. of which, in the Rue A.-P. Alliès, is the *Museum Vulliod-de-St-Germain*, with Provençal furniture and faïence; a fine staircase; 17C Aubusson tapestries; souvenirs of Molière; and preserving important archives, etc.—Uphill to the l., the turreted *Ilot des Prisons* is passed beyond which is a tower of the medieval enceinte.—To the l., the

Rue Montmorency bears round the site of the old castle, razed by Richelieu in 1632, after Montmorency's execution at Toulouse.—Further W. is the former *Ghetto*, not much altered since the 14C; and the doorway to the *Ancienne Prison Consulaire*, and the *Porte Faugères* (1597), off the N. end of the Cours Jean-Jaurès, in which No. 20, the *Hôtel des Grasset*, preserves a fine staircase.—In the Rue Henri-Reboul, leading W. off the Porte Faugères, is the *Chapelle de Penitents Noirs* (1590), transformed into a *Théâtre* in 1804; near by is 17C *Ste-Ursule*, containing a 13C 'black' Virgin, said to have originated in Rhodes.

Note, at the junction of the Rue Alfred-Sabatier (leading from the N.W. corner of the Pl. Gambetta) and the Rue de la Foire, the Renaissance niche of 1511 on the *Hôtel de Flottes de Sébasan*.—Turning l. down the latter street (r.), the *Hôtel de Wicque*, with remarkable Renaissance windows, and (l.) the *Hôtel de Carrion-Nizas*, with a 15C tower and 17C doorway, are passed.—Bearing round to the l., we reach *St-Jean* (1740), immediately behind which (r.) is the 16C courtyard of the *Sacristie des Pénitents Blancs*, while opposite is the former *Commanderie of St John of Jerusalem*.—A few paces to the S. is the *Pl. de la République*.

Hence the Rue Victor-Hugo leads S., to the r. of which at its far end is the *Hôtel Malibran*, with a fine facade and 17C staircase; while No.

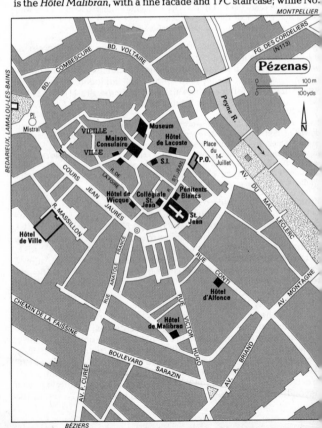

36 in the Rue Conti, leading S.E. from the square, is the *Hôtel Alfonce*, in the inner courtyard of which, overlooked by arcaded balconies, Molière acted in 1654.

At *St-Thibéry*, 8km S., are remains of a Roman bridge across the Hérault.

AT 23km S.W., we enter **BÉZIERS** (78,500 Biterrois), the prosperous centre of the wine trade of the Hérault and Aude, standing on an escarpment above the river Orb (the Roman *Orobis*) and the adjacent Canal du Midi.

The Celtiberian city of *Betera* became the Roman colony of *Julia Beterrae* in 120 B.C. During the first twelve centuries of the Christian era its history was very similar to neighbouring Narbonne; until July 1209. Having refused to hand over some 200 known Cathars to the ecclesiastical authorities, whose crusading forces were approaching the place, it was taken by storm and its citizens indiscriminately slaughtered, whether orthodox or heretic: 'Kill them all; God will know his own', exhorted Arnald-Amaury, the intransigent Abbot of Citeaux, as the timbers of the cathedral collapsed in flames on those who had sought safety within. As many as 20,000 are said to have died in Beziers' smoking ruins. The massacre remains the worst single blot of the Albigensian crusade, and the town is still haunted by the tragedy, a subject on which Catholic apologists have chosen not to dwell.

Its story has since been comparatively uneventful. Here in 1656 Molière's early comedy, 'Le Dépit Amoureux' was first performed. it was the birthplace of Pierre-Paul Riquet (1604 – 80), constructor of the Canal du Midi (see p 490), on visiting the port of which, just below the town, Arthur Young remarked: 'This is the best sight I have seen in France. Here Louis XVI, thou art truly great'. Young also observed that it was becoming 'a favourite residence for the English, preferring the air to Montpellier'. Among its other natives were Jacques Esprit 1611 – 78), and Paul Pellison (1624 – 93), 'hommes de lettres'; and Jean Moulin 1899 – 1944), founder of the 'Conseil National de la Résistance'.

The most interesting approach to the view of Béziers is from the S.W. as we cross the *Pont-Neuf* (1846), just below the 17-arched *Pont-Vieux* (13C) while those from the E., and from the motorway, lead more directly into the long *Allées Paul-Riquet*, a wide and umbrageous esplanade separating the old town from the new, and overlooking the gardens of the 'Plateau des Poètes', while off its W. side opens the *Pl. Jean-Jaurès*.

At its N. end is the *Théâtre* (1844), behind which is the *Pl. de la Victoire*, a busy junction of streets.

The plan of the older town is complicated. To the N.W. of this Place are two church of slight interest: *La Madeleine* (12C, but radically altered in the 18C), and *St-Aphrodise* (13-15C, with a Romanesque crypt).

From the W. side of the Allées, one may follow the narrow Rue du 4-Septembre, passing (r.) the 16C *Pénitents-Bleus*, to reach the central *Pl. Gabriel-Peri*, with the 18C *Hôtel de Ville* on the r.—The Rue Viennet, ahead, leads to the *Pl. de la Révolution*, with the 17C *Palais de Justice*, occupying the former *Bishop's Place* abutting the cathedral apse; and to the S.E., the *Musée des Beaux-Arts*; see below.

The former **Cathedral of St-Nazaire**, partly fortified and recently restored, dates mainly from the 13C (transepts), and 14C; only fragments of the choir and tower antedate the holocaust of 1209. Some good 14C glass is preserved, together with murals of 1347 in some chapels, while the 15C octagonal sacristy and chapter-house are noteworthy. The organ-case dates from 1623. The 14C cloister contains sculptural fragments.

Its terrace commands extensive views over the Orb, and towards the *Monts de l'Espinouse* to the N.W.

The **Museum**, in the *Hôtel Fabregat*, contains: attrib. *Hans Holbein the younger*, Male portrait; *School of Van der Weyden*, Portrait of an Abbé; *Goya*, Pietà; *Sebastien Bourdon*, Queen Christina of Sweden; and representative works by French 18-19C artists. it has recently been enriched by several 20C works of interest, by *Othon Friez, Dufy, Soutine, Utrillo*, and *Suzanne Valadon*, among others, together with a room devoted to the art of *Maurice Marinot* (1882–1960). An important collection of Greek vases is also preserved here.

The Rue de Bonsi leads E., to the r. of which, in the Rue Massol, is the **Musée du Vieux Biterrois**, containing interesting collections illustrating the history of Béziers from prehistoric times, with some notable Graeco-Roman sculptures and ceramics (some from *Ensérune*; see below). bronzes, etc. recovered from wrecks near Agde, in 1964; medieval antiquities, including parts of 14C facades; 17C Aubusson tapestries; a reconstruction of a room in the 'Auberge du Coche d'Eau (1855), a reminder of the passenger-carrying days of the Canal du Midi (from Toulouse via Béziers, to Sète); and a section devoted to Wine.

Further S., approached by the Rues des Drs-Bourgouet and St-Jacques (to the E. of which are the slight remains of a Roman arena) is *St-Jacques*, notable for its 12C apse, standing on a fortified promontory of the old town.

For roads from Béziers to **Carcassonne**, and **Castres**, see Rtes 88A and B, respectively, in reverse.

A l.-hand turning on the far bank of the Orb leads to the *Écluses de Fonseran-nes* of the Canal du Midi, where it descends 25m in 350m by means of eight successive locks.—15km S.E., at the river-mouth, is the resort of *Valras-Plage*.

Continuing S.W. from Béziers, at (10 km) *Nissan*, with a 14C church (l.), a r.-hand turning leads across the Canal du Midi and a section of a Roman road before ascending to the *Oppidum of Ensérune, ◇ with a view (r.) of the unusual circular 'Ancien Étang de Montady', with its fields, cultivated since 1248, radiating from the centre.

The Graeco-Iberian oppidum, one of the most important archaeological sites in France, stretches along the summit of the long hill, and dates from the 6C B.C. to the early Christian era, and three successive periods of settlement have been discerned. The partially wooded hill, providing extensive views, was fortified, and on either flank of the central part are seen ranges of habitations. Much of the site, but not all areas, is open to the public, while numerous objects excavated there since 1915 are well displayed in the site **Museum**.
    These include an extensive collection of ceramics, huge storage jars (dolia) Greek, Etruscan, and Rhodian pottery, and other examples from the Balearics Roman and Greek lamps; Celtic, Gaulish, and Visigothic jewellery; Roman glass and bone objects; coins; cinerary urns, etc. On the 2nd floor are further collections of Iberian ceramics, and bronze and iron weapons, etc.
    Close to the museum one may see a well-constructed stone cistern; to the l. of the road as we make our descent is a terrace containing some 76 storage silos. The far W. end of the ridge is occupied by a necropolis.

On regaining the main road, at 6km we cross a canal known as the *Nazour des Anglais* and enter the department of Aude, crossing that river at (4km) *Coursan*, where the Gothic church has a Romanesque tower, and 7km beyond, enter **Narbonne**; see Rte 146.

A DETOUR may be made from Coursan to *Fleury*, 7km E., with a ruined castle once owned by Card. Fleury, some 12km S.E. of which is *Narbonne-Plage*, whence one may reach Narbonne either by a hilly road over the *Montagne de la*

*View of the Étang de Montady from the oppidum of
Ensérune*

Clape (214m) or, continuing S., via the old village of *Gruissan*, on its lagoon,
15km S.E. of Narbonne.

B. Via Sète and Béziers

100km (62 miles). N113, off which fork l. onto the N112 3.5km
S.W. of **Montpellier**—24.5km **Sète**—23km **Agde**—22km
Béziers—N113. 27km **Narbonne**.

Maps: IGN 65, 72, or 114. M 240.

The N112 from **Montpellier** (Rte 144) improves shortly after crossing the A9, with as we descend parallel to the coast, a view S.E. of the
church of *Maguelone* on a wooded hillock of a sandspit beyond a
lagoon; see the latter part of Rte 152C.—To the r. is the ridge of the
Montagne de la Gardiole.

10.5km. *Vic-la-Gardiole* (l.) has a fortified 12C church.

7km. *Frontignan* (15,000 inhab.), famous for its muscatel dessert
wines, and preserving Romanesque fragments in its Gothic church,
is traversed as Sète is approached.

7km. **SÈTE** (formerly *Cette*; 40,500 Sétois), an important commercial and fishing port, its prosperity dating from the construction of
the *Canal du Midi*, of which it is the Mediterranean terminus, lies on
a narrow sand spit beneath the isolated *Mont St-Clair* (175m) and between the *Étang du Thau* and the sea. It is divided up into islands by
several canals, which are about the only things of interest to see.

The harbour was established in 1666–73 by Riquet, enlarged in the 19C, and its installations have been modernised since destruction caused by bombing in 1944. It was briefly occupied by Adm. Sir John Norris in 1710. Its most famous native was the poet Paul Valéry (1871–1945).

The *Canal de Sète*, spanned by several bridges, and bisecting the town, is skirted by boulevards which are the main centres of animation, especially to the S. near the *Vieux Ports*, above which, between the *Cimetière St-Charles* (or Marin) and *Fort Richelieu*, is a new *Museum* devoted largely to souvenirs of Valéry, and of the *Canal du Midi*, and containing a collection of miscellaneous paintings.

Circling round the S. side of the *Mont St-Clair*, we skirt the shore for 20km, following a sand bar (the Isthme des Onglous), to the N. of which is the *Bassin de Thau*, a salt-water lagoon. The road then bears inland, leaving the development of *Cap d'Agde* to the l. Passing (l.) the balsitic Mont St-Loup, an ancient volcano from which building stone is quarried, we enter (3km) *Agde*, also by-passed to the S.

Agde (13,200 Agathois), although of very ancient origin, having been founded in the 6C B.C. by Phocaeans under the name of *Agathé Tyché*, and a seat of a bishop from 400–1790, is an unprepossessing place. Previously described as 'a dirty little fishing port', it has changed little in recent decades. The only edifice of interest is the fortress-like *Cathedral*, the machicolations of the parapet being among the earliest existing examples of their kind. A keep-like tower surmounts the N. transept, while on the S. side are slight traces of a cloister. The choir is at right-angles to the nave; the interior was restored in the 17C.—A Renaissance house in the S. part of the old town contains local antiquities; the *Musée Agathois*.

The Hérault is crossed some 4km from its mouth, and the road drives due W. via (4km) *Vias*, with a lava-built 14-15C church.—13km. *Villeneuve-lès-Béziers*, on the S. bank of the Canal du Midi (see p 787), preserves a massive Romanesque church tower.—Passing beneath the A9, we enter **Béziers** 5km beyond; see Rte 145A, and for the road hence to **Narbonne**.

146 Narbonne to Perpignan and Le Boulou (for Figueras, and Girona)

83km (51 miles). N9. 46km *Salses*—16km **Perpignan**—21km *Le Boulou*.

Maps: IGN 72, or 114. M 240.

The B9 motorway provides a rapid route to the Spanish frontier, avoiding the Perpignan bottleneck, and is in many ways preferable to the N9. It should be joined S.W. of Perpignan, or at least at Le Boulou, after visiting Elne, by travellers crossing into Spain at the Col du Perthus.

NARBONNE (42,700 Narbonnais), lying in a dusty vine-covered plain some 12km—as the crow flies—from the Mediterranean, and once a flourishing Roman port, is a town of fallen fortunes, preserving few vestiges of its Imperial past although retaining certain medieval monuments of interest. It straddles the *Canal de la Robine* (1787; a branch of the Canal du Midi), which divides the Cité from the Bourg on its S. bank, the latter only 3-4km from the salt-water *Étang de Bages*. It is famous for its white honey, and is a market for Corbière wines.

Narbo Martius, founded c. 600 B.C., and capital of the Volcae Tectosages, was the principal Roman colony in Transalpine Gaul from 118 B.C. until the rise of Lugdunum (Lyon) in the 2C A.D. It was the chief city of the province of *Gallia Narbonensis*, and the 'pulcherrima Narbo' of Martial. It is said to have been evangelised in the 1C by Sergius Paulus, proconsul of Cyprus, who became its first bishop. It was certainly the seat of a bishop from the 4C until 1790. It was occupied by the Visigoths in 462, and in the 8C by the Saracens, becoming in the 9C capital of the duchy of *Gothia* or *Septimania* (see p 434). Its government was shared between its archbishops and its viscounts, while an important part of the town's intellectual life was played by the Jewish comnmunity; at the university which they founded in the 12C taught the learned rabbi Moses Khimkhi (before 1250).

It was annexed by Raymond III Pons, Count of Toulouse, c. 924, but the area was devastated between 1179–85, and again in the ensuing Albigensian crusade, during which the redoubtable Arnald-Amaury became archbishop of Narbonne, where later a form of Inquisition was established to combat heresy. The expulsion of the Jews in 1306, and the breaking of a dyke in 1340, which had diverted the Aude from its artificial course through the town, and the subsequent silting up of its port, put an end to its prosperity, while the Black Prince burnt its suburbs in his 1355 campaign. Being a frontier town its reputation also suffered: Symphorien Champier, writing in the early 16C, considered it 'La Latrine du Monde, et la plus basse cité que on sache des autres pays de France'. Its walls, in which numerous Roman fragments had been incorporated, were largely demolished in 1867, and their site laid out as boulevards, and any relics of interest were deposited in a disused church.

Narbonne was the birthplace of Publius Terentius Varro (82–37 B.C.), author of the 'Argonautica'; the 3C emperors Carus, Carinus, and Numerianus; St Sebastian, the martyr (250–88); the troubadour Guiraut Riquier (fl. 1254–92); and Henri Cros (1840–1907), the artist.

From the Blvd Frédéric Mistral, with its neighbouring gardens (where once the croaking of frogs drowned the whistle of trains), not far W. of the cathedral, one may follow the Rue Jean-Jaurès, skirting the N. bank of the canal, and turn l.

The **Cathedral of St-Just** is in fact only a huge unfinished choir (1272–1340), in the Northern Gothic style, to which insignificant towers were added in the 15C. An abortive attempt was made to complete the nave in the 18C, which when seen by Stendhal in 1838, was let out to a cooper! The pinnacles and flying buttresses of its apse can only be seen with difficulty, being hemmed in by adjacent building.

It would have been a magnificent church if it were finished, remarked Stendhal, who was suitably impressed by the height of the vaulting (40m; only exceeded by Amiens, Beauvais, and Metz).

The apse contains some good 14C glass, and in the E. chapel is a 14C alabaster Virgin. Notable among the tombs are those of Card. Briçonnet (d. 1514), and of the Chevalier de la Borde (1607), with a kneeling statue. Also notable are an early 16C terracotta Entombment from Rodez, and the Organ of 1741 backing onto the W. wall. Above the *Chapter-house* is the *Treasury*, containing a Flemish tapestry of the Creation, among other cult objects; adjacent is the 15-16C cloister.

From the apse, the Rue Rouget-de-Lisle leads N., in which (r.) stands the so-called **Horreum**, an underground storage depot of Roman origin, now displaying relics of the Roman occupation of Narbonne.—A short distance further N.E. is the *Pl. Bistan*, site of the Capital, where Roman columns have been re-erected.—Further E. stands Flamboyant *St-Sébastien*, with a good 15C vault.

From the Place one may return S. by the Rue Droite to reach the *Pl. de l'Hôtel de Ville*. The *Hôtel de Ville* itself is accommodated in the fortified **Archbishop's Palace**. The corner tower (1318, in which

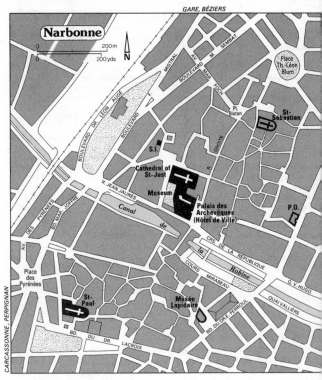

Louis XIII, at the instance of Richelieu, signed the order for the arrest of Cinq-Mars and De Thou in 1642; see p 697), is connected with the *Tour St-Martial* (1375) by a building in the 13C taste by Viollet-le-Duc. On the N. side is the *Tour de la Madeleine* (1273?), with a Romanesque doorway.

The **Museum**, described almost a century ago as 'much superior to the average of local museums', is reached by a monumental staircase of 1620. It contains a good ceramic collection, including some Gallo-Roman ware; an archaeological section containing several mosaics; and a somewhat miscellaneous collection of paintings, notably portraits by *P.* and *N. Mignard*, *Philippe de Champaigne*, *Oudry*, and *Rigaud*, among others, and a Bust of Louis XVI by *Pierre Puget*.

Just S. of this square, the narrow Rue du Pont-des-Marchands is in fact built on a bridge of Roman foundation, which may be seen from either the animated *Cours de la République*, overlooking the canal, or the *Cours Mirabeau* (with its adjacent market) on its S. bank, also crossed by a foot-bridge.

To the W. is an area 'en cours de rénovation', and so far the results display more taste than usual.—A short distance to the S. stands the deconsecrated *Église Lamourguier* (12-13C), which Freda White considered was 'a good deal more interesting than its contents', an extensive Gallo-Roman lapidary collection of some importance to the antiquarian, including a lintel dated 445 from the church of St-Rustique.

By turning W. along the adjacent boulevard, a short stretch of the ancient *Walls* is passed, and the *Hospital* is approached. Just before reaching this, turn r. to observe the quaintly sculptured so-called *Maison des Trois-Nourrices* (1558), claimed to be the rendezvous of Cinq-Mars and his fellow-conspirators. It in fact supports five, not three, amply-endowed caryatids.

Further W. is the apse of **St-Paul**, just W. of which is the busy *Pl. des Pyrénées*, from which one may regain the centre. The church is an interesting 12-14C edifice dedicated to Sergius Paulus (see above), with massive pillars in its nave preserving some curious capitals, while the S. stoup contains a stone frog fabled to have been petrified as a punishment for interrupting mass with its croaking.—A Paleo-Christian cemetery may be entered from the N. doorway of the church.

For the road to **Toulouse**, via **Carcassonne**, see Rte 88A, in reverse.

NARBONNE TO QUILLAN (97km). The D613 turns l. off the N113 5km W. of Narbonne, after 3km passing under the A61 motorway.—At 3km a l.-hand turning leads 2km to the Benedictine abbey of **Fontfroide*, delightfully sited in a sequestered valley. Groups are conducted round the extensive dependencies, including the 12C Church, 13C cloister, a late-12C Chapter-house, cellars, and courtyard, the lower part of which is Romanesque, the upper, Renaissance, etc. The abbey, suppressed in 1791, was re-occupied by Cistercians in the second half of the 19C, and has since been well restored.

The main road continues S.W. across the vine-growing *Corbières*.—At 13km the D611 leads S. via *Durban* to (36km) *Tuchan*; see Rte 85.—5km. *St-Laurent-de-la-Cabrerisse*, 11km N.W. of which lies *Lagrasse*, a fortified village, preserving several old houses and a medieval bridge, while the 14C church contains seven paintings by G. M. Crespi, among others. The former abbey buildings (10-18C), in part an old people's home, are of some interest.—*Carcassonne* lies 35km

The former abbey of Fontfroide

N.W.—The route may be regained 8.5km to the S., or by the minor D112, turning r. 3.5km S. of Lagrasse, passing (l.) at 12km the ruined castle of *Durfort*, 5km S. of which is the ruined border stronghold of *Termes*, which held out for three months in 1210, when besieged by De Montfort.—One may also continue S.W. via (8km) *Montjoi*, and thread a wooded gorge to reach the D613 at the *Pont de l'Orbieu*.

From St-Laurent we continue S.W. via (13km) *Villerouge-Termenès*, with a castle of the bishops of Narbonne, 3km beyond which a l.-hand turning leads S. through the gorges of the river Torgan to (18.5km) *Padern*, with a ruined castle, from which the D117 may be reached via *Queribus*, to the S.W., or *Tuchan*, to the N.E.; see Rte 85.—13.5km. *Pont de l'Orbieu*, beyond which the *Col du Paradis* (622m) is crossed to (13km) *Arques*, with its splendid 14C castle-keep.—6km. The small spa of *Rennes-les-Bains* lies 3km S.—The ruins of *Blanchefort* (l.), and later (r.) those of the castle of *Coustaussa*, are passed before joining the D118 at (5.5km) *Couiza*, commanded to the S. by *Rennes-le-Château*, for which, and for the road S.W. to (12km) **Quillan**, see Rte 89.

Driving S. from Narbonne, the N9, after crossing to the E. of the B9 motorway, skirts the *Étang de Bages et de Sigean*, and begins undulating through inhospitable coastal hills before circling to the S.W. above the *Étang de Leucate* and *de Salses*.

To the E., beyond the lagoon, are several recently planted summer resorts strung out along the coast from *Leucate-Plage* to the N. to *Argelès-Plage* to the S.—Between *Port Leucate* and *Port Barcarès* is the additional attraction of a beached liner, the 'Lydia', serving as a casino.

W. of the lagoon, between its village and the motorway (which provides a good view, and an approach from a convenient lay-by) is the remarkably complete red-brick ***Fort de Salses** ◊ (1497–1503), designed by Francisco Ramirez on the site of an 11C castle, and recently restored after centuries of neglect. It is one of the earliest built specifically to resist artillery, and consists of a quadrilateral (84m by 110m) with towers at each corner, and three main outworks, with a keep—reduced in height by Vauban—in the centre of its W. side, overlooking a huge courtyard. The whole is surrounded by a wide moat, at present dry, but which could be filled at short notice. Guided visits take place regularly, and the guides are better informed than most.

After 5km the river Agly is crossed, beyond which is the old province of *Roussillon*, annexed to France at the Treaty of the Pyrenees (1659), but the influence of Catalonia is still noticeable in its dialect, etc, and in local place-names the x is pronounced sh; u as oo; final g as tch; and ch as k.

To the S.W. we get a progressively closer panorama of the E. end of the Pyrenees, at this point dominated by the *Massif du Canigou*, rising to 2784m.

2.5km to the W. lies *Rivesaltes*, a busy market-town with a characteristic church tower of Roussillon, and known for its white Grenache wine. It was the birthplace of Marshal Joffre (1852–1931).—6km further S.W. lies *Baixas*, with a fortified Romanesque church and three old gates.

Passing (r.) the airport, the outer industrial suburbs of Perpignan are traversed as the centre, on the S. bank of the Têt, is approached.

PERPIGNAN (113,600 Perpignanais; 21,800 in 1851; 70,100 in 1901), once capital of *Roussillon*, and now préfecture of the *Pyrénées-Orientales*, is a busy, and dusty, frontier town, and has grown very considerably in recent decades, but this is only partially due to the influx of Spanish, and particularly Catalan refugees after the fall of Barcelona to Fascist Spain in Jan. 1939. The old centre, ly-

ing on the S. bank of the Basse (a tributary of the Têt), the banks of
which have been laid out as gardens, retains some characteristic
streets, but most of the rest of the modern brick-built town, although
preserving some buildings of interest, is hardly attractive, indeed
Henry Swinburne thought it 'a villainously ugly town' even in 1775.
It was once a flourishing port, but is now some 3km from the sea.

The countship of Roussillon passed to the house of Aragón in 1172, but in 1276
Jaime I included it in the kingdom of Majorca created for his son, which also
comprised the recently conquered Balearic islands, but after a succession of
disputes Jaime II of Majorca was deprived of his throne by Pedro IV of Aragón in
1344. Philippe le Hardi died here in 1285 after an unsuccessful expedition
against Pedro III of Aragón. In 1462 the province was invaded by Louis XI, and
Perpignan was taken in 1475, but in 1493 Charles returned it to the Catholic
Kings (after which the Fort of Salses—see above—was built to protect the place
from further incursions from France). In 1641 Louis XIII espoused the cause of
the Catalans, who had rebelled against the centralising policy of Castile, and in
1659, by the Treaty of the Pyrenees, Perpignan finally became French. When
the Grande Mademoiselle visited the place, she remarked that its nuns were 'co-
quettes et fardées'. Its 14C ramparts were largely demolished at the turn of this
century, although relics remain in the N.E. quarter.

Its most famous native was the artist Hyacinthe Rigaud (1659–1743).

The centre of animation is the *Pl. Arago*, with its statue of the
astronomer (born at *Estagel*, 22km N.W.), with the S.I. a short
distance W.—By following the Quai Sadi-Carnot to the N.E., the
Castillet is soon reached, a massive brick fort of 1367, enlarged in
1483, when the *Porte Notre-Dame* was added. it now houses the attractively displayed *Musée d'Arts et Traditions Populaires du
Roussillon.*

Hence the Rue Louis-Blanc leads S. to the **Loge de Mar** (Spanish

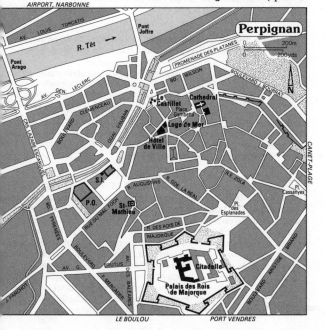

Lonja, or exchange), a Gothic structure of 1397, almost entirely rebuilt in the Renaissance style in 1540, the arcades of which now shelter cafés. Adjacent is the *Hôtel de Ville* (16-17C), and next door is the former *Palais de la Députation*, with a 15C courtyard.—The early Renaissance *Maison Julia*, with its interior courtyard, lies a few paces to the N.E.

The Rue St-Jean leads E. from the Loge to the Pl. Gambetta,providing a view of the curious (unfinished) W. front of the **Cathedral**, of rolled flints and brick bonding, preceded by a 17C porch, and surmounted by a tower with an 18C wrought-iron belfry. it was begun in 1324 on the site of an older church, but was not completed until 1509. A restored Romanesque doorway of *St-Jean-le-Vieux*, with its 12C sculpture, facing the N. side of the cathedral, should not be overlooked.

The dark interior, displaying much red and white mottled stone, is remarkable for the breadth of its nave and for the series of ornate *retablos* in the Catalan manner, the High Altar of 1620 being by Bartolomé Soler of Barcelona. Notable is the retable of the Virgin (or de la Magrana) of c. 1500. The organ-loft is dated 1604, a passage beneath which admits to the chapel of N.-D.-del-Correch, which occupies the 11C S. transept and apse of St-Jean-le-Vieux. By the N. transept is the Tomb of Bp Louis de Montmor (d. 1695). On the S. side of the choir is the Gothic Chapter-house.

It is worth passing through the S. door of the cathedral, with its 14C reliefs, to see the realistic crucifixion (1307) in the adjacent chapel (l.), brought to Perpignan in c. 1528, probably from the Rhineland.

Some distance S.E. of the Loge (approached by the Rue de l'Argenterie to the Pl. Rigaud, and continuing S.) is 14C *Ste-Marie-la-Reál*, preserving two 17C altar-pieces, one depicting Perpignan. Here the Spanish anti-pope Benedict XIII (Pedro de Luna) excommunicated Gregory XII at a council in 1408, but with no effect.—*St-Jacques*, on the E. side of the old town, contains an elaborate 15C retable.

The **Musée Rigaud** has been moved to the *Hôtel de Lazerme*, a 17C mansion at 16 Rue de l'Ange, leading S.E. from the Pl. Arago.

Here, apart from portraits by Rigaud, one may see works of the Catalan School, including a Retable of the Trinity (1489; by the Master of Canapost?), and of the Valencian School; also *Juan de Sevilla*, Coronation of the Virgin; *Lucas*, Ladies on a balcony; *Marguerite Gérard*; Summer (?); *Pillement*, Landscapes; *Largillière*, Baron, the actor; *J.-L. David*, Self-portrait; *Ingres*, The Duc d'Orléans; *Géricault*, Male studies; *Greuze*, Child's head; *Rigaud*, Portraits of Card. Bouillon, Card. Fleury, and the Duc de Chartres, among others; and Self-portraits, wearing a turban, wearing the Order of St Michel, and painting M. de Castagnier. Other rooms contain works by *Dufy*, and *Maillol*, etc.

Some minutes of zigzag walk S. from the Pl. Arago will bring one to the main W. entrance, with sculptures of 1577, of the brick-built bastions of the ***Citadel** (also approached by car from the western boulevards). The huge fortress, the present appearance of which is due to Vauban, embodies earlier work, some raised by the Emperor Charles V. Stepped ramps ascend to the recently restored 13C *Palace of the Kings of Majorca*, the entrance of which, beneath a tower, admits to a large courtyard, two sides of which contain elegant loggias above arcades. On the E. side are two superimposed chapels, with a facade of bands of mottled stone and marble; to the S. is a large vaulted hall, 32m long. The rest of the fortress is still in military hands, which in the past so mutilated the building. The terrace to the W. commands a good view of the *Canigou*.

For the road to **Foix**, see Rte 85, in reverse; for **Bourg-Madame**, see Rte 147.

Canet-Plage lies 13km due E. of Perpignan, approached by the D617 parallel to the S. bank of the Têt, which after 5km passes (l.) *Castel Roussillon*, with a round 12C tower, which with the ruined Romanesque church and the excavated forum, is all that remains of *Ruscino*, the Iberian and Gallo-Roman capital of the province.

PERPIGNAN TO CERBÈRE (47km), VIA ELNE AND COLLIOURE. The N114 leads S.E. across the plain, the landscape dominated by the *Canigou* to the S.W.—14km. **Elne** (6,200 inhab.) was known as *Illiberis* until the 4C, when it was renamed *Castrum Helenae* or *Helena* in honour of the mother of the Emperor Constantine, and was the seat of a bishopric from 571 to 1602, when it was transferred to Perpignan. In the upper town stands the former cathedral of *Ste-Eulalie*, a fortified 11C church with two towers, one Romanesque, the other a 19C addition. The chapels on the S. side, added in the 14-15C, contain some old paintings and the tomb of Bp Raymond Costa (d. 1310); note the cant of the walls. To the N. is the remarkable *Cloister* of two sets of twin columns alternating with square piers of white marble, supporting capitals carved with scriptural scenes of extraordinary realism. Only the S. walk (1175) is wholly original, the rest being rebuilt with old material after the sack of the town in 1285. The upper storey was demolished only in 1827. On the S. side is the tomb of Bp Guilhem Jordan (d. 1186). From the E. side one may visit a small museum, containing Gallo-Roman sarcophagi, etc. The terrace, beyond the 14C foundations of a projected apse, commands a pleasant view.

The Tech is shortly crossed, as (7km) *Argelès-sur-Mer*, with its 14C church tower, is approached, 2km W. of its Plage.—For the road hence to *Le Boulou*; see below.

The road bears S.E. along the base of the Pyrenean foothills, the summits of some bearing ruined towers, and climbing briefly prior to entering (6km) **Collioure**, an attractive but now somewhat commercialised fishing-village and resort, retaining a 12C castle and other fortifications of ancient *Cauco Illiberis*. The church is 14C. Near the harbour the *Hôtel Les Templiers* preserves an interesting collection of paintings by artists who have frequented the place in recent decades. The Spanish poet Antonio Machado (1875–1939), who with other Republican refugees was pursued across the frontier, died here, where he is buried. Its anchovies are delicious.—A minor road leads c. 8km inland to the ruined abbey of *Valbonne* (13C), in the valley of the Ravane.

4km. **Port-Vendres** (5,300 inhab.), the ancient *Portus Veneris*, with a fine harbour, damaged in 1944, is traversed, 5km beyond which lies *Banyuls-sur-Mer*, producing a strong red wine. It also has a fishing harbour, and was the birthplace of the sculptor Aristide Maillol (1861–1944), whose work is much in evidence in the area. The *Aquarium* is part of a marine biological station of the University of Paris.—The *Col de Banyuls* (357m), on the frontier to the S.W., was the scene of a Spanish victory over the French Revolutionary army in 1793.—The road continues to wind above the coast to (10km) *Cerbère*, the frontier village, with an international railway station, beyond which, on either side of the *Col des Bilitres* (170m), here marking the border, are French and Spanish Customs.—The road descends to the fishing-village of *Portbou*, for which see *Blue Guide Spain*.—*Figueras* lies 41km to the S.W.; *Port Lligat*, 35km S.E.

ARGELÈS TO LE BOULOU (19km). Following the D618 due W. (with the *Canigou* ahead), after 4.5km *St-André* is entered, with a church (r. of the road) dating from 1121; note the mutilated Roman masonry by the window.—After another 4.5km we reach *St-Genis-des-Fontaines*, where (l. of the road) the lintel over the church door bears the earliest dated Romanesque carving (c. 1020).—To the S. rises *Pic Neulos* (1256m), on the frontier, and the highest in this section of the *Chaine des Alberes*, the most easterly extension of the Pyrenees.—8km beyond St-Genis we meet the N9 just S. of *Le Boulou*; see below.

Leaving Perpignan, the N9 bears S., roughly parallel to and E. of the motorway, crossing the flat Roussillon plain, always dominated to the S.W. by the *Canigou*, after 13km passing near (r.) *Villemolaque*, with the cloister (1307) of the former Augustinian priory of *Monastir del Camp*, further W.; and then (l.) *Banyuls-dels-Aspres*, preserving ancient fortifications.

8km. **Le Boulou**, with a curious Romanesque portal to its church, where it is recommended to join the motorway to cross the frontier; but see below for the old road.—For the road to *Prats-de-Mollo*, see below.—The road climbs steeply above the valley of the Rome, with good views W. towards the *Canigou*, and of the village of *Le Perthus* below us, to reach the French and Spanish Customs. At the *Col du Perthus*, the main pass in this E. ridge of the Pyrenees, known as the *Chaine des Alberes*, with the Pic *Neulos* (1256m) to the E., and the *Roc de France* (1450m) to the W., the frontier is marked on the Spanish side by a curious pyramidal construction (1976; by Ricardo Bofill). The exit for **Figueras** is 29km from *Le Boulou*, and that for **Girona** is 35km beyond; for which see *Blue Guide Spain*.

The old road (N9) from Le Boulou, crossing the Tech, at 2km passes (r.) the former church of *St-Martin-de-Fenollar*, with its 11C apse preserving 12-13C murals (key at adjacent farm).—The road passes under the motorway and ascends the valley of the Rome, its three narrows or *cluses* fortified in Roman or medieval times. Traces of the Roman Via Domitia are visible at the bottom of the valley. To the r. are the ruins of the feudal castle of *L'Écluse*.—7km. **Le Perthus** (290m), a village straddling the frontier, on either side of which are the French and Spanish Customs. it was here that in 218 B.C. Hannibal crossed the Pyrenees on his march from Spain to Italy. The road descends to (6km) La Junquera, and some 13km beyond, *Figueras*, for which and for the road S., see *Blue Guide Spain*.

It has been estimated that in total some 460,000 Spanish refugees crossed from Catalonia into France and exile between 27 Jan.– 10 Feb. 1939, including 220,000 men of the Republican army, 170,000 women and children, and 10,000 ill or wounded, most of them to spend some uncomfortable weeks in French clearing centres set up at short notice for their reception.

LE BOULOU TO PRATS-DE-MOLLO (38km). The D115 bears S.W. up the valley of the Tech, passing (l.) *St-Jean-Pla-de-Cors*, with a Romanesque church, and (7km) crosses the river near the early 14C *Pont de Céret*, with a span of 45m, restored in the 18C. The upper valley of the Vallespir here was devastated by floods in 1940.—To the S. lies **Céret**, an old town preserving relics of fortifications, in the period c. 1910– 20 frequented by Picasso, Braque, and other artists, which gave it the name 'the Barbizon of Cubism', and a *Museum* of 20C paintings may be seen.—The road continues up the valley, with the *Roc de France* (1450m) to the l., and with a view (r.) of *Palada*, with its old castle, perched on the hillside, and of the *Canigou* (2784m), to enter (8km) **Amélie-les-Bains**, a small spa known to the Romans, and an ancient pavement is preserved in the so-called 'Thermes Romains'. Life here a century ago was 'indescribably dull . . . the same limited society necessarily meeting all day long'. The village, previously *Arles-les-Bains*, changed its name in 1840 to flatter Louis-Philippe's consort—To the W. rises a fort built by Louis XIV; to the S. are the *Gorges du Mondony*, beyond which lies *Montalba*, in a mountain basin; to the N.W. is the hill-top village of *Montbolo*.

4km. **Arles-sur-Tech**, the market-town of the Vallespir, contains an *Abbey church*, founded in 1046, and rebuilt and vaulted in 1157. Here is the Tomb of SS Abdon and Senned, two Persian nobles martyred in 250, whose remains were conveyed here to free the valley of the wild beasts then said to infest it. Note also the effigy of a knight (1210), and a Romanesque Christ in glory; the 16C tower and 13C cloister are likewise noteworthy.—*St-Sauveur*, in an old square, preserves a good Romanesque tower; and to the N.W. is disused *St-Pierre* (13C).—There is an abandoned church at *Corsavy*, 7.5km N.W. At 6km the quaint old village of *St-Laurent-de-Cerdans* lies to the S., beyond which is the Romanesque church of (14km) *Coustouges* (826m), one of the most interesting in the district; another may be seen at *Serralongue*, 7km W. of *La Forge-del-Mitg*, between St-Laurent and the main road.

The D115 continues to climb S.W. to (6km) *Le Tech*, with hydro-electric works.—*Montferrer*, 8km N.E., has an old church and ruined castle; while *Lamanère*, some 10km S., beyond Serralongue, and overlooked by the three *Tours de Cabrens* (13-14C), is the most southerly commune in France.—Threading the defile of *La Baillanouse*, at 7km **Prats-de-Mollo** (745m) is entered, a small winter resort and old fortress town of some interest, with 17C ramparts and a 17C church preserving a Romanesque tower.—8km W. is the high-lying spa of *La Preste* (1130m), beyond which rise the *Pic de Costabonne* (2465m), and *Roc Colom* (2507m), between which is the source of the Tech. From the latter a ridge leads N.E. to the *Canigou* massif.—The D115 climbs steeply S. to the Spanish frontier at (14km) the *Col d'Ares* (1513m; Customs).—*Camprodón* lies 18km to the S.W., on the C151 to *S. Joan de les Abadesses* and *Ripoll*, 24km beyond, for which see *Blue Guide Spain*.

147 Perpignan to Bourg-Madame

108km (67 miles). N116. 17km *Millas*—7km *Ille-sur-Têt*—19km **Prades**—6km **Villefranche-de-Conflent**—30km **Mont-Louis**—D618. 9km **Font-Romeu**—20km *Bourg-Madame*. The direct road between Mont-Louis and Bourg-Madame via *Saillagouse* is 8km shorter.

Maps: IGN 71, 72, or 114. M 240, 235.

The main, but uninteresting, road leads directly W. from **Perpignan** (Rte 146) along the S. bank of the Têt, a river subject to sudden and disastrous floods.

A slightly longer ALTERNATIVE is that via *Thuir*, the D612A leading S.W. from Perpignan, with a view ahead of the *Canigou* massif conspicuous above the Aspres hills.—13km **Thuir**, noted for the manufacture of a ubiquitous apéritif known as 'Byrrh'; the church contains a pewter Virgin and Child of c. 1200.—The D615 leads 13km W. to regain the main road at *Ille-sur-Têt*, but a short recommended detour is that to *Castelnou*, 5.5km S.W., a picturesquely sited walled feudal village, dominated by its restored 10C keep.

Ille-sur-Têt, preserving its fortified gate, is traversed, and 4km beyond, we pass (l.) *Bouleternère*.

Hence a hill road climbs S. c. 8km, from which a track ascends S.W. (enquire at a house here regarding adm.) to the Augustinian priory of *Serrabone*, where the 11-12C church preserves remarkably carved Romanesque capitals.

The Têt reservoir is shortly skirted, overlooked by old perched villages, and (l.) *Vinça*, to enter **Prades** (6,500 inhab.), once the capital of the district of *Conflent*. In the labyrinth of its streets is a Gothic *Church* with an older tower, and containing Catalan-type retables, the high altar being by Joseph Sunyer. it was here that the exiled 'cellist Pablo Casals (1876–1973) organised music festivals during the 1950s.—7km N.W. lies the small spa of *Molitg-les-Bains*.

Some 3km S. of Prades is the abbey of *St-Michel-de-Cuxa*, founded c. 900 for Benedictine monks, and which rose to prominence under a series of abbots more enlightened than most. In 987 Doge Pietro Orseolo I, one of the builders of St Mark's in Venice, died here. After a gradual decline the abbey was burned at the Revolution, and later further despoiled, many of the capitals of its 11-12C cloister now embellishing 'The Cloisters' at New York. Re-occupied by Cistercians, it is in the process of restoration. The church, dedicated in 975, is notable for its horse-shoe-shaped Mozarabic arches, unusual in W. Europe outside Spain, while the apses, tower, and crypt—vaulted from a central pier—are probably 11C work.—The road (D27) may be continued hence along the N. foothills of the

Canigou (2784m) to *Vernet-les-Bains*, c. 16km S.W.; see below.—An approach to
the summit may be made from this road.

6km. *Villefranche-de-Conflent (432m),** an imposingly fortified
village, defends a defile in the valley, above which towers a ruined
fort. Its heavy ramparts date from the 16C, and were later, in 1665,
improved by Vauban. *St-Jacques* dates from the 12-13C; several of
its medieval houses are in the process of restoration.

Hence a road climbs S. via *Corneilla-de-Conflent*, with a remarkable Romanesque
church containing a marble altarpiece of 1345, to (5.5km) **Vernet-les-Bains**
(650m), an old spa 'discovered' by the English c. 1850, among others by the
mountaineer Charles Richard Weld (1813–69), where in 1910 Lord Roberts laid
the foundation-stone of the English Church. Among its visitors was
Kipling.—Above the more modern town stands a restored castle and 12C
church. It is a convenient base for the ascent of the Canigou.
From *Casteil*, 2.5km S. in the Cady valley, one may walk up to the abbey of
St-Martin-du-Canigou, on the summit of a rugged spur (1065m), founded in
1007 by Count Guifred of Cerdagne in expiation of the murder of his son, and
who died here in 1049. The building, with a Romanesque *Church* above an aisled
crypt, has been the object of restoration, but the capitals of the 11C cloister are
remarkable, and little can spoil its site.
    The usual ascent of the **Canigou** is that from a point 5.5km E., on the Vernet-
Prades road (D27), where a r.-hand turning, a narrow mountain road, ascends
steeply to (15.5km) the *Chalet-Hôtel des Cortalets*, whence the summit (2784m),
attained by an easy climb of 2 hours, commands a superb *View* of the serried
ranks of the Pyrenees extending to the W. (indicator), while to the S. the ridge of
Montserrat is visible; to the N., behind the Corbières, rise the Cévennes.
    An alternative return to the N116 may be made by climbing W. from Vernet
to (4.5km) *Sahorre*, which with *Thorrent*, further W., have Romanesque churches, the latter also with a restored château.—From the former we turn N. down
the valley past the 11C church of *Ste-Eulalie*.

From Villefranche the main road climbs to (10km) *Olette*, passing (l.)
the battlemented towers of *La Bastide*.

There are Catalan retables in the church at *Evol*, 2km N., beyond which is a ruined castle; and a restored castle at *Nyer*, c. 3km S. of Olette.

At 6km we pass the entrance to the *Gorges de Carança*, and below
(4km) *Fontpédrouse*, the ruined castle of *Prats-Balaguer*, and later the
railway suspension-bridge of *Pont Gisclard*, before reaching **Mont-
Louis** (1600m), the highest garrison-town in France, surrounded by
ramparts built by Vauban in 1681. A monument commemorates
Gén. Dagobert, who died of wounds here after conducting a successful campaign against the Spaniards in 1793.

Some 6.5km to the S.E., at *Planès*, is a church built on the unusual plan of a
triangle intersecting a trefoil.

Another excursion from Mont-Louis is to follow the D60 N.W. to (14km) the *Lac
des Bouillouses*, a reservoir overlooked to the N.E. by the *Roc d'Aude* (2377m)
and to the W. by the *Pic Carlit* (2921m), the highest of the Eastern Pyrenean
peaks within France; see also the latter part of Rte 87.
    For the road from *Axat* (11km S.E. of Quillan) to *Mont-Louis*, see the latter part
of Rte 89.

MONT-LOUIS TO BOURG-MADAME VIA SAILLAGOUSE (21km). The N116
continues the ascent to (2.5km) the *Col de la Perche* (1579m) on the watershed
separating the Têt from the Sègre basin, and enters the *Cerdagne*, an area anciently inhabited by the Ceretani, and which originally included the three
baronies of Céret, St-Laurent-de-Cerdans, and Puigcerdà, but now restricted to
the upper valley of the Sègre, a tributary of the Ebro. The villages of the upper
Cerdagne were ceded to France, together with Roussillon, in 1659, but its capital

from 1177, *Llivia*, being dignified with the title of 'town', was by a Spanish quib-
ble not included in the cession, and thus remained Spanish, being connected to
Spain by a 'neutral road'; see below.—9.5km. *Saillagouse*, with an altered
Romanesque church.—To the S.E. is *Llo*, with an old church and ruined castle,
beyond which the *Gorges du Sègre* lie in the valley leading to the *Col de Llo*, between (l.) the *Pic de Fenestrelles* (2826m) and *Puigmal* (2910m). On the far side of
the frontier lies *Nuria*.—From Saillagouse one may take the alternative neutral
road through the enclave of **Llivia**, the ancient *Julia Livia*, with balconies in the
Spanish style, a fortified church, and a 15C pharmacy.—9km. *Bourg-Madame*;
see below.

The D618 forks r. from Mont-Louis through forests to (9km) **Font-
Romeu** (1800m), a popular winter-sports station and summer resort
since c. 1910, passing before entering the town the 17C chapel and
spring, the 'Font Roméu' from which the place is named, the chapel
formerly containing a 12C Virgin and an elaborate altarpiece by
Joseph Sunyer (1707). It is a pleasant centre from which to explore
the wooded valleys to the N. in summer, and commands some extensive views. The road descends through adjacent *Odeillo*, with a fine
Romanesque portal to its church, and a huge solar-energy mirror
(1969), part of the experimental complex of (6km) *Targasonne*, with
its 'Centrale Solaire' (1982). Beyond, we traverse a chaos of tumbled
granite boulders, and skirt the N. boundary of the Llivia enclave (see
above), before descending through *Angoustrine*, where the
Romanesque church contains an old altarpiece and a 12C Crucifixion.—After 10.5km the N20 is met at *Ur* (the church of which has a
richly gilt interior), and turn l. for (3.5km) **Bourg-Madame** (1130m),
the frontier village, formerly called La Guinguette, only receiving its
present name in 1815 to flatter the Duchesse d'Angoulême.—The
church at *Hix*, immediately to the E., dates from the 12C.

The bridge across the Raour, which joins the Sègre just below the town, marks
the frontier, with French and Spanish Customs, on the far side of which
Puigcerdà lies on the slope to the r.—*Ripoll* lies 63km S.E. on the N152, and **Seo
de Urgel** 51km to the W. on the C1313, for which see *Blue Guide Spain*.
  For the road from Bourg-Madame to *Toulouse*, see Rte 87, in reverse.

148 Avignon, and Villeneuve-lès-Avignon

AVIGNON (91,500 Avignonnais), préfecture of the *Vaucluse*, and
the prosperous centre of a fertile countryside, is, with Arles and Aix,
one of the more attractive and interesting towns of Provence. The
imposing Palace of the Popes remains one that it was long the
residence of pontifs exiled from Rome, while the Museum of the
Petit Palais contains one of the most remarkable collections of Italian
painting in France. Although occasionally scourged by the *Mistral*,
its climate is healthy, and its life animated.

Roman *Avenio*, at first of slight importance, became sufficiently strong by 1129
to constitute an independent republic under the nominal suzerainty of the
counts of Toulouse. In 1226 it was besieged by Louis VIII on account of its
Albigensian sympathies, eventually surrendering, but was spared the horrors of
a sack, although its old fortifications were levelled. The Count of Toulouse, after
this defeat, pledged the *Comtat Venaissin* (Comitatus Avennicinus) with the Holy See as a security against his treaty obligations, although Avignon itself was
excluded from the pact.

Influenced by its proximity to the Comtat, Pope Clement V (1305–16), when driven from Rome by sedition, established his court here in 1309, where his successor, John XXII, a former bishop of Avignon, converted the episcopal palace into the papal headquarters. In 1348 Clement VI bought the town for a derisory sum from the 20-year-old Queen Joanna of Naples and Countess of Provence, and the 'Babylonian Captivity' continued until 1377, when Gregory XI, the last of the seven popes resident there, returned to Rome. The following year saw the beginning of the Great Schism, and the anti-popes Clement VII and Benedict XIII migrated to Avignon, the latter only being driven out after the seige of 1398–1403 undertaken by Geoffrey de Boucicaut. The city and Comtat continued to be governed by papal legates until 1791, but in 1797 Pius VI renounced all papal claims. In the 18C it was a refuge for English Jacobites.

Rabelais called Avignon 'la ville sonnante' on account of its numerous and incessantly ringing church bells, and a high proportion of its inhabitants remained ostensibly dedicated to the church until the Revolution, when it was annexed to France. This was followed by anti-clerical destruction, and the massacre of La Glacière, while in 1815 the craven populace, Royalist and reactionary in their sympathies, coldly assassinated Marshal Brune, one of Napoleon's generals. Mérimée, and Stendhal, visiting the place in the 1830s, both remarked on its non-French atmosphere, comparing it to a Spanish or Italian town, respectively. Avignon was flooded in 1840. By 1846 its population was 35,200. It received only slight damage when bombed in 1944.

Among its natives were the sculptor Antoine Le Moiturier (1425–1500); members of the Parrocel family of painters (17-18C); Joseph Vernet (1714–89), the marine artist; the félibre Théodore Aubanel (1829–86); the actress Mme Favart (1727–72); and Olivier Messiaen (1908–   ), the composer.

Among residents have been Petrarch (1304–74), who condemned the town as a sink of vice, having lived there from 1313 to 1337, when he retired to Vaucluse, to which he returned frequently although he spent much time in Italy after 1341. He last visited Avignon in 1353. It was here in 1327 that he first saw Laura, the object of his poetic passion, probably Laure de Noves (d. 1348), wife of Hughes de Sade. Lady Mary Wortley Montague here spent the years 1742–46; John Stuart Mill retired here in 1858, where he died in 1873 (and is buried in the Cimetière St-Veran); Mallarmé taught at the Lycée here in 1867–71.

Perhaps the most attractive approach ɩo the walled city is the road from the N.E., skirting the Rhône, and providing a view of the *Tour de Philippe le Bel* and the twin towers of *St-André* at *Villeneuve-lès-Avignon*; or alternatively by approaching from the W. The complete circuit of the well-preserved **Ramparts** (4.3km) by car will give a good idea of the extent of the medieval city. They were constructed by the popes between 1349–70, and the S. section was thoroughly restored by Viollet-le-Duc.

From the N.W. corner, part of the **Pont St-Bénézet** crosses the Blvd de la Ligne. Only four arches of the original 22 remain of the original bridge built in 1177–85 by the shepherd-boy Bénézet (according to legend), who was then canonised. The rest were destroyed by flood and war, and the last attempt to replace them was abandoned in 1680. The 16C *Chapelle St-Nicolas* is preserved, standing on a 13C base. The famous rhyme about dancing 'sur le pont d'Avignon' should probably run 'sous le pont', i.e. on the *Île de la Barthelasse*, lying between two arms of the Rhône, and once spanned by the bridge. On the far bank rises the *Tour de Philipe le Bel* (see below), defending what was the French bridgehead.

On entering the town just E. of the bridge, we shortly ascend to the *Pl. du Palais* (parking). To the N. stands the **Petit Palais**, dating from 1317–35, a residence of archbishops, the facade of which was rebuilt in the late 15C by the legate Guiliano della Rovere, later Pope Julius II.

To the N.E. is the *Rocher des Doms*, a hill now laid out as gardens, which was the site of the earliest settlement. One of the rampart towers here was fitted up by Lady Wortley Montague in 1743 as a belvedere. To the N. the terrace commands an extensive view over the river, with *Villeneuve* to the N.W., and with *Mont Ventoux* in the distance to the N.E.

The ****Musée du Petit Palais**, installed here in 1976, contains paintings previously in the Musée Calvet (see below), the majority originating in the collection of the Marquis Giampietro Campana (1807–80). Largely devoted to Italian Primitives, the collection is of outstanding importance, and is exceptionally well displayed in the restored palace, of interest in itself. It also contains a Library and an International Documentation and Research Centre.

From the entrance stairs ascend r. to **R1**, containing frescoes from Sorgues (c. 1370) of hunting scenes, etc.; capitals from the cloister of N.-D.-des-Doms; a reclining figure of Urban V (1370) from his tomb; sculpture from the Chartreuse de Bompas (Vaucluse); and Christ chastising St Elzéar (c. 1373).—**R2** displays larger examples of sculpture, some from the tomb of Card. Jean de Lagrange.—**R3** *School of the Master of the Magdalen*, Last Supper (Florence, c. 1270); *Paulo Veneziano*, Virgin and Child (c. 1340); *Master of Santa Maria dei Servi*, Virgin in Majesty; *Pseudo 'Jacopino di Francesco'*, Crucifixion; *Taddeo Gaddi*, Virgin and Child; *Giovanni Bonsi*, Calvary, with four saints; *Master of 1310*, Virgin in Majesty.

R4 Examples of the work of *Taddeo di Bartolo*; *Angelo Puccinelli*, The Baptist and the Magdalen; *Bartolo di Fredi*, Adoration of the Shepherds; *Cecco di Pietro*, Crucifixion; *Turino Vanni*, Assumption of the Virgin.—**R5** Works by *Lorenzo di Niccolo Gerini*, including St Eloi; *Nardo*, Virgin in Majesty (note musicians playing a portative organ); attrib. *Ambrogio di Baldese*, Scenes from the Legend of St Laurence.—**R6** Works by *Gherardo Starnina*; note also the *anon.* Young Falconer.—**R7** *Master of the Crucifixion de Pesaro*, Crucifixion.

R8 *Antonio Alberti*, Virgin and Child between St Dominic and the Magdalen; *Pietro Lianori*, St Hommebon (patron of tailors and drapers) and St Christopher; *Ottaviano Nelli*, St Jerome; *Giovanni di Paolo*, Angel of the Annunciation; Triptych of the Nativity, with SS Vittoino and Ansano; and St Augustin; *Paolo da Visso*, Virgin and Child; Lucrecia and Collatin (Siena; mid 15C), and Four scenes from the History of Dido.—**R9** *Master of the Buckingham Palace Madonna*, Virgin and Child and six saints (part of the retable of St Jerome); *Francesco d'Antonio*, Virgin and Child with St Jerome and the Baptist; *Domenico di Michelino*, Scenes from the History of Suzanne; Scenes from the History of Cephalus and Pocris (Florence, mid 15C); *Neri di Bicci*, Coronation of the Virgin, Virgin and Child, and Virgin and Child with six saints; *Pier Francesco Fiorentino*, Virgin and Child with St Laurence, and other saints; *Andrea di Giusto*, Crucifixion.—**R10** (rest room), retaining its late 18C decoration, and displaying documents relating to the palace and the Campana collection.

R11 *Bartolomeo della Gatta*, Annunciation; *Cosimo Rosselli*, Annunciation and four saints; Virgin and Child (Florence; c. 1425–50); and Florentine Deposition mid 15C); *Botticelli*, Virgin and Child.

Stairs ascend to **R12**. *Ludovico Urbani*, Virgin and Child with angels, and attrib. to the same artist, Calvary, with St Severin; *Nicola de Maestro Antonio*, St James; *Carlo Crivelli*, Four saints.—**R13** *Niccolo da Foligna*, Nativity, Ascension, and Pietà; *Cristoforo Scacco*, The Baptist; *Francesco di Gentile*, St Nicolas de Tolentino; *Liberale da Verona*, The Rape of Helen. (The view from this room should not be overlooked). *Benvenuto di Giovanni*, Massacre of the Innocents, and Martyrdom of St Fabian; *Matteo di Giovanni*, St Catherine of Siena; *Girolamo di Benvenuti*, St Jerome; *Francesco di Giorgio*, Virgin and Child; *Antoniazzo Romano*, Virgin and Child with the Baptist and the Evangelist, and (after Giotto) Walking on the water (La 'Navicella'); *Louis Brea*, Presentation in the Temple, and Assumption; *Giovanni Massone*, Triptych of the Nativity.—**R14** *Master of Marradi*, Virgin and Child; *Jacopo del Sellajo*, Virgin and Child; *School of Botticelli*, Virgin and Child with young St John.

Stairs descend to **R15**. *Master of Cassoni Campana*, Mythological scenes of the Siege of Athens by Minos; The Amours of Pasiphae; Theseus and the Minotaur;

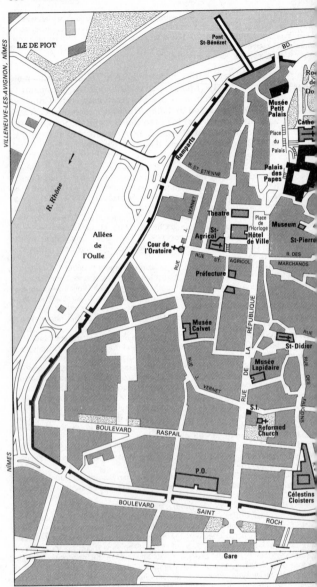

and Ariadne, etc.; The Judgements of Solomon, and of Daniel (Umbrian; earl
16C).—**R16** *Master of the Csartoryki Madonna*, Virgin and Child with young S
John and St Margaret (?); *School of Filippino Lippi*, Holy Family with shepherd
'*Johannes Hispanus*', Adoration of the Magi; *Ridolfo Ghirlandaio*, Coronation o
the Virgin; a Nativity (Umbrian, late 15C); *Cima da Conegliano*, Virgin and Chil
with the Baptist and St Francis; *Marco Palmezzano*, Calvary with the Virgin an

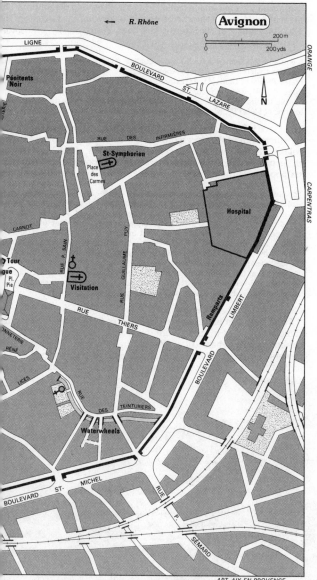

St Jerome; *Francesco Zaganelli*, Christ carrying the cross.—**RR17-19** contain examples of the work of *Enguerrand Quarton*, and *Josse Lieferinxe*, and other works of the School of Avignon.—Our exit is made through courtyards.

Overlooking the Place to the E., and approached by steps, is **N.-S.-des-Doms**, its Romanesque tower (restored in 1431) deplorably disfigured by a gilt image (added in 1859) deserving demolition. The present building, on the site of a much older church, dates from the 12C, but much of its interest has been destroyed by uninspired alterations, mainly 17C.

It contains the *Tomb of John XXII*, the 'English' style of which makes it probable that the sculptor was Johannes Anglicus, known to have been working on the Popes' Palace in 1336–41. Its restoration in 1840 did little to conceal the mutilations of 1791, and the recumbent statue is not that of the pope. Here also is a marble throne, and cenotaph of Louis de Crillon (1543–1615), the companion-in-arms of Henri IV, who died at Avignon.

The Place is dominated to the S.E. by the huge ***Palace of the Popes**, ◇ which, externally, has more the appearance of a fortress than a palace, and in itself is a magnificent specimen of 14C military architecture, with lofty buttressed walls of remarkable thickness. Here six popes held their court.

The old bishop's palace enlarged by John XXII (1316–34) was demolished by his austere successor, Benedict XII (1334–42), who built the whole of the N. part of the present palace, the work being completed by Clement VI (1342–52), who added the W. and S. wings in a more sumptuous style, including the Audience Chamber; the Tour St-Laurent was added by Innocent VI (1352–62), and the Great Court was levelled and its well dug by Urban V (1362–70). Although restored by Leo X in 1516, and occupied by papal legates until 1791, the palace gradually fell into disrepair. Conversion into a prison and barracks saved it from destruction at the Revolution, but wrought considerable havoc to the interior. Only in 1906 was this cleared, and from 1920 its thorough restoration undertaken, which continues. The majority of the rooms are still empty.

Guided tours take place regularly.

From the main entrance, or *Champeaux Gate*, with its pinnacled turrets, we enter (r.) the *Guard-room*, with murals of the 17C, including one of Urban VIII, and await the next tour, which starts by traversing the *Cour d'Honneur* and ascending a ramp on its N. side to enter the *Consistory Court* (damaged by fire in 1413), now contain

View of the E. facade of the Palace of the Popes, Avignon

ing portraits of the nine popes who resided at Avignon, numerous papal ordinances, and three large tapestries of 1759. Off its E. side, in the *Tour St-Jean*, opens a chapel decorated with frescoes of 1347 of the Baptist and Evangelist attrib. to Matteo Giovanetti of Viterbo. Hence steps are ascended in the courtyard of the old palace to an upper gallery, providing a view of the *Tour de la Campana*, and the exterior wall (r.) of the *Chapel of Benedict XII* (no adm.), which will accommodate Archives.

The *Banqueting Hall* or *Salle des Festins* is next entered, also known as the *Grande Tinel*, an imposing vaulted room some 35m by 9m, with a large fireplace at the S. end.—Off the N. end is the upper *Kitchen*, with its huge central chimney. Adjacent (no adm.) is the *Tour de la Glacière* which was the scene of a massacre in Oct. 1791, when 60 citizens wee hurled into an oubliette and buried beneath a load of quicklime; it is also said to be the scene of Daudet's tale 'La Mule du Pape'.—Further N. is the large *Tour de Trouillas*, where it is probable that Cola di Rienzi, the 'Last of the Tribunes' was imprisoned by Clement VI in 1352.—Before leaving the Salle des Festins we are shown the *Chapelle St-Marcial*, with interesting frescoes of the saint's life, also by Giovanetti (c. 1345).

An antechamber is traversed, containing a maquette of the palace, while on the walls hang five Gobelin tapestries, one illustrating the meeting at Fontainebleau of Louis XIV and Card. Chigi.—Off this, in the *Tour des Anges*, are the pope's private apartments; firstly his 'bed-room', in which the original tile floor was discovered in 1963, its walls decorated in blue tempera with foliage: note the bird-cages painted in the window recesses.—Adjacent, in the *Tour de la Garde-Robe*, is the *Chambre du Cerf, likewise tiled, preserving mid 14C frescoes of country life, probably supervised by Giovanetti, and inspired by Flemish tapestries: note the stag-hunting scene, and others depicting hawking, ferreting, etc., and also the ceiling, in its original unrestored state.

Adjoining, at a lower level, is a *Vestry*, from which one enters the *Pontifical Chapel* (of Clement VI), with a restored altar of 1352, and to the S., in the *Tours St-Laurent*, another vestry. The porch of the chapel is lit by the damaged so-called 'Window of the Indulgence', whence the pope gave his blessing to the crowd in the courtyard below.—The *Escalier d'Honneur* is descended to enter the *Salle de la Grande Audience, a vaulted hall divided into two aisles by a row of five pillars, and built for Clement VI by Jean de Loubières. The vault-paintings, by Giovanetti (c. 1353) were completed only as far as the first bay. The rota, or tribunal of the papal court of justice, sat in the E. aisle.—Passing through the vaulted *Salle d'Audience des Contredites* (appeals against papal edicts) in the basement of the *Tour de la Gâche*, the Guard-room is regained.

The narrow Rue de la Peyrolerie, immediately to the S., affords a curious view of the massive foundations of the palace.

On the S.W. side of the Place is the *Hôtel des Monnaies* (1619), once the Mint, and now a School of Music, bearing the arms of Card. Borghese, a former legate.

Walking S., the *Pl de l'Horloge* is entered, the main centre of animation of Avignon, with numerous cafés, flanked by the classical *Théâtre* (1847), and adjacent *Hôtel de Ville* (1845), retaining a clock-tower of 1354, with 15C additions, all that remains of the palace of the Cardinals Colonna, which became the Hôtel de Ville in 1447.

The Rue de la République (see below), the main thoroughfare, leads due S. towards the Railway Station.

A street behind the theatre leads N. towards the *Quartier de Balance*, in which several houses have been restored, off which (l.), at 18 Rue St-Étienne, lived the Montgolfiers, where in Nov. 1782 Joseph discovered the principle of aerostatics.—To the N.W. is the *Quartier de Fusteries* ('fustiers' were once engaged in the timber trade), also retaining several fine old mansions, as does the Rue Petite Fusterie, leading S.

The Rue Joseph-Vernet, parallel to the W., likewise leads S., off which the Rue St-Agricol leads E. to regain the main square, passing (l.) the dark *Church* of that name of 1320–1420, with a Renaissance retable to the r. of the altar.

Continuing S. in the Rue J.-Vernet, and passing (r.) the 18C *Chapelle de l'Oratoire*, a short walk brings one to (l.; No. 67) the **Musée Calvet**, occupying the *Hôtel de Villeneuve-Martignan* of 1742. It is named after Esprit Calvet (1728–1810), a professor of medicine, who left his 'cabinet d'amateur' to the town.

The Museum is at present undergoing a drastic transformation, and it is likely that many rooms will be shut for some time ahead. Among the more important paintings on view are: *Le Nain*, Portrait of a nun; *Santerre*, The Marquise de Moulins; and Self-portraits of *Bourdon*, and *Mignard*. Other rooms are devoted to the art of *Joseph Vernet*, and portraits of his family, by *Van Loo*; also several works by *Hubert Robert*, and of members of the *Parrocel* family; *William Marlow* (1740–1813), view of Villeneuve; *P. Bonnard*, View of Avignon, c. 1700; and other *anon.* views. Among modern paintings are canvases by *Utrillo*, *Dufy* *Vlaminck*, and *Soutine*.

The archaeological collection is of interest, including stylised stellae from Senas; Chalcolithic pottery (2000 B.C., found in 1972 when excavating the underground car-park adjacent to the Palace of the Popes).—Part of the extensive Noël-Biret collection of ironwork is also on view.—Adjacent is the *Muséum Requien*, with natural history collections, and an important herbarium.

The street curves to the l. to meet the Rue de la République opposite the S.I., immediately to the S.E. of which, seen from the gardens, is the octagonal 14C tower of the abbey of *St-Martial*, the chapel of which is now a Protestant church.—A lane from the S.E. corner of the gardens leads to the former *Celestine Convent*, founded in 1393 with a Northern Gothic *Chapel* (under restoration), and cloister.

For *St-Ruf*, see p 816.

Turning N. from the S.I., the Pl. de l'Horloge may be regained, first passing (r.) the *Musée Lapidaire*, housed in a baroque chapel, containing Roman inscriptions, sarcophagi, and reliefs, including some from Vaison; the Venus of Pourrières; figures of Gallo-Roman warriors, etc., and later collections, mostly of local provenance.

Continuing up the Rue de la République we pass (l.) the Rue Viala leading to the *Préfecture*, which occupies two facing 18C mansions. In the Rue Dorée (l.) is the 16C *Hôtel de Sade*, while an alley to the N. leads past the late 15C entrance and courtyard of the *Hôtel de Baroncelli-Javon*, or *du Roure* (della Rovere), with a library of Provençal history, to regain the main Place.

The district immediately to the S.E. of the Pl. de l'Horloge is now a pedestrian precinct. Hence the Rue Galante and Rue Devéria lead S.E. to the *Pl. St-Didier*, overlooked by Gothic *St-Didier* (1325–59) containing a Renaissance altarpiece of 1478 by François Laurana.

Hence the narrow Rue du Roi-René leads due E., in which No. 7 is
the *Hôtel de Crillon* of c. 1625, and No. 8 that of *Fortia de
Montreal*.—We then turn r. down the Rue Petramale and l. along the
Rue des Lices, passing (r.) the arcaded relics of the *Casern des
Passagers* (1753), with four storeys of galleries, beyond which turn r.
to reach the remains of the *Church of the Cordeliers*, destroyed at the
Revolution, where Petrarch's Laura was interred in 1348.

Hence one may follow the charming tree-shaded Rue des Teinturiers, passing (r.)
the chapel of the *Pénitents-Gris* (15-17C), on the far side of a stream, an arm of
the Sorgue, on which are several old water-wheels, once used to drive the
dyeworks here.

The Rue Bonneterie leads N.W. from this turning to the modern
Market, there bearing r. to the *Pl. Pie*, with the tower of *St-Jean-le-
Vieux*, a former commandery of the knights of St John, and then l.,
shortly passing (l.) the *Synagogue*, and then (No. 42 Rue des Marchands) the 15C *Hôtel de Rascas*.—We now reach the apse of **St-
Pierre**, built in 1258–1525, with an elegant belfry, a W. front of
1512, and doors of 1551, and containing 17C woodwork.
    From just N. of the apse the Rue Banasterie leads N. past (l.) the
17C *Hôtel de Madon de Châteaublanc*, among other fine mansions of
the period, while some distance beyond, facing the end of the street,
is the curious 17C facade of the chapel of the *Pénitents-Noirs*, displaying the Baptist's head, and with a rich interior of 1739–55 (apply S.I.
for adm.).—Hence the Rue des Trois Colombes leads E., later bearing
r., off which we turn l. along the Rue des Infirmières, and then r.
down the wide tree-lined *Pl. des Carmes*.—To the l. stands the former
Carmelite church of *St-Symphorien*, with a 14C tower and relics of a
cloister, and ahead, the 14C *Clocher des Augustines*.
    Further E. is the 17C *Hôtel-Dieu* or *Hôspital Ste-Marthe*, preserving
its old *Pharmacy*.
    By following the Rue Carnot and the Rues des Marchands to the
W., we regain the Pl. de l'Horloge.

Villeneuve-lès-Avignon

VILLENEUVE (9,500 inhab.), situated on the opposite bank of two
arms of the Rhône, and dominated by *Fort St-André* on *Mont Andaon*,
is approached with ease via the *Pont Daladier* (1960; replacing the
19C suspensions bridge), crossing from the *Porte de l'Ouille*, and
then turning r. It is a charming small town, often overlooked by
visitors to Avignon, which grew in importance as being the
bridgehead on French territory as opposed to the Comtat Venaissin,
and with the establishment of the papacy at Avignon, some cardinals
chose it as a convenient summer residence.
    Above the river bank (l.) opposite the remains of the medieval *Pont
St-Bénézet* (see p 802) stands the 32m-high ***Tour Philippe le Bel**
1307; heightened c. 1360), guarding the bridgehead, and worth
ascending for the *View.—Those on foot can continue directly N.
    Following the main road, we shortly turn l. towards the *Church*.

It was founded in 1333 by Arnaud de Via, nephew of John XXII, as the col-
legeiate church of Notre-Dame, but assigned to the parish of St-Pons in 1791
when the old parish church was demolished. it was completed in 1355, and contains a reconstruction of the founder's tomb, with the original effigy by Jean de
Lavenier, and a 10C epitaph of St Casaria (d. 586). The *Sacristy* (fee) contains an
early 14C ivory Virgin; to the N. is a plain cloister.

A few paces to the S. along a partially arcaded street is the *Museum* in a 17C *Hospice*.

It contains several paintings by the *Mignards*, and *Simon de Châlons*, Deposition *attrib. to Philippe de Champaigne*, Crucifixion; *Bourgeois*, François I at the Fontaine de Vaucluse; an *anon.* St Bruno; and *Enguerrand Quarton's* masterpiece *The Coronation of the Virgin (1453), the details of which deserve close study

The Rue de la République, preserving several old mansions, leads N. from the church, on the r.-hand side of which is the entrance to the extensive **Chartreuse du Val de Bénédiction*, ◊ founded by Innocent VI in 1356, who is buried there (d. 1362). The monastery was severely damaged at the Revolution, its contents scattered, and its dependencies divided up as tenements. In the process of a thorough restoration, it is now a centre for the promotion of culture.

From the entrance vestibule one may visit the two naves of the church (containing Innocent VI's tomb, by Thomas de Tournon and Barthélemy Cavalier), two cloisters, and a chapel preserving frescoes by Matteo Giovanetti. A third and larger cloister, with its 17C fountain, may be explored before making our exit.

Returning towards the *Pl. Jean-Jaurès*, we turn l., shortly passing the remains of the palace of Card. Giffon (1380), to reach the **Fort St-Andre*, ◊ a partially ruined stronghold of 1350–64, dominating the town and once enclosing a Benedictine abbey. The Romanesque chapel of *N.-D.-de-Belvézet* and the *Tour des Masques* lie to the l.; to the r. is the entrance of its 17C buildings (private property), the attractive **Gardens* of which should be visited both for themselves and for the superb panoramic **Views* they command. At the highest point stands the 10C *Oratory 'of St Casaria'*, tastefully restored.

149 Nîmes to Marseille

A. Via Arles and Salon

122km (75 miles). N113. 30km **Arles**—12km, then fork l. for (29km) **Salon**—51km **Marseille**.

Maps: IGN 66, 67, or 115. M 93 or 245.

It is recommended that the A7 motorway is followed from just S.E. of Salon to central Marseille. A section of motorway is under construction between Nîmes and Arles.

The road between **Nîmes** (see Rte 143) and Arles is of slight interest, *Bellegarde* being by-passed at 15km, on a hill above the Canal du Rhône à Sète.—Travellers wishing to take in *St-Gilles* en route will drive S.E. on the D42, shortly passing (l.) the airport.—For **Arles**, and **St-Gilles**, see Rtes 152A, and B, respectively.

The fast N113 drives E. from Arles, from which we fork l. after 12km (not well indicated), but a peasanter road is the old tree-lined N453 (a continuation E. of the Blvd des Lices), which joins the main road just beyond this fork.

5km. *St-Martin de-Crau*, beyond which the *Alpilles* hills to the N. come into view, as the **Crau** is traversed.

This plain, some 200km^2 in extent, littered with rolled stones (*galets*) and small boulders brought down by the Durance during millennia, was known to the

Romans as the *Campus Lapidus*, and later as *Campus Cravensis* or *Cravus*. Much of its vegetation is grass, the pasture of large flocks of sheep, but when ir-rigated by the canals of the Craponne and others, it is very fertile, and is characterised by long lines of cypresses, forming a protection against the Mistral.

At 9km the unattractive town of *Miramas*, (20,700 inhab.) with railway marshalling yards, lies 10km S.E., beyond which, *Miramas-le-Vieux*, on its hill, and preserving some restored old houses, pro-vides a view over the N. end of the *Étang de Berre*; see below.

Further S. is the old port of **St-Chamas**, now somewhat derelict, with the Roman *Pont Flavien*, which carried a branch of the Aurelian Way from Marseille to Tarascon, crossing the Touloubre; the town, with a 17C church, is bisected by a ridge pierced by prehistoric caverns; also in the vicinity (near *Calissanne*) is the oppidum of *Constantine*.

On approaching the W. outskirts of (13km) *Salon*, the main road bears r. to meet the A7 motorway; see below.

SALON-DE-PROVENCE (35,700 inhab.) is a flourishing market-town and important junction of roads, which since 1937 has been a training centre for French airforce pilots. The old centre is dominated by the Château de l'Empéri, with its military museum. It was the birthplace of Adam de Craponne (1525– 76), creator of the canal which bears his name, which irrigates the *Crau* (see above); the new Durance Canal, with its power-stations, has also increased the importance of the town.

Not far N. of the older town lies *St-Laurent* (1344), containing the tomb of Michel Nostradamus (1503– 66), born at St-Rémy, whose 'Centuries' (1555) attracted the attention of the superstitious Catherine de Médicis, who here received the astrologer in 1564.—Hence the Rue Maréchal-Joffre leads to the tree-lined Cours Victor-Hugo, from which the 13C *Porte Bourg-Neuf* (adjoining the *Hôtel de Ville*, in a 17C mansion) leads shortly to 13C *St-Michel*, the tympanum of the W. door of which is of interest. The centre of the enceinte has recently been gutted.

Steps ascend to the **Château de l'Empéri** (13-15C), a residence of the archbishops of Arles.

It was first visited by François I in 1516; in 1590 it was besieged during the wars of the League; in 1600 Marie de Médicis stayed there; and in 1660 Louis XIV and Mazarin were entertained there by Monseigneur de Grignan. From 1831 it was used as barracks, but was severely damaged by the earthquake of June 1909, since when it has been gradually restored, and since 1972 its vaulted galleries surrounding two courtyards have accommodated a notable ***Musée d'Art et d'Histoire Militaires**.

The firearms displayed, of which there are over 200 examples from 1650 on-wards, many of them from the Brunon collection, are of particular interest, apart from numerous uniforms, including those of marshals Davout, and Macdonald. A section is devoted to the American campaign of 1778– 83, and another to the 1914– 18 War; among portraits are those of Gén. Meyronnet (born at Martigues), and of a Gendarme de la Guarde du Roi playing a violin (c. 1775).

Hence one may turn N. to regain the outer boulevard via the Rue de l'Horloge, passing through a *Clock-tower* of 1630.

THE OLD ROAD TO AIX (N572) meets the N7 16km E. of Salon, at *St-Cannat* see Rte 156A), first traversing (4km) *Pélissanne*, Roman *Pisavis*, a pleasant town 6,200 inhab.) which was the birthplace of the poet J.-E. Esménard (1769– 1811), and the orientalist Amadée de Jaubert (1779– 1847), who imported Tibetan goats into France.—5km beyond, the restored château of *La Barben* (12th and

14Cs), is passed to the l.

The A7 motorway for *Marseille* may be entered S.E. of Salon, off which, after 13km, the A8 bears E. for *Aix* and the *Côtel d'Azur*.

The N113 drives S. from Salon, later veering S.E., at 20km skirting the E. side of the *Étang de Berre*, and (4km r.) what was once the old fishing-village of *Berre*, said to retain arched streets and a Romanesque church with Gothic additions, but the whole is entirely engulfed by oil refineries, chemical factories, and a naval air station, etc.

The *Étang* is a large salt-water lagoon, unexpectedly deep, surrounded by low limestone hills, which during recent decades has been radically transformed by the exigencies of commerce and industry. It is fed by the rivers Arc and Touloubre, and by the E.D.F. Canal linking it with the Durance.

To the l. rises the *Chaine de Vitrolles* and the village of *Vitrolles* on its hill, and (r.) the airport of *Marseille-Marignane* is shortly passed. The *Mairie* of the adjacent town of *Marignane* was once the château in which Mirabeau and Emilie de Marignane lived just after their marriage in 1772. The road commences to climb the N. flank of the *Chaine de l'Estaque*. Near the summit we have the choice of joining the motorway into Marseille, the centre of which is c. 14km distant, which will avoid having to traverse its unattractive suburbs. For **Marseille**, see Rte 158.

B. Via Arles and Martigues

120km (74 miles). N113. 30km **Arles**—12km, where we fork r. for (29km) *Fos*—9km **Martigues**—40km **Marseille**.

Maps: IGN 66, 67, or 115. M 93 or 245.

It is recommended that the A55 motorway is followed between Martigues and central Marseille.

See Rte 149A for the road from Nîmes to a junction 12km beyond **Arles**, where we bear r. across the *Crau*, at 21km reaching the extensive industrial and oil-refining zone N.W. of *Fos*.—The r.-hand turning here (N268) leads to (15km) *Port St-Louis-du-Rhône*, dating from 1871.

4km. The l.-hand turning (D51) leads c. 15km to Martigues round the N. end of the *Étang de Lavalduc* to the **Chapelle de St-Blaise** (12th and 17C), beside which are walls dating from a Phocaean settlement of 4-1C B.C., and probably reoccupied in the 4C; a 5C church has been discovered near the centre of the ramparts. It was abandoned again in the 9C, and again re-occupied in the 13-14C.—There is another oppidum at *Istres*, 4km N., with a small archaeological collection of local finds.—Traversing *St-Mitre-les-Ramparts*, preserving some 15C walls, but named after earlier fortifications, the road descends to Martigues (see below), with a view (l.) of the *Étang de Berre*; see Rte 149A.

4km. The village of **Fos**, with a Romanesque cemetery chapel and ruins of a 14C castle, takes its name from the *Fossae Marianae*, a canal cut by Marius in 104 B.C., but the Roman port at its mouth is now submerged. Amphorae brought to the surface during excavations have revealed how from the 2C B.C. onwards the Romans had used cork stoppers.

Passing cement works, *Port-de-Bouc* is skirted, an old-established commercial port on the N. side of the Canal de Caronte, connecting the *Étang de Berre* with the *Golfe de Fos*. On the S. side is a medieval fort strengthened by Vauban, which contrasts with the tubular jungle of the oil-port of *Lavéra*, the S. terminus of the S. European Oil Pipeline (oléoduc).—The canal has since 1972 been spanned by an impressive *Bridge*, part of the A55 motorway, which by-passes (l.) Martigues, approached from the N. bank.

Martigues (42,000 inhab.), an old fishing port, occupies both banks of the Canal, and the intermediate *Île Brescon*.

It was the birthplace of Gérard Tenque (d. 1040), founder of the Order of St John of Jerusalem, and of the reactionary writer Charles Maurras (1868– 1952). It was once a haunt of artists, such as Félix Ziem (1821 – 1911; whose work may be seen in the local museum in the N. quarter of Ferrières), and Augustus John, who entertained E.J. Moeran and Roy Campbell here.

The town still preserves one or two picturesque corners, particularly on the island, and views from the central *Pont St-Sébastien*. Adjacent *Ste-Madeleine* is under restoration; while to the S. is the 17C *Hôtel de Ville*. A collection of by-gones is displayed in the *Musée du Vieux-Martigues*, opposite the church of *Ferrières*. In the S. quarter of *Jon-quières* is *St-Geniès* (1625– 69), behind which is the baroque *Chapelle de l'Annonciade* (1636).

The motorway may be entered just E. of the town, which leads E. at a higher level along the *Chaine de l'Estaque*.

The little fishing-port of *Carro* (9.5km from Martigues) on the S. side of this peninsula may be visited, with other small resorts. A neolithic settlement has been discovered on adjacent *Cap Couronne*.—Hence its S. flank may be skirted to (26km) *l'Estaque*, at the S. end of the *Tunnel du Rove* (see below), and now contiguous with *La Madrague* and Marseille itself.

The N568 leads E. from Martigues along the S. bank of the *Étang de Berre*, with a view N.E. towards the airport of *Marignane* (see Rte 149A), at (15km) *Gignac* crossing the N. end of the *Tunnel* (or *Souterrain*) *du Rove*, a disused barge-tunnel over 7km long pierced in 1927 through the range of hills here to connect the lagoon with the *Rade de Marseille*.—At 6km we have another opportunity of entering the motorway, to reach central **Marseille** 18km S.; see Rte 158.

150 Nîmes to Cavaillon

61km (38 miles). D999. 24km **Beaucaire**—24km **Tarascon**—N99. 16km **St-Rémy**—14km the N7 crossroads, 5km S.W. of **Cavaillon**.

Maps: IGN 66, or 115. M 93 or 245.

This route overlaps to a certain extent Rte 151, but is described for the convenience of those travelling from W. to E. rather than from N. to S. Several variations may be made, and are pointed out en route.

The D999 drives due E. from **Nîmes** (Rte 143) to (24km) **BEAUCAIRE** (13,000 inhab.), an ancient town on the W. or r. bank of the Rhône at its junction with the Canal du Rhône à Sète.

It was long an important river-port, with a privileged corporation of boat-men who monopolised the river crossing, charging passengers exorbitantly before the bridge of boats was built; see below. It was also the scene from 1217—if not earlier—until the coming of the railway, of a famous fair, with the falling off of which the place declined in importance. Murray reported that even in the 1840s some 100,000 people might congregate there each July, when it was attended by merchants 'not only from all parts of France, Spain, Italy, Portugal, but by many Jews, Turks, Armenians, Greeks, and even Moors from Barbary, who sell dates, etc.'. It also once had a talmudic school; in 1174 it was a residence of Raymond V of Toulouse, and here took place the principal scene of the romance 'Aucassin et Nicolette' (the MS of which was not rediscovered until 1752). During the Albigensian crusade it was taken by Raymond VII, who was in turn besieged there by Simon de Montfort (1216). It was, with Tarascon, damaged in 1944.

The fair-ground, shaded by plane trees, is on the river-bank beyond an embankment to the N. of the bridge. Further N. is the *Arènes*, for bull-fights. To the W., on a hill rising steeply from the river, is the finely placed *Castle*, but most of the present building—including the chapel, in a Romanesque style—dates only from the 13-14C. It was largely dismantled in 1632. Passing round its N. end we see relics of the triangular keep. The ascent—for the view—may be made from the *Pl. du Château* to its S.W.

Hence one may also enter the medieval and somewhat neglected town, turning r. along the narrow Rue de la République, at No. 23 in which is the 17C *Maison des Cariatides*. Opposite is a gateway, passing through which one gets a view of the curious 12C frieze on the E. side of *N.-D.-des-Pommiers* (early 18C).—Turning l. in the adjoining square, and then r., we reach the ornate *Hôtel de Ville*, an interesting edifice of 1683, by Mansart.—Further S., off the Rue de l'Hôtel de Ville, stands Gothic *St-Paul*. In the parallel Rue Barbès, nearer the river, is the *Musée*, of local interest, particularly with regard to the once-celebrated fair.

From Beaucaire, in Languedoc, the Rhône is crossed to Provençal **TARASCON** (11,000 inhab.), on its E. or l. bank. They have little in common except the new bridge (1958; 426m long), which replaced the suspension bridge of 1829, before which travellers had to cross by a bridge of boats, which Wraxall traversed with some temerity, being informed that it was not uncommon for carriages to be swept into the river when the wind was violent! It provides a good view of the river-lapped castle.

It is said to derive its name from a fabulous dragon, the 'Tarasque', from which the town was providentially delivered by St Martha, after her landing at *Les Saintes-Maries* (cf.), a miracle annually celebrated by mummers well into the 19C, when it was suppressed on account of the practical jokes and acts of violence it engendered, to be revived in a different form on the last sunday of June. The earlier castle was acquired by marriage in 990 by Raymond III Pons, count of Toulouse. From 1872 the name was immortalised by Daudet's satirical tales of 'Tartarin of Tarascon'. In 1944 it suffered severely in Allied air-raids directed against the Rhône bridges. It produces early vegetables and fruit.

Almost opposite the bridge is *Ste-Marthe*, with a late 12C portal, but otherwise rebuilt between c. 1380– 1420, and restored since 1944. There is also a fine Romanesque S. doorway. In the *Crypt* are the *Tomb of Jean de Cossa* (d. 1476), governor of Provence under King René, with a statue attrib. to Francesco Laurana; a stone tomb with a recumbent statue said to be of St Martha, and a 17C marble tomb containing a 5C sarcophagus, claimed to be the first tomb of the saint.

While the Tarasque is legendary, the lion of the town is the *Castle*, ◊ guarding the bridgehead.

This well-preserved and imposing fortress, with its seven towers, was begun c. 1400 on older foundations by Louis II of Anjou, and completed by King René in the mid 15C. It later became a prison, and remained so until 1926, and was the scene of a massacre in 1794. It contains some fine vaulted rooms, particularly those overlooking the Rhône, but they can only be visited on a long-winded guided tour, during which one is locked in (cf. Blois), an objectionable procedure.

The 16C *Porte Jarnègues*, in the Blvd Itam, to the E., admits to the old town. Close-by is the restored *Hôtel de Ville* (1648), from which the Rue des Halles, with several arcaded houses, leads S.—On the S. boulevard is the *Porte St-Jean* (18C), a few steps to the E. of which is the *Hôspital St-Nicolas*, preserving a 15C chapel and an unusually complete 18C *Pharmacy*.—To the N.E. is the 14-15C *Porte Condamine*.

The N570 leads to **Avignon**, 23km N.E.; and **Arles**, 18km S.—At 5km S.E., by driving ahead past the *Chapelle de St-Gabriel* (on the site of ancient *Ernaginum*), the road skirting the S. flank of the *Alpilles* provides an alternative approach to *Les Baux*; see Rtes 151A and B.—Continuing E., the D17 traverses the pleasant villages of *Paradou* and *Maussane* (the latter on the road between St-Rémy and Arles; see Rte 151A).—The D17 leads S.E. to (30km) **Salon**, via (6km) *Mouriès*, on the site of Roman *Tericias*, beyond which we climb l. past (7km) *Aureille*, named after the Roman Via Aurelia, with a ruined castle, and (8km) *Eyguières*, passing a tower on *Les Opiès* (493m), the highest of the Alpilles chain.

The N99 leads E., at 4km crossing the direct Avignon-Arles road, and shortly by-passes (r.) *St-Étienne-du-Grès*, to approach (11km) **St-Rémy**; see Rte 151A.

A minor road from St-Étienne skirts the N. flank of the *Chaine des Alpilles* to (6km) *Le Mas Véran*, where Daudet once lived, with the 16C *Tour du Cardinal*, (whence the D27 climbs S. to *Les Baux*), to enter **St-Rémy** 3.5km further.

The main road continues E.; at 9km a r.-hand turning leads past the Renaissance *Mas de la Brune* to (3km) *Eygalières*, a pleasant village, just E. of which is the 12C *Chapelle St-Sixte*.—At 8km the Durance is crossed, 2km beyond which lies **CAVAILLON** (20,800 inhab.), a very ancient town, and seat of a bishop until 1790, and now an important market for fruit and vegetables, particularly melons. It is overlooked on the W. by a chapel (rebuilt in the 17C) on the summit of the *Colline St-Jacques*, on which stood an oppidum.

At the N. end of the older centre, now by-passed by a boulevard, is a *Gateway* of 1740, adjacent to which is the small but interesting *Archaeological Museum*, partly installed in a mid 18C hospital chapel. Notable are a Paleo-Christian altar and a Celtic funerary stele with Greek characters (2C B.C.).

Continuing down the Grand-Rue we reach **St-Véran** (12-13C), once the cathedral, with an octagonal tower on a drum base; the belfry dates from 1496. Adjacent is a small cloister. The interior, suffering from 19C restorations, preserves an organ-case of 1653.—Continuing S., in the *Pl. du Clos* is the so-called *Arc de Marius*, a curious Roman relic consisting of two sets of decorated piers united by arches. It was moved here from its original site in 1880, having previously stood, half embedded, nearer the cathedral.

By turning l. beyond the E. end of this square, we pass the mid 18C *Hôtel de Ville* and follow the Rue Raspail, parallel to and E. of which is the Rue Hébraique. Here, in a fine state of preservation, stands the *Synagogue* of 1774, containing good boiseries, and ironwork by François Isoard, etc., below which is a collection of mementoes of the once flourishing Jewish community, the foundations of whose earlier synagogue may also be seen.

For roads leading E., and S.E. from Cavaillon, see Rtes 153, and 156.

151   Avignon to Arles

A.   Via St-Rémy and Les Baux

50km (31 miles). N571. 10km *Châteaurenard*—11km **St-Rémy**
—9.5km **Les Baux**—5.5km D17. 3.5km *Fontvieille*—4.5km the
Abbey of Montmajour—6km **Arles**.

Maps: IGN 66, or 115. M 93 or 245.

Following the Tarascon road (opposite the *Porte St-Michel*, E. of the
Railway Station of Avignon; see Rte 148), we shortly pass near the
ruins of the abbey of *St-Ruf, founded in the 9C, rebuilt in the 12th
and destroyed in the 18th.

On crossing the Durance, fork l. for *Châteaurenard* (11,100
inhab.), taking its name from the *Castle* of the Counts of Provence
where Benedict XIII took refuge after his escape from Avignon in
1403, and which provides panoramic views.—*Noves*, 4.5km E., with
old town gates and a 12-13C church, was the birthplace of Laure de
Noves, wife of Hughes de Sade, beloved by Petrarch.

Traversing (5km) *Eyragues*, with a partly Romanesque church, we
enter (6km beyond) the small town of **ST-RÉMY-DE-PROVENCE**
(8,400 inhab.), the sleepy centre of an extensive market-gardening
area. Although preserving one or two quaint streets within its circle
of boulevards, it is of slight interest in itself. It was the burthplace of
Nostradamus (1503–66; cf. Salon), and the félibre Joseph
Roumanille (1818–91).

Opposite the *Pl. de la République*, W. of the enceinte, stands *St-
Martin*, rebuilt in the early 19C, preserving a tower of 1330. A lane
to the N.E. leads shortly to the *Musée des Alpilles* in a 16C building
of local interest, and the *Hôtel de Sade* (likewise 16C), containing objects excavated at *Glanum* (see below), including the marble heads of
Octavia and Julia (sister and daughter of Augustus), etc., and from *St-
Blaise* (see Rte 194B), which will interest the professional.

The road gently ascends S. from the Pl. de la République, in 1km
reaching the *'Plateau des Antiquités'*, where stand the two most conspicuous relics of the Greek and Roman town of *Glanum*.

The *Triumphal Arch* has lost its upper parts, but the six-sided
panels of the vaulting are well-preserved. The sculptures of the piers
represent chained captives accompanied by women, and the monument is believed to commemorate Julius Caesar's subjugation of the
Gallo-Greeks of Massilia (Marseille) in 49 B.C.

The *Mausoleum*, over 19m high, stands on a square pedestal,
above which are two main storeys, crowned by six Corinthian columns supporting a cupola.

The reliefs of the lower storey represent Greeks and Trojans quarrelling over
the body of Patroclus; Achilles killing Penthesilea; the massacre of the Niobids
and the death of Adonis. The upper is pierced by four arches and has a frieze of
gods and sea-monsters. The heads of the statues beneath the cupola are modern.
They probably represent Gaius and Lucius Caesar, adopted sons of Augustus
(both of whom died young; cf. *Maison Carrée*, Nîmes), for whom this cenotaph
which dates from the first years of the Christian era, was constructed. The inscription on the N. side stating that it was set up by three members of the Gens
Julia in honour of their parents in almost certainly an addition.

On the far side of the road, just to the S., is the entrance to the site of

*Glanum, ◊ excavated since 1921, and containing the oldest civilis-
ed buildings known in France, dating from a Greek (Phocaean) col-
onisation of the 2C B.C., together with remains of previous settlements of the Celto-Ligurian Glanici, dating back to the 6C.

The town appears to have been burnt c. 100 B.C. (? by the Teutons), but was immediately re-occupied, by which time the Romans were there, as an inscription
of 96 B.C. marks one building as belonging to C. Sulla. After 49 B.C. (see above)
numerous Hellenistic houses were replaced by larger Roman constructions. The
place was destroyed during the Barbarian invasions of the 3C, and it later served
as a quarry for the town of St-Rémy which replaced it.

The site, in a narrowing valley, is divided by a street running N. to S.
The N.W. section is the richest in Hellenic remains, with two houses
similar to those of Delos, separated by a little square which later serv-
ed as a sanctuary of Cybele, with an altar dedicated to her.—To the
E. are remains of Roman *Thermae*, and the *Maison du Capricorne*, on
Hellenic foundations, preserving a Roman mosaic.
    Further S. are the *Forum* and the *Maison de Sulla*, also with a
mosaic pavement. To the E. is a restored Roman *Theatre*, built on a
Hellenistic one. We now come to two temples (r.) probably dedicated
to Gaius and Lucius Caesar (see above), and the foundations of a
Hellenistic meeting-place. Further on, beyond a fortified gate, steps
descend to a sanctuary and sacred spring.—The walls of the *Nymphaeum* were restored by Marius Agrippa (20 B.C.), who added the
temple of *Valetudo*, while near-by is a temple of *Hercules*, dating
from the earlier Roman occupation.

On returning to the main road, one may visit (r.) the priory of *St-Paul-de-
Mausole*, preserving a church and charming cloister of the 12C. The buildings
have long accommodated an asylum, and it was here that Vincent van Gogh was
confined for a year from May 1890. Albert Schweitzer was apparently interned
here during the First World War.

Continuing S. from Glanum, the road ascends through the rocky
Chaine des Alpilles, 3km beyond the summit turning r. for Les Baux.

View of the site of Les Baux

Les Baux-de-Provence, perhaps more imposing in the not too distant past when it was largely deserted and derelict, is built on an
abrupt spur of the Alpilles, surrounded and buttressed by bare rock
and surmounted by a ruined castle. Its charms are in danger of over-
exploitation: too many of its reviving population of c. 300 Baussencs
are now engaged in selling souvenirs and attempting to compete
with the much-rosetted 'Baumanière' in the valley below. Many of its
houses, some hewn out of the rock, retaining Romanesque, Gothic,
and Renaissance details, are in the process of restoration.

Although long a strongly fortified site, the castle of *Les Baux* ('*bau*' meaning
escarpment in Provençal), a refuge from Saracen raids in the 8C, rose to importance during the 12C. Its seigneurs (claiming descent from Balthazar, one of the
three Magi, even placing the Star of Bethlehem on their coat of arms) held lands
throughout Provence, rivalling the house of Barcelona. They boasted—either
successively or simultaneously—the titles of Princes of Orange, Kings of Arles,
and of Vienne, and even Emperor of Constantinople. They enjoyed the flattery
of troubadours attending their 'Cour d'Amour', indulged in debauchery, and the
house declined, in 1426 – shortly after the death of the predatory Raymond de
Turenne—dying out. Its lesser nobles and their retainers dispersed, and the lordship was merged with the country of Provence; but revolts led to its castle being
dismantled by Louis XI in 1483, and its support of Protestantism provoked its
final demolition in 1632. The ruins were generously presented by Louis XIII to
the Prince of Monaco, but the *cité* repidly decayed. Mérimée reported that only
a few beggars lived there; by the turn of this century the population had risen to
111. Rose Macaulay, in her 'Pleasures of Ruins' (1953) remarked that 'No 19C
"Rambles in Old Provence", illustrated with little drawings, was complete
without it ... To-day, though grown vulgar, it still makes its flamboyant
dramatic effect'.

Parking (fee) is provided near the entrance of the town, the narrow
Grande Rue of which ascends past (r.) the old *Hôtel de Ville* (17C) and
then the new (l.), installed in the 16C *Hôtel de Manville*, now containing a collection of contemporary art. Further uphill is the *Musée
Lapidaire* (r.) in the 14C *Tour de Brau*.

A gate (fee) admits to the '*Ville Morte*', and *Castle* on the summit of
the escarpment, now little more than a formless heap of ruins, the extent of which is impressive, some towers commanding wide views. It
is occasionally dramatically lit up at night. The S. end of the plateau
provides another good viewpoint.

Returning to the Hôtel de Manville, we turn l. past the Renaissance
window (1571) of a Protestant oratory to gain the *Pl. St-Vincent*. The
nave and S. aisle of the *Church* (in which is a 10C font) are 12C; the
N. chapels were added in the 16C. Adjoining is the *Hôtel des
Porcelets* of 1569, the vaulted rooms of which preserve 17C frescoes.
Opposite is the restored 17C *Chapelle des Pénitents Blancs*, unfortunately decorated.

The square commands a view into the valley towards the so-called *Pavillon de la
Reine Jeanne*, a gem of Renaissance art (1581), but in fact erected by Jeanne de
Quiqueran, baroness of Baux, not by a queen. It is approached either by road, or
by a path descending from the *Porte Eyguière*, the original entrance to the
stronghold, which is passed (l.) on threading the Rue de l'Église, leading N., to
regain the present entrance.

We follow the road leading S.W. to (9km) *Fontvieille*, an attractive
village with a watch-tower of 1353, and the occasional residence of
Alphonse Daudet, just S. of which is the so-called *Moulin de Daudet*,
although in fact his 'Lettres de mon moulin' (1866 – 68) were mainly
written in Paris. it contains a small museum devoted to Daudet.

Some 2km S. are the ruins of a Roman *Aqueduct*, and near by, a Gallo-Roman flour-mill.

Continuing S.W. from Fontvieille, the road passes near several late-Neolithic tomb-chambers, and at 4.5km approaches the well-sited Benedictine abbey of **Montmajeur*, ◇ just prior to which (l.) is the curious 12C *Chapelle Ste-Croix*.

Montmajeur was founded on this height above a tract of reclaimed marshland in 949, although few of the present buildings are older than the 12C. Re-colonised by reformed Benedictines in 1683, it was later extended, until suppressed in 1786 because Card. Édouard de Rohan, involved in the scandal of the diamond necklace, was the titular abbot. Restoration of the ruins began in 1872.

Steps mount l. to the *Church*, never finished, consisting of a broad aisleless nave and apsidal choir and transepts. On the N. side are two 15C chapels and a 14C chapel with tombs of the Malsang family. To the r. steps descend to the admirable *Crypt*, with an ambulatory and five radiating chapels. The adjacent *Cloister*, with double columns and historiated capitals, notable in the S. walk, is a good example of 12C work. Off the E. side opens the *Chapter-house*; off the S., the *Refectory*. To the S.E. of the church is the battlemented *Donjon* of 1369, beside which is the partly rock-hewn *Chapelle de St-Pierre* (closed for restoration).

We shortly meet the N570 and turn l. for *Arles*; see Rte 152A

B. Via Tarascon

44km (27 miles). N570. At 5km turn r. onto D35 for (5.5km) *Barbentane*—15.5km **Tarascon**—N570. 18km **Arles**.

Maps: IGN 66, or 115. M 93 or 245.

An ALTERNATIVE road to that described is the direct N570, which continues ahead on crossing the Durance, traversing *Rognonas* to approach (13km) *Graveson* (l.), 2km S. of which lies *Maillane*, birthplace of the félibre Frédéric Mistral (1830–1914; cf. Font-Ségugne, Rte 153A, and Museon Arlaten, Arles), whose mausoleum (reproducing the Pavillon de la Reine-Jeanne at Les Baux) is in the cemetery. The *Museon Mistral*, in a house he built and lived in from 1876, is devoted to the poet.—*St-Rémy* lies 6km to the S.E.

Just to the S.W, of Graveson one may either fork l. direct to *Arles*, regaining the N570 near (10km) the *Chapelle de St-Gabrielle* (see below), or r. to *Tarascon*, 9km S.W.; see Rte 150.

Almost immediately a turning off the latter road ascends into the hills of *La Montagnette* (r.) to (3km) the former Premonstratensian abbey of *St-Michel-de-Frigolet*, where among the mid 19C buildings are a simple 12C church and cloister, and an 11C chapel (N.-D.-du-Bon-Remède), incorporated into the modern church, which preserves boiseries presented by Anne of Austria in 1638 in gratitude for the birth of a son, the future Louis XIV. Readers of Daudet will recall the history of Père Gaucher and his elixir.

Turning r. on crossing the Durance, the old fortified village of *Barbentane*, a fruit-growing centre, is traversed, preserving a charming *Château* of 1654 with the interior re-decorated in the 18C. Notable also are the 14C *Tour Angelica*, built by the brother of Urban V on a steep rock; and the *Maison des Chevaliers*, with a Renaissance facade.

Skirting the hills of *La Montagnette*, at 6.5km the ruined château of *Boulbon*, and the Romanesque cemetery-chapel of *St-Marcellin*, containing sculptures of interest, are passed on approaching (8km) **Tarascon**; see Rte 150.

Bearing S.E. hence, at 5km a road-junction is reached, where the N570 turns r. direct to (13km) *Arles*; but the more interesting road is the D33 continuing S.E. passing (l.) almost immediately the remarkable **Chapelle de St-Gabriel* (late 12C), with a well-sculptured facade; key at the nearby auberge.—After 2km one may fork r. to (3km) *Fontvieille* (see Rte 151A), and follow the road hence to **Arles** via *Montmajeur*.

152 Arles to Montpellier

A. Arles

ARLES (50,800 Arlésiens), an ancient city of considerable charm, on the l. bank of the Rhône, is famous for its Roman remains and medieval cathedral, and its museums, and is a pléasant centre from which to explore the several places of interest in its vicinity.

Arles (Arelate; the 'Gallula Roma Arelas' of Ausonius), being connected by canal with the Golfe de Fos, flourished under the Romans as a naval and commercial port (being then closer to the coast), particularly after Caesar's sack of Marseille in 49 B.C. Christianised in the 1C, according to tradition by St Trophimus, a disciple of St Paul (2 Tim. iv. 20), who is said to have here dedicated an oratory to the Virgin even before her death, it became an influential ecclesiastical centre, and several councils were held here in the 4-5Cs. From 480 it was sporadically pillaged by waves of Barbarians, and in 730 was occupied by the Saracens. From 879 to 1150 it was the capital of the Kingdom of Burgundy, later known as that of Provence or 'of Arles', after which, for a century, it was ruled by a 'podestà' like the Italian civil republics. In 1110 Gibelin of Arles became Patriarch of Jerusalem; and in 1209 Gervais of Tilbury was made Marshal of Arles by the Emperor Otto IV. In 1239 it was handed over to the counts of Provence.

In 1535 the Emperor Charles V, in an attempt to re-establish the power of Burgundy, was crowned 'King of Arles' at Aix-en-Provence, but was unable to take the city from the French. It suffered severely in the plague of 1720. In 1789 its archbishopric was suppressed, and its last holder, Jean-Marie Dulau, was murdered in Paris in 1792. Although by then 'shrunken up into a dull provincial town' it was frequently visited by English travellers in the late 18th and early 19C, for, as Murray's 'Hand-Book' suggested: 'the stranger who succeeds in threading its labyrinth of dirty narrow streets . . . will be duly rewarded, if he takes an interest in antiquities'. It was heavily bombed in 1944 prior to its liberation, much damage being caused in the N. quarter, in which Van Gogh's home in 1888 was destroyed, and in the transpontine suburb of *Trinquetaille*.

Among its natives were the Emperor Constantine II (315–40), and the artists Antoine Raspal (1738–1811), and Jacques Réattu (1760–1833).

From the broad Blvd des Lices, the main thoroughfare, the Rue Jean-Jaurès leads to the central *Pl. de la République*, embellished since 1676 by an obelisk of Egyptian granite from the spina of the Roman Circus (cf. Vienne), which stood some distance to the W., in the vicinity of the church of *St-Césaire*.

The E. side of the square is dominated by the magnificent **W. Porch* (1190) of **St-Trophime*, the former cathedral, perhaps the finest Romanesque church in Provence. Frederick Barbarossa was crowned emperor here in 1178.

The tympanum, lintel, and jambs are covered with elaborate reliefs: the tympanum represents Christ surrounded by emblems of the Evangelists; below, on the lintel, the Apostles flanked by angels; on either side are the Elect and Damned. The Adoration of the Magi, and of the Shepherds (r.), and the Magi before

Herod, and the Massacre of the Innocents (l.) are seen below on a narrower frieze; while among the large figures of saints, those of Trophimus and Stephen (3rd from the door on each side) are noteworthy, although the whole deserves cleaning.

Interior. The narrow aisles are vaulted in the Auvergnat style, and date from the 12C, although the transepts are a century older; the rebuilt choir is 15C; the side chapels 14C, and the lower part of the tower, 12C. The *Chapelle des Rois*, on the S., was added in 1625. In the N. transept, the altar is an antique sarcophagus representing the Crossing of the Red Sea (4C); there is another behind the high altar, together with a 16C Entombment.

The *Cloister is normally entered from an adjacent lane. Its E. and N. walks (the capitals in the arcade of the latter being mostly 19C restorations) date from the 12C; the W. walk from the early 14C, and the S. from some decades later. The most interesting sculptures (c. 1175) are in the N. walk, the best of which are the statues of saints on two corner piers, Trophimus and Stephen again prominent. They are characteristic of Provençal work of the period, evidently inspired by antique bas-reliefs, without any Byzantine or Gothic stiffness.

To the N. of the square is the *Hôtel de Ville* of 1684, based on plans by Mansart, with a public passageway beneath, and incorporating a 16C clock-tower surmounted by a statue of Mars (1555), popularly known as the 'Homme de Bronze'.

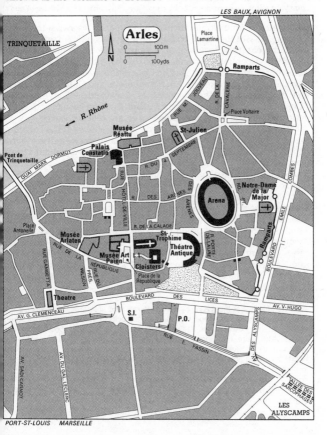

Opposite St-Trophime is the **Musée lapidaire païen**, installed in the former church of *Ste-Anne*, an early 17C building in the Gothic style. The extensive collection includes sculptures of Augustus; two charming dancing-girls; a lion from Les Baux, a provincial Greek work of the 2nd or 3C; several well-carved sarcophagi (1-4C); and among the mosaics, Europa and the Bull, and Orpheus, etc.

Hence one may follow the pedestrian Rue de la République from the S.W. corner of the square, shortly passing (r.) the *Museon Arlaten* (sic), a most interesting collection illustrating local life and history, to which some time can be devoted.

It was founded by Mistral in 1896, and opened here in 1909, the poet having devoted his Nobel Prize money to its improvement. Here also, in the 16C *Hôtel de Laval-Castellane* (taken over by the Jesuits as a college in 1648, and later enlarged), took place meetings of the 'félibres'. A series of rooms on the FIRST FLOOR illustrates life in the region of Arles, and the Camargue, with costumes—the arlésienne guardians are also in costume—characteristic interiors; musical instruments; santons, and ex-votos; naive portraits; old photographs and prints; furniture (including Mistral's crib); tools and utensils, etc. Note the 'cabeladuro d'or', a head-dress discovered in a tomb at Les Baux. Rooms on the SECOND FLOOR are in the process of re-arrangement. In the courtyard a Roman exedra has been unearthed, with niches for statues of gods.

On turning r. on making our exit, and r. again, we reach the large *Chapel* (1652) of the Jesuit college, now accommodating the *Musée lapidaire chrétien*, containing a remarkable collection of early Christian sarcophagi, particularly of the 4C, including the so-called Tomb of Constantine II; that of Bp Concordius; and that depicting an olive harvest, etc. Here also are Romanesque and Gothic sculptures, and artefacts from the dolmens of Fontvieille.—The extensive *Crypto-porticus*, or underground galleries of the Forum, with foundations of Roman *horrea* or grain-stores, are reached hence.

Between this point and the Hôtel de Ville are relics of the *Palace of the Kings of Provence*, opposite which we may descend a street to the *Pl. du Forum*, into the S. side of which two Corinthian columns have been built.—Continuing N. and bearing r., the extensive remains of Roman baths are reached, known as the *Thermes de la Trouille* or *Palais de Constantine*, partly restored, notable for their characteristic bands of brickwork.

In the next r.-hand turning (Rue du Grand Prieuré) is the *Musée Réattu*, tastefully accommodated in the old Commandery of the Knights of Malta, containing the collections of the Arlésian artist *Jacques Réattu* (1760–1833), including a Self-portrait; a charming series of paintings by *Antoine Raspal* (1738–1811), mostly of Arlésiennes in traditional costume; also of a Young Man; the Artist's Family; a Dressmaker's workroom at Arles (c. 1760), and Interior of a Paris Kitchen.

Also notable is a Self-portrait by *Simon Vouet*, and among more modern paintings, sketches, and drawings, representative works by *Henri Rousseau*; a series of drawings by *Picasso* (from 31 Dec. 1970–4 Feb. 1971); and tapestries by *Jean Lurçat*. Also some 17C Brussels' tapestries, and sculptures by *Zadkine*. Do not miss the river view from a room overlooking the Rhône. Other collections—including pre-Roman art—are to be housed here.

A short distance to the E., in the Rue du 4-Septembre, stands *St-Julien* (restored after damage in 1944), a 17C example of the Southern Gothic style.

Hence we ascend the Rue de l'Amphithéâtre to the entrance of the

The Roman Theatre and Amphitheatre at Arles

Roman ***Amphitheatre** (Les Arènes), the largest edifice of its kind N. of the Alps (136m by 107m), but not so well preserved as that at Nîmes, which is fractionally smaller (133m by 101m). Each of its two storeys is pierced by 60 arches, the exterior of the lower being decorated with Doric columns, the upper with Corinthian. The attic storey has entirely disappeared. The arena, which holds 20,000 spectators, is used for bull-fights in summer.

An inscription records a 4C restoration, and it must have been founded in the 2C. Its present condition was caused by the fact that it was fortified in the 8C, and again in the 12C, three watch-towers of the period remaining. As late as 1724, according to John Breval, it was 'crowded with beggarly tenements that compose a sort of dirty little town and quite obstruct the view of one of the most magnificent fabrics of the kind that is to be met with anywhere out of Italy'.

Some distance N. of the arena stands the *Porte de la Cavalerie*, and a small section of walls, just beyond which stood Van Gogh's house, destroyed in 1944 from which he was removed—ear-less—to St-Rémy in Dec. 1888.—Hence a Roman bridge once spanned the Rhône, slight remains of which can be traced on its far bank, approached by the new *Pont Trinquetaille*, replacing an iron bridge, and where once stood a bridge of boats.

To the E. of the arena stands *N.-D.-la-Major* (12th and 16C), on the site of an earlier building in which was held a Council in 452.

To the S.W., at a higher level than the arena, is the Roman **Theatre** (1-3C A.D.). Two columns of the proscenium, with a section of the entablature, are still standing; the semicircle of seats (104m across; holding 7000 spectators), has been restored. Like the amphitheatre, is served at once time as a fortress. During its earlier excavation many works of art were discovered, including the Venus of Arles, presented to Louis XIV, and now in the Louvre. It is likewise the site of spectacles in summer.

From the Rue du Cloitre, to the W., one may regain the Pl. de la

République, but a recommended excursion, too often overlooked by the tourist in a hurry, is that to the *Alyscamps*, some ten minutes' walk to the S.E.

From the Roman Theatre, it is best approached by following the N. side of the adjacent public gardens, skirting the S.E. corner of the medieval walled town, with the most interesting section of the *Ramparts* extending to the N., parallel to the Blvd Émile Combes, and which stand on Roman foundations. Here entered the Roman aqueduct, to reservoirs between the *Pl. de la Redouté* and N.-S.-la-Major (see above).

Within this corner of the ramparts are the remains of the *Abbey of St-Césaire* (12-14C), and the foundations of the apse of a Paleo-Christian church of the 4th or 5C have been uncovered. Adjoining is the former church of *St-Blaise* (12-14C), and near-by, the Romanesque apse of *St-Jean-de-Moustier*.

Crossing the Blvd des Lices, we turn down the Av. des-Alyscamps and over the Canal de Craponne to reach the entrance to the *Alyscamps* (*Elysii Campi*, or Champs Élysées), all that remains of the once extensive necropolis of ancient Arles. This remarkable avenue of marble tombs formed the approach to Arles by the Aurelian Way.

St Trophimus was buried here, and the miracles performed around his tomb brought great honour to the site, and from the 4C several princes and prelates chose to be interred near his tomb, and citizens from towns along the Rhône used to float the coffins of their dead downstream, bearing money to pay the expense of burial near this sacred spot. Both Dante (Inferno, ix, 112) and Ariosto, in 'Orlando Furioso', allude to the cemetery.

The translation of Trophimus to the cathedral in 1152 deprived the Alyscamps of its magnet, and many of the most beautiful monuments were carried off to other cities; several were later removed to the Musée Lapidaire, and with the construction in 1848 of the adjacent railway and its workshops, the remainder were assembled along the avenue as we now see it.

On the l. is the *Chapelle St-Accurse* (1521), adjoining the Romanesque entrance of a vanished church known as St-Césaire-le-Vieux; further on (r.) is the *Tomb of the Consuls*, who died during the plague of 1720; and l., the *Oratoire des Porcelets* (14C), a noble provençal family, and a wall of the chapel of *N.-D.-des-Guerres* (? 10C). At the far end is the partly ruined church of *St-Honorat* (12C, with 17C additions). Its huge columns are notable, and the Romanesque bell-tower is one of the finest in Provence.

Among relics of slighter interest in Arles are the former *Dominican Church* (15-16C), now a storehouse, with remnants of a cloister; *St-Césaire* (15-17C), containing the tomb of Honoré de Quiqueran de Beaujeu, grand prior of the Order of Malta; and a *Tower* at the S.W. extremity of the old town, adjacent to the fly-over.

Part of another 4C Christian cemetery founded on the site of 2C Roman baths was excavated in 1962 near the former church of *St-Genès*, in the suburb of *Triquetaille*, on the far bank of the Rhône; and also an extensive mausoleum: apply at the S.I., at a central point in the Blvd des Lices, for information with regard to admission to such sites, etc.

B.   From Arles to Montpellier via St-Gilles and Lunel

71km (44 miles). N572. 16km **St-Gilles**—18km *Vauvert*—13km *Lunel*—N113. 24km **Montpellier**.

Maps: IGN 66, or 114, also 303. M 240.

Crossing the Rhône, the N572 drives due W., later crossing the Petit-Rhône and the Canal du Rhône à Sète prior to entering **St-Gilles** (10,800 inhab.), a small town of great antiquity but dubious origin, lying among vineyards, and famous for the mutilated but still remarkable W. Front of its church.

Its present name is taken from the 8C hermit-saint, whose tame doe was wounded by Wamba, king of the Visigoths. Pursuing his quarry to the saint's cell, the king repented, and bequeathed the district to the church. The first prior in Europe of the Knights of St John was founded here in the early 12C. The town was a favourite residence of the counts of Toulouse, and Raymond IV called himself Raymond of St-Gilles; its market was of some importance for silks, perfumes, and spices, and an ordinance of 1178 reveals the existence of over 100 money-changers in the place. Count Raymond VI erected a fort on land then claimed by the abbot, which brought him into conflict with the church, and in 1196 he suffered the first of many excommunications. In Jan. 1208 the papal legate, Peter of Castelnau, was murdered near-by. His assassin was 'recognised' as a servant of the count, who was forthwith again excommunicated by Innocent III, and the interdict was only provisionally removed at St-Gilles the following June on Raymond VI submitting to the papacy and agreeing, reluctantly, to join their crusade against the heretics of Languedoc he had previously tolerated.

It was the birthplace of Guy Foulques Le Gros, Pope Clement IV (1265–68), but with the decline of the Church the town also declined in importance, and during the Wars of Religion it further decayed.

From the *Pl. F.-Mistral*, on the W. side of the main street, we pass through a medieval town gate to approach the *Abbey-church*, fortified by the Huguenots in 1562, and almost entirely destroyed in 1622, with the exception of its *W. *Front* (c. 1180), which was comparatively little damaged.

Its reliefs and statues, a curious blending of both Byzantine and Classical inspiration, are all remarkable. The tympanum of the N. portal displays the Adoration of the Magi; the S. portal represents the Crucifixion; while in the centre is Christ in Majesty surrounded by the symbols of the Evangelists. The *Crypt*, with strongly carved rib-vaults; fragmentary ruins of the original choir, and the spiral-stair or *Vis de St-Gilles, in the N. E. tower, may also be seen, but the 17C Gothic church is otherwise of slight interest.

The so-called *Maison de Clement VI*, E. of the church, has been seriously disfigured by restoration, but several other Gothic and Renaissance features may be noticed in the squalid little lanes on the hillside.

The D42 leads 19km N.W. to **Nîmes**; see Rte 143.

We continue W., later climbing, with views S. over the *Camargue* (see Rte 152C), before descending to (18km) *Vauvert*.—The *Château de Candiac*, 3.5km N., was the birthplace of the Marquis de Montcalm (1712–59), the defender of Quebec against Gen. Wolfe in 1759.

At 5.5km the D979 leads S. to (14km) **Aigues-Mortes**; see Rte 152C.—Continuing W., we shortly meet the N113 and turn r. to (7.5km) *Lunel* (see p. 780), and enter **Montpellier** 24km beyond; see Rte 144.

Cain and Abel; reliefs from the abbey-church of St-Gilles

C. From Arles to Montpellier via Les Saintes-Maries-de-la-Mer and Aigues-Mortes: the Camargue

108km (67 miles). N570. 40.5km **Les Saintes-Maries**—on returning on our tracks 14.5km, turn l. onto the D58 for (21km) **Aigues-Mortes**—D62. 13km *La Grande-Motte*—19km **Montpellier**.

Maps: IGN 66, or 114; also 303. M 240.

The **Grande Camargue**, a flat marshy tract of some 70,000 hectares, lies between the two branches of the Rhône, extended to the W. by the *Petite Camargue*, an additional 10,000 hectares, and separated from the Mediterranean by a line of low dunes. About half the area is occupied by unreclaimed mosquito-infested swamps and lagoons, the largest of which, the *Étang de Vaccarès*, is a Nature Reserve. Its pastures nourish large herds of sheep, and black fighting bulls on their 'manades' or ranches, and the small white horses of Arab type, said to have been introduced by the Saracens. The herdsmen are known as 'guardians'. The area abounds in wild-fowl, among them wild duck (macreuse), rose flamingoes, egrets, and ibises. The cultivation of rice (introduced in the 16C) has ben successfully improved, and extensive areas, particularly in its N. half, continue to be drained, de-salinated, and cultivated.

To visit the *Réserve zoologique et botanique de la Camargue* it is necessary to apply in advance to the Director, Rue Honoré-Nicolas, Arles.

The main entrance road through the public area is the N570, leading S.W. from Arles to (15km) the village of *Albaron*, 11km S.E. of *St-Gilles*.

The l.-hand turning here leads 18km E., skirting the N. rim of the *Étang de Vaccarès*, to meet the D36, following the r. bank of the Rhône from Arles to (32.5km) *Salin-de-Giraud*, the southernmost village of this E. lobe of the delta, from which

a ferry crosses to the l. bank to a point 6km N. of *Port-St-Louis*, on the D35. Rough
or windy weather may well make the threading of the narrow dyke roads between Salins and the Étang de Vaccarès a hazardous proposition.

The N570 continues S.W. and then S. from Albaron, briefly skirting
the Petit Rhône, to (25.5km) **Les Saintes-Maries-de-la-Mer** (*Li Santo*
in Provençal), a desolately sited fishing-village and summer resort
amidst a waste of sand and marsh, the boats of which, drawn up on
the beach, were painted by Van Gogh in June 1888. It preserves a
fortified church of some interest, the goal of a gypsy pilgrimage
(24-25 May), now somewhat commercialised.

It is here, according to legend, that Mary, sister of the Virgin, Mary, the mother
of the apostles John and James, and Mary Magdalen were said to have landed in
c. 40, in company with their servant Sarah—represented as an Ethiopian—Martha (cf. Tarascon), Lazarus, Maximinus, and Sidonius, having fled from persecution in the Holy Land. Maximinus and Mary Magdalen were later buried in St-
Maximin (cf.), while the other two Marys, together with Sarah (whose dusky hue
made her a suitable figure of devotion to the superstitious Romany) were said to
have been buried here. Their relics were providentially 'discovered' by King
René in 1448, and enshrined in the upper church, oppressively filled during the
vigils and religious ceremonies held in Sarah's honour by the influx of gypsies;
the place is then given over to characteristic and raucous entertainment prior to
the dispersal of the tribes, who, it is said, take the opportunity to elect their
'queen' here every few years. A less important gathering takes place at the
weekend after 22 Oct.—Mistral places the tragic denoument of his 'Mireille' at
Les Saintes-Maries.

The imposing battlemented *Church* (12C), to which a tower and
belfry was added in the 15C, was built on the site of a pagan temple
(wrongly assumed to have been Mithraic). It consists of a large nave,
containing a well, and three superimposed E. chapels. The capitals in
the ground-floor apse are notable. In the *Crypt* are the relics of 'St'
Sarah; those of the two Marys in the upper *Chapelle St-Michel*.
   Just S. of the church is the *Musée Baroncelli*, with collections illustrating the life, flora, and fauna of the Camargue; and further S.,
near the shore of the *Golfe de Beauduc*, is a bull-ring.
   We return to a junction 14.5km N. of Les Saintes-Maries, and fork
l., crossing the Petit Rhône after 4km, after 11km passing (r.) the
Tour Carbonnière, guarding the land approach to Aigues-Mortes,
2km N. of which the *Mas de Psalmody* is a farmhouse on the site of a
former convent.
   3km. **AIGUES-MORTES**, no longer a dead town—being too easily
approached from Montpellier or Nîmes—is famous for its authentic
medieval ramparts rising from the marshy flats (*aquae mortuae*, or
eaux mortes) from which it was named.

Aigues-Mortes owes its foundation to Louis IX, who required a Mediterranean
port in which to assemble his crusading fleet, and most of the rest of the coast
was held by untrustworthy vassals. He bought the site from the monks of
Psalmody (see above), erected the Tour de Constance, and dug a channel to the
sea at Le Grau-Louis. Hence he embarked for Cyprus (on the 7th Crusade) in
1248, and again on his fatal expedition to Tunis in 1270.
   A town had meanwhile been laid out on a regular bastide plan adjacent to the
harbour, and in 1272 Philippe le Hardi commissioned the Genoese engineer Boc-
canegra to built the range of ramparts which still stand, possibly similar to those
of Damietta. Another ship-canal was excavated, but both channels soon silted
up, the port stagnated, and by the time the Burgundians took the town in 1418, it
was virtually dead. Royal troops recaptured the place and the Burgundians were
massacred, their bodied being hurled into the S.W. tower and covered with
heaps of salt to prevent putrefaction and pestilence breaking out.
   The Emperor Charles V and François I met here in 1538, and four years later

the latter's ally, Barbarossa, anchored his fleet off the coast here. it became a Protestant stronghold, but with the revocation of the Edict of Nantes the Tour de Constance was used as a prison for captured female Huguenots, and the malaria-breeding moat which once surrounded it was drained and filled in.

The **Ramparts* ◊ form a rough rectangle, with the Tour de Constance at its N.W. corner, the usual approach to which is the *Porte de la Gardette*, one of five twin-towered entrances in the walls. A walk (c. 30 minutes) round the 'chemin de ronde' may be made from the *Tour de Constance.*

This fine cylindrical keep contains on its ground floor the *Salle des Gardes*, with the *Salle des Chevaliers* above, the staircase connecting them cut into the thickness of the wall. At its foot are the cells in which the Comte de Pézenas and the Duc d'Alençon were confined, in 1375–77 and 1457 respectively. At the top is an oratory with foliated capitals. The Huguenot Camisards were incarcerated in the upper rooms, in which the heroic Marie Durand spent 37 years. The roof, where a beacon used to burn as a 'light-house', commands a view over the surrounding salt-marshes, to the hills to the N., and now to the pyramids of La Grande-Motte.

The town itself is of slight interest. The Rue Jean-Jaurès leads to the *Pl. St-Louis*, with the restored church of *N.-D.-des-Sablons*, while the arcaded remains of a hospital founded in 1347 may be seen in the N. half of the Rue Gambetta.

The main road is gained 2km N. of the enceinte, where we turn l. to by-pass (11km) *La Grande-Motte.*—This may also be traversed by turning S.W. from Aigues-Mortes on the D979 (good retrospective view) to (6km) *Le Grau-du-Roi*, now a small fishing-port and resort at the mouth of a branch of the Canal du Rhône à Sète.

La Grande-Motte, one of several planned holiday 'unités' on this coast, is characterised by a series of pyramidal structures which have been compared to ziggarats apart from other less complimentary erections. They should be seen to be believed.—Hence parallel roads traverse a sandy isthmus, on the N. side of which is the *Étang de Mauguio* or *de l'Or*, to (8km) *Carnon-Plage*, virtually contiguous with *Palavas-les-Flots*, another popular seaside development 6km further S.W., which in 1890 *had* 'all the picturesqueness which red balconies and green shutters give, and possesses every kind of café, from the best to the humblest, and two little stone piers jutting out into the blue Mediterranean at the mouth of the Lez', according to Augustus Hare.

5km beyond the latter, deserted on its sandspit, stands the ***Church of Maguelone**, all that survives of an ancient seaport entirely destroyed by Louis XIII in 1633 on account of its Protestant proclivities. Formerly a cathedral, it is a fortified 12C building with a sculptured doorway, interesting capitals, bishops' tombs (including a 6C sarcophagus), and 12C marble reredos. Its huge gallery served as the canons' choir.

Montpellier (see Rte 144) lies 11km N.W. of Carnon-Plage, first passing (r.) its airport of *Fréjorgues*, but may also be approached from Palavas.

153 Avignon to Castellane

A. Via Apt, Forcalquier, and Digne

175km (109 miles). N100. 23km **L'Isle-sur-la-Sorgue**—10km
Gordes lies 8km N.E., and the abbey of *Senanque* 4km
beyond—33km *Apt*—26km *Manosque* lies 14km E.—16km
Forcalquier—D12. 11km to meet the N96 and turn l.—9km
Peyruis—D4 and N85. 29km **Digne**—54km **Castellane**.

Maps: IGN 60, 61, or 115. M 245.

Driving almost due E. from **Avignon** (Rte 148), the A7 motorway is
shortly crossed, beyond which the château of *Font-Ségugne* lies to
the l.

Here in 1854 the 'Félibrige' was founded by Roumanille and Mistral, together
with Mathieu, Aubanel, Brunet, Giera, and Marcellin. This was the name chosen
by Mistral for the group of poets, later joined by Tavan, who endeavoured to
stimulate an interest in the preservation of the language, literature,
characteristics, and customs of Provence.

At 17km *Le Thor* is traversed, famous for its dessert grapes, and with
a beautiful late Romanesque church, 2.5km N. of which is the stalactite cave of *Thouzon*, and a ruined castle.

5km. **L'Isle-sur-la-Sorgue** (13,200 inhab.), a small carpet-making
town of some character, surrounded by tree-lined boulevards, one of
which, to the W. of the centre, is lined with pictureque old *Water-
wheels*. In the centre is a profusely decorated 17C church, while the
18C *Hôtel-Dieu* retains its *Pharmacy*, containing 17C faïence from
Moustiers.

From a point just N.E. of the town the D25 turns r. to (7.5km) the contaminated
village of **Fontaine de Vaucluse**, mostly visited by trippers who have never
heard of the poet whose sylvan haunt it once was, 'happy to have the Muses for
his companions and the song of the birds and the murmur of the stream for his
serenade'. Petrarch (cf. Avignon) spent the years 1334–41 in retirement here,
and visited it occasionally afterwards. The *Fountain* itself, a still pool at the foot
of a cliff, is a resurgence of an underground stream, and not in fact the source of
the Sorgue. Above rise the ruins of a castle of the bishops of Cavaillon. The
village has an 11C church, a *Musée Spéléologique* (the collection of Norbert
Casteret), and another devoted to Petrarch.—Some 2km N. of the approach road
is the château of *Saumane*, once belonging to the de Sade family.

The N100 bears S.E. from L'Isle-sur-la-Sorgue to crossroads at (10km)
Coustellet.

The D2 forks l. here, ascending to (8km) **Gordes**, an attractively sited village, and
more picturesque prior to being smartened up. Its Renaissance *Château* now
houses examples of the decorative art of *Vasarely* (cf. Aix).—Of more interest is
the abbey of *Sénanque*, hidden in a valley 4km N., on the road to which several
'bories' are passed, curious primitive constructions in dry-stone walling with corbelled roofs similar to the 'trulli' of Apulia or the Irish 'clochán', some 5-6000 of
which, often designated 'clapiers' are scattered through Haute-Provence.

Sénanque was founded in 1148, and of the three 'Cistercian sisters of Provence', is the most well-endowed. (The others are Silvacane and Le Thoronet). It
was attacked by the Waldensians in 1544, and sold at the Revolution, but from
1854 until 1969 (with a break in 1901–26) it was re-occupied by the order, who
did much work of restoration. The fireplace in the *Monks' Hall* is notable, but

one no longer finds here the serenity one might have expected. The buildings also house a museum devoted to the Sahara Desert.—The main road may be regained via *Roussillon*, 9km E., so-named for its ochre quarries, 5km N. of *Pont Julien*.

An alternative DETOUR may be made along the S. side of the valley from a point 2km. E. of Coustellet, to (4km) *Oppède-le-Vieux*, one of the many curious old fortified villages of ruined mansions, or castles, along the N. flank of the **Montagne du Lubéron**, a long ridge running parallel to the route.—Hence one may continue E. via (4.5km) *Ménerbes*, on a ridge, with a 14C church; *Lacoste*, 6km further E., with a ruined castle of the de Sade family; and, 5km beyond, **Bonnieux**, with a 12C church, 13C walls, and several 16-18C houses, from which one may approach Apt, 12km N.E.—*Lourmarin* (see Rte 156C) lies 11.5km S.E. of Bonnieux, on the S. side of the Lubéron ridge.

Driving E. from the Coustellet crossroads, at 14km we pass (r.) the 3-arched Roman bridge of *Pont-Julien, one of the best preserved in France, on the Via Domitia.—*Bonnieux*, see above, lies 6km S.

8km. **Apt** (11,600 Aptois or Aptésiens), a small town on the Calavon, was the Roman *Apta Julia*; it manufactures sulphur products, candied fruit, and nougat, and its ochre deposits stain the neighbouring roads and hillsides. In the town centre, with its tower built over the Rue des Marchands, is the former cathedral of *Ste-Anne* (1056–c. 1120, and 14C), with a nave-vault and other alterations of the 18C, and a 16C chapel in the N. aisle. In the S. apse is a 12C Byzantine altar; a 5C Gallo-Roman sarcophagus is also preserved, together with a small Treasury. The reputed relics of St Anne lie in the lower of two crypts, roofed with slabs with Carolingian ornamentation; the upper is 11C.—There is a small archaeological collection not far N. of the church.

Two excursions may be made: to the S.E. via (4km) *Saignon*, a village preserving a partly 12C church, and the Romanesque church of the abbey of *St-Eusèbe*, now a farm, just to the E. Hence the road ascends to (5km) *Auribeau*, from which a track mounts steeply S. to (5.5km) the ridge of the Lubéron just W. of its highest point, the *Mourre Negre* (1125m).

Driving N.E. from Apt on the D22 up the Dôa valley, with its ochre quarries, one reaches (23.5km) *Simiane-la-Rotonde*, its ruined castle with a curious 12C chapel. Hence one may climb E. to (3km) *Carniol*, there turning r. past (l.) the ruined Cistercian abbey of *Valsaintes*, and through (6km) *Oppedette*, standing above a narrow gorge, to regain the main route 10km beyond, 3km before *Céreste*.

The N100 continues E. from Apt, at 15.5km crossing the Calavon for the last time, with two Roman bridges in the area, and other traces of Roman occupation, including (1.5km S.) the *Tour d'Embarbe* (? Turris Ahenobarbi).—3km. *Céreste*, 1.5km N.E. of which is the Romanesque chapel of *Carluc*, with its necropolis.—The hill-town of *Reillanne* lies 2.5km N. at 7.5km.

The r.-hand turning (D907) climbs over the N. end of the Lubéron to (14km) **Manosque** (see Rte 154), providing attractive views.—From a point 3km up this road, those wishing to return W. may follow the D956 (views) via (21km) *La Tour d'Aigues* (see Rte 155) to meet the D973 at *Perthuis*, 6km beyond.

4.5km. *Lincel* (l.) preserves a late 12C church.

3km N. is **St-Michel-l'Observatoire**, just S. of which is the Romanesque church of *St-Michel*, with 13-16C additions, containing some fine mosaics, including a Christ in Majesty, probably 14C (restored). The *Tour de Porchères* (12C) is an unaltered example of a military tower.—A road leads 2.5km N. to the *Astrophysical Observatory 'de Haute-Provence'* (begun 1938), one of the best equipped in Europe (650m). The main road may be regained 3km E. of St-Michel.

t is an interesting coincidence that the first observatory in France was built in 1603, by the Flemish astronomer Godefroy de Wendelin, on the *Montagne de Lure*, c. 25km further N.

We shortly pass (r.) the *Château de Sauvan* (1719; by J.-B. Franque), once owned by the Marquise de Janson, beyond which (l.) is the Romanesque priory church of *N.-D.-de-Salagon*, before entering (8km) *Mane*, with a restored feudal castle, attractive church tower, and several old houses in the Grand-Rue.

3.5km. **Forcalquier** (550m), once the capital of Haute Provence, taking its name (*Furnus Calcarius*) from its ancient lime-kilns, preserves a number of medieval buildings in its picturesque narrow lanes. To the N. of the old centre is the *Pl. du Bourguet*, with the *Hôtel de Ville* and a small museum, from behind which a road leads N. to the *Cemetery*, remarkable for its topiary work. Here lie the Drummond family, assassinated near Lurs in 1952. Raoul Dufy (1877–1953) died at Forcalquier.

The Place is dominated by the former cathedral of *Notre-Dame* 12-17C), with a good 18C organ.—The adjacent fountain bears a plaque commemorating the marriage of the unpopular Eleanor of Provence (d. 1291) with Henry III of England (1235). From the *Pl. Vieille*, S. of the church, a lane descends to the medieval *Porte des Cordeliers*, beyond which is the *Couvent des Cordeliers*, a Franciscan foundation of 1236, considerably reconstructed in 1963.

In the old centre, which had a Jewish quarter and synagogue, is the *Pl. St-Michel*, with a Gothic fountain, from a few steps S. of which one may ascend to the former terrace of the *Castle*, seat of a powerful Provençal family in the 12-13C, and demolished in 1601 by Henri IV, but commanding pleasant views over the countryside from the modern octagonal chapel.

The road shortly descends E. into the Durance valley, at 8.5km passing (l.) a lane ascending to *Lurs*, a well-sited village of arcaded streets, 2.5km beyond this turning meeting the N96, where we turn l.

At 3km a lane ascends steeply to the l. to approach the important ruins of the Cluniac priory of *Ganagobie* (12-13C), commanding, at 660m, a fine view over the valley of the Durance. The church, with its lobular decoration and curious tympanum, and cloisters similar to those at Montmajour, near Arles, are noteworthy. The sanctuary contains restored mosaics of oriental inspiration (1122), and in the nave is a Virgin and Child by Monticelli, who lived here during part of his childhood.—A path leading towards Lurs passes a 2-3C Roman bridge.

5km. *Peyruis*, known for its fruit, olive-oil, and nougat, has a 16C church with gargoyles, ruins of a castle, and a former Jewish quarter.

For the road hence to **Sisteron**, 24km N., see Rte 154 in reverse.

We fork r. and cross the Durance to (4.5km) *Les Mées*, at the foot of the fantastic *Rochers des Mées*, a curious limestone formation c. 2km long and rising to 150m, whose name has been ascribed to their vague resemblance to Roman boundary stones (metae). Pasteur researched into the diseases of silkworms at the *Château de Paillerol*, 7km S.

At the 16C château of (5.5km) *Malijai*, where the Bléone is crossed just E. of its confluence with the Durance, Napoleon spent the night of 4 March 1815 en route to Grenoble.—The N85 (Route Napoléon) is followed to the E. along the N. bank of the narrowing Bléone valley to (19km) **Digne**, and **Castellane**, 54km beyond; for both, see Rte 155.

B. Via Carpentras and Sault to Forcalquier

226km (140 miles). D942. 24km **Carpentras**—45km _Sault-de-Vaucluse_—D950. 40km _Le Rocher_—14km **Forcalquier**—D12, after 11km meeting the N96 and turning l.—9km _Peyruis_—D4 and N85. 29km **Digne**—54km **Castellane**.

Maps: IGN 60, 61, or 115. M 245.

For the road between Avignon and **Carpentras**, see the last part o Rte 141B, in reverse.

The D942 leads due E. through (6.5km) _Mazan_, preserving two medieval gateways, and a cemetery containing Gallo-Roman sar cophagi.—After (10km) _Villes-sur-Auzon_ we commence to climb above the _Gorges de la Nesque_.

28.5km. _Sault-de-Vaucluse_, a large village with a 12-14C church and a small museum of Gallo-Roman antiquities, pleasantly sited on the limestone _Plateau de St-Christol_, abounding in potholes further S

Hence the D942 leads N. between the ridges of _Mont Ventoux_ and the _Montagne de Lure_, further E., to (13km) _Montbrun-les-Bains_, with a picturesque medieval quarter culminating in the imposing ruined 16C château.—14km beyond crossroads are reached 2km S. of _Séderon_, noted for its honey, whence the r.-hand turning leads down the valley of the Jabron to meet the Durance after 36.5km, 4km S. of **Sisteron**; see Rte 154.—Another road descends N.E. from Séderon into the valley of the Méouge, after c. 6km passing near (r.) the fine 12C church of _N.-D.-de-Calma_, and later threads a gorge below the _Montagne d Chabre_ (1393m) to reach and cross the Durance at (28.5km) _Laragne-Montéglin_ see Rte 138B.

From Sault the D950 leads E. to (29km) _Banon_, where the old village perches on a rock above the new, preserving ramparts and arcaded streets, and producing an excellent local goat cheese.

The D51 leads S.W. to (31km) _Apt_, after 4km passing (r.) _Montsalier_, N. of which is a deserted village with a Romanesque church and mills, and near-by, the famous pot-hole of the _Gouffre de Caladaire_, 487m deep, explored in 1949.—S miane lies 5.5km S.W.; see Rte 153A.

From Banon one continues E. to (11km) _Le Rocher_.

Hence the D951 bears N.W. via (7km) _St-Étienne_, from which the D113 climbs steeply, later passing the former Benedictine abbey of _N.-D. de Lure_, to the _Signal de Lure_, the highest summit of the range (1826m; panoramic views).—The N96 is met 19km E. of St-Étienne, opposite _Les Mées_; see Rte 153A.

The D950 forks r. at Le Rocher to (14km) **Forcalquier**, for which, and the road beyond, see Rte 153A.

154 Sisteron to Aix-en-Provence

108km (67 miles). N85. 24km _Peyruis_—31km N96. **Manosque** —22km _Pont de Mirabeau_—31km **Aix-en-Provence**.

Maps: IGN 60, 67, or 115. M 245.

SISTERON (500m; 7,600 Sisteronais) is an ancient town built beneath an imposing rocky height in a defile (the 'gate of Provence') just S. o the confluence of the Buëch and Durance.

Roman *Segustero* was the seat of a bishop from the 5C until the Revolution, and was often in dispute during the Religious Wars. Jean-Casimir of Poland was imprisoned here for six months in 1639. Napoleon passed through on 5 March 1815 en route to Grenoble. it was heavily, and needlessly, bombed on 15 Aug. 1944 by the Americans during the German retreat, and subsequent building has much altered its appearance, although parts of it are still 'composed of narrow dirty streets, cooped up within useless ramparts'.

It was the birthplace of the 12C troubadour Albert de Sisteron, and of J.-B. d'Ornano (1581 – 1626), marshal of France.

Just S. of the town centre, facing the Allée de Verdun, are three *Towers* of the 14C ramparts; another lies to the W. of the main road, from near which the ascent to the citadel may be made.

Notre-Dame, the former cathedral, is a handsome 12C building, the main door of which preserves marble columns with sculptured capitals. The belvedere above the apse will be noted.—Steps behind the apse descend towards the medieval *Porte de la Nière* and a huddle of narrow arched and stepped lanes.

The main road passes (r.) the *Pl. du Dr-Robert*, and crossing the Rue Droite, traverses a tunnel of 1957 pierced through the massive rock surmounted by the *Citadel*, which may also be approached by turning l. shortly beyond the tunnel. The present fortress dates from the 13C, with additions of 1597 by Jean Erard, a precursor of Vauban, who also had a hand in later works. it commands interesting views, particularly of the contorted strata of the defile. The 15C chapel has been restored.

In the transpontine suburb of *La Baume* is a Romanesque house of the bishops, restored *St-Jacques* (12C), and the Romanesque belfry of the former church of *St-Dominique*, belonging to a convent founded in 1248 by Beatrice of Savoy. A good view of the old town may be obtained from a short distance downstream.

An excursion may be made from Sisteron to the N.E., following the D3 which climbs and skirts the S. slope of the *Montagne Gache* to the *Défilé de Pierre-Ecrite*, at the farther end of which is a Roman inscription in honour of the consul Dardanus and his wife Nervia, who opened the passage in the 5C. The road continues E. through *St-Geniez*, S.E. of which rises the *Rocher de Dromont* (view); *Authon*, further E., lies S.W. of summit of *Les Monges* (2115m).

For roads from Sisteron to *Gap* and **Briançon**, to **Grenoble**, and to **Valence**, see Rtes 137, 138, and 140 respectively, in reverse.

For the more attractive road S. (D4) along the E. bank of the Durance, crossing the river just S. of *Château-Arnoux*, see Rte 155.

The main road leads S., at 8km having a view across the valley to *Volonne*, dominated by two tall castle-towers, and 2km beyond, traverses *Château-Arnoux*, with its mutilated château, after which the N85 forks l. over the *Barrage de l'Escale*, part of the complicated hydro-electric works of the Durance valley scheme, to *Malijai* (see Rte 153A), and **Digne**.

We bear r. past the large chemical works of *St-Auban*, and the confluence of the Bléone and Durance, to (10km) *Peyruis*, for which, and for the following 10km (after which the D12 turns r. for *Forcalquier*), see Rte 153A.

4km. *La Brillanne*, where the river is crossed by a bridge from *Oraison*, with its underground hydro-electric stations. The Canal d'Oraison is shortly carried across the W. bank of the Durance.—7.5km. *Voix*, above which is the hill of *Bellevue* (791m).

8.5km **Manosque** (19,100 inhab.), the older centre of which lies on a slope 1km to the W. within a ring of boulevards, is a characteristic Provençal town, behind which rise olive-clad hills.

It was once known as 'Manosque la pudique' (the modest) from the story that when François I visited the place in 1516, the daughter of the 'consul', Antoine de Voland, in order to avert the usual embarrassing attentions of that gallant king, disfigured her face by holding it over a chafing-dish of burning sulphur. It was the birthplace of Jean Giorno (1895–1970).

The imposing battlemented *Porte Saunerie* (14C) admits to the narrow Rue Grande, passing (r.) *St-Sauveur*, partly Romanesque, and beyond, *Notre-Dame*, containing a 6C sarcophagus and 12-13C Virgin. In the neighbouring *Hôtel de Ville* is the head of a 16C silver reliquary bust of Gérard Tenque (cf. Martigues). The Rue des Marchands continues N. to the *Porte Soubeyran*.

MANOSQUE TO AIX VIA PERTUIS (58km). This pleasant alternative road (D907) ascends W. to (11km) the *Col de Montfuron* (645m), there turning l. past the hamlet of *Montfuron*, with a ruined castle, before descending the S. flank of the *Montagne du Lubéron* (fine views) past the perched village of (15km) *Grambois*, and (6km) **La Tour d'Aigues**, with a Romanesque church and the splendid *Ruins* of its moated castle (c. 1570; but burned in 1780) of the Barons de Cental, with a remarkable monumental gateway of Corinthian columns, and 12C keep of its predecessor.—The Durance is crossed shortly beyond (6km) *Pertuis* (see Rte 156C), whence the N556 bears S. to (20km) *Aix*; see Rte 157.

The N96 continues S. from Manosque, to a narrows of the Durance valley at (22km) the *Pont-de-Mirabeau*, for which and the village of *Mirabeau*, to the r. at the previous fork, see Rte 156C.—The road traverses (9km) *Peyrolles*, and *Meyrargues*, 6km beyond (see Rte 156B), and bears S. to meet the road from Pertuis some 10km N. of **Aix-en-Provence**; see Rte 157.

AIX TO MARSEILLE. The recommended route to follow is the A51 motorway (29km), by-passing (l.) *Luynes*, the ancestral home of the ducal family, which gave its name to the castle in Touraine inherited in 1619 by Charles d'Albert, Duc de Luynes, the favourite of Louis XIII.—The perched village of *Cabriès*, with remains of fortifications, is later passed to the r., while to the l. rises the *Pilon du Roi* (670m).—For **Marseille**, see Rte 158.

155 Sisteron to Grasse via Digne, and Castellane, for Nice or Cannes

158km (98 miles). D4 and N85, 22km *Malijai*—19km **Digne** —30km *Barrême*—24km **Castellane**—63km. **Grasse.**

Maps: IGN 60, 61, or 115. M 245.

Crossing to the E. bank of the Durance immediately N. of **Sisteron** (see Rte 154), we turn S. with an interesting retrospective view across the river and defile, to (13km) *Volonne*, commanded by two towers of its ruined castle, and 4km beyond, by-pass (l.) *l'Escale* to meet the N85.

5km. *Malijai* (see p 831), whence the N. bank of the Bléone is followed to (19km.) Digne. **DIGNE** (600m; 16,400 Dignois), préfecture of the *Alpes de Haute-Provence*, the lower ranges of which partly surround it, is a somewhat sombre town on the E. bank of the Bléone. It is known for its lavender, honey, dried fruits, and pentacrinites, a fossil found in the local shale.

Roman *Dinia* grew rapidly after the 10C, and had its share in the Religious Wars of the 16C, in which the poet Antoine Héroët took part in the siege of 1552. Some 80 per cent of its population was carried off by plague in 1629. Napoleon traversed the place—one is reminded—on 4 March 1815 en route from the coast to Grenoble; see pp 748 and 874. The astronomer Pierre Gassendi (1592–1655), born at *Champtercier*, 9km W., was long 'prévôt' of the cathedral.

From the *Pl. du Tempinet*, by the N. bridge, the tree-lined Blvd Gassendi leads N.E. through the *Pl. Gén. de Gaulle* (S.I.), beyond which (r.) is a small *Museum* of art and archaeology.—From the square, a lane ascends the hill surmounted by the *Cathedral of St-Jérôme* (1490–1500), drastically restored in 1846 and again the object of restoration. The 16C belfry has a top storey of 1620. The episode of the bishop's candlesticks in Hugo's 'Les Misérables' (in which Monseigneur Myriel was based on Bp Miollis of Digne) may be recalled.

Some distance further N., past the *Grande-Fontaine* (1829) is the former cathedral (*N.-D.-du-Bourg*; 1200–1330), now a cemetery church, with a rose-window above the Romanesque W. portal, preserving its lions, while the interior contains 14-15C murals and a Merovingian altar.

For the road N.E. hence towards *Barcelonnette* or *Embrun*, see the last part of Rte 137B, in reverse.

The N85 climbs steeply to the S.W. and then S., before descending to (12km) *Châteauredon*.

Hence the D907 descends the valley of the Asse for 14km to *La Bégude-Blanche*, from which the D953 mounts steeply across a plateau of lavender-fields before climbing down to (16km) *Riez*; see Rte 156C.

The road bears S.E. and threads the *Clue de Chabrières*, ascends the upper valley of the Asse, and traverses (18km) *Barrême*, where the N202 (to *Nice* via *Entrevaux*) turns l.; see Rte 165, in reverse. The town lies in a basin at the confluence of the Asse de Blieux, de Moriez, and de Clumanc. Opposite the bridge is a rock-perched 12C chapel.

5km. **Senez** (r.) has an early 13C church, formerly a cathedral, resembling Notre-Dame at Digne, but in a better state of preservation, and containing a 17C altarpiece and tapestries.

The road shortly starts to climb between the *Castellard* (l.; 1725m) and the *Mourre de Chanier* (1930m), traversing the *Clue de Taulanne* to reach (14km) the *Col des Lèques* (1146m), beyond which we climb down in zigzags, with plunging views towards Castellane, dominated by its Roc, entering the town after 10km.

Castellane (724m) is a strikingly sited town on the Verdon, crossed by a narrow old bridge, and a new one. It is commanded by a massive limestone cliff rising to 184m, on which is perched the chapel of *N.-D.-du-Roc*.

The place, still retaining parts of its 14C fortifications, including a conspicuous tower to the N., resisted sieges by the troops of the Emperor Charles V in 1536, by Lesdiguières in 1586, and by Imperial forces in 1746–47. From N. of the central *Pl. Marcel-Sauvaire* two gates admit to the old town, in which stands *St-Victor*, of various dates. Castellane is a convenient base from which to visit the *Canyon du Verdon*; see the latter part of Rte 156C.

The N85 shortly commences to climb again, at 9km crossing the

Col de Luens (1054m), passing (l.) 10km beyond the modest summer resort of *Le Logis du Pin*.

The D21 leads S.W. hence past (9km) *Bargème* (r.; 1094m), a fortified village under restoration, dominated by its ruined castle, and with a Romanesque church of some interest, to *Comps-sur-Artuby*, 7km beyond; see Rte 156C.

LE LOGIS-DU-PIN TO VENCE (55km). The D2 leads E. past (r. at 16km) the summer resort of *Thorenc*, 6km beyond which a l.-hand fork ascends to (11km) *Gréolières-les-Nieges*, a ski-station on the *Montagne du Cheiron*, rising to 1777m (view).—The D2 continues E., first threading its 'clue' to (7km) *Gréolières*, in the upper valley of the Loup, the church of which contains a Retable of the late 15C Nice school, and a 14C carved Virgin, while the village is dominated by ruined castles both to the N. and S.

At 3km a junction is reached, the r.-hand D3 leading S., where at 5km it again divides, the r.-hand fork leading via (7km) **Gourdon**, a perched village (758m commanding a fine view, with a 14C castle containing a collection of naive art beyond which it descends to (8km) *Le Pré-du-Lac*, 6km E. of *Grasse*; the l.-hand fork descends through the picturesque ravine of the *Gorges du Loup*, with their cascades, to (5.5km) *Pont-du-Loup*. Hence we may turn r. to *Le-Pré-du-Lac*, via (3km) **Le Bar-sur-Loup**. a picturesquely sited village dominating the lower valley and the birthplace of the Adm. Comte de Grasse (1722–88), a hero of the American War of Independence. Its partly Gothic church contains a large retable of 14 panels and a Dance of Death (both 15C Nice School).—Alternatively, by bearing l. we skirt the N. side of the valley to (15km) *Vence* via (8km *Tourette-sur-Loup*, still comparatively unspoilt, curiously built against a cliff preserving its old walls and three towers, and a 14C church containing 16-17C retables.

The l.-hand fork below Gréolières (D2) climbs in 8km to a point just below *Coursegoules*, where both prehistoric and Roman remains have been found, and bears S.E. to (8km) the *Col de Vence* (970m; views) beyond which its descends steeply to (10km) **Vence** itself; see Rte 161.

The N85 circles E. from *Le Logis-du-Pin*, ascending to (10km) the *Co de Valferrière* (1169m).

Hence the D2563 leads to (12.5km) *Mons*, a picturesquely sited village, 13.5km S. of which, above the valley of the Saignole, lies *Fayence*; see Rte 156B.—About 6km S. of Mons, off the minor road to *St-Cézaire*, are relics of the Roman aqueduct of *Roche Taillée*.

Descending from the Col (views), *Escragnolles* is traversed, commanded by the *Montagne de l'Audibergue* (1642m), beyond which the road makes a sharp turn to the W., before mounting again to (17km) the *Pas de la Faye*, providing an extensive view, as does the next sharp turn to the E., before reaching (5km) *St-Vallier-de-Thiey*

A DETOUR may be made hence on the D5 to (11km) *St-Cézaire*, a village preserving a medieval aspect, with its towers and gateway, its ruined castle, ancient cemetery-chapel, and old houses. In the Mairie is a Roman sarcophagus.—Hence, by turning E. via (10km) *Cabris* (view; Corsica may be discerned occasionally), *Grasse* is approached, 6km beyond.

The N85 once more ascends, to the *Col du Pillon* (786m; views) before climbing down to (12km) *Grasse*.

GRASSE (333m; 38,400 Grassois), well situated on the S. slope of the *Roquevignon*, with a distant prospect of the Mediterranean preserves a picturesque old centre which has little changed since the 18C, and its exploration is preferable to visiting the much-promoted perfume-distilleries, for which the town is reputed. The golden blossom of the mimosa is best seen during Jan. and Feb., while fragrent fields of violets, jonquils, lavender, roses, mignonette

jasmine, and tuberoses, etc. are also farmed in the vicinity to feed its
factories, although chemicals are now added. Other specialities are
crystallised flowers and fruits, and olive oil.

An independent republic in the 11C, it was absorbed by the Count of Provence
in 1227; and it was long the seat of a bishopric transferred from Antibes in 1243.
The perfume industry was introduced by an Italian named Tombarelli during the
reign of Catherine de Médicis. It was by-passed by Napoleon in March 1815,
who followed what is now known as the 'Route Napoleon' to Grenoble; see also
Rte 138A. Grasse was made fashionable as a health resort by Pauline Borghese,
and was later frequented by Queen Victoria.
    It was the birthplace of the Provençal poet Bellaud de la Bellaudière
(1532– 88); the 'gallant' artists J.-B. Mallet (1759– 1825), and Jean-Honoré
Fragonard (1732– 1806), and the latter's sister-in-law, Marguerite Gérard
(1762– 1837); and the naturalist Geoffroy Saint-Hilaire (1772– 1844). Maeterlinck wintered here c. 1900– 14, as did Mary Cassat in 1911– 27.

The Blvd du Jeu de Ballon is the town's main thoroughfare, with the
S.I. at its N. end, and the *Pl. du Cours Honoré Cresp* to the S. (view).
From the N. end of the boulevard one may descend to the 18C arcaded *Pl. aux Aires*, whence the narrow stepped lanes of the older town
may be explored, the Rue Droite in which leads S. to gain the *Pl. du
Cours.*—Approaching it from the Cours, we shortly reach the entrance, in the Rue Mirabeau, of the **Museum of Provençal Art and
History*, attractively arranged in a late 18C mansion built by the Marquise de Cabris, Mirabeau' sister, and containing interesting collections of furniture, glass, ceramics, and paintings, and a maquette of
Grasse.
    A small *Naval museum* devoted to Adm. de Grasse (1722– 88;
born at neighbouring Le Bar-sur-Loup) may be visited in the *Hôtel de
Pontevès* in this street.
    Three minutes' walk to the S.W., beyond the adjacent gardens, is
the new *Musée Fragonard*, installed in a restored 17C villa once owned by a Freemason and perfume-manufacturing cousin of Fragonard,
in which the artist took refuge in 1790. Copies of panels executed for
Mme du Barry by Fragonard (the originals of which are in the Frick
Collection, New York) are displayed on the ground floor, together
with other representative drawings and paintings by the artist.
    The Rue Jean-Ossala, just to the N. of the Rue Mirabeau, leads E.
from the Cours, off which the Rue Trecastel turns r. (with
Fragonard's birthplace at No. 23) to approach the *Pl. du Petit-Puy*, in
which is the *Hôtel de Ville*, retaining part of the bishop's palace, and
a Romanesque tower. Adjacent is the former Cathedral, **N.-D.-du-
Puy**, a heavy early 13C building with thick ogival vaulting, preserving Fragonard's Washing of the feet (a rare example of his religious
painting), the Triptych of St Honoratus, attrib. to Louis Bréa, and
three early works by Rubens (Rome; 1601). The notice to the faithful
should be read.—The *Pl. du 24-Aout* (the date of its liberation in
1944), E. of the church, provides an extensive view.

For the road from Grasse to (17km) *Cannes*, see Rte 161, in reverse.

GRASSE TO NICE (39km). Driving N.E., the D2085 traverses (6km) *Le Pré-du-
Lac*, where we may diverge directly to *Vence*; see above.—The main road passes
(r.) *Châteauneuf-de-Grasse*, a pleasant old village (views), below which is *Opio*,
with a 12th and 15C church built on a Roman site.—1.5km further S. is *N.-D.-de-
Brusc*, a partially ruinous 11C church in which Roman masonry has been re-
used, and preserving a relic of a 6C baptistry converted into a porch.
    The main road continues its sinuous descent into the valley of the Mardaric to
(18km) *Villeneuve-Loubet*, birthplace of Auguste Escoffier (1846– 1935), the

chef, whose home is now a museum devoted to the culinary arts. There is also a restored 12-13C castle.—The road provides a view E. towards *Haute-de-Cagnes* see Rte 161. On reaching a T-junction we turn l. and then r. to mmet the coast road, there turning l. again, shortly crossing the mouth of the Var, and passing (r.) *Nice airport*, later following the Promenade des Anglais into **Nice** itself; see Rte 162.

An ALTERNATIVE road (D7) forks l. 7km from *Le Pré-du-Lac*, descending into the valley of the Loup, crossing the river to (8km) *Le Colle-sur-Loup*, 3km S.W. of *St-Paul-de-Vence*.—The above-mentioned T-junction is reached 8km beyond.

156 Avignon to Cannes

A. Via Aix-en-Provence and Fréjus

228km (142 miles). N7. 34km *Sénas*—24km *St-Cannat*—16km **Aix-en-Provence**—36km **St-Maximin-la-Ste-Baume**—20km **Brignoles**—23km *Le Luc*—40km **Fréjus**—35km **Cannes**.

Maps: IGN 67, 68, or 115. M 245.

The A7, and then A8 motorways provides a rapid and often attractive route, with convenient exits to the main points of interest en route, and are recommended even to those travellers who prefer older main roads to motorways for the difficult stretch through the Massif de l'Esterel between Fréjus and Cannes.

The N7 leads S.E. from **Avignon** (Rte 148), at 11km crossing the Durance by the *Pont de Bonpas* (1953), replacing the older bridge destroyed in 1944, with a view (l.) of the ruins of the 14C *Chartreuse de Bonpas*.—**Cavaillon** (see Rte 150) lies 13km S.E.

16km. *Orgon*, at a narrows between an eastern spur of the *Chaîne des Alpilles* (r.) and the W. end of the *Montagne du Lubéron*, is overlooked by a ruined castle and the modern chapel of *N.-D.-de Beauregard*. It preserves slight remains of its 14C ramparts.

At (7km) *Sénas*, with a Romanesque and Gothic church, we bear S.E.

The N538 continues ahead, at 5km passing (r.) *Lamanon*, with a remarkably large plane-tree, to (7km) *Salon-de-Provence*, part of the way between (r.) the Canal de Craponne, and the new Canal E.D.F., connecting the Durance with the Étang de Berre; for *Salon*, and the roads hence to *St-Cannat*, or *Marseille*, see Rte 149A.

9km. *Pont-Royal*, 3km W. of which is *Alleins*, with a 17C belfry, and a Romanesque cemetery-chapel containing fragments from the Roman temple near *Vernègues* (see below); a minor road climbs up to its ruined 16C *Castle*, providing wide views.—The N561 forks l. at *Pont-Royal*; see Rte 156B.

3km. *Cazan*, 1km W. of which is the *Château-Bas*, in the gardens to the S. of which are the attractively sited ruins of a *Roman Temple* and Romanesque chapel.

7km. *Lambesc*, by-passed, a small market-town and the seat of the Provincial Assembly in 1639–1788, 5km beyond which *St-Cannat* is traversed, the birthplace of Pierre-André, Bailli de Suffren (1726–88; cf. St-Tropez).

13km. The N296, turning l. here, leads shortly to the site of *Entre* mont; the main road continues downhill, with a view (l.) of the *Vasarely Foundation building*, to (3km) **Aix-en-Provence**; see Rte 157.

For the road from Aix to *Marseille*, see the latter part of Rte 154.

AIX TO VAUVENARGUES AND POURRIÈRES (32.5km). The **Montagne St-Victoire** is the most commanding physical feature in the vicinity of Aix, a long limestone ridge made famous by the paintings of Cézanne, rising to 1011m at the *Pic des Mouches*, towards its E. end. Below it to the N. is *Vauvenargues*, approached by the D10 leading 14km N.E. from Aix, which passes near (l.) the so-called *Tour de César*, providing panoramic views, and (r.) the *Château de St-Marc*, with one square and three round towers, and a reservoir in the wooded Infernet valley. The **Château of Vauvenargues* (16-17C), flanked by two large towers and 14C fortifications, was where Luc de Clapiers, Marquis de Vauvenargues (1715–47) wrote his 'Maximes' in 1744–45; and where since 1958 until his death in 1973 lived Pablo Picasso, who daubed its interior walls with paintings. He is also buried here (no adm.).—From a point c. 1.5km W., at *Les Cabassols*, a track mounts the N. flank of the ridge to the hermitage of *N.-D.-de-la-Victoire* (17C; restored), in a convent adjoining which took place the interview between Arthur Vere and Margaret of Anjou in Scott's 'Anne of Geierstein'. Near-by is the *Croix de Provence* (1103m; *View).—The circuit of the ridge may be made by continuing E. from Vauvenargues, turning S. after 11.5km past (l.) the oppidum on the hill of *Pain du Munition*, thence descending to (7km) *Pourrières*, said to take its name (*Putreirae* or *Campi Putridi*) from the rotting corpses left on the battlefield, when Marius defeated the Teutons and Cimbri here in 102 B.C.—The N7 lies 2.5km beyond; or the return journey to Aix may be made by following, in the reverse direction, the sub-route below.

AIX TO LE THOLONET AND POURRIÈRES (27km). The D17 leads due E., providing attractive views of the *Montagne St-Victoire* ahead (see above), shortly passing (l.) the *Château Noir*, part of it rented by Cézanne between 1887–1906.—6km. *Le Tholonet*, with marble quarries worked since Roman timbes, is a picturesquely sited hamlet with an 18C château, from which the S. side of the mountain is skirted to (7km) *St-Antonin-sur-Bayon*, with remains of a Roman aqueduct, and 8km beyond, *Puyloubier*, with a ruined castle.—6km. *Pourrières* (see above), from which the main road (N7) may be gained 2.5km beyond.

Leaving Aix by the Cours Gambetta, we pass under the A7 motorway three times before forking l. at 8.5km.

The r.-hand fork (N96) leads S.E. towards the N8 for **Toulon**, but it is better approached by the B52 motorway, which may be joined near here.

We drive due E., parallel to the A8 and the *Montagne Ste-Victoire* (see above), which dominates this stretch of the road.—16km. *Pourrières* (see above) lies 3km N.E.; 5km to the S.W. lies *Trets*, an old town with a 12-17C church, a synagogue with a 13C façade, and part of its 14C town wall.—Further S. rises a chain of hills culminating in *Mont Aurélian* (880m), a reminder that we are following the Roman *Via Aurelia*.

13km. **St-Maximin-la-Ste-Baume** (5,600 inhab.) is a curious and somewhat derelict market-town deriving its name from an involved legend concerning Mary Magdalen and a certain Maximinus; the resulting abbey-church is the most complete example of a Northern Gothic structure in Provence.

According to tradition, the town was the burial-place of Mary Magdalen and Maximinus, who c. 40 had landed at Les Saintes-Maries-de-la-Mer, having fled from persecution in the Holy Land (cf. Rte 152C). Mary Magdalen subsequently retired to the Sainte-Baume (see Rte 159), but died here later in the 1C, where Maximinus, who had meanwhile been the first bishop of Aix, was also buried. An oratory was built on the site of their graves, which became a goal of pilgrimage, and an abbey of Cassianites was later erected. This was destroyed by the Saracens in the 8C, and the area became depopulated. The relics had been so carefully hidden that it was rumoured in the 11C that they had been conveyed to Vézelay in Burgundy. In 1279 the Benedictines (who had replaced the Cassianites in the 11C), on the instructions of Charles d'Anjou (later Charles II) started excavations, which brought to light what they claimed to be the sarcophagi of the saints, and the promotion of pilgrimages was promptly organised by the Dominicans, who had taken over the abbey in 1295, and a basilica was founded.

The town was known as *Marathon* during the Revolutionary period.

The heavily buttressed *__Church__ ◇ was begun by Jean Baudici, but was never completed, lacking towers, transepts, and ambulatory, and even its W. front remained unfinished.

The austere interior is remarkable for its elegance of line and proportions, while its polygonal apse seems almost wholly constructed of glass. The decorated organ-case (1773) is a particularly fine example, which was saved from destruction at the Revolution by Lucien Bonaparte, who was then a resident.

The sumptuous *Choir* (17-18C) and huge altar of 1683 (by Lieutaud, a pupil of Bernini and Puget) are likewise notable. The iron grilles display the arms of France and the emblem of Louis XIV; the 94 stalls of 1692 illustrate the history of the Dominican Order. In the apse of the N. aisle is an imposing 16C *Altarpiece of 22 panels depicting the Passion, by Francesco Rozen, a Venetian; the backgrounds include the earliest known view of the Palace of the Popes at Avignon.—In the N. aisle is the entrance to the Crypt, a 5C burial-chamber, heavily restored, containing Gallo-Roman sarcophagi, etc., and a 19C casket purporting to preserve relics of the Magdalen.

To the N. of the church, behind the *Hôtel de Ville*, is a seminary built round a large 15C cloister; while elsewhere in the town are fragments of medieval ramparts, and a few disfigured 16-18C houses.

The N560 leads 21km N.E. to *Barjols*; see Rte 156B, and S.W. towards (12km) *Nans-les-Pins*, a convenient approach to the *Massif de la Ste-Baume*, rising to 1147m; see p 861.

At 7km, where the road from Marseille joins the route, *Tourves*, with a ruined 18C château, is by-passed, while after 2km a r.-hand fork leads S. skirting the *Montagne de la Lube* (830m), with its strange limestone formations and commanding splendid views, to (11km) *La Roquebrussanne*, with a castle destroyed in 1707.—The road continues S. towards *Toulon* or *Hyères*; see first part of Rte 160.

6km. A r.-hand turning leads 3km E. to *La Celle*, where in the grounds of an hotel are the remains of a Benedictine abbey; the scandalous conduct of its nuns occasioned an inquiry by Mazarin which led to their removal to Aix.

5km. **Brignoles** (10,900 inhab.), with important bauxite mines in its vicinity, was earlier famous for its plums. it was the birthplace of St Louis of Toulouse (1274–97; son of Charles II d'Anjou, king of Naples); the artist Joseph Parrocel ('des batailles'; 1646–1704); and François Raynouard (1761–1836), the medievalist.

In the centre of the old town, preserving some ramparts to the S.W., twice sacked by troops of the Emperor Charles V (in 1525 and 1536), are the characterless remains of the winter palace of the counts of Provence (15-16C), housing a *Museum* of local history. Its most interesting exhibits are the *Sarcophagus from nearby La Gayole (late 2nd or early 3C), possible Greek work, and a 4C Paleo-

Christian altar.—The nearby church preserves a Romanesque doorway.

Brignoles is a convenient point from which to make the DETOUR to *Le Thoronet*.
The D24 leads N.E. up the Caramy valley to (14km) the *Lac de Carcés*, where we
continue E., after 2km forking l. through an area spoilt by open-cast bauxite min-
ng, to (4km) the ***Abbaye du Thoronet**, ◇ hidden in the trees (l), in typical
Cistercian solitude. Founded in 1146, it is perhaps the most interesting of the
three 'Sisters of Provence' (cf. *Sénanque*, and *Silvacane*). The plain Romanesque
Church has four apses at the E. end; and on the N. is the cloister, at three levels,
with a charming polygonal lavatory; off the E. walk opens the early Gothic
Chapter-house, with the dormitory above. Beyond the S. transept is the
.ithebarn, and to the N.W., other dependencies.—The road continues through
4.5km) the village of *Le Thoronet*, to regain—by the D17—the main route 7km
beyond, or by the more attractive D84 leading l. down the pretty valley of the
Agents to (16km) *Vidauban*; see below.

The N7 continues E. from Brignoles.—At 12km the D13 leads 4km r.
o *Besse-sur-Issole*, an old 'ville forte' beside a round lake; and N. to
7km) the village of *Cagasse*, 7km beyond which is the *Abbaye du
Thoronet* (see above), for which this road is an alternative approach.
    The main road bears N.E., passing (r.) *Flassans-sur-Issole*, and
descends towards (11km) *Le Luc*, where the N97 from Toulon joins
the route, passing (r.) a Celtic oppidum on a rocky spur.—**Le Luc**, an
old town of crooked streets, with a 15-16C church, and dominated
by a ruined castle known as the 'Pigeonnier des Mascs', is by-passed
o the l., and 2km beyond, *Le Cannet-des-Maures* is traversed,
overlooked (l.) by the 12C church of *Le Vieux-Cannet*, and the
château of *Bouillidon*.

LE CANNET TO GRIMAUD (28km). The D558 forks r., after 10km ascending the
valley of the Neuf-Riaux and climbing through corkwoods into the *Massif des
Maures* (see below) to (8km) **La Garde-Freinet** (405m), an old village guarding
this pass in the range, and commanded by a height bearing the ruins of a 15C
ort. From an earlier eyrie the 'Saracens' harried extensive areas of Provence,
until expelled c. 973.—Hence the road descends steeply (views) to (10km)
Grimaud; see Rte 160. Cogolin lies 3km S., and *St-Tropez* 10km E.
    The **Massif des Maures**, the wooded range of hills extending from Hyères to
the S.W. to Fréjus to the N.E., comprises three parallel ridges, rising to 779m at
La Sauvette, some 20km S.W. of *La Garde-Freinet*, whence it is approached by
the ridge road. For the most part they are thickly covered with dark green
orests of Aleppo pines and cork-oaks, and with an undergrowth or maquis of
ree-heath and other aromatic shrubs, areas of which have been repeatedly
devastated by fires in hot dry summers. The brown schist rocks are less striking-
y coloured than those of the *Estérel* further E.
    The name is derived from the Greek word 'amauros', dark, whence the Pro-
vençal *Maouro*, pine wood. The connection with the Moors is fanciful—it is only
incidental that the district was briefly occupied in the 9C by 'Saracen' invaders
of doubtful origin, although Algerian pirates frequently descended on the coast
down to the 18C, in search of slaves, and loot, which caused its shores to be prac-
ically deserted (except for such fortified ports as St-Tropez, and a few inland
villages perched on inaccessible hilltops) until the habit of sea bathing
transformed the coastal strip. Previously the only local industries were the
manufacture of corks from the bark of its oaks (chênes-lièges), and of 'briar'
pipes from the roots of its heaths (bruyères).

The N7 bears N.E. beneath the A8, with a view (half-r.) of the hill-top
Chapelle de Ste-Brigitte, through (9km) Vidauban—also by-
passed—an ancient town trading in silkworms' eggs ('graines'),
overlooked to the N.W. by the Château d'Astros, once a commandery of the Knights of Malta, while on a hill due N. is an oppidum.

At 5km the Argens is crossed by a widened bridge of 1625, some 275m below which are remains of a Roman bridge, where Marius Antonius is supposed to have encountered Lepidus in 43 B.C.

The D555 forks l. here for (12km) **Draguignan** (see Rte 156B) via (2km) *Les Arcs* an old town conserving a 13C castle-tower in the walled enceinte and an altar piece attrib. to Louis Bréa in its modern church.—Some 3km N.E. is the château of *Ste-Roseline*, with the chapel of the former Carthusian nunnery, in which is the tomb of Roseline de Villeneuve (1267–1329) and a fine altarpiece of 1635

A road junction is reached in 6km, whence the improved D25 turns S.E., crossing the E. end of the *Massif des Maures* to (25km) *Ste-Maxime* (see Rte 160) via the *Col de Gratteloup*, some kms to the E. of which is the deserted village of *Vieux-Revest*.

2km. **Le Muy**, on the E. side of which is the *Tour de Charles-Quint*, from which some men lying in wait for Charles V on his retreat from his disastrous expedition of 1536 shot Garcilaso de la Vega by mistake, being misled by the splendour of the Spanish poet's attire.

The precipitous N. face of the *Montagne de Roquebrune* (372m, marking the N. limit of the Massif des Maures), is passed, and 6km beyond, the village of *Roquebrune-sur-Argens* (2.5km S.), in the 16C church of which is a Roman milestone from the Via Aurelia; another is preserved in the church of *Puget-sur-Argens*, which is traversed 4km before entering Fréjus.

FRÉJUS (32,700 Fréjusiens or Forojuliens), the ancient *Forum Julii*, once a seaport, but now 1.5km from the sea, preserves considerable Roman remains, while its suburbs now join with those of St-Raphael. When Smollett passed that way he described it as 'very inconsiderable, and indeed in a ruinous condition', but he was well-lodged and 'treated with more politeness than we had met with in any other part of France'. Its W. quarters were badly damaged when the Malplasset dam (c. 10km N.) burst in 1959, a catastrophe claiming 420 victims. It is the centre of a peach-growing district.

Forum Julii was founded c. 50 B.C. by Julius Caesar to rival Marseille, which favoured Pompey, and in 31 B.C. Augustus won the sea-battle of Actium with galleys built in its yards. It was partially destroyed by Saracens in the 10C, burnt by Barbary corsairs in 1475, and pillaged by the troops of Charles V in 1536. St Francis de Paule landed here during a plague in 1483, but by the 16C the harbour had entirely silted up.

It was the birthplace of Cornelius Gallus (66 B.C.—A.D. 26), the poet and soldier; Agricola (c. 37-93), conqueror of Britain; and the Abbé Sieyès (1748–1836), the statesman. Card. Fleury (1653–1743) had been bishop of Fréjus from 1698–1715 before becoming chief minister to Louis XV.

It is perhaps convenient to first visit the Christian remains, by following the Rue Sieyès E. from crossroads in the town centre, in which the best of the 17-18C mansions are preserved, to the *Pl. Formigé*, to the E. of which is the former *Bishop's Palace* (now the *Hôtel de Ville*), behind which are remains of its 14C predecessor.

The square is overlooked by the **Cathedral**, an example of early Provençal Gothic (13C), with an 11C N. aisle, and containing a polyptych of the Apotheosis of St Margaret by Durandi of Nice (c. 1450). The see was founded in the late 4C, but the bishop's seat was transferred to Toulon in 1957.

The doors, baptistry, cloister, and museum, are shown by a guide. The *Doors (protected) of the principal entrance (1530) are elaborately adorned with Renaissance carvings of the Life of the Virgin, Nativity, etc., which may be compared with those of the cathedral at Aix. To the l. is the 5C octagonal *Baptistry*

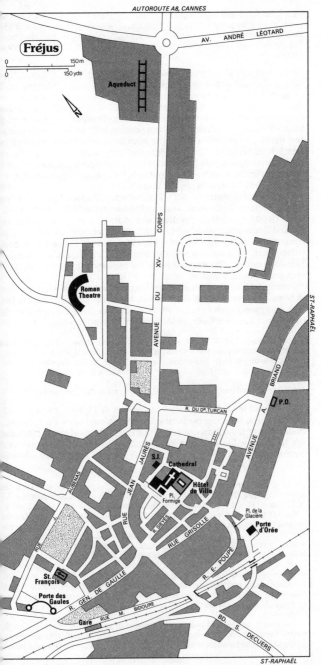

AUTOROUTE A8, CANNES

AV. ANDRÉ LÉOTARD

Fréjus

0 ___ 150 m
0 ___ 150 yds

Aqueduct

CORPS

XV-

DU

AVENUE

Roman
Theatre

ST-RAPHAËL

R. DU Dr. TURCAN

BRIAND

A.

P.O.

AVENUE

AUBENAS

RUE

JEAN

JAURÈS

S.I.

Cathedral

Hôtel
de Ville

Pl.
Formige

R. SIEYÈS

Pl. de la
Glacière

Porte
d'Orée

RUE GRISOLLE

St.
François

R. E. POUPÉ

RUE

R. GEN. DE GAULLE

RUE M. BIDOURE

Porte des
Gaules

Gare

BD. S. DECUERS

ST-RAPHAËL

with four apses and eight monolithic antique granite columns with marbl
capitals.—Stairs ascend to the 12C *Cloister, ◊ with elegant arcades and 15
pine ceilings (painted). On one side is an upper gallery containing a collection
Roman and Gallo-Roman antiquities, and documents illustrating the history
Fréjus.

Few traces remain of the Roman *Walls*, perhaps best seen on eithe
side of the N.E. gateway, which stood adjacent to the *Aqueduct*,
of the N7, which conveyed hence via the Reyran valley the waters o
the Siagnole, near Mons, 50km N.—S.E. of this point stood th
Praetorium or military headquarters, with cisterns and grain-stores
to the S.W. (approached by a lane turning off the Rue Jean-Jaurè
not far N. of the cathedral) is the *Roman Theatre* (72m by 30m), o
which little remains.—Of more interest is the *Amphitheatre*, N.W. c
the centre (approached from hence by retracing our steps and takin
a r.-hand turning), well-seen from the N7 if approaching from Aix, o
from the D37 leading N. to the motorway.

The ***Amphitheatre** (c. A.D. 210), which measures 114m by 82m
small compared to those at Arles and Nîmes, but which could contai
over 10,000 spectators, retains parts of its vaulted galleries on th
ground floor, and tiers of seats with their supporting arches are als
evident, but as Smollett observed in 1765, 'part of the wall now con
stitutes part of a monastery, the monks of which, I am told, hav
helped to destroy the amphitheatre, by removing the stones for thei
own purposes of building'.

Returning S.E., the Roman *Porte des Gaules* is passed, semi-circula
in plan, from which the Decumanus Maximus lead directly to the
N.E. gate; see above.—By the *Pl. de la Glacière* (S. of the cathedral) i
the restored *Porte d'Orée*, probably part of a monument.

The area immediately E. of this was once the Roman harbour, while to the S. o
the adjacent railway, on the *Butte St-Antoine*, stood a fort of which three roun
towers remain. A mole protecting the port lead E. to the so-called *Lantern
d'Auguste*, a stone turret which served as a landmark to its entrance.

For the coast road hence via *St-Raphael* to *Cannes*, see the latter part of Rte 160

The 'old' N7 leads N.E. to cross the *Massif de l'Esterel*, but althoug
this slow and winding route provides occasional views, it is recom
mended that travellers not following the coast road should join the
A8 motorway 5km N. of Fréjus, which provides a peasanter an
easier journey of 23km to join the N7 7km W. of **Cannes** (see Rt
161).

Those making directly for **Grasse** may turn l. off the motorway at (11km) Le
Adrets, to follow the E. bank of the *Lac de St-Cassien*, after 8.5km meeting th
D562 some 17km S.W. of Grasse. See the latter part of Rte 156B for this road.
    The N7 drives N.E. past the remains of the Roman *Aqueduct* (l.) and shortl
beyond (r.) a curious *pagoda* in memory of Indo-chinese soldiers who fell in th
First World War.—The laborious ascent of the W. flank of the *Massif de l'Estere
is now commenced, reaching the summit level at (14km) *Le Logis de Pari*
(316m).—3km before this point a track to the r. climbs to *Mt Vinaigre* (618m
view), the highest peak of the range; see below.—On the descent—passing th
Auberge des Adrets, an old posting-house—we have a view (l.) of the *Massif du
Tanneron*, rising to 519m, and later (r.) the *Îles de Lérins*, on approaching (14km
Mandelieu, 7km from the centre of **Cannes**, preferably entered by turning r. to
La Napoule, and following the coast road, which avoids the industrial suburb o
La Bocca.
    The **Massif de l'Esterel** is an isolated group of porphyritic hills between St
Raphael and La Napoule, rising to 618m at *Mt Vinaigre*, on its N. side; see above
Its thickly wooded interior is practically uninhabited, except for fire-guards, for,

unhappily, conflagrations are as frequent here as in the *Massif des Maures*. It only became accessible after 1903, with the opening of the coast road, and until the
early 19C had a reputation for being the haunt of highwaymen and other lawless
types. Even now the roads there are little more than tracks, and require cautious
driving. The range provides numerous walks for the strenuous armed with a
good map, such as the path traversing the rocky gorge of the *Mal-Infernet*, while
two of the finer view-points are the *Pic de l'Ours* (496m), and further S., the *Pic
du Cap Roux* (452m), on its S.E. side, dominating the coast road; see Rte 160.

B. Via Silvacane, Barjols, Draguignan, and Grasse

241km (150 miles). N7. 34km *Sénas*—9km *Pont-Royal*—N561.
11km **Silvacane**—16km *Meyragues*—N96. 6km *Peyrolles-en-
Provence*—D561. 17km *Rians*—D561 and D554. 24.5km
Tavernes—5.5km **Barjols**—D560. 16km *Sillans-la-Cascade*—6km
Salernes—23km **Draguignan**—D562. 30km *Fayence* is 5km
N.—26km **Grasse**—N85. 17km **Cannes**.

Maps: IGN 67, 68, or 115. M 245.

The A7 motorway may be followed as far as Sénas.

This indirect route traverses a comparatively unfrequented part of
the interior of Provence, which may avoid the sometimes crowded
main roads.

Rte 156A is followed as far as *Pont-Royal*, there turning l. onto the
N561 through (9km) *La Roque-d'Anthéron*, 2km beyond which (l.) is
the Cistercian abbey of *Silvacane* ◊ (1145), with *Sénanque* and *Le
Thoronet* one of the 'three Cistercian sisters of Provence'. Its Church
is imposing in its simplicity, and it has a good Cloister and Chapter-
house of the period, and a vaulted refectory of 1420.

The next r.-hand turning (N543) leads 25km S. to *Aix-en-Provence* via (6km)
Rognes, a pleasant village known for its stone-quarries, the church of which
preserves notable carved altarpieces (15th and 18C), beyond which the *Chaine
de la Trévaresse* is crossed, to meet the N7 9km from **Aix**; see Rte 157.

We continue to ascend the Durance valley, with the *Montagne du
Lubéron* to the N., at 16km crossing the N556 (from Pertuis to Aix)
and 3km beyond passing below (r.) the well-sited 13C castle of
Meyrargues, refurbished in 1638 (now a hotel), and 5km beyond,
traverse *Peyrolles*, where the Romanesque church has a late Gothic
aisle, and the *Hotel de Ville* occupies a 17C château.

The r.-hand fork is followed 1km E., through *Jouques*, and then
between the *Montagne de Vautubière* (659m; N.) and the ridge of the
Montagne des Ubacs, beyond which rises the *Montagne Ste-Victoire*
(1011m; cf. Rte 156A), to approach (17km) *Rains*, its church containing several small rose-windows, 11km beyond which is *St-Martin*,
with its dour château.

At (8km) *Varages*, 6km S.E. of *La Verdière*, with a château of interest, we ascend to (5.5km) *Tavernes*, 6km to the E. of which, in the
château of *Barras*, was born Paul Barras (1755–1829), the revolutionary.—The road turns S. to (5.5km) **Barjols**, an attractively sited
village, once called 'the Tivoli of Provence' on account of its fountains and the cascades in its wooded environs. It has two tree-shaded
squares; the *Hôtel de Pontevès* has a Renaissance doorway, and its
church (rebuilt in the 16C), a Romanesque tympanum.

BARJOLS TO DRAGUIGNAN VIA LE THORONET (c. 60km). This recommended detour follows the D554 S. to (8km) *Châteauvert*, pleasantly situated on the Argens, the shady ravine of which is threaded via *Correns* to (17km) *Carcès*. Here we take the D13, turning l. after 1.5km to follow a by-road to (7km) the **Abbaye du Thoronet**, hidden in woods to the l.; see Rte 156A.—At the village of (4.5km) *Le Thoronet* we turn l. to the *Pont d'Argens*, and (8.5km) *Lorgues*, a pleasant little town preserving its 14C gates, thence bearing N.E. across country before descending to (13km) *Draguignan*; see below.

From Barjols the road turns E., at 9km passing some 5km S. of *Fox-Amphoux* on its height, to (7km) *Sillans-la-Cascade*, preserving part of its walls, to the S. of which, on the Breque, is its waterfall; 6km S.W. lies *Cotignac*, with two 15C towers, a church of 1514, and tree and fountain-lined streets; *Carcès* (see above) lies 7km beyond.

From Sillans the D22 leads N. via (9km) *Aups*, an attractive little town, to (23km) the W. end of the road following the S. bank of the *Gorges du Verdon*; see Rte 156C.

6km. *Salernes*, where 'tomettes', or floor-tiles, are manufactured, has a Romanesque church and ruined 13C castle.—The large 17C château of the navigator Bruni d'Entrecasteaux (1740–92), with gardens attrib. to Le Nôtre, is 8km to the S.; in the village are relics of a Gallo-Roman aqueduct, and a 13C bridge.

From Salernes, we continue E. across country to (16km) *Flayosc*, descending shortly to (7km) **Draguignan** (28,200 Dracénois), occupying a sheltered position at the foot of the *Malmont* (557m), no longer the departmental capital, which is now Toulon, but still a centre for artillery training. It was anciently known as *Draguinianum* or *Dracoenum*; among its préfets was Baron Haussmann (in 1849), while Clemenceau was a deputy for 25 years. Augustus Hare thought it 'wholly without interest'!

The wide Blvd Georges-Clemenceau is the main thoroughfare, near the N. end of which are grouped most of the main public buildings. The Rue de la République leads to the *Museum* and *Library*, containing Gallo-Roman antiquities, Marseille and Moustiers faïence, and a bust of the Comte de Valbelle attrib. to Houdon; also a collection of MSS, incunables, and fine bindings.

From the N.E. corner of the adjacent *Pl. du Marché* one may enter the older town by a medieval gate, ascending towards the *Tour de l'Horloge* (17C), replacing a belfry demolished by Louis XIV in 1660 to punish the town for its share in the 'Semestre' or Fronde of Provence.—Hence one may descend W. to the 13C *Porte Aiguière*, abutting the Rue de la Juiverie, in which is the facade of a 13C *Synagogue*.

The Blvd Jean-Jaurès leads E. off the Blvd Clemenceau, to the l. of which are relics of an *Augustinian church* (12-13C), beyond which is an *American Military Cemetery*, containing the graves of paratroopers who landed between Le Muy and Draguignan on 15 Aug. 1944, and others who fell in the disembarkment.

The D955 leads N.E. to (32km) *Comps-sur-Artuby* (see Rte 157C), shortly passing (l.) the *Pierre de la Fée* dolmen, and later threading the *Gorges de Châteaudouble*.

The N555 leads 13km S.E. to meet the N7 just W. of *Le Muy*; see Rte 156A.

From Draguignan we climb E., following the contour of the hills above the Endre valley.

At 11km a DETOUR to the N., via *Callas*, may be made (c. 10km longer than the main road) to visit the hill villages of (9km) *Bargemon*, preserving parts of its ramparts and a good Gothic church containing 17C paintings, (13km) *Seillans*, with a

13C gate, ruined 12C castle, and Romanesque church, later altered, and 7.5km beyond, *Fayence*, with a 14C gate and 18C church, providing fine views S.—The main route may be regain in the valley below, 5.5km S.E.

The D562 turns E., at 18.5km passing below *Fayence*; see above.—At 4.5km a l.-hand turning climbs to the villages of *Callian*, with its 15C castle, reconstructed in the 17C, and church of 1685, and *Montauroux*, both providing extensive panoramas, whence one may regain the route 4.5km further E.—The r.-hand turning here leads across the *Lac de St-Cassian* to (8.5km) the A8 motorway at *Les Adrets*, 19km W. of *Cannes*; see the latter part of Rte 156A.

The main road shortly makes a wide bend in the wooded valley of the Siagne, and continues N.E., with the Tanneron hills rising to the S., and to the N. a ridge on which *Cabris* is perched, to approach (15km) **Grasse**; see the latter part of Rte 155.

For the road from Grasse to *Cannes*, 17km S.E., see Rte 161, in reverse.

C. Via Cavaillon, Riez, Moustiers-Ste-Marie, the Gorges du Verdon, and Castellane

267km (166 miles). N7. 11km—D973. 13km **Cavaillon**—33km *Cadenet*—12km *Pertuis*—16km *Pont-de-Mirabeau*—D952. 22km *Gréoux-le-Bains*—20km **Riez**—15km **Moustiers-Ste-Marie**—45km **Castellane** via the N. bank of the **Gorges du Verdon**—N85. 63km **Grasse**—17km **Cannes**.

Maps: IGN 60, 61, 67, 68, or 115. M 245.

At c. 11km the road from **Avignon** (Rte 148) passes beneath the A7 motorway and (l.) the 14C *Chartreuse de Bonpas* to follow the r. bank of the Durance to (13km) **Cavaillon**; see Rte 150.

From Cavaillon, the road bears round the W. end of the *Montagne du Lubéron*, rising here at the *Tête des Buisses* to 619m.—13.5km. To the l. is the remarkably narrow *Gorges de Régalon*, 2km beyond which (r.) is the old suspension bridge across the Durance to *Mallemort* and *Pont-Royal*, whence we may visit the abbey of **Silvacane**; see Rte 156B.

2km. *Mérindol*, with ruins visible of the old Waldensian village which was destroyed and its inhabitants massacred in 1545 by order of the reactionary Parlement of Aix, an atrocity which led to the union of the 60 reformed churches of Provence in 1560.

A DETOUR may be made from just beyond (9.5km) *Lauris*, where the D27 forks l. to (4.5km) **Lourmarin**, an attractive village notable for its 15-16C Château (since 1925 a study centre of the University of Aix). Albert Camus (1913–60) is buried in the cemetery.—The detour may be continued via (7km) *Cucuron*, with a 14C gateway, 14C tower to its château, and a part Romanesque, part Gothic, church containing a huge 17C retable.—Hence a track climbs steeply to the summit of the Lubéron ridge just W. of the *Mourre Negre* (1125m; view).—At **Ansuis**, 4.5km S.E. of Cucuron, the village is commanded by the 17C *Château* of the Duc de Sabran-Ponteves (1285–1325) and his wife Delphine de Signes, both of whom were canonised in 1369 for their good works. Part of the building date from 1160, but it was seriously damaged in the 14C and again in the late 16C, after which the Renaissance S. front was added. It contains some good Flemish tapestries, a portrait of the Archduke Albert and the Infanta Isabel, attrib. to Rubens, a kitchen of character, and is surrounded by formal gardens.—*La Tour d'Aigues* (see Rte 154) lies 8km further E., from which the main route may be regained at *La Bastidonne*, 3km S.E.

The D973 continues E. from Lauris through (6km) *Cadenet*, the church of which has an antique marble vase as its font, and a bell-tower of 1538; it was the birthplace of André Étienne (1774–1838), 'the drummer of Arcole'.

12km. **Pertuis** (12,400 inhab.), noted for its seed-corn and potatoes, was the birthplace of the elder Mirabeau (1715–89), author of 'L'Amis des hommes' (1756), but harsh father of the more famous orator. It possesses a 13C *Clock-tower*, and *St-Nicolas*, restored in 1537.—Traversing (5.5km) *La Bastidonne*, at 7.5km the village of *Mirabeau* is reached, a pleasant little place, whose 17C château gave the name to the family; it was acquired earlier this century by Maurice Barrès (1862–1923).—A defile is entered 2km beyond, just S. of which is the *Pont-de-Mirabeau*, with a Romanesque chapel to the E.

Manosque (see Rte 154) lies 21km N.E., from which our route may be regained at *Vinon-sur-Verdon*, 16km S.E.—*Corbières*, on the approach to Manosque from this direction, provides some attractive views towards the N.E., with *Mont Pelat* in the distance.

Crossing the rebuilt suspension bridge near the relics of the old one spanning this narrows of the Durance, we turn l., shortly skirting (r.) the *Centre d'Études Nucléaire de Cadarache* (no adm.!); to the l. stands the 15C château of *Caderache*, overlooking the confluence of the Durance and Verdon, and the start of the E.D.F. canal, some 85km long, providing a considerable volume of irrigation water and hydro-electric power before entering the *Étang de Berre*; see Rte 149A.—13km. *Vinon-sur-Verdon*, where we cross the river and turn r. to (8km) *Gréoux-les-Bains*, an old thermal spa, known to the Romans, with a ruined castle of the Templars (14C), beyond which the valley of the Colostre, with its vines, olives, and lavender-fields, is ascended via (12km) *Allemagne-en-Provence*, with a restored 14-15C castle, to (8km) *Riez*.

Riez (528m), a decayed episcopal town, preserving some remains of its medieval walls, two *Gates*, and several mutilated mansions, is principally of interest for its *Baptistry (c. 600; reconstructed in the 12C), just S.W. of the centre, containing a lapidary collection; a short distance further W. are four Corinthian columns, part of a 1C Temple, a relic of the Gallo-Roman city of *Reia Apollinaris*.

At *Valensole*, 14km W., noted for its almonds, was born Adm. de Villeneuve (1763–1806), Nelson's opponent at Trafalgar.

We continue N.E. for c. 10km before descending and climbing again to (5km) **Moustiers-Ste-Marie** (631m), named from a monastery founded in 432, with steep arcaded streets and quaint old houses clinging picturesquely to the sides of a defile, down which the Rioul descends in cascades. Across it is suspended an iron chain from which hangs a gilded star, said to be a votive offering of a crusading Chevalier de Blacas.—Immediately below is a chapel rebuilt in the 12th and 14C, possessing Renaissance doors.—The *Church is a notable Romanesque structure with a Gothic choir (12-13C).—Moustiers faïence of the 17-18C is now highly prized, and may be seen in the *Musée des Faïences*; the art was revived in 1925, examples of which, for sale, are displayed at every turn.

The route hence follows the N. bank of the *Gorges** (or *Cañon*) **du Verdon** to *Castellane*, a good centre from which to make detailed explorations, and the S. bank is therefore described from E. to W., for those who may want to make the complete circuit.

The *Grand Cañon du Verdon* is perhaps the most remarkable natural feature of the Provençal Alps, and is wilder, deeper, and narrower than the *Gorges du Tarn*. The swiftly flowing Verdon has here hollowed out a series of deep gorges, in some places 700m below the plateau, in the soft Jurassic limestone. The road encircling the gorge provides several magnificent plunging views into its depths, which may be explored on foot, preferably keeping to the marked footpath, as rapid variations in water level can occur. The walk takes c. 8 hours, and should not be attempted without adequate clothing and heavy boots, and food, and an electric torch (for the threading of tunnels) will not come in amiss. Only experts should attempt a more thorough exploration of the river-bed, first made in 1905 by a party led by E.A. Martel.

AT 2.5km from Moustiers the D952 forks l., gradually ascending, with good views over the extended *Lac de Ste-Croix*, and of the lower end of the *Grand Cañon*, later passing the *Belvedere de Mayreste*, to the *Col d'Ayens* (1032m), there bearing away to the village of *La Palud*.

Here the D23 turns r. to make the smaller circuit (23km) of the N. bank, known as the *Route des Crêtes,* providing numerous characteristic views of the gorges, notably from the belvederes of *La Maline* (beyond which a track descends to the river bed) and those facing E.—From the *Trescaire belvedere* one turns W. to regain the main road just E. of *La Palud*.

7.5km. *Point Sublime*, commanding a fine view of the upper end of the cañon, above which is the old village of *Rougon*, noted for its fossil deposits, whence the *Mourre de Chanier* (1930m; N.W.) may be ascended.—We continue to follow the r. bank of the river, shortly joined by the footpath from the gorge, and at 5.5km meet the D955 (see below), to enter **Castellane** 12km beyond; see Rte 155.

The S. bank of the *Gorges du Verdon* may be followed by turning onto the D955 here, to (16km) *Comps-sur-Artuby*, passing (r.) the ruined castle of *Trigance*. Comps is dominated by a good early Gothic church in the local style.

The road continues S. over the military *Camp de Canjuers* to (32km) **Draguignan** via the *Gorges de Châteaudouble*; see Rte 156B.

From Comps (which may also be approached by the D21 from the Route Napoléon from near *Le Logis du Pin*—19km. S.E. of Castellane— by those driving from Grasse), we turn N.W. on the D71 to (c. 14km) the *Balcons de la Mescla*, commanding a magnificent * View of the confluence of the Verdon and Artuby, 3km beyond which the chasm of the latter, with its vertical walls, is crossed by the *Pont de l'Artuby* (1947), 175m above the river. We get another fine plunging view from between two tunnels further W., and from the nearby *Falaise des Cavaliers*, beyond which a section of the road known as the 'Corniche Sublime' is reached, running high above the narrowest part of the gorge, later mounting to the *Col d'Illoire* (964m) and (20.5km) the village of *Aiguines*, on the edge of the lonely causse-like *Plans de Canjuers*.—Hence the road descends, at 7.5km meeting the D957 on the bank of the *Lac de Ste-Croix* 9.5km S. of *Moustiers*.

The D957 skirts the lake-side before turning S. to (15.5km) crossroads 7.5km N. of Aups, from which the less frequented *Basse Gorges du Verdon* may be explored.—*Aups* lies 9km N.E. of *Sillans*; see Rte 156B.

For the road from Castellane to **Grasse**, 63km S.E., and **Cannes**, 17km beyond, see the latter part of Rte 155; and Rte 161, in reverse.

157 Aix-en-Provence

AIX-EN-PROVENCE (124,600 Aixois), the historic capital of Provence, and seat of a university and court of appeal, although it has lost its political importance, retains its distinction thanks to its vital cultural life, and its handsome 17-18C mansions. Charming features are its tree-shaded boulevards and squares, and their many fountains. It certainly no longer has the 'air of silence and gloom, so commonly characteristic of places destitute of commerce and industry', which so depressed Sir Nathaniel Wraxall two centuries ago. Its 'Calissons', iced almond-paste confection, are a speciality. It has been the site of a Summer Music Festival since 1948.

In 123 B.C. the Celto-Ligurian stronghold of *Entremont* (on a height N. of the town; see below) was destroyed by the Roman consul C. Sextius Calvinus, who founded the first Roman settlement in Transalpine Gaul on the site of the present town, doubtless attracted by its thermal springs, and called it *Aquae Sextiae*, eventually contracted to Aix. It was enriched by Marius after his victories over the Cimbri, and was made a colony after Caesar's sack of Massilia (Marseille), later becoming the capital of *Gallia Narbonensis Secunda*.

Its first bishop was St Maximinus (cf. St-Maximin-la-Ste-Baume), and it became an archbishopric in the 5C. Although it was sacked by the Lombards in 574, the inhabitants were saved by paying a ransom, but the devastated city was abandoned. By the end of the medieval period little of the Roman city remained, having long been used as a quarry. Although subordinate to Arles, Aix emerged as a city of the County of Provence, and the Catalan dynasty of counts made it their principal residence, as did the Angevins who succeeded them. The cultured and genial Count René (called from his titular kingdom of Naples 'le bon roi Rene'), who introduced the muscatel grape, made Aix his headquarters from 1471 – 80. On the death of his successor some seventeen months after his own demise, the County was merged with France. By the second decade of the 15C the university was established; and the Parlement of Provence—with the Mistral and the Durance one of the three 'scourges' of the province—had its seat here from 1501 to 1790. In 1536 the town was captured by the Emperor Charles V, who was crowned 'King of Arles' in the cathedral, although Arles never fell to him.

The 17-18Cs were a period of great expansion, when the Cours, and a whole new quarter to the S. were laid out; the spa was developed; and it was visited by a number of distinguished travellers, many of them English. Some remained, a certain William Wilson was made an honorary citizen in 1790 after 14 years of charitable work in the town. Thicknesse described it as 'a well built city', although Arthur Young observed that many houses lacked glass windows, while Smollett, who took the waters, had to admit that 'as many of its inhabitants are persons of fashion, they are well bred, gay, and sociable'; but he also noted that some English travellers had complained that the Duc de Villars, then governor, gave them a cold reception when they were presented to him, for the French could not conceive of a man of fashion not having a title, and that to be introduced as a mere *monsieur un tel* made them assume he was 'some plebian, unworthy of any particular attention'. Jefferson was there in 1787. Mirabeau was elected deputy in 1789. In 1801 its population was 23,700.

Its 19C history was uneventful when compared with Marseille. Some have noticed an erosion of its elegance during recent decades due to the proximity and brash prosperity of that port, and its natives.

Among Aixois were Joseph Pitton de Tournefort (1656– 1708), the botanist; the philosopher Marquis de Vauvenargues (1715– 47); the historian F.-A. Mignet (1796– 1884); the artists J.-B. Van Loo (1684– 1745), François-Marius Granet (1775– 1849), and Paul Cézanne (1839– 1906); the composer André

Campra (1660– 1744); and Louise Colet (1808– 76), authoress and friend of de Musset and Flaubert.

Émile Zola spent his childhood and youth at Aix (1842– 58), living first in a house in the Impasse Silvacane (occupied earlier by Thiers) and later in the Rue Mazarine. His lifelong friendship with Cézanne began at the Lycée Mignet, then the Collège Bourbon. Darius Milhaud (1892– 1974), born at Marseille, is buried in Aix.

Roads from the N. and W. converge on the *Pl. du Gén. de Gaulle* (to the S. of which is the S.I.), dominated by its fountain of 1860, at the W. end of the stately ***Cours Mirabeau**, laid out after 1650, and lined with plane trees, which extends E. towards the *Pl. Forbin*, and which is the main centre of animation.

Unfortunately too many of the once dignified 17-18C mansions which lined this wide boulevard have been degraded to house banks and offices. Beyond the *Hôtel de Villars* (1710; No. 2) is the *Hôtel des Princes* (1785; No. 3), long the only hotel in the Cours, and which until its sale in 1870 was much favoured by English travellers. The *Hôtel d'Isoard* (1710; No. 10) was once the home of the navigator Bruni d'Entrecasteaux. No. 20, the *Hôtel de Forbin* (1656); the *Hôtel d'Arbaud-Jouques* (1647; No. 19), now the *sous-préfecture*; the disfigured *Hotel d'Estienne d'Orves* (No. 27), and No. 38, the *Hôtel d'Espagnet*, of 1647, with its colossal caryatids, are notable.

From the last the Rue du Quatre-Septembre leads S. into the elegant quarter laid out for Abp Michel Mazarin, brother of the Cardinal. At the corner of the Rue Mazarine is the *Musée Arbaud*, containing a good ceramic collection (especially Moustiers ware), portraits of the Mirabeau family, and a Self-portrait by Granet, together with documents relating to Provence and the félibres in the Library (note boiseries).—Further S. is the charming *Pl. des Quartre Dauphins*, with its *Fountain of 1667.

Turning l. here, the Rue Cardinale is followed to 13C *St-Jean-de-Malte*, with a belfry of 1376 altered in the 17C. It contains several 17-18C paintings, and a reconstruction of the tomb of the counts of Provence, destroyed at the Revolution (with statues of Alphonse II, Raymond Bérenger V, and his wife Beatrice of Savoy).

Adjacent, occupying the dependencies of the priory of the Knights of Malta, where in 1600 Marie de Médicis lodged, is the **Musée Granet** (or *des Beaux-Arts*), *still* undergoing drastic and long overdue re-organisation. Most of the contents, including the Gaulish antiquities from Entremont, are not on display, but are no doubt in 'reserve'.

Among the more notable at present on view are: **R1** *Cuyp*, Margaretha de Geer; and Landscapes attrib. to *Van de Hagen*, and *Rembrandt*.—**R2** *School of Fontainebleau*, 'Repas galant'; *Jerome (Hieronymus) Franken*, Self-portrait; *Jean Capassin*, Diane de Poitiers as Peace; attrib. *Quesnel*, Portrait of Henri III; *Philippe de Champaigne*, Portrait, of 1648; *Jean Daret*, The artist playing a guitar; *Le Nain brothers*, Card-players; *Parrocel*, Battle for a bridge, and Boarhunt; *Mignard*, Mars and Venus.

R3 *Van Willel, Largillière*, Adelaide de Gueidan and her sister playing the clavichord, Mme de Gueidan as Flora, Gaspar de Gueidan writing; *Rigaud*, Gaspard de Gueidan playing bagpipes, and as Advocat-general, Portrait of an officer; *Quentin Delatour*, Pastel portrait of the Duc de Villars; *J.-B. van Loo*, Mme d'Albert picking grapes.—**R4** Works by *Germain Drouais*; *Ingres*, Portrait of F.-M. Granet, Jupiter and Thetis, and other studies; *F.-M. Granet*, Views of Rome and Tivoli, and Death of Poussin; *J.-R. Brascassat*, Landscape with Argus guarding Io (turned into an heifer); *Marguerite Gérard*, Mother and Child; *David*, Portrait of a youth; *J.M. Langlois*, Portrait of Remi Gérard.

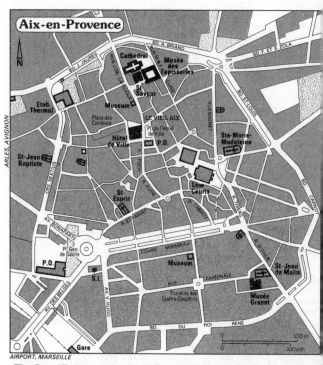

AIRPORT, MARSEILLE

The Rue d'Italie, just to the N.E., leads to the *Pl. Forbin*, to the l. of which is the *Chapelle des Oblats* (1695); to the r. is the Rue de l'Opéra, in which Nos 18, 24, and 26 are notable. No. 28 was the birthplace of Cézanne, who died at 23 Rue Boulegon, off Rue Mignet.

The *Hôtel de Carcès*, at the intersection of the Rue Lacépède (leading N. from the Place) with the Rue Eméric-David, is the oldest of the aristocratic town houses of Aix (1590); No. 16 in the latter street is the *Hôtel de Panisse-Passis* (1739); No. 33 has interior decoration by Van Loo. At the corner is the *Hôtel d'Agut* (1676), with caryatids, mentioned by Mme de Sévigné in letters written from the old palace of the governors which stood opposite.

The classical *Palais de Justice* (1822–32), overlooking the *Pl. de Verdun*, occupies the site of the old Palais Comtal, later the palace of the governors, demolished by 1786 as unsafe. Ledoux' designs were not implemented, and those of a departmental architect were later followed.—Behind the building is the *Prison*, the two connected by an underground passage.

To the N.E., beyond a fountain of 1762 by Chastel, stands *Ste-Marie-Madeleine* (1703; with a mid 19C facade), containing the central part of an anon. triptych of 1449 of the Annunciation; the wings are copies of the originals (in London, and Brussels). The 18C organ is notable.

The police occupy the *Hôtel de Valbelle* (1655) in the Rue Mignet, leading N., next to which is the *Chapelle de la Visitation* (1647), in which Mme de Sévigné's grand-daughters were buried.

The Rue de Montigny leads N.W. opposite the church, from which one may turn l. along the Rue Jaubert (passing the curiously named Rue Rifle-Rafle) to reach the *Pl. Richelme* (previously the Pl. aux Herbes), on the N. side of which is the *Post Office*, occupying the *Halle aux Grains* of 1759.

To the N. is another square, on the W. side of which is the *Hôtel de Ville* (1670), with a belfry of 1510.—It houses the *Bibliothèque Méjanes*, founded in 1786 by the Marquis de Méjanes, and containing c. 300,000 volumes, some bindings and MSS from which are displayed.

The Rue Gaston-de-Saporta continues N., in which No. 17, the *Hôtel d'Estienne de St-Jean*, houses the *Musée du Vieil-Aix*, with collections of local interest, including puppets representing the 'Fête-Dieu' procession, discontinued in 1851, and views of Aix, furniture, etc.—In No. 19, the *Hôtel de Châteaurenaud*, with a staircase painted by Daret in 1654, Louis XIV lodged in 1660. No. 23 is the *Hôtel d'Oppède*, accommodating the Faculty of Letters from 1846– 1950, and now departmental archives. The new faculty buildings are in the *Cité Universitaire*, S. of the town.

Opposite is the **Cathedral of St-Sauveur**, a curious edifice of several periods, as reflected in its W. front. The elaborately carved and decorated *W. Doors* (covered, but shown on application), by Jean Guiramand of Toulon (1510), represent the four major prophets and the twelve sibyls. The door of the S. aisle is 12C, but the rest of the facade is 15C, crowned by a 15C octagonal tower restored in the 19C. The lower statues are copies of those destroyed at the Revolution.

Off the S. aisle, in fact the nave of a late 11C church, opens the late 4th or early 5C *Baptistry*, restored in 1579, supported by eight antique monolithic columns.—The central nave is a good example of late 13C Gothic, and contains several interesting paintings, including Nicolas Froment, *The Burning Bush* (du Buisson Ardent), a large triptych with wings representing (l.) King René, with the Magdalen, and SS Anthony and Maurice, and (r.) Jeanne de Laval, René's young second wife, with SS John, Catherine, and Nicholas: the background of the central subject depicts Tarascon and Beaucaire.—Adjoining is a 15C triptych of which only the central panel is original. The green and gilt organs, one mute, will be noted.

In the N. aisle is an altarpiece showing St Martha with the Tarasque (cf. Tarascon), and the tomb of Abp Olivier de Pennart (1484). In the apse is the *Chapelle St-Mitre*, with the saint's 5C sarcophagus, while tablets recording earlier English residents will be noted at the E. end of the S. aisle.

The *Brussels Tapestries* of 1511 which were displayed in the *Choir* (and may be so again, although some were stolen in the late 1970s) were looted from the choir of Canterbury cathedral during the Civil War, and during the Commonwealth were sold to a canon of Aix.

Passing through the S. door, the charming little *Cloister* (late 12th-early 13C; restored) replacing an 11C cloister, is traversed.

To the l. on making our exit, is the former *Archbishop's Palace* (rebuilt between 1650– 1730, and redecorated in 1780), the courtyard of which is used for open-air performances during the July Music Festival.

It contains an excellent collection of *Tapestries*, and also furniture. The finest series (Beauvais) depict 9 (of the original 10) scenes from 'Don Quixote' (1735– 44), after Oudry and Besnier, from designs by Natoire preserved at Compiègne; also Rustic Games (1769), after Leprince; and Grotesques (1689), after Berain and Monnoyer. The *Salon Jaune* is said to have been the scene of the reconciliation of Louis XIV with the Grand Condé in 1660.

On the far side of the boulevard just N. of the cathedral, extends the Av. Pasteur, on the r. of which is the supererogatory monument to Joseph Sec (1792), beyond which stands the *Hôpital St-Jacques*, founded in 1519, enlarged in 1565 and again in the mid 18C, the chapel preserving a door of 1542.—Uphill to the E. of the hospital, in the Av. Paul-Cézanne, is Cézanne's former studio, '*Les Lauves*', containing several souvenirs of the artist.

The Rue du Bon-Pasteur leads W. from the cathedral to the *Établissement Thermal*, built in 1705 and rebuilt in 1923, with a Roman bath in its central hall.—To the N., in the Blvd Jean-Jaurès, is the 14C *Tour de Tourreluque*, sole survivor of the town's 39 rampart towers.

From the far side of the Cours Sextius, the Rue Célony continues W., shortly reaching the entrance (r.) to the fine gardens of the *Pavillon Vendôme, built by Rambot in 1667 for the Duc de Vendôme, governor of the province from 1654; a later owner was J.-B. van Loo, the artist, who died here in 1745. The caryatids on the garden front are notable, while the interior, with its collection of furniture, may also be visited. It has also suffered from the depredations of art thieves.

Following the Rue Van Loo on making our exit, we re-cross the Cours Sextius (in which stands *St-Jean-Baptiste*, of 1692) and continue E. along the Rue des Cordeliers to regain the *Pl. de l'Hôtel de Ville*.

Turning r. down the Rue du Maréchal-Foch, and following the Rue Aude, the Rue Espariat is reached, on the S. side of which is the charming little *Pl. Albertas*, surrounded on three sides by the *Hôtel d'Albertas* of 1745.—By turning r. along the Rue Espariat, the Pl. du Gén de Gaulle is regained, first passing (r.) *St-Esprit*, where Mirabeau married Mlle de Marignane in 1772, while the Gothic *Tower* opposite, with an iron belfry, is a relic of an Augustinian convent of 1494.—By turning l. in the Rue Espariat, we pass (l.) the imposing *Hôtel Boyer d'Eguilles* (by Puget; c. 1675), housing a *Natural History Museum*, containing dinosaur eggs found at Roques-Hautes, c. 8km E. of Aix.—By turning r. at the adjacent *Pl. St-Honoré* along the Rue Clemenceau, the Mirabeau is regained.

Two short excursions (by car) from the centre are those to the site of *Entremont* (see below), while admirers of the art of Victor Vasarely (1908–   ) will visit the *Vasarely Foundation*, some 4km W., and conveniently approached by the Av. de l'Europe, leading W. from the Av. des Belges (S. W. of the Pl. du Gén. de Gaulle).

The characteristic building (1975), a glass, marble, and metallic structure of eight hexagonal cells, is entirely devoted to his designs, other examples of which may be seen at *Gordes*; see Rte 153.

Some 9km further W. (on the D64), beyond the A8, is the imposing *Aqueduct of Roquefavour* (1847), spanning the valley of the Arc, and constructed by the engineer François de Montricher (1810– 48) to carry the waters of the Durance to Marseille.

Entremont lies some 2.5km N. of the cathedral, approached by a continuation of the Av. Pasteur, which climbs steeply to the *Plateau d'Entremont*. It is convenient to park just before a bridge crossed by the N296 and then walk up a signposted path to the r.

Here are the partially excavated ruins of the fortified oppidum of the Salluvian Celts, probably founded early in the 4C B.C., and destroyed by the Romans in 125 B.C. The remains of dry-walled ramparts, of streets, and dwellings, are extensive. Most of the remarkable sculptures unearthed, including numerous characteristic decapitated heads, are preserved in the Musée Granet, Aix.

For the *Montagne de Ste-Victoire*, see Rte 156A; likewise for the road from Aix

to *Fréjus* and *Cannes*; and in the reverse direction, to *Avignon*. For roads from
Sisteron to Aix, and to *Marseille*, see Rte 154.

158 Marseille

MARSEILLE (anglicised as **Marseilles**; 878,700 inhab.; 111,100 in
1801; 491,200 in 1901), the second largest town in France, and its
principal commercial port, is the préfecture of the *Bouches-du-
Rhône*. Although an animated and cosmopolitan city—it being the
'gateway to the Orient', and Africa, has caused its crowds to be colourful—it has few of the attractions of a great metropolis. Writing
two centuries ago, Thicknesse had noted that the city was 'crouded
with men of all nations, walking in the streets in the proper habits of
their country'. Its streets are usually clogged with traffic. It retains
most of the venal characteristics concomitant with being a Mediter-
ranian port, is spite of the fact that parts of the once notorious harbour area were demolished during the last war. '. . . it has few fine
public buildings or sights for strangers' wrote Murray in the 1840s,
and this is still true, while Arthur Young somewhat unkindly referred to the Vieux Port as a 'horse-pond' when comparing it to the
Garonne at Bordeaux! It has a reputation for its sea-food, and here
'Bouillabaisse' is claimed to be found at its best.

The *Massalia* of the Greeks and the *Massilia* of the Romans was founded c. 600
B.C. by a colony of Phocaeans. The settlement, commanding the natural trade
route of the Rhône valley, prospered, soon becoming the rival of Carthage, and
the ally of Rome. Caesar besieged and took the city in 49 B.C. as it had espoused
the cause of Pompey, and partially demolished its fortifications, while Arles and
Fréjus thrived during its temporary eclipse. As a seat of learning it was praised
by Cicero and Tacitus.
   The medieval city was rich enough, in 1249, to furnish all the galleys required
by Louis IX to transport his army in the 7th Crusade. It was taken by Charles
d'Anjou, Count of Provence, in 1252, but was soon outstripped in maritime importance by Genoa, Pisa, and Venice. it was sacked by Alfonso of Aragón in
1423, who carried off the chain across the harbour mouth; it now hangs in the
cathedral of Valencia. However, it repulsed the Constable of Bourbon in 1524,
and held out against Henri IV long after Paris had submitted, while in 1660 Louis
XIV was constrained to enter the city through a breach in its walls. Its Chamber
of Commerce was established in 1599.
   Bp Belsunce and the Chevalier de Roze were the heroes of the plague in 1720,
which carried off half of its 80,000 inhabitants, burying the dead when galley-
slaves had fled in terror. At the Revolution its populace supplied many radical
supporters, led by Barbaroux, while the revolutionary hymn 'to the Army of the
Rhine', composed by an Alsatian officer, Rouget de Lisle (1760 – 1836), sung by
troops marching thence to Paris in 1792, thus became known as the
'Marseillaise'. The Reign of Terror at Marseille itself, lead by Fréron and Barras,
was characterised by frightful atrocities and was prolonged even after the death
of Robespierre.
   In the 19C its commerce increased rapidly with the French occupation of N.
Africa and the opening of the Suez Canal (1869), and its harbour was extended to
accommodate great liners. It suffered considerably from air attacks during the
Second World War (by the Germans and Italians in 1940, and by the Allies in
1943–44), while its once picturesque but profligate port quarter, a focus of
Resistance, was partly razed during the German occupation. In Aug. 1944, prior
to evacuating the city, the Germans mined the harbour, and wrought havoc with
its installations, destroying also the transporter bridge crossing the Vieux-Port.
But the place was then encircled, and the garrison of 17,500 German troops
capitulated.
   The harbour works have been replaced and very considerably extended dur-

ing the last four decades, with larger dry docks and improved railway communications, etc., and an underpass has replaced the bridge. Subsidiary ports were created on the *Étang de Berre*, to the N.W., at *Lavéra* (an oil port), and at *Fos* (see Rte 149B), but they have not expanded entirely as planned, and their prosperity is still in the balance.

Marseille was the birthplace of Petronius Arbiter (d. A.D. 66); the troubadour Folquet de Marseille (d. 1231); Honoré d'Urfé (1567–1625); the sculptor Pierre Puget (1620–94); Désirée Clary (1777–1860), who married Gén. Bernadotte and became queen of Sweden; Adolphe Thiers (1797–1877), and Émile Ollivier (1825–1913), statesmen; Honoré Daumier (1808–79), the caricaturist; the artist Adolphe Monticelli (1824–86); the dramatist Edmond Rostand (1868–1918); and Darius Milhaud (1892–1974), the composer. Arthur Rimbaud (1854–91), died in the Hôpital de la Conception here.

The approach most likely to bring one without undue delays into the centre of Marseille is the A7 motorway from the N., or the branch off this leading to and under the Vieux-Port, which will be extended under the hill of N.-D.-de-la-Garde to join the A52 from the E.

Passing at the *Pl. Jules-Guesde* an *Arc de Triomphe* of 1832 (on the axis of the main transverse thoroughfare—with one-way traffic coming from the opposite direction), we bear r. and turn to descend to the *Quai des Belges*, on the E. side of the **Vieux-Port**, with parking facilities—notably expensive, *déférence aux ordres*—in the vicinity.

The *Old Harbour*, the *Lacydon* of the Greeks, was until 1844 the only harbour at Marseille, its mouth guarded on the S. by *Fort St-Nicolas* (1665), and on the N. by *Fort St-Jean*, a former castle of the Knights of Malta, with a tower of 1447, enlarged in 1664.

There is a S.I. at the lower end of the broad *Canebière* (from the Provençal 'canabé', hemp, from the rope-walk which once occupied its site), which ascends gradually almost at right-angles to the port, and which shortly intersects the N.—S. artery of the city at the Cours St-Louis.—On the N. side of the Canebière stands the *Bourse* (1860) with its Corinthian colonnade. The Ground Floor is now occupied by the *Maritime Museum*, with a good collection of ship models, paintings and prints, etc. Above is the *Chamber of Commerce*, with a notable library.

It was near here that Alexander I of Yugoslavia was assassinated in 1934.

Immediately behind the Bourse is an area recently excavated and laid out as gardens, where considerable relics of the *Greek Ramparts* may be viewed, while a *Musée d'Histoire* has also been inaugurated, in which a Roman merchant ship of the 2C, discovered in 1974, is displayed.

From the N.E. corner of the port, the *Quai du Port* leads W., shortly passing the *Hôtel de Ville* (1672), built by Pierre Puget's brother, Gaspard, incongruous among the dull uniformity of the arcaded blocks of apartments which have replaced the characteristic tenements previously overlooking the busy harbour.—On a height to the N. stands the huge *Hôtel-Dieu*, mainly 17C, preserving a 14C belfry.

Immediately N. of the Hôtel de Ville stands the *Maison Diamantée* (1576;) deriving its name from its diamond-pointed facade), housing the **Musée du Vieux-Marseille**, with an interesting collection of plans and prints; maquettes of Marseille in 1848 and of the port; a model of the old Transporter bridge; Provençal furniture; local costumes; santons; numismatic collections; and an important section illustrating the manufacture of playing-cards by the firm of Camoin. Note also the wood and stucco staircase.

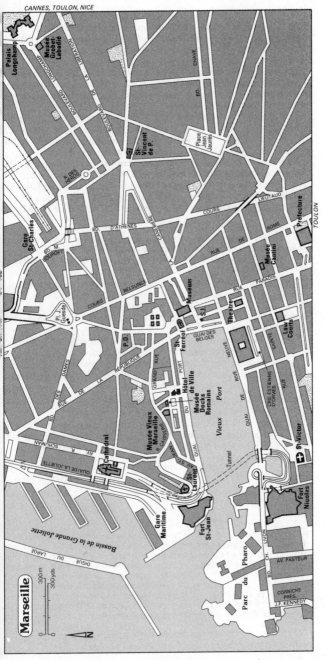

CANNES, TOULON, NICE

Marseille

Palais Longchamp

Musée Grobet-Labadié

St-Vincent de P.

Place Jean Jaurès

CHAVE

BD

BD. DE LA VALETTE

BOULEVARD LONGCHAMP

R. DES HÉROS

LIEUTAUD

Gare St-Charles

BD. M. BOURDET

BD. D'ATHÈNES

CANEBIÈRE

COURS

RUE DE ROME

Préfecture

TOULON

Musée Cantini

COURS BELSUNCE

PL. Guesde

RUE DE LA RÉPUBLIQUE

BD. DES DAMES

COURS

P.O.

Museum

St-Ferréol

QUAI DES BELGES

PARADIS

RUE

S.J.

Théâtre

Law Courts

RUE NEUVE

RUE SAINTE

CRS. ESTIENNE D'ORVES

GRAND' RUE

RUE CASSERIE

Hôtel de Ville

Musée Docks Romains

QUAI DU PORT

Vieux Port

QUAI DE RIVE NEUVE

AV. R. SCHUMAN

Cathédral

Musée Vieux Marseille

R. ST-JEAN

St-Laurent

QUAI

Tunnel

St-Victor

QUAI DE LA JOLIETTE

Gare Maritime

Fort St-Jean

Fort Niccolas

BD. CH. LIVON

Bassin de la Grande Joliette

DIGUE DU LARGE

Parc du Pharo

AV. PASTEUR

CORNICHE PRÉS. J.F. KENNEDY

300 m

300 yds

N

A few paces further W. brings on to the **Roman Docks Museum**, where, in situ, one may see their remains, dating from the 1C A.D., discovered in 1947. A number of artefacts found here—lead anchors, amphorae, etc.—are grouped around the huge storage jars (dolia) which are in their original positions.

Continuing W., the quay is regained just S. of slight traces of a *Roman Theatre*, built in the Greek manner.—Steps ascend to restored *St-Laurent* (on the site of a Temple of Apollo), mainly Romanesque, with an octagonal 18C belfry.

On turning N., we obtain a view of the modern dock area, and the conspicuously ugly '*New' Cathedral* (known as *La Major*; 1852–93), designed by Léon Vaudoyer in a neo-Byzantine style on a Gothic ground plan, with alternative courses of green and white stone.

Immediately to the E. are the remains of the *Old Cathedral*, a 12C Provençal-Romanesque structure, with two 14C chapels beside the apse. The unremarkable interior contains statues of Lazarus and his sisters by Francesco Laurana (1483), an altar of c. 1175, and a plaque by Luca della Robbia.—Relics of the late 17C *Bishop's Palace* lie to the S.E.

From the apse end of the New Cathedral a bridge crosses the once-famous *Quai de la Joliette* to an esplanade over the *Gare Maritime* (1953), providing a general view over part of the new harbour extending N., and protected by an immense artificial breakwater.

From the E. side of the Old Cathedral, one may ascend steps to the E., and fork l. and l. again to reach the main entrance to the 17C **Hospice de la Vieille Charité**, under restoration, with a chapel designed by Pierre Puget; temporary exhibitions are held in the W. wing of the building.

To the S. is a colourful warren of alleys which are better avoided after dark, all that remains of this vitiated *Quartier de Vieux-Port*.

By working our way E. from the Hospice, the Rue de la République is soon reached, uniting the *Pl. de la Joliette* with the Quai des Belges, which is regained by turning downhill to the r.

At the S. end of the Quai du Belges is the *Cours Étienne-d'Orves*, formerly the Quai du Canal (filled in), isolating the warehouses between it and the Quai du Rive Neuve, now a tastefully restored area; here also are a covered market, several restaurants, and a good bookshop.

Towards the W. end of the quay is the *Théâtre de la Criée* (1981), previously the fish-auction house.—Steps ascend to a higher level, where on turning r., the ancient abbey-church of **St-Victor** is approached.

Founded in the 5C, it was one of the two oldest monastic foundations in France; the other was at *Lérins* (cf.). It was destroyed by the Saracens in 923, and rebuilt in the 11-12C, in the 14C being furnished with battlemented square towers. During the Revolution the cloister and conventual dependencies were demolished.

The upper church (early 13C) reveals the transition from the round to pointed arch, and the porch has one of the earliest Gothic vaults in Provence (mid 12C). The sacristan, if available, will show the earlier and lower church (or crypt), a 'martyrium' erected c. 415 in the pagan necropolis by St Cassianus to honour the relics of St Victor, and containing several sarcophagi of interest.

Below the church lies the *Bassin de Carénage*, now circled by the exit and approached roads of the Vieux-Port tunnel.

On a height to the S.E. is **N.-D. de la Garde**, built on the site of a chapel of 1214, which since 1864 has figured too prominently in photographs of Marseille. It was erected by Espérandieu in the then fashionable neo-Byzantine style, and is sur-mounted by a belfry crowned by a gilded image. Its interior is remarkable only for the mariners' ex-votos which line it, and for the models of ships that are there suspended. The ascent to its terrace can be made by car for the view it commands. The famous funicular no longer runs.

For the road beyond St-Victor, see below.—One may return to the centre by the Rue Sainte, leading E.

Some minutes' walk will bring one to the Rue Paradis, which with the parallel Rue St-Ferréol (pedestrians only), are the principal shopping streets (in which curiously inelegant clothes are fashionable); further E. is the Rue de Rome, the main transverse thoroughfare.

The *Opéra* is just N.W. of the junction of the Rue Sainte with the Rue Paradis, while at No. 19 Rue Grignan, to its S.E., a mansion of 1694 houses the **Musée Cantini**, with excellent collections of Marseille and Moustiers ceramics, among others, but the building is mainly important for the loan exhibitions held there.—Facing the S. end of the Rue St-Ferréol stands the *Préfecture* of 1867.

The *Musée des Beaux-Arts* may be approached (preferably by car) by following the Canebière and its extension, the Blvd de la Libération, for c. 2km inland, to reach a road junction, where by turning abruptly l. along the Blvd Philipon the *Palais Longchamp* is reached.

Built by Espérandieu in 1870, it consists of two wings united by Ionic colonnades, in the centre of which is the *château d'eau* of the aqueduct bringing water from the Durance to Marseille. in front are a cascade, and sculptured groups by Cavalier and Barye.

The **Musée des Beaux-Arts**, in the N. wing, is in the process of re-organisation, but among the more notable works at present on display are: *Rubens*, Boar-hunt; *Brueghel de Velours*, Air and Fire; *Jean van Bylert*, Male, and Female portraits; *Ribera*, Juan de Procida; *David Teniers*, The Monkey Guard; *Martin Faber*, two Self-portraits; *Louis Finson* (*Finsonius*), The Magdalen in ecstasy; *Jean Daret*, A Magistrate; *Largillière*, A Gentleman; *Rigaud*, Louis Boucherat; *Michel Serre* (1658–1733), two Views of Marseille (including one of the Hôtel de Ville) during the plague of 1720–23.

Other rooms are devoted to the sculpture and paintings of *Pierre Puget*; also a section of African ethnography, and it is probable that among rooms to be opened in the near future will be one devoted to the work of *Daumier*.

The S. wing contains a *Natural History Museum*, while behind the building is a *Zoological Garden*.

No. 140 Blvd Longchamp (first on the l. of the street descending opposite the Palais) houses the ***Musée Grobet-Labadié**, with varied collections of art and furniture, tapestries, and musical instruments, etc., donated to the municipality in 1920, and reflecting the personalities of those who assembled them. Among the paintings are charming portraits of Arlésiennes by *Antoine Raspal*, Portraits by *Roslin*, *Drolling*, and *Nattier*, etc., and representative works by *Monticelli*.

Parc Borély (by car)

Although this may be approached more directly from the centre by following the umbrageous Av. du Prado, the S. extension of the Rue de Rome, an alternative is along the coast from the S. quay of the Vieux-Port, passing *Fort St-Nicolas* (l.) and (r.) the *Parc du Pharo*, beyond which the rocky cove of *Anse des Catalans* is reached, providing a view of the offshore islands, including the *Château d'If*; see below.—The Corniche Président J.F. Kennedy is followed, later passing new beaches and yacht basins, etc. prior to turning l. into the Av. du Prado.—The coast road continues to *Cap Croisette*, the extremity of the *Massif of Marseilleveyre*.

Just S. of the Avenue, beyond the little river Huveaune, is the *Parc Borély*, with a racecourse and botanical gardens.

The **Musée Borély** is installed in an imposing château built by Joseph Esprit Brun (1710–1804) for Louis de Borély during the years 1766–78, which preserves several splendidly decorated rooms, among them the Galerie Parrocel, containing 14 paintings of the story of Tobias by *Pierre Parrocel*; and the Dining-room, decorated with plaster plaques; while notable among the paintings is a St Peter, attrib. to *Zurbarán*, in the Chapel.

The Clot-Bey collection of *Egyptian Antiquities* is of importance, containing a black granite statue of the goddess Neith, and numerous smaller statuettes, together with a bronze of the cat-goddess Bastet, etc.; the mummies of Noub-en-Ouseret, and Tentamon; several well carved stellae; cult objects, talismans, and chaouabtis, etc.; canopic vases; Greco-Roman funerary masks; Coptic fabrics, etc.

Other rooms contain collections from Susa, and Cyprus; while in adjacent galleries are Phoenician, Greek, and Roman antiquities found in the neighbourhood of Marseille, including finds from Roquepertuse, among them Celtic statues.

Upper floors display the Feuillet de Borsat donation of *Drawings*, largely of the French School, with rooms devoted to the art of *Hubert Robert, Boucher, Fragonard, Lancret, Greuze*, et al, together with examples of other European Schools; also paintings and pastels, among the former a Portrait of a young girl, attrib. to *Goya*.

Driving N.E. along the Av. du Prado, the Rondpoint is reached, to the E. of which is the *Parc Amable-Chanot*, site of trade fairs, radio and T.V. studios, and a sports stadium, etc.—Further S., to the W. of the Blvd Michelet, is the *Cité Radieuse* (1952), which will be visited by admirers of the vertical art of *Le Corbusier*.

The Château d'If

Allow 1½ hours for this excursion by launch from the Quai des Belges. Leaving the Vieux-Port, the *Château du Pharo* (l.) is passed, to approach the *Îles du Frioul*, the bare islet of *Ifs* backed by the larger *Île Ratonneau* and *Île Pomègues*, the last two now connected. The **Château d'If**, ◇ a good specimen of 16C military architecture, was built for François I in 1524, and was long used as a State prison. It is best known from its description in 'The Count of Monte-Cristo', by Dumas *père*, and the gloomy dungeons of Edmond Dantès and the Abbé Faris are duly pointed out.

More historical are the condemned cell on the staircase, and the cells, airy and with sea views, in which were confined the Marquis de la Valette; the 'Man in the Iron Mask' (cf. Îles de Lérins); Glandèves de Niozelles, imprisoned for six years for failing to 'uncover' before Louis XIV; Mirabeau, mewed up at the request of his father; and Prince Casimir of Poland, etc. The terrace commands a wide view, while to the S.W. one may discern the *Phare du Planier*.

For roads from Marseille to *Nîmes*, see Rte 149, and to *Aix* and *Sisteron*, Rte 154, both in reverse; for *Toulon*, and *St-Maximin*, see Rte 159.

159 Marseille to Toulon

There are three main routes: **A.**, the B52 motorway, which drives through some very attractive country, and provides wide views; **B.**, the inland N8; and **C.**, the coastal N559. The latter can also be used in conjunction with the motorway, which also provides an easier access to the N8.

Maps: IGN 67, or 115; also 269 for the 'Calanques'. M 245.

A. A52 and then B52; 64km (40 miles). Perhaps the best way to join the motorway is to follow the Av. du Prado S. to the main roundabout, there turning l. along the Blvd Rabatau. We then bear due E. through industrial suburbs towards (16km) *Aubagne*, birthplace of Marcel Pagnol (1895–1974), with potteries, and after 1962 the H.Q. of the obsolescent French Foreign Legion. Here the motorway divides: the l. branch leading towards the A8, or the N7 at *St-Maximin*; see below. We bear r.

AUBAGNE TO ST-MAXIMIN (34km). The alternative hill-road via *Gémenos*, perhaps better approached from the N8, is first described. The D2 ascends steeply from *Gémenos* towards the *Roque Forcade* (936m), at the W. extremity of the *Massif de la Ste-Baume*.

The Sainte-Baume is a white limestone ridge c. 15km long, with *Bertagne* (1041m) at its W. end, and rising to 1147m at its E. end, with the crest of *St-Pilon* (994km) at a central point. Its main cliff protects from the hot S. wind a deciduous forest, remarkable at this latitude, which may have once been a sacred grove before it acquired its Christian sanctity.

At 3km the *Parc de St-Pons* (r.), with the remains of a 13C abbey, is passed. After crossing the *Col de l'Espigoulier* (728m) at 15km the D80 is followed to the E. for 6.5km to reach the *Hostellerie de la Ste-Baume*, in a former convent, also approached by the track from *St-Zacharie*; see below.—A marked path ascends steeply hence through the forest towards the peak of *St-Pilon*, which may be ascended for the view, to the W. of which (path marked) is the *Grotte de la Ste-Baume* in the face of the limestone cliff, where Mary Magdalen is traditionally said to have spent here latter days; cf. St-Maximin. Hermits and monks who later established themselves here were scattered by the Barbarians, and the spot was forgotten until the revival of the cult in the 13C. Angels conveyed her daily to the summit of St-Pilon to pray: mere mortals will have to climb, for their sins.—Returning to the Hostellerie, we continue E., after 1km turning l. down to (8km) *Nans-les-Pins*, a pleasant village among pine-woods, with ruins of an older settlement to the N., and 3km beyond, crossroads on the N560 are reached 9km S.W. of *St-Maximin*.

The main road (A52) merges after 12km with the N560, almost immediately after which the first of several hill-roads climb to the S. into the *Massif de la Ste-Baume*; see above. Another ascends from (5km) *St-Zacharie*, and after 6km a third mounts r. through *Nans-les-Pins*; see above.—At 3km beyond the latter turning, we fork l. to (9km) *St-Maximin-la-Ste-Baume*; see Rte 156A.

The B52 motorway veers S., avoiding (r.) the new town of *Carnoux-en-Provence*, built to house the opprobriously named 'pieds-noirs' from French N. Africa, and winds through the *Pas d'Ouillier* and then the *Pas de Bellefille*, with an exit to and view of **Cassis** to the S.W. (see below), and shortly beyond, an exit to **La Ciotat**, just past which (l.) is *Ceyreste*, once the Greek colony of *Kitharista*. The bay of *La Ciotat* is briefly approached before the road makes a wide circle inland, passing between the hilltop villages of (r.) *La Cadière*, and *Le Castellet*, again nearing the sea at **Bandol** (exit).—To the l. rises the ridge of *Le Gros Cerveau* (429m); to the r. lies **Sanary**, and beyond, the *Îles de Embiez*, as **Toulon** is approached, dominated to the N. by *Mont Faron*.—To the r. rises the *Fort of Six-Fours*, and beyond, at the

W. end of the *Petite Rade*, lies *La Seyne*, as the W. suburbs are traversed, passing (r.) the old *Fort of Malbousquet*, and the *Arsenal Maritime*; see below.

B. A52 for 16km, then B52 for c. 2km before turning onto the N8. 64km (40 miles).

Rte A is followed past (l.) *Aubagne*. The first l.-hand turning off the N8 leads 2km to *Gémenos*; see above. The road ascends to the *Col des Anges*, with the main limestone ridge of the *Massif de la Ste-Baume* rising to the N.; see above. Traversing *Cuges-les-Pins*, we climb again before descending to *Le Beausset*, with a distant view of the bay of *La Ciotat*. Ahead rises *Le Gros Cerveau* (429m), and to the l., *Mont Caume* (801m). The *Gorges d'Ollioulles*, where the Reppe has gouged its way through the limestone hills, is threaded, with the deserted village of *Évenos* on the l., and *Ollioules*, with a Romanesque church and arcaded houses, is traversed. To the N.E. rises the *Bau de 4 Heures* (576m), and ahead, *Mont Faron*, above **Toulon**, which is shortly entered; see below.

C. N559. 68km (42 miles). A slow and hilly road, offering numerous sea views, traversing (22km) **Cassis**—10km **La Ciotat**—17km **Bandol**—4km **Sanary**—to (15km) **Toulon**.

Driving S. along the wide Av. du Prado, continued by the Blvd Michelet, with its triple lines of plane trees, we later veer E.—To the S.W. rises the rugged and waterless *Massif de Marseilleveyre* (432m), beyond which are several barren offshore islands; to the S.E., is the *Massif de Puget* (564m). Between the two are several *Calanques* or rocky creeks, approached by minor roads.

The road commences to climb, with a view (r.) of *Luminy*, with a new *Cité Universitaire*, perhaps the cradle of future luminaries, and with a good retrospective view on the ascent to the *Col de la Gineste* (327m), with *Mont Carpiagbe* (646m) to the N. A bare upland plateau is crossed, skirting (l.) a military camp, while ahead, on the descent to Cassis, is the towering cliff of *Cap Canaille* (362m), rising precipitously from the bay.

Cassis (6,300 Cassidiens), a lively fishing-port and crowded summer resort, is overlooked to the E. by a ruined château built by François des Baux in 1381. Cassis was the birthplace of the Abbé J.-J. Barthélemy (1715–95), author of 'Voyage de jeune Anacharsis en Grèce'. The ancient *Carsici Portus* was rebuilt in the 18C, and several houses of this period survive around the *Pl. Baragnon*, just E. of the harbour. The excursion by boat, in calm weather, may be made to the neighbouring calanques, to the W.—Those with heads for heights may follow the cliff-top road to *La Ciotat*.

The N559 climbs steeply to the N.E., past vineyards producing a good white wine, before turning S., and descending below the motorway to **La Ciotat** (31,700 Ciotadens), with important ship-building yards to the S. nearer the *Cap de l'Aigle*, off which lies the *Île Verte*. The church, of 1626, on the N. side of the harbour, contains a Deposition by Finsonius.

4km inland, just N. of the motorway, is the village of *Ceyreste*, once the Greek colony of *Kitharista*, of which La Ciotat was the port.

We bear inland behind the resort of *Les Lecques*, to the S. of which is a small *Archaeological Museum*, and turn r. in *St-Cyr-sur-Mer*, passing as the road ascends the 17C *Château des Baumelles*, surrounded by vineyards.—The N559 climbs down to **Bandol**, once a pleasant sheltered resort, now with 6,700 inhab., where Katherine Mansfield wrote 'Prelude' in the spring of 1916, and where died Louis Lumière (1864–1948), who was the first to exhibit cinema films (1895).—The offshore *Île de Bendoe* sports a pseudo-Provençal tourist complex.

Skirting the bay, with a view of the *Gros Cerveau* ridge to the N., **Sanary-sur-Mer** is shortly entered, a frequented resort with a palm-shaded quay and fishing harbour. Aldous Huxley passed some time here.

To the S. lie the *Îles de Embiez*, with a light-house, and a power-boat complex promoted by a pastis-manufacturer, overlooked by the ruined medieval *Château de Sabran.*—On the adjacent coast is *Le Brusc*, possibly the site of the Greco-Roman port of *Tauroentum*; slight relics of a subterranean aqueduct can still be seen near the Six-Fours road.

The N559 turns inland between (l.) the old village and *Fort of Six-Fours*, on the site of 5C or earlier buildings, the church of which, partly 17C, but partly Romanesque on much earlier foundations, contains a 16C polyptfch attrib. to Jean de Troyes.

Some 5km S. is *N.-D.-du-Mai* (1625), erected on an earlier look-out tower (328m) above *Cap Sicié*, commanding a wide view.

Industrial *La Seyne*, with ship-building yards, is traversed on approaching Toulon.

TOULON (181,400 Toulonnais; 20,500 in 1801; 101,600 in 1901), which has replaced Draguignan as the préfecture of the *Var*, is, with its fine roadstead, protected by the peninsula of *St-Mandrier*, the principal naval base of France. Behind it is an amphitheatre of hills, and the town itself is dominated by the fortified heights of Mont Faron. Although most of the picturesque 18C centre survived the damage caused to the harbour during 1943–44, the tasteless rebuilding of the quays has destroyed much of its colour and charm.

Telo Martius was a Roman naval station, also noted for its purple dyes obtained from the murex. Its bishopric dates from 514. Sibylle, last descendant of the Viscounts of Marseille, bequeathed the lordship of Toulon to Charles d'Anjou, and in 1481 it passed to France. Louis XII fortified the place, and his Tour Royale still stands, while further extensive works erected in the 17C enabled Tessé to withstand the combined attacks of an Austrian and Sardinian army under Prince Eugène and an English and Dutch fleet commanded by Sir Cloudesley Shovell in 1707, during the War of the Spanish Succession. Nevertheless, most of the French fleet was scuttled or put out of action by Shovell's bombardment. In 1720–21 some 17,000 of its 26,000 inhabitants died of plague.

At the Revolution Toulon was handed over to the British by its Royalist citizens, but after a three months' siege, during which Bonaparte, a 24-year-old artillery officer, distinguished himself, the Republican army under Dugommier captured the forts of *Mulgrave* (or *Petit Gibraltar*), *Eguillette*, and *Faron*, which commanded the roadstead, and compelled the British fleet under Hood to withdraw (13 Dec., 1793), leaving the city to the savage vengeance of the Conventionals under Fréron and Fouché.

It was bombed by the Italians in 1940, and in Nov. 1942 some 60 ships of the French Mediterranean fleet were scuttled in the harbour to prevent them from falling into German (or British) hands. In the following year the town and port, strongly fortified by the occupying Germans, were heavily bombed by Allied aircraft until on 25 Aug. 1944 Toulon was recaptured by the French relief forces under Gén. Lattre de Tassigny, who had landed further E.

Among its natives were Louis-Michel van Loo (1707–71), the artist; Ferdinand Brunetière (1849–1906), the literary historian and critic; and Jules Muraire Raimu'; 1883–1946), the actor.

Toulon handed over to the British

The transverse Av. Gén. Leclerc, continued by the Blvd de
Strasbourg, bisects central Toulon. Near the W. end is the *Jardin
Alexandre-Ier*, adjacent to which is the **Museum** and *Library* (the latter preserving an important numismatic collection). The collection
of paintings (including works by *Carraci, Brueghel, Fragonard,* and
David, among others, and more modern works) is at present closed
for extensive re-organisation, as is the archaeological section.

Some distance further E. is the *Théâtre* of 1862, to the S. of which
are the narrow alleys of old Toulon (now partly a pedestrian
precinct). To the S.E. is the *Pl. Puget*, with its dolphin fountain of
1782, whence the Rues Hoche and d'Alger are followed to reach the
Quai Stalingrad, now flanked by ugly arcaded concrete structures
overlooking the old harbour or *Darse Vieille* of 1589.—To the r. a
modern building is supported by telamones carved by Pierre Puget

A short distance to the W. brings us to the entrance to the *Naval
Arsenal* (no adm.), immediately to the S. of which is its old monumental *Gateway* (1738), four marble columns supporting an attic storey
in which figure Mars and Bellona. It now provids the entrance to the
new **Naval Museum** (1981), containing a good collection of ships
models, marine paintings, etc., illustrating the history of the port
and the development of the French Navy; see also *Tour Royale*
below.

To the N. is the *Pl. d'Armes*, laid out by Colbert in 1683.

Towards the E. end of the Rue de la République, parallel to the
Darse Vieille, stands 18C *St-François-de-Paule,* where one may turn
N. along the tree-lined Cours Lafayette, with its colourful morning
market.—The Traverse de la Cathédrale (l.) approaches the
Cathedral of Ste-Marie-Majeure, three bays of which date from the
13C, the rest from 1661. The dark interior is of slight interest.

At No. 69 in the Cours is the *Musum of Old Toulon* (rarely open)
with local collections, almost opposite which the Rue Garibaldi lead
E. to the *Porte d'Italie,* a relic of Henri IV's town wall.—Thence, turning N., the W. end of the Blvd de Strasbourg is soon regained.

From the Rond-Point Bonaparte (at the E. end of the *Av. de la République*) on

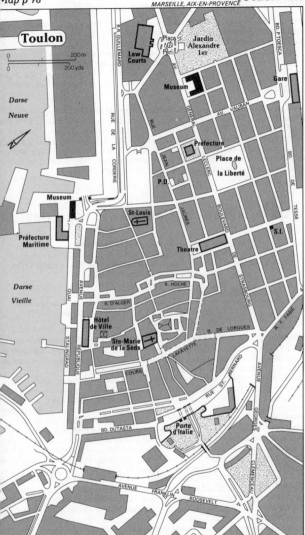

AIRPORT, FRÉJUS

may follow—preferably by car—an avenue leading S. and skirting the *Port Marchand* (1840; with the *Gare Maritime*), to traverse the suburb of *Le Mourillon* to the **Tour Royale** (or *Grosse Tour de la Mitre*; 1524). Previously used as a prison, its seven cylindrical casements now house an extension of the naval museum. Built on a promontory between the *Petite Rade* (W.) and the *Grande Rade*, it commands a wide view, while to the S. extends a long breakwater.—By returning N. and shortly turning r. a small harbour is reached, protected by *Fort St-Louis* (1697), beyond which the Littoral Frédéric-Mistral leads E., with its beaches, overlooked by *Fort Lamalgue*; *Cap Brun* rises further E.

A longer EXCURSION (18km) is that to *Mont Faron*. This is best approached by car by following the D46 N.W. from the W. end of the Av. Gén. Leclerc, and then turning r. onto the steeply mounting V40 to the *Tour Beaumont* (507m), an old fort enlarged to form the *Memorial to the Allied landings in Provence* in Aug. 1944, with a small museum containing an explanatory diorama, etc. The coastal views are splendid as the circuit is continued (on the V41) before descending towards central Toulon.—The excursion may also be made by taking the Télépherique, its lower terminus just N. of the Blvd du Faron, which ascends directly to the Tour Beaumont.

Another view over the Toulon roadstead may be obtained from the peninsula or *Presqu'île de St-Mandrier*, S. of the port, approached directly by launch from the Quai Stalingrad, or by road by turning l. off the main Marseille road through *La Seyne*, and later passing the forts of *L'Eguillette* and *Balaguier* (containing a small naval museum) to reach the old resort of *Tamaris*, title of a novel written near-by in 1861 by George Sand. On the sandy isthmus connecting St-Mandrier to the mainland lies the resort of *Les Sablettes*, rebuilt since 1944.

160 Toulon to Cannes via the Coast

148km (91 miles). C52 and N98. 18km **Hyères**—17km N559.—6km *Le Lavandou*—20km *Cavalaire*—13km *La Roux* crossroads, 5.5km E. of which on N98. 9km **St-Tropez**—N98. 9km **Ste-Maxime**—21km **Fréjus**—3km **St-Raphael**—41km **Cannes**.

Maps: IGN 68, or 115. M 245.

A faster direct, but inland, road is N97 from Toulon to (58km) *Le Cannet-des-Maures*, on the N7 or A8 motorway; see Rte 156A. This is first described.

TOULON TO LE CANNET-DES-MAURES (58km). The C52 motorway drives N.E., circling below *Le Courdon* (702m), with its fort, to (15km) *Solliès-Pont*, noted for its cherries, while the 12C church of *Solliès-Ville* is built on the foundations of a Roman temple, and contains an organ-case of 1499.
  Hence the D554 turns l. towards St-Maximin, ascending the Gapeau valley.—After 11km the D202 turns W. to a lane (l.) to the Carthusian monastery of *Montrieux-le-Jeune*, founded in 1117, rebuilt in 1843 (adm. to chapel only).—1km further W. are the slight remains of the original monastery (Montrieux-le-Vieux), abandoned in the 12C. The surrounding woods hide the curiously weathered 'cité dolomitique' of *Valbelle*.—The main road continues N. via (2km) *Méounes-lès-Montrieux* to (7km) *La Roquebrussanne*; see Rte 156A.
  The N97 bears N.E. at Solliès to by-pass (6km) *Cuers*.—Hence the D14 leads E. via (6.5km) *Pierrefeu-du-Var*, picturesquely sited, ascending the Collobrières valley to (15km) the old village of *Collobrières*, a centre of the cork industry in the heart of the *Massif des Maures* (see p 841), overlooked to the N.E. by *La Sauvette* (779m).—A minor road winds 25km further E. to *Grimaud* (see below), off which, after 5.5km, a track (r.) leads c. 5km to the beautifully situated but dilapidated ruins (mainly 18C) of the *Chartreuse de la Verne*, founded in 1170 and abandoned at the Revolution.
  Puget-Ville (8km from Cuers) lies at the foot of a hill crowned by a 12C tower, 8km beyond which *Pignans* is traversed, to the E. of which, in the mountains at a height of 771m, stands the hermitage of *N.-D.-des-Anges* (with a crude image attrib. to the anchoress Nymphaea, sister of St Maximinus; see St-Maximin), providing a wide view, from which a hill-road climbs down to *Gonfaron* (6.5km from Pignans), 12km beyond which the N7 is met just prior to *Le Cannet-des-Maures*, for which, and for the road beyond, see Rte 156A.

The C52 motorway drives N.E. from **Toulon** (Rte 159), commanded to the N. by *Le Courdon* (702m), with its fort, passing (l.) the suburb of *La Valette-du-Var* (the church preserving a 12C choir), where Mme Mère (Letizia Bonaparte) retired in 1793 during the troubles caused by Paoli in Corsica.—The N98 shortly bears r., passing to the S., the

old village of *La Garde* perched above the modern town, and continues due E. to *Hyères*; by-pass under construction.

It may also be approached by a coast road (N559) via the small
resort of *Carqueiranne*, beyond its cape, the E. limit of the *Grande
Rade de Toulon.*

HYÈRES (41,700 Hyérois), although one of the older winter resorts
on the Riviera, and with a resident English colony until 1939, gives
the appearance of a town of fallen fortunes—at least the upper town.
Following Lady Craven's advice, Arthur Young went 'upon a wild-
goose chase to Hyeres', adding 'one would think this country, from
her's and many other descriptions, was all a garden; but it has been
praised much beyond its merits'. And the landlord of the Hôtel de
Necker worried him 'with a list of English that pass the Winter at
Hyeres; there are many houses built for letting ...'. Murray
reiterated that apart from its mild climate it had 'certainly been too
much cried up in other respects'; it continued to be visited, nevertheless, by Tolstoy, in 1860 (his brother Nicholas died here); by Edith
Wharton; by R.L. Stevenson, in 1888 (who here wrote the 'Child's
Garden of Verses', and the 'Black Arrow'); and Queen Victoria
honoured it with her presence. Jules Michelet died here in 1874, and
Ambrose Thomas lived here from 1883–95.

The first settlement was that of a Greek colony from Marseille, and known as
Olbia, 5km S. The inland fortress was also of early foundation, and it was here in
1254 that Louis IX landed on returning from the 7th Crusade. it was occupied by
Sir Cloudesley Shovell during the blockade of Toulon in 1707. Here was born
J.-B. Massillon (1663–1742), the preacher.

A narrow main road separates the modern resort, with its villas and
palm-lined boulevards, from the older town of steep lanes, which
may be conveniently explored from the *Pl. Clemenceau*, to its E. A
few steps to the N.W. is the shady *Pl. de la République*, with *St-Louis*,
(13C, altered in the early 19C), with a plain wide nave in which Louis
IX made his devotions after disembarking.—From the *Porte de la
Rade* the Rue Massillon ascends to the *Pl. Massillon*, dominated by
the former *Commandery of the Templars*, flanked by the *Tour St-
Blaise*.—The Rue Ste-Catherine climbs hence to the *Pl. St-Paul* (view),
from which steps ascend to the disused church (16C, with a
Romanesque facade), abutting which is the 13C *Porte de Baruc*,
through which one enters the Rue Paradis, preserving a restored
13C house.—The *Porte des Princes* stands a short distance to the W.
of the Place.—On the summit of the hill (240m) are the ruins of the
castle, dismantled in 1620, within a fortified enceinte of the 13C.

The Rue du Portalet descends S. from the Pl. Massillon to regain
the main road, crossing which is the long Av. Gambetta; to the S.E. is
the *Museum*, with finds from the excavations of Olbia.

Some 3km S. lies *Costebelle*, likewise favoured by the English, where the 16C
chapel has been rebuilt since its destruction in 1944.—The r.-hand fork here
leads 2km to *L'Almanarre*, with the extensive but indefinite ruins of *Olbia*, later
a Roman settlement, probably *Pomponiana*. Underwater exploration has revealed part of an ancient port. Also here are the ruins of the medieval nunnery and
chapel of *St-Pierre*.

Hence (in good weather) one may follow the Route de Sel past the salt-pans of
Pesquiers to reach the *Giens peninsula*—once one of the *Îles d'Hyères*—the
village of which preserves a ruined castle (view).—From the pier near the *Tour
Fondue*, further E., named after a tower erected by Richelieu, launches cross to
Porquerolles (5km S.E.: see below).

The road N. traverses the narrow isthmus, passing the beach of *La Capte* to

Hyères-Plage, with its port and airport. For launches hence to Porquerolles, Port Cros, and the Île du Levant, see below: apply at the local S.I. for times of sailings.—Hence one bears 8km N.E., skirting the *Rade d'Hyères* to regain the N98 beyond the fishing-port of *Port-Pothuau*, and a Provençal-style village built for workers in the adjacent salt-pans. The *Massif des Maures* rises ahead; see below.

The offshore **Îles d'Hyères**, known to the ancients as *Stoechades* from the lavender (Lavendula stoechas) which flourished there, have a sub-tropical flora and equable climate. A haunt of pirates in the 16-17C, they were successfully assaulted by a British fleet in 1793, while in Aug. 1944 the German garrison was overwhelmed by an American landing force.

Porquerolles, the largest and most westerly of the group (c. 7.5km by 2km) has one small village and sandy beaches on the N., and steep cliffs on the S., and provides some pleasant walks among its vineyards and pinewoods. The *Phare*, 2km S. of the port, commands a general view.—*Port-Cros*, to the E., is the loftiest and steepest of the islands (c. 4.5km by 2km), and has the richest vegetation, being designated a Nature Reserve, preserving also the surrounding sea-bed, with rare rock-fish and seaweeds. To the N. of the harbour is the 16-17C *Fort du Moulin*.—A narrow strait separates it from the *Île du Levant* (8km long), the most barren of the three, with a cliff-bound coast accessible at only two points. At its W. end is the village of *Héliopolis*, with a long-established nudist colony, whose privacy is respected.

Driving E. from Hyères, the N98 shortly skirts salt-pans, and by passes *La Londe-les-Maures* before ascending to (6km) *La Verrerie* 1km beyond which we bear r.

LA VERRERIE TO (25km) COGOLIN, AND THE LA FOUX CROSSROADS, for *St-Tropez* or *Ste-Maxime*. The N98 diverges l. just E. of the village, mounting through the *Forêt du Dom*, one of the many ravaged by fires in this area, to (3.5km) the *Col de Gratteloup*, beyond which gradually descending the Môle valley to (21.5km) **Cogolin**, a pleasant village with a Romanesque church enlarged in the 16C, containing a triptych of 1540. It manufactures carpets, silk yarn from 'graines' (silkworms' cocoons), and 'briar' pipes.—*Grimaud*, 3km N., was an ancient Grimaldi stronghold, preserving a dark Romanesque church founded in 960, an arcaded house of the Templars, and a partially ruined castle.—For the road hence to Le Cannet-des-Maures, see Rte 156A.—The *La Foux* crossroads lie 4km E. of Cogolin; for **St-Tropez**, 5.5km further E., see below.

The N559 descends past (l.) *Bormes-les-Mimosas*, where the artist Charles Cazin (1841–1901) is buried, to (6km) **Le Lavandou**, a fishing-village and flourishing resort with a sandy beach.—To the S. extends *Cap Bénat*, with the 17C *Château du Retz*, and 16C fort on the *Cap de Bregançon*, further W.—Offshore lie and islands of *Port Cros* and *du Levant* (see above), for launches to which from Le Lavandou, enquire at the S.I.

The road now skirts the *Corniche des Maures*, the most southerly ridge of the *Massif des Maures* (see p 841), rising abruptly to the N., and traverses several minor resorts on the indented coast, among them *Cavalière* (perhaps the ancient *Portus Alconis*), with a pine shaded beach, and a small collection of antiquities preserved in a reconstructed 'Temple of Hercules'.—*Cape Nègre* is passed (r.), scene of the landing of the left wing of the invasion forces on 14 Aug 1944, which in less than a fortnight achieved the liberation of most of Provence.—Shortly beyond is *Rayol*, still an attractive resort which is passed before descending to (20km) *Cavalaire-sur-Mer*, a larger resort on a sheltered bay, with *Cap Lardier* to the E., straggling up the lower slope of *Les Pradels* (528m). It was perhaps the ancient *Heraclea Kakkabaria*.—The road now begins to climb inland to (6km) *La Croix-Valmer*.

Hence the D93 winds E. to (11km) crossroads just S. of the old village of

amatuelle, with a 17C church. The main road approaches the beaches on the
Anse de Pampelonne, with *Cap Camarat* to the S., before reaching, (16km) **St-
Tropez**; see below.—Between Ramatuelle and *Gassin* to the N.W., rise the
Moulins de Paillas (326m; views), the highest point of the peninsula.

The N559 leads N. past (r.) *Gassin*, before descending to the *La Foux*
(pron. Fousse) crossroads, 5.5km W. of St-Tropez.

ST-TROPEZ (6,200 Tropéziens; increased by many thousands in
search of sophistication during the season), even if unprotected from
the Mistral, has become an increasingly 'fashionable' summer resort
since the third decade of this century. It was occasionally visited as
early as the 1890s by artists in search of the picturesque, but even in
1789 Young had noted that it was 'prettily situated and tolerably
well built on the banks of a noble inlet of the sea'.

It claims to be named after a 1C Christian martyr from Pisa called Torpes, but
more certainly it was a trading post of the Greeks at Marseille. it was repeatedly
attacked by Saracens, and was eventually repopulated by Genoese in the late
15C. Mariners from St-Tropez assisted in the recapture from the Spanish of the
Îles des Lérins in 1637, and their repulse of a Spanish fleet of galleys soon after is
still commemorated by noisy processions, etc. on the 16-18th of each May,
known as the 'bravade'. The Suffren family were Seigneurs de St-Tropez in the
17-18C, although their most famous member, Pierre-André, Bailli de Suffren
(1726– 88), the naval commander against the English in Indian waters, was in
fact born at St-Cannat.

On 15 Aug. 1944 the occupying Germans blew up the quay in an attempt to
hamper American landing forces, and then surrendered the same day. Some 6
battleships, 21 cruisers, and 100 destroyers were involved in the Allied invasion
of the coast here, the code-name for which was originally 'Anvil', later changed
to 'Dragon'. Here Gén. Lattre de Tassigny met Gen. Patch to co-ordinate the attack on Toulon.

Parking space may be found near the approach road. At the S.W. corner of the Old Harbour is the ***Musée de l'Annonciade**, an important
collection of mostly 20C art, so-called as it has since 1955 been attractively displayed in a former chapel, dating from 1568. The collection was largely assembled by Georges Grammont. 56 paintings
were stolen in 1961, but were later recovered.

It includes representative works, many of them paintings of St-Tropez and the
area before it was irremediably ruined, by *Bonnard, Braque, Maurice Denis,
Derain, Dufy, Dunoyer de Segonzac, Orthon Freisz, Albert Marquet, Rouault,
Utrillo, Suzanne Valadon, Van Dongen, Vlaminck, Vuillard, Charles Camoin,
and Charles Dufresne*; and among sculptures, works by *Maillol*. Among in-
dividual canvases may be listed: *Maximilian Luce* (1858– 1941), View of St-
Tropez in 1892; *Matisse*, Corsican landscape (1898), among other works; and
Signac, two Views of St-Tropez, of 1896 and 1899.

23 blocks of Carrara marble were discovered in the roadstead off the adjacent
Quai de l'Épi in 1950, which it has been suggested may have been intended for
the Temple of Augustus at Narbonne.

From the S.E. corner of the port (S.I.), the Rue de la Citadelle leads up
to the massive 16-18C fortress, now housing a *Naval Museum* containing a reconstructed Greek galley, and a section devoted to the
Allied landings in 1944; it also offers extensive views.

Returning towards the harbour, one may bear r. along the Blvd
d'Aumale and Rue des Ramparts to the *Port de Péche*, to enter the
town by an old gate.—S. of the Rue de la Mairie is the 18C parish
Church; to the N. is the small cove of *La Glaye*, at both extremities of
which are defensive towers.—From the *Tour Daumas* (W.) the quays
may be regained near the entrance to the protective mole.

The beaches of St-Tropez are mostly on the wide *Anse de Pampelonne*, on the E
side of the peninsula, approached by the Route de la Belle-Isnard or the Route
des Plages (D93), turning S.E. from the D98A on the S.W. outskirts of the
town.—The latter also leads to (11.5km) *Ramatuelle*; see above.

From the La Foux crossroads, 4km to the W. of which is *Cogolin* (see
above), the N98 leads N. past (r.) exclusive *Port-Grimaud*, a bogus
fishing-village described as a 'cité lacustre', or modern lake
dwellings, similar to the Irish crannógs, whose amphibious community have each their individually designed but luxurious habitation,
jetty, and yacht (or coracle).

Bearing round the *Golfe de St-Tropez*, the road flanked by a succession of camping-sites, we reach (9km) **Ste-Maxime** (7,400 inhab.), a
popular resort, with a view across the bay to St-Tropez. A monument
to the Allied landings at *Cap Sardinaux*, just to the E., on 15 Aug
1944, will be noted.—For the improved road N.W. to *Le Muy*, see Rte
156A.

The road continues to skirt the coast, dotted with resorts, to
(15km) *St-Aygulf*, beyond which the wide Argens valley is entered.
A small airport is shortly passed, from which Roland Garros made
the first trans-Mediterranean flight (to Bizerta) in 1913.

For **Fréjus**, to the l. at the next main junction, see Rte 156A, and
likewise for the A8 to **Cannes**.—Turning r., the N98 enters **St
Raphael** (24,300 inhab.), lying at the foot of the *Massif de l'Esterel*
see p 844. It is a well-sited summer and winter resort, above which
among pine-trees lies the more exclusive *Valescure*, frequented by
English visitors from the turn of the century.

Napoleon landed at the harbour on his return from Egypt in 1799, and embarked
hence for Elba in 1814. it was the residence from 1864 of the novelist and wit
Alphonse Karr (1808–90), who first brought the town to notice. Gounod composed his 'Roméo et Juliette' here in 1866.

The main church, near the port, is in the neo-Byzantine style of the
1880s. The Blvd Félix-Martin leads N., from which, passing beneath
the railway bridge, the older town is reached, preserving a *Templar
Church* of the 12C, adjacent to which is a small local *Museum*.

After St-Raphael begins the *Corniche de l'Esterel* (once known as
the Corniche d'Or, but the gilt has worn thin), skirting the rocky
base of this range, the crossing of which requires caution. It was constructed c. 1903 at the instigation of Abel Baillif (1845–1934), the
first president of the Touring Club de France, who died near the *Col
de l'Esquillon*.

The *Cap du Dramont* (r.) is shortly passed, inland from which are
porphyry quarries, and a monument of the landing of the 36th U.S.
Division in Aug. 1944, before circling the sheltered harbour of *Agay*
overlooked by the jagged ridge of the *Rastel d'Agay*. There are
several hill-roads climbing N. hence into the Esterel, all requiring
caution.

The lighthouse on the *Pointe de la Baumette* is next passed, with a
commemorative tablet recording the disappearance of Antoine de
Saint-Exupéry in July 1944, when flying on a reconnaissance operation. In a villa just W. of the adjoining resort of *Anthéor* lived Vincent
d'Indy between 1922–31, beyond which the *Pic du Cap Roux*
(452m) is approached, rounding the promontory of which we get a
view of the *Îles de Lérins*. Inland rises the *Pic d'Ours* (496m).

The *Pointe de l'Esquillon* is next rounded, shortly beyond which
the road turns W. to skirt the *Golfe de la Napoule*. Near here the

French right wing landed during the disembarkment of Aug. 1944.
We descend to the fishing-port of *Théoule-sur-Mer* and enter *La
Napoule*, retaining two towers and a gateway of its 14C castle,
erected by Raymond de Turenne. Part of the building houses works
by an American sculptor, Henry Clews (d. 1937).—The A8 motorway may be entered 3km to the N.

The N98 bears r. across the mouths of the rivers Argentière and
Siagne, with an alluvial plain to our l. on which is a small airport, and
skirts the long beach which extends to **Cannes**; see Rte 161.

Panorama of Cannes, with the Îles de Lérins in the distance

XIII   THE CÔTE D'AZUR

The **Côte d'Azur**, also known as the *Riviera*, is the narrow coastal strip protected by the Maritime Alps, extending from Hyères to Menton, with its serene winter climate and numerous resorts with pretensions to luxury. They are still fashionable, although the dense crowds of *vacanciers* who converge there in the summer may well be described as the fourth scourge of Provence; see p 761. It was the stretch between the Var (just W. of Nice) and the Italian frontier, which was the former *Comté de Nice*.

See also introduction to Section XII; p 761.

161   Cannes to Nice; and from Cagnes to Vence

33km (20 miles). N7 or N98. 11km **Antibes**—9km **Cagnes**. **Vence** lies 11km. N.—13km **Nice**.

Maps: IGN 68, or 115. M 245 or 195.

The A8 motorway, entered just N. of Cannes, provides a rapid inland road, which will avoid the often crowded coast road, from which one makes an exit at Nice airport. Travellers wishing to drive directly E. to Menton and Italy are advised to follow the motorway; see Rte 163.

CANNES (72,800 Canois), one of the oldest of the Riviera winter resorts, and once described as 'the hospital of all the world and the flowery cemetery of the aristocracy of Europe'. Modern Cannes and its suburbs sprawl well beyond its bay and into the amphitheatre of hills behind it, rising to and engulfing *Le Cannet*. With its growth and rebuilding, it has lost much of its character, although the port, and the older town clinging roud *Mont Chevalier* to the W., retain a certain charm, while the Blvd de la Croisette, leading E. to its 'Pointe' (off which lie the *Îles de Lérins*) will have its sophisticated devotees. it is the venue of an international film festival and numerous other distractions.

Although a place of ancient foundation, it was long merely an insignificant dependency of the abbots of Lérins. Smollett found it 'a little fishing town, agreeably situated on the beach of the sea', which he again passed through on his return from Italy, when he remarked that he 'would rather live here for the sake of the mild climate, than either Antibes or Nice. Here you are not cooped up within walls, nor crouded with soldiers and people: but are already in the country, enjoy a fine air, and are well supplied with all sorts of fish'. Lord Brougham, on his way to Nice in the autumn of 1834, but prevented from crossing the then Italian frontier on account of an epidemic of cholera in Provence, bought land on the Fréjus road just W. of Cannes, and later built a villa there, where he spent some months of every year from 1840, eventually dying in Cannes in 1868, by which time the place was becoming fashionable. T.R. Woodfield laid out a croquet lawn on his property, and obtained permission to build an English church at his expense. Speculative building commenced c. 1850, and with the advent of the railway in 1863, its fate was sealed. By 1914 its resident population was 30, 000.

Mérimée died there in 1870, having embraced Protestantism on his deathbed in gratitude to the English ladies who nursed him. Louis Blanc, the left-wing politician and historian, died here in 1882; and Leopold, Duke of Albany, the youngest son of Queen Victoria, in 1884; the tragic actress Mme Rachel died at Le Cannet in 1858, as did Pierre Bonnard in 1947.

The artist Charles Ginner (1878–1952) was born here, as was the actor Gérard Philipe (1922–59).

There are S.Is at the Railway Station and Palais des Festivals.

The *Allées de la Liberté* (with its morning flower-market), skirting the *Vieux Port*, from which launches ply to the *Îles de Lérins* (see below), leads W. to the old town, known as *Le Suquet*, where steep lanes and steps ascend to the *Pl. de la Castre* and *N.-D.-de-l'Esperance* (1521–1648), behind which is a disfigured Romanesque chapel. Close-by are the *Tour Suquet* (14C on 11C foundations; view), and the adjoining *Museum*, containing Egyptian and general antiquities (including sculpture from Cyprus), ethnographical collections, and Pre-Columbian ceramics.

Bearing E. from the harbour, where the Jetée Albert-Edward is named after Edward VII, who when prince of Wales was a frequent visitor, the new '*Convention Centre*' (1982) is passed, replacing the characteristic fin de siècle Casino, to gain the pullulating palm-lined *Blvd de la Croisette*, overlooking the beach.

Further E. in the boulevard is the *Palais des Festivals* (1949). Some distance beyond is the new yacht harbour, while on the promontory stands the '*Palm Beach' Casino* (1929). The *Pointe de la Croisette* provides a view of the built-over bay, and offshore *Île Ste Marguerite*, beyond which is the *Île St Honoret*; see below.

The immediate environs of Cannes are of slight interest: the panoramic view from the *Observatoire de Super-Cannes* (325m), to the N.E., to which the funicular has been discontinued, has been described as 'chastening'.

CANNES TO GRASSE (16km). The wide Blvd Carnot climbs due N. from the town centre, and after 2km we bear l. To the r. lies *Le Cannet*, preserving a 16C church and two disfigured medieval towers. The motorway is shortly crossed, and, 2.5km beyond, the road passes (l.) the ancient fortified village of **Mougins** (now with 10,200 inhab.), with a polygonal chapel rebuilt in the 17C. After joining the N85 we traverse *Mouans-Sartoux* with its 16C castle, and commence the ascent towards **Grasse**, on the slope of the Roquevignon; see Rte 155.

The **Îles de Lérins**, approached by a regular ferry from Cannes, comprises two main islands, *Ste-Marguerite*, the *Lero* of the ancients, the nearest and largest (3300m by 950m) lying 1100m S. of the Pointe de la Croisette.

It is covered by a forest of evergreen oaks and Aleppo pine; on *Pointe Bataignier*, its W. extremity, excavations have revealed traces of a Roman port. We disembark adjacent to the *Fort*, on the N. side, built by Richelieu and altered by Vauban, in which one is shown the cell of 'the Man in the Iron Mask' (d. 1703 in the Bastille), imprisoned here for 11 years (1687–98) by Louis XIV. Various have been the attempts to solve the mystery of the identity of this unfortunate fellow, whose mask was in fact of silk or velvet, not iron, and most of the theories advanced have been quite discredited. He was probably Count Mattioli, a diplomatic agent who had offended both his master the Duke of Mantua and Louis XIV by revealing secret negotiations. Among other prisoners mewed up here were six Huguenot pastors who had rashly returned to France after the revocation of the Edict of Nantes; the Marquis de Jouffroy d'Abbans (1773), a pioneer of steam navigation in France; Marshal Bazaine, who surrendered Metz to the Germans in 1870, interned here in Dec. 1873, succeeded in escaping by boat to Spain the following June with the help of accomplices.

Of more interest is the small *Île St-Honoret*, Roman *Lerina*, adjacent to the S., where the convent, founded c. 410 by St Honoratus, was a centre of Christian culture in the Dark Ages. Among those who studied here were St Lupus of Troyes (d. 479), and almost certainly St Patrick. In the 7C its community is said to have numbered 3700, but it declined due to the sporadic raids of pirates and later occupation by Spaniards (1635–37), who had seized it in 1524, etc., and was dispersed in 1788.

The re-occupied monastery comprises a tasteless *Church* (1880–1930) and cloister, preserving sculptured fragments, adjoining a Romanesque cloister.—Further S. is the sea-lapped fortified *Monastery* (11C; restored in the 14C), with a cloister of two storeys, to whose confined quarters the community retreated on the approach of corsairs. Two ancient chapels, possibly of 6C foundation, survive on the shores of the islet, and also three of the 12C.

Following the N7 E. from La Croisette, with a view across the bay of Golfe Juan towards *Cap d'Antibes*, at 5km the resort of **Golfe-Juan** is reached, in the sheltered roadstead of which Napoleon, sailing from Elba with some 800 men and the expletive Gén. Cambronne, landed on the evening of 1 March 1815, and begain his forced cross-country march to Grenoble, which he entered on the 7th; see Rtes 155 and 138A, in reverse.—An inland by-pass is under construction, but one may here bear r. to skirt the shore on the N98.

The D135 climbs steeply from the town centre to (2.5km) **Vallauris** (21,200 inhab.), lying at 122m, noted for its potteries, both industrial and artistic (particularly since 1947, when Picasso worked there in the Madoura pottery). In the main square is Picasso's bronze Man and Sheep. To the E. is the *Priory of Lérins*, founded 1227 and rebuilt in the 16C, except for the chapel, once used as an oil-mill, three walls of which now display Picasso's War and Peace, an unexceptional work painted on ply-wood in the 1950s. An exhibition of modern ceramics may be seen in the adjacent museum.

4km. **Juan-les-Pins**, a fashionable resort since the mid 1920s, when it was promoted by Frank Jay Gould, an American millionaire, imperceptibly merges with *Antibes*, on the N. side of the *Cap d'Antibes* peninsula. Their combined population is 63,200; see below.

The circuit of the rocky peninsula, with its numerous sumptuous villas, may be made by following the Blvd du Littoral. In the 17C *Tour du Graillon*, near its S.W. extremity, is installed a *Naval and Napoleonic museum*. The Blvd du Cap later bears l., traversing the centre of the peninsula, from which one may turn r. to visit the restored chapel of *La Garoupe* (preserving numerous ex-voto paintings, etc.) and the adjacent lighthouse, to pass (l.) the *Jardin Thuret*, an exotic garden founded in 1856 by G.-A. Thuret (1817–75), a Dutch Huguenot botanist. Continuing N., the Anse de la Salis is skirted, on the S. outskirts of Antibes.

The N98 leads to the central *Pl. Gén. de Gaulle* in **ANTIBES**, whence the Blvd Albert-Ier turns r., at the far end of which turn l. to approach the *Bastion St-André*, displaying local archaeological collections, including anchors, amphoras, ceramics, coins, and a Greek inscription recording a certain Terpon's gratitude to Aphrodite of Cyprus.

Antibes, originally *Antipolis*, named from its position 'facing the city' (of Nice), was founded by Massiliot Greeks c. 340 B.C., and was of some importance under the Romans. Ruins of a theatre existed until 1691. It was the seat of a bishop from the 5C until 1244. Its ramparts resisted attack in 1746, and again in 1815, when besieged by an Austro-Sardinian army. It was the birthplace of Marshal Reille (1775–1860); here died the artist Nicholas de Staël (1914–55), and the Cretan novelist Nikos Khazantzakis (1883–1957).

The Rue de la Touraque is followed to the N. into the old town. Turning r. between the market and the 19C *Hôtel de Ville*, we reach the 17C Church, with notable doors, a Romanesque E. end, and with a tall Romanesque tower adjacent, serving as a belfry. It contains a good altarpiece of 1515 of the School of Louis Bréa in the S. transept.

Steps ascend to the 16C **Château** of the Grimaldi, preserving a 14C tower. It now accommodates a *Museum devoted to Picasso, including tapestries, 25 paintings, 44 drawings, and 76 ceramics (produced at Vallauris in 1947–48), many of them executed here in 1946 and having mythological themes, apart from goats. The terrace commands a pleasant view.

Further N. is a promenade built on the 16C ramparts, dominating the *Port Vauban* and the *Anse St-Roche*, defended to the N. by the 17C *Fort Carré*, in which is the tomb of Gén. Championnet (1762–1800), organiser of the Parthenopean Republic; cf. Soyons.—A short distance W. of the market is the Pl. *Nationale*, from which the Rue de la République leads back to the central Pl. Gén. de Gaulle.

The N98 leads N., skirting a dreary beach and later a race-course, to (10km) *Cagnes;* see below. The Var is crossed 8km beyond, with the airport of Nice on the flat headland to the E. of its month.

Some 4km from Antibes the D4 turns l., shortly crossing the motorway, and the next r.-hand turning leads immediately to the *Musée Fernand Léger*, devoted to the work of that artist (1881–1955), and designed by A. Svetchine (1960), with a colourful mosaic on its facade.—The D4 continues W. through *Biot*, with two polyptyches in its church, one attrib. to Louis Bréa.—9km further W. lies *Valbonne*, with an attractive arcaded square.—3km S. of Valbonne is the reconstructed 'Provençal' village of *Castellaras*, once a deserted 17C and Gallo-Roman site.—9km. W. of Valbonne lies *Grasse*, and 4.5km N.W., *Opio*; see Rte 155.

Cagnes (or *Cagnes-sur-Mer*; 35,400 inhab.) comprises three parts: seaside *Le Cros-de-Cagne*; *Cagne-Ville*, to the N.E. of which, in the *Villa des Collettes*, lived Renoir from 1907 until his death in 1919, which now contains some works and souvenirs of the artist; and **Le Haute-de-Cagnes**, on a height to the N.W. The last, the old town, a maze of narrow stepped lanes, and preserving much of its ramparts (for it *was* the nearest town to the Italian frontier until 1860), is dominated by a massive battlemented *Castle*, until 1789 owned by the Grimaldi family. Dating from the 14C, its courtyard was refaced c. 1630; the tower was an unfortunate 19C addition.

On the ground floor is the *Musée de l'Olivier*, devoted to the cultivation of the olive; the principal rooms of the first floor contain ceiling-paintings by G.-B. Carlone (c. 1624); the 2nd floor displays 20C paintings.—To the N. is *N.-D.-de-Protection* (14th and 17C), with naive 16C frescoes.

For the main road from Cagnes to *Grasse*, see the latter part of Rte 155, in reverse.

CAGNES TO VENCE VIA ST-PAUL (11km). The D236 ascends directly to (9km) *Vence*, but a recommended alternative is to follow

the road further W. to (4.5km) *La Colle-sur-Loup*, with a hotel in the
ruins of an old priory.—Here we bear r. for (3km) *St-Paul*, just prior to
which a l.-hand turning leads to the **Fondation Maeght** (signposted).

The Maeght Foundation is devoted to the promotion of contemporary art, and
was set up in 1964 by a Parisian art-dealer. The complex of buildings is a not entirely successful design by José Luis Sert, although attractively sited among
pine-woods. It is laid out on an open plan, and displays to advantage numerous
sculptures in its courtyards and gardens, in which are pools embellished by
mosaics designed by *Braque*, and *Miró*, but it may disappoint those who are not
devotees of modern art. The main block contains the *Museum* and temporary
exhibition rooms, libraries, and cinema, etc., and here reproductions of the
works of art displayed may be bought.—To the l. of the entrance is the permanent collection, with a room devoted to works by *Picasso*, including a Portrait of
Jacqueline with crossed hands (1954), Paul 'en pierrot' (1925), Mother and child
(1922), and Portrait of Olga Khoklova (c. 1917). Another room displays the at-
tenuated sculptures of *Giacometti*, et al. Notable among sculptures are works by
Barbara Hepworth, Chillida, Miró, and *Arp*, and 'stabiles' by *Calder*. The *Chapel*
contains glass by *Braque*.

St-Paul-de-Vence, an ancient, well-sited, and once picturesque fortified village which has succumbed to exploitation, lies to the r. Its
Gothic *Church*, with 17-18C additions, contains a St Catherine of
Alexandria attrib. to Tintoretto, and a Treasury. The 16C town
walls, with their wall-walk, are well preserved, and several houses retain traces of former prosperity. The *Auberge de la Colombe d'Or*
contains paintings by, among others, *Bonnard, Braque, Derain, Dufy,
Matisse, Utrillo,* and *Vlaminck*.

Continuing N., the Malvan is crossed beneath a broken aqueduct,
and we climb to (3.5km) *Vence*.

VENCE (325m; 13,400 inhab.) with its mild climate, attracted an
English colony at the turn of the century, but the town has grown
very considerably in recent decades. Its old centre nevertheless still
preserves some attractive corners, although it is also now much commercialised.

Roman *Vintium* was the seat of bishops from the 4C until 1790, two of whom
were canonised; among later incumbents were Alessandro Farnese (Pope Paul III
from 1534–49), and Antoine Godeau (1605–72), the poet and 'précieux', and
one of the first members of the Académie. D.H. Lawrence died here in 1930, as
did Count Michael Korolyi, the deposed president of the first Hungarian
republic, in 1955.

From the road junction of the new town the Av. de la Resistance is
followed E. to the *Pl. du Grand Jardin*, immediately N.E. of which is
the *Pl. du Frêne*, with its ash-tree. Hence the walled town is entered
by the *Porte du Peyra*, one of five medieval gateways remaining,
abutted by the massive 15C *Tower* of the castle of the lords of
Villeneuve, seigneurs of Vence. From the S.E. corner of the adjacent
Place, with its charming fountain, the Rue du Marché is followed. A
turning to the l. enters the *Pl. Clemenceau*, with the former
Cathedral, which with its Romanesque nave and aisles, preserving
some earlier work, and greatly extended in the 17C, is more picturesque than impressive. To the l. of the main door is an inscription
in honour of the Emperor Gordianus (c. 230) set up by citizens of
Vintium. The pillars of the S. aisle retain early Romanesque panels,
while in the S.E. chapel is a Gallo-Roman relief. In the main gallery
(adm. on application) are a 15C lectern and 51 choir-stalls carved in
1460 by Jacotin Bellot of Grasse, the misericords of which are
notable.

From the above-mentioned junction the Blvd Tuby, contined by the Av. Henri-Matisse, leads up to the *Chapelle du Rosaire*, decorated by Matisse in 1947–51 for the Dominican nuns of the convent who had nursed the artist through a long illness; times of adm. should be checked first.

Several EXCURSIONS may be made from Vence. The D2210 leads W. via (5km) *Tourette-sur-Loup* and (8km) *Pont-du-Loup* to *Grasse*, 12.5km beyond; see Rte 155.—The D2 climbs N.W. via (10km) the *Col de Vence* (970m) to *Courségoules*, 6km beyond; see Rte 155.—The D2210 leads N.E. below (6km) *St-Jeannet*, whose vineyards produce a wine of local repute, standing on the slope of the *Baou de St-Jeannet* (800m), to *Gattières*, 4km beyond.

From *St-Jeannet* the D18 and D118, passing a research centre of IBM, designed by Marcel Breuer and Richard Laugier (1960), follow the *Corniche du Var* S., parallel to the river, to (11.5km) *St-Laurent-du-Var*, rebuilt after its destruction in 1943–44, to regain the coast road by the Var bridges.

From *Gattières*, an old village perched high above the Var valley (views), one may descend to (5km) the *Pont de la Mande* to gain the N202 (see Rte 165), or continue N. via (5km) *Carros*, with a ruined castle, to reach the same main road 11km below, at the *Pont Charles-Albert*.—From *Carros* a minor road (D1) leads to (4km) *Le Broc*, with a church of 1489, and (8km) *Bouyon*, where the church contains a polyptych of the Nice school (1460). The D8 continues W. past (5km) *Bézaudun-les-Alpes* to *Courségoules*, 6km beyond; see Rte 155.

162 Nice

NICE (338,500 Niçois; 53,400 in 1876; 105,100 in 1901), préfecture of the *Alpes-Maritimes*, and the fifth-largest town of France, is an animated city now extending, with its suburbs, along the *Baie des Anges* from the Var (to the W., once marking the French frontier), with the airport at its mouth, to *Mont Boron*, to the E. beyond the port. The river Paillon, which once separated the old town from the new, and largely filled in, is now—with the recent demolition of the century-old casino—a spacious boulevard providing views of the surrounding hills and the mountains beyond. Although it has some industrial quarters, it has been described as 'the chief pleasure-city of the Riviera', and its mild climate has made it a popular if expensive resort, in spite of its shingly beaches.

In competition with other resorts on the Côte d'Azur, it sets out to provide an extensive range of festivals and other distractions, the most famous being its Spring Carnival (revived in 1878), while the ski-slopes not too far inland are an additional attraction in winter. Since 1966 it has had a university.

Ancient *Nicaea* or *Nikaia*, commonly derived from Nike, the Greek word for victory, was founded by Phocaeans from Marseille in the 4C B.C., but after the Roman intervention in the affairs of Gaul (154 B.C.) it was temporarily eclipsed by the Roman foundation of *Cemenelum* (Cimiez). By the 4C it had a bishop and was of some commercial importance, but suffered from piratical raids, from the rivalry of the counts of Provence and Savoy, and from such feuding families as the Lascaris of Tende and the Grimaldi of Monaco. In 1388 it placed itself in the hands of Savoy.

In 1543 it was besieged by a Franco-Turkish fleet, and sacked. It was decimated by plague in 1631; captured by the French in 1691, again in 1705/6, by the Duke of Berwick, and in 1744. In 1748 Nice was restored, at the Peace of Aix-la-Chapelle, to the House of Savoy, then Kings of Sardinia, when it was known as *Nizza*. Temporarily annexed by the French Republic in 1792, it served as a base for Napoleon's Italian campaigns, but in 1814 reverted to Sardinia. In 1860, in a plebiscite it voted for union with France (Treaty of Turin). Its population was then c. 40,000.

Its reputation as a winter-resort dates from the mid 18C. The first esplanade
was laid out in 1770; the first casino opened in 1777. Edward Young, author of
'Night Thoughts', spent the winter of 1736–37 here. Arthur Young, travelling
through Nice in 1787, stated that 57 English and 9 French had passed the
previous winter there. In the following year Sir James Smith, President of the
Linnaean Society, remarked that the 'whole neighbourhood had the air of an
English watering-place', adding: 'The town is much enlivened and enriched by
the concourse of strangers, who resort hither for the sake of the climate in
winter, and great numbers of people are supported by their means'. Henry
Cavendish, the chemist (1731–1810), was born there, where his parents were
on holiday.

In Jan. 1764 Tobias Smollett rented a ground floor there at the rate of £20 a
year, making it his base for 15 months, but an altercation with his landlord on
leaving caused him to observe that 'A stranger must conduct himself with the utmost circumspection to be able to live among these people without being the
dupe of imposition'. Here he would bathe, which he found beneficial to his
health, but remarked that there was 'no convenience for this operation, from the
benefit of which the fair sex must be intirely excluded, unless they lay aside all
regard to decorum'. It is curious that a street is named after him, considering

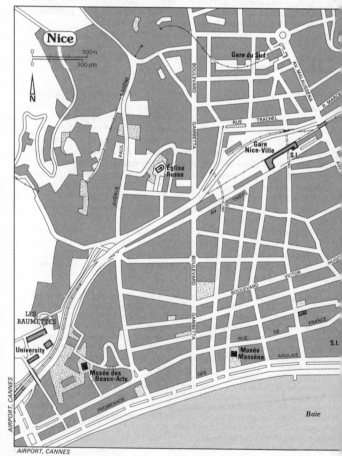

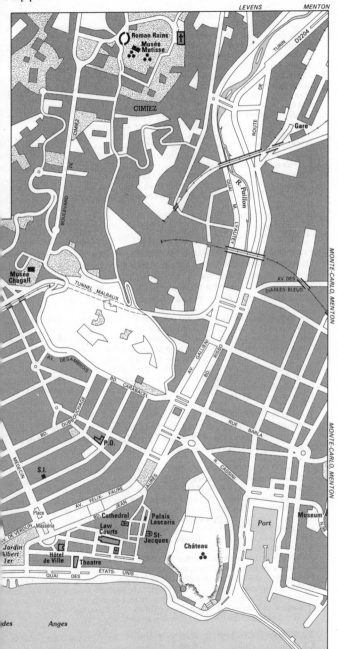

LEVENS   MENTON

Roman Ruins
Musée Matisse

CIMIEZ

TURIN D2204

DE

ROUTE

Gare

QUAI

M.

LYAUTEY

R. Paillon

BOULEVARD

DE

CIMIEZ

Musée
Chagall

TUNNEL MALRAUX

AV. DES
DIABLES-BLEUS

MONTE-CARLO MENTON

AV.
DESAMBROIS

BD. CARABACEL

AV.
GALLIENI

BD.
RISSO

BD.
DUBOUCHAGE

P.O.

RUE
BARLA

MONTE-CARLO MENTON

BD.
MÉDECIN

S.I.

R. CASSINI

AV. FELIX- FAURE

JEAN

BD.
JAURES

Cathedral

Palais
Lascaris

Museum

Place
Masséna

Law
Courts

St-
Jacques

Port

NEB

AV. DE VERDUN

Jardin
Albert
Ier

Hôtel
de Ville

Theatre

Château

QUAI   DES   ÉTATS- UNIS

des   Anges

Smollett's withering condemnation of its 'greedy, and over-reaching' shopkeepers; and its artisans, who 'lounge about the ramparts, bask themselves in the sun, or play at bowls in the streets from morning 'till night'. Here 'There are no tolerable pictures, busts, statues, nor edifices . . . There is not even a bookseller in Nice . . . they are unacquainted with music'; 'you may peruse dean Swift's description of the Yahoos, and then you will have some idea of the *porcheria*, that distinguishes the gallantry of Nice', where the noblesse would 'play at cardes for farthings', and on summer evenings might be seen 'seated in ditches on the highway side, serenaded with the croaking of frogs, and the bells and braying of mules and asses continually passing in a perpetual cloud of dust'. He was not alone: Baretti, his contemporary, likewise condemned the place: 'so ugly a town, and affords so small a number of amusements . . .'.

Among Niçois are the artists Louis Bréa (1443– 1520), and Carle van Loo (1705– 65); Marshal Masséna (1758– 1817), Duc de Rivoli and Prince d'Essling; Giuseppe Garibaldi (1807– 82); and Albert Calmette (1863– 1933), inventor of a vaccine against tuberculosis. James Paterson (a general in the king of Sardinian forces) was commandant of Nice from 1752 to 1765.

Among those who have died there were Nicolo Paganini (1784– 1840); the Rev. Henry Francis Lyte (1793– 1847), author of 'Abide with me'; J.F. Hálevy (1799– 1862), composer of 'La Juive'; Maurice Maeterlinck (1862– 1949); 'La Belle Otero' (Caroline Puentovalga; 1868– 1965), 'grande horizontale' of the '90s; and Henri Matisse (1869– 1954; at Cimiez). Marie Bashkirtseff lived here (at No 63 Promenade des Anglais) from 1872– 76.

From the *Jardin Albert-Ier*, built over the mouth of the Paillon, the famous **Promenade des Anglais**, flanked by hotels and blocks of apartments, extends over 4km to the W., and the Quai des États-Unis leads E., over-looked by buildings of the old town, to the base of the wooded hill still known as the *Château*.

The former thoroughfare was laid out in 1820– 24 as far as the river Magnan (now covered by the Blvd de la Madeleine) by the English colony, who used to take their constitutional there. It was perhaps partially financed by the Rev. Lewis Way, a wealthy clergyman who had passed the winters of 1822 and 1823 at Nice. It is recorded that a fund was started by British residents in Dec. 1825 and used for many years 'for the repair of the English Walk by the Unemployed Poor'. It passed close to the first Protestant cemetery (known as Le Cimetière de la Vallée de Mantéga, which stood near the Blvd Gambetta), in use since 1766, but already full by 1820.

Before reaching the Blvd Gambetta we pass the gardens of the lavishly decorated *Villa Masséna*, built by the marshal's grandson in 1902, which has since 1921 housed the **Musée Masséna** (entrance in the parallel Rue de France, once the main approach to Nice).

On the GROUND FLOOR is the *Bibliothèque Cessole*, an important library of local history, and several rooms contain furniture of the Directory and First Empire periods. On the FIRST FLOOR is a collection of retables, triptychs, and other paintings, mostly 15C, from churches in the area, some attrib. to *Louis Bréa*, and one by *Durandi*; also rooms devoted to the history of Nice, with an interesting collection of maps and plans, and drawings and paintings of the town and district, including a View of 1543. Note also the 15C Marriage-coffer. Another room is devoted to Marshal André Masséna, with a portrait by Hersent painted prior to 1769.

On the staircase ascending to the SECOND FLOOR are water-colour copies of wall-paintings from 14-16C chapels in the district made before 1914 by *Alexis Mossa* (1844– 1926). They include those of St-Étienne de Tinée, Lucéram, Clans, Reillon, La Brigue, and Venanson.—Rooms are devoted to local costume; the Nice Carnival, and musical instruments; arms and armour; to Garibaldi; ecclesiastical art, including ex-voto silver fishes, etc.; furniture; ceramics; more water-colours; and the Chapsal collection of jewellery.

By following the Rue de France to the W. we approach the **Musée Chéret**, an extensive collection of paintings installed since 1928 at

33 Av. des Baumettes, leading N.W.; steps to the l. provide a short cut. This large villa of 1878, erected for Princess Kotschoubey, is largely devoted to the art of *Jules Chéret* (1836–1932), who died at Nice after many years of residence there.

Many of the other canvases displayed are characteristic of his era, such as 'Slave in a harem' by *Paul-Désiré Trouillebert* (1829–1906), and the symbolist works of *Gustav-Adolf Mossa* (1883–1971), but the museum also contains representative works by *Albert Besnard, Boudin, Degas, Dufy, Lazlo, Monet, Renoir, Sisley, Van Dongen*, and *Ziem*, etc.; some of the Impressionists were previously in the Musée Masséna. Among earlier paintings are some by *Battoni, Hubert Robert*, and *Fragonard*; and among individual works: *School of Caravaggio*, David and Goliath; *L.-M. van Loo*, Self-portrait; *Lawrence*, Mrs Brandt; *Allan Ramsay*, Portrait of George III, and an *anon.* Portrait of Queen Charlotte (? copies). A bust of Victor Hugo, by *Rodin*, a second casting of his 'Age d'Airain'; and a collection of Gobelins tapestries are notable.—The museum also contains a collection of Oriental art, sometimes displaced by temporary exhibitions.

The university quarter of *Les Baumettes* lies to the N.W., with a mosaic by Chagall in the Faculté de Droit.

One of the curiosities of Nice, conveniently approached by turning N. up the Blvd Gambetta, and then l. into the Blvd du Tzarewitch just beyond the overpass, is the characteristically ornate *Russian Orthodox Cathedral* (1912), and the adjoining chapel on the site of a villa in which the Grand-Duke Nicholas-Alexandrowitch died in 1865.

Returning E. along the Rue de France, and passing the Musée Masséna, one shortly reaches the *Croix de Marbre*, commemorating the arrival in 1538 of Pope Paul III to act as an intermediary between François I and the Emperor Charles V in arranging a peace settlement, the two monarchs declining to meet each other.

In the parallel street to the N. stands the Anglican church of *Holy Trinity* (consecrated 1860), on the site of an earlier chapel. The district between this point and the Pl. Masséna, further E., was known by the English colony as 'Newborough'.

The N. side of the arcaded *Pl. Masséna* (1835; S.I. on the E. side), one of the main centres of animation, is laid out in the Genoese style of the 17C, its buildings picked out in terracotta and pistachio green.—Hence a tree-lined avenue leads N. towards the *Railway-station*.

From the S. side of the Pl. Masséna, one may enter the characteristic **Vieille Ville**, turning r. into the Rue St-François-de-Paule, in which is the disfigured *old Hôtel de Ville*, and the *Church of St-François-de-Paule* (1736), and opposite, the *Opéra* (1885; modernised 1961). The street is continued by the Cours Saleya, with its morning flower-market, on the N. side of which is the *Gallery of Malacology* of the Natural History Museum, with a remarkable collection of shells and molluscs, together with specialist aquariums.

The Cours is separated from the Quai des États-Unis, parallel to the S., by two rows of low houses, the roofs of which formed terraces, and once provided a fashionable promenade. Facing the quay is the *Galerie des Ponchettes*, used for contemporary art exhibitions.

To the N. of the Cours opens the attractive Italianate *Pl. Pierre-Gautier*, with the *Préfecture* in the old *Governor's Palace* (1611; restored 1907).—To the r. is the *Chapelle de la Miséricorde* (1736), with an oval nave and apsidal chapels, containing an early 15C retable by Jean Miralhet.

A lane leading E. behind the Préfecture approaches *St-Giaume*, in the 17C Italian Baroque taste, while a l.-hand turning off this lane leads to the *Cathedral of Ste-Reparate* (1650; restored 1901), facing a small square from which the Rue Rossetti leads E.—To the S. of this lane, in the Rue Droite, is *St-Jacques* (1607–50), built in imitation of the Gesù at Rome.

To the N., at No. 15 in the Rue Droite is the **Palais des Lascaris**, a well-restored mid 17C mansion in the Genoese style, with an elaborate stone stair-case embellished with statues, and another room with baroque decoration. On the first floor are two ceilings by J.-B. Carlone. The portative organ of 1700 from the N. of England will be noted. On the r. of the entrance is a Pharmacy from Besançon (1738).

Continuing N., the *Pl. St-François* is reached, preserving a 17C *Town Hall.*—Beyond, to the r., is baroque *St-Martin*, containing a Pietà attrib. to Louis Bréa.

A short distance further N. is the *Pl. Garibaldi* (1750), just N.W. of which, at 60 Blvd Risso, is the *Musée Barla*, with palaeontological, and mineralogical and mycological collections of the city's Natural History Museum.

The Rue Cassini leads S.E. from the Pl. Garibaldi to the little Harbour, known as *Port Lympia*, flanked by the *Pl. Île-de-Beauté*, beyond which, at 25 Blvd Carnot (which later circles Mont Boron), is the new *Musée Terra Amata*, where a prehistoric site has been excavated and its artefacts imaginatively displayed.

From the W. side of the port one may regain the Quai des États-Unis by following the Quai Rauba-Capéu ('rob-hat') round the sometimes gusty S. end of the umbrageous hill known as the **Château** (although little remains of the fortress razed by Berwick). Excavations have brought to light the foundations of a 12C cathedral built over earlier edifices. On the N.W. side of the hill is the old cemetery in which Gambetta is buried. To the S.W. is the 16C *Tour Bellanda*, containing a *Naval Museum*. Berlioz twice visited this site, once when orchestrating 'King Lear', and a second time in 1844, after which he was inspired to finish his 'Corsair' overture. The museum and summit (views) can be reached by a lift from the quay S.W. of the hill.

Cimiez

The mst convenient approach (by car) is by turning l. into the Blvd Carabacel at the Pont Barla (some distance N.E. of the Pl. Masséna), shortly forking r. to follow the Blvd de Cimiez uphill.

Beyond the *Pont Barla*, built over the bed of the Paillon, stands the *Palais des Expositions* (1957), venue of numerous trade fairs.

After c. 1km the *Musée Chagall* is passed to the l., built in 1972 to house that artist's series of works on biblical themes.—The avenue continues to climb for c. 1km before bearing r. by the former *Hôtel Regina*, Queen Victoria's favourite, in which Matisse died.

Cimiez is the Roman *Cemenelum*, previously an oppidum of the Vediantii, and an important station and administrative centre on the Via Julia. By the mid 5C it had its own bishop, often in conflict with that at Nice, but the place was razed during later Barbarian invasions. By the time Smollett visited the site, where he measured the arena with packthread and noted down several inscriptions, there was little visible above ground, those ruins remaining being used as a dwelling and stable by the peasant taking care of the charming 17C villa there.

Abutting the road is the small arena or *Amphitheatre* (65m by 54.50m; seating 6000). Close-by is the *Villa des Arènes*, accommodating both an *Archaeological museum*, and (on the first floor), the *Musée Matisse*.

The latter contains a representative selection of the work of Henri Matisse, from his early paintings (including a Breton village scene of 1896) to his last ('Fleurs et Fruit'); also some 300 drawings; pottery; sculpture; and designs from the chapel at Vence (see latter part of Rte 161), etc.

The archaeological collections include artefacts found on the site, among them jewellery; coins; bronze statuettes; glass objects; Corinthian, Attic, Etruscan, and Roman pottery; a statue of Antonia, niece of Augustus; a 3C sarcophagus; milestones from the Via Julia (from Menton to Cimiez); a replica of the 4C B.C. phial of repoussé silver, found at Èze in 1870 and now in the British Museum; and lead anchors, votive altars, and funerary inscriptions unearthed in the region.

The site, systematically excavated in recent decades, has so far revealed three Roman *Baths* (3C), possibly the best examples of their kind found in Gaul. Those to the E. and S.E. of the villa include a frigidarium; the former, with its alternate stone and brick courses, was once erroniously called the 'Temple of Apollo'. Between the two is a 1C wall. To the S.W., beneath the baptistry and *Paleo-Christian basilica* of Cimiez (5C), lie the *Women's Baths*.

Hence, crossing a small park in an olive-grove to the E., we approach the 17C *Church* (with a mid 19C facade) of a re-occupied Franciscan convent, containing a Pietà and Crucifixion by *Louis Bréa*, and a Deposition by *Antoine Bréa*. The convent houses a small *Franciscan museum*. In the cemetery to the N. are the graves of Dufy, Matisse, and Martin du Gard.

For *Falicon*, and the road to *Levens*, see Rte 165.

For roads from Nice to *Grasse*, and to *Vence* and *Cannes*, see Rtes 155, and 161, in reverse; for *Menton*, Rte 163, for *Tende*, Rte 164, and for *Digne* via *Entrevaux*, Rte 165.

163 Nice to Menton

The Corniche roads and the autoroute

With the completion of the motorway (1980), there are four main routes along this mountainous stretch of the Riviera, approx. 30km or 18 miles in length, which are described below.

Maps: IGN 61, or 115. M 245 or 195.

The *Motorway* (**A.**; see below) is the fastest, but is not cheap, although saving considerable nervous strain; it also provides some extensive views, and is preferable if driving direct to Menton, or Italy. It also avoids the bottleneck of Monaco-Monte-Carlo, which is of slight interest anyway.

The *Grande Corniche* (**B.**). 'The Corniche' par excellence—the word meaning a road carried across the more or less precipitous face of a height, as it were a shelf or cornice—is the upper road, part of a military road to Italy constructed by Napoleon in 1806, which partly follows the Roman road. It avoids all towns and villages except *La Turbie*, and conforms to the contour of the rugged mountain face, commanding—except in hazy wather—the constantly varying panorama of the coast, with its promontories and bays. *Èze* may also be approached by a steeply descending road leading off it.

C.; the *Moyenne* (or Middle) *Corniche*, was completed in 1937, designed to ease traffic congestion—even then—on the upper and lower roads. It is the best means of access to **Èze**, between which and *La Turbie* it is connected to the upper road. This middle road is also provided with broad side-walks for pedestrians.

The *Corniche Inférieure* or *Littoral* (**D.**), as its name implies, leads along the coast, providing direct access to all the towns and their extensions, including *Monaco* and *Monte-Carlo*, which are described on this route.

All four roads require careful driving, and cross-winds must be taken into account on the motorway, particularly between its numerous tunnels, and on its viaducts. They can of course be followed in either direction, but are all here described from W. to E. In the 18C and earlier many travellers preferred to make the journey by sea, coast-crawling from harbour to harbour all the way to Genoa . . . as did Smollett in 1765.

A. A8 motorway; 38km (from Nice airport to the frontier); 23km from Nice-Est to **Menton**.

Travellers wishing to avoid *Nice* altogether may continue on the A8 from *Cannes* (see Rte 161), which turns abruptly N. on crossing the Var, and which may be joined with ease near Nice airport, W. of the town. It may also be entered directly at *Nice-Est* from the E. end of the Promenade des Anglais by the road skirting the E. side of the Paillon valley (later becoming the D2204); or at *Nice-Nord*.

The westerly road climbs to the r. after 4km to enter the first of the 16 tunnels traversed before its pierces the frontier ridge into Italy. From its first viaduct one gets a brief glimpse across the *Baie des Anges* before plunging into the next tunnel, and later there is a view of the *Observatory* on *Mont Gros* (375m) on crossing the Paillon valley (*Nice-Est*).—8km brings us to the turning (r.) for *La Turbie* (see B.), while ahead is fort-topped *Mont Agel* (1110m), on the slope of which are the transmitters of *Radio Monte-Carlo*. It is worth stopping at a *Belvedere* on the r. for the plunging *View of *Monaco* and *Monte-Carlo* which it commands—in the opinion of some, perhaps the best way of seeing the principality, spread out like a game of 'Monopoly' below.—The road descends gradually, with a view (half-r.), of *Roquebrune*, with the promontory of *Cap Martin* beyond, before bearing inland again to circle behind *Menton*, passing (l.) the perched villages of *Gorbio* and *Ste-Agnes*, with (l.) the *Pic de Baudon* (1264m), and *Mont Grammont* (1378m) marking the border beyond.—The exit for **Menton** is approached, the resort itself, 3km S., reached by turning down the narrow Carei valley; see p 889.

The A8 veers round to the E., nearing the coast, and at 4km plunges into a tunnel beneath the *Roche Longue*, its ridge marking the frontier, on the far side of which (on the A10; autostrada dei Fiori) we are in Italy. Customs (French and Italian) are 6km beyond, 2km N. of *Ventimiglia*; see *Blue Guide Northern Italy*. **Genoa** lies 107km beyond, via the motorway.

B. The *Grande Corniche*. D2564; 31km 18km **La Turbie—Menton** lies 13km beyond.

Following the boulevards on the E. side of the Paillon valley from the Promenade des Anglais, we turn r. near the Palais des Exposi-tions, and shortly commence the ascent N., making a loop round *Mont Gros* (375m), surmounted by an *Observatory* (built by Garnier, and presented to the University of Paris in 1899).—The road now commands a view of the peninsula of *Cap Ferrat* before bearing N.E. well above *Beaulieu*, with *Mont Leuze* (577m) and *Mont Fourche* (570m) to the l. as the *Belvedere d'Èze* is approached, and soon after, the *Col d'Èze* (512m). The village of **Èze** may be reached directly hence by taking a steeply descending road; but see C.

We continue E., with a view of the *Tête de Chien* (556m) ahead, above *Cap-d'Ail*, to reach **La Turbie** (480m), an ancient village preserving medieval gateways and an 18C church. it commands the famous *View of the Alpis Summa* of the Antonine Itinerary, and once marked the boundary between Italy and Gaul: ('huc usque Italia, abhinc Galliae').

Its modern name is derived from the *Tropaea Augusti*, a *Tower* ◊ erected in honour of Augustus in 6 B.C. to celebrate his final subjugation of the Ligurian tribes. it was injured by the Barbarians and by St Honoratus in the 5C, as the statue was still considered as a god by the natives. It was converted into a fortress in the 13C, which was thoughtlessly blown up by Gén. de la Feuillade in 1705. A skilful and conservative restoration of the shattered ruin was completed in 1933, largely at the expense of Edward Tuck, an American philanthropist, who also established the neighbouring *Museum*, containing fragments, and documents relating to its history and restoration, and models of what may have been its original appearance.

The tower originally stood on a square base, above which was a circular storey surrounded by 24 marble Doric columns, providing a 45m high plinth for a colossal statue of the emperor.

Some 2.5km N.W. of La Turbie lies the village of *Laghet*, with an Italianate church of 1656, with a cloister and some hundreds of naive ex-votos. It was here in March 1849 that Charles Albert of Sardinia passed his last night on Italian soil after his defeat at Novara: he travelled on to Portugal, where he died not long after.

A steep road descends S. from La Turbie to both the lower corniche roads not far W. of *Cap-d'Ail* and *Monaco*.

The D53 ascends N., skirting (r.) *Mont Agel* (1110m) to (10km) *Peille*, whence one may climb the *Pic de Baudon* (1264m) for the panoramic view. The sombre village preserves a 12-13C church and the imposing ruins of its castle. Hence one may descend to *La Grave* in the Paillon valley; see Rte 164.

Continuing E., the *Mont des Mules* (r.), site of a prehistoric camp (views) is passed, and the road skirts the hills above *Monte-Carlo*, at 5km reaching a point at which the motorway may be joined.—The road gradually descends, turning S.E. below *Roquebrune*.

Roquebrune is an ancient fortress-village of narrow arcades and stepped lanes, preserving the 17-18C church of *Ste-Marguerite*, adjoined by charming gardens. In Jan. 1592 Lavalette was mortally wounded in the siege undertaken by Lesdiguières. The centre of the system of fortifications erected in the 10C against Saracen raids is the ruined **Donjon*, substantially a building of the 13C with later additions by the Grimaldis, in whose hands it remained until 1848. Sir William Ingram, a later owner, presented it to the municipality. Roquebrune was one of the favourite retreats of Winston Churchill.

The Grande Corniche shortly meets the *Corniche Moyenne* just prior to bearing round *Cap-Martin*, and 4km W. of **Menton**; see D.

C. The *Corniche Moyenne*.—N7; 28km. 11 km **Éze**—5km **Monaco** —12km **Menton**.

We turn r. at the *Pont Barla* in the Paillon valley, or from the roundabout a short distance N.E. of the port of Nice, and ascend the side of *Mont Alban* in curves (222m; the summit provides a panoramic view of Nice) to the *Col de Villefranche*, overlooking the *Rade de Villefranche* and the peninsula of *Cap Ferrat*.

Bearing N.E. above *Beaulieu*, at 11km the turning for Èze (r.) is reached. **Èze**, an ancient—but now commercialised—perched village, stands on the summit of a pyramidal rock crowned by a ruined 13C castle. Its restored houses, now largely inhabited by potters and others engaged in trading to trippers, piled close together, seem to be parts of a single dilapidated citadel, although separated by a labyrinth of narrow stepped lanes.—A mule-track descends precipitously to *Éze-sur-Mer*.

Just beyond the village the l.-hand fork ascends to the *Grande Corniche* and *La Turbie*; see above.—We descend towards the *Tête de Chien*, and bearing round the *Cap-d'Ail*, skirt the upper boundary of the Principality of *Monaco*; see D.—A l.-hand fork shortly diverges to the upper road and the motorway.—The gradual descend is continued to *Cabbé*, there merging with the *Corniche Inférieure*. *Roquebrune* (see B.) is seen on a height to the l. as the road circles S.E. to meet the descending Grande Corniche on the outskirts of *Cap-Martin*, for which and the road ahead to **Menton**, see D.

D. The *Corniche Inférieure*. N98; 27km.

The lower road, also known as the *Corniche Littoral*, skirts the indented Mediterranean coast, ascending just E. of the port of Nice to circle the foot of *Mont Boron*, with a view ahead of the rocky but wooded peninsula of *Cap Ferrat*, and shortly enters the outskirts of **Villefranche** (7,400 inhab.).

It was founded in the early 14C by Charles II d'Anjou, Count of Provence, who granted it commercial privileges. Here the Emperor Charles V stayed while negotiating with François I in 1538. In 1691 it was bombarded and captured by the Comte d'Estrées.

The old town lies below the massive *Citadelle* (late 16C), facing the protected roadstead, the only considerable haven between Golfe-Juan and Genoa. Its stepped arcades streets descend steeply from its late 17C church to the fishing-port, on the quay of which is the restored *Chapelle St-Pierre*, decorated with queer frescoes by Cocteau.

The road bears round the bay, at the far side of which a r.-hand turning admits to **St-Jean-Cap-Ferrat**, which here merges with *Beaulieu*; see below.

A very sharp l.-hand turning after c. 1km leads to the villa built for Baroness Beatrice Ephrussi de Rothschild in 1912, which with its contents was bequeathed in 1934 to the Académie des Beaux-Arts and designated the *Musée 'Île de France'*. Its gardens are very pleasant; a few items of quality stand out among the effusion of furniture, porcelain, and paintings, etc., patently acquired with more money than taste.

Further S. (r.) is the *Villa des Cèdras*, with its botanical garden, once owned by Leopold II of Belgium (d. 1909), and later by a liqueur-manufacturer. Somerset Maugham resided in the *Villa Mauresque* from 1928 until his death in 1965.—The round of the promontory with its lighthouse (views) may be continued before descending to the old fishing-village, facing E., protected by the *Pointe St-Hospice*.

The direct road to adjacent Beaulieu passes near (l.) the *Villa Kerylos*, a curious edifice constructed in 1900 by the archeaologist Théodore Reinach (1860–1928) in the antique Greek taste, and left to the Institute of France; it contains some authentic Greek antiquities.

Beaulieu, probably ancient *Anao*, is attractively situated, and contains luxurious hotels: those who can afford them have few reservations. The resort was patronised by the English, who built a church. The third Marquis of Salisbury built a villa there, as did James Gordon Bennett (1800–72), founder (in 1835) and proprietor of the 'New York Herald'.

A mid 19C view of Monaco, by Harry J. Johnson

The road soon traverses *Èze-sur-Mer*, 350m above which is perched **Èze** itself (see above), and approaches *Cap-d'Ail*, dominated by the
cliffs of the *Tête de Chien* (556m), just before which a l.-hand turning
climbs to the *Moyenne Corniche* (conveniently allowing one to by-
pass Monaco and Monte-Carlo), and thence continues to ascend
steeply in zigzags to *La Turbie* on the *Grande Corniche*.

Bearing round the cape we enter *Monaco*, denominated 'a dwarf-
fish kingdom' by Baretti.

MONACO and MONTE-CARLO (with c. 25,000 Monégasques), a
miniature independent sovereign state, whose anomalous position as
a tax haven has caused its survival, lies on the lower slopes of the
Mont des Mules, only separated from its French suburb by the Blvd
de France. In recent years its total area of some 150 hectares has
been extended by land reclamation schemes, but even so this leaves
little room for its opulent population (with their portfolios), who
have congregated in cliffs of apartment blocks which have
mushroomed on almost every space available. This toy enclave
within the French department consists of three district: the old
capital of *Monaco* on a promontory to the S.; *La Condamine*, a commercial quarter around the harbour below it; and *Monte-Carlo*, to the
N.E., laid out since 1828 on the bare rocks of the *Spélugues*. One
would hardly notice the existence of this pocket principality was it
not for the difference in the uniform of its police endeavouring to
keep the dense traffic from grinding to a standstill. French currency
is valid there, although it issues coins of its own, and also stamps. The
Casino is no longer the main source of its income, for both the
French and other foreigners also flock there to attend its various activities, from car rallies and races (when its streets form part of the
circuit) to T.V. festivals, concerts, regattas, and what not. The only
objects worth visiting—although the problems involved in approaching them are getting progressively more complex—are the
Palace, Oceanographic Museum, and the Galéa Collection of dolls,

automata, and—appropriately—puppets.

An 18C rhyme went: 'Son Monaco Sopr'uno scoglio; Non semino, e non ricoglio; Eppure mangiar voglio'. (I am Monaco seated on a rock; neither do I sow nor gather anything; yet I will not starve).

It was called by the Romans *Portus Herculis Monoeci*, from an ancient Phoenician temple on the headland dedicated to Melkarth, known to the Greeks as *Herakles Monoikos*. The Genoese built a fort here in 1215, and by the 14C the Genoese family of Grimaldi, under Carlo I (d. 1363; who had been wounded at Crécy), had established themselves there as lords of Monaco. In 1525 commenced a period of Spanish 'protection', which on the accession of Honoré II, a minor, in 1604, developed into domination. The Spaniards were only thrown out in 1641, to be replaced by French protectors. In 1715 the Grimaldi heiress married Jacques de Matignon, Comte de Thorigny (1689–1751), who assumed the name of Grimaldi, whose descendants still reign. From 1793 until 1814, when its sovereignty was recovered, the principality was absorbed into the Alpes-Maritimes department. In 1848 Roquebrune and Menton, formerly subject to Monaco, renounced their allegiance. Albert I granted a constitutional government to the Monégasques in 1911. From 1911 (when 'Le Spectre de la Rose' was first performed) until 1922, when it became their headquarters, it was frequently the base of Diaghilev's Ballets Russes. Col de Basil's company was launched here in 1932. In 1949 Rainier III succeeded his grandfather Louis II, and in 1956 married the American film-star Grace Kelly (1928–82), who brought glamour to the place. It was the birthplace of the composer Franz Schreker (1878–1934).

From the main road junction below a precipitous rock projecting boldly into the sea one may ascend the Rampe Major to the *Pl. du Palais* and Promenade Ste-Barbe, overlooking a dusty area recently reclaimed from the sea to accommodate a Heliport, etc. The square, preserving bronze cannon presented by Louis XIV, and the 18C barracks of the carabiniers, is flanked by the **Palace**, over the main gate of which (1672) are the family arms supported by armed friars (for Francesco I Grimaldi captured the place in 1297 having gained entrance disguised as a Franciscan). The building has been much altered since it was first enclosed in the 13-14C fortress.

From the Cour d'Honneur a double staircase ascends to an arcaded gallery (1552), with restored 17C frescoes of the Labour of Hercules by *Orazio Ferrari* on the ceiling, and others on the walls by Francesco *Mazzuchelli* (1571–1626?); those on the facade of the wing opposite are by *Luca Cambiaso* (1573), much restored.

The *State Apartments* contain a collection of family portraits, by *Rigaud, Toquè, Gobert, Van der Meulen, Philippe de Champaigne*, and *Largillière*, etc.—The Chambre de l'Alcôve contains The Music Lesson, attrib. to *Giorgione*; the Chambre d'York is named after Edward Augustus, duke of York (brother of George III), who died here in 1767, 'of malignant fever'.—A small Napoleonic collection has been installed in a new wing. The gardens are laid out on ramparts of 1560.

Passing beneath an arch at the S.E. side of the Place, off which the narrow lanes of the old town lead, we approach the nondescript late 19C *Cathedral*, built in a neo-Romanesque style, but containing the retable of St-Nicolas, and a Pietà, both attrib. to the *Bréas*.

The Av. St-Martin, overlooking luxuriant gardens, leads E. to the **Oceanographic Museum**, founded in 1910 by Albert I to illustrate his deep-sea explorations, and since enlarged. it contains skeletons or models of marine mammals and other fauna; and sections devoted to marine zoology, and models of yachts and oceanographic apparatus, etc. The *Aquarium* in the basement is notable. The museum, directed by Cdr Jacques Cousteau, is an important centre for Mediterranean underwater studies.

By continuing E. and turning l. through a fortified gate, the descent may be made to *La Condamine*.

On the hillside opposite is a *Jardin Exotique*, notable for its cacti. It contains an *Anthropological Museum* illustrating the evolution of man from Pithecanthropus via Neanderthal, Grimaldi, and Cro-Magnon developments, and includes bones found in the Baoussé-Roussée caves near Menton, among others; gold ornaments found at La Condamine, and a few Roman antiquities. The nearby *Grottes de l'Observatoire*, may be visited.

Following the Av. du Port, the ostentatious yacht harbour is shortly reached, and the Blvd Albert-Ier approaches *Monte-Carlo* proper, at the N.W. corner of the port, where we ascend the Av. d'Ostende.

Near this corner stands *Ste-Dévote* (1870; on earlier foundations). This Corsican virgin-martyr, the patron of the town, was guided here in a dying state by a dove which issued from her mouth, and when in 1070 some Florentines attempted to carry off her relics, their boat remained becalmed in spite of a favourable breeze, a miracle annually celebrated by the devout Monégasques.

The **Casino** is now reached, standing in well-tended and colourful gardens, and long the centre of activity in the town, and of the various fêtes organised by the Société des Bains de Mer, etc. It is an elaborate structure of various dates, the earliest (1879) being designed by Charles Garnier, and contains a theatre and ballroom apart from gaming rooms, all characteristic of the period.

The first casino in the principality was opened in 1856, and moved to this site in 1862, but it was not a financial success until François Blanc's arrival from Homburg in the following year. Its fortunes were consolidated by the arrival of the railway in 1868. Its concession passed into the hands of a joint-stock company paying an annual tribute to the Monégasque government, and it was managed from 1877 by Camille Blanc (d. 1927).

Hence, by descending N.E. to the Av. Princesse-Grace, the extensive *Galéa Collection* of 'poupées' and automata may be visited in a villa built by Garnier. An adjacent 'ascenseur' mounts to the main Blvd des Moulins.—Beyond lies the *Plage du Larvotto*, but *Monte-Carlo Beach* lies further N., in French territory.

On a height ahead on leaving Monte-Carlo is seen the perched village of *Roquebrune*; see B.—The neck of the wooded peninsula of *Cap-Martin* is crossed, off which the architect 'Le Corbusier' (Édouard Jeanneret; 1887–1965) was drowned. In a garden near the Hôtel de Ville of Cap-Martin is a small ruin, a relic of Roman *Lumone*. W.B. Yeats (1865–1939) died at the Hôtel Idéal-Séjour here, and was buried at Roquebrune until the transference of his remains to Ireland in 1948. Claude Grahame-White (1879–1959), the aviator, spent his last years in a villa here, dying in Nice. The accomplished forger Van Meegeren retired here in 1932. The resort, once described as 'an aristocratic annexe' now merges imperceptibly with Menton.

MENTON (25,400 Mentonaisse) enjoys perhaps the mildest climate on the Riviera, sheltered from the Mistral by a semicircle of mountains, a ridge just E. of the town forming the frontier with Italy. The older centre of narrow lanes, rising on a promontory, divides the modern resort which has extended to flank two shallow bays: the more sheltered E. bay, with the yacht harbour, is known as *Garavan*; that to the W. is skirted by the long Promenade du Soleil. It is reputed for its lemons, oranges, and olives.

It appears to have been a possession of the Counts of Ventimiglia at the end of the 10C, and by the middle of the 12C it had passed into Genoese hands. In 1364 Carlo Grimaldi bought it, and with various interruptions it remained with that family until 1848, when Roquebrune, and Menton (or *Mentone* as it was then known) revolted against fiscal extractions, and declared themselves free towns. Its first president was Charles Trenca (d. 1853), and it remained a republic until 1860, when together with Nice it was annexed to France. In the following year the prince of Monaco sold his hereditary rights to France.

In 1940 it was occupied by the Italian army, and later by the Germans, and suffered some damage during and after their retreat.

Its climatic virtues having been extolled by Dr James Henry Bennet (d. 1891), it became a haunt of English valetudinarians, among them R.L. Stevenson, who wrote 'Ordered South' when wintering there in 1873–74, and Katherine Mansfield was later a visitor (1920–21). But, according to Augustus Hare, by 1890 the two bays had already 'filled with hideous and stuccoed villas in the worst taste' . . . 'pretentious paved promenades have taken the place of the beautiful walks under tamarisk groves by the sea shore. Artistically, Mentone is vulgarised and ruined . . .'. Among those who died here were the historian J.R. Green (1837–83); the artists Narcisse Diaz (1808–76), and Aubrey Beardsley (1872–98); William Webb Ellis (1807–72), the 'founder' of Rugby football; and the Spanish novelist Vicente Blasco Ibáñez (1867–1928).

Its most famous native was Gén. J.-B. Bréa (1790–1848), killed by insurgents in Paris.

Facing the lower end of the central *Jardin Bioves*, laid out above the torrent of the Careï, with the old casino of 1909 (S.I.), is the *Casino* of 1935, beyond which is the Promenade du Soleil (previously de George-V), overlooking a pebbly beach. The Av. Félix-Faure leads E. from the casino and parallel to the front. To the N., in the Rue de la République, stands the *Hôtel de Ville*, with a Salle des Mariages decorated by Jean Cocteau in 1957. (A *Museum* devoted to Cocteau's art is housed in an early 17C fort near the jetty at the E. end of the Promenade.)

A short distance to the N. is the *Musée Municipal*, with important prehistoric collections, including the Grimaldi Skull, discovered in the neighbouring caves of Roches Rouges in 1884; see below. Other rooms are devoted to local history, etc.

Continuing E., from the Hôtel de Ville, the chapel of the *Pénitents-Noirs* (1617) is passed (l.) to enter the crooked stepped alleys of the old town, in the centre of which, facing the charming Italianate *Pl. St-Michel* (in which concerts of chamber-music are given in the season) stands *St-Michel*, in the Italian Jesuit style (1675), with an altarpiece of 1565 by André Manchello of Monaco.—Higher up is the chapel of the *Pénitents-Blancs*, similar in style, containing 18C statues. Further N. is the *Old Cemetery*, on the site of a castle, below which a road tunnel has been pierced.

Steps descend from the Place to the narrow Rue Longue, at the S. end of which is the 14C *Porte St-Julien*, a relic of medieval fortifications. No. 123 in the street is a mansion restored in 1650, with an interior vaulted staircase.

Another flight of steps descends to the Quai Bonaparte, and the *Plage des Sablettes*. Graham Sutherland apparently designed the Coventry Cathedral tapestries in a garage near here.—Hence the Quai Laurenti leads E., to the l. off which is the *Villa Isola Bella*, where Katherine Mansfield stayed, and *Tropical Gardens*. Another garden, '*des Colombières*', laid out by Ferdinand Bac (d. 1952) may be visited off the Blvd de Garavan, at a higher level.

The quay continues to skirt the Garavan as far as the *Pont St-Louis* and the Italian frontier (Customs). Those with their passports may cross the border to visit the caverns of *Baoussé-Roussé* (Balzi Rossi), in the *Roches Rouges*, in which important prehistoric remains have been found.

Some distance W. of the Casino, approached by the Av. Carnot (after passing the *English Church*), and to the r. some distance beyond gardens laid out above the channel of the Borrigo, is the **Musée du Palais Carnolès** (3 Av. de la Madone). This early 18C Grimaldi residence, sumptuously decorated by the Vento brothers (but mutilated by an American, Dr Allis, who lived there from 1896 to 1947) has since 1977 contained a small but interesting collection of paintings.

Notable are: *Louis Bréa*, Virgin and Child with St Francis; *M. de Nardo*, St Matthew and an angel; attrib. *Andrea d'Orcagna*, SS Peter and Paul; *School of Corneille de Lyon*, Female portrait; attrib. *Antonio Moro*, Woman with a Dog, and The Count of Sussex (1525); *B. Maineri*, Portrait of Urbain Bologna; *F. Voet*, Male portrait; *anon. Italian* Passage of the Rhine (1606); *Benjamin West*, The Sacrifice of Iphigénie; also drawings by *Rodin*, and a section of 20C art.

Several short EXCURSIONS may be made from Menton. Among the picturesque perched villages in the hills behind, all approached by steeply mounting minor roads, are *Castellar* (365m), 7km N.; *Ste-Agnès* (650m), 11km N.W., with ruins of its 10C castle; and *Gorbio* (359m), 9km W., also with a ruined castle, and old arcaded houses. They all command wide and plunging views.

   For excursions into Italy, see *Blue Guide Northern Italy*.

   For the D2556 to *Sospel*, 21km N., see Rte 164, in the reverse direction. A lane climbs to the l. off this, on the outskirts of Menton, to the convent and chapel (1703) of the *Annonciade* (225m), providing a good view over the town.

164 Nice to Tende (for Cuneo)

83km (51 miles). D2204. 21km *L'Escarène*—22km **Sospel**—21km N204. 7km *Saorge*—12km *Tende*.

Maps: IGN 61, or 115; also 258–9 for the mountains on the frontier. M 245 or 195.

The road from **Nice** (Rte 162) is followed up the Paillon valley, probably to be paralleled by another further W., past (r.) *Drap*, which has given the title of count to the bishops of Nice since the 13C, to (12km) the *Pont de Peille*.

Here the D21 leads r. up the Paillon valley, passing (r. at 4km) the hilltop village-fortress of *Peillon*.—2.5km. A. by-road zigzags r. up to (6.5km) *Peille* (630m), a sombre village with a 12-13C church of interest and an imposing ruined castle.—The D21 threads the *Gorges du Paillon* to (7.5km) *l'Escarène*; see below.

We continue on the main road for 1.5km.

The D15, turning l. of the D2204, ascends the valley of the Paillon de Contes to the N.W. via (3.5km) *Contes*, whose Italianate church contains a good 16C polyptych, to (11km) *Coaraze*, inhabited by artists and potters, later circling to the E. round the *Cime du Savel* (1015m) to (19km) *Lucéram*; see below.

After a further 6.5km we reach the *Col de Nice* (412m), 4.5km W. of which, on a height, stands *Berre-des-Alpes* (675m).—The road descends steeply to (1km) *L'Escarène*, an old village at the junction of two streams, with a large 17C church.

Hence the D2566 ascends l. to (6.5km) **Lucéram** (665m), passing (r.) on the approach, the *Chapelle de St-Grat*, with 16C frescoes. Lucéram, once a Roman colony, and a free commune as early as 1271, lies in a cup-like depression, and preserves some old houses, remains of a castle and other fortifications, and a church of 1487 with six 15-16C altarpieces, including a *St-Margaret attrib. to Louis Bréa, and a treasury of some interest.—Hence the road commences to climb in zigzags to (10km) *La Cabanette* (1327m), and the summer and winter resort of *Peira-Cava* (1450m), 2.5km beyond, curiously placed on a narrow ridge, and formerly a military post.—7km. further N. is the *Col de Turini* (1607m), from which one may descend W. into the Vésubie valley; see Rte 165.—Some 6km N.E. of the col is the commanding summit of the *Authion* or *Pointe des Trois Communes*, rising to 2082m, crowned with forts which guarded the old frontier, where in 1793 Gén. Brunet with an army of 12,000 Republicans was repulsed by the Sardinians.

From l'Escarène the D2204 climbs N.E. in zigzags to (10km) the *Col de Braus* (1002m), to descend round the slope of *Mont Barbonnet* (847m), with its fort, to (12km) **Sospel** (349m), an ancient little town on the Bévéra, with an 11C bridge and watchtower (rebuilt since damaged in 1944–45), arcaded square, classical church and Romanesque belfry; the *Church* contains an altarpiece attrib. to François Bréa, as does the *Chapelle des Pénitents-Blancs*, on the far side of the river.

The D2566 climbs N.W., and then N. through the *Gorges du Piaon* to (12km) *Moulinet*, a village pleasantly sited in an expansion of the valley, and continues to climb steeply to (13km) the *Col de Turini*; see above.

SOSPEL TO MENTON (22km). The D2566 ascends S. to (10km) *Castillon* (548m), between *Mont Grammont* (1378m) on the frontier, and *Mont Ours* (1239m), to the W. The former village was destroyed in 1944, and the hill-top settlement of *Vieux-Castillon* was ruined by an earthquake in 1887. The descent is made past (l.) the horseshoe-shaped *Viaduc du Caramel* to (7km) the hamlet of *Monti*, between (S.E.) *Castellar*, and (S.W.) *Ste-Agnès*, both approached directly from Menton, and the road continues to climb down, beneath the motorway, to (7km) **Menton** itself; see the latter part of Rte 163.

The D2204 leads N.E. from Sospel, at 2km passing a r.-hand turning for (8km) *Olivetta*, a frontier crossing, and climbs N. to (10km) the *Col de Brouis* (879m), where a pocket of German troops was finally defeated in April 1945. The road descends steeply to (9km) the hamlet of *La Giandola*.

2km S., at *Breil*, is an 18C church, 5km beyond which are French Customs, and 3km further S., on the frontier itself, Italian Customs.—*Ventimiglia*, on the coast at the foot of the Roya valley, lies 17km S.E.; see *Blue Guide Northern Italy*.

From La Giandola the N204 ascends the Roya valley via the *Gorges de Saorge*, impressively narrow and tortuous, on emerging from which we have a striking view (r.) of the fortified village of **Saorge** (520m), its dark houses clinging to the hillside like swallows' nests. It may be approached by car, but not traversed, preferably from (7km) *Fontan*, 2.5km further N.

The *Gorges de Bergue* are now threaded, later passing power-stations, and through chestnut woods, before entering (8km) *St-Dalmas-de-Tende* (696m).

The mountain village of *La Brigue*, 2.5km E., has a good 13-14C church with a Lombardic tower, and 4km beyond (enquire first at the Mairie of La Brigue for key), the woodland chapel of *N.-D. des Fontaines (1492), and Giovanni Baleisoni.
The D91 leads W. from St-Dalmas to *Les Mesches*, in the *Vallon de la Minière*, some 9km. beyond which, approached by a rough signposted track, is the

remote *Vallée des Merveilles*, with its lakes, and a remarkable series of c. 36,000 late Bronze Age grafitti in the vicinity of *Mont Bégo*. (Special transport may be hired at St-Dalmas.) Near the head of the mountain-encircled valley rises *Mont Clapier* (3045m), on the frontier. Passes to the W. of the valley lead into the upper valley of the Gordolasque; see Rte 165.

4km. **Tende** (791m; French Customs) stands at the foot of the frontier range of mountains, a strange old town of dark slate-roofed houses and with a *Church* of 1518 preserving a remarkable facade designed by the Varences brothers of Genoa. Above the town are the curious ruins (dismantled 1692) of the 15C *Castle* of the Lascaris, a celebrated member of the house being Beatrice de Tende, whose cruel fortunes at the hands of the Visconti inspired an opera by Bellini.

The district of *Tende* and *La Brigue* (together with sections of the upper Tinée and Vésubie), although parts of the County of Nice, were expressly reserved to Italy by the Franco-Italian treaty of 1860 in a rare moment of liberality by Napoleon III, a great part of the chamois-haunted territory being a favourite hunting-ground of Victor Emmanuel II. In 1947 they were rejoined to the rest of the country by treaty, an act confirmed by a local plebiscite in favour of France. The frontier now runs across the Col de Tende and the minor passes further W. at the head of the Vésubie and Tinée basins.

The main road to (45km) *Cuneo*, and **Turin** (85km beyond) traverses a tunnel 9km N. of Tende, penetrating the ridge below the *Col de Tende*. The old road over the top of the pass (1871m), constructed by Victor Amadeus III, is for pedestrians only, and provides an extensive mountain view. Italian Customs are at the far end of the 3km-long tunnel, beyond which the road descends to (6km) *Limone*, for which see *Blue Guide Northern Italy*. Among many others who crossed this pass was Arthur Young, in Sept. 1788.

165 Nice to Digne via Entrevaux

142km (88 miles). N202. 20km *Plan-du-Var*—7km *Gorges du Tinée*—19km *Gorges du Clan*—8km *Puget-Théniers*—7km **Entrevaux**—6km *Gorges du Dalius*—7km. *Annot* lies 2km N.W.—17km *St-Julien-du-Verdon*—(**Castellane** lies 13km S.) —8km *St-André-les-Alpes*—13km *Barrême*—N85. 30km **Digne**.

Maps: IGN 61, or 115; also 258 for the mountains near St-Martin-Vésubie. M 245, 195.

A number of digressions from the main route may be made into side valleys, where several churches contain altarpieces of the 15-16C Nice School, and which preserve some impressive mountain-scenery.

An excursion in this direction is first described, from NICE TO ST-JEAN-LA-RIVIÈRE (c. 36km). The D19 bears l. beneath the A8 motorway as it crosses the Paillon valley at *Nice-Est*.—At 3.5km the D114 descends from Falicon to joint the road.—*Falicon*, an attractive village commanding extensive views, is also approached with ease from **Cimiez**, beyond which the r.-hand turning is taken at *Aire-St-Michel*.—The D19 ascends the valley of the Garbe, passing below (r.) at 5km, *Tourrette-Levens*, an old perched village with remains of ramparts and a 12C church.—The D719 climbs W. to (4.5km) a col (530m) E. of the village of *Aspremont*, S. of which rises *Mont Chauve*, with its ruined fort (854m), and *Mont Cima* (879m) to the N.—1km beyond Tourrette the D815 climbs E. over the *Chaine de Férion* to (13km) the road below *Contes* (see Rte 164), passing at 8km the ruins of medieval *Châteauneuf* to the r.—*Mont Férion* (1413m) rises to the N.E. as the road approaches (9km) *Levens* (570m), the ancestral home of the Masséna family, beyond which we turn N.E., high above the gorge of the Vésubie valley 'en corniche', with the hamlet of *Gros-d'Utelle* on the far bank, later passing the *Saut des Français* (see below) before descending steeply to *St-Jean-la-Rivière*, on the D2565, 10km N.E. of *Plan-du-Var*; see below.

From the W. end of **Nice** (Rte 162), by the airport, the valley of the Var is ascended, overlooked to the l. by *Gattières, Carros,* and *Le Broc* (see last section of Rte 161), to (18km) the *Pont Charles-Albert,* on approaching which are the perched villages of *La Roquette* (r.), and *Gilette* (l.), near the mouth of the Estéron valley.

High up to the l., 9km by road from the bridge, is *Bonson* (plunging views), where the church has two good Niçois altarpieces.—21.5km beyond (7km) Gilette lies *Roquesteron*, once a frontier village, and 4.5km beyond, *Sigale*, with medieval houses, gateway, and tower, whence the caverns and waterfalls of the upper valley of the Estéron may be explored, notably the *Clues du Riolan* and *d'Aiglun*.—A ridge road (D27) climbs N.W. and W. from Bonson to (41km) *Puget-Théniers*; see below.

2km. *Plan du Var.*

PLAN DU VAR TO ST-MARTIN-VÉSUBIE (34km). The valley of the Vésubie, at the head of which rise several peaks of over 3000m, is visited for its scenery, and by both climbers and winter-sports enthusiasts, its alpine character earning it the name of 'the Switzerland of Nice'. The D2565 turns r. through the *Gorge of the Vésubie* between cliffs 240m high. After a brief expansion the rock walls again converge. From the *Saut des Français*, on a height to the r., a number of Republican troops were hurled into the gorge in 1793.—The road from *Levens* (see above) descends from the r. just prior to (10km) *St-Jean-la-Rivière* (285m), which stands at the foot of a zigzag road climbing l. to (9km) *Utelle*, an old fortified village, where the church, with carved 16C doors, contains an Annunciation of the Nice School. The ascent mày be continued to (6km; 1174m) the sanctuary of *Madone d'Utelle*, providing a wide view.—9km. *Lantosque* (510m) an ancient village of stepped lanes, is built on a ridge that bars the valley, 2km beyond which the road descending from the *Col de Turini* (1607m) is met; see Rte 164.—*La Bollène-Vésubie*, 3km up this road, is a small summer resort in chestnut woods, with ruins of a castle, and church containing 15C paintings.—*Roquebillière*, to the l., by-passed, has a church with an altarpiece of six panels and a predella. It was built after the old village of tall dark houses, which is traversed at 4km, was partly destroyed by a landslide in 1926.—From *Belvédère*, a mountain village to the r., a track ascends the Gordolasque valley towards the *Grand Capelet* (2935m), N. of which rises *Mont Clapier* (3045m), on the Italian frontier.

9km. **St-Martin-Vésubie** (960m), surrounded by pine and chestnut forests, and at a junction of valleys, although a busy summer and winter resort, preserves little of interest apart from the dilapidated mansion of the Comtes de Gubernatis in the main street, and a fragmentary retable of the Bréa School in the church of 1694, providing a good view from its terrace.

4km S. lies *Venanson*, with a chapel containing frescoes of 1481.—A road climbs N to (8km) *Le Boréon* (1500m), a base for ascents in the *Mercantour* range (with a Game Reserve), while another climbs steeply N.E. to (11.5km) *Madone de Fenestre* (1903m), base for the ascent of the *Cime des Gélas* (3143m), further N.E., the highest peak in the region.

From a point 3km N. of St-Martin the D2565 climbs W. to (5km) the *Col St-Martin* (1500m), before descending through (3km) *St-Dalmas*, with a primitive 11C church containing 15-16C retables, and the *Vallon de Bramafan* to meet the D2205 (to *St-Étienne-de-Tinée*; see below) after a further 14km, passing (r.) the high-lying hamlet of *Rimplas*, astride a rocky chapel-crowned ridge.

At 7km beyond Plan-du-Var the main road narrows, and turns abruptly W. at the *Pont de la Mescla*, strikingly situated at the confluence of the Tinée and the Var.

THE PONT DE LA MESCLA TO ST-ÉTIENNE-DE-TINÉE (53km). The D2205 turns r. to penetrate the *Gorges de la Mescla*, the first of a succession of defiles alternating with fertile basins, perched above which are several small mountain villages providing attractive and convenient refuges from the coastal heat in summer, among which *Auron*, in particular, offers winter-sporting facilities.—5km. At *La Tour*, 7km E., a chapel contains curious frescoes of 1491; and more may be seen in the *Chapelle St-Jean*, 1 hour's walk further N.E.—5.5km. *Pont-de-Clans*, 6.5km N. of which is the small resort of *Clans*.—At 10.5km the D2205 from St-Martin-Vésubie descends from the r.; see above.—4km. *St-Sauveur-sur-Tinée* (497m), its church with a Romanesque tower (1333) and a retable of 1483 by Guillaume Planeta.—Hence a mountain road (D30) climbs W. to (24km) *Beuil*, in the Cians valley (see below) via the *Col de la Couillole* (1678m), passing (r.) *Roure*, with a 13C chapel with 16C frescoes, and an Assumption attrib. to François Bréa (1560), and (12km) *Roubion*, with traces of 12C fortifications, and surrounded by precipices.—The *Chapelle St-Sébastien*, a short distance beyond, has some well-preserved 15C frescoes.

Beyond St-Sauveur the *Gorges de Valabres* are traversed before entering (14km) *Isola* (873m), a large village whose ruined church has a fine tower.—Hence the D97 ascends the steep *Vallon de Chastillon* to (17km E.) *Isola 2000*, a modern—British promoted—ski station (French Customs), 5km below the frontier pass of the *Col de la Lombarde* (2350m), 25km S. of *Vinadio*; see *Blue Guide Northern Italy*.

Just S.W. of Isola is the *Cascade de Louch*, while further N. rises *Mont Mounier* (2817m).—14km up the valley to the N.W. lies **St-Étienne-de-Tinée** (1144m), a small summer and winter resort, with a handsome 16-17C church with a Romanesque belfry; the *Chapelle St-Sébastien* preserves frescoes by Canavesi and Baleisoni (c. 1492), and the *Trinitarian Convent* and *Chapelle de St-Maur* also contain frescoes.—There are winter-sporting facilities at *Auron* (1608m), 7km S., with an 18C church and Romanesque tower, and also the Romanesque *Chapelle de St-Erige*, with remarkable frescoes of 1451.—From St-Étienne a difficult mountain road (D64) ascends to (26km) the *Col de la Bonette* (2802m), beyond which it climbs down to (24km) *Jausiers* (1220m), 8km N.E. of *Barcelonnette*; see Rte 138A.—At mountain-girt *St-Dalmas-le-Selvage*, 7.5km N.W. of St-Étienne, the church contains a 16C triptych of the Life of St Pancras.—*Mont Ténibré* (3031m), one of the highest peaks in the Maritime Alps, rises to the N.E. of St-Étienne, below which are several small mountain tarns.

Continuing W. from the Pont de la Mescla, the village of *Malaussène* is passed (l.) opposite which are some contorted and tilted strata, and to the r. at 11km is picturesque *Villars-sur-Var*, with two good altarpieces in its church.—6km. *Touët-sur-Var* (r.), huddled against a high cliff, has a ruined Romanesque chapel, and at a higher level, a church built over a waterfall.

2km. *Pont de Cians.*

PONT DE CIANS TO BEUIL (22km). The D28, turning r., threads two defiles of the *Gorges du Cians* as it ascends the valley to Beuil, passing after 5.5km a track mounting to (5km) *Lieuche*, where the church contains a polyptych of 1499 attrib. to Louis Bréa.—**Beuil** (1450m), an ancient village amid alpine pastures, was once a Grimaldi stronghold; the stones from their castle were used to construct the Renaissance *Chapel des Pénitents-Blancs*; the 17C church contains a small collection of ecclesiastical art.—*Mont Mounier* (2817m) rises to the N.—The skiing resort of *Valberg* (1669m) is 6.5km W., just S. of which the *Croix du Sapet* (1829m) may be ascended for the view.—The D28 descends W. from Valberg to (13.5km) *Guillaumes* in the upper valley of the Var; see below.

8km. **Puget-Théniers**, a village of old houses and a ruined château, with a church containing a good painted altarpiece of 1525, was the birthplace of Auguste Blanqui (1805–81), the revolutionary, commemorated by a statue by Maillol.

7km. **Entrevaux** (515m), named from its strong position on a spur which seems to bar the valley, is an old frontier fortress with ramparts of 1695 on Vauban's system. Its 16C *Church* served as a cathedral of the diocese of Glandèves until 1789; its 17C doors and altar-screen are notable, as is the treasury. A small museum may also be visited.

6km. *Pont de Gueydan.*

PONT DE GUEYDAN TO BARCELONNETTE (83km). The D902, threading the
ruddy *Gorges de Daluis* in the upper Var valley, leads 20km N. to *Guillaumes*
(819m), with a church of 1699 and an earlier Lombardic tower, and overlooked
by ruins of a 15C castle.—For the road to *Valberg* and *Beuil*, 20km E., see
above.—The road continues N., at 4km passing a road (r.) to (6.5km)
Châteauneuf d'Entraunes, with an interesting altarpiece ascribed to François
Bréa, before reaching *St-Martin-d'Entraunes*, where the church preserves
Renaissance woodwork and an altarpiece of 1555, also by François Bréa.—To
the W. rise the *Aiguilles de Pélens* (2523m).—The D902 mounts to the *Col de la
Cayolle* (2327m), descending below (l.) the towering cliffs of *Mont Pelat* (3051m),
and *Le Cimet* (3020m), on which the violinist Jacques Thibaud was killed in an air
crash in 1953.—Threading the *Gorges du Bachelard*, we turn N. again below (l.)
the *Col d'Allos*, to approach **Barcelonnette**; see Rte 138A.

The main road continues 7km W. to a junction 2km S.E. of *Annot*
(700m), a small town founded in the 12C, preserving a loopholed
14C tower serving as apse to its church of 1363, with a belfry of
1574, beyond which one may ascend the valley of the Vaïre, abounding in caverns and eccentric rocks.

The N202 ascends past the *Clue de Rouaine* to the *Col de Toutes-
Aures* (1124m), and then descends past the *Clue de Vergons* to reach
(17km) a lake formed by the dam of Castillon.—Here the D955 turns
l. for (13km) **Castellane**; see Rte 155.—We bear r. to (8km) *St-André-
les-Alpes*, a small summer resort among orchards and lavender-
fields.—For the road hence via *Colmars* to *Barcelonnette*, see Rte
138A, in reverse.

Crossing a ridge to the W., the road descends to (13km) *Barrême* to
meet the N85, where we turn r. for (30km) **Digne**; see Rte 155, in
reverse.

LIST OF THE PRINCIPAL FRENCH ARTISTS, ARCHITECTS, ETC.

This reference list includes those whose *works* are referred to frequently in the text, together with their dates (and including certain foreign artists working in France). The abbreviations A., P., and S. indicate Architect, Painter or draughtsman, and Sculptor, respectively.

Abadie, Paul (1812—84), A.—392, 404, 430, 431
Aved, Joseph (1702—66), P.—189, 782

Baldung Grien, Hans (1476—1545), P.—625
Barye, Antoine-Louis (1795—1875), S.—144, 460, 581
Baugin, Lubin (1612—63), P.—250, 307, 661
Bazille, Frédéric (1841—70), P.—782
Bellegambe, Jean (1470—1543), P.—86, 96, 99
Blanche, Jacques-Émile (1861—1942), P.—120, 128, 625, 640
Boeswillwald, Jacques Émile (1815—86), A.—458, 492, 617
Boilly, Louis-Léopold (1761—1845), P.—86, 93, 119, 530, 606, 661, 698
Bonnard, Pierre (1867—1947), P.—198, 340, 500, 581, 674, 698, 720, 732, 774, 782, 808, 869, 876
Bonnat, Léon (1833—1922), P.—460, 674
Boucher, François (1703—70), P.—110, 144, 161, 307, 326, 353, 500, 544, 581, 606, 614, 661, 674, 726, 860
Boudin, Eugène (1824—98), P.—82, 96, 119, 128, 170, 178, 198, 250, 280, 340, 368, 445, 460, 581, 640, 698, 720, 727, 881
Boulogne, Jean de (Valentin; 1591—1632), P.—96, 170, 235, 623, 725
Bourdelle, Antoine (1861—1929), S.—326, 386, 625, 727, 743, 779
Bourdon, Sébastien (1621—76), P.—197, 672, 782, 788, 808
Braque, Georges (1882—1963), P.—123, 128, 661, 698, 798, 869, 876
Bréa, Louis (c. 1443—c. 1520), P.—530, 837, 843, 875, 880, 883, 891, 892
Brosse, Salomon de (c. 1562—1626), A.—112, 141, 157
Buffet, Bernard (1928—   ), P.—86
Bullant, Jean (c. 1510—78), A.—150, 151, 152

Caffieri, Jean-Jacques (1725—92), S.—120, 144, 671
Caillebotte, Gustave (1848—94), P.—120
Callot, Jacques (1592—1635), P.—342, 417, 614
Carmontel, Louis (1717—1806), P.—666
Carpeaux, J.-B. (1827—75), S.—82, 727
Carrière, Eugène (1849—1906), P.—625, 698
Cézanne, Paul (1839—1906), P.—727, 854
Chagall, Marc (1887—   ), P.—720, 732, 882

Champaigne, Philippe de (1602—74), P.—86, 99, 151, 168, 189, 198, 235, 250, 307, 450, 485, 544, 581, 616, 647, 674, 685, 698, 718, 753, 792, 810, 851, 888
Chardin, J.-B. (1699—1779), P.—110, 144, 207, 250
Clouet, François (c. 1520—72), P.—119, 151, 317
Colson, J.-F.G. (1733—1803), P.—250, 671, 726
Corneille de Lyon (1505—74), P.—147, 151, 314, 460
Corot, Camille (1796—1875), P.—82, 86, 96, 119, 198, 280, 368, 418, 450, 581, 671, 698, 727, 782
Cotte, Robert de (1656—1735), A.—147, 588
Courbet, Gustave (1819—77), P.—82, 198, 368, 450, 530, 581, 586, 637, 674, 677, 698, 726, 782
Coypel, Charles-Antoine (1694—1752), P.—307, 657, 674
Coypel, Noël (1628—1707), P.—251
Coysevox, Antoine (1640—1720), S.—140, 144, 357, 671, 699

Daubigny, Charles-François (1817—78), P.—368, 460, 581, 586, 674, 758
Daumier, Honoré (1808—79), P.—149, 581, 661, 698
David, Jacques-Louis (1748—1825), P.—86, 96, 119, 144, 147, 235, 307, 460, 581, 661, 674, 698, 782, 792, 851, 864
David, d'Angers (1788—1856), S.—80, 141, 353
Degas, Edgar (1834—1917), P.—445, 460, 698, 727, 782, 881
Delacroix, Eugène (1798—1863), P.—96, 110, 119, 144, 147, 258, 430, 460, 581, 601, 614, 636, 677, 698, 782
Delatour, Maurice-Quentin (1704—88), P.—101, 110, 418, 430, 671, 706, 851
Delorme, Philibert (c. 1515—77), A.—155, 156, 161, 166, 701
Denis, Maurice (1870—1943), P.—582, 654, 698, 869
Derain, André (1880—1954), P.—661, 698, 720, 869, 876
Desportes, François (1661—1743), P.—250, 661, 698, 718
Diaz de la Penam Narcisse (1807—76), P.—674, 758
Doré, Gustave (1832—83), P.—446, 720
Drolling, Martin (1752—1817), P.—198, 280, 307, 623, 672, 859
Drouais, François-Hubert (1827—75), P.—191, 450, 606
Dufy, Raoul (1877—1953), P.—120, 128, 171, 178, 198, 581, 613, 625, 661, 698, 720, 788, 792, 808, 869, 876, 881

INDEX

In an attempt to keep this index within reasonable bounds, it concentrates on topographical entries; but see also the list of the principal French artists on p 897.

Villages are not included if only mentioned in passing, nor are all churches, monasteries, chapels, and châteaux in the vicinity of places listed; nor every lake, reservoir, river, and canal, island, and cape; peak, pass, *causse*, and *cirque*, or every valley, gorge, cave, forest, *pays*, and ruin, etc. While thus being to an extent selective, it should contain more than enough points of reference for the traveller to find his way about.

Îles and *Monts* are indexed as such.

Typeset by Cold Composition Ltd, Tonbridge
Printed in Great Britain by Fletcher & Son Ltd, Norwich